Gallaudet Encyclopedia of DEAF PEOPLE AND DEAFNESS

1

A–G

John V. Van Cleve, Editor in Chief
Gallaudet College

McGraw-Hill Book Company, Inc.

New York • St. Louis • San Francisco • Auckland • Bogotá • Hamburg
Johannesburg • London • Madrid • Mexico • Milan • Montreal • New Delhi
Panama • Paris • São Paulo • Singapore • Sydney • Tokyo • Toronto

1 2 3 4 5 6 7 8 9 0 HAHA 8 9 4 3 2 1 0 9 8 7

ISBN 0-07-079229-1

Library of Congress Cataloging in Publication Data

Gallaudet encyclopedia of deaf people and deafness.

   Includes bibliographies and index.
   1. Deaf—Dictionaries.   2. Deafness—Dictionaries.
I. Van Cleve, John V.   II. Gallaudet College.
HV2365.G35   1987   362.4'2'0321   86-15396
ISBN 0-07-079229-1 (set)

Gallaudet Encyclopedia of DEAF PEOPLE AND DEAFNESS

1

A–G

Associate Editors

Contributors

Contributors are listed in volume 3, beginning on page 355.

McGraw-Hill Staff

Sybil P. Parker, Editor in Chief
Patricia W. Albers, Editorial Administrator

Edward J. Fox, Art Director

Patrick J. Aievoli, Graphic Arts/Production
Supervisor
Diane T. Kraut, Art Production Assistant

Joe Faulk, Editing Manager
Frank Kotowski, Jr., Editing Supervisor

Art supplied by Eric G. Hieber, EH Technical Services, New York City; Howard Friedman, New York City

Composition by Waldman Graphics, Inc., Pennsauken, New Jersey

Printed and bound by Arcata Graphics/ Halliday

Foreword

In 1857 Edward Miner Gallaudet envisioned a new world of opportunity for deaf people. Amos Kendall had invited the young man to become president of the Columbia Institution for the Deaf and Dumb and Blind, an elementary school in Washington, D.C. Gallaudet accepted this offer with the provision that he be permitted to create as well an institution of higher education, a college, for deaf students. He quickly set forth to make Kendall's small school into an institution of national importance and influence. Opening in 1864, the college gradually grew in purpose and stature, firmly establishing a tradition of higher education and academic achievement among deaf people.

Gallaudet College's sponsorship of the *Encyclopedia of Deaf People and Deafness* is in keeping with the tradition Edward Miner Gallaudet established. Like the institution, the Encyclopedia is unique; it is possible only because of the efforts and successes of deaf individuals; it is expected to have broad importance and influence; and its ultimate purpose is to enhance the quality of life of persons with hearing impairments.

The Encyclopedia also symbolizes a broadening of the institution's traditional concerns. It is international in scope and participation, as Gallaudet College has become. The Encyclopedia addresses topics related to individuals of diverse age, varied hearing loss, and heterogeneous cultural characteristics, while the College, too, has become more inclusive in its mission. It is fitting, then, that this work is sponsored by Gallaudet College at a time when the institution is reaching out to new constituencies and strengthening its commitment to research and dissemination activities.

Gallaudet College is proud of the many members of its community, deaf and hearing, its faculty, staff, and alumni, who have contributed to this Encyclopedia. The result of their collective effort is a reference source that can serve to open minds and to enhance the opportunities of all people, whatever their auditory abilities, to achieve a satisfying life.

JERRY C. LEE
President
Gallaudet College

Preface

The *Gallaudet Encyclopedia of Deaf People and Deafness* stands alone in its field. No comparable reference source exists, for this Encyclopedia combines two different categories of analysis and information. These volumes pertain both to an identifiable group of people, those with hearing impairments, and to a physical attribute, deafness. The information herein has been selected from studies in the sciences, the social sciences, and the humanities. Fields as methodologically disparate as otolaryngology and art have contributed, thus creating a comprehensive work useful to generalists and to specialists in many endeavors.

While the approach to entry selection has been inclusive, the actual process of selecting entries varied somewhat among disciplines. In most cases the process began when the associate editor responsible for a particular discipline compiled a preliminary list of topics that was then shared with the editor in chief. Negotiation followed to add entries that seemed relevant or to eliminate any on topics about which too little was known to justify an article; however, topics of particular importance to the deaf community or to the advancement of scholarship were included whenever enough information could be gathered about them to assist further research. Many of the articles about sign languages are examples of this guideline. While most sign languages have not received the close linguistic scrutiny applied to American Sign Language, for instance, entries about them are important for comparative purposes and for illuminating areas where more study would be fruitful.

Biographical entries presented unusual selection challenges. At the outset, general criteria were de-veloped, and an advisory committee made recommendations to the editor in chief. The criteria included an individual's impact on the general society and the person's importance specifically to deaf people. Thus individuals such as the deaf teacher Laurent Clerc, who committed his life to the advancement of deaf people, and the astronomer John Goodricke, who was deaf but left no record of personal or professional links to other deaf people, are both included. Generally, people who met the criterion of impact were excluded if their careers were not finished, if they were hearing, or if their hearing impairment was so slight that it did not interfere significantly with aural-oral communication. Some exceptional individuals, however, such as Regina Olson Hughes and Edward Miner Gallaudet, are the subjects of biographical entries despite their ineligibility according to the stages of their careers, as in Hughes's case, or their auditory condition, as in Gallaudet's case.

The editor in chief functioned without an associate editor for the biographical and historical entries, but in all other instances the ten associate editors had major responsibility for the ultimate shape and content of the entries. Nine associate editors were each responsible for a particular discipline, or group of related disciplines, with a particular relevance to deaf people or deafness. The other associate editor assumed responsibility for all the entries about deafness and deaf people in countries other than the United States. For each associate editor, the responsibilities were to compile the initial topic lists, recommend contributors, and review manuscripts for appropriateness and content accuracy.

In many instances, though, the associate editors did much more than this simple list of duties implies. They sometimes worked under the pressure of other commitments and short deadlines. Often they had to encourage and hurry contributors or ferret out new ones to replace original choices. They handled the queries and complaints of contributors or would-be contributors who were frequently personal acquaintances or professional colleagues. Problems created by contributors, the publishers, or the editor in chief landed in the hands of the associate editors. Yet they did superb work, putting together the best scholarship in their fields and guiding the editor in chief through the complexities and controversies of their respective disciplines.

Studies of deaf people and deafness have been marked by intense controversy since the eighteenth century. While no scholarly work, even the most comprehensive, can resolve all substantive controversies, this one tries to clarify them by presenting the best-substantiated research from diverse disciplines, disciplines that often are in conflict. The editors selected topics to be comprehensive, not to fit a preconceived methodological or ideological viewpoint. The only criteria consistently applied were that the entries must reflect the best research and thinking within their field and that they must treat deaf people respectfully.

To help assure that all aspects of the Encyclopedia respected deaf persons, early in its gestation an advisory board recommended the present title. A previous working title had been the "Encyclopedia of the Deaf and Deafness." Several individuals, deaf and hearing, suggested that the use of "deaf" as a noun was inappropriate and disrespectful, that what the Encyclopedia was about was *people* who were deaf. The logic of this recommendation convinced the editor in chief and the board, and led to the use of "deaf" as an adjective throughout the Encyclopedia. Where "deaf" does occur as a noun, it is in a proper name, such as the National Association of the Deaf.

The use of the terms deaf and deafness in the title may be controversial, but they are appropriate. The Encyclopedia has entries about hearing impairments that could not, by any definition, be termed deafness. It also discusses people who are hard-of-hearing, who have not attended schools with deaf children, who do not have deaf relatives, and who do not know sign language. These people are neither audiologically nor culturally deaf. Still, the preponderance of material within this Encyclopedia is about people with hearing impairments severe enough to prevent purely aural-oral communication. Most individuals who have had this condition since childhood refer to themselves as deaf, not as hearing-impaired. The latter term, they believe, is euphemistic and unnecessary.

Deaf and deafness, then, are terms with social and cultural implications. Their usage herein reflects this Encyclopedia's commitment to the proposition that persons with hearing impairments must be respected for who they are in all their complexity, diversity, and cultural integrity.

JOHN V. VAN CLEVE
Editor in Chief

Acknowledgments

In today's highly specialized world the creation of an important reference work requires collective and, in this case, international effort. During the seven years from this Encyclopedia's gestation to its publication, many individuals and institutions assisted in its development. Their help sustained this work's progress through to fruition.

The idea for this work sprang from the fertile mind of Gallaudet graduate Albert Berke. With Eugene Bergman, he put together the original proposal that gained planning funds from the National Endowment for the Humanities. Berke also convinced the eventual editor in chief of the project's viability and proposed the general form and some of the Encyclopedia's specific topics.

In addition to the Division of Research Programs of the National Endowment for the Humanities, which provided a planning and assessment grant, Armand Hammer and the Bernard Lee Schwartz Foundation both gave financial assistance. The foundation's contribution was especially generous and important. It paid many of the research and editorial expenses of the editor in chief, his staff, and some of the contributors.

When the Encyclopedia was no more than wishful thinking, two sources were especially helpful in defining problems and suggesting ways of meeting them. The editors of the Professional and Reference Division of the McGraw-Hill Book Company explained the details of encyclopedia making from the viewpoint of the publisher. Warren T. Reich of Georgetown University, the editor in chief of the *Encyclopedia of Bioethics*, gave valuable advice from the viewpoint of both academic scholar and editor.

Administrative support for this project was al-

ways forthcoming from Gallaudet College. Edward C. Merrill, Jr., president of the college during the first few years of the Encyclopedia's development, was interested in and enthusiastic about it. Jerry C. Lee, president as the work was finished, was supportive also. John S. Schuchman, provost of the college during most phases of the project, provided both material assistance and wise counsel. The latter was also provided by Jean Shoemaker, formerly dean of the College of Arts and Sciences. Former deans James Madachy and Catherine Ingold allowed the editor in chief sufficiently free rein to accomplish his other activities around the needs of the Encyclopedia project.

Ausma Smits's role in the Encyclopedia's development was pivotal. As a deaf person, fellow historian, and chair of Gallaudet's history department when the Encyclopedia began, she provided advice and encouragement on which the editor in chief quickly came to depend. She enthusiastically allowed released time to work on the Encyclopedia; without that grant of numerous hours the project could not have been undertaken.

Other colleagues at Gallaudet College contributed as well. Francis Higgins, Harold Domich, Jerald Jordan, Leon Auerbach, and Jack Gannon provided historical information about the deaf community. They also recommended contributors, helped select subjects for the biographical entries, and provided congenial criticism on a number of topics. The members of the Gallaudet College history department, Kurt Beermann, Anne Butler, Barry Crouch, Joseph Kinner, Donna Ryan, Ausma Smits, and John Schuchman, all assisted in some way, by contributing entries, offering constructive criticism, and creating a supportive atmosphere in which the editor in chief could function.

Able clerical and research assistance facilitated the editor in chief's task. At various times, Anita Hart and Valerie Dively handled these matters in a competent and thorough manner. The greatest burden was carried by Lynne Payne, the secretary of the history department and, for three years, of the Encyclopedia as well. She handled this extra work with skill and her usual professionalism.

David de Lorenzo, head Gallaudet College archivist, and his staff members Corrine Hilton and Michael Olson provided many services necessary for the Encyclopedia's preparation. They exerted themselves to make Gallaudet's archival collections accessible to people writing for, or in other ways associated with, the Encyclopedia. They helped locate rare sources, and they provided photographs to accompany many of the biographical entries. In a larger sense, their efforts to save the rare books, papers, and artifacts of the deaf community's past make possible all serious studies of this community.

The 364 contributors and ten associate editors are most responsible for the content of the Ency-

clopedia. Their knowledge and willingness to devote themselves to this project despite their heavy commitments, and their agreement to follow the Encyclopedia's demanding guidelines, have assured its quality. Two associate editors, Charlotte Baker-Shenk and Robert Lee Williams, joined the project after it was well under way; consequently the pressure under which they labored was extraordinary and exceeded only by their skill in meeting it.

The National Association of the Deaf, a venerable institution that has strengthened the deaf community for over a hundred years, generously permitted the use of the international symbol of deafness in the design of these volumes. The stylized blocked ear is instantly recognizable and appropriate to identify this unique work.

Special thanks are due to my friends and family and to my students. The latter, through their successes and their failures, showed again and again why this work is necessary. The former provided the emotional support essential to anyone embarking on such a long, difficult, and exhausting project.

JOHN V. VAN CLEVE
Professor and Chair
of the History Department
Gallaudet College

Using the Encyclopedia

The 273 entries in the Encyclopedia are arranged alphabetically in continuous sequence in the three volumes. In turn, many of the entries are divided into sections and subsections about particular aspects of the topic; typographically distinctive headings flag these organizational blocks for the reader. The entry "Sign Languages," for example, has 41 sections, from Facial Expression, Origins, and American Sign Language to Yugoslavian Sign Language, and the entry "Audiometry" has 13 sections covering topics from Principles of Audiometry to Tests of Central Auditory Dysfunction.

When looking for information covering a particular topic, therefore, the reader may choose to turn first into the volume pages for the entry. Biographies of significant individuals, important organizations and periodicals, and national summaries about deafness and deaf people over the globe all appear as entries, alphabetically arranged. If the topic does not comprise an entry, the reader should turn to the Index in volume 3. The Index indicates quickly and easily where information about hundreds of topics can be found in the Encyclopedia.

In addition to the entries and the Index, cross-references and bibliographies that accompany most entries provide leads to other valuable information. The cross-references refer to other entries in the *Gallaudet Encyclopedia of Deaf People and Deafness* that contain related or more detailed information about subjects raised in a particular entry. The reader will benefit by pursuing them. With the exception of a few entries based solely on personal experience or unpublished research, all entries, and sometimes sections, are followed by bibliographic references to assist further research. Whenever possible, the references are to English language publications readily available in larger libraries. Judiciously selected, and sometimes rare, illustrations enhance the text.

A

ACOUSTICS

Acoustics is the science that pertains to the generation, transmission, reception, and control of sound, and sound is a detectable disturbance in an elastic medium. In the following, the sound of interest is that which is audible to a normal human listener and the medium of interest is air. Because speech communication is important for both normal and impaired listeners, the principles of acoustics often will be illustrated with examples that relate to speech production and reception.

BASIC FEATURES OF SOUND

Air consists of particles or molecules that are in a constant state of random motion. The particles have mass and some average distance between them depending on the ambient atmospheric temperature and pressure; the density (mass per unit volume) of the air varies inversely with the average distance between molecules. The air also has elasticity; a volume of air requires force to compress it into a smaller volume, and if the force is removed, the original volume is restored. This elasticity is quite evident if one closes off the hose of a tire pump with the finger of one hand and pushes on the plunger with the other hand.

To illustrate sound propagation, the air particles, each with a particular mass, can be imagined to be separated from each other by the same distance and tethered to each of the immediate neighbors by springs. Now imagine that a large wall with air about it is forced to move first to the right and then back to its rest position. Particles on the immediate right side of the wall first will be forced to the right closer to neighboring particles to compress the springs in the direction of motion and then will bounce back again. Energy given to the medium by the wall propagates to the right successively from one layer of particles through the compressed springs to the next layer. The energy in this compression wave travels uniformly to the right, while the particles simply move short distances first to the right and then back to their rest positions. In like manner, particles on the immediate left of the wall will be pulled to the right and then back again as the wall moves. Springs to the next layer of particles to the left will be extended to pull them to the right. Energy given to the medium by the wall propagates to the left successively from one layer of particles through the extended springs to the next layer. The energy in this rarefaction wave travels uniformly to the left, while the particles simply move short distances first to the right and then back again to their rest positions. If the wall were to move from rest position to the left and then back again, a compression wave of acoustic energy would be transmitted to the left and a rarefaction wave would be transmitted to the right.

In most instances, the moving surface is part of a larger object such as the vocal cords of a person or the diaphragm of a loudspeaker. Then, the acoustic energy propagates radially away from the vocal cords or diaphragm in successive, ever-expanding, spherical wave fronts of compression and rarefaction, while the particles oscillate radially back and forth about their rest positions.

The propagation velocity of sound in air is about 345 meters (1130 feet) per second. The displacement of the particles about their rest positions depends on the intensity of the sound, but by most standards it would be considered small. For example, tones that are just detectable by young adult listeners at frequencies where their hearing is most sensitive cause particle displacements of only about a trillionth of a meter (10^{-12}m). This is significantly less than the diameter of a hydrogen atom. Even for the most intense sounds, those that cause discomfort to the listener, particle displacements at these frequencies are less than the diameter of a human hair.

DESCRIPTORS OF SOUND

In the absence of sound, the temperature, density, and pressure of the air are constant over space and time and represent the ambient or atmospheric conditions. Under the influence of a sound wave, the particles move and the temperature, density, and pressure vary above and below their ambient values. Any of these features could be used to describe the sound wave. However, the one that is most easily measured is the incremental change in pressure. This sound pressure, therefore, is the feature that is most often used in describing sound.

Pressure has dimensions of force per unit area. In the MKS (meter, kilogram, second) system of units pressure values are specified in pascals (Pa) or newtons per square meter (N/m^2; 1 Pa = 1 N/m^2). The pressure of the atmosphere at sea level is about 100,000 or 10^5 Pa. The pressures of the most intense sounds of interests, those that cause

obvious discomfort, are about 10 Pa, and the faintest sounds that are just detectable by a young adult have pressures in the order of 0.00001 or 10^{-5} Pa.

FREQUENCY, WAVELENGTH, AND SPECTRA

A signal that is often used to test the response of many types of acoustic systems is a sine wave or pure tone. It is the kind of wave that is produced, for example, by an audiometer to test hearing sensitivity. Like all progressive acoustic waves, its basic shape is the same when viewed at some point in space as a function of time or at some instant of time as a function of space or distance from the source. In the illustration, notice that the wave is periodic; it oscillates above and below the horizontal axis and completes one oscillation after each T seconds. The period of this wave is T seconds per cycle, and its frequency (f) or rate of oscillation is $f = 1/T$ cycles per second. The unit "cycle per second" is called the hertz and abbreviated Hz. For example, a pure tone with frequency $f = 500$ Hz has period $T = 1/500$ or 0.002 s.

When viewed as a function of space, one cycle is completed in a distance of λ meters. The wavelength (λ) has dimensions of meters (per cycle). Thus, if the wave travels at a velocity of c meters per second, the wavelength and frequency are related by

$$\lambda = c/f$$

Recall that in air sound propagates at $c = 345$ m/s (1131 ft/s). Thus, the wavelength of sound in air at $f = 500$ Hz is $\lambda = 345/500 = 0.69$ m (2.26 ft).

Like the pure tone, the complex tone is periodic. However, the complex tone consists of a series of discrete frequencies. Because of the manner in which complex tones typically are generated, these frequencies usually are integral multiples of the lowest or fundamental frequency. The higher frequencies are called harmonics. Complex tones are produced by many musical instruments and by sirens and whistles. Usually, power in the fundamental frequency of a complex tone is large compared to power in the harmonics. The voiced sounds of sustained vowels in speech also are complex tones, but the ratio of fundamental to harmonic powers is much lower. The display of the magnitude of the energy or power in a wave as a function of frequency is called the spectrum of the wave.

Some continuing sounds have no repetitive character or periodicity; the power in these sounds is distributed continuously over a band of frequencies rather than being concentrated in a discrete set. These are called random signals because information about the waveform of their past does not enable precise prediction of the waveform in the future. Examples are the sounds of a waterfall,

Wave fronts of acoustic energy showing spatial variations in sound pressure above and below atmospheric pressure.

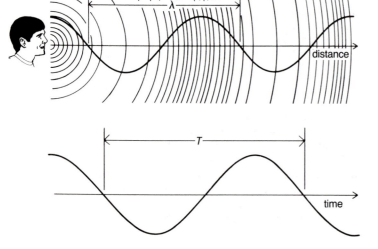

highway traffic, and the unvoiced sounds of "s" and "sh" in speech.

THE DECIBEL

The values of the most intense sound pressures relevant to human audition are more than 1 million times those that are just detectable, that is, from 10^{-5} Pa to 10^1 Pa. Manipulation of such a large range of numbers is cumbersome. To reduce this problem and to simplify some aspects of acoustical analysis, values of sound pressures or, more precisely, values of sound pressure ratios are transformed through the logarithm into a much smaller range of values. The transformed values have units of decibels (dB). Specifically, a sound pressure (p) in pascals is transformed into a sound pressure level (L_p) in decibels by the equation

$$L_p = 20 \log_{10} (p/p_r)$$

where p_r is the reference sound pressure and equal to 20 micropascals (20 μPa), and $\log_{10}$ is the logarithm to the base 10 of the number within the parentheses, (p/p_r). The reference pressure (p_r) is at the very low end of the range of audible sound pressures. Thus, the ratio (p/p_r) will be greater than unity for most sound pressures of interest, and corresponding sound pressure levels in decibels will be positive (greater than zero). The million-to-one range of pressure ratios from hearing threshold to discomfort is transformed into a range of just 120 decibels. Some common benchmarks of sound pressure levels are 120 dB: auditory discomfort, jet takeoff at 60 m; 90 dB: diesel locomotive at 15 m; 60 dB: conversational voice level at 1 m; 30 dB: quiet conference room (ambient sound level); and 0 dB: threshold of hearing (1000 to 6000 Hz).

In addition to drastically reducing the range of numbers used to specify sound pressures, use of the decibel has several other advantages. First, it simplifies some of the routine calculations of acoustics such as those that predict changes in sound levels with distance from a source and with transmission through acoustical materials and acoustical systems. For example, the acoustical gain (amplification) in decibels or loss (attenuation) in a system is simply added to the input sound pressure level to determine the output sound pressure level. Thus, if the speech input level is 65 dB to a hearing aid with 35 dB acoustic gain, then the output sound level will be 65 + 35 or 100 dB. Likewise, if the sound reduction through the wall between two rooms is 40 dB and the sound pressure level in the source room is 90 dB, then the sound pressure level in the receiving room is 90 − 40 or 50 dB. Second, people perceive the loudness of sound almost as though they had a logarithmic (pressure-to-decibel) converter built into their sensory system. Thus, changes in perceived loudness are highly correlated with changes in sound pressure level in decibels; to be specific, loudness approximately doubles with each 10 dB increase in sound pressure level.

A concept that is difficult, both to understand and to use, concerns the addition and subtraction of sound levels from independent sources. If source 1 operating alone produces at some location L_1 decibels sound pressure level and an independent source 2 operating alone produces L_2 decibels sound pressure level at the same location, then the total sound pressure level L_T is

$$L_T = 10 \log [10 \lambda (L_1/10) + 10 \lambda (L_2/10)]$$

where 10 λ is the antilogarithm to the base 10 of the number in brackets or, equivalently, 10 raised to the number in brackets. Likewise, if the two sources operating together produce sound level L_T and source 2 is turned off, then the sound level of source 1 is given by

$$L_1 = 10 \log [10 \lambda L_T/10] - 10 \lambda (L_2/10)]$$

The extension of these equations to accommodate more than two sources is straightforward, and the calculations can be easily handled with an electronic calculator.

From the above discussion, it can be shown that if sources 1 and 2 produce the same sound pressure level (say 70 dB) when operating alone, the sound level with both operating will be 3 dB greater (73 dB) than the level of either. This would be perceived as a noticeable change in loudness, but it would not be dramatic. Now suppose that when operating alone the level of source 1 (say 70 dB) is 10 dB greater than the level of source 2 (60 dB). Then the sound level with both operating together will be 70.4 dB or only 0.4 dB greater than the level of the larger. In this case, the loudness of both will be imperceptibly (about 3 percent) greater than the loudness of the larger (1) but more than double the loudness of the smaller (2).

SOUND MEASUREMENT

The sound level meter is used to measure sound pressure level. This instrument has a microphone to transform the acoustic wave into a corresponding electric wave, an amplifier to increase the signal amplitude, weighting networks or filters to selectively weight or emphasize some frequency regions more than others, and a display or meter system that indicates the value of the sound level at the microphone input.

Sound level meters are classified according to the kinds of measurements that can be made and the expected accuracy of these measurements. For example, some instruments have for display a simple electromechanical meter with a needle that deflects according to an average signal level; others have thermometer displays using columns of lights;

and still others have digital displays in which the actual numeric value of the sound level is shown. Most instruments have slow and fast modes that enable the user to select a relatively long (1.0 s) or short (0.125 s) averaging time. In some of the newer instruments the averaging and measurement functions are accomplished using digital electronic microprocessors. Then the averaging times can be made very long, and the averaging process is very precise. Such instruments are called integrating sound level meters.

The accuracy of a sound level meter is indicated by a type number. The Type 0 or Laboratory instrument is the most accurate, the Type 1 or Precision instrument is less accurate, and the Type 2 or General-Purpose instrument is least accurate.

Three electronic weighting networks or filters often are provided in sound level meters. They are designated A, B, and C and are distinguished principally by the degree to which they exclude low-frequency sounds. These networks have transmission characteristics that simulate equal-loudness curves of low-, moderate-, and high-level tones, respectively, and were developed so that the indicated response of the meter would emulate the subjective response of a listener to the loudness of the sound being measured. The A-weighting network is used, almost to the exclusion of the others, whenever a measurement of sound is required that is highly correlated either with subjective judgments such as loudness, noisiness, or annoyance, or with the risk of hearing damage. A-weighted sound levels have units of decibels, just as do other measures of sound level.

Speech spectra of groups of 10 men, 10 women, and 7 children measured at 1 m (3.3 ft) in the free field. Speech of individual talkers was mixed electronically and then analyzed in third-octave bands. Average overall sound pressure levels per talker were 57.2 dB for the men, 61.5 dB for the women, and 60.0 dB for the children.

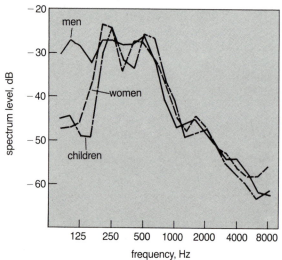

A common way of describing a sound is by its spectrum. The spectrum of a sound must be known whenever engineering measures are used to control it, because the materials and devices used to control sound typically are frequency dependent and because human perception of sound also is frequency dependent. Spectrum measurement is done with a spectrum analyzer. Usually, the spectrum is specified by the sound pressure levels in a set of contiguous frequency bands. These bands are defined by their center frequencies and by their bandwidths in fractions of an octave. The most common bandwidths are full (1/1) and third (1/3) octaves. Band center frequencies are specified at frequencies that are separated by full or third octaves above and below the index frequency of 1000 Hz. Portable hand-held instruments usually are capable of measuring the sound level in only one band at a time. In larger, more complex, more costly instruments, the band levels simultaneously are measured and graphically displayed with selectable integration times from very short, where the spectrum appears to change simultaneously with the acoustic event, to very long.

SOUND POWER

While sound pressure is useful in defining the sound field about a source in a particular location, the source itself usually is better described by its radiated sound power (W) in watts and its sound power level (L_w) in decibels. A source that radiates W watts of acoustic power has sound power level L_w in decibels given by

$$L_w = 10 \log (W/W_r)$$

where the reference power W_r is 10^{-12} watt. The sound power radiated by a source often is relatively independent of the acoustical environment about it. In contrast, the sound pressure about the source can vary drastically with the acoustical environment.

SOUND RADIATION

In the study of sound radiation, it is convenient first to consider radiation from a simple or point source and then to show how radiation from more complex sources can be predicted by the additive radiation from a suitably chosen array of simple sources. A simple source is spheric in shape with a surface that oscillates uniformly like a pulsating balloon and with a radius that is very small compared to the wavelength of sound being radiated. Radiation from a simple source is uniform in all directions. It is described as nondirectional or omnidirectional. Its directivity pattern, the polar graph of sound pressure level as a function of angle about the source, is circular. The directivity factor (Q) of a source is the ratio of sound intensity radiated in a particular direction relative to the intensity averaged over all directions. The directivity factor for a simple source is constant and equals one for all directions.

Sound power from a simple source radiates outward in spherical waves. As a wave spreads, the area of the spherical wavefront increases, the sound power is distributed over a larger area, and the sound pressure, which relates to the power per unit area, decreases. This is expressed approximately by

$$L_p = L_w - 20 \log r - 11$$

where L_p is the sound pressure level in decibels at a distance of r meters from the source, and L_w is the sound power level of the source. For the simple source in a free sound field, one in which there are no reflecting objects, the sound pressure level decreases by 6 dB for each doubling of distance r to the source. For an actual source in a free field where the distance to the source is large compared both to the dimensions of the source and to a wavelength of the radiated sound, the sound pressure level also decreases by 6 dB per doubling of distance. When this is true, the actual source appears like a simple source, and the observer is said to be in the far field of the source.

DIRECTIONAL SOUND SOURCES

Most actual sources of sound have relatively large radiating surfaces that vibrate often in very complex ways. As one segment of the surface moves outward, another may move inward, and still another may not move at all. Thus, the actual source can be imagined to be composed of a large number of simple sources or surface segments whose sound radiations add together in a constructive way in some directions and in a destructive or canceling way in others. Sound radiation from such a source will be more intense in some directions than in others; then the source is described as directional. Its directivity pattern is not circular, as with the spherical or simple source, but rather will have lobes in those directions in which radiation is particularly strong, and the lobes will be separated by troughs in directions where the radiation is relatively weak. Typically, at low frequencies where the wavelength of sound is long compared to the dimensions of a source, radiation is relatively uniform in all directions. As frequency increases, the source becomes more directional and a lobe usually forms in the direction of the principal axis when such an axis can be identified. For direct-radiator loudspeakers, the principal axis is the axis of symmetry of the driver cone, and for the human talker, it is a line through the center of the mouth directed radially outward from the head in the horizontal plane. As frequency increases so that the source

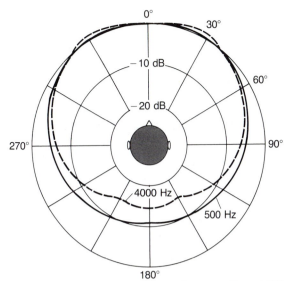

Directivity patterns for an average human talker at 500 and 4000 Hz. Curves represent third-octave band data averaged over a group of three men and three women.

dimensions are comparable or large when compared to a wavelength, the directivity along the principal axis usually increases and both the number and sharpness of the side lobes increase.

DIRECTIONAL SOUND DETECTORS

Detectors of sound such as microphones and human ears generally are directional, that is, they are more sensitive to sounds coming from some directions than from others. The generalizations about directivity that were advanced for sound sources apply as well to sound detectors. Typically, detectors are nondirectional at low frequencies where the wavelength is long compared to the receiver dimensions; and typically, the directivity increases with increasing frequency. However, comparison of the directivity patterns for nondirectional and directional hearing aids shows that the directional aid is noticeably atypical; it is quite directional at low frequencies and quite nondirectional at high frequencies. This response is by deliberate design; high-frequency directivity is already built into the human head and external ear, and greater directivity is provided by the hearing aid only where it is needed at middle and lower frequencies.

ACOUSTICAL PROPERTIES OF MATERIALS

Whenever sound waves impinge on a panel of solid or fibrous material, part of the acoustic intensity in the incident wave is reflected into the space containing the source, part is absorbed or transformed into heat within the panel, and the remaining portion is transmitted into the space beyond. The intensities of sound reflected, absorbed, and transmitted relative to the incident intensity are specified

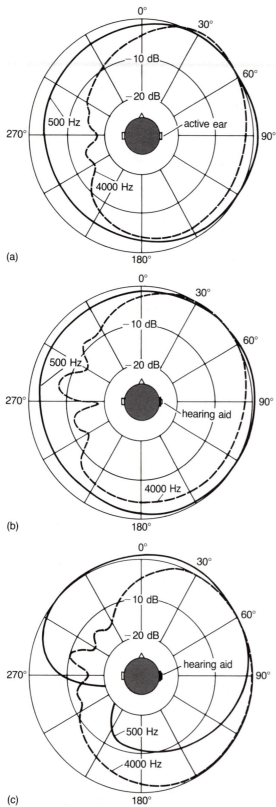

Directional responses of an acoustic research manikin to third-octave noise bands. (a) Unaided. (b) With nondirectional behind-the-ear hearing aid. (c) With directional behind-the-ear hearing aid.

for any material respectively by its reflection, absorption, and transmission coefficients. Because the intensities of sound reflected, absorbed, or transmitted must be greater than zero and less than the incident intensity, the values of the respective coefficients must lie between 0 and 1. The values of all coefficients typically are dependent on the composition of the material, on its thickness, and on the frequency and angle of incidence of the sound. Also, because the sum of reflected, absorbed, and transmitted intensities must equal the incident intensity, the sum of the reflection, absorption, and transmission coefficients must equal one. Therefore, a knowledge of any two coefficients enables calculation of the third. Typically, the absorption coefficient and the transmission loss, a quantity directly related to the transmission coefficient, are used to describe the acoustical properties of materials used in buildings.

Porous Materials Sound absorption is a dominant characteristic of porous materials. These include fibrous materials and open-cell foams in which the pores are open and interconnected. Sound absorption, characterized by the transformation of acoustic energy into heat, is achieved through viscous friction between the mobile air molecules that move at relatively high velocity near the center of the pores and the constrained low-velocity molecules near the boundaries. Porous materials with relatively high sound absorption include heavy carpeting, heavy draperies, and wall and ceiling panels made of mineral and glass fibers. Open-cell foam plastics often are used to absorb sound, for example, in enclosures for mechanical equipment and in rooms, when a durable nonfibrous material is required.

Both the absorption and the transmission coefficients of porous materials are relatively high. Thus, they usually perform well when used as sound absorbents but are not suitable as a sole means of sound isolation.

Typically, porous materials have low absorption at low frequencies and relatively high absorption at high frequencies. The absorption at low frequencies generally increases with the thickness of the material or with the depth of air space between the material and nonporous structural surface behind it. Absorption coefficients usually are measured in a way that averages over all possible angles of incidence. The noise reduction coefficient (NRC), defined as the average absorption coefficient over the octave frequencies from 250 to 2000 Hz, allows comparison of the absorption of materials within a particular class. Approximate NRC ratings of some common finish materials are carpeting, 0.2; draperies, 0.3; mineral fiber ceiling panels, 0.6; and glass fiber wall panels, 0.7.

Usually the range of NRC ratings of materials

within a particular class is broad. For example, NRC ratings for carpeting vary from about 0.1 to 0.5, depending on the density, height, and type of the pile and on the pad and the coating that backs the carpet.

The total absorption provided by a patch of material with area S and absorption coefficient α is $S\alpha$ absorption units. A room with n distinct patches of absorbents with areas $(S_1, S_2, \ldots S_n)$ and respective absorption coefficients $(\alpha_1, \alpha_2, \ldots \alpha_n)$ will have total room absorption R given by

$$R = S_1\alpha_1, + S_2\alpha_2, + \ldots + S_n\alpha_n$$

Nonporous Materials Sound isolation between spaces usually is achieved with nonporous (solid) materials such as wood, glass, steel, gypsum board, concrete, and lead. When sound waves strike a nonporous panel, it is set into motion. Typically, a large portion of the incident sound intensity is reflected into the source room with only small amounts being either absorbed in the panel or transmitted beyond into the receiving room. Thus, nonporous materials generally are poor absorbers of sound but provide good isolation between enclosed spaces.

The ability of a panel to isolate is specified by its transmission loss (TL). Transmission loss usually is measured at third-octave frequencies between 125 and 4000 Hz in a way that averages overall angles of incidence. The units of transmission loss are decibels, and TL is expressed in terms of the transmission coefficient (τ) by

$$TL = 20 \log (1/\tau)$$

Typically, the transmission loss of a solid panel is low at low frequencies and high at high frequencies, and the curve of TL as a function of frequency usually has one or more sharp dips at frequencies where the tranmission loss is particularly low. One such dip, called the coincidence dip, occurs at the frequency where the velocity of the shear wave that travels along the panel coincides with the velocity of the airborne sound wave along the panel. Other dips occur at resonant frequencies of the panel.

The sound isolation of a panel often is specified by its STC (sound transmission class) rating. This single-number rating results from a weighted average of transmission loss values at third-octave frequencies from 125 to 4000 Hz. The weighting is applied to account for the decreased sensitivity of the normal human listener at frequencies below about 1000 Hz. Approximate STC ratings of some common materials are ⅛-in. glass, 20; residential interior drywall partition, 35; 4-in. reinforced concrete slab, 45; and 12-in. brick wall, 55.

SOUND IN ROOMS

When the source and receiver of sound are enclosed in a room, the total sound at the receiver is the instantaneous sum of the direct sound plus the reflected or reverberant sound. The direct sound is the same as would exist in a free sound field; its intensity varies directly with the acoustic power and directivity factor (Q) of the source and inversely with the square of distance (D) between source and receiver. The reverberant sound intensity varies directly with the sound power of the source and inversely with total acoustic absorption (R) in the room. Close to the source, the direct sound dominates. With sufficient level, the sound is perceived as clear and distinct, and speech intelligibility would be expected to be high. Far away, where reverberant sound dominates, the sound will be less precise with less definition, and speech intelligibility likely will be lower. The distance from

Direct and reverberant (reflected) sound in a room; the source is a talker and the receiver is a listener.

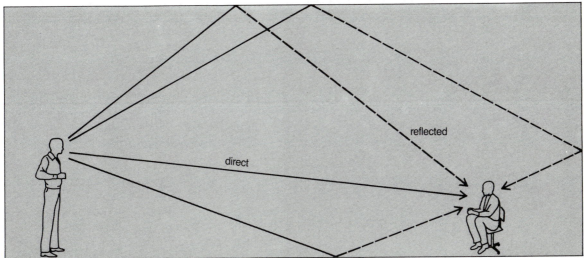

the source to a point where the direct and reverberant sound levels are equal is called the critical distance. This distance increases with room absorption (R) and source directivity (Q).

ACOUSTICAL STRATEGIES FOR GOOD LISTENING

The primary goal in the acoustical design of rooms for speech is to achieve high speech intelligibility by providing adequately low noise levels and adequately low reverberation. The criteria for adequacy are stricter for hearing-impaired listeners than for normal listeners but the strategies for acoustical design are the same.

Low noise levels in rooms are achieved by providing sufficient sound isolation in the walls, floor, and ceiling and by assuring that noises generated within the room are insignificant. Greater sound isolation results with the use of heavy nonporous construction panels; this isolation is further improved if two mechanically independent panels are used and if these are separated by an air space filled with a porous acoustical absorbent. A common construction technique that simulates this strategy is to apply drywall (gypsum wall board) to both sides of resilient steel studs and to fill the stud cavities with glass fiber batts. Many other constructions are used; differences among them relate principally to the surface density (mass per unit area) of the nonporous panels and to the degree to which mechanical independence of the panels is achieved. Greater independence, and therefore greater sound isolation, results with larger distances between the panels and with the use of separate studs for each panel system.

Low reverberation in a room is achieved by ap-

plying absorbent materials, with sufficient area and absorption coefficient, to the walls, floor, and ceiling. For example, classrooms for deaf students often have carpeting on the floor, absorbent acoustic panels at the ceiling, and fabric-covered glass fiber panels on at least one of each pair of parallel opposing walls.

Speech communication in a room can be optimized by adopting strategies that give maximum speech level to the listener while minimizing noise and reverberation. For example, talker and listener should face each other for maximum directional gain. They should be as close as possible for maximum speech level and maximum ratio of direct-to-reverberant sound, and they should locate themselves as far as possible from noise sources for minimum noise level. In addition, an acoustically reflective wall often can be used behind the talker to enhance sound projection, and absorbent panels can be used behind the listeners to reduce reverberation and to avoid the production of echoes.

Bibliography

Beranek, L. L.: *Acoustics*, McGraw-Hill, New York, 1954.

Bess, F. H., B. A. Freeman, and J. S. Sinclair (eds.): *Amplification in Education*, Chap. 10, A. G. Bell Association for the Deaf, Washington, D.C., 1981.

Durrant, J. D., and J. H. Lovrinic: *Bases of Hearing Science*, Chaps. 1, 2, and 3, Williams and Wilkins Company, Baltimore, 1977.

Knudsen, V. O., and C. M. Harris: *Acoustical Designing in Architecture*, Acoustical Society of America, New York, 1980.

Peterson, A. P. G., and E. E. Gross: *Handbook of Noise Measurement*, 8th ed., General Radio Company, Concord, Massachusetts.

Arthur F. Niemoeller

ALCOHOLISM AND DRUG ABUSE

Alcoholism and drug abuse is a serious problem in the United States. Individuals, families, and social life are affected when persons become dependent upon chemicals to alter their emotional moods. While treatment programs are available to teach people to live free from drug and alcohol dependency, minority group clients are often at a disadvantage in these programs that are generally designed for middle-class Americans. People with disabilities who are abusing chemical substances face special difficulties when they seek help. They encounter many programs that are inaccessible due to attitudinal and architectural barriers. New, specially designed advocacy programs for deaf substance abusers have proven to be successful wherever they are established. Since advocacy programs are few, it is vital that deaf people and their families know the underlying dynamics of substance abuse and how to use existing treatment and pre-

Direct and reverberant sound pressure levels (SPL) in a room. The two are equal at the critical distance D_0. L_w is the source sound power level in decibels for 10^{-12} watt; Q is the directivity factor of the source; R is the room constant in square meters, a measure of acoustic absorption in the room; and D is distance to the source in meters.

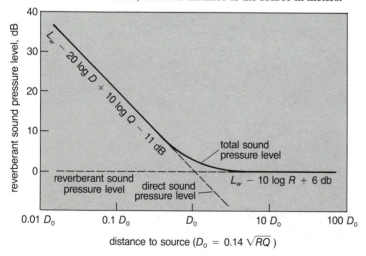

vention services to meet their unique needs. Otherwise, alcohol and drug abuse can become another disability to be faced by the deaf person.

GENERAL CHARACTERISTICS OF ABUSE

Alcoholism is a dependency on the anesthetic aspect of alcohol to reduce awareness of one's difficulties. This evolving process produces serious physical, social, and economic malfunctioning in the drinker's life. These problems are manifested in different ways. Of all adults who drink, approximately 1 drinker in 10 is likely to be a problem drinker. The National Institute of Alcohol Abuse and Alcoholism estimates that 19 percent of adolescents (14 to 17 years of age) are also problem drinkers. The economic cost of alcohol abuse in the United States is over $42 billion a year.

There are also many social implications of alcohol abuse: between 35 and 64 percent of drivers in fatal accidents have been drinking prior to the accident; between 45 and 60 percent of all fatal crashes with a young driver are alcohol-related; between 50 and 68 percent of drowning victims have been drinking; between 25 and 37 percent of successful suicides involve alcohol; a divorce rate of 40 percent occurs among families experiencing alcohol problems; almost 26 percent of adult fire deaths involve alcohol; almost 45 percent of deaths from falls involve alcohol; estimates suggest that alcohol may play a role in as many as 33 percent of all reported cases of child abuse; and finally, it is estimated that between 3000 and 6000 births in 1980 evidenced the full fetal alcohol syndrome, which is characterized by mental retardation, slow growth rate, small head, distinctive facial features, and heart and genital organ defects.

Alcohol is the most common drug choice of Americans. Professionals working with deaf persons estimate that alcohol abuse and substance abuse is similar to the patterns of hearing people. The complications and pathologies of alcohol abuse are also comparable.

More is known about drug abuse among hearing people than is known about drug abuse among deaf people. In general, drug abuse is the compulsive, uncontrolled, and continued use of a drug in spite of adverse consequences. Many drugs are in use today, such as narcotics, barbiturates, and other hypnotic-sedative drugs, tranquilizers, antihistamines, and phencyclidine (PCP). When used simultaneously with alcohol, these drugs can grossly exaggerate the usual responses expected from alcohol or from the drug alone.

Contrary to popular beliefs, prescription drugs are more frequently abused than street drugs such as heroin, lysergic acid (LSD), or cocaine. In 1975 a White House Drug Abuse Task Force reported that 7 to 8 million Americans were abusing amphetamines, barbiturates, and tranquilizers. Consequences of drug abuse may be addiction, withdrawal, involving paranoia, painful muscle contractions, blackouts, convulsions, memory and concentration difficulties, and contemplation of suicide. Since deaf persons often face inadequate communication with medical personnel, it is absolutely necessary that deaf patients understand the correct usage of prescribed drugs in order to avoid disastrous effects.

The mixing of alcohol and drugs is common today. Experts have agreed that alcoholism in combination with tranquilizer dependency is a major public health problem. Such cross-addictions are referred to as substance abuse or chemical dependency.

With only a few studies completed on substance abuse problems among deaf people, conclusions are necessarily tentative. In general, deaf people follow the same drinking patterns as most Americans. Their one significant departure is the use of the deaf club by members of the deaf community as a social gathering place. As with other Americans, 1 out of 10 deaf drinkers will seriously abuse alcohol. However, deaf substance abusers are less apt to come from the deaf community where sanctions are imposed by a concerned membership. Deaf alcoholics known to treatment programs generally come from the deaf population with few or no ties to the churches, organizations, and clubs of the deaf community. These substance abusers are marginal to both the hearing and deaf communities. Their inability to find acceptance in either community leaves them with a sense of alienation and despair. They use alcohol and drugs to reduce awareness of their difficulties, rather than take more constructive actions to solve these problems. *See* DEAF POPULATION: Deaf Community.

Substance abuse has been reported to be present with deaf high school youngsters to the same degree found among their hearing peers. The manner of alcohol usage, type, and extent of consequences are similar between both groups. Deaf students prefer beer or wine, occasionally becoming intoxicated, with a minority arrested for traffic violations. All these drinking deaf students also experience such adverse effects from excessive drinking as extreme sleepiness, difficulty in controlling impulses, and prolonged nervousness.

BARRIERS TO TREATMENT

Great advances in the treatment of alcoholics have been made since the 1930s. The development of the self-help philosophy of Alcoholics Anonymous expanded the resources of fellow alcoholics. A variety of professional organizations emerged to consolidate the work of helping alcoholics recover from their chemical dependencies. Governmental involvement in financing and planning services for substance abusers provided needed programming for special populations such as inner-city blacks, women, youth, and neglected ethnic groups. Alcoholism and drug addiction prevention programs that focus on school-age children have increased dramatically since the mid-1970s.

A number of methods have been found to be successful in treating substance abusers: (1) a treatment of substance abuse that is well organized and logically implemented; (2) the existence of inpatient medical care and relevant nonmedical rehabilitation; (3) a well-planned postdischarge follow-up; (4) the direct involvement of significant people in the counseling of the substance abuser; (5) a persistent outreach to bring substance abusers into treatment through community contacts and to effect transition back into community resources; (6) in the case of alcoholics, the adjunctive use of Antabuse drugs for aversion therapy; (7) the use of behaviorally oriented interventions along with verbal therapies.

These seven methods of treatment, along with the self-help organizations of Alcoholics Anonymous, have improved the recovery rates for members of the general population. However, substance abusers from minority groups have not fared as well. Although the percentage of drinkers increases with higher social status, the actual rates of pathological drinking are highest among those citizens who are of lower socioeconomic status. Consequently, untreated alcoholism seriously jeopardizes many minority group members in attempts at full integration and upward movement in the mainstream of American society economically, educationally, and socially. The latest challenge facing the field of substance abuse is how to make methods of treatment more responsive to the minority of citizens who are physically disabled.

Utilizing existing programs proves to be especially difficult for deaf alcoholics. One major barrier to treatment exists within the deaf community itself. Many deaf people living in large cities may associate with each other through their own churches, clubs, friendship circles, and various organizations. Through these personal social interactions, deaf people share a common identity and destiny. Hence, they fear being labeled by the actions of a few deviant members. Many deaf persons have suffered the stigma of "deaf and dumb" and now fear the added label of "deaf and drunk." For reasons of self-protection, the deaf community is reluctant to admit that any deaf persons have an alcoholism problem. Referrals from the deaf community to alcoholism agencies are rare.

In addition, since alcoholism is defined by many deaf persons as a sin, deaf alcoholics are unwilling to admit to themselves or to others that they need outside help for a drinking problem. Self-referrals to treatment are lower among deaf people than with the general population. A very efficient and devastating deaf gossip network further inhibits any public admissions of pathological drinking. With little support from the deaf community for the treatment of deaf alcoholics, the prognosis for professionally attended problem drinkers is very poor.

Another important barrier to treatment exists within the alcoholism agencies. These programs have been designed for verbal, hearing clients. Alcoholism counselors do not understand the psychosocial aspects of deafness, nor do they have manual communication skills. Agency budgets do not include funds for interpreters. Neither do substance-abuse counselors have a regular working relationship with rehabilitation workers who provide specialized services for deaf persons. The deaf alcoholic, with a double disability, is misunderstood and ignored by both the rehabilitation and alcoholism experts. The professional specialist on deafness is untrained to deal with alcoholism. Similarly, the alcoholism specialist cannot deal with the communication problems encountered with deaf clients. Encountering such confusion and ambivalence, deaf alcoholics learn to avoid agencies, which only increase the individual's frustration in being different.

As a consequence, although the probability of becoming an alcoholic among deaf persons approximates the rate for the general population, it is rare to find deaf persons in alcoholism treatment programs. As a result of the attitude barriers that keep the deaf alcoholic hidden within the deaf community or protected in parental homes, and the barriers of professional indifference that exclude him or her from agency treatment, it is difficult to estimate the real numbers of deaf alcoholics needing service in any geographical area. When a conscious effort is made to seek them out by tracing clues of concerned friends and coworkers, the numbers of deaf persons needing help for their drinking problems begin to accumulate and reveal a compounded tragedy of neglect and hopelessness.

PROGRAMS

The first real attempt to overcome barriers in finding and treating deaf alcoholics occurred during the mid-1970s. The initial program that specialized with deaf alcoholics was the Alcoholic Treatment Unit of St. Mary's Extended Care Center in St. Paul, Minnesota, begun in 1973. The San Francisco Bay Area's Alcohol Project for the Deaf began in 1974 with volunteers and was funded in 1976 by the San Francisco Foundation. The pioneering Workshop on Alcoholism and the Hearing Impaired was held in Cleveland, Ohio, attracting participants from five states and Canada in 1975. During this period, St. Paul–Ramsey Hospital and Medical Center of St. Paul, Minnesota, developed inpatient treatment for deaf alcoholics. The Cleveland Foundation funded a 2½-year outreach advocacy project, Addiction Intervention with the Deaf (AID), in 1978. About the same time, a group counseling program for deaf alcoholics was started in Flint, Michigan.

These pioneer programs developed in isolation from each other. Their founders met for the first time at a joint meeting during the 1978 national conference of the American Deafness and Rehabilitation Association in San Antonio, Texas. From these original leaders, a larger group emerged later in the same year to form the Task Force on Drugs and the Disabled at the National Drug Conference in Seattle, Washington. AID went on to produce national conferences on deaf alcoholics at Kent State University in 1979 and in Cleveland, Ohio, in 1980. The quarterly *AID Bulletin* was started in 1979 to provide updated information to a national membership about research, service, and advocacy for multidisabled alcoholics. *See* AMERICAN DEAFNESS AND REHABILITATION ASSOCIATION.

By 1985 there were programs for deaf alcoholics in California, Illinois, New York, Ohio, Maryland, Minnesota, and Massachusetts. Success with deaf alcoholics has encouraged the development of programs for other disabled people throughout the country. All these efforts are worthwhile and demonstrate progress, but they are only a beginning. Much more needs to be done before disabled people receive equal treatment for their substance abuse problems.

TRENDS AND IMPLICATIONS

The early programs for deaf alcoholics established a general model of intervention that became a trend. The essential core of these efforts is an outreach advocacy program staffed by paid specialists who are knowledgeable about substance abuse and the psychosocial communication problems presented by deaf persons. These advocates help to bridge the gap between rehabilitation and substance abuse services through substance abuse awareness presentations to deaf groups and inservice technical assistance to agencies serving deaf clients. Although separate programs for deaf alcoholics are desirable, the more cost-effective strategy of mainstreaming with the use of interpreters is acceptable when monitored by the advocacy team. With such modifications of treatment services, deaf alcoholics recover at the same rate as hearing coclients in the same programs.

A strong continuous effort will be required to maintain progress in successfully treating deaf persons who are abusing alcohol and drugs. A number of lessons have already been learned; future programming can build upon conclusions drawn from earlier programs. There is general agreement on the following points:

1. The rate of alcoholism among deaf drinkers is at least as high as it is for hearing drinkers.

2. Drinking problems are more severe among deaf persons who do not benefit from the meaningful, integrative experiences of organized deaf community life.

3. Without special services aimed at the unique communication needs of deaf people, deaf alcoholics will go on being undiscovered, uncounted, and untreated.

4. A dependency on the anesthetic aspect of alcoholism is a late indicator that the deaf person's attempt at self-therapy is not working in an adaptable manner.

5. Prevention education for deaf people on alcohol and drug abuse as part of good mental health must be improved considerably in public schools, adult education classes, and deaf community awareness sessions.

6. Without recovery from alcoholism, deaf alcoholics will continue to encounter progressive losses in their health, family, employment, and social relationships.

7. Any psychiatric examination of mental disorders in deaf clients should include an alcoholism and drug abuse assessment by trained substance-abuse specialists who are familiar with the psychosocial aspects of deafness.

8. With appropriate safeguards to assure that the deaf client is not ignored because of her or his communication disability, mainstreaming deaf alcoholics can be successful and cost-effective.

9. In mainstream programs, deaf clients may require one-to-one discussions of the treatment materials with a deafness specialist immediately after the therapeutic group sessions.

10. Outreach in places where deaf persons regularly go is mandatory for the discovery of bypassed deaf problem drinkers and bringing them into treatment.

11. Until alcoholism programs are completely accessible to deaf people (socially, psychologically, and communicatively), deaf alcoholics will require an advocate to help them obtain responsive services.

12. Program personnel who treat deaf substance abusers must adapt to the disability of deafness. Special communication skills are required to treat deaf clients. The use of manual or oral interpreters can be effectively used by therapists and group facilitators in most circumstances. Visual aids have to be developed for some deaf clients whose ability to use language is limited.

13. An active, continuous education program for deaf community leaders and agency personnel on early signs of substance abuse will generate more referrals of clients in the beginning stages of their illness.

14. There currently is no evidence that integrated programs that mainstream deaf alcoholics with interpreters are superior to separate programs for deaf clients only. The major reason for integrated programs has been the cost.

15. Any impetus for making substance abuse agencies more responsive to deaf persons should come from the educators of deaf students, personnel in deaf residential schools, Bureau of Vocational Rehabilitation counselors, parents, and leaders of deaf organizations. Specialists in the deafness field must be knowledgeable about early signs of substance abuse and the workings of treatment services.

16. Given the present difficulties in obtaining adequate treatment from traditional substance abuse agencies, the major advocacy effort must come from those persons knowledgeable about the situations faced by deaf clients.

Bibliography

Armour, D. J., et al.: *Trends in U.S. Adult Drinking Practices*, Rand Corp., Santa Monica, 1977.

Boros, A.: "Alcoholism Intervention for the Deaf (AID)," *Alcohol Health and Research World*, vol. 5, no. 2, Winter 1980/81.

Isaacs, M., G. Buckley, and A. Berman: "Patterns of Drinking Among the Deaf," *American Journal of Alcohol Abuse*, vol. 6, no. 4, 1979.

Locke, R., and S. Johnson: "A Descriptive Study of Drug Use Among the Hearing Impaired in a Senior High School for the Hearing Impaired," in E. H. J. Steed (ed.), *Drug Dependence and Alcoholism*, vol. II, Plenum, New York, 1981.

Mendelson, J. H., and N. K. Mello (eds.): *The Diagnosis and Treatment of Alcoholism*, McGraw-Hill, New York, 1979.

National Clearinghouse for Alcohol Information: "Fact Sheet: Selected Statistics on Alcohol and Alcoholism," National Institute on Alcohol Abuse and Alcoholism, Rockville, Maryland, 1981.

Woodward, J.: *Signs of Drug Use*, T. J. Publishers, Silver Spring, Maryland, 1980.

Alexander Boros

ALEXANDER GRAHAM BELL ASSOCIATION FOR THE DEAF

The American Association to Promote the Teaching of Speech to the Deaf was founded in 1890 at the Convention of American Instructors of the Deaf held in New York. The association changed its name in 1948 to the Volta Speech Association for the Deaf, and then in 1953 to the Alexander Graham Bell Association for the Deaf. *See* CONVENTION OF AMERICAN INSTRUCTORS OF THE DEAF.

Since its inception, the association has had one primary purpose: to promote the use of speech, speechreading, and residual hearing by hearing-impaired persons.

The majority of the 62 first members of the association were articulation teachers. Many of them had met in 1874 at the first convention of speech teachers ever held in America. These teachers used the method of visible speech, developed by Alexander Graham Bell's father, Alexander Melville Bell, with their deaf pupils. Visible speech consisted of written symbols which presented the anatomical formation of individual speech sounds. *See* VISIBLE SPEECH.

Rather than have this new association consist wholly of professional persons, membership from the beginning was extended to the general public and included "all who were interested in oral instruction, including the parents and friends of deaf pupils who have been taught to speak." Since 1890, the association has developed into an international organization with 4500 individual members in 38 countries, and affiliate members totaling some 4500 more persons in parent groups across the United States. Its annual budget of unrestricted and restricted revenue was close to $1 million in 1983. Revenue is acquired through dues, publications, and donations. No federal money supports its activities.

Membership in "A. G. Bell" consists of four major categories: professionals, parents of hearing-impaired children, oral deaf adults, and anyone who supports the teaching of speech to deaf persons.

INTERNATIONAL PARENTS' ORGANIZATION

To accommodate the interests and needs of the diverse membership, three sections have been developed. In 1958 the International Parents' Organization (IPO) section was formed. While the objects of this section are the same as those for the association as a whole, there is special emphasis on aiding families of hearing-impaired children, with particular interest in fostering oral/aural education for these children. Any A. G. Bell member may join the IPO by notifying the IPO Executive Committee. Affiliate groups may join through application to IPO.

Activities of the IPO include publication of *Our Kids Magazine*, which is an A. G. Bell membership benefit, family workshops, a parent-to-parent network throughout Canada and the United States, and financial support of a scholarship for a child of an IPO parent.

ORAL DEAF ADULTS SECTION

In 1964 the Oral Deaf Adults Section (ODAS) was formed. This section as "a voluntary nonprofit service organization is to encourage, help, and inspire all concerned with hearing impairment so that hearing impaired children and adults may improve their educational, vocational, and social opportunities in the hearing environment through cultivation of their speech, speechreading, and residual hearing." Membership in this section is through application to the ODAS.

Activities of the ODAS include publication of a newsletter to its members and an ODAS membership directory, family outings designed to assist parents of hearing-impaired children, and scholarship support.

INTERNATIONAL ORGANIZATION FOR THE EDUCATION OF THE HEARING IMPAIRED

The International Organization for the Education of the Hearing Impaired (IOEHI) is the most recently formed branch of the association, and was established in 1967. Its purpose is to promote excellence in the education of hearing-impaired children and adults. It is dedicated to "(1) the teaching of oral communication and the development of quality oral programs, (2) the encouragement of scientific study of the educational and verbal communicative processing, (3) the exchange of information among educators through publications, dissemination of research findings, professional meetings and seminars." Membership to this section is through application to the IOEHI.

In 1982 the association's board of directors, consisting of 18 voting members, approved the formation of chapters. A major purpose of these chapters is to assist members with updated information about the communities. Michigan, Alabama, Virginia, and Pennsylvania have developed state chapters.

Since its beginning, the association has reflected the influence of its leadership. Alexander Graham Bell was its founder and first president. Names such as Mrs. Calvin Coolidge, Gilbert Grosvenor, Helen Keller, Mrs. Spencer Tracy, and Caroline Yale have been closely linked with the association's message. *See* BELL, ALEXANDER GRAHAM; KELLER, HELEN.

VOLTA BUREAU

In 1909 a significant advancement to the future of the association occurred when the Volta Bureau was presented to the association. The Volta Bureau was founded and endowed by Bell in 1887 for the "increase and diffusion of knowledge relating to the deaf." The building housing the bureau was built in 1893 and was part of the gift to the association. The directors of the association were "left free to expand the work the Bureau had been doing in whatever way changing conditions might make desirable."

The Volta Bureau, funded by the money of the

Volta Bureau, headquarters of the Alexander Graham Bell Association for the Deaf, Washington, D.C. (Alexander Graham Bell Association for the Deaf)

Volta Prize which was conferred on Bell by the Republic of France for his invention of the telephone, included a reference library containing literature on deafness. Much of this archival collection remains housed at the Volta Bureau.

ACTIVITIES

Over the years, the association expanded its efforts beyond speech for the deaf and "through its active agent, the Volta Bureau and its official organ, the *Volta Review* encouraged the conservation of hearing, the elimination of causes that lead to deafness, the study of the art of lip-reading by the hard-of-hearing child and adult, and the correction of defects in speech in children and adults."

Current activities emphasize subjects concerning hearing impairments with concentration on profound hearing losses (90 dB and above in the better ear). A major program is financial support to oral profoundly hearing-impaired children, youth, and young adults for schooling with hearing peers. Information services for members are available through children's rights coordinators in each state and province; regional workshops are provided on such subjects as amplification, use of the telephone, and note taking. Oral interpreters have been professionally prepared to assist the oral deaf adolescent and adult in large gatherings or in environments not conducive to the use of residual hearing. A biennial convention brings members together for information, encouragement, and social activities. *See* INTERPRETING.

A publications department of the association presents texts for teachers of hearing-impaired students, parents, and deaf adults. Subjects include the use of speechreading, teaching of speech to deaf children, curriculum for science and reading, and mainstreaming hearing-impaired students.

Hearing Alert! is a public education program to encourage early identification of hearing loss and to promote prompt remedial actions. Brochures and guidelines are available in English and Spanish.

The *Volta Review*, published six times a year plus one monograph, has been the professional journal of the association since 1899, when it was known as the *Association Review. Newsounds* is the newsletter published 10 times a year. All individual members receive the periodicals plus the two issues per year of the *Our Kids Magazine.* Other publications are sold to members and nonmembers primarily through catalogs. *See* VOLTA REVIEW.

For nearly a century, the Alexander Graham Bell Association for the Deaf has focused on the promotion of oral/aural education. Today, it provides educational research, guidelines, and encouragement for a unique "family" composed of educators, parents, and oral deaf adults. Working together, these groups strive to provide the best possible opportunities for deaf individuals to realize their maximum potential as fully participating members in the hearing world.

Bibliography

Breunig, H. Latham: *Bell Revisited*, Clarke School for the Deaf, Northampton, Massachusetts, 1977.

Bruce, Robert V.: *Bell: Alexander Graham Bell and the Conquest of Solitude*, Little Brown, Boston, 1973.

Conlon, Sara: "Shattering Silence the Alexander Graham Bell Way," *The Quotarian*, pp. 2–3, November 1982.

Miller, Lawrence W.: "Pioneer in Children's Rights," *Bell Telephone Magazine*, 57(4):44–45, 1978.

Sara E. Conlon

AMBROSI, GUSTINUS
(1893–1975)

Gustinus Ambrosi was born on February 24, 1893, in Eisenstadt, Austria. Working primarily in bronze and marble, he created sculptures in the classical tradition. Europe's political, cultural, and financial giants flocked to Ambrosi, because he was also a master of the portrait bust. As sculptor, poet, graphic artist, and philosopher, Ambrosi symbolized to

Gustinus Ambrosi. (Gallaudet College Archives)

many the Renaissance man who had surmounted his fate.

An accomplished pianist and violinist by the age of six, August Arthur Matthias Josef Ambrosi dreamed of becoming a musician. Shortly before his seventh birthday, he was stricken with meningitis. He lived but was left deaf.

As a student at the Prager Privat-Taubstummenanstalt, the eight-year-old Ambrosi began to model and to study woodcarving. In 1907 he became an apprentice at the firm of the sculptor Jakob Kozourek in Prague. After the death of his father, Ambrosi moved with his mother to Graz. While employed with the firm of Suppan, Haushofer and Nikisch, Ambrosi was working on a building when a coworker plunged to his death. Overwhelmed by the accident, the 16-year-old Ambrosi created the sculpture *Mann mit dem gebrochenen Genick* (Man with the Broken Neck), which won him great critical acclaim.

In 1912 Ambrosi received both the National Prize for Sculpture and the Felix von Weingartner Medallion. The following year, Emperor Franz Joseph awarded him the use of an atelier for the rest of his life. At that time Ambrosi decided to give his future noncommissioned works to the Austrian people so that all could enjoy his art.

An extremely prolific sculptor, Ambrosi created approximately 3000 works. His masterpieces, some of monumental proportions, often embody classical and biblical themes and heroes, such as his *Kain* (Cain) and *Promethidenlos* (The Lot of Prometheus). He was ever conscious of humankind's struggle wtih fate. In *Der Mensch und das Schicksal* (Man and Fate) gargantuan hands envelop a small writhing human figure. The hand of God in his 9-foot-high (2.7-meter) sculpture *Erschaffung Adams* (The Creation of Adam) is as much a heavy fist weighing upon the first man as it is a life-giving force. In another sculpture, it is not Icarus soaring but rather the plummeting figure that Ambrosi molded.

The naturalistic portrait busts show Ambrosi's attention to fine anatomical detailing. He created uncommonly lively, highly individualistic and sensitive portraits of Richard Wagner, Friedrich Nietzsche, Georges Clemenceau, August Strindberg, Stefan Zweig, Rainer Maria Rilke, Benito Mussolini, and Popes Pius XI, Pius XII, and John XXIII, to name only a few of his subjects.

Ambrosi was recognized by governments and his fellow artists. His many awards included Knight of the French Legion of Honor, the Commander's Cross of the Italian Crown, the Vatican's Golden Medal of Honor, Corresponding Membership in the National Sculpture Society in New York, and numerous honors in his native Austria. Ambrosi was, however, controversial among critics because he championed what some perceived as a bygone style. He declared that he would be ashamed to produce some of the art now considered modern, and charged that the Futurists, Cubists, and Surrealists were not real artists because they were incapable of creating portraits.

Throughout his life, Ambrosi wrote many poems. Five collections of his sonnets have been published (in German only): *Sonette an Gott* (Sonnets for God; 1923), *Sonette vom Grabe einer Liebe* (Sonnets from Love's Grave; 1926), *Einer Toten* (To One Who Has Died; 1937), *Sonette an Beethoven* (Sonnets for Beethoven; 1948), and *Das Buch der Einschau* (Introspections; 1959). However, the majority of his poems, short stories, drafts of novels, and tragedies remain unpublished in the Ambrosi family library in Vienna. Parts of his diaries have been included in exhibition catalogs; they set forth Ambrosi's philosophical principles and optimistic world view. The Gustinus Ambrosi Museum in Vienna houses the majority of the sculptor's work. Many pieces are also in private collections throughout the world.

Ambrosi was not preoccupied with his deafness. The child prodigy, who smashed his beloved violin when he realized he was deaf, later said that deaf-

Detail of *Der Engel und die Seele* (The Angel and the Soul), Ambrosi's sculpture for the Wiedner family grave monument. (Gallaudet College Archives)

ness was a blessing—the sense of hearing for the language of nature. He considered his deafness a source of creativity. Ambrosi did not know sign language. Although he could lipread to some extent, as he became older he insisted upon communicating by means of written notes in an effort to preserve his eyes for his work. *See* Sign languages; Speechreading.

As advancing age weakened him, it became increasingly difficult for Ambrosi to handle his heavy materials. He committed suicide on July 1, 1975, in Vienna.

Bibliography

Catalog of the Gustinus Ambrosi Museum, Vienna.

"Mitteilungen der Gustinus Ambrosi Gesellschaft," Gustinus Ambrosi Gesellschaft, Vienna.

Parkes, K.: "Gustinus Ambrosi: Sculptor and Poet," *Apollo*, vol. 2, 1927.

Vance, Yandray Wilson: "Gustinus Ambrosi, Sculptor in Vienna," *The American Era* (school paper of the American School for the Deaf, West Hartford, Connecticut), vol. 31, no. 5, February 1945.

———: "Triumphant Soul of Austria," *The American Era*, vol. 35, no. 3, December 1948.

Evelyn McClave

AMERICAN ANNALS OF THE DEAF

The *American Annals of the Deaf* is the oldest surviving professional educational journal in the United States. Except for the years 1861 to 1867, when the

Civil War interrupted, the *Annals* has been published every year since its founding in 1847. It was published originally by the faculty of the American School for the Deaf in Hartford, Connecticut, because no other journal published in English was concerned with the education of deaf children. The faculty's ambitions for the journal were very broad: its first editorial noted, "In short, we mean that our *American Annals* shall constitute, when completed, a perfect treasury of information upon all questions and subjects related, either immediately or remotely, to the deaf and dumb." *See* AMERICAN SCHOOL FOR THE DEAF.

SPONSORS

The lofty ambitions for the journal did not last beyond three years and two volumes. In 1850 the journal passed from the aegis of the American School for the Deaf to the Convention of American Instructors of the Deaf (CAID), which carried the burden of its publication from 1850 to 1895. The Conference of Executives of American Schools for the Deaf (formerly the Conference of Superintendents and Principals of American Schools for the Deaf and now the Conference of Educational Administrators Serving the Deaf, or CEASD) joined the Convention of American Instructors in 1895. In 1917, the latter decided that it could no longer afford its contribution to the costs of publishing the *Annals*. The Conference of Educational Administrators then assumed responsibility for its publication until 1940, when the Convention of American Instructors again resumed its contributions to the journal's subsidy. Since 1940 the *Annals* has been the official organ of the Convention of American Instructors and the Conference of Educational Administrators—the two major organizations involved in the education of this country's deaf children. In 1961 an agreement between the organizations made them joint owners of the *Annals*. They have since administered it through a committee composed of four members from each organization. *See* CONFERENCE OF EDUCATIONAL ADMINISTRATORS SERVING THE DEAF; CONVENTION OF AMERICAN INSTRUCTORS OF THE DEAF.

FEATURES

Through the various sponsorship and financial arrangements, the *Annals* has essentially retained its initial purpose of broadly publishing material of interest to those concerned with the education of deaf people. Its articles have included historical sketches, techniques of instruction, and accounts of political factors affecting the education of deaf people. Readers of the *Annals* look to it for statistics on deafness, research reports on the psychology and sociology of deafness, philosophical treatises, and reports of conferences of importance to those professionally involved with deafness.

The *Annals* features "Comments, Questions, and Answers," a section containing quotations from other sources, queries from readers, which are answered by the editor, and occasional editorial expressions. Reviews of tests and books of interest in the deafness field are a regular part of the publication. The *Annals* also has a section "Teacher to Teacher," in which new techniques and materials, submitted by the readers or from the editor's own knowledge, are presented.

Since 1967 the *Annals* has devoted one issue to the *Directory of Services for the Deaf*. Statistical reports on services for deaf people first appeared in 1858. The material was greatly expanded over the years until an entire issue was devoted to summaries of information about deafness. The January issue contained the statistical summaries until 1967 when they were moved to the May issue, because it required a full year to process the data and ready it for the printer. The annual directory issue now appears in April. The directory issue details information about each school and program for deaf children in the United States, including the address and telephone number of each, the number of teachers, the size of the enrollment, distribution of students by ages, numbers graduating, and counts of those having multiple handicaps. Other sections of the April issue have listings of postsecondary facilities for deaf students, university programs training personnel in deafness, programs for deaf-blind students, federal and state rehabilitation programs, religious programs, homes and housing for deaf persons, athletic programs, summer camps, national organizations of deaf people, national professional organizations and centers of information about deafness, selected government-sponsored research programs, and doctoral programs on deafness. The directory also contains a roster of Convention of American Instructors of the Deaf membership and the professional committees of the journal's sponsoring organizations. Each year the directory issue also features review articles devoted to summaries of research and statistics on major topics of interest to professional educators, such as recent legislation, multiply handicapped students, and academic integration. Among educators, the directory issue of the *Annals* is considered an invaluable tool. In 1969, in recognition of the importance of the directory, a separate editorship was established: William Craig, superintendent of the Western Pennsylvania School for the Deaf in Pittsburgh, became the editor of the directory. In 1974 his wife, Helen Craig, also on the staff of the Western Pennsylvania School for the Deaf, joined him as a coeditor.

EDITORS

The first editor of the *Annals* was Lucerne Rae, a member of the faculty of the American School for the Deaf. When the Convention of American Instructors became the publisher of the *Annals*, Rae continued as editor. He was succeeded in 1855 by Samuel Porter, the initiator of the *Annals's* statistical reports on the education of deaf persons. After six years Lewellyn Pratt replaced Porter. A professor at the National Deaf Mute College (later called Gallaudet College), Pratt served only from 1868 to 1870.

For the next 50 years, from 1871 to 1920, Edward Allen Fay was the editor of the *Annals*. Like his predecessor, he was a professor at the National Deaf Mute College, and toward the end of his career he became vice-president of the college. Fay held the *Annals* to high standards of literacy. He was himself a master of the English language and a scholar in foreign languages and in deafness. Not afraid of controversy, Fay made the *Annals* a lively publication, though his 50-year tenure speaks for the evenhanded way in which he managed those controversial articles that appeared in the journal. He frequently published views that were contrary to his own. His leadership brought great respect to the *Annals* from authorities within and outside the field of the education of deaf students. *See* FAY, EDWARD ALLEN.

Another vice-president of Gallaudet College, Irving S. Fusfeld, succeeded Fay as editor of the *Annals*. Fusfeld held a doctorate in psychology, so the increase in the articles reporting on the results of psychological testing of deaf students is not surprising. Responsibility for that publishing trend also reflected a trend in the field of education, especially in special education. When Fusfeld resigned in 1943, he was replaced for two years by Ignatius Bjorlee, superintendent of the Maryland School for the Deaf. In 1945 Leonard Elstad assumed the editorship of the *Annals* and the presidency of Gallaudet College. He passed on the editorship in 1948 to Powrie Vaux Doctor, who had become an assistant editor in 1940.

In 1969 Doctor was replaced by McCay Vernon. Vernon introduced the "Comments" and "Teacher to Teacher" sections of the *Annals* and continued the efforts to extend the positive influence of the journal. He was particularly sensitive to the political-cultural nuances in the education of deaf children.

The *Annals* was originally a quarterly publication. From 1895 to 1900 it was issued bimonthly. From 1900 on, however, it has appeared in January, March, May, September, and November. The sixth issue is the directory issue, which appears in April.

SIGNIFICANCE

The *Annals* has tripled in circulation during the twentieth century, a period in which the numbers of teachers of deaf children about doubled. For years the schools that belonged to the Conference of Educational Administrators Serving the Deaf were charged for the number of subscriptions that reflected the size of their teaching staffs. That arrangement changed in 1969, after which time all members of the Convention of American Instructors have received a subscription to the *Annals* in return for a portion of their dues payments. When Fay resigned the editorship in 1920, the *Annals* had 1100 subscribers; for its 1985 fiscal year, the *Annals* reported that it printed 4400 copies for distribution to its 3615 subscribers. The circulation figures do not, however, reflect the importance that the journal has in the education of deaf students. Its long publication record makes its collective issues an authoritative record of the education of deaf children in the United States. Moreover, for those who hold professional concerns with deafness, reflection of current practices in the field make the *Annals* one of the few indispensable publications.

Jerome D. Schein

AMERICAN ATHLETIC ASSOCIATION OF THE DEAF

The American Athletic Association of the Deaf (AAAD) has helped athletics become a unifying force for the progress of deaf individuals in the United States. It was founded to provide a means whereby the athletically inclined graduates of schools for deaf people could continue competition at a level consistent with their skills, and to encourage camaraderie among the many deaf clubs in the nation. The traveling done by the deaf teams (and their adherents) from one locality to another has carried ideas from club to club; thus, the AAAD can be viewed as an inspiration to all deaf organizations, for it is the one with the greatest number of participants on all levels.

HISTORY

In the early years of the twentieth century, many deaf leaders talked about a national basketball tournament for teams representing deaf clubs. The idea did not progress, however, until Art Kruger, a Pennsylvania native working in Akron, Ohio, during World War II, determined to attempt such a tournament. Given free rein to carry out his ideas and having the complete backing of the Akron Club of the Deaf, Kruger, who had previous experience in arranging tournaments for adult deaf persons in New York City, set about preparing for a tournament truly national in scope. Wartime restrictions made travel difficult, but in 1945 arrangements were made for top teams from Buffalo, New York; Philadelphia, Pennsylvania; Kansas City, Missouri; and Los Angeles, California, to come to Akron to compete along with the host team for the title of National Champion of the Deaf.

More significant than the outcome of that first tournament was the meeting that took place the day before. On April 13, 1945, approximately 30 representatives of various deaf clubs met at the Akron Club of the Deaf and voted to form a national organization with the hope of making the basketball tournament an annual affair. The name selected for the fledgling organization was the American Athletic Union of the Deaf (AAUD). Kruger was chosen as first president. Stated objectives were to foster and regulate uniform rules of athletic competition among member clubs; to provide adequate competition for those members primarily interested in interclub athletics; to provide a social outlet for deaf members and their friends; to provide a means of creating better relationships among member clubs; and to establish a regulated means of determining athletic championships among member clubs. The first bona fide national basketball tournament was held the next day in Goodyear Gymnasium. It was a tremendous success, with an attendance of some 2000 fans. Buffalo won the first tournament, defeating Akron in the finals, 53–51.

Kruger moved to Los Angeles following the end of World War II, but by means of correspondence kept things moving in the AAUD. By the time of the second tournament in Chicago, he had arranged for the establishment of regional organizations and tournaments. More than 40 years later, although membership has increased from 58 to over 150 clubs, the essential structure and modus operandi remain unchanged.

By 1947, at the request of the Amateur Athletic Union of the United States, the American Athletic Union of the Deaf changed its name to American Athletic Association of the Deaf in order to avoid confusion between the initials of the two organizations—AAU and AAUD.

The AAAD was the first national group among deaf persons to eliminate and prohibit discrimination because of a person's race or creed. At one time there were small pockets of resistance to nondiscrimination in a few regional areas, but all regional tournaments and the national tournament now are fully integrated.

In 1948 the *AAAD Bulletin* got under way, with Kruger as the first editor. It is published four times a year. In 1948 the AAAD became affiliated with the Comité International des Sports des Sourds (CISS), which recognized it as the only national athletic association of deaf individuals to coordinate the participation of American deaf athletes in international competition. The influence of the CISS enabled the AAAD to stage three successful World Games for the Deaf; the summer games in Washington, D.C., in 1965, the winter games in Lake Placid, New York, in 1975, and the summer games

in Los Angeles, California, in 1985. *See* COMITÉ INTERNATIONAL DES SPORTS DES SOURDS.

Another milestone was reached in 1952 with the establishment of the AAAD Hall of Fame. Since 1955 the AAAD has also selected an "Athlete of the Year."

ACTIVITIES

Each year the basketball tournament is held in a different city and seldom in the same region. Sites of the more than 40 consecutive tournaments have ranged from coast to coast and border to border. Sites are not limited to larger clubs; some of the most successful and financially profitable tournaments have been staged by clubs with a very small membership. These five-day annual affairs are a blend of sports, business meetings, and social gatherings, and are arranged and conducted by deaf people themselves. All bona fide deaf clubs in the United States are managed without interference or assistance from persons with normal hearing. Deaf Americans are proud of and grateful for this independence of action; the national tournaments have become a highlight of deaf social activity, and attendance has been so consistently large that they are rarely a financial failure.

Currently, the AAAD serves as parent organization of eight regional athletic associations promulgated by the AAAD. The regional associations conduct their own year-end tournaments for their member clubs in basketball, softball, and volleyball. In turn, the AAAD sponsors a national tournament for the regional winners. The first National Softball Tournament was held in Detroit, Michigan, in 1967, and Westchester, New York, was the first national champion.

The AAAD also is affiliated with the United States Olympic Committee (USOC), as a member of the USOC/Handicap in Sports Committee, and the Amateur Softball Association. The AAAD has more than 150 affiliated clubs; there are also four national athletic organizations (skiing, ice hockey, tennis, and volleyball) affiliated with the AAAD. The United States World Games for the Deaf Committee is a committee of the AAAD; it has the responsibility of selecting deaf athletes to represent the United States in the CISS-sponsored World Summer and Winter Games for the Deaf.

The elected officers of the AAAD are president, vice president, secretary-treasurer, publicity director, softball commissioner, and chairperson of the USA World Games for the Deaf Committee. All of the officers are elected every year, except the AAAD/WGD committee chairperson who is elected every four years. The AAAD is a nonprofit organization made up of volunteer officers, and money raised to send American athletes to participate in the World Games for the Deaf is collected on a voluntary basis. Unlike its hearing counterpart, the USA World Games for the Deaf trials in different sports are always held one year before the Games themselves to allow sufficient time for individual fund raising.

Many star players have contributed to the excitement of the annual tournament games and international competitions. Similarly, there have been many men and women whose dedication and sacrifices have helped to build the AAAD into the strongest and the largest national deaf sports organization in the world. Deaf Americans take pride in and are grateful for the accomplishments of all these people.

Art Kruger

AMERICAN COALITION OF CITIZENS WITH DISABILITIES

The American Coalition of Citizens with Disabilities, Inc. (ACCD), is a national nonprofit organization of organizations composed of national, state, and local member groups. Members include the major disability rights organizations and many professional associations. The coalition is governed by a Delegate Council Assembly made up of delegates representing each voting member organization. The assembly meets yearly and sets policies, goals, and directions. It also elects a 14-member board of directors which establishes policy and governs the coalition's operation between meetings of the Delegate Council Assembly.

The coalition is the only national membership organization of and for all disabled people with so broad a mandate to be directed by disabled people themselves. It strives to enhance the human and civil rights of disabled people through promotion of consumer and professional involvement in decision making on national, state, and local levels; research and training; and information and referral programs. Its goals are to: (1) promote the involvement of disabled people in policy making at all levels: local, state, and national; (2) represent disabled people and advocate for their human and civil rights; (3) provide information and referral services relating to disability; (4) establish a viable and effective linkage and networking system of disabled people throughout the nation; and (5) provide leadership for the disability rights movement.

The coalition publishes a quarterly newsletter, the ACCD *NewsNet*, which provides updates and information on current disability-related issues and events and is disseminated to its members. It also publishes and sells several books that focus on disability and related issues.

The Rehabilitation Act was vetoed twice in the early 1970s by President Richard Nixon. These ve-

toes spurred disabled people into taking control of their own lives. It shocked them into uniting and taking action to get the Rehabilitation Act of 1973 passed; many went on to establish the American Coalition of Citizens with Disabilities. *See* REHABILITATION ACT OF 1973.

HISTORY

The coalition was founded in 1974 by 150 leaders of major disability groups during the annual meeting of the President's Committee on Employment of the Handicapped. These leaders recognized the need for a strong, free-standing umbrella organization capable of speaking for all of the nation's 36 million citizens with diasabilities to project a unified voice before the media, the federal administration, Congress, and the public at large. The intent was to create a powerful and representative force for the involvement of citizens with disabilities in public policy making through the concept of cross-disability communication and cooperation. The coalition now comprises more than 170 organizations, representing a total membership base of over 8 million.

In 1974 a steering committee was formed to provide leadership during the developmental stages of the coalition. This steering committee was led by Albert Pimentel, with members including Frederick Schreiber, Eunice Fiorito, Frederick Fay, Judy Heumann, Louis Rigdon, and Roger Peterson. Fiorito was the coalition's first president from 1975 until 1978, followed by Terrence J. O'Rourke from 1978 to 1982, and Phyllis Rubenfeld for the first of two elected terms beginning in 1982. *See* SCHREIBER, FREDERICK CARL.

In 1974 and 1975 work was done only with volunteers. In 1976 the coalition hired its first full-time executive director, Frank G. Bowe, and received its first research grant to develop and test a model for cross-disability communication and cooperation from the Rehabilitation Services Administration. Reese Robrahn followed as executive director from 1981 until 1983. *See* REHABILITATION.

In 1976 the coalition placed several volunteers who researched disability issues on President Jimmy Carter's transition team. This was the first time that disabled people had been brought in to help plan a transition from one federal administration to the next.

During 1977 the coalition played a leading role in getting the Secretary of the U.S. Department of Health, Education and Welfare (HEW) to sign regulations implementing Section 504 of the Rehabilitation Act of 1973. Acting as a focal point for communication between disabled people and officials from HEW, the coalition kept both disabled people and officials informed regarding critical issues. It also coordinated successful nationwide sit-ins and demonstrations demanding the regulations be promulgated.

In 1979 the organization successfully coordinated nationwide activities for a National Solidarity Day, and on October 20th events took place throughout the country to bring attention to the need of disabled people for full enforcement of civil rights legislation.

TRAINING

The coalition has been instrumental in the training and development of persons with disabilities as advocates in their own communities. An example was the coalition's Section 504 Citizen Training and Technical Assistance Project, conducted from 1979 to 1981, to train disabled citizens about their rights and responsibilities under Section 504 of the Rehabilitation Act. Many of these conferences have provided the link between disabled consumers; professionals in the disability field; and national, state, and local administrators. The coalition has provided technical assistance and training in the areas of disability rights, coalition building, career and vocational education, sensitivity training, and resource development. In presidential election year 1984, the coalition developed and compiled *A Basic Guide to Voter Registration/Education in the Disability Community* in response to often-asked questions about disabled people's voter registration and voting.

ACCOMPLISHMENTS

The coalition's interest and achievements have included: (1) implementation of Public Law 94-142, the Education for All Handicapped Children Act of 1975; (2) training disabled citizens and their representatives about rights and services; (3) enforcement of Title V of the 1973 Rehabilitation Act, including Section 504; (4) organizing and building coalitions among disability groups at the state level; (5) consumer involvement of disabled people in government, business, education, and the media; and (6) provision of technical assistance to industry on outreach and recruitment of disabled job seekers.

The coalition recognizes distinguished individuals and organizations that have made a contribution to the disability rights movement through annual awards. Those that have been honored in the past include Senator Lowell P. Weicker; Frederick Schreiber; Justin Dart, Jr.; Paralyzed Veterans of America; and the American Association for the Advancement of Science Project on the Handicapped in Science.

In 1984 the coalition elected representatives to the North American Regional Assembly of the Disabled Peoples' International (DPI), an international organization that brings together representatives from all over the world to work toward equal opportunity for disabled people.

MEMBERSHIP

The coalition has three types of membership. Active members are nonprofit consumer organizations with governing bodies made up of a majority of people with disabilities. National consumer organizations have 10 votes at the Delegate Assembly, state coalitions have three votes, state organizations have one vote, and local groups have one vote. Associate members are organizations that do not meet the qualifications for active membership but wish to support the work of the coalition. Associate members can take part in the work, but are not entitled to vote at the Delegate Assembly. Individual members are persons, disabled or nondisabled, who wish to support the coalition's work. Fifty individuals from any one state may caucus at the Delegate Assembly to cast one vote.

Bibliography

Bowe, F.: *Handicapping America: Barriers to Disabled People*, Harper and Row, New York, 1978.

Bowe, F., J. E. Jacobi, and L. D. Wiseman: *Coalition Building*, American Coalition of Citizens with Disabilities, Inc., Washington, D.C., 1978.

Bowe, F., and J. Williams: *Planning Effective Advocacy Programs*, American Coalition of Citizens with Disabilities, Inc., Washington, D.C., 1979.

Phyllis Rubenfeld

AMERICAN DEAFNESS AND REHABILITATION ASSOCIATION

The American Deafness and Rehabilitation Association (ADARA) began its organizational existence as the Professional Rehabilitation Workers with the Adult Deaf (PRWAD). It was founded at a national meeting entitled "The Vocational Rehabilitation of Deaf People: A Workshop on Rehabilitation Casework Standards for the Deaf," in St. Louis, Missouri, in May 1966. The participants agreed that in order to develop and maintain standards a professional organization that stood outside the rehabilitation system would be essential. It was for that purpose that they joined to form the Professional Rehabilitation Workers with the Adult Deaf.

The timing of the conference and its sponsorship are key factors in understanding how the organization came into being. The conference was sponsored by the Rehabilitation Services Administration (RSA), which played a major role in starting and maintaining the organization, and which has also been a component of the Social and Rehabilitation Service. The birth year of the Professional Rehabilitation Workers with the Adult Deaf is significant because that year also saw the founding of the Registry of Interpreters for the Deaf (later the National Registry of Interpreters for the Deaf) and the establishment of the first Rehabilitation Research and Training Center on Deafness, at New York University. *See* REGISTRY OF INTERPRETERS FOR THE DEAF; REHABILITATION: Administration.

All three enjoyed the support of the Rehabilitation Services Administration, then headed by Mary E. Switzer. As a federal administrator, Switzer saw the need for these organizations and provided the impetus and the funding that led to their creation. She had aided in the establishment of the National Rehabilitation Association and the merger that led to the American Speech and Hearing Association (ASHA). Switzer realized the latent political potential in the disabled population, a potential that could not be effective until it was brought together in a cohesive body. That reasoning led her to assist, through federal grants, efforts to organize the disabled population and those who served them. Thus, she furthered professionalization in rehabilitation in general, and deafness rehabilitation in particular. *See* AMERICAN SPEECH-LANGUAGE-HEARING ASSOCIATION.

No organization existing at that time made any specific provisions for professionals serving adult deaf persons. The Convention of American Instructors of the Deaf confined its interests to teaching and to the teachers of deaf students; the National Rehabilitation Association (NRA) had no section for those who worked with deaf clients, and offered no particular attraction to those whose duties solely encompassed deafness; the American Speech and Hearing Association, bent on bolstering the professional qualifications of audiologists and speech pathologists, did not welcome members from deafness rehabilitation. The emergence of the Professional Rehabilitation Workers with the Adult Deaf made available to rehabilitation counselors, psychologists, social workers, and other professionals whose clientele were largely or entirely made up of deaf persons, the benefits of association with colleagues who shared their interests and concerns. *See* CONVENTION OF AMERICAN INSTRUCTORS OF THE DEAF.

For several years, various proposals had been made to change the name of the organization. Some objected to "professionals" being such a prominent part of the organization's title; others disliked the term "workers," feeling that it carried servile connotations that were not in keeping with the desire for more professional status. The most telling argument seemed to be that professionals in disciplines other than rehabilitation counseling actually outnumbered the rehabilitators. After much deliberation, the 1978 convention chose the name American Deafness and Rehabilitation Association, with the pronounceable acronym ADARA. This name placed "deafness" ahead of "rehabilitation," thus indicating the numerical degree of representation among the membership, while retaining the focus on rehabilitation in the title as well as in the activities of the association.

PURPOSES

The bylaws of ADARA state six purposes for the association. Over the years, these basic objectives have remained in force, though emphasis has shifted from time to time.

The first purpose is "to promote the development and expansion of professional rehabilitation services" for the adult deaf client.

The second calls for ADARA "to provide a forum and a common meeting ground so that the organization may be instrumental in bringing about a better understanding of deaf people as a whole by encouraging students, professional persons, and laymen to develop more than a superficial understanding of the needs and the problems of this group—especially the problems related to communication techniques needed to work effectively with the adult deaf in a rehabilitation setting."

Third, ADARA is "to promote and encourage scientific research of the needs and problems engendered by deafness which inhibit in important ways the successful overall functioning of a deaf person."

Fourth, ADARA should "promote and develop recruitment and training of professional workers for the deaf."

Fifth, ADARA's bylaws state that it should publish a journal that will promote inter- and intradisciplinary communication among those persons who have a professional interest in deafness, particularly as it affects those who are adults.

The sixth purpose is "to cooperate with other organizations concerned with deafness and rehabilitation of the deaf and with allied services in promoting and encouraging legislation pertinent to the development of professional services and facilities for the adult deaf."

ACTIVITIES

The activities of ADARA have been in keeping with its purposes. Regarding the first purpose, ADARA has sponsored, often with support from the Rehabilitation Services Administration, conferences that have been directed at perceived gaps in services for deaf adults. Many of these meetings have had as their theme the improvement or expansion of some aspect of the rehabilitation-service-delivery system. For example, the fifth biennial conference focused on serving severely handicapped deaf persons and the eighth convention on interagency cooperation (networking). At any of the conventions, the interests of those who are concerned with special groups within the deaf population (for example, deaf-blind persons) or who have particular professional interests (such as vocational assessment) are usually satisfied by various presentations that are made in the form of learned papers or panel discussions. ADARA also assists individual programs in their efforts to improve or expand services. In 1970 it assisted in securing permanent certification for teachers of deaf students in California. The existence of the national organization is helpful in bringing into focus the diverse problems that confront deaf people and providing a vehicle for assisting in alleviation of them.

The biennial conferences fulfill the second stated purpose of ADARA, "to provide a forum and a common meeting ground." The bylaws specify that ADARA must hold at least one convention every two years for all of its members. The first meeting was held in 1967 in Washington, D.C., as part of the convention of the National Rehabilitation Association. It is the only time that ADARA has met in conjunction with another organization. The leadership has felt that conjoint meetings diminish and distract from ADARA's purposes. The biennial conventions generally begin with a keynote address from a prominent figure in government or the professions. Other major addresses, paper sessions, and open meetings are regular features of the conventions. Their principal objective is to inform the memberships about developments in the field, special problem areas, and new treatments and advances in service delivery. The meetings also provide an opportunity for informal contacts between the members, affording them occasions in which to broaden their professional acquaintances, to strengthen their identification with the field, and to encounter others with knowledge that is not yet codified.

While ADARA does not itself conduct research projects, its conferences and publications are invaluable to researchers, providing them with useful information and bibliographical support, which thus fulfills ADARA's third purpose. The four volumes of *Deafness Annual*, which were published in 1969, 1972, 1973, and 1974, and which contain summations of research and substantial reference material, have been of special value. Each volume held listings of then-current research projects, thus enabling researchers to identify others working on the same or related problems. At the conclusion of the 1974 volume, the Rehabilitation Services Administration, which had supported these publications, withdrew its financial aid. ADARA has subsequently been unable to afford continuation of the project.

Regarding ADARA's fourth purpose, recruiting personnel to enter services for deaf persons has largely been addressed through the conventions. For example, the fourth convention, held in Washing-

ton, D.C., in 1972, was largely devoted to papers on the education and training of personnel, addressing cooperative education, religious services, social work, psychology, short-term training, and many such areas bearing upon the development of personnel to serve the deaf population.

In accordance with its fifth purpose, ADARA publishes the *Journal of Rehabilitation of the Deaf*. It has appeared quarterly since 1967. ADARA also publishes monographs, most of which arise out of the biennial conventions or from other conferences that it sponsors. These monographs are sold as separate publications intended to enlighten those with a professional interest in deafness. *See* JOURNAL OF REHABILITATION OF THE DEAF.

Cooperation with other agencies has been facilitated by ADARA's location in the National Association of the Deaf headquarters building, which helps to fulfill ADARA's sixth purpose. ADARA was a member of the Council of Organizations Serving the Deaf (COSD) when it was active. While the formal mechanisms for coordinating ADARA's activities with those of other rehabilitation organizations and agencies no longer exist, ADARA has maintained its relations with them through less efficient, informal contacts, such as its relationship with the Council of State Administrators of Vocational Administration. The eighth biennial convention devoted its entire agenda to discussions of ways to promote cooperation between agencies and individuals interested in deafness; Monograph No. 9 (*Networking and Deafness*) grew out of this convention. Other activities of ADARA include testimony by its executives before the U.S. Congress and state legislatures to further the purpose of "promoting and encouraging legislation pertinent to the development of professional services and facilities for the adult deaf." *See* COUNCIL OF ORGANIZATIONS SERVING THE DEAF; NATIONAL ASSOCIATION OF THE DEAF.

GOVERNANCE

ADARA is a nonprofit, nonpolitical organization, structured along the traditional lines of a professional group. It originally elected a president, first and second vice-presidents, secretary, treasurer, and a four-member board. This arrangement varied slightly over the following years, with the combining of the secretary and treasurer positions in 1972 by action of the ADARA board, and the addition of a member to the board. With its name change, ADARA's organizational structure also changed to its present roster of a president, president-elect, vice-president, secretary-treasurer, and five-member board.

In 1971, with the assistance of additional funding from the Rehabilitation Services Administration, ADARA was able to hire an executive secretary (now called the executive director). The purpose of the grant from the Rehabilitation Services Administration was to publish the *Deafness Annual*, but the funding enabled ADARA to hire a full-time director. The first was Arthur J. Norris, a son of deaf parents and an engineer who, upon his retirement, became actively involved in the rehabilitation of deaf people. His full-time successor, Sharon H. Carter, herself deaf, pursued a career in deafness education and rehabilitation. In addition to the executive director, the central office staff consists of only one secretarial employee. Volunteer assistance has enabled the organization to function far more effectively than its slender resources would suggest it could.

After its establishment grant from the Rehabilitation Services Administration expired, the Professional Rehabilitation Workers with the Adult Deaf has occasionally received other funding from the agency for various specific projects; however, fiscally it is now independent of government support for its continuation as a professional organization. From its membership of about 300 in 1967, ADARA has grown to over 2000 members, which has provided a foundation for a surprisingly large and influential structure within the field of deafness rehabilitation. The headquarters since 1971 have been located in Halex House, the building owned by the National Association of the Deaf which also houses other organizations concerned with deafness.

Several states have chapters of ADARA that attempt to carry on the work of the national organization at the local level. Chapters in Ohio and Indiana, for example, followed the national organization in changing their names. They hold regular meetings and work to carry out the objectives of ADARA within their states.

ADARA's bylaws also permit it to form sections devoted to special interests within deafness rehabilitation. Over the years, separate sections have been formed on deaf-blindness, mental health, and vocational and psychological assessment. These sections aim at developing and expanding services in particular areas, which is consistent with the first objective of the organization to develop and expand professional rehabilitation services, and with the organization's effort to increase its overall impact on the welfare of deaf people.

Jerome D. Schein

AMERICAN PROFESSIONAL SOCIETY OF THE DEAF

On November 4, 1966, nine deaf people, including psychologists, engineers, and other professionals, gathered in New York City with the dream of founding a unique organization for people who were both deaf and professionals. The outcome was the American Professional Society of the Deaf (APSD).

OBJECTIVES

The APSD was organized with ten objectives: (1) to show society that there were deaf persons in the various professions, and so to help eliminate certain persistent misconcepts of deaf people as a whole; (2) to provide a setting for the congregation and socialization of deaf professional persons, and to stimulate and encourage their sharing of professional and intellectual experiences; (3) to promulgate among its members the concept of professionalism and professional behavior; (4) to encourage members of the deaf community who have the potential to pursue professional careers, and to aid them in the attainment of their professional goals; (5) to serve as an advisory body for promising young deaf students and to offer them educational and vocational guidance and other assistance with respect to career goals; (6) to serve by example as inspiration to deaf persons in the pursuit and attainment of professional goals; (7) to encourage, promote, or collaborate with endeavors designed to build, augment, and increase a pool of sophisticated and knowledgeable leaders for the deaf community; (8) to encourage and actively participate in the cultural development and enrichment of deaf people at large; (9) to serve as a valid representative or voice for deaf professional persons, and for other deaf persons as well, in matters dealing with their education, civil rights, vocational rehabilitation, and social welfare, and in legislation; (10) to serve as a volunteer or resource group, providing services and information to schools, facilities, agencies, projects, and other special programs serving deaf people.

The diversity of professional interest and unusual accomplishments of the APSD's membership are striking. The first four officers, for example, Albert Hlibok, Edgar Bloom, Francis Celano, and John Seidel, were respectively a cost engineer, a chemist, a teacher, and an insurance and mutual fund agent. Only Celano, who taught at the Lexington School for the Deaf, held what would be considered a traditional or typical position for a deaf individual. *See* DEAF POPULATION: Socioeconomic Status.

MEMBERSHIP

By 1978 the APSD consisted of 50 members with even more diversified professional backgrounds. They included a professor of experiment surgery, a research chemist, a lawyer, a system engineer, an art designer, a librarian, a programmer, and psychologist. There were also a few prominent hearing people, such as Edna Levine, who were honorary members.

ACTIVITIES

Following the initial meeting in 1966 and the election of temporary officers, the APSD wrote and adopted a constitution and bylaws. The first officers elected under the constitution were Edgar Bloom, Albert Hlibok, Donald Ballantyne, Martin Sternberg, Barbara Brauer-Sachs, John Seidel, and Allen Sussman. At this early stage in the APSD's existence, and into the early 1970s, monthly dinner meetings were held at the Engineer's Club in New York City. Later, they usually took place in the Volunteer's Conference Room at the Institute of Rehabilitation Medicine of the New York University Medical Center.

APSD was incorporated under the laws of New York State on April 30, 1970, and became recognized as a tax-exempt organization on November 18, 1971. The latter was an important occasion as it facilitated the setting up of a scholarship fund to encourage members of the deaf community to pursue professional careers. By 1978, the last year in which the APSD was fully active, 38 awards totaling over $5000 had gone to deaf students with academic potential and financial need.

To the general public, APSD was perhaps best known for its sponsorship of an annual forum, during which the presentations of the scholarship awards were made. Afterwards, a pertinent and controversial topic of the day was debated among the panelists, with audience participation welcome at the end. The subjects were sometimes of special interest to the deaf community, such as the "deaf power" movement and the issue of a special tax exemption for deaf people. At other times, subjects such as the space program or premarital sex—of interest to both hearing and deaf people—were debated.

The APSD also published its own newsletter several times a year. The newsletter consisted of membership profiles and local activities of interest to deaf professionals.

In 1975 the American Association for the Advancement of Science had its annual meeting in New York City, during which was held the symposium "The Physically Disabled Scientist: Potential and Problems." The symposium panelists were invited to attend a luncheon sponsored by APSD. On April 16, 1977, APSD took an active role, along with other organizations in New York City, in activities that led to the formation of a new organization, the New York Center for the Law and the Deaf.

CHANGES

In 1979 APSD revised its constitution and bylaws in order to become a national organization, thus encouraging chapters to be established in different parts of the country. The New Jersey Chapter and the New York City Chapter were formed, each with its own officers and activities.

This reorganization did not have the desired effect; APSD lost momentum and became inactive. The members have considered reorganizing APSD into a foundation. Whatever shape it assumes in the future, however, the APSD served to unite deaf professionals in and around New York City at a time when the professional deaf person was viewed as an anomaly.

Clifford R. Rowley

AMERICAN REHABILITATION

American Rehabilitation is the official quarterly publication of the Rehabilitation Services Administration, one of three agencies housed within the Office of Special Education and Rehabilitative Services, of the U.S. Department of Education. (The other two agencies within the Office of Special Education and Rehabilitative Services are the National Institute on Handicapped Research—which, until separated from the Rehabilitative Services Administration in 1980, was its research division—and the Special Education Programs. All three agencies are concerned with the rehabilitation and habilitation of disabled people.) *See* REHABILITATION: Agencies.

While *American Rehabilitation*'s publishing policy accommodates articles on all facets of disability, articles about severely disabled people of working age receive priority. This is mandated under the rules that require the Rehabilitative Services Administration to serve severely disabled people first, as described in the Rehabilitation Act of 1973 as amended (the basic legislative authority governing the rehabilitation of disabled people through the State-Federal Vocational Rehabilitation Program). Deaf people usually meet the criterion of severe disability, and the categorical importance of this disabled population is recognized in the Rehabilitative Service Administration through its Deafness and Communicative Disorders Branch. *See* REHABILITATION ACT OF 1973.

HISTORY

The evolution of *American Rehabilitation* is understood best in relation to the history of vocational rehabilitation programs. Federally funded vocational rehabilitation began in 1920 with the passage of the Smith-Fess Act (Public Law 236). Only a few years passed before the need was recognized for a communications vehicle among professionals serving disabled individuals. Consequently, *Rehab Review* was launched in January 1926 as a joint venture of the state directors of the New Jersey and New York programs. *See* REHABILITATION: History.

The National Rehabilitation Association, a private organization of rehabilitation professionals, was launched only a few years after the Smith-Fess Act. However, it was not until January 1935 that the *National Rehabilitation News* started publication, to continue until March 1945, when it was replaced by the National Rehabilitation Association's present publication, the *Journal of Rehabilitation.*

These early publications addressed the state and professional needs of the rehabilitation movement, which is a cooperative effort of the federal government and the states. In 1960 Mary E. Switzer, administrator of the Vocational Rehabilitation Administration in the Department of Health, Education and Welfare and perhaps the best known of its federal administrators, saw the need for a publication at the federal level to disseminate information about the expanding commitments of the movement, both at the program level and at the level of research and training. Consequently, the *Rehabilitation Record* was founded and continued bimonthly publication until October 1973. *American Rehabilitation* is a direct descendant of this inaugural federal publication.

On August 15, 1967, The Vocational Rehabilitation Administration was renamed the Rehabilitation Services Administration. At this time it was transferred to the newly formed Social and Rehabilitation Service, and Mary Switzer became its first administrator. Since the rehabilitation philosophy had worked so well with disabled people, the process would be infused into the welfare and social programs administered by the Department of Health, Education and Welfare.

Rehabilitation Record continued publication until October 1973, when its function was transferred to the parent organization, Social and Rehabilitation Service, where it was combined with the service's former publication, *Human Needs*, to become the *Social and Rehabilitation Record*. The *Record* continued until the disbanding of the Social and Rehabilitation Service and the transfer of the Rehabilitation Services Administration to still another umbrella agency of Health, Education and Welfare, called the Office of Human Development Services. With transfer of the Rehabilitation Services Administration, the rehabilitative segment of the *Social and Rehabilitation Record* was reestablished in the Rehabilitation Services Administration, and the present *American Rehabilitation* was inaugurated in September 1975. *American Rehabilitation* continues publication today. Its schedule was changed from bimonthly to quarterly in January 1983.

PURPOSE AND AUDIENCE

While *American Rehabilitation* publishes materials that appeal to a mix of professional people who deal with disabled clients, it accents program materials, legislative enactment at the federal level, innovations in program administration, research trends, and professional development areas. It occasionally prints articles on counseling technique, accommodation innovations, and concerns affecting handicapped people in other areas such as transportation and housing.

American Rehabilitation also serves as a resource index by presenting lists of new reports, new publications, and program news of other agencies, both public and private. Its letters-to-the-editor column, called "Commentary," provides a forum for the expression of readers' opinions.

Because of its programmatic accent, its prime recipients are the administrators, supervisors, and counselors who work for the general state vocational rehabilitation agencies and the state agencies for blind people. It is also sent to research and training centers and rehabilitation engineering centers supported by the National Institution on Handicapped Research, to all United States depository libraries, to colleges and universities which conduct professional training in rehabilitation, and to many other public and private organizations whose services include rehabilitation. A mid-1970s survey established a probable readership of 20,000. The Superintendent of Documents, U.S. Government Printing Office, maintains a paid subscription list to the magazine.

CONTRIBUTOR'S INFORMATION

Since *American Rehabilitation* is a public document, its articles are in the public domain. Except where prior copyright has been obtained, its material may be freely reproduced, although most reprinting organizations seek prior author and editor permission and credit the source.

The editor receives unsolicited articles that deal with any phase of the rehabilitation process. All manuscripts are reviewed by the editor and by one or more assigned experts in the subject field. A special edition that concentrates on one phase of rehabilitation is occasionally scheduled. Articles for these concentrated areas are usually solicited by the editor.

Ron Bourgea

AMERICAN SCHOOL FOR THE DEAF

The first permanent school for deaf children in the United States was the Connecticut Asylum for the Education and Instruction of Deaf and Dumb Persons (now called the American School for the Deaf), established in Hartford on April 15, 1817. It had for its model the National Institution for the Deaf of Paris, France, the first known free school for deaf students in the world, founded in 1755 by Charles Michel Abbé de l'Epée. (The first school for deaf people in Great Britain followed in 1760, under the auspices of the Thomas Braidwood family, and the Abbé Silvestri was credited with the establishment of the first Italian school in Rome in 1784.) *See* BRAIDWOOD, THOMAS; L'EPÉE, ABBÉ CHARLES MICHEL DE.

A number of earlier attempts had been made to educate deaf children in the United States, since it was expensive and distressing for families to send their deaf children to Europe for an education. Around 1811 the Reverend John Stanford attempted to teach a group of deaf students in a New York City almshouse. A year later John Braidwood, an alcoholic member of the English Braidwood family, tried to launch a program in New York and later in Baltimore. Both attempts were short-lived. *See* EDUCATION: History.

The American School for the Deaf owes its beginnings to a Hartford physician, Mason Fitch Cogswell, who had a profoundly deaf daughter. Cogswell was a man of means and vision who saw beyond his own child to other deaf children and wanted to provide them with a genuine educational environment similar to schools in Europe. Among his neighbors were the Gallaudet family, whose eldest child, Thomas Hopkins, showed a great interest in Alice and her need for an education. One of his earliest efforts to teach her was by tracing in the dirt "HAT" and placing his own hat beside it. After Gallaudet graduated from Andover Academy, he spent a great deal of time with Alice during the fall and winter of 1814. Dr. Cogswell had formed a committee to raise funds to sponsor an individual to go to Europe and learn about educating deaf children; Gallaudet was selected. *See* GALLAUDET, THOMAS HOPKINS.

After a frustrating year in England and Scotland, Gallaudet accepted an invitation from the Abbé Sicard to study at the National Institute in Paris. Upon completion of his observations and practicum, he returned to America with Laurent Clerc, one of the deaf teachers of the renowned French school. Clerc and Gallaudet spent seven months giving talks and demonstrations and raising funds for the new school, which opened with 7 students and grew to 21 students within a couple of months. The new program received a great deal of publicity and attention, as instruction of deaf children was quite unusual at that time. Among dignitaries visiting the Hartford school were President James Monroe, Henry Clay, Andrew Jackson, and Charles Dickens. Clay was at that time Speaker of the House in the United States Congress and engineered a bill to grant the foundling school 23,000 acres of land in Alabama, which was later sold to establish a permanent endowment fund. The state of Connecticut also authorized funds. *See* CLERC, LAURENT.

Gallaudet and Clerc were the initial faculty members for the pioneer program. The school had 31 students by year's end, with ages ranging from 10 to 50 years. Both instructors eventually married deaf students from this beginning group—Gallaudet to Sophia Fowler and Clerc to Eliza Boardman.

The American School for the Deaf began in a small three-story building, and not only was the first school for deaf children but was the very first school for handicapped children in the Western Hemisphere. The second year, with over 100 students enrolled, it was necessary to secure larger quarters. The school purchased seven acres of land and erected new buildings. In 1921 it moved to its present location in West Hartford, where today it enrolls over 200 day and residential students.

Bibliography

American Annals of the Deaf (directory), vol. 129, no. 2, April 1984.

Gannon, Jack R.: *Deaf Heritage: A Narrative History of Deaf America*, National Association of the Deaf, Silver Spring, Maryland, 1981.

Lane, Harlan: *When the Mind Hears: A History of the Deaf*, Random House, New York, 1984.

Mervin D. Garretson

AMERICAN SOCIETY FOR DEAF CHILDREN

The American Society for Deaf Children (ASDC) was called the International Association of Parents of the Deaf until 1984. The new name better reflects the services provided by the organization, removes the negative connotation of "the deaf," and identifies the primary area of service, the United States and Canada.

FOUNDING

At the 1965 meeting of the Convention of American Instructors of the Deaf (CAID), a proposal was made that the convention establish a parent section. The convention conducted a survey to determine the need for, and the interest in, a parent organization. The survey was sent to parents and educators and other professionals. As a result, the convention moved to encourage the establishment of a parent organization at their meeting in 1967. *See* CONVENTION OF AMERICAN INSTRUCTORS OF THE DEAF.

The late 1960s was a time of transition for deaf people and their families. Sign language was used more publicly, and studies were being conducted into the academic and emotional levels of deaf children. Parents were questioning the results of oral education and many were beginning to use manual communication or the new method of total communication, the combination of speech and sign language. Parents who were using sign language with their children began communicating with each other, gathering at meetings and sharing their experiences of raising a deaf child. From the sharing came the concept of a parent organization that would represent families who believe in the philosophy of total communication and the need for parent networking. *See* SOCIOLINGUISTICS: Total Communication.

More than 90 percent of parents with deaf children have normal hearing. They often feel alone and confused when the diagnosis of deafness is made. Many know nothing about deafness. A parent organization provides these parents with resources and is a source of information and support from which they gain knowledge and confidence.

In 1969 the first edition of the CAID Parent Section newsletter was published and distributed. The first convention of the parent section was held at the California School for the Deaf in Berkeley, with parents from 16 states attending. The following resolution was passed: "We the parents of deaf children assembled in the First National Convention at the California School for the Deaf, Berkeley, do accept the kind invitation of the Convention of American Instructors of the Deaf to form a national parent organization. We do move that a committee be appointed to prepare a constitution in harmony with the objectives of our host organization, the CAID." This meeting was the first formal meeting held by parents in the United States and Canada.

PURPOSES

The aims and objectives of the CAID Parent Section were voted on and passed at the convention in California. They were as follows: (1) to strive toward total communication; (2) to orient parents; (3) to promote understanding of deafness; (4) to stress the needs and importance of summer school facilities for young deaf children; (5) to publish and distribute important documents, including laws; (6) to maintain a good Speakers' Bureau; (7) to encourage the use of proper terminology pertaining to deafness; (8) to help promote legislation that would benefit the welfare and education of all deaf children; (9) to support adult education programs; (10) to institute and help maintain health measures and programs that will aid in the prevention of deafness; and (11) to promote and help institute educational programs and facilities for multiply handicapped deaf children.

Since 1984 the purposes of the American Society of Deaf Children have been condensed to four major points: (1) to educate the public, especially families of children who are deaf or hard-of-hearing, about opportunities for, and problems encountered by, people who are deaf or hard-of-hearing; (2) to improve the education, recreation, health, and employment opportunities of all children who are deaf or hard-of-hearing; (3) to unite deaf and hearing parents, professionals, and friends to promote the general welfare of children who are deaf or hard-of-hearing; (4) to provide information and support to parents and families with children who are deaf or hard-of-hearing.

The second annual meeting of the CAID Parent Section was held in 1971. At this convention, the membership voted to change the name of the organization from Parent-Section-CAID to the International Association of Parents of the Deaf-Parent Section of the CAID (IAPD). Lee Katz, the parent of a deaf daughter, was elected first president of IAPD.

IAPD committed itself to communication that included deaf children and adults as equal members of their families and society. It worked to unite parents, professionals, and deaf adults in efforts to improve the lives of children who are deaf or hard-of-hearing. IAPD also set up a network through which members could provide each other with information and support.

IAPD business continued on a voluntary basis until the end of 1972 when the office was moved to Halex House, owned by the National Association of the Deaf. The National Association of the Deaf covered the salary cost for a staff member and provided office space as well as strong support for the concept of the parent organization. NAD provided IAPD/ASDC with an annual subsidy until 1985, when ASDC became financially independent. *See* NATIONAL ASSOCIATION OF THE DEAF.

At the third biennial convention, Lee Katz became the first executive director; Larry Newman, who had a deaf daughter, became president. The membership increased, with parents, professionals, and friends joining to support the needs of parents with deaf children.

Between 1974 and 1976 IAPD developed communication kits which were sold to families, schools, libraries, and professionals. The kit provided books and guides about deafness for parents, books and toys for children, and "Someone Just Like Me" dolls with hearing aids. Books for parents about deafness were sold through the office. Mary Ann Locke, the parent of a deaf daughter, became executive director upon the death of Katz.

During this time, IAPD was instrumental in launching several different programs. The I LOVE YOU campaign made the international sign for "I love you" known throughout the world and encouraged the use of sign language for deaf people and their families as well as for the general public.

The Key Network is IAPD/ASDC's system of networking parents and professionals around the United States and other parts of the world. It was used the first time to help override the presidential veto of the Rehabilitation Act of 1974. The Key Network is presently used to alert parents and families of important legislative issues that need congressional

INTERNATIONAL ASSOCIATION OF PARENTS OF THE DEAF

Universal sign for "I love you."

attention and action. Through the Key Network, the voices of parents are heard to advocate or protest a particular political action.

REORGANIZATION

In 1975, with individual and family membership increasing and the building of affiliate groups (IAPD/ASDC's local chapters), IAPD held its fourth biennial convention. IAPD was incorporated as an independent organization, and was no longer the Parent Section of CAID. Bylaws were adopted and a national executive board was installed, which consists of voluntary members who meet twice a year. The board includes an executive committee, all of whose members must be parents of deaf children, and the executive board at large, which is composed of parents and professionals. Regional representatives and resource consultants also participate in establishing goals and directions for ASDC.

Affiliate groups consist mainly of local parent groups and are IAPD/ASDC's link with local communities, families, and issues. Affiliate groups pay annual dues to ASDC but function independently. Groups hold meetings, plan fund-raising events, and provide activities for parents and families. Affiliate groups aid in biennial conventions as well as keep ASDC informed of legislative issues of importance on local levels. ASDC provides affiliate groups with newsletters, special mailings, literature on how to begin and maintain parent groups, and information and support as well as speakers for meetings. In 1985 ASDC had 95 affiliate groups.

PUBLIC LAW 94–142

IAPD was deeply involved in the development of the Education for All Handicapped Children Act (Public Law 94–142). Board members served on committees and advisory boards to ensure that parents of deaf children were heard. A close partnership with the Gallaudet Task Force on P.L. 94–142 was formed. A three-day seminar was presented for parents about the new law. Testimony was given and continues to be given before Congress not only pertaining to P.L. 94–142, but advocating the rights of deaf children and their families. *See* EDUCATION OF THE HANDICAPPED ACT.

POSITION PAPERS

IAPD position papers were developed in 1976, and were written on topics including early intervention, mainstreaming, interpreters, and most appropriate education. Position papers have been used by individuals and groups to support positions in individual educational program meetings, town councils, and before the Supreme Court, as well as in due process hearings. They have been used to provide parents with information about the rights of their children and about the positions of a national organization on classroom placement, communication, and support services.

PUBLICATIONS

In 1977 IAPD turned over the sales of all books to the National Association of the Deaf. New publications that were written and distributed by IAPD include: *Years of Challenge: A Guide for Parents of Hearing Impaired Adolescents*; *Need an Interpreter?*; *Learning Disabilities and Deafness*; *Annual Summer Camp Directory*; *In the Beginning: A Guide for Parent Groups*; and the *Endeavor*.

The *Endeavor* is the official publication of IAPD/ASDC. The first edition was distributed in 1969. Today the *Endeavor* is printed and distributed six times a year. *See* ENDEAVOR.

NEW DIRECTIONS

In 1979, a new executive director of IAPD/ASDC, Jacqueline Z. Mendelsohn, the parent of a deaf son, was hired and began reorganization to improve delivery of services to members and families. A trust fund was established. The seventh biennial convention was held in conjunction with the National Association of the Deaf Centennial Convention. The IAPD Speakers' Bureau was established with speakers attending 87 conventions, conferences, workshops, and meetings. The Key Network was expanded to improve the relay of information among members on timely issues pertaining to deaf children and their families. Legislative testimony increased and advocacy for parent's and children's rights became a priority.

A new publication was written by the executive director and the past president of IAPD/ASDC, Bonnie Fairchild, titled *Years of Challenge: A Guide for Parents of Hearing Impaired Adolescents*. Workshops were presented around the United States and Canada specifically addressing the needs of hearing-impaired adolescents and their families.

A new program was developed by IAPD/ASDC called Two Years of Love, which is a program of personalized services paid for by a service organization or a school and presented to a family with a deaf or hard-of-hearing child. A family receives membership in ASDC, books, toys, letters, and journals on a monthly basis for two years. This monthly support for families provides them with education, support, and confidence in raising their deaf child. A family with a deaf child is located by ASDC or a local school so that the family falls within the location of the service organization.

Legislative awareness for ASDC members and for members of Congress is accomplished through membership in the Council of Representatives. The council is an organization of representatives of associations involved with deafness which focuses on legislative issues that will affect individuals who are deaf, families with deaf individuals, and those working in the field of deafness.

ASDC is influential in decisions affecting education and mental health. Through task forces, conventions, regional meetings, local meetings, publications, position papers, special mailings, and the newsletter, ASDC keeps its members and others informed and educated. The Medical Awareness Campaign informs doctors and other health-care providers about the importance of early diagnosis of deafness. ASDC also provides information and support to parents and families with children who are deaf or hard-of-hearing. Through information, parents can make confident choices about their deaf children and their needs.

Jacqueline Z. Mendelsohn

AMERICAN SPEECH-LANGUAGE-HEARING ASSOCIATION

The American Speech-Language-Hearing Association (ASHA) is the national professional and scientific association for speech-language pathologists and audiologists concerned with communication behavior and disorders. The official date of the founding of the association is December 29, 1925, when formal action was taken by a group of 11 men and women at the eleventh annual meeting of the National Association of Teachers of Speech. The concept of this organization, known for the first 11 years as the American Academy of Speech Correction, was developed in the spring of 1925 when Carl E. Seashore sponsored a weekend conference on the causes, symptoms, and methods of treatment of speech disorders. During several meetings held by Lee Edward Travis and Robert West, the concept of an exclusive association for research scholars and heads of state and city programs evolved.

The purpose of the academy was defined as "the promotion of scientific, organized work in the field of speech correction." Membership was limited to individuals who were doing actual corrective work, teaching methods of correction to others, or con-

ducting research which "has as a leading purpose the solution of speech correction problems." Robert West was elected president and Sara M. Stinchfield secretary. Two years later, the 25 members changed the name of the organization to the American Society for the Study of Disorders of Speech.

In 1930 several significant developments occurred: a major convention program was offered on the subject of therapy for stuttering; the society developed its first official publication; and the Constitution Committee reported its recommendations regarding membership requirements. "Fellows" were required to hold a master's degree and to have published original research. "Associates" were required to hold the bachelor's degree. At this convention a constitutional amendment was approved which detailed practices that would be considered "unethical."

In 1935, with a membership of 87, the society introduced the *Journal of Speech Disorders*, and allocated 75 percent of the budget for its support. The first issue contained articles relating to cleft palate, foreign accent, and stuttering, and a bibliography on speech, voice, and hearing disorders.

A year later the society adopted a new name, the American Speech Correction Association. In 1947 the society became the American Speech and Hearing Association, making official the long-recognized link between speech and hearing. The name of the quarterly publication was changed to *Journal of Speech and Hearing Disorders*, and a new publication, *Monograph Supplements*, was introduced to handle some of the good, but lengthy manuscripts being submitted. *See* JOURNAL OF SPEECH AND HEARING DISORDERS.

In 1950 the association celebrated its Silver Anniversary by holding its first independent convention; more than 700 people registered for the meeting. By 1957 the Code of Ethics had been revised and expanded; the membership had grown to 4500; the first executive secretary was appointed; and ASHA moved into its first national office (officially opened on January 1, 1958). With establishment of a national office, increased attention was given to the dissemination of knowledge within the profession and to the establishment of appropriate professional standards. In 1958 the second quarterly, the *Journal of Speech and Hearing Research*, was introduced, and the American Speech and Hearing Foundation was incorporated into the National Office. The foundation had been established in 1939 as the Stuttering Research Foundation under the guidance of Wendell Johnson, who served as chairperson until his death. *See* JOURNAL OF SPEECH AND HEARING RESEARCH.

In 1959 the association's monthly house organ, *Asha*, was founded. It was designed to serve as a major vehicle of communication between the National Office, the leadership, and the members. Over the next four years, the association began accrediting academic programs and clinical facilities. Membership requirements were set at the master's level in 1965, and certification standards for persons performing clinical work were strengthened. By the end of 1965 ASHA was building a new national office. *See* ASHA.

In 1966 the American Speech and Hearing Association moved into new headquarters in Washington, D.C. The association symbolized the solid foundation of an organization which would nearly double its membership in the next decade. New national office programs were developed to improve and expand services to the membership and communicatively handicapped individuals. Professional needs were met through meetings, conventions, and publications, including the addition of a third quarterly journal, *Language, Speech, and Hearing Services in the Schools.* Programs were established to deal with matters relating to schools, clinics, and urban and ethnic affairs. Programs of public information and governmental affairs were initiated to promote a better understanding of communicative disorders by the general public and legislators. *See* LANGUAGE, SPEECH AND HEARING SERVICES IN THE SCHOOLS.

By the end of 1976 membership was over 24,000, and the National Office was preparing to move into temporary quarters where it remained from 1977 through the first half of 1981. In 1978 ASHA took an unprecedented step for a professional association by recognizing the National Association for Hearing and Speech Action (NAHSA), a consumer association founded in 1910, as its consumer affiliate.

The National Association for Hearing and Speech Action began in New York City, when a small group formed to teach lipreading to persons with hearing problems. Some members believed that the variety of organizations and individuals interested in hearing-impaired persons should be bound together by a national association. As a result, the American Association for the Hard of Hearing was organized in 1919; Thomas Edison was an early member of the board of directors. In 1922 the National Association was relocated to Washington, D.C. Hearing screening programs were established for school children, and efforts were begun to stop discrimination against hard-of-hearing drivers. During the 1920s, the National Association president urged members to mount an "aggressive campaign of education among the public to arouse interest in deafness prevention." National Hearing Week, the forerunner of today's Better Hearing and Speech Month, was introduced in 1927. Hearing Week grew to a national event during the 1930s, and support was gained from Franklin and Eleanor Roosevelt.

World War II brought new concepts of service.

Professional staff members were employed, and the National Association prepared instructions for hard-of-hearing individuals to follow during practice air raid blackouts. These instructions were adopted by the U.S. Office of Civilian Defense and broadcast across the country.

In 1958 Hearing Week was extended into the full month of May. Speech problems, programs, and services related and unrelated to hearing disorders were formally included in the Certificate of Incorporation and bylaws of the National Association in 1962.

In 1966 the board of directors reestablished the organization as the National Association of Hearing and Speech Agencies. Its purpose was to assist and represent its members in promoting high standards of professional service and community organization and identification, diagnosis and assessment, treatment, education, and research in the various areas of communication disorders. *Hearing and Speech News* was the official publication of the National Association.

In 1972–1973, a new name and new purposes were selected. It was now to be known as the National Association for Hearing and Speech Action. The primary objective was to "promote the interests of persons with hearing and speech handicaps and related disorders—including deafness—by means of enlightened public understanding, stimulation of consumer advocacy, direct assistance to hearing and speech agencies, extension and upgrading of services, fostering needed social action, and launching a program of prevention."

In 1980 NAHSA was reorganized with increased emphasis on consumers' control of the association. It also formally requested affiliation with ASHA and the designation of "consumer affiliate." The reorganized board of directors met for the first time in 1983 and reconfirmed NAHSA's dual purpose of serving as public informant and advocate. Since that time NAHSA has initiated a toll-free speech and hearing Helpline (1-800-638-TALK), produced several television public service announcements promoting hearing health and aphasia, and printed a series of brochures.

The affiliation of these two national associations—professional and consumer—has forged a historic and unique partnership. As an affiliate of ASHA, NAHSA has ready access to ASHA's professional staff for input into NAHSA's growing list of publications, as well as assistance in handling some of the calls received on its toll-free consumer line. ASHA, in return, has a ready communication channel with the consumer of its services. NAHSA does retain autonomy and operates under the direction of a board of directors made up of consumers.

When ASHA moved into its permanent Rockville quarters, the membership had topped 35,000 and ASHA had a new name (but retained the previous acronym)—the American Speech-Language-Hearing Association—reflecting the profession's historic involvement with language disorders.

Today, with over 40,000 members, ASHA has five major goals: it strives to maintain high standards of clinical competence for professionals providing services to the public; encourages the development of comprehensive clinical service programs; promotes investigation of clinical procedures used in treating disorders of communication; stimulates the exchange of information about human communication through its publications, conventions, and other continuing education activities; and encourages basic research and scientific study of human communication and its disorders.

ASHA requires that new members hold a graduate degree or the equivalent in speech-language pathology, audiology, speech and hearing science, or an allied discipline. Members who provide clinical services on an independent basis must meet requirements for the Certificate of Clinical Competence. And all members and certificate holders subscribe to a Code of Ethics.

ASHA's publications include a monthly house organ, *Asha*; three quarterly publications: *Journal of Speech and Hearing Disorders*; *Journal of Speech and Hearing Research*; *Language, Speech, and Hearing Services in Schools*; and *ASHA Monographs*; *ASHA Reports*; *ASHA Directory*; *Guide to Professional Services in Speech-Language Pathology and Audiology*; *Governmental Affairs Review*; and career and public information literature.

ASHA is governed by a legislative council selected by members in each of the 50 states and the District of Columbia, members residing outside of the United States, and two members elected by the National Student Speech Language Hearing Association; an executive board composed of nine elected officers; and the executive director of the association.

Bibliography

American Speech-Language-Hearing Association: *Information About American Speech-Language-Hearing Association*, ASHA, Rockville, Maryland, 1981.

Paden, E. P.: *A History of the American Speech and Hearing Association, 1925–1958*, ASHA, Washington, D.C., 1970.

Van Riper, C.: An early history of ASHA, *Asha*, 23:855–858, 1981.

Russell L. Malone

ANNALS OF OTOLOGY, RHINOLOGY, AND LARYNGOLOGY

The *Annals of Otology, Rhinology, and Laryngology* publishes original manuscripts dealing with clinical and scientific aspects of otolaryngology, bronchoesophagology, head and neck, maxillofacial and plastic surgery, audiology, speech pathology, and related specialties. The privately owned journal is published bimonthly and circulates to nearly 6000 researchers and clinicians.

James P. Parker served as editor when the journal was first issued in January 1892 under the title *Annals of Ophthalmology and Otology*. The journal grew quickly from 212 pages in the first volume to 1380 pages in the fifth volume in 1896, when it was separated into the components of ophthalmology, neurology, otology, and rhinology and laryngology. The publication devoted to the ear, nose, and throat appeared in 1897 as volume 6, under the title *Annals of Otology, Rhinology and Laryngology*. Volume 6 contained 25 original communications and 528 pages, almost half of which were case reports or descriptions of new instruments. Abstracts constituted a large part of the earlier volumes, as did proceedings of the American Laryngological Association; the American Laryngological, Rhinological and Otological Association; the French Otological Society; and the Section of Laryngology and Otology of the British Medical Association.

The balance shifted rapidly, however, and original communications soon became the primary feature of the journal. In 1900 there were 34 papers published along with the journal's first photomicrographs. Five years later, the lead article was illustrated with the first color page, depicting four drawings of mucous membranes and glands. From 1895 to 1899, Hanau W. Loeb served as a member of the editorial board. In 1896 the demand for more rhinology and laryngology articles made a special editor imperative, and Loeb assumed charge of these areas; he later purchased the journal and was its editor and publisher until 1926.

In 1927 L. W. Dean was appointed editor in chief; he immediately asked Arthur W. Proetz to become his associate editor. After nine years, Dean named Proetz coeditor and transferred major responsibility for the journal to him. After gradually assuming greater editorial responsibility, Proetz became editor after Dean's death in 1943. Ben H. Senturia served as associate editor under Proetz for eight years before assuming editorship in 1966. During Senturia's term of service, the *Annals* initiated changes to a bimonthly and larger journal format and also began including longer papers as supplements. In 1890, as part of a national trend to make journal titles reflect the more comprehensive nature of their specialty, the name of the journal was expanded to *Annals of Otology, Rhinology and Laryngology—Annals of Head and Neck Medicine and Surgery*. Brian F. McCabe assumed the position of editor in 1982.

The *Annals* has become a fully international journal, with authors and subscribers around the world. It reflects the evolution and expansion that have characterized science, medicine, and otolaryngology in this century. The journal is well illustrated using the sophisticated technology of both medical science and the printer's art, and includes color illustrations.

Articles that are too long for publication in the journal may be considered for supplements, providing separate identification and more rapid publication than the regular, shorter, journal articles. Each year three issues publish papers read at meetings of the three senior societies: the American Laryngological Association, the American Otolaryngological Society, and the American Broncho-Esophagological Association. Regular features include an x-ray study of the month, ENG (electronystagmography) of the month, pathology consultation, and book reviews.

Volunteered articles are peer-reviewed. Contributors are not paid, and anyone may submit papers.

Brian F. McCabe

ARCHITECTURAL BARRIERS ACT

The U.S. Congress passed the Architectural Barriers Act (Public Law 90-480) in 1968 to direct the federal government to ensure physical accessibility and usability in certain public buildings. This law applies to buildings constructed for the United States or financed by a construction loan or grant by the United States after 1968. Under this law, these buildings must be designed, constructed, and altered so as to be accessible to and usable by handicapped persons—those in wheelchairs; those with sight, hearing, or coordination impairments; or those who through aging, accident, or disease move with difficulty.

BACKGROUND
Prior to the passage of the act, public buildings and structures were designed for the average young and able-bodied adult. The buildings presented architectural barriers to persons with disabilities, thus adversely affecting the person's ability to get a job, obtain social and health services, benefit from education, or vote.

In 1961 the American National Standards Institute issued standards for making buildings accessible to physically handicapped persons. Despite efforts of the federal government to eliminate physical barriers through education and awareness, many buildings remained inaccessible when built or altered. In 1968 Congress passed the Architectural Barriers Act to require physical accessibility in public buildings and structures.

APPLICABILITY
In general, the act applies to any building that may be used for the employment or residence of handicapped persons and that is designed, constructed, or altered by or on behalf of the United States or in whole or in part with federal funds. Buildings subject to the law include newly constructed federal office buildings and schools or public housing construction which are financed with federal funds. Excluded from the act are most privately owned housing projects. Partial or entire alterations (such as remodeling or restoration) to a building should make it accessible to and usable by disabled persons.

UNIFORM FEDERAL ACCESSIBILITY STANDARDS
The Barriers Act also directed four federal agencies to establish minimum standards for design, construction, and alteration of particular types of buildings and facilities. Those agencies are: the General Services Administration for federal office buildings and courthouses, the Department of Housing and Urban Development for residential structures, the Department of Defense for defense installations, and the U.S. Postal Service for postal facilities.

In implementing the act's mandate, the four agencies jointly issued accessibility standards known as the Uniform Federal Accessibility Standards (UFAS). They are consistent with or exceed the minimum guidelines and requirements established by the U.S. Architectural and Transportation Barriers Compliance Board. UFAS is similar to technical specifications of the American National Standards Institute as well.

UFAS defines a physically handicapped individual as having a physical impairment, including an impaired sensory, manual, or speaking ability, which results in a functional limitation in access to and use of a building or facility. This definition applies to those suffering from deafness or hearing impairments.

UFAS contains specifications for space allowances, accessible routes, parking spaces, curb ramps, elevators, doors, drinking fountains, bathrooms, restrooms, entrances, alarms, telephones, and assembly areas. Federal buildings or federally funded facilities subject to the act must at least meet these specifications. For example, there must be visual warning signals in rooms where deaf individuals may work or reside alone. For assembly areas without amplification systems and for spaces used primarily as meeting and conference rooms, a permanently installed or portable listening system must be provided. If public telephones are provided, at least one telephone must be equipped with a volume control.

ENFORCEMENT
When Congress realized that there was no agency charged with the enforcement of the Architectural Barriers Act, it created the Architectural and

Transportation Barriers Compliance Board under Section 502 of the Rehabilitation Act of 1973. The board may conduct investigations, hold hearings, and issue orders to comply with the Architectural Barriers Act. An order may include withholding or suspending federal funds for any noncomplying building or facility. *See* REHABILITATION ACT OF 1973.

Any person who has reason to believe that there has been noncompliance with the Architectural Barriers Act may file a written complaint with the board. The complaint should describe the barrier-related problem and give the name and address of the building. The board investigates every complaint it receives. First, the board tries to resolve complaints amicably and informally. If no informal resolution is achieved, the board's executive director may begin legal action by filing a citation before an administrative law judge. A hearing may be held on the disputed issues. The complainant need not be present at the hearing and will remain anonymous unless written permission states otherwise.

The administrative law judge will make a final decision for the board. It may require an agency to correct problems within a given period of time. The judge may order that funds be suspended or withheld.

In addition to enforcement of the Architectural Barriers Act, the board is given a wide range of responsibilities, including the development of advisory standards and provision of technical assistance to groups affected by regulations prescribed pursuant to the civil rights sections of the Rehabilitation Act. This responsibility applies to communication barriers, particularly with respect to telecommunication devices.

REHABILITATION ACT (1973): SECTION 504

Section 504 of the Rehabilitation Act of 1973, as amended, can be used to eliminate architectural barriers in federal and federal-assisted programs. It prohibits discrimination against otherwise qualified handicapped persons on the basis of handicap in these programs. The section has been interpreted as requiring, among other things, that each building constructed for the use of a federal agency or with federal financial assistance be accessible to and usable by handicapped persons. Thus, an overlap between the Architectural Barriers Act and Section 504 exists. Federal agencies have adopted the ABA standards for Section 504 compliance. In Section 504 cases, complaints about architectural barriers should be filed with the responsible federal agency.

Bibliography

Minority Staff of Senate Committee on Environment and Public Works, 96th Cong., 1st Sess., Architectural Barriers in Federal Buildings (Comm. Print 1979).

Uniform Federal Accessibility Standards, 49 *Federal Register* 31528 (1984).

Robert J. Mather

ARCHIVES OF OTOLARYNGOLOGY

The *Archives of Otolaryngology* is one of nine specialty journals that are published along with the *Journal of the American Medical Association* as the major educational program in medical science of the American Medical Association. The *Archives of Otolaryngology* publishes scientific information that is international in scope and includes both basic science and clinical topics pertaining to the causes of deafness, assessment of hearing loss, and treatment of patients.

EDITORIAL POLICY

The *Archives of Otolaryngology* has 10 editorial goals: (1) To publish the highest-quality, most widely read journal in the specialty of otolaryngology and head and neck surgery, emphasizing the publication of important, new scientific information that is useful to the readers. (2) To publish basic science information that is useful in support of clinical decisions and to provide continuing insights in medical practice. (3) To publish research information that will forecast important advances and issues in otolaryngology and head and neck surgery. (4) To publish clinical case review reports that bridge the gap between medical training, textbooks, and the bedside. (5) To strive for the highest standards of excellence in medical science and journalism. (6) To attract the very best original work through the process of rigorous peer review. (7) To seek to improve the quality of otolaryngology and head and neck surgery medical care. (8) To assist in the promotion and development of complete physicians. (9) To serve as a forum for the scientific, social, economic, and political concerns of physicians in this specialty. (10) To take editorial stands that will protect and improve the health of the public generally and encourage the highest ethics within the profession of medicine.

DESCRIPTION

The audience for *Archives of Otolaryngology* consists of physicians and research scientists whose work is related to the specialty of otolaryngology and head and neck surgery, audiologists, speech pathologists, teachers, and other professionals whose activities overlap the boundaries of these specialties. The *Archives of Otolaryngology* is issued monthly. It serves as the official publication organ of the American Society for Head and Neck Surgery and of the American Academy of Facial Plastic and Reconstructive Surgery. In its relationship with these latter two organizations, the journal is provided with the initial opportunity for publication of the papers presented at the national meetings of these organizations, but is not obliged to accept material that is not acted upon favorably in the peer review process. The *Archives of Otolaryngology* is provided as a benefit for those members of the American Medical Association who elect to receive it. It is available to all others by subscription; there are no restrictions on outside subscriptions. The journal has 2500 foreign subscriptions, and there are almost 5000 subscribers who are nonphysicians (audiologists, speech pathologists, organizations, and libraries). Total circulation is approximately 14,000 for the English version. The *Archives of Otolaryngology* also is translated and published in French, and it is widely distributed in Europe on a quarterly basis.

HISTORY

The board of trustees of the American Medical Association established the *Archives of Otolaryngology* as a monthly journal pertaining to the specialty of otology and laryngology in response to a resolution from the association's Section on Laryngology, Otology, and Rhinology at the time of its annual meeting in 1923. The first volume was published in January 1925, and publication has continued without interruption. The journal became quite popular during its early years, particularly because of its association with the American Medical Association.

EDITORS

The American Medical Association board of trustees selected George Elmer Shambaugh, Sr., as editor when publication commenced in 1925. After 12 years as the senior editor, Shambaugh stepped down and was replaced by George Morrison Coates, who was appointed editor in chief in January 1937. Coates served for 23 years, longer than any editor before or since his tenure. He was succeeded by George E. Shambaugh, Jr. (1960–1970), Bobby R. Alford (1970–1980), and Byron J. Bailey (1980–   ).

Editors are selected by an appointed search committee that is charged with the responsibility of identifying candidates suitable for the position and recommending one or more of them to the senior editor of the full-time American Medical Association editorial staff and the board of trustees for the final selection. The term of the editorship is five years, with a second term of five years if mutually agreeable.

The manuscript selection and editorial process is begun initially in the locality of the chief editor, with the final stages of editing and publication being coordinated by the professional staff. The chief editor of the *Archives of Otolaryngology* also serves as

a member of the editorial board of the *Journal of the American Medical Association*, an appointment that permits broader familiarity with the activities of this general medical publication.

CONTENT

The *Archives of Otolaryngology* publishes a number of different types of editorial material. The backbone of the publication consists of original articles—reports of basic science or clinical investigations and experience. Also published are case reports featuring new approaches to diagnosis or treatment (clinical notes), clinical pathological quiz and learning exercises (residents' pages), book reports, announcements, and letters to the editor. Information is included concerning scheduled meetings and teaching conferences in the field and reports of new officers and other information of general interest concerning professional organizations.

The original articles, clinical notes, and residents' pages are selected on the basis of review by two experienced scientific reviewers and by the chief editor. A balance is maintained between the number of articles accepted for publication and the amount of space in order to keep the time to publication at a minimum of six months. All the published material is volunteered; writing tasks are not assigned to any authors, nor is any material accepted from meetings without strict peer review. Contributors are not paid for their manuscripts.

Byron J. Bailey

ARNOLD, HILLIS
(1910–   )

Hillis Arnold is an American sculptor and teacher. Despite losing his hearing at the age of six months from spinal meningitis, Arnold taught sculpture and ceramics for 32 years at Monticello College in Godfrey, Illinois. Now Lewis and Clark Community College, Monticello was a private junior college for women during Arnold's tenure. Some of his pupils have become well-known sculptors, attesting to his influence, dedication, and ability to communicate his artistic knowledge despite hearing loss.

EARLY YEARS

Hillis Arnold was born June 10, 1906, in Beach, North Dakota. During his first 12 years he lived on a farm and received no formal education. His parents kept him out of school because of his poor health and because they wished him to have an oral education, at that time unavailable to deaf children in North Dakota. Arnold's interest in sculpture began when he was about 10 years old and "sculpted" farm scenes from mud. Recognizing this interest, his mother bought him modeling

Hillis Arnold.

clay, which proved to be the catalyst for a long and productive career.

Arnold's formal education commenced when his family moved to Minneapolis, Minnesota, in 1918. He attended public school and graduated from Minneapolis Central High School, and in 1933 graduated cum laude from the University of Minnesota. He also attended the Minneapolis School of Art and the Cranbrook Academy of Art, where he studied with and assisted renowned sculptor Carl Miles. Arnold joined the Monticello College faculty in 1938 as a professor of sculpture.

CHARACTERISTICS

Arnold is an advocate of symbolism, and his art reveals a debt to expressionism—an art style involving the artist's personal thoughts and expressing his or her soul and innermost beliefs. Though often less obvious in his more abstract sculptures, symbolism never disappears completely from his work, for he believes that art should elicit an emo-

tional response in its spectators. While he dislikes purely abstract, nonsymbolic art, Arnold also disapproves of the opposite extreme, that is, art that imitates life too faithfully. Arnold thinks that this imitative style lacks form, and in his figures there are no clearly defined muscles or tendons. He believes that art should be a vehicle for stimulating the spectators' interest in the world of form, color, and line—the three building blocks of art.

The Lord Is My Shepherd illustrates characteristics of Arnold's sculpture. Located in the garden of Cardinal Joseph Ritter in St. Louis, Missouri, it is made of Georgia marble and stands 7 feet tall, including the column. The sculpture represents God, in Arnold's words, by a "symbolic mystic form." The artist's intention is that onlookers gain various impressions—admiration, judgment, and protection—as they walk around the sculpture and view it from different perspectives.

Although Arnold works in all the traditional sculpture media, he also experiments with new techniques. For example, he is the only noted sculptor to use extensively the relatively new medium of plastic aluminum. An acetylene torch is used to construct a base of metal pipes, rods, galvanizing mesh screen, and brass screen, and the plastic aluminum is then applied to the meshed form and

The Lord Is My Shepherd by Hillis Arnold, in Cardinal Joseph Ritter's garden in St. Louis, Missouri.

shaped by the artist. To learn this unusual technique, Arnold trained to become an accomplished crafts worker and expert welder, did experimental studies in polyester resin casting on a large scale as well as in plastic aluminum, and studied methods of molding for polyester resin casting.

HONORS AND EXHIBITIONS

In 1960 Arnold was honored with the title Live Fellow of the International Institute of Arts and Letters. The institute, headquartered in Switzerland, has a limited worldwide elected membership of 760, including artists in the performing arts, the plastic arts, and literature.

Arnold's work has been exhibited in the United States and abroad. In 1956 his angel of polyester resin was included by the United States Information Agency in the "Plastics USA" exhibit in Leningrad, Moscow, Yerevan, and Baku in the Soviet Union. Arnold's *Abraham and Isaac* in mahogany was one of 16 examples of American liturgical art shown at the International Biennale of Contemporary Christian Art in Salzburg, Austria, in 1948. It may now be seen in the private chapel of Cardinal Ritter in St. Louis, Missouri.

Two of Arnold's most popular pieces are also in St. Louis. One is the *World War II Memorial* in the Aloe Civic Center area—an impressive 32-foot-high limestone shaft portraying soldiers on one side and sailors on the other, leaving home, in combat, and emerging from death. The other is a giant wooden eagle with a 5-foot wingspan—the symbol of Manifest Destiny—and is part of the Museum of Westward Expansion.

Bibliography

Arnold, Hillis: "A Deaf Sculptor," *Volta Review*, pp. 378–380, June 1967.

"Expressing the Sounds of a Silent World," *Monticello College Alumni Bulletin*, pp. 7–9, 1963.

Kowalewski, Felix: "Hillis Arnold's American Deaf Sculptor," *Deaf American*, pp. 3–5, November 1972.

Missouri Life Magazine, pp. 42–43, November–December, 1979.

Deborah M. Sonnenstrahl

ASHA

Asha is the monthly house organ of the American Speech-Language-Hearing Association. Introduced in September 1959, *Asha* had a circulation of under 6000 which grew to nearly 50,000. Its readership is composed primarily of speech-language pathologists, audiologists, and students. About 900 copies are sent to libraries and other individual subscribers.

The purpose of *Asha* is to serve as a channel for communication between members and association leadership. *Asha* prints material related to the professional and administrative activities of speech-language pathology, audiology, and the association.

For the first 20 years of its publication, *Asha* was printed in one color, with limited use of graphics. In the latter part of 1978, the magazine was redesigned. Full-color covers were initiated, color was introduced within the text, and an emphasis was placed on graphics. New features were introduced and writers were encouraged to adopt a more informal style of writing, including less reliance on jargon and increased attention to communicating with readers.

Asha accepts contributed manuscripts in the form of articles, features, news, committee reports, guest editorials, reviews of books and clinical materials, and letters. Committee reports are restricted to members of ASHA committees, but contributors to other departments need not be affiliated with ASHA. No fees are paid to authors.

Asha publishes articles or features of broad professional interest, including those of a philosophical, conceptual, historical, or synthesizing nature. Articles are distinguished from features in their content. Manuscript of a technical nature requiring review by members of the profession is considered an article and is referred to a minimum of three assistant editors for review. A feature does not generally require such review and is handled in the same manner as other sections of the magazine.

Readers may express their opinions on any subject relating to communicative disorders by writing letters to the editor. *Asha* seeks a wide variety of subject matter and opinion, and reactions, contrary views, opinions, and problems are all appropriate when stated in 200 words or less. Unsigned letters cannot be published, although names are withheld on request if the identity of the writer is known to the editor and there is a valid reason for anonymity. Guest editorials serve essentially the same purpose as letters, but may run between 1000 and 2000 words. Book reviews and clinical material are also published, subject to certain guidelines, and news items are welcomed.

All manuscripts are subject to stylistic editing after acceptance for publication, and only accepted articles will be returned for author approval. No manuscript that has been published or is under consideration elsewhere should be submitted.

Asha's editorial policy stresses the importance of effective writing in all materials published, since the major purpose of printing material in *Asha* is to communicate. *Asha* is the most frequently read publication of the American Speech-Language-Hearing Association. Jargon which will not be readily understood by all readers is eliminated wherever possible, and the first person is used in lieu of "the present writer" or "the investigator."

Asha attempts to keep readers current on news related to the profession or association with legislative reports in "Capitol Hill"; current activities of the American Speech-Language-Hearing Foundation and the National Association for Hearing and Speech Action, ASHA's consumer affiliate; and major events in the lives of members. Interviews with leading personalities within and outside the profession are printed about six times a year. A calendar of events and classified section are published monthly. Each issue contains listings of new products on the market, and "Ask *Asha*" responds to readers' questions.

Special features each year include: an interview with the new president (January), review of the November convention highlights (February), index of books and materials reviewed (variable), Annual Directory of Manufacturers/Publishers (July, August), annual report (variable), auditors report (summer), committee members and charges (winter), code of ethics (January), call for papers for the annual convention (February), accredited academic and clinical programs (variable), legislative council report of actions taken (March), national office salaries (December), and lists of newly certified members (variable). October's issue is devoted to the November convention, and contains abstracts of each technical session to be given, details on all special events, and a guide to the city.

Throughout the year, certain issues are focused on particular topics; for example, the role of minorities in the profession, research assistive listening devices, and speech pathology in prisons. *See* AMERICAN SPEECH-LANGUAGE-HEARING ASSOCIATION.

F. Spahir

ASHLEY, JACK
(1922–   )

Jack Ashley is probably the only totally deaf member of any legislature in the world. His story is an inspiring record of coping with restricted educational and vocational opportunities and with the impact of total deafness.

Born in the English industrial town of Widnes on December 6, 1922, the son of a laborer, Ashley was only five years old when his father died. An elementary education ended at the age of 14, and for the next four years he was employed as a laborer by several firms. Then he joined the Royal Army Service Corps, in which he lasted less than one year since he was discharged because of a hearing impairment due to a perforated eardrum. He resumed employment at Bolton's Copper Works, initially as a laborer and later as a crane driver.

Involvement in trade union and political activities stemmed from Ashley's personal experiences.

A foreperson's refusal to give him a light job following an operation for appendicitis caused Ashley to organize fellow employees as part of the Chemical Workers' Union. The appalling condition of his mother's rented residence led him to a wider interest in housing problems and his election to Widnes Town Council. When only 21, Ashley was a member of the National Executive of his union and one of the youngest municipal councillors in the country.

The chance reading of a newspaper article led Ashley to apply successfully in 1946 for a scholarship to Ruskin College, Oxford, awarded on the basis of an essay and interview. Two years later he was awarded the Oxford Diploma in Economics and Political Science and a further scholarship to Gonville and Caius College, Cambridge, where he read economics and graduated in 1951. At Cambridge he became the first person from a working class background to be elected president of the Union Society. He also participated in a debating tour of universities in the United States. At Cambridge Ashley met Pauline Kay Crispin, whom he married in 1951.

From 1951 to 1966 Ashley was employed by the British Broadcasting Corporation. For the first six years he was a radio producer, but in 1957 became a senior television producer concerned with current affairs programs, including *Panorama* and *Gallery*. In 1955 he was awarded a Commonwealth Fund Fellowship for a year of study in the United States.

After unsuccessfully contesting the Labour Party candidate in 1951, Ashley entered no other elections until 1966 when he was returned to Parliament as the member for Stoke-on-Trent South. The following year he became parliamentary private secretary to Michael Stewart at the Department of Economic Affairs.

Ashley's career was threatened in 1968 when he became totally deaf after a supposedly minor operation for the repair of the perforation in his left ear. His moving autobiography, *Journey into Silence* (1973), describes Ashley's feelings on returning to Parliament following this disaster: "I sat alone on the terrace watching the Thames . . . It was early evening and although I did not expect the river to be busy it seemed exceptionally still and silent. I thought I had known despair but now I felt a chill and deeper sadness as if part of me were dead. After a while I went back to the chamber where the debate was continuing but as speakers made their points there was for me total and unbelievable silence . . . At that moment I felt in my heart that I had begun a lifetime of tomb-like silence. I took a final look round the chamber before leaving . . . to prepare for my resignation from the House of Commons."

The support of his constituents and members of

Jack Ashley.

all political parties dissuaded Ashley from resigning. A particularly significant reason for remaining in Parliament was the suggestion that the House itself would benefit from having a person with first-hand experience of disability. This argument has been amply justified. With Alfred Morris, Ashley was responsible for the Chronically Sick and Disabled Persons Act of 1970, which requires local authority social services departments to provide many forms of assistance for disabled persons if a need exists. Ashley was, among other things, responsible for the clause requiring the secretary of state for health to collate and present evidence to the Medical Research Council on the need for an institute of hearing research. Despite initial opposition from the Medical Research Council, the institute was established in 1976. Ashley was also prominently associated with measures for improving the safety of drugs and vaccines, most notably in the campaign for the compensation of victims of the drug thalidomide. The outlawing of discrimination in respect to employment and a quota scheme are examples of Ashley's concern for disabled persons. Legislation relating to rape, battered wives, child cruelty, vandalism, contempt of court, and the control of the legal profession also prompted Ashley to campaign vigorously inside and outside Parliament. In 1975 he again became a

parliamentary private secretary, this time to Barbara Castle at the Department of Health and Social Security.

Ashley would be the first to concede his indebtedness to four influences: his wife, his constituents, his parliamentary colleagues, and technology. In the latter context a Palantype transcription unit was developed for Ashley's use by Professor Alan Newell. The unit consists of a Palantype shorthand machine connected to a computer-type display screen. Palantype script, phonetically based and split into syllables, is converted into a form that a trained deaf person can read. Ashley sits in the Commons with his screen close by. The typist who acts as his ears is located in the press gallery with the Palantype machine and electronic processing unit.

It is, however, not only for his work but his personal courage that caused Ashley to be the recipient of many honors. He was made a Companion of Honour for his services to handicapped people in 1975 and became a privy councillor in 1979. Fellowships and honorary degrees have been conferred by the Open University, Manchester College of Science and Technology, Keele, and Gallaudet College. He was Midlands Man of the Year in 1974, and in 1980 received the Harding Award for services to the disabled. A new London secondary school was named after him in 1976. He also was a member of the General Council of the Royal National Institute of the Deaf, vice-president of the National Deaf Children's Society, and a patron of the Council for the Advancement of Communication with the Deaf. *See* GALLAUDET COLLEGE; UNITED KINGDOM: Organizations.

Bibliography
Ashley, J.: *Journey into Silence*, Bodley Head, 1973. *Who's Who*, 1983.

Kenneth Lysons

AUDECIBEL

Audecibel is the official journal of the National Hearing Aid Society (NHAS). NHAS was founded as the Society of Hearing Aid Audiologists, but in 1952 it changed its name and also initiated publication of *Audecibel*. The journal's name is a neologism created from "audible" (to be heard) and "decibel" (the unit of the relative measure of the loudness of sounds). The name also invokes the Latin *auditus* (to hear), a euphonic coincidence that figured in its choice. The editorial offices were first in Detroit, but since 1975 they have moved to Livonia, a suburb of Detroit. The journal continues to be published quarterly.

Audecibel's principal purpose is contained in the editorial statement accompanying each issue: "to bring to the otologist, the clinical audiologist, the hearing aid audiologist and others interested in the field of hearing and audiology, authoritative articles, papers and data concerned with research, techniques, education and new developments in the field of treating and assisting the hard of hearing." A substantial portion of the space in *Audecibel* is devoted to research on hearing aids and their use.

While the main concern of the journal is electronic amplification, it does publish articles more broadly related to the interests of those with impaired hearing, such as discussions of the education of deaf children, lipreading instruction for adults with newly acquired hearing impairments, treatment of tinnitus, and other such topics. The majority of the content, however, focuses on hearing aids and related problems. Particular attention is paid to legislation and regulations concerning their distribution, sales, fitting, and repair, and to the problems of relations with the other professions that serve the hearing-impaired population. Such interests naturally reflect those of NHAS, which is "dedicated to the goal of reaching and maintaining the highest possible standards in the field of hearing aid audiology." To do so, *Audecibel* strives to bring together a rather diverse group of professionals with markedly different backgrounds.

In a further explication of its editorial policy, the journal notes, "*Audecibel* is dedicated to the goal of rapport among all those concerned with the hard of hearing so that mutual and overlapping problems may be recognized and outstanding ideas, skills and experience be shared for the benefit of all." The emphasis on good professional relations appears repeatedly in the journal's pages. Of particular concern has been the lack of rapport between NHAS and the American Speech–Language–Hearing Association (ASHA). NHAS does not appear to have similar difficulties relating to the medical professions or with the hearing aid industry, which largely supports NHAS activities through the advertising carried by the journal. *See* AMERICAN SPEECH–LANGUAGE–HEARING ASSOCIATION.

Another NHAS activity that is reflected in *Audecibel* is the certification of hearing aid dealers and their salespeople. NHAS issues certificates attesting to the qualifications of those "who meet strict standards of experience, training, competence, knowledge and character" and granting such individuals the right to the title Certified Hearing Aid Audiologist. The use of the term audiologist by NHAS has been one of the problems in relations with ASHA, which feels that the terms should be restricted to those with extensive graduate study leading to a degree in audiology. In addition to their diploma, Certified Hearing Aid Audiologists are granted membership in NHAS. A substantial

portion of the editorial matter in *Audecibel* is devoted to this activity by NHAS.

Though *Audecibel* is NHAS's official publication, the journal invites articles from NHAS members and nonmembers alike. The content of these submitted articles may vary from reports of research projects to reviews of published research and theoretical discussions of relevant issues. While the journal has an editorial board, which is a part of the NHAS administrative structure, *Audecibel* does not make explicit its review policy. Apparently the editor's discretion determines whether peer review is sought for the various submissions.

Audecibel strives to be more than a house organ for NHAS. In addition to articles presenting new research and summarizing other published studies, *Audecibel* carries (1) the programs of NHAS conventions, (2) reviews of books of interest to the hearing aid profession, (3) notices of pertinent national activities, especially legislative and regulatory, and (4) comments on a wide variety of topics by its elected presidents. The journal has urged its readers to submit case histories that illustrate points about hearing aid dispensing and that bear upon issues of importance for selling and maintaining aids. *Audecibel* regularly contains a section by its editor called "Hear and Now," which reflect the matters that are of interest to NHAS's leadership at any particular time and provide concise statements of the organization's policies regarding these various issues. The editor also fills the role of NHAS Executive Secretary.

Originally, *Audecibel* was printed in a pocket-sized format. Beginning with volume 30, number 4, 1982, the journal emerged with a larger page size, resembling more closely that of professional journals in the field. The larger format has facilitated improvements in the illustrations accompanying research articles and has permitted more detailed tabular materials to be presented. Also, the larger page size can accommodate advertisers with less difficulty. The journal, however, continues to carry about the same amount of editorial and research content.

In keeping with NHAS's desire to promote cooperation and understanding among the professionals who serve hearing-impaired people, *Audecibel* is circulated without charge to Certified Hearing Aid Audiologists and to United States and Canadian audiology clinics, hearing aid retail and manufacturing firms, medical libraries, otologists, schools for deaf and hard-of-hearing students, speech and hearing centers, and teachers in university speech and hearing departments. Those not qualified to receive *Audecibel* free may subscribe to the journal.

Jerome D. Schein

AUDIOLOGIC CLASSIFICATION

In addition to classification of hearing losses into conductive, sensorineural, and mixed categories, hearing losses are classified in terms of degree or extent of hearing loss. Labels of mild, moderate, severe, and profound often are used and are based primarily on difficulty in hearing speech.

The audiogram below shows average hearing losses and complaints associated with such losses based on a large survey. Persons who have hearing thresholds on the order of 25–45 dB HL (curve 1) for the frequencies of 500 through 4000 Hz (the frequency region most important for hearing and understanding speech), and who report difficulty hearing soft or distant speech such as in church or the theater, have a "mild" hearing loss. Individuals who have thresholds of hearing at 45–65 dB HL (curve 2) from 500 through 4000 Hz, and who have difficulty in hearing even normal levels of speech, are labeled as having a "moderate" hearing loss. Those who have hearing losses of 65–85 dB HL (curve 3) and who cannot hear loud speech or use a telephone satisfactorily but can hear shouted speech, have a "severe" hearing loss. Persons whose hearing thresholds are 85 dB HL (curve 4) or greater have a "profound" hearing loss, because they have difficulty hearing even shouted speech. The label "hearing-impaired" is often applied to individuals who have mild, moderate, or severe hearing losses; those who have profound hearing losses often are said to be "deaf." *See* AUDIOMETRY.

These categories are general classifications of degree of hearing loss relative to ability to hear speech. Such definitions do not consider ability to understand speech that is heard. Estimates of speech understanding often are based on spoken word recognition scores for test lists of one-syllable words (monosyllables). Scores of 90–100 percent correct indicate that the individual should have "no practical problems" understanding speech that is loud

enough to be heard easily. In like conditions, scores of 70–90 percent suggest "occasional difficulty" in circumstances where it is necessary to understand information exactly. Hearing-impaired individuals whose word recognition scores for monosyllables loud enough to be heard easily are 60–70 percent have "definite difficulty" in understanding speech. "Severe difficulty" in understanding the speech heard is encountered by individuals who obtain word recognition scores of 40–60 percent. Scores below 40 percent correct indicate "extreme difficulty" in understanding speech by hearing alone. The percentage scores assigned to each category depend to a considerable extent upon the difficulty of the particular word-recognition test used.

With these definitions the difficulty of a hearing-impaired individual can be described on the basis of degree of hearing loss and estimated ability to understand speech. A person who has a mild hearing loss, 25–45 dB in the frequency region of 500–4000 Hz, and a word recognition score of 92 percent should have less difficulty than an individual with a similar hearing loss and a word recognition score of 64 percent. These definitions are based on test results. The categories described above do not take into account the listening and communication demands of the individual in his or her daily activities. Therefore, the hearing difficulties reported by the hearing-impaired individual also must be considered in conjunction with the test results. Nevertheless, results of hearing tests and definitions such as those outlined above can help explain the hearing and communication problems experienced by hearing-impaired individuals.

Wayne O. Olsen

AUDIOLOGY

Audiology is a comparatively young discipline. The term first appeared in the 1940s, and was used often to mean "the science of hearing." This broad interpretation of audiology encompassed essentially all aspects of normal and disordered hearing. These included the study of acoustics; the structure and function of the ear in both natural and abnormal states; sound perception and its assessment; diagnosis of auditory disorders; implications of impaired hearing in human life; and the medical, surgical, prosthetic, behavioral, and educational strategies for managing hearing loss.

In the intervening years, especially in the United States, audiology has come to describe more specific activities having a common focus: the amelioration of impaired speech, language, and hearing associated with medically irreversible auditory impairment. Modern audiology is a discipline circumscribed by two unique objectives: the study of hear-

Audiogram showing average hearing losses and associated complaints.

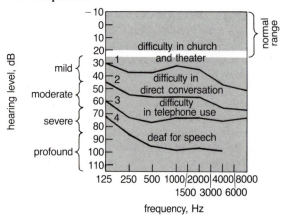

ing, whether normal or disordered, as a fundamental component of human communicative behavior; and the development and application of effective strategies leading to optimal use of sensory and oral expressive skills in hearing-impaired children and adults. The latter includes selection of hearing-aid amplification; using educational techniques to enhance visual perception of speech (speechreading) and to improve auditory discrimination; developing and maintaining optimal speech and voice skills; and counseling regarding educational, social, or vocational concerns that may occur as a consequence of hearing impairment. *See* SPEECH TRAINING; SPEECHREADING.

The scope of audiologic practice includes the design and implementation of programs for hearing conservation, and for the prevention of reduced auditory function. Such activities are particularly relevant in certain industrial environments, and apply to the early identification of impaired hearing in children. The audiologist administers a wide variety of behavioral and physiologic tests to better understand the nature and extent of auditory dysfunction.

Audiologic research is conducted in many areas having relevance to the understanding of normal and impaired audition, and to the development of evaluation techniques and procedures for the improvement of communicative behavior. Close experimental and clinical collaboration with allied disciplines is maintained, particularly with otology, psychology, and special education.

The American Speech–Language–Hearing Association (ASHA) has established voluntary standards for the practice of audiology and of speech-language pathology. Accreditation of professional education and of service programs is offered by the association. Clinical certification is awarded to individuals meeting specific education, knowledge, and supervised experience requirements. The Association maintains a code of ethical conduct subscribed to by its members. Licensure statutes defining the practice of audiology were enacted in 34 states by 1983. Many of these laws are modeled after the ASHA certification requirements. In general, the minimum academic preparation needed for independent professional practice is at the master's degree level. The doctor of philosophy degree in audiology is also conferred by a number of universities. *See* AMERICAN SPEECH–LANGUAGE–HEARING ASSOCIATION.

Bibliography

Canfield, Norton: "Audiology: The Science of Hearing," *Acta Oto-laryngologica* (Stockholm), Suppl. 76, 6–19, 1949.

Davis, Hallowell, and S. Richard Silverman: *Hearing and Deafness*, 4th ed., Holt, Rinehart and Winston, 1978.

Phillip A. Yantis

HISTORY

Contemporary audiology as a cohesive area of study, professional training, and service about hearing impairment owes its development to a number of distinctive historical but not wholly unrelated influences. The most prominent among these are: advances in middle ear surgery; technological refinements in audiological instruments, especially audiometers and hearing aids; increasing sophistication of investigative methods; expanding awareness of the noxious effects of noise; the comprehensive service model growing out of World War II military rehabilitation programs; and heightened public appreciation of the value of rehabilitative services for handicapped persons. Although isolated activities that may properly be labeled audiological were carried on prior to 1930, it was from then on that the bases were being established for audiology as an area of academic and professional concentration.

Middle Ear Surgery A common condition, resulting in hearing impairment is otosclerosis, a change in the bone adjacent to the stapes that conducts sound into the inner ear. Since the latter part of the nineteenth century, in the absence of any validated cure for the condition, ear surgeons have sought means to circumvent the fixated stapes. About the mid-1930s the effort led to the development of an endaural (into the ear) rather than a postauricular (behind the ear) approach. A fenestra (window) was made in a semicircular canal and provision was made for placing the eardrum membrane over the created opening, permitting sound to be conducted to the sense organ in the inner ear. *See* AUDITORY DISORDERS, REMEDIATION OF: Surgical Treatments; EAR: Anatomy, Physiology.

In order to deal with the challenges of this elective procedure, surgeons sought the guidance of workers from other fields whose knowledge and skills were germane to the purpose of the surgery. Among areas of study were physiological acoustics involving particularly the biomechanics of the normal and abnormal middle ear. Operators posed such questions as size, shape, and location of the fenestra and the structural alterations which would result in maximum conduction of sound to the inner ear. Methods also were devised for increasing efficiency and reliability of diagnosis, prognosis, and evaluation. Conventional methods of diagnosis up to that time were case history, ostoscopic examination, and emerging bone conduction audiometry, the last succeeding classical tuning fork tests. These were significantly supplemented by the introduction of speech audiometry. Word tests that had been developed to assess communication systems and hearing aids were presented to the ear well above threshold to be repeated by the patient. This additional procedure contributed to clinical confidence and efficiency. Experience gained in this use of speech audiometry pointed the way to its application in a variety of other clinical needs for both children and adults, including subsequent surgical procedures—stapes mobilization, stapedectomy, plastic reconstruction in the ear, diagnosis and removal of acoustic tumors, and cochlear implantation.

What is historically important about the kind of collaboration detailed here is that it suggested a pattern for cooperative attack on the problems of hearing impairment, in this case not only by medical specialists but also by acoustic and electronic engineers, experimental physiologists, speech scientists, and biostatisticians. The pattern was to be repeated in diverse but essentially similar responses to the other conditions that adversely influence hearing. Audiology was evolving nationally and internationally, and the knowledge, skills, and attitudes required by its practitioners began to be progressively delineated and refined, a process that is as cogent now as it was in the late 1940s and 1950s.

Instruments Audiology is no exception to the rule of the history of science that the emergence of new and valuable instruments attracts people to their constructive use. The development of the electric pure-tone audiometer was one of the major audiological forces of the 1930s and 1940s. As the manufacture of many kinds of audiometers, including speech instruments, kept pace with technological advances extending to the computer era, so did their uses increase to include diagnostic, prognostic, and evaluative information, screening, monitoring, and legal adjudication. Although not technically an audiometer, the impedance bridge used to assess the condition of the middle ear came into clinical use in the 1950s. See AUDIOMETRY.

In the 1930s speaking tubes and bulky, hardly portable hearing aids gave way to wearable vacuum-tube instruments that were substantially accepted by hearing-impaired individuals; such design improvement has continued with the technological progression to microcircuitry. During World War II, in conjunction with military rehabilitation programs, and thereafter, the question of optimum design characteristics for hearing aids was vigorously addressed along with the associated problem of their selection for individual needs. Tailored design, valid selection procedures, and systems of distribution have remained major concerns for audiology. See HEARING AIDS.

Methods of Investigation A prime audiological activity is the assessment of auditory function. Procedures for this derive from the methods of psychoacoustics. Sophisticated methods of measuring responses to quantifiable attributes of many kinds of sounds have contributed to an understanding of the way in which the auditory system works and to identification and description of its aberrations. Similar methods aided by improved instruments have been helpful in studies of tinnitus (head noises) and balance mechanisms housed in the inner ear. See AUDITORY DISORDERS, EVALUATION AND DIAGNOSIS OF; PSYCHOACOUSTICS.

Electrical phenomena occurring in the body, called potentials, can be recorded from the brain, from nerve fibers, and from nerve cells. In the case of the brain and various neuronal way stations, trains of electrical impulses are transported from one place to another and take part in processes of sorting, recording, reduction, and classification of information. Methods of electrophysiology have been adapted to clinical use, greatly enhanced by computers. This has made possible assessment of points in the auditory pathways from the periphery to (and including) the brain, even in infants. In research, methods have progressed from recording from gross regions to recording from intracellular sites, the latter in animals. Findings using these methods promise to yield information basic to an understanding of various pathologic conditions, particularly of the sensory-neural variety, including effects of noise, aging, drugs, and deprivation of sound stimulation. They should be helpful, too, in studies of metabolic factors in deafness using recently developed techniques of biochemical assay.

A complement to electrophysiological approaches has been electron microscopy, which enables examination of structures at greatly refined levels of magnification. Correlation of minute structural changes with recordings from neural elements constitutes a significant historical theoretical and clinical advance.

Since 1968 methods of investigating responses to sound by behaving, intact animals have advanced dramatically. Fine control of stimulus conditions, automated experimental paradigms, and computerized analysis of data have contributed to knowledge in such diverse areas as the effects of noise and the basics of speech perception.

Language is central to the education of hearing-impaired children. The burgeoning activity in the study of the description, acquisition, and measurement of normal and disordered language since the 1970s has commanded the increasing attention of audiologists, especially in counseling parents and in guiding school personnel.

Hereditary deafness is now understood as a genetic problem, and its associated syndromes and linkages have been studied extensively since the early 1960s. Expanding knowledge may raise the level of confidence in diagnosis and counseling about genetic matters. See HEARING LOSS: Genetic Causes.

Noise The post–World War II period witnessed an intense unabating public anxiety about the noxious effects of the environment on people. Hazards of noise exposure to hearing, particularly in certain industries, have claimed the active attention of management, labor, lawyers, legislators, physicians, psychologists, and acousticians, and has given rise to the specialty of industrial audiology. The audiologist is called upon to deal with acoustic hygiene, hearing conservation, definition of risk, preemployment and monitoring audiometry, causal relations between noise exposure and hearing impairment, and the provision of rational bases for estimating handicap and compensation for noise-induced hearing loss. Concern, too, for noise as an annoying environmental pollutant (for example, around airports) has been increasingly expressed. *See* HEARING LOSS: Noise-Induced.

Public Sensitivity The activities cited above reflect rising public sensitivity to the problem of hearing and associated impairments. As much as anything, the military audiology program during World War II laid the groundwork for audiology as it has been carried on. An estimated 15,000 service men and women received help for their hearing impairments in military centers established specifically for their needs. Services consisted of diagnosis, medical treatment where indicated, and rehabilitative measures, including vocational and psychiatric counseling. On returning to civilian life, military personnel who had worked in these programs applied this experience to the establishment of comprehensive services, to the development of academic and professional curricula for preparation of professionals, and to stimulation of basic and applied research. In the United States, wide-ranging legislative sanction and public fiscal support secured these programs.

Bibliography

Békésy, G. von, and W. A. Rosenblith: "The Early History of Hearing-Observations and Theories," *Journal of the Acoustical Society of America*, 20:727–748, 1948.

Davis, H., and S. R. Silverman (eds): *Hearing and Deafness*, 4th ed., 1978.

Jerger, J. (ed.): *Modern Developments in Audiology*, 1963.

Silverman, S. R.: "Historical Foundations of Speech Audiometry," in D. F. Konkle and W. F. Rintelmann (eds.), *Principles of Speech Audiometry*, 1983.

————: "Update, 1960–1980 in the United States," in R. E. Bender, *The Conquest of Deafness*, 1981.

S. Richard Silverman

CERTIFICATION

The Certificate of Clinical Competence (CCC) in audiology is widely acknowledged as evidence that the holder is qualified to provide independent audiologic services to hearing-impaired children and adults. This voluntary standards program was established for its members by the American Speech–Language–Hearing Association (ASHA) in 1952. The certificate in audiology is one of two certificates offered by the association; the other is in speech-language pathology.

The purpose of the ASHA certification program is to provide a means for the public to identify competent individual practitioners. The certificate signifies that the applicant has specific knowledge and clinical skill considered necessary for the delivery of professional services to communicatively impaired individuals.

The requirements for the Certificate of Clinical Competence are divided into three areas: (1) Educational preparation: Satisfactory completion of an academic program leading to a master's degree or its equivalent is mandatory. A minimum number of credits is required in various areas covering the normal and disordered processes of hearing, speech, and language. (2) Clinical practice: At least 300 hours of supervised clinical experience must be obtained within the academic program, at least half of which must be at the graduate level. The applicant must then obtain the equivalent of nine months of full-time professional experience under the supervision of a certified audiologist. (3) Examination: The applicant must pass the National Examination in Audiology. This written examination is administered periodically throughout the United States. It covers the applicant's knowledge of the basic auditory sciences as well as factors associated with clinical skill in the field. The maintenance of active membership in ASHA was a requirement for the Certificate of Clinical Competence until 1980. Certification by the association is now available to anyone meeting the above standards.

The certification standards of the association are set by the Council on Professional Standards in Speech-Language Pathology and Audiology. The Standards Council was established by the governing body of the ASHA in 1980 as a semiautonomous group. In addition to the requirements for the Certificate of Clinical Competence, the council establishes standards for the accreditation of educational programs at the master's level, and of professional service programs in audiology and speech-language pathology. The Standards Council monitors the administrative activities of three operating boards and evaluates appeals of board decisions. The Clinical Certification Board determines whether applicants meet the standards of individual competence established by the council.

ASHA maintains a voluntary program to recognize those who continue to participate in approved learning experiences following the completion of their formal education. Continuing Education Units are awarded, and a registry of program participants is maintained by the association. This program represents a commitment to continuing education in preserving and improving the clinical skills of Certificate of Clinical Competence holders throughout their professional careers.

Bibliography

American Speech–Language–Hearing Association: *Requirements for the Certificates of Clinical Competence*, 1983.
Phillip A. Yantis

SERVICE SETTINGS

The audiologist works in a wide variety of service settings. The precise activities of individual audiologists depend on the type of service facility in which they work (see table).

Universities Audiologists who work in university settings are involved primarily in teaching students to be audiologists or speech-language pathologists. In addition to classroom instruction, they supervise student clinical practicum and direct student research projects. Audiologists often conduct or direct ongoing clinical services and research projects as part of their academic responsibilities and as a means to provide opportunities for students to have clinical and research experiences.

Medical Centers and Hospitals In most medical centers, hospitals, and rehabilitative agencies, a major role of audiologists is to perform hearing testing services, including the pre- and postoperative evaluation of otologic surgical patients. The audiologist receives referrals from a wide variety of medical specialists and surgeons, including otolaryngologists, neurologists, neurosurgeons, pediatricians, family practitioners, and internists. In hospitals with active intensive care infant nurseries, the audiologist may be responsible for directing and supervising a hearing screening program for at-risk infants to identify those babies who may have a hearing loss. Audiologists in hospital-based

ASHA Audiologists by Primary Employment Setting (1983)[a]

Setting	Number	Percentage[b]
College or university	660	12.1
School	525	9.7
Nongovernmental health service[c]	1401	25.8
Governmental health service	252	4.6
Private practice	478	8.8
Other setting	602	11.1
Unknown	1513	27.9
Total in United States	5431	100

[a]From J. Punch, Characteristics of ASHA Members, *Asha*, 25(10):31, 1983. [b]Based on total unknown. [c]Includes nonuniversity clinics, hospitals, and rehabilitation facilities.

clinics often dispense hearing aids as part of their total aural rehabilitation services. The Veterans Administration hospitals and medical centers employ audiologists for diagnostic and therapeutic work with the large number of military service veterans who have hearing impairment.

Schools Most states mandate some sort of hearing screening program in public and private schools. These school hearing screening programs are directed and supervised by audiologists. Children receive hearing tests at various times during their primary and secondary school years to identify educationally handicapping hearing loss. The children with hearing losses are referred for medical treatment to improve their hearing problem, or are fitted with hearing aids if their hearing loss is not amenable to medical treatment. Audiologists also work with classroom teachers in accommodating the special educational needs of their hearing-impaired children.

When there are special classes for hearing-impaired children within the school, the audiologist may be responsible for the selection, installation, and adjustment of amplification systems for the classroom. Some audiologists also participate in the instructional programs for those classes. An audiologist may perform these same functions in a school for deaf children and, in that same setting, may do periodic hearing evaluations of all children in the school and work with them with their individual wearable hearing aids.

Medical Office Settings Many audiologists are employed by or are partners in private practice medical offices or group medical clinics. The audiologists in these work settings spend most of their time in direct patient contact, conducting a full realm of diagnostic audiologic hearing tests, vestibular evaluations, and hearing-aid dispensing. Usually the audiologist in a medical practice works most closely with an otolaryngologist, a physician who specializes in diseases of the ears, nose, and throat.

Private Practice A trend has been growing for audiologists to establish themselves in private practice offices. So far, the largest activity for these audiologists is the retail dispensing of hearing aids directly to hearing-impaired consumers. Those audiologists who distinguish themselves from the traditional commercial hearing-aid dealers also provide a full program of aural rehabilitation for those persons who do purchase hearing aids. Other prominent aspects of private audiologic practice are diagnostic services and hearing conservation consultation and service to industry. The audiologist in private practice, in addition to drawing upon special knowledge of hearing, hearing impairment, and hearing aids, must possess additional skills in business-related activities such as financial planning, marketing, and public relations.

Community Hearing and Speech Centers These centers employ audiologists to work with adults and children with hearing impairments. In this employment setting, the audiologist more often is a rehabilitation specialist rather than a medically oriented diagnostician. The audiologist performs hearing tests, selects and fits hearing aids, and guides the rehabilitation of hearing-impaired individuals fitted with personal amplification. Many such facilities include special education programs for hearing-impaired children who benefit from the audiologist's special training and understanding of pediatric problems. The audiologist's duties may include helping individuals use their hearing aids better, working to improve speech and reading skills of hearing-impaired listeners, or assisting in community public service health education programs.

Industry Excessive noise in the workplace contributes substantially to employee hearing loss. The audiologist plays a major role in dealing with hearing problems related to overexposure to noise. Governmental influences, through the Occupational Safety and Health Act and the Workman's Compensation Program, require that employers with noisy work environments provide for employee hearing protection. Many industries employ audiologists to conduct hearing conservation programs which involve periodic employee hearing tests, development of noise reduction plans, and the issue and maintenance of ear protectors for hearing protection of employees.

Bibliography

Davis, H.: "Audiology," in H. Davis and S. R. Silverman (eds.), *Hearing and Deafness*, 4th ed., Holt, Rinehart and Winston, New York, 1978.

Punch, J.: "Characteristics of ASHA Members," *Asha*, 25(10):31, 1983.

Jerry L. Northern

AUDIOMETRY

Audiometry is the measurement of hearing. This broad term includes many procedures and tests used to define the type, degree, and communicative consequences of hearing loss. The major diagnostic purposes of audiometry may be grouped under two areas: medical diagnosis and communicative ability. In terms of medical diagnosis, audiometry is used to determine whether there is a reason to suspect an underlying pathologic condition or disorder based on audiometric test findings. Certain characteristics of hearing losses, for example, are associated with disorders in relatively specific anatomic locations within the auditory system. In the case of communicative function, audiometry is aimed at a description of the perceptual abnormalities associated with any presenting hearing loss. Audiometry is used to understand a patient's ability to hear and understand speech and to communicate effectively in everyday listening situations.

Clinical hearing tests are designed to evaluate two basic aspects of audition: sensitivity and discrimination (or acuity). Hearing-sensitivity measures determine the weakest signal level at which a person can just detect the presence of sound. The subject is only required to judge the presence or absence of a test sound. The minimum sound levels (dB SPL, or decibels sound pressure level) required at threshold for tones are hearing-sensitivity measures. Measures that require an identification response or judgments of sound differences on the part of a listener are tests of auditory discrimination or acuity. Tests of loudness perception and the identification of words or other speech material are examples of discrimination tasks.

Test procedures used in clinical audiometry result in relative measures, in the sense that responses or test findings for a given individual are classified according to norms collected for a control group of subjects with normal auditory function. If a person is said to have a hearing loss, for example, it means the person's hearing sensitivity is less than that for an average individual.

In considering the purpose and results of audiologic tests, it is important to distinguish the terms hearing loss and hearing handicap or impairment. Hearing-sensitivity measures provide estimates of hearing loss (in dB). The degree of communicative handicap or impairment associated with a given amount of hearing loss, however, may differ across individuals depending on many factors such as the extent of damage to, or lesion of, the anatomic structures and the age of the person at onset of the hearing loss. There is a poor predictive relation, for example, between hearing-sensitivity measures and speech discrimination performance. Accordingly, two individuals with the same degree of hearing loss (in dB) may demonstrate substantially different abilities to communicate effectively in everday situations.

There are numerous specific audiometric test procedures and techniques. In addition to routine tone and speech audiometry based on behavioral responses, for example, there are electrophysiologic procedures. Here, no behavioral response is required on the part of the listener; judgments regarding auditory function are based on changes in ongoing electric activity of the central nervous system in response to sound. This type of procedure is useful in auditory diagnosis for patients (such as babies and mentally retarded children) who are unwilling or unable to provide appropriate behavioral responses to test signals. Specialized audiometric procedures are available for determining the anatomic site of a lesion or insult to the auditory system. Acoustic-immittance measures, for example, are particularly powerful in evaluating middle-ear function. The battery of tests used will depend on the presenting symptoms and the response capabilities of the individual. In addition, the outcome for one test procedure may dictate the need for further tests.

Terry L. Wiley

Principles

In audiometry, pure tones (single frequencies from 125 to 8000 Hz) and speech are most commonly used to determine an individual's hearing thresholds, that is, levels necessary for the sounds just to be audible. Responses to speech at levels above threshold often are evaluated also.

Test signals usually are presented to listeners via earphones and via a bone vibrator. Use of earphones allows each ear to be tested individually by air conduction; the vibrations from the earphone are conducted through the air in the ear canal to set the eardrum and three attached tiny bones (ossicles) into motion to transmit the stimulus to the inner ear (cochlea). The cochlea converts the stimulus to nerve impulses to be directed to the brain for interpretation. Bone-conduction testing uses a bone vibrator held tightly against the skull to transmit the vibrations directly to the skull and to the cochlea, bypassing the ear canal, eardrum, and ossicles. Comparison of thresholds obtained by air conduction and bone conduction provides diagnostic information on the status of the ear canal, eardrum, ossicles, cochlea, and auditory nerve. *See* EAR: Anatomy.

The audiogram is a chart reporting tests results for routine audiometric testing. The 0 line on the audiogram represents the average hearing sensitivity (threshold levels) for young individuals having "normal" ears. The sound levels for normal hearing (0 dB HL, or decibels hearing level) are agreed upon nationally by the American National Standards Institute (ANSI) and internationally by the International Standards Organization (ISO). The normal range includes persons whose hearing thresholds for 125–8000 Hz are within the range of −10 to 25 dB HL and who rarely report any difficulty with hearing. However, it must be noted that thresholds of 15-25 dB may still signify that something about the hearing mechanism is not normal.

Hearing losses may be conductive, sensorineural, or mixed. A conductive hearing loss is due to one or more problems in the air-conduction route of the ear canal, eardrum, or ossicles. A sensorineural

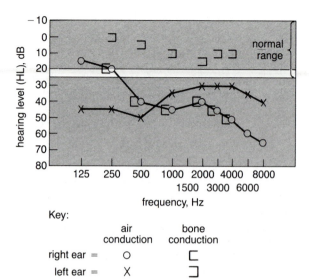

Audiogram (pure tone) for routine audiometric testing. The test results for the right ear show hearing sensitivity within normal limits for 125 and 250 Hz, but below normal for 500 to 8000 Hz, indicating a hearing loss across the latter frequency range. The bone-conduction symbols for the right ear are at the same levels as the air-conduction symbols, indicating that the hearing loss is sensorineural. All thresholds for the left ear are below normal from 125 through 8000 Hz. However, the bone-conduction thresholds for the left ear are better, within normal limits, indicating that the cochlea and auditory nerve probably are normal. These results indicate that the hearing loss for the left ear is conductive.

hearing loss is due to damage to the cochlea (sensory) or auditory nerve (neural). For a mixed hearing loss, the thresholds for air-conducted sounds are poorer than for the same signals presented via bone conduction, but one or more bone conduction thresholds also are greater than 25 dB HL.

Routine speech audiometry evaluates thresholds (speech reception threshold) for two-syllable words (spondees) and ability to understand speech (word recognition scores) for one-syllable words (monosyllables), at one or more levels above the speech reception threshold. The speech reception thresholds are at levels similar to the air-conduction thresholds for one or more frequencies between 500 and 2000 Hz. In the audiogram shown here, the word recognition scores at 25 dB sensation level (25 dB above the speech reception threshold) show less-than-perfect understanding of monosyllables (76 percent) for the right ear with the sensorineural hearing loss. The score for the left ear is perfect, 100 percent. These results reveal that speech loud enough to be heard easily is understood perfectly by the left (conductive hearing loss) ear, but not by the right (sensorineural hearing loss) ear. Such differences are expected for the two types of hearing losses. *See* AUDIOLOGIC CLASSIFICATION.

Bibliography

Davis, H., and S. R. Silverman (eds.): *Hearing and Deafness*, rev. ed., Holt, Rinehart and Winston, New York, 1960, and 3d ed., 1970.

Newby, H. A.: *Audiology Principles and Practice*, Appleton Century Crofts, New York, 1958.

Wayne O. Olsen

Pure-Tone Audiogram

The pure-tone audiogram reflects the ear's sensitivity to the various frequencies (tones) tested. Frequency in cycles per second is designated by hertz (abbreviated Hz). The audiogram form is arranged so that octave frequencies and some half-octave frequencies are represented across the top. The frequency increases from left to right. The audiologist samples hearing sensitivity at several specific frequencies within that range. The range 125 to 8000 Hz includes the important frequencies for hearing and understanding speech. For example, the main frequency of a man's voice is about 125 Hz, while the main frequency of a woman's voice is around 250 Hz. The voice actually is a complex sound wave made up of a set of evenly spaced frequencies, called harmonics, based on the main or fundamental frequencies. The harmonics resonate in the oral and nasal cavities, which gives the vowels and consonants their particular characteristics. Certain consonant sounds such as "s" and "sh" contain frequencies up to, and beyond, 8000 Hz.

The hearing-level (HL) scale on the left axis of an audiogram shows the strength of the test sound in decibels (dB). The sensitivity of the ear to each frequency tested is recorded in dB HL. The usual range on the audiogram is between −10 dB HL at the top to 110 or 120 dB HL at the bottom.

It has been recommended that the octave frequencies be evenly spaced across the top of the audiogram so that each octave spacing is equal to 20 dB on the hearing-level scale. This provides a grid upon which a person's hearing sensitivity across the frequencies may be displayed.

Threshold of sensitivity is usually defined as the weakest level at which a person responds to a test frequency 50 percent of the time that it is presented. The threshold sensitivity is the measure of interest for the pure-tone audiogram.

PURE-TONE STANDARDS

A pure tone cannot be perfectly pure (that is, a single frequency), but its degree of purity can be specified. Current standards specify that all of the harmonics of a pure tone must be at least 30 dB below (that is, 1000 times less intense than) the level of the specified frequency of the tone.

In order to be meaningful, the decibel must have a reference level. A common reference for physical sound measurement is 0.0002 microbar or dyne/

Table 1. Reference Levels for 0 dB HL in dB SPL (Referenced to 0.0002 microbar)*

Frequency (Hz)	dB SPL
125	45.0
250	25.5
500	11.5
1000	7.0
1500	6.5
2000	9.0
3000	10.0
4000	9.5
6000	15.5
8000	13.0

*These values apply to a standard earphone and earphone cushion (Telephonics TDH-39 with the MX-41/AR cushion).

cm^2, or, depending on the units of measure, 20 micropascals. This is an extremely small sound pressure. If a signal occurs that equals 0.0002 microbar in sound pressure, it is by definition 0 dB sound pressure level (SPL).

The ear is most sensitive in the middle frequencies (500 through 4000 Hz) and less sensitive to lower and higher frequencies. The HL scale is a decibel scale based on the hearing sensitivity at each frequency of a large number of normal people. On the audiogram, 0 dB HL represents the level at each frequency that young adults with normal hearing can just barely hear. The intensity level in dB SPL equal to 0 dB HL for each frequency is shown in Table 1.

A significant proportion of hearing losses are not flat (about the same across all frequencies). Older people and those exposed to loud noise over a period of years typically have a greater loss in the high frequencies than in the low frequencies. These people have greater difficulty than would be expected from the categorization of hearing based on 500, 1000, and 2000 Hz. They have difficulty hearing high-frequency consonant sounds. Because English is highly dependent on consonant recognition, their ability to understand spoken English is reduced.

CALCULATION OF HEARING LOSS

The percent hearing loss calculation is a medicolegal tool used to adjudicate compensation cases involving hearing. In the past, at least, it was based on the threshold results at 500, 1000, and 2000 Hz and therefore subject to problems of applicability to hearing losses that are not flat. Hearing sensitivity that is better than 26 dB HL is not considered a loss, and hearing worse than 93 dB HL is considered a total loss. Thus, the range from 0 to 100 percent hearing loss covers a range of 67 dB. Each decibel step above 26 dB HL, therefore, is rated to 1.5 percent. In order to calculate the percent hearing loss, the thresholds at 500, 1000, and 2000 Hz are averaged, then 26 dB is subtracted from the average, and the remainder is multiplied by 1.5 percent. This is done for both ears. An additional calculation will give the binaural percent hearing loss. The binaural percent calculation assumes that one ear is about as good as two. In some compensation rules, the better-ear percent is multiplied by five and then added to the poorer-ear percent. The sum is then divided by six to give the binaural percent hearing loss.

What has been described is for medicolegal purposes. It is difficult to estimate the degree of difficulty a person has with a hearing loss based only on pure-tone results. The pure-tone results give threshold sensitivity but do not provide suprathreshold information such as loudness growth or clarity of pitch perception.

AIR-CONDUCTION TESTING

In order to test hearing sensitivity to 0 dB HL, certain precautions must be taken to ensure that the noise level in the test area will not interfere. A noise survey should determine the amount of noise within an octave band surrounding each frequency that is to be tested. Table 2 shows the maximum allowable noise levels for testing air-conduction threshold to 0 dB HL by using standard earphones and earphone cushions.

Preparation   After the patient is seated comfortably, the ears should be checked visually to determine if the ear canal could close when the ears are pushed against the head by the earphones. Collapsible ear canals result in a hearing loss that is not present normally, without earphones. If this condition is present, it should be corrected prior to testing.

Table 2. Maximum Allowable Octave-Band Noise Levels in dB SPL for Air-Conduction Threshold Measurement*

Frequency, Hz	dB SPL
125	28.0
250	23.0
500	21.5
1000	29.5
1500	29.0
2000	34.5
3000	39.0
4000	42.0
6000	41.0
8000	45.0

*These values apply when using an earphone with a standard earphone cushion (MX-41/AR).

Instructions to the patient should be brief and clear. The patient is told what will be heard and what types of response should be given, that is, pressing a button, raising a hand, or responding verbally to each tone that is heard. For young children, responses such as dropping marbles or stacking rings may be used.

The earphones are placed so that the red right earphone and the blue left earphone are on the right and left ears, respectively. The hole in each earphone cushion is placed directly over the ear canal.

Testing   The Hughson-Westlake method for acquiring threshold is a modified ascending psychophysical technique described graphically by a threshold-seeking flow chart. Testing is initiated at 40 dB HL. If there is a response, the test sound must descend in 10-dB steps until there is no response. If there is no response at 40 dB HL, the test

Threshold-seeking flow chart; threshold is the lowest level at which responses occur at least 50 percent of the time.

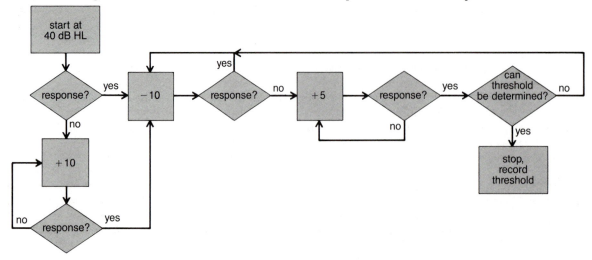

sound must ascend in 10-dB steps until there is a response. The initial search for a response may be done in 15- or 20-dB steps, except above 80 dB HL where 5- or 10-dB steps are used. This should bring the testing within 10 to 20 dB of the threshold. The threshold search consists of descending 10-dB steps and ascending 5-dB steps. The judgment of threshold is made on the basis of the ascending 5-dB steps.

Threshold is defined clinically by the lowest ascending 5-dB step at which responses occur at least 50 percent of the time. Because of the use of 5-dB rather than 1-dB steps, the actual 50 percent level of response may not be found. Often, responses may occur 60–70 percent of the time at one level and only 0–25 percent at 5 dB below that.

The threshold level obtained is recorded on the audiogram on the vertical line representing the frequency tested and at the level found on the dB HL scale. The right ear is represented by a red O and the left ear is represented by a blue X. Straight lines may be drawn between the symbols for each ear. The lines are red for the right ear and blue for the left ear.

Test Protocol The test ear is selected. The threshold measure starts at 1000 Hz and proceeds through 2000, 4000, and 8000 Hz. The half-octave steps may be tested if there are large differences in threshold between the octave frequencies. Then 1000 Hz is retested as a validity check, followed by 500, 250 Hz, and sometimes 125 Hz. This procedure is then completed for the other ear.

Masking In many cases of hearing loss, there is a difference in sensitivity between ears. If the difference is large enough, there is a possibility that the better ear may hear the tone that is being presented to the less sensitive ear. In order to prevent the better ear from participating in the test of the poorer ear, a masking noise is introduced in the better ear. When the proper amount of masking noise is used, it raises the threshold of the nontest ear so that the responses that are given reflect the hearing of the test ear.

Limitations Measuring hearing via air conduction shows the overall sensitivity of the peripheral auditory system. It does not distinguish between the various types and combinations of disorders which could contribute to a hearing loss. A disorder at one or more points along the route between the outer ear and the brainstem could result in a sensitivity loss.

Bibliography

AAOO Committee on Conservation of Hearing: "Guide for the Evaluation of Hearing Impairment: A Report of the Committee on Conservation of Hearing," *Transactions of the American Academy of Ophthalmology and Otolaryngology*, 63:236–238, 1959.

American National Standards Institute. *Standard Criteria for Permissible Ambient Noise During Audiometric Testing*, ANSI-S3.1-1977, 1977.

————: *Standard Specifications for Audiometers*, ANSI-S3.6-1969, 1969.

ASHA Committee on Audiometric Evaluation: "Guidelines for Audiometric Symbols," *Asha*, 16:260–264, 1974.

Goodman, A.: "Reference Zero Levels for Pure-Tone Audiometer," *Asha*, 7:262–263, 1965.

Robert G. Ivey

BONE-CONDUCTION TESTING

Sound waves may reach human sensory receptors directly through the bones of the skull. Hearing by bone conduction occurs when a tuning fork or a mechanical vibrator (from an audiometer) is placed in direct contact with the skull. This mode of sound transmission is, however, far less efficient than the usual air-conduction route. Except for certain theoretic considerations, the principal interest in bone conduction has been its usefulness in the clinical diagnosis of middle-ear or conductive hearing loss. Together with air-conduction measurement, the measurement of bone conduction has been an integral part of almost all auditory diagnostic routines.

In most auditory evaluations, air-conduction thresholds are obtained initially to determine whether the individual has a hearing loss. Traditionally, the classical test to distinguish conductive (middle-ear) from sensorineural (inner-ear) impairment is the difference between air-conduction and bone-conduction threshold hearing levels. The distinction between conductive and sensorineural hearing loss is critical since the causes, prognosis, and medical treatment of the two types of hearing loss differ substantially.

Clinical Measurement In practice, bone-conduction measurements are usually performed with a vibrator applied to the mastoid bone (part of the skull bone located directly behind the auricle of the outer ear). A metal headband holds the vibrator in a fixed location with sufficient application force. The procedure for measuring bone-conduction thresholds is essentially the same as used for obtaining air-conduction thresholds. Tests are conducted at several representative frequencies (using a simple or pure tone) within the most useful range of human hearing. The intensity of the tone is varied on the audiometer either manually by the tester or automatically if a self-recording audiometer is used.

When testing an individual for air- and bone-conduction thresholds, there are potentially three outcomes of diagnostic importance. First, both the air- and bone-conduction thresholds may be normal, indicating that there is no hearing loss. Second, both air- and bone-conduction thresholds may be equally reduced from normal hearing, suggesting a sensorineural hearing loss. Last, the bone-conduction threshold may be normal or, at least, not as severely elevated as the air-conduction threshold. This last result indicates that the hearing loss is either totally or partially conductive, depending on the hearing level of the bone-conduction threshold.

The clinical utility of the difference between air- and bone-conduction thresholds (the so-called air-bone gap) is based primarily on two assumptions: (1) that the air-conduction threshold depends on the function of the entire hearing system, both conductive (external and middle ear) and sensorineural (receptors in the cochlea and auditory nerve); and (2) that the threshold for bone conduction is a measure of the integrity of only the sensorineural auditory system. The second principle assumes that sound transmitted by the skull bones bypasses the middle ear and travels directly to the cochlea, resulting in stimulation of the sensory receptors. Investigators have demonstrated, however, that both the external and middle ear contribute to hearing by bone conduction. However, as a first approximation, the bone-conduction threshold primarily measures the sensorineural impairment, and the air-bone gap is an estimate of middle-ear or conductive impairment.

Because the bone-conduction threshold is a reasonable approximation of the integrity of the inner ear, ear surgeons often use bone-conduction threshold levels as an estimate of the potential success of an operative procedure. *See* AUDITORY DISORDERS, REMEDIATION OF: Surgical Treatment.

Limiting Factors   The measurement of bone-conduction threshold usually is more complicated than the assessment of air-conduction thresholds. The

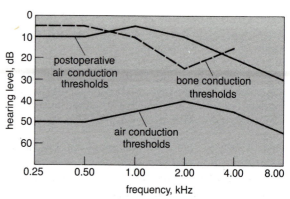

Air- and bone-conduction thresholds of a patient with surgically confirmed stapes fixation due to otosclerosis. The patient has a moderate hearing loss by air conduction but essentially normal auditory thresholds by bone conduction. The difference between the air- and bone-conduction thresholds indicates that there is an air-bone gap, suggesting the presence of a conductive loss. For this particular auditory impairment, surgery was performed and the hearing was eventually returned to normal.

complications are related to two major difficulties: (1) listening by bone conduction is, in most instances, a special case of binaural hearing (stimulation of both ears simultaneously) and requires elimination of one ear through masking in order to measure the other ear; and (2) the specification of the physical intensity level from a bone vibrator is more difficult to standardize than from an air-conduction receiver.

1. Masking. When a test signal is applied to the skull via a vibrator or tuning fork, the entire skull is set into vibration. The two cochleas, embedded within the same skull, are stimulated almost equally regardless of the location of the vibrator or tuning fork on either side of the head. Thus, most thresholds obtained by bone conduction are really binaural (listening with two ears) measurements. The implication is that the ears of an individual cannot be tested separately by bone conduction unless one ear (nontest) is eliminated from the test. In order to isolate the test ear, a masking noise is presented simultaneously to the nontest ear.

The rules for masking (the required intensity level and other characteristics of the noise) are reasonably well understood today; however, the practical application of the appropriate level of noise can be a problem in some patients with hearing loss. The masker is usually presented to the nontest ear via an earphone so that the masking noise is restricted to that ear. In some patients with moderate-to-severe hearing loss, the noise must be presented at an intense level before the masker becomes effective. As the noise level is raised, eventually the masker itself begins to vibrate the skull and affect the threshold of the test ear. This is known as over-

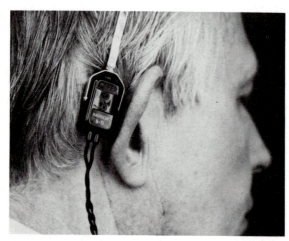

Conventional bone vibrator located on the mastoid process of a subject during testing.

masking. There are also instances of moderate-to-severe hearing loss in which the level of the masker cannot be made intense enough to completely eliminate the nontest ear. Problems of insufficient masking or overmasking sometimes limit the use of bone-conduction measurements in clinical diagnoses. In those cases, other test procedures must be used in order to demonstrate the presence of a middle-ear impairment.

2. Standardization of testing system. As in air-conduction audiometry, it is necessary to adjust or calibrate the bone-conduction system so that the appropriate electric voltage is delivered to the vibrator when the intensity dial on an audiometer is set to zero decibels. Bone-conduction vibrators, however, are more difficult to standardize than air-conduction earphones. The mechanical vibrations transmitted by a bone vibrator from sound stimulation are altered by the characteristic of the skull and skin. Unfortunately, these characteristics vary greatly among individuals.

For many years it was standard practice to determine if the bone-conduction system of an audiometer was in calibration by testing bone-conduction thresholds on a group of listeners who had normal hearing by air conduction. The scale for bone-conduction hearing levels was then set so that no air-bone gap was determined for the normal listeners. However, "artificial headbones" have become available, which contain mechanical characteristics that simulate an average normal skull. It will be possible to calibrate a bone-conduction vibrator physically by measuring the vibrator's mechanical output on a standard artificial headbone. This development should lead to accurate and reliable standardization of bone-conduction testing systems among clinics and laboratories.

Summary Bone-conduction thresholds have been used primarily in clinical diagnosis to determine the presence or absence of a middle-ear hearing loss. These measurements can also be used by surgeons for prognostic purposes, that is, to estimate the potential success for restoring hearing for air conduction through surgery treatment. Bone-conduction thresholds are somewhat more difficult to measure than air-conduction thresholds because both ears are stimulated when the skull is set in vibration and because there is inadequate standardization of bone-conduction testing systems. Despite such problems, the measurement of bone-conduction thresholds makes an important and useful contribution in almost every auditory diagnostic examination.

Bibliography

Békésy, G. v.: "Bone Conduction," *Experiments in Hearing*, chap. 9, McGraw-Hill, New York, 1960.

Dirks, D. D.: "Bone-Conduction Testing," in Jack Katz (ed.), *Handbook of Clinical Audiology*, chap. 10, Williams and Wilkins, Baltimore, 1978.

Tonndorf, J.: "Bone Conduction: Studies in Experimental Animals," *Acta Otolaryngol.*, Suppl. 213, 1966.

Donald D. Dirks

Acoustic-Immittance Measures

Acoustic immittance is an encompassing term defined as either acoustic impedance or acoustic admittance, or both. Impedance represents the opposition to the flow of energy, and admittance is the ease with which energy flows through a system. The associated term "acoustic" indicates the form of energy under measurement. Acoustic impedance and acoustic admittance are reciprocal terms. A system that offers high acoustic impedance (opposition) to the flow of sound has low acoustic admittance. Acoustic-immittance measures in human ears characterize the energy-transfer function of the ear (at the tympanic membrane) when sound is delivered to it.

Clinical acoustic-immittance measures are used as routine adjuncts to audiometric tests. The rationale for acoustic-immittance measures is based, in part, on the finding that persons may present significant ear disease with little or no hearing loss. Audiometry results will determine the degree and type of any presenting hearing loss, but may not necessarily reflect existent otic (ear) disease. It has been demonstrated, for example, that active middle-ear disease (such as otitis media) may be present in a significant proportion of young children who have normal hearing. Here, acoustic-immittance measures are particularly valuable. In contrast to routine audiometry, acoustic-immittance measures are effective in detecting the presence and character of middle-ear disorders. In addition, acoustic-immittance procedures require no behavioral response on the part of the patient. This is an advantage because the measures can be obtained in clinical patients (such as infants, very young children, and mentally retarded persons) for whom behavioral response techniques are not always feasible.

INSTRUMENTAL PRINCIPLES

Acoustic-immittance measures in human ears are based on the measured sound-pressure level of a probe signal in the ear canal. A probe unit is sealed (airtight) in the ear canal by means of a rubber cuff. The probe unit contains openings connected to the three subsystems of the instrument. One subsystem provides for the introduction of a tone in the ear canal space between the probe tip and the tympanic membrane (eardrum). A separate microphone and meter system monitors the sound-pressure level of the probe signal in the ear canal.

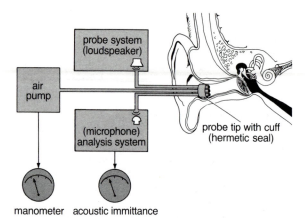

probe system
(loudspeaker)

air
pump

(microphone)
analysis system

probe tip with cuff
(hermetic seal)

manometer   acoustic immittance

Simplified block diagram of an electroacoustic-immittance instrument and its coupling to the human ear. (After J. Katz, ed., *Handbook of Clinical Audiology*, 3d ed., Williams and Wilkins, Baltimore, 1985)

The acoustic immittance offered by the ear under test is proportional to the sound-pressure level of the probe signal. The higher the acoustic impedance, for example, the higher the measured sound-pressure level of the probe signal. Another opening in the probe tip, the third subsystem, allows for the introduction of air-pressure changes in the ear canal, used in tympanometry.

TYMPANOMETRY

Tympanometry is the measure of acoustic immittance in the ear canal as a function of air pressure in the canal. Acoustic-immittance measures are made as air pressure is varied above (+) and below (−) atmospheric level in the ear canal. The tympanogram is a graphic representation of acoustic admittance or acoustic impedance as a function of ear canal pressure. In the case of a normal middle-ear system, the opposition to sound flow (or acoustic impedance) is least at air pressures close to ambient or atmospheric level (0). As air pressure is increased or decreased from atmospheric condition, the acoustic impedance is increased (or the acoustic admittance is decreased). The positive or negative air-pressure changes effectively stiffen the tympanic membrane and connected ossicular chain, resulting in a reduction in energy transfer through the middle-ear system.

The normal variation in acoustic immittance with air pressure is altered in middle-ear disorders. Characteristic tympanogram configurations are identified with specific pathologic conditions of the middle ear. In cases of serous otitis media with effusion (fluid), the tympanogram may be flat in configuration. The middle-ear fluid severely dampens the ossicular chain, and since the middle-ear transmission system is already stiffened by the presence of fluid, there is little or no change in acoustic immittance with alterations in ear canal pressure. In direct contrast, a disruption of the ossicular chain typically will result in a tympanogram whose peak is of greater amplitude than normal. The discontinuity in the ossicular chain results in less-than-normal opposition to sound flow, resulting in greater changes in acoustic admittance with ear canal pressure.

Tympanometric measures can be used to estimate the resting-state or static acoustic immittance at the tympanic membrane. Static measures are those acoustic-immittance values demonstrated under two concurrent conditions: (1) when the air pressure in the ear canal is at atmospheric or ambient levels, and (2) when the middle-ear muscles are relaxed (not contracted). Conventionally, static measures are referenced to the lateral surface of the tympanic membrane. During tympanometry, however, the probe tip is remote from the tympanic membrane. The portion of the ear canal separating the probe tip and eardrum contributes to the acoustic-immittance measure at the probe tip. In order to reference the static acoustic-immittance measures to the tympanic membrane, the clinician must extract the effects of this ear canal volume. This is done by subtracting the acoustic-immittance value (taken from the tympanogram) at a high negative ear canal pressure [such as − 400 dekapascals or millimeters of water (mm H_2O)] from the value at ambient (zero) ear canal pressure. Effectively, the high negative pressure stiffens the middle-ear transmission system, and the acoustic-immittance value approximates that offered by the residual ear canal volume between the probe tip and the eardrum. The value at zero pressure represents this volume plus the

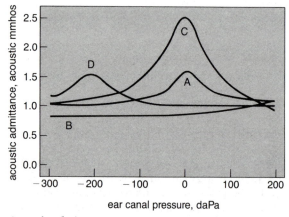

Acoustic-admittance tympanograms typically observed in: A, subjects with a normal middle-ear system; B, cases of serous otitis media (middle-ear fluid); C, cases of ossicular chain disruption; and D, cases of eustachian tube obstruction. The probe frequency is 220 Hz. Acoustic admittance (in acoustic millimhos) is shown as a function of ear canal pressure (in dekapascals).

contributions of the eardrum and middle-ear system. The resultant (after subtraction) is an estimate of the acoustic immittance offered at the tympanic membrane.

Like tympanograms, static acoustic-immittance values are altered in cases of middle-ear disorders. In cases of serous otitis media, for example, the middle-ear fluid stiffens the middle-ear transmission system, resulting in static acoustic-impedance values much higher than normal. A similar, but less dramatic, finding is observed in cases of otosclerosis with associated stapedial fixation. Disruptions of the ossicular chain, in contrast, result in acoustic-impedance values much lower than normal. Here, the ossicular discontinuity results in less opposition to sound flow at the eardrum. Accordingly, acoustic impedance is decreased (or acoustic admittance is increased) compared to normal.

Tympanometry can be used as an indirect measure of eustachian tube function. This is an important adjunct to the assessment of middle-ear function because tubal dysfunction often is a precursor of middle-ear disease. Eustachian tube obstruction, for example, is often associated with initial stages of otitis media.

The tympanogram pressure at which acoustic admittance is greatest (or acoustic impedance is at its minimum) is a rough approximation of the resting pressure in the middle ear. The opposition to sound flow is least when the pressure on both sides of the tympanic membrane is equal. This indirect measure of middle-ear resting pressure provides a means of evaluating the ventilatory function of the eustachian tube. In normal subjects, with proper eustachian tube function, the tympanogram peak occurs near ambient (atmospheric) pressure. The normal ventilatory function of the eustachian tube maintains equilibrium between atmospheric and middle-ear pressure. In early stages of otitis media, however, the eustachian tube may be obstructed, resulting in a negative middle-ear resting pressure. Tympanometry, then, provides a means of tracking eustachian tube function. This is important diagnostically as well as for evaluating the success of treatment for middle-ear disease.

STAPEDIAL REFLEX MEASURES
The stapedius muscle will contract in response to an acoustic signal of sufficient intensity and duration. This is termed an acoustic reflex. When the stapedius muscle contracts, it pulls the head of the stapes down and away from the oval window. This, in turn, stiffens the ossicular chain, resulting in a decrease in sound transmission through the middle ear. The acoustic immittance measured at the tympanic membrane, then, will change with a stapedial contraction. Under stapedial contraction, the acoustic admittance will decrease, whereas its re-

ciprocal, acoustic impedance, is increased. Thus, stapedius muscle function can be monitored indirectly by measuring acoustic-immittance changes at the tympanic membrane. Because the measure is indirect, the integrity of the measure is dependent on: (1) a normal middle-ear system; (2) a normal, neuronal afferent (sensory) auditory system; and (3) a normal, neuronal efferent (motor) system associated with the stapedial reflex arc. Abnormalities in any of these three systems may result in abnormal stapedial reflex measures.

The acoustic reflex is bilateral in normal subjects. An acoustic activating signal that produces a stapedial reflex in one ear also will cause an acoustic reflex (stapedius contraction) in the opposite ear. Ipsilateral acoustic reflex measures are those in which acoustic-immittance changes are monitored in the same ear that receives the acoustic activator. Contralateral acoustic reflex measures are performed by presenting an acoustic activator to one ear and monitoring acoustic-immittance changes in the opposite ear. The application and results of ipsilateral and contralateral acoustic reflex measures will depend on the functional integrity of the middle ear and of afferent-efferent neural systems for the two ears. In cases of unilateral middle-ear disease, for example, acoustic reflexes will usually be absent for ipsilateral and contralateral reflex measures with the acoustic-immittance probe in the affected ear. The presenting middle-ear disorder precludes the observance of acoustic-immittance changes with stapedius contractions. In cases of unilateral VIIIth nerve lesions, acoustic reflexes are often absent for those ipsilateral and contralateral acoustic reflex measures that involve activator presentation to the involved ear. Lesions of brainstem structures of the central auditory nervous system often are associated with abnormalities in one or both contralateral acoustic reflex measures.

Presently, three primary acoustic reflex characteristics are evaluated in audiologic diagnosis: (1) presence or absence of the reflex; (2) reflex threshold; and (3) reflex adaptation (or decay). The significance of absent acoustic reflexes has already been mentioned. The absence of an acoustic reflex means that no acoustic-immittance changes were observed with presentation of the acoustic activator at the highest intensity level available. If the reflex is present, further diagnostic information may be provided by determining the reflex threshold. This is the weakest level of the acoustic activating signal that produces a just-noticeable change in acoustic immittance. In normal subjects, the acoustic reflex threshold for tones occurs at 70–90 dB above the threshold of audibility. The acoustic reflex threshold may be elevated in cases of cochlear and VIIIth nerve disorders. In cochlear disorders, reflex thresholds for tones usually are elevated in direct proportion to the degree of sensorineural hearing loss. Reflex thresholds for patients with VIIIth nerve lesions, however, may be absent or disproportionately elevated in threshold based on the presenting sensorineural hearing loss. Indeed, the absence or threshold elevation of the acoustic reflex in the presence of normal hearing or a mild sensorineural hearing loss (with normal middle-ear function) is a positive sign for VIIIth nerve involvement.

Acoustic reflex adaptation or decay is defined as a reduction in reflex magnitude over time during presentation of a sustained acoustic activator. An acoustic activating signal is presented at a given level above reflex threshold for a specified time period (for example, 10 dB above reflex threshold for 10 seconds), and acoustic-immittance magnitude is monitored during the presentation interval. A low-frequency (500 or 1000 Hz) tone usually is used as an adaptation activator because normal subjects do not evidence reflex decay for these activators, whereas they will evidence reflex decay for activators of higher frequency. In contrast to normal subjects, patients with VIIIth nerve lesions typically demonstrate rapid reflex decay for 500- and 1000-Hz tonal activators. Patients with cochlear lesions also may demonstrate reflex decay, but the decay pattern will evidence less change (decay) in acoustic immittance and a slower time course of decay compared to the pattern for patients with VIIIth nerve involvement.

Bibliography

Katz, J. (ed.): *Handbook of Clinical Audiology*, 3d ed., Williams and Wilkins, Baltimore, 1985.

Silman, S. (ed.): *The Acoustic Reflex: Basic Principles and Clinical Applications*, Academic Press, Orlando, Florida, 1984.

Terry L. Wiley

Speech Sensitivity

A common component of a hearing evaluation is some measurement of a person's sensitivity to speech. This is defined as the lowest level at which speech is barely heard. Normally hearing listeners can detect very faint speech (10–15 dB SPL) and can recognize words or sentences at slightly higher levels (20–25 dB SPL). Hearing impairment results in a reduced ability to hear speech. A reduction in sensitivity to speech is called a hearing loss for speech and is expressed in dB HL. Thus, normal sensitivity to speech would be quantified as 0 dB HL (no hearing loss for speech), and the number of decibels above that level required to make speech audible to the listener would reflect the amount of hearing loss for speech.

MEASUREMENT

Speech sensitivity may be measured by means of establishing a threshold either for recognition of speech or for awareness of speech. The term speech reception threshold (SRT) is applied to the level at which speech can be recognized and repeated with 50 percent accuracy. The term speech awareness threshold (SAT) or speech detection threshold (SDT) is used for the level required for 50 percent accuracy in responding to the presence of speech.

The speech reception threshold is estimated by using easily recognizable speech materials so that if any part of the word or sentence is heard, one can accurately predict the remainder of the message. Frequently two-syllable words are used to establish the speech reception threshold. English language words such as baseball, duckpond, airplane, and cowboy are spondaic words. In order to increase the probability of recognition of the words at faint levels, the listener is familiarized with the list of words that he or she will hear before testing begins. The use of familiar, easily recognizable words makes it possible to assess sensitivity to speech with minimal influence by difficulties in understanding speech. The ease of recognition tends to give a whole list of words homogeneity of audibility. This implies that there is a relatively sharp division between sensitivity and audibility: if one word is understood, other words on the list will probably be understood. Simple, everyday sentences can also be used to determine a speech reception threshold. Recorded versions of standard speech materials are commercially available for speech reception threshold testing; however, amplified, monitored live-voice presentations are most common.

The level at which speech detection thresholds occur is slightly lower than the speech reception threshold. Rather than having to recognize the word or sentence heard, the listener merely has to be aware that something was spoken. Speech awareness levels often are used when speech reception thresholds cannot be obtained. For example, infants, who cannot be expected to recognize words, can be trained to respond in a way that indicates whether a sound was heard. Materials used for determination of speech detection thresholds are less rigorously specified than materials for speech reception thresholds. Sentences, short phrases, or single familiar words are presented variously from tape recordings or live voice.

RELATION TO PURE-TONE SENSITIVITY

The hearing loss for speech has been found to be closely related to hearing loss for pure tones in the frequency region from 500 to 2000 Hz. If a hearing loss is relatively flat and pure-tone thresholds are similar at the octave frequencies 500, 1000, and 2000 Hz, the speech reception threshold will be approximately equal to the average of the hearing loss in dB HL for those three tones. The pure-tone average (PTA) at 500, 1000, and 2000 Hz will overestimate the loss for speech if the pure-tone threshold is significantly worse for one of the three tones. In that case, the speech reception threshold is expected to be approximately equal to the average pure-tone threshold for the two tones for which there is less hearing loss (Fletcher's average). The close relation between pure-tone thresholds and speech reception thresholds is due to the predominance of speech sounds falling in the frequency region from 500 to 2000 Hz.

CLINICAL USE OF SPEECH SENSITIVITY MEASURES

Speech sensitivity measures may be used to estimate the severity of hearing loss. Classifications based on severity of hearing loss for speech parallel classification of pure-tone thresholds. Hearing loss for speech is rated as mild from 25 to 35 dB HL, as moderate from 40 to 55 dB HL, as severe from 60 to 85 dB HL, and as profound if over 90 dB HL. In normal conversation, speech occurs at an average level equivalent to approximately 55 dB HL. Therefore, with a mild loss for speech, conversational speech would sound faint. With a moderate loss, conversations would barely be detected, and with a severe hearing loss only very loud speech would be audible. A profound hearing loss for speech would require amplification in order for speech to be heard at all. *See* AUDIOLOGIC CLASSIFICATION

A comparison of the pure-tone average and the speech reception threshold can provide insight into the reliability of the two measures. Also, in cases where incomplete evaluation information is available, the appropriate pure-tone average or the speech reception can be used to predict the other.

Measurements of sensitivity to speech may be helpful in some instances in determining benefits from amplification. Comparing the speech threshold obtained without a hearing aid to a speech threshold obtained with a hearing aid yields a measure of the gain provided by the hearing aid. The level at which the speech threshold is obtained when the aid is worn also provides a gross estimate of the way that a hearing-impaired person may be expected to function with a hearing aid. For example, if a young child has an unaided speech detection threshold of 90 dB HL and an aided speech detection threshold of only 60 dB HL, the child would not be expected to be able to use the hearing aid to hear conversational speech. On the other hand, if the speech detection threshold while wearing the aid was at 30 dB HL, it would be assumed that speech at conversational levels was audible.

In medicolegal or compensation cases, a combination of sensitivity to speech and ability to understand clearly audible speech may be used to determine the handicapping nature of a hearing loss. In many systems, a choice may be made as to whether the ability to hear soft speech and understand louder speech or the loss of sensitivity for pure tones is a more accurate reflection of the handicap. Also, the validity of test results may be scrutinized carefully in such cases, and the agreement between the speech reception threshold and the pure-tone average will be relied upon heavily for mutual substantiation.

LIMITATIONS OF MEASUREMENTS

Measurements of speech sensitivity are not designed to provide information regarding the ability to understand speech. Instead, they are designed to be as free as possible from influence by speech-understanding abilities. Thus, they provide information regarding the audibility, but not the clarity, of speech to the listener. In extreme cases, a hearing impairment may cause sufficient distortion of speech sounds that even the simple materials used for speech reception thresholds are not easily recognizable. In that case, the speech reception threshold will be elevated relative to the pure-tone average. In general, however, nothing about understanding of speech can be inferred from the levels at which speech can barely be heard.

The precise levels at which speech can be detected or words and sentences can be recognized with 50 percent accuracy are dependent upon the specific speech message used for testing. Speech is a complicated acoustic signal that varies rapidly in loudness, pitch of the voice, and the frequency range of particular sounds. For example, vowels, such as the "a" in "cat," are made up of lower-frequency sounds than is a consonant such as the "t" in "cat." If test materials consisted of words like sister, thistle, shift, and fish, there would be relatively more high-frequency sounds than if the list consisted of words like all, man, wound, rain, and lore. If the former list was used to determine speech sensitivity for a person with a high-frequency hearing loss, the individual might show a greater loss for speech than if the latter list, with more low-frequency sounds, was used. The standard materials used for clinical measurement of speech thresholds are selected so as to be relatively representative of all sounds of speech rather than being heavily weighted toward either high frequencies or low frequencies.

Bibliography

Davis, H., and R. Silverman: *Hearing and Deafness*, 3d ed., Holt, Rinehart and Winston, New York, 1970.

Hopkinson, N.: "Speech Reception Threshold," in J. Katz (ed.), *Handbook of Clinical Audiology*, Williams and Wilkins, Baltimore, 1978.

Olsen, W., and N. Matkin: "Speech Audiometry," in W. Rintelmann (ed.), *Hearing Assessment*, University Park Press, Baltimore, 1979.

Rose, D.: *Audiological Assessment,* 2d ed., Prentice-Hall, Englewood Cliffs, New Jersey, 1978.

M. Jane Collins

Speech Discrimination

Speech discrimination is one of many terms applied to measurements of the responses of human listeners to speech stimuli. Other terms for the same or similar measurements include speech recognition, speech intelligibility, and articulation.

Speech discrimination most commonly refers to the task in which a listener repeats words that are presented through earphones or a loudspeaker. The term speech recognition is more appropriate for this task, and there is a trend in audiology to adopt it. Recognition refers to the selection of a response from a closed set of possible responses. The speech-recognition task (repeating words) involves the selection of a response (the word) from a closed set that may include all the words known by the listener. The set may be restricted by instructing the listener that all of the test stimuli are from a certain category (such as one-syllable words) or by the use of multiple-choice procedures.

Discrimination refers to a comparative judgment among two or more stimuli. By this definition, the speech-recognition task is not properly referred to as discrimination. The more correct and older use of speech discrimination refers to experiments in which two or more speech stimuli are presented and the listener is required to make a comparison. For example, two words may be presented and the listener must respond "same" or "different."

Speech intelligibility has been used synonymously with speech recognition. However, the distinction is that speech intelligibility refers to a property of the speech material (how understandable a specific speech sample is to a group of listeners), speech recognition refers to a property of the listener. Speech-recognition ability is an individual's general ability to repeat spoken words, in comparison to norms obtained from groups of normal listeners.

Articulation is a term which was used by early speech-recognition investigators. Due to the common usage of the term to refer to characteristics of speech production, the term is seldom used in current speech-recognition literature.

In the remainder of this section, the term speech recognition will be used; it is the most correct term for the test commonly referred to in audiology as speech discrimination.

Speech-recognition tests typically consist of standardized lists of speech materials that are either tape-recorded or presented by a live talker. The speech materials may be nonsense syllables, monosyllabic words, multisyllabic words, or sentences, but are most commonly monosyllabic word lists. Several monosyllabic-word-recognition tests have been developed, varying primarily in the average difficulty of the test words. Difficult tests are desirable for assessing relatively mild impairments,

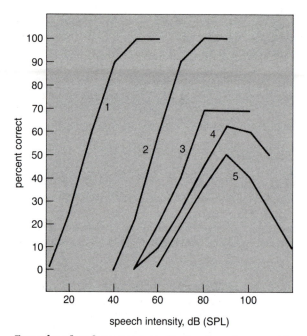

Examples of performance-intensity functions for monosyllabic materials for five listeners: normal hearers (1), conductive hearing losses (2), sensorineural impairments (3 and 4), and retrocochlear lesions (5). (After F. H. Bess, "Clinical Assessment of Speech Recognition," in D. F. Konkle and W. F. Rintelmann, eds., *Principles of Speech Audiometry*, University Park Press, Baltimore, 1983)

while easier tests are useful for evaluating persons with more severe hearing losses. The tests are typically administered through a clinical audiometer. The audiometer is capable of presenting the speech stimuli to an earphone or loudspeaker at controlled intensity levels.

The use of speech recognition in audiometry can best be understood by the concept of the performance-intensity function, a graph depicting the relationship between the percentage of words correctly repeated and the intensity at which the speech material was presented to the listener. For a normal-hearing listener (listener 1 in the graph here), when the speech is at a low-intensity (below 10 dB SPL) the words are too soft to be understood and the listener scores 0 percent. As the intensity is raised, the words become louder and some of them can be correctly repeated. At higher intensities (50 dB SPL and above) the listener can repeat all of the words correctly. From the performance-intensity function, several measures of performance can be extracted. The intensity at which the listener achieves a score of 50 percent is called the speech-recognition threshold (also called the speech-reception threshold). For listener 1, the speech-recognition threshold is about 27 dB SPL. The percentage of words correctly repeated at a specific intensity is the speech-recognition score for that intensity. Listener 1 achieved a speech-recognition score of 90 percent at 40 dB SPL. The maximum speech-recognition score achieved by a listener is sometimes referred to as the PB Max. PB stands for phonetically balanced, a characteristic of the word lists that comprised the early speech-recognition tests. Listeners 1 and 2 achieved PB Max scores of 100 percent; listener 3, 70 percent; listener 4, 62 percent; and listener 5, 50 percent.

Speech-recognition tests in audiometry are used for several purposes, including estimation of auditory sensitivity, diagnosis of auditory disorders, hearing aid evaluation, and medicolegal considerations.

ESTIMATION OF AUDITORY SENSITIVITY
The speech-recognition threshold is used as a measure of auditory sensitivity. It is traditionally measured by using two-syllable words spoken to place nearly equal stress on the syllables (for example, hotdog, baseball, cowboy). The measure is highly correlated with the pure-tone audiogram. When the validity of the pure-tone audiogram is in doubt, the speech-recognition threshold is used as a check. For listeners for whom the pure-tone audiogram cannot be obtained, such as young children, the speech-recognition threshold substitutes as a crude estimate of auditory sensitivity. It is crude because it does not provide information at specific frequencies as the pure-tone audiogram does.

DIAGNOSIS OF AUDITORY DISORDERS
The illustration demonstrates how speech-recognition measurements can be used for the diagnosis of auditory disorders. Listener 1 has normal hearing. A PB Max of 100 percent is achieved at a relatively low speech level (50 dB SPL). Listener 2 has a conductive hearing loss. The performance-intensity function is shifted to the right with no reduction of PB Max. Listeners 3 and 4 have sensorineural hearing losses due to cochlear pathology. Their performance-intensity functions are shifted to the right with reduced PB Max scores. Listener 4 achieved lower scores at intensities above PB Max; this effect is called rollover. Listener 5 has a retrocochlear (neural) disorder. The performance-intensity function was shifted to the right with a reduction in PB Max and a large degree of rollover. Examination of the performance-intensity functions can help determine if the listener has normal hearing or else has some pathologic condition of the external or middle ear, cochlea, or auditory nerve.

HEARING AID EVALUATION
Performance-intensity functions can be obtained when the listener is wearing a hearing aid. A comparison of scores obtained under aided and unaided (no hearing aid) conditions can be helpful in measuring the benefit provided by the hearing aid.

Speech recognition scores also can be compared for different hearing aids. In general, however, speech-recognition scores are not sufficiently sensitive to be useful for selecting hearing aids. Measurements of speech recognition, then, are useful for determining if aided performance is better than unaided performance, but not very useful for determining which hearing aid is best for an individual.

MEDICOLEGAL CONSIDERATIONS
For purposes of evaluating the extent of disability resulting from a hearing impairment, speech-recognition scores are sometimes incorporated into a medicolegal evaluation. Because the most important use of hearing is speech communication, it is desirable to know the extent to which an auditory disorder impairs a person's ability to understand speech. Speech recognition scores, then, may be considered in determining eligibility for and amount of compensation that may be awarded to a person when another party (such as employer or insurance company) may be legally responsible.

Bibliography
Konkle, Dan F., and William F. Rintelmann (eds.): *Principles of Speech Audiometry*, University Park Press, Baltimore, 1983.

Robert H. Margolis

Loudness Recruitment
Loudness recruitment is an abnormal growth in loudness for an acoustic signal with increases in the physical strength or level of the signal. Normal listeners experience a relatively even or uniform (monotonic) growth in loudness with increases in the level of sound. Over a substantial dynamic range, psychologic loudness perception is directly proportional to the physical intensity or level of the acoustic signal. This normal relation between signal level and loudness perception is altered, however, in cases of insult to the cochlea or VIIIth (auditory) nerve. Listeners with cochlear disorders experience loudness recruitment. Loudness growth increases at a disproportionately rapid rate with increases in the intensity level of the signal. By contrast, loudness decruitment is typical of patients with VIIIth nerve involvement. Here, loudness growth with increases in signal level is abnormally slow. In some cases of VIIIth nerve disorders, loudness may actually remain constant or decline as signal level is increased. These differences in loudness perception are diagnostically useful for distinguishing cochlear and VIIIth nerve disorders and form the bases for loudness recruitment tests in audiologic practice.

TESTS

Clinical tests of loudness recruitment are based on loudness balance measures. One of two different loudness balance procedures is used, dependent on the characteristics of hearing loss. In unilateral hearing loss, the Alternate Binaural Loudness Balance (ABLB) Test is used. Here, loudness growth in the ear with hearing loss is compared to loudness growth in the normal ear. The subject's task is to judge the relative loudness of a tone (at a specific frequency) in the two ears. A reference tone of a specific frequency is presented to the better ear at a level slightly above threshold (such as 10 dB SPL). The tone is then switched alternately between the normal ear and the ear with hearing loss. The level of the tone in the bad ear is varied up and down in discrete steps based on equal-loudness judgments of the patient. In this manner, the

level of the variable tone in the bad ear that results in equal loudness with the reference tone at a set level in the good ear is determined. This process is then repeated at successively higher reference levels in the good ear until the complete loudness function is determined. In addition, it is often useful to evaluate loudness balance measures for different signal frequencies.

The Monaural Bi-Frequency Loudness Balance (MLB) Test is used in cases of equal hearing loss in both ears. This test is particularly useful in measuring loudness recruitment in cases of bilateral, high-frequency hearing loss. The basic procedure and response task are similar to those for the ABLB, except MLB is a monaural (one-ear) procedure. Specifically, loudness judgments are made for two tones of different frequency in the same ear. The reference tone is set at a frequency for

Illustrative laddergrams (left) and Fowler plots (right) for the Alternate Binaural Loudness Balance (ABLB) Test at a signal frequency of 4000 Hz. (a–c) Different degrees of loudness recruitment: (a) complete, (b) partial, and (c) hyperrecruitment. (d) Loudness decruitment. The patterns shown in (a–c) are all associated with sensorineural hearing loss of cochlear origin. The pattern in (c) is a dramatic example of the abnormal loudness growth that may be associated with a cochlear disorder. Note that at the highest signal level, less intensity level is required for a tone in the variable ear (with a hearing loss) to be judged equal in loudness to the same tone at a higher level in the normal ear. (After J. Katz, ed., *Handbook of Clinical Audiology,* 3d ed., Williams and Wilkins, Baltimore, 1985).

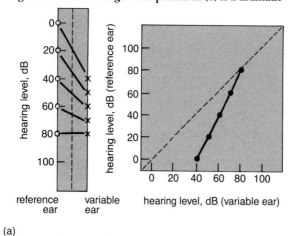
(a)

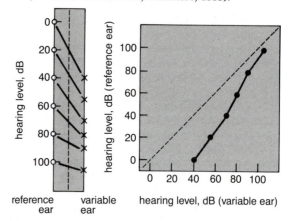
(b)

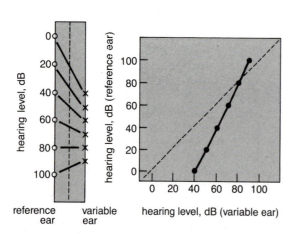
(c)

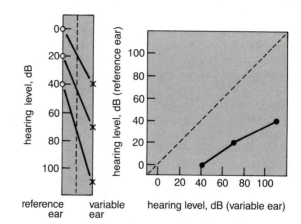
(d)

which hearing sensitivity is within normal limits. The variable tone is set at a frequency for which a hearing loss is evident. Here, the examiner determines the level of the variable tone that is judged equal in loudness to the reference tone at a set level.

INTERPRETATION OF TEST RESULTS

The interpretation of test results is basically the same for both ABLB and MLB procedures. Either a laddergram or a Fowler plot is used to represent loudness balance measures for a given set of test conditions. These are simply two different types of graphs that may be used to display the same test results.

As noted above, loudness grows in a monotonic fashion with the intensity level of a tone in normal listeners. This relation is represented by a diagonal line on the Fowler plot. In general, a similar relation is true for patients with conductive hearing loss and a normal cochlea and VIIIth nerve. Here, a similar diagonal function would result except that the line would be displaced along the horizontal axis in direct proportion to the degree of conductive hearing loss.

A cardinal sign of sensorineural hearing loss due to cochlear insult is the presence of loudness recruitment. As described above, this is an abnormally rapid growth in loudness with signal level. In direct contrast with findings in cases of cochlear disorder, patients with VIIIth nerve lesions often demonstrate a reduced rate of loudness growth, or loudness decruitment. Loudness growth is slower than normal. Larger changes in intensity level are required in the affected ear to maintain equal loudness with the same tone in the good ear. Loudness does not grow monotonically with the intensity level of the signal. Although loudness decruitment is often associated with VIIIth nerve lesions, some cases may demonstrate results similar to those for normal subjects or patients with conductive hearing loss. This finding is still diagnostically significant in cases of sensorineural hearing loss due to VIIIth nerve involvement, however, because loudness recruitment is expected in cases of sensorineural hearing loss due to cochlear disorder.

Bibliography

Hood, J. D.: "Basic Audiological Requirements in Neuro-Otology," *J. Laryngol. Otol.*, 83:695–711, 1969.

Katz, J. (ed.): *Handbook of Clinical Audiology*, 2d ed., Williams and Wilkins, Baltimore, 1978.

Terry L. Wiley

Loudness Adaptation

Loudness adaptation is a perstimulatory decrease (that is, decrease with respect to stimulation) in loudness for a sustained acoustic signal. It is a loudness decline that occurs while the sound is on. In clinical audiology, auditory adaptation measures usually involve threshold estimates for a sustained sound, and the term tone decay refers to the increase in threshold (or adaptation) with time observed for patients experiencing auditory adaptation. Auditory adaptation or tone decay typically is measured monaurally for tones. Within practical limits, it is absent in persons with a normal auditory system. Patients with lesions of the cochlea or VIIIth nerve, in contrast, commonly will demonstrate appreciable tone decay. A major diagnostic distinction between cochlear and VIIIth nerve disorders is the more extensive and more rapid tone decay observed in cases of VIIIth nerve lesions. Clinical tests of auditory adaptation can be classified under two major methods: Békésy audiometry and conventional tone-decay tests.

BÉKÉSY AUDIOMETRY

Békésy audiometry is a form of automatic audiometry. The Békésy audiometer provides for automatic tracking of auditory thresholds for tones on a moving chart. Thresholds can be charted as a function of frequency (sweep-frequency Békésy audiometry) or as a function of time at a given frequency (fixed-frequency Békésy audiometry). In either case, the listener's task is simply to indicate (by pushing a button) when she or he just detects the presence of the tone. The button presses (threshold responses) are automatically recorded on the moving chart paper. Auditory thresholds for pulsed and sustained tones are recorded, and the tracings are classified or evaluated on the basis of the separation between threshold tracings for pulsed and sustained tones. Because neither normal nor pathologic listeners demonstrate auditory adaptation for pulsed or interrupted tones, this procedure is basically an evaluation of auditory adaptation for the sustained tone. In normal-hearing persons or those with conductive hearing loss, the threshold tracings for pulsed and sustained (or continuous) tones interweave. There is no appreciable auditory adaptation. The two tracings are separated in cases of cochlear and VIIIth nerve lesions, however, in direct proportion to the degree of auditory adaptation. The greater the adaptation effect, the greater the shift in threshold for the sustained tone. Greater intensity levels are required to maintain audibility of the sustained tone over time. In the case of VIIIth nerve disorders, the continuous-tone tracing rapidly separates from the pulsed-tone tracing, and the amount of separation (or adaptation) may be extreme. Indeed, in some cases of VIIIth nerve lesions, shortly after signal presentation the patient may not hear the sustained tone at the highest level available on the audiometer. It may not be possible to achieve a level at which the patient can hear the sustained tone for any appreciable period of time.

Patients with cochlear disorders also demonstrate auditory adaptation with associated separation in threshold tracings for pulsed and continuous tones. The amount of separation (or adaptation), however, is considerably less than that observed for patients with VIIIth nerve lesions. In addition, the time course of adaptation is slower in cochlear disorders. In most cases of cochlear disorders, as the level of the continuous tone is increased, the patient will hear the tone for longer periods of time. The continuous-tone tracing typically levels off, and the total separation (in dB) between pulsed-tone and continuous-tone tracings is significantly less than that observed in cases of VIIIth nerve disorders. Over a given period of signal presentation, then, the amount of auditory adaptation (in decibels of threshold shift for the sustained tone) is greater in cases of VIIIth nerve disorders.

TONE-DECAY TESTS

The basic principles of conventional tone-decay tests are similar to those for Békésy audiometry. Tone-decay tests, however, require no special instrumentation; usually they can be performed with a simple pure-tone audiometer and a stopwatch. Although there are several different tone-decay procedures, the basic task for the person under test is similar for all tests. The listener is instructed to judge the presence (audibility) of a sustained tone over time. A tone of a given frequency is presented at or slightly above threshold, and the listener is instructed to signal (for example, by pushing a button or raising a hand) for as long as the tone is heard. If the subject indicates that the tone is no longer audible before 60 seconds has elapsed, the level of the tone is increased by 5 dB and the process is repeated. For some tests, a rest period is provided between each successive tonal presentation. This test sequence continues until a tone level is reached at which the subject indicates audibility for the full 60 seconds. Test results are expressed in terms of the amount (dB) of intensity-level change from threshold required for the listener to hear the tone for the criterion time period (60 seconds). This is the amount of tone decay. Certain tests also incorporate a record of the time that the tone was audible at each intensity level. This provides a profile of the tone decay or auditory adaptation over time.

As noted earlier for Békésy audiometry, persons with normal hearing or conductive hearing loss evidence no appreciable auditory adaptation or tone decay. For tone-decay tests, then, these subjects hear the tone indefinitely (less than 60 seconds) at levels slightly above threshold. In patients with cochlear or VIIIth nerve disorders, significant tone decay is usually evident. The characteristics of tone decay are different for cochlear and VIIIth nerve lesions, however, and these distinctions are used diagnostically to differentiate the two potential lesion sites. In most cases, the amount (dB) of tone decay is greater for VIIIth nerve disorders. Indeed, some patients with VIIIth nerve disorders may demonstrate total tone decay. That is, they may never hear the tone for a full 60 seconds at the highest signal level. In addition, the tone decay may be quite rapid. Patients with VIIIth nerve lesions often hear the tone for only a few seconds at each successively higher level, and the time to inaudibility remains relatively constant across levels. Listeners with cochlear lesions, in contrast, typically demonstrate less tone decay with a slower time course. Specifically, fewer intensity-level steps are required to reach a level at which the tone can be heard for the full 60 seconds. In addition, the time to inaudibility increases with successively higher intensity levels. This latter temporal distinction in tone decay or auditory adaptation is particularly significant in differentiating cochlear and VIIIth nerve disorders.

Bibliography

Katz, J. (ed.): *Handbook of Clinical Audiology*, 2d ed., Williams and Wilkins, Baltimore, 1978.

Rintelmann, W. F. (ed.): *Hearing Assessment*, University Park Press, Baltimore, 1979.

                                                    Terry L. Wiley

Electrophysiologic

Tests of hearing sensitivity that incorporate recorded changes in the electric properties of the body as direct or indirect responses to auditory stimuli are termed electrophysiologic audiometric tests. Electrophysiologic tests of hearing have been regarded as objective tests, because electric auditory responses are free from the willful control of the listener. However, for a test to be fully objective, the tester and the procedure used to assess the integrity or measure the sensitivity of the auditory system also must be objective.

ELECTROPHYSIOLOGIC AUDITORY RESPONSE SYSTEMS

An electrophysiologic auditory response system includes anatomic structures and neurophysiologic mechanisms that respond to sensory stimulation or mediate the final auditory response. Some of these systems are auditory-specific, while others may respond to any kind of sensory or cognitive stimulation.

Specific   Specific auditory response systems are the sensory receptors and neural pathways that are arranged anatomically and physically to respond only to auditory stimulation. Those that are being employed most to obtain electric auditory responses for clinical purposes include the cochlea, the auditory nerve (cranial nerve VIII), and specific auditory pathways and nuclei within the brainstem and the brain. The electric signals evoked from these systems are of very low voltage (microvolts), and it is necessary that sophisticated instrumentation and computers be used to amplify and extract them efficiently from irrevelant background electric brainwave activity. These electric auditory responses are recorded from electrodes placed on the promontory of the middle ear or in the external ear canal, or from scalp electrodes placed appropriately. Specific electric auditory response systems are not influenced by cognitive activity in the brain and only minimally by the effects of drugs. If the integrity of the auditory system beyond the cochlea is disrupted in the presence of a normal cochlea, however, absent or poor neural synchronization will result in either no identifiable response or one that is distorted in its waveform.

Nonspecific Nonspecific electrophysiologic response systems are not tuned to respond only to auditory stimulation. They include body systems that respond to all types of sensory stimuli, cognitive stimuli or, in general, any external or internal stimuli that produce emotional arousal. Electric responses evoked from these systems by auditory stimuli are indirectly related to the auditory stimulation. The cortex, central autonomic centers, or spinal autonomic mechanisms are first excited by auditory stimuli via neural collaterals from the auditory sensorineural pathways. These systems, in turn, stimulate neural activity or motor reflexes that alter the electrical activity of other mechanisms. Nonspecific response mechanisms that have been incorporated into auditory tests as electrophysiologic response systems include the sweat glands, the heart, and the brain. Electric activities generated by these mechanisms that have been used as auditory response indicators include electric potential or resistance of the skin as influenced by sweat gland activity, electric recordings of heart rate, and ongoing electroencephalic activity.

CLINICAL APPLICATION

Electrophysiologic audiometric procedures are used clinically to gain estimates of auditory threshold in persons who will not or cannot respond voluntarily to auditory stimuli for reasons unrelated to the integrity of their auditory systems. These procedures are of primary value when assessing the auditory sensitivity on newborn babies, young infants, and individuals with pseudohypacusis (nonorganic hearing loss).

In the late 1940s, the first electrophysiologic audiometric procedure was introduced for clinical use on a systematic basis. It incorporated the nonspe-

cific electrodermal response system, which terminates with recordable changes in the electric properties of the skin as influenced by sweat gland activity. This activity is controlled by the autonomic nervous system, which is excited when the listener is aroused in anticipation of a coming event. Through classical conditioning, a listener is conditioned to anticipate sensing a noxious stimulus (usually a shock) upon hearing a sound. Electrodermal response audiometry was popular throughout the 1950s and early 1960s, but lost favor in the mid and late 1960s. It was most effective when used with pseudohypacusic adults and least effective with very young children, children with central nervous system disorders, and retarded children.

The electrocardiac response to auditory stimulation is most frequently quantified by computing the difference between pre- and poststimulus recordings of the electric activity of the heart. Early investigations into the use of heart rate change as an auditory response for chemical purposes appeared in the literature between the late 1950s and early 1960s. During this time period, research interests were directed toward the effects of suprathreshold auditory stimulation upon heart rate change and patterns. Studies conducted during the late 1960s and 1970s were designed to explore the habituation of heart rate change evoked by sounds in children with central nervous system disorders, the effects of speechlike sound upon heart rate in normal infants, and the feasibility of using heart rate change as an auditory response for the measurement of auditory sensitivity. The incorporation of heart rate change into auditory test designs administered in audiology clinics is not common practice.

In the early 1960s exploration into the clinical use of brain-wave electric activity recorded on the electroencephalogram as an auditory response began in several clinical research laboratories. This research was terminated in the mid-1960s, however, with the introduction of the signal-averaging computer. At this time, the development of evoked response audiometry was initiated with the extraction of an auditory evoked response (late components) from ongoing brain-wave electric activity by using the averaging computer. Later, it became feasible to amplify and average lower-voltage electric responses from specific auditory systems in the brain which have since been employed in auditory threshold procedures. It is now possible to employ other specific electrophysiologic responses in auditory threshold, as well as other types of audiologic test paradigms, due to the averaging computer and technologic advances that were made in the 1970s. Currently, fairly reliable estimates of auditory sensitivity in difficult-to-test individuals may be gained by using brainstem evoked response audiometry or electrocochleographic audiometry. The former incorporates electric activity generated from the VIIIth nerve and levels of the brainstem as auditory responses. The latter uses electric responses evoked from the cochlea to estimate auditory thresholds, as well as to gain information relative to the physiologic integrity of the cochlea.

VALIDITY OF ELECTROPHYSIOLOGIC MEASURES

The validity of electrophysiologic measures of auditory sensitivity has been based upon research findings that reveal how closely they agree with behavioral auditory thresholds, when both measures are gained at the same frequency, or frequencies, from the same persons. Agreement, and therefore validity, has been considered satisfactory if the decibel values of the electrophysiologic thresholds fall within the same normal, mild, moderate, severe, or profound range (in decibels) of hearing impairments as do the behavioral thresholds. A more stringent requirement specifies that, to be valid, the decibel values of the electrophysiologic thresholds should equal those of the behavioral thresholds within certain more restricted decibel limits. The clinical validity of auditory thresholds based upon changes in the electroencephalogram or heart rate activity has not been clearly demonstrated. Several studies have presented data supporting the validity of electrodermal response auditory thresholds which have been reported to fall within approximately ± 10 dB of behavioral thresholds at all audiometric test frequencies. Thresholds based upon the brainstem evoked response or the VIIIth nerve (action potential) response have gained greater empirical support as valid measures of auditory sensitivity than have thresholds based upon other specific electrophysiologic responses. These thresholds, however, are only valid when measuring auditory sensitivity at frequencies from about 1000 to 8000 Hz.

Bibliography

Eisenberg, Rita B.: "Cardiotachometry," in L. J. Bradford (ed.), *Physiological Measures of the Audio-Vestibular System*, Academic Press, New York, 1975.

Goldstein, Robert: "Electrophysiologic Audiometry," in J. Jerger (ed.), *Modern Developments in Audiology*, Academic Press, New York, 1963.

Katz, J. (ed.), *Handbook of Clinical Audiology*, 2d ed., Williams and Wilkins, Baltimore, 1978.

Shepherd, David C.: "Pediatric Audiology," in D. Rose (ed.), *Audiological Assessment*, 2d ed., Prentice-Hall, Englewood Cliffs, New Jersey, 1978.

David C. Shepherd

Auditory Evoked Potentials

Auditory evoked potentials are small electric signals that can be obtained from the brain in response to repetitions of identical sounds. These signals have a characteristic pattern or waveform that is related to the way they are elicited and recorded. The waveform can provide information about whether the brain has responded to a test sound. If the brain has responded, then, by inference, the test sound must have been above the listener's threshold of hearing.

ELECTROENCEPHALOGRAM

In animals and in humans, it has been shown that the brain acts like a generator, emitting a variety of low-voltage electric signals. These constantly changing electric signals may be written out in the form of an electroencephalogram (EEG). The EEG represents the electric activity or waxing and waning potentials of the brain. During the 1930s, investigators discovered that they could see sudden changes in the EEG if they presented loud sounds (auditory signals, such as hand clapping) to sleeping subjects. These changes were called evoked potentials because they were elicited or evoked by the presentation of a stimulus, and auditory evoked potentials because the eliciting signal was sound. However, it was soon discovered that if several similar sounds in a row were presented to a listener, the auditory evoked potentials became too small to be seen in the ongoing EEG activity. Therefore, this technique could not be used readily as a hearing test. It was not until the 1950s that technical developments in computers progressed sufficiently to allow investigators to detect the tiny responses to many identical clicklike sounds in a row. Computers were used to add up and average small segments of the EEG activity following the presentation of each click to form a pattern called the averaged auditory evoked potentials (AAEP).

Because of the way that they usually are recorded and elicited, these evoked potentials generally are regarded as stimulus-related potentials: their properties bear predictable relations with the physical properties of the eliciting sounds, such as intensity. They are distinguished from event-related or endogenous potentials which can be recorded in association with some internal psychologic process. The focus of this section is on hearing testing for which stimulus-related potentials ordinarily are used. Therefore, no further mention will be made of the event-related potentials.

ADVANTAGES

Averaged auditory evoked potentials are of interest because they provide clinically useful information about the integrity of the ear and about how the brain responds to sound. These small electric signals accompany physiologic events that occur in the various parts of the auditory system, including pathways within the central nervous system. Abnormalities of the AAEPs may help to detect and locate disorders of the ear or of the central nervous system, so that hearing loss and other disorders may be detected and evaluated. One of the principal advantages of the AAEPs is that they may be obtained from many subjects who cannot or will not cooperate during conventional hearing testing procedures. For example, patients who are too young or too severely multiply handicapped to give reliable behavioral responses to sound may be tested with these techniques. In addition, AAEP measures have been applied to a broad range of neurologic problems as a means of identifying both discrete and diffuse lesions of the brain, as well as serving as a method of monitoring the progress of neurosurgical procedures.

TIME DOMAINS

A typical AAEP that was recorded in response to a large number of clicks (very brief sounds) presented to a normal-hearing listener at a moderate or comfortable listening level is illustrated. The electric activity of the listener's brain, also referred to as the EEG, is recorded by affixing small disk-shaped electrodes to the surface of the head, one on top (the vertex) and the other directly behind the right ear at the bump called the mastoid. Then

EEG activity is routed to a computer for averaging following the presentation of each click. The portion of the response at the bottom of the figure contains the entire response pattern (or waveform or trace) over a period of 800 milliseconds (ms). [Time is shown on the horizontal axis.] A series of smaller deflections or bumps is seen in the left portion of this trace. This left portion, expanded by the computer, is seen in the trace in the middle of the figure; and again, a series of smaller bumps is seen in the left portion of this middle section of the trace. This portion, computer-expanded, is seen as the trace at the top of the figure. The time represented in the top portion is 12.5 ms. The middle portion represents the time from the click onset to about 50 ms, or the beginning of the bottom trace. The AAEP has been divided in various ways by different people into arbitrary time segments. For purposes of discussion here, the AAEP will be divided into the auditory brainstem response (ABR), early, or fast components (0–12.5 ms after the arrival of the stimulus at the ear), the middle components (12.5–50 ms after the arrival of the stimulus at the ear), and the slow or late components

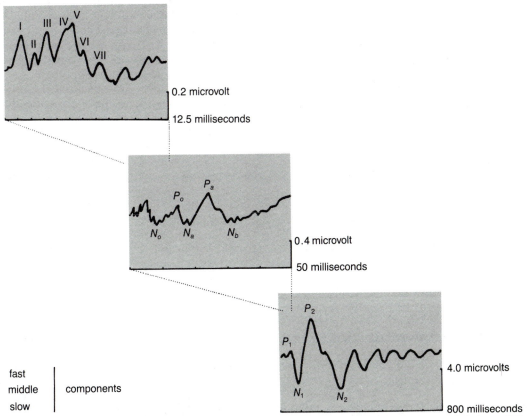

Typical averaged auditory evoked potentials of normal-hearing listener. Clicks of 60 dB SL intensity were presented once every second to the right ear. Responses were averaged over 1536 trials from vertex to right mastoid electrodes at three different time bases and three different amplitude calibrations. Negativity at the vertex is shown by downward deflection, and is labeled N.

(50 ms and later). The earliest research on the changes in the ongoing EEG in response to sound during the 1930s focused on the late components. The first practical computer-averaging techniques in the late 1950s examined what are now called the middle components, and it is only since the early 1970s that the auditory brainstem response has been recognized. While a great deal of research has been carried out on each of these three time domains, most clinical AAEP hearing testing today focuses on the early components, or ABR.

AUDITORY BRAINSTEM RESPONSE

Examples of ABRs obtained from a normal-hearing adult in response to clicks are also illustrated. As shown, a series of bumps or waves may be recorded within a 10-ms window following the presentation of the stimulus. The top trace represents the ABR obtained with the loudest clicks (65 dB sensation level, or 65 dB above the subject's behavioral audiometric threshold, which is defined as the level where the stimulus can just be detected or heard). The series of waves is labeled with roman numerals I through VII. As the level of the clicks gets softer (from top to bottom in decreasing 10-dB

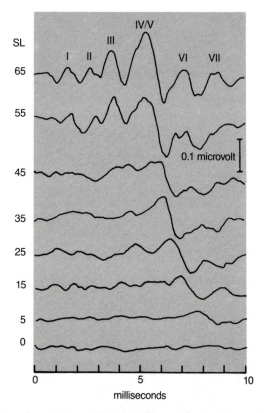

Examples of the auditory brainstem response (ABR) obtained for a normal listener. Positivity at the vertex is shown as an upward deflection. The sensation level is noted beside each trace. (After T. J. Glattke, *Short-Latency Auditory Evoked Potentials,* **University Park Press, 1983)**

steps), the waves get smaller and the pattern less distinct. In addition, some individual waves drop out of the pattern, and the remaining wave or waves shift to the right (later in time) as the clicks get softer. The largest and most distinctive peak is the middle of the waveform, and is labeled "wave V." At levels of 45 dB and below, it is the only wave that may be seen in the pattern, and it remains identifiable down to 5 dB. At the bottom of the illustration (0 dB), there are no identifiable waves or bumps, and the pattern is essentially a straight line. In this example, then, there is a response down to 5 dB, with wave V identified at this level (5 dB) with a latency or time of occurrence of about 8 ms. At the loudest level (65 dB), wave V occurs with a latency of about 5 ms. In this series of traces, therefore, wave V can be seen to shift in latency by about 3 ms to the right, from the loudest level to the softest level at which it can be identified (5 dB). In this example, the threshold of detection of the ABR, determined as the lowest level at which wave V may be identified, is 5 dB.

In the topmost trace of the illustration, waves or multiple response peaks are labeled from I to VII. One of the chief reasons that the ABR has achieved such widespread clinical use is that several clinical investigators suggested that the multiple response peaks could be associated with sequential activation of the individual parts of the auditory pathway: the auditory nerve, brainstem, and midbrain structures. The origin of wave I was attributed to the activity of the auditory or VIIIth nerve, and each successive wave was associated with successively higher auditory pathway structures. More recent evidence, however, continues to suggest that while wave I does appear to reflect electric activity generated by the auditory nerve, the concept of individual sequential generators for the later response peaks is not totally appropriate. However, this association between the peaks shown in the illustration and the underlying anatomic structures responsible for their generation has aided in the clinical acceptance of the ABR evoked potential. Abnormalities of the response latency and waveform pattern often correlate well with the presence of a disorder of hearing or with some neurologic disorders in the central nervous system.

STIMULATION AND RECORDING TECHNIQUES

The principles underlying the stimulation and recording of responses, as well as analysis techniques, will be reviewed briefly in the following paragraphs to provide a basis for understanding how clinical judgments may be made with the ABR. Of course, analysis techniques are changing rapidly, and changes certainly will occur in clinical applications, but the principles described below probably still will apply in the future.

Expected Latencies (in Milliseconds) of Peaks I Through V of the Auditory Brainstem Response*

Stimulus Level, dB	Wave I	Wave II	Wave III	Wave IV	Wave V
65	1.4	2.6	3.7	4.6	5.4
55	1.8	3.0	3.9	5.0	5.8
45	†	3.3	4.3	5.4	6.0
35	†	†	4.7	†	6.6
25	†	†	5.1	†	7.1
15	†	†	†	†	7.7

*Modified from A. Starr and J. Achor, "Auditory Brain Stem Responses in Neurological Disease," *Archives of Neurology*, 32:761–768, 1975.
†There was no identifiable peak in the waveform.

The basic measures obtained from the ABR consist of latency, and amplitude or vertical size. Typically, latency is measured as the time after the arrival of the stimulus at the ear to the peak or peaks that are of interest. Amplitude is measured as the difference between the top of a peak (such as wave V in the illustration of ABRs, p. 64) and the following negative minimum or trough. Once latencies of individual peaks have been determined, the intervals between peaks may be computed by subtracting the latency of one peak from the other. As illustrated by the ABR example, at softer levels not all peaks are present. The absence of peaks I, II, and IV is typical of these softer levels. Also, as shown, wave V is the most frequently occurring peak in the ABR, and consequently it is used most frequently in clinical judgments. The expected latency of waves I–V for stimuli at the levels shown in the illustration are presented in the table. The table shows that the latency for the major response peaks varies systematically with the level of the stimulus; that is, as the stimulus gets softer, the latency of each response peak increases in a regular manner. Another factor that may be seen in this table is that the interval from wave I to wave III is approximately 2.0 ms (3.7 minus 1.4

The effect of stimulus intensity on the peak latency of wave V of the onset brainstem potentials reported from four laboratories. Wave V latency-intensity curves are shown from two patients on the right. (After J. N. Gardi and M. I. Mendel, in S. Gerber, ed., *Audiometry in Infancy*, Grune and Stratton, 1977)

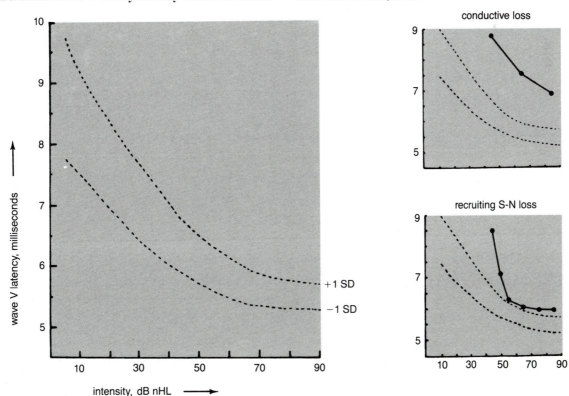

ms at 65 dB) and the interval from wave I to wave V is approximately 4.0 ms (5.4 minus 1.4 ms). This measure is called central transmission time or interpeak interval, and the measure is sensitive to the presence of some disorders beyond the cochlea or inner ear.

As in the illustration (p. 64) of ABRs and the table, wave V is the largest and most distinctive peak of the ABR. The most striking characteristic of the ABR is the latency sensitivity to the insensitivity of the stimulus. For clicks, the latency of wave V in adults increases from 5.4 to 9.0 ms as stimulus intensity decreases from 90 dB sensation level to threshold. This latency-intensity function for wave V is highly repeatable within and across subjects as well as among laboratories. In the illustration (p. 65), results from four different laboratories provide values which all fall within plus or minus one standard deviation of the mean, that is, between the broken line curves.

By using a standard graph such as the latency-intensity function, the results from an individual subject can be compared to the expected values of wave V latency obtained for different stimulus levels. The results for a normal-hearing individual would be expected to fall within the area between the standard deviation limits. Failure to fall within these limits may be interpreted as an indication of hearing loss. For example, an individual with a conductive hearing loss would be expected to give a pattern such as that shown in the upper right portion of the illustration (p. 65), while a sensorineural-type loss would be expected to show a steeply falling pattern such as that in the lower right portion. In general, conductive hearing loss produces a shift in the response to the right on the intensity axis, but the general slope of the function will be normal, or will parallel the normal area within plus or minus one standard deviation. Sensorineural hearing loss often results in the steep latency-intensity function shown, with the wave V latency approaching near-normal values for strong stimuli. A graph such as that illustrated is used routinely in many hearing clinics as a way of summarizing results of ABR evoked-potential tests in a shorthand manner.

In contrast to the general agreement that has been shown with response latency, measures of response amplitude appear to show wide variability. While there is a general trend for the size of the response amplitude to increase with the level of the stimulus, the amplitude of individual waves is quite variable. Different techniques, such as calculating ratios between the size of wave I compared to wave V, have been proposed as a diagnostic index. However, no standard clinical technique is available to use amplitude information routinely in the analysis of the ABR.

The waveform amplitude and latency of the ABR are influenced by variables associated with recording techniques and subject characteristics. These factors are reviewed briefly in the following paragraphs.

RECORDING TECHNIQUES

Changes in the waveform of the ABR have been noted as the rate of stimulus presentation was increased from 2.5 to 50 clicks per second. In general, as the rate of stimulus presentation increases, individual waves of the ABR drop out of the pattern, peak amplitude decreases, and the latency of the remaining peaks increases. A pattern such as that at the top of the illustration (p. 64) is typically seen when clicks are presented at a rate of about 10 per second. However, when the rate of stimulus presentation is increased to 100 clicks per second, the latency of wave V may be increased in normal listeners by as much as 0.9 ms. In routine clinical practice, rates between 10 and 30 clicks per second are used to ensure optimal response patterns and clarity of waves I, III, and V, whereas higher rates are used for measures that are restricted to wave V.

Thus far, the auditory stimulus used to elicit the ABR has been described as a click, a brief sound that has energy at all frequencies ordinarily used to test hearing. In reality, when a click is presented through an earphone, which is the technique most often used to obtain the ABR, the major energy peaks are in the mid- to high-frequency region. This means that the information obtained with the ABR is indicating primarily how well a person hears sounds that are in the region of about 2000 to 4000 Hz, the middle-frequency range. A great deal of research has been devoted to the goal of obtaining information with the averaged auditory evoked potentials about hearing in the lower-frequency regions. Several interesting techniques have been used with the ABR. These include the use of sounds such as tone bursts that are longer than clicks and are more frequency-specific. Another technique involves derived responses that are obtained in a complicated manner by mixing the clicks with various bands of noise and then using a computer to subtract one response from another. A final technique employed is embedding a click in a specially shaped band of noise in order to obtain responses to low-frequency stimuli. None of these techniques has yielded a clinically accepted method for obtaining low-frequency information. Therefore, investigators have explored the use of other time domains such as the middle components as a way of obtaining low-frequency information. This means that normal ABR thresholds determined with clicks appear to predict normal hearing in the mid-to high-frequency region. A significant ABR threshold shift is probable evidence that a hearing loss exists in the high-frequency region. However, it is difficult to make determinations of the shape of the audiogram based only on ABR information derived from clicks.

SUBJECT CHARACTERISTICS

Subject characteristics that have been studied extensively are age and its effect on the ABR. Major changes in the waveform, latencies, and thresholds of the responses have been described during the first few weeks and months of life. Investigators generally have reported that waves I, III, and V may be recorded reliably at birth, but that waves II and IV are less obvious, even for intense clicks. The latencies of the response from newborns are prolonged when compared with responses obtained from adults for similar sounds. The latency-intensity function illustrated (p. 65) must be adjusted to somewhat prolonged values when testing the hearing of newborns and infants less than 18 to 30 months of age. In addition, the interpeak intervals for newborns are prolonged when compared with adult values, and well-defined ABRs are more difficult to obtain in premature infants than in term babies.

At the other end of the age spectrum, reports indicate that the latency of the ABR is prolonged in individuals over 60 years of age, even in the presence of what is judged to be normal hearing, and that the latency of the ABR may show systematic increases in latency throughout the intermediate years from age 20 to 50. Overall, a single set of response threshold and latency norms probably may be applicable to individuals from the third year through the sixth decade of life without adjustments.

With regard to gender, studies have shown that responses obtained from women have shorter latencies than those obtained from men, and that responses from women tend to be larger than those from men These differences may be due to head size. Research in this area continues to clarify the basis for the gender differences.

RETROCOCHLEAR DISORDERS

Retrocochlear disorders refer to lesions that lie central to the cochlea. With the ABR, it is possible to begin this distinction between disorders that are peripheral to the cochlea and those that are retrocochlear. Retrocochlear disorders include space-occupying lesions such as VIIIth nerve tumors, degenerative disorders, and those secondary to malformation or trauma. Specific findings with the ABR do not permit identifying characteristics peculiar to any specific disease entity. Instead, ABR findings permit initial categorization of patient disorders into broad peripheral or central categories, roughly divided at the level of the cochlea. In very general terms, disorders of the peripheral hearing mechanism are reflected by alterations in wave I and subsequent peaks. Disorders at the level of the auditory nerve and more centrally are associated with alterations of the ABR beyond wave I. Therefore, for neurologic purposes, interwave interval measures and changes in response waveform caused by other than simple shifts of latency are of interest. Prolonged interwave intervals may occur, for example, in multiple sclerosis, hypothyroidism, and barbiturate overdoses.

Bibliography

Beagley, H. A., and J. B. Sheldrake: "Differences in Brain Stem Response Latency with Age and Sex," *British Journal of Audiology*, 12:69–77, 1978.

Buchwald, J. S.: "Generators," in E. J. Moore (ed.), *Bases of Auditory Brain-Stem Evoked Responses*, Grune and Stratton, New York, 1983.

Davis, P. A.: "Effects of Acoustic Stimuli on the Waking Human Brain," *Journal of Neurophysiology*, 2:494–499, 1939.

Eggermont, J. J., and M. Don: "Analysis of the Click-Evoked Brainstem Potentials in Humans Using High-Pass Noise Masking, II. Effect of Click Intensity," *Journal of the Acoustical Society of America*, 68:1671–1675, 1980.

Gardi, J. N., and M. I. Mendel: "Evoked Brainstem Potentials," in S. Gerber (ed.), *Audiometry in Infancy*, Grune and Stratton, New York, 1977.

Geisler, C., L. Frishkopf, and W. Rosenblith: "Extracranial Responses to Acoustic Clicks in Man," *Science*, 128:1210–1211, 1958.

Goldstein, R., and L. B. Rodman: "Early Components of Averaged Evoked Responses to Rapidly Repeated Auditory Stimuli," *Journal of Speech and Hearing Research*, 10:697–705, 1967.

Hasimoto, D.: "The Auditory Brainstem Responses and Acoustic Reflex Thresholds in a Normal-Hearing Elderly Population," unpublished master's thesis, University of California, Santa Barbara, 1983.

Jewett, D. L., M. N. Romano, and J. S. Williston: "Human Auditory Evoked Potentials: Possible Brain Stem Components Detected on the Scalp," *Science*, 167:1517–1518, 1970.

Jewett, D. L., and J. S. Williston: "Auditory-Evoked Far Fields Averaged from the Scalp of Humans," *Brain*, 94:681–696, 1971.

Meged, D.: "The Effects of Aging on the Auditory Brainstem Evoked Potentials in Normal-Hearing Adults," unpublished master's thesis, University of California, Santa Barbara, 1985.

Picton, T. W., et al.: "Evoked Potential Audiometry," *Journal of Otolaryngology*, 6:90–119, 1977.

———— and A. D. Smith: "The Practice of Evoked Potential Audiometry," *Otolaryngology Clinics of North America*, 11:263–282, 1978.

Starr, A., and J. Achor: "Auditory Brain Stem Responses in Neurological Disease," *Archives of Neurology*, 32:761–768, 1975.

Stockard, J. J., J. E. Stockard, and F. W. Sharbrough: "Detection and Localization of Occult Lesions with Brainstem Auditory Responses," *Mayo Clinic Proceedings*, 52:761–769, 1977.

Maurice Mendel

Conditioned Play

As audiometric test equipment has become more sophisticated, testing techniques have been developed to include reliable and valid procedures for younger and younger people. Now, identification of hearing impairment in early childhood is possible. A young child, however, does not show extended interest in raising a hand or saying "yes" upon the presentation of a sound, responses expected of adults, so audiologists have incorporated behavioral modification techniques into a test procedure called conditioned play audiometry. In this procedure, a child is taught to respond to a sound, presented through either an earphone or a loudspeaker, by manipulating a toy, for example, placing a peg in a pegboard each time the child hears a sound. The child is consequently rewarded through play for attentiveness and, it is hoped, will respond appropriately for the duration of the hearing test.

Reliable test results are possible only if a child has sufficient mental, emotional, and physical maturity to be interested in and able to respond to the play technique, criteria usually found in children from about 2½ to 5 years of age. Beyond 5 years, the method often becomes boring to a child, and adult procedures can be used. As a young child's attention span is short, the testing must be completed quickly, yet in a relaxed manner. Two examiners, an audiologist and a trained assistant, usually work with a child in a two-room test suite. One person is involved with the child and the child's responses to the sounds, while the other delivers controlled sounds from instruments in the other room of the test suite. Many experienced audiologists, however, are able to work with the parent as the assistant, and prefer to do so.

Prior to introducing the child to the test suite, the audiologist observes an informal play situation to assess the child's maturity and to determine the responses to sound that the child is capable of making. This observation assists in determining the level of sophistication of the conditioned play technique to be used and to give a rough estimate of the loudness levels at which to begin the testing. The types of sounds used to assess a young child's hearing can be simple two-syllable words, bursts of narrow-band noise (which have some tonality), or pure tones. It is often preferable to derive a threshold for speech prior to attempting a pure-tone evaluation because of a child's potentially short attention span and general higher level of involvement with words rather than with pure tones.

SPEECH RECEPTION THRESHOLD TESTING

Simple toys, or pictures of toys, with two-syllable names can be used for the speech reception threshold (SRT) testing. These words approximate the two-syllable words, called spondaic words, used in testing adults and older children. Objects have more apparent interest to a child than do pictures, and toys such as a baseball, airplane, bathtub, football, or toothbrush can be used. First, however, it must be determined that the child knows the name of each object or picture so that vocabulary confusion does not contaminate the hearing-test results. When this has been determined, the earphones are placed on the child in a matter-of-fact manner, and if one is fortunate enough to have a child leave them on, testing of each ear separately (monaural SRT) can proceed. The audiologist asks the child through each earphone to point to the various toys, one at a time, recording the signal level at which the child responds correctly 50 percent of the time. If a child is persistent in refusing to wear the earphones, speech testing can be done in the sound field over a loudspeaker. Once SRTs are recorded for each ear, the audiologist can continue with conditioned play pure-tone audiometry.

PURE-TONE TESTING

With knowledge of the SRT results, the audiologist presents a tone that is sufficiently loud to elicit a response from the child. The assistant working with the child also is wearing earphones and can hear the same tone. When the assistant is sure that the child has heard the tone and is not just reacting randomly, the assistant places a peg in the child's hand, takes the child's hand, and assists the child in placing the peg in the pegboard. Each time the peg is placed correctly after the tone presentation, the assistant displays much praise and enthusiasm for the child's listening skill and performance. Several suprathreshold trials are given until the child apparently has grasped the idea of the listening task. The child is then allowed to proceed alone, placing the peg in the pegboard each time the sound is heard until a threshold estimate is reached for a particular pure tone. Because the child may tire of placing pegs in a pegboard after several threshold derivations, other toys are made available. Transfer of the learning task, however, may be difficult for some children, and a new conditioning session may be necessary for each new toy introduced. Some commonly used toys are blocks in a box, simple wooden puzzles of four to six pieces, and rings on a peg. Care must be taken that the child does not become so involved in play, however, that she or he forgets the listening task.

At the earliest possible age of testing with conditioned play audiometry, it is unlikely that exact speech or pure-tone thresholds will be derived or will be necessary. At that age, the audiologist is usually interested in an estimate of a child's hearing sensitivity, and because attention spans are short, approximating threshold is quite appropriate. As a child gets older, however, reliable threshold results are possible with this test method.

OLDER PATIENTS

The play conditioning test technique also can be used with persons who are mentally retarded or neuromuscularly disabled, or who display other adult cases of central nervous system insult such that a traditional test procedure may be too difficult. In the case of adult testing with these methods, the reinforcement technique remains similar to that used with children, while the actual objects or pictures used as toys are graded to a person's intellectual level, if known.

Bibliography

Hodgson, William R.: "Testing Infants and Young Children," in Jack Katz (ed.), *Handbook of Clinical Audiology*, 2d ed., Williams and Wilkins, Baltimore, 1978.

Martin, Frederick N.: *Introduction to Audiology*, 2d ed., Prentice-Hall, Englewood Cliffs, New Jersey, 1981.

——— (ed.): *Pediatric Audiology*, Prentice-Hall, Englewood Cliffs, New Jersey, 1978.

Northern, Jerry L., and Marion P. Downs: *Hearing in Children*, 3d ed., Williams and Wilkins, Baltimore, 1984.

Carol C. McRandle

Visual Reinforcement

Infants as young as six months and up to two years of age are now given hearing tests by a technique called visual reinforcement audiometry (VRA), that is, pairing a visual reward, such as a lighted toy, with a sound coming from a loudspeaker or an earphone. Although the original VRA method was quite definitive in the steps for its execution, the term has become almost generic among professionals for any technique that uses visual reinforcement of the test sound signals.

Responses to sound vary according to the age of the infant, but by six months a normal baby reacts to sound by moving the head or eyes toward the sound source (localization or orientation response). Later, the infant may attempt to reach the sound by body movements or by crawling toward the sound source or, more subtly, may respond by smiling or vocalizing shortly after it is presented. Still later, babies will recognize their own names and those of close family members and pets. At about 18 months an infant can point to body parts or clothing when asked to do so, and by 2 years of age should be able to identify familiar objects by name, such as kitty, airplane, and baseball.

These responses are used by audiologists to assess the hearing sensitivity of the infant through a variety of VRA methods. One of the simplest techniques is to place the baby in an infant seat or on a parent's lap midway between two loudspeakers having lighted toys on or near them (see the illustration). Lap placement, however, is less desirable than the infant seat because of possible inadvertent movement (at the sound signal) of the parent or

Two-room sound suite for visual reinforcement audiometry testing.

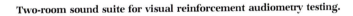

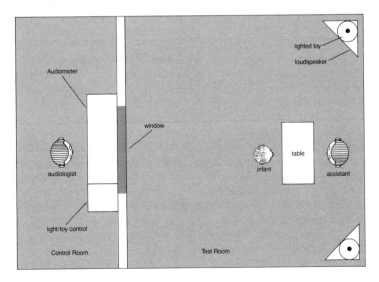

other adult who is holding the child. Positioning the infant should also be done so that a clear localization response can be seen by the observer when the baby searches for the sound. An assistant facing the baby in the test room keeps the baby occupied with a quiet toy, a soft doll, for example, so that the view of the baby may be kept in the midline. Sounds such as warble tones, pure tones, or narrow-band noise bursts are presented through a loudspeaker. The infant may show an orientation response to the sound by turning the head to look at the loudspeaker. At that time, the lighted toy on the speaker is activated to reinforce the baby's searching response. Once the conditioned response is established, each loudspeaker is used randomly at different frequencies and loudness levels without the light, or with the light only as a reinforcer until an estimate of hearing sensitivity is achieved.

Testing one ear at a time (monaural testing) is not possible with a sound field test, however, as the better ear will respond to the sound even if a slight hearing loss exists in only one ear. In the original VRA sound field procedure, an ear plug was placed in the infant's nontest ear so that monaural test results could be approximated. The success of this technique is dependent upon the severity of loss in the test ear, as a loss exceeding the sound attenuation value from one ear to the other might result in the nontest ear hearing the test sound, thus negating the assumed monaural unplugged ear response. Some infants will tolerate earphones, however, so that after the conditioned response has been established in sound field, a VRA method can be employed monaurally under earphones, care being taken to establish a strong head-turning response in the infant. In this manner, bone-conduction testing is also possible.

With an older infant, it may be preferable to get an estimate of a speech detection threshold (SDT) prior to the pure-tone test, because speech seems to hold the attention of young children better than pure tones. Further, a speech reception threshold (SRT) can be estimated by adding 10 dB to the SDT score, thus making the SDT a particularly useful test. Placement of the infant and the assistant in the test suite for speech VRA is the same as in pure-tone VRA. Using speech, either through loudspeakers or through earphones, the audiologist may say the child's name or ask the child to point to body parts or to toys on the table in front of the child, again rewarding the child with a lighted toy when the desired response is given. Even though adequate speech detection responses are attained through this method, pure-tone testing is still advised, as the SDT results do not give an adequate identification of high-frequency sensitivity, a prerequisite in relating hearing loss to speech discrimination skills.

TANGIBLE REINFORCEMENT OPERANT CONDITIONING

Other sensory modalities used in reinforcement paradigms include those of touch and taste, having been tapped in tangible reinforcement operant conditioning audiometry (TROCA). With this test method, an infant or an older difficult-to-test child faces a loudspeaker and a device that automatically dispenses a piece of candied cereal or a token, for example, under certain predetermined rigid test conditions. Most often, the child is conditioned to press a lever or button in response to a sound presented over the loudspeaker. If the lever is pressed within a set time interval after the sound presentation, the child is rewarded with the cereal piece or token. On the other hand, if the child presses the lever out of step with the preset latency period, this false response is negatively reinforced through a time-out period.

BEHAVIORAL OBSERVATION

The least restrictive VRA test procedure with regard to response acceptance by the audiologist is that of behavioral observation audiometry (BOA). This technique does not rely upon formal response reinforcement but upon the audiologist's observation of an infant's normal responses to sound presentation. Responses to sound can include reflexive activity commensurate with the child's developmental age, such as an eye blink, localization or orientation responses, or smiling and vocalizations. For BOA testing, a baby is placed in the test room with an assistant, as in the illustration, and moderate-to-loud sounds are presented through a loudspeaker or earphone. An animated or lighted toy may be activated in conjunction with the child's response to the sound, but usually this method is used only to keep the infant's interest in the test proceedings and not as a reinforcement device. The audiologist subjectively evaluates any of a variety of responses to the sound presentation and praises the infant for the response. The BOA technique is reliable only when replicable responses can be observed and only when an experienced and knowledgeable audiologist interprets the baby's response activity. The method is also limited because an infant quickly adapts to short-duration sound presentations in a relatively sterile test environment. Thus, without formal reinforcement methods, only limited screening results may be possible with BOA and the very young child.

Several techniques have been devised to extend the BOA test period with the infant. In one method, the baby may be allowed to breast- or bottle-feed during the evaluation with careful observation being made of sucking, respiration, or other reflex changes occurring upon presentation of the sound. Letting the child drift off into light sleep after nursing can also extend the test duration. Often, in infants, reflexive responses to sound adapt less during the onset of light sleep than they do in the wakened state.

Bibliography

Hodgson, William R.: "Testing Infants and Young Children," in Jack Katz (ed.), *Handbook of Clinical Audiology*, 2d ed., Williams and Wilkins, Baltimore, 1978.

Jaffee, Burton F. (ed.): *Hearing Loss in Children*, University Park Press, Baltimore, 1977.

Martin, Frederick N.: *Introduction to Audiology*, 2d ed., Prentice-Hall, Englewood Cliffs, New Jersey, 1981.

———— (ed.): *Pediatric Audiology*, Prentice-Hall, Englewood Cliffs, New Jersey, 1978.

Moore, John M., Wesley R. Wilson, and Gary Thompson: "Visual Reinforcement of Head-Turn Responses in Infants Under Twelve Months of Age," *Journal of Speech and Hearing Disorders*, 42:328–334, 1977.

Newby, Hayes A.: *Audiology*, 4th ed., Prentice-Hall, Englewood Cliffs, New Jersey, 1979.

Northern, Jerry L., and Marion P. Downs: *Hearing in Children*, 3d ed., Williams and Wilkins, Baltimore, 1984.

Carol C. McRandle

Tests of Central Auditory Dysfunction

Assessment of the central auditory nervous system is a difficult task that has challenged researchers for many years. The primary reason for the difficulty is that the central auditory nervous system is an extremely complex structural network highly resistant to breakdown on auditory tasks (tests). Anatomically, both ears are represented bilaterally in the brain by multiple ipsilateral and contralateral pathways, nuclear centers, and intra- and interhemispheric connections. This intricate system leads to the primary, secondary, and perhaps additional auditory cortical areas.

The central auditory tests discussed here are those found to be sensitive to dysfunction or pathologic conditions of the auditory pathways in the brainstem at the level of the cochlear nuclei and olivary centers up to and including the higher auditory pathways in the cortex.

Conventional auditory tests are highly redundant and offer too much information to provide a challenge for the central auditory nervous system. For example, persons with known damage to it but intact peripheral auditory systems (normal hearing) typically exhibit normal performance on both conventional tonal and speech tests. Because of this, clinical researchers have chosen to degrade, or make more difficult, the conventional tonal speech stimuli in an attempt to tax the central auditory nervous system and thereby to provide more sensitive indicators of central auditory dysfunction.

Most of the tests designed for central auditory assessment use speech rather than tones as the stimuli. Conventional speech tests are made more difficult by changing one or more of the basic acoustic parameters of speech, namely, time, intensity, or frequency. These features of speech are altered in various ways to reduce the redundancy of the signal and, hence, make the task for the central auditory nervous system more difficult. Another method of degrading or distorting speech is to present various forms of competition simultaneously with the conventional test. Examples of both methods are discussed below.

Tests of central auditory dysfunction can be presented monaurally or binaurally. In a monaural test situation, one or more signals are delivered to a single ear. Binaural presentation can be divided into two test conditions: (1) Diotic presentation is when identical signals are presented to both ears simultaneously. (2) Dichotic presentation is when both ears receive different signals simultaneously.

The following discussion deals with individual tests of central auditory dysfunction. The tests have been divided into subsections according to type of stimuli and method of presentation. Because of the difficulty in assessing central auditory dysfunction, site of lesion should not be determined from a single auditory test. A test battery approach using conventional and central auditory tests is necessary for obtaining a complete audiologic profile. In addition, results of central auditory tests in patients with peripheral (outer, middle, inner ear) hearing loss should be interpreted cautiously.

MONAURAL SPEECH TASKS

Conventional speech tasks have proven to have limited use in detecting central auditory nervous system lesions. One task using ordinary speech that occasionally suggests central auditory nervous system damage is the Performance Intensity Function for Phonetically Balanced Word Lists (PI-PB). In this test, monosyllables with a carrier phrase (such as "say the word pick") are presented at various intensity levels ranging from low to high to each ear. Speech recognition (discrimination) ability in percent correct is measured at each intensity level. Thus, a performance intensity function is obtained, with the expected outcome of improvement in scores as the speech signal level becomes higher (more audible). This task has been suggested to be valuable as a screening test in assessment of central auditory disorders; however, it is most sensitive to lesions of the VIIIth cranial nerve or peripheral brainstem.

A degraded speech test that has proven useful as a screening test for central auditory dysfunction is the speech-in-noise task. In this test, speech recognition materials, such as monosyllables with a carrier phrase, are presented to a single ear and simultaneously noise is presented to the same ear at a level at or near the intensity of the primary (speech) message. Results show this test to be useful in detecting abnormalities of the auditory system from the cochlea through the temporal lobe, but not in localization of a specific lesion site.

Another speech test that uses same-ear competition is the Synthetic Sentence Identification–Ipsilateral Competing Message task (SSI-ICM). In this test the primary message presented to the test ear consists of third-order approximations of English sentences (for example, "Small boat with a picture has become"). Continuous discourse (such as someone reading a story) is the competing message presented to the same ear at varying intensities. Normal hearers have no difficulty recognizing and reporting the primary message. However, patients with brainstem lesions may demonstrate a reduced score on the ear ipsilateral to the lesion, whereas patients with temporal lobe damage may show reduced performance in the ear contralateral to the lesion.

The filtered speech test is an example of a degraded task that uses elimination of information as the method of distortion. The test signal is speech recognition materials (monosyllables with a carrier phrase) that have been altered, usually with a low-pass filter, to make the speech less intelligible. Low-pass filtering is accomplished by filtering out that portion of the signal that is above a designated frequency such as 2000 Hz. Thus low-frequency information of the speech is maintained, while high-frequency components of the speech signal are eliminated. Listeners report that filtered speech sounds as though the speaker is talking in a rain barrel. Because filtering eliminates some of the acoustic information of the speech signal, this task can be made quite difficult depending upon how much filtering is done. Filtered speech tests have been used with some success in detection of cortical lesions and occasionally brainstem lesions.

Accelerated speech and time-compressed speech are two forms of time-altered speech that have been used to assess central auditory function. Early investigators used accelerated speech, which simply involves fast playback on a tape recorder of a conventional speech task. Not only does this method make the speech faster, but it changes the frequency characteristics of the signal and produces a "chipmunklike" quality to the speech. Time-compressed speech, however, uses speech recognition materials (usually monosyllables) that have been compressed in such a manner that the rate of speech is quite fast but the frequency characteristics of the speech have not been altered. Time-compressed speech is the most popular time-altered speech task, and results have shown it to be sensitive to lesions in the temporal lobe. Time-expanded speech has also been investigated in assessing central auditory dysfunction, but results have not proven to be very successful.

Interrupted speech is another example of a signal-altering task that has proven to be effective in identification of temporal lobe damage. In this task, portions of the speech signal are actually removed at very rapid rates so that the speech has been interrupted (chopped) and made less intelligible. Results show reduced performance in the contralateral ear in patients with temporal lobe involvement.

BINAURAL SPEECH TASKS

As stated above, binaural speech tasks can be divided into dichotic (two different messages, both ears) and diotic (same message, both ears) tasks. Both auditory tasks provide a challenge to the central auditory nervous system; however, many more dichotic stimuli are available as test signals. Dichotic speech tasks are especially sensitive to lesions in the higher auditory pathways of the temporal lobes. Diotic speech tests are most sensitive to brainstem lesions.

Competing messages may be used in dichotic speech tasks just as in their monaural counterpart. However, in a dichotic situation the competing message is presented to the opposite ear rather than the same ear. The patient is instructed to concentrate on the primary message being delivered to the test ear and ignore the competing message in the nontest ear. The Synthetic Sentence Identification with Contralateral Competing Message (SSI-CCM) is an example of this type of test. Third-order approximations of English sentences (for example, "Battle cry and be better than ever") are presented to the test ear, while meaningful connected discourse (such as reading a story) is presented to the nontest ear. Normal listeners find no difficulty with recognizing and reporting the primary message; however, patients with cortical lesions experience difficulty when the primary message is in the ear that is contralateral to the lesion. The ear ipsilateral to the lesion is unaffected by this test.

Other dichotic tasks that use a competing message are Northwestern University (NU) Auditory Test No. 2 and the NU-20. These tasks were originally used in the evaluation of binaural hearing aids. However, the potential use of NU-2 in patients with temporal lobe damage was discovered. These competing message tasks (NU-2 and NU-20) use monosyllables with a carrier phrase (such as "say the word dog") as the primary message. The competing message consists of meaningful English sentences (for instance, "How many colors in the rainbow?") that usually are presented at a slightly higher intensity level than the primary message. Results have shown that persons with diffuse temporal lobe damage (for example, cerebral vascular accident) exhibit poor performance when the primary message is delivered to the ear opposite the lesion. Normal listeners have no difficulty identifying the primary message.

The final competing message task in popular use is the Competing Sentence Test. In this task two meaningful sentences are presented dichotically, one sentence to each ear. The primary message is presented to the test ear (for example, "I think we'll have rain today") and the competing message to the nontest ear (such as "There was frost on the ground") at a higher level than the primary message. The listener is instructed to attend to the primary message and ignore the competition. This test also demonstrates abnormal performance in the ear contralateral to a temporal lobe lesion.

Another type of dichotic task requires the listener to respond to the stimuli presented to both ears instead of concentrating on one ear. An example is the Staggered Spondaic Word Test. In this test a different two-syllable word, with nearly equal stress on both syllables (such as airplane, hotdog) is presented to each ear. The words are aligned so that the last syllable of one word is presented simultaneously with the first syllable of the second word. The listener must repeat as many of the syllables as possible, and a percent correct score is obtained. Results from this test show that in temporal lobe lesions the ear contralateral to the damage has a reduced score compared to the ipsilateral side. Research also has shown this test to be sensitive to lesions located in the auditory pathways in the parietal lobes as well as the temporal lobes.

Two dichotic tasks that are very sensitive to lesions in the higher auditory pathways are dichotic digits and dichotic consonant-vowel (CV) syllables. These tests have been used primarily as research tools; however, the dichotic digits task is gaining popularity as a successful clinical tool.

In the dichotic digits task one-syllable digits (such as one, five) are presented to both ears with a different digit or digits to each ear. The listener is asked to repeat all digits heard. A percent correct score for each ear is obtained, and results between ears are compared. As in other dichotic tasks, persons with involvement of the temporal lobes exhibit a poor score in the ear that is contralateral to the damaged lobe.

Dichotic consonant-vowel syllables consist of the English stop plosives and the vowel /a/ (for example, pa, ba, ta, da, ka, ga). The syllables are aligned precisely to allow for correct dichotic presentation of two different syllables (one to each ear). The subject is asked to report the two syllables presented. If only one syllable is perceived, the subject is asked to guess the second syllable. This is an extremely difficult task and therefore is not used with much success in a clinical setting. Research has shown, however, that as in other dichotic tasks, the ear contralateral to a damaged temporal lobe shows a reduced score. In addition, this test has proven successful in helping identify central auditory nervous system lesions in the deep left parietal lobe and crossing pathways (corpus callosum) between the two hemispheres of the brain.

Filtered speech tests also have been used with success as dichotic or diotic tests in patients with brainstem lesions. In a dichotic test situation two different signals of electronically filtered speech are presented to both ears. For example, a speech message that distorts the low frequencies (high-pass filter) is presented to one ear, and the same speech message that distorts the high frequencies (low-pass filter) is presented to the opposite ear. It has been demonstrated that persons with normal central auditory nervous system function are able to "fuse" both speech segments and obtain a normal speech-intelligibility score. However, persons with brainstem lesions are unable to fuse the two complementary segments of the signal to form a whole or undistorted message. In a diotic test condition, high- and low-pass filtered speech is presented simultaneously to both ears. Persons with brainstem lesions are unaffected by this task.

Another binaural phenomenon used in central auditory nervous system testing is the speech masking-level difference. In this task, speech (two-syllable words) and noise are presented simultaneously to both ears either in phase or out of phase by 180°. Results of various combinations of the signal and noise are obtained and compared with one another. This test has been successful in assessing patients with brainstem lesions. Patients with cortical lesions do not show unusual findings. A puretone (usually 500 Hz) masking-level difference also is available as another test of central auditory nervous system function. Results are similar to those of the speech masking-level difference.

The auditory tests discussed above are primarily speech measures designed specifically for assessment of the central auditory nervous system. Other audiologic procedures have potential in central auditory nervous system assessment. Acoustic reflex measures, auditory brainstem response audiometry, auditory adaptation tasks, alternate binaural loudness balance, and simultaneous binaural median-plane localization have been successful in determining involvement of the auditory system, especially at the level of the VIIIth cranial nerve or brainstem. Limited results of alternate binaural loudness balance also have suggested involvement of the higher auditory pathways in patients with temporal lobe lesions.

CONCLUSION

The auditory tests discussed herein have been used successfully in the assessment of central auditory nervous system dysfunction. These tests, used in conjunction with conventional auditory tests, and a case history can provide information to aid in the diagnosis of lesions in the auditory pathways of the brainstem through the temporal lobes. Neurologic, otologic, and radiologic findings typically also are required to complete the patient profile and arrive at a diagnosis.

Bibliography

Berlin, C. I., et al.: "The Construction and Perception of Simultaneous Messages," *Asha,* vol. 10, 1968.

Jerger, J.: "Auditory Tests for Disorders of the Central Auditory Mechanism," in B. R. Alford and W. S. Fields (eds.), *Neurological Aspects of Auditory and Vestibular Disorders,* 1964.

———, R. Carhart, and D. Dirks: "Binaural Hearing Aids and Speech Intelligibility," *J. Speech Hear. Res.,* vol. 4, 1961.

——— and S. Jerger: "Diagnostic Significance of PB Word Functions," *Arch. Otolaryngol.,* vol. 93, 1971.

———, C. Speaks, and J. Trammell: "A New Approach to Speech Audiometry," *J. Speech Hear. Disord.,* vol. 33, 1968.

Katz, J.: "The Use of Staggered Spondaic Words for Assessing the Integrity of the Central Auditory Nervous System," *J. Aud. Res.,* vol. 2, 1962.

Kimura, D.: "Cerebral Dominance and the Perception of Verbal Stimuli," *Canad. J. Psychol.,* vol. 15, 1961.

———: "Some Effects of Temporal Lobe Damage on Auditory Perception," *Canad. J. Psychol.,* vol. 15, 1961.

Matzker, J.: "Two New Methods for the Assessment of Central Auditory Functions in Cases of Brain Disease," *Ann. Otol.,* vol. 68, 1959.

Noffsinger, P. D., and S. Kurdziel: "Assessment of Central Auditory Lesions," in W. F. Rintelmann (ed.), *Hearing Assessment,* 1979.

Olsen, W. O., and R. Carhart: "Development of Test Procedures for Evaluation of Binaural Hearing Aids," in *Bulletin of Prosthetics Research: Prosthetic and Sensory Aids Service,* Department of Medicine and Surgery, Veterans Administration, Washington, D.C., 1967.

Rintelmann, W. F., and G. E. Lynn: "Speech Stimuli for Assessment of Central Auditory Disorders," in D. F. Konkle and W. F. Rintelmann (eds.), *Principles of Speech Audiometry,* 1983.

Speaks, C., and J. Jerger: "Method for Measurement of Speech Identification," *J. Speech Hear. Res.,* vol. 8, 1965.

Willeford, J.: "Central Auditory Function in Children with Learning Disabilities," *Audiol. Hear. Educ.,* vol. 2, 1976.

Sabina Kurdziel Schwan

AUDITORY DISORDERS, EVALUATION AND DIAGNOSIS OF

Auditory disorders are manifested in many forms and degrees of impairment and can occur at all life stages. The specific disturbances in auditory function will depend on the degree and location of injury or disease in the underlying auditory system.

Disorders of the outer and middle ear often result in conductive hearing loss. This is primarily an attenuation problem caused by interference with the normal transmission of sound to the inner ear; thus sounds are heard at a softer level than normal. Pathologic conditions of the cochlea or auditory nerve (VIIIth cranial nerve) will usually result in sensorineural hearing loss. Here, because the receptor mechanisms are not functioning properly, sounds are not only attenuated but also considerably distorted. In disorders of the central auditory nervous system, the auditory disorder often is more subtle and complex. Persons with disorders of the auditory brainstem or cortex, for example, may have normal hearing sensitivity. However, they often manifest a poor ability to understand speech in a degraded listening environment such as in background noise or in the presence of a competing message. Persons with or without hearing losses may also complain of noises (tinnitus) in the ears and head. In addition, pathology of the auditory system may be associated with nonauditory symptoms such as dizziness and pain. *See* TINNITUS.

The diagnosis of auditory disorders encompasses both medical and communicative concerns. Medical diagnosis is usually made by an otolaryngologist, a physician who specializes in disorders of the ear, nose, and throat. For example, the otolaryngologist determines the need for surgery or other medical treatment based on the symptoms and test findings. The diagnosis of hearing or communicative impairment is the function of an audiologist, who determines the type and degree of hearing loss and its potential effect on everyday communication. If the presenting problem cannot be treated medically, the audiologist evaluates the need for amplification (hearing aids) and rehabilitation services such as counseling or speech and language therapy. Effective diagnosis and treatment of auditory disorders requires cooperative efforts on the part of the audiologist and otolaryngologist.

Diagnosis is based on determining the history, symptoms, signs, and test results that profile a patient's disorders and complaints. By combining information from a patient's historical accounts of an auditory disorder with presenting complaints (such as hearing loss, dizziness, and ringing in the ears), otoscopy (visual inspection of the ear canal and eardrum), and formal test results, the examiner often can get a picture of the nature and likely underlying cause of the disorder. This process results in a preliminary diagnosis. Often, a diagnosis cannot be exact because the cause of a disorder cannot be pinpointed. Medically, diagnosis is concerned with a determination of the existence, nature, and anatomic location of a pathologic condition of the auditory system. Audiologically, the principal diagnostic issue is communicative function—for example, how well a person hears and understands speech. Ultimately, both the audiologic and medical diagnostic impressions serve as the primary determinants of recommended treatment.

Terry L. Wiley

SYMPTOMS

A symptom may be broadly defined as something that indicates a bodily disorder. It constitutes the patient's description of a particular problem; symptoms of an auditory disorder may be described as having difficulty hearing, experiencing ringing in the ear (tinnitus), or dizziness (vertigo). By asking appropriate questions, the clinician may discover specific information about each of these symptoms and be significantly assisted in determining a diagnostic approach. This section will address the following symptoms that accompany auditory disorders: hearing difficulty, paracusis Willisiana, tinnitus, vertigo and dizziness, pain, and facial weakness.

Sometimes an accurate history of symptoms cannot be obtained directly from the individual because of infancy, mental retardation, senile dementia, or similar problems. The next best source is the observant parent, spouse, or guardian. For instance, it is not uncommon for parents to have a child examined because the child will not talk. Lack of speech development, delayed speech development, or poor speech may be a symptom of auditory disorders. Consequently, all children with a speech or language problem should have a hearing test as part of the diagnostic process.

A cluster or group of symptoms that resemble those of a known disorder constitute a syndrome. A syndrome is not a diagnosis; it is a description. For example, Ménière's syndrome means that the person has symptoms similar to those presented by a person with Ménière's disease. Either the clinician does not have enough information to make a diagnosis, or the symptoms mimic those typically associated with the disease. Consequently, the description Ménière's syndrome satisfies the patient's need to know and the physician's need for closure until a precise diagnosis can be made.

Richard H. Nodar

Hearing Difficulty This section will be presented in two parts: symptoms associated with unilateral vs. bilateral hearing losses and symptoms associated with different types of hearing loss.

Unilateral vs. Bilateral Hearing Loss. Individuals with a unilateral hearing loss usually will complain about three things: they have difficulty hearing people who are on the side of the nonhearing ear (off side); they have difficulty determining where sound is coming from (localization); and they have great difficulty understanding speech in noisy sit-

uations (reduced speech discrimination). On the other hand, an individual with the same amount and kind of hearing loss in both ears (bilaterally symmetric) will not have a better ear and will usually not have the localization problem. If the bilateral hearing loss is not severe, such persons' complaints are more likely to be that people mumble or do not speak loudly enough; or they claim that they hear only what they want to hear.

Individuals may have a hearing loss in both ears, but with different levels of sensitivity in each (bilaterally asymmetric). Then the person will have a better ear but will manifest the symptoms of a person with a unilateral hearing loss. Finally, an individual may have a conductive hearing loss in one ear and a sensorineural hearing loss in the other ear. In this case, the person may manifest symptoms associated with each disorder, or with the hearing loss of the greater magnitude.

Types of Hearing Loss. A person with a bilateral conductive (mechanical) hearing loss may have the following symptoms and signs: (1) They may speak in a soft voice because the conductive loss causes them to hear their own voice more loudly than it would seem to them normally. (2) They may hear better in noisy situations than in quiet ones, as in paracusis Willisii. (3) They may understand women better than men if the loss is greater in the low frequencies. (4) They can tolerate very loud sound better than individuals with no hearing loss or those with sensorineural hearing loss because the mechanical block reduces the level of sound reaching the ear and, thus, its loudness. (5) They may experience a low-pitch tinnitus (described as a hum, roar, or buzz). (6) They may feel pressure or "fullness" in the ear. (7) They only need amplification, that is, they hear a sound if it is loud enough.

In general, people with sensorineural hearing loss (1) speak louder than necessary to be heard to overcome their own hearing loss; (2) have difficulty understanding speech even when it is loud; (3) have additional difficulty understanding speech in noisy situations; (4) understand men better than women; (5) experience pain or severe discomfort when exposed to very loud sounds (loudness recruitment); (6) hear two pitches when only one note is being sounded (dyplacusis); (7) hear noises, which are often high-pitched, in their ear (tinnitus); (8) respond inappropriately during conversation; (9) request a speaker to repeat; or (10) withdraw from conversations completely.

A mixed hearing loss occurs when the person has a conductive hearing loss and a sensorineural hearing loss in the same ear. The person with the bilateral, symmetrical mixed hearing loss exhibits symptoms of the type of hearing loss which is greater in magnitude.

Richard H. Nodar

Paracusis Willisiana   Paracusis Willisiana is the ability to hear better in background noise than in quiet. The phenomenon was named for Thomas Willis, an English physician who recognized and described it in 1672. This phenomenon occurs in individuals with conductive hearing losses. In contrast, individuals with normal hearing or sensorineural hearing losses have more difficulty hearing in background noise than in quiet. The phenomenon occurs in all forms of conductive hearing losses, including fixation of the footplate of the stapes in otosclerosis, middle-ear effusion in otitis media, perforation of the tympanic membrane in chronic otitis media, ossicular discontinuity, tympanosclerosis, and adhesive otitis media.

Individuals with conductive hearing losses tend to have equivalent threshold elevations throughout the frequency range of hearing, while individuals with sensorineural hearing losses tend to have a greater elevation of thresholds in the higher frequencies than in the lower frequencies. *See* AUDIOMETRY.

Background noise tends to mask hearing. There is a natural tendency to raise the intensity of the voice to approximately 30 to 40 decibels (dB) above the background noise so that the listener can hear the voice at a comfortable listening level. For example, if the background noise is at the equivalent 45 dB hearing level (HL), a speaker will naturally raise the intensity of the voice to deliver to the listener's ears an intensity of approximately 80 dB HL. The individual with a conductive hearing loss at all frequencies of 45 dB HL cannot hear the background noise below the intensity of 45 dB HL, but is able to hear the speaker's voice well at 80 dB HL, which is 35 dB above the hearing threshold. Assuming that the listener has a pure conductive hearing loss, the sense organ will be normal and the speech reaching the inner ear will be completely intelligible. The individual with a sensorineural hearing loss that averages 45 dB but is greater in the higher frequencies than the lower frequencies can hear the low-frequency background noise at an intensity of 45 dB and will have the hearing masked by the low-frequency noise. Therefore, an individual with a conductive hearing loss often hears better in background noise than in quiet, while an individual with a sensorineural hearing loss has greater difficulty hearing in noise because of the masking effect. The person with normal hearing also is more handicapped in noise than the person with a conductive hearing loss because the full range of background noise is audible to the normal-hearing listener.

James B. Snow

Vertigo and Dizziness   Vertigo and dizziness commonly accompany diseases that cause hearing impairment. These symptoms most frequently are the result of disease of the balance (vestibular) system. This system is in such close anatomic proximity to the hearing system that localized diseases usually affect both. *See* EAR: Anatomy.

Vertigo may be defined as a hallucination of movement. Most frequently, the sensation is one of spinning, either of oneself (subjective) or the environment (objective). Because the semicircular canals in the inner ear contain sense organs designed to detect head rotation, it is logical that activity, either spontaneous or induced, within these sense organs or their connections within the central nervous system will produce a sensation of rotation. On the other hand, spontaneous or induced activity within the macular organs of the inner ear (the utricle and the saccule), which are designed to detect linear acceleration (such as the effect of gravity), or within their connections in the central nervous system, will produce a sensation of tipping, tilting, tumbling, or unsteadiness (dysequilibrium).

Dizziness is a more nebulous symptom. It may be defined as a sensation of loss of immediate contact with one's surroundings. A hallucination of motion (vertigo) obviously is one such mechanism that might disrupt one's sense of orientation. Thus, it may be seen that vertigo is a much more specific symptom, connoting a disturbance of the vestibular system, whereas dizziness is not a well-defined concept and can arise from a wide variety of causes, including low blood pressure, diabetes mellitus, anxiety, hypertension, hyperventilation, cataract and glaucoma, or ototoxic drugs. In one study of this symptom, over 60 different and distinct diseases were found to be capable of causing dizziness. Many of the causes have no direct connection with the labyrinth or the rest of the balance system.

In trying to determine the cause of the individual's complaint of vertigo or dizziness, therefore, it is important to ascertain whether there are any associated hearing symptoms (hearing loss, tinnitus) or ear symptoms (pressure, fullness, pain). Generally, the more definite the sensation of vertigo, the more likely is the disease to be in the inner ear. Conversely, the less definite the sensation, the more likely the problem is in the central nervous system. Also, ear disease is usually of short duration; central nervous system disease generally is prolonged.

Examination. Balance relies heavily upon three main inputs known as the equilibrium triad: the eyes, the labyrinth, and the proprioceptive system (joint and muscle sensation, and so on). Not surprisingly, therefore, eye movement signs are quite common in individuals with vertigo and dizziness. The most common eye movement seen with disturbances of the balance system is nystagmus. This is an involuntary, alternating, to and fro (fast in one direction, slow in the opposite) eye movement.

This is usually one of the first signs to be sought in the clinical evaluation of the individual. It may occur spontaneously and be seen when the individual looks straight ahead (spontaneous nystagmus), or on voluntary deviation of the eyes from center (gaze nystagmus). Occasionally, it may be of congenital origin, when the to-and-fro movements, on gaze ahead, assume a more simple sinusoidal oscillatory pattern. Fixation may affect its intensity; in peripheral disease the effect of fixation is to tend to suppress the nystagmus, and the opposite is true in central disease. Fixation may be minimized by placing +20 diopter (Bartel's) lenses (also known as Frenzel's glasses when illumination is added) in front of the eyes. Fixation may be abolished by having the individual close the eyes, or keep the eyes open in darkness.

Another common sign of disturbance of the vestibular system is a problem with balance. Tests of gait, such as walking forward or backward, with the eyes open or closed, may reveal evidence of disease.

Simple clinical tests of hearing are important, and a careful examination of the ear, including visualization of the ear drum or tympanic membrane with an operating microscope, is essential. In addition, a brief examination of the structures served by the other cranial nerves, and a simple general medical examination, should be performed.

Tests. In addition to hearing tests, there are a number of balance system tests that may be most informative. The best known and most useful is the ENG test battery. ENG is short for electronystagmography, that is, the electrical recording of nystagmus. The result of an ENG test is called an electronystagmogram.

The electrical recording of eye movement is often known as EOG, that is, electrooculography, because this technique allows the electrical recording of a wide variety of eye movements in addition to nystagmus.

In the eye, there is a physiologic electric field, the corneoretinal potential. When the eye moves, this electric field also moves. Electrodes placed on each side of the eye will pick up this change in electrical activity, which is then amplified and displayed as a pen movement.

X-rays of the ear (film or more detailed polytomogram x-rays) may be helpful. Computerized tomography (CAT scans) of the brain or of the ear itself have proved valuable, and it seems as if NMR (nuclear magnetic resonance) studies of the soft tissues may prove a useful additional test in the future.

If systemic disease is suspected, more generalized laboratory tests may be indicated. These include a complete blood count (CBC) for anemia, leukemia, and other blood disorders; FTA-absorp-

tion test for syphilis; Survey-20 for a wide variety of diseases; glucose tolerance test for diabetes mellitus or hypoglycemia; and psychologic tests for emotional disturbances. Frequently, consultations with various medical specialists may be necessary.

Cause and treatment. Because of the physical proximity of the hearing and balance organs and systems, middle-ear disease may spread to the inner sense organs of hearing and balance. Children with acute or chronic middle-ear infections may complain of balance symptoms, or be seen to stagger and fall easily. Such impairment of the labyrinths in childhood, although it may become permanent, usually is compensated for by other body mechanisms, but these patients are especially prone to dizzy spells late in life.

Ménière's disease is a well-known but relatively uncommon disturbance. It consists of vertigo–dizziness, hearing loss, and tinnitus, and usually occurs in spells. Typically, the attacks occur in clusters that often begin early in the morning; are associated with nausea and vomiting; are aggravated by movement; and are accompanied by a low-pitched tinnitus and a low-frequency hearing loss. Episodes last a few hours, and the patient is well between attacks. Spells may frequently be triggered by emotional stress. Treatment is usually medical, although surgery may occasionally be necessary where medical treatment fails to control the attacks. The same clinical picture may also be caused by circulatory disorders, syphilis, diabetes, and so on, so that a careful medical evaluation of the individual is necessary.

Another disease that may produce both hearing loss and dizziness or unsteadiness is an acoustic neuroma, a small benign tumor that grows in the vestibular (balance) nerve in the inner-ear canal (internal auditory meatus) leading from the inner ear to the brain. In this disease, however, the dizziness often is less marked than the hearing loss.

Vertigo or dizziness occurring without auditory-ear symptoms often can be quite difficult to explain. Episodic attacks identical to Ménière's disease but without the auditory-ear symptoms are commonly attributed to vestibular neuronitis. This deliberately vague term is meant to describe a disturbance of the vestibular system anywhere between the labyrinth and the furthest limits of its pathways within the brain. A common cause is a viral infection, especially if there is only one episode. If the episodes are recurrent, the diagnostic possibilities are essentially the same as those that can produce the picture of Ménière's disease.

Another common, purely vestibular disorder is benign postural vertigo. The patient feels fine until bending over, stooping, rolling over in bed, and so on, whereupon after a few seconds there is a transient violent whirling sensation, possibly with nausea. Often, the cause is thought to be due to a condition known as cupulolithiasis. For whatever reason (head injury, vascular disease, age, and so on), the small calcium carbonate crystals (otoconia) normally lying on the macular organs (utricle and saccule) fall off and float around in the labyrinth, settling on the posterior (inferior) semicircular canal. This changes a rotation sense organ into a linear acceleration (gravity) sense organ. Fortunately, the condition is usually self-limiting and clears up in 6 to 12 weeks.

Bibliography

Elia, Joseph C.: *The Dizzy Patient*, Charles C. Thomas, Springfield, 1968.

Finestone, Albert J. (ed.): *Evaluation and Clinical Management of Dizziness and Vertigo*, John Wright PSG, Boston, 1982.

Spector, Martin (ed.): *Dizziness and Vertigo*, Grune and Stratton, New York, 1967.

Cecil W. Hart

Pain Pain in the ear is referred to as an earache or otalgia, and is most commonly caused by an infection in the ear canal (external otitis) or the middle ear (acute otitis media). Earache also may occur with a virulent infection in a middle ear with a long-standing perforation of the tympanic membrane resulting from chronic otitis media. It also may be a symptom of an impending intracranial, infectious complication of chronic otitis media such as meningitis, brain abscess, epidural abscess, subdural empyema, or lateral sinus thrombosis.

Infections in the ear canal and the middle ear usually are caused by bacteria and require prompt treatment by a physician with antibiotics to relieve pain, to prevent serious complications of the infection, and to preserve hearing.

Earaches caused by viral infections may result in blister formation on and inflammation of the tympanic membrane (bullous myringitis). Shingles of the ear (herpes zoster oticus) is another painful ear condition caused by a virus infection. The herpes zoster virus can cause inflammation of the facial nerve and the nerve of hearing and balance, and there may be any combination of hearing loss, tinnitus, vertigo, facial weakness, earache, and blister formation in the ear canal, outer ear, or postauricular area. Neoplasms of the external or middle ear are rare causes of ear pain.

Disease processes such as infections or neoplasms in the paranasal sinuses, nasopharynx, tongue, teeth, jaws, pharynx, hypopharynx, larynx, or parotid and submandibular glands may cause pain to radiate to the ear or to be perceived as an earache. Temporomandibular arthritis (inflammation of the jaw joint) also may cause pain that is perceived as an earache.

James B. Snow

Facial Weakness Weakness of one side of the face occurs if the function of the contralateral motor cortex of the brain (the pathway from the cortex to the facial nerve nucleus), the ipsilateral facial nerve nucleus, or the facial nerve (the seventh cranial nerve) is compromised by disease or injury. After leaving the brainstem, the facial nerve travels through a long canal in the temporal bone (the bone that houses the ear). The facial nerve is particularly vulnerable to damage because swelling of the nerve within the bony canal (the fallopian canal) results in compression of the blood supply to the nerve. After leaving the temporal bone, the nerve divides into many branches that supply motor control to the muscles of facial expression, including the muscles that close the eyes and move the mouth.

Lesions of the motor cortex such as cerebrovascular accidents (strokes) may result in weakness of the lower half of the face on the opposite side. This incomplete paralysis of the face occurs because the portion of the nucleus of the facial nerve that controls the upper part of the face receives innervation from the motor cortices of both sides of the cerebrum, while the portion of the nucleus that controls the lower part of the face receives innervation only from the contralateral cerebral cortex.

Infections or injury to the nerve within the fallopian canal are likely to cause weakness or paralysis of all branches of the facial nerve. Bacterial infections of the middle ear may cause sufficient inflammation of the nerve to cause paralysis. Viral infections of the facial nerve such as acute idiopathic facial paralysis (Bell's palsy) and herpes zoster oticus (shingles) cause paralysis of the face that usually disappears in two or three weeks. The facial nerve can be injured by neoplasms (such as acoustic neurinomas) in the internal auditory canal (where the nerve of hearing and balance enters the inner ear), or in the fallopian canal. Fractures of the temporal bone due to head injury may result in facial paralysis. Injuries to the facial nerve also may occur as complications of ear operations such as mastoidectomies. In all of these instances, hearing loss often is a concomitant symptom.

Branches of the facial nerve on the face may be damaged by neoplasms of the parotid gland and by trauma to the face. In these cases, hearing is not likely to be affected.

Facial paralysis results in a loss of protection of the eye by the eyelids, difficulty in moving food in the mouth, difficulty in articulating labial sounds, and cosmetic deformity. Protection of the eye with the use of artificial tears and taping the eye shut should be carried out immediately. If there is no recovery of facial strength, decompression of the facial nerve, nerve grafts and transpositions, and operations to reanimate the face can be performed.

James B. Snow

OTOSCOPY

To detect a variety of ear diseases, many of which are manifested by hearing loss, a careful visual examination is essential. The external ear canal may be inspected directly. Although the tympanic membrane (eardrum) seals off the middle-ear space, it provides a convenient semitransparent window to gather information about the status of the middle-ear and mastoid tissues.

Method   Examination of the ear by otoscopy permits direct inspection of the external ear using a speculum and light source. The otoscope consists of an electric or battery-powered bulb, magnifying lens, and a speculum with side port for insufflation of the external auditory canal. The speculum straightens and dilates the soft outermost portion of the external auditory canal. Illumination may be provided by headlight, mirror, or operating microscope, but the compact hand-held otoscope is most widely used.

The otoscope is used by first tilting the patient's head toward the opposite shoulder to bring the ear canal into the horizontal plane. Further alignment is accomplished by gently pulling the ear pinnacle upward and backward, or slightly downward in an infant. Optimal illumination is achieved by wedging the largest possible speculum into the outer cartilaginous ear canal. A common error is to insert a speculum that is too small. This compromises exposure and risks inadvertently advancing into the sensitive, easily damaged skin lining the bony ear canal.

Diagnostic Signs   When the tympanic membrane is perforated, the middle ear can be seen directly through the tear, but more often the status of the middle ear is deduced by subtle changes in the tympanic membrane. Successful diagnosis is based on methodical examination of the drumhead, with identification of landmarks and changes in color, texture, thickness, and mobility. The malleus is the only ossicle normally attached to the tympanic membrane. Most consistent of the landmarks is the malleus manubrium, which roughly divides the tympanic membrane surface along a vertical axis. The inferior end of the manubrium is at the apex of the cone-shaped eardrum, and this rounded surface forms the umbo. A funnel-shaped light reflex is seen extending downward and forward from the umbo in the normal ear. A thick, white, fibrous annulus marks the periphery of the tympanic membrane. The upper end of the manubrium protrudes as the short process of malleus. A thin and vulnerable portion of tympanic membrane is the pars flaccida, which is just above the short process and conspicuous by its lack of a fibrous annulus.

Normally, the tympanic membrane exhibits a whitish-gray ground-glass appearance with prominent vessels running along the manubrium and around the periphery. Increased redness suggests inflammation, but may also occur in excited states such as when crying. White deposits in the tympanic membrane commonly result from degeneration or calcification. However, opacity and discoloration may suggest a middle-ear mass. The tympanic membrane may look blue if blood or a vascular mass is in the middle ear. Yellow or amber is the most common abnormal color and indicates middle-ear fluid or pus buildup.

Examination of the ear by pneumootoscopy allows identification of tympanic membrane landmarks.

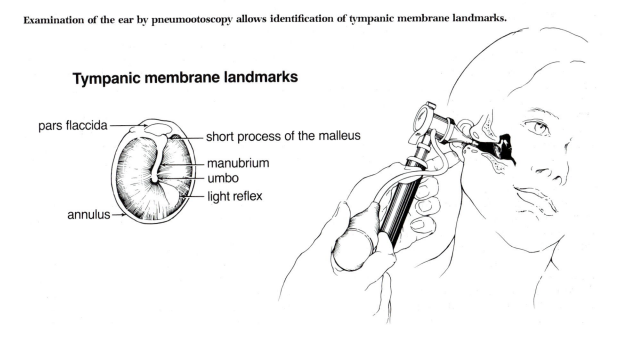

Tympanic membrane landmarks

pars flaccida —
short process of the malleus
manubrium
umbo
light reflex
annulus →

A change in the normally concave surface of the tympanic membrane can also signal a problem. An accumulation of fluid or pus in the middle ear may cause the drumhead to bulge outward. By contrast, an accentuated tympanic membrane concavity also indicates middle-ear pathology, usually associated with impaired aeration of the middle ear due to inadequate opening of the eustachian tube. The resultant negative middle-ear pressure sucks the drum inward, accentuating the concavity, increasing prominence of the short process, and creating the illusion of a foreshortened manubrium.

Pneumootoscopy   Pneumatic otoscopy (pneumootoscopy), accomplished by alternating pressure with a bulb syringe attachment, allows more accurate assessment of position and mobility of the tympanic membrane. Slightly decreased motion may indicate negative middle-ear pressure; absence of obvious excursion suggests fluid in the middle-ear cavity. Malleus motion also may be assessed by using careful pneumootoscopy with adequate magnification.

Serious Diseases   There are a few signs that should alert the examiner to the possibility of serious underlying ear disease. Any perforation of the tympanic membrane, especially along the margins, may indicate skin or epithelial growth into the middle ear and mastoid. Such epithelial proliferation is referred to as cholesteatoma and often is associated with a putrid discharge. Debris on the tympanic membrane is abnormal. Earwax is excreted in the outer ear canal and moves outward naturally because the external auditory canal is self-cleaning by the peripheral migration of surface cells. Unless debris is manually pushed into the canal, the finding of cerumen or debris on the drumhead indicates underlying disease.

Charles N. Ford

TUNING FORK TESTING

Tuning forks were introduced in the early nineteenth century. They are called the poor man's audiogram by ear, nose, and throat residents because they are simple, quick, and inexpensive to use, and can be used to support the results obtained by the more formal testing done by an audiologist.

After being struck, a metal tuning fork vibrates, producing a pure tone. The standard octave frequencies used are 128, 512, 1024, and 2048 Hz, and the 512-Hz fork is the most useful tool for testing. Four standard tuning forks are routinely used today; they are named after their German inventors: Weber, Rinne, Schwabach, and Bing.

In the Weber test, if the hearing is not the same in both ears, the fork's tone will appear to be displaced to one side of the head or to be in only one ear. Therefore, if the sound is displaced from the center of the head toward one ear, some hearing loss is indicated. If the individual has already complained of a hearing loss in one ear and the tuning-fork tone is heard in the good ear, then the otolaryngologist suspects a sensorineural hearing loss in the poor ear. However, if the sound is lateralized to the poorer ear, then a conductive loss in the poorer ear is suspected. Unfortunately, if the individual has a mixture of conductive and sensorineural hearing loss, the Weber test results are not as helpful diagnostically.

The Rinne test is commonly used by ear, nose, and throat physicians. It compares the individual's bone-conduction hearing with his or her own air-conduction hearing. The vibrating hilt of the tuning fork is placed alternately on the mastoid and then positioned 1 to 2 inches (2 to 5 centimeters) from the opening of the external ear canal. The former tests bone conduction, and the latter tests air conduction. The individual is asked to indicate where he or she hears the sound louder. In normal-hearing individuals, sound is heard better by air, or for almost twice as long by air as by bone. This is called a positive Rinne. Persons who have a sensorineural hearing loss also will hear better or longer by air conduction. The tone will not be heard as loud, or for as long, as in persons with normal hearing. On the other hand, if the individual has a conductive hearing loss, the tone will be heard better or longer by bone conduction (tuning fork on the mastoid). This is recorded as a negative Rinne. Hearing is shorter by air conduction because of the mechanical blocking of sounds traveling the normal air-conduction route. The bone-conducted sound bypasses the conductive block and is heard normally by the intact cochlear mechanism. A negative Rinne test with the 512-Hz tuning fork suggests a conductive hearing loss of at least 25 to 30 decibels (dB); with the 1024-Hz tuning fork, a negative Rinne implies a 35-dB hearing loss.

The Schwabach test was developed by a German otologist in 1885. The hilt of the vibrating tuning fork is placed on the mastoid, and the individual is asked to indicate when the tone is no longer heard. The examiner then applies the tuning fork to her or his own mastoid. A sensorineural hearing loss is indicated if the examiner hears a tone longer than the individual (Schwabach-prolonged). In contrast, if bone-conduction hearing time is longer by the individual (Schwabach-shortened), a conductive hearing loss is indicated. The validity of the test is dependent on the normality of the examiner's hearing.

In 1895 the Bing test was developed. It is designed to detect middle-ear impairment and is valuable in differentiating between conductive and sensorineural hearing loss. The hilt of the tuning fork is placed on the mastoid. The ear canal is then gently blocked, without causing pressure on the eardrum. The individual indicates whether this causes the sound intensity to increase. The procedure is then repeated on the other ear. In a normal ear, or in one with sensorineural hearing loss, the sound transmitted intensifies with occlusion of the ear canal. Blockage of the ear canal does not intensify sound transmission in this fashion in an ear with a large conductive hearing loss.

Tuning forks are useful in a complete analysis of hearing loss. There are several drawbacks to their applicability, including inaccurate measurement of the intensity of the fork's tone, limited benefit in younger children, distortion of sound if the fork is struck too hard, and difficulty in isolating the response of the test ear. Tuning forks are, however, helpful in supporting pre- and postoperative audiometric results.

Bibliography

Davis, Hallowell, and S. Richard Silverman (eds.): *Hearing and Deafness*, 4th ed., Holt, Rinehart, and Winston, New York, 1978.

English, Gerald (ed.): *Otolaryngology*, Harper and Row, Hagerstown, 1976.

Shambaugh, George, and Michael Glasscock, III: *Surgery of the Ear*, 3d ed., W. B. Saunders, Philadelphia, 1980.

Sheehy, James, Gale Gardner, Jr., and William Hambley: "Tuning Fork Tests in Modern Otology," *Arch. Otolaryng.*, 94:132–138, 1971.

Judith N. Green

NASOPHARYNX EXAMINATION

Examination of the nasopharynx is important in the evaluation and diagnosis of auditory disorders because the eustachian tubes open on one end into the respiratory tract in the nasopharynx and into the middle ear on the other end.

The nasopharynx is located posterior to the nasal cavities, superior to the soft palate, and inferior to the base of the skull. The cervical vertebrae contribute to the skeleton of the posterior wall of the nasopharynx. The nasal cavities communicate with the nasopharynx. The eustachian tubes enter the nasopharynx through its lateral walls at an angle of 45 degrees to the sagittal plane, which divides the right and left sides of the head.

The nasopharynx is lined with mucous membrane that has respiratory epithelium (pseudostratified, columnar, and ciliated) in some areas and stratified squamous epithelium in other areas where there is abrasion from the movement of the soft palate. Beneath the mucous membrane is the superior constrictor muscle of the pharynx which, with the musculature of the soft palate, forms a sphincter called the velopharyngeal valve. The valve closes the nasopharynx from the oropharynx during swallowing and during the production of all phonemes (speech sounds) except those represented by the letters *m* and *n* and *ng*. The sphincteric action prevents regurgitation of food and fluids into the nose during swallowing and excessive emission of air through the nose during speaking.

The adenoid tissue (pharyngeal tonsil) is located on the posterior (back) wall of the nasopharynx. Adenoid tissue is lymphoid tissue. It reaches its greatest absolute and relative size at the time of puberty and normally atrophies by adulthood. The adenoid tissue is adjacent to the eustachian tubes and, during childhood, plays an important role in the development of the infectious and inflammatory conditions that occur in the middle ear.

The nasopharynx may be examined by inspection through the mouth with a mirror placed posterior to the free edge of the soft palate. Light may be directed into the mirror which is held at an angle of 45 degrees to the horizontal plane, and the light is reflected into the nasopharynx. The light is reflected from the nasopharynx back to the mirror and from there back to the eye of the examiner. A right-angle telescope may be used through the mouth to look around the soft palate into the nasopharynx; or a nasopharyngoscope, a thin right-angle telescope that is passed through the nose, may be used. The nasopharynx also may be inspected through the nose or through the mouth with a flexible fiber-optic endoscope. Palpation (feeling with the finger) of the nasopharynx can be very informative, too, and is usually performed under general anesthesia.

The nasopharynx can be examined radiographically and with other imaging techniques. Lateral radiographs of the nasopharynx are helpful in determining the size of the adenoid tissue in children and in detecting neoplasms of the nasopharynx. Tomography of the nasopharynx can provide additional evaluation of the contour of the nasopharynx. Also, computerized tomography (CAT scans) of the head is an effective way of evaluating the nasopharynx for neoplasms.

Disease processes such as infections and neoplasms in the nasopharynx can produce obstruction of the eustachian tubes and thereby cause abnormalities of the middle ear. For this reason examination of the nasopharynx is important in evaluating middle-ear abnormalities such as middle-ear effusion, retraction of the tympanic membrane, acute otitis media, and chronic otitis media. Some basic causes of ear disease, such as infection in the nasopharynx, sinusitis, allergy, adenoid hypertrophy, adenoiditis (infection of the adenoid tissue), and neoplasms of the nasopharynx, can be detected on examination of the nasopharynx. The appropriate management of the condition in the nasopharynx may allow the function of the eustachian tubes to return to normal, and thereby may eliminate the middle-ear abnormality.

James B. Snow

VESTIBULAR EXAMINATION

The most common symptom of vestibular dysfunction is dizziness, and the most common signs are spontaneous nystagmus and abnormal voluntary eye movements. Dizziness or some form of dysequilibrium or disorientation can be produced by other nervous system or organ lesions, so the patient's history is a crucial part of the vestibular evaluation when ascertaining the origin of dizziness. A physical examination and vestibular and other laboratory tests (x-ray, audiometry) are necessary to determine if the site of the lesion is in the inner ear, the vestibular centers, or the pathways in the central nervous system.

Dizziness   The individual's description of the dizziness can be of help in determining which part of the systems involved in orientation is responsible for the symptoms. An illusion of movement is specific for vestibular system disease, and rotation is most commonly described. The illusion of linear displacement or rocking is less frequently experienced. Other terms used by persons to describe disorientation are less specific: giddiness, one's head is swimming, lightheadedness, floating, a feeling of drunkenness. These sensations can be associated with disorders of other systems. The intensity, duration, and frequency of attacks, the precipitating or relieving factors, and the characteristics of associated symptoms (tinnitus, hearing loss, ear pain, and infections) are all important factors in evaluating the underlying cause of dizziness.

Nystagmus   Nystagmus can be induced in normal subjects, where it is termed physiologic. Physiologic nystagmus is induced by vestibular (caloric or rotatory) or visual (optokinetic) stimulation, or it can occur on extreme lateral gaze (end-point nystagmus). Pathologic nystagmus, spontaneous or induced, occurs in individuals with vestibular disorders, and its analysis (direction, intensity, shape) often offers clues to the involved pathology. It can be spontaneous (present with the head erect and the gaze centered), positional (induced by a change in head position), or gaze-evoked (induced by a change in eye position), and can be affected by interference with fixation (darkness, use of special lenses). Spontaneous nystagmus can be caused by lesions of the peripheral or central vestibular system or lesions of other central nervous system pathways involved in the control of eye movements, or it can be visual-ocular in origin (congenital). The combined effects on the nystagmus of vision (or its absence), the position of the head, and the direction of gaze are helpful in elucidating its origin.

The recording and quantitative measurement of nystagmus form the basis of many vestibular tests and provide documentation of vestibular function.

Vestibular Tests   There has been a renewal of interest in vestibular testing since the mid-1970s. This is due both to the realization of its important diagnostic value in various neurologic disorders (in addition to those of the inner ear) and to the introduction of new techniques that have enabled accurate quantitative analysis of vestibular function.

Vestibular tests can be based on subjective responses as reported by the individual, or based on

Record of eye movements during a caloric response showing the appearance of left-beating nystagmus from 40 to 60 seconds after the beginning of irrigation.

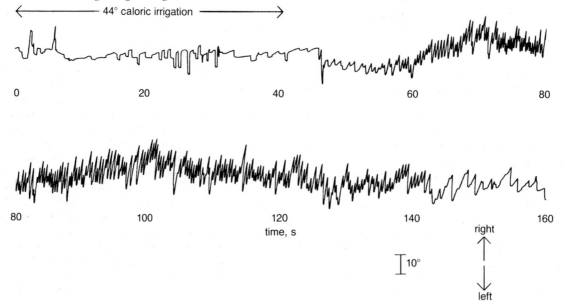

reflexes which can be evaluated more objectively by the tester, such as vestibuloocular reflexes (VOR) and postural reflexes:

1. Tests of vestibular subjective sensation. Contrary to most auditory evaluations, which depend on subjective responses to sound, tests based on the subjective sensation of motion have limited clinical value. This is due largely to the difficulty of isolating a purely vestibular sensation from that induced by the additional proprioceptive, visual, or auditory cues, which also occur during any type of rotational or translational movement.

2. Tests of VOR function. Electronystagmography, a technique for recording eye movements based on the corneoretinal potential, has been successfully used in clinical VOR tests for more than 50 years. Electrodes are placed on the skin around the eyes to measure an electric potential, generated by the pigmented layer of the retina, whose magnitude is proportional to the position of the eye in the orbit. During a nystagmus reaction the direction and amplitude of the slow component are the parameters believed to reflect most accurately the nerve activity generated by stimulation of the vestibular end organs. With the aid of small laboratory computers, continuous measurement of the

slow-component velocity during the nystagmus reaction can be performed automatically and precisely to obtain quantitative information on vestibular function.

Caloric test. Introduced by Robert Bárány at the beginning of the twentieth century, the caloric test remains one of the most useful methods for evaluating peripheral labyrinthine lesions. The individual's head is positioned so that the horizontal semicircular canal is vertical. Each ear is then individually irrigated with water at temperatures 7°C (12.6°F) above and below that of the body for 30 to 40 seconds. Heat or cold is transferred from the external ear canal to the semicircular canal within the temporal bone. A convection current is established in the semicircular canal fluid which deforms the cupula and stimulates the hair cells of the crista. The resulting complex nystagmus reaction is evaluated by a computer-generated plot of the slow-component velocity as a function of time. The greatest advantage of the caloric test is that it allows the evaluation of each ear independently. Because caloric irrigation is not a natural physiologic stimulus and because the transmission of temperature change varies greatly from subject to subject (influencing the magnitude of the stimu-

Plots of the eye velocity during the slow component of the nystagmus reaction to caloric irrigation in a normal subject. The four traces correspond to irrigations of the left (L) and right (R) ears, each at water temperatures of 30 and 40°C (86 and 104°F). The arrowheads point to the maximum intensity of each response.

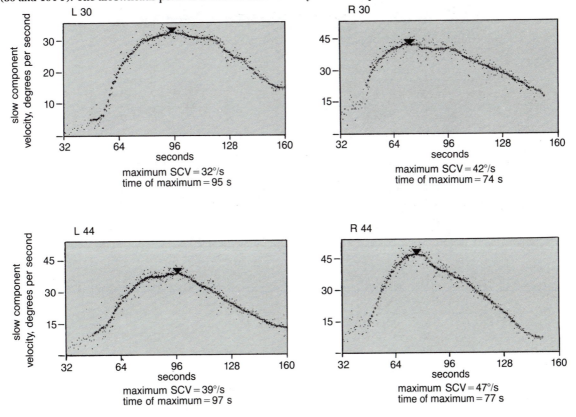

maximum SCV = 32°/s
time of maximum = 95 s

maximum SCV = 42°/s
time of maximum = 74 s

maximum SCV = 39°/s
time of maximum = 97 s

maximum SCV = 47°/s
time of maximum = 77 s

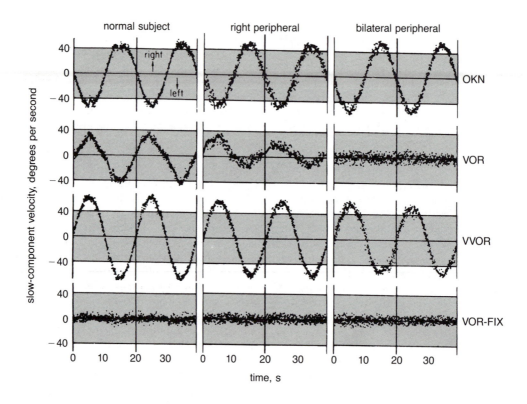

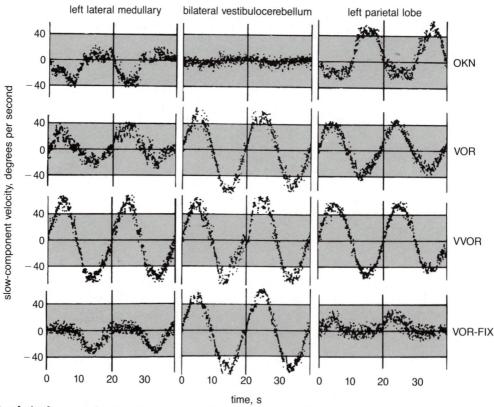

Computer-derived curves showing the responses of a normal subject and patients to a variety of rotatory stimuli as indicated on the right. In all cases the test consisted of a sinusoidal stimulus of 0.05 Hz at 60 degrees per second peak velocity. (From R. W. Baloh et al., *Nystagmus and Vertigo: Clinical Approaches to the Patient with Dizziness*, Academic Press, New York, 1982)

lus), the quantitative evaluation of the caloric test results depends on a comparison of responses from each ear in the same subject. The technique, while simple, requires experience and meticulous execution. In routine clinical practice, when quantitative evaluation is not possible, the caloric test is often conducted by irrigating each of the ear canals with 1 to 5 cubic centimeters of ice-cold water, with the objective being only to demonstrate the presence or absence of excitability as detected by direct visual observation of the induced, usually strong, nystagmus response.

Rotatory tests. A more accurate assessment of VOR function can be achieved with the use of rotatory stimulation because it more closely resembles natural stimulation. The individual is seated in a chair that rotates about its vertical axis. The head is tilted 30 degrees forward so that angular rotation takes place in the plane of the horizontal semicircular canals. During sinusoidal rotations, the gain, defined as the ratio of the peak velocity of the nystagmus slow component to the peak velocity of the chair, is used to characterize the response for each direction of rotation. With modern techniques the slow-component velocity can be monitored precisely and the sinusoidal trajectory of the response quantified. The only disadvantage of the rotatory test is that it acts simultaneously on both ears so that the response represents the combined ouput of receptors on both sides.

Because eye movements during natural head motion are the result of interaction of visual and vestibular reflex responses, it is important to test the subject for each of these reflexes alone as well as during their interaction. Rotatory tests are particularly useful when combined with quantitative tests of voluntary visual-ocular control, for example, tests of smooth-pursuit and saccadic (sudden) eye movements or optokinetic nystagmus (OKN). Computer-derived curves obtained by these tests show the velocity of the eye during the slow component of nystagmus. Four standard tests are OKN (a vertically striped drum rotates around a stationary subject in the light), VOR (the subject is rotated in complete darkness), visual-vestibuloocular reflex (VVOR; the subject is rotated in the light), and fixation suppression of VOR (VOR-FIX; the subject is rotated in the dark while fixating on a small dot of light rotating with the subject which suppresses the vestibular nystagmus).

The test data consist of sinusoidal eye velocity records with magnitudes dependent on the type of stimulus used and the type of pathology. The pattern of normal and abnormal vestibular responses is often of great value in the differential diagnosis of peripheral and central nervous system lesions. Patients with unilateral or bilateral peripheral vestibular lesions have normal OKN, VVOR, and VOR-

FIX responses but asymmetrical or absent VOR responses. However, the individual with bilateral peripheral labyrinthine paralysis (A, right side, VOR), as expected, does not react to VOR testing, but has normal VVOR responses. Abnormal reactions may be governed by where the lesion is located in the neural pathways involved in visual-vestibular interaction reflexes: the brainstem (left lateral medullary syndrome), the cerebellum (bilateral vestibulocerebellar lesion), or the cerebrum (left parietal lobe lesion).

3. Posture test. Platforms with sensors to detect the body's center of force are used to evaluate the instability of individuals with vestibular disorders. These methods measure the interaction of the three systems that participate in the maintenance of posture and equilibrium: the proprioceptive, the vestibular (including both the semicircular canal and otolithic receptor components), and the visual. Standards for the evaluation of these tests, which are presently in the experimental stage, have been difficult to develop because the human brain adapts quickly to changes in any of the systems in order to maintain equilibrium and orientation.

Bibliography

Baloh, R. W.: *Dizziness, Hearing Loss, and Tinnitus: The Essentials of Neurotology*, F. A. Davis, Philadelphia, 1984.

———— and V. Honrubia: *Clinical Neurophysiology of the Vestibular System*, F. A. Davis, Philadelphia, 1979.

Honrubia, V., and M. A. B. Brazier (eds.): *Nystagmus and Vertigo: Clinical Approaches to the Patient with Dizziness*, Academic Press, New York, 1982.

Vicente Honrubia

CRANIAL NERVE SCREENING

Several causes of hearing impairment involve cranial nerves in addition to the auditory nerve (cranial nerve VIII). The results of cranial nerve screening can give the diagnostician insight into the hearing impairment. There are some simple basic examinations available to persons without neurologic specialization that facilitate the recognition of involvement of these nerves. These are described below except for the auditory nerve, whose function is measured by audiometry. *See* AUDIOMETRY.

Olfactory nerve (cranial nerve I). These nerve fibers are sensory; they come from the olfactory mucosa and function in the sense of smell. Nerve reaction is assessed by using a set of substances that produce different odors, such as alcohol, perfume, coffee, gasoline, camphor, or mint. Irritants such as ammonia which stimulate trigeminal endings (cranial nerve V) should be avoided.

Optic nerve (cranial nerve II). These nerve fibers are sensory; they come from the retina of the eye and function in vision. Visual acuity (near and distant) and color vision are determined by using test cards. The confrontation method may be used for testing visual field. In this test the examiner and subject face each other and the examiner compares both visual fields. The study of the fundus of the eye is reserved for a specialist.

Oculomotor, trochlear, and abducens nerves (cranial nerves III, IV, and VI). These nerve fibers are motor; they carry information about motility of the eyeball and aperture of the pupil. The nerves are studied together by asking the subject to look in different directions. Alteration of conjugated eye movements or individual dysfunctions of muscles may be found. Pupil changes are studied by the accommodation reflex and the light reflex.

Trigeminal nerve (cranial nerve V). This is a mixed nerve; motor fibers carry information about masticator muscles, while sensory function is in touch, temperature, and pain sensitivity of the face. Motor function is studied by observing the movements of mastication, lateralization, projection, and retrocession of the jaw. Sensitivity is determined by comparing one side of the face with the other. A straight pin and a tube of warm water are sufficient for stimulation. Lack of corneal reflex (blinking on irritation) is an early sign of impairment.

Facial nerve (cranial nerve VII). This is a mixed nerve; motor fibers carry information about facial expression muscles and the stapedial muscle, and the sensory function is in taste in the front two-thirds of the tongue. Motor function is studied by asking the subjects to wrinkle their forehead, close their eyes, smile, whistle, and so on. Taste is examined by application of different flavors: sweet (sugar), acid (vinegar), salt (salt), bitter (quinine). Taste sensitivity and acoustic immitance studies of the stapedial reflex help to localize a peripheral lesion topographically.

Disorders of the facial nerve often accompany hearing impairment because portions of this nerve accompany the auditory nerve in the internal auditory meatus and travel separately in and through the middle ear.

Glossopharyngeal nerve (cranial nerve IX). This is a mixed nerve; motor fibers carry information about the stylopharyngeal muscle only, while sensory fibers come from the back of the tongue and part of the pharynx, and function in taste for the back third of the tongue. Pharyngeal and lingual sensitivity is studied by a light touch with a cotton applicator. The gag reflex is provoked by heavier pressure; the motor part of reflex is vagal. Taste in the back third of the tongue is studied as in the front two-thirds.

Vagus nerve (cranial nerve X). This is a mixed nerve; the motor fibers innervate the musculature of the thorax, abdomen, larynx, pharynx, and soft palate, while sensory fibers function in laryngeal, epiglottal, and hypopharyngeal sensitivity. The motility of the soft palate is determined by provoking the gag reflex or asking the subject to say "ah." The motility of the vocal cords require study by a specialist. A dysphonia may point to an alteration in function of the vagus nerve.

Spinal accessory nerve (cranial nerve XI). These nerve fibers are motor; they transmit information about the sternocleidomastoid and trapezius muscles. Response is determined by asking for a lateral flexing of the head or movement of the shoulder against resistance given by the examiner.

Hypoglossal nerve (cranial nerve XII). The nerve fibers are motor, innervating the musculature of the tongue and anterior throat. Response is determined by studying the lingual motility, and deviations in the protrusion, atrophies, and fasciculations of the nerve fibers.

Bibliography
Gilroy, J., and J. S. Meyer: *Medical Neurology*, Macmillan, New York, 1974.
Vinken, P. J., and G. W. Bruyn (eds.): *Handbook of Clinical Neurology*, vol. 2: *Localization in Clinical Neurology*, North Holland Publishing Co., Amsterdam, 1969.
Benjamin Rosenblüt

AUDITORY DISORDERS, PREVENTION OF

In general, prevention of auditory disorders is defined as the elimination of those conditions that interfere with the acquisition, development, or use of normal auditory skills. Failure of prevention may lead to the development of communicative disorders, because audition is an important input of the communicative process. Some auditory disorders are progressive; others are not. A definition of prevention, therefore, should reflect the potentially progressive nature of an auditory disorder.

Prevention may be defined in three phases; primary, secondary, and tertiary. Primary prevention is the elimination or inhibition of the onset and development of an auditory disorder by altering susceptibility or reducing exposure for susceptible individuals. For example, a rubella vaccination can be given to women prior to conception to prevent bearing a child with congenital rubella syndrome. Secondary prevention is the early detection and treatment of auditory disorders. Early detection may lead to the elimination of the disorder or the retardation of the disorder's progress, thereby preventing further complications. For example, a school auditory screening program can be instituted to test systematically the hearing of all pupils in order to identify those who have a significant hearing loss. Tertiary prevention is the reduction of the severity of disability of an auditory disorder by the use of procedures that restore effective function. For example, a hearing-impaired person can be supplied with a hearing aid to provide more effective sound levels for communication.

PRINCIPLES OF PREVENTION

Prevention of auditory disorders is a public health responsibility. While local health care programs are important, and in many locations may be the only health services available, state or national public health institutions often are better equipped to evaluate the problem, establish priorities for and institute control, and assess the results of preventive or corrective measures. Because auditory disorders can become communicative disorders that in turn produce disruption of the learning process, educational institutions also have a significant interest in prevention of auditory disorders in students.

To be effective, preventive measures must have defined objectives; the latter may be developed after an analysis of the causes of auditory disorders. An important axiom is that the effectiveness of preventive measures will vary according to the specific cause of the disorder.

REPORTED CAUSES OF AUDITORY DISORDERS

Surveys generated by the World Federation of the Deaf, the National Census of the Deaf Population (United States), the International Congresses on Noise as a Public Health Problem, and others have indicated that the auditory disorders of greatest significance are caused by: infectious diseases (including otitis media, mastoiditis, meningitis, pre- and postnatal viral infections), aging, prematurity and certain perinatal problems, goiter, hazardous noise exposure, hereditary and genetic factors, toxic drugs and chemicals, and trauma. *See* WORLD FEDERATION OF THE DEAF.

PUBLIC HEALTH MEASURES

In considering how to prevent auditory disorders from a particular cause, the following public health factors must be reviewed and weighed.

Definition of the Problem   Auditory disorders imply disease or disorder of the auditory system that is associated with impairment of the sense of hearing, in contrast to otologic disorders, which may or may not be accompanied by hearing loss. The degree of disability caused by the hearing loss is an important factor for the definition of cases and for the determination of risk.

Epidemiologic Surveys   The major causes of auditory disorders are reasonably well identified, but knowledge of the populations involved varies by disease and country. Health surveys are needed to develop the statistics from which priorities for prevention and care can be established.

Case Finding   Because hearing loss often is unaccompanied by outward physical abnormalities, especially in younger children, its presence usually has to be detected by an evaluation of auditory function. The search for the presence of potential hearing losses in a given population often is called identification audiometry. Screening audiometry is a simpled test for this purpose to select persons with potential hearing loss according to certain predetermined criteria. Other case-finding procedures include the use of at-risk information to identify persons who may be likely to have or to develop auditory disorders. Examples include the perinatal high-risk registry, a listing of those conditions that may predispose the newborn infant to hearing loss, and the identification of industrial workers who are exposed to hazardous noise.

Establishment of Priorities   Primary followed by secondary and then tertiary preventive measures (in order of importance) should be pursued when feasible. Many preventive programs develop priorities by age group, such as, maternal and child health, neonates, preschool, school, adult, and aged. Some factors affecting prioritization are the extent and severity of the problem, the effectiveness of preventive measures, the availability of resources, cost, and cost-to-benefit ratio.

Direct Preventive Action   Preventive measures may be broad in scope, such as implementation of general hygienic measures or improvements in nutrition; or they may be more specific, such as immunization programs for specific viral infections. Several avenues of prevention may be used: legislative regulation of hazardous noise exposure, school hearing screening programs, medical and surgical treatment of diseases that produce auditory disorders, aural rehabilitation, control of exposure to ototoxic substances, genetic counselling, and others.

Followup   Successful, preventive health programs must have some mechanism to assess the effectiveness of preventive measures. Because changes in hearing are often difficult to assess, auditory measurements are needed.

FUTURE PROSPECTS

The inadequacy of international statistics of auditory disorders presents an obstacle to the formulation of an international strategy for prevention. Agreement upon the definition of what constitutes a disabling auditory disorder followed by sampling surveys to determine prevalence would provide a basis for formulation of preventive programs. The United Nations Development Program estimates that 80 percent of disabled persons live in developing countries, mostly in the poorest communities of

Asia, Africa, and Latin America. UNICEF estimates that in the 60 poorest countries of the world a third of those disabled are children. In these countries, the need is for massive delivery, through general health programs, of simple measures to combat malnutrition, poor hygiene, and infectious diseases, rather than elaborate technology. Here, the shortage of trained personnel and the unaffordable cost of medical equipment, including hearing aids, make solutions difficult.

Even the technologically advanced countries face problems, although on a lesser scale. Infectious disease remains a primary cause of auditory disorders, and increased industrialization has led to more extensive exposure of their populations to hazardous noise. Better health care and hygiene have prolonged life and resulted in a population of more older people than before, and older people are more likely than younger people to have hearing losses. Improved technology has made diagnosis and treatment increasingly expensive. Clearly, the prevention of auditory disorders presents a major challenge for all countries.

Bibliography

Catlin, F. I.: "The Public Health Aspects of Deafness," in Donald B. Tower (ed. in chief), *The Nervous System*, vol. 3: *Human Communication and Its Disorders*, pp 313–324, Raven Press, New York, 1975.

Schein, J. D., and M. T. Delk: *The Deaf Population of the United States*, National Association of the Deaf, Silver Spring, Maryland, 1974.

Tobias, J. V., G. Jansen, and W. D. Ward (eds.): *Proceedings of the Third International Congress on Noise as a Public Health Problem*, Rockville, Maryland, ASHA Rep. 10, April 1980.

Francis I. Catlin

Prevention of Hearing Loss

Action to prevent hearing impairments may take various forms, including avoiding conditions that place hearing at risk, or followup, such as medical evaluation. Further, it is necessary to be aware of the reasons for preservation of hearing.

WARNING SIGNS

Knowledge of the following warning signs that indicate possible malfunction of the ear is a first step in prevention of auditory disorders.

Pain Pain is not always present in auditory disorders. Disturbances of the inner ear, for example, are not accompanied by pain because there are no pain receptors located in that region. Pain in the ear is an indication that problems have begun to develop in the external- or middle-ear regions. For example, middle-ear infection can cause the tympanic membrane to be stretched beyond its comfortable limits, sometimes causing sharp pain. Young children often experience this when excessive adenoid tissue interferes with normal air-pressure equalization in the middle-ear by the eustachian tube. Physicians now hesitate to remove adenoids, but if recurrent pain occurs, they have no choice. Another common cause of pain in the ear is the so-called swimmer's ear. Here, the skin lining the external ear canal has become inflamed, often due to overexposure to treated water while swimming. There is very little tissue between the skin lining and bony support for the canal; therefore, with inflammation and the concurrent swelling, pain results. In any case, pain in the ear region signals the need for medical attention. *See* EAR: Anatomy.

Vertigo or Dizziness The balance sense shares many of the same components of the inner ear with the hearing sense. Problems in one of these senses may be accompanied by problems in the other. Therefore, if vertigo is ever experienced, medical consultation is imperative. In many cases, the symptoms are mild and become self-correcting. However, recurrent balance system malfunction can be a harbinger of significant health problems. Causes of dizziness include chemical or fluid imbalances in the inner ear, allergies, interference with or pressure on the vestibular nerve in the central nervous system, vascular disturbances affecting the balance receptors, motion sickness, and tension resulting from emotional upsets.

Tinnitus (Head Noises) Another common indicator of inner-ear disturbance is the ringing sensation experienced by nearly all people at some time in their life. For some, this ringing is pervasive and incapacitating. Tinnitus takes many forms. Patients have given dozens of descriptions for these head noises, including the sound of whistles or the chirping of crickets. Episodes of tinnitus can be of short or long duration. Two types of tinnitus have been described: objective and subjective. Objective tinnitus is caused by muscle spasms in the middle ear. The tympanic membrane is moved rapidly in and out, creating a low-pitched sound heard not only by the person but by others who place their ear next to the ear of the tinnitus sufferer. Subjective tinnitus is due to inner-ear or central nervous system conditions and can be heard only by the tinnitus sufferer. A ringing sound that lasts about 20 seconds occurs in the ears of many people and usually is not cause for concern. If the tinnitus lasts for longer periods of time or is recurrent, medical consultation is advised. *See* TINNITUS.

Fullness Sensation Certain abnormal ear conditions cause a feeling of fullness at one or both ears. The sensation is as if a small pump increased the quantity of air behind the tympanic membrane. This symptom can be associated with both middle-ear and inner-ear disorders. It warrants medical attention.

Distortion When the volume of a cheap radio is increased beyond its normal limits, the sound generated becomes "tinny." This loss of sound quality is due to distortion of the original acoustic signal. If the ear is overdriven by sound, it will distort the sound and quality of perception suffers. Some abnormal inner-ear conditions can cause distortion of sound that negatively influences one's ability to accurately perceive speech and other sounds. For some, the first indication of a hearing problem comes from recognizing that sound is becoming distorted.

CAUSES OF IMPAIRMENT

The many causes of hearing impairment are discussed elsewhere; thus, only some of the more prominent ones will be reviewed. They include: external-ear infection (swimmer's ear); tympanic membrane perforation; cholesteatoma; middle-ear air-pressure imbalance or fluid accumulation; infection of the middle ear (when the fluid has become infested with bacteria); adhesions and residue in the middle ear; otosclerosis; dislocation of the ossicles; ossicular necrosis (pathologic degeneration); inner-ear disturbance due to excessive endolymphatic fluid accumulation (Ménière's syndrome, endolymphatic hydrops, fluctuant hearing impairment); vascular inadequacy or interruption; sensory cell deterioration due to vascular insufficiency, noise exposure, drug toxicity, ingestion of other toxic substances such as aspirin or alcohol; and central nervous system disorders, including brain tumors, degenerative disease processes, and stroke. *See* HEARING LOSS.

It is generally acknowledged that noise exposure is the most common cause of hearing disorders in the industrialized world. Occupational and nonoccupational exposure to high-level sound has increased to the point that estimates by the United States Environmental Protection Agency suggest that as many as 20 million workers in the United States are exposed to dangerously intense sound. Hazards to hearing in the workplace have been recognized for decades. But in recent years the recreational environment has matched or exceeded occupational exposure potential with common exposure to personal listening devices (up to 114 dBA), recreational vehicles (snowmobiles and motorcycles, over 100 dBA), recreational shooting (140 dB or greater peak impulse sound), and lounges with bands playing at levels approaching 110 dBA. With the frequent opportunities for high-level noise exposure in the nonoccupational and recreational environment, it is not surprising that significant numbers of persons are experiencing reduced hearing ability due to noise-induced damage. The unfortunate fact is that most of this damage is preventable by simple and appropriate conservation practices. Knowledge of the three danger signs can help one to avoid the inevitable loss of hearing where the noise exposure continues to be excessive: (1) if it is not possible to carry on a conversation without yelling, the noise environment is probably over 90 dBA and should be regarded as dangerous; (2) if, after leaving the noise, tinnitus is noticed, the ears have been overexposed and that type of experience should be avoided; and (3) if, after leaving a noisy environment, sound seems distorted as if one's head is in a barrel, the exposure has been extreme and should not be repeated.

In noise exposure conditions, two results are possible: temporary threshold shift (TTS), a nonpermanent reduction of hearing sensitivity that reverses in a few hours; and permanent threshold shift (PTS), from which recovery is never complete. The latter is to be avoided. If it is not practical to avoid noise exposure, hearing protective devices, when properly fitted and used, are quite effective in reducing deleterious effects. These devices are grouped into three classifications: (1) insert plugs that fit snugly into the ear canal; (2) earmuffs which enclose the ear and are held in place by a headband; and (3) canal caps, something of a compromise between the first two types in that their tips are placed at the entrance of the ear canal and are held by a small band. Safety-equipment supply outlets or sporting goods departments stock numerous types of these devices.

SUMMARY

Knowledge of the warning signs of hearing-impairment conditions, proper approaches to hearing health, medical consultation when necessary, and avoidance of those activities and environments that put hearing at risk are the necessary components in the prevention of hearing impairment.

David M. Lipscomb

Screening

Hearing screening is designed to sift out from a population those persons most likely to have hearing impairments that may interfere with educational development or communication. There are three major considerations regarding auditory screening: (1) valid auditory screening and assessment may be accomplished with any age population; (2) early identification, diagnosis, and remediation generally result in better individual prognosis; and (3) screening is cost effective for all populations regardless of age or complicating pathologic conditions.

Hearing function spans a continuum from pathologic condition to the complete lack of auditory function. Screening tests, however, do not assess the deficit but, instead, use a pass-fail criterion to group those warranting further evaluations to determine if a hearing impairment does exist and, if so, its extent. Screening accuracy is less than perfect. False-positive and false-negative identifications are inevitable in any economically feasible procedure. Controversy exists regarding acceptable procedures and pass-fail criteria to keep false-positive and false-negative errors to a minimum.

Infant screening is most efficient when using a High Risk Register. In 1982 the Joint Committee on Infant Hearing Screening (made up of representatives from the American Speech-Language-Hearing Association, American Academy of Otolaryngology-Head and Neck Surgery, American Academy of Pediatrics, and the American Nurses Association) recommended seven factors for identifying infants at risk. Screening of all infants manifesting any factor on the list is recommended prior to age three months. Methods of obtaining and using a High-Risk Register and appropriate behavioral and physiologic testing criteria are documented. The use of the auditory brainstem response (ABR) as a screening tool with infants is considered to be highly valuable. *See* AMERICAN SPEECH-LANGUAGE-HEARING ASSOCIATION.

Pure-tone screening in the public schools has been an accepted procedure for over 30 years. A serious limitation has been the inability to test below 20–25-dB hearing level due to the masking effects of ambient noise in the usual school testing environment. While pure-tone testing is effective in measuring hearing loss, the 20-dB-plus screening criterion may pass more than half the children with middle-ear disorders. The American Speech-Language-Hearing Association (ASHA) in its "Guidelines for Identification Audiometry" includes a combination of acoustic-immittance measures and pure-tone testing in its recommended screening protocol. The guidelines are intended for children functioning at a developmental level of three years and above. Specifically, the procedure requires testing 1000, 2000, and 4000 Hz at 20 dB HL in each ear, and acoustic-immittance screening by the procedure recommended by ASHA. Rescreening is required for those who fail, and appropriate audiologic, medical, and educational follow-up is recommended. By using these procedures, middle-ear disorders as well as mild to moderate hearing losses may be detected.

To emphasize the importance of screening, it is generally agreed that about 10 percent of children between birth and ten years will have measureable hearing losses when tested. Most will go unnoticed without a screening program, and once detected and confirmed the majority will respond to medical treatment.

The American Academy of Otolaryngology defines a hearing handicap as a loss exceeding an average of 25-dB for the frequencies of 500, 1000, 2000, and 3000 Hz. Consequently, most tests for adults use the 25-dB criteria and often include frequencies up to 8000 Hz.

Hearing conservation programs in industry mandated by the Occupational Noise Exposure Hearing Conservation Amendment of the Occupational Safety and Health Administration (OSHA) require audiometric testing on an annual basis for all employees whose noise exposures equal or exceed an eight-hour time-weighted average sound level of 85 dB measured as the A scale. The audiometric test is to determine pure-tone air-conduction thresholds for the frequencies of 500, 1000, 2000, 3000, 4000, and 6000 Hz. Each annual test is checked against the initial (baseline) audiogram to determine if a standard threshold shift has occurred. In the event the defined threshold occurs, employees must be so notified and required to wear ear protection devices, and further audiological-otological evaluations may be recommended. The OSHA requirements are designed to decrease the risk of permanent hearing loss related to noise exposure.

Bibliography

American Academy of Otolaryngology Committee on Hearing and Equilibrium and the American Council of Otolaryngology Committee on the Medical Aspects of Noise: "Guide for the Evaluation of Hearing Handicap," *Journal of the American Medical Association*, 251:19, 2055–2059, 1979.

American Speech-Language-Hearing Association: "Guidelines for Acoustic Immittance Screening of Middle-Ear Function," *Asha*, 21:283–288, 1979.

———: "Guidelines for Identification Audiometry," *Asha*, 22:49–53, 1985.

———: "Joint Committee on Infant Hearing Position Statement," *Asha*, 24:1017–1018, 1982.

Federal Register, March 8, 1983, pp. 9737–9785. Department of Labor, Occupational Safety and Health Administration: Occupational Noise Exposure, Hearing Conservation Amendment, Final Rule.

Galambos, Robert, Gayle E. Hicks, and Mary Jo Wilson: "The Auditory Brain Stem Response Reliably Predicts Hearing Loss in Graduates of a Tertiary Intensive Care Nursery," *Ear and Hearing*, 5:254–260, 1984.

Jacobsen, John T., and C. Robin Morehouse: "A Comparison of Auditory Brain Stem Response and Behavioral Screening in High Risk and Normal Newborn Infants," *Ear and Hearing*, 5:247–253, 1984.

Mencher, George T., and Sanford E. Gerber: *Early Management of Hearing Loss*, Grune and Stratton, New York, 1981.

Northern, Jerry L., and Marion P. Downs: *Hearing in Children*, 3d ed., Williams and Wilkins, Baltimore, 1984.

Martin S. Robinette

Screening: Newborns

The developing child has a prescribed period of time in which to learn the rudiments of oral language. The success of this learning experience will depend largely on the status of the child's auditory system. If the child's hearing is impaired, the sensory experience is altered to the detriment of associated oral language acquisition and use, and the ability to develop and function in society is compromised.

To avoid potentially insurmountable lags in the child's linguistic development, hearing loss that is present at birth (congenital hearing loss) must be detected and managed at the earliest opportunity. To be maximally successful, efforts should be initiated in the first year of life.

SCREENING PROGRAMS

The identification of hearing impairment early in life was facilitated by the acceptance in the 1960s of hearing screening in the newborn nursery of many hospitals in the United States. At no other place and time are such large groups of infants so readily available for testing. However, initial attempts encountered many obstacles. The infants were unable to respond to sound in a reliable fashion, and it was difficult to test large numbers of infants quickly and economically.

The initial screening programs used volunteers who tested thousands of newborns by visually observing sound-induced, behavioral reflexes. These mass screening efforts demonstrated that the prevalence of severe congenital hearing loss was low (approximately 1 child in every 1000 births), and that test reliability was poor due to the variability in responsivity of even normal-hearing infants. As a result, false positive identifications were frequent. In fact, far too many babies had to be retested to detect a truly impaired child, which was quite costly, and far too many families were unnecessarily alarmed about the status of their newborn baby's hearing.

The difficulties encountered with the mass screening approach motivated the development of more sophisticated tests and new approaches to the identification of hearing loss in the newborn baby.

HIGH-RISK OR AT-RISK GROUP

In 1973, a Joint Committee on Infant Hearing recommended identifying infants at risk for congenital hearing loss by using five high-risk categories and following the identified infants over time until a definitive hearing evaluation could be done. By definition, high-risk newborns have a significantly greater likelihood of congenital hearing loss than members of the general newborn population. Included are newborns who have one or more adverse conditions associated with insults to the auditory system. In 1982, the Joint Committee expanded these categories to seven: neonatal asphyxia; bacterial meningitis, especially *Hemophilus influenzae*; congenital infection such as syphilis,

toxoplasmosis, rubella, cytomegalovirus, and herpes; defects of the head or neck, such as craniofacial abnormalities associated with various genetic and metabolic syndromes, cleft palate, and malformations of the pinna; elevated bilirubin to an extent which requires an exchange transfusion; a family history of childhood hearing loss; and a birthweight of less than 1500 grams (3 pounds 3 ounces). In the high-risk group, the risk of severe, congenital hearing impairment is perhaps 1 in 20 or 1 in 50 instead of the 1 chance in approximately 1000 usually expected for the general newborn population. Most high-risk newborns are found in the newborn intensive care unit. Referral of infants based on the high-risk criteria alone, however, still results in a high over-referral rate.

One new test, the CRIB-O-GRAM, uses a sensitive detector placed under the mattress of the infant in the nursery and records movement in response to sound. The auditory response cradle is similar to the CRIB-O-GRAM, but in addition has detectors for head movement and changes in respiration. The auditory brainstem response (ABR) test, a computer-analysis of electric activity from the auditory nervous system in response to specific sounds, is still another approach. These techniques are neither invasive nor do they require active participation of the infant. Unfortunately, even the use of these new procedures has not succeeded in overcoming completely the problem of false positive identification in many newborns. As in any screening program, follow-up is required for those failing to respond according to criteria. *See* AUDIOMETRY: Electrophysiologic, Evoked Potential.

SCREENING TESTS FOR HIGH-RISK INFANTS

During the latter 1970s, two international conferences on newborn screening were convened in Canada. The conferees resolved that the auditory brainstem response was a reasonable test for screening this select group of high-risk newborns. It has been suggested that nearly every newborn with hearing impairment could be identified by administering an auditory brainstem response screening test to those who (1) are graduates of the newborn intensive care unit; (2) appear on a high-risk register; (3) fail behavioral screening; or (4) are considered suspect for whatever reason.

Thus far, it would appear that the auditory brainstem response is the best tool available to exclude congenital hearing loss in both ears of the suspect newborn. Previous experience suggests that between 10 and 20 percent of high-risk newborns will fail an auditory brainstem response screen. However, as learned with mass screening experience, failure on this screening test cannot be interpreted as de facto evidence of hearing loss. Failure indicates the need for subsequent evaluation and, if necessary, diagnosis, as it should in an appropriate screening program.

CURRENT RECOMMENDATIONS

The Joint Committee now endorses the audiologic testing of high-risk newborns because of the 2 to 5 percent associated prevalence of moderate-to-profound hearing loss, and suggests that the initial screening of these newborns should include the observation of behavioral or electrophysiologic (for example, auditory brainstem response) responses to sound. The message is clear. With selected screening via a high-risk registry and tests such as the auditory brainstem response test, identification of virtually all congenitally hearing impaired infants is now possible. The ability to identify those infants who require more complete diagnostic workups has been especially important in initiating the special attention that the infants and their families need as early as possible. Conversely, the knowledge that congenital hearing loss has been ruled out with a high level of confidence in an at-risk infant may greatly influence specific aspects of management during early life.

Bibliography

American Academy of Pediatrics, Joint Committee on Infant Hearing: "Position Statement 1982," *Pediatrics*, 70:496–497, 1982.

Galambos, R.: "Use of the Auditory Brainstem Response (ABR) in Infant Hearing Testing," in S. E. Gerber and G. T. Mencher (eds.), *Early Diagnosis of Hearing Loss*, Grune and Stratton, New York, 1978.

Jacobson, J. T., et al.: "Auditory Brainstem Response: A Contribution to Infant Assessment and Management," in G. T. Mencher and S. E. Gerber (eds.), *Early Management of Hearing Loss*, Grune and Stratton, New York, 1981.

Stein, L. K., and T. J. Jabaley: "Early Identification and Parent Counseling," in L. K. Stein, E. D. Mindel, and T. J. Jabaley (eds.), *Deafness and Mental Health*, Grune and Stratton, New York, 1981.

Thorner, R. M., and Q. R. Remein: "Principles and Procedures in the Evaluation of Screening for Disease," in J. B. Chaiklin, I. M. Ventry, and R. F. Dixon (eds.), *Hearing Measurement: A Book of Readings*, 2d ed., Addison-Wesley, 1982.

Robert J. Nozza; Thomas J. Fria

Screening: Preschool Children

Identification of potentially handicapping hearing impairment of any degree must be accomplished at the earliest possible age. Hearing screening for preschool children is a simple, appropriate, and efficient method for such identification.

With some modifications, the processes involved in hearing screening are not different for children and adults. Essentially, the task involves determining whether the individual can or cannot hear across the frequency spectrum at predetermined, weak intensity levels. When a tone is presented, a cooperative adult or an older child can be requested to indicate (by raising a hand or other means) whether he or she hears the tone. Because preschool children cannot necessarily be expected to respond the same way in such a test situation, however, their responses to hearing screening sounds may have to be determined in an indirect manner.

TWO TO FIVE YEARS

Children between two and five years of age usually can be engaged in a play situation. For such youngsters conditioned behavior audiometry methods are recommended. These methods can be used when screening either by earphones or by a loudspeaker in a sound field. After the child is conditioned to respond to readily audible test tones, the tones are lowered in intensity, until the screening level is reached, with predetermined pass-fail criteria.

In play audiometry a team of two audiologists is used, one working at the audiometer and one with the child. The latter teaches the child to respond to auditory stimuli, with various play activities. In this manner the hearing screening stimuli and the child's play responses become integral parts of a game. *See* AUDIOMETRY: Conditioned Play.

For less mature, distractible, hyperactive, mentally retarded, or generally difficult-to-test children, tangible reinforcement operant conditioning audiometry (TROCA) can be used. TROCA employs tangible, positive reinforcement (candy, raisins, and such) for appropriate responses to test sounds. The child's behavior is conditioned to push a release mechanism on a feeder box when the tone is heard.

In screening the hearing of children in this age group, it is important to work as quickly as possible, because the child might quit before the procedure has been completed. Children may be easily distracted; they may be fearful of the situation; or they may not be comfortable away from a parent in unaccustomed surroundings. It can be helpful to screen one child while two or three others (quiet ones) look on. When it is their turn, those who have observed another child being tested may be more cooperative.

In the two-to-five age range the test sounds should be pure tones of 500, 1000, 2000, 3000, and 4000 Hz, at a screening level of 20 dB. Failure to respond to a 20-dB signal at any one frequency, in either ear, constitutes a failure. Failures on rescreening should be referred for an audiologic evaluation.

Perhaps most important to the success of the hearing screening process, with children aged two to five, is that the audiologist must be sensitive to the varying developmental levels. Even the seemingly simple task of learning to place a peg in a hole when a tone is presented may turn out to be unexpectedly difficult for a particular youngster. In that case the audiologist must know how immediately to modify the task so that it falls within the child's developmental grasp.

UNDER TWO YEARS

Hearing screening of children younger than 24 months can best be accomplished by using behavioral observation audiometry methods. Very young children usually exhibit a variety of reflexive behaviors in response to auditory stimulation. These include eye closing, startle, and orienting (localizing) reflexes as well as generalized body movement or cessation of movement. Such behaviors have been chronicled as following a developmental sequence so that professional observers can make use of their appearance in screening the hearing of infants. However, because testing in this age group primarily involves the use of relatively intense auditory signals, because infants with normal hearing may be unresponsive, and because reflexive responses tend to extinguish fairly rapidly, the notion that screening should be used only to identify possible hearing impairment is of special import when using behavioral observation. Stimuli can include calibrated noise makers, filtered environmental sounds, and narrow bands of noise. The use of warble tones across frequencies in a sound field is recommended.

Visual reinforcement audiometry (VRA) combines behavioral observation with conditioned behavior audiometry. VRA makes use of the infant's orienting or other reflexive responses to audible sounds. When the child responds to the stimulus tone, that reflexive response is reinforced with a visual stimulus (bright light, illuminated toy, colorful projection, and so on). Because the visual reinforcement is provided after the child has already responded to the test signal, VRA can be used successfully in determining minimal response levels. *See* AUDIOMETRY: Visual Reinforcement.

Prestimulus behavior can be a critical factor in judging responses when screening preschool children. Whereas older children and adults can be expected to attend to weak or soft sounds, very young children who are involved in play or are otherwise active may not be responsive at the screening levels.

MIDDLE-EAR FUNCTION

Whereas pure-tone audiometric screening is essential in the identification of moderate-to-profound sensorineural hearing loss, it is not the most efficient means of detecting mild middle-ear dysfunction, common in preschool children. The function of the middle-ear cavity and surrounding structures, containing the conductive mechanism for hearing, can best be evaluated by acoustic-immit-

ance measures. These measures provide a quick, simple, cost-effective screening method for identifying possible middle-ear dysfunction—often the cause of mild hearing impairment. The instruments are used to evaluate the flow of acoustic energy through the eardrum, and provide a reliable assessment of the integrity of the middle-ear mechanism. *See* EAR: Pathology.

Disagreement still exists on otologic referral criteria, on the validity of results of impedance tests on the youngest infants, and on whether acoustic-immitance measures should be used routinely in mass screenings. There is total agreement, however, that these measures are an irreplaceable supplement to audiometry in hearing screening with the preschool child.

PROBLEMS

Although the potential to do so exists, hearing-impaired children are still not being identified early enough. The question seems not to be how to screen the hearing of preschool children, but who should do it, where it should be done, and which children should be screened.

While screening older children and adults might be left to astute, trained volunteers, preschool screening should only be in the hands of audiologists or specially trained allied professionals. All preschool children should be screened annually. Those with whom earphones can be used may be screened in any setting, provided that a calibrated audiometer is used and that ambient noise is demonstrated not to be an interference. Those who need to be screened in a sound field must be seen in a professional setting where a specially constructed, sound-controlled environment exists. At the very least, an acoustic-immitance battery can be administered, with no need for environmental modifications. Special attention must be paid to those youngsters who fall into the category of high risk for hearing impairment.

Finally, a major problem in screening preschool children is the seeming lack of commitment on the part of individuals and agencies responsible for the health and educational needs of these children. Audiometric capabilities are in place, the research has been published, and trained professionals are available to do the screening and to follow up on the recommendations.

Bibliography

Brooks, D.: "Impedance in Screening," in J. Jerger and J. Northern (eds.), *Clinical Impedance Audiometry,* American Electromedics Corp., 1980.

Hodgson, W.: "Testing Infants and Young Children," in J. Katz (ed.), *Handbook of Clinical Audiology,* 2d ed., Williams and Wilkins, 1978.

Matkin, N.: "Assessment of Hearing Sensitivity During the Preschool Years," in F. Bess (ed.), *Childhood Deaf-*

ness: Causation, Assessment, and Management, Grune and Stratton, 1977.

New Jersey Department of Education: *Screening Children Ages 3 to 5.*

New Jersey Speech and Hearing Association: *Guidelines for Hearing Screening*, 1978.

Northern, J., and M. Downs: *Hearing in Children*, 2d ed., Williams and Wilkins, 1978.

Zaner, A., and J. Purn: "Auditory Problems in Children," in R. Rieber (ed.), *Communication Disorders*, Plenum Press, 1981.

Annette Zaner

Screening: School Children

Audiologic identification programs in public schools have evolved over a long time. Screening programs date back to the 1920s, when group speech tests of hearing became popular. Group pure-tone screening tests became popular following the development of the electroacoustic pure-tone audiometer. Later, individual pure-tone screening procedures became more prevalent and now are the accepted means of screening hearing sensitivity. Finally, acoustic-immittance procedures became part of some audiologic identification programs as a means of supplementing information obtained from hearing-sensitivity screenings. *See* AUDIOMETRY: Acoustic Immittance Measures, Pure-Tone Audiogram.

POPULATION

It is important to administer individual pure-tone screenings and, whenever possible, acoustic-immittance screenings to all children functioning at a developmental level of three years through grade three, and to any high-risk children, including those individuals above grade three. High-risk students are those who: (a) repeat a grade, (b) are enrolled in exceptional-education programs, (c) are new to the school system, (d) were absent during a previously scheduled screening, (e) failed a threshold test during the previous year, (f) have speech or language problems or obvious difficulty in communication, (g) are suspected of hearing impairment or have medical problems commonly associated with hearing impairment, (h) are involved in coursework that places them at risk for noise exposure (for example, band, woodworking, and auto mechanics).

In addition, it is important to monitor annually students having a previously documented hearing impairment or students whose families have a history of hearing impairment. Monitoring for this particular group of students may consist of threshold audiometry and acoustic-immittance screening, or a referral to a local agency that provides complete audiologic assessment.

PROCEDURES

Pure-tone audiometric screening procedures are used to identify students needing further audiologic assessment. Acoustic-immittance procedures are used to identify students with middle-ear disease and are intended to supplement the information obtained from pure-tone air-conduction hearing-sensitivity screenings.

Hearing sensitivity is screened at 1000, 2000, and 4000 Hz when pure-tone testing is used in combination with acoustic-immittance screening procedures. When acoustic-immittance procedures are not used, 500 Hz can also be screened, if ambient noise levels are acceptable, to provide some of the information ordinarily derived from acoustic-immittance testing. Students are screened at 20 dB HL (hearing level) at each test frequency. Each student is to be screened individually. Instructions given to the student are important. Time spent in proper instruction of students will save time spent on retests.

Acoustic-immittance measures incorporate two procedures, tympanometry and acoustic-reflex testing. Tympanometry measures changes in acoustic impedance or admittance at the eardrum as air-pressure changes are artificially induced into a hermetically sealed ear canal. The recorded results are known as a tympanogram. Acoustic-reflex screening procedures measure a change in the acoustic impedance or admittance at the eardrum after a suprathreshold stimulus is administered; reflex contraction of the stapedius muscle in the middle ear causes the impedance change.

PASS-FAIL CRITERIA

Pass-fail criteria for pure-tone audiometric and acoustic-immittance screening may be combined to provide a comprehensive audiologic identification program for school children. Such a program will help identify students with potentially educationally significant hearing loss and students with medically significant problems. The criteria are divided into three categories: pass, at-risk, and fail.

Category I: Pass. A student in category I responded consistently at 20 dB HL at 1000, 2000, and 4000 Hz for each ear; and the tympanograms for that student revealed normal middle-ear pressure (pressure peak ± 50 mm H_2O), and the acoustic reflex was present for each ear. Students in category I are dismissed from further screening at that time. Students from the high-risk group noted earlier will need to be monitored periodically even though they may have passed one comprehensive screening.

Category II: At Risk. A student in category II passed the pure-tone audiometric portion of the screening (20 dB HL at 1000, 2000, and 4000 Hz) for each ear, middle-ear pressure was mildly positive or negative ($+50$ to $+100$ mm H_2O; -50 to -200 mm H_2O), and the acoustic reflex was either present or absent; or middle-ear pressure was normal and the acoustic reflex was absent.

Students in category II are at risk and need to be rescreened in three to five weeks. If the test findings are the same upon rescreening, the student should be referred for further evaluation.

Category III: Fail. The student in category III did not respond at 20 dB HL at any one or all of the test frequencies for either ear, but middle-ear pressure was normal; the acoustic reflex may have been present or absent; or the student failed the pure-tone screening, middle-ear pressure was abnormal (peak outside -200 to $+100$ mm H_2O), and the acoustic reflex was absent; or the student responded consistently at 20 dB HL at each test frequency for each ear, but acoustic-immittance findings were abnormal (peak outside -200 to $+100$ mm H_2O, acoustic reflex absent).

Decisions made about students in the at-risk and fail categories constitute an area of controversy and of unending work for the clinician in the public schools. Sometimes problems identified during a screening are not present during followup screening. The problem identified earlier may have resolved spontaneously, or there may have been an error in the original findings. Feedback from local physicians, nurses, and parents as well as shortages in school and medical staff and equipment may dictate the need to modify criteria in any particular school district. Feedback from area physicians concerning specific criteria for treatment may determine whether a referral or further testing in the school is warranted. Changing the retest interval from three to five weeks to six to eight weeks also may be considered. Feedback from parents regarding a particular student's otologic or audiologic history and present status may help determine the need for referral or for further monitoring. The number of other high-risk factors that a student has also can help determine the need for referral or further monitoring.

PERSONNEL

Ideally, an audiologist should administer an audiologic identification program. A well-trained audiologist should be skilled in screening procedures and the subtle points of screening school children, and have knowledge of educational programming for hearing-impaired students. Considering the limited number of audiologists currently in the public schools, it is apparent that identification programs will, in fact, be administered in many districts by other personnel such as nurses and speech and language clinicians. A well-organized program run by a knowledgeable and skilled clinician can be effective and efficient whether it is run by an audiologist or by another clinician. Support personnel should complete an appropriate course of training or achieve a certain level of proficiency. Inaccurate screening results, which can be described as large numbers of false positive failures

and false negative passes, can be avoided when an identification program is supervised by properly trained professionals.

EQUIPMENT AND CALIBRATION

American Speech-Language-Hearing Association (ASHA) guidelines specify that audiometers used for screening purposes meet American National Standards Institute (ANSI) S3.6-1969 requirements in all areas. It is important to ensure that audiometers meet all specifications when delivered. Audiometric calibration to ANSI specifications must then occur at least once a year. Sound-pressure output must be checked at least every three months. Daily calibration checks will help to ensure that audiometers are at least grossly within calibration specifications.

ASHA guidelines specify that acoustic-immittance instruments used for screening programs must have the capability for tympanometry and for monitoring of an acoustic reflex at a specified intensity level. The equipment also must have an automatic recording system so that permanent records of tympanograms can be obtained. Monthly electroacoustic calibration according to manufacturer's specifications is recommended. Daily calibration checks using a standard test cavity are recommended during periods of heavy use. Further assessment of the equipment is recommended when immittance results appear inaccurate. ASHA guidelines also provide information regarding monthly calibration of the acoustic-reflex eliciting signal, the air-pressure system, and the recording system. Information also is provided regarding the air pump system, air-pressure range, probe-tone frequency, rate and direction of air-pressure change, measurement units, frequency and level of the acoustic-reflex eliciting signal, and pressure at which the acoustic reflex is to be tested.

ENVIRONMENT

The administrator of a screening program must evaluate the acoustic environment in which hearing screening is conducted. Usually, ambient noise levels in school environments are acceptable for screening hearing sensitivity at frequencies above 1000 Hz. Sometimes, however, noise levels will interfere with frequencies 1000 Hz and below. Screening the 1000–4000-Hz range is specified, because it is less affected than lower frequencies by ambient noise levels and because most significant hearing impairment will include failure in this range.

COMMUNICATING RESULTS OF SCREENINGS

The program administrator coordinates and supervises the communication of test results to parents, school personnel and, when appropriate, community agencies. Procedures regarding protection of confidentiality are detailed in the Family

Educational Rights and Privacy Act (1976). The law requires that notices about the audiologic identification program be provided to parents or guardians of the students to be screened. Generally, this is accomplished by written informed consent, that is, notices are sent home with each student, and parents have the right to comment or to exclude their children from participation. The agency responsible for conducting the screening is responsible for ensuring that consent is obtained. Notification of the screening must be in a style and language understandable to the responsible adult.

SUMMARY

Early identification of communication disorders in school-age children is essential in order to forestall potential educational problems and to provide the greatest chance for habilitation or rehabilitation of problems identified. An effective audiologic program will assist in this process by identifying students in need of further audiologic or otologic assessment. In order to be effective, audiologic identification programs must be an integral part of a comprehensive hearing-conservation program that also includes prevention, ongoing assessment, and management of hearing impairment within the school setting.

Bibliography

"Guidelines for Acoustic Immittance Screening of Middle-ear Function," *Asha*, vol. 21, no. 4, April 1979.

"Guidelines for Identification Audiometry," *Asha*, vol. 27, no. 5, May 1985.

Kenworthy, O. T.: "Integration of Assessment and Management Processes: Audiology as an Educational Program," in Bob Campbell and Victor Baldwin (eds.), *Severely Handicapped Hearing Impaired Students*, Paul H. Brookes Publishing Co., Baltimore, 1982.

"A Survey of Audiological Services Within the School System," *Asha*, vol. 27, no. 1, January 1985.

Wilson, Wesley R., and Wendel K. Walton: "Public School Audiometry" in F. N. Martin, *Pediatric Audiology*, Prentice-Hall, Englewood Cliffs, New Jersey, 1978.

Janice Lange Gavinski

Screening: Military

When applied to audiometric testing in the military, the term hearing screening is a misnomer. Screening tests generally involve some pass-fail criterion; a given suprathreshold standard is exceeded, met, or failed. While audiometric test results may be used as a basis for selection for active duty or retention in the service, the screenings are not simply pass-fail measurements; they are actual threshold determinations. Using traditional methods of threshold management, audiologists or trained technicians conduct such screenings for a variety of purposes. The audiometric data obtained are used for administrative purposes, to determine the need for diagnostic referrals, and as a baseline

and monitoring system for the hearing-conservation programs. This section will focus on administrative and hearing-conservation uses of audiometric screening data.

HEARING THRESHOLDS AND ADMINISTRATIVE DECISIONS

Prior to induction of an individual into the Armed Services, the person's hearing ability, as well as other physical conditions, is assessed to determine fitness for duty. As part of the induction physical examination, pure-tone air-conduction audiometry is performed. Pure-tone thresholds are compared to an audiometric "fence" or set of audiometric criteria that establishes the individual's fitness for duty. The audiometric criteria are essentially the same throughout the United States Armed Services. The Army standards for hearing levels for acceptance into the service are: the average of 500, 1000, and 2000 Hz will not be greater than 30 dB (ANSI, 1969), with no level greater than 35 dB, and at 4000 Hz the thresholds may not exceed 55 dB. These criteria apply to both ears. If one ear does not meet these criteria, fitness standards can be met only if the threshold values in the better ear are no worse than 30 dB at 500 Hz, 25 dB at 1000 and 2000 Hz, and 35 dB at 4000 Hz. If the better ear meets these criteria, the poorer ear may be anacusic or totally deaf.

Following induction, audiometric data are used for another administrative purpose, the assignment of a military occupational specialty or MOS. Individuals are assigned to occupational areas in which they are physically capable of performing. For the purpose of these assignments and to determine fitness for retention on active duty, hearing ability is classified into four categories or profiles: H-1 through H-4. The H-1 profile essentially indicates hearing within normal limits. Thresholds in each ear must not be poorer than 30 dB at 500 Hz, 25 dB at 1000 and 2000 Hz, and 45 dB at 4000 Hz. The H-2 profile corresponds to the induction standards described earlier, which indicate a mild bilateral impairment or a unilateral impairment of even profound degree. If a service member's hearing becomes poorer than the standards for the H-2 profile, an H-3 profile is assigned. Hearing ability is within the limits of the H-3 profile unless the better speech reception threshold (SRT) exceeds 30 dB. When this is the case, a hearing aid that yields an aided SRT of 30 dB or better (hearing aid set at "comfort level" to 50 dB speech noise) must be worn to meet fitness standards. The profile is then H-3 aided only. When the hearing loss is such that an aided SRT of 30 dB or better cannot be obtained, an H-4 profile is assigned, and the service member is boarded (medically discharged) from the military. *See* HEARING AIDS.

Each profile encompasses a wide range of thresholds. To adjust for the variety of impairments possible within a given profile range and to protect the service member from an inappropriate job classification, one of four specific modifying codes may be assigned to soldiers having H-2 or H-3 profiles. Specific military occupation specialties cannot be assigned to individuals with certain physical profiles so as to ensure duty limitations such as those described in the following code (Code J):

1. No exposure to noise in excess of 85 dBA or weapon firing without use of properly fitted hearing protection (not to include firing for pending-overseas-assignment, or POR, qualification or annual weapons qualification). Annual hearing test required.

2. Further exposure to noise is hazardous to health. No duty or assignment to noise levels in excess of 85 dBA or weapon firing (not to include firing for POR qualification or annual weapons qualification with proper ear protection). Annual hearing test required.

3. No exposure to noise in excess of 85 dBA or weapon firing without use of properly fitted hearing protection. This individual is, for definition purpose, deaf in one ear. Any permanent hearing loss in the good ear will cause serious handicap. Annual hearing test required.

4. Further duty requiring exposure to high-intensity noise is hazardous to health. No duty or assignment to noise levels in excess of 85 dBA or weapon firing (not to include firing for POR qualification or annual weapons qualification with proper ear protection). No duty requiring acute hearing. A hearing aid must be worn to meet medical fitness standards. (Code J is from Army Regulation 40-501, Change 34, 1 December 1983, p. 9-4.)

HEARING-CONSERVATION SCREENING AUDIOGRAMS

Hearing conservation is an integral part of all operational elements within the Armed Services. The Department of Defense has directed the military to enforce hearing conservation measures for all service members exposed to steady-state noise of 85 dBA or greater or to impulse noise equal to or greater than 140 dB peak sound-pressure level. To ensure effective monitoring, pure-tone air-conduction audiograms are obtained for individuals in such areas either semiannually or annually. The preinduction audiogram serves as a baseline or reference point. All subsequent audiograms are then compared to the original. Audiometric tests are conducted by trained personnel utilizing audiometers. A significant threshold shift is operationally defined as a change of ± 20 dB or more in the frequency range of 1000 to 4000 Hz in either ear relative to the reference audiogram or to the most recent audiogram. If a significant shift in hearing is suggested, a complete diagnostic workup and appropriate medical referral are indicated. At times, it is necessary that the soldier be reclassified. This means that the soldier is given another MOS in which continued noise exposure is not likely. In rare cases, the individual may be subject to dismissal from the military.

Audiometric data are computerized and stored in a central data repository. At the time of discharge or retirement from the service, audiograms are used as a basis for determining service-connected hearing impairment and possible disability or compensation.

In summary, audiometric pure-tone threshold tests are administered to all service members from the time they enter the military until the time they retire or separate. On the basis of these tests, prudent occupational, administrative, and diagnostic decisions are rendered.

Bibliography

Hearing Conservation, Department of the Army Technical Bulletin 501, March 1980.

Specifications for Audiometers, American National Standards Institute S36-1969.

Standards of Medical Fitness, Department of the Army Regulation 40-501, December 1, 1983.

Roy K. Sedge

Screening: Industrial

Industrial, or more accurately occupational, hearing-conservation programs require testing and referral procedures that are more detailed than and qualitatively different from those used to screen the general population for auditory disorders. The final Hearing Conservation Amendment entered into the Federal Register by the Occupational Safety and Health Administration (OSHA) on March 8, 1983, requires that employers establish and maintain an audiometric testing program for all employees whose noise exposures equal or exceed an eight-hour time-weighted average of 85 dB measured on the A scale slow response of a sound level meter or, equivalently, a dose of 50 percent on a personal audio or noise dosimeter (OSHA's action level). Audiometric testing and related services must be provided at no cost to the employees. The audiometric tests performed on noise-exposed workers are pure-tone, air-conduction threshold hearing examinations, with test frequencies including as a minimum 500, 1000, 2000, 3000, 4000, and 6000 Hz taken separately for each ear. Audiometers for these tests must be maintained and used in accordance with the American National Standard Specification for Audiometers, S3.6-1969. The audiometers used may be manual, self-recording (automatic), or microprocessor-controlled.

Noise-exposed employees must be tested at least annually after the baseline audiogram is obtained. A valid baseline audiogram must be obtained within six months of a worker's first exposure at or above the action level. Where mobile test vans are used to meet the audiometric testing requirements, the baseline audiogram must be obtained within one year of the worker's first exposure at or above the action level. In cases where baseline audiograms are obtained more than six months after the first exposure, employees are required to wear personal hearing protective devices for any period exceeding six months after the first exposure until the baseline audiogram is obtained. If the annual audiogram shows that an employee has sustained a standard threshold shift (STS), a retest may be performed within 30 days, and the results of the retest may be considered as the annual audiogram. An STS is defined as a change in hearing threshold relative to the baseline audiogram of an average of 10 dB or more at 2000, 3000, and 4000 Hz in either ear. Written notification of the occurrence of an STS must be sent to the employee within 21 calendar days of this determination.

QUALIFIED TESTING PERSONNEL

Air-conduction audiograms may be performed by a licensed or certified audiologist, otolaryngologist or other physician, or by a technician who is certified by the Council for Accreditation in Occupational Hearing Conservation (CAOHC) or who has satisfactorily demonstrated competence in administering audiometric examinations, obtaining valid audiograms, and properly using, maintaining, and checking calibration and functioning of the audiometers being used. OSHA states that the technician who operates microprocessor audiometers does not need to be certified but must be responsible to an audiologist, otolaryngologist, or physician. Many specialists and the CAOHC view the microprocessor exception as gratuitous and contrary to the interests of quality occupational hearing conservation, because personnel who operate such equipment may be called upon to test workers with other types of equipment and to perform other vital services in the program, such as issuance and monitored use of hearing protection, record keeping, and employee education for which certification is essential. Furthermore, personnel performing audiometry with any type of audiometric equipment may demonstrate on-the-job competence to a professional in the absence of a formal certification program.

Problem audiograms are reviewed by an audiologist, otolaryngologist, or physician to determine if there is a need for further evaluation. The reviewer must have access to: (1) OSHA's requirements for hearing conservation as described in relevant sections of the amendment; (2) the baseline and most recent audiogram of the employee to be evaluated; (3) measurements of background sound-pressure levels in the audiometric test rooms to determine whether they conform to the maximum allowable octave-band sound-pressure levels for audiometric test rooms (40 dB sound-pressure level at 500 and 1000 Hz, 47 dB at 2000 Hz, 57 dB at 4000 Hz, and 62 dB at 8000 Hz); and (4) records of audiometric calibrations (at least annual acoustic calibration including sound-pressure output and linearity checks and, at least once every two years, exhaustive calibration conforming to sections 4.1.2 to 4.5 of the American National Standard Specification for Audiometers, S3.6-1969.

REFERRAL SYSTEM

Unless a physician determines that the STS is not work-related or aggravated by occupational noise exposure, the employer must take the following steps when an STS has occurred: (1) employees not using hearing protectors shall be fitted with them, trained in their use and care, and required to use them; and (2) employees already using hearing protectors shall be refitted and retrained in the use of hearing protectors and provided with hearing protectors offering greater attenuation if necessary. The employee shall be referred for a clinical audiological evaluation or an otologic examination as appropriate, if additional testing is necessary or if the employer suspects a medical pathologic condition of the ear unrelated to the use of hearing protectors.

While OSHA mandates the above referral procedures for employees who have sustained an STS, no requirements have been established for referral of workers who show evidence of significant pathologic conditions of the ear or hearing on the baseline or preemployment audiogram. However, other groups have addressed this important problem. The Subcommittee on the Medical Aspects of Noise of the American Academy of Otolaryngology–Head and Neck Surgery Foundation recommends that otologic referral be made when the average hearing level on the baseline audiogram at 500, 1000, 2000, and 3000 Hz is greater than 25 dB in either ear. Referrals also should be made when the difference in average hearing level between the better and poorer ear is greater than 15 dB at 500, 1000, and 2000 Hz, or more than 20 dB at 3000, 4000, and 6000 Hz. The academy also recommends that if workers exhibit any of the following medical problems, they be referred directly to an otolaryngologist: history of ear pain or drainage; dizziness; severe, persistent tinnitus; sudden, fluctuating, or rapidly progressive hearing loss; or a feeling of fullness or discomfort in one or both ears within the preceding 12 months. The academy further recommends that a person who has received otologic evaluation previously on the basis of the foregoing criteria should be reevaluated if any of the following conditions develop: ear pain or drainage; dysequilibrium or imbalance; severe, persistent tinnitus, or significant changes in hearing levels defined as a change in average hearing level, in either ear, compared with the baseline audiogram of more than 15 dB at 500, 1000, and 2000 Hz, or more than 20 dB at 3000, 4000, and 6000 Hz.

Bibliography

Miller, M. H.: *Manual for Training Occupational Hearing Conservationists*, Council for Accreditation in Occupational Hearing Conservation, pp. 59–62, Fischler's Printing, Cherry Hill, New Jersey, 1978.

———— and C. A. Silverman: *Occupational Hearing Conservation*, pp. 174–180, Prentice-Hall, Englewood Cliffs, New Jersey, 1984.

Maurice H. Miller

Genetic Principles

Minor hearing losses, whether of childhood, adolescence, or adult life, often are not sufficiently severe disabilities to motivate people to seek genetic advice. Thus, in this section, deafness will be taken to connote profound hearing impairment of childhood, though, of course, the laws of Mendelian inheritance, and the other principles of which mention will be made, are equally applicable to other types of genetically determined hearing loss.

RECESSIVE GENES

The most common type of Mendelian inheritance governing the determination of profound childhood deafness is autosomal recessive. The human genetic material consists of 22 pairs of autosomes and a pair of sex chromosomes (XX in females, XY in males), or 46 chromosomes in all. Thus, genes exist in pairs, and a chromosomal site or locus will contain two examples of the gene that occupies it. Furthermore, such a Mendelian gene can exist in variant forms, known as alleles. If the two alleles at a chromosomal locus are the same (AA, aa), the individual is said to be homozygous at that locus. If the two alleles are different, the individual is said to be heterozygous. If A is the normal allele, and a the abnormal allele responsible for autosomal recessive deafness, normal homozygotes (AA) and heterozygotes (Aa) have normal hearing, and aa individuals, homozygous for the abnormal allele, are deaf. In general, therefore, when normal parents have one or more deaf children, the situation when autosomal recessive inheritance is operative is that they are both heterozygotes (Aa), and the deaf children have inherited one a allele from each of the parents and are abnormal homozygotes (aa).

The situation is more complex in practice, because there are many different chromosomal loci at which deafness may be determined. Conceptually, however, the situation is similar in each case, and the different forms of autosomal recessive deafness may be represented as aa, bb, cc, and so on. Each child has an equal chance of inheriting the A or the a allele from each parent so that the probability that he or she is an abnormal homozygote and deaf is $\frac{1}{2} \times \frac{1}{2}$, or $\frac{1}{4}$.

If the usually normally hearing parents of a deaf child had a $\frac{1}{4}$ chance of recurrence in any subsequent pregnancy, the genetic situation would be simple. However, especially when there is only one deaf child, many unrecognized causes for the deafness other than autosomal recessive inheritance may be operating. Such a recurrence chance can be given, however, in the following circumstances.

1. When there is more than one deaf child and no family history suggestive of autosomal dominant inheritance.

2. If the parents are related to each other, often as first cousins, sometimes more distantly. This is because such consanguinity between the parents is one of the hallmarks of autosomal recessive inheritance. The abnormal alleles a, b, c, and so on, are each individually rare in the population, and a heterozygous male who is carrying one of these alleles (genetic constitution Aa, Bb, Cc, and so on) is more likely to marry a woman who is also carrying the same abnormal allele if she is related to him than if he chooses his wife from the general population. This is because there is a likelihood that the marriage partners have each inherited the abnormal allele from a heterozygous common ancestor.

3. If the deafness in the child, who may be the only affected one, is part of a syndrome known to be inherited in an autosomal recessive manner. Among the better known of such syndromes are Pendred's, Usher's, Jervell's, and Lange-Nielsen's. *See* HEARING LOSS: Genetic Causes.

A situation in which both parents suffer from the same type of autosomal recessive hearing loss is one of the very rare occasions where the risk of a child being affected is 100 percent. However, although autosomal recessive hearing impairment is the most common among inherited forms, marriages of persons with matching genes are extremely rare because there are so many different genes which can cause this condition. Thus, in the vast majority of cases, marriages between persons with autosomal recessive hearing impairment involve two distinct genes, and the offspring will be carriers for both and will enjoy normal hearing.

DOMINANT GENES

Less often, the inheritance of deafness is autosomal dominant. In such cases one abnormal allele is sufficient to cause deafness even if it is paired with a normal allele. Thus, the deaf individuals have one abnormal allele at one of many possible chromosomal loci (D_1, D_2, and so on) and one normal allele (d_1, d_2, and so on). They are heterozygous at that locus (D_1d_1, D_2d_2, and so on). A deaf male D_1d_1 may marry a woman who is either hearing or deaf. If she is deaf, it is unlikely that her deafness is due to the same cause because there are so many causes which can be responsible for deafness. At the chromosomal locus in question, she is, therefore, a normal homozygote (d_1d_1). The male produces gametes (sperm), each of which carries with an equal probability ($\frac{1}{2}$) the normal (d_1) or the abnormal (D_1) allele. The female will produce only d_1 gametes. Thus, half the children will be heterozygotes like the father (D_1d_1) and will be deaf, and half will be normal homozygotes like the mother (d_1d_1) and will have normal hearing. This type of transmission may give rise to the classical pedigree of autosomal dominant inheritance, stretching back for many generations with half the children, on average, of a deaf individual being deaf.

The situation just described is not, however, so simple in practice, and this classical type of transmission is the exception rather than the rule. The main complicating factor is that the abnormal alleles (D_1, D_2, and so on) do not have the same effect in all the individuals to whom they are transmitted. Some such individuals may be only mildly or moderately, rather than profoundly, deaf and others only unilaterally deaf (this is known as variable expressivity of the abnormal allele), while in others hearing may be spared altogether (failure of penetrance).

Sometimes, as in the case of the autosomal recessive variety, autosomal dominant inheritance may be inferred because the deafness is associated with clinical abnormalities known to be characteristic of a syndrome inherited in this way, the most common being that of Waardenburg. It should be noted, however, that variable expressivity and failure of penetrance are particularly marked with respect to the deafness component of the syndrome. Thus, an affected individual, even though profoundly deaf, will have a 50 percent chance of passing on the abnormal allele, but of the children who inherit this allele only a third or less may be bilaterally profoundly deaf, though they may show other features of the syndrome, including mild bilateral or profound unilateral deafness. The risk of transmitting bilateral profound deafness is, therefore, 10–20, rather than 50, percent.

The abnormal allele responsible for deafness may occasionally be situated on the sex (X) chromosome rather than on one of the autosomes. This gives rise to a pattern of inheritance that is well known in the case of color-blindness and of hemophilia, conditions that occur almost exclusively in males but are transmitted by unaffected hetero-

zygous (Aa) females. Thus, if a deaf male has a deaf maternal grandfather or deaf maternal uncles, great-uncles, or male first cousins (children of a maternal aunt), this type of inheritance (X- or sex-linked recessive) may be inferred. Because the mother is a heterozygote (Aa) while the father has the normal (A) allele on his unpaired X chromosome, half the sons will be affected and half the daughters will be heterozygous carriers. In all, the chance for further affected children (sons only) will be $\frac{1}{4}$, exactly as in the case of recessive inheritance.

The most difficult common situation encountered in genetic counseling in connection with deafness occurs when normal-hearing parents with a single affected child ask about risks of recurrence, and there is no unequivocal evidence implicating any of the three modalities of Mendelian inheritance discussed above. Such a child may suffer from recessive deafness, autosomal or, if male, X-linked, with a recurrence risk of $\frac{1}{4}$ in future pregnancies, or the disability may be due to any one of a number of undetected causes where the recurrence risk is essentially zero. When no indication whatsoever of the true cause exists, a recurrence risk of 10–15 percent may be given, reflecting an approximately equal admixture of these two types of cases.

MARRIAGES OF TWO HEARING-IMPAIRED PERSONS

The prognosis for the children of two deaf parents is difficult to establish, but contrary to common opinion, the risk of hearing impairment is not very elevated. Thus, Edward A. Fay (1898) in his monumental study of more than 4000 marriages of hearing-impaired persons in North America came to the surprising conclusion that the proportion of hearing-impaired offspring arising from marriages where one partner had normal hearing (151 out of 1532, or 9.9%) was fractionally greater than the proportion where both parents had hearing impairment (492 out of 5072, or 8.5%). Neither figure is very large, though considerably more substantial than that prevailing in the general population. When one of the parents owes his or her disability to autosomal dominant inheritance, it matters little whether the spouse has normal or impaired hearing. The risk among the offspring is substantially less than 50 percent because of the phenomena of variable expressivity and reduced penetrance mentioned above. *See* FAY, EDWARD ALLEN.

Bibliography

Boughman, J. A., and K. A. Shaver: "Genetic Aspects of Deafness: Understanding the Counseling Process," *American Annals of the Deaf*, 127:393–400, 1982.

Fay, E. A.: *Marriages of the Deaf in America*, Volta Bureau, Washington, D.C., 1898.

G. R. Fraser

Genetic Counseling

Genetic counseling is a complex process, especially since it affects the feelings of those who seek counseling related to childbearing. To function effectively, the counselor needs a formidable store of knowledge. First, the counselor must master the technical information derived from studies of genetics and allied disciplines which bear upon the wide variety of problems presented. Equally important is the ability to impart this information, to share it fully with the counselees, and to participate actively in their doubts and self-questioning.

Due to its complexity, genetic counseling usually has evolved as a group effort in countries at an advanced level of economic development. It involves individuals having widely differing specializations and most often affiliated with a medical school or a large medical center. In many such places the need has been accepted to make special arrangements within the counseling group to deal with restricted classes of diseases and disabilities. Deaf persons have been recognized as one such constituency. This means that, in some regions at least, the services of specially qualified personnel have been made available to deal with large groups of deaf persons such as are found in residential educational institutions. In such a setting, deaf individuals can be instructed in the general principles of the genetic (and other biologic) laws and guidelines that may influence their attitudes toward future reproduction. In addition, such special expertise will be available to deal with the specific problems of deaf people when they marry and with the common problem of a hearing couple who have had one or more deaf children.

HEREDITARY AND EXOGENOUS FACTORS

As presented here, deafness connotes a severe form of hearing impairment in childhood (profound childhood deafness), usually of such an extent as to necessitate special educational methods. Moderate degrees of hearing impairment in childhood are often due to illness, trauma, or other external (exogenous) factors. Genetic counseling is most effective when simple Mendelian factors are operative and when the handicap is substantial as in the case of profound childhood deafness.

The most important application of the rules of Mendelian inheritance is that there is a 25 percent risk of recurrence if parents give birth to a child with a hearing impairment that is caused by inheritance of two copies of the same abnormal gene, one from each parent (autosomal recessive inheritance). This is the most common type of hereditary hearing loss, and such individuals are said to be homozygous for the abnormal gene. Because chromosomes exist in pairs, the locus, or chromosomal site, where a form of deafness of this type is determined is occupied by the two abnormal genes,

and no compensating normal gene is present. In some instances a single gene is inherited that causes hearing impairment (autosomal dominant inheritance), and in a very few cases the pathologic gene causing hearing loss is situated on the X chromosome (X-linked inheritance) and affects only males. In both autosomal dominant inheritance and X-linked inheritance, severe hearing impairment may occur in several generations. Autosomal recessive inheritance usually is confined to a single generation.

Genetic counseling in families with deaf children is complicated by the numerous distinct causes that can underlie severe hearing impairment. In addition to the inherited causes, the condition may be due to exogenous factors, and these may act in the pre-, peri-, or postnatal period. Examples of such factors are rubella infection of the pregnant mother, rhesus blood-factor incompatibility, and meningitis. Hereditary and exogenous factors are of approximately equal importance in the causation of severe hearing impairment in childhood.

Often the counseling is a simple one. If a cause can be unequivocally determined to be exogenous, the hearing prognosis for further children is excellent. In cases where clear indications exist that the hearing impairment is of a hereditary nature, the advice appropriate for that type of inheritance may be given. The main difficulty rises in the substantial proportion of cases where a child represents an isolated case of hearing impairment in the family and where there is no clear indication of cause. The importance of early diagnosis must be stressed at this point, because counseling loses much of its efficacy if the couple embarks on another pregnancy before hearing loss is detected in a previously born child.

In all cases of severe hearing impairment, a thorough medical investigation of the family history is necessary. This is especially important where the cause is difficult to define. Even after such an investigation, identification of cause when there is only one hearing-impaired child in the family is often probabilistic rather than absolute. In a substantial proportion of cases the counselor and the family may be left in a situation where no exact numerical risk of recurrence can be given.

The operation of Mendelian inheritance can be detected in various ways. The family history provides the most important information in this connection. Thus, when multiple affected individuals are found only in one sibship, autosomal recessive inheritance may be strongly suspected. When such affected individuals are found in two or more generations, inheritance is more likely to be autosomal dominant, each child having an equal chance of inheriting the normal or the abnormal gene, except in the rare cases when the familial occurrence is characteristic of X-linked recessive inheritance. Autosomal dominant deafness in one or the other parent is by far the most frequent reason for the birth of deaf offspring to a marriage between deaf persons.

In the regular pattern of dominant transmission from parent to child, half the offspring are affected. This may be modified, however, because of variable expressivity or failure of penetrance of the gene involved, meaning that this pathologic gene may not have the same effect in all the individuals who carry it. Thus, the effects of the gene may vary from profound bilateral deafness, through mild or unilateral forms (variable expressivity), to the total sparing of hearing (failure of penetrance). Allowance must be made, of course, for this variation in the effects of pathologic genes when giving advice during the counseling process.

Even when a case of deafness is isolated in the family, important clues may reveal the probable operation of Mendelian inheritance. Thus, if a blood relationship exists between the hearing parents of a deaf child, such as when they are first cousins, autosomal recessive inheritance is probable since the marriage partners are more likely to share rare pathologic genes than are unrelated persons.

Thorough clinical studies often reveal that the deafness is part of a syndrome that is known to be determined in a Mendelian manner. For example, the deafness may be associated with goiter in Pendred's syndrome or with retinitis pigmentosa in Usher's syndrome, both syndromes being inherited in an autosomal recessive manner, or with heterochromia iridum (eyes of different color) and other disorders of pigmentation in Waardenburg's syndrome, which is inherited in an autosomal dominant manner.

The most satisfying counseling situation is, of course, one in which an acquired cause can be unequivocally demonstrated and the parents can be reassured that the recurrence risk is negligible. This may happen, for example, when there is good evidence of an attack of rubella in pregnancy. Careful examination of the fundi (eye grounds) with an ophthalmoscope may reveal evidence of such infection having been transmitted to the fetus even when the mother is unaware of a subclinical episode of rubella in pregnancy. Untoward turbulent events in the perinatal period, often associated with low birth weight, may point to an acquired cause. Sometimes this can be identified with virtual certainty, as when the medical records show that streptomycin or another ototoxic drug has been administered; in other cases, the exact nature of an acquired cause can only be suspected.

It is clearly impossible in the perinatal period to establish a cause-and-effect relation on the basis of direct observation, because there is no evidence that hearing was normal at the time of birth. It is possible that severe illnesses, especially with a meningitic or encephalitic component, may be responsible for deafness without the possibility of convincingly demonstrating such an acquired cause.

All these considerations involving the heterogeneity of the causes of deafness, both genetic and acquired, lead to special difficulties in the counseling process in the common situation in which only one individual is affected in the family and there is no firm evidence about cause after careful evaluation of clinical and anamnestic evidence. An empiric recurrence risk of 10–15 percent may be given, reflecting an approximately equal admixture of autosomal recessive cases with others where the risk of recurrence is essentially zero.

ETHICS OF GENETIC COUNSELING

Counseling should involve only the giving of advice in a nondirective manner and allowing the counselees to make their own decision concerning reproduction on the basis of this advice. Ideally, the skillful counselor imparts knowledge in such a way that the information is readily understandable to the counselees. The counseling session is a two-way process and should lead to the formulation of questions on the part of the counselees. The counselor will answer questions to the best of his or her ability, taking into account the completeness of the information available. A directive attitude on the part of the counselor is not appropriate in that it may override the desires and autonomy of the individual counselee about such a basic right as that of choosing whether to reproduce. This view does not exclude the possibility that the counselor should give an opinion if asked to do so, and that the potential advantages and disadvantages of the choices open to the counselees should be discussed. In the case of deaf people, in particular, the counselor would be wise to defer to their perception of the degree of handicap to which this disability gives rise.

There are, however, subjective elements that affect the decision-making process on the part of the counselees, even if the counseling session is fully successful according to the criteria outlined above. First, the concept of risk does not have a uniform and standard meaning, and even if an accurate figure can be given, it will not have the same significance in all cases. Thus, a risk of 25 percent of recurrence may be perceived as enormous by one couple and small by another, especially when related to the average risk of serious disability, perhaps as high as 3–4 percent, which any parents take in having a child.

Then again, an exact risk of recurrence often cannot be given. Moreover, in the case of a condition such as profound childhood deafness which, though a major handicap, is still compatible with a life of normal duration and acceptable quality, couples will differ widely in their perceptions of the extent to which their desire for a child should be affected by any specified risk figure.

There is, in addition, the apparent paradox that when the counselees are a deaf couple they may be concerned as much about the risks of having a hearing child as those of having a deaf one. This is a reflection of the vastly improved economic status of deaf people and of the problems which deaf parents fear a hearing child may face in the first few years of life in the home environment. Such couples should be reassured on this last point. There can be no doubt that the situation of hearing children of deaf parents is an unusual one, but it is not one that can be shown to give rise to any long-term harmful effects. *See* DEAF POPULATION: Socio-economic Status.

In some cases the counseling session may reveal the existence of family members who face problems and risks of which they may be unaware. The counselor should establish a sufficient rapport with the counselees and inspire sufficient confidence that they themselves inform their relatives of the situation and the availability of advice. The counselor should encourage such referral but should not take steps to contact family members without the specific consent of the actual counselees. Such consent may often be easier to obtain if the counselor agrees to transmit information to the relatives through their own medical advisers.

There has been a great deal of discussion of the responsibility of the counselor to society as well as to individual counselees. For example, in the case of dominant deafness, there is a potential cost to society in general, as well as to the counselees, in view of the high risk of the birth of a deaf child who will need special education and rehabilitation. There is a consensus, although dissenting opinions are being heard, that reproduction is a right rather than a privilege, in the same way that all forms of medical treatment should be a right. Thus, no one would think of withholding treatment from a patient with carcinoma of the lung because the individual had been smoking heavily for 20 years and had known throughout that period of its potential dangers. Education is society's main weapon in reducing the avoidable burden of births of severely handicapped children and that of avoidable disease unconnected with pregnancy. The counselor's primary responsibility should be to the counselees or patients and in economically developed countries at least, both the counselor and the counselees have the right to assume that society will provide facilities for the rehabilitation of a handicapped child.

Economically developed countries do not in general have the problem that their resources are being strained by overpopulation. On the other hand, underdeveloped countries do have such problems, and there is evidence that strong persuasion, if not actual coercion, is being applied in some to limit reproduction. Even within such a context, efforts can be made to distribute the burden of restrictions of this type with justice throughout the population, and without discrimination on the basis of such factors as a moderate risk of a tolerable disability such as deafness in the unborn child, or even on the basis of sex choice.

Economic progress over the last two centuries has been accompanied by the introduction of educational rehabilitation of deaf individuals and their integration into society. Quite independently of the availability of counseling, deaf persons have been encouraged to make a home and family, whereas previously they were regarded as outcasts, and rarely reproduced. Concern has been expressed about such dysgenic trends, in that genes for deafness are being perpetuated in the population whereas previously they would have been lost.

It can be shown, however, that whether the deafness is dominant and deaf children are born, or whether it is recessive with only the gene rather than the disability being transmitted, such dysgenic effects are very small. Thus, the problems caused by an increase in the incidence of genetically determined deafness as a result of the improved economic circumstances of deaf people should not strain the resources of future generations. It would, in any case, be totally impractical to aim at an eradication of deleterious genes, in general, because each normal individual is liable to be carrying several such genes, which, though without effect in single dose (heterozygous), give rise to severe recessive diseases in double dose (homozygous).

In particular, the popular prejudice against marriages between deaf persons is especially ill-founded because, as explained above, in most cases where transmission occurs from parent to child, the deafness is dominant and the hearing status of the spouse makes no difference to the number of affected offspring to be expected. Although, with the increased integration of deaf individuals into hearing society, this tendency for assortative mating within the deaf community may be diminishing, such marriages have much to commend them in terms of compatibility and chances of success.

The resources available to the genetic counselor have been increasing substantially. Previously, the role of the counselor was restricted to giving advice concerning the risks of reproduction. Virtually the only proposed alternative to taking these risks was adoption, and this has become increasingly difficult in economically advanced countries because of a lack of available children. Artificial insemination by donor has been used for some time in cases of male infertility, and it would seem logical to extend its use to situations where the male is voluntarily infertile because he fears the risks of transmitting a hereditary condition such as autosomal dominant deafness. It is also relevant after the birth of a child with an autosomal recessive condition (including many forms of deafness) because it is unlikely that the donor would be carrying the same abnormal gene as the father (and the mother also). The acceptance of artificial insemination by donor as a potential solution to such problems has been slow and by no means uniform, but counselees should undoubtedly be informed of this possibility.

Counselors have placed much more emphasis on antenatal diagnosis, another method which has become available. This technique is combined with the option of selective abortion. An increasing number of defects and diseases in the fetus can be diagnosed prenatally using the technique of amniocentesis, a needle puncture of the uterus in the second trimester of pregnancy to obtain fetal cells from amniotic fluid to test for the presence of chromosomal aberrations or biochemical defects. This method is being replaced to an increasing extent by transcervical biopsy of chorionic villi, which has the great advantage that results can be obtained earlier in pregnancy, during the first trimester. These techniques for the antenatal diagnosis of chromosomal or biochemical abnormalities have been supplemented by methods involving direct viewing of the fetus. During such fetoscopy, specimens of fetal tissue, including blood, can be obtained. Information about the fetus can also be obtained by x-ray or by ultrasound scanning, a technique whose powers of resolution are already sufficient to detect even minor malformations of the fetus and are rapidly improving. Finally, in the case of open neural-tube defects in the fetus, examination of the alpha-fetoprotein levels of the maternal serum may be useful as a screening method for detection which must, however, be supplemented by amniocentesis and testing of the amniotic fluid when serum levels are suggestive.

None of these methods is currently applicable to common types of deafness, though this may change in the future, both because of advances in the understanding of the biochemical basis of some types of hereditary deafness and because of advances in the application of recombinant DNA techniques to the problem of gene location. Accompanying gross malformations of the outer or middle ear may be detected by ultrasound scanning or fetoscopy, as may malformations affecting other organs which are found in combination with deafness in various syndromes. A nonhereditary type of deafness due to maternal rubella may be suspected if the virus is isolated from amniotic fluid. However, the large majority of cases of congenital and hereditary deaf-

ness cannot be detected prenatally. Even if it were possible to test auditory nerve function in the fetus, the timing of the neuronal degeneration associated with the various forms of hereditary deafness is unknown; such degeneration may in many cases be postnatal in origin.

ETHICS OF ANTENATAL DIAGNOSIS AND SELECTIVE ABORTION

Antenatal diagnosis is linked to the practice of selective abortion, that is, to giving the parents the option of aborting the fetus after an abnormality has been detected. This practice has raised a host of moral and ethical problems. It is very different from the practice of abortion for social or economic reasons, which the laws of many countries permit today (usually at an earlier stage of pregnancy). The very nature of the counselor-counselee relationship implies that selective abortion involves a wanted child. An extreme and formalistic ethical point of view might hold that this practice represents the antithesis of all the accepted principles of medicine in that in no other case can the deliberate killing of the patient be considered as a therapeutic procedure.

Ethical arguments revolve around the question of whether the fetus can in fact be regarded as a patient. This question leads to an insoluble metaphysical and moral problem—whether the fetus has human attributes or even a human nature, and how much protection society owes to the fetus at various stages of growth. These issues cannot be discussed adequately within the limitations of this article. Selective abortion has, in general, been accepted in medical and legal circles in those countries that permit abortion for social reasons and even in some that do not. The counselor has no right to withhold information about the availability of this approach from the counselees even if the approach is inconsistent with the counselor's own moral and ethical views. In any case, such moral attitudes might not be absolute but may be modified by the gravity of the defect. In this connection it has been stressed that profound deafness cannot be regarded as belonging to the more severe categories of childhood handicap.

In logic, it is a relatively facile step to argue that when a condition is readily recognizable at birth even without any tests, such as Down's Syndrome, the costly and laborious mechanism of prenatal diagnosis followed by selective abortion is not worthwhile in that it is equivalent to infanticide, which is easier to institute on a systematic basis. Morally, however, the newborn infant is a separate human being, whereas the interests of the fetus are inseparable from those of the mother. Thus, it seems improbable that this justification for infanticide will be legally recognized. Many people think this is fortunate because to them it would represent a major victory for nonsupporters of one of the cardinal ethical tenets of society, namely respect for the sanctity of human life—a tenet which in their view is not threatened by abortion, selective or otherwise.

No one would regard selective abortion as a definitively acceptable solution for the problems under discussion. Thus, one may speculate on the approaches and techniques which may replace it in the immediate (and even distant) future as adjuncts which may add true therapeutic modalities to the counseling process. Much work is being done on the development of intrauterine therapy. This has long been known to be effective in disease due to rhesus blood-factor incompatibility that can be treated by intrauterine blood transfusions. Fortunately, these are no longer often necessary, since this disease has ceased to be a major problem because of the introduction of preventive measures.

Possibly, other conditions will prove amenable to intrauterine therapy in the future. In the case of hereditary childhood deafness, it would be important to define when the damage to the auditory apparatus occurs. If, in some cases at least, it is postnatal rather than intrauterine, the chances of the development of therapeutic measures, applicable after birth and early detection, would be much greater.

The contentious question of the choice of the sex of offspring may be profoundly affected by methods that have been under development for a long time and now show some signs of success. These methods center on the partial or complete separation of sperm into X- and Y-chromosome-bearing fractions and the use of the appropriate fraction for artificial insemination. Such an advance would be important in genetic counseling because it would replace the selective abortion of all males which now occurs when the mother is known to be a carrier for a variety of X-linked diseases, even though only half of the aborted male offspring may be expected to be affected. X-linked types of profound childhood deafness are rare, however, only 1–2 percent of cases being attributable to this type of inheritance.

Other, more speculative directions for potential advances lie within the scope of genetic engineering. Thus, it may become possible to modify the phenotype of the fetus or infant, or even the actual genotype, replacing the defective gene with a normal one in all cells. In the field of gametic selection, it may become possible to separate sperm and ova into classes according to whether they possess a defective gene or not, and then discard those gametes which do.

These are just speculations at the moment, but future generations will find ways of dealing with these problems, whether following the avenues mentioned above or others that will be medically and ethically more satisfactory than the present methods that mainly involve selective abortion.

Bibliography

Boughman, J. A., and K. A. Shaver: "Genetic Aspects of Deafness: Understanding the Counseling Process," *American Annals of the Deaf,* 127:393–400, 1982.

Fay, E. A.: *Marriages of the Deaf in America,* Volta Bureau, Washington, D.C., 1898.

Fletcher, J. C.: "Prenatal Diagnosis: Ethical Issues," in W. T. Reich (ed.), *Encyclopedia of Bioethics,* pp. 1336–1346, Macmillan and Free Press, New York, 1978.

Fraser, G. R.: *The Causes of Profound Deafness in Childhood: A Study of 3,535 Individuals with Severe Hearing Loss Present at Birth or of Childhood Onset,* Johns Hopkins University Press, Baltimore, 1976.

Konigsmark, B. W., and R. J. Gorlin: *Genetic and Metabolic Deafness,* Saunders, Philadelphia, 1976.

President's Commission for the Study of Ethical Problems in Medicine and Biomedical and Behavioral Research, *Screening and Counseling for Genetic Conditions,* Government Printing Office, Washington, D.C., 1983.

G. R. Fraser; J. C. Fletcher

Hearing Loss Compensation

Compensation for hearing loss generally refers to Workers Compensation laws enacted by the various states to provide monetary reimbursement for hearing impairment sustained as a result of workplace noise exposure or an industrial accident. Before such laws were enacted, employees' rights were governed by common law, a situation that still exists in jurisdictions that have not enacted Workers Compensation statutes for hearing impairment. Under the common law, several legal defenses were used by employers, such as maintaining that the injury was associated with the nature of the job, negligence of a fellow employee, or the worker's own negligence. Even if the workers were successful in proving their cases, they had no assurance that their employers were financially able to pay damages.

The first Workers Compensation law in the United States was enacted in 1908. Such laws were based upon legislation adopted in Prussia in 1854, Germany in 1884, and Great Britain in 1897. The original intent of these laws was to provide a portion of the wage loss and medical expenses to employees who sustained an occupational injury. To establish a claim, the worker had to demonstrate actual wage loss or a reduced earning capacity as a result of the occupational injury. Because most cases of occupational hearing impairment involve long-term exposure to high-intensity workplace noise while the employee continues to earn normal wages, such losses were originally regarded as not constituting a compensable injury.

LANDMARK DECISIONS

Gradual loss of hearing secondary to occupational noise exposure was first regarded as an occupational injury subject to compensation benefits in May 1948. The New York Court of Appeals ruled that compensation was payable although no loss of earning was involved or anticipated. Similar decisions were made in Wisconsin in 1953 and Missouri in 1959.

There is no uniformity from state to state for occupational hearing loss benefits, and procedures and awards in various jurisdictions are subject to constant change. M. S. Fox and J. H. Bunn identified six factors which contribute to the determination of benefits awarded employees: (1) the method for computing hearing handicap; (2) whether partial impairment is compensable or whether the hearing loss must be total in one or both ears; (3) the prescribed length of time a claimant has to be separated from his employment (if any); (4) the deduction in hearing handicap attributed to aging and prior noise exposure (if any); (5) the amount of weekly benefits prescribed by the state, and the number of weeks scheduled for hearing loss; (6) whether hearing loss was caused by either accident (traumatic) or chronic noise exposure, or a combination of both.

DEFINITIONS

Occupational hearing loss or impairment, also called noise-induced hearing loss, refers to partial (or, rarely, complete) hearing loss in both (occasionally one) ears arising out of and in the course of one's employment. The loss usually is bilateral and sensorineural.

Acoustic trauma is hearing loss of sudden origin resulting from exposure to intense acoustic energy, often from blasts, explosions, or direct injury to the head or ear. It may be partial or complete, unilateral or bilateral, conductive, sensorineural, or mixed. Pseudohypacusic (nonorganic hearing loss) factors need to be evaluated.

Hearing impairment is any deviation or change for the worse in structure or function and may range from mild to profound. Any audiometric configuration, type, or degree of loss may be involved.

Hearing handicap is the disadvantage imposed by an impairment sufficient to affect adversely one's personal efficiency in carrying out activities of daily living.

Hearing disability is the actual or presumed inability to remain employed at full wages. In effect, disability relates to how much the worker is paid for the handicap.

ASSESSMENT AND AWARDING OF DISABILITY

Hearing loss has moved from a state of virtual nonrecognition in the 1950s, to legislation for compensation in the 1960s, to possibly the largest liability factor in the 1980s and in future decades. In some states, compensation in excess of $66,000 is granted for a bilateral, total loss of hearing that is determined to be industrially related. For such total losses, the Federal Employee Compensation Act and the Longshore Act allow a maximum of $144,500 and $91,200, respectively. The U.S. Chamber of Commerce estimates that 1.7 million American workers between 50 and 59 years of age have sufficient hearing loss to qualify for compensation. If only 10 percent of these persons file claims at an average amount of $3000 per claim, the potential cost to industry is more than $500 million. G. Bugliarello estimated compensation payments in the United States for noise-induced hearing loss to be about $6 billion if all eligible claims are filed.

Control of actual or potential Workers Compensation claims for industrially related hearing loss has become the major factor in convincing employers that occupational hearing conservation programs are warranted. When the cost of not implementing these programs exceeds the cost of implementing them, budgetary allowances begin in earnest. The passage and implementation of regulations by the Occupational Safety and Health Administration (OSHA) of the U.S. Department of Labor to control occupational noise exposure also has been a major factor in the establishment of programs to protect the hearing of noise-exposed employees. There is no direct relationship, however, between the adjudication of a Workers Compensation claim for occupationally related hearing loss (state) and the existence of an OSHA-compliant occupational hearing conservation program (federal). However, employers generally are in a more advantageous position when a Workers Compensation claim is filed if they can show that a continuing, effective hearing conservation program that equals or exceeds OSHA requirements has been in operation during the period when the hearing impairment was allegedly sustained.

Formerly, the most commonly used formula to calculate percent hearing impairment in settling Workers Compensation claims was that developed by the Committee on Conservation of Hearing and Equilibrium of the American Academy of Ophthalmology and Otolaryngology (AAOO) and endorsed by the American Medical Association. The three pure-tone frequencies of 500, 1000, and 2000 Hz are averaged; for these frequencies a low fence of 25 dB is subtracted because no impairment is assumed to exist in the ability to hear everyday speech under favorable conditions until the average hearing level exceeds 25 dB (a concept increasingly questioned by some workers). The 25-dB fence includes the average presbycusis factor for persons up to the age of 65. After 25 dB is subtracted, the remainder is multiplied by 1.5 percent, the high fence of 93 dB at which the impairment for hearing ordinary speech is considered total, to obtain the monaural percent hearing impairment. To obtain the binaural hearing impairment, the monaural percent hearing impairment in the better ear is multiplied by 5, the monaural percent hearing impairment of the poorer ear is added once, and the total is divided by 6. In 1979, the American Academy of Otolaryngology–Head and Neck Surgery (formerly the AAOO) and the American Council of Otolaryngology modified their formula to include the hearing level at 3000 Hz in addition to the level at 500, 1000, and 2000 Hz. This altered procedure, which parallels changes adopted in several states to include higher frequencies in the formulas used, will make more employees eligible for benefits, and the benefits awarded will be significantly higher than was the case when the previous AAOO formula was used. Compensation awards are generally determined by multiplying the maximum compensation award for occupational hearing loss (weekly compensation benefit multiplied by the scheduled number of weeks) by the percent hearing handicap. *See* PRESBYCUSIS.

Bibliography

Background for Loss of Hearing Claims, Alliance of American Insurers, Loss Control Department, Chicago, 1982.

Cudworth, A. L.: "Hearing Loss: Legal Liability," in C. Harris (ed.), *Handbook of Noise Control*, 2d ed., chap. 13, McGraw-Hill, New York, 1979.

Davis, H.: "Hearing Handicap, Standards for Hearing, and Medicolegal Rules," in *Hearing and Deafness*, 4th ed., chap. 9, Holt, Rinehart and Winston, New York, 1978.

Fox, M. S., and J. H. Bunn, Jr.: "Worker's Compensation Aspects of Noise-Induced Hearing Loss," *Otolaryngol. Clinics of North America*, 12:705–724, 1979.

Ginnold, R. E.: *Occupational Hearing Loss: Workers Compensation Under State and Federal Programs*, prepared for U.S. Environmental Protection Agency, Office of Noise Abatement and Control, Washington, D.C., 1977.

Miller, M. H., and J. D. Harris: "Hearing Testing in Industry," in *Handbook of Noise Control*, 2d ed., chap. 10, McGraw-Hill, New York, 1979.

———— and C. A. Silverman: "Audiometric and Audiologic Aspects of Occupational Hearing Conservation Programs," in *Occupational Hearing Conservation*, chap. 8, Prentice-Hall, Englewood Cliffs, New Jersey, 1984.

Teplitzky, A. M.: "Noise Abatement: Historical and Legislative Background," in M. H. Miller and C. A. Silverman (eds.), *Occupational Hearing Conservation*, chap. 1, Prentice-Hall, Englewood Cliffs, New Jersey, 1984.

Maurice H. Miller

Noise Control Principles

Exposure to noise may have several adverse consequences upon humans. Noise may interfere with sleep, it may affect a person's ability to understand what someone is saying, it may cause general aggravation and annoyance, and it may permanently damage the hearing mechanism. Noise is referred to as unwanted sound for these reasons. This section describes principles and approaches for controlling noise.

The first consideration is how sound is produced and transmitted. The process may be thought of in the following sequence: sound source—transmission medium—receiver. The sound source, or the generator of sound, must be set into vibration. It transfers the vibrations to the transmission medium, usually air. The vibrations are propagated through the transmission medium as a sound wave and eventually arrive at the receiver, which in this context is the ears of a listener. Thus, when one hears the sound of a lawnmower, for example, the mower engine and other vibrating parts are the sound source, air is the transmission medium, and the hearing mechanism is the receiver. *See* ACOUSTICS.

Before considering specific noise control approaches, appropriate physical measurement of the noise must be made to determine if there is indeed a need for noise control. The physical characteristics of noise that are most important in dictating the need for control are the intensity of the noise and the duration of exposure to it. Greater noise intensity and longer exposure duration indicate a greater need for noise control. Three noise control approaches are outlined below.

MODIFY THE SOUND SOURCE

By modifying the sound source the noise intensity or duration is reduced. An example for reducing noise intensity might involve an engineering redesign of a noisy machine so that it has fewer vibrating parts. Another example involves changing a noisy production process such as riveting to a less noisy welding process. Control of noise at the source so that the duration is reduced may merely involve turning off a noisy machine during times when its operation is not necessary.

ALTER THE TRANSMISSION PATH

Another noise control approach involves alteration of the sound-transmission path so that the intensity of the noise arriving at the person's ears is reduced. This approach may take many forms. First, the distance between the noise source and the person may be increased. A noisy machine may be moved farther from a group of workers, or the workers may be moved farther from the machine. This approach is more effective in outdoor environments or in large rooms where sound reflections from the walls, floor, and ceiling do not affect the sound intensity. Second, use of sound-absorbent material on walls, ceiling, and floor of a room may reduce the intensity of noise that arrives at a person's ears. Noise sources located in rooms with hard surfaces generally are more intense because the sound is reflected from the surfaces. Thus, the reflected sound arriving at a person's ears adds to the direct sound from the source, resulting in a greater intensity. Treatment of the walls and ceiling with acoustic tile, for example, reduces the amount of sound and therefore the intensity of sound arriving at the person's ears. Finally, the sound-transmission path to a person may be altered by incorporating sound-reducing enclosures or barriers between the sound source and the person. A sound-reducing enclosure may be placed around a noisy machine, or the enclosure may be placed around the person. If total enclosures are not practical, partial sound-reducing barriers may be installed between the noise source and the person. Enclosures and barriers result in less intense sound arriving at the person's ears.

A special application of alteration in the sound-transmission path involves the use of personal hearing protectors to control noise. These devices, which are worn by an individual and may fit over or in the ears, are designed to reduce the intensity of noise that arrives at the person's eardrum. Various types of hearing protectors are available, and each has advantages and disadvantages. The major types are described below and a few advantages and disadvantages noted for each.

Earmuffs consist of two domes that fit over the ears and seal against the side of the head with a soft cushion. The muffs typically are connected by a headband that holds them in place. Earmuffs have the advantage of good sound reduction and consistency of reduction each time they are worn. They have the disadvantage of being somewhat uncomfortable when worn for long periods.

Earplugs are devices designed to fit into a person's ear canal. They are available in various types: moldable, premolded, and custom-molded. Moldable earplugs are made of pliable material that conforms to the shape of a person's ear canal. Most moldable plugs are disposable and are composed of materials that are effective in reducing sound; some have the appearance of cotton or foam rubber. Premolded earplugs have a more stable shape than the moldable variety and are made of soft material such as silicone rubber and plastic. They are designed to fit snugly into the ear canal and are available in several sizes to accommodate small and large ears. Custom-molded earplugs are designed to fit an individual's ears and require that an impression be made of the ear canal. Custom-molded earplugs are only effective for that specific person.

Earplugs are more comfortable to wear than earmuffs, and except for custom-molded plugs, they are less expensive than earmuffs. The major disadvantage of most earplugs is that if they are improperly fitted and inserted into the ear canal, a sound leak may result, thereby reducing their effectiveness.

The sound-reduction capability (attenuation) of personal hearing protectors is determined according to test procedures specified by the American National Standards Institute. A useful index for judging the effectiveness of hearing protectors is the Noise Reduction Rating (NRR) developed by the Environmental Protection Agency. Most hearing-protector manufacturers provide the NRR for their devices. The NRR is expressed in decibels and, for most hearing protectors, ranges from 15 to 30 dB. The larger the NRR, the more effective the protector. Thus, for persons exposed to intense noises, a hearing protector with an NRR between 28 and 30 dB should be chosen.

REDUCE EXPOSURE TIME

A final noise control approach involves a reduction of an individual's exposure time to noise. This may be accomplished by scheduling an employee in and out of a noisy workplace throughout the day so that daily noise exposure does not exceed permissible noise-exposure standards in the federal Occupational Safety and Health Act. In an occupational work environment, this approach is often called an administrative control of noise.

Bibliography

Berendt, R. D., E. L. R. Corliss, and M. S. Ojalvo: *Quieting: A Practical Guide to Noise Control*, National Bureau of Standards, U.S. Department of Commerce, 1976.

Botsford, J. H.: "Ear Protectors: Their Characteristics and Uses," *Sound and Vibration*, 6:24–34, 1972.

Burns, W.: *Noise and Man*, Lippincott, Philadelphia, 1973.

Edwards, R. G., et al., "Effectiveness of Earplugs as Worn in the Workplace," *Sound and Vibration*, 12:12–23, 1978.

Lipscomb, D. M. (ed.): *Noise and Audiology*, University Park Press, Baltimore, 1978.

Miller, M. H., and C. A. Silverman (eds.): *Occupational Hearing Conservation*, Prentice-Hall, Englewood Cliffs, New Jersey, 1984.

"Personal Ear Protection," in *Council for Accreditation in Occupational Hearing Conservation manual*, chap. 10, Fischler's Printing, Cherry Hill, New Jersey, 1978.

Peterson, A. P. G., and E. E. Gross, Jr.: *Handbook of Noise Measurement*, General Radio Co., Concord, Massachusetts, 1972.

Raymond S. Karlovich

Noise Control Regulations

In the United States, federal efforts to control noise by legislative means began in 1968 when the Congress enacted the first federal noise-related law, an amendment to the Federal Aviation Act. Prior to that time, the only noise control legislation was an inconsistent scattering of local and state ordinances which largely dealt with the "nuisance" aspect of certain noises. Once federal legislation was initiated, three additional laws followed in rapid succession.

OCCUPATIONAL HEARING CONSERVATION

In 1969, hearing-conservation regulations for industrial workers were contained in a revision of the Walsh-Healy Act, but the regulations were limited in scope. Authority extended only to those businesses engaged in trade with the federal government. At the time, it was unusual to include safety directions for the workplace, but inclusion of the hearing-conservation section had a dramatic impact on industrial hearing-conservation activities. The noise regulations in the Walsh-Healy Act caused a flurry of activity and numerous expressions of concern. For the first time, industry was being told that effective hearing-conservation programs would be required. At the time of its passage, the Walsh-Healy regulations affected only the approximately 70,000 plants involved in products and services that were part of federal contracts.

As the safety movement continued, the omnibus Williams Steiger Occupational Health and Safety Act of 1970 (OSHA) became law. This comprehensive statute incorporated a multitude of safety regulations that heretofore were scattered throughout several governmental agencies and state enforcement bureaus. In the main, there were no new regulations in this legislation, since the bulk of guidelines for such things as handling toxic materials, control of dust and fumes, and use of protective guards on equipment were in practice throughout industry. A significant exception was the noise portion of OSHA, Section 1910.95. The authors of OSHA included the noise control and hearing-conservation section of the 1969 Walsh-Healy Act word for word, thus extending hearing-conservation regulations to all workers in all industries. The section was limited in detail, leading to a decade of guideline development during which relatively little was accomplished in industrial hearing-conservation practices compared to later progress once the guidelines were written into law on March 8, 1983. The essential contents of the noise control and hearing-conservation portion of OSHA in the order of priority can be summarized as three key words signifying important concepts: qualify, abate, and protect. A brief discussion of these concepts follows.

Industries were required to define, or qualify, those areas in plants in which time-weighted noise exposure to workers exceeded an equivalent of 90 dBA for an eight-hour workday. This was established using a 5-dB time-intensity trading relation. Therefore, if 90 dBA exposure is allowed for eight hours, a 95-dBA sound can be allowed no more than 4 hours. Each time noise level increases 5 dBA, the allowable time of exposure is halved.

When excessive noise exposure conditions are discovered, it is incumbent on the employer to reduce, or abate, employee exposure by lowering noise levels if technically and economically feasible.

When noise exposure conditions are in excess of those prescribed by OSHA and noise abatement is not sufficient, workers are to receive a two-part protective program: (1) monitoring audiometry on an annual basis is to be instituted to identify workers who experience progressive hearing impairment; and (2) hearing protective devices are recommended to reduce exposure conditions at the ear until noise control procedures adequately reduce worker noise exposure.

ENVIRONMENTAL NOISE CONTROL

The final major noise-related federal activity was enacted by the Congress as the Noise Control Act of 1972. It charged the United States Environmental Protection Agency (EPA) with oversight of all federal noise regulatory action with two exceptions: the Department of Labor retained control over enforcement of OSHA, and the Federal Aviation Agency (FAA) in the Department of Transportation still held authority over aircraft noise regulatory action.

As a small part of the Clean Air Act of 1968, the EPA had been mandated to initiate an Office of Noise Abatement and Control (ONAC). With the Noise Control Act, this small group of persons was expanded into a sizable force of professionals assembled to carry out the act's provisions. Essentially, ONAC was to develop information systems, evaluative procedures, product noise output regulations, community-environmental noise control procedures, and to offer technical assistance to communities and other jurisdictions. Further, ONAC was to provide input for all noise control activities of other governmental branches. For example, ONAC took an active role in the early discussions that ultimately led to the 1983 noise control and hearing-conservation guidelines for OSHA, and they commented on numerous aircraft noise control proposals of the FAA.

The contributions of ONAC are impressive. An extensive review of pertinent literature on noise and its effects led to publication of two key documents: the *Criteria Document* outlined the state of knowledge on deleterious effects of noise exposure, and the *Levels Document* set forth those levels of sound determined to be safe to the ears and insufficient to interfere with speech communication.

ONAC also specified a hierarchy of noisy products, identifying those which should be considered first for design and manufacturing specifications. Labeling of noisy products was initiated, and some products are labeled now according to the guidelines that ONAC established. Of vital interest to community noise concerns was the preparation of a Model Community Noise Ordinance (EPA 550/9-76-003). The office also established the ECHO (Each Community Helping Others) program wherein cities were encouraged to work together to enact community noise codes or to update and revise existing codes.

In 1980, funding for ONAC was discontinued, ending its brief but significant existence. Some of the activities formerly undertaken by ONAC are being carried on by other agencies or local jurisdictions, but the demise of this office ended the only centralized federal noise control operation.

LOCAL NOISE REGULATIONS

Most cities have noise regulations. Some regulations have been updated in recent years, incorporating state-of-the-art technology. Most, however, still rely on subjective nuisance provisions that are difficult to enforce. A major shortcoming in many local noise codes is the lack of adequate guidance for evaluation of regulated noise sources. Another common problem is that mandated allowable noise levels are so unrealistic as to be unenforceable. Acceptable levels are occasionally set so low that they are unattainable, or levels are excessively high, undermining purpose. The ONAC Model Community Noise Code can be of valuable assistance in writing or updating local noise regulations.

David M. Lipscomb

AUDITORY DISORDERS, REMEDIATION OF

This article addresses, for the most part, treatment of hearing loss. The difference between hearing loss and deafness is considerable. While remarkable progress has been made in the management of some types of hearing loss, restoration from deafness is not yet achievable.

In recent times, most of the advances in the treatment of hearing loss have been surgical rather than medical. If a hearing problem is due entirely or partly to a failure of sound to reach the inner ear, there is a good chance that it can be fixed, at least partially. In medical terms such losses are called conductive hearing losses because of the interference with the sound energy as it is conducted through the outer and middle ear on its way to the inner ear. The most common interference with sound conduction, and the easiest to fix, is wax in the ear canal. The most difficult to fix is an interruption of transmission created by the loss or erosion of a middle-ear bone caused by chronic infection. In between are the repair of eardrum perforations and replacement of the stapes bone fixed in place by otosclerosis. The success rate for the vast majority of these operations is good, but there are disappointments and even small risks of increased hearing loss.

The nonsurgical or medical management of hearing loss is of considerably broader scope, be-

ginning with genetic counseling even before conception of a child if there is a history of childhood hearing loss in potential blood relatives. During pregnancy, certain drugs (notably some antibiotics) can cause hearing loss in the fetus. Deafness or severe hearing loss is relatively rare in infants and babies, occurring about twice for every 1000 births. Because it is rare, pediatricians often dismiss the possibility when parents (or, more often, grandparents) suspect that there might be a hearing problem in a young body. Quite often, and particularly when deafness is not total, delay in the development of speech beyond one year is the first sign. To encourage identification of potentially handicapping hearing loses, many hospital nurseries have hearing-screening programs for early detection, and a few have programs for habilitation. *See* HEARING LOSS, PREVENTION OF: Screening.

In early childhood (six years and younger) mild degrees of hearing loss are common, approaching perhaps 15 percent of all children in cold climates. Typically, these losses are caused by collection of fluid in the middle ear. Most are painless and quite often go unrecognized, resolving spontaneously in a few weeks. Others do not, and treatment of these may be more important than some physicians believe. There is at least some statistical evidence that these mild hearing losses over many months may cause permanent decrements in reading ability and in some hearing-related intelligence-test achievement.

The prevention of noise-induced hearing loss can become a problem in adolescence, remaining so throughout the individual's life. A mild loss through sound damage quite often goes unrecognized until the later years when additional losses, perhaps secondary to aging, compound the hearing loss. In adults (and sometimes in children, too) there are a variety of other causes for hearing loss. Few are truly correctable, or even arrested, by medical management. The chances are only about 50/50 for establishing a cause even after considerable detective work. Ménière's disease leads this list. Autoimmune disorders, toxic drugs, neurosyphilis, inner-ear membrane ruptures, viral infections, an occasional tumor, late-onset genetic hearing loss, and the rare patient faking a hearing loss for financial gain appear from time to time. Patients complaining of ear noises (tinnitus), with or without significant hearing losses, are an enigma and in constant search of a solution. *See* HEARING LOSS; TINNITUS.

Hearing loss associated with aging (presbycusis) often has its special problems. Hearing aids do not cure all such problems but they usually help. Occasionally a person in later life will develop a conductive hearing loss, and these are just as reparable as earlier on. The automatic assumption that a hearing loss is the result of irreparable inner-ear damage related to aging is not wise. Only a high-quality audiometric test can reveal the difference. *See* PRESBYCUSIS.

F. Blair Simmons

Medical Treatment

Although many auditory disorders are due to degenerative or traumatic changes of the inner ear for which no known medical treatment exists, a number of auditory disorders are helped by medical therapy. The auditory disorders that are considered medically treatable involve both the middle ear (acute otitis media and middle-ear effusions) and the inner ear (syphilis, autoimmune hearing loss, sudden hearing loss, otosclerosis, Ménière's disease, and hearing loss from certain drugs). Even though medical treatment is recommended for these disorders, convincing proof of effectiveness is lacking for some of the therapeutic measures.

MIDDLE EAR

Acute Otitis Media This is the middle-ear infection that is common in childhood but also affects adults. Acute otitis media frequently follows an upper respiratory infection and results in ear pain and decreased hearing. Untreated, it may cause perforation of the eardrum or spread to the mastoid bone and beyond. Medical therapy in the form of antibiotics is effective in reversing the disease process and eliminating the pain and hearing loss. Since the advent of antibiotics, there has been a dramatic decrease in hearing losses and other complications as sequelae to or aftermaths of acute otitis media. Generally, one of the pencillin-derived antibiotics is administered, but other effective antibiotics are available for individuals allergic to penicillin. A one- to two-week course of the antibiotic usually is sufficient to clear the infection, but it may take several weeks before hearing returns to normal. Decongestant medications are also sometimes prescribed for acute otitis media. They may relieve some of the symptoms of the accompanying upper respiratory infection, but there is no proof that they aid in the resolution of the ear infection.

Middle-Ear Effusions Collections of fluid (effusions) in the middle ear are the most common cause of hearing loss in childhood, and they sometimes occur in adults with respiratory infections and other disorders that interfere with Eustachian tube function. Most children who are prone to chronic or recurrent middle-ear effusions outgrow the problem when they are between six and eight years of age. Until then, however, the effusions can cause repeated bouts of acute otitis media and can produce a hearing loss that is especially harmful during important developmental years. Surgical drainage of the fluid by making an incision through the eardrum (myringotomy), followed by insertion of a small ventilating tube through the eardrum, is an effective means of providing long-term relief

from the fluid collection. In order to avoid the necessity for this frequently performed operation, several types of medical treatment have been advocated. Allergic management, decongestant medications, and long-term antibiotic therapy have been recommended.

Scientific studies that support the effectiveness of allergic management or decongestive therapy are lacking, and good results from prolonged treatment using these methods probably are due to the natural inclination for effusions to clear. Unfortunately, the hearing loss that exists while the effusion is present may cause developmental problems that make it risky to await slow resolution of the disease.

Long-term (six to eight weeks or more) antibiotic therapy may be effective in clearing some cases of middle-ear effusion in children. Preliminary studies strongly suggest that this may be an effective treatment, but long-term studies on large numbers of children are needed before final conclusions can be drawn.

INNER EAR

Syphilis An inner-ear type of hearing loss may develop from a congenital syphilis infection or from one acquired later in life. Children often have severe hearing losses that affect both ears symmetrically, while adults frequently develop the hearing loss gradually, and the loss may fluctuate in intensity and affect one ear more than the other. Diagnosis of hearing loss from syphilis depends on blood tests that identify the patient as having been infected by syphilis-causing bacteria.

Medical treatment consists of penicillin and a steroid medication given over a period of months. If hearing improves on these medications, the steroids may be continued indefinitely to prevent relapses of hearing loss. Some syphilitic hearing losses improve dramatically on medication; others fail to respond in spite of prolonged treatment.

Autoimmune Hearing Loss This entity was described only recently as an uncommon but reversible type of inner-ear hearing loss. The hearing loss occurs usually in young and middle-aged adults and is bilateral, asymmetric, and rapidly progressive over weeks or months. An inflammatory response in the inner ear is suspected and is thought to be due to the body's attempt to reject its own tissue. Diagnosis is made by recognizing the unusual manifestations of this hearing loss and by a blood test available in only a few research laboratories. Medical therapy consists of prolonged (months to years) administration of a steroid drug and a powerful drug used in cancer chemotherapy.

Sudden Hearing Loss Hearing loss can develop quite suddenly (minutes to hours) in one ear, and this devastating but uncommon occurrence affects persons of all ages. The cause of the hearing loss is not known, but there is some evidence that it results from a viral inner-ear infection. Blockage or spasm of an inner-ear blood vessel also has been suspected, but there is little evidence to support this.

Approximately two-thirds of patients with sudden hearing loss recover without treatment. A multitude of types of drugs have been used to treat patients with sudden hearing loss to improve the natural recovery rate. Blood vessel–dilating drugs, histamine, antihistamines, diuretics, carbon dioxide inhalations, and steroid medications are just a few of the many treatments that have been proposed in the management of sudden hearing loss. Because of the high rate of spontaneous recovery and the lack of scientific studies on the effectiveness of drug therapy on sufficient numbers of patients, medical management of sudden hearing loss remains controversial. Although recent reports suggest that steroid medications or carbon dioxide inhalations may be beneficial, many physicians still do not find enough convincing evidence of drug therapy effectiveness to warrant medicating their patients who have sudden hearing loss.

Otosclerosis The abnormal bone of otosclerosis causes fixation of the stapes bone of the middle ear and interferes with sound conduction into the inner ear. Additionally, patients with otosclerosis often have an accompanying inner-ear type of hearing loss. Surgery (stapedectomy) is successful in restoring the sound-conducting mechanisms of the middle ear, and medical therapy has been proposed to treat the inner-ear hearing loss of otosclerosis.

The combination of sodium fluoride, calcium, and vitamin D has been proposed to stabilize the hearing loss from otosclerosis. This treatment must be given for years and can cause skeletal changes (fluorosis) in some patients. Other complications of this regimen are stomach upset, skin rash, kidney stones, and arthritis. There have been clinical reports suggesting that this medical therapy may be effective in stabilizing the hearing loss of otosclerosis. However, the scientific, controlled studies necessary to convince the Food and Drug Administration (FDA) of fluoride efficacy in otosclerosis are lacking, and fluoride has not been granted FDA approval for treatment of otosclerosis. Nevertheless, some physicians prescribe fluoride (as a dietary supplement) for otosclerosis, and this treatment remains controversial. It should not be given to pregnant women.

Ménière's Disease The cause of the episodic vertigo, progressive hearing loss, and tinnitus (ear noises) of Ménière's disease is unknown. Ménière's disease has been treated with many different types of drugs. Because the natural progress of this disease is so episodic and unpredictable, it is difficult

to assess the effectiveness of these drugs. No drug has been found by controlled studies to be effective in halting the episodes of vertigo or in arresting the progressive hearing loss of Ménière's disease. Drugs that suppress the inner-ear balance mechanisms are useful to control or shorten dizzy spells. Although evidence suggests that diuretic medications may reduce the frequency of dizzy spells, no medication has been proved effective in controlling the hearing loss from Ménière's disease.

Aspirin Various drugs are toxic to the ear and cause a permanent hearing loss by killing the delicate sensory tissues of the inner ear. Fortunately, most of these toxic drugs are not used commonly and are reserved for very ill patients. The inner-ear damage that they may cause is not reversible when the drug is stopped, nor is it treatable.

Aspirin is different in that the inner-ear hearing loss it causes when given in large doses is reversible. In general, 12 or more tablets per day must be taken before hearing loss develops, but individual sensitivity to the drug is variable. Tinnitus usually accompanies the hearing loss from aspirin. Medical treatment consists of discontinuing the aspirin and substituting a nonaspirin-containing drug for the condition being treated. Hearing recovers rapidly over a few days after aspirin ingestion is discontinued. Quinine-containing drugs may cause a similar, reversible hearing loss.

Bibliography

Lim, D. (ed): "Recent Advance in Otitis Media with Effusion," *Annals of Otology, Rhinology and Laryngology*, suppl. 69, vol. 89, May–June 1980.

McCabe, B. F.: "Autoimmune Sensorineural Hearing Loss," *Annals of Otology, Rhinology and Laryngology*, vol. 88, March–April 1979.

Mattox, D. E., and F. B. Simmons: "Natural History of Sudden Sensorineural Hearing Loss," *Annals of Otology, Rhinology and Laryngology*, vol. 86, July–August 1977.

Torok, N.: "Old and New In Ménière's Disease," *Laryngoscope*, vol. 87, November 1977.

Zoller, M., W. R. Wilson, and J. B. Nadol: "Treatment of Syphilitic Hearing Loss," *Annals of Otology, Rhinology and Laryngology*, vol. 88, March–April 1979.

Edward L. Applebaum

Surgical Treatment

Theoretically, once the diagnosis of a conductive-type hearing loss has been made, the problem can be corrected surgically. In practice, it is important to determine the exact abnormality needing correction so that the patient can be advised about the advantages and disadvantages (including risks) of surgical correction. These can then be compared with results expected from an aid.

One of the most challenging problems is the undeveloped ear canal. After the integrity of the inner ear has been established by audiometric testing and the course of the facial nerve, the development of the middle and inner ears, and the structure of the external auditory canal and mastoid process have been determined radiographically, the surgeon will have a reasonable idea of what can be accomplished surgically. It may be desirable to create an ear canal even if normal hearing cannot be achieved, for this will allow the patient to wear an air-conduction hearing aid rather than a bone-conduction aid. In addition to an ear canal, one needs a membrane separating the ear canal from the middle ear. This may be constructed of fascia (sheets of fibrous tissues that envelop muscle and other parts of the body), vein, or perichondrium, (connective tissue around the cartilage), or from a tympanic membrane or eardrum transplanted from a cadaver and available in the operating room in a freeze-dried state. The transplanted eardrum usually has a malleus (hammer bone of the middle ear) attached. Another alternative is to use the patient's own malleus, if present, or use a sound transmission mechanism that does not require a malleus.

Similar materials may be used to repair perforations of the tympanic membrane from whatever cause. In addition, small perforations may be closed with sclera obtained from an eye bank or with fat. Either fixation or disarticulation of parts of the ossicular chain interferes with hearing. Fixation of the head of the malleus can be bypassed by removing the head and interposing it between the handle of the malleus and the head of the stapes. At other times, a prosthesis is placed from the stapes to the eardrum. The prosthesis is usually covered with cartilage or perichondrium to decrease the chance that it will be extruded or pushed out. The most common site of disarticulation is between the stapes head and the incus. It is repaired as mentioned above with natural or plastic material from the stapes head to the malleus handle or tympanic membrane.

If the ossicular chain is working and the stapes is fixed, the stapes can be removed (stapedectomy), the oval window sealed with tissue, and a prosthesis of wire or plastic attached to the incus to transmit sound to the oval window. An alternative approach is to make a small hole in the stapes footplate (stapedotomy) and to attach a prosthesis to the incus that protrudes just through the footplate hole into the vestibule.

The most difficult situation to correct is stapes fixation with no lateral ossicular chain for attachment of a prosthesis. In theory, the problem can be solved by using a homograft tympanic membrane with a malleus attached and then, at a second stage, removing the stapes and attaching a prosthesis to the malleus. In practice, long-term successful results for this situation are unusual.

Fenestration surgery is now being reconsidered for this problem.

In considering whether or not to proceed with surgery, one needs to know the hearing status of both ears, the result that can be reasonably anticipated from surgery, and the chances that the hearing may worsen as a result of surgery.

Whereas surgery is an option for many patients with conductive hearing loss, patients with sensory-neural hearing loss rarely are candidates for surgical procedures. An acoustic tumor usually manifests itself by producing a progressive unilateral sensory-neural hearing loss. The tumor is benign, but is serious because of its location. Because the tumor usually originates on the vestibular portion of the auditory nerve rather than on the cochlear portion, it is theoretically possible to save the hearing. Unfortunately tumor size, tumor or operative interference with the cochlear blood supply, or the route selected for tumor removal often destroys whatever hearing is still present in the ear at the time the tumor is diagnosed. Although acoustic tumors can be removed via the middle cranial fossa if they are small, most teams of neurotologists and neurosurgeons choose other approaches.

The cochlear implant is now being placed in patients who lost their hearing after they developed speech and who are not helped by a combination of amplification with a hearing aid and speech reading. On an experimental basis, some children who lost their hearing before they developed speech are being implanted. The implant consists of a part that is implanted in the temporal bone and a part that is external to the skin. The implanted part consists of one or more electrodes that are placed into the middle ear or via the round window into the inner ear. These electrodes emanate from an induction coil embedded in the temporal bone deep to the skin. The external device is positioned with skin and subcutaneous tissue separating it from the buried coil. Often magnets are used to keep the external and internal coils lined up. A number of different strategies are used to code the auditory signal and transmit it from the external to the implanted device, from where it is transmitted via one or more electrodes to surviving portions of the inner ear or the auditory nerve. The resulting transmission coupled with speech reading facilitates communication (both speech reception and voice modulation). The device does not usually allow recognition of open set words without speech reading.

One side benefit of the cochlear implant has been its effectiveness in suppressing tinnitus in some patients. Only rarely has it been used exclusively for this purpose. Other procedures for intractable tinnitus depend upon specific problems amenable to surgery. Many kinds of conductive hearing loss are associated with tinnitus. Appropriate surgical correction of the problem relieves the tinnitus in about half of these patients. The specific problems causing surgically correctable tinnitus without conductive hearing loss include tensor tympani spasm (the tensor may be cut), glomus tympanicum (this may be removed), and vascular causes (small vessels may be ligated, and arteriosclerotic plaques in the carotid may be removed). Additionally, some of the surgical procedures used in the treatment of Ménière's disease (destructive labyrinthectomy and saccus shunts) may improve or eliminate tinnitus.

Surgery to alleviate sensorineural hearing loss has been attempted, but it has not been successful; many creative approaches have been used.

Bibliography

English, Gerald M.: *Otolaryngology*, Harper and Row, New York, 1976.

Goodhill, Victor: *Ear Diseases, Deafness, and Dizziness*, Harper and Row, New York, 1979.

Paparella, Michael M., and Donald A. Shumrick: *Otolaryngology*, W. B. Saunders, Philadelphia, 1980.

Schuknecht, Harold F.: *Otosclerosis*, Little, Brown, Boston, 1962.

Shambaugh, George E., and Michael E. Glasscock: *Surgery of the Ear*, W. B. Saunders, Philadelphia, 1980.

James A. Donaldson

MASTOIDECTOMY

A mastoidectomy is an operation to remove the mastoid portion of the temporal bone. Mastoidectomy is usually performed for chronic otitis media and cholesteatoma. It may be used in the repair of facial nerve paralysis. Because of the success of antibiotic treatment, it is performed less frequently than previously in acute otitis media and acute mastoiditis.

The approach to the operations may be (1) permeatal (through the ear canal as in atticoantrostomy) without an external skin incision, (2) endaural (through the ear), or (3) postauricular (behind the ear). Most operations are performed from behind the ear, usually under general anesthesia, but they may also be performed under local anesthesia. The bone removal is facilitated by the use of high-speed drills, electrically driven or pneumatic, and by the use of the binocular operating microscope. Continuous lavage, or washing, and suction are used to keep the operating field clear of bone dust and prevent undue heating of tissues.

Several types of mastoidectomy are described below: antrotomy, cortical, radical, modified radical, and combined approach.

Antrotomy In infants where the mastoid air cells and mastoid process have not yet developed, the operation has been called antrotomy because the largest mastoid cell or antrum is always present from birth. During gastrointestinal epidemics, which often led to mastoiditis in the affected person, the infected bone was cleared and drained; and many believed the operations to be life-saving. This operation was performed frequently in the 1930s and 1940s but has now become almost obsolete.

Cortical In cortical mastoidectomy, also termed simple or Swartze mastoidectomy, all cells of the mastoid process are removed, making one cavity. The middle-ear cavity is not entered. Swartze in 1873 described the technique and indications for this operation in resistant otitis media, although Wilde in 1853 described an incision behind the ear for drainage in fluctuant mastoiditis. It is important to open and clean all of the cells as failure to do so may lead to a poor result. Superiorly, the dura or membranous covering of the brain is exposed; the venous lateral sinus is exposed posteriorly and the incus anteriorly.

Indications for cortical mastoidectomy are acute mastoiditis, profusely draining ear, recurrent otitis media, and masked mastoiditis. Possible complications of the surgery are facial nerve injury, dislocation of incus with resulting hearing loss, and penetration of lateral venous sinus or dura.

Radical This operation leads to a conversion of the mastoid and middle ear into a single disease-free cavity, easily accessible and communicating freely with the external ear opening. The tympanic membrane, the three ear ossicles, and the posterior wall of the external canal all are removed together with the diseased tissue and mastoid. Radical mastoidectomy has been recommended for cholesteatoma, which is controversial, and for complicated otitis media to cure the suppuration or discharge and to render the ear safe. The operation allows good visualization and complete removal of cholesteatoma or of other diseased tissues. The disease is exteriorized, and the ear is rendered safe. Recurrence may be visualized for convenient treatment. The cavity may require frequent cleaning and may continue to discharge. Entrance of water into the ear may be troublesome and should be avoided. There is a justifiable reluctance to perform this surgery in every case of cholesteatoma.

A possible complication of the procedure is facial nerve paralysis, for the nerve is at risk both in the middle ear and mastoid. Some loss of hearing is inevitable. A 50-decibel conductive loss can be predicted because of removal of middle-ear ossicles. There is also a possibility of sensory-neural hearing loss which can even be complete if the footplate of the stapes is displaced. Some of the conductive hearing loss may be offset by an immediate or delayed reconstructive operation (tympanoplasty).

Modified Radical In this procedure, also termed Bondy operation, the bony wall between the anterior antrum and attic is removed to allow withdrawal of disease which is confined to this area, while most of the middle-ear contents are preserved. Classically, the operation for removal of disease is performed from behind forward, from mastoid to attic, but it may be performed in a retrograde fashion, from attic to antrum (atticoantrostomy). The operation is recommended for cholesteatoma confined to attic and mastoid and not involving the middle ear. Complications similar to those attendant to radical mastoidectomy can occur. In addition, the desire to conserve functional tissue may allow some diseased tissue to remain with consequent recurrence of the disease.

Combined Approach In this method, also termed intact canal wall mastoidectomy or canal UP mastoidectomy, the mastoid cavity and the middle ear are both cleared of cholesteatoma disease while preserving the intervening posterior canal wall, usually as a preliminary to tympanoplasty. The procedure avoids leaving a mastoid cavity that requires cleaning. Also, it is easier to reconstruct a functioning middle-ear cavity than in the other procedures. Its disadvantage is that some of the cholesteatoma may be left behind and concealed from view; therefore, follow-up observation is mandatory. Some surgeons perform second-look operations routinely in one or two years; possible complications are injury to the facial nerve and even sensory-neural hearing loss. The early enthusiasm for this operation has been replaced by a sober reappraisal by some otologic surgeons.

TYMPANOPLASTY

Tympanoplasty is subdivided into types 1–5 according to the nature of the defect to be treated. As a rule, the larger the number, the greater the problem. Tympanoplasty involves reconstruction of the sound-conduction mechanism of the middle ear. While most operations in the past were performed for the eradication of disease, the trend since the 1950s has been a gradual stress on the surgical repair for the conductive hearing loss based on physiologic principles. An important prerequisite is that the cochlea and auditory nerve should have sufficient reserve to benefit from the improvement in conductive function. Tympanoplasty may be performed on an ear in which there is no active disease, or concurrently with the removal of disease, or subsequent to the removal of the disease.

Myringoplasty Myringoplasty, or type 1 tympanoplasty, means surgical repair of perforation of a tympanic membrane. Sometimes an attempt may be made to promote closure of a tympanic membrane perforation with a cauterizing agent such as silver nitrate. In most cases of long-standing perforation, surgical repair is necessary. The patient's motivation for the closure of a perforation is to

prevent recurring infections and to improve hearing. The perforation is closed with a graft, most frequently an autograft, that is, tissue taken from the patient's body. The commonest tissue used is temporalis fascia, a thin covering of connective tissue removed from the surface of the temporalis muscle, which is adjacent to the ear and may be included in the original ear incision. Alternative autograft material may be perichondrium, the outer thin covering of cartilage taken usually from the tragus. Vein is preferred less commonly. Skin, which was the original graft material, is seldom used today. Homograft materials removed from donors and placed in a special bank have the advantage that they can be stored ready for use. Homografts are being used more often today.

The two methods for laying the graft are known as overlay and underlay. In the overlay method, the graft is placed on the outer remnants of the eardrum, the recipient bed being first freshened and prepared by removing the outer tympanic membrane or epithelial layer of the drum and baring the adjacent skin of the external canal. The graft may be kept in position, by tethering it to the malleus, by external packing, or even by tissue adhesive. In the underlay method, the graft is placed under the drum and under the skin of the external canal. In the overlay, the graft is easier to lay and is better visualized. There is a danger, however, of squamous epithelium remaining under the graft, and the graft can become displaced. In underlays, the graft may retract and be displaced under the drum, especially in anterior perforations.

Ideally, tympanoplasty is performed when the ear has been dry for at least a number of months. Results may be predicted and generally are good. The middle-ear ossicles are inspected, and ossicular surgery may be performed simultaneously. The postoperative change in hearing may be anticipated by the preoperative temporary closure of the perforation with cigarette paper and performing threshold audiometry.

Ossiculoplasty Ossiculoplasty is surgical repair for the hearing loss caused by a defect in the mechanical transmission of sound by the middle-ear ossicles. The defects usually result from chronic otitis media or cholesteatoma, but may result from head trauma with temporal-bone fracture. Ossiculoplasty may be combined with myringoplasty or mastoid surgery.

There are many variables both as to the problem and solution. Frequently, the incus is partly destroyed and fails to make adequate contact with the head of the stapes. There is general agreement that, when possible, the remains of the incus should be removed, sculptured, and replaced to fill the defect between the malleus and the head of the stapes. Results are good. If the patient's incus can-the head of the stapes. There is general agreement that, when possible, the remains of the incus should be removed, sculptured, and replaced to fill the defect between the malleus and the head of the stapes. Results are good. If the patient's incus cannot be used, then a homograft incus or sculptured cortical bone may be used. When the malleus or stapes is diseased or missing, the problem is more complex and the solution less predictable. The gap may be bridged by human cartilage or bone, either autograft or homograft. Manufactured prostheses are used; these are solid or porous plastic materials or, more recently, ceramics. In general, the chronically discharging ear tends to extrude or push out these foreign materials, but improvements in materials and techniques may minimize this problem. The latest additions, ceramic prostheses, are easy to handle and appear to be well tolerated.

These prostheses are sometimes known as TORP's (total ossicular replacement prostheses) or PORP's (partial ossicular replacement prostheses). Homograft ossicles, from another person, with or without the entire tympanic membrane may be specially prepared and preserved in a bank ready for use. Total en bloc transplants are being used successfully and may be used also in the reconstruction of a radical mastoid cavity. The difficulty in removing the homograft, and the problems related to its storing, may partially account for a lack of popularity among many surgeons. Principles and techniques developed in otosclerosis surgery are also applied to the solving of problems connected with the immobile footplate in otitis media. In these cases, the inner ear is at risk.

Bibliography

Ballantyne, John, and John Groves: *Scott-Brown's Disease of the Ear, Nose & Throat*, 4th ed., Butterworths, 1980.

Paparella, M. M., and D. A. Shumrick: *Otolaryngology*, 2d ed., vol. 2: *The Ear*, W. B. Saunders, Philadelphia, 1980.

Shambaugh, G. E., and M. E. Glasscock: *Surgery of the Ear*, 3d ed., W. B. Saunders, Philadelphia, 1980.

I. Gay

AUDITORY NERVE TUMORS

Auditory nerve tumors usually cause hearing loss on the affected side and can result in other cranial nerve weaknesses. However, most tumors can be cured by surgical removal. Although several types of growths may be associated with the auditory nerve, the most common tumor found there is an acoustic neuroma, sometimes termed a neurinoma and schwannoma. This growth is benign (noncancerous) and arises on the VIIIth cranial nerve.

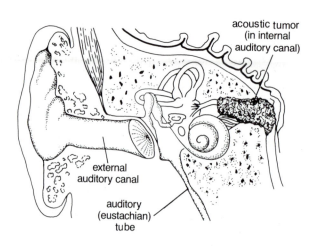

Medium acoustic tumor.

The VIIIth cranial nerve is really two separate nerves, one part associated with transmitting hearing messages, and the other with sending balance information to the brain from the inner ear. These parts are closely intertwined as they pass through the bony canal leading from the brain to the inner ear. This tiny connective opening, called the internal auditory canal, varies from 0.4 to 1.2 centimeters long, and it is there that acoustic neuromas usually begin to grow from the sheath surrounding the VIIIth nerve. The VIIth or facial nerve that serves facial movement, as well as important blood vessels, also passes through this internal auditory canal.

Characteristics The cause of acoustic neuroma is unknown, except for a small percentage of individuals in whom both sides are involved. This bilateral involvement may indicate a form of neurofibromatosis, a separate neurologic disorder in which there often is a hereditary factor.

Acoustic neuromas usually grow slowly, sometimes over a period of many years. They characteristically remain within their lining (encapsulated) and displace normal tissue very slowly, and the body accommodates a long time to this abnormal growth. An acoustic neuroma first distorts the VIIIth nerve, then presses on the adjacent VIIth nerve. As the tumor grows, it protrudes from the canal into the area of the brain (about behind the region of the mastoid bone) called the cerebellopontine angle. As it expands, it presses on the Vth cranial nerve, the one of facial sensation, and on other parts of the brain, causing more intense symptoms, and finally damages a portion needed to maintain life.

These tumors are found more commonly in women than men, and most removal surgery is performed between the ages of 30 and 60.

There is not a typical pattern of symptoms caused by a developing acoustic neuroma, thus making early diagnosis a challenge. However, persons with what seem to be inner-ear problems should be evaluated completely to eliminate acoustic neuroma as the cause of the symptoms.

Studies have shown that over 90 percent of those with tumors experience one-sided hearing impairment caused by nerve failure, often accompanied by ear noise or ringing. Some people also feel a fullness in that ear. The lessening of hearing capacity may be gradual or sudden. Other symptoms may include unsteadiness and balance problems, change in facial sensation, facial spasms, and headaches.

Auditory tests usually are given as a first step in detecting or ruling out an acoustic neuroma. These may be followed by other tests of balance and hearing, including a brainstem auditory evoked response (BAER) test and a computerized tomography (CAT) scan that may be done with materials that enhance radiologic contrast. *See* AUDIOMETRY: Evoked Potential.

Removal Procedures Surgical removal of these tumors is a complex and delicate procedure. In general, the smaller the tumor at time of surgery, the more satisfactory are the results. In the decades since the 1950s, microsurgical techniques have been pioneered and refined. Alternate cutting and tumor-reducing equipment such as the laser and the operating microscope, used by surgeons trained and experienced in this process, have made possible an extremely low mortality rate and minimal contact with nerves and tissue near the tumor.

The location and size of the tumor, and the surgeon's preference, will determine the approach to the tumor site. The commonly used approaches and the incision locations are translabyrinthine (just behind the ear), suboccipital or posterior fossa (base of the skull), or middle fossa (immediately above and in front of the ear). Often an ear surgeon (otologist) and a neurosurgeon work together as a team to remove an acoustic neuroma.

Postoperative Conditions Postoperatively, one to several days may be spent in intensive care. Immediate postoperative problems may include headache, decreased mental alertness due to development of a blood clot or obstruction of flow of cerebrospinal fluid, cerebrospinal fluid leak, and meningitis.

There may be incomplete removal of the tumor, either elected preoperatively by the patient and physician or decided by the surgeon during surgery. Incomplete removal reduces the risk of complications, but at a later date further surgery may be needed.

Postremoval problems may be caused by unavoidable damage to, or necessary sacrificing of, cranial nerves involved with the tumor. In small tumors (usually under 1.5 cm), it may be possible to save still present hearing. Monitoring of hearing function during surgery is a technique being perfected to assist in this preservation. However, in medium or large tumors the hearing usually has been partially or totally lost already, and cannot be restored. This means that the problems in locating the direction of sound, hearing a person speaking softly on the deaf side, and understanding speech over a high level of background noise will continue.

Ear noises usually remain the same as before surgery. In a few instances internally produced sounds begin after tumor removal.

Because the facial nerve, which controls muscles of facial expression, is in close contact with most acoustic neuromas, it usually is necessary for the surgeon to manipulate, and sometimes to remove, portions of this nerve. In some instances, even though the nerve is still anatomically intact after surgery, nerve damage or swelling may cause temporary— or in a small percentage of cases, permanent— facial paralysis. If facial control does not return after a time, a second operation may be performed to aid in toning or reanimating the sagging face.

Long-term eye discomfort and other eye problems affect at least half of those who have had an acoustic neuroma removed, particularly if the tumor was medium or large. These eye problems may be loss of eyelid function or altered tear production, weak eyelid blink, or double vision. Other discomforts may include taste disturbance and decreased or excessive salivation, difficulty in swallowing, throat and voice problems, balance problems, fatigue, or persistent headaches.

For some, adjustment to a new self after acoustic neuroma removal is challenging. In addition to the changes in hearing, there may be other impairments present. However, studies have shown little correlation between self-perception of disability and actual amount of physical incapacity.

Bibliography

Diagram Group: *The Brain: A User's Manual*, 1982.

Hart, R. G., D. P. Gardner, and J. Howieson: "Acoustic Tumors: Atypical Features and Recent Diagnostic Tests," *Neurology*, vol. 33, 1983.

House, W. F., and C. M. Luetje (eds.): *Acoustic Tumors*, vol. 1: *Diagnosis*, vol. 2: *Management*, 1979.

Ojemann, R. G.: "Microsurgical Suboccipital Approach to Cerebellopontine Angle Tumors," *Clinical Neurosurgery*, vol. 25, 1978.

Virginia D. Fickel

ATRESIA

Atresia (the absence or pathological closure of an anatomical opening) of the ear results from a congenital arrest in the development of the auricle, external-ear canal, or middle ear. The inner ear usually is not involved, because of its different embryologic origin. Generally, only one ear is affected, but bilateral malformations are occasional occurrences. Beside arrest in development during early fetal life, defects of the auricle could be induced by a variety of factors like mechanical trauma, burns, tumors, infections, and hematoma.

Surgical management of ear atresia may have two purposes: (1) improvement of the patient's appearance by correcting the deformed auricle; and (2) restoration of hearing by creating a new, open passage for airborne sounds to reach the inner ear. If the inner ear is also involved in a pathologic process, reconstructive surgery of the middle or outer ear would not be beneficial in restoring hearing, but still might be considered for cosmetic purposes. In the infrequent cases of bilateral ear atresia, the indication for surgery is evident, whereas in cases of unilateral atresia, corrective surgery is less imperative. In the latter event, additional factors are considered, such as severity of damage, chances of success, and the patient's age, physical condition, necessity for binaural hearing, and socioeconomic level.

In atresia of the external-ear canal, airborne sounds cannot reach inner-ear receptors, but at high intensities they set the whole head in vibration and reach the inner ear as bone-conducted sounds. Complete external- and middle-ear atresia, with unaffected inner ear, generally results in a 55–60-decibel hearing loss for speech sounds. This is the maximum degree of loss that is observed in pathologic conditions of the conductive mechanism of the ear.

The extent and severity of pathologic findings can vary greatly among cases. Thus, the surgical procedure must be flexible, allowing for adaptation to circumstances that may become evident only during surgery. The surgical principle is to obtain an ear canal closed at its inner end by a compliant membrane separating it from the middle-ear cavity. Within this cavity a rigid structure is created, connecting the inner drum surface to the oval window. Hearing should be corrected before the cosmetic procedure is performed.

Hearing Restoration The skin is incised and the bony surface of the mastoid bone exposed. If the canal is restricted by fibrous tissue, this is cleared and the canal enlarged to greater than its normal size to prevent postoperative narrowing and closure. Attention also should be given to the facial nerve crossing the posterior wall of the newly created ear canal. If no remnant of an ear canal is visible on the mastoid surface, its cavity and the antrum with the attic extension are opened and connected to the middle-ear cleft.

The middle ear is then inspected, as are the oval and round windows and eustachian tube. The new ear canal is lined with skin graft obtained from a nonhairy donor site of the patient. The part of the graft closing the middle-ear entrance serves as a new eardrum. From the rudimentary auditory ossicles, a simple, shortened ossicular chain is created. The structure is positioned to form contact with the new drum's inner surface at one end and with the stapedial foot at the other.

Results in terms of hearing restoration depend on the severity of malformation, but at least a 20-decibel gain is obtained in nearly half of the patients.

Cosmetic Procedure Atresia of the auricle is an uncommon anomaly, occurring in 1 out of every 20,000 to 30,000 live births. It can be observed as an isolated pathologic condition, or associated with atretic ear canal and middle-ear involvement. If the developmental arrest occurs after the third gestational month, the auricle may appear normal.

If surgical reconstruction of the auricle is decided upon, it should be performed before the age when the child moves from the safe home environment to the outside world of school. Some people consider complete surgical reconstruction to be disappointing, at least with respect to long-term results.

The normal position of the ears on the head interferes with their being simultaneously observed; thus accurate comparison between the auricles from both sides is difficult. This is advantageous, because no surgery can create an auricle identical to an existing one. Even when reconstruction is performed on both sides by the same surgeon, using the same method, the healing process itself may induce significant differences between the two sides.

The most common congenital deformity of the auricle is protruding, or bat, ear. The angle between the scalp and the auricle, which is normally 30 degrees, may be as great as 90 degrees in this pathology. This is caused by hypertrophic development of the conchal cartilage or insufficient folding of the antehelix ridge. The cosmetic surgical procedure begins with the skin on the posterior aspect of the auricle being incised vertically, exposing the conchal cartilage. An adequate ellipsoidal portion of the cartilage is excised, breaking the anatomic continuity of conchal cartilage with the antehelix. The antehelix can then be displaced medially closer to the mastoid bone and fixed in this position by sutures. If the upper part of the auricle is overdeveloped, this can be corrected by additional excision of cartilage and skin parallel to the free margin of the helix curvature.

Another relatively frequent deformity of the auricle in which corrective surgery is indicated is macrotia (an overdeveloped auricle with otherwise normal shape and appearance). Generally, both auricles are affected but, exceptionally, the deformity can be limited to one side only. The surgical procedure giving satisfactory cosmetic results consists of excision of a triangular segment from the free part of the auricle. The excision, performed in the superior-posterior part of the auricle, includes the two skin layers with the cartilage in between. When the borders are sutured, the surface of the auricle is diminished by the amount of the excised segment, and at the same time the lateral projection of the auricles is also slightly decreased.

When total reconstruction of the auricle is required, it is performed in several stages. First, the vertical rudiment that is found in most cases is divided horizontally, and the two halves are transposed so that one will include the superior-anterior end of the planned new auricle, and the other half its inferior part. The space between the two portions is filled by a curved piece of costal (rib) cartilage inserted under the skin covering the mastoid bone. Some surgeons prefer using, instead of costal cartilage, a pediculated tubular skin graft prepared from the skin of the neck. This is followed by freeing the posterior margin of the new auricle from the mastoid bone. The posterior raw surface is covered with free skin graft, and efforts are made for the structure to protrude laterally from the mastoid plane by 30 degrees. In some instances a plastic stent is temporarily used to prevent the postauricular crease from filling with scar tissue. During this procedure, the opening of the external ear canal should be placed in the correct position relative to the newly created auricle.

Bibliography

Bauer, B. S.: "Reconstruction of Microtic Ear," *J. Pediat. Surg.* 19(4):440–445, August 1984.

Crabtree, J. A.: "Congenital Atresia Case Selection; Complication Prevention," *Otolaryngol. Clin. North Amer.*, 15(4):755–762, November 1982.

Fraser, A. G., and A. C. Watson: "The Surgical Treatment of Microtia: Long-term Review," *Brit. J. Plast. Surg.*, 35(2):185–194, April 1982.

Hanus, S. A., N. R. Bernstein, and K. A. Kapp: "Immigrants into Society; Children with Cranio-Facial Anomalies," *Clin. Pediat.* (Phila.), 20(1):37–41, January 1981.

Marquet, J.: "Congenital Malformation and Middle Ear Surgery," *J.R. Soc. Med.*, 74(2):119–128, February 1981.

Portman, M., and P. Le Grignou: "Surgery of Major Agenesis of the Ear: 100 Cases," *Rev. Laryngol. Otol. Rhinol. Bord.*, 103(5):347–352, 1982.

Tumasaka, S.: "Congenital Ossicular Anomalies Without Malformation of External Ear," *Arch. Otorhinolaryngol.*, 224(3-4):231–240, 1979.

Wegner, H. E.: "Correction of Protruding Ears in Combination with Reduction Surgery of Hyperplastic Auricles," *Aesthet. Plast. Surg.*, no. 1, pp. 57–62, 1981.

Moshe Rubinstein

OTOSCLEROSIS

Prior to 1938, a variety of surgical procedures were attempted. One of the major difficulties that physicians had with their contemporary treatment methods was the tendency of otosclerosis to recur. In 1938 Julius Lempert proposed the first successful one-stage surgical approach to otosclerosis, thus initiating the first treatment that could safely be used for a large group of patients.

Fenestration Lempert suggested that otosclerosis could be cured by ignoring the fixation at the stapes (the most common site) and creating a new sound pathway to the end organ of hearing, the cochlea. In effect, he planned to bypass the normal sound conduction system of the ear (eardrum, malleus, incus, stapes) and devise a new oval window, or fenestra, through which sound waves could be transmitted to the inner ear. The otosclerosis would still be present, but the new window would be put in a location with an extremely low incidence of otosclerosis—avoiding recurrence of hardening and the accompanying hearing loss. The site that Lempert chose was the horizontal semicircular canal (balance center) of the labyrinth, or inner ear.

In the classic Lempert fenestration approach, the mastoid and middle ear are exposed via an ear canal incision. Only enough mastoid air cells are removed to uncover the horizontal semicircular canal dome, and great care is taken to keep the skin of the ear canal intact. A flap of tissue made up of eardrum and ear canal skin is created and protected. The back wall of the ear canal is then removed. The chorda tympani nerve, tendon of the stapedius muscle, incus, and head of the malleus are exposed. First the incus is separated from the head of the malleus and stapes, and removed. Then the head and neck of the malleus are detached from their handle and removed. The bone of the horizontal semicircular canal dome is carefully drilled down to its thin inner layer, forming a fenestra approximately 2 by 6 millimeters. The eardrum–ear canal skin flap is then brought into position to cover this window, and the operation is completed by packing the ear canal with a sterile material to keep the flap in place, and closing the wound. The last step in the fenestration procedure is the removal of the packing 10 days after surgery.

This approach, done primarily between 1938 and 1958, marked an advancement in the treatment of otosclerosis. However, results obtained from the fenestration procedure were far from ideal. Patients stood a good chance for some initial improvement of their conductive hearing loss; but it was also likely that this improvement would deteriorate with time. Because both eardrum and ossicles (ear bones), which ordinarily act together to magnify sound waves, had been removed, patients were left with an uncorrected hearing loss of at least 25 decibels (dB). Patients who have undergone fenestration will have an external ear canal with a large posterior fenestration cavity because of the removal of the mastoid air cells. When their ears are being cleaned, suction should be used gently and irrigation should not be used at all unless absolutely necessary. If these patients develop suppurative otitis media, they should be treated immediately in order to prevent the occurrence of labyrinthitis. Other complications of fenestration include a mastoid cavity that requires periodic cleaning; injury to the facial nerve with resultant facial paralysis; and dizziness, either immediately or after several years delay, usually due to wax or debris in the area of the new window.

Since 1951 fenestration has not been the treatment of choice for otosclerosis. There are, however, still a few patients who would benefit from the fenestration operation. This is true of those in whom the disease is so active that the entire oval window turns solid; and those who have already undergone more than one stapedectomy due to closure of the oval window by recurrent otosclerosis. Other patients who might benefit from the fenestration approach are those at high risk for damage to the nerve that controls the facial muscles or those born without an oval window or stapes. However, for patients for whom fenestration has proved unsuccessful, and for the vast majority of patients with otosclerosis, the most satisfactory results can be obtained from a procedure called a stapedectomy.

Stapedectomy In 1952, while palpating the stapes to determine the amount of stapes fixation present before performing a fenestration operation, S. Rosen accidentally moved the stapes too much, effectively loosening the otosclerosis and mobilizing the stapes. Postoperatively, the patient had near-normal hearing—much better than from a routine fenestration procedure. Unfortunately, while this mobilization approach initially looked promising, the original disease process (otosclerosis) continued to be active in most patients. Eventually the stapes again became fixed to the oval window and all benefits were lost. In addition, there are many patients with otosclerosis whose stapes are too sclerotic or fixed to be simply mobilized. Mobilization is now used primarily in patients with congenital anomalies of the region (stapes itself or oval window) that preclude a safe approach, or in patients in whom the tissue overlying the bone in the area to be operated on has too many blood vessels.

It remained for J. Shea in 1956 to reintroduce and refine the major operation used for otosclerosis today—stapedectomy. He removed the stapes, sealed the oval window with a thin piece of connective tissue, and placed a prosthesis (strut) from the incus to the oval window. Since that time many surgeons have developed modifications of Shea's technique but still employ his basic principles. Some of these modifications are discussed below.

A patient can be considered a candidate for stapedectomy if the otosclerosis disease process is advanced enough to firmly fix the stapes. Clinically, a conductive hearing loss (air-bone gap) of at least 20 dB should be present with a speech discrimination (understanding) score of at least 60 percent. The Rinne test should be negative for both 256-hertz (Hz) and 512-hertz tuning forks. Even patients with severe hearing loss from otosclerosis might be candidates for surgery if only to bring the hearing up to a level where a hearing aid can be used. Stapedectomy is rarely, if ever, indicated if the patient has only one hearing ear.

Most ear surgeons prefer to perform stapedectomy under local anesthesia, using a combination of intravenous sedation with narcotics or Valium and local injections of a xylocaine-adrenaline solution in the ear canal. A connective tissue graft is then "harvested." Many operators prefer to use tragal perichondrium because it is available and in the operating field. Other surgeons prefer the loose fatty tissue that lies on top of the temporalis muscle that is directly above the ear, or a vein graft (generally obtained from the back of the hand). Whatever graft is chosen, it is generally taken at this time and set aside for later use.

The operating room microscope provides adequate magnification (up to 40 power) and lighting. A large ear speculum is used to examine the ear and perform the remainder of the surgery. A flap of tissue made up of eardrum and ear canal skin (U-shaped) is created in the same fashion as for the Lempert fenestration procedure. (The ear canal skin is cut with microscopic angled instruments and then elevated to the bony tympanic annulus. At that point the round knife or Rosen pick is used to separate and raise the fibrous annulus from the bony sulcus. By carefully elevating the fibrous annulus and eardrum–ear canal flap forward, the middle ear is exposed.) The stapes, stapedial tendon, incudostapedial joint, part of the incus, and oval window will be visible, although in many people a small amount of bone on the back wall of the ear canal must be drilled or cureted away to provide enough exposure for surgery.

The mobility of the ossicular chain is then gently tested by using a fine probe—examining the malleus, incudomalleal joint, incudostapedial joint, and stapes individually. If the diagnosis of otosclerosis is confirmed, the surgeon proceeds with the stapedectomy. The incudostapedial joint is first sectioned with an angled knife and the stapedial tendon then cut. The arch (crura) of the stapes is fractured and removed. The distance from the footplate to the top of the incus is measured. With a very fine pick, an opening (perforation) is made in the footplate and the footplate is removed in two sections (anterior and posterior). The tissue graft is placed over the oval window immediately to seal it. The prosthesis (strut) is brought into place and crimped onto the long process of the incus. The ear drum–ear canal skin flap is brought back into position, and the ear canal packed with gelfoam, surgical silk, surgical rayon, or another appropriate material.

Many surgeons now prefer the small-fenestra technique in which the footplate perforation (hole) is enlarged enough for a 0.6-millimeter-diameter Teflon piston prosthesis. The remainder of the stapes footplate is left in place. Other operators will use the laser to create the fenestra rather than the sharp pick and microhooks. If the footplate is obliterated (completely covered) by otosclerosis, the drill must be used to remove the larger mass of otosclerosis before the regular technique can be used.

Many prosthetic stapes have been developed, including the Teflon and stainless steel pistons, Shea cup piston, Schuknecht Teflon wire piston, tantalum wire loop, platinum ribbon loop, and Teflon-wire prosthesis.

Antibiotics are generally used from the day of surgery to two to five days postoperatively to prevent infection. The patient should be kept at bedrest for 18 to 24 hours following the procedure and should keep his or her head elevated for the first 48 hours. Packing and sutures will be removed five to seven days after surgery. The ear should be kept dry for one month. Possible air travel should be discussed with the patient's surgeon.

While the hearing thresholds are improved at two weeks, they are usually at their optimum at three months postoperatively. At this time approximately 80 percent of patients will have an improvement in hearing of at least 15 dB, and 90 percent will have an improvement of at least 10 dB. The highest gains are usually from 250 to 1000 Hz. Interestingly, patients who have surgery also have an improvement in sensory-neural (bone conduction) hearing levels at 2000 Hz (elimination of the Carhart notch). One to two percent of patients undergoing stapedectomy are at risk for injury to the cochlea and a resultant "dead ear." The remainder of the patients will receive no benefit from the surgery.

Complications that can occur during stapedectomy include injury to the chorda tympani nerve with decrease or change in taste, perforation of the eardrum, fracture of the long process of the incus, and damage to the ossicular chain. In the immediate postoperative period Bell's palsy (facial nerve paralysis) can occur, with complete recovery the general rule with appropriate treatment. Otitis media and otitis externa are now rare complications with the use of sterile technique and antibiotics.

Dizziness (vertigo) that occurs immediately after surgery generally disappears with treatment; in those patients in whom the dizziness persists, surgery may be necessary, especially if hearing loss, hearing change, or increased tinnitus (ringing) develops. During these reexplorations, the operator may discover a slipped prosthesis, a prosthesis that is too long, or a fistula (communicating hole connecting inner ear and middle ear) caused by failure of the tissue graft to seal the oval window. Delayed complications can also occur. A fistula can develop many years after surgery; the patient suffers from dizziness and hearing problems or loss. Granulomas ("proud flesh") of the middle ear or vestibule are uncommon complications now. More common when the wire-gelfoam prosthesis was used, they cause dizziness, tinnitus, and either no improvement in hearing after surgery or a profound hearing loss. If the granuloma is removed in time, the ear tissue and hearing loss may recover. Despite these possible complications, stapedectomy can be highly beneficial—notably, for the patient's hearing.

Bibliography

Davis, H., and T. Walsh: "The Limits of Improvement of Hearing Following the Fenestration Operation," *Laryngoscope*, 60:273, 1950.

Goodhill, V.: "Complications of the Surgical Treatment of Otosclerosis" and "Surgical Treatment of Otosclerosis," in G. M. English (ed.): *Otolaryngology*, vol. 1, Harper and Row, Philadelphia, 1984.

Goin, D. W.: "Otospongiosis," in G. E. English (ed.), *Otolaryngology*, Harper and Row, Hagerstown, Maryland, 1976.

Lempert, J.: "Improvement of Hearing in Cases of Otosclerosis: A New One Stage Surgical Technique," *Arch. Otolaryngol.*, 28:42, 1938.

Rosen. S.: "Palpation of the Stapes for Fixation: Preliminary Procedure to Determine Fenestration Suitability for Otosclerosis," *Arch. Otolaryngol.*, 56:610, 1952.

Shambaugh, G. E., and M. E. Glasscock: *Surgery of the Ear*, W. B. Saunders, Philadelphia, 1980.

Shea, J., Jr.: "Fenestration of the Oval Window," *Ann. Otol. Rhin. Laryngol*, 67:932, 1958.

Judith N. Green

Quack Cures

Deafness is no exception to the general rule that unwary and uninformed sufferers of all kinds of ailments are tempting targets for predatory quacks. As far back as the thirteenth century Saint Albertus Magnus wrote, "Lion's brain, if eaten, causes madness; but remedies deafness, if inserted in the ear with some strong oil." The rationale for the remedy, advanced a century earlier, was "the keen virture of a lion's hearing." Albertus was a great figure in the natural science of the time and should not be thought of as a quack, but his kind of claim is suggestive of the bases of deliberate quackery practiced in the centuries thereafter. In modern times rationales tend to be more plausible, and quacks still appeal to those of the lay public experiencing the chronic stress of hearing impairment who desperately seek not just amelioration but cure. Quackeries can reasonably be classified as medication, prostheses, manipulation, and stimulation.

Medication is best illustrated by the variety of ear oils said to penetrate the ear, thereby clearing up the source of "catarrhal" conditions that presumably cause deafness. Sometimes, the injection of the claimed therapeutic substance was accomplished through an instrument that was placed in the mouth and nose to blow material into the ear. Frequently, the substances exuded an aromatic quality undoubtedly intended to impress the unsuspecting consumer with its medicinal value. Among ingredients in such mixtures were camphor, eucalyptus, oil of wintergreen, and mustard.

Prosthetic devices usually were claimed to transmit sounds to the nerve of hearing by way of the ear canal and vibration of the eardrum. Such devices were quite legitimate in very select cases when applied by early otologists and before the advent of more feasible and effective measures. These were generally small disks of rubber or paper to cover perforations of the eardrum when there was no suppuration (running ear). Sometimes, pledgets (small flat masses) of cotton were applied over the round window, an elastic membrane between the middle ear and the inner ear. Occasionally, improvement in hearing, not cure, was noted. This approach was seized upon by quacks and specially shaped devices were offered as cures. The possibility, too, of transmission of sound by bone conduction was exploited. A device would be held against the teeth with one flat surface facing the source of sound.

Among the more egregious quackeries advanced to alleviate or cure deafness was the manipulation of the eustachian tube by finger surgery. The air-filled cavity of the middle ear and the mastoid air cells that lead from it are ventilated periodically by the eustachian tube. The tube connects the middle ear with the back of the nasal cavity, called the nasopharynx. The function of the eustachian tube is to equalize the pressure inside and outside the eardrum and to replenish the air in the middle ear. Frequently, hearing is reduced by adhesions of the eustachian tube, with subsequent pus in the middle ear and involvement of the ossicles, the small bones in the middle ear that conduct sound. The finger surgeon claimed that he normalized and reconstructed the eustachian tube by feeling the lesions (the adhesions and pus pockets) with his finger and subsequently removing them. This procedure is especially dangerous because it has been known to injure delicate tissues and to worsen pathologic conditions.

Quack stimulatory devices based their appeal on the notion that some form of excitation can revive nerves and other pertinent structures of the ear. Usually, the stimulus was claimed to be electricity. An example was an "electro-magnetic head cap" that consisted of an arrangement of straps and metal pieces to be worn on the head of the deaf person. The legitimate purposes and demonstrated value of auditory training of those with some residual hearing also have been exploited by the unscrupulous. Auditory training when carried out by qualified professionals aims to enable the hearing-impaired person to make full use of auditory cues and to facilitate speech production especially in those severely and profoundly deaf, but reputable workers have never claimed it as a cure for deafness. On the other hand, fakers have promoted the idea that listening to recorded sounds elegantly "tailored to individual needs" would cure deafness by stimulation of appropriate neural elements.

Perhaps the most dramatic example of the appeal of stimulation resulting in cure was the airplane spin and dive. In the inner ear, structures containing sense organs for sensing turning in space and for sensing the acceleration due to the pull of gravity are connected to the snaillike structure (the cochlea) that is involved in hearing. The intense, even violent, stimulation by rapidly changing spatial excitation was presumed to stimulate the hearing portion of the inner ear because of its connection to the structures serving space-orienting functions. The claim for the cure of deafness following the afflicted person's airplane experience rested on this unfounded notion.

The increase of government agencies and private organizations committed to protect consumers from fraud promises to reduce, if not to eliminate, the practice of quackery.

Bibliography
Davis, H., and S. R. Silverman (eds.): *Hearing and Deafness*, 4th ed., Holt, Rinehart and Winston, New York, 1978.
Goldstein, M. A.: *Problems of the Deaf*, Laryngoscope Press, St. Louis, 1933.
Thorndike, L.: *A History of Magic and Experimental Science*, Columbia University Press, New York, 1923.

S. Richard Silverman

AUDITORY TRAINING

Auditory training involves the use of procedures and instruments by competent professionals to develop, restore, and enhance the auditory speech perception of children and adults for the purpose of improving their listening skills, speech, and overall communication ability. Auditory refers to the sense of hearing, including both the sensitivity to a variety of sounds and the ability to understand a spoken message without looking at the speaker. Understanding through listening includes the rhythm and intonation (pitch changes), the speech sounds (consonant and vowels), and the meaning of the spoken words, phrases and sentences. The listener's ability to understand others is affected by their own use of rhythm, intonation, and speech sounds.

Training is used to develop the person's rhythm, intonation, and speech sounds by using auditory training units. These units allow the person either to hear or to feel (vibrotactile input), while the therapist stimulates and corrects the patterns of speech. Then, the person's memory for the correct speech sounds and movements helps the person to correct his or her errors and to underststand the speech of others. The hearing-impaired person also becomes more intelligible to others. Training should be administered by a competent therapist or teacher who has good listening skills and the ability to correct the speech of others. *See* SPEECH TRAINING.

Auditory training units provide a good speech-to-noise ratio by increasing the intensity of the speech signal through proper microphone placement and a high-quality amplifier, and presenting the speech signal to the person through stereophonic headsets or through a vibrator. In the early stages of training, a wide high-fidelity frequency response that includes low (bass) and high (treble) frequencies enhances the development of rhythm and intonation. Later, filters can be used to attenuate some frequencies while allowing other frequencies to pass. For example, a 6-dB-per-octave attenuation of low frequencies reduces the masking of the high-pitch speech sounds. The optimum frequency response through filtering usually makes the speech sound clearer without making it too loud.

A hardwired training unit has the microphone attached to the amplifier-and-filter system for the input, and the vibrator or headset attached for output. A hearing aid is worn outside the training sessions and is set to the frequency response similar to that of the training unit. As the person's listening ability improves, a wireless amplification system usually enhances listening in classrooms and other situations where the speech-to-noise ratio may not be ideal. The wireless system allows the proper placement of the microphone near the speaker because the microphone and amplifier can be separated. In the final stage of training, the person should be able to understand speech at a distance of 15 to 20 feet (4.5 to 6 meters) without visual clues. This is usually evaluated in rooms with both favorable and unfavorable speech-to-noise ratio and reverberation times.

Auditory training is mostly used to improve the listening skills of hearing-impaired people, ranging from a minimum to a profound hearing loss. The training also can be used to improve listening skills of normal-hearing people who have a speech problem related to poor listening skills. Included are people who have difficulty hearing and understanding the speech sounds of a foreign language.

Carl W. Asp

Procedures

The primary purpose of auditory training is to enable the person to both comprehend and produce speech. With an intact hearing mechanism, the ability to detect, recognize, comprehend, and use speech is accomplished in a relatively brief interval starting at birth. This is not the case when the hearing is impaired. The older the child when training is begun, the longer the interval between awareness of sound and spontaneous use of speech.

Research in infant perception has confirmed the hypothesis that auditory function, like other sense perceptions, is learned. Furthermore, it is normally learned in infancy and relates to listening experiences. The necessary stimuli are the parents' voices, and the critical reinforcement is the affection that they extend. These facts remain the same for many hearing-impaired children. They may not distinguish spectral features of speech, but they may be able to differentiate gross variations in the acoustic pattern. The material, however, should have some meaning and be of importance to the child, and promptly his or her attention should be rewarded. This is the formula for programming the mind of the hearing-impaired child to comprehend and use speech.

HISTORY

Using the residual hearing of deaf children for speech and language development is an ancient procedure. In his text of 1939 Max Goldstein reviewed the historical development of auditory training, and recently S. Richard Silverman gave a more detailed account by translating Victor Urbantschitsh's material. He reported that as early as the first century Archigenes advocated the use of a hearing trumpet and intensified sound to stimulate latent hearing function. Similarly, Alexander of Trailles in the sixth century and Guido Guidi in the sixteenth century encouraged shouting into the ear, thereby providing auditory stimulation to defective ears. *See* GOLDSTEIN, MAX AARON.

By 1761, a method was being demonstrated with hard-of-hearing subjects by Ernaud, who showed that they could differentiate speech sounds. Six years later J. R. Periere claimed the same accomplishment by using a peculiarly constructed trumpet.

Gaspard Itard was the first to show systematic unisensory exercises to improve the hearing-impaired person's sound perception. Goldstein, however, credits Urbantschitsh, professor of otology at the University of Vienna, with contributing the most profound investigations and actual accomplishments in auditory training. It was this work that motivated Goldstein, who had done postgraduate work in Vienna, to found the Central Institute for the Deaf in St. Louis, Missouri. During those early years there was no auditory equipment other than the conversation tube. The tube was modeled somewhat after a stethoscope and enabled pupils to hear the teacher's voice speaking into the mouthpiece, with the child's own voice speaking into another. The significance of auditory feedback was recognized even then as an important dimension for speech development through audition. *See* CENTRAL INSTITUTE FOR THE DEAF; HEARING AIDS: History.

Because of the range of hearing losses within a classroom, where the selection of pupils is usually based upon academic achievement, the unisensory approach declined. To be successful, the unisensory system requires a one-to-one setting of teacher and pupil. In this way the material can be adapted to each child's hearing ability.

A dichotomous situation eventually arose with the multisensory "look and listen" technique occurring in the classroom while the unisensory system thrived in clinical settings. In the tutorial-type program the unisensory system has sometimes been called the acoupedic method as a result of the impact of people such as Wedenberg, Huizing, and Whetnall. Beginning in 1964 and continuing to the present is a system called Auditory Global, which is primarily an auditory approach, but permitting speechreading, in order to program in the mind the complete linguistic pattern of the individual's environment.

AUDITORY GLOBAL

The Auditory Global approach is broad but also comprehensive. The concern is with the total child, his or her hearing ability, developmental age, interests, cognitive experiences and social functioning. The content of the auditory stimuli is the global language rather than discrete sounds or noisemakers. The connected spoken language which is appropriate to the situation contains all the suitable nuances of speech, the rhythmic structure, intonation, and stress, as well as the natural rate of utterance of the connected phonemes.

In order for hearing-impaired children to build up a knowledge of the probabilities of language, they must hear enough speech. It has been proposed that the quantity of speech must be greater than that heard by the normally hearing child.

Therefore, if the child is to develop an ability to predict the events in language—the phoneme, the word, the next sentence—the code information must be processed through the receptive and expressive systems, that is, hearing and speech. By giving the natural connected linguistic code the teacher programs the statistic information of language that the child induces. The child receives not only the speech sounds but sentences that differ in length, pitch, and intonation. It is the differences that provide the cues to the listener.

Much of language, such as structural words, morphemic forms, and word order, can be made meaningful only through first-hand experiences. The Auditory Global system is built upon seizing spontaneous experiences for auditory input. This is true if the "trainer" is either the parent or the teacher. In a clinical or school setting, however, the activity may have to be contrived in order for it to appear spontaneous.

Over a period of time the same structural words and morphemic forms are frequently used in a variety of ways. Through imitation the child stores the memory of sequencing and meaning. Since the meanings grew out of first-hand experiences, the semantic, cognitive information is understood.

If the auditory perception has been too faulty, the child may get assistance from watching the speaker's lips as well as listening. Although bisensory modalities are exploited fully, audition is given priority. The auditory stimulus, however, should not be strange to the child. Auditory training is not auditory testing. Training needs to involve familiar material.

The language of the experience is printed for the children to follow while listening to the auditory patterns, which they in turn repeat. This listening and watching of the print allows the child to perceive something in print even though it is not audible. The structure words "if," "can," "the," "but," and so on, and the grammar forms "s," "ed," "er," and so on, are low in acoustic powers but extremely significant in language meaning. Referral to the experience chart from previous days requires memory for the auditory cues of any given sentence and the context in which it occurred. Auditory memory also is enhanced when more than one sentence is given for retrieval. The sequencing of the words in sentence order and the resulting sentences in their order serve to increase the memory span.

There is a purpose in repeating sentences given through hearing alone. The repetition provides auditory feedback for speech; it gives practice for stringing phonemes together to make morphemes, words, and sentences; and it provides opportunity to use the important prosodic aspects of speech.

In order to ensure that the language being given for auditory training is meaningful to the child, the teacher matches the child's thoughts about the experience they shared. Experiencing clarifies meaning. The child will be more concerned with content if the material is about the child's activities. The training then becomes a pleasurable task. In this way the child can store vast amounts of information about the language and have untold opportunities to differentiate speech.

The Auditory Global approach allows the child to attain important acoustic characteristics of language, at the same time instinctively acquiring the rules for spoken communication. It provides the material whereby the hearing-impaired child can collect knowledge of the probability of word and sentence formation while giving the rhythm and acoustic cues of connected spoken speech. Thus the mind is programmed to utilize the communicative sounds that the ear receives.

Bibliography

Calvert, D., and S. R. Silverman: *Speech and Deafness*, A. G. Bell Association, 1975.

Goldstein, M. A.: *The Acoustic Method for Training of the Deaf and Hard-of-Hearing Child*, Laryngoscope Press, St. Louis, 1937.

Ling, D., and A. Ling: *Aural Habilitation*, A. G. Bell Association, 1978.

Mulholland, A. M. (ed.): *Oral Education Today and Tomorrow*, A. G. Bell Association, 1981.

Pollack, D.: *Educational Audiology for the Limited Hearing Infant*, Charles C. Thomas, 1970.

Silverman, S. R. (trans.): *Auditory Training for Deaf Mutism and Acquired Deafness*, by Victor Urbantschitsh, A. G. Bell Association, 1981.

Simmons, A. A.: "Teaching Aural Language," *Volta Review*, 70:26–30, 1968.

Whetnall, E., and D. B. Fry: *The Deaf Child*, Charles C. Thomas, 1964.

Audrey Simmons-Martin

Instruments

Auditory training is a process in which emphasis is on improving listening skills and communication of hearing-impaired children and adults. The training to enhance listening and perceiving is often part of a larger or broader program of aural rehabilitation. Auditory training for adults with acquired hearing loss can be defined in terms of three processes: (1) learning to recognize auditorily those sounds that initially are incorrectly discriminated; (2) pre- and posthearing-aid orientation, including adjustment to amplification; and (3) improvement of tolerance for strong amplification. Auditory training for children emphasizes the development of speech, language, and academic contact in addition to improvement in listening skills.

For adults, auditory training usually is accomplished with a personal, wearable hearing aid or aids. Hearing aids are discussed elsewhere. For children, training may be done with special am-

plification systems, personal hearing aids, or both. The following is a description of special amplification systems for use in classrooms for hearing-impaired children.

HARD-WIRED SYSTEMS

The first auditory training system was hard-wired. This system consists of an amplifier, a microphone (worn by the teacher), and listening stations (headphones worn by the students). Hard-wired refers to the physical connection of wires between the microphone, the amplifier, and the headphones at the listening stations. Hard-wired systems can provide good amplification characteristics with frequency responses to 8000 Hz. Electroacoustic characteristics also may be modified to meet the gain needs of individual children. The hard-wired system has the disadvantage of lack of mobility for students and teachers because of the wire connections. These systems are still used in some school settings.

INDUCTION-LOOP SYSTEMS

The induction-loop system was developed to overcome hard-wired system shortcomings. The loop system allows for: child-teacher mobility; the monitoring of one's own speech, in addition to hearing both teacher and classmates; and the use of the child's personal hearing aid in the auditory training process. In the induction-loop system, the child's own hearing aid serves as the receiver. The system contains a wire loop around the room, under the carpet, or on the ceiling, connected to an amplifier. The teacher's microphone is connected to the amplifier. The setting on the personal hearing aid is on the telephone (or the telephone-microphone) switch. This loop system will work only if the hearing aid contains a telecoil to receive speech through magnetic induction. The disadvantages of this system are limited output, poor low-frequency emphasis, and reduced sensitivity to high frequencies. Overspill also is a major difficulty because the child may receive signals from adjacent classrooms. The loop system, however, may be successful in the individual's home where competing systems are not a factor.

RADIO-FREQUENCY (RF) SYSTEMS

The most used auditory training system for education of children is the free-field FM (frequency-modulation) system. This system functions as a regular hearing aid as well as a pretuned radio receiver. It was designed to provide a better-controlled sound-pressure level for the instructor's voice as well as to eliminate overspill. The RF system has two primary advantages over previous auditory training systems. First, no installation is necessary; the system can be used in different classrooms and in the home environment; the extended range over several hundred feet allows the child to engage in a variety of auditory situations. Second, the radio-frequency FM system allows normal placement for hearing-impaired children in a regular classroom. The frequency band between 72 and 76 MHz has been allocated by the Federal Communications Commission for the education of hearing-impaired students. Thirty-two frequencies are available in the allocated band, allowing a school thirty-two different teacher microphones, thereby avoiding overspill. Disadvantages of the RF system include a lack of true binaural FM amplification, because there is only one input signal. In addition, the units are body type, which is cosmetically unacceptable for some children. Very young children may have difficulty and need continuous adjustment by the teacher with input-selection controls. The decision to use personal hearing aids, auditory trainers, or both needs to be made by professionals dealing with hearing-impaired children in conjunction with the parents.

Bibliography

Alpiner, Jerome G.: *Handbook of Adult Rehabilitative Audiology*, Williams and Wilkins, Baltimore, 1982.

Ling, Agnes, H., and Daniel Ling: *Aural Rehabilitation*, Alexander Graham Bell Association for the Deaf, Washington, D.C., 1978.

Mussen, Ethel F.: "Hearing, Listening, and Attending Techniques and Concepts in Auditory Training," Ross J. Roeser and Marion P. Downs, (eds.), *Audiology Disorders in School Children*, Thieme-Stratton, New York, 1981.

Sanders, Derek A.: *Aural Rehabilitation, a Management Model*, Prentice-Hall, New York, 1982.

Jerome G. Alpiner

AUSTRALIA

Australia, with a land area of 2,968,000 square miles (7,717,000 square kilometers), has a population of only a little over 15 million people. It is largely an urban nation, with almost three-quarters of the people living in cities or towns. These facts must be taken into account in any survey of services to hearing-impaired people in Australia. Delivery of service is relatively easy for those who live in the major urban complexes, but is very difficult for those who live in the sparsely populated rural areas. Some of the latter may be several hundred miles from the nearest hearing-aid supplier or service for the hearing-impaired individuals.

Politically, Australia is a federation of six self-governing states and two territories. It has a mixed economy, with certain services being provided by governments and others by the private sector. This is reflected, for example, in the provision of hearing aids: children and government pensioners receive hearing aids and have them serviced free by a federal government agency, but all other people must buy them from private suppliers. Similarly, adults who receive their hearing aids from a government agency have rehabilitation services provided by that agency, but those who buy from private suppliers have rehabilitation services provided by voluntary agencies, most of which are assisted by government subsidies. The same is true in provision of educational services, where the majority of pupils attend free government schools, while a small number attend private programs that require their parents to pay fees.

PREVALENCE

Hearing impairment is the second most prevalent disabling condition in Australia (exceeded only by musculoskeletal diseases such as arthritis and rheumatism). Depending on the criteria developed for definition of a hearing problem, between 500,000 and 750,000 Australians report having a hearing problem. In a survey, approximately 750,000 Australians (5% of the total population) reported a hearing loss great enough to occasionally cause them some degree of difficulty, particularly in noisy conditions. Of those who report a hearing loss, 168,000 have difficulty understanding speech, even with a hearing aid. The great majority of people with hearing impairment (575,000) are elderly and become deaf after leaving school, generally late in life. About 40,000 were born hearing-impaired or acquired a hearing loss early enough in childhood that they required special education services. *See* DEAF POPULATION: Demography.

Generally speaking, the hearing-impaired population has losses that are sensorineural in origin, although there is the usual amount of conductive-hearing impairment in the community, particularly in childhood, due to both bacterial and viral invasions. Conductive-hearing impairment is particularly high among the aboriginal people, for most aboriginal children have chronic suppurative otitis media for lengthy periods. This constitutes a major health and educational problem, and has proved difficult to solve. *See* EAR: Pathology.

EDUCATIONAL SYSTEM

Education in Australia is largely provided by the states, although there has been a great deal of decentralization of administrative control of schools since the mid-1970s. There are only eight school districts for the six states and two territories. While there are differences among the states in the range and variety of provisions, the overall pattern is similar. Each state education department has a parent-guidance service which operates with the families of hearing-impaired children from the age of diagnosis. The department is usually centered upon the metropolitan capital city, occasionally with either full-time or itinerant services in smaller rural cities. In states where distances between the state capital and outlying towns are very great, parent-guidance services may often be provided by the generalist (usually elementary-trained) teacher of hearing-impaired children who runs the elementary or secondary provisions in that district.

Provisions at this level are generally satisfactory, with most families having access to a reasonable level of guidance during the child's earliest years. In several states, there are also private parent-guidance services for those who elect to use them. All states provide a kindergarten or preschool service for hearing-impaired children, often with a relatively large center in each capital city, and small programs are usually associated with units for elementary-age children in rural districts. These services are usually separate preschools for deaf children, but in all states children may also be enrolled in regular preschools and provided with additional services by an itinerant teacher of hearing-impaired pupils.

Among programs for elementary-age children, the pattern becomes more diverse. Most states have a large school or schools for hearing-impaired students in the major metropolitan area, with relatively smaller units (often within the grounds of a regular elementary school) in country towns. In two states, however, there is no longer a central school for hearing-impaired students, but relatively small units within the grounds of regular schools are established in the suburbs as well as in country towns. As for secondary-level programs, the tradition in Australia has been to create an upward extension of elementary-school programs. This has meant that academic subjects are largely taught by elementary-trained teachers of hearing-impaired pupils, and specialist secondary teachers have been employed mainly for vocationally oriented areas such as commercial and business studies and manual arts. Subsequently, specialist secondary teachers in the sciences and humanities have begun to be recruited and trained. In smaller country towns, the provision is likely to be a unit, usually within the structure of a local regular high school. Once again, at both elementary and secondary levels, there is a much smaller private provision of schools and units for hearing-impaired children. A Catholic school for deaf girls was established in 1875 and one for deaf boys in 1922. Since World War II, a small number of other private programs have been established.

Several of the large state schools for deaf pupils have passed their centenaries, as provisions for education of deaf children were initially established in most states between the late 1860s and the end of the nineteenth century. The present metropolitan schools for hearing-impaired youngsters grew out of these large state schools, and were in their early days largely residential. However, since World War II, the proportion of pupils in residential placement has decreased dramatically, and there are now very few pupils in residence; almost all pupils travel to schools and units from home. Most services provide the pupils with basic literacy, number skills, and social skills in order to prepare them for a career. Increasingly, pupils are also being prepared for work in computer science and other technologies, and the variety of opportunities available for hearing-impaired people has broadened considerably. Most schools and units provide full-time programs for all the educational needs of the pupils, with occasional integration into regular classes, particularly where the provision is a unit, normally within the grounds of a regular school. However, all state education departments provide a large itinerant teacher service, the responsibility of which is to oversee the placement of (mostly partially hearing-impaired) pupils within regular classes. There would normally be only one such pupil per regular class, and the itinerant teacher could make up to four one-hour visits per week to that pupil (ranging down to perhaps an annual visit for some pupils whose needs were felt to be less). The itinerant teacher would provide a consultancy service to the hearing-impaired child's regular class teacher, or would provide special tutorial assistance to the pupil if necessary, as well as provide for hearing-aid checks, battery replacement, and so forth. About half of all pupils wearing hearing aids in Australia are so placed in regular schools.

About 25–35% of all hearing-impaired pupils have a severe handicap secondary to their hearing impairment, and all state services make special provision for them, whether within the programs of the schools and units for hearing-impaired students, or by the provision of special classes for hearing-impaired pupils within schools for students who are blind, intellectually handicapped, physically handicapped, or behaviorally disturbed. These classes would normally be taught by specialist teachers of hearing-impaired persons. In most states a deaf-blind unit is also provided.

Given this pattern of provision of services, the academic achievement of hearing-impaired children within Australian educational systems varies from superior to well below normal. For those pupils placed in full-time services for hearing-impaired students, the usual lag in academic achievement noted in other English-speaking countries is found. *See* EDUCATION: Problems.

Increasing emphasis is now placed upon a type of education provided in all states, called Technical and Further Education (TAFE). This sector is responsible for apprenticeship and technical training and transition-to-work programs, and increasing use is being made of its programs by those responsible for delivery of services to hearing-impaired people. Several states now have classes within TAFE colleges for hearing-impaired pupils, and these colleges often provide vocational preparation and follow-up programs for pupils in their first years of employment. It is anticipated that greater use will be made of these kinds of programs.

There are no specialist higher-education programs for hearing-impaired students in Australia. Those pupils graduating from regular schools under the services of itinerant teachers could go on to regular universities and colleges. Very few graduates of the full-time schools and units for hearing-impaired students do go on, particularly if manual communication is their preferred mode. Accordingly, only a very small number of hearing-impaired people have graduated from universities and colleges of advanced education.

TEACHERS

Typically, teachers of the hearing-impaired in Australia would be graduates of a teachers college with a three-year diploma of teaching in elementary education, and a one-year graduate diploma in education of hearing-impaired pupils. Most would have had some experience in regular schools before becoming teachers of hearing-impaired pupils, although a small number of teachers graduate directly into education of hearing-impaired students. A small but increasing number of teachers would have had their initial training in early-childhood education or a secondary specialization. Training programs for teachers of hearing-impaired students exist in colleges of advanced education in four Australian states, and advanced training (including graduate research degrees) is available from several Australian universities.

DEAFENED ADULTS

As noted above, the majority of hearing-impaired people in Australia are elderly. Frequently, these people are unaware of the services available to them, or even of the benefit of a hearing aid. They often do not seek out such services and aids, and are conservative about accepting them. Thus these older people become withdrawn and isolated, even from their families. A number of government and voluntary agencies attempt to meet the needs in this area, but they are reaching only a very small proportion of the potential users. The government service which provides hearing aids to pensioners, most of whom are elderly, also provides a limited rehabilitation service. In all states, there are branches of a voluntary organization known as Better Hearing Australia, which provides lipreading and lim-

ited auditory rehabilitation services for its members. More federal funding has become available for this and similar voluntary agencies.

Because they are elderly, most deafened individuals are beyond the age of normal employment. No research has been done into the employment of these individuals. It is a commonly accepted view that individuals have limitations imposed by their hearing impairment, and among employers and the public there is a general lack of awareness of the ability of hearing-impaired people to hold jobs in most areas which do not require normal hearing. In general, deafened people still in employment can be found in all sorts of situations. *See* DEAF POPULATION: Deafened Adults.

PRELINGUALLY DEAF PEOPLE

Many graduates of schools for hearing-impaired pupils form a recognizable deaf community in adult life, with familial, social, and recreational activities taking place largely within that community. All states have a well-established Deaf Society, which grew out of the traditional mission to deaf people. Deaf Societies provide a range of services to prelingually deaf people, including interpreting, welfare, and recreation. Some Deaf Societies have extended their range of services from their traditional base in prelingual deafness to rehabilitation services for deafened adults and certain welfare activities.

Traditionally, the Deaf Societies also provided religious services to deaf people, but most denominations have begun to establish chaplaincies for deaf persons, with either interpreted regular services or services in sign language. These are not ordained prelingually deaf clergy, but those denominations that use lay ministers and preachers have a number who are deaf.

No research has been done into the vocational and socioeconomic status of prelingually deaf people, but there is a general opinion among them and those working with them that, largely because of limited academic achievement, they are not employed at a level commensurate with their capacities. Prelingually deaf individuals are not at all represented in professional and semiprofessional activities as their proportion in the general population would warrant.

There has been considerable resistance among state education departments to employing prelingually deaf teachers, although this attitude is noticeably beginning to soften. It is now considered that in most states, when appropriately qualified deaf individuals come forward, they will be employed as teachers of hearing-impaired students. However, the availability of such teachers is limited by the fact that there is no provision for interpreting and other services in higher education, and until better higher-educational opportunities are available for prelingually deaf people, their vocational aspirations will not be realized.

Among prelingually deaf people, most of the men are employed in unskilled labor or process work or skill trades in the metal and building areas, with increasing employment becoming available in electronics and data processing. Most women in the work force are employed in clerical work or process work in factories. An increasing, though still small, number of deaf people are being employed by organizations that work with deaf people. Traditionally, prelingually deaf people in Australia have always been highly employable, but because of their lack of formal skills and qualifications, deaf school-leavers are finding it increasingly difficult to obtain appropriate employment. *See* DEAF POPULATION: Socioeconomic Status.

METHODS OF COMMUNICATION

Most hearing-impaired people in Australia were deafened later in life, and accordingly their methods of communication are oral-aural. Most rely on amplified residual hearing and speechreading for ordinary communicative purposes. Among the prelingually deaf, a little under half spent all of their educational career in regular educational settings, where they were taught purely orally-aurally. Although no research-based evidence is available, it seems likely that most such people continue to communicate only orally-aurally in adult life.

With few exceptions, the schools and services for pupils who spend most or all of their education in settings for deaf people use a manual supplement to oral-aural education. A little less than half of all deaf children requiring full-time special education are educated by using a manual supplement. In the majority of cases, this manual supplement is a mixture of signs and fingerspelling which enables the child to use Signed English, as far as he or she can. In a small number of cases, the manual complement is cued speech. Graduates of programs using Signed English mostly continue to use manual communication for their intimate personal and social activities throughout life and as such constitute a distinct group—the deaf community. It is estimated that there are approximately 7000 such individuals in Australia who rely for their daily activities mostly on manual communication. The form that manual communication would take among deaf people themselves is Australian Sign Language. *See* MANUALLY CODED ENGLISH; MOUTH-HAND SYSTEMS: Cued Speech.

Australian Sign Language was brought to the country by deaf men who founded the two large state schools for deaf pupils in Victoria and New South Wales. The Australian Sign Language is a direct descendant of British Sign Language. There are slight dialectal differences among Australian states, because the two deaf men who introduced sign languages brought the variants of British Sign Language which were used where they were educated. For many years, the Catholic schools for deaf students in Australia used the Irish Sign Language, which was brought in by the founders of the Catholic schools in 1868 and 1922. These schools became purely oral just after World War II, and now use cued speech. There are relatively few users of the Irish-Australian Sign Language still living, and it seems likely that its use will die out within a generation or two. A one-handed fingerspelling alphabet was used in conjunction with that sign language. Existing diagrams of that fingerspelling indicate that it was somewhat different from the one-handed alphabet now used in the United States. The fingerspelling used in conjunction with Australian Sign Language is the British two-handed system. *See* SIGN LANGUAGES: British, Irish.

Teachers of hearing-impaired pupils, being aware of the limitations of Australian Sign Language for educational purposes (because its grammar, like all sign languages, is not that of English), formed the Australian Sign Language Development Project together with representatives of the deaf community. This project has been active since about 1980, and aims to extend the use of Signed English by adding to Australian Sign Language various fingerspelled markers for tense, plurality, adverbial markings, and so forth, as well as invented signs. It is not intended to supplant Australian Sign Language in use among adult deaf people but to provide a basis for Signed English use in schools. A dictionary based upon the efforts of the project was published in 1981, and is used widely in all schools and services for hearing-impaired people in Australia which use Signed English. *See* EDUCATION: Communication.

A major breakthrough occurred when Australian Sign Language was accepted as a "community language" by the National Authority for the Accreditation of Translators and Interpreters, giving it the same status and rights as spoken non-English languages. This means that officially recognized standards and examinations for both sign language and oral interpreters for deaf people have been established, which will lead to upgrading of professional standards and recognition for interpreters.

The Australian aboriginal people had an extensive system of signs which they used for communication under certain conditions, and this is beginning to be used with aboriginal deaf children, particularly in remote communities. A dictionary of one such system (Walpiri) has been published.

NATIONAL ACOUSTIC LABORATORIES

One of the most important influences in provision of services to hearing-impaired people in Australia has proved to be the creation in 1948 of what is now called the National Acoustic Laboratories (NAL). Its task then was to provide hearing aids for deafened veterans of World War II and for the large number of children deafened by the rubella outbreaks of the early 1940s. Since that time, NAL has developed into the second-largest provider of hearing aids and services to hearing-impaired individuals in the world. It is a branch of the Australian Department of Health, and has offices in all major metropolitan and many larger rural cities, as well as providing regular visiting services to more remote rural areas.

The National Acoustic Laboratories provides and maintains hearing aids free of charge for all military and civil pensioners in Australia, as well as for all persons under the age of 21 diagnosed as hearing-impaired. It also offers limited rehabilitation services to its adult clients. It has always maintained its own technical and audiological research and development services, and has extensive facilities for engineering, acoustic, electronic, and audiological research and development at its Sydney headquarters. Publications of NAL are models for other such services around the world.

In metropolitan and some rural areas, NAL is able to provide a regular hearing-aid maintenance service to schools for hearing-impaired pupils, and it fits all Australian deaf children with radio-frequency hearing-aid systems. This is a new type of system, developed by NAL and the Commonwealth Scientific and Industrial Research Organization. Largely because of NAL services, virtually every child in Australia who can benefit from a hearing aid has one provided and serviced free of charge for life, and the impact of this service upon education of hearing-impaired children has been great. *See* HEARING AIDS.

ORGANIZATIONS AND INFORMATION

A number of organizations represent points of view and professions active within the field of hearing impairment in Australia. There are, for example, the Australian Association of Teachers of the Deaf, the Association of Welfare Workers with the Deaf, the Federation of Australian Deaf Societies, the Audiological Society of Australia, the Australian Caption Centre (for television captioning), and the Oto-Laryngological Society of Australia, as well as numerous smaller groups representing many interests of hearing-impaired persons. Most of these organizations served the prelingually deaf population; Better Hearing Australia is one of the few that provides auditory rehabilitation services for deafened people. All these organizations have come together under the Australian Deafness Council, which has a permanent secretariat in Canberra, the national capital. Thus, the council is able to represent the views of the hearing-impaired community and those working for and with them to both federal-government and private interests.

A number of periodicals are produced by associations for deaf persons in Australia, including the *Australian Teacher of the Deaf, Journal of the Oto-Laryngological Society of Australia*, and *Journal of the Audiological Society of Australia*. Research is undertaken by a number of organizations, including the National Acoustic Laboratories, Melbourne University, and the Brisbane College of Advanced Education, Centre for Human Development Studies. A national Deafness Research Foundation has been established.

Bibliography
Australian Journal of Audiology, Australian Society of Audiologists.
Australian Teacher of the Deaf, Australian Association of Teachers of the Deaf.
Better Hearing Australia.
Centre for Human Development Studies, Brisbane College of Advanced Education, Reports and Occasional Papers.
Hearing Technology Review, Australian Deafness Council.
Jeanes, R. C., and B. E. Reynolds (eds.): *Dictionary of Australasian Signs for Communication with the Deaf*, Victorian School for Deaf Children, Melbourne, 1982.
Journal of the Oto-Laryngological Society of Australia.
NAL News, National Acoustic Laboratories.
National Acoustic Laboratories, *Reports.*
Supertext News, Australian Caption Centre.

D. J. Power

B

BEETHOVEN, LUDWIG VAN
(1770–1827)

Ludwig van Beethoven, composer and piano virtuoso, has become symbolic of music in its highest form. He is viewed as the typical artist, and his art was his life. For his art, he sacrificed much and suffered much, partly because of progressive deafness, partly because of his personality.

Beethoven was born into a musical family of Flemish origin, probably on December 16, 1770; he was baptized on December 17 in Bonn, in the Electorate of Cologne. Beethoven early showed an interest in and great ability for the piano. Like his father and grandfather before him, he obtained a position as court musician in Bonn, at the early age of 12. Aside from music, which he practiced assiduously, his education was limited. Although he educated himself in later years by voracious reading, he had constant difficulties with orthography and punctuation and was unable to do simple multiplication. While his musical education and his compositions prospered among aristocratic supporters and friends at the electoral court, Beethoven had to become the provider for his family. His mother died in 1787, his father in 1792; his two younger brothers continued to look to him as the head of the family.

In 1792, with the financial support of the prince elector of Cologne, Maximilian Franz, Beethoven left Bonn for Vienna. For the rest of his life, he lived and worked in Vienna, enjoying patronage and the friendship of aristocratic musical connois-

seurs and musicians. Not least among them was Archduke Rudolph, a brother of Emperor Francis II (Francis I of Austria after 1804), who remained his staunchest supporter and, also, music student. Beethoven dedicated his *Missa Solemnis* to him when Rudolph became archbishop. Beethoven had great musical successes in Vienna and, except for slight reverses, also financial security.

In all else, his life was a constant struggle. He suffered from a series of medical disorders, now diagnosed as connective tissue immunopathy. Beginning in his twenty-eighth year, he had a progressive hearing loss due to otosclerosis. He had a violent temper, fantasized about his birth (both as to his exact age and to being the bastard of a king of Prussia), was given to melancholia, and may have had an Oedipal complex. He also had difficulties in forming genuine love relationships with women. Probably Beethoven did not want to marry in spite of numerous proposals that he made. He seemed to pursue unavailable women: their social position was superior to his, or they were already married or about to be married. With only one did he apparently achieve a full, honest love. This was Antonie Brentano, whom Maynard Solomon has identified as the Immortal Beloved, a term Beethoven used in his letters. She was an aristocrat by birth, married, and ready to leave her family and children for Beethoven; yet he drew back (1812). Between 1815 and 1820 Beethoven was involved in lengthy litigation about custody of his nephew Karl, son of his late brother Kaspar Karl and Johanna van Beethoven. During the custody battle, Bee-

Ludwig van Beethoven, an etching from a chalk drawing (about 1818) by August von Kloeber.

thoven acknowledged in court that he was not of noble birth, that the "van" was not the equivalent of the German noble "von." In his own view, Beethoven did not require any patent of nobility—he was a noble in his head and heart, an aristocrat because of his musical genius. If this was arrogance, elitism, perhaps Beethoven was entitled to it. *See* EAR: Pathology.

Such struggles and conflicts were largely of his own making, but the same was not true for his deafness. When he first realized its incurable nature, Beethoven contemplated suicide. In the Heiligenstadt Testament (1802) which was found among his possessions after his death, he particularly laments the loss of hearing to a musician who, so he wrote, possessed the musical gift in a completeness few in his profession had. At the same time, his devotion to his art, to which he could contribute so much, restrained him from ending his life.

Beethoven came to terms with his deafness by 1806, without, however, being able to overcome its social effects. Whether or not it was owing entirely to his declining hearing, he was viewed as hostile, stubborn, and misanthropic. In what is regarded perhaps as his greatest single creation, the Ninth Symphony (1824), based upon J. C. F. von Schiller's "Ode to Joy," the words speak of the brotherhood of mankind. The language is still that of the *Sturm*

and Drang, the language of universals, freedom, brotherhood, and an all-loving deity, not pertaining to a particular denomination. Beethoven could empathize with humanity in general more easily than with individuals. His friendships were many, but not all endured uninterruptedly. Some were only restored near his death, which came on March 26, 1827, in Vienna. By that time, even the stormy relationship with his sister-in-law Johanna had come to its resolution.

Beethoven was rough, somewhat unpolished, suggested J. W. von Goethe, but, nevertheless, a genius. What was this genius creating? Symphonies, sonatas, an opera, overtures, all exhibiting great sensitivity to people and nature. Beethoven found solace in nature and solitude. And based on what he felt within and could communicate only through his music, Beethoven rivaled the range of Shakespeare.

Deafness was an important factor in Beethoven's artistic and personal life. In May of 1814, Beethoven gave his last public performance as a solo pianist; in January of the following year, he accompanied for the last time. By 1817, the beginning of the last decade of his life, he was completely deaf in the right ear and practically so in the left ear. His loss of hearing intensified his inward search and his musical expression, resulting in his greatest achievements. However, socially his deafness was a limitation, though it did not isolate him completely. His friend Johann Nepomuk Maelzel, an inventor, provided him with an ear trumpet, probably about 1814. In the same year, another friend, Aloys Weissenbach—a deaf surgeon and poet—wrote the libretto of Beethoven's *The Glorious Moment*, a cantata in celebration of the Congress of Vienna. By 1817, Beethoven used conversation books for social intercourse. Since Beethoven spoke, these conversation books more often included questions and answers by others than by the composer. In 1823, at a rehearsal of his opera *Fidelio*, which he conducted, Beethoven noticed confusion in the orchestra. He requested an explanation from his friend, Anton Schindler, who wrote in the conversation book, "It's no good anymore." Beethoven could not hear the orchestra.

In spite of these limitations, Beethoven could still enjoy two visitors singing to him: his hearing gone, the music was within. Even his portraits show it. There is the famous upward glance. Some view it as the characteristic look of deaf persons who frequently gaze upward to maintain face contact with other people. Indeed, with a height of about 5½ feet, Beethoven would have looked upward quite often. But Beethoven ascribed the gaze to a mental habit, and as music was his life, we must accept that he was listening with his inner ear. *See* MUSICIANS.

Bibliography

Cooper, Martin: *Beethoven, The Last Decade 1817–1827,* 1970.

Larkin, Edward: "Beethoven's Medical History," appendix A in Martin Cooper, *Beethoven,* pp. 439–466, 1970.

New Grove Dictionary of Music and Musicians, vol. 2, 1980.

Oxford Companion to Music, 10th ed., 1970.

Solomon, Maynard: *Beethoven,* 1977.

Kurt Beermann

BELGIUM

Belgium is a small, densely populated, highly industrialized, and linguistically divided nation. Slightly more than half the population are Flemish-speaking, while the rest are French-speaking. This linguistic and cultural division has important ramifications for deaf Belgians, who are themselves divided by linguistic identification. The provision of services to them, especially education, is deeply affected by differences between the two sectors.

PRESCHOOL SERVICES

Early diagnosis and habilitation of deaf children are stressed in Belgium. Systematic auditory screening of newborns and infants is common in several maternity wards. Many deaf children are now diagnosed during the first year of life, and most of those who are profoundly deaf are recognized before the age of two. Habilitation, including hearing aid fitting and family counseling in communication methods, is carried out by speech and hearing schools and centers. *See* AUDITORY DISORDERS, PREVENTION OF: Screening.

SCHOOLS

The total number of deaf pupils in Belgian schools is unknown; however, there are about 1500 pupils in special schools for deaf children. Eight of these schools are Flemish-speaking and seven French-speaking. Pupils are in one of three levels: maternal, primary, or lower secondary. The majority of students in both Flemish- and French-speaking schools are day students. All schools are state-supported, but most of the Flemish-speaking schools belong to the Roman Catholic school network and are run by Congregations. One Flemish-speaking school is operated by a province (county) and another by a city. The French-speaking schools are under various authorities: private (3), province (2), city (1), and Roman Catholic Congregation (1).

Career preparation is stressed in most schools. Eighty-eight percent of the students take vocational programs of the lower secondary level. The other 12 percent are in technical sections of lower secondary level, in which they can obtain a degree giving access to the higher secondary and eventually to postsecondary education. There are no higher secondary sections in the special schools for deaf children. Those students who go beyond this level must do so in integrated programs with hearing students.

EDUCATION METHODS

As in most European countries, sign language was discarded as a pedagogic instrument after the 1880 Milan Congress. It continued, however, to thrive in the residential institutes and in successive generations of some deaf families. Although never repressed, it was considered by educators as an inferior type of communication, so that its diffusion always remained very local, limited to the alumni of the different institutions. *See* HISTORY: Congress of Milan.

Integration or mainstreaming of hearing-impaired children in classes or schools for the normally hearing has been widely advocated, and actively practiced by some schools or centers. These have obtained rewarding results mostly for the moderately and severely hearing-impaired, though some profoundly deaf persons have also succeeded and achieved higher standards of education, owing to the integration system.

The oral methodology has been considerably influenced by, and has in some cases deliberately followed, either the methods advocated in Sint Michielsgestel (Netherlands) by A. van Uden or the verbo-tonal method of P. Guberina. The use of electroacoustic technology also has been stressed since the middle of the twentieth century. *See* NETHERLANDS.

The realization that an exclusively oral education does not enable all deaf children to acquire efficient oral language has prompted many educators in Belgium to reassess their methods. Several of them have concluded that some forms of manual communication, combined with the oral pedagogy, can help most deaf children to acquire a good command of spoken language and reach a much higher level of overall linguistic competence.

Since 1980, some of the French-speaking schools for deaf children have resolutely moved in these new directions while others are keeping to oralism alone. Cued speech, demonstrated in France and Belgium by Dr. Orin Cornett and his collaborators, has attracted wide interest and is now applied intensively in some schools. Another system called AKA (Alphabet des Kinèmes Assistés—alphabet of assisted kinemes, or lip movements of speech) has been developed in Belgium by W. Wouts and R. Cerise and is applied in their school. It is a manual complement of spoken language intended to disambiguate speechreading, like cued speech, while simultaneously bringing information about mode of articulation and prosody. *See* MOUTH-HAND SYSTEMS: Cued speech.

Bimodal communication, a form of total communication in which Signed French is used simultaneously with speech, has been introduced as an alternative to cued speech or in combination with it. The Signed French is based on signs of the Belgian Sign Language utilized by French-speaking deaf. *See* SIGN LANGUAGES; SOCIOLINGUISTICS.

There has been a consensus between French-speaking educators and leading deaf Belgians that, at least in the school system, Signed French is preferable to French Sign Language as a means of acquiring a good command of the French language. Adult deaf teachers, however, are now teaching French Sign Language to deaf students to enable them to acquire it correctly.

Most Flemish-speaking schools are exclusively oral or limit communication to fingerspelling for multihandicapped, dysphasic deaf children. Total communication is rarely used except with small groups of children considered incapable of coping with the oral pedagogy. One school is developing a unified Signed Flemish and considering using it systematically from nursery school onward. The use of Signed Flemish for education instead of Flemish Sign Language is supported by the Deaf Community.

There are no sign-language or cued-speech interpreters to help deaf students in ordinary schools or universities. Mainstreamed students must learn through speechreading, residual hearing, and written material. The State University of Mons is beginning to train oral, sign, and cued-speech interpreters and adapting written, video, and computer-programmed materials for deaf students at all levels. *See* INTERPRETING.

Few educational services specifically for multihandicapped deaf children are available. Since September 1981, however, a special center for psychotic and autistic children has operated. The staff use sign language.

Special education, like general education, is free of charge, including special remedial measures required by any child. Transportation of handicapped children to special schools is organized by the schools, which are reimbursed by the State Education Ministry. The National Health Insurance system (INAMI) and the National Fund for Social Adaptation of the Handicapped (FNRSH) support 60–80 percent of the cost of hearing aids. Their combined intervention results in the funding of 80 percent of the cost of stereophonic adaptation (that is, fitting with two hearing aids).

Parents receive family allowances for all children, and these are more than doubled for deaf children. For purposes of income tax declaration, each deaf child counts as two children in charge.

SOCIOECONOMIC STATUS

Deaf Belgians have often remained confined to occupations requiring qualifications inferior to their intrinsic intellectual capacities. Their socioeconomic status is therefore usually not on a par with the latter. Typically, they hold manual-labor, service, or low-level technical jobs. Deaf teachers are almost nonexistent. Although no official statistics are available on unemployment of deaf persons, probably there is no more unemployment among them than in the general population.

There are some legal provisions for reserving jobs for handicapped persons: all state-controlled organizations are obligated to employ 2 percent handicapped people. However, to be eligible for these jobs, they must pass a state examination in addition to their education certificates or degrees.

Besides their professional income or their unemployment wages, handicapped people may receive an allocation to compensate for their underemployment and for their difficulties in social integration.

SOCIOCULTURAL LIFE

There are numerous associations for deaf adults which organize sociocultural activities. In most of these, sign language is the major mode of communication. No data are available concerning the percentage of the deaf population as a whole who are active members of these associations. Pleas for unity are often made but have not eradicated the divisions along linguistic (Flemish–French), philosophical (Roman Catholic–non-Catholic), and local cleavage lines.

There is an increasing tendency toward linguistic separation in Belgium as a whole, and this is reflected in the sign languages, which are drifting apart more and more. In each deaf linguistic community a commission is studying, unifying, and promoting the sign language of that community. A dictionary of the French-speaking deaf community's sign language is currently (1983) in preparation. This language differs from, but has many features in common with, France's sign language, with which it shares about 50 percent of its vocabulary.

There are only a few self-taught sign-language interpreters, either teachers or hearing people with deaf relatives, who assist deaf people on some social occasions and for legal proceedings. There is one association of oral deaf and hard-of-hearing adults who do not use signs, most of the deaf members having lost their hearing after language acquisition. This association sponsors courses in speechreading. There are also a number of oral deaf people who do not participate in the activities of deaf groups and do not feel the need for sign language, being satisfied with the degree of integration within the hearing society which they have achieved. They communicate by speech, speechreading, residual hearing when present, and written language.

Deaf people tend to marry more often with others who are deaf, but no numeric data are available.

MEDIA

Little has been done to make either telephones or television accessible to deaf Belgians. Only a few private lines are equipped with graphic telephones (TDD). However, the Ministry of the French-speaking Cultural Community has begun using them. Since 1981, the national French-speaking television network has provided sign interpretation five days a week with the main early evening news, and shows a weekly program consisting of a course in speechreading for deafened adults and general information of interest to deaf people. *See* TELECOMMUNICATIONS: Telephone Services.

The national Flemish-speaking network has a weekly news magazine for deaf and hard-of-hearing people, consisting of captioned slides, photos or maps for the headlines, pages of written text, and captioned extracts of moving pictures. There are also pages of teletext about deafness and deaf persons which are edited by this network.

There is no systematic captioning program, so that for most deaf people access to television is very limited. They can follow only foreign movies which are shown with subtitles, but these are rare in the French-speaking Belgian or French networks, most films being shown in a French-speaking version. The situation is a little better in the Flemish and Dutch networks, where more films are shown in their original versions with subtitles; however, these films are usually of poor quality.

Bibliography

Degand, J.: *L'éducation des enfants déficients auditifs dans les structures de l'enseignement des entendants*, Bulletin d'Orientation Scolaire et Professionnelle, 28:45–71, 1979.

Lepot-Froment, C.: *L'enfant sourd raconté par ses parents*, Louvain-la-Neuve, Cabay, 1981.

Marquet, J., et al.: *Het gehoorgestoorden-probleem in Vlaanderen*, Universiteit Antwerpen, 1979.

Perier, O., and A. Bochner-Wuidar: "Manual Aids: A Must for the Psychotic Deaf and a Fail-Safe Measure for Other Deaf Children," in G. T. Mencher and S. E. Gerber, (eds.) *The Multiply Handicapped Hearing Impaired Child*, 1983.

Verslag van het internationaal symposium van 6 tot 8 november 1981 te Gentbrugge (België), "Communicatie bij doven," Federatie van Nederlandstalige Dovenverenigingen vzw, Jules Destréelaan 67–9219 Gent-Gentbrugge, België.

Wouts, W., and R. Cerise: "AKA, Alphabet des Kinèmes Assistés," *Proceedings of the Ninth Congress of the World Federation of the Deaf*, Palermo, July 1983.

O. Perier

BELL, ALEXANDER GRAHAM
(1847–1922)

Alexander Graham Bell is famous the world over as the inventor of the telephone. It was on March 10, 1876, shortly after his twenty-ninth birthday, that Bell made his brief historic telephone call to Thomas A. Watson. Refinement and marketing of his invention made him rich and secured his fame. However, he was far more than the inventor of the telephone. Philosopher, philanthropist, editor, farmer, architect, teacher of deaf children—he was all of these, and more. History has rarely seen a more industrious or accomplished human being.

Born on March 3, 1847, in Edinburgh, Scotland, to Melville and Eliza (Symonds) Bell, Alec (as the younger Bell was known) showed early signs of exceptional intelligence and creativity. He produced his first invention before the age of 13, a device for husking wheat. Such experiments continued throughout his life, including not only the telephone but such things as kites, gliders, boats, metal detectors, respirators, an improved phonograph, and even designs for a heavier-than-air flying machine. Bell also followed his father's lead and took an active interest in elocution and the remediation of speech disorders. This interest eventually blossomed into his lifetime occupation, and indeed Alexander Graham Bell should be considered first and foremost an educator of deaf children.

Alexander Graham Bell. (Library of Congress)

Inasmuch as Bell's interests were numerous, this article concentrates on his involvement with deafness and deaf people. First, his development as a teacher of deaf pupils is outlined, culminating with his leadership in the movement to establish day schools for deaf children. Next, his views on sign language and his position in the communications debate are discussed. Third, his work as a eugenicist in the Social Darwinism movement is examined. Finally, the effects of Bell's Social Darwinian philosophy upon his educational philosophy are analyzed.

TEACHER OF DEAF CHILDREN

Bell's first exposure to deafness was through his mother, Eliza Bell, who had lost much of her hearing during childhood, but retained good speech and language throughout her life. Contributing to her skill in these areas is the strong likelihood that her hearing impairment was severe but not profound (accurate hearing testing had not yet begun, since Bell did not invent the audiometer until 1879). Records show that she used an ear trumpet, could carry on conversations (though not easily), taught her sons to play the piano, and played the piano herself.

While Bell's relationship with his mother greatly affected his attitude toward deaf people, it was his father, Melville Bell, who actually served as the link between Bell and education of the hearing-impaired. The elder Bell was a pioneer of Visible Speech, a system that described oral sounds through written symbols. Melville Bell, like his father before him, was an elocutionist, and was intensely interested in the improvement of speech. Visible Speech was developed as a method for such improvement. In order to demonstrate its benefits, the younger Bell learned it and assisted his father in public demonstrations. *See* EDUCATION: History; VISIBLE SPEECH.

The Visible Speech system was not designed as a teaching tool for use with deaf people, but this usage was eventually discovered. Susanna Hull, the director of a small school for deaf children in Great Britain, recognized the system's potential, and in May 1868 the 21-year-old Bell began working with two of her deaf pupils. This was his first experience with deaf students, and according to his own account it was almost immediately successful. In 1870 the director of the Boston School for Deaf Mutes, Sarah Fuller, asked Melville Bell to visit her school and teach Visible Speech. He refused but his son did not, and the younger Bell soon had a class of about 30 pupils. By 1871 Bell was writing his parents that he was planning upon the establishment of a good profession at the school. He even began talking of founding a training school for teachers of deaf children.

In late 1872 Bell's inventive genius began asserting itself, in the form of the multiple telegraph, allowing the transmission of multiple messages over a single telegraph wire. His work on it was a tremendous drain upon his time, and limited his work as an educator. However, he by no means abandoned the latter. For instance, in 1872 Bell started tutoring George Sanders, a five-year-old deaf boy. When he visited the elder Bells in Ontario during the summer of 1873, Sanders went as well. And when Boston University made him professor of vocal physiology and elocution, Sander's grandmother gave Bell free room and board in her Salem home in return for continuing the instruction. The Sanders case is but a single instance of Bell's dedication to his work with deaf children. No matter how far afield his interests spread, and regardless of the demands upon his time related to the development of and patent on the telephone, Bell never discontinued an active interest in deafness.

Bell's relationship with George Sanders continued for many years, not only as a teacher but as a friend and financial backer as well. However, one other teacher-student relationship that Bell made lasted longer, and with far more consequence. Boston lawyer Gardiner Greene Hubbard had a deaf daughter named Mabel, and when Bell began private tutoring in 1873 to supplement his income, Hubbard enrolled her. The 15-year-old Mabel at first disliked her teacher, complaining about his "old-fashioned suit and shiny hair." Her feelings soon changed to respect, and eventually to love—feelings shared by Bell. In 1877 the two were married, and their partnership lasted for 45 years. Mabel Hubbard Bell had a significant impact upon Bell's approach to deaf education, and indeed upon his entire life. She was his most valued critic and his staunchest supporter, and through her writing and her management of family affairs she showed herself to be a remarkable woman in her own right.

The year 1877 was also when Bell began his campaign to establish day schools for deaf children. At that time, almost all schools were residential; that is, students actually lived at the schools for days, weeks, or even many months at a time. Bell felt that residential schools prevented students from developing good relationships with members of their families, or with hearing people in their own communities. He was able to put these feelings into practice when a Scottish businessman asked his assistance in starting a day school in Greencock, Scotland. Bell not only organized the school, but was also one of its first teachers. While it opened in 1878 with only three pupils, it was seen by Bell as a pilot project, and did much to whet his enthusiasm for establishing such schools in North America. *See* EDUCATIONAL PROGRAMS: Day Schools, Residential Schools.

His next direct involvement with day schools came

five years later, this time in Washington, D.C. He limited his class to six pupils, and arranged for a kindergarten class of normally hearing children to occupy the first floor of the building. Bell hoped that the children would mix at certain times of the day, thus enhancing the deaf children's desire and ability to speak and to read lips. In addition, a class for parents and friends of deaf children was formed in order to help them support what the children had learned. Despite Bell's enthusiasm over the results of the school, it lasted only about two years. Problems in retaining a teacher, added to heavy demands upon Bell's time, forced the closing.

The biggest roadblock to day schools for the deaf was the unwillingness of state governments to pay for them. In the early 1880s states supported only residential schools, so that a family wishing to send a child to a day school was forced to pay the tuition. Wisconsin led the way in state support for day schools, prodded by the lobbying of a group of concerned parents and citizens, and the forceful testimony of Bell. In time, other states launched similar efforts, and Bell was frequently called upon for support. Thus, while his own school was short-lived, the day school movement flourished, a movement Bell described as "the most important movement of the century for the benefit of the deaf." It is unlikely that the campaign to establish day schools would have met with such success had it not been for his leadership and support.

CHAMPION OF ORAL EDUCATION

For many years a controversy has existed over how best to communicate with deaf children in the classroom. This argument pits advocates of the oral method against advocates of the combined method. The difference between the two methods centers on the use of sign language. The oral method asserts that almost all people process language auditorally, and thus stresses this mode of language acquisition for deaf children. The formal use of sign language is not allowed in oral programs. *See* SIGN LANGUAGES.

The combined method is based upon the belief that many deaf children are unable to learn language auditorally, and that visual methods should be added to the auditory approach used by oral educators. To speech, speechreading, and the use of residual hearing, the combined method adds some sort of sign language, which is a visual representation of language.

The communications debate had been in full swing for many years before Bell entered it, but he quickly became an influential voice in favor of oralism. Indeed, by the late 1880s he was the acknowledged leader of oral education in America. Normal society, he maintained, is made up of people who speak and hear, making use of the English

Bell and his wife, Mabel Hubbard. (Library of Congress)

language. It was therefore the job of educators to prepare deaf children to make their way in the world, to use English, and to communicate in English by speaking and by reading lips. Society was clearly uppermost in his mind when he defined his philosophy of education of deaf children: "The great object of education of the deaf is to enable them to communicate readily and easily with hearing persons. That is what is meant by 'restoring the deaf to society.'" *See* HISTORY: Sign Language Controversy.

Bell strenuously opposed sign language because of the importance he attached to standard English. This, to him, was the key to successful integration. If a student could communicate only in sign language, he or she would never be able to be integrated into the hearing world. He did approve of fingerspelling with young children, and accepted nonformalized gestures. It was the formal gestures that, to Bell, were harmful, specifically the sign language developed in France by the Abbé de l'Epée. This was the sign language used, in much revised form, by the American deaf population. *See* L'EPÉE, ABBÉ CHARLES MICHEL DE.

Some educators, such as Edward Miner Gallaudet, claimed that the sign language of l'Epée was the natural language of the deaf. Bell disagreed, stating that sign language is no more natural to the deaf than English is natural to all hearing children. "It is natural only in the same sense that English is natural to the American child. It is the language of the people by whom he is surrounded." Bell never argued that sign language was a poor teaching tool. In fact, he admitted "the ease with which a deaf child acquires this language and its perfect adaptability for the purpose of developing the mind." Intellectual development was simply not Bell's major concern. For him, one goal was of paramount importance—integration. *See* GALLAUDET, EDWARD MINER.

While sign language might be educationally effective, so too, in Bell's estimation, were speech and lipreading. He was totally convinced that deaf children would be able to acquire these oral skills. His complete confidence in the oral system appears somewhat naive when examined with today's knowledge and experience. "It is not generally known," he wrote, "that the experimental stage has passed, and that all deaf-mutes can be taught intelligible speech." Bell's belief regarding lipreading skills was similarly unrealistic: "All who are deaf from infancy can certainly achieve . . . results." Unfortunately, history has not borne out Bell's confidence in the oral approach. All deaf children cannot be taught intelligible speech, at least not yet. Modern-day oralists know this, but they still share Bell's conviction that such instruction must be given, or at least attempted.

Many oralists today also share Bell's aversion to sign language, and would probably agree with his opinion that, if signing has any use at all, it is "as a means of reaching and benefitting adults who are unable to communicate with the hearing world . . . The adults referred to represent our failures. Let us have as few of them as we possibly can." Labeling a person a "failure" because he uses sign language instead of standard English might seem harsh to some, as it did to the adult deaf population in the 1890s. To them, attempts to eliminate sign language were tantamount to stripping them of their identity, their community, and their culture, and many of them hated Bell as a result. He knew of this feeling and lamented it, but his convictions were never shaken.

Bell worked hard and effectively to promote the cause of oralism, and he wrote and spoke in its support in the United States and abroad. He also supported oralism with his pocketbook. Profits from the telephone and other inventions eventually equaled close to a million dollars, a most substantial sum by nineteenth-century standards. In 1886 Bell used his money to establish what eventually was called the Volta Bureau, an organization sponsoring research and dissemination of information regarding deafness, and oral education for deaf children. In 1890 he gave $25,000 to fund the new American Association for the Promotion of the Teaching of Speech to the Deaf (AAPTSD). This organization still exists, though its name was changed in 1956 to the Alexander Graham Bell Association for the Deaf. The association, through its meetings, lobbying, and journal, the *Volta Review*, stands at the center of the oral education movement in the United States. *See* ALEXANDER GRAHAM BELL ASSOCIATION FOR THE DEAF; EDUCATION: History; VOLTA REVIEW.

SOCIAL DARWINIST

Bell was a major figure in the intellectual movement known as Social Darwinism, particularly that branch of it known in the nineteenth century as eugenics. Social Darwinists applied Charles Darwin's theory of the survival of the fittest to the social structure of the day. Darwin saw different species of plants and animals in a constant struggle to survive, success coming through the adjustment known as evolution. Social Darwinists applied this analysis of nature to human society. Competition was a social law, as well as a law of nature, and survival was the reward of the fittest. They were concerned with one species—*Homo sapiens*—and with the different classes and cultures that make up humankind.

Eugenicists applied Darwin to the task of selecting a fitter race, advocating selective breeding and a program to keep America free of "inferior" and "lower" peoples. They were not concerned as much with individuals as with society, hoping to improve it through selective marriage, childbearing, and immigration—primitive forms of today's genetic engineering.

Bell believed firmly in the need to strengthen American society by increasing the number of "desirable" people and reducing the number of "undersirables." To this end, he encouraged control on both marriage and immigration. He saw the encouragement of "good" marriages as a positive approach to race improvement, envisioning the development of a "thoroughbred strain" of humans who would intermarry to improve the entire race. These thoroughbreds would be strong, healthy, and without mental or physical handicap.

It was also important, in Bell's opinion, to control immigration. What was the sense of trying to improve the race from within, he asked, when undesirables from outside were pouring into the country? In his view, the wave of immigration hitting America's shores in the late nineteenth and early twentieth centuries required careful government control in order to maintain "the standard of manhood" and to "eliminate undesirable ethnical elements." He saw the issue as being one of self-preservation. "The only hope for a truly American race," he wrote, "lies in the restriction of immigration." As to who should and should not be allowed into the country, the variables Bell chose were literacy and nationality.

In 1915 an effort was made in Congress to require all potential immigrants to take a literacy test. Failure on this test would mean a trip back to the country of origin for the unlucky immigrant. Proponents of the test contended that illiterates put too great a strain on society. Opponents countered by noting that many immigrants were escaping some sort of persecution, and that once denied entry into the United States they would face imprisonment or worse back home. Bell saw both good and bad in the literacy requirement, but decided that American society needed this safeguard, and recommended its passage.

In addition to literacy, national origin was a concern of Bell's. He suggested that the United States would do well to copy Canada's immigration policy. At that time, Canada accepted all immigrants on three years' probation and could expel them at any time during that period. What most impressed Bell about Canada's system was its policy of favoring northern Europeans, such as Finns, Germans, British, Russians, and Dutch, over southern Europeans such as Italians, Portugese, Spaniards, Turks, and Greeks. He considered the southerners to be less cultured, less educated, and less American-like than their northern neighbors. Their arrival in America thus represented a pollution of the clean and pure elements that America needed to maintain its superior stock.

Before continuing, it is important to view Social Darwinism in its proper historical perspective. One might easily dismiss its adherents as self-interested and racist. True, the movement did have its share of crackpots and demagogues. Men such as the Reverend Josiah Strong used it to "prove" the superiority of Anglo-Saxons over all other peoples, and Theodore Roosevelt used it to rationalize the near-genocide of the American Indian. However, many intelligent and thoughtful people supported the philosophical precepts of Herbert Spencer and William Graham Sumner, two of the leading Social Darwinian thinkers. Alexander Graham Bell was merely one of many who saw life as a struggle for survival, with the strongest elements within society having the upper hand. One must take care to separate intent from effect. Bell did not intend to harm specific groups or individuals, but sought to strengthen society for the good of all. The effect of his intentions, had they been realized, might well have inflicted hardship upon those deemed weak or undesirable. Bell's views on deafness should be viewed in this light.

THE DEAF AND EUGENICS

Bell's work in eugenics reveals more concern for society than for individual human needs. When his life's work is so analyzed, it is clear that his interest in deafness was eugenic as much as it was educational. This is not to say that he lacked empathy for the individual deaf children whose lives he so profoundly affected. However, he seems to have thought more about the effect of deafness on society than on the lives of the deaf themselves.

After a lengthy study of statistics on deaf families collected by Edward Allen Fay, Bell concluded that deafness was in many cases an inheritable trait. This disturbed him since deaf people were not, in his opinion, members of what he labeled the "desirable class." He did not consider deaf persons themselves to be bad. Rather, it was the trait that was undersirable, and its transmission from generation to generation was a problem in need of a solution. The obvious solution, in Bell's mind, was rational marriage and child bearing. Individuals whose deafness might be hereditary should marry hearing people, as should their offspring and their children's offspring. *See* FAY, EDWARD ALLEN.

In 1893 Bell wrote his *Memoir upon the Formation of a Deaf Variety of the Human Race.* In it, he asserted that "evidence shows a tendency to the formation of a deaf variety of the human race in America." While he could not alter the inheritability of deafness, he could address the issue of intermarriage among deaf people. He suggested two types of measures—preventive and repressive. Among the preventive measures were an end to the segregation of deaf children in special schools, an end to the employment of deaf teachers for deaf students, and an end to the use of sign language. These three practices "produce an environment that is unfavorable to the cultivation of articulation and speechreading," and without those skills, how could deaf people expect to attract hearing mates?

Bell also described repressive measures meant to foster integration. He called upon friends of deaf people "to prevent undesirable intermarriages," though he doubted that friends would be willing to interfere in this way. He suggested a law banning all intermarriage among deaf people, but immediately rejected it as impractical since it would only foster immorality. Another law he suggested would have banned intermarriage only in cases where one or both partners were congenitally deaf, but this too he rejected as unworkable, since establishing such etiology was impossible in many cases. The most workable law, wrote Bell, would forbid the intermarriage of deaf persons from families with at least one other deaf member. It is important to note that Bell did not advocate immediate passage of any of these laws. He called first for more data collection and more study, and concluded that "a due consideration of all the objections renders it doubtful whether legislative interference with the marriage of the deaf would be advisable." He believed legislative restrictions to be a good idea, but felt that the furor they would create would cause more problems than the restrictions themselves would solve.

Bell's *Memoir* deeply offended the deaf community, which rightly regarded it as an argument that would legislate them out of existence. His statement that such legislation was not "advisable" did not soothe them, and the majority of deaf adults would thereafter view Bell with disdain and fear. For his part, Bell maintained that he did not advocate legislative interference, and accused the deaf community of misinterpreting his writing. Perhaps the deaf community did misinterpret Bell. Or perhaps they were reading between the lines, seeing not a moral aversion to restrictive laws but instead a practical view that such laws were politically unfeasible.

Legal prohibitions aside, Bell did speak out forcefully against intermarriage of persons who were deaf. He tried to convince educational leaders to join him, but was generally frustrated. So strongly did Bell believe in the negative effects of intermarriage that he requested and received permission to speak on the subject to students at the National Deaf-Mute College in Washington, D.C. (Since renamed Gallaudet College). Bell failed to comprehend that, to many deaf people, deafness was not an affliction but a simple fact of life. Bell the scientist saw deaf people as different, as less well equipped than those who could hear. It never occurred to him that there were some deaf people who were satisfied with their condition, who considered themselves normal, and who saw nothing wrong with having deaf children. To be told by a hearing person that they were "afflicted," and that none of them would want to pass on this affliction, was surely an insult. One may argue whether deafness is an affliction, but has anyone the right to make that decision for others? This is what Bell did, and doubtless his view had the backing of society in general. It did not have the backing of deaf people themselves. *See* Gallaudet College.

While clearly giving priority to what he viewed as society's needs, Bell honestly believed that he was working in the best interests of deaf people. Bell the eugenicist thought it best for the race that all people be able to hear, and short of that, that all people should at least be able to understand speech and communicate orally. Thus Bell the educator espoused the oral method, which stressed integration while at the same time addressing the academic needs of deaf children. His vision of an improved society, added to a family background that placed great importance on oral communication, completes the profile of a man born to be an oralist. It is impossible to know how much of Bell's philosophy was affected by his world view

and his expectations for society, but it does seem certain that his emphasis upon humankind as a group, as opposed to a more individualist perspective, played an important role.

One final Darwinian application requires note. Bell, like all Social Darwinists, was convinced that the fittest would ultimately survive. He applied his belief not only to different races, but to educational programs as well. He was certain that in a struggle for ascendancy between oral and combined methods, the oral method (the fittest) would prevail. Indeed, after examining the state of affairs in 1894, Bell was convinced that evolution had already made its mark. After the Milan Convention of 1880 had voted overwhelmingly to support oral education, Bell was moved to comment: "Natural selection, operating on the continent of Europe for more than a century, has brought about the survival of the pure oral method and the almost total extinction of the French system of signs. The verdict of time is therefore conclusive as to the superiority of the oral over the sign method of instructing the deaf." If Bell were alive today he would realize that the verdict is still very much in doubt. While oralism was in ascendancy in the late eighteenth and early nineteenth centuries, it was on the decline in the 1980s.

CONCLUSION

While Bell's scientific approach to life favored a social perspective, he clearly had important, positive effects upon many individuals. A good example is that of the meeting he had in 1887 with a deaf and blind girl. Her father had nearly given up hope of finding a competent teacher for her. During the course of their meeting, Bell did his best to communicate with the six-year-old child, and though complete words were not exchanged, feelings apparently were. Eighteen years later, describing this encounter, Helen Keller wrote that their meeting was "the door through which I should pass from darkness to light." Through Bell, inquiries were made of other professionals in the field, leading to the recruitment of Anne Sullivan as Keller's teacher, and to her eventual success and fame. *See* Keller, Helen.

Alexander Graham Bell died on August 2, 1922, in Beinn Bhreagh, near Baddek, Nova Scotia. By any standard, he was a remarkable man. His personal characteristics included unquenchable curiosity, boundless energy, great dignity, superior intelligence and creativity, and a remarkable sense of confidence in his ability to take on problems and solve them. Of all his many interests, none received more of his attention than the education of deaf children. His success in this field, added to the prestige he gained in the scientific world, made him the perfect standard-bearer for the oral movement. As a result of his early successes with Visible Speech, his tireless efforts to promote oral education within the field of deafness and in the political arena, and his financial and moral support, Alexander Graham Bell surely qualifies as the nineteenth century's most important leader in oral education for deaf children.

Bibliography

Bell, Alexander Graham: "Fallacies Concerning the Deaf," *American Annals of the Deaf*, 29:32–60, January 1884.

———: "A Few Thoughts Concerning Eugenics," *National Geographic*, 19:119–123, February 1908.

———: *Graphical Studies of Marriages of the Deaf*, Volta Bureau, Washington, D.C., 1917.

———: "Growth of the Oral Method of Instructing the Deaf," Press of Rockwell and Churchill, Boston, 1896.

———: "How to Improve the Race," *Journal of Heredity*, 5:1–7, January 1914.

———: "Is Race Suicide Possible?", *Journal of Heredity*, 11:339–341, November-December 1920.

———: *Marriage; an Address to the Deaf*, Sanders Printing Office, Washington, D.C., 1898.

———: "Professor A. Graham Bell's Studies of the Deaf," *Science*, pp. 135–136, September 1890.

———: *The Duration of Life and Conditions Associated with Longevity*, Genealogical Record Office, Washington, D.C., 1918.

———: *Upon the Formation of a Deaf Variety of the Human Race*, Government Printing Office, Washington, D.C., 1884.

———: "Utility of Action and Gesture," *Volta Review*, 17:13–18, January 1915.

———: "Utility of Signs," *Educator*, 5:3–23, May 1894.

———: "Visible Speech as a Means of Communicating Articulation to Deaf-Mutes," *American Annals of the Deaf*, 17:1–21, January 1872.

———: "Who Shall Inherit Long Life?", *National Geographic*, 35:505–514, June 1919.

"Bell Family Papers," Library of Congress, Manuscript Division, Washington, D.C.

Bruce, Robert: *Alexander Graham Bell and the Conquest of Solitude*, 1973.

Burlingame, Roger: *Out of Silence into Sound: The Life of Alexander Graham Bell*, 1964.

Costain, Thomas: *The Chord of Steel*, 1960.

Curry, Samuel: *Alexander Melville Bell: Some Memories, with Fragments from a Pupil's Notebook*, School of Expression, Boston, 1909.

Grosvenor, Elsie: "My Father, Alexander Graham Bell," *Volta Review*, 53:349, 386–388, August 1951.

Grosvenor, Mrs. Gilbert: "Mrs. Alexander Graham Bell: A Reminiscence," *Volta Review*, 59:299–305, September 1957.

Grosvenor, Melville: "Memories of My Grandfather," *Volta Review*, 42:621–622, October 1940.

Mackenzie, Catherine: *Alexander Graham Bell, the Man Who Contracted Space*, 1928.

Mitchell, Sue: "The Haunting Influence of Alexander Graham Bell," *American Annals of the Deaf*, 116:349–356, June 1971.

Waite, Helen: *Make a Joyful Sound*, 1961.

Yale, Caroline: "Mabel Hubbard Bell, 1859–1923," *Volta Review*, 25:107–110, March 1923.

Richard Winefield

BERTHIER, JEAN-FERDINAND
(1803–1886)

Born in 1803 at Louhans, France, Ferdinand Berthier was the most outstanding advocate of deaf people in nineteenth-century France. He was the mobilizer of the large and influential deaf community in Paris and a vigorous campaigner for better public information about deafness. He was also a firm supporter of educational methods which used "natural sign language" to develop the intellectual potential of deaf students and to facilitate the learning of written French. While he was recognized both by deaf people and by hearing people as the persistent political leader of what he called the deaf "nation," he was also the kindly old father figure who acted out the fables of La Fontaine at deaf gatherings. He published numerous papers and books in defense of his people and their language. The first deaf man to receive the medal of the Legion of Honor, he was elected in 1849 to the Société des Gens des Lettres, France's most prestigious literary fellowship.

By some accounts, Berthier was deafened at the age of four. He himself said that he was born deaf. At any rate, he was sent to the National Institute for Deaf-Mutes (the school made famous by the Abbé de l'Epée and the Abbé Roch Sicard), where his teacher was Auguste Bébian. Though hearing, Bébian was fluent in natural signs, and it was Bébian who led the movement to replace methodical signs with sign language. The most distinguished of a long line of deaf graduates educated with the bilingual philosophy of Bébian, Berthier was appointed to a professorship at the age of 26. *See* L'EPÉE, ABBÉ CHARLES MICHEL DE; SICARD, ABBÉ ROCH AMBROISE CUCURRON.

In 1834 Berthier instituted the tradition of celebrating the anniversaries of the birth of the Abbé de l'Epée with annual banquets. Designed to perpetuate the memory of the greatest publicist for deaf people of all time, the banquets became the rallying point for the deaf community for the rest of the century. The Société Centrale des Sourds-Muets (probably the world's first formal association of deaf persons) recognized officially in 1838, was founded to organize the banquets and promote the welfare of deaf people.

The famous deaf banquets in Paris united not only the educated elite of French deaf society—writers, painters, sculptors, teachers—but also the laborers—gardeners, mechanics, carpenters, printers—and, as the years went by, many deaf foreigners who traveled to Paris for what became the international family reunion of deaf people in the nineteenth century. Berthier presided (he was almost always elected banquet president) over these gatherings where sign language was the undisputed champion: "minutes, reports, letters, speeches, everything is read in this language which is admirably understood by the deaf from all corners of the earth." In the beginning, entrance to the banquet was offered only as a rare privilege to hearing people, and only to those who had proven their fidelity to the deaf "nation." Through the years, however, government officials and reporters were invited and provided with interpreters.

The banquets were grand social events, but they were also very serious business (women were not even admitted until after Berthier's death) and, as was common in France, the banquets were a forum for political activism.

The core committee of the Société Centrale, in their monthly meetings, discussed strategies for increasing public information about deafness, for safeguarding their gains since the time of the Abbé de l'Epée while countering the arguments of militant oralists, for planning the continuing education of graduates of French deaf schools, and for teaching the rights and duties of citizenship to deaf persons who had not gone to school.

The goals of the Société Centrale, later renamed the Société Universelle des Sourds-Muets, were for the intellectual and moral advancement of deaf people from around the world and for the unity of the deaf nation (Berthier never ceased to emphasize the need for concerted efforts in the face of periodic quarreling among factions). Of Berthier's part in the progress of the situation of deaf persons since the days before the Abbé de l'Epée, Claudius Forestier, another of the Paris Institute's great deaf teachers, announced to the 1839 gathering: "You have been restored to a place in the social hierarchy where you have the *right* to intelligence. You're always meeting, among your hearing brothers, men eager to offer you their friendship, their services, their talents. And where does this great change come from? It is that you have become a nation and that you have a leader worthy to represent you."

After 1840 Berthier addressed numerous research papers to the parliament on the subject of civil and criminal laws dealing with, or omitting mention of, deaf people. He appeared before the Academy of Moral and Political Sciences and the Academy of Medicine to defend sign language, to criticize the narrow medicopedagogical approach to deafness, and to argue that deaf persons as citizens were worthy not only of equality but of respect.

Though an elite in the deaf community had won recognition and respect, Berthier would never be able to cease fighting the negative attitudes toward deaf people, not only in the general public but even from within his cherished Paris Institute where he became the senior faculty member. Several attempts at the suppression of natural signs in favor of oral methods were vetoed by the signing teachers under his leadership.

Berthier spent years searching for the remains of the body of the Abbé de l'Epée and was a fervent supporter of the erection of memorials to the Abbé de l'Epée in Versailles, at the church of Saint-Roch in Paris, and in the courtyard of the Paris Institute. He was the grand defender of the memory of him "to whom an unhappy people owed its intellectual and moral emancipation." However, Berthier, with his usual candor, was not afraid to denounce the system of methodical signs which was created by the Abbé de l'Epée and then carried to extremes by the Abbé Sicard. Berthier venerated the Abbé de l'Epée, who used his methodical signs only in the classroom, as the loving father of his people; he detested Sicard, a grammarian who simply never learned to communicate with deaf people, Berthier felt, because he lacked respect for this "exceptional" people. The man Charles Michel de l'Epée was an important character in deaf history, but the myth of the Abbé de l'Epée, the godlike "father" of the deaf, was in part a result of the work of Berthier.

Berthier's writings include research into the history and heritage of deaf persons; biographical research on the lives of Bébian, the Abbé de l'Epée, and Sicard; defenses against attacks on the moral and intellectual capacities of deaf people; and even the Napoleonic Code translated into simple French to allow deaf people to understand clearly their rights and duties as French citizens. His writing style was clear and penetrating, honest, and elegant. His signing style, according to contemporaries, was even more elegant.

The fight for genuine equality for his people, for his "family", had made great strides during Berthier's lifetime, but the fight was never won. Berthier died in Paris on July 12, 1886, and in the year afterward as the last students taught in sign language graduated from the Paris Institute, the last deaf teachers at the Institute were forced into early retirement. Ernest Dusuzeau, one of those teachers, said of Berthier at the fifty-second banquet in 1886: "He brought light into the spirit of his students, and it is through him that a great many of my friends and myself have experienced the joy of counting for something, of living thoughtfully and with the heart." *See* HISTORY: Sign Language Controversy.

Bibliography

Berthier's writings include:

Examen Critique de l'opinion de feu le Docteur Itard, 1852.

Histoire et Statistique de l'Education des Sourds-Muets, 1839.

L'Abbé de l'Epée, 1853.

L'Abbé Sicard, 1873.

Le Code Napoleon mis a la portée des sourds-muets, 1868.

Les Sourds-Muets avant et depuis l'Abbé de l'Epée, 1840.

Notice sur la Vie et les Ouvrages d'Auguste Bébian, 1839.

Observations sur la Mimique, 1852.

William Moody

BOOTH, EDMUND
1810–1905

Edmund Booth was an impressive man: nearly 6 feet 3 inches in height, over 200 pounds, blind in one eye, and profoundly deaf. For most of his working years, from 1856 to 1895, he edited an Iowa newspaper, the *Anamosa Eureka*. Before settling down to this career, he was a teacher, farmer, post-

Edmund Booth. (Gallaudet College Archives)

master, county recorder, enrollment clerk in the Iowa territorial legislature, and California gold miner. Booth also played an active role in the deaf community. He was instrumental in furthering the education of deaf people in South Carolina, Georgia, and Iowa; he took part in the debate over a deaf commonwealth in the 1850s; and he helped to organize the National Association of the Deaf (NAD) in 1880.

Booth was born on August 24, 1810, to a farming family in Chickopee, Massachusetts, a small town near Springfield. When he was 4½, his father died from "spotted fever," probably meningitis. The same disease struck him three days later, leaving Booth without sight in his left eye, without hearing in his right ear, and with only slight hearing in his left. Four years later that remnant of hearing disappeared too. At age eight, Booth was completely deaf, and his family was forced to live with relatives who apparently had little concern for the deaf boy's future.

Still, he acquired an education. Before all his hearing was gone, his mother patiently taught him to read, instilling a valuable life-long habit. When 16, he learned from a neighbor's son that Connecticut had a special school for deaf persons that accepted students from Massachusetts. After submitting letters of endorsement from local citizens—and after overcoming the objections of his nephew who wished Booth to remain as his farmhand—Booth received in 1828 a certificate of admission to the Connecticut Asylum for the Deaf and Dumb. There he studied with Laurent Clerc, Thomas Hopkins Gallaudet, and Lewis Weld, the principal who succeeded Gallaudet. *See* AMERICAN SCHOOL FOR THE DEAF; CLERC, LAURENT; GALLAUDET, THOMAS HOPKINS.

In 1832 Booth began his teaching career at the Connecticut school, substituting for the ill F. P. A. Barnard. One of Booth's students was 14-year-old Mary Ann Walworth, who eventually became his wife. Booth's substitute teaching so pleased Weld that the principal appointed him a full-time instructor in 1833, regularly increased his pay, and took him along on speaking engagements to state legislatures in South Carolina and Georgia, where he helped convince the legislators to send the states' deaf children to the Connecticut school. Booth remained a teacher until 1839, when a combination of pneumonia, desire for more money—despite a $600 annual salary—and wanderlust caused him to move west to Iowa where, not coincidentally, Mary Ann Walworth's family then lived.

In his usual creative fashion, Booth quickly became involved in the life of frontier Iowa, building dams, mills, and houses, farming, and working for the post office and the territorial legislature. His mother, brother, sister, their spouses, and two nephews joined him in 1839. The next year, he married Mary Ann. The life of a frontier farmer was not satisfying to Booth, however, so in 1849 he and another deaf man, named Clough, left Mary Ann and the Booths' two children, Thomas and Harriet, with his brother's family and joined a group of forty-niners on the way to the California gold fields.

Booth was away from home for the next five years. In California he held a variety of jobs but spent most of his time mining for gold near Sonora. His earnings were sufficient to enable him to send money home to support his family and to save a substantial amount. Still, this must have been a difficult time for Booth as he sought unsuccessfully the elusive strike that would make him a wealthy man. He survived, he believed, because of his love for a habit acquired as a young boy: "If I had not a relish for reading," he wrote home in 1851, "I should be as wretched as are many others who, to relieve themselves, plunge into vice." Instead he kept up with the eastern papers, read *Uncle Tom's Cabin*, and advised Mary Ann to encourage the children, especially Thomas, to broaden themselves with reading the best periodicals and books. At his wife's insistence, Booth left California and returned home via Nicaragua early in 1854.

Booth began his newspaper career two years later when he became editor of the *Anamosa Eureka*. In 1858 Booth used $1000 saved from his gold mining to buy a half share of the newspaper. In 1862 he finally sold his farm and bought out his newspaper partner to become the *Anamosa Eureka*'s sole proprietor and editor until 1868, when he took in his elder son, Thomas, as his new partner.

During his long years in Iowa, Booth was active in a variety of causes. In the 1840s he encouraged the Iowa legislature to send Iowa's deaf children to the Illinois shool in Jacksonville. Later, he was instrumental in establishing the Iowa School for the Deaf. In the 1850s he became embroiled in the discussion among John J. Flournoy of Georgia and other people over a proposed deaf commonwealth. Ever a practical man, Booth opposed Flournoy's idea of a separate state, or commonwealth, for deaf persons. He argued that it would not have enough people to be economically viable; that deaf people improved their minds by being forced to read and write in hearing society; that suitable land in the West was too expensive for deaf people to purchase; that most deaf people, like him and his wife, had hearing children; and that life—at least in the North—was not really so bad for deaf people. *See* HISTORY: A Deaf Commonwealth.

Booth's remark about life in the North was characteristic of his thinking. In 1853 he had praised

Uncle Tom's Cabin, writing to Mary Ann that it fit well his observations of the South when he had visited there in 1834. In the 1850s he was recognized as an abolitionist, and in 1858 he published a long antislavery poem. After the Civil War, Booth in 1871 published an article in the *Annals of Iowa* criticizing the United States census of 1840 for its proslavery bias. The census had listed all four deaf residents of Jones County, Iowa, including Booth, his wife, and two other graduates of the Connecticut school, as black, blind, idiotic, and insane. In this way, Booth believed, the census preparers had attempted to show that freedom was detrimental to the physical and mental well-being of blacks.

Though somewhat isolated from other deaf people, Booth took an active role in national affairs. In 1880 he received an honorary master of arts from Gallaudet College and traveled to Cincinnati to chair the convention of deaf Americans that established the NAD. Booth's younger son, Frank Walworth Booth, became a teacher of deaf persons, head of the Alexander Graham Bell Association for the Deaf, principal of the Nebraska School for the Deaf, and later the president of the Conference of Superintendents and Principals of American Schools for the Deaf. Ironically, though, Frank Booth became an ardent oralist (opponent of sign language) who consistently opposed the leaders of the NAD, which his father had helped found. *See* ALEXANDER GRAHAM BELL ASSOCIATION FOR THE DEAF; GALLAUDET COLLEGE; NATIONAL ASSOCIATION OF THE DEAF.

Booth finally retired from the editorship of the *Anamosa Eureka* in 1895, when he was 85 years old. Mary Ann died three years later, but Booth, despite having suffered from meningitis as a child and cholera and smallpox as an adult, lived on until March 24, 1905, in Anamosa. Throughout his long life he exhibited energy, independence, compassion for his fellows, and a firm commitment to education and reading as the factors that would free other deaf people, as they had freed him, from ignorance and dependence.

Bibliography

Booth, Frank W.: "Edmund Booth: A Life Sketch," *Association Review*, 7:225–237, 1905.

Braddock, Gilberg: *Notable Deaf Persons*, Gallaudet College Alumni Association, Washington, D.C., 1975.

Edmund Booth, Forty-Niner, San Joaquin Pioneer and Historical Society, Stockton, California, 1953.

Fay, Edward Allen: "Edward Booth," *American Annals of the Deaf*, 50:320–321, 1905.

Gallaher, James E. (ed.): *Representative Deaf Persons of the United States of America*, James E. Gallaher, Chicago, 1898.

John V. Van Cleve

BOVE, LINDA
(1945–   )

When deaf people watched the *Sesame Street* program before closed-captioned television, they often complained of the difficulty in lipreading the assorted cast of characters. What they did not realize was that Linda Bove, the pretty brunette who talked with her hands and regularly interacted on the show with "Big Bird" "Kermit" and "Ernie" had to cope with the same problem. *See* TELECOMMUNICATIONS: Captioned Television.

Bove, who is totally deaf, started making guest appearances on *Sesame Street* in 1971, and in 1976 she became a permanent resident member of the popular children's show. She portrayed an ordinary person, as do all the human characters on the program—she just happened to be deaf.

Bove was born in 1945 in Garfield, New Jersey, to deaf parents. Congenitally deaf, she attended St. Joseph's School for the Deaf in the Bronx, New York, and then transferred to the Marie Katzenbach School for the Deaf in Trenton, New Jersey, from which she graduated. Enrolling in Gallaudet College, she majored in Library Science and took an active part in dramatics, wherein she was acclaimed for her performances as "Polly Peachum" in *The Three Penny Opera* and as the female lead in *Spoon River Anthology*. *See* GALLAUDET COLLEGE.

Upon graduation, Bove was invited to join the National Theatre of the Deaf in 1968, having participated in their Summer School Program the year before. Also joining the company was Edmund Waterstreet, a fellow graduate from Gallaudet College. Their marriage two years later made them the first deaf husband-wife team with any professional group. *See* NATIONAL THEATERS OF THE DEAF: United States.

Since 1968 Bove has performed in leading and supporting roles for many of the National Theatre of the Deaf's repertory of plays which have toured the United States and abroad. Among her major triumphs were "Mrs. Webb" in *Our Town*, "Canina" in *Volpone*, "Belissa" in *The Love of Don Perlimplin and Belissa in the Garden*, "Lauretta" in *Gianni Schicchi*, and "Polly" in *He Who Gets Slapped*. As "Priscilla", the girl who turns into Wonder Woman in *Priscilla, Princess of Power*, she electrified audiences with her dexterous and melodramatic acting in this hilarious drama of pop art and comic strip, which was directed by Edmund Waterstreet.

Bove has also contributed greatly to the development of children's theater. As one of the five company members who started the Little Theatre of the Deaf as a branch, she has directed and starred in many of its productions. "LTD" as it is known,

Linda Bove of *Sesame Street*

has brought delight and wonder to children of all ages. After its Christmas week success on Broadway in 1972, the *New York Times* called it "the most rewarding kid's show in town!"

In 1973 Bove successfully auditioned for the role of a deaf character ("Melissa Hayley") in the longest-running CBS serial, *Search for Tomorrow*. She characterized some of the problems that deaf people have in the world, communicated by means of sign language and by reading lips, and found romance with a young doctor at the hospital where she worked (his mother was deaf and he knew sign language). For a period of 26 weeks Bove won the hearts of millions on television and helped the hearing public to develop a better understanding of deaf people and deafness.

Bove was also blazing new pathways for deaf people by her increasing appearances on primetime television. She appeared as a guest star on the *Dick Cavett Show* on PBS and on ABC's *Omnibus* series; also, with the National Theatre of the Deaf, she had the role of "Jim" in *A Child's Christmas in Wales*, a CBS special that was nationally broadcast during Christmas week 1973.

In 1974 Bove was honored with the AMITA (Italian-American) Award for her outstanding work on television, along with Marlo Thomas. Two years later, Bove was given the status of permanent resident of the *Sesame Street* program and was awarded a long-term contract. In 1980 she performed with

Henry Winkler on *Happy Days*, ABC's popular serial. As "Allison," the deaf girlfriend of "Fonzie," she not only won his heart but also made him declare his love in sign language.

Along with her talent and personality, Bove proved to be very photogenic; these qualities yielded many spinoff benefits. She was frequently featured in *Sesame Street Magazine*, which contained color photographs of Bove making the signs for words or fingerspelling the manual alphabet. In 1980 *Sesame Street* and the National Theatre of the Deaf cooperated in publishing a book, *Sign Language Fun with Linda Bove*, which was illustrated by Tom Cooke and featured Jim Henson's *Sesame Street* Muppets. Thus, by communicating with sign language, Bove helped children become more aware of the many cultures in American society while also enhancing the image of deaf people.

Bove continued to be active in live theater. During 1980–1982, she was the understudy and stand-in for her National Theatre of the Deaf colleague, Phyllis Frelich, as "Sara Norman" in *Children of a Lesser God*, the Tony Award-winning Broadway play. When the National Tour Company was formed, Bove was billed as the deaf heroine of the play in major theaters throughout the United States and Canada. *See* FRELICH, PHYLLIS.

In the fall of 1979, Bove played a major role in the National Theatre of the Deaf's world tour which covered 30,000 miles. The theater's visit to Japan was the climax of the tour. It had been arranged in advance by Tetsuko Kuroyanagi, Japan's celebrity of television, stage and screen, who had invited David Hays, founder and artistic director of the National Theatre of the Deaf, and Bove to come to Japan and appear on her television show, *Tetsuko's Room*. Later, the National Theatre of the Deaf company made its debut in the famed Shinjuku Bunka Center of Tokyo, which was attended by the Crown Prince, his wife, and Prince Hitachi. Tetsuko, Hays, and Bove met with the royal family during the intermission.

Two years later, the deaf people of Japan succeeded in establishing a professional theater along the lines of the National Theatre of the Deaf. For Bove and Hays, the world tour helped fulfill another of the objectives of the National Theatre of the Deaf—the successful exchange of cultural experiences in theater arts between the deaf people of America and those of foreign lands. In 1979, and for the next three years, Japan sent 10 deaf students to the Summer School Program of the National Theatre of the Deaf, one of whom later became a member of the professional company. *See* NATIONAL THEATERS OF THE DEAF: Japan.

In 1984 Bove continued to perform regularly on *Sesame Street*, which had implemented closed captions for its deaf viewers. Additionally, Bove had a featured role in a special movie made for television, *Follow That Bird!*

Bove also branched out to do freelance work in Los Angeles for Beyond Sound, a deaf television production company. Showcasing her talent, Beyond Sound not only featured her as a guest on several programs but also had her perform as the hostess for their videotaped documentary celebrating the 15 years of service to the deaf community by the Greater Los Angeles Council on Deafness. The documentary premiered at the Convention of the National Association of the Deaf at Baltimore in 1984 to enthusiastic reviews. *See* GREATER LOS ANGELES COUNCIL ON DEAFNESS, INC.; NATIONAL ASSOCIATION OF THE DEAF.

By covering such a wide range of interests in theater and television, Linda Bove established herself as one of the most influential women in the performing arts. Furthermore, as a founding member of both the National Theatre of the Deaf and the Little Theatre of the Deaf, she could take pride in helping to open doors for other deaf performers. By 1984 her work was internationally recognized, and although by then she functioned mostly as a consultant to the National Theatre of the Deaf, she remained their popular ambassador-at-large.

Bibliography

"Beyond Sound," *Silent News*, October 1984.

Panara, Robert, and John Panara: *Great Deaf Americans*, T.J. Publishers, Silver Spring, Maryland, 1983.

Robert Panara

BRAGG, BERNARD
(1928–   )

Bernard Bragg, who has been called the "prince of players on the silent stage," is an actor, mime, theatrical director, and lecturer. He was one of the original members and a cofounder of the National Theatre of the Deaf. One of his major contributions to deaf theater was the development of sign-mime, a classical variation of sign language that delicately translates from one language to another, utilizing nuances of movement and motion that visually illuminate the dialogue.

Born deaf on September 27, 1928, in Brooklyn, New York, Bragg was the only child of deaf parents, Jennie Stoloff and Wolf Bragg. His father had an amateur theater company in New York, which gave Bragg an early exposure to the stage. He entered Fanwood School for the Deaf in 1933, which had become the New York School for the Deaf by the time he graduated in 1947. Encouraged by his first deaf teacher, Robert F. Panara, Bragg developed an interest in writing poetry, and began performing in and directing plays at the school.

Bernard Bragg.

After graduating as class valedictorian, he entered Gallaudet College, where he majored in English and education. His interest in drama and poetry continued, and when he graduated from Gallaudet in 1952, he received the Teegarden Award for poetry. While attending college, he played the lead roles in Molière's *The Miser*, *The Merchant Gentleman*, and *Tartuffe* and directed John Galsworthy's *Escape. See* GALLAUDET COLLEGE.

After graduation from Gallaudet, Bragg accepted a teaching position at the California School for the Deaf in Berkeley, where he taught for the next 15 years. In 1956 when Marcel Marceau was appearing in San Francisco, Bragg performed for him. Marceau was so impressed that he invited Bragg to study with him in Paris, so Bragg spent the summer of 1957 in Europe.

Returning to the United States in the fall, Bragg began performing in small clubs in the San Francisco area, and in 1958 he was selected one of the best small night club performers of the year by *Life* magazine. In 1959 he received a master's degree in special education from San Francisco State University, and from 1960 to 1964 he had his own weekly television show, *The Quiet Man*. He went back to Europe in 1962, where he appeared on television in England and Yugoslavia and performed in Paris and Madrid to rave reviews.

In 1967 the noted psychologist Edna Levine, who first conceived the idea of the National Theatre of the Deaf, brought its future director, David Hays, together with Bragg. This meeting led to the organization of a professional theater made up of deaf performers. In addition to playing leading roles with the company, Bragg adapted the scripts to sign-mime, directed, taught in the theater's summer school for deaf performers, and served as an administrator for the theater. He was also a founding member of the Little Theatre of the Deaf, which made its debut in 1968. *See* NATIONAL THEATERS OF THE DEAF: UNITED STATES.

In 1973, Bragg served as artist in residence with the Moscow Theater of Sign Language and Mime, as part of the United States–Soviet cultural exchange. In 1977 he was invited by the U.S. Department of State to serve on the U.S. Intelligence Agency's Overseas Speakers Program, and in that capacity he traveled all over the world, performing and giving workshops in sign language to mixed deaf and hearing audiences. Later that year, after reducing his relationship with the National Theatre of the Deaf to a minimum, he accepted the post of artist in residence at Gallaudet College.

Bragg has since appeared in numerous television shows, including *A Child's Christmas in Wales*, *And Your Name is Jonah*, *Can Anybody Hear Me?*, and *My Third Eye*. He has toured the country giving solo performances, and has served as a consultant at Gallaudet College.

Bibliography

Powers, Helen: *Signs of Silence*, Dodd Mead, New York, 1972.

Helen Powers

BRAIDWOOD, THOMAS
(1715–1806)

Thomas Braidwood, a pioneer educator of deaf children, was born in Scotland in 1715 and educated at Edinburgh University. After employment as an assistant master in a grammar school at Hamilton, he opened a mathematical school in Edinburgh.

In 1760 Charles Shirreff, a deaf boy without speech, who was then aged nine but had lost his hearing at three, was placed in Braidwood's care to learn writing. After some years Braidwood taught Shirreff to speak and to understand language. This and other successes prompted Braidwood to concentrate on teaching deaf children. By 1766 Braidwood's Academy for the Deaf and Dumb was advertising in *Scots Magazine*. In 1769 a letter in the same publication stated that since only a few pupils could be taught at a time, such education for deaf children was expensive, and suggested that a fund be established to help parents who could not afford Braidwood's fees. The letter also recommended that Braidwood should "communicate his skill to 3 or 4 ingenious young men." Apparently, no response was received to either proposal. Indeed, Braidwood taught his skill only to family members who swore not to reveal his methods. One was his nephew John Braidwood, who joined him in 1775 and later married Thomas's daughter. By 1779 Braidwood's academy had about 20 pupils, including some from the United States.

The most famous account of the Braidwood establishment is given in *The Journey to the Western Isles of Scotland* by Samuel Johnson, written in 1773: "There is one subject of philosophical curiosity to be found in Edinburgh, which no other city has to shew; a college of the deaf and dumb, who are taught to speak, to read, to write and to practice arithmetick, by a gentleman, whose name is Braidwood. The number which attends him is, I think, about twelve . . . The improvement of Mr. Braidwood's pupils is wonderful. They not only speak, write and understand what is written, but if he that speaks looks towards them and modifies his organs by distinct and full utterance, they know so well what is spoken, that it is an expression scarcely figurative to say, they hear with the eye . . . It is pleasing to see one of the most desperate of human calamities capable of such help . . ., after having seen the deaf taught arithmetick who would be afraid to cultivate the Hebrides?"

Another early account of Braidwood's academy was given by Francis Green, in *Vox Oculis Subjecta—A Dissertation on the Most Curious and Important Art of Imparting Speech and the Knowledge of Language to the Naturally Deaf and (Consequently) Dumb; with a Particular Account of the Academy of Messrs Braidwood of Edinburgh*, published in 1783. (The Latin title of the book was the Braidwood motto.) Green, an American, sent his deaf son to Braidwood's academy in about 1780 and visited it frequently. His book mentioned the absence of any harsh discipline, as was sometimes practiced upon deprived persons, and that the children, individually taught, loved both the school and their lessons.

Braidwood's method was a development of that devised by Thomas Wallis (1616–1703), which emphasized articulation and the use of speech organs according to the sound that each letter required. Green noted, however, that Braidwood did not preclude the use of natural signs and the manual alphabet as useful aids. *See* EDUCATION: Communication.

In 1783 the Braidwoods moved to London, King George III having promised them £100 from the royal purse for educating deaf children, and set up at Grove House, Mare Street, Hackney. Braidwood's high fees, beyond the reach of poorer persons, were brought to the notice of John Townsend, a Congregational minister, by a former pupil at the academy. Assisted by Henry Cox Mason, Rector of Bermondsey, Townsend collected funds to provide an independent institution for poor deaf children. This was opened in Grange Road, Bermondsey, with six pupils in 1792. The foundation stone of a larger building was laid by the Duke of Gloucester on a site in the Old Kent Road in 1807. The first master there was Joseph Watson, another nephew of Thomas Braidwood, who had joined him in 1794.

Braidwood had two grandsons, Thomas and John, from the marriage of his daughter and his nephew John. Both became teachers of deaf people. Thomas opened a school at Birmingham in 1814 and remained there until his death in 1825. John was the first headmaster of the Edinburgh Institution, opened in 1810, but in 1812 he emigrated to the United States.

The oath of secrecy, imposed on his family by Braidwood, had far-reaching consequences. In 1815, Thomas Hopkins Gallaudet, who had studied the manual communication system perfected by the Abbé Sicard, was sent to Britain to learn the oral method. He found the three English schools—London Hackney, London Old Kent Road, and Birmingham—controlled by the Braidwood family. The head of the Edinburgh Institution, Mr. Kinniburgh, agreed to teach Gallaudet the oral method if the junior Thomas Braidwood agreed. The terms were unacceptable to Gallaudet, who continued to study the French manual system under Sicard in Paris. Thus, the French system became the basis of communication in American schools for deaf children. *See* EDUCATION: History; GALLAUDET, THOMAS HOPKINS; SICARD, ABBÉ ROCH AMBROISE CUCURRON.

Braidwood has perhaps been unfairly castigated for his secrecy, but at that time it was common practice for ideas to be adopted without any reward to their originator. Although he was not directly connected with the establishment of the first English public school for deaf children, he had an indirect influence. His work showed that it was possible to educate deaf children, and he and his family established a tradition of doing so. On October 24, 1806, Braidwood died in London.

Bibliography

Fay, Edward Allen: "The Braidwood Family," *American Annals of the Deaf*, vol. 23, January 1878.

Green, Francis: *Vox Oculis Subjecta*, 1783.

Johnson, Samuel: *The Journey to the Western Isles of Scotland*, 1773.

Pritchard, D. G.: *Education and the Handicapped*, Routhledge and Kegan Paul, London, 1963.

Kenneth Lysons

BRAIN

The brain is the upper extension of the central nervous system, which includes the spinal cord. The brain serves all of the sensory modalities (vision, touch, smell, taste and so on) and all muscular or motor-output functions. It also is involved with regulation of many bodily functions over which a person has no control, such as heart rate, temperature adjustment, and contraction and dilation of the pupil of the eye.

Structure and Function

When sound stimulates the ear, the sensory structures of the inner ear convert the acoustic energy into electrochemical energy that eventually causes neurons (nerve cells) of the auditory nerve to discharge. Hearing does not take place, however, until the nerve discharges are delivered to the brain and the brain's mechanisms act to convert the discharges into awareness of the sound, followed by recognition and understanding.

LEMNISCAL SYSTEM

All systems within the brain interact to some extent during any activity, including hearing. Nevertheless, some structures (groups of nerve fibers or their cell bodies) within the brain are more clearly identified than others with specific functions. They consist of bundles of nerve fibers that are large because they are covered with a whitish myelin sheath. A bundle or ribbon of large nerve fibers is referred to as a lemniscus.

The portion of the brain most closely identified with hearing is called the primary auditory projection system or the auditory lemniscal system. The fibers in the lemniscal pathway interact with other fibers along the pathway through specialized contacts called synapses. The synapses occur at three or four "way stations" or nuclei from the point of entry of the auditory nerve in the lower brainstem to the termination of the pathway at the primary auditory reception area in the cerebral cortex. The lemniscal system transmits the same message from the ear to the several way stations along the ascending pathway. Transmission is rapid and with minimal change in the characteristics of the message. The lemniscal system also contains pathways from higher way stations to lower way stations.

The lemniscal system is more easily identified than are other portions of the brain involved with hearing. Therefore, when references are made to the central auditory nervous system, they usually imply the lemniscal system. Because of the relative ease of identifying the lemniscal system anatomically and electrophysiologically, it is used extensively in neurologic diagnosis and in evoked-potential audiometry. *See* AUDIOMETRY: Auditory Evoked-Potentials.

Despite its anatomic prominence and its physiologic importance, the auditory lemniscal system probably is not involved directly with the actual conscious awareness or perception of sound. Studies of the lemniscal system indicate only minimal differences in its electric activity, whether the experimental animal or human subject attends to or is aware of the sound, or whether the subject is in reverie, ignores the sound, or even sleeps. Laboratory and clinical studies also have shown that damage to the lemniscal system may lead to impairment in the way that sounds are perceived, understood, or interpreted, but that it does not reduce auditory sensitivity (that is, cause a permanent hearing loss as depicted in an audiogram) or prevent conscious awareness of sound.

GRAY MATTER

The major perceptual functions and the total operational control of the brain seem to be in the gray matter that, in the lower part of the brain, lies around a fluid-filled canal running through the central part of the brain. The nerve cells appear gray because they have little or no whitish myelin covering their many extensions. Within the spinal cord and the brain, the central gray matter is surrounded by interconnecting pathways and nuclei. With no pathways to surround it at the top or rostral end of the head, the gray matter extends over the top of the rest of the brain as the cerebral cortex. Although the white matter neurons occupy the majority of space in the brain because of their large size, they constitute only about 3 percent of the number of the brain's nerve cells. The smaller unmyelinated cells of the gray matter make up most of the remaining nerve cells.

It is probable that the nerve discharges initiated in the ear and transmitted along the auditory lemniscal pathway do not enter directly into the central gray matter. Rather, the discharges probably are modified or processed by computerlike groups of cells or nuclei at each of the way stations of the lemniscal system and then passed on to the central gray matter—the core of the brain—for further processing, perception, recognition, and understanding.

FUNCTIONAL CHARACTERISTICS

The brain is not a single functional unit, but rather a series of brains, each superimposed on the older one during the process of evolution. All auditory functions seem to be negotiated at each brain level, but with increasing sophistication at successively higher levels. The auditory functions range from primitive unconditioned reflexes, such as startle reactions to loud noises, to sophisticated pragmatic evaluation of spoken messages. Auditory functions do not take place in isolation from other sensory and motor functions. At the highest levels, auditory function is virtually inseparable from language and speech function.

The brain is generally symmetric, as is the entire body, with neural pathways connecting both sides of the brain at all levels. However, small but important sidedness differences in the central auditory nervous system anatomy appear to lead to significant functional sidedness differences. For example, in the mature human brain, the left side seems to play a more dominant role than the right side in the processing of speech messages.

Consequences of Brain Damage

Because of the overwhelming complexity of the brain, specific dysfunctions or lesions have not been correlated closely with specific disorders of auditory function, and vice versa. Nevertheless, some generalities are at least partially defensible. The closer a central lesion is to the input of the auditory nerve in the brainstem, the more likely it is that the resulting dysfunction will be primarily auditory. However, there will be no impairment of auditory sensitivity, as depicted in an audiogram, if the lesion is beyond the initial input to the brain. The higher the lesion in the brain, the subtler the resulting auditory dysfunction is likely to be, and the more likely the lesion is to result in a disorder involving more than hearing. Another defensible generality is that in lesions affecting only one side of the brain, the resulting dysfunction is more likely to be manifest from responses to sounds presented to the ear opposite to the affected side of the brain than to sounds presented to the ear on the same side.

The brain is remarkably plastic or programmable at birth but gradually loses much of its plasticity with maturation. Therefore, auditory disorders resulting from brain damage are contingent to a great extent on the age at which the damage occurred. For example, massive lesions to one side of the brain that may have devastating effects on auditory function in the adult may affect auditory function only minimally in a child born with an equivalent lesion.

Bibliography

Eagles, E. L. (ed.): *Human Communication and Its Disorders*, 1975.

Goldstein, R.: "Neurophysiology of Hearing," in N. J. Lass et al. (eds.), *Speech, Language and Hearing*, 1982.

Hanard, S., et al. (eds.): *Lateralization in the Nervous System*, 1977.

Møller, A. R.: *Auditory Physiology*, 1983.

Robert Goldstein

Diseases

Diseases of the developed brain known to cause impaired auditory functions may be classified under the categories of cerebrovascular disorders, demyelinating and degenerative diseases, tumors, infectious diseases, and trauma. This discussion describes briefly the general features of the most common brain diseases in these categories and the associated auditory disorders.

CEREBROVASCULAR DISORDERS

There are two basic pathologic conditions affecting the brain as a result of vascular disease of various causes: infarction and hemorrhage. Infarction refers to necrosis (death) of tissue produced by reduction of blood supply (ischemia) to the affected area, while hemorrhage refers to bleeding into the region involved. Whether there is associated auditory dysfunction associated with the infarction or hemorrhage depends on the location of the affected blood vessels. In the brainstem, which receives its blood supply from the vertebrobasilar arterial system, disordered detection of signal phase and various types of speech discrimination disorders may occur, depending on the level and extent of involvement of the brainstem's auditory system. At the cortical level, supplied primarily by the carotid arterial vessels, understanding of speech may be affected when the tests are administered under specific conditions, depending on the region of involvement at this level.

DEMYELINATING DISEASES

Demyelinating diseases cause either a breakdown or an injury to normally developed central myelin or a failure of myelin to develop normally with relative preservation of axons. There are a number of diseases in this category with varied causes. The leukodystrophies, for example, are conditions occurring mainly in childhood as a result of metabolic abnormality. The cause of multiple sclerosis, the most common demyelinating disease, is unknown. Scattered plaques of myelin loss may be found in the brainstem, spinal cord, cerebellum, and cerebrum. Lesions also may involve the cranial nerves. Usually, they are confined to the proximal central portion of the nerve, which is covered by an extension of central nervous system myelin. Hearing loss is not common in multiple sclerosis. When it is present, it is usually a mild high-frequency sensorineural impairment with some evidence of fluctuation consistent with the relapsing and remitting course characteristic of the disease. Although central processing of speech and detection of changes in signal phase may be affected, the patterns of abnormality vary considerably among patients, depending on the status of the disease process, the location of the pathologic tissue, and the type of auditory tests used to evaluate auditory function.

DEGENERATIVE DISEASES

This category of central nervous system diseases includes a considerable number of conditions in which progressive dementia often is an early and predominant finding. Most of the diseases in this category are associated with neuronal degeneration resulting from a biochemical defect. Among these diseases are Alzheimer's disease, Pick's disease, Huntington's disease, Jakob-Creutzfeldt disease, kuru, progressive supranuclear palsy, disorders of involuntary movements such as in Parkinson's disease, and the spinocerebellar degenerations including Friedreich's ataxia and olivoponto-cerebellar atrophy. The neuronal atrophy may be widespread throughout the cerebellum, brainstem, and cerebrum, although in some conditions certain areas of the central nervous system may be relatively uninvolved, especially in early stages of the disease process. In time, the disease process becomes more extensive. High-frequency sensorineural hearing loss and speech discrimination abnormalities have been reported to be associated with some of these conditions, possibly because of extension of the disease to include part of the peripheral neural system.

TUMORS

About 80 percent of all central nervous system tumors involve the brain, including the gliomas (glial cell origin), meningiomas (arachnoid cap cell origin usually attached to the meninges), pituitary adenomas, neurilemmomas (Schwann cell origin), metastatic tumors, and blood vessel tumors. The number of known etiologic factors having to do with the development of tumors are few. Tumors arising within the substance of the brain (intra-axial) may occur anywhere in the brain and may involve remote areas via infiltration or pressure effects. Tumors arising outside the brain (extraaxial) may displace brain tissue, causing effects in other areas via secondary pressure or compression. Effects associated with intracranial tumors include increased intracranial pressure; papilledema; transtentorial, temporal lobe, or cerebellar tonsil herniation; compression of arteries and veins; and bony erosion. Associated symptoms include headache, vomiting, seizures, alterations in consciousness level, changes in mentation, and a variety of abnormal sensations in the head. Hearing loss is a rare symptom in intraaxial brain tumors. Various types of speech discrimination disorders may be associated with intracranial tumors, depending on the location of the mass and type of tests used.

INFECTIOUS DISEASES

Infectious diseases of the central nervous system often are widespread, affecting many areas of the brain, including the central auditory system. Peripheral and central components may be difficult to differentiate in many cases, such as in meningitis, encephalitis, and neurosyphilis. A brain abscess is a well-localized infection that may involve

any region of the cerebrum, and neurologic signs and symptoms are the same for any expanding mass in the brain. Speech discrimination under specific test conditions may be affected, with involvement of auditory areas of the temporal and parietal lobes of the brain, depending on test techniques. The auditory disorder may be the result of either primary involvement of the auditory system or secondary pressure effects from a lesion located in another region of the brain, such as the occipital or frontal lobes.

TRAUMA

The types of brain injuries that can affect the central auditory system from forces acting on the head are skull fractures, closed head injury without fracture, and penetrating wounds. Mechanisms by which the brain is injured are compression of brain tissue, tearing of tissue, or shearing action (the sliding of tissue past other tissue). These effects on brain tissue may occur simultaneously or in succession. In instances of minor head injuries without fracture, neurologic dysfunction may be temporary, with full recovery over a short period of time. However, severe and irreversible damage to the brain, brainstem, cranial nerves, or blood vessels also may occur. Head injury may occur without loss of consciousness. In cases with loss of consciousness, recovery may be rapid in mild concussion or more prolonged in cases with moderate to severe injury. Hearing loss does not occur following damage to the cerebrum unless there is associated involvement of the peripheral auditory system (external or middle ear, cochlea, or eighth cranial nerve). However, various types of auditory disorders involving the ability to understand speech under different stimulus conditions may be present in cases with damage to the brainstem or temporal lobes.

AUDITORY DISORDERS OF CENTRAL ORIGIN

The particular features of auditory disorders associated with lesions of the central auditory nervous system depend primarily on the location of the brain abnormality and the types of tests employed. The nature of the auditory disorder is related to the anatomic region involved, not the type of lesion. The major auditory disorders are difficulty in understanding degraded or low-redundancy speech delivered monaurally, impairment in the ability to fuse or resynthesize segmented speech when a separate segment of speech is delivered simultaneously to each ear (binaural fusion), difficulty in understanding different speech samples delivered to both ears simultaneously (dichotic), and reduced ability to appreciate subtle changes in signal phase at the two ears under certain test conditions. A number of tests are available to detect the presence of these functional abnormalities. Other functions, such as the ability to detect faint signals (pure tones, speech, or noise) and the ability to understand high-fidelity speech, usually are unaffected by lesions of the central auditory system. Possible exceptions are cases with lesions involving the most caudal portion of the central auditory system (the region of the cochlear nuclei, for instance). The effect of central lesions on the ability to detect loudness and pitch changes is not well understood.

Patients with brainstem lesions involving auditory centers or pathways at the pontomedullary junction may demonstrate during testing some degree of high-frequency sensorineural hearing loss, difficulty in understanding normal and low-redundancy speech, abnormal perception of subtle signal phase changes at the two ears, and abnormal binaural fusion of segmented speech. Discrimination of dichotic material may be normal or only mildly affected, depending on the sensitivity of the tests employed. The auditory disorder may be demonstrated in only one ear (ipsilateral or contralateral to the affected side) or both ears, depending on the extent of the lesion. Patients with brainstem lesions localized to higher regions of the pons or midbrain level may show similar types of auditory dysfunction except there may be no effect on hearing threshold sensitivity, discrimination for normal, undistorted speech, binaural fusion processes, or signal phase differences between the two ears. *See* EAR: Anatomy.

Patients with unilateral temporal lobe lesions involving either the auditory projections from the thalamus or the auditory cortex of either hemisphere may demonstrate, depending on the particular tests used, abnormal discrimination for monaural low-redundancy and dichotic speech material in the ear contralateral to the affected temporal lobe. Generally, hearing threshold sensitivity, discrimination for ordinary speech, binaural fusion for segmented speech, and binaural signal phase remain unaffected.

Patients with lesions involving the interhemispheric auditory pathways localized to the region of the corpus callosum (mainly the posterior region) or its lateral extensions in the right or left hemisphere may demonstrate with special test procedures an abnormal understandng of dichotic speech material in the ear ipsilateral (left ear in most cases) to the dominant hemisphere for speech and language. Other speech discrimination functions, when tested monaurally, usually are normal unless auditory centers of the brainstem or temporal lobes also are involved. *See* AUDIOMETRY: Tests of Central Auditory Dysfunction.

Bibliography
Gilroy, J., and J. S. Meyer: *Medical Neurology*, 3d ed., Macmillan, New York, 1979.

Jerger, J., and S. Jerger: "Clinical Validity of Central Auditory Tests," *Scandinavian Audiology*, 4:147–163, 1975.

Jerger, S., and J. Jerger: "Neuroaudiologic Findings in Patients with Central Auditory Disorder," in J. L. Northern and W. H. Perkins (eds.), *Seminars in Hearing*, 4:133–159, 1983.

Lynn, G. E., and J. Gilroy: "Effects of Brain Lesions on the Perception of Monotic and Dichotic Speech Stimuli," in M. D. Sullivan (ed.), *Central Auditory Processing Disorders*, University of Nebraska Medical Center, Omaha, 1975.

———: "Evaluation of Central Auditory Dysfunction in Patients with Neurological Disorders," in R. W. Keith (ed.), *Central Auditory Dysfunction*, Grune and Stratton, New York, 1977.

Mathog, R. H., and G. Viscomi: "Otologic Manifestations of Retrocochlear Disease," in M. M. Paprella and D. A. Shumrick (eds.), *Otolaryngology*, vol. 2: *The Ear*, W. B. Saunders, Philadelphia, 1980.

Neely, J. G.: "Disorders of the Central Auditory System," in J. L. Northern and W. H. Perkins (eds.): *Seminars in Hearing*, 4:97–107, 1983.

George E. Lynn

BRAZIL

Brazil, the largest country in Latin America and the only Portuguese-speaking one, covers over 3.2 million square miles (7.3 million square kilometers). Inhabited by approximately 120 million people, half of them under 19 years of age, it is a federal republic of 23 states and three territories divided into five regions: the north, the northeast, the midwest, the southeast, and the south. The capital is Brasília.

FUNDS AND PROVISION OF SERVICES
The federal government allocates funds through various departments for the diagnosis, treatment, education, and rehabilitation of deaf persons. Free diagnosis of simple cases of deafness and routine prescription of hearing aids are provided by the Instituto Nacional de Assistência Médica e Previdência Social (INAMPS) through its own otolaryngologists or through its agreements with private audiological clinics. Little attention is given, however, to correctly prescribing hearing aids, and so deaf people may receive inappropriate ones. *See* AUDITORY DISORDERS, EVALUATION AND DIAGNOSIS OF; HEARING AIDS.

Minimal provision for education, habilitation, and rehabilitation is provided by the Centro Nacional de Educacão Especial (CENESP), formed in 1973 by the Ministério de Educacão e Cultura (MEC), and by the Legião Brasileira de Assistência (LBA).

The CENESP maintains a special school in Rio de Janeiro, the Instituto Nacional de Educacão de Surdos (INES), and finances the training of teachers in the states that have neither the financial nor technical means. The LBA subsidizes some clinics and private schools so that they can attend to needy deaf individuals. State governments and some cities work through their departments of education to set up special classes and a few schools.

Private charitable organizations, religious institutions, and some institutions connected with universities also serve deaf Brazilians. The Associacão des Pais e Amigos de Excepcionais (APAE) provides special classes in cities in various states. Some special schools, such as the Instituto Santa Therezinha in São Paulo, belong to religious orders. The Pontificia Universidade Católica de São Paulo (PUCSP) has a diagnosis center, clinical programs, and a school for hearing-handicapped persons in its Instituto Educacional São Paulo, part of its Divisão de Educacão e Rehabilitacão dos Distúrbios da Comunicacão (DERDIC).

There are good private clinics and professionals trained in diagnosis, habilitation, and rehabilitation in the large capital cities (mainly São Paulo and Rio de Janeiro), where there are universities with courses in communication disturbances. However, their costs are often prohibitive for most Brazilian families.

TRAINING OF SPECIALISTS

The quality of specialists has improved greatly with the introduction of phoniatrics (a medical specialty) and phonoaudiology in 1960. There are now five university courses in phonoaudiology in São Paulo, four in Rio de Janeiro, and one each in Paraná, and Pernambuco. These courses train professionals in speech therapy and audiology and emphasize work with deaf persons.

Traditionally, teachers for deaf pupils were trained while in service, or in rare specialized high school extension courses. Now there are three- and four-year university programs and one-year post-high school courses.

The training for phonoaudiologists and for teachers includes courses in anatomy, physiology, auditory pathology, speech and language development, acoustical physics, and hearing aids. The courses in phonoaudiology stress language development methods, audiologic tests, and the selection of hearing aids; while those for teachers emphasize curriculum development, speech improvement, and the education of deaf students. *See* AUDIOLOGY: Certification; TEACHING PROFESSION: Training.

TEACHERS AND STUDENTS

There has not been a census of Brazil's deaf population or an accurate count of the total number of deaf people who receive special attention in schools or clinics. However, profound hearing loss is thought to occur in 0.5 to 1.0 percent of those under 20 years old, that is, from 300,000 to 600,000 persons. *See* DEAF POPULATION: Demography.

Private institutions and the departments of education of eleven states and two territories gathered data for their regions. The area studied covers more than half of the country and 66 million inhabitants, a little more than 50 percent of the country's population. Special services reach only about 7000 school-age deaf people in these states and territories. Thus, more than 95 percent of the school-age deaf population receive no special help at all; of those who do, approximately 65 percent receive it from the states. Federal agencies and private organizations each serve about 10 percent; and state-subsidized institutions serve about 15 percent.

The number of properly trained teachers keeps rising because of the university courses being offered and because of other training programs. A 1974 study indicated that half of the 1159 teachers identified were not sufficiently trained. Of the estimated 3000 teachers in 1983, 2000 were university-trained specialists or had been trained in special courses.

EDUCATIONAL PROGRAMS

Government services favor both special and integrated classes. Approximately 55 percent of the deaf students who receive government services are in special classes, 25 percent are in integrated classes, and 20 percent are in special schools. In Santa Catarina in the south and Pará in the north, integrated classes are strongly preferred; in these, the children receive support through auditory training and speech programs either in the school itself or at Department of Education centers. *See* EDUCATIONAL PROGRAMS.

The special classes are often made up of children of very different ages and of very different degrees of hearing loss. Some children who are not able to communicate are diagnosed as being deaf, but in fact are not.

There are at least 20 special schools in Brazil. Seventeen are day schools; the other three (one in Rio de Janeiro and two in São Paulo) are both residential and day schools, but the number of residents is decreasing. Most of the schools have programs for two- to seven-year-olds and classes through the fourth grade. Few have a complete elementary course. Furthermore, there are no special high schools or universities.

The objective of the majority of the special schools is to lead the students to achieve sufficient ability in oral and written communication that they can enter regular schools and be successful in classes with hearing students—a difficult and rare accomplishment.

Other special schools have a different aim. For example, DERDIC's Instituto Educacional São Paulo regards education as a program that should not be interrupted up through the eighth grade, that should be organized to develop successive stages in the acquisition of academic knowledge, that provides preparation for social adjustment, and that gives some base for a future profession.

The predominant philosophy in schools and clinics is the integration of the deaf person in the world of the hearing by developing speech and lipreading skills and utilization of residual hearing, which should be achieved through early diagnosis, binaural amplification, intense auditive stimulation, and techniques for cognitive and verbal development. *See* AUDITORY TRAINING; SPEECH TRAINING.

There are no extensive or regular programs for the detection of hearing loss in babies or preschool children. Some private schools in the important capitals give routine hearing tests to five- or six-year-olds. Diagnosis is being made earlier, however, and increasingly so, in both private and government clinics, some of which are equipped for electrocochleography and evoked-response audiometry. *See* AUDIOMETRY: Auditory Evoked Potentials.

Clinic and school programs for speech development favor multisensory methods, even though the unisensory approach was highly regarded in the 1970s. Some schools and clinics use Guberina's verbotonal method.

Although sign language is the principal form of communication among deaf persons, it was practically abolished by specialists between 1950 and 1970. In the late 1970s total communication was studied and utilized; it is spreading slowly throughout the country, and is being tried out in some private clinics in São Paulo and Rio de Janeiro and in one school in Paraná. Among the state-run centers, the Fundação Catarinense de Educação Especial is the only one that deviates from the strict oralist tradition. *See* SIGN LANGUAGES: Brazilian SOCIOLINGUISTICS: Total Communication.

Oralists and total communication proponents try to involve parents in their programs, often as collaborators. The only services organized especially to train parents to work in these programs are the Centro de Audiologia Educacional da Santa Casa de São Paulo and the Audiology sector of the Hospital Regional de Sorocaba. *See* PARENT EDUCATION.

PROFESSIONAL TRAINING AND WORK OPPORTUNITIES

The INES in Rio de Janeiro and the Instituto Santa Terezinha in São Paulo train deaf students for simple or middle-level jobs such as design copying, computer work, typography, photography, tailoring, manicuring, hairdressing, and carpentry.

There are sparse data on the work status of deaf Brazilians. Counselors think that the majority of deaf individuals do not have access to the job market because of lack of adequate training. In rural areas, profoundly deaf persons do simple manual tasks or work in the home. In industrial centers, those who go through primary and vocational schools can become middle-level technicians; some

students reach higher positions owing to better education, while others do so because of their own creativity and intelligence.

Bibliography

Almanaque Abril, Editora Abril, São Paulo, 1983.

Anuário Estatístico do Brasil, Instituto Brasileiro de Geografia e Estatística, Brasília, 1981.

Bevilacqua, M. C.: "Audiologia Educacional: considerações sobre a audicao em crianças da 1ª serie do 1º grau de escolas publicas," Master's thesis, PUCSP, São Paulo, 1981.

Bueno, J. G. S.: "Alfabetização do deficiente auditivo: estudo sobre aplicação de abordagem analitica," Master's thesis, PUCSP, São Paulo, 1982.

Cervellini, N. G. H.: "A criança deficiente auditiva e suas reações à musica," Master's thesis, PUCSP, São Paulo, 1983.

Educação Especial: dados estatísticos: Ministério de Educação e Cultura, Brasília, 1975.

Educação Especial—Tabelas: Secretaria de Estado da Educação, São Paulo, 1981.

Ficker, L. B.: "Alguns aspectos da comunicação entre mães ouvintes e crianças deficientes auditivas," Master's thesis, PUCSP, São Paulo, 1983.

Goldenberg, M.: "O deficiente auditivo no mundo do trabalho: um estudo sobre a satisfação profissional," Master's thesis, PUCRJ, Rio de Janeiro, 1980.

Mangabeira Albernaz, P. L., M. M. Ganan123, and W. F. House: *Surdez Neurosensorial*, Editora Moderna, São Paulo, 1978.

Novais, B. C. A. C.: "Organização de um procedimento para a avaliacao da função semiótica visando a sua aplicação em crianças deficientes auditivas," Master's thesis, PUCSP, São Paulo, 1981.

Oates, E.: *A linguagem das mãos*, Gráfica-Editora Livro, Rio de Janeiro, 1969.

Rabelo. A. S.: "Aplicação de abordagem oralista e de Comunicação Total em deficientes auditivos: Estudo comparativo de duas crianças." Master's thesis, PUCSP, São Paulo, 1982.

Spinelli, M.: *Foniatria*, Editora Moraes, São Paulo, 1983.

Sprenger, A. M. A.: "Estudo do comportamento articulatório em crianças com deficiência auditiva," Master's thesis, PUCSP, São Paulo, 1980.

Yoshioka, M. C. C. P., et al.: "Utilização de Comunicação Total em sujeitos com deficiência auditiva severa," in A. F. Paiva, M. Spinelli, and S. M. M. Vieira (eds.), *Distúrbios de Comunição: Estudos interdisciplinares*, Cortez, São Paulo, 1981.

Mauro Spinelli

BREUNIG, H. LATHAM
(1910–   )

H. Latham Breunig has been committed to opportunities for deaf people through the use of speech and a philosophy of self-help. Realizing that his own freedom of movement as a professional chemist and statistician was due in great part to his ability to speak and speechread, as well as to the environment of encouragement during his school years, he worked persistently for the cause of oral education and broadening opportunities for deaf youth among hearing people.

Born November 19, 1910, in Indianapolis, Indiana, Breunig suffered a partial hearing loss at age three for an unknown reason. A bout with scarlet fever at age five increased the loss to 60 percent. Finally, an accident involving a skull fracture at age seven resulted in a 115-decibel loss.

From 1920 to 1927 Breunig attended the Clarke School for the Deaf in Northampton, Massachusetts. He served as president of its alumni association for 16 years, was appointed to the board of trustees in 1946, and became vice-chairman of the board in 1961. He met his wife, then Nancy D. Tyree, at the Clarke School. *See* CLARKE SCHOOL.

After attending Clarke, Breunig went to Shortridge High School, a public school in Indianapolis. Breunig was an active high school student, working as an associate editor on the school newspaper, achieving the rank of Eagle Scout, and excelling in his studies. He was named a member of the National Honor Society in his junior year.

Breunig was no less active in college. As a student at Wabash College in Crawfordsville, Indiana, Breunig was a member of the Beta Theta Pi fraternity and the Science Club, and also worked on the newspaper. He received a bachelor's degree in chemistry in 1934.

Pursuing his interest in chemistry, Breunig went to Johns Hopkins University, which awarded him a doctor of philosophy degree in 1938. He was a member of Sigma Xi and Phi Lambda Upsilon, both honorary research societies.

Breunig then began full-time work as a research chemist at Eli Lilly and Company in Indianapolis, where he had worked as a laboratory assistant the previous eight summers. After 18 years as a researcher, Breunig spent a year at Purdue University studying theoretical and applied statistics, enabling him to use statistical methods in Lilly's laboratories to analyze the company's chemical procedures. As a result, the company's quality control, evaluation procedures, and efficiency in this area were significantly improved. By the time Breunig retired from the company in 1975, he had achieved the title of senior statistician and had published a number of papers concerning quality control in the pharmaceutical industry.

Running parallel to his career at Lilly was Breunig's increasing involvement in organizations of and for deaf people, both locally and nationally, and with issues in special education. In Indiana, he was the director of the Indianapolis Speech and Hearing Center for 21 years, and president for two terms. As a testament to Breunig's commitment to the use of speech, he was a member of Toastmasters Inter-

H. Latham Breunig.

national for 10 years, serving as the president of the Eli Lilly Club during 1954.

On the national level, Breunig contributed extensively to the work of the Alexander Graham Bell Association for the Deaf in various capacities. In 1964, when he had already been on the auxiliary board and the board of directors for 10 years, Breunig cofounded and became the chairman of the Oral Deaf Adults Section (ODAS) of the association, a post he held until 1968. (Another cofounder was Robert Weitbrecht, who engineered the acoustic coupler that links the teletypewriter, or TTY, to the standard telephone.) ODAS, an organization that promotes expressive and receptive speech for deaf people, makes its members available for speaking engagements, conferences, or other activities designed to present these individuals as role models for deaf young people and their parents. The group raises money for scholarships that each year allow young deaf adults to attend colleges with their hearing peers. The idea for this organization may well be attributed to Helen Keller, who in 1952 said to Lillian Jones, granddaughter of Alexander Graham Bell: "You need to get outstanding oral deaf adults—

those who can speak really well and clearly—to be leaders. They will attract people's attention and dramatize what can be done." *See* ALEXANDER GRAHAM BELL ASSOCIATION FOR THE DEAF; BELL, ALEXANDER GRAHAM; KELLER, HELEN.

Breunig served on the board of directors of the Bell Association for the period 1960–1982, as president (the first deaf person to do so) for the years 1976–1978. During his presidential term, he dedicated his efforts to the goals of early detection of hearing loss, early intervention for hearing-impaired infants, and parent counseling. Public Law 94-142, the Education for All Handicapped Children Act, had not yet seen its first anniversary when Breunig took office, and he hailed it as an important means toward realizing the goals of the Bell Association for hearing-impaired children. *See* EDUCTIONAL LEGISLATION.

While Breunig was a member of the board of the Bell Association in 1968, American Telephone & Telegraph agreed to donate surplus TTYs to the association. Since the association itself could not handle the acquisition of the machines, Breunig, with his wife and Jess Smith, editor of the *Deaf American*, set up Teletypewriters for the Deaf, Inc. (TDI), independent of the association, for this purpose, and to recondition the machines. TDI has devoted itself to the distribution of surplus TTYs to deaf people and publishes a yearly TTY directory. As executive director of this organization, Breunig gave testimony before a Senate subcommittee calling on the federal government to make its several thousand surplus TTYs available to TDI. In addition, he advocated the installment of TTYs in legislative and executive offices commonly contacted by the public. The TTY network in the United States now numbers more than 75,000 stations, of which approximately 6000 are member stations of TDI. Breunig resigned his position in 1978 to protest the relocation of TDI to the headquarters of the National Association of the Deaf, a move he saw as a threat to TDI's independence. *See* DEAF AMERICAN; NATIONAL ASSOCIATION OF THE DEAF; TELECOMMUNICATIONS: Telephone Services.

Breunig was also appointed to the National Council on the Handicapped, a 14-member body charged with studying the effectiveness of federal programs serving handicapped people. He remained active with the Alexander Graham Bell Association for the Deaf as the chairman of its Governmental Relations Committee and a member of the ODAS Council. *See* ORGANIZATIONS.

Bibliography

Breunig, H. L.: "The Challenge of Higher Learning for the Deaf," *Volta Review*, 68:653–654, 1966.

Jones, L. G.: "History and Activities of the Alexander Graham Bell Association for the Deaf," *Otolaryngologic Clinics of North America*, 8(1):219–231, 1975.

"Oral Deaf Adult Named President-Elect of A. G. Bell Association," *Volta Review*, 76:399, 1974.

Shaw, J. P.: "Latham Breunig—A Deaf Boy Without a Handicap," *Volta Review*, 32:161–166, 1930.

Star, R. R: *"We can! #2,"* Alexander Graham Bell Association for the Deaf, 1980.

Timberlake, J. B.: "Deaf Graduates: The Eighth List," *Volta Review*, 36:715–716, 763–764, 1934.

Gina Doggett

BREWSTER, JOHN, JR.
(1766–1854)

John Brewster, Jr., was born to Dr. John and Mary (Durkee) Brewster on May 30, 1766, in Hampton, Connecticut. The only member of his family to be born deaf, he was to become one of New England's most successful traveling artists during the first 35 years of the nineteenth century.

The earlier personal references to Brewster appear in the manuscript diary of the Reverend James Cogswell of Scotland Parish, Windham, Connecticut. On December 13, 1790, he recorded: "Doctor Brewster's Son, a Deaf and Dumb young man came in in the Evening, he is very Ingenious, has a Genius for painting & can write well, and converse by signs so that he may be understood in many Things. He lodged here." On February 7, 1791, Cogswell wrote again: "Brewster, the Deaf & D. young Man was at my House when I came home . . . he appears to have a good Disposition & an ingenious Mind. I could converse little with Him, being not enough acquainted to understand his Signs." It is not now known from whom Brewster received this specialized instruction.

During the late eighteenth century the young man studied portrait painting for a short time with the Reverend Joseph Steward of Hartford, and despite a minimum of formal training he executed several early commissions in Connecticut for family and friends. However, it was the marriage of his brother Royal in 1795 to Dorcas Coffin of Buxton, Maine, that led to his professional career as a traveling artist. Royal became the only physician in Buxton, and in 1798 John joined him there and eventually made his permanent home with his brother's family in Maine.

The life of a traveling artist was not easy in the early nineteenth century. It necessitated continuous travel by horseback or on foot, and constant communication with strangers in unfamiliar surroundings such as crowded inns or clients' busy homes. Considering his lack of speech and hearing, Brewster's ability to become totally independent is a tribute to his courage and perseverance. In pursuit of his career he advertised in various small-town newspapers, traveled the winding back roads of northern New England, and visited and revisited

John Brewster, Jr.'s portrait of Junia Loretta Bartlett, Kingston, New Hampshire, 1821.

the coastal towns of Massachusetts and Maine. On March 24, 1823, Hezekiah Prince, Jr., of Thomaston, Maine, recorded in his diary: "Mr. Brewster a deaf and dumm man came this morning to take my portrait . . . price $10 and boarded."

The features of Brewster's sitters are clearly drawn, his brushwork skillful and precise, his flesh tones tinted a delicate rose pink with subtle gray overtones. The most distinctive aspect of his sensitive likenesses, however, is an evocation of close personal relationship with his subjects resulting, perhaps, from complete concentration while painting in a silent world of his own.

In the spring of 1817 occurred an event that must have occasioned a momentous decision for Brewster. On April 15, the Connecticut Asylum for the Education and Instruction of Deaf and Dumb Persons opened in Hartford. Brewster no doubt heard of the school through Dr. Mason Fitch Cogswell, son of the Reverend James Cogswell, because of the deafness of the doctor's small daughter Alice. Dr. Cogswell was a leading spirit in founding the asylum, and the initial class of seven students included both little Alice Cogswell and John Brewster, Jr. Admitted as the sixth pupil, Brewster was then 51, a man who had been successful and independent for at least 20 years. As he was taught to write and use signs when young, it seems probable that he hoped to learn through professional instruction the practice of lipreading and speech. *See* AMERICAN SCHOOL FOR THE DEAF; COGSWELL, ALICE.

During the three years that he lived at the asylum, Brewster supported himself, as few of the pupils were then able to do, leaving in 1820 to continue his painting in Maine and elsewhere. Although no inscribed pictures by him have been recorded during his asylum years, the portrait of Junia Loretta Bartlett of Kingston, New Hampshire, is signed by him in pencil on the top stretcher: "John Brewster Jr. pinxt, May 28th, 1821. 11 years old." In his lifetime he may well have painted several hundred portraits and miniatures, and today he is considered one of New England's most accomplished folk artists. He died in Buxton Lower Corner, Maine; and there in the Tory Hill Cemetery, behind the old Congregational Church, stands a simple headstone that bears the brief epitaph: "John Brewster Died Aug. 11 1854 Aged 88."

Good examples of Brewster's paintings are in the York Institute Museum, Saco, Maine; Historical Society of Old Newbury, Newburyport, Massachusetts; and New York State Historical Association, Cooperstown, New York.

Bibliography

Cogswell, Reverend James: "MS Diary" (unpublished), Library, Connecticut Historical Society, Hartford.

Jones, Emma C. Brewster: *The Brewster Genealogy*, 2 vols., Grafton Press, New York, 1874–1880.

Little, Nina Fletcher: "John Brewster, Jr., 1766–1854," *Connecticut Historical Society Bulletin*, vol. 25, no. 4, October 1960.

Nina Fletcher Little

BRIDGMAN, LAURA DEWEY
(1829–1889)

Laura Dewey Bridgman was the first deaf and blind person to be successfully educated in the United States. She was born December 21, 1829, in Hanover, New Hampshire, the third daughter of Daniel and Harmony Bridgman, intelligent people of New England heritage. Her father served two sessions as a New Hampshire legislator.

Bridgman was a sensitive, delicate child, apparently subject to convulsions until about 18 months of age. She then recovered and seemed to be normal. At age two, however, she had an attack of scarlet fever which destroyed her sight and hearing and dulled her senses of taste and smell. She was ill for two years. She had learned to speak a few words before her illness, but she now forgot them and no longer spoke.

Bridgman's busy farm family had little time to spend with her after she recovered. Her best friend and companion between her recovery and the age of eight was Asa Tenney, an old man with a speech impediment. Kind and gentle with Bridgman, he took her on trips to the woods and fields, showing her the things of nature and providing her with exercise and fresh air. There was no formal communication between them; they did not find it necessary. In fact, Tenney disapproved of the idea of sending Bridgman to school. Still, he played an important part in her early development.

In 1837 Bridgman came to the attention of Samuel Gridley Howe, the founder and first director of the Perkins Institution for the Blind in Boston, Massachusetts. He went to visit her and found her to be a highly intelligent child, with a need for more sophisticated communication than she then had. Her communication with her parents was very limited. She understood approval (they patted her head) or disapproval (they rubbed her hand). A push or a pull meant to go or to come. She had respect only for strength; she had experienced no moral and little intellectual development. She was a stubborn child, reluctant to yield to the demands of others, although she did recognize her father's stomp on the floor as a sign that she must obey. Despite this sketchy communication, her mother taught her to do some sewing and knitting and simple household chores. Bridgman also developed an extremely acute sense of touch, upon which she depended all her life to maintain contact with others.

Laura Dewey Bridgman. (Perkins School for the Blind)

Howe persuaded Bridgman's parents to bring her to Perkins in October 1837. He was determined to try to educte her despite the odds against him. When Bridgman first arrived at Perkins, she was allowed to familiarize herself with her new surroundings thrugh touch. Howe had tremendous patience with Bridgman and worked with her constantly, trying to establish communication between her and other people, so she could enjoy social relationships.

At first, the process of educating Bridgman was slow and tedious. Labels with raised letters were pasted on common objects; she soon learned that the word formations differed with various objects. Next, detached labels were used, and she learned to match these with the correct objects. These labels were then cut into their individual letters and mixed up, whereupon Laura learned to combine them again into the proper formats. At first, this process was a meaningless one in which Bridgman simply imitated her teacher. When she finally understood that these efforts represented the means by which she could communicate her thoughts to other people, the greatest obstacle had been overcome. She increased her vocabulary for several more weeks and was then taught to fingerspell. She could soon spell very rapidly and meticulously with her fingers. *See* SIGNS: Fingerspelling.

Bridgman enjoyed learning, and acquired new skills or improved former ones (such as sewing, knitting, and crocheting, and performing housework) and studied various subjects (reading, writing, mathematics, geography, history, astronomy, and philosophy) at Perkins. She became an accomplished seamstress, making many of her own clothes, and later in life learned to operate a sewing machine. She could deftly thread a needle with her tongue. Although sometimes irritable and temperamental as a child, she was taught to control herself as she grew older, and acquired a pleasant disposition. If she could not find someone to talk to by fingerspelling, whe would conduct her own "conversations," with her own two hands talking to each other. She even enjoyed music, "listening" to a piano or an organ by laying her hands on it or by feeling the vibrations through the floor. She read what books were available in raised print, particularly the Bible.

Bridgman enjoyed writing, kept a journal, and wrote letters to her mother and other relatives and friends. These letters may be naive, but they offer interesting insights into Bridgman's character. The thoughts expressed often seem more those of a child than of an adult. Bridgman also wrote three poems: "Holy Home," "Things Spiritual," and "Light and Darkness."

Bridgman seemed to have an innate knowledge of "proper" behavior, even as a child. She was very affectionate with women friends, but shied away from familiarity with men, although she did enjoy their friendship. Howe, her guardian, was the only man toward whom she was comfortable showing affection, probably because she regarded him as her second father.

Charles Dickens visited the Perkins Institution in 1842 during his first trip to the United States. He was very much impressed with Bridgman, being struck by her obvious intelligence and the manner in which she conducted herself. He recorded his observations of her in his *American Notes.*

Bridgman's religious education presented much more difficulty, but it was accomplished. She became a member of her parents' Baptist church in 1863 and remained a devout Baptist for the rest of her life.

Bridgman had four teachers especially appointed for her at successive tmes during her youth since she required a great deal of individual attention and thus nearly the entire time of one teacher during each period. The situation was very exhausting because Bridgman was a very inquisitive child and was always asking questions about everything around her.

Bridgman was able to recognize people she knew by touching them or their clothes, or by feeling the vibrations of their footsteps on the floor. She could detect when someone was nearby through these vibrations or by the movement of the air. She made sounds to show she recognized a person. Each of her acquaintances was identified by a different sound, and according to Howe, she had over 50 of these sounds. Although she learned to say a few words, she never really learned to talk.

When Bridgman was 23, Howe decided it was time for her to return to her home in Hanover permanently. She had learned as much as could be expected at Perkins, and was thought to be self-reliant for all practical purposes. It was supposed she could keep herself occupied with household activities. After the busy and interesting life at Perkins, however, home was too dull for Bridgman. She longed so for her former life that she began to waste away and was confined to bed. She was brought back to Perkins near death, but recovered and resumed her former happy routine there. Howe made a provision in his will for her to remain at Perkins for the rest of her life. She went home to join her family each summer, a visit she enjoyed since she knew she would return to Perkins in the fall.

Howe died in 1876. Bridgman was so grief-stricken that her friends feared she would soon die also, but she recovered. She kept herself busy with different activities at the institution, helping to teach the children and sewing various items. She was honored with a jubilee celebration of her 50 years at

Perkins in 1887, She died quietly on May 24, 1889, in Boston at the age of 60, and was buried in Hanover.

Although Bridgman was important in the field of education as proof that it was possible to educate a deaf and blind person, the success of her education must be qualified. Her sheltered life at Perkins could hardly be compared to a normal existence; she never became truly independent of Perkins. This independence remained for Helen Keller to achieve later. *See* KELLER, HELEN; DEAF-BLINDNESS: Education.

Bibliography
"The Anne Sullivan Legacy," *The Lantern*, vol. 35, no. 3, March 1966.

Howe, M., and F. H. Hall: *Laura Bridgman: Dr. Howe's Famous Pupil and What He Taught Her*, 1903.

Kiddle and Schem, *Cyclopedia of Education*, 1877.

Lamson, M. S.: *Life and Education of Laura Dewey Bridgman: The Deaf, Dumb, and Blind Girl*, 1881.

"Laura D. Bridgman: A Name That Is Very Familiar to American People," *The Silent Worker*, vol. 3, no. 18, November 28, 1889.

Queen, S. A., and D. M. Mann: *Social Pathology*, 1925.

Richards, L. E.: *Laura Bridgman: The Story of an Opened Door*, 1928.

Melanie Yager Williams

BRODERSON, MORRIS
(1928–   )

Born in Los Angeles, California, in 1928, Morris Broderson is a noted figurative painter. He gained national recognition with the inclusion of *The Chicken Market* (1960) in the "Young America USA 1960" exhibit at the Whitney Museum of American Art in New York City. Broderson began his career as an artist in the late 1940s and early 1950s, when abstract expressionism dominated the contemporary art field, yet he developed a realistic style of painting. The acceptance of his figurative work in the 1960 Whitney show was a testament to the fact that he was talented enough to challenge the prevailing tenets of modern art and to pursue his own vision.

Deaf at birth, Broderson was educated at the California School for the Deaf in Berkeley and at schools in Los Angeles. He had an early interest in art which was encouraged by his aunt, who gave Broderson at the age of 14 a book of Leonardo da Vinci's drawings for inspiration and Nicolaïdes' *The Natural Way to Draw* as a study guide. At 15 he entered Francis de Erdley's life drawing class at the Pasadena Museum of Art. The next year, when de Erdley was made an associate professor of art at the University of Southern California, he insisted that Broderson be granted admission as a special

The Sound of Flowers (1960) by Morris Broderson. (Gallaudet College Collection)

student to the university. Broderson was admitted and remained for four years.

He later enrolled at the Jepson Art Institute in Los Angeles, where he was influenced by the institute's director, Rico Lebrun, whose emphasis on the importance of draftsmanship in the Renaissance and Baroque traditions has had a lasting effect on Broderson's work. When the institute closed, he began experimenting on his own, principally with new silk-screen and mixed-media techniques.

Broderson had his first one-person show in 1954 at the Dixi Hall Studio in Laguna Beach, California, and by the age of 35 had eight such shows to his credit, including ones at the Stanford University Museum of Art in 1957, the Santa Barbara Museum of Art in 1958, and in 1960 a major exhibit at the M. H. de Young Memorial Museum in San Francisco. He has since exhibited at the Phoenix Art Museum (1964), the Fine Arts Gallery of San Diego (1969), the University of Arizona Museum (1975), and Gallaudet College (1981). In 1963 *The Rape* (1963) was in the prestigious Whitney Museum annual in New York.

In 1975 *Angel and Holy Mary after Leonardo da Vinci* (1960) was included in the inaugural exhibition of the Hirshhorn Museum and Sculpture Garden in Washington, D.C.; this work is representative of Broderson's series of paintings in the

1960s which were based on religious themes. Throughout this period his paintings were characterized by sculptural effects, which he achieved by placing static figures against simple backgrounds and modeling their forms through light and shadow. The surreal quality of these isolated, poignant figures was further enhanced by his use of multiple views of a single image, a device which was a legacy from some of Picasso's (1881–1973) female figures of the 1930s.

In addition to biblical sources, many of Broderson's themes have grown out of his travels to Europe, Asia, and Mexico. During a trip to Japan in 1963 he became fascinated by the traditional Japanese theater form of Kabuki, which incorporates stylized and exaggerated gestures and expressions. *The Rape* (1963) is from this series and combines Kabuki figures with references from his own culture, sign language. The inclusion of the manual alphabet is a motif in a number of his works. The bullfights in Tijuana and Garcia Lorca's poem about the death of the famous toreador Ignacio Sanchez spawned a series of powerful, allegorical paintings throughout the 1960s, such as *Ignacio Sanchez Mejias' Home* (1966). Modern myths, such as that of Lizzie Borden from Agnes de Mille's ballet *Fall River Legend*, also captured Broderson's imagination, and inspired a number of paintings on this subject in the late 1960s and early 1970s. One of his most sensitive series of works, *The Sound of Flowers*, is based on a friend's story of seeing a small child wander through the fields, "listening to the sound of flowers." For these children, as for the artist, images are both sight and sound. *See* SIGNS: Fingerspelling.

Since the mid-1970s Broderson's works have become less introspective. *Madonna* (1979), for example, is an interpretation of a familiar theme in Broderson's works—Mary the Mother of Christ—but it is stylistically quite different from his earlier religious paintings. Muted tones and sculptural massiveness have been replaced by brilliant clear colors, rich textures, and intricate patterns. Broderson's extraordinary talents as a draftsman and colorist are given free rein in his current decorative style. His continuing interest in Asian art is evident in both his images and techniques.

Broderson's work is represented in public collections, which include the Container Corporation of America, Chicago; Fine Arts Gallery of San Diego; Fresno Arts Center, California; Hirshhorn Museum and Sculpture Garden, Washington, D.C.; Honolulu Academy of Arts; Joslyn Art Museum, Omaha; Kalamazoo Institute of Arts, Michigan; La Jolla Museum of Contemporary Art, California; Los Angeles County Museum of Art; Museum of Fine Arts, Boston; Phoenix Art Museum, Arizona; San Fran-

Broderson's *The Answer (Self Portrait)*, a watercolor from 1982. (Ankrum Gallery, Los Angeles)

cisco Museum of Modern Art; Santa Barbara Museum, California; Stanford University Museum of Art, California; Whitney Museum of American Art, New York City; and Yale University, New Haven, Connecticut.

Bibliography

Frankenstein, Alfred: "Kollowitz and Broderson—Artists of Similar Conviction," *San Francisco Chronicle*, pp. 23–24, January 22, 1961.

Hines, Diane: "Morris Broderson Speaking Through His Art," *American Artist*, pp. 46–51, October 1980.

Seldis, Henry J.: "Southern California," *Art in America*, no. 4, pp. 57–59, 1960.

Steadman, William: *Morris Broderson*, University of Arizona Art Museum, Tucson, 1975.

Judy P. Mannes

CALIFORNIA STATE UNIVERSITY, NORTHRIDGE

California State University, Northridge (CSUN), is a relatively new campus, having celebrated its twenty-fifth anniversary in 1983. One of 19 campuses in the California State University system, it is located in the San Fernando Valley, approximately 20 miles (32 kilometers) from the center of the city of Los Angeles. The original bungalows, set among orange and walnut trees, that constituted the campus in 1958 have gradually been replaced by 50 modern structures on 350 landscaped acres (142 hectares). CSUN offers undergraduate degrees in 46 fields and graduate degrees in 36 fields to more than 28,000 hearing students. Disciplines range from liberal arts and sciences to engineering and the arts.

NATIONAL LEADERSHIP TRAINING PROGRAM

University programs for hearing-impaired persons include the National Leadership Training Program (NLTP), begun in 1961, which initiated the university's service in the field of deafness. The National Leadership Training Program continues as a cooperative effort between the National Center on Deafness (NCOD) and Department of Educational Administration and Supervision (EAS) to train leaders in deafness. Funded since 1962 by the Rehabilitation Services Administration, it provides graduate training to established professionals in the fields of deafness who wish to become administrators. Participants, selected on the basis of national competition, receive a federally funded traineeship. Each receives a master's degree in administration and supervision at the conclusion of 8 months of training.

Major strengths of the program have been its integration of trainees from the fields of rehabilitation, education, community service, and business and industry; and its integration of deaf and hearing trainees. Approximately one-third of the program's graduates are deaf. The program has been very successful in placing its graduates in leadership positions in rehabilitation and education throughout the United States and several other countries. For five years (1974–1979), a counterpart program [the National Leadership Training Program in the Area of the Deaf-Blind (NLTP-DB)] was in operation, funded by the Bureau of Education of the Handicapped; 41 students successfully completed the program.

SUPPORT SERVICES

What began as an informal effort to support two deaf trainees in the National Leadership Training Program class of 1964 became a full-fledged program of support services for about 200 deaf students, who came to CSUN each semester from nearly every state. The students are enrolled, both on an undergraduate and graduate level, in more than 500 university classes encompassing nearly every discipline.

Support services for these students include interpreting services by full-time staff interpreters and interpreters assigned by the hour. Most of them have been trained at CSUN, and many are preparing for careers working with deaf people as teachers and counselors. Note-taking is also provided to deaf students. *See* INTERPRETING.

Student personnel specialists offer academic, career, and personal counseling, as well as other valuable services to deaf students, including orientation to new students and coordination of student activities in conjunction with the CSUN Associated Students. Speech and audiological services are provided by a communications specialist in conjunction with the university's Language, Speech and Hearing Center. Remedial courses in English and mathematics are taught by staff of the National Center on Deafness.

INTERPRETER TRAINING

Begun as a formal sign language class in 1964, today the program involves extensive coursework in both sign language and interpreter training. Approximately 400 hearing students per semester enroll in sign language or interpreting coursework, and many go on to serve as interpreters for deaf students in CSUN classes. Media materials, especially video tapes, have been developed on campus to support the sign language-interpreter training program. In addition, numerous instructional 16-mm films have been adapted for hearing-impaired viewers by transferring to video tape and adding a sign language insert or captioning. *See* INTERPRETING: Interpreter Training.

TEACHER PREPARATION PROGRAM

Begun in 1969 by the CSUN Department of Special Education to prepare teachers to work at the secondary school level, the Teacher Preparation Program originally provided a summer program for experienced teachers who wished to strengthen their academic preparation for credential requirements. Today, the program prepares teachers for both elementary and secondary deaf education credentials, and a considerable number of deaf students have completed it. *See* TEACHING PROFESSION: Training.

In addition to current programs on deafness, CSUN has pioneered a number of projects which have been widely emulated throughout the United States. Among these are Adult Education (1963), Telephone Communications (1964), Parent Education (TRIPOD; 1967), Legal Rights of the Deaf (1964), and community information and referral services for the deaf (1966).

The success of deaf students at CSUN has clearly established that, given reasonable support services, many deaf students can succeed in regular university classes at both graduate and undergraduate levels. They can successfully complete degree requirements, and they can achieve competitive professional employment. *See* EDUCATIONAL PROGRAMS: Higher Education.

Ray L. Jones

CANADA

Canada is an officially bilingual country which prides itself on its multicultural nature and actively supports linguistically and ethnically diverse groups. However, the Canadian deaf population, which views itself as holding minority group status, has been largely ignored. In the past, prejudice perpetuated deaf people's isolation from one another and from the general community. Deaf people have historically evoked unflattering stereotypes, have been stigmatized by pejorative characterizations, and have received insensitive, if not cruel, treatment. While the early perceptions of deaf persons as deviant, defective, and dependent have disappeared, there still persists in Canadian society a lack of awareness and understanding of the implications of deafness and the richness of deaf culture.

About 2 million Canadians, or 1 in 10 citizens, suffer some form of hearing impairment. About 40,000 adults have hearing losses of such a nature as to preclude the processing of information auditorally. Nearly 4000 children and youths are in special programs for hearing-impaired individuals. Of this number, almost half have profound losses. Six percent come from families where one or both parents are deaf. These rates are approximations, as no national survey on deafness has been undertaken. Moreover, they fail to include the native population of the far north among whom hearing loss is reportedly endemic.

Forming such a minute segment of the population, deaf Canadians command the interest of only a small number of professionals. There are not many trained personnel in psychology, vocational counseling, and social work in Canada. Rapid advances have been made in interpreting services, but no comprehensive certification for interpreters currently exists.

The problems of a small and scattered deaf population served by few trained professionals are compounded by the autonomous nature of Canadian legislation. Under the 1867 British North America Act, the provinces were ceded sole jurisdiction over education and social services, a right tenaciously guarded. The inherent decentralization has engendered a proliferation of often uncoordinated services for deaf individuals. Across the country, services are delivered in a variety of ways, with vast differences in their comprehensiveness and degree of association. Similarly, education has developed untidily, and there is a general lack of a systematic approach to the education of deaf children.

Generalizations regarding education, social services, and the deaf community are difficult to make. Research is sparse—apart from purely educational projects, barely a dozen contemporary studies exist and most are regional in nature. Little attention has been directed to the genesis and evolution of educational and social services, deaf associations, and the deaf community in Canada. The outstanding contributions of pioneers, both deaf and hearing, are not well documented, and these distinguished achievements have generally not received the acclaim they deserve.

Nevertheless, some favorable patterns can be seen emerging. There has been a resurgence of deaf groups involved in political, fund-raising, social, and sporting activities. Deaf Canadians have won battles to become teachers, to hold government positions, to have interpreters in court, and to become adoptive parents. However, lags continue to exist in postsecondary education, the socioeconomic status of deaf adults, the structure of service delivery, research activities, and the awakening of the general public to an appreciation of the unique needs and contributions of deaf Canadians.

HISTORICAL PRECEDENTS

The correlates of the development of the education and socialization of deaf Canadians are complex. Although deeply influenced by British and French factors, Canada's association has been most clearly with the United States. In the development and maintenance of services, Canadians have traditionally placed great faith in the American system and a heavy reliance on American precedents; the two countries have been linked together in exploring and delivering services for deaf people.

Demography determined the development of educational services for deaf Canadians 40 years after philanthropy initiated the venture in the United States. The first permanent Canadian institution was established at Halifax in 1856. By 1900 seven institutions were in operation, three founded by deaf men. With the exception of the two Quebec schools established under the auspices of the Catholic Church, each became provincially sponsored and funded. In their development and progress, the early schools each progressed through designations of philanthropic venture to social welfare to education, and all made a gradual shift from allegiance to the manual modes of communication to oral philosophies. *See* EDUCATION: Communication.

The tentatively evolving pioneer Canadian schools aligned closely with their American counterparts. They adopted similar pedagogical techniques; personnel was recruited from American institutions; Canadian teachers were trained at American centers; Canadian educators held office in the Convention of American Instructors of the Deaf and served on the executive board of the *American Annals of the Deaf*; professsional conferences were hosted at Canadian institutions, and the annual reports of Canadian schools were larded with excerpts from American educators, with detailed explanations of their philosophies and practices. While the Halifax School for the Deaf flirted briefly with the British manual system, the American signs were rapidly adopted and American Sign Language (ASL) has remained the preferred mode of communication for deaf persons in Canada. *See* AMERICAN ANNALS OF THE DEAF; CONVENTION OF AMERICAN INSTRUCTORS OF THE DEAF; SIGN LANGUAGES: American.

Schooling and the development of the deaf community were intertwined in Canada. Prior to the establishment of educational services, there is no evidence of the existence of any community. The great majority of deaf Canadians in the midnineteenth century lived in isolated farming communities. Marriage rates of the deaf population were low, and one educator reported in 1880 that there were only "about a dozen deaf-mute married couples in the Dominion of Canada."

Within the early schools, education was chiefly a training process by which deaf students were directed into social and vocational roles determined by what hearing educators presumed was consonant with their handicap. With the development of an industrial society, there was little room for those who could not compete in earning a living, so the schools stressed industrial training, supplemented by a restricted literary curriculum.

Graduates were inevitably impelled toward urban areas in search of gainful employment in school-taught trades (printing, shoemaking and carpentering), and thus became part of the urbanization movement that characterized late-nineteenth century eastern Canadian society. Scattered throughout metropolitan areas, deaf communities emerged in the 1870s. Cities such as Toronto, Halifax, and Montreal witnessed the growth of churches, soci-ties, newspapers, and social clubs which arose, much like the American networks founded earlier, to cater to the special needs and sustain a way of life for an emerging deaf urban group. The deaf community provided for its members identification with others of similar experience, financial and moral support, and links to the countryside.

Organized religious and social associations rapidly arose. The Ontario Deaf and Dumb Christian Association was founded by a deaf man in Toronto in 1878 and rapidly spread to the other provinces. This group provided Bible study, literary groups, and mutual help missions in outlying areas. Provincial Deaf Mute Associations, which fulfilled social, recreational, and political functions, arose in the same period.

As the railway opened up western Canada, educators of deaf people rapidly followed and deaf communities appeared. The Manitoba School for the Deaf was opened in 1884 and, by mandating free and compulsory education by 1890, established a dominance in providing services. Manitoba's early commitment remains imprecise, but may be associated with the unique deaf community formed in Wolseley, Manitoba, in 1884.

Deaf Americans had explored the possibilities of buying tracts of land and settling in separate areas in the 1850s, but the Wolseley project brought the idea to reality. A deaf female missionary, encouraged by the Canadian government and the Canadian Pacific Railway, conceived a plan for transporting deaf colonists to Manitoba. At least 40 deaf English immigrants settled in the Wolseley community to learn to farm in order to buy land in the area. The Winnipeg press railed against the "consignment of deaf mutes," although others applauded them as being "desired acquisitions to the country." The community apparently flourished for about four years, but its final fate is unknown. *See* HISTORY: A Deaf Commonwealth.

By the opening decades of the twentieth century, associations of deaf people in eastern Canada were actively lobbying both the federal government and the provincial legislatures. Many of the causes they espoused are still remarkably relevant—postsecondary education, equality in hiring practices, and the right of deaf individuals to have some say in programs and communication policies initiated in the schools developed to cater to their unique needs.

CONTEMPORARY CONSIDERATIONS

A high percentage of deaf Canadians today report either full or partial membership in the deaf community. Reflecting the multicultural nature of Canadian society, the deaf community is a spectrum of social classes, religious affiliations, and racial and ethnic groups. These differences lead to divisions based on such factors as signing type and ability, social class, ethnicity, and the perceived differences between deaf people and hard-of-hearing people. While ASL is the overwhelmingly preferred mode of communication of the deaf community in English Canada, the small and relatively isolated French community employs French Canadian Sign Language.

Deaf Canadians prefer to socialize with other deaf persons and regard ASL as their native language. Deaf English Canadians report that they use ASL consistently in communicating with deaf friends, and a majority use ASL in the home. English (school-based) signs are not popular, although deaf individuals under 30 years of age appear more accepting of them. The primary means of communication on the job or with neighbors is speech, writing, and lipreading. Writing is the most popular mode in communicating with hearing persons, and one-third of deaf people report that they depend on writing to give or receive messages.

The majority of deaf persons are not adverse to using interpreting services in order to establish a communication link. The willingness is situational, and demand increases according to the complexity of the activity. Interpreters are valued in legal and medical matters, in business and religious activities, and in educational endeavors such as night school and continuing education. If an interpreter is needed, the preference is for a professional; family members are acceptable, but friends are not.

Across the Dominion, regional differences in sign are apparent. Currently, some deaf Canadians are proudly proclaiming the development of Canadian Sign Language. The Canadian Co-ordinating Council on Deafness is creating a bilingual dictionary that will codify a basic vocabulary of sign languages used in Canada. This will be a first attempt at an in-depth study and codification of the sign language used in French Canada, thereby shedding light on the distinctive cultural traits of the French deaf community.

Given their preference for sign language, it is not surprising that many deaf Canadians disagree with the school-based English sign systems incorporated as part of total communication in the schools. Input from the deaf community has not been a factor in determining how signs are to be incorporated into the framework of the educational system. While educators have been slow in their efforts to examine ASL as a potentially effective educational tool, most deaf adults believe it should hold an important place in school instruction. They support a bilingual approach to language acquisition, viewing ASL as the first language to be learned but appreciating English signs as an important addition to the child's communication. *See* SOCIO-LINGUISTICS: Total Communication.

Technological innovations have opened up new communication vistas for the scattered Canadian deaf community. At least 80 percent of deaf adults own or have access to teletype machines for personal and business communication. However, long-distance calls are rarely made, due to the prohibitive costs. Message relay centers are available in urban areas. Hearing aids are not a high-priority item, and a maximum of 20 percent of deaf persons report using an aid full- or part-time.

Captioned television has wrought major changes in the structure of recreational activities. In 1981 the federal cabinet approved funding for the Canadian Captioning Development Agency, which became operational in 1982. They initially captioned French language telecasts because French-speaking people, worldwide, had no closed captioning available to them. A wide variety of Canadian programs and commercials are now captioned in both official languages.

Socioeconomic Status Deaf persons in Canada demonstrate a relatively poor employment record in both the availability and nature of work. The lowest employment rates appear to be in Atlantic Canada. Many deaf individuals do not know how to locate jobs, or even the type of job they want. These difficulties are compounded by the low skill levels of many deaf individuals, and by the false assumptions, unfounded myths, and misunderstandings held by many employers. Once on the job, deaf persons tend to be underemployed; they cannot find positions commensurate with their skills and abilities. Opportunities for advancement are limited, and deaf adults express pessimism concerning their chances for promotion.

While deaf persons now occupy many more positions than were once thought consonant with their disability, the majority tend to cluster in manual and manufacturing enterprises. They are in low-skill-level jobs and show a lack of occupational diversity. Many work at trades that were introduced in school or in jobs related to those trades. Deaf Canadians are far behind in professional, technical, clerical, sales, and service positions, and are grossly underrepresented among managers, officials, and proprietors.

An insufficient number of deaf persons fill the professional ranks. Most professionals are teachers who have earned degrees in the United States. They work in provincial schools for deaf students, but not in mainstreaming programs operated by school boards. The number of deaf teachers differs dramatically in each province. For example, in 1982 Alberta had 19 hearing-impaired teachers; Ontario, the most populous province with seven times more deaf children, had only three deaf teachers. Within the schools, deaf employees have little involvement in decision making. There are no deaf administrators; all administrative positions connected with the education of deaf children are held by hearing persons.

The underrepresentation of deaf people in professional and managerial positions is directly correlated to the availability of and the person's preparedness for higher education. Fewer than 5 percent of Canada's deaf students proceed to postsecondary or university education. Access to continuing education is extremely limited: the handicap prevents the individual from making use of the facilities and materials that are available through public programs. Interpreting services are fragmented and difficult to obtain and maintain.

Canada has traditionally depended upon American postgraduate institutions to provide tertiary education for its deaf population. In 1983 the first postsecondary preparatory program for deaf students opened in London, Ontario, in order to accommodate the students from the "rubella bulge." Gallaudet College lent much assistance to the neophyte program, providing curricula, course objectives, and course materials. Upon successful completion of the preparatory program, students are eligible to apply for the first year at Gallaudet College. Community colleges are beginning to address the technical and vocational interests of the deaf. A number of special programs, providing tutors, notetakers, and counseling, are in place. *See* GALLAUDET COLLEGE.

A clear-cut measure of the penalty of deafness is personal income. The average income of the Canadian deaf population is approximately half of that of the hard-of-hearing and markedly lower than that of hearing families. However, more than 60 percent of deaf persons are reported to own an automobile. Insurance is not a problem, but some deaf persons have met difficulties in obtaining a driver's license. Credit card usage is relatively low, but whether this is because credit is unavailable or because of personal preference is unknown.

Only about 10 percent of deaf persons are reported to own their homes; the majority rent, or live with parents. Marriages appear to occur later, possibly related to economic conditions, occupational status, or the availability of compatible partners. In the Maritimes it was found that only 36 percent of a sample were married; of these, 64 percent had chosen deaf mates.

As deaf Canadians have problems as producers, they also meet difficulties as consumers. They find that access to stores and facilities is restricted by communication and attitudinal barriers, and have expressed suspicions regarding price gouging and unethical business practices.

Deafness is not recognized as a disability by the Canadian government. Tax deductions are allowed blind persons, crippled individuals, and those confined to bed, but none may be claimed by deaf people. Expenses incurred in the purchase and maintenance of teletype machines, hearing aids, batteries, medical bills, diagnostic evaluations, special school costs, and transportation all place extra burdens on day-to-day survival. Deaf lobbying groups are actively addressing this issue. Some deaf persons in the past have argued against special tax dispensations, but deaf Canadians have been advised that they can ignore the proposed deduction if they so wish.

Social and Legal Services Canadian legislation concerning deaf people has assumed principally one form—the education of deaf children. Currently, each of the 10 provinces and 2 territories has some form of legislative arrangement directed toward deaf students. Mandatory legislation in regard to the education of exceptional children is found only in Ontario and Manitoba.

Sign language interpreters are provided by the courts in criminal cases. In civil proceedings the use of an interpreter is left to the discretion of the judge who holds the residual responsibility for deciding if an interpreter has the requisite degree of skill to serve. When in circumstances of practical necessity it is not possible to locate an interpreter who can communicate effectively and still be a disinterested person, the law seems to attach priority to effective communication.

The Canadian Charter of Rights (effective April 1985) provides that deaf persons have the right to the assistance of an interpreter in any proceeding (Section 14). It is difficult to anticipate how the courts will interpret the new charter. Questions revolve around the availability of an interpreter at the arrest, at the review before the officer in charge, and upon application for interim release.

In other situations, interpreting services are available in the cities, although many deaf persons do not appear to be aware of them. Moreover, deaf persons rarely utilize such existing professional and social services as legal aid or family counseling.

Organizations   In the opening decades of the twentieth century, deaf groups and associations lobbying for improved social and educational conditions were relatively prominent and wielded some influence. Recently, organizations of deaf persons have again formed cohesive bodies in order to enhance the societal and educational status of deaf Canadians. While there is a movement toward centralization, deaf people are presently organized at the local, provincial, and national levels and are well represented on international bodies.

The Canadian Co-ordinating Council on Deafness and the Canadian Association of the Deaf are major national organizations with provincial bodies to carry out their mandates. In 1970 the national Canadian Cultural Society of the Deaf (CCSD) was formed by a deaf man in order to enrich the cultural lives of deaf individuals and to bring to the general public an awareness of deafness and deaf culture through publications and other activities. The CCSD hosts a deaf Biennial National Festival of the Arts, for example, which attracts participants and audiences from across Canada and the United States. Access to sporting events by deaf persons is encouraged by the Federation of Silent Sports, which was founded in 1963 by a deaf man.

A plethora of groups operate at the local level. Deaf groups create and operate four TV companies which present weekly programs and publish their own newsletters and journals. They arrange social and recreational activities which include sports teams, bingo nights, and dance and theatrical groups.

The Ontario Mission for the Deaf is an organization of deaf persons which has recently established a facility unique in North America. The Bob Runball Centre for the Deaf in Tronoto, operated totally by deaf persons, is a place where deaf people live, work, learn vocational skills, worship, play, socialize, and are nursed, educated, and counseled. To finance this unique concept, the deaf persons raised $90,000. The Ontario Mission also operates a foster home, 7 group homes, and 14 churches, and is planning an alumni house for multiply handicapped young adults.

Public Attitudes   Awareness of hearing loss has certainly occurred among the general Canadian public, but an appreciation of the implications of deafness and even the existence of the deaf community is lacking. In 1976, for example, many deaf people were aghast when the Census of Canada Instruction Booklet referred to "deaf-mutes." Paternalism persists, especially in relation to education; deaf people have little input into policies and programs implemented in the schools designed to meet their needs. Nevertheless, inroads on negative public perceptions and attitudes are being made, albeit in slow and halting steps, largely through the efforts of deaf people themselves.

Bibliography

Clarke, B. R., and M. A. Winzer: "A Concise History of the Education of the Deaf in Canada," *ACEHI Journal*, 9: 36–51, 1983.

Darbyshire, J. O., and D. A. Vaghy: *Final Report on the Communication Needs of Hearing-Impaired Youths and Adults*, Queen's University, Kingston, Ontario, 1979.

Fraser, S., and P. J. Owsley: "A Study of Graduates at the Atlantic Provinces Resource Centre for the Hearing Handicapped, *ACEHI Journal*, 7: 86–93, 1981.

Stewart, D.: *The Opinions of the Adult Deaf Community towards Methods of Communication in the Education of the Deaf*, M.A. thesis, University of British Columbia, 1982.

Winzer, M. A.: *An Examination of Some Selected Factors that Affected the Education and Socialization of the Deaf of Ontario, 1870–1900*, doctoral dissertation, University of Toronto, 1981.

                                                Margret A. Winzer

Canadian Co-ordinating Council on Deafness

The Canadian Co-ordinating Council on Deafness (CCCD) was established in 1975 in response to a need felt by the deaf and hard-of-hearing community across Canada. For many years, organizations had been working with deaf persons on a local or provincial level, but there was no umbrella organization enabling them to unite in a national coalition to express their concerns and to press for solutions to the problems of people with a hearing loss.

The Council is more than a single office—it is a network of organizations concerned with the welfare of Canada's hearing-impaired citizens. Local organizations and service agencies belong to provincial councils which meet regularly to discuss matters of provincial concern. About 121 organizations belong to the CCCD through their memberships in the provincial councils. Each provincial council elects representatives to the national board of directors, which is responsible for promoting effective national policies on those matters that affect hearing-impaired individuals. Half of the members of the national board must be deaf. The other delegates may be either hearing or hard-of-hearing, depending upon the wishes of each provincial council.

ROLE

The CCD occupies a unique place in the Canadian consumer movement of disabled persons. It believes that the most constructive way to remove the barriers between the hearing-impaired and the hearing community is to work in an integrated setting with consumers, agencies, and professionals. While membership in the Council is open to any interested person, the philosophy basic to the CCCD's work is "consumer advocacy" to help deaf and hard-of-hearing Canadians realize their full potential and to remove the barriers hindering their integration into society.

In addition to the CCCD's role as an advocate for the rights and interests of deaf and hard-of-hearing Canadians, it acts as an umbrella group for consumer groups and the agencies which serve deaf and hard-of-hearing people. The Council provides these organizations with information and support and acts as a forum for the discussion and exchange of views. The Council also carries out a public education program to make Canadians more aware of the problems that can result from a hearing loss. As part of this program, the Council produces educational videotapes and pamphlets, and publishes a quarterly magazine, *Communication*. The magazine has a circulation of about 2500, which includes about 1200 subscribers in Canada and about 100 exchange subscribers in the United States, Europe, and other foreign countries. The magazine is also distributed to all Canadian senators and members of Parliament. *Communication* and all other CCCD publications are produced bilingually, in French and English, to serve both of Canada's official languages.

The short existence of the Council has been marked by growth in the number and quality of its publications and the number of requests made to it by government and private industry for consultation. Its higher visibility means that the public's expectations of the Council are increasing. In the early 1980s the Council produced a new five-year plan to state its goals for the future. While organizational development was a high priority in the first plan, advocacy and public education are emphasized more strongly in the second.

The Council's areas of concern are: captioned television, technical aids for deaf and hard-of-hearing persons, prevention and early detection of hearing impairment, noise pollution and industrial noise, postsecondary education, employment, access to public services, telecommunications, human rights, and public education.

NATIONAL OFFICE

The CCCD maintains an office with full-time staff in Ottawa. This office serves to carry out the policies of the CCCD board of directors and acts as the hearing-impaired community's link to the national government. The staff maintains regular contact with government departments, crown corporations, national corporations, service agencies, and international organizations in the field of hearing impairment. Through regular contacts as well as special briefs and presentations, the CCCD monitors changes in policy, legislation, and regulations, and is able to voice the concerns of deaf and hard-of-hearing Canadians to the policy makers.

PROVINCIAL COUNCILS

The CCCD's provincial councils perform much the same function as the national office, but at the provincial level. They coordinate the activities of groups within their provinces and serve to express the views of deaf and hard-of-hearing people, the parents of deaf children, and agencies serving the deaf community. The provincial councils make their views known to their respective governments, which have jurisdiction over important issues such as health care delivery, education, vocational training, rehabilitation, and social welfare programs. Most of the provincial councils are voluntary and do not have paid staff. One of the CCCD's goals is to strenghten the provincial councils.

MEMBERSHIP AND SUPPORT

The CCCD is funded by a combination of public and private sources. It receives sustaining support from the Department of National Health and Welfare, and carries out a fund-raising campaign in the private sector. It is the Council's practice to apply all private sector contributions toward its public education activities. The Council's goal is to increase its fund-raising program and to expand its membership at the grass-roots level.

The CCCD is an associate member of the International Federation of the Hard of Hearing. At the 1982 Annual General Meeting, the CCCD sponsored a workshop on the organizing of Canada's hard-of-hearing population. This resulted in the formation in 1982 of the Canadian Hard of Hearing Association (CHHA), an organization the CCCD hopes to work with closely.

Bibliography

Canadian Co-ordinating Council on Deafness: *Can Your Baby Hear?* (pamphlet), Ottawa.

———: *Equal Access* (booklet), Ottawa.

Carbin, Clifton F.: "Deaf History: Long Neglected," *Communication*, 7(3):6–7, February 1983.

David, Michel J.: *Deafness in the Family* (booklet), Canadian Co-ordinating Council on Deafness, Ottawa, March 1982.

Huebener, Alrick: *Psychology of Deafness* (booklet), Canadian Co-ordinating Council on Deafness, Ottawa, March 1983.

Rebick, Judy: *Deafness, the Invisible Handicap* (booklet), Canadian Co-ordinating Council on Deafness, Ottawa.

Alrick Huebener

Mental Health

The mental health status of all deaf Canadians has not been examined. A careful study of deaf children and adolescents in the Vancouver area of British Columbia, however, presents a picture that may be applicable nationwide. The study indicates that deaf children and adolescents were more likely than their hearing counterparts to have been hospitalized in the first two years of life; that the diagnosis of hearing impairment was often seriously delayed; that parental concerns about hearing loss were frequently rejected by physicians; that parental "shock" on hearing of the diagnosis was less frequent than suggested by studies conducted in the United States; that deaf students showed a constellation of behaviors that might be loosely described as aggressive or hyperactive; that one in five of the respondents was rated as having a "persistent psychiatric disorder of moderate or severe degree"; and that cerebral dysfunction was present frequently in a number of the respondents. *See* Psychology: Mental Health.

Services

Unfortunately, the findings of this study have not resulted in major growth in services. There are only two main centers in Canada where reasonable services are available for deaf people or students with mental health problems—the facilities at the Children's Hospital Diagnostic Centre in Vancouver and those developed in the Deafness Clinic at the Clarke Institute of Psychiatry in Toronto. Other centers, such as the Atlantic Provinces, the University of Alberta, or the McKay Centre in Montreal, have some interest in the mental health of deaf people, but they have not developed extensive and comprehensive services. As a result, there is little understanding of the mental health needs of deaf people and children in general psychiatric services, and patients or clients are frequently misdiagnosed or inappropriately treated. Incorrect diagnosis of deaf people as schizophrenic or retarded is common. Even when patients or clients are known to be deaf, they rarely receive counseling or other appropriate help. *See* Psychology: Psychotherapy.

There are some specialized services that are attempting to develop positive preventive treatment programs to reduce the prevalence of mental health problems. For example, in Vancouver an excellent preschool program using total communication has been developed. A number of vocational programs such as DECSA (Distinctive Employment and Counselling Services of Alberta), SHIP (Saskatchewan Hearing Impaired Program), and George Brown College in Toronto are attempting to foster good prevocational skills and increased social sensitivity in deaf adolescents and adults seeking employment. Most of the residential schools are developing better training programs for residential care staff, but sometimes educational objectives seem to prevail over other perspectives. Vocational schools, particularly those in Atlantic Canada and Ontario, are also showing increased awareness of the need to incorporate "mental hygiene" into their programs so that students are able to cope better with stressful situations. Finally, academic school programs themselves are showing increased sensitivity to mental health problems, although there is still a desperate shortage of trained counselors.

Counseling

A first line of defense in mental health programs has to be adequate and appropriate counseling of parents. Unfortunately, Canadian programs with a focus on parents are often dominated by an educational and an oral philosophy. The program in Vancouver, by contrast, attempts to move away from counseling as didactic advice about teaching. It focuses on family-centered counseling, which provides families with opportunities and skills to explore choices and make their own decisions about education and other family needs. It is exceptional and, partly as a result, Canadian services are being threatened by an unobjective commitment to wholesale mainstreaming which pays little attention to the psychosocial needs of differing groups of deaf students. Certainly, anybody in clinical practice in Canada is seeing more adolescent deaf children who could be loosely described as "mainstream failures," that is, the students are described as "behavior-disordered" or "situationally maladjusted" when, in fact, they are showing behavioral reactions to extreme psychological stress.

COMMUNICATION

The use of sign language with deaf students and its effect on self-image and educational achievement is as big an issue in Canada as in the United States or the United Kingdom. Studies in both the Vancouver and Toronto areas indicate that the inability of most parents to communicate with their children in either an indigenous sign language or a form of manually coded English was an issue of concern. The problem continues at the adult level, and for adults or for problem children there are few residential facilities with an empathetic environment and a staff who can communicate fluently in natural sign language. Even less available are trained psychologists and psychiatrists who can also communicate fluently or who understand the effect of deafness on psychological, educational, and social skills. The Lions Home in Belleville, Ontario; the Bob Rumble Home in Toronto; the Lauderdale House in Edmonton, Alberta; the McNab Home in Saskatoon, Saskatchewan; and similar facilities in other cities provide supportive environments, but the necessary national network of services and staff is only just beginning to develop. Deaf people and the parents of deaf children are more likely to meet the "gifted amateur" rather than the fully trained professional. If they are hard-of-hearing, they will probably find even less support available. However, more active involvement of audiologists in adult aural rehabilitation can sometimes help maintain the self-esteem of the adventitiously deafened or hard-of-hearing adult. *See* PSYCHOLINGUISTICS.

DEAF COMMUNITY

The impact that the deaf community itself is beginning to have on mental health programs of deaf people in Canada cannot be ignored. The activities of the Canadian Association of the Deaf (CAD) and the Canadian Cultural Society for the Deaf (CCSD) have led to an increased awareness of the needs of deaf people. They have also led to the provision of better role models for deaf students. The Canadian Deaf Youth Development Programme and the National Festivals of the Arts organized by CCSD are good examples of how a first line of prevention is found in the positive values that deaf people transmit to hearing people and to each other. Evidence presented by the Alberta Association of the Deaf (AAD) to a provincial Committee on Tolerance and Understanding provides an excellent synopsis of the need and importance of the deaf community in positive mental health programs: "The deaf community with its own language and culture provides immeasurable positive impact upon the daily lives of the deaf and hearing impaired people; it is safe to say that the deaf community provides a safety valve for thousands, without which they might end up in isolation, in mental hospitals, or in jails. Yet, many professionals working in the area of deafness continue to perpetuate misconceptions and stereotypes about the deaf community." A collective involvement by the deaf community in positive mental health programs will do much to prevent the overlay of induced problems which are the tragedy of deafness. However, it will be some time before Canadian deaf people are accepted as fully equal partners in the service delivery system, or before they are given opportunities for professional training comparable to those provided for hearing people.

Bibliography

Carbin, C. F.: "A Total Communication Approach: A New Program for Deaf Infants and Children and Their Families," *British Columbia Medical Journal*, 18:141–142, 1976.

Carver, R.: *Deafness: A Study in Silent Frustration*, evidence submitted to the Committee on Tolerance and Understanding, Alberta, February 1984.

Denmark, J. C.: "Mental Illness and Early Profound Deafness," *British Journal of Medical Psychology*, pp. 117–124, 1966.

Freeman, R. D.: "Psychiatric Aspects of Sensory Disorders and Intervention," in P. J. Graham (ed.), *Epidemiological Approaches in Child Psychiatry*, Academic Press, 1977.

McLaughlin, J. R.: "Counselling at the High School Level," *ACEHI Journal*, 6:54–62, 1979–80.

————: *Proceedings of the Fourth Conference of the Association of Canadian Educators of the Hearing Impaired*, Canadian Deaf Youth Development Program, Association of Canadian Educators of the Hearing Impaired, Amherst, Nova Scotia, pp. 218–229, 1979.

Nix, G. W.: "Mainstreaming: Illusion or Solution?", *ACEHI Journal*, 8:7–14, 1981–82.

Pyke, J. M., and S. K. Littman: "A Psychiatric Clinic for the Deaf," *Canadian Journal of Psychiatry*, 27:383–389, 1982.

Rodda, M.: "An Analysis of the Myth that Mainstreaming and Integration are Synonymous," in A. Boros and R. Stuckless, *Deaf People and Social Change*, Gallaudet College, Washington, D.C., 1982.

Schlesinger, H. S., and K. P. Meadow: *Sound and Sign: Childhood Deafness and Mental Health*, University of California Press, Berkeley, 1966, 1972.

Sussman, A. E.: "Comprehensive Counselling Needs of Deaf Persons," *Hearing and Speech News*, 38:12–13, 22, 24, 1970.

Michael Rodda

Parent Guidance and Preschool Programming

A prerequisite to good preschool and parent guidance programs is the early diagnosis of hearing loss. Canada lags behind the United States in the age at which the deaf child is diagnosed and intervention commences. The Saskatoon Conference on the Early Diagnosis of Hearing Loss recommended routine infant screening programs through "well baby clinics" and other health units. Nevertheless, it is generally not before two years of age, and frequently much later, that any intervention, remediation, or habilitation begins. Significant numbers of hearing-impaired children are not diagnosed or provided with intervention programs prior to entry into school. Therefore, the programs described below serve a relatively small number of all preschool hearing-impaired students. In fact, services are not provided because students are not identified, which in turn establishes that there is no demand for services.

SPECIFIC SERVICES

Even when children are diagnosed early, the existing services are highly variable in availability and quality—many are excellent; some are nonexistent. Also, with the exception of British Columbia, there are no clearly documented records of past or contemporary preschool programs for Canadian hearing-impaired students.

The rural nature of much of Canada has led to the development of special programs designed to cope with providing services over large distances—it is not without cause that Canadians are among the most prolific users of telephones in the world. They also make extensive use of the John Tracy Correspondence Courses offered through the John Tracy Clinic of Los Angeles. Memorial University of Newfoundland and the Newfoundland School for the Deaf developed a "distance education" package for the parents of preschool hearing-impaired children. The hardware for this package is a video playback unit and a speech trainer. Support is provided by a qualified teacher of deaf pupils, by occasional home visits, by an on-campus workshop, and by telephone support. A carefully controlled study of the effectiveness of the program has not been possible, but the evaluation clearly indicated that if the families were able to adapt to the use of this method, positive and beneficial results were obtained. Programs of this type which are developed even further can be effective and viable alternatives to separating very young children from their families. There are now few, if any, technological barriers to "on-line" communication with even the most geographically isolated family.

In contrast to the rural isolation of Newfoundland, the metropolitan areas of Canada have urban-style preschool programs that are comparable to any in North America. These include the program at the Children's Hospital in Vancouver, British Columbia; the Glenrose Hospital and the Association for the Hearing Handicapped in Edmonton,

Alberta; the program in the Audiological Unit in Toronto's Hospital for Sick Children; and programs organized in various metropolitan areas of the Maritime Provinces (New Brunswick, Nova Scotia, and Prince Edward Island) by the Atlantic Provinces Resource Centre for the Hearing Handicapped from Amherst, Nova Scotia. Characteristically, these programs are either completely oral (usually but not exclusively those organized by the audiological units) or they use total communication (those organized by parents or groups of deaf people). Staff training varies—in some programs all are trained teachers of hearing-impaired people, while in others none are trained. In some cases, the programs (particularly those in western Canada) use staff with training in "early childhood services" rather than those with special expertise in the area of hearing impairment. When trained teachers of hearing-impaired persons are used, they are sometimes used as itinerant teachers in a similar way to the use of peripatetic teachers in Great Britain (Ontario, in particular, has well-developed services of this type). Most of the programs are exclusively for hearing-impaired students, but a few have practiced a small amount of reverse integration. In at least one case (the Association for the Hearing Handicapped, Edmonton), an interesting program involves intervention with the families of hearing children with deaf parents (as well as some deaf children of deaf parents), and another (the Children's Hospital and Diagnostic Centre, Vancouver) has an innovative program directed by a deaf man.

In Quebec, there are two programs—one English and one French. The English language program is an oral program at the School of Human Communication Disorders, McGill University, Montreal. The second program is also an oral program, but more importantly, it is a francophone program similar to some programs for anglophone families in other areas of Canada. The program is organized by the Centre de l'Ouie et de la Parole de l'Hotel-Dieu de Québec. It is small and includes a number of different services. It provides the regional Assessment Centre for Eastern Quebec, serving children and their parents in individual or small group settings, and it has a major impact on the development of preschool services for francophone, hearing-impaired preschool children.

PARENT COUNSELING

Despite the richness and wealth of preschool educationally based programs in Canada, parent counseling services are lacking. In fact, the areas of family counseling and hearing impairment have rarely made contact. This may reflect the dominance of European and American models in preschool practice and a shortage of trained psychologists with the necessary skills to work in this area. Moreover, the provincial structure of services may lead to a certain conservatism in educational programs, which is hard to break in the absence of some outside agent for change. As a result, family counseling tends to be rejected as inappropriate for both educational and early childhood services.

This pattern has been showing signs of change, particularly in the western provinces, which have tended to make greater use of agencies with an early childhood focus rather than audiological or educational services for preschool children. Through these agencies, it is easier to introduce what are often perceived to be innovative approaches from the more traditional perspective of deaf education. In particular, the Children's Hospital and Diagnostic Centre in Vancouver, British Columbia, developed nondirective, supportive, parenting-skills programming oriented around the family of the hearing-impaired child. Furthermore, the Department of Educational Psychology at the University of Alberta offered the first training course in parent counseling for families of hearing-impaired children in the summer of 1982, and in tandem with this, the Association for the Hearing Handicapped in Edmonton worked on developing a program of parent education and counseling for hearing parents of deaf preschoolers and another for deaf parents. These programs tend to be less instrumentally based and less directive than the more traditional programs in eastern Canada.

Bibliography

Anderson, J.: "Education of the Hearing Impaired in British Columbia: The Changing Scene," personal communication, unpublished paper, 1978.

Carbin, C., Roger D. Freeman, and Robert I. Boese: "A Counselling and Home Training Program for Deaf Children," *ACEHI Journal/La Revue ACEDA*, 7:128–130, 1981.

Csapo, M.: "A Collect Call to Ottawa: Will Someone Accept the Charges?", in M. Csapo and L. Groguen, *Special Education Across Canada: Issues and Concerns for the 80's*, Centre for Human Development, Vancouver, British Columbia, 1982.

—— and L. Groguen: "Introduction," in *Special Education Across Canada: Issues and Concerns for the 80's*, Centre for Human Development, Vancouver, British Columbia, 1982.

Cumming, C.: Counselling with Parents of Hearing Impaired Students, unpublished paper, University of Alberta, 1982.

Freeman, R., C. Carbin, and R. Boese: *Can't Your Child Hear?*, University Park Press, Baltimore, 1981.

Lawrence, Sister Maria: "One Teacher's Work Week," *ACEHI Journal*, 7:205–209, 1981.

Ling, D., and A. Ling: *Aural Rehabilitation*, A. G. Bell Association, Washington, D.C., 1978.

Luterman, D.: *Counselling Parents of Hearing Impaired Children*, Little, Brown, Boston, 1979.

Lyon, D. J., and M. E. Lyon: "The Importance of Early Detection," *ACEHI Journal*, 8:15–37, 1982.

Neville-Smith, C., and B. P. O'Reilly: "Home Centred Video-Tape Counselling Program for Parents of Pre-school Hearing Impaired Children," *ACEHI Journal*, 7:172–184, 1981.

Reich, C., and L. Johnson: "Canadian Services to Hearing Impaired Adults," *American Annals of the Deaf*, 127:80–88, 1982.

Vachon, Jeanne d'Arc: "Le Centre de l'Ouie et de la Parole de l'Hotel Dieu de Québec," *La Revue ACEDA*, 7:185–188, 1981.

Williams, D. M. L., and J. O. Darbyshire: "Diagnosis of Deafness," *Volta Review*, 84:24–30, 1982.

                                    Michael Rodda

Education

Canadian education has been influenced by several main factors: geography, colonialism, religion, language, and the structure and function of government. These same factors have affected the education of hearing-impaired people and make generalizations difficult.

Canada has 10 provinces and 2 territories, and because education comes under provincial and not federal jurisdiction, each province has its own educational legislation and school system. Although the provincial governments directly control a few schools (including provincial schools for deaf students), local school boards administer most schools. Local property taxes and provincial government grants provide most educational funding.

In some provinces public education reflects not only the language but the religious affiliation of the family; for example, the five major religious groups of Newfoundland operate their own schools. In Alberta, Ontario, Saskatchewan, and the Territories, communities provide public schools that are open to all, but school law enables a religious minority to set up its own separate schools. Although no such law operates in British Columbia, Manitoba, New Brunswick, Nova Scotia, or Prince Edward Island, these provinces provide public support for English- or French-language Catholic or private schools.

EARLY HISTORY

The first school for deaf people in Canada was opened in 1831. The founder, Ronald McDonald, visited schools for deaf people in the United States and spent a year at the American Asylum at Hartford, where he trained under Thomas Gallaudet and Laurent Clerc. McDonald then established a school in Champlain, Quebec, which functioned for about five years. *See* AMERICAN SCHOOL FOR THE DEAF; CLERC, LAURENT; GALLAUDET, THOMAS HOPKINS.

The earliest extant school was founded by the Bishop of Montreal at Mile-End, Quebec, in 1848. Under the auspices of the Community of Clerics of St. Viator and supported chiefly through private benevolence, the Institution Catholique des Sourds-

Muets largely served French Catholic deaf boys. At first fingerspelling and signing were used, but shortly after the Milan Conference in 1880, oral instruction was introduced. The curriculum was modeled on the French schools of that time in Quebec and had a strong emphasis on vocational training. *See* HISTORY: Congress of Milan.

In 1851 another Catholic school, this time for deaf French girls, was opened at Longue-Pointe, Quebec, by the Sisters of Charity of Providence. Initially the methodology was manual, but it changed to oral after the school's resident chaplain visited European schools for deaf pupils.

William Gray, a deaf graduate of the Braidwood Academy in Edinburgh, started a class for a small group of deaf children in Halifax, Nova Scotia. Public interest in his work led to the appointment of James Scott Hutton, an instructor at the Edinburgh School for the Deaf and Dumb, as principal of the Halifax School in 1856. Funds were obtained at various times from the other Maritime Provinces, but the school remained for many years a private corporation administered by a board of management.

Little is known about a school that opened on Prince Edward Island in 1866 except that its existence was short-lived; and in New Brunswick an Institution for the Deaf and Dumb struggled for survival between 1869 and 1890 under a deaf principal named Abell, but did not succeed.

The first school for deaf children in Ontario was opened in 1870. Twelve years earlier, J. B. McGann, an Irish immigrant who had worked as a clerk in the New York Institution for the Deaf, set up and taught a class of deaf children in Toronto. Politically astute, tenacious, and zealous, McGann obtained the patronage of some of Toronto's most prominent citizens; this led to the opening of the Ontario Institute for the Education and Instruction of the Deaf and Dumb at Belleville on the Bay of Quinte.

Two months after the opening of the Ontario school, the Protestant Institution for Deaf-Mutes was established in Montreal by Thomas Widd, a former pupil at the Yorkshire School for the Deaf. Manual methods were used, but in contrast to Hutton in Halifax who used the British two-handed system, Widd introduced the single-handed alphabet. The school moved to new quarters in 1877 and was renamed the Mackay Institution for Protestant Deaf Mutes to honor a generous benefactor. The school also admitted blind children, and has enrolled deaf students from Newfoundland, New Brunswick, and Alberta. It also took in crippled children until 1980, when the deaf students were moved to their own building on a separate site.

In Manitoba a small class was started in 1875 by a son-in-law of McGann at the pleadings of deaf parents. It attracted not only public support but government action. In 1888 Manitoba became the first province to legislate free education for deaf people, and two years later mandated compulsory education for all deaf children. The Manitoba school has housed children from Alberta, British Columbia, Saskatchewan, and the North-West Territories.

A second school was established in New Brunswick in 1882, but it perished from lack of funds and other problems. A fifth Quebec school at St. Marie Beauce had a short and poorly documented existence in the early 1880s.

TWENTIETH CENTURY

In the late nineteenth century, the population of the west gradually increased and the provinces of Alberta, British Columbia, and Saskatchewan began to gain strength. In 1888 a school for deaf people in Vancouver survived only one year, and, although the Vancouver School Board operated classes as early as 1901, it was not until 1915 that the British Columbia School for the Deaf opened under the superintendency of C. H. Lawrence from the Halifax school. It was moved seven years later, together with the school for the blind, to the then vacant Boys' Industrial Home.

Prior to the Vancouver classes and the British Columbia Institution, deaf children had traveled some 1500 miles (2500 kilometers) to Manitoba. Children from Alberta and Saskatchewan made a similar journey. When Manitoba raised its fees in 1914, the Saskatchewan government opened its own school under Thomas Rodwell from the Institution of Belleville, Ontario. However, when he enlisted in World War I, the school closed and the children returned to Manitoba. It was not until 1931 that the Saskatchewan government, in response to pressure from deaf individuals and parents of deaf children, established a new school under the superintendency of E. G. Peterson, who had trained in the United States.

Alberta children were admitted to the Saskatchewan school until 1956 when, after prolonged and intense lobbying by the Calgary and Edmonton Association for the Deaf, a new provincial school was opened at Edmonton.

Following World War II, the Manitoba School was converted to a teachers' college, but in 1951 the school was reestablished on its original site at Tuxedo, largely due to prolonged pressure group activities of deaf people and of parent bodies.

In Ontario, the Belleville school, like the others, had been occupied during World War II by the Armed Forces and its pupils scattered throughout the community. At the war's end, the Ministry considered replacing the school with a day school system, but the resultant storm of protest, particularly from deaf adults, led to the summary shelving of such plans. As the population of deaf children increased, a second school was opened at Milton in 1963 and a third in London in 1972.

In the Atlantic Provinces, the Newfoundland government withdrew its deaf children from the overcrowded Halifax school in 1958 and arranged for them to be sent to Mackay in Montreal. Three years later, through the cooperative efforts of the provinces of Nova Scotia and New Brunswick, the Interprovincial School at Amherst was opened and legislation was enacted to cover a cost-sharing agreement, joint participation in the board of management, and the closing down of the Halifax School for the Deaf. Some children from Newfoundland attended the Interprovincial School for a short time until the Newfoundland School was opened in ex-Air Force buildings at Torbay, St. John's. Deaf children from Prince Edward Island were accommodated in a day program attached to a regular school in Charlottetown.

During this period there were significant changes in the development of the provincial school systems, in the acceptance of public responsibility for the education of handicapped persons, and in the theory and practice of teaching deaf children. However, the system was still in a state of flux, reflected by the differences between provincial schools. Some employed deaf teachers and deaf supervisory staff; others did not. Some became aggressively oral (for example, Saskatchewan); others relied more heavily on manual communication, particularly in senior classes. The ratio of day and residential pupils varied; some schools sent all residential students home on weekends, others did not.

About this time the schools came under heavy fire when a group of new professionals began to encroach on the hitherto remote and isolated world of education of deaf people. More emphasis was to be placed on the use of residual hearing; some of these neophytes regarded signing and fingerspelling as unnatural and harmful. They were joined by teachers who, due to their basic training, had a close affinity to the oral method. An interesting thesis has been developed by M. A. Winzer stating that "oralism was an educational reform initiated, brought to fruition and eventually dominance by female teachers," most of whom were trained in oral institutions. There were also parents who did not want to send their child away from home to a school for deaf children, and other parents who demanded a different kind of program for their hard-of-hearing child. While school and provincial administrators were trying to cope with pressures for an aural-oral approach, deaf adults and organizations working with deaf people were bitterly denouncing the schools for failing to ensure that manual skills were adequately developed in their pupils. These circumstances prepared the ground

for the rise of alternative programs, the establishment of oral schools, and for the eventual introduction of total communication, which appeared in Canadian provincial schools in 1968.

ALTERNATIVES TO RESIDENTIAL SCHOOLS

Ontario was the first to make systematic attempts to provide day classes. Toronto followed in 1924, Ottawa in 1928, Hamilton in 1944, and eventually the Metropolitan Toronto School Board built the largest Canadian day school for deaf children in 1964.

During the 1960s, school boards across Canada, reacting to professional and particularly parental pressure, began to assume more local responsibility for the provision of services to deaf and hard-of-hearing pupils. In a piecemeal way, three distinctive types of program were developed: (1) Special classes for hard-of-hearing children were generally organized on the basis of partial or gradual integration of the hard-of-hearing child into a regular classroom. At first they operated largely at the elementary level but eventually extended to the secondary level. Teaching methods were predominantly oral. (2) Special classes for deaf children tended to function as separate classes but permitted some degree of social and academic integration. Essentially they were organized as an alternative to special school placement particularly for younger children and for those in remote areas. Instruction was either oral or total communication. (3) Itinerant services or resource room facilities for tutoring, remediation, and counseling were made available to hearing-impaired children enrolled in regular schools, generally on an individual basis.

Some early classes for deaf children which were located in regular schools had been set up and administered by provincial schools for deaf students. For example, off-campus classes have been operated in Vancouver schools by the provincial school since 1953, and in several other communities by the provincial school in Amherst since 1969. Schools for deaf students have also developed other functional plans for merging the deaf child and the community. The Atlantic Technological Vocational Centre offers a wide range of programs to older hearing-impaired students from the provincial school who are expected to live in the community—a stipend is provided to cover living costs and individual expenses. In Alberta, students over 18 years of age are expected to participate in an independent living program and to live off campus. In Manitoba, after age 16 academic students are integrated part-time into one high school and vocational students into another. A further variation is seen at Milton, Ontario, where a large regular secondary school has been built right on the campus of the deaf school. This enables a considerable amount of integration to take place, particularly in the technical areas.

W. Cory has suggested that much of the early impetus for alternative programs stemmed from direct pressure on the local school districts or on the provincial schools themselves rather than from expressed policy on the part of administrators. However, since the 1970s, provincial policies have generally supported integrated rather than segregated placements, and this has led to the proliferation of many small local programs; however, there is little or no comprehensive evaluation of the nature of this integration or its quality. Apart from one seminal study in Toronto, alternative programs in Canada have not received the careful study they warrant.

ORAL SCHOOLS

Oral schools have not flourished in Canada as they have in other countries. The reasons for this are varied. In response to pressure from interest groups, the provincial schools in the past have declared themselves on occasion to be partially or even entirely oral. Furthermore, alternative programs, such as those offered by local school boards, have taken this concern away from provincial schools and permitted a variety of oral-aural settings. However, a group of English-speaking parents in Montreal did start a small oral program in 1950 that offers parent guidance services, a preschool and elementary program, and itinerant services. Ten years later a similar development took place in Vancouver, and much the same services are provided by this oral center. Calgary also has established two programs: an oral elementary program in one regular school and a total communication program in another elementary school; few of their students are sent to the provincial school in Edmonton. On the other hand, at the provincial school in London, Ontario, deaf children have been separated into three separate streams; one of these is oral-aural.

HIGHER EDUCATION

The provincial schools provide programs either on or off campus for vocational and academic students up to the college level. At some Canadian universities, notably the University of British Columbia, a handful of deaf and hard-of-hearing students have managed to complete undergraduate and graduate programs with the aid of interpreters and other services. Most Canadian deaf students must go to American universities, in particular to Gallaudet College or the St. Paul Technical Vocational Institute.

MULTIHANDICAPPED

Generally, special programs for multihandicapped persons are housed in the provincial schools. In some instances, the latter act as resource centers for the province so that their expertise can be deployed over larger geographical areas. There is one program for deaf-blind persons in Brantford, Ontario, and others at the Atlantic Provinces Special Education Authority in Amherst, and the Saskatchewan School in Saskatoon. The Belleville school in Ontario maintains a fairly large program for aphasic children. The lack of hard data in Canada and elsewhere warrants a systematic study of the precise nature and extent of additional handicaps in the hearing-impaired population.

Teacher Training

Canada was late to begin training teachers of deaf students. At first, trained teachers were recruited from other countries, particularly Great Britain and the United States; this was followed by student teachers or in-service training supplemented by summer school courses at home or abroad. The first formal program in teacher training on a staff basis was begun at the Belleville School in 1924, but it was more than 40 years before this one-year program came under a principal independent of the school superintendent. The program consists of 25 weeks of lectures and 13 weeks of practica. Candidates, who must have a teaching certificate, are selected for employment by the provincial schools or school boards prior to training. A specialist certificate is issued after two years of supervised teaching. Not until 1972 was any form of manual communication introduced to the curriculum, and two years later the first deaf candidate was admitted.

In 1968 the first university-based program for teachers of deaf people was established at the University of British Columbia (UBC). Candidates must hold a degree from a recognized university, and preference is given to those who have a teaching qualification and who have experience with deaf people. There is a core curriculum in education of deaf persons, with electives available from other departments. Students are expected to become proficient in both oral-aural and total communication settings and are awarded a university diploma that satisfies provincial requirements.

The Université de Québec in Montreal has offered a few elective courses in education of deaf students since 1971, and these units may be applied to a degree in special education.

At Amherst, Nova Scotia, the school began a program in 1972 to enable French and English-speaking teachers to become qualified as teachers of deaf pupils for the four Atlantic Provinces. Applicants, who must be qualified to teach in a regular school and possess a university degree, apportion their time between the Learning Assistance Centre at the school and the University of Moncton, which confers a master's degree on successful candidates.

At McGill University in Montreal an exclusively oral-aural two-year master's program was offered in 1975 by the School of Human Communication Disorders in collaboration with the Department of Educational Psychology. Applicants must have teacher certification, and a working knowledge of French is mandatory for those intending to work in a clinical setting in Quebec. A maximum of six students per year is admissible. A great deal of emphasis is placed on the application of audiological knowledge to optimize residual hearing and the facilitation of intelligible spoken language. Extensive and intensive practical training occupies seven months of full-time teaching or clinical work at spaced intervals over two years.

The University of Alberta in September 1980 began to offer both a diploma in the education of hearing-impaired students and a master of education degree with a specialization in working with hearing-impaired people. York University in Ontario set up a program in 1981.

Apart from the above training centers, a number of Canadians have acquired their training in the United States or England. The resulting eclecticism overcomes any form of inbreeding which can so easily be fostered by a few small programs, particularly if future teachers are trained by the same administrative organization that employs them.

For many years, Canadians have been members of American organizations, for example, the Conference of Educational Administrators Serving the Deaf (CEASD), the Convention of American Instructors of the Deaf (CAID), and the Alexander Graham Bell Association of the Deaf. In 1971 a national publication, the *Canadian Teacher of the Deaf*, was issued at the school of Amherst. Two years later the First National Conference of Canadian Teachers of the Deaf met at the Belleville School, and a national organization was founded and named the Association of Canadian Educators of the Hearing Impaired (ACEHI). The journal was renamed the *ACEHI Journal/la Revue ACEDA*, and the first issue under this name came out in March 1974. The association has national and regional directors, and national conferences are held biennially. In 1983 ACEHI planned a joint convention in Winnipeg between ACEHI and its American counterparts, CAID and CEASD.

As yet, Canada has no national policy regarding training and certification of teachers of deaf students. In some provinces, teacher organizations themselves are strongly opposed to specialist certification. With the exception of Ontario, Nova Scotia, and British Columbia, the provinces also lack regulations concerning qualifications required to teach deaf children. ACEHI has drawn up a model for national certification and established a committee to certify teachers at a national level, but it is conjectural whether provincial governments are prepared to accept this standard.

Bibliography

American Annals of the Deaf, 41:47, 1896.

Boyd, J.: "Structure of Canadian Institutional Systems for the Hearing Impaired," *American Annals of the Deaf*, 127:74–79, 1982.

British Columbia School: *American Annals of the Deaf*, 34:291–292, 1889.

"Catholic Institution for Deaf Mutes in the Province of Quebec, under the Direction of the Clerics of Saint-Viator, Mile-End, Montreal, P.Q., Canada," in *Histories of American Schools for the Deaf, 1817–1893: Denomination and Private Schools in Canada and Mexico*, vol. 3, supplement, Volta Bureau, Washington, D.C., pp. 13–15, 1893.

Clarke, B. R.: "A Study of Canadian Programs in Education of the Deaf," *ACEHI Journal*, 1:3–21, 1972.

———: "Total Communication," *Canadian Teacher of the Deaf*, 2:22–30, 1972.

——— and D. C. Kendall: "Communication for Hearing-Impaired People in Canada," in H. J. Oyer (ed.), *Communication for the Hearing Handicapped: An International Perspective*, University Park Press, Baltimore, pp. 73–129, 1976.

Cory, W.: "Education of the Deaf in Canada," master's thesis, University of British Columbia, 1959.

Hutton, J. Scott: "Statistics of the Deaf and Dumb in the Lower Provinces of British North America," *American Annals of the Deaf and Dumb*, 14:65–82, 1869.

"Institute for the Female Deaf and Dumb in the Province of Quebec," in *Histories of American Schools for the Deaf, 1817–1893: Denominational and Private Schools in Canada and Mexico*, vol. 3, supplement, Volta Bureau, Washington, D.C., pp. 1–7, 1893.

McGann, J. B.: *The Deaf Mute of Canada: A History of Their Education with An Account of the Deaf Mute Institutions of the Dominion, and a Description of All Known Finger and Sign Alphabets*, C. J. Howe, Toronto, 1888.

Rae, L: "Education of the Deaf and Dumb in Canada," *American Annals of the Deaf and Dumb*, 2:32–37, 1849.

Reich, C., D. Hambleton, and B. Klein: *The Integration of Hearing Impaired Children in Regular Classrooms*, Board of Education, Toronto, 1975.

Report of the Department of Education, no. 17. Government Printer, Toronto, 1921.

"Saskatchewan School," *American Annals of the Deaf*, 61:380, 1916.

Widd, T.: "History of the Protestant Institution for Deaf-Mutes, Montreal, Canada," *American Annals of the Deaf and Dumb*, 22:193–204, 1877.

Wilson, J. D., R. M. Stamp, and L. Audet: *Canadian Education: A History*, Prentice Hall, Scarborough, Ontario, 1970.

Winzer, M.: "Historical Perspectives on the Education of the Deaf in Canada: To Nova Scotia Belongs the Honour," *ACEHI Journal*, 6:15–19, 1979.

———: "Talking Deaf-Mutes: The Special Role of Women in the Methodological Conflict Regarding the Deaf, 1867–1900," *Atlantis*, 6:123–133, 1981.

Bryan R. Clarke

CARLIN, JOHN
(1813–1891)

John Carlin, born in Philadelphia on June 15, 1813, lost his hearing and speech in infancy. He became an outstanding artist, writer, poet, and speaker, and was knowledgeable in many fields.

Carlin was largely self-educated and early demonstrated a talent for drawing. He attended the Pennsylvania School for the Deaf in Philadelphia, graduating in 1825 at the age of 12. One of his instructors was the renowned Laurent Clerc, a deaf teacher from the American School for the Deaf at Hartford, Connecticut, who was helping the Philadelphia school get started. In later years, Carlin painted portraits of Clerc. *See* AMERICAN SCHOOL FOR THE DEAF; CLERC, LAURENT.

Carlin's father, an indigent cobbler, was unable to provide financial support for the boy to remain in school, so Carlin secured employment as a sign and house painter. In his leisure time, he studied art and the English language, and by the time he was 19 years old he had mastered five languages.

In 1833 and 1834, Carlin studied drawing under John Rubens Smith and portrait painting under John Nagle in New York City. These experiences strengthened his belief that painting was his forte.

John Carlin. (Gallaudet College Archives)

With money earned from a personal business venture, in 1838 Carlin took up the formal study of art, first in London at the British Museum, and later in Paris, where he studied portrait painting under Paul Delaroche. His knowledge of the French language stood him in good stead.

Carlin returned to New York City in 1841, making it his home. He established a studio and devoted himself to producing miniature paintings of members of the Knickerbocker families. The advent of photography turned his attention to painting landscape and genre subjects and to portraits in oils.

In December 1843 Carlin married Mary Wayland, a former pupil of the New York School for the Deaf; they had five children, all with normal hearing.

Carlin painted miniature portraits of the most famous men of the day, including a number of Washington diplomats. He knew Jefferson Davis personally and painted his son.

Carlin wrote poetry and once earned the praise of William Cullen Bryant. He was also a prolific writer, and lectured before deaf audiences on many topics. In 1868 he wrote a children's book, *The Scratchsides Family*.

Beginning in the early 1850s, Carlin took an active interest in the public affairs of deaf people. He helped to raise considerable money for the building fund of St. Ann's Church for the Deaf in New York City. Erected in 1852, it was the first church for deaf parishioners in the United States. For 40 years, Carlin was a member of the church. The first monument to Thomas Hopkins Gallaudet, the pioneer educator, was erected in Hartford at Carlin's suggestion. He contributed a side panel for the monument and gave an oration at the unveiling of the memorial column in 1858. *See* GALLAUDET, THOMAS HOPKINS.

In 1854, ten years before Gallaudet College was founded in Washington, D.C., Carlin wrote an article in which he favored higher education for deaf persons. He delivered a speech at the inauguration of the college (then known as the National Deaf-Mute College) on June 28, 1864. He was the first recipient of an honorary degree from the college in recognition of his services to the deaf community. *See* GALLAUDET COLLEGE.

Other accomplishments included the founding of the Manhattan Literary Association of the Deaf in 1864, the first such organization in the United States, and the chairing (1873–1881) of a committee to raise funds for the building of the Gallaudet Home for Aged and Infirm Deaf.

Following an illness of six months, Carlin contracted pneumonia and died on April 23, 1891, at the age of 78 in New York City. He was buried in Woodlawn Cemetery.

Bibliography

Braddock, Guilbert C.: *Notable Deaf Persons*, Gallaudet College Alumni Association, Washington, D.C., 1975.

Carlin, John: "The National College for Mutes," *American Annals of the Deaf*, 6:179, 1854.

Deaf Mute Journal, April 30, 1891.

Domich, Harold: *John Carlin: A Biographical Sketch*, Gallaudet College Press, Washington, D.C., 1939.

Gannon, Jack R.: *Deaf Heritage: A Narrative History of Deaf America*, National Association of the Deaf, Silver Spring, Maryland, 1981.

National Deaf Mute Gazette, April 18, 1868.

Panara, Robert, and John Panara: *Great Deaf Americans*, T. J. Publishers, Silver Spring, Maryland, 1983.

The Silent Worker, vol. 2, no. 6, September 27, 1888, and vol. 4, no 31, April 30, 1891.

Francis C. Higgins

CARRIÓN, MANUEL RAMÍREZ DE
1579–1652(?)

Manuel Ramirez de Carrión was a teacher, a pioneer in the early education of deaf people, and the immediate successor in the work of the Spanish Benedictine monk Pedro Ponce de León. Born in 1579 in the town of Hellín, province of Murcia, Spain, Carrión (more properly, Ramírez de Carrión) first taught a deaf child in his native town. Later he moved to Montilla and entered the service of the Marquis of Priego in order to teach his deaf son, Don Alonso Fernández de Córdoba y Figueroa. *See* PONCE DE LEÓN, PEDRO.

EARLY CAREER

Carrión settled for life in Montilla, province of Córdoba (Andalucía), where he married Doña Elvira de Godoy. In 1606 Carrión's deaf pupil, Don Alonso, became Marquis of Priego when he was 18 years old. His legal right to the inheritance was not questioned, indicating that his education was successful. A relative of the marquis, the Abbot of Rute, said that "in spite of the natural handicap of hearing and speech, Don Alonso governs his estates prudently, availing himself of zealous administrators . . . whose decisions are supported by the Marquis, not orally but in writing, the method that he uses in order to answer all questions."

In approximately 1615 Carrión went to Madrid at the request of the Duchess of Frías in order to teach her deaf son, Don Luis Fernández de Velasco, then six years old. Don Luis was the grandson of Don Iñigo de Velasco, 4th Condestable of Castile and Duke of Frías, who had two deaf brothers, Don Francisco and Don Pedro, former students of Fray Pedro Ponce de León.

TEACHING METHOD

Carrión, like most early teachers of deaf pupils, surrounded his teaching method with extraordinary secrecy, presumably in order to ward off competition and keep his privileged position among the princes and noblemen who competed for his services. He refers to this secrecy in the prologue of a book he wrote entitled *Maravillas de la naturaleza* (*Wonders of Nature*), which deals with bits of curious information about natural phenomena listed alphabetically and collected from classical and medieval authors. In this work, Carrión discussed at length his correct assumption that the cause of muteness is deafness. He wrote that a child who is born deaf or becomes deaf when young will be mute but that deaf mutes have normal speech organs and can be taught to articulate sounds.

Carrión's method of teaching deaf children to speak is closely connected with his method of teaching children how to read in a very short time. He cited the case of the Condestable of Castile, Don Bernardino Fernandez de Velasco, whom he taught how to read in "fifteen days or at the most a month" when he was only six years old. The reading technique invented by Carrión was explained by Juan Bautista de Morales, his friend and publisher.

Morales wrote a book entitled *Pronunciaciones generales de lenguas, ortografia, escuela de leer, escribir y contar y significación de las letras de la mano* (*General Pronunciation of Languages, Spelling, School of Reading, Writing, Counting, and Meaning of the Manual Alphabet*) in 1623. Giving full credit to Carrión, it tells that the technique was based on teaching the letters by the sound they stood for, not by their regular names. This method was called reduction (that is, simplification) of the letters. In this manner, the teacher would refer to "h" not as /āch/ but just as /h/, that is, by producing only the voiceless glottal fricative that it stands for. *See* SPEECH TRAINING.

The use of this fundamental principle of reducing the names of the letters to just the sounds they represent was likely used as well by Fray Pedro Ponce in teaching his deaf pupils to speak. This was also the method used by Juan Pablo Bonet, who wrote the first book ever published on the education of deaf persons, *Reduction de las letras y arte para enseñar a ablar los mudos*, published in Madrid in 1620. Pablo Bonet was at that time Don Bernardino's secretary. As such, it is possible that he had knowledge of the method used by Ponce in the teaching of Don Bernardino's granduncles. Neither Carrión nor Pablo Bonet, however, mentions the other in their respective works, in spite of the fact that both served the condestable in Madrid during the years 1615 to 1618. It is more probable that Pablo Bonet benefited from Carrión's knowledge than vice versa. *See* PABLO BONET, JUAN.

Another chapter of Morales's book deals with the manual alphabet that Carrión used in order to communicate with deaf students. While there are no pictures of the position of the hand for each letter, there is a description of the manner in which each letter is to be formed. There are only small differences between this manual alphabet and the one published by Pablo Bonet in his *Reduction de las letras*. *See* SIGNS: Fingerspelling.

As was the case with Ponce and Pablo Bonet, Carrión devoted special care to teaching his students to speak and speechread. The success of his technique has been documented by a contemporary, Sir Kenelm Digby, who accompanied the Prince of Wales to Madrid in 1623. Digby met Don Luis de Velasco, who was 13 years old at the time, and also his secretive teacher, Carrión. He was so impressed by Don Luis that, 23 years later, he gave an account of Don Luis's abilities in his book *Of Bodies and of Man's Soul . . .* (London, 1658), in the chapter entitled "Sensible Quality Sound."

Carrión was also summoned to the court by express order of King Philip IV of Spain to teach Emmanuel Filibert Amadeus, the deaf son of the Italian Princess of Carignan, wife of Thomas Francis of Savoy, Marquis of Priego. After these stays at the court, Carrión always returned to the marquis's service in Montilla, where he was still living in 1652.

Carrión should be considered as the most important continuator of Pedro Ponce de León in the history of the education of deaf persons. However, his method was incorporated into the history of western culture only when Juan Pablo Bonet, who must have borrowed information about his method, put it in writing and published it in 1620.

Bibliography

Carrión, Manuel Ramírez de: *Maravillas de naturaleza, en que se contienen dos mil secretos de cosas naturales, dispuestas por abecedario a modo de Aforismos faciles, y breves de mucha curiosidad, y provecho, Recogidos de la leccion de diversos y graves Autores.*

Chaves, Teresa L., and Jorge L. Soler: "Manuel Ramírez de Carrión (1579–1652?) and His Secret Method of Teaching the Deaf," *Sign Language Studies*, vol. 8, 1975.

Navarro Tomas, Tomas: "Manuel Ramírez de Carrión y el arte de enseñar a hablar a los mudos," *Revista de Filologia Española*, vol. 11, pp. 225–266, 1924.

Jorge Soler

CENTRAL INSTITUTE FOR THE DEAF

The Central Institute for the Deaf (CID) was founded in 1914 in St. Louis, Missouri, by Max A. Goldstein, M.D. It operates as a private nonprofit organization designed to improve the condition of humanity as related to hearing impairment and disorders of human communication. The beneficial interaction of research, professional training, and service is accomplished through the activities of a number of interrelated divisions. *See* GOLDSTEIN, MAX AARON.

RESEARCH DEPARTMENT

The laboratories of the Central Institute conduct both basic investigations and applied research. Knowledge-seeking basic studies have included analysis of the nature of the cochlea and the auditory nerve, the perception and production of speech, and a description of human capacity for hearing. Applied projects have involved the effects of noise and toxic substances on hearing, development of tests to identify and describe impaired hearing from birth through old age, creation and application of sensory aids to assist speech perception and speech production, and evaluation of testing and teaching procedures for hearing-impaired children and adults. Funding for research is from private contributions, foundation grants, and government grants and contracts.

PROFESSIONAL TRAINING PROGRAM

Classes, observation, and practical application within this program have prepared students from the United States and abroad to become teachers of hearing-impaired children, audiologists, speech-language pathologists, and research scientists. In 1931 the Central Institution for the Deaf set up the first training program for teachers of deaf students in the United States to be affiliated with an accredited university, Washington University of St. Louis. College credit is given for courses, and the degrees of bachelor of science and master of science in speech and hearing are granted. The degrees of master of arts and doctor of philosophy in communication sciences may also be given to those who study for careers in scientific research and college instruction. The institute's Professional Training Program is accredited by the National Council on Accreditation of Teacher Education, the Council on Education of the Deaf, and the American Speech-Language-Hearing Association (ASHA). *See* AMERICAN SPEECH-LANGUAGE-HEARING ASSOCIATION; AUDIOLOGY: Certification; TEACHING PROFESSION: Certification.

PUBLICATIONS DEPARTMENT

The information and training functions are extended beyond the institute by this division, which prepares and distributes reprints of articles; books; tests of hearing, language, and speech; computer software; and materials for testing and teaching deaf children. The publication *Historic Devices for Hearing* describes the CID-Goldstein Collection of Hearing Devices, located at the institute. The Professional Library of the institute includes more than 9500 volumes and 96 periodicals on hearing, speech, psychology, and on medical and engineering literature relevant to concerns of staff and students. The CID-Goldstein Rare Book Collection, with volumes dating to the fifteenth century, is housed in the Washington University School of Medicine.

HEARING, LANGUAGE, AND SPEECH CLINICS

Persons of all ages, primarily from the Missouri-Illinois area, are served by the clinics. Through the institute's Independent Educational Evaluation Program, school-age, hearing-impaired children throughout the country have been examined. Testing and evaluation procedures include those for hearing, language, speech, speechreading, intelligence, visual perception, and academic achievement. Among the treatment and rehabilitation services are hearing-aid consultation and fitting, speechreading and aural rehabilitation, speech therapy, and language therapy. The parent-child programs of the clinics include a Parent-Infant Program for deaf babies and their families, and language development classes for children of preschool age with retarded language but normal hearing. "Hearing Central" is an information and referral service related to noise exposure and hearing loss. Many procedures used in the clinics were developed through collaboration with the institute's Research Department. The Hearing, Language, and Speech Clinics are accredited by the American Speech-Language-Hearing Association.

SCHOOL

The school for hearing-impaired children, from its inception in 1914, has been distinguished by the following features: enrollment of deaf children beginning at age 3; oral communication; and intensive auditory training. A 3-to-1 pupil-teacher ratio and a grouping-by-ability management pattern permit individualized instruction. Enrollment of children from 3 to 15 years of age may be on either a day-student or residential basis. Throughout the school's history, enrollment has consisted of about one-third day students from the St. Louis area, one-third day students whose parents have moved to St. Louis to enroll the children, and one-third residential students who live in the institute's dormitories during the school year. Tuition is charged at a level well below actual cost, and about two-thirds of the children have significant scholarship assistance. Geographic representation of enrollment has included all 50 states and many foreign countries. Integral to the school classrooms is the Sensory Abilities Center, which includes a full-time educational audiologist and a hearing-aid technician for the 100–120 students. Vision tests are conducted routinely by the school nurse. A Computer Instruction Center is available for children 10 years and older, and Individual Learning Centers where children follow self-directed courses of study are available for middle- and upper-school children. Typing is taught beginning at age 9 to permit ac-

cess to telecommunication devices and computers. A description of the educational program is contained in the report of the Experimental Project in Instructional Concentration (EPIC). A high proportion of students leave the school before the eighth-grade level to enroll in classes with hearing children, and many children attend colleges with hearing students. *See* EDUCATIONAL PROGRAMS: Private Schools.

The Central Institute for the Deaf is affiliated with Washington University as the Speech and Hearing Department of the Graduate School of Arts and Sciences. The institute is a member of the Washington University Medical Center and a member agency of the United Way of Greater St. Louis.

Bibliography
Calvert, Donald R. (ed.): "Experimental Project in Instructional Concentration," *American Annals of the Deaf*, vol. 126, November 1981.

Koelkebeck, Mary Lou, Colleen Detjen, and Donald R. Calvert: *Historic Devices for Hearing: The CID-Goldstein Collection*, Central Institute for the Deaf, St. Louis, 1984.

Lane, Helen S.: *The History of Central Institute*, Central Institute for the Deaf, St. Louis, 1981.

Donald R. Calvert

CHINA, PEOPLE'S REPUBLIC OF

China has a long history. Documents mentioning deafness extend over 2000 years. For example, the fourth century B.C. Zuo Commentary on Tso Chiuming's *Spring and Autumn Annals* says: "Ears unable to hear the harmony of five-tone are deaf." The five-tone of ancient China was a pentatonic scale of five pitches in an octave, and the statement defined deafness as the inability to hear over a certain range of frequencies, a concept close to the current understanding of deafness. *The Book of Rites*, a second century B.C. codification of Confucian ceremonies, when discussing the idea of the Great Harmony (a utopian ideal), mentions the ideal that "all handicapped people have received special care." This was a progressive thought, that Chinese society should take good care of all its handicapped people.

EDUCATION

The first school for deaf children in China was established in 1887 at Dengchou, Shandong Province; later it was moved to Yantai. Other schools were begun in several large cities and in coastal China. By 1948, China had 23 schools for deaf children and 9 for blind and deaf children; only 7 of these were public, and the others were privately owned. Altogether they taught more than 1700 students and employed more than 260 faculty and staff.

On October 1, 1949, the People's Republic of China was founded, and major changes began in the education of deaf Chinese. In October 1951, in a document entitled "Decision on Reforming the Education System," the Chinese government specified that "governments of every level shall establish schools of special education for the deaf and the blind and offer education to handicapped children, youth, and adults." This had the effect of accommodating deaf education into the national education system and spurring its growth.

With this policy as basis, relevant government departments took a series of measures related to deaf education. (1) The government took control of and reorganized the existing schools for deaf students and adopted certain textbooks. (2) The government established a Bureau of the Deaf and the Blind within the Central Education Ministry, which was to be in charge of educational affairs of deaf people and blind people. (3) The government specified policies and missions for the schools for deaf students and required that deaf people be fully educated in mind and body, to promote their overall moral, intellectual, and physical development. These policies stipulated that deaf schools should complete the curriculums used in normal primary schools and should instruct students in vocational skills. From these requirements, teaching plans for the deaf schools were drawn. (4) The government performed research and experiments in oral teaching methods and promoted the use of improved methods nationwide. (5) The government established budget levels and personnel systems for the schools, and specified that the number of students in each classroom should be between 12 and 15. The budget levels for schools for deaf students were higher than those for regular schools. To encourage service to deaf people, the government specified that principals, deans, and teachers of these schools would receive 15 percent more in wages than those in regular schools. (6) The government edited and compiled language and mathematics textbooks for the schools for deaf children.

Since the establishment of these policies, education programs for deaf people and blind people in China have grown considerably. The People's Republic of China has over 33,000 deaf or blind students enrolled in over 300 schools employing nearly 9000 faculty and staff. Annually, primary schools admit about 5600 new students and graduate about 3000, while secondary-school figures are substantially less. Deaf students are found in three different school settings: combined schools for deaf students and blind students, schools for deaf students only, and special classes in hearing schools. The largest percentages are in the special schools for deaf students only.

Most of these schools are supervised by local education boards, and only a few by civil administrations. There are two main types of schools for deaf students: full-time schools and work-study schools. In the former, primary education comprises eight years and secondary education three years. Students either live on campus or commute to school. In the work-study schools, students work part-time and study part-time. There are also vocational schools for deaf youth. For deaf adults there are evening schools, continuing-education courses, vocational skill training workshops, and other such programs.

Deaf students are instructed in the fundamentals of general education as well as vocational skills and knowledge to prepare them to cope with their hearing impairment and to be productive. The curriculum of the elementary schools consists of language, mathematics, morality and meditation, general science (natural science, geography, history), rhythm exercise, art, handicrafts, and vocational training. The language and mathematics textbooks in the primary schools are specially designed. In general, however, the secondary schools for deaf students use the same textbooks as regular secondary schools. Students are required to learn pronunciation, speech, fingerspelling, and writing after they are admitted to schools. Spoken language is the primary method used in teaching, but sign language and fingerspelling are used as supplementary classroom tools in schools for deaf students.

Since the Chinese economy is still in a developmental stage, deaf education is imperfect. The school enrollment rate of deaf children is very low. The system of education for deaf people is not satisfactory. Preschool education for deaf children is still in an experimental stage, and it is not popular. However, the government already has taken further steps to develop special education and is making good progress.

RIGHTS AND EMPLOYMENT

There are about 3 million deaf people in the People's Republic of China. They play the same roles in the nation as their hearing counterparts. After reaching the age of 18, they have the right to vote, to run for election, to work, to rest, and to receive an education. All of these rights are endowed by the Constitution. Due to their hearing impairment, deaf people are considered to deserve more care and concern from Chinese society. Article 45 of the Constitution, which was enacted in 1982, stipulates that the state and society should help make arrangements for the work, livelihood, and education of blind, deaf, and other handicapped citizens.

Deaf people in China contribute their own efforts to the national economy. They have assumed positions as representatives in the People's Congress or in the Chinese People's Political Consultative Conference at every level, as leaders on various political levels, as specialists in different fields, as engineers, and as skilled workers.

There are three types of employment arrangements for deaf people in Chinese cities: (1) They may work in government bodies, public enterprises, or public organizations. (2) They may work in welfare facilities or services. Their wage scales are the same as their hearing coworkers, according to the principle "from each according to his ability, to each according to his work." The civil administration supervises about 1200 production units, employing 48,000 workers who are deaf, blind, or have other handicaps. In these facilities they produce electronic elements, electric appliances, textiles, rubber and plastic products, hardware, wooden furniture, handicrafts, rugs, clothes, and other light goods. (3) They may participate in the small factories or service organizations of Neighborhood Committees. Some big enterprises have organized collective production factories for their employees' handicapped dependents.

The government gives tax incentives to factories that employ handicapped workers. If 35 percent of its total employees are handicapped, a factory is exempted from paying all its factory income tax (there are no personal income taxes in China). A factory with some handicapped workers, but less than 35 percent, can be exempted from paying 50 percent of its income tax. Newly established factories that employ handicapped workers, but have not reached the required percentage for a normal tax exemption, also have one year of income tax exemption. The government allows deaf people to be self-employed as well.

In the cities, deaf workers can receive government-paid medical care and pensions. People who are deaf and blind and without the capability for self-support can receive an appropriate amount of financial aid from the government. Old deaf people can move into homes for the aged to have a peaceful and respected life.

The government has special stipulations for deaf people who violate criminal law. Article 16 of the Penal Code, which has been in effect since 1980, stipulates that if "deaf or blind violate the criminal law, they can be lightly punished, the punishment can be reduced, or they can be exempted from punishment."

SOCIAL LIFE

The communication method used by deaf people in China was not well unified in the past. Research in the reform of sign language was started only after the establishment of the People's Republic of China in 1949. In 1958, the Sign Language Reform Committee was founded, consisting of various specialists and deaf people. In 1963, based on the principles of the Chinese pronunciation scheme, the

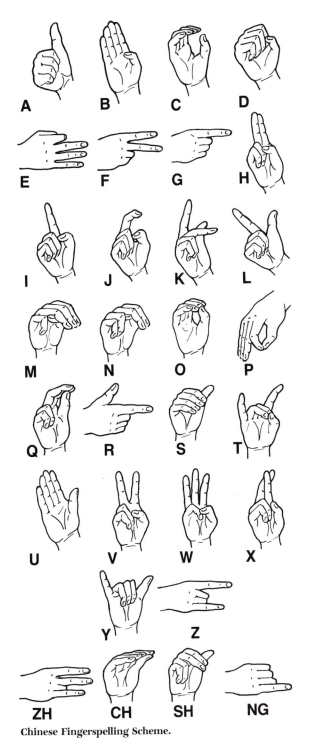

Chinese Fingerspelling Scheme.

government adopted the Chinese Fingerspelling Alphabet Scheme. This scheme consists of 30 separate fingershapes; it provides significant distinguishability among the shapes, and it is easy to remember. Almost half the letters are similar to the written alphabet. Some are similar to the handshapes of daily life, making them easy to understand and to remember. Most use outward finger-shapes, which are easily made, and some fingerspelling letters are the same or similar to other nations' fingerspelling alphabets. *See* SIGNS.

ORGANIZATIONS AND PUBLICATIONS

Deaf people in China have their own organizations. In 1956 the Chinese Deaf Welfare Association was founded. In 1960 the first National Blind and Deaf Representative Assembly convened and founded the Chinese Association for the Blind and the Deaf (CABD). The CABD, headquartered in Beijing, is a member of the World Federation of the Deaf and publishes the bimonthly periodical *Chinese Deafness*. Every province and municipality in the nation has its own local blind and deaf association. *See* WORLD FEDERATION OF THE DEAF.

Two organizations conducting research in the prevention of deafness are the Otolaryngological Institute of the Chinese Medical Institute and the Beijing Municipal Otolaryngology Research School. The latter publishes the *Chinese Otolaryngology Journal*.

Piao Yong-xin

CHINA, REPUBLIC OF

Education for deaf persons in the Republic of China began during the last dynasty of China, the Ch'ing (1644–1911). In 1888 Annetta Thompson Mills, the wife of American Presbyterian missionary Reverend Charles Rogers Mills, sister of a deaf student at the Rochester School for the Deaf, and former teacher at the same school, established the first school for deaf Chinese in the city of Teng-chow in Shantung Province in China's northeast. The school struggled throughout its short existence, and following the death of her husband in 1895, Mrs. Mills was forced to close the school in February 1896. However, she continued her work, and in 1898 she reopened the school in the city of Chefoo (now known as Yantai), also in Shantung Province. Her school grew from 7 students when it reopened to 50 by the year 1941.

MAINLAND BACKGROUND

Mrs. Mills had two major goals for the schools. One was to establish it on a firm financial foundation. To this end she worked tirelessly, soliciting donations from friends in Europe and the United States in order to establish an endowment fund, the interest from which could support the activities of the school over an extended period of time. Her other major goal was to improve the quality of teaching, not only at her own school, but at all future schools for deaf pupils in China. To accomplish this goal, she founded within her school a teacher training division which for over 50 years provided prospective teachers with the kinds of skills they needed to educate properly the large number of deaf children that were being identified almost daily throughout China.

Mrs. Mills was a close friend of both Edward M. Gallaudet and Alexander Graham Bell, and she was a firm believer in the philosophy of oral communication. Through her association with Bell, she became interested in Visible Speech, invented by Bell's father, and developed it for use in writing the Chinese language phonetically. She envisioned using it in teaching Chinese deaf children how to speak. However, she apparently was not opposed to the use of some manual communication in her teaching, as exemplified by a glance at any page of her *Deaf-Mute Primer*. This was the first attempt to develop special instructional materials for deaf children in China, and it became the backbone of language instruction at her school for years. (A copy of this book is available at the Gallaudet College Archives.) *See* BELL, ALEXANDER GRAHAM; GALLAUDET, EDWARD MINER; GALLAUDET COLLEGE; VISIBLE SPEECH.

Largely due to her efforts, schools for deaf people gradually began to spring up in other areas of China. One of the first schools established after the founding of the Republic of China in 1912 was the Hwei-Ai School for the Deaf in Hangchow, founded in 1914 by a Mr. Tse and his deaf son Tse Tien-fu, a former pupil of Mrs. Mills and eventually the first deaf principal in China. Soon after, a school was established in Peiping (now Beijing) by Tu Wen-chang. Many of the teachers at these schools were trained under Mrs. Mills's supervision, and before long her trainees were serving in schools as far away as Shanghai and Canton.

As she grew older, Mrs. Mills became less able to handle the affairs of the entire school, so she enlisted the assistance of her niece, Anita E. Carter, to come to China and help with the administration of the school. One of Carter's first steps was to establish the girls' department of the school, which previously had served only boys. Mrs. Mills retired in 1923, leaving the school in the hands of her niece. Under her guidance, the school continued until the mid-1940s to be the guiding force in the training and cultivation of teachers for schools for deaf students throughout China. Although the province of Taiwan was cut off from China under the Japanese occupation from 1895 to 1945, even the schools in that province of China were influenced by the efforts of Mills and Carter, since teachers trained at this school were among those who came to Taiwan between 1945 and 1949 in the wake of the communist revolution on the mainland.

As of 1947 there were 44 special schools in mainland China and 2 in the province of Taiwan, 35 of which were privately run. Taken together, the schools served 963 blind students and 1624 deaf students. There were a total of 413 teachers and other staff members. By that time schools had been established in the cities of Nanking, Peiping, Canton, Chungking, Chengtu, Yangchow, Wuchin, Chenkiang, Nantung, Mukden, and Hong Kong; Shanghai had as many as eight privately operated schools. Nevertheless, these schools served only a fraction of the total deaf population of China. The outbreak of civil war in China forced the closing of many schools, but since 1949 most have reopened, and many more have been established. *See* CHINA, PEOPLE'S REPUBLIC OF.

EDUCATION

There are three public residential schools for deaf pupils in Taiwan, located in the cities of Taipei, Taichung, and Tainan, and one private elementary school, located in Kaohsiung. These schools serve a fairly large number of students: over 1000 at the Taipei school, about 700 at the Tainan school, and approximately 100 in Kaohsiung.

Schools for deaf Taiwanese students are mostly run by the government at various levels, although a small number of programs are privately supported. The Taipei municipal government oversees the Taipei Municipal Ch'i-ts'ung School for the Deaf, a residential school that also has a large number of commuter students.

The history of the school goes back to 1917, during the Japanese occupation of the island, when a Japanese physician named Kimura Kingo petitioned the Japanese government for permission to establish a school for blind pupils, and was urged by the parents of deaf children to include them in his plans. This was done, and one of the earliest teachers of deaf students at the school was a deaf native Taiwanese, Lin Wen-sheng, born in 1895 and educated between 1904 and 1917 at the Tokyo School for the Deaf. When the Japanese were defeated in World War II, Lin became the first principal of the school under Chinese administration, a position which he retained until 1951.

The history of the Tainan School for the Deaf began in 1890 when a school for blind people was founded in that city by the English Presbyterian Mission under the supervision of the Reverend William Campbell. In 1915, during the Japanese occupation, deaf students were enrolled in the school for the first time, and the school continued to serve both populations until 1968 when the name of the school was changed to Taiwan Provincial Tainan Ch'i-ts'ung School for the Deaf.

Taiwan's third public school for deaf pupils began as an offshoot of the Tainan School in 1956. It became independent in 1960 and was located for many years in Weng-tzu Li, near Feng-yuan, Taiwan. In 1979, the school relocated to a new site within the confines of Taichung city.

The fourth major school for deaf Taiwanese is the privately run elementary school located in Tsoying, near Kaohsiung. The principal of the school, Chiang Ssu-nung, is deaf. Graduates of the school generally continue their studies at one of the island's three public schools for deaf people.

A recent trend in the education of hearing-impaired individuals in Taiwan has been the shift in emphasis toward programs that aim at integrating deaf children with their hearing peers in school situations. This generally takes the form of special classes for deaf children established within the general public school system, such as the highly successful program at the Hsin-hsing Junior High School in Taipei. The emphasis in the majority of these classes is on oral and auditory training. Students in these classes frequently are the products of, or continue to be assisted by, numerous privately run speech training centers located primarily in the major cities that offer speech training to hearing-impaired young children.

Although opportunities for advanced studies are available, the emphasis in educating deaf people in Taiwan has traditionally been on preparing them for a particular career. This is reflected by the fact that the official name of the high school program at all three schools is Senior Vocational School. Among the courses taught in these programs are printing, typing, baking, sewing, home economics, rattan weaving, wood carving, art, haircutting, tailoring, and photography.

COMMUNICATION IN EDUCATION

In contrast to the situation in most schools for deaf individuals throughout the world, the schools in Taiwan largely employ manual communication systems. Although lip service is paid to the philosophy of total communication, it falls short of its goal because of the generally poor quality of speech training offered to students at the schools. Teachers generally employ a form of Signed Mandarin during actual classroom instruction, that is, speaking while signing in the word order of Mandarin. Students at the schools, however, communicate with each other in what may be regarded as a totally different language: Taiwan Sign Language. *See* EDUCATION: Communication; SIGN LANGUAGES: Taiwanese.

Education programs for preschool-age hearing-impaired children focus on developing aural-oral abilities. One of the most successful of these programs is supervised by Huang Teh-yeh of the Department of Health Education at National Taiwan Normal University. Other similar programs are operated within both public and private hospitals, and still others are operated in cooperation with YMCAs, churches, and so on. As children enter the public schools for deaf pupils, the emphasis on speech training is lost, and many children who had previously developed some facility in oral communication frequently lose it during their elementary school years. Secondary schooling places more and more emphasis on vocational training.

POSTSECONDARY EDUCATION
Upon graduation from high school, a small number of deaf students are able to further their education in the limited number of college and university programs that are open to them. Some of the areas of study which they may pursue are art, physical education, home economics, history, horticulture, and veterinary medicine. Significantly, deaf students are not allowed to major in education and are thereby officially excluded from obtaining teaching jobs at schools for deaf pupils.

For those deaf people who do not go on to college, opportunities for further learning and training generally end with their secondary school courses. Although a few job training centers exist, most are geared toward persons who have orthopedic disabilities or are mentally retarded.

INCOME
In virtually all aspects of life, deaf people in Taiwan are second-class citizens. When compared to hearing people, their income is on the average lower, their unemployment rate is higher, and when they do find employment they are frequently stuck in a fixed position with little or no opportunity for career advancement. Many deaf people in Taiwan are printers, artists, painters, copyists, designers, cartoonists, barbers, and laborers. Unfortunately, there are a large number of deaf peddlers, most of whom can make much more money asking for donations than they can by working.

SIGN LANGUAGE
The predominant method of communication among deaf people in Taiwan is their own language, Taiwan Sign Language. Over the years it grew out of the daily interaction of members of the deaf community in both school and social settings. It traces its roots to three distinct sources: Old Taiwan Sign Language, or the language as it existed during the last century before the occupation by Japan; Japanese Sign Language, which was introduced as part of the educational system by teachers from Japan; and Mainland Chinese Sign Language, introduced over the past 40 years by immigrants and refugees from the Chinese mainland. In addition, deaf people in Taiwan are constantly adding new vocabulary in the form of new coinings and recent bor-

rowings from other sign languages such as American Sign language. See SIGN LANGUAGES: American, Chinese.

INFORMATION
There are several important sources of information concerning deaf and hearing-impaired persons in Taiwan. The government organization officially charged with administering all special education is the Department of Social Education of the Ministry of Education in Taipei. The department supervises all three public schools for deaf children, as well as schools for blind persons and for people with other handicaps. Classes for deaf pupils in regular public schools fall under the jurisdiction of the Department of Elementary and Junior High School Education, which supervises and administers the free nine-year compulsory education offered in Taiwan.

Another important clearinghouse of information on special education in Taiwan is the Special Education Center at National Taiwan Normal University. The center, in addition to maintaining an up-to-date library of information on all handicapping conditions, publishes the *Special Education Quarterly* and a wide variety of scholarly works and bibliographies on deafness and special education in general. The center is also headquarters of the Special Education Association of the Republic of China, which periodically holds meetings and sponsors international symposia.

ORGANIZATIONS
Organizations dealing specifically with deaf people are few, yet are gradually gaining strength largely due to the increasing numbers of deaf young people who are assuming more and more leadership roles in them. Two of the oldest organizations are the Taiwan and Taipei City Welfare Associations for the Deaf, the first established in 1958. The expressed purposes of these organizations include collecting information about deaf people such as educational and occupational data, and working toward improving the protection and livelihood of the deaf citizens of Taiwan. The organizations have also been active in welfare work. For example, their efforts have enabled deaf people to enjoy half-price charges on public transportation and at the movies, and have gained educational benefits for the children of deaf parents.

These organizations have also been active in aid and relief ventures. They provide funds to their members when they are sick or when someone dies or has a child; they sponsor an emergency mutual aid fund; and they organize winter relief drives which provide food and necessary household supplies to needy deaf families. Although their capacity to offer job training is limited, they do conduct classes in such things as leatherworking, sewing, and painting, and they operate a ballpoint pen factory which sells directly to the local schools. Other areas in which the welfare associations provide assistance are matchmaking, legal advice, assistance in filling out various application forms, sign language interpreting services, and babysitting services for the children of members. The associations are funded partly through government subsidies, but largely through voluntary donations and the profits of the ballpoint pen factory.

In March 1980 the Deaf Sign Language Research Association of the Republic of China was established, with several goals in mind. The primary purposes of the organization were to promote the use and acceptance of natural Taiwan Sign Language as a language, through such methods as conducting sign language classes for the general public; to sponsor a highly successful Deaf Theatre Group, which has put on four major performances (including one in Hong Kong); to bring together deaf college graduates into an active alumni association; and to sponsor periodic sports and recreational events for mixed groups of hearing and hearing-impaired people. These activities are designed to help eliminate communication barriers and thereby assist deaf people in becoming more accepted in the hearing society. One of the interesting by-products of all of this is the fact that learning sign language is now popular among young people in high schools and colleges. One weekly television program even donates approximately 15 minutes to a sign language song competition, but unfortunately participation is limited only to those people who can hear so that their signs will keep time with music.

Wayne H. Smith

CLARKE, JOHN LOUIS
(1881–1970)

John Louis Clarke was born on January 20, 1881, in Highwood, Montana. His Indian ancestry and environment provided him with the background that ultimately led to his fame as a master wood sculptor. His father, Horace John Clarke, was half Blackfeet; his mother, Margaret, was a full-blooded Blackfeet, known as First Kill, and her father was Chief Stands Alone; his paternal grandfather was Malcolm Clarke, a classmate and friend of General William T. Sherman.

Malcolm Clarke migrated west in 1841 to head the American Fur Trading Company at Fort Benton, Montana Territory. He was shrewd in dealings with the warring Blackfeet and gained their confidence. They looked to him as their mediator when trouble brewed between them and white men.

John Louis Clarke displaying some of his carvings.

During this time, Malcolm Clarke married a Blackfeet by the name of Cutting Off Head Woman, the daughter of Chief Talking. One of their four children was Horace John Clarke.

At the age of two, John Louis was afflicted by a severe attack of scarlet fever; when the disease subsided, he was deaf. His Indian friends named him Cutapuie—Man Who Talks Not. At an early age, Clarke began to show artistic talent, fashioning the likenesses of animals from the clay of the riverbanks near his home. Since he was not able to hear or speak, his visual perception became unusually keen; his unspoken thoughts flowed from his hands to the medium with which he worked.

Clarke's education began at the Fort Shaw Indian School. He then entered the North Dakota School for the Deaf, Devils Lake, in 1894, left there in 1897, and entered the Montana School for the Deaf at Boulder for one year. Realizing his potential as a great artist, friends sent him to the St. Francis Academy for the Deaf in Milwaukee, Wisconsin, where he learned the rudiments of wood carving.

In 1913 he returned to the Indian Reservation in East Glacier, Montana, then known as Midvale, where he established an art studio. Clarke maintained his studio in Glacier Park for 57 years. Woodcarvers from the world over came to learn his techniques. During the winter months when the park was closed, he resided in Great Falls. In 1918 he married a hearing white woman, Mary (Mamie) Peters, who gave him much support during the remainder of her life (she died in 1947). In 1931 they adopted a daughter, Joyce Marie.

Clarke's works number in the thousands. His success as a sculptor was due to his ability to depict the animals of the wild with realistic accuracy. He was known among American sculptors as "The Bowie Knife Sculptor." His best medium was wood; cottonwood was his favorite because its rough texture and soft fibers shaped easily into shaggy fur. He also modeled in clay, painted in oil and watercolor, and drew in crayon and charcoal. His favorite subjects for carving were goats and bears.

In 1958 Clarke carved a panel for the Veterans and Pioneers Historical Building in Helena, Montana. This masterpiece was carved from one ton of cottonwood. Other well-known works are his 14-foot carving *A Blackfeet Encampment* and the Philippine mahogany panels at the entrance to the Blackfeet Indian Hospital, Browning, Montana.

Clarke's works have been exhibited in New York City at the Roerich Museum, Ferargil Galleries, American Institute of Sporting Art, and New York Academy of Design; in Montana at the Butte Art Center (Butte), Museum of the Plains Indians and Craft Center (Browning), Charles M. Russell Art Gallery (Great Falls), and Montana Institute of Art and Montana Historical Society (Helena); Vose Gallery, Boston; The Little Galleries, Tulsa; in Chicago at the Arts Club of Chicago, Chicago Women's Club Gallery, and Chicago Art Institute; Nooan and Koochin, Kansas City; Baltimore Salon, Los Angeles; Children's Art Museum, Detroit; and in Philadelphia at the American Art Gallery and the Philadelphia Academy of Fine Art. His *Lady Elk* was exhibited in the 1934 World's Fair, Chicago.

Clarke worked until his death on November 20, 1970, in Cut Bank Montana, at the age of 89. Several years earlier, his eyes became so clouded with cataracts that he could barely see. His work was then done by touch and feel; nevertheless the fine detail of his work was still evident.

John L. Clarke is buried in East Glacier Cemetery, Glacier National Park, Montana.

Bibliography
Anderson, Mary McCourt: "John Clarke's Artistry Established Worldwide," *Montana Standard–Butte Daily Post*, Butte, Montana, January 7, 1973.

Clark, H. McDonald: "Sculptor John Clarke Speaks with Hands," *Great Falls Tribune*, Great Falls, Montana, January 5, 1958.

Ege, Robert J. "Montana Wood Hawks," brochure, Lloyd P. Morton, Great Falls, Montana.

"Indian Carver Deaf and Dumb," *Billings Gazette*, Billings, Montana, June 20, 1923.

International Exhibition of Fine and Applied Arts by Deaf Artists, Roerich Museum, New York, 1934, Papers: Correspondence Between Mamie Clark and Eleanor Font, 1934–1941.

"John Clarke Carving Scene from Ton of Cottonwood," *Cut Bank Pioneer*, Cut Bank, Montana, April 26, 1956.

"John L. Clarke, Deaf Indian Sculptor," *The Pelican*, Louisiana School for the Deaf, Baton Rouge, vol. 58, no. 4, December 1937.

Letter: Joyce Clarke to Mrs. Jewett, Glacier Park, Montana, December 20, 1947, Montana Historical Society Library, Helena.

"The Man Who Speaks Not, John L. Clarke, Noted Deaf Indian Sculptor, Passes Away," *Mont-As-De News*, Montana Association of the Deaf, Inc., vol. 9, no. 4, December 1970.

"Margaret Spanish, Born in 1849 at Fort Benton, Passes Away," *Great Falls Tribune*, September 29, 1940.

Rowell, Agnes Sherburne, "Malcolm Clarke, Fur Trader, was a Power Among Blackfeet Indians," *Great Falls Tribune*, Great Falls, Montana, May 15, 1932.

Tschache, J. W.: "J. L. Clarke, J. W. Tschache's Reminiscences," unpublished.

Corrine Hilton

CLARKE SCHOOL

The Clarke School, located in Northampton, Massachusetts, is a private residential school that provides an educational program for children who, because of profound or partial deafness, require a special education to prepare them for future study with hearing students. Since its establishment, Clarke has exclusively employed the oral method of instruction. Children are taught in small classes and receive individual instruction. Each classroom is sound-treated and equipped with modern group hearing aids. The students study the same academic subjects as students at other elementary and junior high schools and receive constant instruction in speech, lipreading, language, and the effective use of their residual hearing.

EARLY HISTORY
The school was founded in 1867 as the first permanent oral school for deaf children in the United States. Its establishment was due primarily to the efforts of Gardiner Greene Hubbard, a prominent Boston attorney. Hubbard's daughter Mabel had been deafened by scarlet fever at the age of four. The Hubbards were told by the leading educators of that day that Mabel would soon lose her speech, could only be trained in sign language, and had to be 10 years old to enroll in school.

The Hubbard's taught Mabel with limited success and soon realized that they had to find a teacher. Hubbard knew that deaf students in Germany were taught to speak and read lips. He was determined to establish a school in the United States using the German method, and went before the Massachusetts legislature in 1864 for permission to do so. However, due to the objections of Lewis J. Dudley, a member of the legislature and father of a deaf daughter who had never spoken, Hubbard's efforts failed. Meanwhile, in Chelmsford, Massachusetts, Harriet B. Rogers had been engaged to teach a little deaf girl named Fanny Cushing. She had no experience in teaching deaf children, although she was somewhat familiar with the manual methods. She taught her pupil to fingerspell and also to speak, but soon became convinced that it was unwise to combine the two methods. Consequently, she relinquished the use of fingerspelling and depended wholly upon speech. Rogers became so interested in this experiment that she sought more pupils. A friend arranged a meeting between Rogers and Hubbard, and through his efforts and financial support, in 1866 a small school was opened in Chelmsford, Massachusetts, with five pupils. *See* SIGNS: Fingerspelling.

Hubbard arranged another meeting with the Massachusetts legislature and invited Rogers and three of her students: Rosco Greene, an 18-year-old student at the Chelmsford School; Jeanie Lippett, who had been trained orally by her mother and whose father was the governor of Rhode Island; and his own daughter Mabel. The legislative body was quite impressed with the conversation among these three young deaf people. After seeing the results of oral teaching, Dudley asked if his daughter could be taught to say "Daddy." Two days later, Theresa Dudley, who for 13 years had never uttered a meaningful sound, said not only "Daddy" but some 16 other words. So convinced was Dudley, he joined Hubbard, and through their combined efforts a charter was granted to establish an oral school for deaf children in Massachusetts.

ESTABLISHED AS A PRIVATE SCHOOL

The governor of Massachusetts learned that a Northampton merchant, John Clarke, had offered $50,000 to establish a school for deaf persons in Northampton. Clarke had become interested in deaf people because of his own gradual loss of hearing. In October 1867 the Chelmsford School moved to Northampton, thus establishing the first permanent oral school for deaf pupils in the United States. One of the first pupils to enroll was Theresa Dudley. Clarke, who had first preferred to remain anonymous, later agreed to have the school named for him.

TEACHER EDUCATION

Due to the success of the new school and in order to accept more children, new teachers had to be found. There were no schools that trained teachers of deaf students at that time, so Clarke decided to train its own. In 1889, under the leadership of Caroline A. Yale, Clarke School's second principal, the first teacher training program in the United States was instituted for members of the Clarke School staff. At the request of the Alexander Graham Bell Association for the Deaf (then called the American Association to Promote the Teaching of Speech to the Deaf), the program was broadened in 1892 to prepare teachers for the profession at large. In 1947

Smith College affiliated with Clarke School, and expanded Clarke's educational resources. In 1962 Smith's board of trustees instituted the only master of education of the deaf (M.E.D.) degree program in America. Over 1100 teachers have graduated from this program to teach deaf children in 47 states and 33 foreign countries. They have worked in residential and day schools, day classes, and mainstream settings. *See* ALEXANDER GRAHAM BELL ASSOCIATION.

LEADERSHIP

Clarke School has earned an international reputation as a pioneer and standard bearer in this special field of education. The school has been fortunate in having outstanding leadership to determine its programs and policies. Gardiner Greene Hubbard, the school's first board chairperson, became president of the Bell Telephone Company, the forerunner of the American Telephone and Telegraph Company.

In 1871 Alexander Graham Bell went to Clarke School to teach the faculty his father's method of visible speech. Bell continued his interest in the school for 51 years, serving on the board from 1898–1922 and as its chairperson for the last five years of his life (1917–1922). He tutored and then later married Mabel Hubbard. *See* BELL, ALEXANDER GRAHAM.

Grace Goodhue trained as a teacher of deaf children at Clarke and taught there from 1902 until 1905. It was there she met a young man from Vermont, Calvin Coolidge, who had graduated from Amherst College and was practicing law in Northampton. They were married in October 1905, and he went on to become mayor of Northampton, governor of the Commonwealth, and president of the United States. Both the President and Mrs. Coolidge retained a very active interest in the school and served on the board. She was president of the board from 1935 to 1952 and remained on it until her death in 1957.

In addition to its international prominence in the oral education of deaf children, Clarke School is recognized as a world leader in the training of teachers of deaf pupils and in research. Over the years, new ideas and new techniques have evolved from research in the hereditary aspects of deafness, the psychology of deafness, and the field of experimental phonetics and audiology.

Clarke was one of the first schools to sponsor summer schools for teachers. More than 1600 teachers and student teachers have been enrolled in this program since its beginning in 1962. Clarke has been a leader in establishing preschool programs, speech laboratories, guidance and counseling services, mainstream support services to assist students in the transition from the special school to the public or private school, captioned television programs, and the use of computers to enrich the education of hearing-impaired people.

PROGRAM AND PURPOSE

Clarke School enrolls deaf children, ages 4 to 17 years, from all over the United States, Canada, and occasionally abroad, and offers them a full academic elementary program stressing oral communication. Residential students live in homelike dormitories under the supervision of qualified teachers.

The goal of the school is to prepare deaf students to join their hearing contemporaries in the mainstream of education in public or private schools as soon as they are able to succeed. Children are accepted into Clarke's program based on commitment from parents and the needs and ability of the child. The child's hearing loss must be so severe that he or she is unable to benefit from instruction provided for children with normal hearing and speech in the public schools. Using modern individual and group hearing aids, pupils are taught to make the best use of their residual hearing, to lipread, and to talk. The method used is strictly oral—no sign language is taught. A professionally trained staff provides an environment where speech and language can be acquired in both oral and written forms, enabling students to acquire the necessary language competence to participate and compete in a world of hearing people. *See* EDUCATION: Communication.

GRADUATES

That deaf individuals can and do compete successfully has been verified by the school's alumni. One study indicates that 95 percent of the alumni attended high school or preparatory school for hearing students; 60 percent of this group went on to over 200 colleges and universities; 24 graduates received master's degrees and 4 have Ph.D. degrees. Those who did not continue academically were still able to compete successfully in the world of business and industry because of an oral education.

Bibliography

Blish, Stanford C.: "A Survey of the Educational and Vocational Experiences of the Alumni of the Clarke School for the Deaf," Clarke School for the Deaf, Northampton, Massachusetts, 1981.

Clarke School: *Annual Reports*, vol. 1, pp. 1867–1877, Northampton, Massachusetts, 1983.

Clarke Institution: *25th Anniversary Report*, Northampton, Massachusetts, 1892.

Numbers, Mary E.: *My Words Fell on Deaf Ears*, Alexander Graham Bell Association Inc., Washington, D.C., 1974.

Yale, Caroline A.: *Years of Building*, Dial Press, New York, 1931.

Bill G. Blevins

CLERC, LAURENT
(1785–1869)

The influence of the deaf teacher Laurent Clerc in the early movement for education of deaf persons in America is incalculable. He was described by a deaf French former student as of pleasant manners, polished and refined, engaging company, in short "a true gentleman." Considered a born teacher, Clerc was an excellent role model for his deaf pupils in both France and America. To the public he was a striking example of what might be accomplished through support for education of deaf persons.

Above all, Clerc strove to influence his pupils to stand on their own feet, to solve their problems in a realistic manner, and never to feel sorry for themselves. Deaf Americans bracketed Clerc with Thomas Hopkins Gallaudet as their benefactors. *See* GALLAUDET, THOMAS HOPKINS.

Louis Laurent Marie Clerc was born December 26, 1785, in LaBalme les Grottes, Dauphiné, France, 26 miles east of Lyons, beside the Rhône and within sight of the Alps. His father, Joseph François Clerc, was village mayor and a justice of the peace. His mother, Elizabeth Candy, was the daughter of a notary public of the canton of Crèmieu. The eldest sons of the Clerc family had held the office of *tubelion*, or king's commissary, for over 300 years.

Laurent Clerc (ca. 1820) in a portrait by Charles Willson Peale. (American School for the Deaf)

At the age of one year, Clerc fell into the fireplace and was burned on the right cheek. His name-sign among deaf people came from the resulting scar —a brushing of the two forefinger tips on the right hand down the right cheek, near the mouth. Clerc's parents attributed his deafness and loss of the sense of smell to the fever which followed. Clerc described himself as deaf from birth.

In his twelfth year, Clerc was taken to the Royal National Institute for the Deaf in Paris by his uncle and godfather, Laurent Clerc, of Lyons. His first teacher and lifelong friend was Jean Massieu, a brilliant deaf man whose five siblings were also born deaf. The two men took part in the frequent exhibits to publicize the school's work, and many stories have come down to us of their strikingly original and perceptive replies to the questions posed to them. *See* MASSIEU, JEAN.

Within eight years, Clerc had completed the school's courses and was advanced to tutor; by 1816 he was teaching the highest class. His years in France encompassed the turbulent period of the French Revolution, the Commune, and the rise and fall of Napoleon. As a priest and suspected Royalist sympathizer, Abbé Roch Ambroise Sicard, the school's head, was imprisoned at least twice, barely escaping with his life. Once he was saved at the last minute by a petition from his deaf pupils, led by Massieu. When Napoleon escaped from exile in Elba in March 1815 and rallied his old soldiers to begin his "hundred days," Sicard felt it prudent to be absent in London with Clerc and Massieu. They supported themselves by giving public exhibitions of their communication skills several times a week. These aroused such a sensation that many notable persons attended, including members of Parliament and the Duchess of Wellington. *See* SICARD, ABBÉ ROCH AMBROISE CUCURRON.

On July 10, 1815, one of those present was young Thomas Hopkins Gallaudet, a Congregational minister who had arrived from Connecticut a few days before. Gallaudet had been sent by Hartford citizens to learn to teach deaf people and then start a school in Hartford. Sicard invited Gallaudet to study at the Paris institution as soon as the political situation might be settled. *See* COGSWELL, ALICE.

In Paris he was welcomed to visit all classes at the school. He took lessons from Sicard, Massieu, and others. With funds running low, Gallaudet realized he could not complete his mission, and he invited Clerc to return to the United States with him.

In spite of heavy pressure to remain with the aged and ailing Sicard, Clerc agreed to come to America for three years to teach and to train other teachers. During the 52-day voyage in the sailing ship *Mary Augusta*, Gallaudet taught Clerc English, and Clerc tutored him in communication and

Clerc (ca. 1850) in a portrait by John Carlin. (Episcopal Mission to the Deaf of Philadelphia)

teaching methods. They altered a few signs to conform to New England customs. Clerc wrote an interesting diary for practice in English. Shortly after his arrival in Connecticut, he was writing fundraising speeches, in practically flawless English, to be read before legislatures and civic groups.

For seven months they toured eastern cities, giving lectures and demonstrating methods, to raise money to start the school. In Clerc, even the most skeptical found evidence that deaf persons could be educated, and educated well. Asked about the benefits of his schooling, he replied that, through his teacher, he had passed from the class of brutes to that of men. The sum of $5,000 was raised, which the Connecticut General Assembly matched— the first such legislative appropriation in the history of the United States.

On April 15, 1817, the school opened in Hartford, with seven pupils present in rented rooms. It soon became evident that steady financial support was necessary for the school to survive. In January 1818, Clerc visited Congress with board member Henry Hudson to seek assistance. Speaker of the House Henry Clay seated Clerc beside him, and Clerc conversed in writing with congressmen in both French and English. By an odd coincidence, both Clay and President James Monroe (whom Clerc met the next day) recognized him. One had seen him at a London exhibition, and the other had observed him conversing in sign language with another deaf man, probably Massieu, at a cafe in Paris.

At the 1819–1820 session of Congress, Clay helped sponsor a bill granting the school a township (23,000 acres) of land from the public domain in Alabama, on part of which is present-day Birmingham. Thus Clerc's visit helped ensure financial stability from the approximately $300,000 realized through the land sales. President Monroe signed the bill, which is now in the American School's historical museum. *See* AMERICAN SCHOOL FOR THE DEAF.

Among the school heads trained by Clerc were Abraham Stansbury (New York), the Reverend A. B. Hutton (Pennsylvania), H. N. Hubbell (Ohio), Roland MacDonald (Quebec), Joseph Dennis Tyler (Virginia), John Adamson Jacobs (Kentucky), and J. S. Brown (Indiana). Many of Clerc's deaf students founded schools or classes for deaf persons in other states or became valued teachers as the United States spread westward. Clerc was in demand as a speaker and his influence among the graduates was tremendous.

On May 3, 1818, Clerc was married to Eliza Crocker Boardman, one of his first pupils, of Whitesborough, New York. She had lost her hearing in early childhood but retained some speech. Attractive, vivacious, intelligent, and of graceful manners, she provided a new incentive for Clerc to remain in America. He revisited France only three times, in 1820, 1835, and 1846.

The Clercs had six children, all with normal hearing, four of whom survived infancy. The Reverend Francis Joseph Clerc was well known among deaf persons and an Episcopal clergyman. Others distinguished themselves in various careers. Guy B. Holt, a great-great-grandson, was president of the American School's board of directors until his death in 1965. High school dormitories at this school are named for Clerc and Holt.

For eight months beginning in August 1821, Clerc was acting principal of the Pennsylvania Institution in Philadelphia. He organized courses and trained the faculty. Charles Willson Peale painted two portraits, one of Clerc and one of Mrs. Clerc holding their baby daughter Elizabeth. A Clerc descendant gave these priceless paintings to the American School.

In 1850, graduates of eastern schools for the deaf held a convocation in Hartford to honor Gallaudet and Clerc. Gallaudet had taught only 13 years, although remaining on the board of directors of the school. Clerc was in his thirty-fourth year in America (including about 9 years in France). They were presented with coin-silver pitchers and trays, artistically engraved with the record of their services.

Clerc had always given credit to Gallaudet and to Divine Providence for blessing the school. He now gave credit to Hartford citizens, the Congress, the directors, and various legislatures and friends for success of the school. It remained for Gallaudet to make clear that the enterprise would not have succeeded without Clerc.

In 1851, after Gallaudet's death, Clerc became president of an association to erect a memorial at the school. This led to organization in 1854 of the New England Gallaudet Association of the Deaf, the first of many associations of deaf citizens in the United States.

In 1858, at the age of 73, Clerc was retired with a pension after teaching half a century in two countries. His last years were spent peacefully. The library and reading rooms of Hartford were favorite haunts, and he enjoyed keeping posted on the progress of the school of his deaf friends.

Clerc Monument at the American School for the Deaf. (American School for the Deaf)

In 1864, when Clerc was 79, he spoke at the inauguration of the National Deaf-Mute College, now Gallaudet College, which was founded by Gallaudet's youngest son, Edward Miner, in Washington, D.C. Although Clerc had never attended college himself, he received an honorary master of arts degree from Trinity College in Hartford, as well as citations from Dartmouth College and the University of Lyons. *See* GALLAUDET, EDWARD MINER; GALLAUDET COLLEGE.

A little more than a year after celebrating his golden wedding anniversary among family and friends, Clerc passed away, on July 18, 1869, in his 84th year. He is buried beside his wife in Spring Grove Cemetery, Hartford.

Besides the Charles Willson Peale portraits, two others were the work of Clerc's deaf friend John Carlin. One is at the Kentucky School in Danville, the other is owned by the Episcopal mission to the deaf in Philadelphia. A charcoal sketch is owned by Gallaudet College. The American School owns an oil portrait of Clerc in his old age, painted from a photograph. *See* CARLIN, JOHN.

In 1874 Clerc's deaf friends unveiled an impressive memorial to him at the Hartford School. His bronze bust is set atop a polished black granite shaft. At the bottom is the name "Clerc," spelled out with bronze hands in the manual alphabet Clerc brought from France. The inscription calls him "The Apostle to the Deaf-Mutes of the New World . . . who left his native land to uplift them with his teachings and encourage them by his example."

Poems and plays are presented at programs in schools for deaf children almost every April and December to honor Clerc and Gallaudet. A high-rise dormitory at Gallaudet College also bears his name. But his best memorials are in the deaf people of America whose lives since 1817 have been influenced by Clerc. Thus a poor deaf boy, born in an obscure village in France, has made a difference.

Loy E. Golladay

Bibliography

L'Abbé Sicard, a biography by an anonymous former student of Clerc's.

Barnard, H. A.: *A Tribute to Thomas H. Gallaudet, LL.D.*, containing an autobiographical sketch by Laurent Clerc, 1852.

Clerc Papers, Yale University and American School for the Deaf, Golladay Historical Museum.

Denison, James: *The Memory of Laurent Clerc*, dedication address for Clerc Memorial, 1874, *American Annals of the Deaf*.

Golladay, L. E.: Laurent Clerc, Pioneer Deaf Teacher in America," *Gallaudet Today*, Summer 1975.

Lane, Harlan: *When the Mind Hears: A History of the Deaf*, Random House, New York, 1984.

COCHLEAR IMPLANTS

Auditory implants or prostheses are electronic aids designed to provide deaf people with sensations of sound via electrodes implanted in the auditory system. Although research for these implants began in the 1950s, the field is still in its early stages of development. This article describes the aims of implant designs, some issues related to their application, further research, and current status.

Auditory implants are presently intended only for profoundly deaf persons. The most common type is the cochlear implant, consisting of a sound pick-up/stimulator unit connected by a small cable so as to activate electrodes implanted in the cochlea. The surgical procedures involve implantation behind the ear of a small receiver from which electrode wires are routed inward and fixed in the cochlea or on its walls. The receiver is activated through the overlying skin by a small transmitter button held against the head (by internal magnets). The transmitter is activated by the stimulator, worn on the belt or in a pocket, via the cable. The cable and transmitter button are easily removed by the patient.

At present two types of cochlear implant are approved for clinical use in the United States; one type employs a single electrode as the stimulator; the other employs an array of electrodes distributed along the cochlea. The single-electrode implant is relatively simple in its surgical and electronic aspects, but it provides only very limited auditory benefits. There are approximately 10 different implant systems under study that provide more auditory information. Some of these employ more electrodes to attempt to distribute sound frequencies from low to high along the cochlea. *See* EAR: Anatomy.

Prime candidates for auditory implants are deaf people whose inner ear (cochlea) is totally ineffective but whose auditory nerve endings are still responsive to direct stimulation. When the implanted electrode is activated with sound, the nerves are stimulated, and the deaf person hears sounds. The sounds are described as noises and buzzes that are quite different from the original sound. Wearers of single-electrode implants—usually adults who formerly had normal hearing—report that they can learn to identify some useful environmental sounds, but that the amount of aid to lipreading is not satisfactory. There is at least a relief from the sense of isolation by deafness.

The basic reason for the abnormal character of the stimulated sound is that the electrical stimulator and electrode do not simulate the normal process by which the ear converts sounds into nerve impulses. This process is extremely complicated, and it is only partly understood, even for the simplest types of sound inputs. Ideally, the highly complex sounds of speech and of the environment should be simulated; these are made up of many components spread over a wide range of frequencies. *See* EAR: Physiology.

MULTIELECTRODE IMPLANTS

It is known that different nerve endings in the inner ear, arranged in a row in the cochlea, respond with sounds that are heard as low to high in pitch, also ordered in a row somewhat like a scale of notes. Thus, if the electrical stimulation could be suitably arrayed over the row of nerve endings, some useful frequency (pitch) representation or discrimination of the original sounds might occur. For this reason, most of the implant research centers have experimented with arrays of implanted electrodes. An external receiver-analyzer worn by the patient converts the sound to its frequency components and distributes stimulation accordingly over the electrodes to the possibly suitable locations in the cochlea. These multichannel implants are now proving to be more beneficial in many cases.

One type of multielectrode arrangement uses eight electrodes. The small top part, or apex, of the cochlear spiral conveys the lower frequencies of sound, the middle turn conveys the frequencies from about 500 to 1500 hertz (cycles per second), and the long turn around the base conveys the frequencies from about 1500 to 20,000 hertz. Implanted electrodes are inserted in the cochlear outer wall to reach the outer boundaries of the turns of the cochlea. The cochlea itself is not penetrated. The sound frequencies received by the microphone of the analyzer system are assigned, by frequency, to the cochlear boundary electrodes for stimulation of an area of the nerves within. Although the stimulation and resulting sensations are not normal, useful partial identification of received words has been reported by the researchers testing this approach.

A second general approach is to insert the electrodes into a window at the end of the cochlea, the round window in the middle-ear cavity. This ap-

Internal and external components of a single-electrode cochlear implant. (Gallaudet Research Institute)

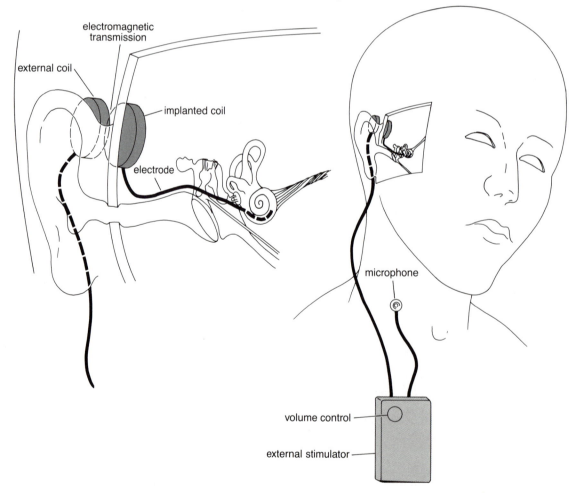

proach entails surgical insertion of a special electrode carrier that curls around along the first turn of the cochlea. The results with this system are highly encouraging. In speechreading tests with this system, the average patient scored 52 percent correct words by speechreading with the aid of the implant system versus 25 percent without it. Simple everyday sentences were often understood perfectly through the implant without speechreading. *See* SPEECHREADING.

ALTERNATIVE SITES
The auditory nerve stem and the auditory lower brain centers are also under consideration as stimulation sites for implanted electrodes. The reason for seeking new sites is the difficulty of providing separate stimulation for the different frequencies due to spread of currents between electrodes in the cochlea. Current spread is believed to be a major cause of the abnormal sound sensations from the multielectrode implants.

DESIGN AND ISSUES OF RISK
The implantation of a foreign object in the cochlea represents an invasion of peripheral parts of the nervous system (those involved in hearing and balance). Thus clinicians have been concerned to minimize the risks both long-term and short-term. So far, there have been very few adverse effects and no unmanageable complications. Nevertheless, the auditory research community is still concerned with this issue.

The least invasive cochlear implants use only one electrode inserted only a few millimeters and fixed in the round window; however, these have no possibility to direct different sound components to different nerve locations as in the multielectrode systems. Nevertheless, some single-electrode systems, when adjusted for the individual, have achieved speech perception results for some of the patients that are nearly as good as with the best multielectrodes. Current implants are predominantly of the single-electrode type.

One group of workers has developed a less invasive stimulator system. Only the lowest component of the input sound, the fundamental frequency, is presented. The electrode is held by spring tension to rest near the round window; it is removable by the patient. The fundamental frequency of speech is the pitch of the voice. Voice pitch alone is known to be a valuable aid to a deaf person in speechreading because it helps to separate the run-together appearance of words and phrases. Thus this system attempts only to provide voice pitch sensations as an aid to speechreading and control of one's own voice. This system has a good chance for success as an effective auditory aid to speechreading because the coding of voice pitch by the auditory system is sufficiently understood, and the surgery is simple and reversible.

CRITERIA FOR PATIENT SUITABILITY
Most of the present implantees are adults who became profoundly deafened after acquiring speech and language (postlingual deafness). Total deafness is also required, insofar as this can be determined. (If there is residual hearing, it is likely that the currents for electrical stimulation would destroy it.) Very young deaf children have not been considered suitable candidates because it is difficult to diagnose total deafness in these cases. Even with adults the value of a hearing aid is difficult to test, and special hearing aids for the severe-to-profound range of hearing loss are not in a high state of development. In one study a special hearing aid that presented only the voice pitch was found to be beneficial for some patients who previously reported that their conventional hearing aid was of no use. To the degree that future implant systems have greater efficacy for most candidates, these issues may become moot for many cases, although the implants would be more costly than hearing aids. *See* HEARING AIDS.

EFFICACY AND COST
A serious problem from the point of view of the patient is that it is not possible to predict how much benefit will result from implant sounds. Similar patients using identical implant systems have exhibited widely different scores when tested for speech perception, scores ranging from zero correct to 90 percent correct with simple messages. The more complex systems, with multielectrodes, are more costly, but may soon come into greater use because of their greater efficacy.

TACTILE AIDS
Even the simplest implanted system is costly and, in view of the implant risks and poor prediction of the attainable level of perception, it has been suggested that tactile aids might be a better alternative to current implants. A simple two-vibrator aid was used by two researchers to learn to identify words by reading phrases of a story to the subject via the vibrators, with prompting when the subject repeated any phrase incorrectly (the tracking procedure). Later they tested themselves in speechreading unrehearsed words of one syllable, with and without the tactile aid; their scores were 66 percent correct when speechreading with the aid, versus 47 percent when speechreading without it. Another tactile aid that represented the frequency range of speech on 16 vibrators demonstrated 80 percent words correct from a pool of 250 words, after extended training. These scores are comparable to some of the better implant scores. Implants pro-

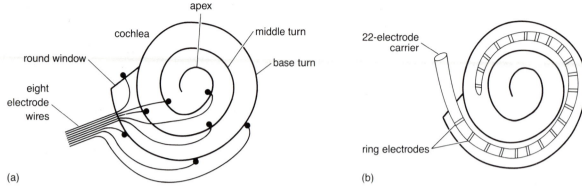

Two types of electrode arrangement for cochlear implants. (a) Eight-electrode extracochlear arrangement (after P. Banfai, S. Kubik, and G. Hartmann, "Our Extra-Scalar Operating Method of Cochlear Implantation," *Acta Oto-Laryngologica* (Stockholm), Suppl. 411:7–12, 1984). (b) A 22-electrode system (after G. M. Clark et al., "Design and Fabrication of the Banded Electrode Array," in C. W. Parkins and S. W. Anderson, eds., Cochlear Prostheses, an International Symposium, *Annals of the New York Academy of Sciences*, 405:191–201, 1983).

vide immediate sensations of sound, whereas tactile stimulation requires experience in order to be interpreted as sound. Possibly implant and tactile aids could be profitably combined. *See* Sensory aids.

Status of Implant Development
The single-electrode implant was introduced into clinical practice in late 1984. It has been approved only for use in persons 18 years or older, and provides only rudimentary hearing via a single electrode in a shallow penetration of the cochlea through the round window. Clinical research trials are under way on child implantees with this system. More advanced multielectrode implants are providing improved efficacy in research studies, and one system has been approved for clinical practice. Issues of efficacy, cost, invasiveness, diagnosis, and long-term viability still motivate considerable further research. It is apparent that auditory implants are well beyond the pioneer stage, in a second phase of development for considerably increased efficacy. However, much research remains to reach the goal of predictable, natural-sounding communication for deaf people.

Bibliography
  Banfai, P., S. Kubik, and G. Hortmann: "Our Extra-Scalar Operating Method of Cochlear Implantation," *Acta Oto-Laryngologica* (Stockholm), Suppl. 411:7–12, 1984.
  Chouard, C. H. (ed.): Second International Symposium on Cochlear Implants, *Acta Oto-Laryngologica* (Stockholm), Suppl. 411, 1984.
  Clark, G. M., et al.: "Design and Fabrication of the Banded Electrode Array," in C. W. Parkins and S. W. Anderson (eds.) Cochlear Prostheses, an International Symposium, *Annals of the New York Academy of Sciences*, 405:191–201, 1983.
  Millar, J. B., Y. C. Tong, and G. M. Clark: "Speech Processing for Cochlear Implant Prostheses," *Journal of Speech and Hearing Research*, 27:280–296, 1985.
  Pickett, J. M., and W. F. McFarland: "Auditory Implants and Tactile Aids for the Profoundly Deaf," *Journal of Speech and Hearing Research*, 28:134–150, 1985.

J. M. Pickett

COGSWELL, ALICE
(1805–1830)

Alice Cogswell inspired the founding of the first permanent school for deaf persons in the United States. She was born August 31, 1805, in Hartford, Connecticut, the third daughter of Dr. Mason Fitch Cogswell and his wife, Mary (Ledyard) Cogswell. Dr. Cogswell, one of the most prominent physicians and surgeons in the United States during his time, made valuable contributions in the field of surgery, such as introducing the operation for cataracts and pioneering an operation on the carotid artery. He was selected as the First Professor of Surgery at Yale University, although he chose not to serve, and played an important part in the formation of the Connecticut State Medical Society.

When Alice Cogswell was two years old, she became ill with cerebrospinal meningitis, or spotted fever as it was then called, which caused her deafness. She had not quite learned to talk, and whatever speech she had at that time was nearly lost by the time she was four years old. She apparently could hear a little, as indicated in a later letter from one of her sisters to their mother, in which reference is made to Alice's ability to hear a bell. Cogswell was an intelligent child and eager to learn, but still fell behind in her development, despite vigorous efforts of her parents and two older sisters to stimulate her.

Cogswell's deafness influenced her father to become deeply interested in the education of deaf people in the United States. He wanted her to have a proper education and the opportunity to develop socially, but at that time there were no schools in the United States for deaf or other disabled persons. He was reluctant to send his daughter to one of the schools for deaf students in Europe, and tried first to stimulate interest throughout Connecticut in deaf education. *See* EDUCATION: History.

Alice Cogswell met Thomas Hopkins Gallaudet about 1813. The Cogswells and the Gallaudets were neighbors, and Alice played with the Gallaudet children, with whom she communicated through her own code of simple gestures. Apparently, it was Thomas who took an interest in her and taught her to spell H-A-T, using his own hat as an example and writing the word on the ground. Cogswell quickly made the connection and, pointing to other objects, asked Gallaudet to spell the name of those objects too. Real communication between Cogswell and other people had begun. Gallaudet and another teacher, Lydia Huntley Sigourney, later taught her more words and sentences. This encounter with Cogswell influenced Gallaudet in choosing his life's work—education of deaf persons. *See* GALLAUDET, THOMAS HOPKINS.

Sigourney, a poet to some extent, may have been Cogswell's first real teacher. Since she mentions Cogswell's use of a manual alphabet, consisting of using both hands to form the letters, and sign language in her "Letters to My Pupils," it seems Cogswell may have gone with her two older sisters to Sigourney's school during the time between her first meeting with Gallaudet and the year 1817. Being eager to learn, Cogswell would ask Sigourney, whenever she had a spare moment, to teach her something new. In addition, her peers learned to fingerspell and to sign, and could communicate with her. Teachers at the school prepared manuscripts to help increase her vocabulary and improve her grammar. *See* SIGN LANGUAGES; SIGNS: Fingerspelling.

Between 1812 and 1815, Cogswell's father and Gilbert, an attorney in Hebron with five deaf children of his own, conducted an investigation to find out how many deaf people lived in Connecticut. The count was 84, a larger number than previously guessed. Their first attempts to obtain financial aid from the state legislature for establishing a school for deaf students were unsuccessful. On April 13, 1815, a group of concerned Hartford citizens, inspired by Cogswell's concern for his deaf daughter, met at his home to discuss methods for establishing such a school in the United States. They agreed to send Thomas Gallaudet, who had just graduated from a theological seminary, to Europe to study methods and bring back knowledge necessary to start a school for deaf persons. Funds collected from the Hartford community financed his trip. While in Europe, Gallaudet wrote simple letters to Cogswell, giving her religious encouragement and ad-

vising her to try to read the lips of other people and imitate their movements. He returned to New York in August 1816, bringing with him Laurent Clerc from France, who became the first deaf teacher of deaf people in America. *See* CLERC, LAURENT.

While Gallaudet was in Europe, friends at home succeeded in obtaining legislation in May 1816 to establish the "Connecticut Asylum for the education and instruction of deaf and dumb persons." The asylum opened on April 15, 1817, with seven pupils. Twelve-year-old Alice Cogswell headed the list. The name of the school was changed to the American Asylum for the Deaf and Dumb in May 1819, as more states were represented by its pupils. Cogswell continued his great interest in the school, and was the physician in charge when it opened. Today this school is known as the American School for the Deaf. *See* AMERICAN SCHOOL FOR THE DEAF.

As a student at the school, Cogswell wrote a number of compositions. Her first efforts contained many grammatical errors, but she improved as she learned more. Many of her compositions had a sober, religious tone, such as: "On the Public Worship of the Deaf and Dumb on Sunday," "On Heavenly Kingdom," "On the Sabbath," and "A Description of the World." Cogswell completed her studies at the asylum in 1823.

Cogswell seems to have been an outgoing person. She was interested in music, leaning on the piano to feel its vibrations. She is said to have carried a slate with her so she could communicate with people who did not know sign language. She did learn to speak a few words in a strained, unnatural voice. She often visited her sister Mary and her husband, Lewis Weld, who was principal of the Pennsylvania School for the Deaf, and wrote long letters to her father describing her activities in Philadelphia. Weld succeeded Gallaudet as principal of the American Asylum in 1830.

Little more is known of Cogswell until 1830, when her father died of pneumonia on December 17. Heartbroken, she became violently ill and delirious, and was unable to attend his funeral. She said that she could not live without him. Thomas Gallaudet came to pray for her in her last hours, and she died peacefully on December 30, 1830, in Hartford, only 13 days after her father. She was twenty-five years old.

Bibliography

Braddock, G. C.: "Notable Deaf Persons: Alice Cogswell," *The Frat*, March 1, 1941.

Lampson, E. R.: "Mason Fitch Cogswell" (reprinted from *Yale Journal of Biology and Medicine*), *The American Era*, vol. 26, no. 5, February 1940.

Root, G. C. (ed.): *Father and Daughter: A Collection of Cogswell Family Letters and Diaries (1772–1830)*, 1924.

Melanie Yager Williams

COMITÉ INTERNATIONAL DES SPORTS DES SOURDS

The World Games for the Deaf are the deaf athlete's "Olympic Games." They have been held every four years since they began in Paris in 1924, and are divided into summer games and winter games. Organizational responsibility for them rests with the Comité International des Sports des Sourds, a group recognized by the International Olympic Committee as having jurisdiction over all sports for deaf athletes throughout the world.

HISTORY

Deaf people generally find sports an appealing outlet for their recreational needs. The rules are clearly defined and, with the exception of some team sports, hearing is not an important factor. While deaf teams have often competed against hearing teams, the greatest benefit of sports results from interaction among participants. Communication barriers frequently prevent this from happening with hearing teams. Thus, the greatest pleasure for deaf people occurs when deaf teams compete against each other. After decades of international competition with other deaf teams, deaf people decided to hold their own "Olympic Games."

In 1924 six nations (Belgium, Czechoslovakia, France, Great Britain, the Netherlands and Poland) convened at Pershing Stadium in Paris and held the first World Games for the Deaf. The athletes competed in track and field, swimming, soccer, cycling, and shooting. At the same time, the representatives decided to form an organization to regulate future Games, and the Comité International des Sports Silencieux (CISS) was established with E. Rubens-Alcais (France) as president and A. Dresse (Belgium) as secretary.

ORGANIZATION

The Comité International des Sports Silencieux (later renamed Comité International des Sports des Sourds) was organized and conducted along the lines of the International Olympic Committee. It consists of national sports federations of deaf people and is run by an executive committee of eight persons, each from a different country. All officers as well as delegates must be deaf. Business at its internal meetings and at its biennial congress is conducted in international sign language (Gestuno) without the assistance of interpreters. See SIGN LANGUAGES: International Gestures.

New federations applying for membership must demonstrate that they represent deaf athletes in their country, that they have the recognition of their National Olympic Committee, and that a majority of the members of the board of directors are deaf.

The members of the executive committee serve four-year terms. There is no limit on the number of terms they may serve. The officers of CISS are selected by the executive committee from its members. CISS is staffed by volunteers, none of whom is full-time or paid. Its revenue consists solely of annual dues, various fines, and competition fees. Records are compiled and published annually. A bulletin is printed quarterly carrying results of international competitions.

In 1966 the International Olympic Committee awarded its prestigious Olympic Cup in recognition of CISS's exemplary service to the cause of sports and the Olympic spirit.

GAMES

The Summer Games are held one year after the Olympic Games, and the Winter Games are held two years later. Host countries are selected by majority vote at the congress six years in advance. The Games follow the rules and principles of the Olympic Games and have the patronage of the International Olympic Committee. Competitors in the Games must have an average hearing level for speech greater than 55dB in the better ear in order to be eligible. An audiogram must be submitted in ad-

Sites of Summer World Games for the Deaf

Year	Site	Nations
1924	Paris	9
1928	Amsterdam	10
1931	Nuremberg	14
1935	London	12
1939	Stockholm	13
1949	Copenhagen	14
1953	Brussels	16
1957	Milan	25
1961	Helsinki	24
1965	Washington, D.C.	27
1969	Belgrade	33
1973	Malmo	32
1977	Bucharest	34
1981	Cologne	31
1985	Los Angeles	28

Sites of Winter World Games for the Deaf

Year	Site	Nations
1949	Seefeld, Austria	5
1953	Oslo, Norway	6
1957	Oberammergau, Germany	8
1959	Montana, Switzerland	8
1963	Are, Sweden	12
1967	Berchtesgaden, Germany	12
1971	Adelboden, Switzerland	13
1975	Lake Placid, New York, U.S.A.	14
1979	Meribel, France	14
1983	Madonna di Campiglio, Italy	16

vance. An audiologist makes spot checks of competitors and retests all event winners. Hearing aids may not be worn during competition. *See* AUDIOLOGIC CLASSIFICATION.

The Summer World Games for the Deaf have been celebrated every four years since 1924 except during World War II. Competitions are held in track and field, swimming, wrestling, cycling, shooting, tennis, table tennis, badminton, soccer, team handball, basketball, volleyball, and water polo. With the exception of wrestling, cycling, soccer, and water polo, all sports are open to women as well as men. Gold, silver, and bronze medals are awarded to the first three finishers and diplomas to the first six places. At the award ceremonies the medal winners' flags are raised and the CISS anthem is played. At the Winter Games, the sports are limited to the alpine and nordic ski events and to speed skating.

The Games are opened with colorful ceremonies that include a parade of athletes and the raising of the CISS flag. The Olympic torch is not used, but patronage by the International Olympic Committee permits the Olympic flag to be flown.

Competitions are conducted under the same rules as the Olympic Games. Modifications are made, however, in order to make auditory cues visible. For example, at the 14th Games held in Cologne in 1981, the starter's pistol also activated strobe lights placed in front of the starting blocks. Referees of some events wave flags in addition to blowing their whistles. Some athletes can hear the whistle and stop play, causing other competitors to follow suit; others notice the motion of the flag. No special equipment is used or worn by the athletes.

Bibliography

Comité, International des Sports des Sourds; *CISS Handbook*, (50th anniversary ed.) 1974, and 1985.

Jerald M. Jordan

COMMUNICATION OUTLOOK

Communication Outlook is an international quarterly publication focusing exclusively on communication aids and techniques for people who cannot speak. These aids and techniques range from simple pictures that a person points at for communicating a basic need, to sign language, to computer-based electronic aids equipped with voice synthesizers which speak the words, phrases, and sentences that the user chooses. These various modes of communication are grouped into a category known as augmentative communication. Cerebral palsy, amyotrophic lateral sclerosis, head injury, hearing impairment, stroke, and illness are just some of the physical limitations that prevent a person

from being able to speak, and often to write. The communication-enhancement field embodies all individuals and organizations interested in people who cannot speak and in augmentative communication. *See* SENSORY AIDS.

Communication Outlook is more than a publication, as it provides a regular forum for individuals interested in augmentative communication to exchange views and establish contacts. Further, it aims to assist the delivery system of communication aids to every individual who needs one.

COMMUNITY OF READERS

The community of readers of *Communication Outlook* spans many backgrounds. Included are users and potential users of communication aids and their parents, family members, and friends, as well as speech pathologists, occupational and physical therapists, social workers, teachers, educational administrators and supervisors, physicians, psychologists, government officials, computer scientists, inventors, manufacturers, distributors, and electrical, mechanical, and rehabilitation engineers.

FEATURES

The main purposes of *Communication Outlook* are improvement of communication for individuals experiencing communication handicaps and promotion of communication among professionals in the communication-enhancement field. Its goal is to communicate to its readers developments and progress in the field. The format consists of regular features combined with articles from readers. Features include: "News on Aids," articles on communication aids that are commercially available and under development, as well as components used to build aids: "New Materials," descriptions of new publications and resources available; "Where the Action Is," reports from readers of centers and groups working on various aspects of communication enhancement; "Interfaces/Accessories," information on interfacing and augmenting communication aids; "Software," descriptions of new computer software written or adapted specifically for use by individuals experiencing handicaps; "Tips," innovative methods, procedures, teaching strategies, and uses of materials shared by readers; "Advocacy Update," pertinent advocacy issues, including new groups, strategies, and successes; "Courses Offered," detailing courses available to professionals in communication enhancement; "Anybody Know?," questions from readers to readers; and "Coming Up," a calendar of events of regional, national, and international interest.

Articles from readers include narratives by people describing their experiences with their communication aids; articles by parents detailing their children's struggles to obtain communication; articles by communication-aid developers stressing the need for research, funding, education, and support; and articles dealing with funding, legal aspects, terminology, research, engineering, and advocacy.

Articles of 2000 words or less may be submitted for publication. Articles should relate to the topic of augmentative communication, and may include opinions, ideas, or technical information the writer would like to share with others in the field. Relevant photographs are welcome.

ISAAC

Communication Outlook is edited and published by the Artificial Language Laboratory at Michigan State University in partnership with the Trace Research and Development Center on Communication, Control and Computer Access for Handicapped Individuals, University of Wisconsin, Madison. It is an official publication of the International Society for Augmentative and Alternative Communication (ISAAC). Before the society was formed in May 1983, *Communication Outlook* was a publication of the International Action Group for Communication Enhancement.

ISAAC enables *Communication Outlook* readers to belong to an organization linking people throughout the world whose common goal is to advance the transdisciplinary field of augmentative communication aids and techniques. As the one international organization for the entire field of augmentative communication, ISAAC is dedicated to: the involvement of consumers, an international information exchange, giving attention to augmentative communication interaction and integration into all life situations, having highly developed countries help developing countries, increased awareness in communities around the world to the needs and accomplishments of individuals experiencing communication handicaps, publications and conferences to upgrade professional knowledge, a greater use of systems to complement one another, professional training, and service standards.

Members of ISAAC are entitled to a one-year subscription to *Communication Outlook*, as well as a special reduced subscription rate to *Augmentative and Alternative Communication*, ISAAC's official international transdisciplinary journal, and to *Communicating Together*, a quarterly publication of the Blissymbolics Communication Institute in Toronto, Ontario, Canada. ISAAC members are also entitled to reduced conference fees for conferences organized by ISAAC and to receive and be included in a registry of ISAAC members and others concerned about or working in augmentative communication. In addition, special arrangements will

be made available to members concerning ISAAC conference proceedings and other ISAAC publications.

Tamara L. Redburn

CONFERENCE OF EDUCATIONAL ADMINISTRATORS SERVING THE DEAF

The Conference of Educational Administrators Serving the Deaf (CEASD) has had three official names. At its founding in 1869 it was called the Conference of Superintendents and Principals of American Schools for the Deaf. By 1928 it had become the Conference of Executives of American Schools for the Deaf; with that name it was incorporated under the laws of the State of Maryland in 1958. The name was changed to the present one in 1980 to eliminate the exclusionary geographic and scholastic references. While the Canadian members have never explicitly protested the use of "American" in the organization's title, the word connotes the United States more often than it does North America. The elimination of "Schools" was necessitated by the tendency to educate deaf students in integrated settings. By 1980, for instance, only half of the deaf students known to the Annual Survey of Hearing Impaired Children and Youth were in residential schools, while almost half were in day classes. Among educators of deaf students, the organization is unofficially known as the Conference in contrast to its companion organization the Convention (Convention of American Instructors of the Deaf, abbreviated CAID). The histories of the two organizations entwine. The Convention of American Instructors of the Deaf was established first, but CEASD has generally been considered the more powerful. The two groups share interests, publications, and personnel. *See* CONVENTION OF AMERICAN INSTRUCTORS OF THE DEAF.

The impetus behind the establishment of CEASD was Edward Miner Gallaudet. Then president of the Columbia Institution for the Deaf and Dumb (later called Gallaudet College), in Washington, D.C., Gallaudet wished to unite school principals behind his approach to the issue of communication methods in the classroom. Although that meeting was referred to as the sixth Convention of American Instructors of the Deaf, all of those invited to attend the inaugural gathering were principals of schools for deaf students. The confusion between the two organizations was rapidly dispelled once CEASD was formed by the 17 executives who attended that first conference. *See* GALLAUDET, EDWARD MINER; GALLAUDET COLLEGE; HISTORY: Sign Language Controversy.

The convening of the fourteenth CEASD in 1928 witnessed a move to reorganize CEASD and merge it with the National Education Association (NEA). Meetings were held with the leadership of the National Education Association Department of Superintendence, which eventually rejected the automatic admission of administrators of day, private, and denominational schools for deaf students, a courtesy that would be extended to the head of any state school. For that reason, CEASD representatives recommended against the merger. Since that time, CEASD has not considered any other efforts to join it with another group.

PURPOSES

CEASD was founded "to promote the management and operation of schools for the deaf along the broadest and most effective lines and to further and promote the general welfare of the deaf." In 1980 the leadership revised the statement of purposes to read "the improvement and advancement of a continuum of educational opportunities which promote the general welfare of the deaf in North America, and to encourage the efficient management and operation of schools, programs, program service centers, and governmental units providing for the needs of the deaf." The objectives remain essentially the same, but the limiting phrase "schools for the deaf" in the first statement has been broadened to "schools, programs, etc.," reflecting the change in constituency that led to the change in the organization's name. The revised statement is also less encompassing than the first, eliminating the commitment to "promote the general welfare," a phrase that would justify almost any beneficial action. Instead, the second statement specifies only "educational opportunities that promote the general welfare."

ACTIVITIES

One of the means by which CEASD carries out its self-imposed mandate to promote educational opportunities is through biennial meetings of its membership. For its first 62 years, the meetings were held sporadically; only 15 were called between 1868 and 1930. By 1930 the members had agreed to meet every three years, but World War II interrupted that schedule. Annual meetings became the rule from 1948 to the present. In odd-numbered years, the CEASD meeting is held in conjunction with the Convention of American Instructors of the Deaf. At those meetings, CEASD usually sets aside one day to conduct its own business, sharing the convention schedule's presentations for the remaining time. The conferences in the even-numbered years include presentations of papers and discussions that are spread over four or five days. The proceedings of these latter meetings are usu-

ally printed by one of the schools and distributed to the membership. Since 1951 the proceedings of the meetings held with the Convention of American Instructors of the Deaf have been included as a section in CEASD's semiannual publication.

Another vehicle for carrying out CEASD's purposes is the certification program for teachers of deaf students. In 1960 CEASD joined with the Convention of American Instructors of the Deaf and the Alexander Graham Bell Association in a confederation called the Council on Education of the Deaf (CED). This organization serves to coordinate efforts by the three groups in teacher certification and related areas. The Council on Education of the Deaf sets the standards for teachers, conducts the evaluations of teacher training programs, and issues the certificates. *See* ALEXANDER GRAHAM BELL ASSOCIATION FOR THE DEAF; TEACHING PROFESSION: Certification.

From 1966 to 1982 CEASD held various contracts with Captioned Films for the Deaf, a division of Special Education Programs in the Department of Education. CEASD set up a distribution center for captioned educational films. This generated sufficient income to enable CEASD to open a permanent office. The office has been located in the National Association of the Deaf building, Halex House, since 1976. As with most of its activities, CEASD shares the office with the Convention of American Instructors of the Deaf.

CEASD has also been active in the legislative arena, particularly at the national level. Its executives have appeared frequently as witnesses before congressional committees and as advocates in congressional offices.

One of CEASD's best-known activities is its joint sponsorship of the *American Annals of the Deaf*. The journal was founded 18 years before CEASD came into being, but occasionally CEASD has been the agency responsible for its publication. Since 1948 a committee of four members each from the Convention of American Instructors of the Deaf and CEASD has administered the journal. *See* AMERICAN ANNALS OF THE DEAF.

GOVERNANCE AND MEMBERSHIP

A president, president-elect, secretary, and treasurer head CEASD. Policies are set by these officers and an 11-member board of directors. The requirement that members must be superintendents or principals heading programs for deaf students has been dropped in favor of the broader inclusion of those who have administrative roles in educational programs for deaf students.

CEASD shares an executive director with the Convention of American Instructors of the Deaf. CEASD also has a large number of standing committees, as well as ad hoc committees. Among the standing committees are ones for educational research, public relations, legislation, statistics, and school accreditation. These committees make possible the broad involvement of the membership in the affairs of the association.

Jerome D. Schein

CONVENTION OF AMERICAN INSTRUCTORS OF THE DEAF

One of the oldest professional organizations concerned with education in the United States, the Convention of American Instructors of the Deaf (CAID) was founded in 1850. In that year it held its first meeting, which was the first national convention of deaf educators held anywhere in the world, at the New York Institution for the Deaf. Germany held a similar meeting in 1884, and Great Britain in 1895, and there were international congresses on education of deaf persons beginning in 1878. The CAID's inaugural occurred four decades after the first state-supported school for deaf students was established in Hartford, Connecticut, in 1817, indicating the degree to which educators of deaf students saw their profession as differing from general education and the depth of their commitment to improving their craft. *See* EDUCATION: History; INTERNATIONAL CONGRESS ON THE EDUCATION OF THE DEAF.

The convention was initiated by educators at the New York Institution for the Deaf, who desired to bring together their colleagues "to compare methods, to impart instruction, explain theories, make acquaintances, and so bring about harmony of design, unity of action, and thus aid in the accomplishment of the object all had in view; namely, the education and betterment of the deaf and dumb." They arranged for the presentation of papers, and the participants responded with resolutions, among which was the one recommending adoption of the *American Annals of the Deaf* as the official and continuing publication of CAID. Four more meetings had convened by 1858, at which convention a sixth was set for 1860. The advent of the Civil War prevented it from occurring until 1868. That meeting, however, was limited to school executives, and it later proved to be the first meeting of the Conference of Educational Administrators Serving the Deaf (CEASD). *See* AMERICAN ANNALS OF THE DEAF; CONFERENCE OF EDUCATIONAL ADMINISTRATORS SERVING THE DEAF.

The next CAID meeting took place in 1870 and every four years thereafter until 1893. The 1893 convention met at the Chicago World's Fair, in conjunction with the International Congress on the Education of the Deaf (ICED). Joint meetings with the International Congress came about again in 1933

and 1963, the other two occasions on which these international meetings have been held in the United States. Since 1893 CAID has met every two years up to the present. The Conference of Educational Administrators Serving the Deaf, the organization of administrators which meets annually, combines its odd-year gatherings with those of CAID.

In 1897 CAID was incorporated by an act of the U.S. Congress. As a result, its biennial proceedings were published at government expense by the Government Printing Office until the 1980s. This unusual move of seeking incorporation from the federal legislature grew out of Edward Miner Gallaudet's success in securing a charter from the college for deaf students, first known as the Columbia Institution for the Deaf and Dumb and later as Gallaudet College. It was through his urging that CAID chose to incorporate in the District of Columbia rather than in one of the states. This decision also shows the extent to which Gallaudet dominated CAID during the beginning of its middle period of development. *See* GALLAUDET, EDWARD MINER; GALLAUDET COLLEGE.

CAID has been involved in efforts to merge with other professional groups that have shared its interests in the education of deaf students. In 1895 overtures were made to the American Association to Promote the Teaching of Speech to the Deaf. The latter organization was headed by Alexander Graham Bell, whose positions on deafness and the education of deaf children conflicted with those of CAID's Edward Miner Gallaudet. The attempts to reconcile the groups failed, but with the death of both men, the merger pressures resumed. In 1920, along with a third group, the Society of Progressive Oral Advocates, a meeting was held at the Mount Airy (Pennsylvania) School for the Deaf. The suggestions to bring the three organizations under a single administration did not succeed. *See* ALEXANDER GRAHAM BELL ASSOCIATION FOR THE DEAF; BELL, ALEXANDER GRAHAM.

PURPOSES

The purposes of CAID are "promotion of the education of the deaf on the broadest, most advanced, and practical lines and to secure the harmonious union in the organization of all persons actually engaged in educating the deaf in America." CAID is clear that, by the phrase "in America," it includes educators in the United States and Canada but not Mexico. Unlike the Conference of Educational Administrators Serving the Deaf, the CAID has not felt it necessary to change its name.

ACTIVITIES

The biennial conventions have been a major vehicle for furthering the objectives of CAID. Attendance, which varies with economic conditions, is usually substantial, representing a large portion of the CAID membership. Meetings are held shortly after the closing of schools in the summer months, thus enabling a residential school to host the event and to provide inexpensive accommodations in its dormitories.

The meeting format has changed from a series of lectures and discussions to an increasing number of workshops led by experts in the focus area. Papers are still given, but the emphasis has shifted to a more active participation on the part of those who attend the conventions. The content remains broad, embracing almost every topic of interest to educators of deaf students, from preschool to higher education, from fingerpainting to mathematics, but with language development a virtual constant among the subjects considered by the participants.

Publication of the *American Annals of the Deaf* supports the organization's goal of advancing education of deaf students. CAID adopted the journal, which had been published for three years by the American School for the Deaf. When CAID found it could not manage the journal, it turned in 1917 to the Conference of Educational Administrators Serving the Deaf, which assumed full responsibility for its publication unti 1942. From that point until 1969, CAID helped to subsidize the journal. Most schools were assessed for the number of teachers they employed, and were sent that number of copies. In 1969 CAID made the *Annals* a benefit of membership, thus regularizing the subscription base of the journal. CAID continues as an equal partner with the Conference in the management of the *Annals* by appointing four members to the eight-member publications committee. *See* AMERICAN SCHOOL FOR THE DEAF.

GOVERNANCE AND MEMBERSHIP

While its title suggests that its members are all teachers of deaf students, CAID also includes administrators among its membership. During the twentieth century, the leadership of CAID has come almost entirely from the executives of schools. This changed in 1974, when Robert Davila, then a professor at Gallaudet College, noted that elections were controlled by those "present and voting" at the biennial conventions. The superintendents had taken advantage of this provision in the bylaws, being assured that they could attend each meeting and being easily organized through their annual contacts at the Conference of Educational Administrators Serving the Deaf. Thus, though the instructors greatly outnumbered the executives, the latter dominated the organization. Davila organized the large number of delegates to the 1974 convention and succeeded in winning the election for president. He became the first deaf person to hold that office.

In addition to the president, CAID officers include the president-elect, secretary, treasurer, and eight directors. Since 1969 CAID has shared an executive director with the Conference of Education Administrators Serving the Deaf. The executive director maintains offices in Halex House, the building owned by the National Association of the Deaf. Staff size fluctuates with funding for additional activities in which the Conference and CAID occasionally engage, such as the contract for selection and captioning of Captioned Films for the Deaf. *See* NATIONAL ASSOCIATION OF THE DEAF.

Jerome D. Schein

CORNFORTH, JOHN WARCUP
(1917–   )

John Warcup Cornforth, distinguished scientist and joint Nobel Prize winner for chemistry (1975), was profoundly deaf from otosclerosis for most of his life. *See* EAR: Pathology.

Cornforth was born on September 7, 1917, in Sydney, Australia. His hearing impairment, perceptible from the age of 10, became serious by the age of 14. Despite this disability, Cornforth entered Sydney University at the age of 16 after studying at Sydney High School. He could not hear the lectures, but he learned chemistry from performing his own experiments and by reading original literature. He graduated in 1937 with a bachelor of science degree and first-class honors and a university medal, and in 1938 received his master's. In 1939 he was awarded one of two 1851 Exhibition Scholarships, open to all the science faculties of Australian universities for doctoral studies in England. The other scholarship recipient was Rita H. Harradence, another organic chemist from Sydney University. They traveled together to Oxford University, and were married in 1941. That same year the Cornforths received their doctor's degrees.

John Cornforth's early research in Australia was principally on natural products from plants. At Oxford, his work with Sir Robert Robinson, a Nobel Prize recipient (1947), on the chemistry of penicillin and steroids culminated in 1951 in a total synthesis of epiandrosterone.

From 1946 to 1962 Cornforth was employed in the Mill Hill Research Laboratories of the British Medical Research Council, where he developed his basic approach to the stereochemistry of enzyme processes. Stereochemistry deals with the three-dimensional architecture of molecules, and it is in the biochemical applications that Cornforth made his most significant contributions. These studies came to fruition during his next appointment in 1962 as joint director, with George Popjak, of the Milstead Laboratory of Chemical Enzymology of

John Warcup Cornforth and Rita Cornforth.

Shell Research Limited, Sittingbourne, Kent. This laboratory was set up by Lord Rothschild, then director of research for Shell, to enable Cornforth and Popjak to work together. Cornforth's contract with Shell stipulated that half his working time be devoted to research specified by the company, and the remaining time spent on personal scientific pursuits. The collaboration between the two scientists spanned 20 years. In 1965 Cornforth and Popjak were jointly awarded the CIBA Medal of the Biochemical Society. The joint award of the Davy Medal of the Royal Society followed in 1968. While at the Milstead Laboratory, Cornforth also held two professorships: associate professor of molecular sciences at Warwick (1965–1971), and visiting professor of chemistry at Sussex (1971–1975). He was Pedler and Robert Robinson Lecturer to the Chemical Society (1968–1969; 1971); Max Tishler Lecturer, Harvard (1970); and Sandin Lecturer, University of Alberta (1977). From 1975 until his retirement in 1982 Cornforth was Royal Society Research Professor at the University of Sussex.

Cornforth received many honors in addition to his Nobel Prize and the Davy and CIBA medals. He was made a Companion of the British Empire in 1972 and was knighted five years later. He became a Fellow of the Royal Society in 1953, and in 1962 received the society's highest honor, the Copley Medal, in recognition of his distinguished research on the stereochemically controlled synthesis and biosyntheses of biologically important molecules. The Chemical Society awarded him its Corday-Morgan Medal and Prize (1953) and Flintoff Medal

(1966). Other distinctions include the Stouffer Prize (1967), the Ernest Guenther Award of the American Chemical Society (1969), and the Prix Roussel (1972). He received honorary doctorates from the universities of Zurich (1975); Oxford, Warwick, Dublin, and Liverpool (1976); and Aberdeen, Hull, Sussex, and Sydney (1977). He became an honorary Fellow of St. Catherine's College, Oxford, in 1976.

Cornforth transmitted his knowledge essentially through literature (approximately 185 publications). However, he did lecture without great difficulty, apart from a certain flatness in his delivery. Deafness did not significantly affect his speech, but he attended meetings and symposia less than most scientists. *See* SPEECH.

Cornforth communicated mainly by lipreading and writing and did not practice sign language. He found compensation for his disability in his intellectual life. He was a strong chess player and held (as of 1985) the Australian record, set up in 1936, for simultaneous blindfold chess against seeing opponents (12 games: won 8, drew 2, lost 2). He read poetry as a substitute for music and collected and wrote limericks. Gardening, however, was his favorite recreation. *See* SPEECHREADING.

The most important influence in Cornforth's life was his wife. An eminent scientist in her own right, Dr. Rita Cornforth was not only his most consistent scientific coworker, but assisted him with his communication problems. On occasion she sat in the front row at lectures, indicating to him by almost imperceptible gestures whether the pitch of his voice was too high or too low, and repeating questions from the back of the hall that he was unable to lipread.

Bibliography
Aural News, no. 132, Summer 1976.
Royal Society News, issue 16, July 1982.
Science, vol. 190, November 21, 1975.
Who's Who, 1983.

Kenneth Lysons

COUNCIL OF ORGANIZATIONS SERVING THE DEAF

The Workshop on Community Development through Organizations of and for the Deaf (the Second Fort Monroe Workshop), which met in Fort Monroe, Virginia, in April 1961, recommended that an organization be developed that would bring together all advocacy groups interested in promoting the welfare of deaf people. The workshop was funded by a grant from the federal agency responsible for vocational rehabilitation, in keeping with the concept that rehabilitation is facilitated by the active participation of the consumers of its services, rather than seeing them as weak individuals who must be assisted at every level of development.

FOUNDING

For the first time in the brief history of federal rehabilitation programs, the workshop brought together a sample of deaf leadership in a national meeting that was completely managed by deaf people. The government did not insist on able-bodied people coordinating a national meeting. This rejection of paternalism encouraged the participants to consider their problems without preconceived notions about what could or could not be done. They recognized that one of the hindrances to achieving the kinds of legislative and administrative responses they desired from the federal level of government was the lack of unity in their approaches. Deaf people lacked an agreed-upon list of priorities; they did not have a unified strategy for attaining these objectives; and they needed a forum in which to mediate disputes between those whose principal interests focused on deafness and deaf people. The workshop called for an organization that would bring together the principal groups involved in the affairs of the deaf community—whether deaf membership organizations or voluntary organizations that provided services to deaf people—so they could discuss issues and resolve differences of opinion about priorities and strategies while outside of the scrutiny of the federal officials and legislators they hoped to influence on their behalf. *See* REHABILITATION: Administration.

An ad hoc group of leaders of six national organizations—National Association of the Deaf, National Congress of Jewish Deaf, National Fraternal Society of the Deaf, International Catholic Deaf Association, Conference of Executives of American Schools for the Deaf, and Registry of Interpreters for the Deaf—plus representatives of the Vocational Rehabilitation Administration met in February 1965. As a result, a one-year grant was awarded to the National Health Council to study the existing organizations of deaf people and to recommend a structure for a national coordinating body or council. A set of proposed bylaws were presented to a meeting of 14 prospective organizations at a meeting held in Chicago in 1966. By the end of the year nine organizations ratified the bylaws, and in New York in 1967, the Council of Organizations Serving the Deaf (COSD) was incorporated. *See* CONFERENCE OF EDUCATIONAL ADMINISTERS SERVING THE DEAF; NATIONAL ASSOCIATION OF THE DEAF; NATIONAL FRATERNAL SOCIETY OF THE DEAF; REGISTRY OF INTERPRETERS FOR THE DEAF.

ORGANIZATION

The federal rehabilitation agency awarded the council a five-year grant to develop cooperation among those agencies interested in the rehabilitation of deaf clients. The membership comprised mostly of those organizations that were concerned with deafness: Alexander Graham Bell Association for the Deaf, American Athletic Association of the Deaf, Board for Missions to the Deaf, the Lutheran Church (Missouri Synod), Canadian Association of the Deaf, Conference of Church Workers among the Deaf (later, Episcopal Conference of the Deaf), Conference of Executives of American Schools for the Deaf (later, the Conference of Educators and Administrators of Schools for the Deaf), Convention of American Instructors of the Deaf, Episcopal Conference of the Deaf, Gallaudet College Alumni Association, International Catholic Deaf Association, National Association of the Deaf, National Association of Hearing and Speech Agencies (later, the National Association for Hearing and Speech Action, now a part of the American Speech-Language-Hearing Association), National Congress of the Jewish Deaf, National Fraternal Society of the Deaf, Professional Rehabilitation Workers with the Adult Deaf (later, the American Deafness and Rehabilitation Association), Registry of Interpreters for the Deaf, and as associate members, the Board of Missions of the United Methodist Church, the Deafness Research Foundation, and the Ephphatha Mission for the Deaf and Blind. Eight of the 19 members and associates were organizations of deaf people; the remaining 11 provided services to deaf people as their sole or principal purpose for existing or advocated on behalf of deaf people. Not all were members at the start of the organization, and as time progressed, some of the original member organizations withdrew their support for the council. For example, between 1970 and 1971 the Conference of Church Workers among the Deaf and the Alexander Graham Bell Association for the Deaf withdrew and the Episcopal Conference of the Deaf joined the council. *See* ALEXANDER GRAHAM BELL ASSOCIATION FOR THE DEAF; AMERICAN ATHLETIC ASSOCIATION OF THE DEAF; AMERICAN SPEECH-LANGUAGE-HEARING ASSOCIATION; CONVENTION OF AMERICAN INSTRUCTORS OF THE DEAF; GALLAUDET COLLEGE ALUMNI ASSOCIATION.

The first executive director of the council was Mervin D. Garretson, a member of the Gallaudet College faculty who had been deafened early in life. Alfred Cranwill, son of deaf parents and a retired administrator of a school for deaf children, joined as the assistant executive director, and Lee Katz, a parent of a deaf child, took the position of administrative assistant. Garretson left the council to become the principal of the Model Secondary School for the Deaf when it opened in 1970. He was succeeded by the council's president-elect, Edward C. Carney. Carney remained as the chief executive of the council until its end. Throughout its few years of existence, the council had a deaf person directing its activities. *See* GALLAUDET COLLEGE; MODEL SECONDARY SCHOOL FOR THE DEAF.

PROGRAMS

The council had two means of achieving its principal objective of providing a single voice on issues of interest to deaf people. The first was to hold meetings of the council at which representatives of the constituent organizations debated the matters brought before it. The second was to hold national and sectional meetings to which all interested persons were invited, at which a particular topic would be covered in depth by experts from within the field and through panel discussions by interested participants, and at which comments and questions from members of the audiences were answered. The council conducted seven forums: New Horizons on Deafness, The Deaf Man and the World, Legal Rights of the Deaf, Medical Aspects of Deafness, Perspectives in Education of the Deaf, The Deaf Child and His Family, and Organizations and Agencies Serving the Deaf.

These meetings were held at various locations throughout the United States, and they attracted increasingly larger attendance. For example, the 1970 conference, The Deaf Man and the Law, was held in Chicago, where over 200 persons registered; the 1973 Memphis, Tennessee, meeting planned for 250 persons but registered over 400 people. Each meeting prior to the Memphis conference had had a keynote speaker, but the COSD planning committee could not agree on one for the sensitive issue of education of deaf children. Instead, the conference opened with a "Love-In," conducted by Leo Buscaglia, who specialized in creating goodwill among participants. The meetings progressed without the anticipated hostilities, and those in attendance expressed surprise and satisfaction at the smoothness and fruitfulness of the discussions.

At the conclusion of the forums, edited transcripts of the papers and the ensuing discussions were published and initially distributed without charge. The forums also provided material for the council members to discuss in their regular meetings. The hope was that the organizational representatives would return to their respective groups and gain support for the actions agreed upon by the council.

In addition to these two activities directed at gaining consensus among the council's member organizations, the council had other objectives. Its grant from the federal government specified that it would: be a clearinghouse for information about deafness; strive to eliminate social and economic barriers for deaf people; coordinate and strengthen the services of its member organizations; act as a liaison between organizations interested in deafness and other organizations; assist efforts to prevent deafness; and mobilize individuals and organizations to improve deaf persons' opportunities for advancement in society. The drafters of those objectives did not anticipate the eventual reaction of the council's member organizations to goals which, in most cases, closely resembled their own. Instead of seeing the council as providing additional support, many of the organizations began to regard the council as a competitor. This attitude was shaped by circumstances outside the control of the council.

DEMISE

When the council's five-year federal grant was coming to a close, Carney negotiated a three-year extension with the federal government. It was intended to carry the council through 1975, but in 1973 the federal government abruptly announced that further funding would be terminated in that year. This unexpected move left the council in desperate financial straits. Its offices had been recently moved to Columbia, Maryland, a city near both Washington, D.C., and Baltimore, Maryland. Because in its original conception the council was to become self-sustaining, it had begun a campaign to seek individual memberships—a move that was probably fatal. The member organizations found that they were in competition on several fronts. First, the council was approaching people who were already pledged to the member organizations or whom the member organizations would have liked to recruit. Second, the council had to seek financial aid through grants, again putting it in competition with its member organizations, many of whom were also vigorously pursuing funding from the same sources. Third, as noted above, most of the secondary objectives of the council overlapped the member organizations' own goals. In a sense, the council was competing for achievement. This competition led to more than one organization claiming credit for actions that an organization might feel, rightly or not, was its sole doing. This led to bitterness between the council and its member organizations. When the federal funds ceased, the organization continued for a brief period, then disbanded when faced with the inability to raise adequate funds.

SIGNIFICANCE

While the organization collapsed nationally, it left a strong legacy. Several states have adopted the council model. Connecticut, for example, still has a Connecticut Council of Organizations Serving the Deaf. Even at the local level there are remnants of the council's philosophy. New York City continues to have a Council of Organizations Serving the Deaf, as does Baltimore. Though these state and local organizations may lack the glamour that a national body has, they can perform the much-needed task of coordination without drawing to themselves attention that, in the long run, might prove to be counterproductive. A part of what led to the destruction of the council might have been its immodesty, an unwillingness to set itself up as a servant to its members instead of as a superorganization.

Under the leadership of Executive Secretary Frederick C. Schreiber, the National Association of the Deaf attempted to establish a replacement for the council soon after its demise. The Mutual Alliance Plan (MAP) began to take shape in 1976, and by 1979 it had been considered by many of the same organizations that had formerly belonged to COSD. The essence of the plan was to promote active discussions among the organizations concerned with deafness and deaf people. In an effort to avoid the mistakes that the council had made, MAP would have no elaborate staff, no expensive headquarters, and no other goals than the promotion of cooperative action among its members, and it would seek no grants or individual memberships. MAP would be solely a means to coordinated efforts on behalf of deaf people. MAP would be able to employ a lobbyist on Capitol Hill, something that the individual organizations could not afford. This action, if it came to pass, would facilitate the single objective of coordination of activities among the various organizations. *See* SCHREIBER, FREDERICK CARL.

Schreiber recognized that the idea had to overcome the council's earlier failure and that he would have to be patient. He worked assiduously to convince the leaders of other organizations to join in MAP. Unfortunately, he died in 1979 before he could bring MAP into being. His devotion to that concept was apparently not immediately shared by his successors, and efforts to create MAP or a similar organization slowed. The idea of coordination at the national level, however, has not passed into complete obscurity. Meetings among various organizations of deaf people have continued, but without success.

Jerome D. Schein

COURT DECISIONS

The decisions in four important court cases have upheld the rights of deaf people to equal treatment under the law.

In *Pyles v. Kamka*, the provision of services to deaf prisoners in the criminal justice system was addressed in a consent decree dated February 27, 1980, between a deaf man, James A. Pyles, Jr., and the State of Maryland. The state agreed to provide a qualified interpreter so that a deaf prisoner could participate in and benefit from on-the-job training,

vocational, or education programs; psychological, psychiatric, or medical care; counseling; and prison disciplinary hearings.

Eckstein v. Kirby dealt with the issue of jury duty; for many years handicapped people in the United States, including deaf people, were automatically excused from serving on juries. In 1978 Teresa Eckstein, a deaf woman living in Arkansas, decided to take legal action after she was rejected for jury duty by an Arkansas court because of her hearing impairment. Like many states, Arkansas has a state law that disqualifies people who have substantially impaired hearing or vision, or who cannot speak or understand English, from serving on juries in Arkansas courts.

In the criminal trials of *People v. Lang* and *Jackson v. Indiana*, the deaf individuals Donald Lang and Theon Jackson were unable to speak, read, write, sign, or understand sign language. Lacking even the rudiments of education and without the ability to communicate effectively in any manner, they presented the legal system with unusual dilemmas. They could neither communicate with their attorneys nor understand the charges brought against them. Thus, they could not participate in their own defense. Lang, in particular, was charged with a very serious offense, making him a potential threat to the community.

Pyles v. Kamka

The deaf individual involved in this precedent-setting case, James A. Pyles, Jr., was a prisoner in Maryland, at a medium-security prison. Following a visit from his brother, he was charged with "improper visitation and attempting to shove an officer out of his way after being told he could not have a visit in this manner." Specifically, the State of Maryland accused Pyles of disobeying a lawful order, cursing or using vulgar language, assault, inciting or creating a disturbance, and resisting or interfering with an officer, Since the charges were thought to be a major infraction, the state scheduled the case to be heard by a prison disciplinary team.

According to the rules of the prison, all prisoners had the following rights: (1) to have representation and to have an inmate or employee of the prison to act as representative; (2) to call one or more witnesses; (3) to question witnesses; and (4) to testify. The rules also provided that no rights could be reasonably withheld or restricted during prison disciplinary proceedings.

Pyles requested a "special deaf interpreter" to be present at the disciplinary hearing. Personnel at the prison advised him that they would arrange for "a person to interpret the incident for you so they will understand." No interpreter was present at the disciplinary hearing, however, and the prison personnel concluded that no one was available to interpret. At the conclusion of the hearing, the state told Pyles that he would lose five days good time and that he would be transferred to a maximum security institution to see a psychologist.

Prior to his transfer, Pyles had performed odd jobs and participated in group recreational activities. Following his transfer, he was precluded from performing any job or participating in any recreational activities. His meals were brought to him in a cell where he was locked except during visits and exercise periods. After his transfer to the maximum-security institution, but before the filing of the lawsuit, Pyles had been visited by medical personnel, but no interpreter had been present.

SUIT

On behalf of Pyles, the Legal Defense Fund of the National Association of the Deaf then filed a lawsuit in the U.S. district court for the District of Maryland. The suit claimed that the state's failure to provide Pyles with a qualified sign language interpreter in the disciplinary proceedings violated his rights under the Civil Rights Act and the due process clause of the Fourteenth Amendment to the U.S. Constitution. Pyles alleged that, without the provision of a qualified sign language interpreter, he was unable to present a defense or testify in his own behalf at the disciplinary proceedings. He could not hear or cross-examine any witnesses who testified. He could not call any witnesses in his own behalf, and even if he had done so, he would not have been able to understand their testimony without an interpreter. Pyles was also unable to request that an inmate or employee of the prison act as a representative because he would have been unable to communicate with any representative. In addition to Pyles's Fourteenth Amendment claim, he alleged that he was subject to cruel and unusual punishment in violation of the Eighth Amendment to the Constitution because his stay in the maximum-security prison amounted to solitary confinement. *See* LEGAL SERVICES; NATIONAL ASSOCIATION OF THE DEAF.

CONSENT DECREE

After the lawsuit was filed, Pyles and the State of Maryland entered into a consent decree which was approved by the court. The state agreed that Pyles's conviction of institutional charges "was obtained in violation of his rights under the Constitution of the United States" and was "therefore, null, void, and of no legal effect whatsoever." All files or records on the institutional charges were destroyed. The state also agreed to restore Pyles's five days of good time.

Furthermore, the state agreed to advise any deaf inmate of the right to a qualified interpreter in a variety of settings: disciplinary hearings; counsel-

ing; psychological, psychiatric, or medical care; or any on-the-job-training, vocational, or educational program. The state also agreed to provide and compensate a qualified interpreter in these settings if a request for an interpreter was made by a deaf inmate or if, in the judgment of prison officials, effective communication was not occurring. An interpreter was deemed qualified only if certified by the National Registry of Interpreters for the Deaf or by the Potomac Chapter of the Registry of Interpreters for the Deaf, or if on a list of interpreters kept by the Maryland State courts pursuant to the state interpreter law, or if on a list compiled by the National Association of the Deaf or the Maryland Association of the Deaf. *See* REGISTRY OF INTERPRETERS FOR THE DEAF.

The state also agreed to provide a minimum of 90 minutes of counseling per week to Pyles, with interpreter services, for the duration of his confinement in prison or until counseling was no longer required in the professional judgment of personnel at the prison. In addition, the state agreed to seek placement for Pyles in a mental health facility with appropriate services, care, and therapy for deaf persons, and to pay reasonable attorneys' fees and costs for him.

IMPACT

The care and treatment of disabled prisoners in local detention centers, state facilities, and federal institutions is an issue of considerable concern to budget planners, government officials, and prisoners and their families. Deaf persons constitute a subgroup of disabled prisoners, and this consent decree marked one of the first successes in implementing a program to provide the special care that deaf prisoners are entitled to under federal law and the U.S. Constitution.

Bibliography

Pyles v. Kamka, Civil No. K-79-1864 (D. Md. Feb. 27, 1980).

Pyles v. Kamka, 491 F. Supp. 204 (Md., 1980).

United States Constitution, Amendments VIII and XIV. 42 U.S.C. 1983.

Marc P. Charmatz

Eckstein v. Kirby

Eckstein had been selected as a prospective juror in Pulaski County, Arkansas, in a criminal trial. When she appeared for jury duty, she had a qualified, certified sign language interpreter with her. First, Judge Kirby, who was presiding, asked Eckstein questions through the interpreter. Then the prosecuting attorney inquired as to whether she would need an interpreter during the entire jury deliberations. When Eckstein said she would need the interpreter, Judge Kirby excused her from serving.

Eckstein appeared voluntarily for jury duty in that same court a few days later. Judge Kirby then permanently excused her from jury duty and stated that Arkansas state law prevented her from ever serving on any Arkansas jury.

FEDERAL COURT PROCEEDING

Eckstein decided to file a lawsuit against Judge Kirby and the State of Arkansas in federal court. Eckstein's lawyers urged several arguments to support the claim that deaf people should have the opportunity to serve on juries. They argued: that the state law preventing hearing-impaired people violated the Due Process and Equal Protection Clauses of the U.S. Constitution; that Arkansas state law was arbitrary and unreasonable in excluding all aurally and visually impaired people rather than providing guidelines to determine which of these persons have other abilities to compensate for their disabilities to enable them to serve as jurors; and that the state law denied handicapped individuals the right to serve on a jury.

The state and Judge Kirby responded that there is no individual right to serve on a jury. Further, the defendants argued that the state could legitimately decide and determine the necessary qualifications for jury service; they maintained that hearing-impaired persons, because of their limited vocabularies, would not receive accurate, word-for word translations even with the assistance of qualified interpreters and that interpreters would be unable to show the witness's voice inflections, thereby preventing deaf people from being able to judge the witness's entire behavior. Furthermore, because the deaf person has to concentrate on the interpreter during testimony in order to understand the witness, the deaf person cannot observe the witness's body movements. Moreover, it was felt that the presence of an interpreter during the jury deliberations would disrupt the discussions and bring up the issue of a possible "13th juror." Finally, they argued that the defendant has a right to be heard by jurors who are able to evaluate completely all the evidence presented at the trial.

JUDGE ROY'S DECISION

Judge Roy, the federal judge who presided over this case, looked at the history of jury selection. Cases challenged successfully state laws that prevented certain individuals from serving on juries because of their race. There are also various groups of people who are automatically excused from serving on juries, for example, individuals whose professions are crucial to the well-being of the everyday life of the community, such as doctors, lawyers, and fire fighters.

Judge Roy looked at the Arkansas state law to see if it violated the U.S. Constitution. She decided that the law disqualifying deaf people from serving on juries was not discriminatory because the prohibitions against hearing-impaired people applied equally to all persons without regard to race, sex, religion, or ethnic background. Also, she found the state law did not violate any fundamental right, such as the right to vote, the right to interstate travel, and the right to privacy.

The U.S. Supreme Court had decided that the Sixth Amendment of the Constitution, that is, the right to trial by jury, is primarily for the protection of the defendant in a criminal case; all a United States citizen could expect was to be considered for jury service. A defendant in a criminal action is entitled to an impartial jury which occurs through the use of peremptory challenges and "for cause" removals.

Defendants and plaintiffs in both civil and criminal court actions that have juries can use the peremptory challenge and "for cause" removals to eliminate potential jurors. Peremptory challenges are made by a party without the need to give a reason for the exclusion. These are usually limited in number. The "for cause" removals mean that if the parties feel that a potential juror may not give a fair consideration to the trial proceedings, the parties may use the "for cause" method of removing people. This method means that an explanation must be given as to why a particular person is not wanted to serve on the jury. These removals are unlimited in number.

Judge Roy also based her decision on personal observation of Eckstein during a hearing in court. Despite Eckstein's intelligence, she had to follow closely and pay attention to the qualified interpreter in order to understand what was going on in court; this prevented her from looking at the speaker's face. The judge determined that this hampered Eckstein's ability to evaluate fully testimony presented by the speaker.

Judge Roy, however, praised Eckstein for her desire to serve on a jury. The judge said that despite her empathy for Eckstein's desire to serve on a jury, she had to make her decision in fairness to the parties to the litigation.

She ended her opinion by stating that the court's responsibility was limited to examining the constitutional requirements of the Due Process and Equal Protection Clauses as well as to determining whether the state law followed the U.S. Constitution. She pointed out that the issue before her was more of a public policy matter which should be left to the states to legislate.

STATE LEGISLATION

Several states have removed the restrictions caused by physical disabilities as a reason for not serving on the jury. California, Colorado, Louisiana, and Iowa have enacted laws that allow deaf people to have the opportunity to serve on juries within their respective states. These state laws caution that deafness is not to be used as an automatic excuse for not serving on the jury, but also that the hearing-impaired person is subject to peremptory challenges or "for cause" removals. There have been reported instances of deaf people serving successfully on juries in Florida, Oregon, Washington, Texas, California, Colorado, Illinois, Kentucky, and New Jersey.

Deaf people in other states have served successfully on juries despite state laws that can be used to disqualify them from jury service. One example is Montgomery County in Maryland, which has allowed qualified deaf and hearing-impaired jurors to serve on juries within that county despite the Maryland state law that prevents individuals who cannot speak or understand English from qualifying for jury duty. However, another county, Prince George's, uses this state law to automatically disqualify hearing-impaired citizens from serving on juries.

In 1984 a deaf New Yorker, Alec Naiman, was called to be in a jury pool for the case *New York v. Guzman*. The defense attorney used a "for cause" challenge to remove Naiman by arguing that his client's right to a fair trial would be denied. The presiding judge issued an opinion refusing to allow the defense attorney to use the "for cause" challenge. Judge Goodman's opinion was very well reasoned and researched. He found that Naiman met the New York statutory requirement of understanding English because he could speak, read, and write in English, and he could communicate with the court through the use of a sign language interpreter.

Judge Goodman further found that deaf people are as capable as others of understanding court proceedings. He pointed out that at least nine other courts throughout the United States had seated deaf jurors. He ended his legal opinion by stating that deaf people should "be considered, evaluated, and finally either accepted or rejected for service as individuals just as any other citizens. The grounds for exempting the deaf from jury service have vanished. People who are otherwise qualified cannot be challenged for cause under New York statutory law or the Constitution of this state, or of the United States, solely on the basis of deafness." Judge Goodman thereby denied the defendant's motion to challenge Naiman "for cause." However, the defendant's attorney then decided to use a peremptory challenge to remove Naiman.

In conclusion, despite Eckstein's and Naiman's failures to be seated on juries, the fact that other deaf and hearing-impaired people have sat on juries indicates that hearing-impaired people have been accepted more and more in the mainstream of American society.

Bibliography
California Code S198 Civil Procedure.
Colorado Revised Statutes S13-71-109.
Eckstein v. Kirby, 452 F. Supp. 1235 (E. D. Ark. 1978).
Iowa Senate File 253/607.1 Service on Jury.
Louisiana Code of Criminal Procedure Art, 401 and 401.1.
The People of the State of N.Y. v. Guzman, Indictment #7213/84 (N.Y. Country).

Seattle (Washington) *Post Intelligence*, August 20, 1979.
The Silent News, 1981 (California juror story).
Louisville (Kentucky) *Times*, March 30, 1981.
Colorado Gazette Telegraph, 1982.
Chicago Tribune, March 13, 1982.
St. Augustine (Florida) *Record*, June 19, 1982.
Montgomery County (Maryland) Circuit Court, *Washington Post*, June 21, 1982.
Portland, Oregon, Mulnomah Country Circuit Court, *Washington Post*, October 22, 1983.

Sheila Conlon Mentkowski

People v. Lang

Donald Lang was born deaf. As a child he received no formal education. At the age of 20 he could not speak or hear; he could not read or write; he did not understand sign language or lipreading. Except for simple gestures, he had no method of communication.

In spite of his handicap, he managed quite well, living with his mother and father in Chicago and working as a truck loader in the wholesale food district. His employer liked him and said that he was very hardworking and dependable. Lang enjoyed sports and bowling, and had many friends in his neighborhood. Prior to 1965, he had a good reputation and no criminal record.

FIRST MURDER

In 1965, when Lang was 20 years old, he was accused of murdering a prostitute. The evidence against him was purely circumstantial: he had left a tavern late at night with the woman; she had been found stabbed to death the next morning in an alley; there were bloodspots on Lang's clothes. However, the bloodspots might have been from a cut on Lang's hand.

The judge appointed a deaf lawyer, Lowell Myers, to represent Lang. A jury decided that Lang's inability to communicate made him incompetent to stand trial; he could not testify or communicate with his lawyer. The trial judge then committed Lang to a state mental hospital in Chester, Illinois, which had no facilities for educating a deaf person.

Attorney Myers appealed the decision, and in 1967 the Illinois Supreme Court decided that the trial judge should not have committed Lang to the mental hospital. The court said that Lang should be put into the general custody of the Illinois Department of Mental Health and taught to communicate, thus allowing him to face trial.

The Department of Mental Health put Lang in a school facility where an attempt was made to teach him sign language. After two years, he still had not learned to communicate. Myers then filed a court petition pointing out that Lang had been kept in custody for over two years, without having been convicted of a crime. Myers demanded that Lang be placed on trial for murder so that he could prove his innocence and be released.

The trial judge ruled, however, that Lang must be kept in custody until he learned to communicate. This meant that if Lang never learned to communicate he would be kept in custody for his entire lifetime, even though he had never been tried and convicted of a criminal offense.

Myers then took a second appeal to the Illinois Supreme Court, arguing that Lang had a right to a trial regardless of his handicap. The Illinois Supreme Court agreed and ruled in 1970 that Lang should be placed on trial for murder. Specifically, the court said: "This court is of the opinion that this defendant, handicapped as he is and facing an indefinite commitment because of the pending indictment against him, should be given an opportunity to obtain a trial to determine whether or not he is guilty as charged or should be released."

However, the case did not go to trial. In the years between the prostitute's murder and the supreme court's decision that Lang must be tried, the main witness for the prosecution died and other evidence was thrown out. The state prosecutor admitted that he could no longer prove any case against Lang. The case was then dismissed, and Lang went home to his parents.

SECOND MURDER

Six months later, on July 26, 1971, a prostitute was beaten to death in a hotel room, and Lang was arrested and charged with this new murder. The case against him was again based on circumstantial evidence: Lang had gone to the hotel room with the woman late at night; later her body was found in the room; there were bloodspots on Lang's clothes.

The court reappointed Myers to defend Lang on the new murder charge. This time a full trial was held before a jury, which found Lang guilty of murder. He was then sentenced to state prison for a term of 14 to 25 years.

This decision was appealed to the Illinois Appelate Court on the ground that Lang could not properly be found guilty of a criminal offense, due to the fact that he could not understand the testimony against him, that he could not testify in his own defense, and that he could not communicate with his lawyer. In 1975 the Illinois Appelate Court decided that, in view of these matters, the criminal conviction was improper. The judgment against Lang was reversed, and the jail sentence was removed.

Although Lang's murder conviction was reversed, he was not set free because the murder charge was still pending against him. Myers withdrew from the case at this point, and the county public defender took over Lang's defense. A tremendous amount of litigation then took place to determine where Lang should be kept, what kind of treatment or education he should receive, and whether he was entitled to be released on bail until such time as a trial might take place.

COURT DECISION

The Illinois Supreme Court reached a decision on these matters in 1979. It decided that when a person such as Lang is unfit to stand trial due to a handicap, is considered to be dangerous, has been given a full trial on the criminal charge, and has been found guilty (even though the judgment was later reversed due to the handicap), the state has the right to keep the person in custody for the purpose of teaching him to communicate. The person can be kept in custody either until he learns to communicate and can stand trial or until he is no longer considered dangerous.

Lang presently is being kept in the Chicago-Read Mental Health Center in Chicago, Illinois, a public institution under the Illinois Department of Mental Health, where he receives an individual program of training in sign language. When Lang has developed enough communication ability to take part in a full court trial, he will then be tried for murder in the criminal court.

Jackson v. Indiana

Two years after the Illinois Supreme Court held that a person, unable to communicate and faced with the possibility of an indefinite commitment, could demand a trial to determine his guilt or innocence, the Supreme Court of the United States handed down a decision in a case presenting the same issue.

The case decided by the Supreme Court involved Theon Jackson, a deaf man who lived in Indiana. Jackson was charged with two robberies of $5.00 and $4.50. He was unable to speak, read, or write; his knowledge of sign language was very limited; and he was judged to be mentally defective.

The Indiana trial court committed Jackson to the custody of the Indiana Department of Mental Health until such time as he should recover from his various disabilities. No trial was held upon the criminal charges.

His attorney pointed out that Jackson was not likely ever to recover from any of his disabilities. Thus, he was being committed into the custody of the department of mental health for his entire lifetime. The attorney pointed out that Jackson had never been tried or found guilty of the two pending criminal charges.

The case was taken to the U.S. Supreme Court. In 1972 the Supreme Court ruled that the State of Indiana, in making a commitment in a case of this kind, could give no weight at all to the fact that criminal charges were pending. Citing the decision of the Illinois Supreme Court in *People v. Lang*, the Supreme Court said that the state "must either institute the customary civil commitment proceedings that would be required to commit indefinitely any other citizen, or release the defendant."

Because of the decisions in the *Lang* and *Jackson* cases, it is an established principle of law that a person may not be confined indefinitely for the possible violation of a criminal statute when such confinement would result from a physical inability to communicate.

Bibliography
Jackson v. Indiana, 406 U.S. 715, 925 Ct. 1845 (1972).
Myers v. Briggs, 1970, 46 Ill.2d 281, 263 N.E.2d 109.
People v. Lang, 1967, 37 Ill.2d 75, 224, N.E.2d 838.
People v. Lang, 1975, 26 Ill. App.3rd 648, 32 N.E.2d 305, Cert. den, 423 U.S. 1079.
People v. Lang, 1978, 62 Ill. App.3rd 688, 378 N.E.2d 1106.
People v. Lang, 1979, 76 Ill.2d 311, 391 N.E.2d 350, Cert. den. 444 U.S. 954.

Lowell J. Myers

COURT INTERPRETERS ACT

In 1978, the U.S. Congress passed and President Jimmy Carter signed into law the Court Interpreters Act. The act assures that hearing-impaired individuals involved in proceedings initiated by the federal government in district courts can understand those proceedings to the greatest extent possible. It requires a judge or other presiding judicial official to appoint an interpreter, either oral or manual, at public expense. Specifically, an interpreter must be appointed when a defendant, witness, or a party to a dispute has a hearing loss that inhibits his or her ability to communicate with the presiding judicial official, understand and present testimony, or communicate with his or her attorney.

BACKGROUND
Previously, judicial rules merely permitted the use of an interpreter when a hearing-impaired person could not understand court proceedings. The decision whether to appoint an interpreter was left to the discretion of the presiding judicial official.

On numerous occasions, presiding judicial officials did not exercise this option, however, and hearing-impaired individuals were left without adequate communication assistance.

Several situations led to appellate court rulings that served as an impetus to the Court Interpreters Act. The rulings declared that a person must be provided with the means to confront witnesses and to communicate with his or her attorney in any case where the federal government brings a person into court and that person stands to lose life, liberty, or property as a result of the court proceedings. Without such means of communication, the appellate courts ruled, hearing-impaired persons would be deprived of their constitutionally protected right to due process of law.

PRESCRIBING INTERPRETERS' QUALIFICATIONS
Under the terms of the act, the director of the Administrative Office of United States Courts prescribes the qualifications of interpreters. The report of the Committee on the Judiciary of the House of Representatives, which accompanied the act, suggests that the director seek assistance from the National Association of the Deaf, the National Registry of Interpreters for the Deaf, state registries of interpreters for the deaf, and state associations of the deaf to identify the qualifications needed by interpreters. The clerk of each United States district is responsible for maintaining a current list of all interpreters within that court's jurisdiction who are certified by the director. The presiding judicial official will choose an interpreter from this list when possible.

APPOINTMENT OF INTERPRETERS
The decision to appoint an interpreter can result from any one of three actions: a decision by the presiding judicial official; a motion or request by the hearing-impaired individual's attorney; or a request from the hearing-impaired person. Although neither the act nor the accompanying reports discuss the matter, it appears that a defendant in a criminal action is entitled to an interpreter at all stages of the criminal process, such as arraignment and appearance before a grand jury.

Hearing-impaired persons may waive their right to an interpreter. This decision must be made by the hearing-impaired individuals themselves, and it must be explained to them by the presiding judicial official. When making such an explanation, the presiding judicial official is required to use an interpreter. Individuals who waive their right to a court-appointed interpreter may select their own interpreters instead. In these cases, the interpreters' fees will still be paid by the public at the same rate as that of interpreters appointed by the court.

Once an interpreter has been chosen, the presiding judicial official determines the interpreter's competence. An interpreter who cannot communicate effectively will be dismissed by the presiding judicial official and a successor appointed. The decision to replace an interpreter can be the result of findings by the presiding judicial official or after motions or requests from hearing-impaired persons or their attorneys.

The interpreter will either interpret simultaneously, that is, without pause; consecutively, with a brief pause after the completion of short intervals; or by means of a summary. The House Judiciary Committee report on the act, however, recommends that the summary method be used only sparingly.

In court actions initiated by a state or by an individual, rather than by the federal government, a hearing-impaired party or witness may seek assistance from the clerk of the court in locating an interpreter. However, in this instance the interpreter is not necessarily provided at public expense. The presiding judicial official, at his or her own discretion, will determine who pays the interpreter's fee.

CONFIDENTIALITY

The report of the House Judiciary Committee states that otherwise privileged communications made through an interpreter remain privileged, and the interpreter cannot be forced to reveal them. For example, statements made by hearing-impaired individuals to their attorneys through interpreters are privileged. The interpreter who transmits such statements cannot be forced to testify about them.

LEGISLATIVE HISTORY

Senator Charles McC. Mathias of Maryland introduced this act into the U.S. Senate as the Interpreters for the Hearing Impaired Act. Subsequently, it was merged with the Bilingual Courts Act, which provided interpreters for non-English-speaking individuals. The merged bill was passed and signed into law as the Court Interpreters Act.

A provision of the act requires the director of the Administrative Office of United States Courts to report annually on the frequency of requests for sign language interpreters under the provisions of the act. Thus, during 1980, sign language interpreters were requested 17 times, but there were no requests for oral interpreters.

Bibliography

Director of the Administrative Office of the United States Courts, *Annual Report*, p. 155, 1980.

House Report No. 95-1687, Committee on the Judiciary.

Senate Report No. 95-569, Committee on the Judiciary.

Terry v. State, 21 Ala. App. 100 (1925).

United States ex rel. Negron v. New York, 434 F.2d 386 (2d Cir. 1970).

Michael A. Chatoff

CRIME AND DELINQUENCY

Social institutions of justice throughout much of history have considered deaf people incapable of legal, adult responsibilities. Under early Hebrew law, for example, deaf persons were classified with children and mentally defective adults. Because all legal testimony was given orally, the deaf person was not considered competent as a witness to any transaction. Deaf people were protected from others, but they were not accountable for their own actions. This condition persisted, to at least some extent, to the twentieth century.

Until the mid-twentieth century, many laws in the United States continued to be based upon the assumption that deaf people were deficient to some degree and incapable of certain civic acts. Discrimination, for example, occurred at one time in the immigration laws. The owners or captains of vessels were required to report deaf passengers to the port authorities and to post bond in some states to prevent the deaf immigrants from becoming public charges. Today, some laws and regulations can restrict or interfere with deaf individuals' rights to drive automobiles or to obtain insurance. *See* DRIVING RESTRICTIONS.

Stereotypic assumptions about the capabilities of deaf people have also been present in the courts. At one time the capacity of deaf individuals to testify in judicial proceedings was regarded as very questionable, especially for those without an education. Today, however, a deaf person may appear as a witness in practically any American court. To take the witness stand, the deaf person must understand the nature and sanctity of an oath, and there must be a satisfactory means of communication, such as a certified interpreter. However, there is still some discrimination against deaf citizens serving on a jury. Formerly, the courts assumed that the law required jurors to possess good hearing, and that court officers had the right to dismiss from jury duty individuals who could not hear. During the 1970s and 1980s, however, the deaf community has argued that deaf people have full rights and obligations as citizens, and that if they are otherwise qualified as jurors, it is inappropriate to exclude them. The courts are reluctantly beginning to agree. Also, in the past a deaf person, especially if uneducated, was not considered to be responsible for misdeeds. Today, deaf people are held accountable for their actions, and can be tried. The courts have held that the deafness of an accused person must be viewed simply as a circumstance to be considered in connection with any other evidence in determining whether the individual is capable of assisting in his or her own defense. *See* COURT DECISIONS: Eckstein v. Kirby.

INCIDENCE

While there are no national statistics on the incidence of deafness among criminals and delinquents, audiological studies of penal populations indicate that the incidence of deafness and severe hearing loss (approximately 1.2 percent) is similar to the incidence rate in the general population when age and sex are considered. In two New York studies, assault, burglary and theft, and disorderly conduct accounted for 67 percent of the crimes committed by deaf perpetrators, rape for 9 percent, and murder and nonnegligent manslaughter another 7 percent. In an Ohio study of deaf victims, burglary and theft accounted for 70 percent of the crimes, sexual misconduct accounted for 15 percent, and robbery and assault for 10 percent. However, these studies are based upon small numbers of known criminals and victims, and the lack of specific information on handicapped populations in the Uniform Crime Statistics makes it difficult and inappropriate to comment on whether crimes associated with deaf persons are similar to or different from the general population. The same is true for the incidence of juvenile delinquency among deaf children.

DEAFNESS AND THE JUSTICE SYSTEM

In every society, social institutions emerge to provide organized ways in which to conduct the affairs of the group. Highly organized societies develop a formal system of laws proscribing unacceptable behavior and prescribing acceptable behavior, and a system must be created to deal with violators. In the United States, this social institution is known as the justice system.

Infractions of the law by deaf people do not appear to be much different from those of hearing people in the general population, but thorough studies are needed to confirm or reject this hypothesis. What is clearly different for deaf people is the ability of the justice system to deal fairly with them. The system was set up with the assumption that citizens who participate can speak and hear. To the extent that an individual does not meet these expectations, the system tends to founder.

Law Enforcement   The first contact an individual has with the justice system is usually with a law enforcement officer. Because of the low incidence of deafness in the general population, many officers are unfamiliar with deafness and do not expect to encounter a deaf person. Inasmuch as communication is of prime importance during initial

contact, this could create a dangerous situation. For example, during a routine traffic stop it is important that a deaf person not make any sudden or unexpected moves. To the officer, a deaf man or woman probably looks like anyone else and is expected to act like anyone else. This situation can be compounded if the officer is not visually identified by a uniform or a patrol car. A plainclothes officer and a deaf citizen could experience a disastrous failure to communicate.

Communication continues to be a potential impediment to the ordinary flow of events if a deaf person is arrested. On criminal charges, for example, the police are required to inform the accused person of his or her constitutional rights before questioning can take place. According to the National Center for Law and the Deaf, many deaf people will not fully understand their rights without an effective means of communication (such as an interpreter), and consequently the requirements of the Supreme Court Miranda Decision will not be met. Similarly, making the alloted one telephone call after being arrested may present a problem. Here a lack of communication can result in unnecessary time spent in jail.

In addition to the possibility of being arrested inappropriately, a deaf person may escape being arrested or ticketed. Sometimes police officers become so frustrated at the lack of communication that they dismiss the person with a warning, ironically a warning that the deaf person does not hear.

Juvenile Justice System   Crimes committed by children are generally brought before a juvenile or family court. Although the process tends to parallel the adult system, there are several significant differences. For example, a youth is "adjudicated a juvenile delinquent," not "found guilty." Likewise, adults are "sentenced" to probation or jail terms for their acts, but with juveniles, a "disposition" is reached by the court to provide appropriate care, maintenance, and treatment to avoid further delinquency. These dispositions may involve a period of probation, individual or family counseling, or placement in a public or private institution for a number of months.

It is during the disposition process that the greatest conflicts arise in planning for deaf youths involved in the juvenile justice system. Generally, probation officers charged with making dispositional recommendations to the court are not acquainted with the needs of young deaf people. The probation officers then sometimes turn to other professionals, such as educators serving deaf youth. But these professionals are often not familiar with the juvenile justice system and its limited resources for deaf children. Thus, the treatment for young deaf offenders may become a matter of compromise between programs that are designed to help delinquents who can hear and programs that do not have expertise in delinquency prevention for hearing-impaired children.

Adult Courts Equal access and due process are critical issues in the court system of the United States. It is important that individuals understand completely the charges brought against them and be able to participate fully in their own defense. The average deaf person in the United States has an elementary school education. This background, coupled with problems of communication, can make it difficult for deaf individuals to comprehend the verbal abstractions of law and court proceedings. It has been noted, for example, that a deaf person with limited concept formation may not understand what an oath is or what the difference is between posting bail and paying a fine. Often deaf people not only do not understand these things but are frequently unable to find a lawyer with whom they can communicate.

The courts can be equally naive about deafness. Too few hearing people understand the range of hearing loss and what the implications are. Many mistakenly assume that all deaf people are expert lipreaders, and very few realize that only 30 to 40 percent of spoken English actually can be seen on the lips of the speaker. Professionals, such as lawyers, also frequently experience great difficulty in simplifying their questions to the level of verbal understanding shown by the average deaf person. Moreover, hearing people are generally unaware of the many different forms of sign language and the need for appropriate, qualified interpreters. The courts often depend too much on an interpreter to translate subtle meanings and intentions. They assume that what is being said is what the deaf person is understanding. As a result, there is often an information problem in the court. At every stage of the judicial process there is a need for qualified legal interpreters. *See* COURT INTERPRETERS ACT.

Lack of sufficient education, language, and communication skills can render deaf persons unable to participate in their own defense. Under the Constitution the courts then have three choices: to provide the defendant with services to enable him or her to stand trial, to issue an order of civil commitment to a mental health facility, or to release the defendant. When a defendant is deaf, none of these alternatives is generally satisfactory. The defendant is incompetent to stand trial because of an inability to communicate, not from mental illness. The court could issue a civil commitment until such time as the defendant is competent to stand trial. However, the mental health facilities are not designed to accomplish this goal, and it is often an unattainable objective. If no further action is taken, such a move is likely to lead to permanent institutionalization, which is unconstitutional in view

of the absence of a demonstrable mental illness. The court can release the defendant but generally refuses because of the nature of the charges that brought the case to court. It is a dilemma, although relatively rare. The situation received considerable media attention in the 1966 case of Donald Lang in Chicago. It is still unresolved, as shown in the 1984 case of Andres Delgado in New York City. *See* COURT DECISIONS: People v. Lang.

Corrections While it is clear that deaf and other people with disabilities commit crimes, little attention has been given to their rights after they have been incarcerated. Their numbers are unknown because there are no national statistics on such prisoners. Although the Civil Rights of Institutionalized Persons Act provides some procedural protections, the law is of very limited use and to date has not been used in any case to protect prisoners' rights. Deaf inmates denied sign language interpreters may be unable to participate in legal proceedings, rehabilitation programs, and counseling sessions. A deaf prisoner in Maryland filed suit in 1980 because he lost his due process rights for lack of an interpreter during a disciplinary hearing. He could not communicate with the board to present his side of the case. Deaf prisoners may also be effectively denied access to work, recreation, and other prison activities. For these kinds of reasons, it has been suggested that handicapped prisoners are being punished not only for their crimes but also for being handicapped. The failure to accommodate to their special needs usually results in a degree of isolation and punishment that is disproportionate to the particular crime. *See* COURT DECISIONS: Pyles v. Kamka.

SOCIAL CHANGE

It was noted above that much has changed over the years in legal discrimination of deaf people. The deaf population in the United States has progressed from strictly limited rights before the law to almost full equality. Much of that progress has occurred since the 1970s through the efforts of the deaf community and its supporters with the authority provided by the Rehabilitation Act of 1973. *See* REHABILITATION ACT OF 1973.

Title V of the Rehabilitation Act has been referred to as a Bill of Rights for people with disabilities. Its purpose is to ensure that programs receiving federal funding can be used by all handicapped people. The major sections of Title V prohibit discrimination and require accessibility in employment, education, health, welfare, and social services. Section 504 of this act prohibits discrimination against qualified handicapped people in federally supported programs or activities and is applicable whether the federal monies were received directly or indirectly.

Most agencies of the justice system receive some form of federal funding. Law enforcement agencies and the courts have received mandates, via regulations from the Department of Justice that interpret Section 504, to provide interpreters, qualified in the deaf person's preferred mode, for communication with hearing-impaired persons in civil and criminal matters within court systems receiving federal financial assistance. This right has been augmented by the Bilingual, Hearing and Speech-Impaired Court Interpreter Act of 1979. Section 504 has also been interpreted to require the installation of telecommunication devices for deaf people in all federally assisted agencies with which the public has telephone contact.

Police departments are becoming more and more aware of the nature of the problems and remedies for communicating with deaf people. Law enforcement training manuals in a number of states now include specific recommendations for dealing with deaf people. Special films and inservice training programs have been developed, and many officers have undertaken basic sign language classes.

In part through stories about deaf street gangs in the press, the public has become more aware of the fact that deaf adolescents encounter adjustment problems in growing up just as hearing adolescents do. Some states are now recognizing the problems of dealing with troubled deaf adolescents and are developing special residential treatment programs for deaf youth with emotional and behavioral problems, including delinquency. Additionally, a lawsuit was filed in New York City demanding adequate special education for all youth detained to await court action, regardless of their handicapping condition. This suit, if successful, would have far-reaching effects on the juvenile justice system.

All of these changes have been beneficial to deaf people in the United States, but there is more to be done to clarify rights and responsibilities of hearing-impaired citizens. Further improvements will come through the efforts of individuals, such as the growing cadre of deaf lawyers, and the educational programs and actions of the deaf community and its supporters through organizations such as the National Association of the Deaf and the Center for Law and the Deaf. *See* LEGAL SERVICES; NATIONAL ASSOCIATION OF THE DEAF.

Bibliography

Baum, Edwin M.: "Handicapped Prisoners: An Ignored Minority?", *Columbia Journal of Law and Social Problems*, 18(3):394–379, 1984.

Bender, Ruth E.: *The Conquest of Deafness*, 3d ed., Interstate Printers and Publishers, Dansville, Illinois, 1981.

Best, Harry: *Deafness and the Deaf in the United States*, Macmillan, New York, 1943.

Collins, John D.: "Crime Reporting as Perceived by the Deaf and Its Educational Ramifications," unpublished doctoral dissertation, University of Cincinnati, 1983.

Collins, Kevin J.: "The Deaf and the Police," *FBI Law Enforcement Bulletin*, December 1973.

Cromwell, Paul F., and George Keefer: *Police-Community Relations*, West Publishing Co., St. Paul, Minnesota, 1973.

DuBow, Sy, et al.: *Legal Rights of Hearing-Impaired People*, Gallaudet College Press, Washington, D.C., 1982.

Flanagan, Timothy J., and Maureen McLeod (eds.): *Sourcebook of Criminal Justice Statistics—1982*, U.S. Department of Justice, Bureau of Justice Statistics, U.S. Government Printing Office, Washington, D.C., 1983.

Gannon, Jack R.: *Deaf Heritage: A Narrative History of Deaf America*, National Association of the Deaf, Maryland, 1981.

Higgins, Paul C.: "Deviance Within a Disabled Community: Peddling Among the Deaf," *Pacific Sociological Review* 22(1):96–114, 1979.

Jacobs, Leo M.: *A Deaf Adult Speaks Out*, 2d ed., Gallaudet College Press, Washington, D.C., 1980.

Klaber, M. Michael, and Arthur Falek: "Delinquency and Crime," in John D. Rainer, Kenneth Z. Altshuler, and Franz J. Kallman (eds.), *Family and Mental Health Problems in a Deaf Population*, Charles C. Thomas, Springfield, Illinois, pp. 141–151, 1969.

Melnick, William: "Hearing Impairment in an Adult Penal Institution," *Journal of Speech and Hearing Disorders*, 35(2):173–181, 1970.

Meyers, Lowell J.: *The Law and the Deaf*, U.S. Department of Health, Education and Welfare, Social and Rehabilitation Service, Rehabilitation Services Administration, Washington, D.C., 1967.

New York Crime and Justice Annual Report—1982, New York Division of Criminal Justice Services, Office of Identification and Data Systems, Albany, New York, 1982.

Schein, Jerome D., and Marcus T. Delk, Jr.: *The Deaf Population of the United States*, National Association of the Deaf, Silver Spring, Maryland, 1974.

Tidyman, Ernest: *Dummy*, Little, Brown, Boston, 1974.

Whalen, Thomas E.: "A Report of a Project To Prepare a Manual of Procedure for Serving Deaf Defendants, Victims and Witnesses," unpublished doctoral dissertation, New York University, 1981.

Wise, Daniel: "Judge Sets Program To Ready Deaf Youth for Arson Trial," *New York Law Journal*, p. 1, July 18, 1984.

R. Greg Emerton; Karen Emerton

CULTURAL PROGRAMS

Cultural programs have always played an important role in the educational and social development of deaf Americans. Offering esthetic and spiritual enrichment, they have provided opportunities to develop skills and innate talent as performing artists, to entertain deaf audiences through the medium of sign language, to enhance sign language's usage by beauty and eloquence of expression, and to bring deaf people together in social communality.

However, until the second half of the twentieth century, cultural programs of this kind and scope had a relatively obscure place in the deaf community at large and in the outside world of hearing people. The pursuit of such interests was commonly referred to as the subculture of the deaf, and the practice of these activities usually happened at the weekly or monthly programs at residential schools for deaf children, including Gallaudet College. Upon graduation and later employment in the working world, deaf persons would usually gravitate to the clubs of the deaf in metropolitan centers and large towns where similar cultural programs were held on a fairly regular basis. These organizations were generally labeled literary societies, and the bill of fare involved the dramatization of stories and the recitals of poems in sign language, with an occasional literary debate comparing the merits of two novels or two authors, or a pantomime show or scene from a play. *See* GALLAUDET COLLEGE.

Deaf Experience

In line with the cultural revolution in America during the 1960s and 1970s, these programs became identified with the deaf experience and deaf heritage. As they grew in stature and expanded their range of activities, they drew a national following. By 1975 a cultural renaissance gave new birth to deaf culture, deaf heritage, deaf folklore, deaf awareness, and American Sign Language (ASL). *See* DEAF POPULATION: Culture and Subculture; SIGN LANGUAGES: American.

This movement by deaf Americans to find their roots and develop a sense of pride in their talents as cultural carriers, as well as to bring deaf awareness to their hearing counterparts, was the result of many contributing events, organizations, and individuals.

The name of Douglas J. M. Burke stands out as the deaf person who could well be called the father of deaf cultural programs. Burke became active in the social and cultural affairs of the District of Columbia Club of the Deaf (DCCD), where he conceived the idea of a guild system. This was a formal organization for deaf club members to share cultural interests common to themselves, as well as a means for safeguarding and maintaining the cultural standards of the group. The first organization was the DCCD Dramatics Guild, which also evolved into the first community theater for the deaf in metropolitan Washington. As the group expanded and its performances became more polished, its audience grew to include hearing theater goers as well. In 1962 the Dramatics Guild reached the finals of the District of Columbia's One Act Play Tournament involving 25 hearing community theater groups, and one of its members won the best

major actor award. Several years later, the Dramatics Guild went on to win the Eastern U.S. Regional One Act Play Competition, defeating all the hearing groups entered. Eventually, the guild assumed independence, and, with reorganization, evolved into the Frederick H. Hughes Memorial Theatre of the Deaf.

NAD NATIONAL PROGRAM

The success of the Dramatics Guild led to the formation of other culturally oriented groups or guilds. As these thrived, Burke conceived the idea of expanding cultural programs on a nationwide scope. This was proposed at the Convention of the National Association of the Deaf (NAD) in 1964, with Burke as chief designer and architect of the master plan that would be known as the National Cultural Program, sponsored by the NAD. Largely through the support of Jess Smith, editor of the *Deaf American*, and with the backing of Robert Sanderson, NAD president, the program design was accepted at the 1966 NAD Convention, and Burke was appointed national director. *See* NATIONAL ASSOCIATION OF THE DEAF.

As Burke envisioned it, there would be a series of competitions beginning at the local club or city level, progressing to state and regional contests, and culminating at the biennial NAD National Convention. Competition would be divided into five areas: physical (including photography, painting, sculpture, dance, and pantomime), recreation (chess, checkers, and bridge), literary (short story and poetry recitals, one-act plays, and journalistic essays or news publications), spiritual (Bible knowledge, Bible story presentation, and hymn signing), and home economics (dressmaking, quilting, and knitting).

To develop the guidelines for the national cultural program, the NAD Cultural Committee was formed, with Douglas Burke as chairperson along with Robert Panara, Alfred Sonnenstrahl, David Neill, Frank Turk, and Francis Higgins. Its first project was to establish a National Theatre of the Deaf, with the Washington-based Frederick Hughes Memorial Theatre Group as its model. This proposal asked for a $10,000 grant from the newly formed National Foundation on the Arts and Humanities to send the Hughes Theatre company to eight major cities within a 500-mile radius of Washington, D.C. In addition to entertaining deaf and hearing audiences, and bringing cultural enrichment to a deprived minority, it would help deaf people establish theater groups in their communities. Furthermore, the National Cultural Committee (NCC) believed this offered a fresh and innovative approach to the theater via a new visual art form.

Although this was similar to an idea originally

proposed by Edna Simon Levine in 1961, the National Cultural Committee was using a different strategy and program design to achieve somewhat similar objectives. Their proposal, though considered meritorious, was not accepted. However, its concept was realized on a larger scale two years afterward, when a proposal by David Hays, the noted hearing stage designer, and George White, president of the Eugene O'Neill Memorial Theatre Foundation, was accepted and granted funding for a five-year period by the Federal Vocational Rehabilitation Administration. Burke and the National Cultural Committee were involved as consultants in this proposal, and they obtained the commitment by the National Theatre of the Deaf to cooperate fully with the deaf community in implementing the program. *See* NATIONAL THEATERS OF THE DEAF: United States.

With Burke as its leader, the National Cultural Committee then began the great task of putting the National Cultural Program into smooth operation. The 50 states were subdivided into nine regional areas, and cultural directors were appointed for each region. These directors, in turn, devised a subset of state and city directors within each region, and voluntary cultural directors were appointed. The success of the publicity for and promotion of the total program was due in large part to the tireless and creative efforts of SallyPat Dow.

Dow conceived the colorful newsletter *NCP Culturama*, which was regularly mailed to all cultural directors and to all NAD members, keeping them informed of cultural programs in progress, of current needs, and of suggestions for implementation. She not only served as editor of *Culturama* but also wrote a regular column in the *Deaf American* and served as a valued consultant and adviser to the National Cultural Committee. Another resourceful deaf woman was Evelyn Zola, director of the Milwaukee Committee, who began staging ingenious cultural program contests in 1968 and did so for many years afterward. Because of her hard work and dedication, Zola was honored with the *Deaf American* Cultural Service Award in 1972. *See* DEAF AMERICAN.

The first national finals were held at the NAD Convention in Las Vegas in 1968, where Zola's state of Wisconsin won more awards than any of the other 12 states represented. The award also reflected the outstanding work of Roger Peacock, who served as State Cultural Director. These national contests became known as the National Culturama Program and were often the highlight of the NAD conventions. They could be compared with Hollywood's Academy Awards program because of the dazzling variety show staged by the finalists and other performers and the manner in which the

winning contestants were honored with the prized Golden NADDY awards.

Usually, however, the National Cultural Committee tried to keep the focus of importance on the local city contests and grass-roots individual participants.

By the time the 1972 NAD Convention was held in Miami, over 2000 deaf people were participating in cultural programs at the various levels. There were also approximately 150 cultural directors involved, which was remarkable in view of the fact that a program of such magnitude could expect a large turnover, especially because of its volunteer status. Yet, over three-fourths of the program personnel continued working.

The last project of the National Cultural Committee, which was also conceived by Douglas Burke, was the Miss Deaf America Cultural Pageant. Burke had been invited by the chairperson of the Miss America Pageant to attend their contest in Atlantic City, but he commissioned SallyPat Dow to go and bring back the system of rules, which the National Cultural Committee later revised. The bathing suit contest was eliminated because, as Burke maintained, "the NAD Cultural Program was set up to promote performing and fine arts." Instead, emphasis was put on talent, personality, evening gown impression, and interviews. In publicizing the first contest to be held at the Miami Convention in 1972, Dow stressed that it would be a "new contest to help us to elevate the image and self-concept of deaf ladies throughout the United States" and that "the big point item is one's cultural talent performance." The Miss Deaf America winner is invited to talk at schools for deaf children and to appear as NAD's representative before social groups such as the Lions, Kiwanis, Chamber of Commerce, and Jaycees. Beginning with the Miami Convention in 1972, the Miss Deaf America Pageant grew bigger and better, often with all the pageantry of the Miss America and Miss Universe competitions as more contests were staged at the local, state, and national level.

This final project of the NAD National Cultural Program proved to be the most enduring. Because of the difficulty of funding expenses for tournaments and travel, the NAD Cultural Program was discontinued in 1976 following the convention in Houston, Texas. However, it made a lasting impact on deaf Americans, and its influences extended into many other cultural programs that later developed.

SPECTRUM: FOCUS ON DEAF ARTISTS

Spectrum: Focus on Deaf Artists is a national non-profit group that was formed in 1975 with offices in Austin and Houston, Texas. At the time, it was little more than a dream by its founder and vice-president, Janette Norman, whose aim was to provide an organization for deaf artists with a viable means for realizing opportunities for success equal to that enjoyed by hearing professionals.

With the full support and guidance of philanthropist and patron of the arts Helen DeVitt Jones of Lubbock, Texas, Norman began to seek funds from federal, state, and private organizations to make her dream a reality. She started a newsletter to contact other deaf artists, and followed this with summer conferences that also served as deaf arts festivals. These brought together dancers, actors, painters, sculptors, writers—someone from practically every area of the arts in which there were working deaf artists. Operating from a 10-acre ranch outside of Austin, with the Spectrum Arts Center as its focus, it began developing cultural programs by promoting the work of deaf artists both locally and nationally.

One of its first creations was the American Deaf Dance Company (ADDC), developed in 1976 by Yacov Sharir, its artistic director and choreographer, who was the only hearing member of the group. The deaf dancers learned to perform independently of music and developed the concept of freed dance. First appearing at the University of Texas, the company performed in many cities of Texas and made several national tours of the United States. *See* PERFORMING ARTS.

Another promotion of its performing arts program was the Spectrum Deaf Theatre, which was coordinated by Betty Miller, director of Spectrum's Visual and Performing Arts School and one of the driving forces behind the organization. Spectrum's theater focused on plays either written or adapted by deaf persons; its first production was *A Play of Our Own* by Dorothy Miles. Another original play by a deaf writer was Gilbert Eastman's *Sign Me Alice*. Among the adaptations were *The Golden Fleece* by hearing playwright A. R. Gurney, and the classic foreign film *The Blue Angel*, reworked by Charlie McKinney, the first deaf president of Spectrum.

Spectrum's acting company also contributed greatly in performing at other theaters throughout the United States and abroad. Among these, Liz Quinn starred in *The Trojan Women* at the Los Angeles Actors Theatre (1980) and as the deaf heroine, Sarah Norman, in the Tony Award–winning play *Children of a Lesser God* during its long run in London. Quinn also has been featured in such television serials as *Trapper John, M.D.*, and *Nurse* by CBS-TV.

Other cultural areas promoted by Spectrum involved the visual arts, whose second coordinator, Charles Baird, later went on to a distinguished career as both actor and scenic designer for the National Theatre of the Deaf. A deaf artist, Baird collected photographs and reproductions of the famed deaf artist Morris Broderson and more than 300 other deaf artists. He also featured collections of the works of deaf artists in sculpture, wood carving, batiks, stained glass, and other forms. Among these were the works of Hillis Arnold, a leading contemporary sculptor of the Midwest. This was the start of what Baird dreamed of developing into a national archive that would feature biographies of deaf artists and their work. He also envisioned the day when it would be possible to exhibit the works of deaf artists on nationwide tours. *See* ARNOLD, HILLIS; BRODERSON, MORRIS.

Spectrum made a valiant attempt to establish a permanent, independent organization to develop cultural arts and artists of, for, and by deaf people. However, when government seed money and grants became scarce, lack of funding and facilities forced it to dissolve in 1981 after six years of existence.

CANADIAN CULTURAL SOCIETY OF THE DEAF

An even bolder and more comprehensive national cultural arts program was conceived in 1970 by the Canadian Cultural Society of the Deaf (CCSD), which endeavored to combine the objectives of both the NAD Cultural Program and Spectrum. The brainchild of its founder, Forrest C. Nickerson, a deaf artist, CCSD set up headquarters in the heart of Canada at Winnipeg. After selecting a national cultural committee and appointing volunteer directors from each of Canada's provinces in 1972, they became incorporated under the federal charter. Its president and executive director was Forrest Nickerson, with Angela Jean Petrone as vice-president and cultural coordinator. *See* CANADA.

In June 1973 the first issue of their semiannual magazine, *Cultural Horizons for the Deaf*, appeared; the publication was initiated and edited by Nickerson. It was a significant breakthrough, as it was to be the only deaf international multicultural magazine in publication. In July CCSD held its first biennial National Festival of the Arts at Calgary in conjunction with the Western Canada Association of the Deaf. These national arts festivals were the culmination of all provincial and local city-level tournaments sponsored by each of the 10 provinces, with the Canadian students at Gallaudet College eligible as a special group known as the Canadian Gallaudet Club.

The cultural programs included competition in the following categories: physical—sculpture, painting, and photography; literary—plays, poetry, and essays; performing arts—one-act plays, pantomime, songs, dance, magic acts, manual signs; recreational—arts and crafts, personal hobbies; home arts—knitting, quilting, sewing, crocheting, weaving. An awards program was the highlight of this first arts festival, as well as all subsequent ones. The national finalists of these contests received the Golden Defty (an acronym for deaf and deft) Trophy. Designed by Leo Mol Moloshanin, an internationally known sculptor, this award consisted of a hand and wrist mold that shaped the letter A of the manual alphabet.

Nickerson, who was voted Canada's Deaf Citizen of the Year in 1974, conceived an ambitious program that would make CCSD the repository of deaf culture in Canada. Affiliated organizations established within the framework of the CCSD would include the Canadian Theatre of the Deaf, the Canadian Art Gallery of the Deaf, the Canadian Hall of Fame and Museum of the Deaf, the Canadian Talent Registry of the Deaf, and the *Canadian Literary Journal of the Deaf*. Along with the CCSD, each affiliated organization would have a permanent home or base of operations in a multipurpose cultural arts center. The center would be built in Winnipeg, where its central location would make it accessible to all of Canada's 1.5 million hearing-impaired people, and it would include a 1000-seat theater, creative drama school, hall of fame, art gallery, museum, gymnasium, library, offices, lecture halls, and exhibit and photographic facilities. Future plans also would include cross-country tours to ensure that the arts would play a vital and continuing role in the lifestyle of every deaf youth and adult.

Many people believe that such exposure to the arts and participation in cultural programs should begin early in life. In his monograph, *Understanding Our Deaf Culture* (1980), which was addressed to the Canadian government, Forrest Nickerson stated that "there is deep concern in deaf communities about the lack of arts activities in our schools for the deaf in Canada" and that "artists with sufficient experience and teaching abilities be permitted to work in schools for the deaf as instructors, demonstrators, resource people and artists-in-residence regardless of their former academic qualifications." He went on to reproach the federal government for its laxity and cutbacks in funding, which had forced the CCSD to stop publishing their arts magazine, *Cultural Horizons of the Deaf*, in 1979, and which caused the Canadian Theatre of the Deaf to close after four years of tours throughout the provinces. Similarly, plans for the cultural arts center had to be put aside.

Despite such setbacks, the CCSD national cultural program forged onward and continued to be productive through the dedication of its volunteer committees at local, provincial, and national levels. In 1984, at the seventh biennial Festival of the Arts in Edmonton, the first Miss Deaf Canada Contest was staged, and the winning contestant went on

to represent CCSD and affiliated deaf associations by making cross-country promotional tours.

At this festival, Nickerson also announced his intention to resign, after 16 years as president and executive director. In January 1985 he was succeeded by Angela Petrone Stratiy, who had so faithfully served the program since its inception. She had previously been honored as Quota's International Deaf Woman of the Year (1979), and at the National Festival in 1980 she had received the Founder's Order of Honor, CCSD's highest award. Nickerson, who had recorded an artistic triumph with the publication of his illustrated semibiography, *A Deaf Artist's Trail* (1982), also was honored for his many sacrifices and contributions with a specially designed plaque depicting his likeness in bronze relief. Among many other deaf Canadians honored for their volunteer leadership in promoting cultural programs were David Peikoff and Roger McAuley, who were elected to the Canadian Hall of Fame.

JUNIOR NATIONAL ASSOCIATION OF THE DEAF
One of the objectives of the NAD was to establish an organization for the deaf youths of the United States to develop and maintain their potential for leadership and service in the education and work world. The foremost advocates in promoting this movement were Mervin Garretson and Frank Turk, who became the first national director of the Junior National Association of the Deaf (Jr. NAD) in 1967 and, together with Gary Olson, nurtured its successful growth. Although the accent was on leadership, scholarship, and service to school and community, the Jr. NAD also initiated and maintained a viable program to promote deaf culture and the arts.

In 1968 the NAD executive board provided the opportunity for the Jr. NAD to compete in the National Cultural Contests. They had the same format of rules and talent categories as that of deaf adults, and the response was enthusiastic and widespread. These cultural programs were usually held during the Jr. NAD regional and national conventions, although almost every school chapter held its own competitive talent programs for the dual purpose of cultural enrichment and selection of representative entrants.

The first national convention of the Jr. NAD was held at Gallaudet College in 1968 with 120 student delegates from 36 chapters in schools for deaf children. During the awards program that climaxed the convention, a Miss Jr. NAD Contest was also staged. Twenty-two teenagers competed and performed in such categories as dramatic readings, poetry, song in sign, pantomime, dance, painting, and dressmaking. With the help of benefactors, prizes had also been established for certain cultural pursuits; these were awarded at this first convention, and regularly each year. The prizes were named in honor of contemporary deaf artists and included the Lawrence Newman Award for journalism, the Robert Panara Award for poetry, the Helen Muse Award for fiction, the Loy Golladay Award for the personal essay, the Robert Greenmun Award for creative writing, and the Robert Welsh Award for photography. An all-star Talent Night entertainment program was frequently another highlight of these conventions. The same type of cultural program has been carried over and presented annually at the Youth Leadership Camp operated by Frank Turk and Donald Padden at Swan Lake Lodge each summer in Pengilly, Minnesota.

WORLD AROUND YOU CREATIVE CONTESTS

Another successful program promoting cultural arts among deaf youth is the Creative Contest, begun in 1979 by Cathy Carroll, a hearing educator who conceived and edits the weekly publication *World Around You*. A product of the precollege programs supported by Gallaudet College, *World Around You* is a popular magazine for school-age deaf and hard-of-hearing readers. It features current events in the world, items of special interest to deaf consumers, articles on deaf culture and deaf heritage, and success stories of deaf and hard-of-hearing people of all ages. It annually sponsors a Creative Contest that encourages originality of expression in poetry, fiction, autobiography, essays on the deaf experience, news or feature articles, illustrative art sketches, and cartoons on deaf humor. Prizes are awarded to students who place first, second, and third, and their creative accomplishments are featured in a special issue of *World Around You* printed at the close of the scholastic year.

DEAF COMMUNITY PROGRAMS

The deaf community has become increasingly active in developing cultural programs involving deaf artists and in promoting accessibility to theater performances, museums, art parks, and other cultural pleasures enjoyed by hearing persons. In the San Francisco Bay area, an organization known as DEAF Media has invited local and nationally known deaf painters, poets, storytellers, and actors to present programs that give a positive view of the unique culture of the American deaf community. Titled Celebration: Deaf Artists and Performers, these programs began in 1980 and coincide with the observance of Deaf Awareness Month. In the last week of May 1985, DEAF Media conducted its fourth such celebration at the University of California, Berkeley.

Another unique enterprise is based in St. Paul and Minneapolis. This group involves the pooling of the collective talents and resources of deaf and hearing persons with organizations serving deaf people, such as CENTS (Community Education and National Training Systems), DEAF (Deafness Education and Advocacy Foundation), CADA (Cultural Arts and Deaf Audiences), and MRID (Minnesota Registry of Interpreters for the Deaf). Much like guilds, these groups work to make the arts accessible to deaf people via interpreted performances in various theaters, interpreted tours in art museums and artpark festivals, and celebrations involving deaf artists. Starting with their festival focusing on deaf heritage in 1981, they have staged annual happenings. The festival of 1984, for example, was called A Festival of Art and Sign; it highlighted deaf culture in literature and theatre, analysis and understanding theater of the deaf, visual arts and the deaf, translating play scripts from English to American Sign Language (ASL), ASL and deaf audiences, and scenes of plays performed by hearing professionals during which several different approaches to sign interpretation were presented.

Alice Lougee Hagemeyer, a deaf librarian in the Martin Luther King Public Library at Washington, D.C., has been most creative in showing the many ways librarians and friends of libraries can help the public appreciate the heritage and cultural contributions of deaf people and how these people have helped benefit society as a whole. Since 1974 she has planned and organized annual Deaf Heritage Week activities to bring deaf awareness to the general community. These programs include displays of books by deaf authors, reproductions and slides of the work of deaf artists and sculptors, and recognition of deaf people who have succeeded in various professions. Such programs have been widely copied by many libraries in other cities. An author of many booklets on library services to deaf people, Hagemeyer also writes a monthly column for the *Silent News* entitled "Library for Deaf Action." *See* SILENT NEWS.

In 1980 Hagemeyer developed a special book for libraries called *The Red Notebook*. A resource book on deaf heritage and culture, deafness, and library services and accessibility, it was endorsed at the White House Conference on Libraries and Information Services and approved by both the American Library Association (ALA) and the NAD. Her many awards include the President's Award from the NAD (1980) and the Andrew Woods Memorial Award for Advocate of the Year (1984) from the District of Columbia Rehabilitation Association.

Bibliography

"A Brief Historical Sketch of Miss Deaf America Pageant," *Silent News*, March 1985.

Burke, Douglas J. M.: "How the NTD Was Launched," *Deaf American*, 28:1, September 1975.

Carroll, Cathy (ed.): "The Creative Contest," *World Around You*, vol. 15, May 15, 1984.

Chitwood, Donna: "Focusing on Spectrum," *Gallaudet Today*, 9:3, Spring 1979.

"Cultural Program and Contest Regulations" (4th rev.), Canadian Cultural Society of the Deaf, Inc., 1984.

Dow, SallyPat: "The National Culturama," *Deaf American*, November 1974.

————: "The National Culturama: How It All Began, from the NTD to the Miss Deaf American Pageant," *Deaf American*, April 1973.

Junior National Association of the Deaf: *Convention Proceedings*, National Association of the Deaf, 1968.

Langham, Barbara: "Focus on Deaf Artists," *Exxon USA*, 19:2, 1980.

Nickerson, Forrest C.: "Tomorrow Begins Today," *Cultural Horizons*, 3:5, Spring/Summer 1975.

————: *Understanding Our Deaf Culture* (monograph), Canadian Cultural Society of the Deaf, Inc., September 1981.

Padden, Donald, and Agnes Padden: "Mileposts," *Gallaudet Alumni Newsletter*, 19:7, February 1985.

Panara, Robert: "Cultural Arts Among Deaf People," *Gallaudet Today*, 13:3, Spring 1983.

Robert Panara

Poetry in American Sign Language

Poetry in American Sign Language (ASL) has grown more self-consciously poetic in the last 15 years: poets have begun working more exclusively in ASL with no original in English; the form has undergone formal study; videotape has been adopted as the predominant means of preservation and of creation; and college classes in ASL poetry have been established.

CHARACTERISTICS

Poetry in ASL may mean very different things to different people. First, many people picture a written poem when they think of poetry. Poetry composed with the help of a written medium is very different, generally, from poetry composed without such help, as is the case with ASL poetry. Poetry that is written allows poets a constant interplay between their inner ear and the written form of the poem, and addition of levels of meaning that would be impossible without that interplay. In fact, the final poem may arise out of just that interplay between the written and spoken forms of English, each form allowing the poet to extend the range and allusions beyond what is possible in one form alone.

However, poetry that remains unwritten and only in the mind is essentially oral (that is, nonwritten), and therefore is composed in a more conservative fashion, without the interplay of two forms of the language. Therefore, it is more likely designed to be understood in one presentation. It will probably contain numerous mnemonic devices such as rhythm and rhyme and consonance, repetition of lines, and emphasis on narrative flow, all making it easy to remember and grasp on one hearing (or viewing). Because it is not written, over time it develops variant forms, and if it is picked up by other poet-performers, the original author may be forgotten. Nonwritten, or oral poetry resembles more the general conception of folklore rather than poetry.

ASL poetry, as a whole, fits the description of folklore, although as a whole it has not yet been studied. What has been studied is the more consciously literary productions of a few educated ASL poets. The focus of this discussion, therefore, is on the three best-known poets: Ella Lentz, Clayton Valli, and Dorothy Miles. These three poets all work with a medium—either film or videotape—that allows them to refine and develop their esthetic imagination. All three have worked with written English at one time, but at least two have stopped, since English interfered with their imagination in ASL. By dropping an English analog, they are leading the way in developing poetry in ASL beyond the status of folklore. See FOLKLORE.

As these poets have worked more consciously and in a more studied way, their ASL poetry has become more like present-day American poetry. It is rich in intentional and consistent symbolic structure, subtle analogical play, complexity of idea, interplay of persona—more of what would be expected of modern academic poetry than of a strictly oral form of literature.

This branch of ASL poetry—academic ASL poetry—represented by Lentz, Miles, and Valli, did not spring out of a vacuum. There were earlier translations of poetry in English into a form of sign language. This translation work was stimulated by deaf drama groups that presented signed versions of classic plays, necessitating development of skill in translating from poetry in English into an interesting and poetic kind of signing. Though this kind of translation started in the nineteenth century with the advent of deaf drama groups, the state of the art was expanded and refined in the 1940s, 1950s, and 1960s, especially at Gallaudet College, where deaf and hearing academics worked strenuously to translate classical Greek drama into successful signed versions. Out of this kind of work grew the poetic refinement in sign that led to the present-day ASL poetry.

DEFINITION

Many elements normally found in written and spoken poetry also occur in poetry in ASL. Symbol, analogy, and tone, for example, and almost all the poetic elements normally found in written poems are also found in ASL poetry; but even though the elements are there, they occur differently. For example, one normally thinks of a poetic symbol as a word for something physical (such as tree) that during the poem comes to stand for some intangible concept (such as organic flow). This type of symbolizing process does go on in ASL poetry, but in addition there is symbolic use of the signing space and of directionality in movement. For example, basic symbolic movements are established where movement straight ahead (from the signer's body) comes to symbolize progress, while movement to the left comes to mean frustration or regression. The signs themselves may not carry symbolic intent, but the directionality of the classifiers will. Or the signing space may itself trace out a symbolic shape, such as a Christian Cross, which supports or reveals the meaning of the poem. *See* SIGNS: Artistic.

ASL works with movement; English works with sound. In both cases, the poet also works within a grammatical structure (ASL poetry is not mime or dance, just as English poetry is not music, although in both cases there is some obvious overlap). The symbolizing process can work in either movement or sound, even though there are certain esthetic differences. A certain sound repeated in an English poem, such as "green," will take on symbolic value; a certain movement repeated in an ASL poem, such as SNOWFLAKE-SPREAD-ON-GROUND, will likewise take on symbolic value. The spoken word "green" can be presented with many intonations and in many contexts; the sign (SNOWFLAKE-SPREAD-ON-GROUND) can also be presented with different tones, and can be signed in different locations. Also, the face (which is also grammar-bound) can do something else, the body can be leaning in a certain way, and so on. ASL poetry has many esthetic resources to work with because it is easier to understand simultaneous stimuli visually than aurally.

Many elements familiar in written poetry are difficult to find in ASL poetry because the latter has not been analyzed in terms of line units. Therefore, it is hard to distinguish between internal rhyme and end rhyme, for example, or to identify one pause as caesura and another as line break. Some elements of written poetry may have no esthetic use in ASL. Also, since ASL poems are always presented by a person (and not written), the poem will not stay the same from one presentation to the next. When there is no written form, it is difficult to distinguish the poet from the poem. (ASL poets have yet to devise a system to identify one particular videotaped version of a poem as the one authentic version; for example, Lentz has at least three different versions of one poem on videotape.)

Dramatic irony, for example, an element that is tricky in written poetry, is relatively easy to do in signed poetry. Since so much linguistic information is transmitted by the face in ASL, making for two centers of meaning, there is a wonderful opportunity for ironic contrast between what is signed on the hands and what is signed on the face. Valli uses a lot of dramatic irony. He will, for example, describe difficult and painful experiences with his hands, but maintain an ironically unemotional expression on his face. In spoken poetry one can achieve such irony; in written poetry the reader has difficulty detecting it.

Another element that occurs in ASL poetry is the repetition of a handshape for esthetic and perceptual purposes. Just as in English where the sound of long *e* (as in teeny) by itself suggests a certain meaning, so do certain handshapes in ASL. The simpler, unmarked handshapes, such as the B shape (flat hand, fingers together, used in signs such as PEACE, or CALM), if repeated often in a poem will give it the tone of restfulness and calm. The sudden appearance of a marked (difficult-to-make) handshape will serve as a sharp point of transition to a new tone. In the poem "My Favorite Old Summer House," Valli describes his favorite retreat, which burned down one winter. The first part of the poem, describing the beach and the water and the sand dunes and the birds, is dominated by the peaceful B handshape, but the part describing the fire uses crooked-finger handshapes, showing tension and anguish.

ASL POETS

Those who inspired contemporary ASL poets such as Lentz, Valli, and Miles, include ASL artists (and translators from English) such as Patrick Graybill, Gil Eastman, Erik Malzkuhn, Robert Panara, and Bernard Bragg. For years they and many others have been developing the expressive ability of ASL. When one of them translates a poem from another language into ASL, they are using ASL materials as richly as the poets. The main difference is that the ASL poets Lentz, Valli, and Miles generate original conceptions and new uses of the language, and they tend to focus on the experience of being deaf. *See* BRAGG, BERNARD.

The Gallaudet Theater Arts Department and later the National Theatre of the Deaf were central in moving ASL poets toward the refined expression of today. In the 1940s and 1950s the Gallaudet Theater Arts Department enjoyed the support and interest of an unusual combination of hearing and deaf people. Out of the work done there, the National Theatre of the Deaf (NTD) developed, and the artistic life of ASL took on new vitality and recognition.

Miles was with the NTD and was one of the first to identify herself as an ASL poet. She is, in a sense, the mother of modern ASL poetry. She served as a bridge between the earlier focus on translation of works in other languages into ASL and the present focus on original composition in ASL. She attempted to create poems that would function in both English and ASL because she still worked mostly from the written word (although some of her signed poems defy transcription). She has published a book of her poems, *Gestures* (1976), and has made films of her poems with her own commentary.

Lentz, who cites Miles as a major inspiration for her poetry, has worked for almost a decade to create a body of poetic works. These works are not readily available, even though Lentz has created about 10 ASL poems that have been preserved on videotape. The poems were created initially in ASL, although inevitably they reflect poetic influences from the hearing culture. They are strongly message-oriented and have a lyricism and poetic strength that even the uninitiated can appreciate.

The third ASL poet, Valli, began his poetic career like Miles and Lentz, writing poems in English and trying to work in sign from the English. He was not aware of the work of Miles or Lentz until 1980, but since then has studied their work while continuing to compose new poems.

Valli's poems are often compared to those of Robert Frost because they use natural settings as symbols for human realities. For example, in one poem dandelions may be seen to represent deaf people and the hearing man mowing the lawn may represent hearing people who are intolerant of differences (the lawn should be UNIFORMLY GREEN!, the mower declares).

In their poems, the three poets lament the barriers between deaf and hearing people. They sign of the denial of deaf identity, comparing it to imprisonment, to killing with love, to the general "if you are different, you must be bad" edict present in all societies. They are working heavily in both linguistic and cultural materials and with the advent of videotape have found a medium that allows them to work with increasing complexity.

Trenton Batson

D

DEAF AMERICAN

The *Deaf American* is the major periodical of the National Association of the Deaf (NAD). Its objective is to provide wide coverage of the interests, problems, and successes of deaf people from teenagers through senior citizens. The magazine's purpose parallels that of the NAD. *See* NATIONAL ASSOCIATION OF THE DEAF.

Usually published eight times each year, the *Deaf American* has a circulation of about 4500. The readership includes deaf people and their families, but it is not restricted to these groups. Trainees and professionals in the areas of education and rehabilitation, for example, use the magazine for information and direction. Providers of health and human services on local, state, and national levels also make use of the *Deaf American* for input and reports. Policy and decision makers are part of the target audience as well.

HISTORY

The predecessor of the *Deaf American* was the "new" *Silent Worker*. The "old" *Silent Worker* started as a school publication of the New Jersey School for the Deaf (now the Marie Katzenbach School) in 1892. In addition to printing school news, the *Silent Worker* evolved into a training medium for innovations in graphic arts, drawing postgraduate students from within and without the state of New Jersey. Expansion into national coverage and readership reached its zenith in the mid-1920s. Increasing costs and the changing nature of the magazine, which was no longer a "little paper" so much as a national publication, led to the New Jersey School's decision to discontinue publication in 1929. *See* LITTLE PAPER FAMILY.

Thereafter, and through the Great Depression and World War II, several tabloid newspapers and a few short-lived magazines for deaf Americans came into existence. In 1948, following a survey to determine the market for a national magazine, the NAD revived the *Silent Worker*, again in the "slick" magazine format.

Subsequently, the publication's fortunes rose and fell with that of the NAD. A financial crisis in the late 1950s made survival questionable. Printing was done at the Tennessee School for the Deaf for four years as the result of funding difficulties.

For several years following its revival, numerous proposals were made to drop "Silent" from the magazine's title. Finally in 1964, a change was made to the present title, the *Deaf American*. Eventually, the subscript "The National Magazine for All the Deaf" was dropped to stress changing readership.

The office of publication, as well as printers, changed quite often. For the initial years of revival, both were located in California, then the headquarters of the NAD. Following the four years in Tennessee, printing was done in Lewiston, Idaho, with the editorial office in Indianapolis. Printing was then done at several locations in Indiana before a shift to the Washington, D.C., suburb of Silver Spring, Maryland.

EDITORS

Six editors have served the *Silent Worker/Deaf American:* George S. Porter, 1892–1929; Bill R. White, 1948–1949; Loel F. Schreiber, 1950–1951; Byron B. Burnes, 1951–1958; Jess M. Smith, 1959–1980; and Muriel Strassler, since 1980. Porter was a member of the New Jersey School for the Deaf staff. The next four editors served in part-time capacities. In September 1980, a full-time editor was appointed as a staff member of the NAD's Home Office.

Appointment of the editor is made by the president of the NAD, subject to the approval of its executive board. This is in keeping with the article in the organization's bylaws authorizing official publications.

CONTENTS

For many years following its inception, the magazine carried mostly school news due to its place of publication. Changeover to a national magazine brought about a preponderance of national news coverage and countless "success" articles, along with an abundance of pictorial and artistic illustrations.

Advertisements tell of forthcoming events, of books and other publications having to do with deaf people and deafness, of the availability of specialty merchandise and devices for signals and various forms of communication—especially telecommunication equipment. Club and religious directories are carried at token advertising rates.

Sports coverage, although not feasible in terms of up-to-date reporting, has long been one of the magazine's leading attractions. Annual summaries of high school football, basketball, wrestling, and track are eagerly awaited by deaf teen-agers. Detailed summaries of the quadrennial World Games of the Deaf were carried in the past but are now assigned to the NAD's tabloid newspaper, the *Broadcaster.*

Local news, once a standby, has been phased out due to space limitations and inappropriateness for a national publication. Regular columns have become fewer. Feature articles concerning outstanding deaf persons have become in-depth presentations.

As an official publication of the NAD, the *Deaf American* no longer prints extensive reports and financial statements, but still carries the listing of the Order of the Georges, the association's standby "Advancing Members." The *Broadcaster* prints such official items.

Changing cover formats and mastheads provide interesting contrasts as to the contents and thrust of the magazine. Likewise, typography and style have followed trends in graphic arts technology.

EDITORIAL POLICIES

The "old" *Silent Worker* had no hard-and-fast editorial policy, with the editorials tending to be middle-of-the-road or non-controversial in approach, because the state-funded New Jersey School for the Deaf sponsored it. Advocacy was apparent, however, in publication of articles emphasizing the capabilities of deaf persons in various walks of life, including the arts.

Revival of the magazine by the NAD was accompanied by an increasingly hard-line editorial policy stressing the rights of deaf people and battling against discrimination, both general and specific. Included was the struggle for acceptance of total communication as a viable philosophy in the education of deaf children. Feature articles, as a part of such a policy, complemented editorial statements. Invariably, the editorial policy has been in keeping with the objectives of the NAD. *See* SOCIO-LINGUISTICS: Total Communication.

The editor decides what material is published, with the president and the executive director of the NAD acting as close consultants. While some features are the result of assignments, unsolicited manuscripts come from a broad range of sources. Timeliness and space limitations dictate that only a small percentage of material submitted will get into print. Since the magazine and the NAD are nonprofit organizations, writers do not receive remuneration. This does not discourage submission of articles and reports, because few publications exist on a national basis as an outlet for material about the deaf community.

The magazine's policy on reprints is flexible, because material is not copyrighted. Use of feature articles about prominent and successful deaf persons in anthologies has long been encouraged. Bound copies in school and other libraries provide readings in deaf heritage.

Jess M. Smith

DEAF-BLINDNESS

The independence of a person without the ability to see and hear is sharply curtailed. Loss of both of the distance-sensing functions, audition and vision, confronts educators and rehabilitators with their most difficult assignment. How can people continue to live without seeing and hearing? What means do they use to communicate? Is mobility possible? Do such people work, marry, and raise families? Education, employment, transportation, social relations, recreation, and most daily activities usually require the ability to see or hear. How can deaf-blind people enjoy television, radio, theater? In what ways are their occupational choices limited? Do they require specially designed living quarters in order to enjoy even a modicum of freedom in moving about?

BEGINNING OF FEDERAL ASSISTANCE

Despite their twin disabilities, deaf-blind people can, and usually do, lead rewarding lives, provided they receive the assistance they must have to function in a complex society. Because deaf-blindness is a rare condition, afflicted people have had comparatively little attention from federal, state, or local government and voluntary agencies. The first federal programs specifically for deaf-blind persons were initiated only in 1968. That year saw the passage of legislation establishing the National Center for Deaf/Blind Youth and Adults, a rehabilitation facility, and the Regional Educational Programs for Deaf-Blind Students, designed to assist the states in educating deaf-blind children. Twelve years elapsed before the first nationwide study of the needs of this population sponsored by the federal government was undertaken. It was jointly sponsored by the Rehabilitation Services Administration and Special Education Programs, two federal agencies with substantial responsibilities for these severely disabled people. "Little" and "late" perhaps characterize the federal efforts to provide specific aids for deaf-blind people of all ages.

The event that stirred the U.S. Congress, and later the federal administration, was the 1964–1965 rubella epidemic that affected many pregnant women. Those who contracted rubella usually suffered only what seemed like a mild cold, but if the infection occurred in the first trimester of the pregnancies, the fetuses frequently developed anomalies in their visual or auditory systems. Of the estimated 30,000 infants who were damaged in that epidemic, an estimated 1500 were born deaf and blind. For 1966–1967, the American Foundation for the Blind's register of deaf-blind schoolchildren in the United States totaled 564. Of the 564, only 177 were enrolled in educational programs. *See* HEARING LOSS: Prenatal Causes.

The dramatic increase in the number of deaf-blind children who would be applying for schooling was certain to stress the limited educational facilities, and the impending crisis led the Congress to appropriate special funds for education in 1968. At the same time, rehabilitation administrators were able to convince federal legislators that efforts on behalf of adult deaf-blind persons would also be needed.

These indications of long-term federal neglect, which have been followed by remedial efforts, typify public reaction to deaf-blind people. With rare exceptions, like Laura Bridgman and Helen Keller, they rarely attract the general public's interest. Even when these two historic examples are cited in the literature, they are not presented as examples of a class of disabled individuals, but rather as significant and rare exceptions. For some lay persons and professionals alike, curiosity about deaf-blindness is replaced by a strong revulsion for the very thought of such a condition. The emotional reaction to losing both senses leads to suppression of thoughts about deaf-blindness. This is particularly true of deaf people and of blind people, who are terrified that they might lose the remaining distance sense and thus reduce their independence. In practical terms, the lack of interest in deaf-blind people translates into a lack of society's attention to their needs: they have clearly been underserved. *See* BRIDGMAN, LAURA DEWEY; KELLER, HELEN.

The earlier efforts to provide deaf-blind people with social services were made by individuals and private agencies, like the Perkins School for the Blind, and by some of the state agencies. Since the federal government has taken the lead in addressing their education and rehabilitation needs, deaf-blind people have begun to receive social services from almost all of the state education and rehabilitation agencies. Nonetheless, services for deaf-blind people are far behind those for most other disability groups.

It is important to note that deaf-blind people share a common loss of their distance senses and little else. Their individuality remains intact. Some are brilliant, like the poet Robert Smithdas, and some are severely mentally retarded. Their socioeconomic conditions vary widely. Deaf-blind people are of all ages, though the majority are in the senescent years. Some are well educated and some have had no schooling at all. Some reside in institutions and some in their own or their relatives' homes. Aside from deafness and blindness, they are as varied as the general population.

The education and rehabilitation of deaf-blind people is entering a new era. In the nineteenth century, teachers like Samuel Gridley Howe, first director of the Perkins School for the Blind and the man responsible for the instruction of Laura Bridgman and Anne Sullivan, Helen Keller's teacher, became famous for accepting the challenge posed by their deaf-blind students. They were regarded as heroes for undertaking what others believed was an impossible task. In the twentieth century, Peter Salmon and his colleagues at the Industrial Home for the Blind (Brooklyn) are equally deserving of praise for initiating efforts to rehabilitate deaf-blind adults. Because of their pioneering, society in the coming era will no longer honor educators and rehabilitators for merely entering work with deaf-blind persons: their predecessors' accomplishments have established the feasibility of teaching deaf-blind children and assisting deaf-blind adults in gaining employment and a large measure of independence in their daily living.

The United States and most of the other developed nations are committed to providing educational services to deaf-blind children and some rehabilitation services to deaf-blind adults. In poorer, underdeveloped nations, deaf-blind people do not fare so well. Working with deaf-blind persons, regardless of their ages, is not easy; nor is it routinely successful. The demands on professionals are substantial, but the rewards can also be great. The following sections contain detailed information about the problems in the education and rehabilitation of deaf-blind persons. It is important, however, to note that the progress made in providing these social services denies any society the right to dismiss expenditures on behalf of deaf-blind people as futile. Those serving them do not find that goals are frequently met, but the failures can be charged as much to limitations of resources and inexperience of personnel as to any inherent lack of ability of deaf-blind people. For deaf-blind people, as for all disabled persons, the coming era should be one of commitment on the part of society to their full citizenship.

DECLARATION OF RIGHTS

At the 1977 meeting of its Committee on Services to the Deaf-Blind the World Council for the Welfare of the Blind set forth a Declaration of Rights of Deaf-Blind Persons. Delegates from the 30 countries attending the conference subsequently adopted it and commended it to the attention of the world. The Declaration reads as follows:

"Article 1. Every deaf-blind person is entitled to enjoy the universal rights that are guaranteed to all people by the United Nations Declaration of Human Rights and the rights provided for all disabled persons by the Declaration of Rights of Disabled Persons.

"Article 2. Deaf-blind persons have the right to expect that their capabilities and their aspirations to lead a normal life within the community and their ability to do so shall be recognized and respected by all governments, administrators, educational and rehabilitation personnel and the general public.

"Article 3. Deaf-blind persons have the right to receive the best possible medical treatment and care for the restoration of sight and hearing and the services required to utilize the remaining sight and hearing, including the provision of the most effective optical and hearing aids, speech training, when appropriate, and other forms of rehabilitation intended to secure maximum independence.

"Article 4. Deaf-blind persons have the right to economic security to ensure a satisfactory standard of living and the right to secure work commensurate with their capabilities and abilities or to engage in other meaningful tasks, for which the requisite education and training shall be provided.

"Article 5. Deaf-blind persons shall have the right to lead an independent life as an integrated member of the family and community, including the right to live on their own or to marry and raise a family. Where a deaf-blind person lives within a family, greatest possible support shall be provided to the whole family unit by the appropriate authorities. If institutional care is advisable, it shall be provided in a surrounding and under such conditions that it resembles normal life as closely as possible.

"Article 6. Deaf-blind persons shall have the right, at no cost, to the services of an interpreter with whom they can communicate effectively to maintain contact with others and with the environment.

"Article 7. Deaf-blind persons shall have the right to current news, information, reading matter and educational material in a medium and form which they can assimilate. Technical devices that could serve to this end shall be provided and research in this area shall be encouraged.

"Article 8. Deaf-blind persons shall have the right to engage in leisure time recreational activities, which shall be provided for their benefit, and the right and opportunity to organize their own clubs or associations for self-improvement and social betterment.

"Article 9. Deaf-blind persons shall have the right to be consulted on all matters of direct concern to them and to legal advice and protection against improper abridgment of their rights due to their disabilities."

Definition of Deaf-Blindness

The term deaf-blindness has been variously construed. Legislators and professionals have not fully agreed on how to differentiate the deaf-blind syndrome from conditions that include both impairments of hearing and vision but not deafness and blindness.

Congress, establishing perhaps the most liberal definition in that it would encompass the largest number of persons, defined deaf-blind children as "children who have auditory and visual handicaps, the combination of which causes such severe communication and other development and educational problems that they cannot properly be accommodated in special education programs solely for the hearing handicapped child or for the visually handicapped." Federal law, then, accepts as "deaf-blind" the children who are neither deaf nor blind but have severe hearing and visual impairments.

At the other extreme, and less inclusive, is the definition used by the rehabilitators who manage the Helen Keller National Center for Deaf/Blind Youth and Adults (HKNC) in carrying out its obligations under the Rehabilitation Act of 1973: "Central visual acuity of 20/200 or less in the better eye with corrective lenses or central acuity of 20/200 if there is a field defect such that the peripheral diameter of visual field subtends an angular distance no greater than 20 degrees, and a chronic hearing impairment so severe that most speech cannot be understood with optimum amplification, and the combination of the two causes extreme difficulty for the person to attain independence in activities of daily living, psycho-social adjustment or in the pursuit of a vocational objective." According to these criteria, the deaf-blind adults served by HKNC must be legally blind and technically deaf. Persons labeled deaf-blind by the federal regulations would not be so called by the principal agency funded by the federal government to implement its rehabilitation policies.

While these definitions indicate the limits within which the term deaf-blindness has been applied, they do not account for all of the variations. Blindness is not uniformly defined throughout the United States; however, the most common definition is embedded in the HKNC definition: "central visual acuity of 20/200 or less in the better eye with best correction or a visual field that subtends an angular distance no greater than 20 degrees." Central acuity of 20/200 means that a person needs to be 20 feet (6 meters) from an object to see what the normal person sees at 200 feet (60 meters). It is sometimes likened to trying to see through glasses smeared with cold cream. A visual field of only 20 degrees is like viewing the world through a slit in a cardboard covering the eyes. (Recall that these examples described the best vision for someone to be labeled blind.) In short, persons with vision as described in the definition are severely visually disabled.

Until the 1968 congressional action, deafness had no legal definition, since it involved no sanctions or benefits under the law. (Deafness is now mentioned in a number of laws at both the federal and state levels, but these laws do not define what is meant by it; they treat deafness as if the term is uniformly regarded by professionals and lay persons alike.) Within the professional disciplines dealing directly with deafness, its meaning has many different constructions, nullifying its usefulness for any scientific or professional purposes unless meaning is carefully specified by the user. However, educators and rehabilitators have now come to agree that deafness is an auditory disability that affects communication; specifically: "Deafness is the inability to hear and understand normal speech through the ear alone, even with best available amplification."

This definition avoids the tendency to include extraneous factors, such as the age at onset of impaired hearing or the ability to speak, both of which have been included in some earlier definitions, oc-

casionally along with other criteria. Lacking in the definition are specific audiometric criteria, such as the better-ear average (BEA), which is the arithmetic average of thresholds for the so-called speech frequencies, 500, 1000, and 2000 hertz. The reason for this seeming oversight is that the BEA does not correlate well with individuals' reports of the ability to use their hearing. The functional qualifications, therefore, have become more acceptable, with the possibility remaining that audiometry will eventually provide a measure of hearing performance satisfactory to practitioners in related disciplines. The deafness referred to in the definition of deaf-blindness, then, means that deaf persons cannot depend on their hearing to carry on a conversation or to listen to a broadcast speech; their hearing alone is inadequate for communication. *See* AUDIOLOGIC CLASSIFICATION.

Aside from their conjoint disabilities, deaf-blind people may have little in common, differing as to the presence of other disabling conditions, educational backgrounds, means of communication, socioeconomic status, and other characteristics. All of these characteristics have a bearing upon social-service delivery, but the initial and governing limitations on providing for deaf-blind people are their twin sensory disabilities. It is, therefore, on those, and only on those, disabilities that the definition adopted for this article is focused: "Deaf-blindness involves visual and auditory disabilities so great that they prevent accommodation in programs for those who are only visually or auditorily impaired." This definition is effectively the same as that recommended by the World Council for the Welfare of the Blind at the 1977 meeting of its Committee on Services to the Deaf-Blind ("substantial visual and hearing losses that the combined impairments cause extreme difficulty in the pursuit of educational, vocational, and avocational goals") and by the U.S. Congress, cited above.

The definition makes up for its lack of mensurational precision by its functional utility. As will be seen, such a definition creates some problems in determining the size of the affected population, but its comprehensibility in practice balances the statistical defect. The Congress, in legislating for children, and HKNC, in serving adults, have chosen different limits for the definition of deaf-blindness. In practice, imposing different criteria for deaf-blind children and adults leads to a discontinuity of services for some persons that is inimical to their welfare. Consider a child who has been educated in programs for deaf-blind students but who is denied rehabilitation services on leaving the school, because either the child's vision or hearing does not qualify for those services under the more restrictive view of deaf-blindness that, for example, is used by HKNC. Being introduced to a different group of service providers who are unfamiliar with deaf-blindness might seriously disrupt the transition from education to occupation.

On the other hand, the broad definition of deaf-blindness may be confusing in that the largest number of new cases occurs in the over-65 age group. Unfortunately, social services for that age group are skimpy, so the more inclusive definition's emphasis on services to define the condition may initially be confusing. Elderly persons whose impaired vision and hearing prevent them from participating in rehabilitation programs might properly be classified as deaf-blind, but when no programs for disabled persons in their age group exist, their numbers might be overlooked. Nonetheless, the definition's intent is clear and its application direct for demographic purposes. The designer of a demographic survey need only bear in mind that the definition of deaf-blindness does not depend upon services being available, but classifies individuals on the basis of their abilities to qualify for participation in potential programs.

In providing estimates of the size of the deaf-blind population, this article provides data on all three variations of the basic definitions of deaf-blindness and has given each a name: (1) Exclusive: Deaf-blind persons cannot hear and understand speech through the ear alone and have vision poorer than 20/200 in the better eye, with all possible correction, or visual fields that subtend an angular distance of 20 degrees or less. (2) Moderate: Deaf-blind persons are either deaf and severely visually impaired, or blind and severely hearing-impaired. (3) Inclusive: Deaf-blind persons are individuals who are neither deaf nor blind but have both auditory and visual disabilities that interfere with their being served as hearing- or vision-impaired persons. These three definitional variations provide optional viewpoints for consideration in program development, suggesting different groups that might be served. They lead to a range of data that can be helpful in understanding the nature of the population and in predicting trends within it. They also lead, as their appellations suggest, to completely different estimates of the size of the deaf-blind population. The Inclusive definition provides the largest estimate of this population, and the Exclusive the smallest estimate.

By having data relating to the three different definitions, the divergences in practices among those now serving the deaf-blind population are confronted. Federal law directs educators to observe the Inclusive definition. Acting under another federal law, rehabilitators have tended to adopt the Exclusive definition; others have put into practice the Moderate definition in selecting clients for programs designed to serve deaf-blind people. Knowledge of this situation should allow a better understanding of conflicting accounts in the literature

and the reaching of conclusions as to which definition (and which policies associated with the definition selected) is most appropriate. With respect to that latter point, definitions are not right or wrong; they serve a purpose in communication. However, in this instance, the definition selected also suggests the kinds of programs that are apt to be followed: which clients are served and which rejected; which persons are entitled to particular benefits and which denied them. The underlying issues, then, are not merely semantic or only of concern to demographers.

Advocates for deaf-blind people will probably want to impress the public and government officials with the large numbers that are found under the Inclusive definition. Estimates of great numbers of affected individuals can aid spokespersons for a group to capture the attention of busy legislators and harassed administrators. But what matters to the affected population, in the long run, are not the numbers counted but the persons served. In thinking about definitions, one should not lose sight of the people behind the terms and numbers.

Deaf-Blind Population

How many people are deaf-blind? Very little comparable data are available on the deaf-blind population outside of the United States. This section will, therefore, concentrate entirely on deaf-blind persons within the United States and will not attempt to reconcile data from other countries with the United States information. The reason is not alone the paucity of information from the other countries but the difficulty in determining how they made the diagnosis of deaf-blindness and, hence, how to make comparisons with the more abundant United States data.

For the United States, the national study of the deaf-blind population commissioned by the Department of Education reported prevalences and prevalence rates (Table 1). The numbers alone are impressive, ranging from almost 42,000 to over

Table 1. Prevalence and Prevalence Rates for Three Categories of Deaf-Blindness in the Civilian, Noninstitutionalized Population of the United States, 1980

Category*	Prevalence	Prevalence per 100,000
Exclusive	41,859	20
Moderate	425,158	201
Inclusive	734,275	346

*Each category includes the numbers in the preceding category, that is, those who are in the Exclusive category are also in the Moderate and Inclusive categories, and the Inclusive category includes those persons counted in the Exclusive and Moderate categories.

700,000 persons. The range of prevalence rates also illustrates the importance of the definition selected in determining the answer to the question: How many people are deaf-blind? The rate for deaf-blindness using the Inclusive definition is 346 per 100,000; by using the Exclusive definition, the rate falls to 20 per 100,000—a 17-fold difference! The criticality of definition in determining the size of the population is thus manifest. The total of 734,275 represents the estimate for all persons who would meet the definitions proposed by the Congress, if they were extended to persons of all ages, and by the World Council for the Welfare of the Blind, which does cover all ages.

Even if one elected to call deaf-blind only those persons in the Exclusive definition, data on the other two groups would be important to planning. Persons in the Moderate and Inclusive categories have a much higher probability of entering the Exclusive category than persons in the general population. By using all three categories in planning educational and rehabilitation services, administrators are more likely to be prepared for periodic shifts in the size of the target population. They can assume, for instance, that a larger proportion of young persons in the Moderate category than in the general population will become deaf-blind by the Exclusive criteria as they grow older. Though to a lesser degree, the same holds true for persons in the Inclusive category. Furthermore, most authorities would contend that providing services for those in the Moderate and Inclusive categories requires strategies and tactics more like those needed for persons in the Exclusive category than for persons who are only blind or only deaf. With both distance senses impaired, clients require modifications of procedures usually followed with blind or with deaf people. Having these three sets of rates can be useful to epidemiologists; the comparisons of rates for the three categories within a given geographical location can provide clues useful to detecting its causes. Additionally, being confronted by the three rates should constantly remind administrators of the need for establishing and maintaining vigorous programs to prevent deaf-blindness. Such programs should be directed particularly at those now in the Moderate and Inclusive categories: providing hygienic practices to protect the residual vision and hearing.

CHARACTERISTICS: UNITED STATES

Being deaf and blind does not assure any other characteristics; that is, the conjoint conditions may occur at any age, at any socioeconomic level, to persons of both sexes, and so forth. Yet some tendencies appear in the data from various national, regional, and local surveys. These statistical regularities have implications for planning, but their

usefulness for heuristic ends, particularly for epidemiology, is not entirely clear. The relationships may have no causal or predictive value. They are discussed here for their descriptive contributions and their applications in drawing plans for serving this group.

Age of Deaf-Blind Persons The highest prevalence rate in each of the four categories of deaf-blindness is for persons in the 65-year-and-over age group. The relationship between age and physical impairments has been demonstrated in other disabilities. As individuals grow older, the statistical risks of impairments increase; that is, older persons have been exposed to more potentially injurious situations than younger people. Individuals who have no impairments in youth may develop them as they age; minor impairments in youth tend to become major impairments in later age. Particularly with respect to deaf-blindness, it should be noted that every blind person is at great risk of becoming deaf-blind, as is true for every deaf person. Having suffered disability of either sight or hearing, a person is halfway toward deaf-blindness.

The influence of an epidemic on the prevalence of deaf-blindness can be clearly seen from data gathered by the Department of Education's Regional Centers for the Education of Deaf-Blind Children. Table 2 shows the "rubella bulge," the excess of deaf-blind children born in 1964–1965, who were from 14 to 16 years of age in 1980. In the adjacent categories, prevalences are much lower,

Table 2. Number of Deaf-Blind Students Known to Regional Centers for the Education of Deaf-Blind Children, by Age, in the United States, 1980

Age, Years	Number
All ages	5761
Under 1	11
2	91
3	144
4	170
5	204
6	263
7	265
8	280
9	303
10	294
11	339
12	308
13	337
14	556
15	625
16	458
17	234
18	184
19	187
20	260
21	248

being 308 and 337, respectively, for ages 12 and 13, and 234 and 184, respectively, for ages 17 and 18.

From these data, an expected prevalence of about 250 to 300 deaf-blind children per year would seem to be the nonepidemic prevalence over this time span, representing genetic, disease, accident, and injury factors leading to deaf-blindness in children. The occurrence of more than 1600 children in the three-year span is about double what would have been projected from the other years' experience. The dramatic increase in numbers of deaf-blind children in the years coincident with the rubella outbreak makes plausible the infectious-epidemic explanation of the substantial excesses above expectation.

Nature of Population Statistics The data on the prevalence of deaf-blindness over time show that a rate established from data for a given period may have little application to another period. As obvious as this becomes when a time series is reviewed, the fact has not often penetrated the planning of educational and rehabilitative services. To be effective, plans should be based upon current information. Obtaining up-to-date statistics for a rare population like deaf-blind people, however, requires highly specialized, relatively expensive techniques. Those responsible for social services must determine whether precision in providing services balances the costs of planning based upon accurate information.

Sex of Deaf-Blind Persons In each of the categories, Inclusive, Moderate, and Exclusive, females have a higher rate of deaf-blindness than males. The female preponderance may be partially attributed to females' longer lifespans. In the younger years, females appear to survive illnesses that prove fatal for males and to incur injuries less frequently than males. Living longer, the females are at greater risk of accidents, illnesses, diseases, and degenerative conditions that in turn lead to deaf-blindness.

Geographical Distribution Consideration of deaf-blindness in a particular locale requires attention to discrepancies in rates from area to area (Table 3). The prevalence rate for the Exclusive category of deaf-blindness is highest in the Northeast region and lowest in the North-Central region. For the remaining two categories, the highest prevalence

rates are in the South and lowest, again, in the North-Central region.

In regarding these breakdowns of prevalence rates by geographical regions and type of deaf-blindness, large sampling errors attached to each estimated rate must be considered. Small differences in estimated regional rates need not be taken too seriously in that a second sample might find a different ordering of results. However, the differences among rates found, where large, make an important point: national prevalence rates cannot be relied upon to provide local prevalence rates with any reasonable precision. For instance, using the national rate for the Exclusive definition of deaf-blindness would result in providing far more services than would be needed in the North-Central and far less than would be needed in the Northeast. The Moderate and Inclusive rates averaged across all states would be too high for all but those in the South, where they would be too low. Even greater discrepancies can be demonstrated when comparing deaf-blindness rates for states, rather than regions, to each other. Note further that, while differences in regional and state rates for deaf-blindness may not have the desirable statistical reliability, they do alert epidemiologists to possible etiological factors that might otherwise be overlooked. Investigating disproportionate prevalence rates in particular sections of the country is one of the epidemiologist's tools with which to uncover etiological circumstances. Without reliable statistics, epidemiology is deprived of a critical means to that end.

A somewhat different set of prevalence rates reinforces these points. Congress established regional programs to serve deaf-blind children. Ten regional and state programs were in operation by 1976, covering all the United States. Each of the programs prepared a census of deaf-blind children in their jurisdictions. Dividing their counts of deaf-blind children by the number of all children in elementary and secondary schools in their areas yields the rates shown in Table 4.

The differences between geographical locations are extreme. The lowest rate for deaf-blindness in this age range is for the Southeastern area (6.4 per 100,000); the highest is for the Mountain Plains (21.3 per 100,000), with the Southwestern region close behind (20.7 per 100,000). Allowing for discrepancies in diagnostic criteria, care in casefinding, and other potential sources of error, the results still show differences in rates too large to be reasonably explained away solely by methodological flaws. A major potential source of the higher rates in the Mountain Plains and the Southwest is the greater potency of the rubella epidemics that occurred in that area. Other factors, such as genetics, may account for additional portions of the almost four-times greater prevalence rate in the Mountain

Table 3. Prevalences per 100,000 for Three Categories of Deaf-Blindness, by Geographical Region, in the United States, 1980

Category	National	North-east	North-Central	South	West
Exclusive	20	32	6	22	21
Moderate	201	177	143	296	145
Inclusive	346	288	285	464	298

Table 4. Rates of Deaf-Blind Children per 100,000 Students in Elementary and Secondary Schools, by Regional and State Centers, in the United States, 1976

Area Served	Rate per 100,000 Students Enrolled
United States	10.9
New England	7.7
Mid-Atlantic North and Caribbean	8.3
Mid-Atlantic	9.2
Southeastern	6.4
Midwestern	7.3
South-Central	12.9
Texas	13.2
Mountain Plains	21.3
Northwestern	15.1
Southwestern	20.7

Plains. As suggested above, epidemiological studies might expose instances of extreme consanguinity or other conditions that can explain, and lead to the reduction in, the high prevalence rate for deaf-blindness in this region. Overall, the states west of the Mississippi appear to have higher rates than those east of it—again suggesting, at least partially, an epidemic explanation for the excess in the rates. Finally, these figures make clear why national rates should not be applied to specific regions within the country. The rate for the United States as a whole (10.9 per 100,000) sharply underestimates or overestimates most of the area's prevalence rates. As shown by the range (6.4 to 21.3), the national rate is nearly twice as high as the smallest rate and half as high as the largest. Basing plans for service delivery on the national rate would introduce serious errors in most areas.

INSTITUTIONALIZATION

The impairment of both distance senses may seem to cause so great a handicap that institutionalization is the inevitable placement for those most severely involved. National data do not bear this out. Of the 747,457 deaf-blind persons estimated nationally in all categories, only 13,182 are residents of institutions—1.7 percent. The rate of institutionalization among deaf-blind persons is much greater than for the general population (deaf-blindness occurs at about 1.0 percent of the total institutionalized population, compared to a presence of 0.3 percent deaf-blindness in the general population, by the Inclusive definition of deaf-blindness). This means that for every deaf-blind person who is institutionalized more than 50 are living outside of institutions. Though relatively small, the institutionalized population requires special consideration in planning, because it presents un-

usual problems and entails generally higher costs than the noninstitutionalized population. Within the institutionalized population, costs for maintaining deaf-blind residents is far greater than for other residents. Economically, at least, the number of institutionalized deaf-blind persons merits the attention of social planners.

CLUSTERING

The principle of clustering applies to deaf-blind persons as it does to other disabled persons. The principle states that having one disability raises the probability of the existence of additional disabilities. This appears to be the case with deaf-blind people. Despite their two disabilities, the probability of yet more physical disabilities is greater than for those who have none or only one disability. The additional disabilities include cardiac disorders and metabolic problems, of which diabetes mellitus is relatively frequently observed. For those developing programs to serve deaf-blind people, careful attention should be paid to their potentially fragile health and frequency of other physical impairments.

MISSING INFORMATION

On a national basis, little reliable information is available about the distribution of deaf-blindness by race, socioeconomic status, education, and a host of other variables that would be of interest to social planners and practitioners. Is deaf-blindness more or less prevalent among Black, Caucasian, Oriental, Spanish-surnamed, or other racial-cultural group? Data that would bear upon this important question have not been reported, with the exception of some highly suspect data published in the decennial censuses from 1870 to 1930. The civil status of the United States deaf-blind population has not been reported, nor has its educational distribution been published. No national data are available on the labor-force status of deaf-blind adults or about their economic standings in the community. The gaps in the information about deaf-blind people in the United States provide one further bit of evidence of how little attention has been given to them by the government. Population surveys are the province of government for reasons of authority and economy. A national survey of deaf-blind persons, in particular, must have federal support, because to determine their characteristics with reasonable precision demands very expensive procedures that no private organization is likely to invest. Until public attitudes toward deaf-blind people change, those curious about their principal characteristics must remain frustrated. Worse, those responsible for planning services for deaf-blind people must depend upon fragmentary and frequently inaccurate data.

Education

The child who cannot see or hear presents a major challenge to the educator who is accustomed to instructing children who have at least one intact sensory modality. The child's lack of audition and vision prevents the teacher from using well-practiced skills and demands approaches to communication that are rarely found among educators. In addition, the task of educating deaf-blind children requires an unusual philosophical stance: while sensory deficits are limiting, they do not preclude academic progress, if teaching and caregiving adults and the deaf-blind child are properly motivated. The National Needs Assessment of Services for Deaf-Blind Persons concluded that a major obstacle to the education of deaf-blind students presently in schools in the United States is the very low levels of expectation for their futures held by their parents, teachers, and school administrators. Where those responsible for education of any group do not anticipate that group will achieve at high, or at least average, levels, a self-fulfilling prophecy is set in motion. Thus, the education of deaf-blind children begins with a handicap as serious as the children's lack of distance receptors: the poor motivation of those adults who are responsible for planning and implementing their schooling.

EARLY HISTORY

Public funding for the education of deaf-blind children in the United States is relatively recent. Until 1968, no federal programs for deaf-blind children existed. Only a few states made any publicly supported efforts to provide for the instructional needs of these children. Indeed, until passage of the Education for All Handicapped Children Act of 1975, they were not required to do so. A local education agency, supported by the state, could deny services to children it deemed too difficult or too expensive to serve. Yet, the public may believe that deaf-blind children have been given the benefits of special education for at least a century. The paradox is simply resolved by noting that there have been some notable efforts to educate deaf-blind children, but these attempts have all been privately supported. *See* EDUCATION OF THE HANDICAPPED ACT.

The first successful report of the education of a deaf-blind person was by Samuel Gridley Howe. Howe was the first director of what is now known as the Perkins School for the Blind (Massachusetts). In 1837, he accepted as a student an eight-year-old deaf-blind girl named Laura Bridgman. She was later to become famous, thanks in part to Charles Dickens, who wrote about her in his popular account of his visit to the United States, *American Notes*. Howe began by teaching Laura the names of objects around her, using her sense of touch to discriminate the names in raised letters pasted on them. Later, she learned the manual alphabet, which she could differentiate tactually, thereby increasing the range and the speed of communication between her and her teacher. She also used the manual alphabet to express herself, as she never learned to speak.

Laura Bridgman's success paved the way for another famous woman, Helen Keller. Keller was originally tutored by Anne Sullivan, then a newly graduated student from Perkins. Later, Keller attended Perkins, where she met Laura Bridgman as an elderly lady. Keller's brilliant career demonstrated the feasibility of educating deaf-blind children, but the notoriety that followed her throughout her adult life did not result in large numbers of programs being established. A likely reason for the lack of response from educators was their belief that the numbers of deaf-blind children were too few to require much attention. The first major publication on the subject in 1904 estimated that the total deaf-blind population amounted to only 94 persons, of whom 16 were in educational programs. That the estimate is too low is supported by the U.S. Bureau of the Census, which reported 491 deaf-blind persons in the 1900 decennial census.

The first school with a formal program for deaf-blind children was Perkins, which established the Deaf-Blind Department in 1931. In the prior 100 years, Perkins had accommodated fewer than a dozen deaf-blind students. Within the next three decades, seven other schools established special programs: New York Institute for the Education of the Blind (1936), California State School for the Blind (1945), Michigan School for the Blind (1949), Washington State School for the Blind (1951), Iowa School for the Deaf (1950–1957), Alabama Institute for the Deaf and Blind (1953), Illinois Braille and Sight Saving School (1957). After Iowa closed its department, the remaining seven constituted the entire educational resource with which the United States had to meet the sudden addition of over 5000 deaf-blind children who confronted educators after the 1964–1965 rubella epidemic. In testimony before Congress in 1968, it was pointed out that these schools were educating only 110 of the estimated 500 then in need of schooling. The remainder were at home or in institutions for the mentally retarded, not receiving suitable education.

ELEMENTARY AND SECONDARY EDUCATION ACT OF 1968

On January 2, 1968, the first direct federal support for the education of deaf-blind children was signed into law. The Elementary and Secondary Education Act contained authorization for the establishment of centers and services for deaf-blind children. This move was in direct response to the newly perceived need for educational services for deaf-blind children. The states were not providing for them.

As a result of the federal infusion of money and provision of leadership, facilities for deaf-blind children rapidly came into being. By the time the Education for All Handicapped Children Act mandated education for all handicapped children, regardless of severity of their conditions, it was not necessary for a single state to improvise. Each had made preparations for whatever number of deaf-blind children resided in its territory. From 1968 to 1980, educational enrollments for deaf-blind students increased from about 110 to nearly 6000!

PERSONNEL PREPARATION

A substantial impediment to providing for deaf-blind students is the lack of skilled personnel to meet their needs. The shortage of professionals is evident when early identification and diagnosis should be made. Misdiagnoses are frequent, and wise advice for parents is difficult to obtain. Early intervention is essential to overcome the serious consequences of prolonged sensory deprivation, with the attendant failure to develop adequate responses to external stimulation and to acquire coping strategies and adaptive behavior of a sufficiently high order to lead eventually to a substantial measure of independence.

Teacher training which specifically addresses these problems is limited to Boston College, Michigan State University, and San Francisco State University. Otherwise, teachers are recruited from programs serving deaf or blind children or those with other severely handicapping conditions. They develop their specialization while employed as teachers of deaf-blind students. This process is not economical for teacher or student, the former often suffering early professional "burnout" and the latter being deprived of appropriate instruction during the teacher's early exposure to them.

Psychological services are seldom provided by persons who have specialized preparation for dealing with deaf-blind children. The usual psychological examination is inappropriate; special procedures developed for deaf and for blind persons need further adaptation and standardization to be appropriately used with deaf-blind persons. There are few instruments specifically standardized for assessment of deaf-blind children. An exception is the Callier-Azuza Scale, which assesses activities of daily living, and motor and cognitive skills. It is norm-referenced for use in programs serving deaf-blind infants and preschool children. Another exception is the Deaf-Blind version of the Behavioral Rating Instrument for Autistic and Other Atypical Children (BRIAAC-DB) developed for use in connection with a curriculum for deaf-blind children from infancy through the elementary years. BRIAAC-

DB has the advantages of (1) beginning assessment at primitive levels of development seldom measured by most psychometric instruments; (2) being responsive to small increments in behavioral change; and (3) not depending upon the cooperation of the individual being measured. As an observational technique, BRIAAC-DB overcomes the great difficulty in establishing rapport with most deaf-blind children, something that usually takes considerable time. By initiating assessment at very low levels and by reflecting miniscule changes in behavior, BRIAAC-DB is suited to the typical deaf-blind child, whose functioning levels are usually very low and improve very slowly. It is important to be able to detect small behavioral increments, in order to maintain the teacher's morale. As noted, a substantial problem in the education of deaf-blind children is the lack of adequate expectations for their future. To some extent, this poor teacher motivation may be due to the failure of most psychometrics to reflect improvements over the course of many months of instruction. Improvement may have been made, but be too small to be detected by the measuring instrument. Such psychometric inadequacies can have the most unfortunate consequences for the education of deaf-blind children.

COMMUNICATION

The key to the education of deaf-blind children is communication. Both Howe, with Laura Bridgman, and Anne Sullivan, with Helen Keller, described the moment of breakthrough in communicating with the deaf-blind pupil. The process of teaching deaf-blind persons to communicate has had the benefits of task analysis. M. Gold and R. Rittenhouse have routinized the insights that the pioneer educators Howe and Sullivan had intuited. What is apparent from the evidence, anecdotal and scientific, is that even congenitally deaf-blind people can communicate if given the proper education.

CURRICULUM

What needs to be taught? What is the scope of material that should be covered in the education of deaf-blind students? In what order? At what pace?

These questions of curriculum have not had as much attention as they deserve. The answers depend upon the individual student. The range of talents among deaf-blind persons is as great as in the general population. In addition to stellar performers from the past, like Keller and Bridgman, there are spectacular achievers in the present. Robert Smithdas, Director of Training at the National Center for Deaf/Blind Youths and Adults, is a published poet. Having earned his master's degree in rehabilitation, Smithdas has been a successful rehabilitator, teacher, orator, and author. The late

Richard Kinney was similarly successful, heading the Hadley School for the Blind (Winnetka, Illinois) for many years. His book *Independent Living Without Sight and Sound* contains substantial wisdom for those who wish to serve deaf-blind people. At the other extreme are severely mentally retarded individuals.

For the high-achieving deaf-blind students, little accommodation in the curriculum is required, beyond assuring for communication. For less able students, the pace of instruction must be slowed. The instructor should never take for granted the previous learning of these students, since they profit little from incidental learning—from information picked up in overhearing conversations with others, in dialogues with parents and friends, by watching television or listening to the radio. Most of their information must come from direct tuition, until they build adequate reading skills to manage braille or other forms by themselves. For the lowest stratum, the curricular demands shift. The problem is partially that most instructional programs start at levels too high for the students. The programs assume that the students, even beginners, bring to the classroom much more information and experience than most deaf-blind individuals have. One of the few curricular approaches that presumes virtually no basic skills is the Assessment-Intervention Model (AIM) developed specifically for low-functioning deaf-blind children. AIM, for example, in teaching the student to manage eating, does not assume the child has learned to swallow: the lessons for that portion of the curriculum begin with the assessment of the child's ability to ingest food. The lesson plans are highly individualized and break learning into very small units. AIM was developed to be coordinate with assessment by BRIAAC-DB.

The scope of any curriculum for deaf-blind students needs no arbitrarily determined "ceiling." The goal of self-care, for example, need not be seen as the epitome of educational progress, but rather as a minimal objective. Competitive employment requires a variety of skills that deaf-blind persons can acquire; there are also specific aspects of daily living that may be impossible for them to manage without assistance. Travel, for instance, may be limited to specific areas, while complete freedom to venture into some territories (like big-city shopping centers) may be too dangerous. Real-life barriers are not the same as intellectual hurdles; the deaf-blind person may be unable to manage some aspects of self-care, yet be able to function cognitively without restrictions.

EARLY INTERVENTION
Early, intensive intervention is essential for deaf-blind children to reach their full educational potential. Intervention should begin as soon after birth

or onset of deaf-blindness as possible. Without direct, vigorous efforts to provide an environment that responds in ways they can apprehend, deaf-blind children depend upon their internal stimuli, leading to undesirable stereotypic, asocial behaviors. Parents and professionals should provide sensorimotor activities that compensate for the lack of external stimulation in a consistent, continuing program that use the remaining olfactory, gustatory, tactile, kinesthetic, haptic, baric, and thermic senses, as well as whatever residual hearing and sight the children may have. Such programs often follow the Piagetian model of early cognitive development. They are designed to overcome the deaf-blind children's difficulties in distinguishing self from nonself, developing an appropriate body image, and achieving a positive self-concept. Communication, social, and self-help skills that most children acquire with little obvious parental or professional attention require special programming for deaf-blind youngsters. Each activity must be task-analyzed and introduced step by step, using behavior modification and related instructional procedures. Deaf-blind children need to be given mobility skills to promote the exploration of their environment and to avoid withdrawal from social contacts.

For those parents unable to get in touch with adequate professional facilities, the John Tracy Clinic (Los Angeles) sends, at no cost, their Correspondence Learning Program for Parents of Preschool Deaf-Blind Children. The materials provide measures the parents can take in early education of these children at home.

SCHOOL YEARS
Approaches to the instruction of deaf-blind children through direct involvement of their remaining senses in carefully structured programs must continue throughout the years of formal schooling. The development of the Individualized Education Program (IEP), mandated by the Education for All Handicapped Children Act, must take into account all of the sensory modalities available to the deaf-blind child, including the assessment of residual vision and audition. Programming must be on a one-to-one basis, until the child becomes self-motivating. To avoid regression, instruction should proceed through the summer months.

LEARNING CHARACTERISTICS
The teacher of deaf-blind children encounters many behaviors that are seldom found in unimpaired students. The communication difficulties are noted above, as are the relatively slow pace with which deaf-blind students tend to acquire knowledge and skills. Certainly, communication skills are related to the ease of learning: the more communication skills the children have, the more rapidly they can

acquire concepts. In addition to these behavioral aspects, deaf-blind children frequently engage in self-stimulatory acts. They may gouge their eyes, rock their bodies rhythmically, shake their hands in front of their eyes, and make other repetitive movements that appear to have no other purpose than to stimulate the individuals making them. Educators frequently note, however, that the more active the teacher and the more engaging the curriculum, the less self-stimulation is found among the students. In other words, these acts are usually indicators that the students are not being given sufficiently interesting tasks to perform. In one sense, then, the teacher can measure the interest level of the particular activity by the extent to which the deaf-blind student engages in self-stimulation.

TEACHING TECHNIQUES

At first glance, it may seem logical to approach the education of deaf-blind people by simply merging the techniques for teaching deaf with those for teaching blind people. The idea is, however, incorrect. The rule to be observed in teaching deaf-blind children is the same one that applies throughout special education: the more extensive the disabilities, the more specific the instructional strategies and tactics. For children with no disabilities, teachers tend to address their effort to a hypothetical "average." Comparatively little attention is paid to individual learning styles and particular achievements and problems. Children with a single disability, like those who are blind or deaf, are usually approached with a more specific curriculum and more individualized communication, but again, the amount of generalized instruction is fairly great in the course of any given day. However, most deaf-blind children require one-on-one attention from the teacher. Tutoring is the rule, at least in the early years of instruction.

The successful teacher of deaf-blind children must constantly assess progress. Learning cannot be taken for granted. The process of testing can be useful in breaking through the child's tendency to be overly passive. Developing initiative in deaf-blind children is often just given lip service. Educators responsible for the child's welfare are often protective, fearing to expose the child to environmental dangers. The fear is not without foundation, but it needs to be dealt with in ways that do not restrict the child and inhibit development unnecessarily. It is a major difficulty in the education of these children—one that is difficult to deal with in practice.

The problems of restraint often become confused with those of discipline. Successful discipline begins with anticipation. The better the teacher is at anticipating actions the child may take, the fewer incidents requiring discipline will arise. Distracting the child or shifting to a new activity before the child acts out are techniques that work well with any child. In teaching deaf-blind children they are essential. Educators agree that punishment without adequate explanation accomplishes little of positive value, but providing deaf-blind children with explanations for complicated rules can try the patience and ingenuity of most teachers. It is far better, at least in the early years, to avoid confrontations by staying ahead of the child, by anticipating problems before they arise.

Speaking from the perspective of a deaf-blind person, Hadley explains the learning process: "A deaf-blind person is a walking, talking, living Sherlock Holmes most of his waking hours. He is forever putting two and two together. He may not always get four, but he certainly has extra incentives to draw as many sound inferences as possible from such clues as he can observe." Understanding this point, the teacher of deaf-blind students can provide substantial practice in how to "play Sherlock Holmes." Equally important, the instructor can verbalize the bases for inferences that the deaf-blind student makes, and in that way can assist the student to discard the unsuccessful and to retain and increase the use of the successful. Deaf-blind persons will, throughout their lives, make decisions from limited cues. To be independent, they must be more often correct than wrong. Using reduced information, deaf-blind persons can manage their homes, hold jobs, and enjoy a productive social life.

USHER'S SYNDROME

Victims of Usher's syndrome are typically born deaf and do not become blind until they are in their late teens or early twenties. Night blindness often manifests itself during their early adolescence, and a significant narrowing of their visual fields begins at that time. However, the significance of these changes is often hidden from the affected individual. Not until the visual loss is too massive to be ignored is the person told of the condition that will lead to irreversible, total or near-total blindness. Educators, who often know the diagnosis while the child is still in the grades, avoid telling the child on the grounds that, since nothing can be done to arrest the visual deterioration, the child is better off not knowing. Deaf-blind adults, however, disagree. They note that they lost many years in which they could have prepared for their inevitable condition. They feel betrayed by parents and educators who did not give them the opportunity to adjust over the early years, when they might have more easily accepted their fate than when in early adulthood, as they prepared for careers and family life that would require radical revision of all plans made in innocence of the impending blindness. *See* HEARING LOSS: Genetic Causes.

Recognizing that it is easier for a sighted person to learn braille and to develop many strategies for mobility than it is for one who is blind, it would seem that advising a child of impending blindness makes better sense. The emotional impact can also be cushioned by spreading it over youthful years rather than condensing it into a few months in early adulthood. Vocational planning and education should be directed toward preparing the individual to live without sight and sound, rather than to deafness only. Failure to take advantage of early diagnosis (Usher's syndrome can usually be diagnosed by six years of age or earlier) cannot be excused on the grounds that it is "better for the child." Manifestly, it is not. As with all of the education of deaf-blind persons, the sooner educational strategies are engaged to aid the afflicted individual to deal with the reduced sensory input, the more likely will be success.

Etiology

The causes of deaf-blindness are varied. Some deaf-blindness is due to genetic factors, some to accidents, some to injuries, some to illnesses, and some to combinations of factors. The importance of etiological investigations is their contribution to prevention and to planning of services. When the causes are known, the possibilities of prevention increase, since the causal factors can often be avoided. For example, as genetic knowledge grows, the genetic counselor can advise couples of the likelihood that their offspring will develop particular conditions. Identification of maternal rubella as a causal factor in deafness, blindness, and deaf-blindness has led to efforts to eradicate this mild-seeming childhood infection and to prescribe gamma globulin to pregnant mothers who are exposed to it. Instructing workers about industrial hazards and protective devices can prevent some industrial injuries that lead to deafness and blindness.

With respect to planning, an appreciation of etiology can improve the projections of the future incidence of deaf-blindness. The present knowledge of causal factors leads to anticipation of a greatly increased number of deaf-blind persons in the population over the period from 1980 to 2050. At the same time, the influence of different preventive measures on the incidence of deaf-blindness can be better assessed as they become more widely or less widely introduced. An epidemic of rubella alerts the planner to make adjustments in plans for deaf-blind children and to prepare for the increase in the number of deaf-blind adults. Similarly, shifts in the age distribution in a state or the addition of a new manufacturing facility in an industry that has a history of frequent accidents involving the eyes and ears should cause planners of services for deaf-blind persons to reexamine their estimates of future numbers to be served. In these ways, a knowledge of etiologies associated with deaf-blindness can be applied to making provisions for the necessary services.

TERMINOLOGY

To understand etiological research, terminological distinctions must be clarified. For one, there is a critical difference between incidence and prevalence data. Incidence refers to the number of new cases arising per unit time, while prevalence refers to the total number of cases existing at a particular point of time. The two figures for the same condition may seem to be related, but it is important to note that one cannot be derived from the other. The mathematics need not be understood if the intuitive basis for the distinction between the two concepts is clear: incidence need not be cumulative, since affected individuals may die. Hence, the prevalences of a condition may remain the same from year to year, despite the fact that in those years there is a high incidence of that condition. Once this and related differences between incidence and prevalence are grasped, their independence is clear.

Another distinction that demographers and epidemiologists make is between accidents and injuries. An accident is an unpredictable event in which damage to persons may occur. An injury is the destruction or damage of tissue that results in loss of structure or impairment of function. Injuries can occur that are not accidental. For example, some drug therapies, like the mycins, lead to loss of hearing when applied in large doses over time. The resulting damage to audition is not accidental (unpredictable), though it may be thoroughly justified where no alternative is available to save the patient's life. In the following discussions, these semantic distinctions will be observed.

AGING

The most common combination of factors associated with deaf-blindness involves aging. That a substantial portion of the deaf-blind population results from deaf or blind persons growing older is beyond doubt, but why this is true is not clear. Is it due to some natural process that is called aging or to being exposed to increasing risks of diseases, accidents, and injuries as the years pass by? Some theorists posit a built-in limit to cellular life that extends to organs and, eventually, to the individuals themselves. This notion of an inherent time limit in all animals, including human beings, confronts an alternative hypothesis that life is continuous and cell replacement basically infinite. The latter position holds that the association between degenerative conditions, such as deaf-blindness, and aging is based upon their shared relation to time;

that is, the increase in deafness and blindness results from the fact that the longer one lives, the greater the probability of disease, accident, and injury and, of course, the greater the age of the individual. Thus, the latter theory believes that the data can be explained by the coincidence of factors rather than their causal relationship.

The arguments between these two theories have more than academic interest: the genetic position (cell death is inherent) reduces the importance of preventive measures that the environmental position (cell life is unlimited) puts in the forefront. The implications for planning are equally clear. If deaf-blind people have a limited life-span, the need to provide for their care beyond, say, 85 years of age diminishes rapidly. But if their life-spans are largely dependent upon the care they receive, then society must make provisions for them for much longer periods of time, provided that they are given good treatment.

GENETICS

The chromosomes that direct the development of the auditory and visual systems may deviate from the norm, leading to deaf-blindness. There are at least 26 genetic syndromes associated with deaf-blindness. The most common is Usher's syndrome, an autosomal recessive condition that consists of severe-to-profound hearing impairment (usually deafness) and progressive visual impairment due to retinitis pigmentosa. Estimates of its prevalence in the general population range from 1.4 to 3 cases per 100,000. Among deaf school children,, from 1 to almost 8 percent have been found to have Usher's syndrome, or a visual condition closely related to it. In the deaf-blind population, the proportion of adults exhibiting this syndrome has been estimated to be as high as 40 percent.

There is no known cure for Usher's syndrome. Its onset is insidious, though an ophthalmologist can usually identify its signs by fundoscopic examination at five or six years of age. The retina displays a characteristic pigmentary change. An electroretinogram provides objective measure of the retina's electrical response to light, which also provides a diagnostic sign of Usher's syndrome.

There are a number of other autosomal recessive syndromes involving deafness and retinal degeneration. They are much rarer than Usher's syndrome, though nonetheless devastating to the affected individuals. Bearing the names of the writers who first described them, some of these syndromes are Cockayne, Refsum, and Laurence-Moon-Bardet-Biedl. Other names simply indicate the two affected functions, as in deafness with optic atrophy and deafness with retinal aplasia, conditions noted with sufficient frequency to warrant several theoretical case studies and papers.

The diversity of potential genetic causes make the study of them particularly difficult. Deaf-blindness is a relatively rare condition; within that condition, many of the genetic syndromes are rare. Assuming that deaf-blindness occurs at a rate of 20 per 100,000 and that a particular genetic anomaly arises only once in 100 deaf-blind children, then a sample of 500,000 children in the general population would be needed to find one child with that particular syndrome. In genetic research this means very large samples of affected individuals must often be studied to establish existence of the various conditions. However, advances in electron microscopy and in biochemical techniques offer a promise of more incisive studies with fewer individuals, shrinking the great bulk of "idiopathic" cases of deaf-blindness in favor of more precisely determining etiology, some large portion of which is suspected to be genetic.

INVASION OF THE FETAL ENVIRONMENT

The developing fetus is subject to a number of potentially damaging circumstances resulting from factors affecting the mother. The most dramatic of these is maternal rubella. The virus may affect any organ system, resulting in mentally retarded, heart-damaged, blind, deaf, or deaf-blind children.

The 1964–1965 epidemic may actually have been a series of rubella epidemics involving different strains of the virus. Their contiguity in time brought into focus the hitherto ignored consequences of "childhood diseases," a phrase that makes them seem mild. Their consequences to the vulnerable fetus, however, clearly are not mild. Congress reacted to the epidemic by enacting legislation "to eradicate rubella." The result has been a massive inoculation program under federal auspices, greater public attention to the disease, and the provision of gamma globulin to pregnant women who are at risk of rubella infection. Because of this federal program, there has been a tendency to consider that rubella epidemics are a thing of the past. Unfortunately, that is not the case. New Jersey had two fairly large rubella epidemics in 1979 and 1982; the Seattle-Vancouver area had a major rubella epidemic in 1981–1982. In each of these epidemics, some number of deaf-blind children were born. Other smaller outbreaks of rubella may have gone unnoticed, since physicians have tended to stop reporting cases of rubella to the Federal Disease Control Center, in Atlanta, incorrectly believing that the disease is now largely eradicated.

The nature of the damage that results from maternal rubella appears to depend upon the developmental stage of the fetus at the time of the viral assault and upon the strain of the virus. Large rubella epidemics a few years earlier in Sweden and England have been intensely studied. In the Swedish epidemic, the single greatest damage was cardiac; in the English, it was cerebral, resulting in many mentally retarded children. While both epidemics produced substantial numbers of deaf children, neither seems to have been associated with a great incidence of deaf-blindness. Follow-up studies of children affected by maternal rubella in the United States epidemic may have shown that the virus remains active in them for years after birth, with continuing potential for damage to them. The greatest damage to the fetus arises from infection that strikes the mother during the first trimester of pregnancy. It was earlier believed that rubella infections of the mother later in pregnancy were without consequence to the fetus; this supposition now appears to be incorrect. Damage to the fetus can result from maternal rubella in the second trimester of pregnancy, though the frequency and extent of the defects appear to be lower than when the infection occurs in the first trimester. About half of children whose mothers had rubella during the first three months of their fetal life suffered damage, which ranged from death through deaf-blindness to growth deficiencies.

Numbers of other maternal factors have been associated with deafness and blindness. Infection of the mother by measles and by chicken pox have been cited as potential causes of deafness, blindness, and deaf-blindness. Noninfective agents—smoking and ingestion of drugs, whether addictive, like alcohol, or therapeutic, like streptomycin—have also been indicted as causal agents. While rare, deafness due to maternal toxoplasmosis and diabetes have been found as probable causes of deaf-blindness.

Perinatal factors must be considered among those responsible for deaf-blindness. A major cause of blindness is maternal syphilis, and where proper precautions are not taken (for example, putting silver nitrate in the eyes of the neonate), the probability of infecting the emerging infant is great. If that child is already deaf, the result would be a deaf-blind person.

ACCIDENTS

Data on the incidence of deafness and blindness that result from accidents have been independently calculated; data on the amount of deaf-blindness due to accidents have not. The difficulties in gathering such information are patent. Such studies would need to distinguish between individuals who are either deaf or blind and who suffer injury to the other sense, and those who lose both senses in accidents. Studies of large samples of deaf-blind individuals do not provide incidence data, since the mortality rate from accidents that cause extensive damage to both vision and audition would be extremely high. Nonetheless, such studies would be

of some benefit to the planners, who could make use of this datum in projecting the likely consequences of various environmental changes in the regions of their responsibilities.

The emerging infant is particularly vulnerable to the hazards of the extrauterine environment. Careless handling and, if the infant is premature, measures to sustain life may result in sensory impairments. Accidental hemorrhages associated with prolonged labors and instrument deliveries sometimes result in deaf-blindness. Use of oxygen with premature infants often leads to retrolental fibroplasia if precautions are not observed; as a cause of blindness, oxygen therapy has been greatly reduced in frequency of occurrence. The immature, metabolically unstable newborn infants must be carefully defended against a great number of insults that can permanently deprive them of sight and hearing.

In adults, industrial accidents that cause deafness, particularly noise-related injuries, and blindness are only infrequently involved in deaf-blindness, except for individuals already deaf or blind who may be working in situations that place them at risk of damage to the remaining distance sense. In the area of prevention, this latter consideration highlights the importance of instructing deaf and blind persons in hygienic practices designed to spare their vision and hearing.

DISEASES AND INJURIES

What portion of deaf-blindness results from disease and injuries? In the course of aging, blind and deaf individuals are exposed to conditions that may damage their hearing and seeing. The debilitating effects of prolonged exposure to intense sound are well documented. The fact that central nervous system tissue does not spontaneously regenerate means that as repeated loud-noise exposures occur, the damage to the cochlea acumulates, resulting in eventual serious impairment of hearing. Similar effects occur with respect to retinal damage. *See* HEARING LOSS: Noise-Induced.

What about diseases that affect vision and hearing? Diabetes mellitus has been associated with visual loss; in a small number of cases, audition is also affected. This combination is particularly difficult to treat, since diabetes also affects the peripheral nervous system, reducing tactual sensitivity. Another rare and difficult syndrome is deaf-blindness associated with multiple sclerosis. Degenerative diseases that involve the central nervous system have not been extensively documented in the literature on deaf-blindness, but their existence cannot be ignored, especially in view of the problems they present to education and rehabilitation. Given more thorough studies of etiology in the deaf-blind population, it is possible that the contribution of these diseases to the prevalence of deaf-blindness might be found to be far greater than is presently suspected.

Infectious diseases that cause high fevers, like spinal meningitis and whooping cough (pertussis), frequently lead to damage to the auditory and optic nerves if not treated promptly and effectively. However, cases in which the disease is allowed to progress to the point that it damages both vision and hearing appear to be rare, at least partly because, having caused that much tissue damage, death would probably result. The incidence of other diseases which formerly made a substantial contribution to deaf-blindness, like syphilis, has been substantially reduced. Early treatment, again, limits their deleterious effects on the central nervous system.

Despite the advances in medical practice, there remain ample potential disease agents which can cause massive damage to the sensory systems. Deaf adults should be particularly alert to cataracts, some of which appear to be inherited, and blind adults should avoid exposure to intense sound over prolonged periods of time.

Communication

Making and maintaining meaningful contact with other people presents severe problems to the person deprived of both vision and audition. Yet, difficult as the task may be, ample solutions are available. Indeed, so many possibilities for effective communication exist that they actually augment the difficulties faced by deaf-blind persons. The individuality of deaf-blind people—their diversity of skills and differences in communication abilities—obviates any one approach to communication.

How a deaf-blind person chooses to communicate depends upon several factors: the extent of residual vision and hearing, the ages at onset of hearing and seeing impairments, educational background, intelligence, and other physical characteristics. These factors can be combined in a great number of ways, each of which is associated with a different way to communicate.

A Complete Guide to Communication with Deaf-Blind Persons by Kates and Schein lists 76 distinct approaches. Since deaf-blind persons may use different combinations of these techniques—preferring one method receptively and another expressively, for instance—the potential selections in a given situation number several hundred combinations. Here only the broad categories and a few examples under each will be considered. They are grouped by the sensorimotor areas they involve.

TACTION AND KINESTHESIS

If residual hearing and sight are not useful for communication, then recourse may be made to touch (taction) and the sense of the movements of one's own body parts (kinesthesis). Tactual sensitivity, measured by two-point discrimination, is greatest on the chest, with areas of the back nearly as sensitive. These parts of the body, however, are inconvenient for daily communication, since people are expected to remain clothed. The hands provide a less sensitive but more accessible area.

Alphabets One of the most frequently employed techniques is to spell in the hand of the deaf-blind person, that is, for the sender to make letters of one of the manual alphabets and for the deaf-blind person to receive the message by touching the sender's hand. This procedure can be accomplished in a variety of ways, depending upon which alphabet representation is used.

1. Amanubet. In the United States the most common manual alphabet code used is the American One-Handed Alphabet (Amanubet). The sender forms the various letters, while the deaf-blind person lightly covers the sender's hand with his or her own. A person familiar with this method is able to read fingerspelling comfortably at a rate of about 50 to 75 words per minute. Since speech usually occurs at rates more than twice these speeds, some shortcuts (abbreviations and conventions) have been invented for use between the deaf-blind persons and those with whom they frequently communicate.

2. British Two-Handed Alphabet. An alternative fingerspelling code is the British Two-Handed Alphabet, used by British deaf people. When used with deaf-blind people, the speller replaces his or her passive hand with the deaf-blind person's hand. Thus, to indicate a vowel, the sender touches the tips of one of the deaf-blind receiver's five fingers: *a*—thumb, *e*—forefinger, *i*—middle finger, *o*—ring finger, and *u*—little finger. Other letters are made by various movements and configurations of fingers placed in the receiver's hand.

3. Lorm Alphabet. In Austria, Germany, and the Netherlands, a different version of the two-handed alphabet is used. Called the Lorm Alphabet after its inventor, it has been adopted by the Committee on Services for the Deaf-Blind of the World Council for the Welfare of the Blind. Though no formal research had been conducted to determine if these two-handed methods are faster to use or easier to learn than Amanubet, the international organization made its decision on the basis of its judgment that Amanubet required the detection of movements too minute for many persons to make consistently. Intuitively, that decision may be correct, but deaf-blind persons in the United States seem to prefer one-handed fingerspelling, if they use fingerspelling in communication. *See* SIGNS: Fingerspelling.

4. Morse Code. If the deaf-blind person is fa-

miliar with International Morse Code, messages can be conveyed in it. A dot is represented by a tap, and a dash by a short stroke, of the sender's forefinger on whatever part of the deaf-blind person's body is used (usually the hand or forearm). It has

Lorm Alphabet. (After L. Kates and J. D. Schein, *A Complete Guide to Communication with Deaf-Blind Persons*, National Association of the Deaf, 1980)

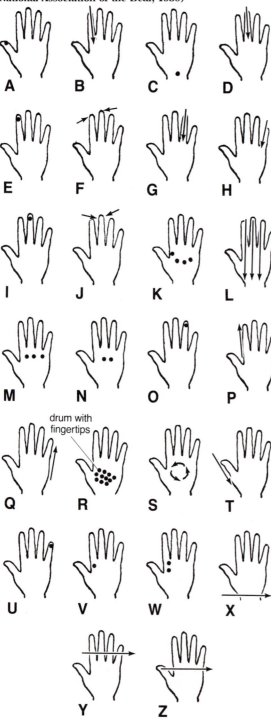

the advantage that many persons already know Morse from membership in the Armed Forces and in the Boy and Girl Scouts or from amateur radio operation. Its use is relatively efficient and inconspicuous, and people generally find it fairly easy to learn. However, like all spelling systems, its continuous use can become tedious.

5. Alphabet printing. For newly deaf-blind persons unfamiliar with any of these finger alphabets, a sender, using the forefinger, can write directly in the deaf-blind person's palm. Standard methods for printing the letters have been devised, to maximize their discrimination and to avoid confusions. The Committee on Services for the Deaf-Blind of the World Council for the Welfare of the Blind has adopted standard instructions for printing the alphabet.

6. Braille. Louis Braille (1809–1852) developed his dot-matrix alphabet code for the French army to use in communicating silently at night. The army did not make much use of it, but blind and deaf-blind people did. Braille letters are made with raised dots arranged in a 3-by-2 cell. To read them, the fingers of one hand are moved across the line of dots while the other hand keeps track of the line being read so that none is inadvertently skipped. To increase speed, braille introduces numerous abbreviations. In Grade 1 braille, each word is spelled out; in Grade 2, 189 contractions are used, along with abbreviations of some words. The deaf-blind person can use braille for notetaking or for writing messages, as well as for receiving them.

While braille is versatile and has the virtue of providing a permanent record that can be referred to again and again, it is limited by the individual's tactile sensitivity. Considerable acuity of touch is needed to make the discriminations that braille reading entails. Only about one-third of blind children learn to use braille. For persons with peripheral neuropathies, such as diabetes, braille reading is largely out of the question. For those who can learn to use the braille code, it provides considerable independence.

7. Other tactual codes. The Moon System or Alphabet is widely used in Great Britain in educating blind and deaf-blind children, but it is not as popular in the United States as braille. Invented by William Moon in 1847, the code retains many of the original forms of the printed alphabet. Basically, Moon has only nine characters that are placed in different positions to represent the 26 letters of the English alphabet. It is reportedly easier to read than braille for persons whose tactual sensitivity is relatively dull, as the discriminations involved are less fine. Another feature is that alternating lines of Moon are read in the opposite direction; that is, the first line is always read from left to right, the second right to left, and the third left to right again.

This makes it easy for the reader to keep track of the text without seeing it. Despite its virtues, Moon has little likelihood of being adopted in the United States, which has too large an investment in personnel familiar with braille, in already brailled texts, and in equipment using braille to discard it.

Similarly, other tactual codes have been invented to improve upon braille. Cross was developed by a deaf-blind man for use with his friends; Fishburne uses large embossed characters; HAIBRL is a pair of 16-dot matrices designed by an engineer. Like Moon, and despite any advantages these codes have over braille, they are unlikely to replace it.

Primitive Indicators In addition to alphabets, primitive indicators can be used—for example, one squeeze of the hand to mean yes and two to mean no. With only these two signals, fairly elaborate conversation can be conducted. The following is a brief illustration, in which the deaf-blind person

International Print Alphabet with which one can write directly on a deaf-blind person's palm. (After L. Kates and J. D. Schein, *A Complete Guide to Communication with Deaf-Blind Persons*, National Association of the Deaf, 1980)

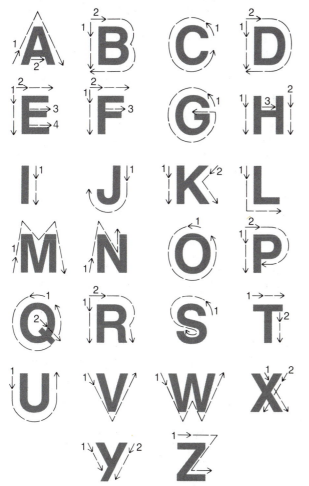

A B C D E F G H I

J K L M N O P Q R

S T U V W X Y Z

Moon Alphabet. (After L. Kates and J. D. Schein, *A Complete Guide to Communication with Deaf-Blind Persons*, National Association of the Deaf, 1980)

speaks and the other person responds entirely by signaling yes or no:

"I'm hungry. Is dinner ready?" Yes.

"Are we eating in the dining room?" No.

"Then are we eating in the kitchen?" Yes.

"Such informality must mean we are having a simple meal. Are we having eggs?" Yes.

"Good. I'll have mine scrambled. Is that agreeable?" Yes.

The limitations of the primitive indicators for conversation are apparent. For one, the deaf-blind person must be sophisticated and able to speak. Names, for example, would have to be guessed—a sizable task—and the deaf-blind person must remain in control of the conversation, reducing the other person's role to that of respondent. Even the addition of some signals (such as three squeezes to mean "I don't know") does not give sufficient range to the conversational possibilities. For that reason, some additional form of communication is requisite for most adults.

Sign Sign language can be used with deaf-blind persons who know it. In order to receive the signs, they face the signer, placing their hands over the signer's. They can then follow the signs as they are made. If, in addition to signing, the person uses Amanubet, it can be received by the deaf-blind person who has cupped the left hand over the sender's right (fingerspelling) hand. This system is often used by persons deaf-blind from Usher's syndrome, since they usually have learned sign as a primary form of communication and, after they have lost their sight, then continue "to think in sign." Because signing is much faster than spelling, this combination of methods is both comprehensive and efficient. See SIGN LANGUAGES.

Alphabet Devices A great many devices have been manufactured to facilitate communication with deaf-blind persons. They are basically of three types: those using a tactile code, those using the visual English alphabet, and those using words and symbols. The most versatile and frequently used are machines for delivering braille.

1. Machines. A number of machines have been developed that take advantage of the compactness of the braille code. The Tellatouch consists of a keyboard that activates a ball on the other side of the machine. As a key is struck, the ball turns to the corresponding representation of the letter in braille. Thus, the sender does not have to know braille to communicate with a deaf-blind person who does. The same principle has been extended to a device that can send typed messages through a modem that produces a signal which is then transmitted over a telephone line to a corresponding device that converts the signal to a braille letter, much as the Tellatouch does. In this way, two deaf-blind people have access to telecommunication. Another variation is the Kurzweil Reading Machine, which scans print and converts the optically imaged letters to braille. The machine enables the deaf-blind person to read newspapers and books independently.

2. Alphabet glove. An inexpensive, easy-to-use device is the alphabet glove. Each letter of the alphabet has a different position on the hand. To spell a word, the deaf-blind person dons the glove and the sighted person presses with his or her index finger the portions of the glove corresponding to the letters. To indicate numbers, the back of the glove is used, the numbers being different positions on the back of the hand. The system is usually learned with little difficulty by the deaf-blind person who has developed good language skills, and it requires no learning on the part of the sighted sender except the ability to read English. It is useful for situations in which the deaf-blind person encounters someone who is unfamiliar with deaf-blind communication. The glove can be homemade for very little expense.

3. Alphabet plate. Alphabet plates are essentially raised versions of the letters of the English alphabet. The deaf-blind person reads them in the same way that braille or Moon is read, by running the finger over the plate. To spell a word, the sighted person moves the deaf-blind person's index finger consecutively from letter to letter. In turn, if the deaf-blind person does not speak but has developed language skills, he or she can point to the letters to spell out responses. The device does not make for speedy communication, and it is seldom used with adults.

4. Letter boards. Individual letters of metal or plastic can be used to spell words that a deaf-blind person can read tactually. The letters can be moved about easily on magnetic board, which can be used with plastic letters if they have metal attached to their backs. This device is inexpensive and easily manipulated even by persons with cerebral palsy, since it does not require the motor coordination of writing.

5. Communication board. The communication board follows the principles of the alphabet plate and glove, in that the sighted person needs to learn very little to use one. There are many variations. Some contain the letters of the alphabet in print, embossed English characters, and braille. Symbols might be included to indicate various objects and activities—for example, a drawing of a plate, knife, and fork to symbolize eating. Such symbols, like sign, can compactly convey a great deal of information quickly, at least centering the conversation on the topic. Then spelling a word or two can specify the aspect of the activity that is desired. The boards can work in both directions, as devices for expression and for reception. Some boards contain Bliss Symbolics, which greatly expands the range of messages that can be conveyed with a minimum of pointing.

Each of the variations places different demands upon the sender and receiver: some require the deaf-blind person to learn quite a few locations; others, almost none. By the same token, some of the systems (such as Bliss Symbolics) require prior orientation to the system before the sighted person can use them efficiently. The conversation boards have the advantage of being quickly and cheaply made at home. Commercially available models are also available.

6. Writing guides. For individuals who learned to write before they lost their sight, writing provides an expressive avenue when a writing guide—any device to help the blind person write in relatively straight lines on the paper—is used. Paper with embossed (raised) lines accomplishes the same purpose as the writing guides.

Alphabet glove. (After L. Kates and J. D. Schein, *A Complete Guide to Communication with Deaf-Blind Persons*, National Association of the Deaf, 1980)

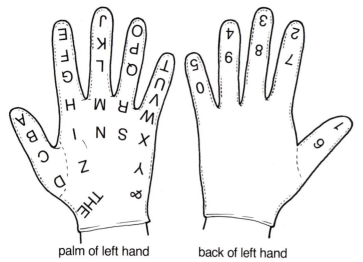

palm of left hand   back of left hand

Tadoma Developed by Sophia K. Alcorn in 1945, this method is a form of tactual lipreading. The deaf-blind person places fingers of the dominant hand across the cheek of the speaker and alongside the windpipe, and the thumb rests lightly on the speaker's lips. This enables the deaf-blind person to feel the shape of the lips and the oral cavity reflected on the cheeks, vibrations in the nasal region, the tongue's position, and, at the same time, the airflow reflected on the surface of the windpipe. Alcorn named the method for the two deaf-blind pupils, Tad and Oma, whom she was teaching at the time. Some deaf-blind persons who have residual vision use Tadoma as a supplementary aid to lipreading. For others, the method takes a great deal of patient instruction to develop adequate skill. As with visual lipreading, some persons seem capable of achieving great proficiency with it.

Electronic Paging Devices Electronic paging devices can also be used with deaf-blind persons. Worn on the belt or on the wrist, these devices vibrate in response to a signal generator activated at a distance from the receiver. In this way, deaf-blind people can have some of the benefits of radio transmission of messages. The signals are limited to simple codes. In a factory, for instance, one vibration might mean that it is break time, and two vibrations, that the receiver should report to the office. The device is particularly applicable to use around the home—for example, to call children to come in from the playground and to signal adults that someone is at the door or that the telephone is ringing. Because skin sensitivity tends to recover slowly after stimulation, the use of Morse code with such a device has not yet proved successful. It is, however, within the realm of probability that some system could be made to serve deaf-blind people in the way that radio and television serve the general population.

AUDITION

If deaf-blind persons can gain any benefit from a hearing aid, it should be issued. The communication function alone is not all that is improved by electronic amplification. The hearing aid allows many deaf-blind persons to remain in auditory contact with the environment. Such contact can mean a great deal to the emotional well-being of the deaf-blind person. The signaling function of audition is also important. Many deaf-blind persons after receiving hearing aids report that their sense of security is greater and their sense of isolation reduced. Being able to anticipate the approach of another person can be very comforting. The ability to detect a doorbell or other environmental sounds can mean much to the daily functioning of the deaf-blind individual. *See* HEARING AIDS.

VISION

Deaf-blind people who have any residual vision should be given the support that will enable them to use it. Large print, low-vision aids, and magnifiers of all kinds, including television projection systems, can be used by some deaf-blind people. If the deaf-blind person only has light perception, he or she may be able to use visual signaling systems. These, like the auditory signals, help deaf-blind persons gain increased control over their environments.

Deaf-blind persons with some useful vision can use it for telecommunication. A visual speech indicator can be used to enable deaf-blind persons to use telephones. The deaf-blind person must be able to speak and to see well enough to detect the deflections of a needle on a sensitive meter. The deaf-blind person advises callers of the code: the hearing person answers either yes or no-no, and yes-yes-yes or no-no-no to convey that the answer is indeterminate. The needle of the speech indicator indicates the number of syllables in response to the deaf-blind person's questions. The system is limited in the ways described above under "Primitive Indicators." It has the advantage of inexpensively providing access to unmodified telephones for those deaf-blind persons who are qualified to use it. Speech indicators can also be made to provide a flashing light in place of the deflecting needle. The latter variation of this idea should make it useful for more deaf-blind people.

INTERPRETERS

Interpreters, or persons skilled in the use of a variety of methods with which to communicate with deaf persons, may be used at various times. Deaf-blind persons attending a meeting cannot participate without the services of an interpreter who conveys what is spoken and also speaks for them if they cannot. Interpreters also function in a variety of one-to-one situations, such as employment interviews, contacts with social service agencies, and medical visits.

The interpreters use whatever of the above methods of communication are preferred by the deaf-blind person. They may spell in the hand, using one of the several alphabet codes. Or the interpreter and the deaf-blind person may use hand-over-hand sign. A professional interpreter first determines what the deaf-blind person is adept at using for expression and reception and then uses these methods, unless the interpreter is not proficient with them. In that case, the interpreter contacts another interpreter who is proficient. Occasionally, deaf persons have been pressed into service at meetings attended by a number of deaf-blind people, because each deaf-blind person must have a single interpreter. The procedure then is to have a hearing interpreter next to the speaker to sign what is spoken. These signs can be seen by deaf persons throughout the room. Each, in turn, spells into the hands of, or signs hand-over-hand with, a deaf-blind person. The procedure may seem awkward, but in practice it makes efficient use of the available interpreting skills. *See* Interpreting.

Individual Differences

If deaf-blind persons have some remnants of vision and audition, it is consequential as to when they lost their hearing and sight. Persons born deaf, for example, will most often depend upon sign language as the principal mode of communication. Even with a 10 degree visual field, signs can be read, provided that the signer takes and holds a position within the narrow confines of the deaf-blind person's vision. Persons who are born blind and late in life become deaf usually prefer to express themselves by speaking and to receive messages through a combination of best available amplification and tactual means. If they have no useful residual hearing, they still can speak but will exclusively use tactual means of receiving communication.

Second, the deaf-blind individuals' education and intelligence will be important factors in determining their preference for communication modes. If they have not learned to read braille in school, they may not learn it as adults. If their language development has been curtailed, losing their hearing and vision will not improve it. Though they may depend upon spelling in the hand, their comprehension will be limited by their poor language.

As noted above, deaf-blind people may have other physical problems in addition to their sensory disabilities. If these impairments include diabetes mellitus, for example, then peripheral sensitivity will likely be reduced to the point that braille cannot be read and that other tactual systems are useless. If the deaf-blind person is also cerebral-palsied, further limitations are placed on communication by the motor impairments. Thus, the combination of degrees of hearing and of visual impairments, the ages at which the impairments occurred, the amount and kind of education, and the presence of other physical impairments contribute to the choice of communication methods. These considerations lead to the general rule that, in approaching a deaf-blind person, one should investigate with that person the choices of methods of communication, expressive and receptive, that are preferred. The deaf-blind person's decisions about how to communicate should govern the initial contacts. Within the limits imposed by deaf-blind persons' sensory and physical disabilities, there are ample choices of effective methods that can be used to communicate.

Rehabilitation

For the education and rehabilitation of deaf-blind people, communication holds the key. However, it is not the only process required for successful rehabilitation. After a brief glimpse at the history of rehabilitation of deaf-blind persons in the United States, this section will review the rehabilitation process with deaf-blind clients and will introduce considerations germane to their successful life adjustment.

Historical Overview

In 1920, the Industrial Home for the Blind, in Brooklyn, began to offer limited services to occasional deaf-blind adults. Not until 1945, however, did the agency institute a department to provide systematic rehabilitation for deaf-blind applicants. This program began under the inspired leadership of a blind rehabilitation specialist, Peter J. Salmon. For the next two decades, Salmon tried to attract the attention of state and federal governments to the lack of any organized efforts to meet the needs of deaf-blind adults. Aided by the rubella epidemic of 1964–1965, he was finally successful when in 1968 Congress appropriated funds for a national center for deaf-blind youths and adults.

In the Rehabilitation Act of 1973, the establishment of the Helen Keller National Center for Deaf-Blind Youths and Adults is authorized. The law provides for regional programs of assistance to state and local agencies, under the national center's direction. The State of New York donated land at Sands Point, Long Island, on which the headquarters of the national center were erected. Until 1983, its operations were supervised by the Rehabilitation Services Administration, but the national center now has a direct appropriation from Congress, without that monitoring. *See* Rehabilitation: Administration.

While facilities are yet sparse, most states now recognize their obligations to rehabilitate deaf-blind adults. The amendments to the Rehabilitation Act of 1973 make clear Congress's intent that states assume these responsibilities. The law mandates that priority in offering rehabilitation be granted in accordance with the severity of the disabilities, and clearly deaf-blindness is among the most severe of the disabling conditions confronting the rehabilitation agencies. Coupled with the Education of All Handicapped Children Act (P.L. 94-142), the federal laws have completely altered the picture of neglect for this disabled population that existed for almost the first 200 years of the United States' existence.

Casefinding and Referral

Because of the communication barriers, deaf-blind people may have great difficulty in making and maintaining contacts with service providers. First of all, the knowledge of available benefits and supports may not reach them and their immediate families. They may remain unaware of programs that can assist them to obtain gainful employment and to live more independently. Worse, agencies may be reluctant to enroll deaf-blind clients in their programs, because of the considerable resources and sizable time investment necessary to properly serve them.

An agency that desires to serve deaf-blind people should, therefore, take an active stance with respect to casefinding and referral. Federal regulations require child-find programs by state education agencies—efforts to identify and bring into public education disabled children who might otherwise remain at home or in institutions without adequate professional instruction. Parents of deaf-blind children sometimes must be convinced that their deaf-blind children are educable; school administrations, too, must sometimes be persuaded to accept deaf-blind students. For adults, casefinding alters in character but not in the need for vigorous efforts. The blind person who becomes deaf and the deaf person who becomes blind can go unserved by personnel and programs designed to alleviate the stress added by the second disability. Getting deaf and blind people accepted as deaf-blind clients is made difficult by their emotional reactions to their changed status and by the obtuseness of agencies that are unprepared to deal with the second disability. Such agencies may continue to treat deaf-blind clients as if they were only deaf or only blind. When aging further complicates the picture, deaf-blind clients may be left unserved altogether. Programs for deaf-blind senior citizens exist in few locales, and programs for senior citizens that can properly serve deaf-blind elderly persons are equally scarce. The needs for active casefinding and prompt, appropriate referral are prerequisites to sound rehabilitation programs for deaf-blind persons of any age.

INTAKE

Agencies recognize that their intake procedures can erect, for some of their potential clients, unscalable barriers to their services. This is particularly true for the deaf-blind person. Rarely does the deaf-blind person attempt to negotiate the intake maze alone, which means that obtaining services often depends upon the sophistication and patience of the person who accompanies him or her. In the case of many deaf-blind adults, the guide is one of their children or parents. The child may be too young and embarrassed by the disabled parent to be effective, and the parent too weary and infirm. The spouse may be employed and unable to take the time to accompany the deaf-blind person to the agency.

These circumstances make the intake process nightmarish for many deaf-blind people. The receptive agency not only must be sympathetic to this client group, but also must provide the communication that is essential to rehabilitation. Where the caseload is too small to justify full-time staff skilled in a range of methods for communicating with deaf-blind people, the agency should make use of professional interpreters who can bridge the communication gap.

DIAGNOSIS AND EVALUATION

Diagnosis and evaluation of deaf-blind persons should be based upon multidisciplinary consultations. As already noted, deaf-blind persons typically have additional disabilities. If deaf-blindness is due to infectious disease or metabolic disorder, then mental retardation, cerebral palsy, and other neurological impairments should be suspected. These disabilities complicate the already difficult planning process, so they must be accounted for in the early stages of rehabilitation programming. Few practitioners of any of the pertinent specialities have much experience with deaf-blindness. Their lack of experience with deaf-blind persons and the difficulties in examining them make busy professionals reluctant to accept them as patients. That is why planning is best accomplished by teams of specialists covering a wide number of disciplines, such as audiology, education (including orientation and mobility instruction), internal medicine, occupational therapy, ophthalmology, optometry, otology, physiatrics, physical therapy, psychology, rehabilitation, speech pathology, and vocational evaluation. The collective wisdom and attention of a group made up of some of these disciplines will likely uncover and cast into proper perspective all of the major factors that need to be considered in rehabilitating deaf-blind clients.

INDIVIDUAL PLANNING

A great handicap to deaf-blind persons' futures is the lack of confidence the educational or rehabilitation planner may have in their ability to succeed. Surveys of the attitudes of professionals who were working with deaf-blind students showed that few professionals regarded the students as being ultimately able to enter competitive employment and live independently. Parents of these same students were equally pessimistic about their futures. Federal laws for education and rehabilitation require individual written plans for every disabled person being served. Developing individual educational and rehabilitation plans for deaf-blind people calls for imagination and ingenuity, as well as a positive outlook. Because planning must have the client's participation, those involved in the process should encourage the deaf-blind client, too, to adopt a positive view of the future. If the planning is realistic and optimistic, it will serve as a motivating factor in promoting the client's progress throughout rehabilitation.

PHYSICAL RESTORATION

Efforts at regaining sensory and motor capacities are as important to the deaf-blind person as to those less impaired. Removal of cataracts, medical-surgical adjustments of malfunctioning limbs, and correction of any organic defects should be carefully considered. Particular attention should be paid to repairing middle-ear anomalies so as to improve the individual's hearing ability, since even small contributions to improved communication are critical to the well-being of deaf-blind people. Any tendency to regard them as "beyond help" should be vigorously fought.

ADJUSTMENT TRAINING

The rehabilitator faced by deaf-blind adolescent clients may regard prospects for their successful vocational placement as dim. Following six months or more of intensive adjustment training, the rehabilitator will likely revise those negative views. The social isolation of the deaf-blind child cannot be overemphasized. Deprived of wide contacts with adults and peers who actively and effectively communicate with them, these individuals lack adequate interpersonal skills. Given the opportunity, however, deaf-blind youths can acquire the empathy, the sensitivity to the needs of others, the self-respect and respect for their fellows' rights, and other elements of well-functioning adults.

VOCATIONAL PREPARATION

While very few in number, some deaf-blind students do go on to higher education. Many are capable of profiting from technical-vocational programs. The preparation for successful vocational preparation should, therefore, include postsecondary education whenever indicated by the individual deaf-blind person's background and ambitions. To make these educational programs work, interpreters will be needed, along with additional support in the form of tutorials and notetaking services. Deaf-blind students in postsecondary courses should also have readily available counseling to assist them. It must not be expected that they will immediately develop strong friendships with other students and that all of the faculty members will be sympathetic. It is important, then, to provide deaf-blind students with counseling that will enable them to weather the social storms, as well as to overcome the academic problems they will encounter.

MAINTENANCE, TRANSPORTATION, AND RECREATION

Whether the deaf-blind client is entering post-secondary training or a sheltered workshop, her or his extracurricular needs must be carefully planned or the rehabilitation effort will certainly fail. Finding suitable living quarters and making arrangements for activities of daily living tax many agencies' resources. Clients who do not continue to live at home with parents must have intensive training to manage their new home environments, after such quarters have been found. Group-living arrangements for several deaf-blind persons have possibilities for solving this difficult problem. Aside from the great advantages of shared expenses for design, construction, and management of such facilities, group living affords the additional advantage of peer companionship.

Those who are newly deaf-blind will also need to be trained, along with their spouses, to adapt anew to their old quarters. Structural and other changes may be needed. A survey of the living area by an independent-living specialist is a worthwhile investment.

Once maintenance has been secured, the rehabilitator's attention turns to transportation. Routes from home to work or school must be studied: Can the client walk the distance? Is public transportation available? Does the community provide special transportation for disabled persons? Once the means for traversing the route have been determined, the deaf-blind client will need mobility instruction specific to that route. In most instances, mobility instructors for blind persons will be able to handle these assignments. Special consideration must be given to the fact that the deaf-blind person may not be able to hear bells, horns, and other auditory warnings and will likely be unable to make use of the sounds reflected by tapping a long cane. Making use of tactual and kinesthetic cues for mobility requires a different perspective than some mobility instructors are accustomed to assuming. In any event, the deaf-blind client must either learn to negotiate the route or be provided with a guide. In the latter option, the rehabilitator has the further problem of locating suitable candidates for the position.

Recreation planning should be thought of as an essential element in the rehabilitation program. If the deaf-blind client's afterclass and afterwork hours are not planned, he or she may regress, and the gains made in adjustment training lost. For deaf-blind people, accessing recreational facilities is difficult. Assistance is required to reach the facilities, and further assistance is usually needed to take advantage of them. In locations where numbers of deaf-blind rehabilitation clients live, the rehabilitator will find that assisting them to establish their own organization will enhance their efforts to develop their own recreational outlets. Directing planning toward the encouragement of social groups makes good sense in terms of agency economics and the individual welfare of the clients.

PLACEMENT, FOLLOW-UP, AND POSTEMPLOYMENT SERVICES

Job development and placement for deaf-blind clients admit of no easy solutions; nonetheless, some deaf-blind persons not only find positions in competitive employment but do so with great success. The majority, however, are not so fortunate.

In placing a deaf-blind client, job tailoring is generally required. The placement specialist usually works with the employer to identify what aspects of the workplace and of the client's occupational activities will require modification to accommodate the particular deaf-blind individual. Then, counseling specific to that placement must be undertaken with the deaf-blind client before work begins. This counseling will likely include (1) specific mobility instruction, learning the particular route to and from the workplace; (2) considerations of the particular situations with other employees that may be encountered in that setting and how best to deal with those situations; and (3) detailed orientation to the work environment, identifying useful landmarks and pointing out various hazards. As these steps would suggest, the placement of a deaf-blind client demands far greater preparation than is usually undertaken for other rehabilitation clients.

To simply place a deaf-blind client and then to provide no further services is to court rehabilitation disaster. The deaf-blind client should have assistance each time there is change in the working or home environment. Counseling should not be discontinued as soon as employment is secured. Deaf-blind workers will need frequent, brief counseling to deal with crises that are nearly certain to develop in their lives. The federal regulations governing rehabilitation make allowances for such services.

CASE MANAGEMENT

Most deaf-blind persons are clients of state agencies for blind people. Their assignment to a blind, rather than a general, rehabilitation agency is required by the regulations of most states, even for cases of Usher's syndrome. Because the latter individuals are usually born deaf, they will have been served through their developing years by education and rehabilitation agencies designed for deaf persons. At the point that their vision deteriorates to legal blindness, their cases are shifted to a different agency. This change is sometimes actively opposed by both the client and the former agency. With some justification, both argue that the client's problems are those of a blind deaf person, not a deaf blind person. The Usher's syndrome client's communication patterns and cultural backgrounds are those familiar to rehabilitators of deaf, rather than blind, clients. As the number of deaf-blind clients increases, this jurisdictional issue deserves a searching examination.

In developing its statewide program for serving deaf-blind clients, the New Jersey Commission for the Blind and Visually Impaired has adopted the concept of lifelong case management, which is a useful model to examine. As noted, deaf-blind clients have difficulty initially accessing services. They also suffer from the lack of personnel who are apt to be familiar with the special problems that deaf-blind people face, since their small numbers mean that few practitioners are likely to even have a single deaf-blind client in their professional careers. Finally, the New Jersey agency reasoned that deaf-blind persons will be candidates for social services throughout their lifetimes. Even after they are placed in employment, they should have follow-up services whenever significant changes occur in the work to which they are assigned, to the personnel with whom they must relate, or to the physical environment in which they work.

The agency's solution to those problems has been to assign to each deaf-blind client a lifetime case manager. The case manager does not attempt to provide all services, indeed may provide none except for information and referral. The case manager, then, becomes the deaf-blind client's social-service broker, determining what the client needs and arranging with the appropriate agency for the delivery of that service. The difficulties of casefinding, referral, intake, diagnosis, and evaluation are greatly attenuated by this approach. The case manager develops an understanding of the deaf-blind client, and the client becomes comfortable communicating with the case manager. In practice it may be necessary to change case managers from time to time as personnel leave the agency, but the deaf-blind client is known to the agency, and it provides the essential continuity in the service-delivery stream.

This concept of case management does not provide a cure for all of the ills faced by deaf-blind persons in their attempts to adjust to society, but it does recognize many of the barriers to obtaining the services offered by the community. It further provides the extra time that deaf-blind people need to develop relationships with others.

COUNSELING

The close professional relationship between deaf-blind client and rehabilitation counselor plays as much of a role for deaf-blind clients as for clients in general. Yet the relationship has had little attention from rehabilitation researchers or practitioners. The experts at the Industrial Home for the Blind, Brooklyn, which pioneered in the rehabilitation of deaf-blind adults, offer their accumulated wisdom in a series of monographs. Every practitioner interested in serving deaf-blind persons should give this collection thorough study. It is particularly rich in insights about the nature of the counseling relationship. The following is a sample:

"If, during the course of the interviews, it is necessary for you to secure supplementary information from others than the deaf-blind client, do not leave him completely out of your thinking and functioning. In talking to another while sitting near him, let him know by firm pressure on the back of his hand or by some motion of your hand on his that you are talking to someone else. If he insists on trying to communicate, break off your discussion with the other person long enough to let him know precisely what you are doing. Keeping him involved in your thinking and planning will help to develop in him, too, a desire to participate in your planning with him. Finally, never leave him without a relatively protracted good-bye, and do not commit yourself to further visitation unless you can be precise about your return. He has learned in the most heart-breaking way how to wait. He has also learned that most of those who have been in touch with him in the past do not return often, and rarely when they say they will. If you are to succeed with him, he must learn that you mean what you say and that he can depend on you."

Another aspect of counseling needs to be emphasized—the extra time needed. For most deaf-blind people, communication is strictly on a one-to-one basis. Information reaches them through another individual who makes direct contact with them. (Occasionally, there may be a series of individuals involved in the communication, as when a deaf person spells to a deaf-blind person what is conveyed by a sign-language interpreter who makes visual a speaker's remarks. This arrangement has arisen in meetings in which the only interpreters for some of the deaf-blind individuals have been deaf people who require interpretation. It would also occur in group counseling where sufficient hearing interpreters are not available for all of the deaf-blind persons present.) Because one-to-one communication is slow, deaf-blind people who are being counseled must be allowed extra time for the reduced pace of communication. A part of the slowness is due to the fact that the deaf-blind person cannot usually determine the context of what is said unless it is specifically described. Counselors and instructors must take the time not only to establish rapport, but also to make explicit many aspects of the particular encounter that are usually taken for granted in communication with persons who can either see or hear.

REHABILITATION GOALS

The potentially handicapping effects of deaf-blindness are perhaps best understood when placed in the context of efforts to eliminate them. They are unquestionably severe and panorganic but not irremediable. The community can make adjustments that enable deaf-blind people to function independently. Some of the adjustments are community-wide and others relate to the individual deaf-blind person. Communities can accommodate to their deaf-blind citizens without major disruptions of communal life and without mammoth expenditures. When contrasted with the costs of long-term institutionalization, the means to achieve independent living for deaf-blind people are very reasonable. Just as a few years ago Western society stopped thinking of crippled and sensorily disabled people as permanent objects of charity, society is now changing its views of deaf-blind persons—recognizing that they have excellent chances for independent living and that providing those opportunities makes good social-economic policy for the communities in which they reside.

Rehabilitation does not have many examples at hand of successfully rehabilitated deaf-blind persons. But even a few are sufficient evidence that, given the resources and the will, deaf-blind persons can achieve high levels of independence.

Bibliography

Braddy, Nella: *Anne Sullivan Macy: The Story Behind Helen Keller*, Doubleday, New York, 1933.

Dantona, R.: "Demographic Data and Status of Services for Deaf-Blind Children in the United States," in Carl E. Sherrick (ed.), *1980 Is Now*, John Tracy Clinic, Los Angeles, 1974.

————: "Demographic Data for Planning of Services for Deaf-Blind Persons," in E. G. Wolf (ed.), *Proceedings on the Delivery of Services to Deaf-Blind Persons*, North and Caribbean Regional Center for Services to Deaf-Blind Children, New York, 1980.

————: *The Development and Growth of Educational Services for Deaf-Blind Children in the United States from 1968 to 1978*, unpublished doctoral dissertation, New York University, 1984.

Dickens, Charles: *American Notes*, Scribners, New York, 1868.

Gold, M., and R. K. Rittenhouse: Task Analysis for Teaching Eight Practical Signs to Deaf-Blind Individuals, *Teaching Exceptional Children*, 10:34–38, 1978.

Howe, Maude, and Florence H. Hall: *Laura Bridgman: Dr. Howe's Famous Pupil and What He Taught Her*, Little, Brown, Boston, 1904.

Industrial Home for the Blind, Brooklyn: *Rehabilitation of Deaf-Blind Persons*, vols. 1–7, 1958.

Kates, L., and J. D. Schein: *A Complete Guide to Communication with Deaf-Blind Persons*, National Association of the Deaf, Silver Spring, Maryland, 1980.

Kinney, R: *Independent Living Without Sight and Hearing*, Hadley School for the Blind, Winnetka, Illinois, 1972.

Salmon, P. J., and H. Rusalem: "The Deaf-Blind Person: A Review of the Literature," *AAWB Annual Blindness*, pp. 15–87, 1966.

Schein, J. D.: *Serving the Deaf-Blind Population of New Jersey*, Commission for the Blind and Visually Impaired, Newark, 1984.

Stillman, R. (ed.): *The Callier-Azuza Scale*, Callier Center for Communication Disorders of the University of Texas, Dallas, 1974.

Wade, W.: *The Deaf-Blind: A Monograph*, Hecker Bros., Indianapolis, 1904.

Wolf, E. G., M. T. Delk, and J. D. Schein: *Needs Assessment of Services to Deaf-Blind Individuals*, Rehabilitation and Education Experts (REDEX), Inc., Washington, D.C., 1982.

World Council for the Welfare of the Blind: *Proceedings of the First Historic Helen Keller World Conference on Services to Deaf-Blind Youths and Adults*, Paris, 1977.

Yoken, C.: *Living with Deaf-Blindness*, National Academy of Gallaudet College, Washington, D.C., 1979.

Enid G. Wolf

DEAF POPULATION

The deaf population in the United States and, to a limited extent, in other countries as well, is examined in this article, which comprises a comprehensive overview of the many facets of this diverse population. The article is divided into sections as follows.

Demography: This section focuses on some general demographic characteristics of the deaf population in the United States, although information about prevalence rates for other countries is included as well.

Deaf Community: This section looks more narrowly at those hearing-impaired people who are part of deaf communities and examines some characteristics of these communities.

Culture and Subculture: This section focuses on the culture of deaf people. With examples from the United States and different countries, especially European nations, an overview of deaf cultural patterns is presented.

Socioeconomic Status: This examines the socioeconomic status of deaf people in the United States in terms of education, occupation, and income characteristics during the twentieth century.

Women; Minorities: Two sections examine distinct subgroups that have historically been victims of discrimination in America: women and members of racial minority groups. While these discussions focus primarily on socioeconomic characteristics of these two groups, other issues, such as the isolation of nonwhite deaf people, are mentioned.

Hard-of-Hearing: This section looks at some sociological characteristics of the many millions of people who are often caught between the world of deaf people living in deaf communities and the world of normally hearing persons.

Deafened Adults: This section examines some of the general characteristics and coping strategies of persons who acquire a significant hearing impairment after age 19.

Aged: This section looks at those deaf persons over age 65 who communicate primarily through sign language and who consider themselves members of the deaf community.

Oralists: Those deaf people who favor the use of speech rather than manual communication are examined in this section, which also includes a discussion of the oralist philosophy.

Attitudes; Advocacy and Political Participation; Social Change: The first discussion examines attitudes that hearing people have traditionally held about deaf people, some reasons why these attitudes have persisted, and the impact of these attitudes. This is followed by a look at the fairly recent effort of deaf people to challenge the negative attitudes and other barriers to full equality. Finally, the impact that social changes in modern society may have on the deaf population is examined.

John B. Christiansen

Demography

Demography is the statistical description of human populations. The characteristics usually covered by demographers include the size of the population, its vital statistics, geographic dispersion, economic status, and similar group data, as well as the trends in these statistics. In this discussion of the demography of deafness, extensive information about deaf persons has been confined largely to the United States, because few other countries have gathered and published such an amount and quality of information on deafness. Where data are known about deaf persons in other countries, references to them have been made.

DEFINITIONS

Deafness has no universally accepted definition. Unlike a disease, deafness cannot be defined in terms of a single etiological agent. The causes of deafness are diverse, including accidents, heredity, illness, and injuries. Deafness is characterized by the results of these causes, and that is why deafness must be defined in functional terms. Herein, deafness is defined as the inability to hear and understand speech through the ear alone. This definition specifies that what is lost is the communication function; thus, it must be noted that the deaf person may hear speech but cannot understand (that is, discriminate) it. By the phrase "through the ear alone," the use of vision, as in lipreading, is not considered in determining if a person is deaf, even though most deaf persons find their vision essential to meaningful interpersonal communication. In other words, the definition does not imply that deaf people are unable to communicate, only that they cannot communicate by means of audition. *See* HEARING LOSS.

Most other definitions of deafness differ in one of two ways. Some require a greater degree of auditory impairment, while others require less. Common parlance tends to use "deaf" to mean any significant loss of hearing, a condition for which the term "hearing-impaired" is preferred. At the other extreme, deafness implies no ability to hear at all, but this degree of impairment is extremely rare; most deaf people can hear some sounds, usually in the low-frequency range. Detection of sounds, however, is not the same as discrimination of sounds. The definition used here accepts the fact that almost all people can hear some sounds, but they are deaf if what they can hear is not useful for effective interpersonal communication.

Another complication is that some definitions include the age at onset of deafness. The individual's age at the time communicative hearing is lost greatly influences the effects of deafness; but including that factor in the definition makes it difficult to compare deafness to other chronic physical disabilities and obscures trends within data on deafness. Here, ages at onset of deafness will be indicated by appending adjectives, such as "prelingual," "childhood," "early," and "prevocational." Where the term "deaf" is used without modification, it should be understood to refer to all ages at onset. Such usage makes the definition of deafness consistent with the way in which blindness, a companion sensory disability, is defined.

SIZE OF DEAF POPULATION

There is no one satisfactory answer to the question of how many deaf people there are. Answers will depend, in part, on how deafness is defined. They also will vary with time and location, that is, the number of deaf people in any given location will differ from other locations and will differ from time to time in the same location.

Deafness is a relatively rare condition, occurring at rates that range from 35 to 300 per 100,000 for prelingual deafness, to about 873 per 100,000 for deafness without regard to age at onset. As the range of estimates in Table 1 demonstrates, each country has a rate that is independent of other countries and that is likely to be different for the country at different periods in its history.

Prevalence Rates The prevalence rates in Table 1 are from countries that have conducted national surveys (censuses) in the last half century. All of the rates in Table 1 are for "deaf-mutes," a term that is no longer in favor among scientists since it implies that there is a necessary relationship between early deafness and mutism. Regardless of the intended implications in the use of the term, the data refer to those deaf persons who do not

speak, from which it can be inferred that their loss of hearing occurred in early childhood, usually in the period from birth to three years of age. Peru reports the highest proportion of prelingually deaf persons in its population, 300 per 100,000, a rate obtained in its 1940 census. Australia shows the lowest reported rate of prelingual deafness (deaf-mutism), 35.1 per 100,000, a figure from its 1933 census. The other countries fall between these tenfold extremes. Though some of the discrepancies in the rates may be due to the ways in which the data have been gathered, these disparities in rates can hardly be reconciled by reference to methodology alone. To a large extent, the various rates for the countries shown in Table 1 likely approximate true differences in the proportions of their populations that have become deaf in early childhood at the time of the surveys. *See* AUSTRALIA; PERU.

The two figures for the United States—47 and 100 per 100,000—indicate the likelihood that the prevalence rate for prelingual deafness greatly increased between 1930 and 1971. The 1930 figure is based on the instructions that the U.S. Bureau of the Census gave its enumerators: to count as deaf those people whose deafness occurred before eight

Table 1. Prevalence Rates per 100,000 Population for Prelingual Deafness[a] in General Population Censuses, 1950–1974

Country	Year	Rate
Peru	1940	300
Honduras	1935	138
Finland	1950	131
Japan	1947[b]	118
	1970	225
Switzerland	1953	94
Sweden	1930	87
Iceland	1948	76
India	1931	66
Canada	1941	63
Egypt	1937	60
Belgium	1950	60
	1974	51
Norway	1930	53
Union of South Africa	1936[c]	49
France	1946	47
United States	1930	47
	1971	100
Northern Ireland	1956	45
Denmark	1940	43
West Germany	1950	43
Mexico	1940	39
	1974	46
Australia	1933	35

[a]Most countries referred to this condition as deaf-mutism. See text for a discussion of terminology.   [b]Census limited to persons 3 to 39 years of age.   [c]Only the European population counted.

years of age. The 1971 rate is for prelingual deafness, defined as deafness occurring before three years of age. Since setting a later age at onset should lead to larger numbers of persons being classified as deaf, the fact that the 1930 count is lower than the 1971 estimate emphasizes the probability that the relative presence of deafness in the United States has grown substantially in recent times. Similarly, Japan appears to have an upwardly accelerating rate for deafness, though the 1947 and 1970 findings are not strictly comparable; the former applies to only a portion of the population, while the latter rate applies to all ages. Nonetheless, the presence of deafness in Japan appears to be growing. Mexico also has found that the rate for deafness has increased from 39 per 100,000 in 1940 to 46 in 1974, a gain of almost 20 percent, which is small compared to the increases shown for Japan and the United States. Belgium, on the other hand, has a declining rate for deafness, reporting 60 per 100,000 for 1950 and 51 for 1974. The difference in the two rates for Belgium, like that for Mexico, may be due to sampling error alone and may not reflect any changes in the population. *See* BELGIUM; JAPAN; MEXICO.

To further illustrate the fluctuations of rates over geographical areas, consider the data in Table 2. These rates are from a study of the United States in which only location varies, since the definition of deafness, the methods of gathering data, and the approximate time are all the same. Note that the difference between the highest rate (242 per 100,000 for the north-central region) is almost 1½ times greater than the lowest rate (173 per 100,000 for the northeast). As startling as these differences are, they are exceeded by the differences found within Peru in its 1940 census. In the Department of Amazonas, a highly mountainous and isolated area of Peru, the rate for early deafness was 843 per 100,000, while in Callao, a province on the seacoast, the rate was 30 per 100,000—28 times less. Studies in Argentina and Chile found similar di-

versities in rates between their mountainous interior areas and those on the ocean. The differences have been explained by such factors as climate, iodine deficiency, and socioeconomic levels that, in turn, reflect upon the incidence of conditions like otitis media, the availability of medical care, and the quality of nutrition. The Finnish survey identified the importance of heredity as another contributing factor to the higher prevalence of deafness among isolated groups in the population.

Table 2 also displays the rates for deafness without regard to the age at onset. For the United States, the increase in the prevalence rates per 100,000 is almost ninefold: from 100 for prelingual deafness to 873 for deafness occurring at all ages. It should be noted that the rate for prevocational deafness (before 19 years of age at onset) is a bit more than double that for prelingual deafness. The high correlation between aging and deafness appears in all studies of general populations; it is discussed below.

When seeking to determine the prevalence of deafness in a specified area at a particular time, extreme caution should be used when applying rates derived from other areas and at other times. The national rate for prevocational deafness in the United States in 1971 was 203 per 100,000. As illustrated by the regional differences in Table 2, that rate would overestimate the prevalance of deafness in the northeast and underestimate it in the north-central region. In addition, without more recent information, one cannot say with any degree of certainty that the national rate remains constant at the last established estimate. The acceleration in the rate of deafness between 1930 and 1971 may be continuing, may have leveled off, or may be declining. Improvements in medical practice, changes in socioeconomic conditions, the occurrence of epidemics, and shifts in migration patterns all have an influence on the prevalence of deafness. To determine the direction of the trend, additional data are needed.

Conclusions The findings with respect to the size of the deaf population so far lead to at least four conclusions. First, the extent of deafness differs greatly, depending upon the age at onset—the earlier the age at onset, the lower the rate. Second, the prevalence rates for deafness are not uniform across the world or within countries. A rate suitable for one locale may be inappropriate for a neighboring one. Third, prevalence rates for deafness vary over time, increasing in some areas and declining in others. Fourth, deafness—especially prelingual deafness—is a relatively rare condition, affecting less than 1.0 percent of general populations, and more typically, having rates closer to 0.1 percent or less for general populations in most countries.

Table 2. Rates per 100,000 for Prevocational Deafness and Deafness Without Regard to Age at Onset, 1971

Region[a]	Deafness[b]	Prevocational Deafness[c]
United States	873	203
Northeast	697	173
North-central	965	242
South	895	196
West	931	194

[a]Regions are those established by the U.S. Bureau of the Census. [b]Deafness without regard to age at onset. [c]Deafness occurring before 19 years of age.

AGE AND DEAFNESS

The prevalence of early (prelingual, childhood, and prevocational) deafness in the general population varies to some extent from year to year, as indicated by the preceding data. It follows, then, that prevalence rates also will vary by age groups; the empirical evidence bears this out. The rates have a jagged appearance, likely reflecting epidemics such as the rubella epidemic in the United States in 1963–1964. However, deafness without regard to age at onset increases dramatically with chronological age. The longer one lives, the more likely becomes impairment of the senses, including audition. In the 1971 survey of deaf people in the United States, the average rate of deafness was about 115 per 100,000 for persons under 6 years of age. The prevalence rates increased slowly, averaging about 370 per 100,000 for those 16 to 54 years of age. Then the prevalence rate jumped to 1273 per 100,000 for persons 55 years of age and older. The age-relatedness of deafness is manifest in these recent data, as it has been in all comparable preceding studies.

SEX AND DEAFNESS

A higher percentage of men than women in the United States are prevocationally deaf. This sex preference for early deafness has been found in studies done at various times and in different places. When deafness is considered without regard to age at onset, however, the sex preference becomes more complex. Women have lower rates for deafness than men in the earlier years, but not when deafness occurs past 55 years of age. Since women generally live longer than men, it has been suggested that this accounts for the greater prevalence rate of deafness among older women. The gross survey data do not permit any conclusive hypothesis testing. The fact remains that deafness has interesting sex-linked features that interact with age.

CIVIL STATUS

Most prevocationally deaf persons have parents with normal hearing. The figures for the United States in 1971 showed that 91.7 percent of prevocationally deaf persons' parents had normal hearing. The typical deaf child, then, was born into a family that had no personal experience with deafness, a fact of considerable significance in the child's development. Studies of the deaf offspring of deaf parents indicate that they do better in school, academically and socially, than deaf children of normally hearing parents. The explanations for this finding seem to include the lesser shock that deaf parents feel after being told their baby is deaf, the greater degree of initial acceptance of the deaf children by their deaf parents, and the deaf parents' better understanding of the condition and greater range of coping strategies for dealing with typical problems confronting a deaf child. The normally hearing parent seldom has any expectation of having a deaf child, so being informed that their child is deaf leads to considerable emotional upheaval that apparently has unfortunate implications for the typical deaf child.

The 1971 survey also discovered that most prevocationally deaf persons married other deaf persons. Deaf males' choices of spouses were 81.5 percent deaf, 6.5 percent hard-of-hearing, and 12.0 percent normally hearing. Deaf females' choices of husbands were 78.9 percent deaf, 6.9 percent hard-of-hearing, and 14.2 percent normally hearing. As with other characteristics of the deaf population, age at onset was a factor in selection of spouse. For both males and females, the later the onset of deafness, the more likely it was that the spouse was normally hearing. Congenitally deaf persons tended to marry each other at a higher rate than did deaf persons with later onsets of deafness.

The 1971 survey examined marital status and found that for deaf males 16 to 64 years of age 40.3 percent were single (never married), 54.8 percent were married, 1.0 percent were widowed, 3.0 percent were divorced, and 0.9 percent were separated. The corresponding percentages for deaf females were 27.5 percent single, 62.8 percent married, 3.3 percent widowed, 4.7 percent divorced, and 1.7 percent separated. For both deaf males and females, the rates for remaining single were almost double that for the general population, and consequently, the marriage rates were much lower. For the remaining categories—widowed, separated, divorced—the rates for deaf persons were closer to those for the comparable groups in the general population. Further analysis indicated that, as had been found in previous studies, deaf persons tended to marry later than persons in the general population. The later age for first marriage suggested some difficulty in completing education and making occupational adjustments. Deaf males married later than deaf females, and because the tendency for deaf females was to be younger than their husbands at the time they married, the probability of widowhood increased for them, as was borne out by the data. Age at onset also played a role in relation to marital status—the earlier the age at onset, the lower the marriage rate. With respect to divorce, the rates for divorce and separation were lower for those whose spouse was also deaf.

FERTILITY

Another factor to be considered is whether the choice of spouse reflects on family size and proportion of deaf children born. The average deaf female in the 1971 survey bore fewer children than the average woman in the general population. These rates differed for white and nonwhite deaf women, but they were lower than for the corresponding averages in the general population. Of all children born to marriages in which one or both parents were deaf, 88.0 parents of the children had normal hearing, 2.9 percent were hard-of-hearing, and 9.1 percent were deaf. These rates altered greatly when the parents were both congenitally deaf as opposed to only one being deaf. In the former case, the proportion of deaf offspring was 17.4 percent, and in the latter case, 4.5 percent. Despite the obviously greater probability of deafness in children born of parents one or both of whom were deaf, the fact remains that the majority of children born of these marriages were normally hearing. Even in marriages in which both parents were congenitally deaf, the average probability of a deaf child being born was less than 2 in 10, a far greater rate than would be expected from matings between normally hearing persons, but still a statistically minor probability.

One contributing factor to the overall fertility data was the finding that the average number of children born to deaf mothers varied by the age at onset of their deafness. Mothers born deaf averaged 0.4 children; those deafened between 6 and 18 years of age averaged 2.3 children; and those outside these two groups averaged a number of children correlated to their ages at onset of deafness. This finding relates to the tendency of prelingually deaf persons to marry less often than those whose deafness was acquired at later ages. It may also reflect the disappointment that some deaf parents feel at having a deaf child, an incorporation of the perceived attitudes of the general public toward congenitally deaf people.

EDUCATION

Earlier in this century, pedagogues reasoned that, because deaf children displayed a slower rate of academic development than children in general, they should enter school later. At the present time, educators believe the opposite, insisting that the slower rate of development requires that provisions be made for the education of deaf children at earlier ages than for those in the general population. This point of view is reflected in the statistics that show deaf persons entering formal schooling at earlier and earlier ages. Many states provide for the education of deaf children to begin at age three. *See* EDUCATION: History.

The type of school attended by deaf students has also tended to shift over the years, away from the residential school to the day school and day class. Earlier in the century about 8 out of 10 deaf schoolchildren were in residential settings; by 1971 that proportion had dropped to about 5 out of 10. The more recent shift has followed the tendency to mainstream children with disabilities, a move supported by federal legislation, which makes it likely that the proportion of children in residential schools may drop still further. It should also be noted that some deaf persons have managed to complete their educations within regular schools and without special support from tutors, interpreters, and so on. This proportion of such deaf students, which was about 9 percent in the 1971 survey, has increased over the years; earlier data estimated the proportion of such deaf persons to be between 1 and 2 percent. The likelihood that a deaf child will attend regular schools had varied with age at onset of deafness, with the later onsets associated with regular school placements. The shift away from residential schools and from special schools and classes may reflect strongly on the nature of the deaf community in years to come, as the schools and classes for deaf children traditionally have been important to the development of deaf leadership. *See* EDUCATIONAL LEGISLATION: Impact of Public Policy; EDUCATIONAL PROGRAMS.

The average deaf adult, 25 to 64 years of age in 1971, completed less than 12 years of schooling. That finding placed deaf adults about one year behind the general population in amount of education. The finding is particularly troubling, since achievement testing reveals that deaf students tend to score much lower than hearing students in general on all measures of academic achievement. Receiving less education (and receiving less rewards from the education obtained) appears to have been the situation for the average deaf adult, a situation which is, however, tending to change. From 1900 to 1960, the proportion of deaf schoolchildren who went on to college remained about constant, while the corresponding proportions for the general population increased after World War I. Since 1965 the proportion of deaf schoolchildren entering higher education has increased markedly, though it remains far below that for the general population. The finding is encouraging, nonetheless, since it suggests that improvements in education are being made. *See* EDUCATION: Trends.

RELIGION

No relationship appears to exist between early deafness and membership in the major religious groups (Catholics, Jews, and Protestants) in the United States; that is, deafness does not appear to be more or less frequent in these religions. However, some minor religious sects that remain isolated from the general population and in which intermarriage is encouraged do have higher proportions of congenitally deaf persons in their congregations as a result of consanguinity. The available evidence suggests that deaf persons of one religious persuasion do not seem to express a greater preference for their religion than do those in other groups. Whatever their religious background, deaf people show no pronounced tendency to shift from it to another religion. In general, deaf persons do not participate to a high degree in the religious life of their community. Instead, a larger proportion of early deafened persons attend special services designed for them, if they attend at all. The study of deaf persons in Washington, D.C., in 1968 found a higher proportion of deaf adults reporting no religious preference (6.2 percent) than is found in similar studies of the general population. Setting aside the generally higher education level of the general population, the finding does seem to expose some dissatisfaction that many deaf people have with the lack of accommodations for them in their respective religions. However, there is a great difference between expressing a preference for an organized religion, which about 94 percent of deaf persons do, and attending the services provided by that religion, which only about 25 percent of deaf persons do. *See* RELIGION, CATHOLIC; RELIGION, JEWISH; RELIGION, PROTESTANT.

MORBIDITY

About one of every three early deafened persons has been found to have an additional physical disability. This finding recurs in various surveys of deaf adults and schoolchildren. Deafness tends to be associated with other physical disabilities. This association is particularly strong with respect to visual anomalies, a matter of utmost importance to deaf persons, since their hearing loss increases their dependence on vision for communication. Federal regulations by the Rehabilitation Services Administration require that all physical examinations of deaf applicants for vocational rehabilitation include a thorough visual examination—a recognition of the demographic fact of higher-than-normal prevalence of visual impairments among persons who lost their hearing at an early age. *See* REHABILITATION: Administration.

Among deaf schoolchildren, the most common secondary disabilities are emotional or behavioral disorders and mental retardation. The studies determining these latter findings have asked for reports from school administrators of "educationally handicapping conditions." About 3 out of 10 deaf schoolchildren are reported to have a secondary disability that interferes with their education. That such high proportions are labeled emotionally disturbed or, alternatively, as having a behavior disorder may reflect more upon the schools than upon the children. In any event, the fact that such a high proportion of deaf students (about 1 in 5) are so classified demands more attention to their mental health than is usually accorded by the school systems.

MORTALITY

Some students of deafness have hypothesized that congenital deafness may be associated with a la-

tent physical weakness leading to early mortality. However, the evidence is admittedly weak. Others have pointed out that for adventitiously deaf persons, the cause of the deafness may also affect other functions that, in turn, lead to reduced longevity. Maternal rubella may cause both deafness and heart damage in the fetus; similarly, spinal meningitis may inflict damage far beyond that expressed by the deafness. It is, therefore, difficult to respond directly to the question of longevity among early deafened persons.

An indirect approach does provide an interesting perspective. By examining the data provided by the National Fraternal Society of the Deaf (NFSD), a company founded in 1903 to provide life insurance to deaf people, it is revealed that insured deaf persons have death rates appreciably lower than those expected from standard mortality tables. Insurance companies in the United States use the mortality tables to establish their life insurance premiums, so they reflect the life expectancies for the general population. The fact that NFSD's experience with its policy holders, all of whom are deaf, is consistently better than the anticipated death rates strongly suggests that at least a portion of the deaf population has a more favorable life expectancy than persons in general. Obviously, like any insurance company, NFSD does not accept all risks. Assuming that the risks it does accept are comparable to those of regular insurance companies, one may conclude that early deafness has no generally unfavorable association with longevity. Indeed, on the average, prevocationally deaf persons may conceivably outlive their normally hearing peers. *See* NATIONAL FRATERNAL SOCIETY OF THE DEAF.

Bibliography

Best, H.: *Deafness and the Deaf in the United States*, Macmillan, New York, 1943.

Schein, J. D.: *The Deaf Community*, Gallaudet College Press, Washington, D.C., 1968.

————: "The Demography of Deafness," in P. C. Higgins and J. E. Nash (eds.), *The Deaf Community and the Deaf Population*, Gallaudet College, Washington, D.C., 1982.

————: "Hearing Disorders," in L. T. Kurland, J. F. Kurtzke, and I. D. Goldberg (eds.), *Epidemiology of Neurologic and Sense Organ Disorders*, Harvard University Press, Cambridge, Massachusetts, 1973.

————, and M. T. Delk, Jr.: *The Deaf Population of the United States*, National Association of the Deaf, Silver Spring, Maryland, 1974.

U.S. Bureau of the Census: *The Blind and Deaf-Mutes in the United States: 1930*, U.S. Government Printing Office, Washington, D.C., 1981.

Jerome D. Schein

Deaf Community

Deaf communities are local groups of hearing-impaired people who, based on common identification and shared experiences, participate together in a wide variety of activities. These local communities, in turn, are linked together in a national deaf network. While the deaf community has been defined in other ways, all definitions stress interaction among people with common ties. Most hearing-impaired people, however, are not involved in deaf communities, and members of deaf communities are not alike in all respects. Moreover, deaf communities are not uniform throughout the United States. The communities vary in their complexity and their ability to meet deaf people's needs.

MEMBERSHIP

More than 14 million people in the United States have a detectable hearing impairment. Approximately 2 million are profoundly hearing-impaired, that is, they cannot hear well enough to understand speech. Prevocationally deaf persons, who were born with a profound impairment or who acquired it before the end of adolescence, comprise approximately 400,000 people. Most people who constitute America's deaf communities are prevocationally deaf. Their youthful experiences with an early, profound hearing impairment often become the basis for an identification with others who share similar experiences; continued interaction of people with similar experiences reinforces that identification.

SHARED EXPERIENCES

Members of deaf communities share many experiences due to the problems of being hearing-impaired in a world dominated by hearing persons. Throughout their lives members of deaf communities, like all deaf people, experience the difficulty of communicating with those who hear. They share the frustrations and embarrassments of the failure to do so. They also share the loneliness of being left out by hearing people—by family members, neighbors, coworkers, and even teachers. Technological devices of the hearing world, such as the telephone, are significant obstacles in their lives. Business, emergency, social, and other transactions, which most hearing people routinely conduct over the telephone, may test the ingenuity and the patience of members of deaf communities. Telecommunication devices for deaf persons are welcome, but they are not panaceas. In a world that assumes that people can hear and speak, members of deaf communities share the experience of being outsiders. *See* TELECOMMUNICATIONS: Telephone Services.

Members of deaf communities also endure the stigma of being disabled in a society that provides little place for those who are different. When signing to each other in public, they are stared at or mocked. The actions of others toward the members of deaf communities often are based on the members' deafness, not their other characteristics, and the actions of some deaf individuals frequently are generalized to all deaf persons. Thus, the traffic accident of a driver who happens to be deaf raises the clamor for stricter regulations governing the driving of all who are deaf, and a deaf employee who does not work out satisfactorily makes it more difficult for the next deaf applicant.

Members of deaf communities also share the experience of unwarranted discrimination. Based on the hearing world's assumptions about the "limitations" produced by a hearing loss, members of deaf communities have to endure questions about their intellectual competence. While "deaf and dumb" originally denoted being unable to hear and to speak, it clearly connotes being senseless as well. Whether being held incompetent to make contracts, as in the past, or encountering difficulties in obtaining jobs that require driving, as in the present, members of deaf communities have been treated as second-class citizens. *See* DRIVING RESTRICTIONS.

However, members of deaf communities also share the camaraderie, easy communication, and sense of belonging that grows out of being educated with other hearing-impaired students in special programs, particularly residential programs. The physical and social isolation of deaf students, many of whom attend residential schools in rural settings, becomes the basis for a beginning identification with the deaf world. The ties that develop in the schools provide a bridge from adolescence into the adult deaf community.

IDENTIFICATION

People who lose their hearing after adolescence are unlikely to identify with the deaf world or deaf communities. Since they have gone through childhood and adolescence with normal hearing, their crucial identities and experiences are as hearing people. With the onset of a hearing impairment, perhaps due to aging or an industrial accident, they remain culturally attached to the hearing community; though they are no longer fully competent hearers, they do not embrace the deaf community.

Even persons who are born deaf or who acquire deafness in childhood do not necessarily identify with the deaf world. Children who have hearing parents and who attend schools without special programs for deaf students (such children constitute perhaps less than 25 percent of hearing-impaired youth and an even smaller proportion of those who are profoundly deaf) often do not identify with the deaf world. Similarly, children whose education was in strictly oral programs with hearing-impaired students may not develop a sense of belonging with members of deaf communities. Those educated primarily with hearing children do not experience the friendship of other hearing-impaired youth, a friendship which slowly builds ties to the deaf world.

Some of those educated in oral programs, like those educated primarily with hearing youth, may share with deaf community members many of the experiences of being hearing-impaired, but they interpret those experiences differently. They are more likely to view the hearing world as the standard against which they measure their competencies and the competencies of others, particularly communication skills. To the extent that they can, they strive to be like hearing people, particularly through an emphasis on speech and speechreading.

Some of these hearing-impaired people live exclusively in the hearing world. Others develop social relations with like-minded hearing-impaired people, perhaps even joining formal organizations such as the Oral Deaf Adults Section of the Alexander Graham Bell Association. They may participate in the activities of deaf communities that they feel are significant to their lives, such as lobbying for captioned television programs, supporting the development of better telephone communication devices for deaf people, or advocating the legal rights of deaf people to serve on juries or gain admittance to colleges and universities. Still, they are not members of deaf communities. They are tolerated by the communities' members but are not fully accepted because they reject sign language and many of the social activities of the deaf communities. *See* ALEXANDER GRAHAM BELL ASSOCIATION FOR THE DEAF.

Yet other people who are hearing-impaired but not profoundly deaf may embrace the deaf community and in turn be embraced by it. One reason is that children with various degrees of hearing impairment, from mild to severe, are educated together in special programs. This was particularly true in the past, when fewer and less specialized educational programs existed. Still having some useful hearing, these deaf youths share many of the experiences of their profoundly hearing-impaired classmates within and outside the educational programs. Those experiences have led to an identification with the deaf world. Children with mild hearing impairments but with profoundly deaf parents or siblings often become members of deaf communities, too. Thus, a hearing impairment is not a sufficient condition for membership in deaf communities; yet neither is a profound hearing loss (deafness) a necessary condition. *See* SOCIALIZATION: Schools and Peer Groups.

The commonality of experiences and the sense of identity of deaf communities are primarily expressed through sign language, especially American Sign Language. In turn, the sign language of the community strengthens the identification of its members with one another. It is an important element of the deaf community's culture, a culture that does not place the same significance on hearing and speaking as does the culture of the hearing world. And it is through the deaf community's culture that the members' shared experiences become meaningful. *See* SIGN LANGUAGES: American.

PARTICIPATION

Members of deaf communities interact with one another in a wide variety of activities and occasions, such as informal gatherings of friends and more structured club meetings, religious services, and athletic tournaments for deaf people only. Identification with one another is strengthened and experiences are shared. Thus, identification, shared experiences, and participation strengthen each other.

Some hearing people also participate in the activities of deaf communities. Children of deaf parents, religious officials, and interpreters are most likely to be involved with the deaf community, though other interested hearing people may participate, too. However, it is not clear to what extent these hearing people are members of deaf communities, for observers of deaf communities differ in their assessment. An individual, deaf or hearing, may be accepted by some members of deaf communities as "one of them," while others will reject the same individual. Thus, although identification of the deaf community may imply a clearly defined boundary, it may be more useful to view individuals as more or less members of a deaf community depending on their own actions and attitudes and those of diverse others in the deaf community.

SOCIAL ORGANIZATION

The deaf community is not homogeneous. Through their attitudes and their actions, members of deaf communities create differences among themselves. Members use these differences in developing social relationships among one another, such as friendships or memberships in particular clubs and organizations. Characteristics such as race or sex, for example, differentiate among deaf community members, as they do among hearing persons. Members also interact with one another according to communication preference.

SOCIAL CHARACTERISTICS

Social relationships are developed along these and other differences. For example, friends tend to have similar levels of educational attainment. Separate clubs for white and black deaf individuals may exist in the same city. Women form coffee clubs, and men play on basketball teams. This should not be surprising; members of the hearing world use these characteristics in organizing their relationships with one another, and members of deaf communities live to a great extent within that hearing world.

Therefore, they learn and use many of those characteristics, too.

Age, which is an important characteristic for organizing social relationships in the hearing world, is also important in deaf communities. Deaf people choose different activities and organizations, depending upon their age. Groups for senior citizens cater to the elderly, while athletic teams usually attract younger persons.

Age, however, holds another significance within the deaf community. Most deaf children, more than 90 percent, have hearing parents. Consequently, while these children may be heavily involved with other deaf youth, primarily in activities that revolve around special educational programs, they are unlikely to be members of deaf communities. They are potential members, for they are beginning to develop the identification and wealth of shared experiences that will lead them to deaf communities. However, because their parents are hearing, most are unlikely to have much contact with deaf adults. Through deaf teachers, through involvement in religious organizations for deaf people, through youth organizations for the deaf such as the Junior National Association of the Deaf, and through other, sporadic occasions, some deaf children develop ties to the world of deaf adults. Yet these are nascent ties that will grow stronger as the youths grow older and become more independent of their hearing parents. Thus, the deaf community is primarily an adult community. *See* NATIONAL ASSOCIATION OF THE DEAF.

Ironically, the members of deaf communities generally are not socialized into the communities by their parents, but rather in opposition to their parents. Desiring that their hearing-impaired children not be different from "normal" youths, sharing most hearing people's misconceptions about deafness, and being unable to communicate well with their children, hearing parents often experience difficult relationships with their deaf children. For those deaf children educated at residential programs, who may come home only for the major holidays and summer vacation, relations with their parents often are difficult and sporadic. Thus, deaf children may be outsiders in their families as well as in the wider hearing world; as the children become adults and members of deaf communities, their parents become outsiders. *See* SOCIALIZATION: Families.

COMMUNICATION PREFERENCE

Members of deaf communities interact with each other on the basis of their communication preference. Members who use sign language interact primarily with others who also sign. Some of these signers may speak and lipread very well, yet they prefer to communicate with fellow members through sign language. In the United States a small minority of deaf community members known as oralists prefer to speak to their deaf friends. In other countries this relative proportion of signers and speakers varies considerably. When communicating with those who rely on sign language, speakers will sign some but not fluently. Those who completely reject signing, called pure oralists, are unlikely to be members of deaf communities, though some may be accepted by the oralists who prefer speaking to each other. Signers and speakers do associate with one another, particularly at communitywide affairs, though not as much as with their fellow signers and speakers; they may even intermarry. However, while signers and speakers recognize each other as part of the same deaf community, they distinguish among one another. Through differential interaction between and among each group, through separate organizations that cater primarily to one or the other group such as social clubs or local divisions of the National Fraternal Society of the Deaf, and through different communication preferences and skills, signers and speakers maintain social distinctions between each other. They may even develop some mistrust of each other, as signers sometimes question speakers' identification with and commitment to the deaf community.

Many older signers were educated, at least partly, in oral programs, which were predominant in the education of deaf children throughout most of this century until the advent of total communication in the 1970s. Oral programs typically stressed speaking and speechreading to the exclusion of sign language. Many of these signers became adamantly opposed to oral education because they perceived themselves as victims of its alleged shortcomings. Consequently, signers may wonder if speakers, who do not embrace sign language, are trying to hide their deafness or if they are still under the influence of hearing educators. Either way, signers may question whether a speaker is indeed "one of them." *See* EDUCATION: Communication.

LOCATION

Deaf communities are found in cities and towns throughout the world. Wherever enough deaf people live to sustain meaningful social activities with one another, deaf communities develop. However, members are scattered throughout the community's locale. Unlike many ethnic or minority group communities, deaf communities cannot be easily located within a specific area of a city. Among deaf communities there is no equivalent to an ethnic neighborhood, barrio, or ghetto. Deaf communities exist in the interaction among and the identification with fellow members, not as easily identified geographical areas of cities.

Deaf communities may vary according to their locations. The population and the social institutions of the area influence deaf communities just as they do hearing ones. The relative characteristics of members and the array of organizations within deaf communities will vary from location to location. The deaf community in a large city will have a greater range of organizations and activities, many of which cater to the interests of special segments of the community, as compared to what is found within a deaf community in a small town. For example, clubs and well-organized social gatherings for elderly members of deaf communities are unlikely to exist in a small town, but they do exist in large cities such as Chicago and San Francisco. Deaf communities in the Southwest and in the West will have Mexican-American members, but deaf communities in the Northeast would be less likely to have such members. Major organizations and institutions, even if they do not provide services and opportunities for deaf individuals, are likely to influence significantly local deaf communities. Due to the variety of institutions in the Washington, D.C., metropolitan area, such as Gallaudet College and the federal government, members of that metropolitan deaf community are better educated and are more likely to be employed in professional and managerial positions than are deaf individuals throughout the United States. However, additional research is needed in order to understand how the locales of deaf communities influence their composition and complexity. *See* GALLAUDET COLLEGE.

Individual deaf communities are interrelated in what might be called a deaf network. Through state, regional, national, and even international organizations and occasions (such as state associations for the deaf, regional athletic tournaments, and the World Federation of the Deaf), through telecommunication devices for the deaf and publications such as the *Deaf American* or the *Frat*, and through former classmates, deaf relatives, and deaf friends who travel or have moved, deaf people and communities that are scattered throughout the country are in contact with one another. These relationships begin at the local level and build up to the regional, national, and international level. *See* PERIODICALS; WORLD FEDERATION OF THE DEAF.

While the specific interconnections among deaf communities and their members are too complicated to be fully charted, they have great significance. Newsworthy events within one deaf community rapidly become widely known within other deaf communities. Consequently, members of deaf communities may find it difficult to escape their past. Yet, this network also helps to develop a larger sense of solidarity and shared identity among a widely dispersed population. Therefore, this national deaf network is both a blessing and a drawback.

THE FUTURE

The deaf community faces an uncertain future. It may continue to be an important part of deaf people's lives, or its significance may change as the larger social world and deaf people's places in it change. For example, as different sign language systems proliferate in educational programs for hearing-impaired youths, will potential members of deaf communities use mutually understandable sign languages? Might these variations in sign systems lead to social distinctions among members of deaf communities as has the preference for signing and speaking? Or, as fewer hearing-impaired children are educated in residential programs and as more are mainstreamed with hearing children, will these hearing-impaired children develop the identification, experiences, and ties to other hearing-impaired people that will lead them to the deaf community? If not, who will become the deaf community's future members? If so, will that commitment to the deaf community be as strong as it has been? If deafness and deaf people become more accepted within the hearing world, if educational, occupational, and social opportunities open more widely for them as they seem to have in the recent past, will deaf people continue to depend as heavily on and be as greatly involved in deaf communities as before? Might economically difficult times keep from opening any wider, or even begin to close, those doors of opportunity for deaf people and other traditionally disadvantaged individuals? As occupations increasingly become professional, technical, and service positions, with increasing educational requirements, will members of deaf communities fall further behind hearing citizens? Or, as may be happening in other minority communities such as among black citizens, may there be a growing gap between deaf individuals who are able to take advantage of those increased educational, occupational, and social opportunities to move into the mainstream and those who are not?

If that greater acceptance and wider opportunity develop for deaf people, that will be due in part to the efforts of deaf communities and their supporters, to their lobbying, legal action, leadership, and determination. It is even possible that in their own successes, deaf communities may alter, even diminish, themselves. Whatever happens, deaf communities face a challenging and uncertain future.

Bibliography

Becker, G.: *Growing Old in Silence: Deaf People in Old Age*, University of California Press, Berkeley, 1980.

Benderly, B. L.: *Dancing Without Music: Deafness in America*, Anchor, Garden City, New York, 1980.

Higgins, P. C.: *Outsiders in a Hearing World: A Sociology of Deafness*, Sage, Beverly Hills, California, 1980.

Nash, J. E., and A. Nash: *Deafness in Society*, D.C. Heath, Lexington, Massachusetts, 1981.

Padden, C.: "The Deaf Community and the Culture of Deaf People," in C. Baker and R. Battison (eds.), *Sign Language and the Deaf Community*, National Association of the Deaf, Silver Spring, Maryland, 1980.

Schein, J. D., and M. T. Delk, Jr.: *The Deaf Population of the United States*, National Association of the Deaf, Silver Spring, Maryland, 1974.

Paul C. Higgins

Culture and Subculture

The term deaf culture is a special term that has appeared in magazines for deaf people, professional journals, panel discussions, and lectures in both the United States and abroad. There are different reasons for the use of this term. Those favoring the total integration of deaf people in society, for example, have argued that the use of sign language or separate educational, recreational, and other facilities have contributed to the emergence of deaf people as a subculture, a deviant group, or even a ghetto, thus isolating them from society. These integrationists also assert that the use of speech and speechreading, as well as school integration (mainstreaming), would prevent such a group formation. On the other hand, those recognizing the existence of social and cultural pluralism in modern societies tend to accept deaf people as a distinctive social group within the society. They are willing to accept a separate deaf culture or deaf subculture.

The restoration of pride in the history of deaf people, popularly called deaf heritage, has become a new social movement among deaf people throughout the world. Several ways have been devised to encourage deaf people to appreciate the uniqueness of their experiences, and a number of countries in Europe also promote deaf heritage by organizing annual theater, art, and dance festivals. The terms deaf power and deaf pride have been used as political slogans in many periodicals that include articles about deaf people. A historical review of the social life among deaf people in different countries may reveal that this social movement is a reaction to recent efforts to integrate people with disabilities in the society. It may also be interpreted as a search for a strong group identity in the face of increasing social and cultural pluralism within the deaf population.

Researchers have tended to accept the terms deaf culture and deaf subculture without any examination. Unfortunately, field or historical studies about the social life of deaf people which could provide evidence on the development of deaf culture are still seriously lacking. Consequently, the best approach at present is to examine briefly the general terms culture and subculture and then discuss the application of these terms to deaf people.

DEFINITIONS

Culture and subculture are among the less precise terms used in anthropology and sociology. However, a comparison of different definitions does indicate an agreement that culture is a process by which the values, norms, language, and technology are shared and transmitted from one generation to another by members of a given human group. Culture is not a concrete thing; it is an abstract design whose characteristics are frequently unrecognized by members of a social group. A group's culture becomes recognized, however, when it is subject to discussion, examination, or comparison with other cultures.

Whenever the values and norms shared by a given group are similar to, yet deviate somewhat from, those of the society where the particular group exists, the group may be called a subculture. The terms cultural group and cultural alternative have also been applied to such groups. If the values or norms of a given group deviate dramatically from the general society, however, the group may be labeled a counterculture. Rock music fans, juvenile gangs, homosexuals, drug addicts, and snake cults have been cited as examples of countercultures because their behavior patterns are not acceptable to the dominant group. Amish communities, circus artists, and physicians and other occupational groups are considered as subcultures since their behavior patterns appear peculiar though acceptable to the dominant group. Plural societies have apparently found it necessary to invent terms for new social categories, while homogeneous societies rarely use categorizing terms. For example, the minority concept has not yet appeared in several European languages.

Deaf people have been called a subculture in many sociological and anthropological studies, but the term deaf subculture seems to be unacceptable to many deaf writers in the United States and abroad. They may have presumed that the prefix sub- implies that values, norms, and language are to be subordinated to those of the society, or what sociologists call the dominant group. The term deaf culture is more widely preferred. The terms cultural group, cultural alternative, or counterculture have not been adopted by deaf people. For these reasons, the term deaf culture will be used here.

TRANSMISSION OF DEAF CULTURE

The school or educational program for deaf people, usually a residential school, is the first place where most deaf children become aware of the special behavior patterns, values, norms, and communication modes demonstrated by older schoolmates and deaf children of deaf parents. Deaf children develop their world view primarily on the basis of what they see, not hear. Perhaps the most important aspect of the deaf culture learned in these educational settings is sign language. The learning of sign language, like any language, requires the observation and internalization of rules and norms. If unsatisfied with or desiring to improve the quality of values and norms, deaf children, like other new generations, may adopt, elaborate, or modify the norms and values of their peers and teachers. Very few deaf children are likely to complete elementary or high school education at a residential or other school for deaf students if they refuse to adopt the method of communication or values favored by most schoolmates. Such children will be labeled as deviants. Statistical surveys consistently indicate that the majority of educational programs for deaf children in the United States use sign language in addition to speech and speechreading; even at oral schools children have been known to use sign language, either openly or in secret.

SIGN LANGUAGE

Deaf children frequently have a very limited interaction with teachers and counselors at school compared to the hearing population; considerably fewer deaf workers and visitors meet deaf children on a daily basis. As a result, the students frequently invent new signs to fill in the gaps in their sign language. In addition, since sign language is highly visible and hence easy to understand when eavesdropping, it may be necessary for students to replace conventional signs with secret ones when signing in front of teachers or counselors. They may also invent signs to emphasize the peculiar features of popular or unpopular persons. Some of these signs can be too graphically offensive or very telling. For example, if a person is known for elegance, children might combine the sign for elegance and the fingerspelled letter for the initial letter of the person's last name to emphasize that person's characteristic. Such richness in sign language has been acknowledged in research studies, but is still underestimated. *See* SIGNS: Name Signs.

Sign language has also been found to be an important guide in indicating the boundaries or the extent of deaf culture. It can, for example, distinguish those who have spent years at a deaf school from those who lost their hearing in adult life. Despite a classic study by K. Meadow (where deaf children of deaf parents were rated more favorably in written English, in speech, and in emotional and social maturity than deaf children of hearing parents), many educators and psychologists persist in sharing the old assumption that the sign language as used by deaf people has delayed the learning of spoken language (such as English) as well as emotional and social development. Instead of suppressing the use of sign language, as those favoring the exclusive use of speech and speechreading have done, many educators and psychologists have attempted to expand or alter American Sign Language by creating new systems such as Signed English, SEE, LOVE, and Cued Speech. They assume that these systems will facilitate the acquisition of English among deaf children. But the fact remains that deaf children today, like other new generations, adopt, invent, change, or abandon every sign, depending on its relevancy to their current interests. The presence of deaf adults could put such changes under control, but deaf children have little access to deaf adults.

Deaf children enrolled in integrated or mainstreamed programs where they interact with hearing schoolmates and have few deaf teachers tend to be awkward or inept in the use of sign language (though probably more fluent in speech and speechreading), compared with deaf children enrolled in separate programs that often employ deaf teachers and counselors. Although studies comparing the sign language competence among deaf children in residential schools versus integrated programs are almost nonexistent, linguists agree that linguistic competence in general depends on not only group interaction but also the knowledge of the group's characteristics.

In several European countries, where strict oral education once was enforced, sign language is not yet standardized. Deaf people from different cities within the country are often unable to understand each other. The absence of deaf adults at schools for deaf pupils in Europe may have been an important obstacle to the learning of standard sign language among deaf children. Compared to European sign languages, American Sign Language is fairly standardized, probably because of the presence of deaf teachers at deaf schools. The standardization of Scandinavian sign language has also been possible, perhaps because teachers are required to be fluent in the use of sign language and do not try to suppress the use of manual communication among deaf students, even though their teaching methods must be oral.

It can then be concluded that the transmission of culture is probably smoother and more complete at separate educational programs than it is in integrated ones.

OTHER SEPARATE ACTIVITIES

As secondary education for deaf people is available only in the United States and very few other countries, and as admission to colleges or universities is open for only an extremely small number of deaf persons, most young deaf individuals enter the work world immediately after elementary school. There they may be exposed for the first time to an environment where they must use methods of communication other than sign language in daily interaction with hearing people. Their acquisition of new values and norms in the world of work is often quite slow because the number of hearing persons able to communicate freely with deaf people is very small. Rehabilitation agencies have been established to facilitate this new acculturation process. Yet, like other minorities or disabled groups, deaf people have frequently experienced the dominant group's inability to modify its behavior patterns to meet the demands of deaf people. Most of these patterns, such as conversations, parties at bars or homes, or group discussions, require the use of normal hearing. For these reasons, it has been necessary for deaf and other disabled groups to develop cultural activities parallel to those in the culture of the dominant group. Thus, separate clubs or organizations have been established to provide a place where deaf people can develop similar patterns. Athletic, religious, educational, theatrical, and other programs, supervised by separate associations, also reinforce the group solidarity among deaf people.

However, recent innovations such as telecommunication devices for the deaf (TDD), telecaptioning adapters (decoders), and the professionalization of interpreters have caused profound changes in the culture and social structure of the deaf community. The installation of TDD stations in hospitals or clinics, government agencies, schools, stores, and other public places, as well as the availability of professional interpreting services and captions on television programs and movies, have considerably expanded the access to the activities of the dominant group for deaf adults. This has permitted deaf and hearing groups to overlap each other and become integrated to some degree, something which never happened prior to World War II. At the same time these innovations have apparently increased independent living and self-reliance among deaf adults. This change has made it necessary for deaf people to reappraise and adapt their culture. However, several traditional or popular activities such as national sports championships and conventions still remain separate for deaf people in many countries.

A cross-cultural comparison also suggests that the structure of organizations of deaf persons and deaf culture is influenced by the culture of the dominant group. Pride in local heritage or community pride is emphasized more in most European countries than in the United States. Consequently, European people, both deaf and hearing, are encouraged to make contributions first at the local level and only later at the regional or national level. However, people in most European nations must also reach a consensus on and observe national policies. As people in the United States come from a much greater variety of cultural and ethnic groups, they are encouraged to make contributions at different levels, from local to national, thus overlapping each other. This important cultural diversity explains why so many national organizations of and for deaf persons and so many methods of communication have appeared in the United States. In addition to the innovations above, the increasing involvement of several professional specialists instead of a single group (teachers of deaf people) as in the past, and the greater participation of deaf adults in the activities of the dominant group, are expected to make deaf culture even more overlapping and less defined than it is now.

Endogamy, or marriage within a social group, is a good indicator of cultural solidarity. The endogamy rate among the deaf population tends to be high in most countries. This is not surprising from the sociological viewpoint because mate selection is based on the abilities of potential spouses to share interests, world views, and lifestyles. A few countries have attempted to forbid or discourage marriages among congenitally deaf persons. These efforts failed, however. This failure may be interpreted as a result of deaf people's resistance to the dominant group's attempt to impose its values on their culture. There are usually comparatively few mixed (deaf-hearing) marriages in most countries.

It is interesting to observe that many hearing children who have deaf parents or close relatives who are deaf return to the deaf world to work as teachers, interpreters, priests, or social workers, which gives evidence about the influence of deaf culture.

CONCLUSION

In conclusion, it can be seen that whenever deaf people find that an activity in the hearing society cannot be shared, they will create an alternative for themselves. A set of values, norms, and behavior patterns usually are developed for each activity. The importance of these values or norms depends to a great extent on the reaction of the hearing society or the new activity of deaf people. If the values are threatening to the dominant group, deaf people may take necessary measures in order to protect their activity. As long as the created activities are regarded as an exclusive concern of deaf people, their acquired values and norms are unthreatened. However, when the hearing society finally agrees to modify their activities to accommodate the demands of deaf people, the latter may then seek ways to preserve their sociocultural identity. Other minorities, disabled groups, and ethnic groups have experienced similar social and cultural situations in most countries. There is an agreement among anthropologists and sociologists that cultures or subcultures are created, sustained, and changed in response to social dynamics within every society, and that they function as important providers of general guidelines for behavior.

Bibliography

Andersson, Yerker: *A Cross-Cultural Comparative Study: Deafness*, unpublished doctoral dissertation, Department of Sociology, University of Maryland, College Park, 1981.

————: "The Deaf as a Subculture," in *An Orientation to Deafness for Social Workers*, Gallaudet College, Washington, D.C., 1975.

————: "Sociologie des Sourdes," in Denis Mermod (ed.), *Entendre avec les Yeux*, Editions Labor et Fides, Geneva, Switzerland, p. 17–29, 1972.

Arnold, David O. (ed.): *The Sociology of Subcultures*, Glendessary Press, Berkeley, California, 1970.

Barnett, H. G.: *Innovation: The Basis of Culture*, McGraw-Hill, New York, 1955.

Gordon, Milton M.: *Assimilation in American Life*, Oxford University, New York, 1964.

Greenbaum, William: "America in Search of a New Ideal: An Essay on the Rise of Pluralism," *Harvard Educational Review*, 44:411–440, 1970.

Hertzler, Joyce O.: *A Sociology of Language*, Random House, New York, 1965.

Keddie, Nell (ed.): *The Myth of Cultural Deprivation*, Penguin, Middlesex, England, 1973.

Meadow, Kathryn: "Early Manual Communication in Relation to the Deaf Child's Intellectual, Social, and Communicative Functioning," *American Annals of the Deaf*, 113:29–41.

Sussman, Marvin B.: "Sociological Theory and Deafness: Problems and Prospects," *Research on Behavioral Aspects of Deafness*, U.S. Department of Health, Education and Welfare, Washington, D.C.

Yinger, J. Milton: *Countercultures*, Free-Press, New York, 1982.

Yerker Andersson

Socioeconomic Status

The socioeconomic status of a group of people usually refers to that group's educational, occupational, and income characteristics. Throughout the twentieth century in the United States, deaf people have generally attended school for a fewer number of years, faced higher levels of unemployment, had more underemployment, been given fewer opportunities for advancement, and earned less than the general, hearing population. Deaf women and nonwhite deaf people have traditionally fared even more poorly than their white male counterparts.

EDUCATIONAL ACHIEVEMENT

During the 1930s a survey of almost 20,000 hearing-impaired people found that approximately half of the deaf and hard-of-hearing population in the United States had completed elementary school; slightly more than a third had attended high school; and approximately one-eighth had attended college. According to the U.S. Bureau of the Census, these percentages were fairly similar to the general population at that time. By the 1960s and 1970s, however, some differences between deaf and hearing people had become apparent. In the early 1970s, for example, while approximately 23 percent of the general population had attended college, only about 12 percent of the deaf population had done so. By this time, while almost half of the deaf population in the United States had completed 12 or more years of education, the median years of schooling completed by deaf adults was 11.1, compared to 12.1 years for the general population. Thus, although the educational achievements of deaf people have improved substantially since the 1930s, the educational achievements of hearing people have improved even more.

Many studies have examined the reading, writing, and mathematical abilities of deaf pupils. Most of these studies have found that the majority of hearing-impaired adolescents who leave school in their late teens are at a severe educational disadvantage compared to their hearing peers.

LABOR FORCE PARTICIPATION

For a variety of reasons, it is difficult to evaluate the accuracy of studies conducted during the early years of this century concerning the participation of deaf people in the civilian labor force in America. However, it is probably safe to conclude that during the first half of the twentieth century deaf people in general were not employed at rates equal to the hearing population. Further, deaf women and nonwhite deaf people probably experienced higher unemployment rates than white deaf males during the years preceding World War II.

In the early 1970s, however, deaf people were employed at rates that were roughly equal to those of the general hearing population. The unemployment rate for hearing males was 4.9 percent in 1972, while it was only 2.9 percent for deaf males. Among females, 6.6 percent of hearing women in the labor force were unemployed in 1972, while 10.2 percent of deaf women were unemployed. Unfortunately, by the late 1970s, the employment picture for deaf Americans was less bright. For both males and females, the unemployment rate for deaf people in the labor force was about 4 percent higher than it was for their hearing peers. Approximately 10 percent of deaf men and 12 percent of deaf women were unemployed in 1977. (It is important to note that the unemployment rate includes only those unemployed individuals who spend time looking for work during the month before the information is collected, and who are available to accept a job should one be offered. It does not include people who have completely stopped looking for work or who have not yet started.)

While it is impossible to know with any certainty why this decrease occurred during the 1970s, perhaps deaf workers were being crowded out of the labor force by hearing members of the baby boom generation seeking full-time employment. It is also probable that in an economy increasingly based on services (where communication skills are at a premium) rather than on manufacturing, employment opportunities for many deaf people are growing very slowly, if at all. While this increase in the unemployment rate during the 1970s is of concern, it is as yet not known if the apparent trend continued into the 1980s.

In addition to having unemployment rates that have traditionally been higher than those found in the hearing population, underemployment has been a persistent problem facing many deaf workers. Underemployment refers to positions that are not commensurate with a worker's training, skills, or aptitudes. For example, slightly more than half of the deaf adults in the United States with 13 or more years of education were concentrated in the following jobs in the early 1970s: clerical work, operatives, farm and nonfarm labor, and service and household labor. In general, it appears that in order to secure a given job in the labor force, a deaf person must attend school for a longer period of time than a hearing person vying for the same position.

PRINCIPAL OCCUPATIONS
Deaf men and women traditionally have been overrepresented in skilled, semiskilled, or unskilled occupations (blue collar positions), and underrepresented in professional and administrative jobs (white collar positions) compared to the general population of the United States. Deaf workers have been concentrated in the manufacturing sector of the economy. In the early 1970s, for example, approximately 60 percent of male deaf workers were either craftsmen or machine operators (both transit and nontransit). Among deaf women, about 70 percent were either machine operators or clerical workers during this period. Even though the proportion of deaf workers in manufacturing has declined in recent years, it still includes about half of the male workers and two-fifths of the female workers.

While most deaf workers, especially males, continue to hold blue collar positions, an increasing number of deaf people are finding professional, white collar jobs. In fact, while the proportion of professional workers in the deaf population is still somewhat less than in the general population, there has been a noticeable improvement in this area during the past 50 years. In 1920, for example, only

about 1 percent of deaf workers held a professional or technical position; by the 1970s, close to 10 percent of deaf workers enjoyed such a position.

Not surprisingly, many deaf professionals tend to depend a great deal on oral communication in their jobs, and the ability to use speech seems to be an important factor in their occupational success. However, not all deaf professionals lost their hearing during their teenage years or after they began training for their chosen profession; many lost their hearing at a very young age. Nevertheless, while professional employment appears to be an increasingly viable option for some deaf people, many deaf professionals may find it difficult to advance to top management level positions where communication is a large part of the job. Deaf workers continue to be underrepresented in those professional occupations where oral communication skills are at a premium: managers, administrators, and sales personnel.

While it is clear that deaf people are overrepresented in blue collar occupations, deaf people are found in almost every occupation in which people are gainfully employed (at least in the United States and England). Apparently, the problem of insufficient representation of deaf people in professional, managerial, administrative, and other white collar positions is due more to environmental factors or structural barriers that make it difficult for a hearing-impaired person to succeed (such as employers who are misinformed about the abilities of deaf workers, or the stereotyping of deaf workers as suitable only for certain positions) than to any inherent limitations of deaf people.

JOB SATISFACTION AND MOBILITY
A variety of studies throughout this century have found that, in general, deaf workers are reasonably well satisfied with their jobs. In addition, employers generally seem to evaluate their deaf employees in a very positive manner. However, even though deaf people as a group seem to be satisfied employees and are judged to be satisfactory or sometimes outstanding workers, opportunities for advancement, even with retraining, appear to be more limited for them than for the general population. Indeed, a general theme that runs through most of the available studies of the occupational performance of deaf persons is that positive job performance evaluations are almost invariably correlated with limited opportunities for advancement.

One of the consequences of limited promotion possibilities is that many deaf workers frequently stay in the same job (often their first job) for a long period of time. One study done in the 1950s found that over 40 percent of deaf workers were employed in the same job for more than 10 years, and approximately 16 percent spent over 20 years in the same position. Another study of deaf adults in Washington, D.C., found that the median number of years in their present job was 5, with some deaf employees working in their current position for more than 35 years. Finally, a study of professional deaf workers conducted during the 1960s found that more than half of the respondents had not changed employers more than once during their entire career.

Findings that document the limited opportunities for advancement for deaf workers suggest that a resigned attitude toward the job rather than job satisfaction may be a more accurate description of what is actually taking place among many deaf workers. If this is true, the traditional picture of the loyal, generally satisfied deaf employee may be somewhat misleading.

While there appears to be limited occupational mobility among deaf workers, the most important predictor of a deaf person's occupational achievement seems to be the amount of schooling he or she has completed. Deaf workers, however, are generally not as effective as hearing workers in converting their education into future occupational success. As noted, it requires more years in school for a deaf student to prepare for a career, professional or otherwise, than it does for a typical hearing student. Thus, deaf workers may be at an initial disadvantage compared with hearing workers simply because of later entrance into the labor force.

Finally, it is important to mention that deaf workers who have deaf parents seem to have higher rates of upward occupational mobility and are more likely to have completed some type of postsecondary education than deaf workers with hearing parents. Presumably, deaf parents of deaf children are more successful than are hearing parents at handling the special problems that must be dealt with if deaf children are to actualize aspirations for higher status occupations.

INCOME DISTRIBUTION
The final factor relevant to the socioeconomic status is income. Information collected during this century indicates that while the incomes of deaf people were fairly comparable to the general population during the 1930s, the situation has deteriorated since then. Studies undertaken since the 1950s consistently have shown that deaf workers do not earn as much as hearing workers. In the early 1970s, for example, deaf workers earned only about 75 percent of the income of their hearing counterparts. As bad as this income situation was, it became even worse. In the mid-1970s it was found that deaf workers earned less than 70 percent of the income enjoyed by their hearing peers. It is not known whether the increasing unemployment rates experienced by deaf workers during the 1970s continued into the 1980s, nor whether the unfavorable income situation in the 1970s persisted into the 1980s.

FUTURE PROSPECTS
Technological change and the emergence of a so-called postindustrial or service-oriented economy in the United States could have profound effects on the socioeconomic status of the deaf population in the future. Despite a growing number of workers in the professional ranks, most deaf people are still confined to traditional manufacturing occupations. However, much of the work previously done by workers in factories is increasingly being done by machines. This process of automation, coupled with the growth of a service industry that often requires frequent contact with the general public, could lead to some major difficulties for deaf workers in the near future. On the other hand, high-growth occupations such as computer programming, accounting, and other fields where hearing is not always necessary for success could provide new employment opportunities for deaf people.

Bibliography

Barnartt, Sharon N., and John B. Christiansen: "The Socioeconomic Status of Deaf People: A Minorities Perspective," paper presented at the annual meeting of the American Sociological Association, San Antonio, Texas, 1984.

Best, Harry: *Deafness and the Deaf in the United States*, Macmillan, New York, 1944.

Christiansen, John B.: "The Socioeconomic Status of the Deaf Population: A Review of the Literature." in J. Christiansen and J. Egelston-Dodd (eds.), *Socioeconomic Status of the Deaf Population*, Gallaudet College, Washington, D.C., 1982.

Crammatte, Alan B.: *The Formidable Peak: A Study of Deaf People in Professional Employment*, Gallaudet College, Washington, D.C., 1965.

Lunde, Anders, and Stanley K. Bigman: *Occupational Conditions Among the Deaf*, Gallaudet College, Washington, D.C., 1959.

Martens, Elise H.: *The Deaf and the Hard-of-Hearing in the Occupational World*, U.S. Government Printing Office, Washington, D.C., 1937.

Schein, Jerome D., and Marcus T. Delk, Jr.: *The Deaf Population of the United States*, National Association of the Deaf, Silver Spring, Maryland, 1974.

Schroedel, John G.: "Variables Related to the Attainment of Occupational Status Among Deaf Adults," unpublished doctoral dissertation, New York University, New York, 1976.

Trybus, Raymond J., and Michael A. Karchmer: "School Achievement Scores of Hearing Impaired Children: National Data on Achievement Status and Growth Patterns," *American Annals of the Deaf*, 122:62–69, 1977.

Wong, Morrison G.: "Socioeconomic Status of the Deaf Population: Issues and Critiques." in J. Christiansen and R. Meisegeier (eds.), *Conference Highlights*, Gallaudet College, Washington, D.C., 1982.

John B. Christiansen

Women

There are no precise figures on the number of deaf women in the United States. Estimating the prevalence of deafness is a task that depends both on how deafness is defined and on how it is measured. Most national studies show a slightly lower rate of deafness for women than for men, but these may give a misleading impression. While there appear to be more hearing-impaired men than women when the only criterion is significant bilateral hearing impairment, there are more women than men who are prevocationally deaf (that is, deaf before the age of 19). Women comprise 52.5 percent of the population of prevocationally deaf adults in the United States, and prevocational deafness is much more important than later deafness in influencing behavior, cultural attributes, and socioeconomic status. Thus, the following discussion focuses on prevocationally deaf adults, the group for whom the best and most recent information is available. The discussion suggests that deaf women are disadvantaged in several important areas (of which income is perhaps the most important) when compared with either deaf men or hearing women.

MARRIAGE AND FAMILY

About 67 percent of deaf women between the ages of 16 and 64 are married, as compared with 75 percent of hearing women. Deaf women marry later and are more likely to remain single than hearing women. This discrepancy in marriage patterns probably is largely a result of the fact that most deaf women marry deaf men. This is especially true of women who became deaf before age three, among whom less than 10 percent marry hearing men. Even though there are slightly more deaf males than females, deaf men are more likely to remain single than are deaf women. Almost 40 percent of deaf men never marry, substantially reducing the number of potential partners available to deaf women, and thereby making marriage less possible for deaf women than for hearing women.

White and nonwhite deaf women differ markedly in marital status. About 67 percent of adult white deaf women are married at any given time, as compared with less than half of nonwhite deaf women. Furthermore, while almost half of nonwhite deaf women remain single, only about a quarter of white deaf women never marry.

Married deaf women have fewer children on the average than do married hearing women, and this might be explained by several factors. One is that deaf women marry later than hearing women, so the amount of time they have for producing children is reduced. Also, deaf women were formerly more likely than hearing women to be working, and they have lower family incomes. These situations all make having large families difficult and therefore probably reduce the number of children born to deaf women.

Two other factors that affect the number of children that deaf women have are race and age at onset of deafness. Black deaf women have, on average, more children than white deaf women. Married women who are born deaf average one child less than women whose deafness began after they were six years old. However, this does not reflect a eugenic attempt to avoid transmitting deafness onto children, but rather, the fact that women of earlier ages at onset are less likely to be married—and so less likely to have children—than are women of later ages at onset.

EDUCATION

Early in the twentieth century, deaf women had less education than deaf men, but since the 1950s this disparity has ended. Deaf men and women both average about 11 years of school. However, there is still a difference in educational attainment between deaf women and hearing women. In 1972, the latest year for which information is available, 60 percent of white hearing women completed high school compared with less than 50 percent of white deaf women. Among nonwhites, however, this difference is reversed: almost 50 percent of nonwhite deaf women completed high school, compared with about 33 percent of nonwhite hearing women. There is also a difference in the average number of years of school completed: the deaf women's median is 11.1 years while the hearing women's median is 12.1 years.

EMPLOYMENT

Deaf women are less likely to work than are deaf men. While about 75 percent of deaf men were labor force participants in 1977 (meaning they were either working or actively looking for work), this was true of only about 50 percent of deaf women; of these, 43.5 percent were working. Although deaf women now participate in the labor force at about the same rate as hearing women, before 1977 a larger percentage of deaf than hearing women were in the labor force. This equalization reflects two concurrent trends: hearing women are increasingly entering the labor force, and deaf women are increasingly leaving it.

The unemployment rate for deaf women is somewhat higher than for deaf men. In 1977 the unemployment rate for deaf women was 12 percent compared with about 10 percent for deaf men. This is, however, a much smaller sex difference than existed in 1972, when the rate was over 10 percent for deaf females and less than 3 percent for males. The discrepancy in the unemployment rate between deaf women and hearing women has remained relatively constant. Although the actual rates have varied over time, the unemployment rate for deaf women always has been higher than for hearing women. In 1977, for example, the unemployment rate was about 8 percent for hearing women but 12 percent for deaf women.

Deaf women, then, appear to be less successful at finding jobs than hearing women. This, in combination with the fact that deaf women appear to be leaving the labor force at a time when hearing women are entering it, suggests that deaf women may not be benefiting as much as hearing women from the social, cultural, and economic changes of the 1970s.

PROFILE OF WORKING WOMEN

Not all deaf women are equally likely to work. Those who are divorced, widowed, or separated are more likely to work than those who are either married or single. This pattern is similar to that of hearing women with one exception: hearing widowed women are least likely to work. Moreover, marital status makes much less of a difference in whether a deaf woman works than it does in whether a hearing woman works.

Both the number of children and the level of education that deaf women have influence their employment status. Women with no children are more likely to work than women who have children, and in general, the likelihood of a woman's working decreases as the size of her family increases. However, this is only true up to five children. After that, the likelihood of a woman's working increases again, probably because of monetary need.

In general, deaf women with more education are more likely to work than deaf women with less education, but there is an intriguing anomaly in this pattern. For some reason, deaf women with a bachelor's degree are the least likely of all deaf women to work. This would be easy to understand if these women had more children than other women, since large families keep women at home. In fact, although they are the most likely to be married of any group, women with bachelor's degrees have about the same number of children as other deaf women. Instead, these women are probably overqualified for most jobs available to deaf women except professional jobs, for which they are underqualified; thus, they work less than other women because they cannot find appropriate jobs.

OCCUPATIONS

Before the 1950s deaf workers were limited, by and large, to working in a very small number of occupations, primarily in the blue collar sector of the economy. The largest single employer of deaf women was the garment industry. However, since the mid-1950s deaf women have been moving out of blue collar work and into white collar jobs, including professional jobs (primarily teaching) and clerical work. By 1977 more than 40 percent held blue collar jobs. The remainder were pink collar or service workers, a category that includes beauticians, waitresses, childcare workers, and other low-status, low-income, traditionally female occupations. In contrast, the majority of employed deaf men are still in blue collar positions. White deaf women have different occupations from nonwhite deaf women. A majority of the latter hold blue collar jobs, and as is the case among hearing women, they are more likely than white deaf women to have pink collar jobs.

As they continue to move out of blue collar work into white collar jobs, the occupations of deaf women are more and more likely to resemble those of hearing women, who are concentrated in white and pink collar jobs. Although this tendency has advantages, it also has disadvantages, since hearing women suffer from occupational segregation by sex, or the concentration of women into a small number of "female" jobs. These usually pay less than those traditionally "male" occupations which require equal or even lower qualifications.

Like their hearing counterparts, deaf women experience sex segregation in the workplace. In 1972 deaf men who responded to one national survey were found in 171 different occupations, whereas deaf women were found in only 104 occupations. It is also true that many, if not most, deaf women are concentrated in occupations in which the majority of their coworkers are female. Those occupations in which the largest number of deaf women work (teaching, clerical work, and various jobs in the garment industry) are all over 70 percent female. This sex segregation has clear negative implications for their salaries.

INCOME

Income is the area in which the disadvantages of being both deaf and female in the United States show up most prominently. Historically, deaf women have earned less on average than deaf men. In 1920, for example, deaf women's median income was 45 percent of deaf men's. By the 1970s the situation had improved only slightly, with deaf women earning about 60 percent of what deaf men were earning.

Deaf women's lower incomes cannot be explained by differences in education. Deaf men earn more than deaf women with the same amount of education at every level except the very lowest where, ironically, deaf women actually have higher average incomes than deaf men. As is the case with hearing workers, deaf women with a college education earn less than deaf men who only completed high school, and deaf women with at least one year of graduate school earn less than deaf men with just a bachelor's degree.

The sex difference in income among deaf workers closely parallels that found among hearing workers, for hearing women earn about 60 percent of the income of hearing men. Deaf women, though, earn even less than hearing women, and the gap seems to be growing. In 1971 deaf women's median income was about 75 percent of hearing women's, but by 1976 it had decreased to about 60 percent of their income. This trend is somewhat puzzling. Although deaf women's income did increase, it did not increase as much as that of hearing women during this period.

The contrast between the income of deaf women and hearing black women illustrates starkly the income disadvantages that deaf women confront. Black women are sometimes described as being doubly disadvantaged, because their incomes are lower than both white women and black men. In this sense, deaf women are triply disadvantaged, because their incomes are even lower than those of black women. In 1971, for example, the median income for deaf women was about 85 percent of that for black women. This is true despite the fact that a larger percentage of deaf women than black women complete high school and that black women are much more likely than deaf women to work in low-paying pink collar jobs.

The two most important factors in determining deaf women's income are their occupation and their number of years on the job, or seniority. Women in white collar jobs earn more than women in blue or pink collar jobs, and women with more seniority earn more than women with less seniority. Also, white women earn more than nonwhite women, and union members earn more than nonunion members, but these differences are much smaller than those based upon occupation or seniority. Finally, women with more education earn more than women with less education but not very much more. (For example, one year of education added only about $150 to women's salaries in 1971.) Clearly, education does not by itself help to improve the incomes of deaf women.

Several factors that affect the incomes of deaf male workers do not affect those of deaf female workers. One factor is communication skill. The only communication-related variable that makes any difference at all in the incomes of deaf females is lipreading ability. However, this makes a very small difference, and it can be explained by the different educational attainments or occupations that more skilled lipreaders have compared with less skilled lipreaders. Signing, fingerspelling, or speaking abilities have almost no impact on the incomes of deaf women. Other insignificant factors include the age at onset of deafness, the women's

hearing level with or without a hearing aid, and whether the women attended a public school, a day school for the deaf, a residential school, or a combination of types of schools.

While factors such as occupation, seniority, education, and union membership influence the incomes of deaf women, they do not account for the disparity between the average incomes of deaf women and deaf men. The only factors on which deaf women differ at all from deaf men are seniority and union membership. Union membership, though, makes only a very small difference in deaf women's incomes, and the sex difference in seniority is small. There are no sex differences in educational level or overall occupational status between deaf men and deaf women.

How, then, can it be explained that deaf women earn only 60 percent of deaf men's salaries? The major cause of the difference between the incomes of deaf women and deaf men is the degree of sex segregation experienced by deaf women. Most women (deaf or hearing) work in jobs that traditionally have been considered to be female jobs. These jobs pay less than do traditionally male jobs requiring the same qualifications. Thus, even though deaf women are approximately equal to deaf men in educational and occupational status, they earn less than deaf men both because of the types of jobs they hold and because those jobs reward their education less than do deaf men's jobs.

The income difference between deaf women and hearing women is not readily explained. Deaf women do average about one year less education than hearing women, and they have somewhat lower occupational status. These small differences alone, however, cannot explain why deaf women's incomes are so much lower, for they are offset by other factors that should raise deaf women's incomes when compared with hearing women's incomes. These include the fact that a larger percentage of deaf than hearing women are union members (16 percent as compared with 12 percent) and the fact that deaf women average almost two years more seniority than hearing women (4.5 years compared with 2.8 years).

The logical explanation seems to be that deaf women experience discrimination. Despite laws (particularly the Rehabilitation Act of 1973) that make such practices illegal, employers may either be paying deaf women less than other women for the same work or be discriminating in the less obvious areas of promotion or occupational retraining. It is impossible to determine exactly how much of deaf women's income disadvantage is due to such overt discrimination, but it seems likely that it is a substantial part. Additionally, discrimination against deaf women may be a large part of the reason why deaf women earn less than black women, since deaf women as a group have more education, higher occupational status, and substantially more seniority (4.5 years compared with 3.3 years) than black women. *See* REHABILITATION ACT OF 1973.

In summary, then, three factors probably account for the very low average incomes of deaf women: (1) occupational segregation and its corollary, the lack of comparable pay for comparable work; (2) the educational and occupational disadvantages that deaf women experience; and (3) discrimination.

THE FUTURE

Deaf women may be in a better position than deaf men to benefit from future changes expected in the labor force. The area of largest growth in the economy for the foreseeable future is expected to be white collar jobs. Specifically, clerical work is expected to continue its growth, although a shift away from such traditional jobs as file clerk and office machine operator toward more computer-based occupations is expected. Pink collar occupations (not including private household work) are also expected to grow substantially. Continuing a long-standing trend, the proportion of the economy that includes blue collar jobs is expected to shrink even further.

It is clear that some of the traditionally female occupations in the white and pink collar segments of the economy are growth areas. About half of deaf women already work in these areas, and they will presumably be able keep their jobs or retrain themselves for new, somewhat similar work. However, those deaf women who work in blue collar jobs may find their job opportunities shrinking, and competition for their jobs will increase in the future. It is those workers who will need to consider looking for work in other sectors of the economy.

Pink collar work has long been the traditional alternative to blue collar work for less educated women, but it will probably never be an option for deaf women. Because pink collar jobs are service jobs, they require contact with people, whether as a beautician talking to clients or as a child care worker interacting with children. Pink collar jobs are therefore really open only to deaf workers who have good oral skills, so white collar jobs will have to be the principal alternative to blue collar jobs for deaf workers without good oral skills. However, most white collar jobs require at least a high school diploma, so they would not be a viable alternative for the approximately half of deaf women who have not finished high school. This suggests that education—at least through high school—will become even more important for deaf women in the future than it is for hearing women, who can continue to use pink collar jobs as their fallback option.

If only small percentages of deaf women continue to work in pink collar jobs, and if they continue to move out of blue collar into white collar jobs, their occupational status should improve. Unfortunately, experience suggests that this will not necessarily improve their income situation. For this to happen, either traditionally female jobs that undervalue and underpay their workers must change their base salary levels, deaf women must start moving into higher-income male jobs, or other factors such as discrimination, which are lowering the incomes of deaf women, will have to be eliminated.

Bibliography

Barnartt, S. N.: "The Socio-Economic Consequences of the Rehabilitation Act of 1973 for Deaf Workers," presented at the American Sociological Association meeting, San Francisco, California, 1982.

Christiansen, J., and J. Egelston-Dodd (eds.): *The Socio-Economic Status of the Deaf Population*, Gallaudet College, Washington, D.C., 1982.

Schein, J. D., and M. T. Delk, Jr.: *The Deaf Population of the United States*, National Association of the Deaf, Silver Spring, Maryland, 1974.

U.S. Department of Labor: *1975 Handbook on Women Workers*, U.S. Government Printing Office, Washington, D.C., 1975.

Sharon N. Barnartt

Minorities

This section examines the sociological and demographic characteristics of black, Hispanic, Native American, and Asian American deaf persons in the United States. While other nonwhite deaf persons could conceivably be included in this list, information is available only about these four groups. In fact, almost all the sociological information available about deaf minority groups is limited to blacks and Hispanics.

INCIDENCE

Except for some general demographic and socioeconomic data about nonwhite deaf people obtained in census reports prior to World War II, little research was conducted on minority deaf people before the National Census of the Deaf Population (NCDP) in the early 1970s. Consequently, even rough estimates of the size of the nonwhite deaf population in the United States prior to the 1970s must be made with some caution.

One recurrent theme that appears in virtually all the studies before the mid-1970s, as well as in the NCDP, is that nonwhites have a lower incidence rate of prevocational deafness than do white persons. One review written in the late 1970s, for example, found that in United States census reports from 1830 to 1930 blacks constituted a much smaller proportion of the deaf population than would be expected, given the number of blacks in America during that period. H. Best, writing in the early 1940s, reported that the 1930 census found that while 9.7 percent of the general population was black, black people made up only 7.4 percent of the deaf population. The late 1970 study, noted above, also mentioned that black deaf people were estimated to comprise 4.2 percent of the deaf population in 1920, but 7.4 percent in 1930. Since an increase of this magnitude among black deaf persons during this 10-year period is quite unlikely, the figures themselves are clearly suspect.

The incidence of deafness was thought to be lower among most other nonwhite deaf people as well. For example, Best reported that Hispanics constituted 1.2 percent of the general population in 1930, but only 0.7 percent of the deaf population. Similarly, while 0.2 percent of the general population in the United States was Asian in 1930, this group was thought to make up only 0.1 percent of the deaf population. Among Native Americans, however, the figures were reversed: deaf members of this minority group comprised about 0.3 percent of the general population in 1930, but 0.5 percent of the deaf population.

Since the late 1970s, however, data have been collected that indicate these earlier estimates are somewhat questionable, and that many minority deaf persons were probably not counted. One important reason for this is that many nonwhite deaf people were socially isolated, and consequently it was very easy for census enumerators to overlook them. Other evidence suggests that the incidence of deafness among nonwhites, particularly children, is much the same as it is for whites.

While this evidence indicates that there are not likely to be systematic differences in prevalence rates among different racial and ethnic groups, it is conceivable that this rate may vary somewhat within each group. Native Americans living on reservations, for example, could very well have a higher incidence of deafness rate than Native Americans not living on reservations. In fact, a study done in the early 1970s estimated that approximately 25 percent of the Indian children at boarding schools in two western states had hearing impairments, a rate more than 10 times the national average. Given this finding, an effort was made to determine whether rates of this magnitude occurred among Native Americans in a large urban community as well. The findings indicated that this extremely high rate was probably not typical of all Native Americans.

Given the above information, it is likely that the estimate of approximately 38,000 nonwhite prevocationally deaf people made after the 1972 National Census of the Deaf Population is an underestimation. Unfortunately, since no national data have been collected since then, it is not possible to specify more precisely how many nonwhite deaf persons there are in the United States at the present time. Perhaps the best estimate can be secured by

assuming that the incidence of deafness is not likely to vary much between whites and nonwhites as long as adequate health care for expectant mothers, infants, and young children is readily available. Unfortunately, this is not always true, and consequently it is possible that the prevalence rate for nonwhites may actually be higher than it is for whites. This is almost certainly true for the Native American children, mentioned above, who were living on reservations. Many of these children lost their hearing due to otitis media, an inner ear infection which, in the absence of prompt medical care, frequently causes deafness. It has been estimated that from 20 to 70 percent of Native American children are victims of otitis media.

EDUCATION

For many years researchers have examined the educational attainment (number of years of schooling completed) of white and nonwhite deaf people in the United States. Virtually all of these national and regional studies have found that nonwhite deaf persons have not completed, on the average, as many years of school as have white deaf people. Since the 1970s, however, this finding seems to be confined primarily to deaf males. In the 1950s, for example, while approximately 10 percent of white deaf persons attended college, less than 2 percent of nonwhite deaf males (90 percent of whom were black) did so. Virtually no nonwhite deaf females attended school beyond high school. By the time the National Census of the Deaf Population was conducted in the early 1970s, nonwhite deaf males attended school for a fewer number of years than white deaf males, but nonwhite deaf women had a slightly higher level of educational attainment than their white counterparts. It is unknown whether this change was due to a sampling bias or whether it actually represents a dramatic improvement by nonwhite deaf women during the late 1950s and throughout the 1960s.

In addition to studies that have examined educational attainment, other reports have consistently documented the lower academic achievement of nonwhite deaf students compared to their white counterparts. A study conducted in 1975, for example, discovered that Hispanic deaf students had lower academic achievement levels than whites in vocabulary and reading comprehension. P. Furfey and T. Harte, in their study of deaf persons in Baltimore, Maryland, found that about half of the nonwhite deaf people in their sample were so poorly educated that they were virtual social isolates: they could not communicate with average ability with either other deaf persons or hearing persons.

Several reasons have been suggested for the relatively poor academic performance of many nonwhite deaf persons. One major problem that confronted nonwhite deaf students, primarily blacks, until at least the 1960s was the system of segregated residential schools established in many states. According to the Babbidge report issued in the mid-1960s, in 1949 there were separate residential schools for white and black deaf students in 13 states. By 1963, almost 10 years after the Supreme Court declared such segregated schools to be unconstitutional, eight states still maintained separated, and inferior, schools for black deaf students. While these eight schools had desegregated by 1970, several states still maintained two residential schools at least into the early 1970s. One of these institutions was invariably smaller, older, and staffed with fewer qualified teachers than the other. Not surprisingly, this was the institution attended by most of the nonwhite deaf children of the state. Nationally, in the early 1970s, at least 5 residential and day programs had no white students, and more than 130 had no minority students. Even Gallaudet College did not accept black students before the 1950s.

Within the segregated residential school system, most of the schools for black students emphasized vocational training in areas such as shoe repairing, tailoring, barbering, or hairdressing. Since the average age of black students who graduated from these schools was 20, most wanted to begin working immediately after they completed their program.

By the late 1970s, programs for deaf students were apparently moving in a direction of increased segregation. Between 1972 and 1983, white enrollment in public residential schools decreased by almost 24 percent. By the 1983–1984 school year, minority students made up almost 30 percent of the student body in these schools, a 10 percent increase from the early 1970s. It is possible that proportionately more white than nonwhite deaf students are leaving residential programs for mainstreamed classrooms. If this trend continues, a de facto segregated school system for deaf students may emerge in the future.

In addition to a segregated educational system, a few other reasons have been suggested to explain the relatively poor academic performance of nonwhite students. Among Hispanic and Native American students, in particular, it has been observed that certain cultural norms and values may lead to problems for the deaf child in school. After age 12, for example, many Native American children are given a great deal of responsibility to make decisions for themselves, and they may not receive constant encouragement from parents to succeed in school. Moreover, deaf Native American children are frequently faced with three different languages with which they must contend: a native language at home, English in public, and English-manual communication at school. This can lead to some confusing communication situations for these chil-

dren. While these problems are likely to be particularly evident if the child lives at home, sending Native American students to a state residential school, where they are likely to be completely cut off from their culture, is not an attractive alternative.

A similar problem has been observed among black and Hispanic deaf children. Since there are few bicultural or bilingual programs for deaf students, Hispanic students from non-English-speaking homes are at a severe educational disadvantage compared with their white peers. There is frequently a great discrepancy between what schools for deaf students are prepared to teach and what Hispanic children and their families need. Hispanic deaf children, like Native American children, also frequently have the problem of trying to deal with three different languages. Moreover, there is a tendency among many Hispanics, as well as among Chinese Americans, to shelter family members with disabilities and to rely on the family rather than on public agencies for support. To the extent that this practice inhibits the family's involvement in the child's educational program, the child's academic achievement could suffer.

While the problem of bilingualism is not usually present, black students, too, frequently face an educational environment which does not take cultural differences into account. Subjects like black history and social problems faced by black people are apparently not discussed in much depth in many programs serving black deaf students.

One major problem facing all four minority groups is the lack of minority teachers in programs for deaf people. While approximately 30 percent of the deaf student population in the United States is made up of nonwhites, about 94 percent of the teachers of these students are white. Clearly, the absence of appropriate role models cannot help having a negative effect on whatever educational aspirations a nonwhite deaf student might have.

Several other factors have been identified that may help explain the low academic achievement of nonwhite deaf students. First, proportionately fewer nonwhite than white deaf children are enrolled in preschool programs. It has been noted that many black deaf children, for example, enter school without much speech or language, deficiencies which might have been addressed in a good preschool program. Second, the hearing loss of minority deaf children is frequently identified at a later date than it is for white children. This oversight becomes particularly important if a child's hearing impairment is not discovered until the optimal period for language development has passed.

It is also apparent that minority deaf children, especially blacks, are disproportionately labeled mentally retarded or learning-disabled, and are frequently seen as having behavioral or emotional problems. While it is possible that there is a higher incidence of these problems among minority deaf children than among whites, it is also possible that such assessments are due primarily to the assessor's lack of familiarity with nonwhite cultures. If this is true, the lower academic achievement of nonwhite students could be explained, at least in part, as a function of the self-fulfilling prophecy.

In the future, the proportion of minority students in programs serving deaf people in the United States is likely to increase. In the 1973–1974 school year, for example, Hispanic students constituted a little less than 7 percent of all students in these programs. By 1983–1984 more than 10 percent of all students were Hispanic. Further, during the 1983–1984 school year Native Americans made up only 0.7 percent of all students in programs serving deaf children. However, since the Native American population is growing rapidly in America (having tripled since 1960), this percentage is likely to increase in the future as well. Blacks and Asian Americans, too, are likely to be found in increasing numbers in programs for deaf students in the future. Approximately 18 percent of the students attending special programs for deaf children in 1983–1984 were black. This figure is a few percentage points higher than it was 10 years earlier, and is higher than the percentage of black people in the general population (again suggesting that the belief, generally held until the mid-1970s, that blacks have a lower rate of prevocational deafness than whites is probably incorrect).

Given these trends, some new initiatives are needed if the academic performance of nonwhite deaf students is to be improved. Two promising efforts are Projecto Opportunidad at the Rhode Island School for the Deaf and the bicultural-bilingual program at the Lexington School for the Deaf in New York City. These programs are designed to ensure that Hispanic and Portuguese deaf students, as well as their families, receive the instructional services they need, and that the students are appropriately placed in educational programs. Other educators of nonwhite deaf students will need to make similar efforts in order to meet the needs of culturally diverse groups of students if the dismal academic performance of the past is to be avoided in the future.

OCCUPATION

Among both males and females, unemployment rates for nonwhite deaf persons in the United States have traditionally been higher than for their white counterparts. In a study of the deaf community in Washington, D.C., conducted in the early 1960s, for example, it was found that the unemployment rate for nonwhite deaf men (predominantly black) was four times the rate for white deaf men. Also, while 10 percent of white deaf women were unemployed, about 50 percent of nonwhite deaf women could not find gainful employment.

The National Census of the Deaf Population discovered that while the unemployment rate for nonwhite deaf women was not as high nationally in the early 1970s as it was in Washington, D.C., 10 years earlier, it was still higher than for white deaf women. Similarly, the unemployment rate for nonwhite deaf men was higher in 1972 than it was for white deaf men. A small follow-up study in 1977 of a sample of those who were included in the original National Census of the Deaf Population study revealed that the unemployment rate was slightly lower in the late 1970s than it was in the early 1970s for nonwhite deaf females, but that it was much higher for nonwhite deaf males. Since the nonwhite sample in this follow-up study was quite small, these apparent changes may be due to sampling error and should consequently be interpreted with caution. Unfortunately, since no national socioeconomic data have been collected since the 1970s, it is simply not known whether unemployment rates of nonwhite deaf persons are still higher than those of their white peers. Further, most of the information about the unemployment rates of nonwhite deaf people is limited to blacks, and virtually nothing is known about specific unemployment rates found among deaf members of other minority groups.

In addition to experiencing higher unemployment rates, nonwhite deaf people have traditionally been found in lower-status occupations than white deaf persons. For example, in 1920 it was reported that while more than 20 percent of white deaf men were employed as craftsmen, fewer than 4 percent of nonwhite deaf men were so employed. Fifty years later, the National Census of the Deaf Population revealed that white deaf men were being employed as craftsmen at a rate that was still twice that of their nonwhite counterparts. Among deaf females, the census found that while nonwhites were more likely to be employed in professional and technical positions than were white deaf women, they were also more likely to be found in semiskilled and unskilled positions than their white counterparts.

A few studies have focused on specific deaf minority groups. For example, it was reported in the mid-1970s that Hispanic deaf people were overrepresented in service, labor, and operative positions. Regional studies in Washington, D.C., Los Angeles, and Milwaukee undertaken in the 1960s and early 1970s revealed that few black deaf persons had professional, technical, or other positions in the labor force. Other studies that have focused on young black deaf workers have found that for a variety of reasons they are quite dissatisfied with their jobs. Another small, regional study in the early 1970s found that clerical work, sales positions, and service occupations were typical jobs found by Native Americans who had sought rehabilitation treatment in Arizona.

While the occupational situation for nonwhite deaf people in the United States appears to be quite dismal, there are some indications that the situation is improving. For example, in one study of deaf professionals in the early 1960s, no black professionals other than teachers were located. By the early 1980s, though, a number of black, Hispanic, Asian American, and Native American professionals were found. While this is a significant improvement in the 20 years separating the two studies, the number of nonwhite deaf professionals is still small compared to the number of white deaf people in professional occupations. Also, as noted, nonwhite deaf females appear to be quite successful in securing professional positions. In fact, one analysis of the National Census of the Deaf Population data found that by the early 1970s approximately 75 percent of deaf women, and slightly less than 20 percent of deaf men, worked in occupations that were racially equal.

However, in spite of this progress, it is clear that in the blue collar occupational world where deaf people have traditionally found jobs, nonwhite males and females are still more likely to be confined to semiskilled and unskilled positions than are their white counterparts.

It is clear that beyond general conclusions about the likelihood of relatively high unemployment rates and the absence of a high proportion of nonwhite deaf professionals and other skilled workers, coupled with the fact that things do seem to be improving a bit, little is known about employment problems faced by various deaf minorities. Further, almost no new information has been obtained about these crucial problems since about 1970.

INCOME

Given this picture of the occupational situation faced by nonwhite deaf people, it is certainly not surprising to discover that their incomes have generally lagged behind those earned by white deaf people throughout this century. In 1920, for example, while approximately one-third of the white deaf male population earned more than $1200 a year, less than 13 percent of the nonwhite deaf male population did so. Nonwhite females also earned less than their white peers in 1920.

The National Census of the Deaf Population found that while the income gap between white and nonwhite deaf persons in the United States is still wide, it is apparently not quite as wide as before. The census also reported that, in general, nonwhite deaf people earn a little over three-fifths of the income

earned by nonwhite hearing persons. White deaf persons, in contrast, earn approximately three-fourths of the incomes of white hearing people in the United States. Further, as perhaps an indirect measure of income, the census found that more than 60 percent of white deaf males who are heads of households own their own home, and that approximately 70 percent of these homes are located in reasonably good neighborhoods. On the other hand, less than 20 percent of nonwhite deaf males who are heads of households own their own home, and less than 30 percent of those homes are found in similar neighborhoods.

As there is little current information available about occupational problems facing deaf people, especially deaf members of specific minority groups, so there is also little contemporary income data available. It is not known whether the income situation for nonwhite deaf people has improved or deteriorated since the mid-1970s.

SERVICES

Many of the occupational and income problems faced by nonwhite deaf people are undoubtedly due to the poor education that many minority deaf persons receive. In addition, the paucity of other services such as vocational rehabilitation make it doubly difficult for minority deaf persons to secure gainful employment. Several studies made during the 1960s and 1970s found that there were few vocational or rehabilitation programs designed to meet the needs of minority deaf persons, and consequently many nonwhite people were frequently underemployed in jobs that offered little opportunity for advancement. One study in Los Angeles in the mid-1960s, for example, found that while there were almost a half million black people in Los Angeles County at the time, only 20 black deaf people were being assisted by one of the two vocational rehabilitation counselors who served a total of more than 130 deaf clients. Another study in the early 1970s found that many agencies serving deaf people in the Los Angeles area, such as vocational training centers, were located far from areas in which many black people lived, while similar agencies in black communities offered few, if any, services for deaf persons.

Other minority deaf people face frustrations with state vocational rehabilitation agencies. For example, vocational rehabilitation counselors must be able to understand Native American or Hispanic culture in order to assist these nonwhite deaf people in an appropriate manner. In addition, while vocational rehabilitation agencies are limited by state boundaries, reservations are frequently located in two or more states. Factors such as these can frequently make it difficult for Native Americans to secure desired vocational services.

SEGREGATION AND ISOLATION

Implicit in much of the information available about the educational and occupational status of nonwhite deaf people is the notion that there seems to be a fair amount of racial segregation within the deaf community. More explicitly, such segregation is frequently found in many large communities that have separate social clubs for white and black deaf people. Further, it has been observed that many nonwhite deaf people are extremely isolated socially, not only from their white deaf peers but, on occasion, from other nonwhite deaf persons, as well as from the larger hearing community.

It has been suggested that one of the major problems facing many nonwhite deaf persons is the lack of communication skills that are needed to interact effectively with others, thus leading to subsequent social isolation. Studies have found, for example, that many nonwhite deaf children often have minimal exposure to communication systems beyond homemade gestures used in the family. Other researchers have observed that an underclass of black deaf persons with very poor communication skills exists in some major communities in America, and that such individuals have little contact with white deaf people or with their better-educated black deaf peers. In one study of black deaf persons in Los Angeles, it was found that few of the people included in the study had any contact with any of the others even though they lived only a few blocks apart. Nor did they have much contact with any other deaf people. Further, many of these individuals were only able to use gestures, rather than American Sign Language or some other sign language system, to communicate with the investigator.

As another indicator of social isolation among nonwhite deaf people, the National Census of the Deaf Population found that nonwhite deaf people marry at a significantly lower rate than their white counterparts. While almost 58 percent of white deaf men marry, less than one-third of nonwhite deaf men have a spouse. Similarly, while approximately two-thirds of white deaf women marry, only about 40 percent of nonwhite deaf women have a marriage partner. Even though these rates are low, more nonwhite deaf people are marrying now than during the first few decades of this century, when only about 20 percent of nonwhite men (predominantly black) and 25 percent of nonwhite women were married.

The isolation that characterizes many nonwhite deaf people is not limited to individuals who have only minimal contact with the wider deaf or hearing community. It also appears that nonwhite and white groups, especially social clubs, have little contact with each other. Further, it has been noted that black deaf people in different parts of the country use signs that are often not used by their white colleagues. While these signs probably do not constitute a separate sign language, their use may make it even more difficult for these two groups to interact with each other. *See* SOCIOLINGUISTICS: Sign Language Dialects.

Social clubs for deaf adults are apparently racially segregated. In some communities, clubs for black deaf people were established because blacks were not permitted to become members of existing clubs. For example, the Washington Silent Society was established in Washington, D.C., because blacks were excluded from the white District of Columbia Association of the Deaf. While strict segregation is no longer the rule, there are still separate social clubs in Washington that cater primarily to deaf people of different races. The Capital City Association of the Deaf is predominantly black, while the Metro Washington Association of the Deaf is largely white.

The National Census of the Deaf Population found that many of the clubs and organizations established by nonwhite, especially black, deaf people were financially quite weak, had few members, and were usually not affiliated with regional or national associations. This, of course, prevents many nonwhite deaf people from learning about educational and vocational opportunities, as well as social activities, which may be available in the community.

In recent years black deaf people have taken a stronger advocacy role, and have sought to merge many of their concerns with those of the larger black community. The first Black Deaf Conference was held in Washington, D.C., in 1981 in order to give black deaf people an opportunity to discuss a variety of issues and to plan an active social agenda for the future. A follow-up conference was held in Cleveland in 1982, which resulted in the election of an executive secretary to coordinate a national effort to advocate the rights of black deaf people. Further, the Black Deaf Associates, a coalition of activist individuals and groups, was formed to do much the same thing, as well as to identify and train young black deaf people for future leadership roles. Thus, while many problems caused by the historical segregation of white and nonwhite deaf people in America remain, there are efforts by members of at least one nonwhite minority group to challenge the status quo.

Bibliography

Alcocer, Anthony (ed.): *Proceedings of the Working Conference on Minority Deaf*, Center on Deafness, California State University, Northridge, 1974.

Babbidge, H.: *Education of the Deaf in the United States: Report of the Advisory Committee on Education of the Deaf*, U.S. Government Printing Office, Washington, D.C., 1965.

Best, Harry: *Deafness and the Deaf in the United States*, Macmillan, New York, 1943.

Bowe, Frank G.: "Nonwhite Deaf Persons: Educational, Psychological, and Occupational Considerations," *American Annals of the Deaf*, 116:33–39, 1971.

Carmel, Simon: "Diversity Within an American Deaf Community," in P. Higgins and J. Nash (eds.), *The Deaf Community and the Deaf Population*, Gallaudet College, Washington, D.C., 1982.

Delgado, Gilbert (ed.): *The Hispanic Deaf*, Gallaudet College, Washington, D.C., 1984.

Furfey, Paul H., and Thomas J. Harte: *Interaction of Deaf and Hearing in Baltimore City, Maryland*, Catholic University of America, Washington, D.C., 1968.

Hairston, Ernest, and Linwood D. Smith: *Black and Deaf in America: Are We That Different*, T. J. Publishers, Silver Spring, Maryland, 1983.

Lombardo, A.S.: "An Examination of the Difficulties Encountered by the Black Deaf," *The Deaf American*, pp. 23–26, March 1976.

Moores, Donald, and Chester W. Oden, Jr.: "Educational Needs of Black Children," *American Annals of the Deaf*, 122:313–318, June 1977.

Nickoloff, Elia George: "The Hearing-Impaired American Indian in the Vocational Rehabilitation Process," unpublished Ed.D. dissertation, University of Arizona, 1975.

Ries, P., D. Bateman, and A. Schildroth: *Ethnic Background in Relation to Other Characteristics of Hearing Impaired Students in the United States*, Office of Demographic Studies, Gallaudet College, Washington, D.C., 1975.

Schein, Jerome D.: *The Deaf Community Study of Metropolitan Washington, D.C.*, Gallaudet College, Washington, D.C., 1968.

———and Marcus Delk, Jr.: *The Deaf Population of the United States*, National Association of the Deaf, Silver Spring, Maryland, 1974.

Schildroth, Arthur: "Public Residential Schools for Deaf Students in the United States, 1970–1978," *American Annals of the Deaf*, pp. 80–91, April 1980.

———: *The School Age Hearing Impaired Population of the United States*, in press.

Smith, Linwood D.: "The Hardcore Deaf Negro Adult in the Watts Area of Los Angeles, California," unpublished graduate project, San Francisco Valley State College, 1971.

Taft, Brenda: "Employability of Black Deaf Persons in Washington, DC: National Implications," *American Annals of the Deaf*, 128:453–457, August 1983.

John B. Christiansen

Hard-of-Hearing

For years the sociology of disabled persons has been a neglected field, although with the advent of the Education for All Handicapped Children Act (Public Law 94-142) and similar legislation the social adjustment of the disabled population in the United States is receiving increased study. However, there is still a scarcity of research and study in the sociology of hearing-impaired persons, particularly those who are hard-of-hearing. This oversight is probably due to the fact that hearing impairment is virtually invisible and as such does not evoke the interest or concern that occurs with visible disabilities.

Hearing impairment is the single most pervasive physical disability in the United States today. The 1980 figures compiled by the National Center for Health Statistics estimated that 15 to 16 million people in the United States had some degree of hearing impairment. There are approximately 2 million deaf and 14 million hard-of-hearing individuals in the United States. While the hard-of-hearing segment comprises the largest component of the hearing-impaired population, its needs and services are also the most ignored educationally, sociologically, and psychologically.

TERMINOLOGY

There is no one generally agreed-upon definition of deafness, hearing impairment, or hard-of-hearing. However, the definition most frequently used in the scant literature related to hard-of-hearing people defines such individuals as "those in whom the sense of hearing, although defective, is functional with or without a hearing aid." This definition fails to take into account the degree of defectiveness and, even more importantly, the functional levels and their effects upon the lifestyle of the individual.

Hearing-impaired, a generic term used to identify hearing loss, is intended to describe any degree of hearing loss, but to some people this term refers only to hard-of-hearing individuals. Moreover, the terms hearing-impaired and hard-of-hearing are commonly used with qualifying adjectives such as mild, moderate, moderately severe, and severe.

FACTORS INFLUENCING SOCIAL ADJUSTMENT

The age at onset and degree of hearing loss have implications for the development of language and communication skills among hard-of-hearing persons, which in turn affect an individual's interaction in the home and the community. Acquisition of language may be hindered if onset is at an early age, especially during the first six years of life, which are crucial for developing language skills. As the age at onset increases and language has already developed, the effect of the hearing loss on language acquisition is reduced; however, problems in communication may become more serious.

Individuals with a mild hearing loss do not have too much trouble with everyday communication activities. There may be a feeling that the world does not talk loudly enough, and there is often an element of strain when trying to hear in a group, but the individual can usually get by.

A moderate hearing loss frequently leads to more difficulty with scanning and the background functions of hearing than with socializing. With a moderate hearing loss, communication usually can be effectively maintained with amplification or by moving closer to the speaker. A moderately severe hearing loss, however, causes an individual problems in social interaction with the normally hearing population. The individual will need to use amplification at all times and will function more effectively in a one-to-one communication situation or in a small group. Such an individual may experience a feeling of isolation from the mainstream and may seek social relationships with others having a similar degree of hearing impairment (that is, with the deaf community) or may tend to withdraw from social interaction.

A severe hearing impairment creates more severe barriers to social interaction and communication with the normally hearing population. In addition to amplification, the individual needs to rely heavily on visual and tactile monitoring of the environment. The most satisfactory personal and social relationships often are with others with a similar hearing loss as well as with the deaf community.

IDENTIFICATION

Early identification of hearing loss is imperative to ensure development of effective language and communication skills among children. Some progress in early identification is being accomplished by screening newborns in hospitals, especially those considered high risk. These screenings are more effective in detecting moderately severe to profound hearing losses than mild or moderate losses, which frequently occur during a child's early years as a result of childhood diseases or chronic ear infections. Preschool-age and young children could be identified earlier if hearing tests were performed routinely as part of the physical examinations conducted by pediatricians and family doctors. *See* AUDITORY DISORDERS, PREVENTION OF: Screening.

Hard-of-hearing children in schools have been called the forgotten children, as teachers are rarely aware of the presence of a hard-of-hearing child in the classroom. Mild to moderate hearing losses in children often go undetected by parents or teachers and may lead to the child being misdiagnosed as lazy, stupid, disobedient, or even faking a hearing loss.

Behavior traits that may suggest a hearing loss are lack of attention; frequent requests for repetition of what has been said; irrelevant answers; frequent mistakes in carrying out oral instructions; peculiar listening behaviors such as cupping the ear, cocking the head, leaning forward to listen, and turning the head to localize sound with the better ear; anxious or listless facial expression; speech defects; indifferent responses to music; restlessness; nervous fatigue; daydreaming; and poor scholarship.

Failure to achieve satisfactory educational or social adjustment may result in the hard-of-hearing children resorting to lying, stealing, truancy, or rowdiness in an attempt to compensate for feelings of inadequacy and a desire to attract attention to themselves. Or some children become extremely withdrawn and introverted, a behavior also exhibited by adults and elderly persons with acquired hearing loss.

Teachers or parents observing any of these behaviors in a child should suspect a hearing problem and arrange for a hearing test for verification. This is especially true in areas where school programs do not have mandatory screening programs for entering children. These behaviors and society's tendency to stigmatize those who are different may be one reason why many hard-of-hearing schoolchildren, especially in nonmainstreamed programs, often are not fully accepted by their peers. Hard-of-hearing children attending mainstreamed programs tend to be better adjusted and accepted because these programs usually provide sensitivity and awareness training for school personnel and children in the school.

Once a hard-of-hearing child is identified, early implementation of educational services is of utmost importance, beginning with preschool planning. Unlike the specialized curricula of residential schools and day schools for deaf pupils, public school programs need to supplement the regular academic program with special services for hard-of-hearing pupils. Students in these programs need auditory training, speechreading (lipreading), speech development, speech reeducation or speech conservation, and language development. These services can best be provided by qualified speech and language pathologists. In addition, school programs have an obligation to provide guidance and counseling for the parents and the hard-of-hearing child. Vocational guidance and training focusing on the assets of hearing impairment rather than its liabilities needs to be built into the curriculum.

IMPACT ON THE FAMILY

The impact of a disabled child on parents and other family members is significant. The reactions of parents, family members, and friends to the disabled member of the family is crucial. The manner in which disabled individuals process these reactions strongly influences their self-perception and self-esteem and consequently their behavior.

Initially, and perhaps for the greater part of the hard-of-hearing child's life, there is a tendency for parental overprotection and overindulgence. Hard-of-hearing children often mistakenly perceive loud speech as an expression of anger. Families with a hard-of-hearing member need to develop tolerance, as does the individual with the hearing loss. The facial and body language that accompanies the frustration of trying to communicate, only to fail or partially succeed, is often misconstrued as annoyance or dislike and may cause the hard-of-hearing person to withdraw from further social interaction. Withdrawal also may occur when the hard-of-hearing person perceives impatience or is told that what is being said is not important. Often the hard-of-hearing person is told to wait until the topic being discussed is completed for an explanation or for clarification, only to be told upon completion that it was not important. Or hearing-impaired people may be told that they would not understand, or they are given a one-sentence summary of a half hour's conversation. Deaf persons constantly experience similar situations.

AMPLIFICATION

Overexpectation of the benefits of amplification, specifically of individual hearing aids, often happens. Both people with normal hearing and hearing-impaired people need orientation to the benefits and the limits of the hearing aid. Frequently hard-of-hearing people are made to feel that they are not trying hard enough to function in the hearing world, when in fact they are receiving and utilizing the maximum benefits possible from their hearing aid given their degree of hearing loss.

Better hearing is only one aspect of hearing aid usage. Noise, lighting, and physical well-being are factors that detract from effective hearing aid usage. A great deal of strain and tension is generated when the hard-of-hearing person interacts with normally hearing people, regardless of whether they are family, friends, or strangers. Sensitive persons can help reduce some of this strain by keeping hands and objects away from the face, by facing the hard-of-hearing person while speaking, by avoiding loud tones or exaggerated speech, and by speaking naturally with clear enunciation. Should the hard-of-hearing person prefer signs along with speech, this needs to be recognized. Preparing ahead of time for activities by providing names of people and places is also helpful. Parents can help children by previewing lessons and preparing them for activities in and out of school. Helping the hard-of-hearing individual develop and maintain a sense of humor is most beneficial for all concerned. *See* HEARING AIDS.

LATE-ONSET HEARING LOSS

Hearing loss that occurs in adults and in the elderly requires psychological adjustment of varying degrees, as it is extremely difficult to adjust to a hearing loss after having had normal hearing. Almost without fail, and regardless of the age at onset or the degree of hearing loss, individuals in this age bracket report feeling isolated from the hearing population. In addition, the hard-of-hearing person's role performance as a family member may undergo drastic changes.

Marital relations may be changed or strained, for example, and relationships with one's children may suffer. Occupational status frequently changes and even may involve a complete change of career.

Changes to hobbies of an individual or visual nature may become necessary. Communication difficulties result in changes or dissolution of old friendships. As communication effectiveness at church, work, home, clubs, and shopping is reduced, there is more and more withdrawal from social situations involving the normal hearing population. In general, life becomes more stressful as individuals find themselves losing their independence and becoming dependent on others for assistance with messages, transacting business and personal affairs, and maintaining friends. There also may be a tendency for the hard-of-hearing person to seek services and associations with hard-of-hearing individuals and sometimes with deaf persons.

Hearing loss among elderly persons (those 65 years of age and over) is approximately 10 times greater than among people in early and late adulthood. This proportion is expected to increase from the effects of noise pollution and because people are living longer than in the past.

Hearing loss interferes with the reception of warning sounds, thereby causing feelings of insecurity. Inhibition of social and cultural interaction leads to withdrawal and introversion by elderly citizens. Participation in vocational and avocational activities may be limited or even curtailed, which further adds to feelings of isolation and stress.

Often the hearing loss is so gradual that the elderly person does not recognize that a loss has occurred or will deny it and accuse others of mumbling or not speaking up. For effective adjustment to the hearing loss, it is important that the elderly person accept the fact and begin to find ways in which to adapt to a new lifestyle. If habilitation is initiated as soon as the hearing loss is discovered, the elderly person may be more adaptable and more willing to learn new skills. Hearing tests by certified audiologists, ideally those specializing in geriatrics, should be arranged in order that an appropriate hearing aid may be selected. Auditory training also needs to be provided in order to help with voice control. Speechreading lessons, as well as instruction in the monitoring of environmental sounds, also are useful. Geriatric counseling is of utmost importance, as is exposure and interaction with other hard-of-hearing senior citizens.

With the increase in the percentage of elderly citizens in the population, the United States government has become interested in the problems of aging and has provided various kinds of help, including the White House Conference on Aging. As a result of the January 1981 Conference on Aging, for example, the report *Elderly Hearing Impaired People* was published. The report mentions the diminishing quality of life and communication hindrances as having the greatest effect on the individual. Other problems identified by the elderly as affecting their lives were that hearing loss restricts the ability to be productive, limits social interaction, and reduces constructive use of leisure time. Hearing loss also was reported as affecting physical and mental health and ultimately the will to live. Some individuals reported poor self-image, isolation, despair, and tension in the family. Some felt that hearing loss was the cause of being placed in nursing homes.

Issues that elderly hard-of-hearing individuals felt need to be addressed in the future are research into physiology, behavioral science, and technology related to hearing deprivation. It was suggested that the behavioral sciences focus more on empathy training, counseling, effects of isolation, denial syndrome, and influence of environmental factors on the individual. Other issues that were identified as needing attention were professional training for the providers as well as for the consumers, special needs such as vocational training programs, devices for environmental control, and social access. *See* Presbycusis.

Organization

Ironically, even though hard-of-hearing people comprise the largest segment of the hearing-impaired population in the United States, they are not as well defined as a social group as are deaf people, and they do not have the organizational network found in the deaf community.

Historically, the lack of organization of, by, and for hard-of-hearing persons has posed problems for individuals seeking to find others with approximately the same level of hearing loss. The oldest and perhaps the most prestigious group is the New York League of the Hard of Hearing; in Canada, it is the Canadian Hearing Society, which also serves deaf persons. More recently established organizations involved in the social welfare of hard-of-hearing individuals are the Suzanne Pathey Speak-Up Institute, Consumers Organization for the Hearing Impaired, Inc., International Federation of the Hard of Hearing, and Self Help for Hard of Hearing People, Inc. These groups generally provide information and support services to adults, while the Alexander Graham Bell Association serves both adults and children who are hard-of-hearing or deaf. The National Association of the Deaf is another consumer organization that includes many hard-of-hearing members. *See* Canada.

These organizations generally provide services such as hearing aid usage and orientation, some auditory training, speechreading lessons, and speech conservation. They also offer counseling and guidance that focuses on resolving identity conflicts, acceptance of the disability, and problems with self-esteem. Unfortunately, there is little vocational guidance material available for hard-of-hearing adults. Publications by these organizations provide information on assistive devices, communication aids, and advocacy.

Conclusion

While profoundly deaf people have been identified as "outsiders in a hearing world," those who are hard-of-hearing can easily be labeled as outsiders in both the hearing and deaf worlds. Hard-of-hearing people belong to two cultural worlds, the hearing and the deaf, but are not entirely a part of either. Instead, they are on the edge of both worlds socially and psychologically. Generally, deaf people make better adjustment to the hearing world than do hard-of-hearing persons, for the former accept the fact that they cannot hear and therefore do not have to undergo the stress of trying to communicate through the auditory process. They do not face the problems of hard-of-hearing persons who fluctuate between hearing and deafness. As hard-of-hearing people start to feel the effects of their hearing loss upon their social interactions, they will seek out individuals like themselves. In this search, they may try to identify with the deaf community. If the hearing loss has occurred after adolescence, however, it is difficult to become a member of the deaf community because of the need for linguistic fluency in manual communication.

Furthermore, the deaf community tends to perceive hearing-impaired individuals with good speech and usable hearing as "hearing" and therefore more a part of the hearing world. This is compounded by the fact that the hard-of-hearing person may not know or may refuse to use signs, which is considered unfavorable by many members of the deaf community. Finally, hard-of-hearing people may stigmatize members of the deaf community in much the same way as those with normal hearing have stigmatized them, which in turns leads to retaliation by members of the deaf community. Thus, hard-of-hearing people may sometimes find themselves without a community. *See* Psychology: Hard-of-Hearing.

Bibliography

Davis, H., and R. Silverman: *Hearing and Deafness*, 3d ed., Holt, Rinehart and Winston, New York, 1970.

Davis, J. (ed.): *Our Forgotten Children: Hard of Hearing Pupils in the Schools*, Audio Visual Library Service, University of Minnesota, Minneapolis, 1977.

Higgins, Paul: *Outsiders in a Hearing World*, Sage Publications, Beverly Hills, 1980.

Myklebust, H. R.: *The Psychology of Deafness*, 2d ed., Grune and Stratton, New York, 1964.

Carol Garretson

Deafened Adults

"Deafened adults" here refers to persons whose hearing impairment became significant after the age of 19. In some ways, descriptive parameters are vague, and this population may be more easily identified by characteristics that are absent rather than by those that are present. That is, members of this group generally would not consider themselves to be part of the deaf community, nor would they know sign language. They are likely to have a good deal of residual hearing rather than to be profoundly deaf. They are present in the population in large numbers and comprise at least 97 percent of those with significant loss of hearing. Even the process of arriving at reasonable estimates of prevalence is a difficult and complicated one, reflecting the complexities of defining and diagnosing the disability itself. However, the attempt to provide this estimate can be instructive for defining the nature of the group.

Prevalence of Hearing Impairment

In the United States, there are approximately 18.7 million persons who have some problem with hearing, making this the largest disability group. This estimate is based on population figures from the 1980 census and is larger than earlier estimates because the Census Bureau had been underestimating the size of the total population in the years from 1971–1979. The most frequent estimate found in the literature is 16.2 million, based on population figures for 1977. In that year, a survey was completed in 40,000 households by interviewers from the Census Bureau and provides additional data on the nature of hearing impairment. Of these 16.2 million persons, about 2 million probably suffered from tinnitus (ringing or buzzing noises in the ears) only. Another 6 million people have trouble hearing in one ear (unilateral hearing loss) only. An additional half million persons had a hearing loss of undetermined extent or nature. Thus, about half of the persons included in prevalence estimates have a hearing loss in both ears (bilateral hearing loss). If population figures for 1980 are utilized, it can be stated that approximately 8.4 million Americans have significant problems with their hearing.

The 1977 nationwide interview survey determined that 56 percent of those with a bilateral hearing loss reported that they could hear words spoken in a normal voice, albeit with difficulty; 32 percent said they could hear words shouted across a room; and 12 percent said they could, at best, hear words shouted in their ear. These estimates are self-reports, which may or may not match results of actual audiological testing.

Prevalence Rates and Aging

There is a sharp increase in prevalence rates of hearing impairment for each successively older age grouping. In 1981 estimated prevalence rates for the total population with a hearing loss in one or both ears was 82.9 persons in every 1000. However, for persons under the age of 17 the rate was 17.7; for ages 17 to 44 the rate was 43.8; for ages 45 to 64 the rate was 142.9; and for persons over age 64 the rate was 283.8. These figures do not include persons residing in nursing homes, where rates of hearing impairment would be even higher. A dramatic illustration of the relationship between aging and hearing impairment is the comparison of an estimated 7 percent of the total population with some trouble in hearing, and 26 percent of nursing home residents judged to have a hearing problem. Another way of demonstrating this relationship between age and hearing loss is to report that 49.3 percent of all people who are able to hear only shouted speech are age 70 or older.

Loss of hearing does not necessarily accompany the aging process, but it certainly may. It is widely recognized that life expectancy is increasing in the United States. As a larger proportion of the total population is found to be over 65 years old, even larger numbers of persons with hearing impairments will also be found.

Characteristics

In addition to the relationship between hearing loss and age, several other characteristics of the deafened adult population can be identified. First, there is a striking preponderance of hearing-impaired men compared with women in every age group. Referring again to the National Health Interview Survey conducted in 1977, it is found that 54 percent of men aged 45 to 64 years report trouble with their hearing compared with 46 percent of women. Of men older than 64 years, 62 percent report trouble in hearing compared with 38 percent of women. Several studies indicate that men may have a more difficult time adjusting to their hearing loss compared with women. This could be because of the likelihood of hearing loss interfering with vocational status or plans.

Hearing loss is also more likely among white people than among black people, among those whose families earn less than $7000 per year, and among those who have completed less than 12 years of education. Those who live in the southern part of the United States, and outside of large metropolitan areas, also tend to be overrepresented among the population with hearing impairments.

Work environments can contribute to increased prevalence rates and to an increased risk for hearing loss in older persons. The hearing acuity of 1000 Swedish workers in two noisy factories has been surveyed. Half of those aged 31 to 35 had some hearing loss, as did 75 percent of those between the ages of 41 and 50, 92 percent of those between the ages of 56 and 60, and 99 percent of workers aged 61 or older. See HEARING LOSS: Noise-Induced.

Characteristics associated with greater risk for hearing impairment may also be related to the quality of health care that is available and used.

People with a hearing loss are likely to be ill more frequently and to have more chronic health conditions than do those without a hearing loss. This relationship of poor health and hearing loss is complicated by the fact that aging persons are also more likely to suffer from poor health as well as from hearing impairments.

GRADUAL VERSUS SUDDEN HEARING LOSS

For most deafened adults, hearing loss is a gradual process, and often almost imperceptible. The individual who loses hearing in this manner may begin to turn the sound up slightly on the radio or television or to ask family members to repeat their remarks. When hearing loss accompanies aging (presbycusis), sounds in the high frequencies are usually more difficult to hear or to understand. For some persons, loss of hearing may come very quickly, even overnight, as a result of injury or accident. Sudden onset of hearing loss may also result from surgery (for example, as treatment for a tumor on the auditory nerve) or from drugs used to treat a serious health condition. Some progressive hearing losses have a genetic base and begin to appear at approximately the same age for many family members.

PSYCHOLOGICAL PROBLEMS

There is a widespread belief that deaf people are likely to be paranoid, that is, that they have a highly exaggerated, even pathological level of suspiciousness that others are discussing them or intend to harm them. This belief may have been partially based on some outdated research studies that used personality tests inappropriate for this population. Recent research using more carefully selected subjects and more appropriate measures indicates that paranoia is no more common among hearing-impaired persons than among other population groups. It is true that deafened persons may take personal offense when companions fail to repeat comments they do not hear and then imagine that the comments were made about them, but this is quite different from the personality disorder known as paranoia. The research evidence indicates that it is more likely that deafened persons may suffer from severe depression or from anxiety. This does not mean that hearing loss causes these disorders, but that changes in work opportunities or in family and social situations create pressures that in turn may trigger severe psychological reactions. One of the difficulties of evaluating the influence of hearing loss on mental disorders resulting in hospitalization is that mental patients with hearing impairments tend to have more lengthy hospital stays and are less likely to receive treatment that utilizes oral communication. *See* PSYCHOLOGY: Mental Health.

Most people who experience severe hearing loss as adults probably have periods of depression and

withdrawal. Decreasing ability to communicate can lead to greater withdrawal and then to increased isolation and loneliness. These circular effects of hearing loss are more likely in middle-aged persons than among the elderly, and loneliness accompanying loss of hearing is felt as severely by those with moderate losses as by those with more profound impairments. Fear of meeting new people is often expressed, and some deafened persons are reluctant to enter social situations with strangers unless accompanied by a hearing companion.

Irritability, fatigue, and nervousness are frequently reported by deafened persons. The strain of following conversations can lead to stress, and eyestrain contributes to fatigue for those who rely on speechreading. For this reason, many deafened people limit social interaction to short periods of time.

Some experiments with simulated deafness have been conducted where subjects wore earplugs producing the equivalent of a 20 to 30 decibels' hearing loss. Nervousness and fatigue were among the symptoms reported. Depression and anxiety were also common. In group situations, conversation may be difficult to follow as one speaker follows another in rapid succession, interruptions are common, or two people may speak at the same time. Background noise at meetings and large parties accentuates whatever problems already exist. Knowledge about these problems and responses comes from personal reports of those who have experienced adult onset of hearing loss. However, there are a few research studies that tend to confirm them. One of these noted that deafened persons were more likely to consult a doctor about nervous problems and worry than were members of a control group. Embarrassment and nervousness in social situations were among the problems listed by participants in another research study.

SOCIAL IDENTITY

Some deafened people report feelings of identity crisis as their hearing becomes more impaired. They have increasing difficulty communicating with others, yet they do not identify with those who have been deaf for many years and prefer sign language to spoken communication. Usually, they know few other people whose hearing loss was acquired late in life. Thus, they are caught between the world of deaf people and the world of hearing persons. They have a sense of being marginal to any group and unable to maintain previous friendships. A number of writers use the analogy of minority group identity, alienation, or self-estrangement. Many of these feelings of estrangement are related to responses of others toward hearing impairment. Deafened persons see hearing people as impatient with their inability to understand; as pitying them; as teasing, taking advantage of, and generally misunderstanding deaf people. Despite the widespread feelings of disparagement among deafened people, there has been little research about actual attitudes of hearing people toward deafness. A few existing studies support the notion of negative attitudes toward deaf people. These feelings vary by the degree of experience hearing people have with hearing impairment. Some deafened people report their own tendency to dominate conversations as one way of dealing with an inability to understand the contribution of others, or of bluffing and guessing what has been imperfectly comprehended. Some view hearing aids as a visible mark of their hearing impairment and try to avoid stigma by refusing to use them. Attitudes toward hearing loss by both deaf and hearing people interact to create a wide variety of response patterns.

EFFECTS OF LATE-ONSET DEAFNESS ON WORK LIFE

Some people deafened in midlife must change their occupations. Others shift from one emphasis to another within the same broad vocational category. Still others may be able to continue with the same job but have fewer opportunities for promotion or less satisfaction through interaction with colleagues. Various studies of deafened workers have reported differing findings. One inquiry in France found that half the deafened workers surveyed had lost their jobs as well as their hearing. A quarter of deafened workers in an English survey reported that either their jobs or their prospects for promotion had changed. Those participating in a Dutch survey emphasized the increased likelihood of needing to work alone rather than with other people.

An interview study conducted in England examined the effects of hearing loss on employment. The researchers reported that 35 percent of respondents between the ages of 25 and 55, with only a moderate hearing loss, felt that job promotions were no longer possible for them. Of comparable groups with prelingual deafness and with normal hearing, 63 percent and 16 percent, respectively, had similar assessments of probabilities for job promotion. Specific deterrents to success in the world of work are seen to be difficulty in using the telephone, in coping with the public, in actually performing the work task, and difficulty with colleagues, in addition to fewer job responsibilities, demotion, or failure to be promoted. Loss of satisfaction in interaction with others at the workplace is not the least of reported problems related to jobs.

As in other areas, the effects on the family life of the deafened individual depend greatly on the degree of hearing loss and the age of the person at the onset of deafness. A number of studies have reported that deafened people have particular trou-

ble interacting with children and teenagers. One report indicates that daughters are especially likely to show impatience with a deafened parent, and that husbands are more likely than wives to feel that their loss of hearing has a negative effect on family relationships. However, many deafened persons report that family members, especially spouses, are extremely helpful in managing contacts with the hearing world and in supporting efforts to maintain previous contacts and lifestyle.

COPING STRATEGIES

Despite the many problems and difficulties encountered by deafened persons, most find practical and creative ways of coping with their loss of hearing. These strategies can be categorized in different ways. For example, the use of hearing aids and other assistive devices are beneficial to many, enabling them to continue their usual lives. President Ronald Reagan's widely publicized acquisition of hearing aids during his term of office was responsible for an increase in those who decided to try a hearing aid.

Many deafened persons study speechreading in an effort to increase their social participation. Most large cities have speech and hearing centers that provide classes in speechreading at little or no cost. Classes can serve as unofficial support groups for newly deafened persons in addition to providing a new skill.

Some people with adult-onset loss of hearing learn systems of visual language to supplement speechreading and residual hearing. These systems include sign language, fingerspelling, and cued speech. Any of these are useful only if there are others in the home or workplace who use them. Sometimes a spouse or friend is willing to learn with the deafened person so that the commitment of time and study necessary for fluency are worthwhile. Some find fingerspelling to be a helpful supplement to speechreading. With the help of an initial letter, a difficult word can be more easily understood. Learning the 26 handshapes representing the American alphabet is much easier than learning an entire sign language vocabulary or the hand shapes and positions of cued speech. Writing as a supplementary system of communication is a strategy that is often overlooked. *See* SIGNS: Fingerspelling; MOUTH-HAND SYSTEMS: Cued Speech.

Many deafened people develop new hobbies or new habits of socializing in adjusting to their reduced ability to hear. Some substitute sports activities, reading, crafts, or birdwatching for previous activities such as lectures, theater, or concerts. Many avoid large parties in favor of smaller groups or even one-to-one visiting. Simple techniques such as facing away from a window to reduce glare can be helpful.

Some persons find organized group activities to

be of help, especially during the period of adjustment to a newly acquired hearing loss. One organization devoted specifically to the needs of deafened adults is Self Help for Hard of Hearing Persons (SHHH), founded by Howard W. Stone, Jr., in the early 1980s. Stone is himself deafened and is an example of the many persons who cope well with hearing loss. For many years he was a senior officer in the Central Intelligence Agency, despite a severe to profound loss of hearing. SHHH emphasizes self-help and assertiveness training, encouraging deafened persons to speak up in work and social situations and to lobby to attain legislative support for their needs. Local chapters have been formed in many states, as well as in some countries outside the United States. Publication of a bimonthly magazine is one of the activities of this organization.

Speech and hearing centers often provide social groups for deafened persons, and some senior citizen centers recognize the special needs of their deafened members by organizing activities for them. Gallaudet College sponsors a two-week summer informational and support session for deafened adults under the auspices of the Elderhostel program. The Alexander Graham Bell Society has a subgroup devoted to deaf or deafened adults and publishes a journal called the *Volta Review*. The National Association of the Deaf publishes the *Deaf American*. (Members of the National Association of the Deaf are more likely to belong to the prelingually deaf populations, but activities might also be of interest to deafened adults.) *See* ALEXANDER GRAHAM BELL ASSOCIATION FOR THE DEAF; DEAF AMERICAN; GALLAUDET COLLEGE; NATIONAL ASSOCIATION OF THE DEAF.

Although late-onset deafness can be a devastating experience for some, leading to withdrawal and social isolation, the positive strengths of many and the outstanding achievements of a few can serve as a source of help and inspiration to others.

Bibliography

Barbara, D. A. (ed.): *Psychological and Psychiatric Aspects of Speech and Hearing*, Charles C. Thomas, Springfield, Illinois, 1960.

Gallaudet College/National Information Center on Deafness/American Speech-Language-Hearing Association: Series on Hearing Loss in Adulthood, Gallaudet College, Washington, D.C., 1984.

Giolas, T. G.: *Hearing-Handicapped Adults*, Prentice-Hall, Englewood Cliffs, New Jersey, 1982.

Hartmann, H. (ed.): *Congress Report*, First International Congress of the Hard of Hearing, Deutscher Schwerhörigenbund, Hamburg, Germany, 1981.

Maurer, J. F., and R. R. Rupp: *Hearing and Aging: Tactics for Intervention*, Grune and Stratton, New York, 1979.

Orlans, H. (ed.): *Adjustment to Adult Hearing Loss*, College-Hill, San Diego, 1985.

Ries, P. W.: *Hearing Ability of Persons by Sociodemographic and Health Characteristics: United States*, National Center for Health Statistics, series 10, no. 140, 1982.

Thomas, A., M. Lamont, and M. Harris: "Problems Encountered at Work by People with Severe Acquired Hearing Loss," *British Journal of Audiology*, 16:39–43, 1982.

Weinstein, B. E., and I. M. Ventry: "Hearing Impairment and Social Isolation in the Elderly," *Journal of Speech and Hearing Research*, 25:593–599, 1982.

Kathryn P. Meadow-Orlans

Aged

The aged deaf population in the United States is only a small proportion of the general population of old people. There are more than 22 million people over the age of 65, of whom over 7 million have some form of hearing impairment. A census of the deaf population reports that there are approximately 119,000 prevocationally deaf people over the age of 65. This figure includes all people who lost their hearing before the age of 18. Thus, only about one hearing-impaired person in sixty over the age of 65 incurred a hearing loss before the age of 18.

Socially, elderly deaf people reflect the overall experience of the larger population of deaf persons. Although a number of persons who may be considered audiologically deaf have integrated themselves into the hearing world or live on the fringes of it, the social patterns described here are those of the majority of elderly deaf persons who communicate primarily through sign language and who consider themselves members of the deaf community.

The great majority of aged deaf people had hearing parents with whom they could not regularly communicate. Most older deaf people did not acquire language until they went to school at the age of five or six. Deaf persons whose parents were deaf are exceptions to this pattern. These persons compose 8 percent of the deaf population as a whole. Most older deaf persons who fall into this category learned sign language from their parents from infancy.

EDUCATION AND SOCIALIZATION

In the early twentieth century, the time when most of today's older deaf people were in school, both oral and manual methods were in use in the United States. The majority of aged deaf people were sent to state schools for deaf persons in childhood, where they lived during the school year. The method used to teach children varied from one state to the next. A smaller proportion of this population attended public and private day schools, where the oral method predominated.

Special education in childhood has had a lifelong effect on deaf persons who are now elderly, as it was instrumental in forming values and lifelong social patterns, regardless of the method used. While the process of socialization and education differed greatly in oral and manual circles, the same basic patterns developed in social relationships. In old age, friendships with other deaf people are based on early childhood association and mutual experiences in the acquisition of language. The shared mutual experiences resulting from the social and emotional context in which individuals first confronted their deafness are the basis of these enduring relationships.

Most elderly deaf persons stayed in school until they were 18 years old, whether or not they graduated. There is some discrepancy between school attendance and graduation figures because of the difficulty deaf people often experienced in mastering English, which in turn affected their ability to perform academically. The great majority of older persons in this age group who went on to college either had deaf parents or had an adventitious hearing loss.

RESIDENCE, EMPLOYMENT, AND RETIREMENT PATTERNS

Certain patterns in daily living situations developed as individuals left school and began to make their way in the world. During the early twentieth century the United States was changing from a rural to an urban society. Coincidentally, the occupations taught in special schools were skills most appropriate to the urban environment. Trades, such as those in the building and printing industries, have the greatest demand in the cities. The traditional difficulties experienced by deaf people in getting jobs then resulted in people moving to the cities where the demand was greatest.

Before retirement, most older deaf men were employed in skilled labor, particularly printing. Other occupations often included carpenter, shoe repairer, machinist, glazier, and clerk. The primary role of older deaf women has been homemaking, as it has been for most of that age group in the general population. Women often worked outside the home, however, especially those without children. They worked in a variety of capacities, especially in trades related to sewing. Both older men and women with college educations worked primarily as teachers and counselors with deaf children.

The deaf person working in industry away from the deaf school tended not to develop friendships with hearing coworkers because of the communication barrier. This factor detracted from job satisfaction and emphasized ingroup sociability. Lifelong involvement in an extensive social life that is not connected with work considerably eases the transition to retirement. Most deaf people thus experience retirement differently from the general population. While individuals may initially miss the sense of accomplishment gained from work, retirement enhances opportunities to socialize with friends. People often begin attending social events of older persons while they are still employed, thus further easing this transition.

In contrast, the experience of retirement for deaf professionals is closer to that of the general population. Since their work environment was often the focus of their social lives, deaf professionals often experienced feelings of loss related to their former productivity as well as the intense social contact they experienced in their work lives. Consequently, deaf professionals often take on retirement jobs or become heavily involved in volunteer and advocacy activities in the deaf community.

In old age, deaf people are dispersed throughout urban areas of the United States, often in the same geographic location in which they have lived since leaving school. Many own their own homes or have owned homes in the past, moving to apartments and housing for senior citizens in later life. A very small proportion reside in nursing homes and other types of sheltered housing, most preferring instead to maintain their independence until extreme physical frailty forces them to change their living arrangements. Housing developments for elderly deaf people exist in several areas of the United States. The pros and cons of living in such close proximity to numbers of other deaf people are frequently debated among this age group.

ETHNICITY AND RELIGION

In terms of religion and ethnicity, older deaf persons as a group parallel the general population who are the same age. There is considerable variation from one geographic locale to another that reflects the ethnic and religious makeup of a given area. Ethnicity and religion are important factors in defining social affiliation in the deaf community, just as they are for the general population, since both factors are used by the group to define its social boundaries.

Little information is available on the ethnic breakdown of this age group. It appears, however, that the proportion of ethnic minority group members who are deaf in this age group is below the proportion one would expect for their numbers in the general population. If so, several factors may account for this discrepancy: (1) high infant mortality rates among ethnic minorities in the early twentieth century; (2) higher mortality rates in later life among ethnic minorities; and (3) exclusion from the majority in deaf communities with consequent forming of separate social groups or increased association with the family. If older deaf persons from ethnic minorities are not excluded from the social group, they often remain marginal to it. In areas where their numbers are sufficiently large, they have formed their own groups.

Religious affiliation is an important consideration for many people, whether or not they are active churchgoers, and plays a part in how they perceive other people. Religious preference is often related to the formation and maintenance of cliques in adulthood. For example, people think of themselves as Catholics or as Lutherans. Their religious identity may affect whom they choose to become their friends and who remain acquaintances. Most of the time, however, there is friendship across religious lines. The small size of the community and the frequency of marriage between persons of different religions help to reduce separatist tendencies. Moreover, religious lines tend to blur as people attend churches other than their own in order to participate in the social life of a church.

In old age, as mobility decreases, church attendance also decreases. The church or temple that offers services in sign language may be at a great distance from a person's home and access becomes a problem. Consequently, one focus of social life often becomes less accessible in old age.

FAMILY LIFE

In old age, the marital couple is the basic family unit in the United States, with approximately one-half of the persons over 65 being married. This pattern is echoed in the deaf community, where the proportion of married couples over the age of 65 may even be slightly higher than that of the general population.

The majority of older deaf persons are married to others who are also deaf. Persons who are now older tended to marry other deaf persons who shared their experiences, especially similar educational backgrounds, and their expectations. Less conflict was anticipated in marriage to another deaf person. An expectation of many older people when they were young was that they would go through life with the person they chose for a mate. In fact, many marriages between deaf persons in this age range are relationships that began in childhood. Schoolmates often married each other when they reached adulthood. Most of these marriages have been enduring, on par with those of older persons in the general population. Considerable homogeneity exists between marriage partners, undoubtedly an important factor in marital success. When couples come from diverse backgrounds, especially when their communication system differs significantly, however, considerable stress is created. Even if they have remained married, these differences are often unresolved and continue into old age.

Limited ties with extended kin tended to reinforce reliance on the marital partner. For persons who had hearing parents, creating a family where deafness was the norm rather than the exception was a major source of personal fulfillment. The process of establishing a family is viewed retrospectively as a major life achievement that fostered greater self-acceptance. These marriages are characterized by a high degree of intimacy and consensus in old age, and reflect a sense of well-being that enhances marital partners' ability to cope with the problems of later life.

Deaf couples who are now older tended to have small families, with an average of two children. In old age, ties with adult children usually remain strong. Involvement of the adult child in the deaf community strengthens these ties. If difficulties exist in communication with the adult child's spouse and with grandchildren, extended family relations may be somewhat affected. Considerable variation exists in social relationships with extended kin. The primary exception to a continuing pattern of social interaction between parents and adult children exists when parents were divorced at a much earlier time. Divorce posed a serious economic and emotional strain on families in an era when divorce was infrequent, and often had the effect of loosening family ties.

Despite the maintenance of close ties with children, older deaf people seldom rely to any great extent on their children for assistance with daily living, except when they become frail in advanced old age. As long as they and their friends remain active, they are much more likely to rely on friends with whom they have developed a lifelong system of mutual support.

One out of 10 persons in the general population never marry, and deaf persons reflect this tendency in the same proportions. Many unmarried deaf persons apparently find adequate companionship when they work in a state school for deaf children or another organization that is central to life in the deaf community. This pattern has been observed among a segment of the older deaf population.

Relationships with siblings take on an added importance in old age for the general population, and there are indications that this is also true for elderly deaf persons. People from this age group came from large families, often with eight or more children. In childhood, hearing siblings of deaf persons were often the only communication link between them and their parents. Consequently this tie often remains strong in old age, even when communication is slow or difficult. If siblings are settled in the same geographic area, patterns of mutual support sometimes develop between them when spouses and close friends die or become infirm. Bonds with deaf siblings are usually strong throughout life and remain so in old age.

SOCIAL PATTERNS

In old age, deaf persons continue a social pattern begun in their youth. The deaf community fosters close interdependence among its members, young and old alike. Aged deaf people share a collective identity with all other deaf people. They, like younger people, are concerned with the social survival of the community, and are tied to it by the language as well as by their personal experiences as deaf persons.

Aged deaf people are settled in urban and suburban areas, rounding out a lifelong pattern of urban living. They developed patterns to cope with the dispersed social environment long before the advent of telephone devices for the deaf (TDDs). In young adulthood, life in the city without a telephone presented a number of problems, such as how to avoid isolation, maximize safety, and maintain contact with friends. As automobiles became an important part of American life, they also became a part of life in the deaf community, a part that continues to be important in old age.

Although it appears that deaf people continue to drive longer than their contemporaries in the general population, both driving and evening activities are curtailed as individuals grow old. Despite an increasing reliance on TDDs for communication, older deaf people continue their lifelong pattern of physical activity and mobility within a limited geographic area to maintain social ties. This pattern is very effective in combating social isolation, a major problem that elderly people in the general population experience.

Voluntary associations and the national network of deaf people have played important roles in the deaf community throughout people's lives. To facilitate social interaction, deaf people set up special meeting places and established deaf clubs in large cities. Having central meeting places is a social institution that has endured through the years and is translated into new settings in old age.

Although older people continue to identify with the deaf community, as they age their social patterns often shift away from participation in evening activities at a deaf club to participation in daytime activities with other older deaf persons. In many urban areas, deaf socials, especially for older people, are held on a regular basis, patterned after social activities in deaf clubs.

In recent years, older deaf people have moved their group activities to various senior citizen centers, recreation centers, and the like in different areas of the United States. Many of these groups meet at a time and place separate from other older people. Increasingly, however, deaf people have developed a tendency to establish socials in senior centers serving the general population of older persons. In these environments, deaf persons can continue to meet in the social pattern established long ago, and also have access to the same services and facilities as the general population. Where such programs exist, elderly deaf persons have demonstrated increased self-confidence in their ability to deal with life problems because of their increased access to services and information found among the general population of older persons.

While the peer group continues to be important during adult life, perhaps more so than in the rest of American society, it is in old age that there is a resurgence of the extremely strong support that membership in this group affords. Involvement in peer group relationships in old age provides an arena in which reciprocity and interdependence can be maintained. Over time, these social exchanges have become increasingly intimate. Because the deaf individual is limited to the deaf community for meaningful communication, intense relationships have developed and are continued through life. These relationships allow the person freedom of self-expression and provide continuity in old age.

FRIENDSHIP

Most older deaf people tend to think of others in their social group as friends. The small size of the group contributes to this feeling of groupwide friendship. Friendship patterns among elderly deaf people are usually based on the couple, reflecting a general pattern in American society. Friends of both sexes are usually recruited from the peer group of childhood or early adulthood. Although the most intimate friendships are invariably between persons of the same gender, many close friendships exist between men and women as well. Single individuals tend to have their closest friends among others of the same gender.

Friendships can be divided in social terms into primary and secondary relations. While the modal number of close friends (or primary relations) in the United States is two, the average number of close friends for elderly deaf people is five or six, an important factor in the life adjustment of deaf people, and particularly significant in old age. Research on aging suggests that such relationships are an important buffer in old age because they reduce social isolation and help people to cope with the problems of later life. Elderly deaf persons are thus particularly well insulated from social isolation as a result of these relationships.

Neighbors (or secondary relations) are especially important in old age in the general population when individuals become more restricted physically, and this is true with elderly deaf persons as well. Many elderly deaf people have one or more deaf neighbors, as well as family members living nearby. Neighborliness often brings people together who would otherwise have little in common, such as persons raised with different communication modes. Neighbors are yet another aspect of the complex social network deaf persons rely on in old age.

In contrast with the general population, secondary relationships (such as neighbors) are significant throughout deaf people's lives and attain particular significance in old age. As the community decreases in size, through death and immobility, those remaining must rely increasingly on secondary relationships to fulfill their social and emotional needs. These relationships have demonstrated their strength over time, and are consequently able to take over many of the functions of primary relationships when needed.

This web of relationships forms complex social networks so that elderly deaf persons may be members of several cliques based on different factors, such as old school friends, ethnicity, degree of education, and geographic proximity. These groups often meet quite frequently and are an extension of the social life of the larger deaf group.

Mutual aid is an important component of social interactions within the group. Although deaf persons provide each other with tangible forms of aid, such as transporting persons without cars, the most significant form of aid deaf people receive in old age is the social and emotional support provided by the group. Group support is a viable, sustaining force in old age that helps individuals to deal with all kinds of problems. Moreover, it brings together people who may have little in common. The social group provides ongoing support for its members on a regular basis. The amount of support that is often available during a health crisis or a period of mourning when a spouse or friend dies is unique, however, and is rarely found in the general population. Long-term group support is particularly significant in old age, since many of the problems elderly people experience become chronic and are often not resolved.

In order to maintain the cohesion that enables the group to provide such extensive social support, social pressure to conform is great. The strong, positive value attached to sociability and group participation that is developed much earlier in the deaf community is kept alive in old age. People are continually encouraged by their peers to participate in social activities, for example, through nagging and gossip. The intensity of this process may even be greater in old age than at younger ages, since the number of participants is gradually dwindling through infirmity and death. Failure to participate without an obvious reason results in a growing coolness on the part of other participants in the group. It is viewed as a lack of commitment to the group as well as lack of identification with deafness.

ILLNESS, DISABILITY AND DEATH
Although no statistics are available on the health status of elderly members of the deaf community, it appears that their lifelong active lifestyle may be a real advantage in both warding off health problems in old age and coping with them when they

do occur. Despite a lack of sophistication about preventive health care, elderly deaf people are concerned about maintaining their health because they observe the relationship between poor health and social isolation among peers who have become frail and homebound or institutionalized. When an elderly deaf person living in the urban environment is no longer able to get around, the dispersed nature of the deaf community precludes extensive social contact. Consequently, the elderly person gradually becomes isolated from the group. Persons in good health are well aware of this phenomenon and are thus highly motivated to stay healthy. Unlike the general population, for whom social isolation is an insidious phenomenon that often occurs for the first time in old age, deaf persons are keenly aware of it after fighting it their entire life.

Having experienced a disability in early life and having consequently dealt with adversity over a lifetime may enable deaf people to cope more effectively with illness. When older deaf persons experience infirmity, they appear to deal with it in a practical, often stoical manner. Catastrophic, life-threatening illnesses and conditions that threaten loss of vision are the most difficult for people to contend with, but even so, coping styles are exhibited that individuals themselves often attribute to the ways in which they have learned to deal with deafness.

Surveys of attitudes about death in the general population of the United States show that people fear the death of others more than they fear their own. This is true of deaf persons in old age as well. Since social isolation is a lifelong enemy that deaf persons have warded off through a complex social network, the decimation of the group's numbers through death is a source of continual concern. While deaf persons fear death, just as it is feared among the general population, there is great concern with the social process that occurs after death and how being deaf may in some way adversely affect what occurs. For example, many older people worry that they will die and hearing relatives will not inform their deaf friends of their funeral. The potential conflict for many deaf people between their families and their friends is thus ever present and remains a lifelong concern.

One particularly valuable role that the group plays in relation to dying is that the high level of intimacy between members of the group allows people to mourn loss and anticipate the future in the company of friends. The close social ties that enable elderly deaf people to discuss such difficult subjects among themselves contrasts with other communities of older people in the United States, such as retirement communities, where the subject of death is often avoided.

Some deaf persons often live to advanced old age

before infirmity sets in. They may in fact be examples of the cross-over phenomenon described for ethnic minority group members in the United States, in which persons have been at higher risk than the general population because of their ethnic minority status, yet have the potential for a longer life than others in the general population once they reach a certain age.

SUMMARY

In summary, elderly deaf people share much in common with the general population of older people. The ways in which they are different are a direct outcome of their participation in a tightly knit community that places great emphasis on social relationships as a means of combating isolation. Deaf people who participate in the deaf community over the course of their lives are therefore at an advantage in old age, as they are insulated from many of the adverse aspects of aging that other Americans experience.

Bibliography

Babchuk, Nicholas: "Primary Friends and Kin: A Study of the Associations of Middle-Class Couples," *Social Forces*, 43:483–493, 1965.

Becker, Gay: *Growing Old in Silence*, University of California Press, Berkeley, 1980.

Becker, Gay, and Gay Nadler: "The Aged Deaf: Integration of a Disabled Group into an Agency Serving Elderly People," *Gerontologist*, 20:214–222, 1980.

Jacobs, Leo: *A Deaf Adult Speaks Out*, Gallaudet College Press, Washington, D.C., 1974.

Riley, Matilda W., et al: *Aging and Society*, vol. 1: *An Inventory of Research Findings*, Russell Sage, New York, 1968.

Schein, Jerome: *The Deaf Community*, Gallaudet College Press, Washington, D.C., 1968.

————, and Marcus T. Delk, Jr.: *The Deaf Population of the United States*, National Association of the Deaf, Silver Spring, Maryland, 1974.

Streib, Gordon F.: "Old Age and the Family: Facts and Forecasts," in Ethel Shanas (ed.), *Aging in Contemporary Society*, pp. 25–39, Sage Publications, Beverly Hills, 1970.

Gay Becker

Oralists

Oralist is a somewhat archaic term used to define individuals (both deaf and hearing) who believe in and promote the use of speech as the preferred communication mode for persons with hearing dysfunction. This philosophy is sometimes referred to as oralism. Advocates of oral communication believe that deaf members of society should be encouraged to use speech, lipreading, and auditory training to find their place among the ranks of the larger world in which they live, because this world is dominated by people who use spoken language.

ORAL EDUCATION

The first recorded accounts of oral education of deaf children are those of Pedro Ponce de Leon (1510–1584), a Benedictine monk. Ponce de Leon worked with children of Spanish nobility at a monastery. His students were reported as being well educated with a good command of languge and speech and were masters at speechreading. A countryman, Manuel Ramirez de Carrion (1579–1652), also used the same methods with apparently the same degree of success. Juan Pablo Bonet (1579–1633) was a third Spaniard who described his teaching of speech to deaf children in his book, which was the first to be published on teaching deaf children. Thus, Spain, at the pinnacle of her power, gave the world the beginning of a systematic means for teaching speech to deaf persons. *See* CARRION, MANUEL RAMIREZ DE; PABLO BONET, JUAN; PONCE DE LEON, PEDRO.

Other teachers followed in France, Germany, and England. The strongest tradition for oral education developed in Germany, where Johannes Conrad Amman (1669–1724) advocated speech exercises which he claimed required only two months to master. Perhaps the best known of the German oralists was Samuel Heinicke (1727–1790). He opened the first German school for deaf pupils in Leipzig in 1778 after having achieved superb results in the oral education of deaf children at Hamburg. Heinicke stated, "Spoken language is the hinge upon which everything turns." He was even against the teaching of the alphabet before the teaching of speech. In England, the Braidwood family, beginning with Thomas Braidwood (1715–1806), made their techniques for oral education of deaf children a family secret as a means to their livelihood. Thomas Hopkins Gallaudet (1787–1851) applied to the Braidwoods to learn their methods during his year spent in Europe in 1815. His lack of success at gaining entry to the Braidwood's school is widely believed to be the reason he then went to France and learned the French sign language (manual) method which he brought back to the United States. *See* BRAIDWOOD, THOMAS; GALLAUDET, THOMAS HOPKINS; HEINICKE, SAMUEL.

ORALIST PHILOSOPHY

In a sense, the traditional debate over communication methods between oralists and manualists and, lately, between oralists and total communicationists centers on differing philosophies about where people with significant hearing impairment should fit in society. In the United States, this point was well understood by Alexander Graham Bell and Edward Miner Gallaudet, two giants in the field who represented the oralist and manualist camps, respectively. Bell announced his opposition to special communities, churches, and social organizations for deaf individuals. He also spoke out at length about the dangers of intermarriage between deaf individuals, predicting "a deaf variety of the human race." Gallaudet, in turn, characterized Bell's ideas as heresy and advocated the need for special accommodation in communication and in many other areas. *See* BELL, ALEXANDER GRAHAM; GALLAUDET, EDWARD MINER; HISTORY: Sign Language Controversy.

Proponents of oral communication today generally feel that Bell was ahead of his time, that the general public and elected government officials are only now beginning to appreciate the value of integrating "different" members of society into the mainstream. The passage of the Education for All Handicapped Children Act, for example, seems to herald a new era of public attitudes regarding disabled persons. Oralists generally hope that attitudes promoting asylums and institutions as preferred places for "different" members of society will be rejected. *See* EDUCATION OF THE HANDICAPPED ACT.

In line with these philosophies, oralists promote the use of speech, speechreading (lipreading), and residual hearing (via hearing aids) to the maximum extent possible as a right for all deaf children. In general, proponents of oral communication do not favor the use of sign language in the teaching process. Most objections to the use of signs center on the undesirability of trying simultaneously to teach two languages, an English sign language and American Sign Language or Pidgin Sign English, to a young child who has a severe language handicap (deafness). The fact that most oralists do not favor sign language as the language of instruction for deaf children does not necessarily mean that all advocates of oral communication reject sign language as a communication mode. Many oralists encourage young people who have acquired a spoken language base and adequate speech and speechreading skills to learn sign language as a social facilitator. Not all oralists are as accepting of sign language as this, however.

TEACHING METHODS

Advocates of oral communication are not a completely homogeneous group. They include orally communicating deaf people, parents of deaf children who want their children to talk, and professionals (teachers, audiologists, and physicians). The three components of the oral camp tend to divide in yet another three ways according to their advocacy of auditory, multisensory, or cued-speech teaching methods.

Auditory oralists are those who focus on the rehabilitation and training of the residual auditory function of hearing-impaired individuals. Other terms tused to describe this approach are auditory-

verbal, auditory-oral, aural-oral, accupedic, unisensory-auditory, and acoustic. Such training utilizes sophisticated amplification equipment (hearing aids and auditory trainers) and specialized instruction that deemphasizes the use of speechreading. The theoretical basis for this approach is that many children with very severe hearing loss can be taught to make use of the minimal auditory cues available via powerful hearing aids.

Another example of the auditory approach is the Verbo-Tonal system. In addition to using sophisticated amplification and intensive training of residual hearing, this system utilizes an involved system of gross body movements to teach and reinforce sound awareness by associating large-muscle-group movements with the finer muscle movements of speech. *See* AUDITORY TRAINING.

In contrast, persons who advocate a multisensory or traditional approach are less concerned about excluding the use of speechreading. In fact, the child is encouraged to use speechreading, natural gestures, facial expressions, body language, as well as tactile means or stimulation through touch to transmit and receive spoken communication. Some practitioners of this oral method will even use a limited amount of fingerspelling to convey words that are difficult to hear or to speechread. Most multisensory-approach practitioners are more concerned with language in a natural context than with teaching methods per se. That is, a rich exposure to real-world events and a highly stimulating environment are encouraged to give the deaf child experience with the concepts that will eventually be expected in communication. *See* SIGNS: Fingerspelling.

The third general category of the oralist camp is cued speech. Cued speech is an oral communication method that supplements the information available via residual hearing with amplification, body language, and speechreading with a system of hand cues made in the vicinity of the speaker's mouth. Cued speech symbols are designed to present information that is not easily visible on the lips. It must, therefore, be used with lipreading because it does not present all of the sounds of speech. This quality separates cued speech from fingerspelling, which is not an oral method because it can exist independently of speech. Cued speech, in contrast, must be used with speech. It does, however, replace residual hearing, making the method useful for children with little or no residual auditory function. *See* MOUTH-HAND SYSTEMS: Cued Speech.

ORGANIZATIONS

In any discussion of oral communication for deaf people, the question of effectiveness is relevant. Usually the question is posed by comparing the relatively small membership (approximately 350) of the Oral Deaf Adults Section (ODAS) of the Alexander Graham Bell Association with the larger membership (approximately 10,000) of the National Association of the Deaf (NAD). The two organizations, however, are fundamentally different. ODAS has little social or grouping purpose; it was formed to act as a resource network for teachers and parents of deaf children. There are no local chapters and members see each other every two years at best. NAD, by contrast, is a federation of local chapters. Many of the chapters have an important community and social function; meetings and social gatherings occur on a regular basis. Some ODAS members also belong to NAD because they recognize the differing functions of two organizations.

Another relevant point is that the basic goal of oralism is assimilation. Successful oral deaf individuals will be members of general service and social organizations such as the Rotary, Sertoma, or Lions Club. Such individuals will probably not join ODAS or NAD, however. Estimates of the current number of profoundly deaf individuals in the United States range from 600,000 to 3 million. Even the lower of these figures indicates that many deaf individuals join no organization of any kind for deaf people.

To conclude, the successful oral deaf person is one who has been assimilated into society at large. This will remain the motivation for advocacy of spoken language, speechreading, and use of technological devices to assist hearing (hearing aids, cochlear implants, and so on) as the birthright of all deaf children. To be sure, not all deaf children are capable of the enormous task of learning to speak a language they cannot hear clearly, nor are all interested in doing so.

Bibliography

Bruce, R. B.: *Alexander Graham Bell and the Conquest of Solitude*, Little, Brown, Boston, 1973.

Mulholland, A. M. (ed.): *Oral Education Today and Tomorrow*, A. G. Bell, Washington, D.C., 1981.

Ogden, P. W., and S. Lipsett: *The Silent Garden*, St. Martin's Press, New York, 1982.

Stoker, R. G., and J. H. Spear (eds.): *Perspectives on Living in the Mainstream*, A. G. Bell, Washington, D.C., 1984.

Richard G. Stoker

Attitudes

Since the 1960s, disabled persons in the United States have witnessed significant improvements in their status as the result of changes in laws concerning public education, equal access, and affirmative job action. However, they continue to experience attitudes and behaviors based on stereotypes. Stereotypes are exaggerated images associated with the individual's specific disabling condition; for example, many people speak quite loudly to blind people (or do not speak to them at all) in the mistaken assumption that all the blind person's senses are affected. Because of the relationship between what people think about a situation and their subsequent behavior in that situation, it is important to examine the origin and consequences of attitudes.

SIGNIFICANCE

Social psychologists define an attitude as a learned evaluative predisposition toward a person, situation, or social circumstance that can influence an individual's response either favorably or unfavorably. Attitudes have three basic components; cognitive—how the object or situation is perceived; affective—the feelings or emotions about the object or situation; and behavioral—the tendency to act a particular way in reference to the object or situation. To translate this into the specific concern of attitudes of hearing people toward deaf people, it should first be recognized that these three components are at work. Hearing individuals have various perceptions of what deafness is like (the cognitive element); they have emotions or feelings about what the deaf experience is like (ranging from fear to pity); and finally, because of these perceptions and feelings, they are inclined to act in a positive or negative way toward a deaf person.

The importance of attitudes is related to this impact on behavior. For disabled individuals, including deaf people, it is not only the association of attitudes and behavior that is important but the fact that attitudes, as reflections of beliefs or perceptions, influence the definition of the situation held by those in the majority. Even if the hearing population does not act on its attitudes toward deaf persons, its attitudes influence what is expected from deaf individuals, and in that way these attitudes have defined the situation. For example, a consistent characteristic of attitudes of hearing people toward deafness is that communication with a deaf person is extremely difficult if they have no speech or interpreter. The hearing person will then expect not to be able to understand the nonverbal deaf person even if an interaction occurs. If deaf people have no chance to demonstrate some nonverbal communication, even paper and pencil communication, the damage is done, and the "definition of the situation" has had its negative impact without actual negative overt behavior.

This definitional aspect of attitudes is particularly important for disabled individuals because it influences their lives at many different levels: in their relationship with family and peers; in their experiences in formal social institutions such as education, employment, and government organizations; and in their everyday life experiences that take them into contact with the general public.

Family and close friends generally have the most positive attitudes toward a disabled person, and they have an important effect on the development of the disabled person's self-concept. Hearing parents of deaf children or walking parents of crippled children all have attitudinal expectations about their offspring and the disabling condition that influence the socialization process that a disabled child experiences growing up in the home. Peers, whether they are from a school, church, or work context, also come into daily contact with the disabled individuals in class or on the job. Attitudes in these circumstances can often be less sympathetic or supportive than the individual may need. Less serious anomalies than deafness or blindness, such as size or stature, have been focuses of ridicule or disparagement in peer situations. Attitudes, therefore, of people with whom disabled individuals have close contact during their formative years can seriously impede or damage the disabled person's self-concept and interaction skills, thereby further complicating the initial disability.

At another level, attitudes of people in positions of authority or responsibility can also influence the lives of disabled individuals. The gatekeepers, as these professionals are sometimes known, can seriously curtail the options available to disabled individuals if they conduct their business based on inappropriate stereotyped images. Physicians who do not recommend surgery or rehabilitation procedures; social workers who do not attempt to find solutions to financial, employment, or family problems; teacher who have a preconceived notion of how much a disabled child can learn or what vocational pursuits are appropriate for such an individual; bankers who have never known successful disabled people—all can be influenced by inappropriate attitudes in their services to a disabled client. In this instance a disabled person's potential is unwittingly circumscribed or limited by the narrowness of the professional's view.

Finally, the attitude of the general public influences the amount of self-consciousness experienced and the degree of difficulty that a disabled person has in conducting ordinary, routine, daily life activities such as grocery shopping, attending a movie, or riding a bus. The public attitude also contributes to how integrated into the community disabled people become in housing, recreation, social interaction, and participation. In addition, the strength of the laws adopted to protect disabled individuals, and the fervor with which they are enforced, is closely related to the responses of the public to their violation. Once again those responses are tied to attitudes.

DEAFNESS

According to J. Nash, the boundaries between deaf and hearing people are maintained by attitudes toward English. To deaf persons, English constitutes the hearing world and their experiences with it. Even if deaf individuals learn to use English, they are nonnative speakers, so that their use of it is as incomplete as are their conceptions of the hearing world. These perceptions influence their attitudes, which may or may not be used as a basis for action by deaf people themselves.

In the same way, the hearing person's conceptions of deaf people are also based on inaccurate perceptions. English is taken for granted as a basic common ground, and it occurs to very few, except for those who have prolonged interaction with deaf individuals, that the assumptions about the uniformity of the communicating medium is the basis for problems, not the ability of the deaf communicator. For hearing people, the focus is on communication and competence: if communication is lacking or garbled, the fault lies not with the hearing recipient of the communication but rather with the incompetence of the deaf communicator. This inaccurate definition of the situation is enough to cause difficulty without any overlay from affective or evaluative reactions to the exchange or further discriminatory or prejudicial behavior.

A very old conception of hearing people about deaf people was the association of deaf with dumb. Because language and speech were so closely associated with thinking and intelligence, the lack of speech, especially for those born deaf, was seen as an indication of their lack of intelligence. While this has been shown to be totally untrue, the tendency to question competence is still an important aspect of hearing people's attitudes toward deaf people. This can be seen in attitudes toward allowing deaf persons to drive or promotion policies toward deaf employees in many organizations.

Much of the research on attitudes toward disabled people does not separate and examine specific conditions but instead uses many types of conditions combined. In many cases the research may combine such divergent conditions as paraplegia, deafness, blindness, mental retardation, and ulcers. In other instances the concern is just with visible physical disabilities. Most of the literature is based on survey questionnaires which assume that answers accurately reflect a respondent's attitudes (cognitive or affective dimension) on the topic of disability. Other studies actually observe behavior toward disabled individuals, assuming that the behavior is a direct reflection of the attitudes the respondent holds.

B. Altman reviewed the methodologies of these studies, pointing out the problem areas and suggesting that the information can be distorted because of those problems. Keeping that in mind, the results of the studies are rather limited. They focus primarily on four aspects of attitudes toward disabled persons: (1) the affective component, which is generally unfavorable; (2) conceptions about disabled individuals, which are usually not entirely accurate; (3) social distance responses, which are inconclusive or somewhat negative; and (4) a ranking of types of handicapping conditions. John Tringo examined this ranking phenomenon with a large sample group ranging from high school to graduate students. The students were asked social distance questions about each of 21 different stigmatizing conditions from alcoholism to old age. Tringo used the scores to rank the group in a disability hierarchy. An individual with an ulcer ranked highest or was most preferred; mental illness received the lowest ranking or the greatest indication of social distance. Deafness ranked eighth, below blindness (seventh) but above stroke, cancer, and old age (ninth, tenth, and eleventh, respectively). The implication from these types of studies is that attitudes toward disabled individuals are not uniform but based on the characteristics of the specific condition. If that is the case, deafness holds the middle ground.

SOURCES OF ATTITUDES

Prejudice is rooted in the social customs and norms which are passed on to children in the rearing process. Great stress is placed on normalcy, health, and conformity in this process and thus gives the child a general conception of what is acceptable and "right." These stereotypes are important for the learning process because it is not possible to teach about every circumstance. A useful generalization is about the best that can be accomplished. For example, even though an adult is aware that police are human, with frailties like everyone else, children are taught to trust the police and seek their help in an emergency. In general this is a useful stereotype. Unfortunately, they are also taught to fear or be careful of those who are "different."

Those who have personal contact with disabled people (for this discussion, specifically deaf people) have the advantage of knowing more about that individual than just a general stereotyped image. Strengths as well as weaknesses are evident, and the person can be known as a whole individual rather than in terms of a specific limitation. Deaf family members, neighbors, or friends can influence the attitudes of those with whom they come into contact, broadening considerably the perception of what is involved with deafness and favorably coloring the affective component of attitudes as well. Research in numerous areas has shown that prolonged contact can favorably modify negative attitudes toward disabled people.

However, most of the population gets their information about deafness or other disabling conditions from secondary sources such as books, movies, or plays. Evil characters are portrayed as flawed (for example, hunchback, missing limbs or eyes, or ugly) while the heroes and heroines are exceptionally strong, intelligent, and beautiful. Unfortunately, children's books are filled with these kinds of misrepresentations that contribute to developing attitudes about deformities and other limitations.

Mass media such as newspapers and television have a particularly strong impact on the general understanding of many phenomena that people do not come into contact with regularly. It is an easily accessible, easily understandable source of information for many millions. When the information is accurate and objective, all is well and good, but too often the attitudes of those responsible for the presentations are reflected. In other instances, a lack of concern or awareness leaves big gaps in the information presented.

Studies of the media as sources of information about disabled people show that the material presented is frequently inconsistent and sometimes inaccurate. An unpublished examination of a large metropolitan newspaper for the period 1960–1980 showed a gradual increase in articles about disabled individuals over that time but very few varieties of disabling conditions and very limited amounts of accurate information about the conditions. The most elaborate articles that were either prominently displayed in the papers or included a picture were of the "individual overcomes great odds" type in which the disabled individual was portrayed as a "super" person and not an ordinary individual. Generally, articles focused on individuals and their successes or problems. Discussions of disabling conditions and useful information about them were presented much less frequently. When such was presented, the stimulus was a new discovery, cure, or procedure related to a specific condition.

In other studies, specifically of the media presentation of deafness, L. J. Gilbert examined both television and newspapers in Los Angeles, California, and Washington, D.C., for the periods of 1972–1975 and 1976–1979. She found that the media personnel in Washington were somewhat better informed about deafness than those in Los Angeles, and that there is more coverage on deafness and deaf people in the Washington paper as well. One reason for this may be that Gallaudet College is located in Washington, which gives deaf people greater visibility. Gilbert also found in both cities a sharp reduction in the use of the terms deaf-mutes or deaf-and-dumb over the period of study. In spite of these favorable aspects of coverage, the two terms still appear in other newspapers around the country. As with previous studies, Gilbert's findings also show that successful individuals are emphasized rather than the more realistic presentation of the problems of deafness and the specific difficulties, such as those with employment, experienced by deaf people.

Television has also increased its inclusion of disabled people as characters in fictional programming and as subjects of special programming. However, compared with newspapers, television's inclusion of information about deaf people has been minimal, and the expansion of signed television for deaf viewers has been very slow. *See* TELEVISION AND MOTION PICTURES.

IMPACT OF ATTITUDES
Attitudes of hearing people toward deaf people affect deaf people at two different levels. At the interpersonal level, attitudes and their associated behavior can influence deaf individuals' self-concept and self-esteem, their integration into a peer group, promotion on the job, or even access to employment. At the societal level, attitudes can become the accepted way of doing things, meaning that the system or structure is not questioned, it is therefore not changed, and the treatment of deaf people remains the same.

During the whole growing-up process, children born deaf are exposed to others whose behavior toward the child influences the child's self-concept. It has been found that a good self-concept, that is, liking oneself, having confidence, and so on, is very important to the success of the individual in the adult world. These feelings of self-worth are very important to any individual—but especially to one who is disabled. Choice of language, nonverbal communication, and facial expressions all can communicate a teacher's or parent's attitude toward a child, even if the actual verbal message appears perfectly harmless. For example, it has been found that deaf children of hearing parents have lower self-esteem than deaf children of deaf parents. This may be due to the deaf children's sensitivity to their hearing parents' conflicting attitudes or the children's awareness that the attitudes underlying the parents' behavior were different for them than for the hearing siblings.

Even for those who develop hearing problems in later life, the impact of the reaction of those close to them is very important to maintaining a good self-concept. Negative attitudes expressed by impatient peers or family can be very detrimental in the adaptation of such an individual to a hearing loss. An example is the refusal of a family to learn sign language and the insistance on verbal communication for the "benefit" of the deaf person. The attitude being conveyed here is that sign language is not good enough or that the individual is not important enough for adaptation to be made.

Attitudes are particularly important in employment situations. Although there are wide variations in the conceptualization of attitudes and their relationship to behavior in the area of employment of disabled individuals, employers in general are less than positive about hiring disabled applicants. There also appears to be a discrepancy between what employers say they will do, that is, hire disabled people, and what they actually do.

Examination of the attitudes and behaviors of employers indicates that they have realistic concerns about higher insurance costs and expenses of accommodating to special needs such as wheelchair ramps, braille computers, or TDDs. These can be dealt with by correcting misconceptions and sharing information. However, employers' attitudes also influence their reactions to the type of working condition and the severity of the working limitation. Stereotyped images of the capacities of different kinds of disabilities seem to be so strong that the individual's unique capacities and suitability do not get the attention deserved. The generalized stereotype so influences the definition of the situation that the appropriate questions do not even get asked. Not all employers are equally oblivious to the strengths of disabled workers. Their demographic characteristics (including education), prior experience, or even psychological traits can lead them to more positive attitudes toward hiring and promotion practices. There are instances, however, where even these individual attitudes are controlled by company policy or organizational attitudes.

The second level of attitudes experienced by disabled persons is not associated with individuals per se but with the way attitudes have been institutionalized or converted into "the way things are done." Examples of this level include hiring policies in organizations, educational policies of school boards, and loan policies at banks, all of which are based on and directed toward the nondisabled majority.

Special needs of the disabled population usually do not figure into these policy decisions, and so by default the attitudes that influenced the policymakers' decision process are transferred to the organizational structure or system. The definition of the situation is thereby translated into written rules and regulations, hiring and promotion procedures, and requirements that are difficult to change.

There are many examples of this process at work. The effort to make buildings accessible, for instance, is a response to years of neglect by decision makers who did not consider that people with mobility limitations would need access to public buildings like anyone else. Deaf professionals are asked to become members of professional organizations that do not even consider the need these members would have for interpreters so they could understand the proceedings at professional meetings. Airlines have specific safety rules that limit disabled people in the use of their necessary devices. Cultural programs fail to recognize the appropriateness of providing signing for deaf people or visual descriptions for blind people. Universities often do not adapt their registration, advising, or testing processes so that disabled students can participate. Many organizations base their acceptance of individuals on physical requirements that have become obsolete because of technological advances. These examples are the result of decision-making processes that at one point or another overlooked their impact on disabled members of society. These are not all direct results of negative attitudes toward any particular groups but rather reflect a lack of information or awareness. However, the attempts to change these situations do directly confront the issue of attitudes, and the varying degrees of successful change effected can be interpreted as indicators of the variety and strength of attitudes toward disabled persons extant in society today.

CHANGING ATTITUDES

The progress that disabled individuals have experienced since the early 1960s is an indication that attitudes can change. Public Law 94-142, the Education for All Handicapped Children Act, is just one example of that progress, and its threatened limitation is an indication that change can move in either a progressive or regressive direction. To keep the changes moving in a positive direction and in a constructive manner, advantage must be taken of what is known about attitudes.

For the cognitive component of attitudes, accurate information is essential. Increased exposure in the media, that is, realistic information, not just information about special disabled people, can educate and reduce the misperceptions that hearing people have about deaf people. Anything that reduces the strangeness of a disabling condition can go a long way toward changing attitudes about that condition. Improvements have been made in the images of deaf people that newspapers and television project.

Contact can influence the affective component of attitudes. It is not clear that short periods of contact influence attitudes positively, but visibility can at least heighten awareness. The current emphasis on mainstreaming can also allow for long periods of contact which can change attitudes of the hearing population and improve integration of deaf people at the same time.

Bibliography

Altman, Barbara: "Studies of Attitudes Toward the Handicapped: The Need for a New Direction," *Social Problems*, 28(3):321–337, 1981.

Gilbert, Laura-Jean: "The Public Media and Deafness," in A. Borow and R. Stuckless (eds.), *Deaf People and Social Change*, Conference: Sociology of Deafness, Gallaudet College, Washington, D.C., 1983.

Higgins, Paul: *Outsiders in a Hearing World: A Sociology of Deafness*, Sage Publications, Beverly Hills, 1980.

Meadow, Kathryn: "Self Image, Family Climate and Deafness," *Social Forces*, 47:428–438, 1969.

Nash, Jeffrey E., and Anedith Nash: *Deafness in Society*, D.C. Heath, Lexington, Massachusetts, 1981.

Schroedel, John (ed.): *Attitudes Toward Persons with Disabilities: A Compendium of Related Literature*, Human Resources Center, Albertson, New York, 1978.

———— and Richard Jacobsen: *Hiring Persons with Disabilities: A Labor Market Research Model*, Human Resources Center, Albertson, New York, 1978.

Tringo, John: "The Hierarchy of Preference Toward Disability Groups," *Journal of Special Education*, 4(3):295–306, 1970.

Vander Zanden, James: *Social Psychology*, Random House, New York.

Barbara M. Altman

Advocacy and Political Participation

Political activism and advocacy among deaf people in the 1980s was the product of a slow evolution. The communication barrier created by hearing loss was certainly the major obstacle hindering deaf peoples' effective political participation, but historical factors were significant as well.

HISTORICAL LIMITATIONS

In America before the nineteenth century, those disabled persons who survived childhood faced a somewhat questionable life as adults. Although disabled people received sympathy from the community as blameless victims of fate, they were also viewed as financial burdens on the township. Local communities in the seventeenth and eighteenth centuries maintained public almshouses where disabled individuals were placed with the poor, incompetent, aged and infirm, and chronically drunk. They were provided with sufficient food and shelter to remain alive but were given little hope or encouragement for self-improvement or eventual self-sufficiency. Parents and protective benevolent and religious organizations assumed some responsibility along with the township, but disability meant dependence, not independence.

Almshouses later were complemented by locally supported workhouses similar to the sheltered workshops operated by Goodwill and other such agencies today. Efforts were begun to provide minimal rehabilitation, but even in the nineteenth century some 80 percent of disabled persons remained institutionalized all their lives. As states formed and joined the Union, they gradually assumed some of the local responsibilities for the disabled population. One of the very first instances of federal assistance to disabled people was a land grant voted by Congress to establish the first permanent school for deaf Americans at Hartford, Connecticut.

Subsequently, a number of American schools were founded by deaf persons who also served as their administrators or principals. With the rise of oralism in the 1860s and 1870s, deaf persons in education began encountering closed doors to teaching as a profession. The deaf population continued to be largely underemployed, underserved, and underrepresented—a silent group with no higher hopes than those of becoming a printer or a factory worker.

In time, with advances in medicine and other developments, more disabled children survived. Adults who had lost or injured their hearing, sight, or limbs through accident or illness were able to benefit from medical treatment and prosthetic devices. As a result, the disabled population grew in size and visibility. Disabled people, their friends, and professionals closely associated with them began to perceive and accept the reality that they could work and contribute to society and that their potential capabilities were similar to those of nondisabled people.

However, at the beginning of the twentieth century, disabled individuals continued to be underemployed, somewhat sheltered, and treated as second-class citizens. The prevailing attitude was paternalistic and at times even patronizing. The nineteenth century had moved a step forward with the advent of special asylums or institutions for deaf, blind, mentally retarded, and mentally ill individuals, but it was a small step.

Institutions for deaf children at that time produced a large number of graduates who were naive, unaware, and afraid of the "outside" world. There were, of course, the usual success stories, the exceptions who went on to the university or otherwise carved a very satisfactory niche in life for themselves. But such people were not typical of the great bulk of the grass-roots deaf population of the 1920s.

Sign language was considered "dirty" and "naked"; it was a mark of low-caste deaf society and not to be used in public. Gradually, a sort of furtive use of signs began to occur, but it was a long time before deaf people felt truly comfortable in using their natural sign language out in the open, and before they became advocates for this chosen mode of communication. While school administrators in most public residential schools for deaf pupils in the United States condoned the use of signs on their campus during the early decades of the twentieth century, when oralism was at its peak, their public face was different. The tendency was to explain apologetically to parents that signs were randomly picked up in the dormitories, but they were not supported in the academic setting except for low-achieving students. In Europe, oralism was all-prevalent and practically all deaf teachers had been removed from their positions. During these years there were no deaf superintendents and only a couple of deaf principals in the United States. Deaf teachers, as a rule, were assigned to vocational classes or to classes for mentally retarded students or slow learners.

EFFECTS OF THE WORLD WARS

World Wars I and II were significant milestones in the climb toward employability of disabled workers. With the exodus of young men and women into the various branches of the military, industry was confronted with a labor shortage, particularly in crucial industries that were producing war materials. Doors opened to the disabled workforce, who demonstrated unexpected skills on the production line and in other levels of industry and government. Many of these workers retained their jobs following the war years.

Returning war veterans with injuries and disabilities led to the rehabilitation movement and the beginning of organized action on the part of disabled individuals. Although the National Association of the Deaf (NAD) had been formed much earlier, in 1880, it had continued to exist primarily as a paper organization with limited resources and influence. The disabled military returnees established the Disabled American Veterans, the Paralyzed Veterans of Foreign Wars, and other groups, which branched out into organizations for every conceivable type of disability.

CIVIL RIGHTS MOVEMENT

In the 1960s equal rights movements among ethnic minorities began to make an impact. The Civil Rights Act of 1964 outlawed racial discrimination, and later Title 9 legislated against discrimination based on sex. The effectiveness of this advocacy signaled to the disabled community that as a minority group they too had rights as citizens for equal opportunity and dignity within society. With this growing awareness and militancy, disabled groups became more articulate and better organized, and began to demand involvement in decisions and policy-making processes in programs and services designed for them by the government, educational agencies, and the private sector. Particularly responsive during the 1960s was the federal Office of Vocational Rehabilitation under its commissioner, Mary E. Switzer, and for the deaf population in particular, Boyce Williams of the Deafness and Communication Disorders Office in the Department of Health, Education and Welfare, *See* WILLIAMS, BOYCE ROBERT.

A major step forward for the legal rights of disabled people in the United States was achieved with enactment by Congress of the Rehabilitation Act of 1973 and its Section 504. Public Law 94-142 (Education for All Handicapped Children Act) guaranteed a free, appropriate public education for all handicapped children of the country. The White House Conference on Handicapped Individuals in May 1977 was another milestone which produced a long catalog of recommendations for action. The International Year of Disabled Persons was proclaimed in 1981, followed in a number of countries by the National Year of Disabled Persons in 1982. On December 3, 1982, the United Nations General Assembly voted unanimously to proclaim the period 1983–1992 as the Decade of Disabled Persons.

NATIONAL ASSOCIATION OF THE DEAF

Like other handicapped and minority groups, it was some time before deaf persons got together as a group to discuss common problems and concerns. The first sizable organization of deaf people in the United States, the New England Gallaudet Association of the Deaf, was established in 1853, but it was nearly three decades before state leaders convened in Cincinnati to create the National Association of the Deaf (NAD). Significantly, although the NAD predates many other organizations of disabled persons and such minority groups as the National Association for the Advancement of Colored People, these organizations moved much more quickly and effectively into the political arena. For one thing, they were not faced with the communication problem which forms the major barrier to deaf people. This communication handicap was aggravated by the thin population density of deaf persons.

With air transportation still in its infancy and later becoming quite expensive, and the continued inaccessibility of the telephone, deaf people were comparatively fragmented and isolated from each other. Job mobility was limited. Faced with the basic hunger for human interaction and ease of communication, deaf persons attending meetings of local and state organizations tended to accent the social aspect of getting together and renewing old friendships. Although their conventions had a business agenda of sorts, the main objective was to have a reunion and an opportunity for the kind of conversational give-and-take that hearing people take for granted as an everyday occurrence.

A few of the more aggressive state associations occasionally became involved in a local cause, as did the national association through the years; most of these advocacy stances resulted in resolutions passed on the floor with little follow-through. In 1956 representatives of some 20 state associations met for a week in Fulton, Missouri, with members

of the board of directors of the national association to overhaul the constitution and by-laws and, in effect, to reorganize the national body into a federation of state associations of the deaf. This marked the beginning of a more active and aggressive role for the organization, which continued to struggle along with only minimal funds. In 1966 the NAD hired its first full-time executive director, Frederick Schreiber. Over the next decade the association increased its staff to some 50 persons. *See* SCHREIBER, FREDERICK CARL.

ACTIVISM

Inherent in the philosophy and practice of educational and rehabilitation programs for deaf people is a commitment to promote the rights and well-being of deaf people so that they achieve their maximum potential and function within society. This assumes a framework of advocacy for deaf persons and a high degree of involvement with and respect for people with hearing losses. It is particularly important that language and cultural considerations as they relate to deafness be understood and accepted.

A growing body of direct and empirical research into deafness began during the 1960s. Involving both people with normal hearing and members of the deaf community, studies were undertaken of communication modalities, of the linguistics of sign language, and of other aspects of hearing impairment. Studies were also undertaken comparing deaf children of deaf parents with deaf children of hearing parents.

As the total communication philosophy of education began to gather momentum, the National Theatre of the Deaf came into being and contributed to the increasing visibility and respectability of signs. Gallaudet College opened its graduate program to deaf students in 1962, adding a deaf clinical professor to the staff. Captioned Films for the Deaf was established in the U.S. Office of Education. The leadership training program in the area of deafness began in 1964 at California State University at Northridge. The NAD received a number of federal grants to conduct the first national census of deaf people in the United States, to implement a Communication Skills Program, to establish a Registry of Interpreters for the Deaf, and to conduct a variety of workshops and training programs, including one on Section 504 of the Rehabilitation Act of 1973. A number of new organizations were born: the International Association of Parents of the Deaf, the American Deafness and Rehabilitation Association, the Council of Organizations Serving the Deaf, and the American Coalition of Citizens with Disabilities. New postsecondary programs sprang up across the country. The legal defense arm of the NAD actively sought and frequently won legal redress on discrimination and other charges involving deaf persons. Training workshops on the political process and leadership seminars were conducted in various parts of the United States and in other nations as well. A number of deaf persons campaigned for state legislatures, having already made some progress at the city and county levels.

The thrust of these combined events helped to open doors and to increase advocacy activities among the deaf population. In addition, technological breakthroughs such as the telecommunications device for the deaf (TDD) and the television decoder helped to reduce communication barriers, as did the advent of certified interpreters and the widespread proliferation of classes in sign language. The World Federation of the Deaf adopted an international symbol of deafness and designated the last week in September as an annual International Week of the Deaf.

During the 1970s and 1980s the international deaf community became more articulate and even militant about the needs of deaf persons. At times they participated with coalitions of other disabled groups in presenting testimony and in protest marches and sit-ins. Demonstrations and marches took place in such diverse geographical areas as Madrid and other large cities in Spain, in Helsinki, Stockholm, Rome, and in different cities of the United States. Over a dozen deaf persons have entered the legal profession; deaf people have testified in courts of law and have served jury duty; and a deaf attorney has appeared before the United States Supreme Court. Deaf persons are serving on school and college boards and in various advisory capacities, including state and federal advisory councils.

Advocacy and political participation among deaf persons continues to face the specter of communication barriers that is inherent in hearing loss: some degree of detachment from the mainstream, lack of resources and visibility due to the low incidence of deafness among the general population, and isolation for those residing in rural areas. Strides have been made in breaking down the communication barrier, but increased advocacy activities will be necessary for a more satisfactory milieu for the average deaf citizen of the world.

Bibliography

Gannon, J. R.: *Deaf Heritage (A Narrative History of Deaf America)*, 1981.

Garretson, M. D.: "Deaf People and the Political Process," *Gallaudet Today*, vol. 10, no. 1, Fall 1979.

———: "Gallaudet College: Its Emerging Advocacy Role," *Disabled USA*, vol. 2, no. 2, 1978.

Greenberg, J.: *In This Sign*, 1970.

Jacobs, L. M.: *A Deaf Adult Speaks Out*, 1980.

Magarotto, C.: "News from the Silent World," *The Voice of Silence*, World Federation of the Deaf Newsletter, no. 2, Rome, 1983.

Merv D. Garretson

Social Change

Change is a fundamental feature of social life. To understand change in the deaf world, it is necessary to know in what ways that world is distinctive and is connected with and influenced by the larger society. Also to be considered is whether the deaf world is going through distinct cycles of change, becoming successively more adjusted to the larger society, or whether through their concerted efforts deaf people and their allies are changing their position in society.

THE DEAF WORLD AS NONMODERN

The experience of deafness is isolating, and early sociological studies interpreted the formation of the deaf community as a response to isolation. Still, deaf social organizations can display a wide range of relationships with their host societies. These vary from an integrative, mutual dependency, as was apparently the case in Martha's Vineyard (Massachusetts) in the eighteenth century, to a highly dependent relationship in societies where the deaf experience originates in state-owned and -operated schools and where welfare and other ameliorative programs provide for impaired individuals. Certainly, no actual group of deaf people conforms perfectly to these extremes, but recognizing extremes shows that the varieties of deaf experiences are responses to the intrinsic, isolating tendencies of deafness. *See* HISTORY: Martha's Vineyard; SOCIOLOGY.

Distinctiveness and isolation are powerful forces that function to form the deaf world into a relatively cohesive whole. Often, a vital social organization referred to as the deaf community results, and this organization, like any minority or ethnic community, tends to set individuals apart from their larger society.

MODERNITY

Modernity refers to the qualities of social life generally found among members of societies that are heterogeneous, economically complex, and highly technological. A modern society is urban, technological, diverse, interdependent, and large. Members of modern society commonly have a typical world view that places a premium on rational deliberation and orders its affairs by the clock.

In modern society, interactions tend to be differentiated. In dealing with others, people tend to focus on specific reasons for being with each other. Since most individual affairs are routine and diverse, people interact with others as if the latter were instruments to achieve their own personal goals. Further, since people deal increasingly with others whom they know only within well-defined situations, they make judgments about people, what they want from them, and what purposes they pursue solely on the basis of appearances. Another way to understand this feature of modernity is to realize that individuals deal with only portions of other people's identities. They are interested in clerks' efficiency in counting change, for example, not in their total personality.

Modernity, then, means styles of thinking, ways of interacting, and modes of social control typifying societies that are highly differentiated according to rational criteria, societies that have technologically sophisticated means of producing goods and services for a highly individualistic population.

Communities of deaf people stand in contrast to most modern social organizations. The deaf world emphasizes face-to-face interaction and continuous and diffuse relationships, while modern social organizations promote different types of interactional skills that result in impersonal, short-term, and specific relationships.

DEAFNESS IN MODERN SOCIETY

A separate deaf world originated as and remains a vital social and linguistic response to isolation from the larger society. The deaf world's vitality depends upon the economic ability of its members to support it and on the relationship it can manage with the larger society.

In a nonmodern society, especially one that changes slowly, it is often possible for deaf people to sustain themselves as a separate collective entity in a fashion not all that different socioeconomically from others in society. Hence, at the outset of the twentieth century, the difference between annual family income for deaf families and hearing families was not particularly significant in the United States. A deaf man could draw wages, along with his hearing coworkers, for manual and semiskilled work. Also, some relatively high-paying jobs, like printing, were open to people with little verbal skill or formal educational background.

Historically, simple, homogeneous communities hosting robust numbers of deaf citizens accommodated deaf customs and communicative needs. Out of these social roots deaf communities arose as natural social organizations exhibiting the same cohesiveness that characterized the larger societies.

Since early in the twentieth century, western societies have undergone massive changes. The major effects of these changes are the transformation of traditional family organization into complicated and varied living and working arrangements; major shifts in population and in centers of power, wealth, and influence; essential changes in the nature of work and play; and the renegotiation of sex roles.

These changes occurred unevenly. Segments of some societies remained relatively untouched by them. In some ways, the deaf world is one such segment. In its organization, it resembles more traditionally organized communities based on class,

racial, or ethnic identities. It is in this sense that the deaf world can be considered a residual form of social organization in modern society.

But in recent times, there have been indications of profound change in the experiences of deaf people. These changes are fostered by technologies of communication, the impact of mainstreaming policies which represent an extension of equalitarian ideologies generally found in modern society, and an increased tolerance in the larger society for social and cultural diversity.

So pervasive are the changes taking place in communications that they have been referred to as revolutionary. Hearing-impaired people experience these changes as they gain increased access to information, for example, closed captioning, real-time interpreting, and the increased availability of information made possible through home computers, networks of information exchange, and the decentralization of control of information.

A communications revolution could provide extensive changes in the deaf experience. Since the deaf social world is a direct response to the lack of easy, natural communication, the new communication technologies will facilitate gaining and understanding information widely distributed in the hearing society. Deaf persons may find that once the barriers of communication with hearing people are overcome through the use of new high-speed communication technologies, their interests can be developed far beyond those commonly found among members of isolated and stigmatized groups. Still, caution is required in assessing the likely consequences of communication technologies. Ethnic and linguistic identities can function as buffers against change. Hence, increased contact between hearing and deaf individuals could also increase conflicts within the deaf world.

A constant and inevitable tension exists between being distinctive and trying to become equal. Many groups who have traveled the route to assimilation have discovered that portions of their heritage fit better with the larger cultural values than do others. Becoming modern has often meant giving up certain behaviors and beliefs and modifying others. Ethnic groups often accomplish this by ritualizing their beliefs. They retain features of their former lives, but only for special occasions and only in highly stylized forms. Similarly, as the deaf world becomes more attuned to modern society, it is likely to retain some of its distinctive features.

Traditional organizational forms have typically either weakened or undergone radical transformations in the process of modernization. To the degree that the deaf social world can be characterized as traditional and to the degree that policies of mainstreaming put deaf people in contact with the modern hearing world, younger members of the deaf world will bring with them ideas and mannerisms, ways of behaving and thinking, that may challenge the foundations of the deaf world. Indeed, while difficult to document, there are already startling differences between young and old deaf people in attitudes toward sexual behavior and marriage, career aspirations, and relationships with the hearing world.

CONCLUSION

Deaf people, then, are confronted with powerful forces of social change. As they participate more fully in modern society, and as the larger society accommodates the increasing diversity of its population, the deaf world might lose some of its distinctiveness. Even with regard to sign language, the linguistic features of deaf communication could be influenced by the technical requirements of other communicative modes. TTD conversational practices already reflect such requirements. American Sign Language could exist primarily as a language of sociability.

It is important to recognize the fact that the precise effects of the changes occurring in modern society will be at least partially influenced by the rational and emotional responses of deaf people themselves. Consequently, it is not possible to say with certainty exactly how the deaf world will mirror or distort larger processes of social change.

Bibliography

Berger, Peter, Brigitte Berger, and Hansfried Kellner: *The Homeless Mind*, Vintage Books, New York, 1973.

Benderly, Beryl Lieff: *Dancing Without Music: Deafness in America*, Doubleday, Garden City, New Jersey, 1980.

Bernstein, Basil: "Social Class, Language and Socialization," in P. Giglioli (ed.), *Language and Social Context*, pp. 157–178, Penguin, Baltimore, Maryland, 1972.

Boros, Alexander, and Ross Stuckless (eds.): *Deaf People and Social Change*, Conference: Sociology of Deafness, Gallaudet College, 1982.

Cuddihy, John Murray: *The Ordeal of Civility*, Basic, New York, 1974.

Erting, Carol: "Language Policy and Deaf Ethnicity in the United States," *Sign Language Studies*, 19:139–152, 1978.

Goffman, Erving: *Stigma: Notes on the Management of Spoiled Identity*, Prentice-Hall, Englewood Cliffs, New Jersey, 1963.

Groce, Nora: "Beyond Institutions: The History of Some America Deaf: An Example from Martha's Vineyard," in Paul C. Higgins and Jeff Nash (eds.), *The Deaf Community and the Deaf Population*, Conference: Sociology of Deafness, Gallaudet College, 1982.

Nash, Jeffrey E., and Anedith Nash: "Typing on the Phone: How the Deaf Accomplish TTY Conversations," *Sign Language Studies*, 36:193–216, Fall 1982.

Novak, Michael: *The Rise of the Unmeltable Ethnics*, Macmillan, New York, 1973.

Stokoe, Jr., William C.: *Sign Language Structure*, Linstok Press, Silver Spring, Maryland, 1978.

Toffler, Alvin: *The Third Wave*, Morrow, New York, 1980.

Williams, Frederick: *The Communications Revolution*, Sage Publications, Beverly Hills, California, 1982.

Jeffrey E. Nash

DENMARK

The Danish welfare system for handicapped members of the population has a tradition nearly 200 years old, initiated by P. A. Castberg. The first headmaster of the Royal School for the Deaf in Copenhagen, Castberg proposed Denmark's first law to provide state education for handicapped children. This law was passed in 1817.

The Danish tradition of helping groups of handicapped individuals was initiated by private persons, who saw the need for schools, institutions, and welfare workers for handicapped persons. Eventually, the government or the local authorities took over the responsibility. In nearly all the Danish institutions, however, private influence remains strong on boards of directors. This influence, through the boards as well as through the direct contact with the authorities, gradually has been taken over by handicapped representatives, who are employed at high levels in the government.

As part of this tradition, all the equipment needed by handicapped individuals is paid for by the government or by local authorities. Equipment that has been approved as an essential aid for a particular handicapped group will be provided at the request of a member of the professional team working within the group. To ease further the financial burden of handicaps, all employed handicapped individuals receive a special monthly stipend to cover extra expenses which their disability may entail.

Another law provides for those who have acquired a handicap in adulthood. These individuals may be reeducated or rehabilitated in order to return to their original jobs or to acquire the skills for a new job. A disability pension is provided for those unable to work. Special apartments in regular housing converted to the specific needs of the handicapped occupant are also available.

EDUCATION

The deaf child usually attends regular nursery school and kindergarten, where some of the teachers are trained by the child-guidance clinic and where there might be a special aide to take care of the deaf children in that particular kindergarten. The teachers are supervised by the child-guidance clinic. The Deaf Center for Total Communication, a private institute established in 1973 to conduct research and teaching related to sign language, arranges sign language courses as well as other special courses in total communication for teachers and parents of hearing-impaired children. *See* SOCIOLINGUISTICS: Total Communication.

There are nursery school classes for five- and six-year-olds. The child-guidance clinic, the kindergarten teacher, and the preschool teacher counsel the parents in making the final decision on which type of school their child will attend: a school for deaf students (the former state schools), a center school for special education (run by the local authorities), or a local public school (in the municipal system). Despite a 100-year tradition of private schools for hearing-impaired individuals, there are no longer any private schools in Denmark for deaf children.

The communication system is different in each of the types of schools. The schools for deaf pupils depend mostly on total communication. All of the teachers make use of manual communication, and several of the staff members are deaf. The center school offers integrated as well as segregated classes for the hearing-impaired child. The teachers are specially trained, but sign language will normally not be used in the class, although some of the teachers may use it outside the classroom. In the local public school, the hearing-impaired child often will be the only handicapped child in the class. He or she may receive lessons with a speech and hearing therapist or may even have an assistant master in the classroom part of the school day, but the technical equipment will be geared to the individual. The teacher is seldom able to communicate with the student in sign language.

A Danish child will normally go to school for nine years, between the ages of 7 and 16. During the last two years of school, the child may attend an after-school or a junior high school. There is also a special junior high school for hearing-impaired children from all Denmark. The student organizations at this school are members of the National Association for the Deaf, so that the young deaf student automatically becomes a member of this organization.

Young deaf adults who complete the required schooling receive instruction from a social worker for deaf persons. Social workers for the 3000 deaf adults are located all over Denmark. The social worker functions as a personal counselor for the young adult, giving guidance in job selection, in starting the job, and in all other social and economic affairs. The social worker helps the client in arranging for interpretation during his or her job training and in assuring that the client's social and economic rights are maintained according to the law. This network of social worker services is provided for deaf adults throughout life.

FACILITIES FOR DEAF PEOPLE

Prenatal care and birth are carefully monitored by nurses and midwives. If there is any indication of a difficult delivery or any risk that the infant will be born with a handicap, the delivery will be performed at the university hospital of Copenhagen or in a hospital with a ward equipped to give special care.

From birth to school age, children are attended by visiting nurses who enter the home and instruct the family in infant care. These nurses also screen infants between the ages of seven and nine months with the Swedish BOEL test, which tests the infants' perceptual skills. New screening procedures are being tested for detecting handicaps in two- and four-year-olds. *See* AUDITORY DISORDERS, PREVENTION OF: Screening.

When the visiting nurse or the family suspect that there may be a hearing loss, the child is referred to a hearing center or clinic for medical observation. The hearing-impaired child will then be taken to the child-guidance clinic or to a school for deaf children, where special training centers have been established to help the family in stimulating the perceptual skills of the child. These institutions have followed the oral tradition, but since the mid-1970s they have changed increasingly to a total communication approach; however, there are slight differences between institutions in different parts of Denmark. The child is treated individually, and at all institutions the choice of communication means for the child is made generally in cooperation with the parents. *See* EDUCATION: Communication.

Besides social-work services, there exists an interpreter service which can be drawn upon when a deaf person needs interpretation in various situations. This service is normally paid for by the local authorities. There are, however, circumstances when the deaf individuals pay for the interpreter services themselves, or when the association for the deaf or other institutions pay for the interpreter.

The National Association for the Deaf, which has 70 percent of the adult deaf population as members, has branches in all major cities in Denmark. This association is supported by the deaf people themselves. But the special activities, evening schools for example, are partly paid for by the state or local authorities.

To enhance deaf people's cultural life, the Danish television regularly broadcasts signed programs, and special programs for deaf viewers are aired once a month. Many programs are also captioned for hearing-impaired viewers. Denmark is the only country in the world where a video recorder is registered as a handicap aid and where bimonthly programs produced by the Deaf Film

Company are mailed directly to the subscriber. A free teletype service has not yet been accepted as a handicap aid by the government.

There is a network of institutions for those adults who cannot provide for themselves. Many of these institutions are located in the Copenhagen area, but there are also several located in other parts of Denmark. The deaf adult is provided with an apartment or a room and can either live there full time or use the facilities in the sheltered workshops during the day. These institutions provide an environment where multiply handicapped individuals can achieve a fulfilling life.

In one of the psychiatric hospitals, there is a special ward offering psychiatric services for the deaf community. The staff has been trained in the communication means of deaf persons as well as psychiatry and psychology for deaf patients.

The Lutheran church, which is the state church in Denmark, employs five ministers who conduct special religious services for deaf Lutherans at the deaf churches.

For the deaf individual, sign language is of the greatest importance with regard to his or her development and mental well-being. Modern life depends on effective communication, from which deaf people are often excluded. With the air of interpreters and through the activities of their organizations, however, deaf persons have been able to move with the times and to live as active, productive members of society while strengthening and developing their own culture.

Lars von der Lieth

DESLOGES, PIERRE
(1747–?)

Pierre Desloges, glue worker and bookbinder, is the author of the first book by a deaf man. Based on his life and the language of a deaf community, his *Observations of a Deaf-Mute*, published in France in 1779, proves that a large deaf community of artisans and unskilled laborers existed in Paris in the eighteenth century and that they communicated among themselves with a highly structured sign language. The French Sign Language was therefore already the principal means of communication among deaf people, well before the founding of the Paris Institute for Deaf-Mutes and the invention of the Abbé de l'Epée's "methodical signs." *See* L'EPÉE, ABBÉ CHARLES MICHEL DE.

Many hearing writers had previously noted that deaf people conversed by gestures, and the sixteenth-century French essayist and philosopher Michel Eyguem de Montaigne even observed that there must be a "gestural grammar" in their communication. But Desloges's book is the first time

that a person who was in the deaf community and who knew sign language provided an inside story.

Desloges was deafened at the age of seven, so his first language was French. His publisher, B. Morin, went to great lengths in his introduction to emphasize that the manuscript was only corrected for grammatical and punctuation errors, that the writing was Desloges's own. In the book, written when he was 32, Desloges said that soon after becoming deaf he could only make himself understood with his faulty pronunciation or by writing. Before he had met any other deaf people, he described his gestures as "disjointed, isolated, incomplete, and without continuity."

His first exposure to sign language was when he met the deaf servant of an Italian actor on tour in France. The deaf Italian taught him, according to Desloges, "the art of putting signs together to form distinct images with which one can represent one's different ideas, transmit them to others of one's kind, converse with them in a continuous and orderly conversation." Though his Italian friend could not read or write, he did teach Desloges how to communicate through gestures.

Desloges considered his case common: as deaf people living alone in their villages or in isolated families began to travel or migrate to the city, they found that their home signs simply were not sufficient. He felt the deaf person needed to associate with others of the same kind: "He meets deaf-mutes more knowledgeable than himself, he learns to combine and perfect his signs . . . he quickly acquires, in interactions with his comrades, the so 'difficult'—so they say!—art of expressing and painting one's thoughts, even the most abstract, by means of natural signs and with as much order and precision as if he knew all the rules of grammar." He went on to say that deaf people, among themselves, could talk fluently about anything.

Desloges never attended the Paris Institute—he was already in his twenties when the Abbé de l'Epée started experimenting with signs—and there is no evidence that the two men ever met. Desloges was aware that there was a growing controversy between the Abbé de l'Epée in Paris, who was advocating methodical signs for educating deaf students, and the Abbé Deschamps in Orléans, who argued that gesturing could never be a viable teaching tool. It was that controversy which inspired Desloges to speak out: "Like a Frenchman who sees his language belittled by a German who only knows a few French words, I thought I was obliged to defend my language against the false charges of this author [Deschamps]."

Desloges had no formal education; he defended his language in simple terms. He wanted only to show that his language was useful and efficient without explaining in detail how it worked. Such a detailed analysis, he said, "would be an immense enterprise which would require several volumes," and he feared that this dynamic and energetic language would only seem weak when explained in words by a novice writer. He did, however, give an example in which he described what today's linguists call size and shape specifiers: after making the generic sign for "pastry," a particular kind of pastry would be expressed by a sign showing its size and shape. *See* SIGN LANGUAGES.

Though Desloges did not try to describe any signs from the vocabulary of the French Sign Language of his time, he did indicate that at least some of the methodical signs described in the Abbé de l'Epée's first book were the same as the signs used in the adult deaf community. This may indicate that there were already some contacts between children in the school and deaf adults in the community. Though the grammatical signs (for articles, genders, and so on) used in the classroom were invented by the Abbé de l'Epée, he apparently accepted many of the natural signs from French Sign Language. The distinction between methodical signs and natural sign language was not made, however, until a generation later. *See* SIGN LANGUAGES: French.

Desloges never addressed the problem of when sign language first appeared in France. His goal was simply to inform the public that deaf people existed and that they found ways to function in society as well as hearing people. It is clear from his writing, however, that deaf people faced strong prejudices from the hearing public—one of his defenses of sign language was that the French church had finally admitted signing nonspeaking deaf people into the sacraments of marriage and the eucharist.

Desloges was not a great leader of the eighteenth-century deaf community: he was simply one deaf worker among many in Paris who lived in a kind of mutual assistance network at a time when there were no recognized clubs or confederations for them. Deaf people searched out the company and help of others who were deaf and, in the need to exchange information and survive in the world together, they refined their language.

The deaf community in France did not formalize these associations until the nineteenth-century. The establishment of large residential schools (as opposed to private oral tutoring, which only the rich could afford) certainly accelerated the evolution of the deaf community and their language. But Desloges's book proves that even before hearing people started seriously paying attention to deaf people as a group, deaf people had already started taking care of themselves as a community.

William Moody

D'ESTRELLA, THEOPHILUS HOPE
(1851–1929)

Theophilus Hope d'Estrella, (born de Rutte) was an extraordinary man, born during an extraordinary time—the gold rush era in California. Presumably born deaf, he chose not to learn to speak. Nevertheless, d'Estrella became a teacher, specializing in art, at the California School for the Deaf, Berkeley (CSDB); a lecturer (using American Sign Language and pantomime); a writer; a world traveler; a naturalist; a mountain climber; and an outstanding amateur photographer.

Born February 6, 1851, in San Francisco, d'Estrella described his childhood this way in an autobiographical sketch: "At the age of five he lost both his parents. This orphan boy had such hard luck with his guardian that he passed four years as a run-away urchin, often living by himself and undergoing the vicissitudes of evil, peculiar to the days of '49." It is little wonder, then, that on May 1, 1860, d'Estrella became the first student of the California Institution for the Education and Care of the Indigent Deaf and the Dumb and Blind in San Francisco (now the California School for the Deaf, Fremont).

The school soon moved to 130 acres across the bay in Berkeley; it became d'Estrella's home. D'Estrella remained in residence at CSDB his entire life. His social development was rapid as he learned the

Theophilus Hope d'Estrella.

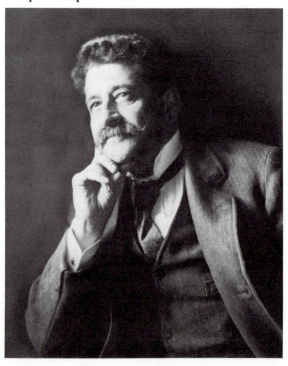

sign language of his peers. When he was 16, d'Estrella chose to change his last name to d'Estrella. *See* SIGN LANGUAGES.

The school's principal, Warring Wilkinson, caught up in the prevailing esthetic milieu of Berkeley as the Athens of the Pacific, believed in the far-reaching effects of art instruction as a means of teaching broader relationships in the education of his visually oriented students. Wilkinson also thought that, properly tutored, selected deaf graduates could succeed in the nearby state university. This unprecedented goal was achieved in part when d'Estrella became the first deaf student to be enrolled at the University of California, Berkeley, in October 1873. Although d'Estrella remained at the university for three years, maintaining his standing in history, nature studies, mythology, and the classics, mathematics proved his stumbling block, and he did not graduate. His English professor, distinguished poet Edward Roland Sill, considered d'Estrella one of his best students.

D'Estrella's talent for drawing and his lifelong interest in art led to his, again unprecedented, enrollment in 1879 as the first deaf student in the West's most prestigious art school, the San Francisco Art Association's California School of Design (now the San Francisco Art Institute), where he studied for five years. Following this, he was appointed art instructor at the California School for the Deaf—a position he held until the art department was discontinued in 1923 because of lack of funds. Following the death of Virgil Williams, director of the art school, in 1887, d'Estrella published a lengthy article which has become a classic reference in California art history circles: "Virgil Williams' Art Notes to a Deaf-Mute Pupil."

Years later, William James, pioneer psychologist of Harvard University, became interested in the thoughts of a person without a formal language. His study led him to a series of communications with d'Estrella and the subsequent publication of "Thoughts Before Language: A Deaf-Mute's Recollections." From d'Estrella's poignant reminiscences, James concluded that abstract thought did indeed occur before the development of a formal language and that moral conscience was intuitive.

In the mid-nineteenth century, California became a mecca for photographers. D'Estrella enthusiastically began the study of photography in 1886. He joined the California Camera Club and worked diligently as a member of the lantern-slide committee to produce slides about the natural wonders of California. He contributed many of his own photographs taken on his summer hiking trips into the Sierra Nevada wilderness with the Sierra Club. He was a popular nightly entertainer, as a pantomimist, for these hearing groups. Today, his photographs are preserved in several California repos-

Rio Chico: Reflections, a photograph made by d'Estrella in California in December 1896. (Archives, California School for the Deaf, Fremont)

itories: Archives, California School for the Deaf, Fremont; Oakland Museum; Santa Cruz City Museum; "Sun House," Ukiah; California Historical Society, San Francisco, Bancroft Library, University of California, Berkeley.

D'Estrella considered the lantern slide an important tool of education, bringing knowledge of the world to his deaf students. Another aspect of his photography was recording his students pursuing their school activities, playing, and fantasizing in an attempt to dispel the prevailing notion that students in an institution were "mentally retarded or insane." His students dubbed him "The Magic Lantern Man." He won first prize in the Animal Section of the first photographic Salon held in San Francisco in 1901.

D'Estrella wrote "The Itemizer" column for the school's news magazine for 44 years, in which he chronicled activities of students, alumni, and faculty, compiling an enormous wealth of information. He wrote numerous additional articles about education of deaf people, summer vacation trips, the Literary Society, and other activities of the West's first school for deaf children.

As a beloved teacher for nearly 50 years, d'Estrella had an incalculable influence on hundreds of students. He discovered and encouraged the talent of his student Granville Redmond, who became one of California's foremost landscape painters. D'Estrella was known throughout his life as the children's friend. He taught his young charges, mostly by example, how to live life fully and joyfully in spite of their disabilities. *See* EDUCATION; REDMOND, GRANVILLE.

D'Estrella died in Berkeley on October 8, 1929.

Bibliography

Albronda, Mildred: *Douglas Tilden: Portrait of a Deaf Sculptor*, 1980.

————: *The Magic Lantern Man: Theophilus Hope d'Estrella*, unpublished manuscript.

Braddock, Guilbert C.: *Notable Deaf Persons*, Gallaudet College Alumni Association, 1975.

Burnes, Caroline H., and Catherine M. Ramger: *A History of the California School for the Deaf*, 1860–1960, 1960.

d'Estrella, Theophilus Hope: "The Itemizer" (column), *California News*, 1855–1929.

————: "Virgil Williams' Art Notes to a Deaf-Mute Pupil," *Overland Monthly*, March 1887.

Gallagher, James E. (ed.): *Representative Deaf Persons*, Chicago, 1898.

James, William: "Thoughts Before Language: A Deaf-Mute's Recollection," *American Annals of the Deaf*, April 1893 (reprinted from *Philosophical Review*, November 1892).

Memorial Issue, *California News*, November 1929.

"Prominent Deaf Persons," *The Silent Worker*, vol. 11, no. 8, April 1899.

Tilden, Douglas: "Higher Education for the Deaf," *Silent Educator*, November 1891.

Mildred Albronda

DIRUBE, ROLANDO LOPEZ
(1928–   )

Rolando Lopez Dirube is considered one of Latin America's greatest plastic artists. Working successfully in various media—painting, murals, prints, sculptures—he has developed innovative, creative artistic styles that have helped make Latin American art among the most exciting in the domain of contemporary art. His works are exhibited in some of the world's most important museums. Dirube also has taught at various universities and has won fellowships from prestigious institutes and museums, including the Cuban-American Cultural Institute, the Brooklyn Museum of the City of New York, the Institute of Hispanic Culture in Madrid, and the Institute of International Education (Cintas Foundation Fellowship).

EDUCATION
Rolando Lopez Dirube was born August 14, 1928, in Havana, Cuba. Deafened by an unknown cause at the age of six, he learned to lipread, and retained articulate speech. He made hundreds of representational drawings when he was a schoolboy, but at 19 enrolled in the University of Havana's College of Engineering and Architecture where he became interested in abstract mathematics and philosophy. There he began working in oils. His paintings from this period reveal an impressionism that characterizes his later work as well. Support from the Cuban government allowed Dirube to study art abroad. At the Art Students League in New York

Rolando Lopez Dirube in 1977. (Editorial Playor)

City he studied drawing with George Grosz and later studied engraving and drawing with Gabor Peterdi, Max Beckman, and other masters.

CHARACTERISTICS OF HIS WORK
Dirube's works do not belong to a defined art movement. They are motivated purely by emotions and a determination to define them. Dirube has insisted that his work does not follow a predetermined plan but grows naturally and subconsciously. His art is influenced by twentieth-century technology and materials.

In 1951, in his third individual show, Dirube exhibited woodcuts in color, using new techniques that combined fire with knife and gauge cut. He used gunpowder, gasoline, flammable gelatin, and acid to achieve the desired effects. As a result, he raised the level of Cuban graphic art to that already achieved in Cuban painting and sculpture.

Dirube's wood sculptures of the 1950s and 1960s show a careful development of conceptual simplification. From his early piece *Casicanecuas* through the later works *Simple Forms*, *Planetariums*, and *Organs*, one can see the artist striving to achieve economy. The essence of all his works is combat, the struggle between the artist and his materials. Dirube has written that he enjoys the challenge of difficult materials, feeling that they provoke him to greater effort and creativity.

As seen in *Organs* and *Altered Spheres*, what identifies his sculpted wood works is how they di-

Dirube's *Haiku VII* (1972); wood and string on plastic laminated panel. (Editorial Playor)

vide, redistribute, and create new forms and spaces, conveying the impression that they are waiting to be united. Despite their small size and simplicity, each is so balanced and unusual that it is not quickly understood. In this sense, they are in marked contrast to his easily grasped cast concrete sculptures, murals, and some of his more rhythmic wood sculptures.

Dirube's artistic growth in the 1950s demonstrated the range of his abilities. In his fourth show, he exhibited drawings using different materials such as graphite, ink, and silver point. In 1953, using his engineering background, Dirube began experimenting with cast concrete sculpture. In addition, he interested the architects of Havana in incorporating murals and sculptures into their designs, and monumental sculpture into the contemporary urban environment. He advocated concrete as the ideal medium for the incorporation of sculpture in architecture and executed concrete murals for private homes.

In 1955, Dirube began his bamboo sculpture series, focusing on the integration of visual concepts with sounds. Relationships between sound and sight are very delicate, and few sculptors succeed in creating an effective merger. Dirube's attempts were considered impossible because of his deafness. Nevertheless, he demonstrated his skill by cutting pieces of bamboo and extending them on very fine tubes, making a mechanism of vibrations whose effects he knows only on an abstract scientific plane.

From 1955 to 1959, Dirube completed various murals in Havana. For the Havana-Rivera Hotel he executed one in mixed media: concrete reliefs,

Bamboo XXI (1956) by Dirube. (Editorial Playor)

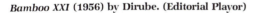

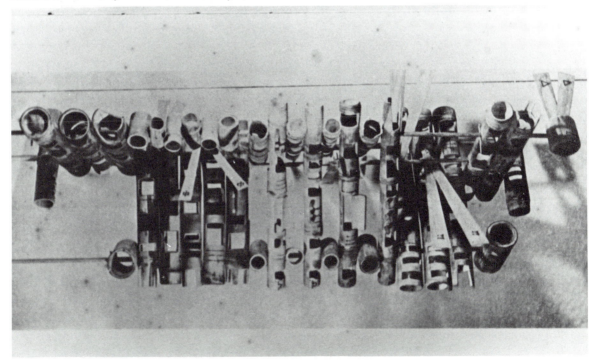

venetian mosaics, bronze structures, glass, and potassium silicate. Others, for the *Prensa Libra* newspaper building and the University of Havana, he did in acrylic paint. He used potassium silicate for the National Convention and Sports Palace at the Plaza de la Republica.

Major Exhibitions and Honors

Dirube's work has been displayed and honored in Latin America, Europe, and the United States. In 1951, for example, he captured first prize in both painting and graphic art at the First Exhibition of Latin American Art organized by the University of Tampa, Florida. In the same year, the Pan-American Union selected his work for an exhibition of Latin American graphic art that toured Germany. His pieces traveled throughout Europe in 1955 as part of the First International Exhibition of Graphic Works in Color, organized by the Victoria and Albert Museum of London.

Dirube's reputation grew in the 1960s. In 1962, the Metropolitan Museum of New York, the Philadelphia Museum, and the Philadelphia Free Library all acquired his works. In 1965, he served as professor of design analysis in the department of architecture of the Inter-American University in San Juan, Puerto Rico, and in 1967 he won the Urbe prize for his monumental sculptures in La Arboleda. Despite his deafness, he was invited to give a series of televised art lectures in 1968.

Bibliography

Pau-Llosa, Ricardo: *Dirube*, Editorial Playor, Santa Polonia, Spain, 1979.

Deborah M. Sonnenstrahl

DRIVING RESTRICTIONS

Hearing-impaired individuals are permitted to drive noncommercial vehicles in the United States, although some states do have certain restrictions, such as the requirement of a passenger-side rearview mirror, or identification of the driver as deaf on the driver's license. However, the majority of states place no restriction on deaf drivers.

Commercial Licensing—State

States have different licensing procedures and standards for drivers of commercial vehicles of a certain size and/or weight, or for drivers transporting passengers commercially. Some states permit hearing-impaired persons to drive trucks or buses within the confines of the state (intrastate), if they meet all other requirements of the license procedure. A state's department of motor vehicles should be contacted to check the hearing require-

ments for a commercial or chauffeur license in any particular state.

Commercial Licensing—Federal

There are different requirements for drivers of commercial vehicles that cross state lines. This type of traffic is interstate commerce, and is regulated by the federal government.

The United States has placed stringent physical requirements on drivers in interstate commerce; these requirements exclude drivers with a moderate or severe hearing impairment. The regulation setting forth the physical requirements for interstate commercial driving states: "A person is physically qualified to drive a motor vehicle (in interstate commerce) if that person—First perceives a forced whispered voice in the better ear at not less than 5 feet with or without the use of a hearing aid or, if tested by use of an audiometric device, does not have an average hearing loss in the better ear greater than 40 decibels at 500 Hz, 1,000 Hz, and 2,000 Hz with or without a hearing aid when the audiometric device is calibrated to American National Standard (formerly ASA Standard)." *See* Audiometry: Pure Tone Audiogram.

The hearing-impaired community has long attempted to revise this regulation so that hearing-impaired drivers could find employment in the lucrative field of interstate commerce. In 1976 and 1981, petitions were presented to the U.S. Department of Transportation to abolish this regulation, or to permit waiver of the regulation for deaf drivers with excellent driving records. These petitions pointed to studies indicating the greater safety records of hearing-impaired drivers. They also cited section 504 of the Rehabilitation Act of 1973 and alleged that the regulation violated the Department of Transportation's responsibility under that law to practice nondiscrimination toward disabled persons. Finally, the petitions noted the relative unimportance of hearing in driving trucks and buses, where the interior noise level is so high as to impair any driver's ability to hear outside noises. *See* Rehabilitation Act of 1973.

The Department of Transportation refused in each instance to grant the hearing-impaired community's petitions. It cited one study of hearing-impaired drivers that found deaf drivers to be less safe than other drivers; so the Department of Transportation stated that it would prefer to err on the side of safety in the important area of interstate commerce.

The refusal of the U.S. Department of Transportation to revise its restriction regarding hearing-impaired drivers constitutes a major setback in the struggle to open more employment opportunities to hearing-impaired workers. Many jobs require the ability to drive in interstate commerce, and many states and employers model their hearing requirements for commercial drivers on the federal interstate commerce requirements. For these reasons, a great number of jobs are closed to hearing-impaired persons due to the Department of Transportation restriction.

A change in the Department's restriction is unlikely in the near future. The safety studies relied upon in the deaf community's petitions are for the most part statistically imperfect. As states do not generally note physical disabilities in their motor vehicle records, accurate figures on the safety records of large numbers of hearing-impaired persons are not generally available. Better studies may be needed to convince the Department to alter its present regulation.

Additionally, better evidence may be needed before a successful court case could be made against the Department of Transportation's regulations based on Section 504. The Supreme Court, in *Southeastern Community College v. Davis*, announced that safety considerations would be given great consideration in Section 504 cases. Moreover, courts traditionally defer to administrative agencies, such as the Department of Transportation, which have the responsibility and expertise to create regulations governing a particular issue. *See* REHABILITATION ACT OF 1973: Southeastern Community College v. Davis.

CASE LAW REGARDING DRIVING RESTRICTIONS

Four recent court decisions clarified the status of rules barring hearing-impaired individuals from employment involving use of motor vehicles. In three cases concerning small Postal Service vehicles, school buses, and forklifts, the courts forbid hearing-impaired persons employment. In the fourth, the courts let stand, on the basis of safety, a U.S. Department of Transportation regulation prohibiting epileptics from driving in interstate commerce; the same regulation applies to hearing-impaired persons.

Flail v. Bolger In response to a lawsuit, in 1981 the U.S. Postal Service dropped its hearing requirement for postal employees driving postal jeeps and small trucks. Prior to settlement of this case, it was difficult for hearing-impaired individuals to secure the desirable "mail carrier" positions with the Postal Service, as these positions required driving small postal vehicles. The Postal Service still requires that drivers of larger postal vehicles (10,000 pounds or larger) be able to hear a conversational voice from 15 feet in one ear, hearing aid permitted.

Strathie v. Department of Transportation This case successfully challenged a Pennsylvania state regulation which denied school bus driver licenses to hearing aid wearers. The lower federal court initially upheld the state's refusal to license an applicant who needed a hearing aid to meet the state's hearing requirements for school bus drivers. The lower court agreed with the state that the hearing aid could become dislodged from the ear, or be subject to mechanical failure, and also expressed concern that the hearing aid wearer might turn the volume of the hearing aid down, or be unable to localize the source of a noise.

The U.S. Court of Appeals for the Third Circuit found that the lower court had not properly considered the evidence presented by the hearing aid wearer. The appeals court directed the lower court to look to the evidence presented, and not to base its decision on unsubstantiated fears. The hearing-impaired plaintiff had presented evidence from expert witnesses to counter each of the lower court's concerns. His hearing aid was built into his eyeglass frame, and was no more likely to become dislodged than regular eyeglasses. To eliminate the possibility of mechanical failure, the plaintiff had suggested requiring periodic inspections and testing of the hearing aid, and the carrying of spare batteries. Moreover, the lower court had not considered his proposal that only hearing aids with preset volume controls be permitted. Finally, the lower court had discounted evidence that stereo hearing aids improve localization of sound, and the plaintiff's suggestion that individuals be tested for ability to localize sound with a hearing aid.

The appeals court ruled that, under Section 504 of the Rehabilitation Act of 1973, the state had to show that accommodations to hearing aid wearers would either modify the essential nature of its program or put an undue burden on the state. Following the decision by the court of appeals, the State of Pennsylvania agreed to lift its ban on the use of hearing aids for school bus drivers.

Kautzky v. Firestone Tire & Rubber Co. The U.S. Department of Labor decided in 1980 that a contractor doing business with the federal government could not disqualify a hearing-impaired worker from using a forklift solely based on his hearing disability. The complainant in this case had, over the period of five years, exhibited an ability to operate a forklift and similar equipment safely for the company. Based on his prior performance, the Department of Labor found that transfer from his position of operating such machinery, based on his disability, was discriminatory and violated Section 503 of the Rehabilitation Act of 1973.

Costner v. United States A U.S. court of appeals found that the U.S. Department of Transportation regulation that forbids all epileptics from driving in interstate commerce does not violate equal protection guarantees, and is not unconstitutional. The court was not swayed by the fact that the individual plaintiff in this case had not had a seizure for 20 years, and had been driving safely in interstate commerce for 15 years. The case is important for the hearing-impaired community as it interprets the same regulation that prohibits hearing-impaired persons from driving in interstate commerce.

Bibliography

Costner v. U.S., 33 Fair Empl. Prac. Cas. (BNA) 292 (8th Cir. 1983).

Federal Highway Administration, Docket No. MC-73, 41 Fed. Reg. 55898 (December 23, 1976).

Flail v. Bolger, No. 80-3259 (D.N.J. 1981) (unreported Consent Order).

Kautzky v. Firestone Tire & Rubber Co., Complaint No. GB/G790065 (U.S. Department of Labor, Employment Standards Administration, Office of Federal Contract Compliance Programs, January 18, 1980).

Southeastern Community College v. Davis, 442 U.S. 397 (1979).

Strathie v. Department of Transportation, 716 F.2d 227 (3d Cir., 1983).

Elaine Gardner

dsh ABSTRACTS

In May 1959 the American Speech and Hearing Association (ASHA; now the American Speech-Language-Hearing Association) and Gallaudet College in Washington, D.C., formed a mutual association called the National Index on Deafness, Speech, and Hearing (NIDSH). Its purpose was to provide information in condensed form from published sources concerning the processes and disorders of human speech and hearing. Four months later this newly formed association agreed to publish a quarterly journal, *dsh Abstracts* (dsh being the initials for deafness, speech, and hearing), which would summarize the relevant literature. In July 1960 the National Index changed its name to Deafness Speech and Hearing Publications, Inc. (DSHP). It is run by a board of directors made up of a president, vice-president, secretary, treasurer, and two or three additional members. Traditionally, half the members of the board come from Gallaudet College and half from the American Speech-Language-Hearing Association. *See* AMERICAN SPEECH-LANGUAGE-HEARING ASSOCIATION; GALLAUDET COLLEGE.

dsh Abstracts was managed by an editor appointed by the Board of Deafness Speech and Hearing Publications. The editor selected a varying number of assistant or associate editors. In addition, from the outset of the journal in October 1960 until 1982, 45 to 60 volunteer abstractors, drawn from professionals (speech pathologists, audiologists, educators, and so on) around the country and abroad, contributed freely of their time, regularly searching assigned journals and summarizing articles of interest to fellow professionals.

dsh Abstracts, appearing in January, April, July, and October, published nonevaluative abstracts of articles dealing with deafness, speech, and hearing. The first two editors of *dsh Abstracts* were from Gallaudet College: Stephen P. Quigley edited the first two issues of volume I in 1960; he was succeeded by Jerome D. Schein, who continued as editor until 1965. Jesse J. Villareal from the University of Texas, Austin, became the third editor and remained until October 1971. Ernest J. Moncada, of Gallaudet College, replaced him in 1972.

From the journal's inception until April 1983, the format and search procedures of *dsh Abstracts* remained fairly consistent. Four to five hundred domestic and foreign journals were regularly searched by editors and volunteer abstractors. Abstracts were usually kept to a maximum of 250–300 words. Relevant books were also abstracted, and in 1964 Ira M. Ventry became the journal's book editor and continued in that office until his death in 1983.

In 1983 a major change was introduced. Prompted by a desire to improve *dsh Abstracts* currency and increase its coverage, Deafness Speech and Hearing Publications entered into negotiations with the National Library of Medicine in Bethesda, Maryland. The result was an agreement under which *dsh Abstracts* would select relevant citations from MEDLINE, the National Library's computerized bibliographic data base. MEDLINE reviews 3000 biomedical domestic and foreign journals monthly. As a consequence of MEDLINE's wide coverage, *dsh Abstracts* was able to increase its own coverage substantially (volume I, for example, contained 1604 abstracts; volume XXIII contained 3536 abstracts). Because of this new and plentiful source of abstracts, *dsh Abstracts* reluctantly disbanded its group of volunteer abstractors. A significant innovation with this new service was the inclusion of a subject index with every issue, in addition to the cumulative annual index in the October issue.

Early in 1985 Gallaudet College and the American Speech-Language-Hearing Association decided, for financial reasons, to discontinue subsidizing *dsh Abstracts*. The last issue they published was in October 1985.

Ernest J. Moncada

DU BELLAY, JOACHIM
(1522–1560)

Joachim du Bellay, one of the great French poets of the Renaissance, was born in the Château de la Turmelière in the province of Anjou about 1522. The youngest son of Jean du Bellay and Renée Chabot, he was orphaned at about the age of 10 and left in the rather indifferent care of his older brother, René. Of his early childhood and adolescence, almost nothing is known. Du Bellay had frail health, and an undetermined illness brought about gradual hearing loss. The details of his early education are not documented, but being the son of a minor noble, it is probable he had some rudimentary knowledge of Latin. He does mention in his poetry that his brother did not take any interest in providing him with a good education. Wishing to further his studies, du Bellay went to the University of Poitiers for the possible opportunity to study law. Whether or not du Bellay actually enrolled in the university remains questionable. What is significant about his sojourn in Poitiers is the early evidence of his interest in poetry. He entered a Latin poetry contest; although he did not win, his enthusiasm for poetry and Latin continued. It is also during those years at Poitiers that du Bellay met Pierre Ronsard, also hearing-impaired, with whom he became a devoted and life-long friend. *See* RONSARD, PIERRE DE.

In 1547 du Bellay joined Ronsard in Paris as a student at the Collège de Coqueret directed by John Dorat, a famous scholar of Greek and Latin. Dorat's erudition and fame as an excellent teacher attracted students, many of whom were to become outstanding poets and writers of the French Renaissance. Under Dorat's tutelage, du Bellay pursued studies in Greek and Latin; he also learned Italian in order to reach Petrarch, Boccaccio, Bembo, and Ariosto. It was during those years that he became friends with other young humanists who together formed a group called the Pléiade with Ronsard as leader. The mission of the Pléiade was to encourage writers to immerse themselves in the literature of classical antiquity and to compose poetry in the French language with classical and Italian poetic forms as models.

In 1548 Thomas Sebillet, a Parisian lawyer, published a pamphlet entitled *Art poétique françoys*. This treatise encouraged poets to write within the accepted poetic tradition, especially that of Mellin de Saint-Gellais, a popular poet of that period. The Pléiade decided that Sebillet's ideas needed to be challenged and chose du Bellay to be their spokesperson. DuBellay's response took the form of *La Deffence et illustration de la langue françoyse*; published in 1549, it defended the French language as capable of great literature in both prose and poetry. Du Bellay further stated that his readers should engage in the study of Greek and Latin, that medieval literary genres be replaced by those modeled on classical Greek and Latin literature, and that France needed a great epic poem in the tradition of Homer and Virgil. Although hastily written and

assembled, du Bellay's document represented an important national declaration. It praised the French language as a medium of great literature and appealed to French pride and patriotism. The year of the publication of the *Deffence* marks the final year of du Bellay's stay at the Collège de Coqueret.

The year 1549 proved especially productive for du Bellay. At Easter he published *L'Olive*, a collection of sonnets written in honor of an ideal woman named Olive. This work is early evidence of du Bellay's skill in the composition of sonnets. In November 1549 du Bellay published the *Recueil de poësie*. Du Bellay hoped through this collection of poems to curry the favor of the wealthy and powerful and to advance his literary career.

Sickly from an early age, du Bellay found himself confined to bed in 1550–1551. The exact nature of his illness is not known, but it resulted in the onset of his hearing loss. However, in spite of being bedridden, du Bellay continued to work on his poetry, publishing a second edition of *L'Olive* in 1550. From time to time he recovered and his hearing improved.

In 1553 du Bellay's cousin Cardinal Jean du Bellay invited him to travel to Rome and to become a member of his household. Du Bellay promptly accepted the invitation and left Paris in April 1553. When he reached the city of Lyons, his fellow poets feted him. After two very pleasant weeks, the Cardinal's entourage left for Geneva. Because of that city's Protestant majority, the Cardinal stayed only briefly and continued his journey through the Alps. During the passage through the mountains, du Bellay suffered another attack of fever. Following the medical practice of the time, he was bled. The fever abated and in June he arrived safely in Rome, the repository of many of the classical world's treasures. Here among the ruins, the poet could commune with those Latin authors whom he loved to read.

Du Bellay's expectations of what life in the Cardinal's household would be like did not coincide with the reality of his position. It soon became apparent to du Bellay that his role was secretary, messenger, and manager of the Cardinal's domestic staff. His daily tasks were particularly onerous because of his hearing impairment. This position of inferiority coupled with his disillusionment with Rome caused him to have feelings of loneliness and homesickness. Du Bellay's ideal vision of a Rome based on the writings of authors of classical antiquity was shattered when he was confronted with the reality of the intrigues and the immorality of some members of the papal court. This rendered him unhappy and cynical. In the spring of 1556, his unhappiness was mitigated somewhat when he fell in love with Faustina, an Italian woman married to an older man. This love affair soon ended when Faustina's husband had her confined to a convent. In August 1557 du Bellay left Rome and arrived in Paris in October. There du Bellay published a collection of poems written in Latin, the third book containing poems honoring Faustina.

Du Bellay's life in Paris became reasonably comfortable thanks to several benefices he had received. He continued in the Cardinal's employ as an administrator of business affairs for the Archdiocese of Paris. This position led him to quarrel with his distant cousin Eustache du Bellay, the vicar of the Archdiocese. The latter complained to the Cardinal that du Bellay was ill-tempered and impossible to deal with because of his deafness. Du Bellay was forced to send letters to the Cardinal defending himself and blaming Eustache for the problems.

However, the fulfillment of his duties, the quarrels with Eustache, and his deafness did not interfere with his literary output. In January 1558 he published *Les Regrets* and in March *Les Antiquités de Rome*.

Les Regrets is a collection of 191 sonnets. He composed the majority of them in his final years in Rome and the remainder upon his return to Paris. This collection is, in many ways, a poetic diary. In them is found his loneliness and nostalgia for his beloved France, his disappointment with Rome, his resulting unhappiness. These highly personal and emotional themes give a lyricism to *Les Regrets* that is not present in his earlier works.

Les Antiquités de Rome is a collection of 32 sonnets composed in solemn and elegant language. The main theme is praise of the ancient city of Rome. In meditating on the greatness, and the ruins, of that city, du Bellay conveys a pathos of lost grandeur.

Another volume published on his return to Paris was *Divers jeux rustiques*, a collection of poems on various themes. It contains his poem on deafness, "Hymne de la Surdité," which is dedicated to Ronsard. The poem is considered to be ironic in tone. Du Bellay reminds Ronsard that deafness in fact may be a blessing in disguise, since the poet is spared extraneous noises thus allowing the poetic muse to function unhampered. The remarkable quality of the poem is du Bellay's ability to make light of his hearing loss, since in his poetry he often complains of his ill health. Perhaps this poem is the poet's way of coming to terms with his own hearing impairment, a loss which caused him to be difficult to get along with, but may have helped to shape him as a great poet of the French language.

In the final months of du Bellay's life, his deafness was so profound that he could communicate only through writing. On the evening of January 1, 1560, du Bellay had dinner with Canon Claude de Bize. On returning home, he began to write some verse but had a stroke and died. Although he had given up the title of Canon of Notre Dame four years earlier, he was buried with all the honors due a canon of the cathedral.

Bibliography

Chamard, H.: *Joachim du Bellay*, 1900.
Keating, L. C.: *Joachim du Bellay*, 1971.
Saulnier, V. L.: *Du Bellay, L'homme et l'oeuvre*, 1951.

T. J. McGovern

E

EAR

Anatomically the ear is an intricate conglomeration of structures. It is much more than the "flap-like appendage" (the auricle) on the side of the head: the term ear refers to the entire peripheral auditory mechanism or apparatus. The auditory mechanism includes everything from the readily visible external or outer ear (of which the auricle is a part) to the intricate structures of the inner ear, located deep in the temporal bone of the skull, and the nerve leaving the inner ear.

The basic principle of anatomy that structure dictates function is certainly true of the ear. The external ear "collects" the sound and directs it to the internal parts, beginning with the eardrum (tympanic membrane). The latter closes off the middle ear, a cavity that houses three small bones or ossicles known collectively as the ossicular chain. The external and middle parts together, often referred to as the conducting apparatus, provide the means by which sound is transformed into mechanical vibration. They conduct sound energy to the internal or inner ear, a complex labyrinth tunneled out of the innermost part of the temporal bone at the base of the skull.

Within the part of the inner ear called the cochlea, sound energy is finally converted into an effective stimulus for the end organ of hearing. This tiny organ, coiled up in the cochlea, is formed in part of thousands upon thousands of delicate hair-bearing cells and supporting structures. The hair cells, which are capable of detecting incredibly minute vibrations, initiate a message to the brain to signal the presence of the sound and to provide detailed information about it. Other organs are also found in the inner ear that help people maintain their sense of balance. These organs form the peripheral vestibular system; they also contain delicate hair cells.

By means of cells called neurons, which make up the acoustic (VIIIth cranial) nerve (and other nerves), auditory information is transmitted to and within the central nervous system (CNS). Auditory neurons are collected together in distinct tracts within the brain, forming the central auditory pathways. These pathways are built up of series of neurons connected more or less in tandem, and the connections between them occur within various nuclei, somewhat like relay stations, along the pathways. The auditory pathways lead from the auditory periphery, through the brainstem, to cortical areas of the brain. While an incredible amount of information processing is carried out by the brainstem auditory system, it is by virtue of the cerebral cortex that one is able to process complex stimuli, such as speech, and interpret them. *See* BRAIN.

The development of the ear begins very early in life, at the end of the third week of gestation. Formation of the intricate and delicate structures of the ear and the equally intricate "wiring" of the auditory system consumes nearly the full term of pregnancy (depending upon what criterion is used to identify a fully operational system). Still, much of the ear is fairly well developed by the end of the first trimester, wherein the auricle, the bones of the middle ear, and the inner ear (including the organ of hearing) all are approaching their adult forms, and even their adult sizes in the cases of the ossicles and the hearing organ. Considering the numerous foci of activity, the diversity of materials involved (soft tissue, cartilage, and bone), and the fact that the different parts of the ear have different embryologic derivations, the timing of the different stages of development is clearly critical. A deformity will result from disruption at any stage. However, because the outer, middle, and inner ears are somewhat independent in their origin and development, a deformity may involve only one part. On the other hand, the fact that parts of different organs or sensory systems have common embryologic derivations explains how multiple handicaps can result from congenital abnormalities (for instance, blindness and deafness).

On a percentage basis, clinically significant developmental defects of the auditory system are relatively uncommon. However, the structures of the peripheral and central auditory systems can be attacked by disease or other adverse factors (for example, exposure to excessive noise, toxic drugs, viruses, or aging) that may cause a defect leading to some loss of hearing. In the peripheral system, two general kinds of problems are possible. One involves the conducting apparatus wherein there is a blockage of the ear canal, damage to the delicate eardrum, or impediment of vibration of the ossicular chain. The result is a decrease in the sound energy reaching the inner ear, and so a loss of hearing sensitivity. The other type of problem involves some aspect of the functioning of hair cells or the neurons attached to them. Such problems also lead to a loss of hearing sensitivity, although other kinds of problems (such as decreased ability to distinguish between words) also may result. However, it is also possible to have both types of problems concomitantly, involving both the conduction and sensorineural mechanisms. Only some of the conductive problems are medically treatable, and the sensorineural defects are largely uncorrectable by medical treatment or surgery.

Defects of the central nervous system also can occur. These generally manifest themselves in terms of the integrative aspects of hearing, for example, two-eared information or demanding conditions of speech perception. Generally, problems that may be involved, other than developmental defects, are tumors, vascular accidents, infections, or breakdowns in the ability of auditory neurons to properly conduct the neural signals.

Like other parts of the body, the auditory system has some ability to mend, although the possibilities are increasingly limited as the site of damage becomes more central. Also, although two-eared listening affords significant benefits over one-eared listening, even the complete loss of functioning of one ear does not create much of a communicative handicap.

John D. Durrant

Fetal Development

In the remarkable chain of events taking place between conception and the emergence of a newborn child, development of the ear presents an interesting progression. Formation of structure in the human ear during pregnancy mirrors historic stages of the evolutionary emergence of the ear.

Sequential Development

Specific stages occur in this sequence of events generating the sophisticated mammalian ear. First, the segmented inner ear and neural connections form. These segments, the semicircular canals, vestibule, and cochlea, are among the earliest complex structures in the developing fetus to reach completion. The inner ear is practically of adult size and complexity by the end of the first trimester and attains full adult size in the fifth month. The possibility of the mother contracting certain diseases or other health problems which can lead to malformation of the inner ear causes deep concern in early pregnancy. Included in an extensive list of extrinsic causes of fetal auditory maldevelopment are infection, tumors, trauma, neurologic disorders, metabolic imbalances, and rubella (German measles). The disease process can interfere with normal structural development of the cochlear region. Further, certain drugs are potentially harmful to normal formation of the inner ear. After the first trimester, however, the inner ear is formed and is somewhat less subject to untoward influences by disease or other factors that cause structural malformation. *See* HEARING LOSS: Prenatal Causes.

The middle ear is the next auditory region to achieve structural completion. This occurs in about the fifth month of pregnancy. Arising from the margin between the head and neck of the fetus, the complex mechanical structure of the middle ear takes form, with its precise relations between bones and membranes and its sophisticated suspension system. In developmental disorders, middle-ear malformations are common collateral problems with clefts of the palate or lip. These malformations occur after the first trimester as the facial region is assuming its final embryonic form.

The external ear is the last of the ear tissues to take shape. Mammals are the only creatures with an external earflap, called the pinna or auricle. Beginning in the second month and continuing into the fifth month, the pinna of the fetus extends as an outcropping of tissue in three directions. This gives rise to the three-sided auricle. This final step in development of the auditory mechanism is the one that has the greatest range of individual variation. Some authorities maintain that the external ear, specifically the pinna, is as definitive for personal identification as are fingerprints. By the end of the sixth month of pregnancy, the ear is formed and the fetus can react to sounds; despite earlier beliefs of many that babies were born deaf.

DETAILED EMBRYOLOGY
A summary outline of the events during the development of the fetal auditory structure is given in the table. An early seed of human hearing structure, the auditory placode, develops from an infolding of tissue, the auditory pit. The approximately 11-millimeter-long six-week-old embryo has a more refined placode that is called the otocyst. At this stage in development, the architecture of the region has already been divided into two separate anatomic and functional areas, the auditory and vestibular (balance) systems. At about the same time, considerable activity begins in the throat region, where several convolutions (arches) can be identified. From these tissues, the external- and middle-ear structures will emerge. Out of view but in the same general area as the throat, the source for the middle ear is beginning to form into an elongated pouch. The construction of ear tissues continues in systematic order until about the thirty-seventh week of pregnancy, at which time the

Summary of Major Steps in Fetal Development of the Ear

Fetal Week	Inner Ear	Middle Ear	External Ear
3d	Auditory placode; auditory pit	Tubotympanic recess begins to develop	—
4th	Auditory vesicle (otocyst); vestibular-cochlear division	—	Tissue thickenings begin to form
5th	—	—	Primary auditory meatus begins
6th	Utricle and saccule present; semicircular canals begin	—	Six hillocks evident; cartilage begins to form
7th	One cochlear coil present; sensory cells in utricle and saccule	—	Auricles move dorsolaterally
8th	Ductus reuniens present; sensory cells in semicircular canals	Incus and malleus present in cartilage; lower half of tympanic cavity formed	Outer cartilaginous third of external canal formed
9th	—	Three tissue layers at tympanic membrane are present	—
11th	2½ cochlear coils present; VIIIth nerve attaches to cochlear duct	—	—
12th	Sensory cells in cochlea; membranous labyrinth complete; otic capsule begins to ossify	—	—
15th	—	Cartilaginous stapes formed	—
16th	—	Ossification of malleus and incus begins	—
18th	—	Stapes begins to ossify	—
20th	Maturation of inner ear; inner ear reaches adult size	—	Auricle is adult shape, but continues to grow until age nine years
21st	—	Meatal plug disintegrates exposing tympanic membrane	—
30th	—	Pneumatization of tympanum	External auditory canal continues to mature until age seven
32d	—	Malleus and incus complete ossification	—
34th	—	Mastoid air cells develop	—
35th	—	Antrum is pneumatized	—
37th	—	Epitympanum is pneumatized; stapes continues to develop until adulthood; tympanic membrane changes relative position during first two years of life	—

After J. L. Northern and M. P. Down, *Hearing in Children*, 2d ed., Williams and Wilkins, 1978.

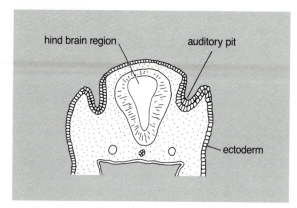

Head region of 12-day-old fetus in frontal section showing the auditory pit.

building blocks are in place, and the only changes that occur are progressive growth of some structures into adulthood.

It is apparent from the table that each subcompartment of the ear follows its own timetable, with apparent independence from the others. However, there is considerable interdependence between subcomponents in achieving structural completion. Maldevelopment of one may lead to structural disorder of a nearby component. Further, a single disease or other extrinsic influence can disrupt development of more than one part of the auditory mechanism simultaneously.

The inner ear achieves adult complexity and configuration first. As the otocyst divides, two sacs in the vestibular portion, the utricle and saccule, form during the sixth week. Around the seventh week, the cochlea begins to elongate, and coils ultimately

Six-week human embryo showing auditory region in context with other significant body parts.

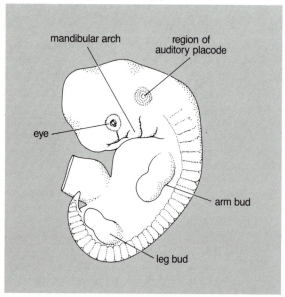

to about 2⅔ turns. By the eighth week, the tube connecting the cochlea and saccule (ductus reuniens) is present, and the semicircular canals produce sensory cells that ultimately will give information on acceleration, deceleration, and rotation. Importantly, during the eleventh week, the auditory nerve and cochlea are approaching final form. During the next week, when sensory cells appear in the cochlea, the structure is complete, and development of the protective bony shell begins (os-

(Top) Closeup of mandibular arch showing six hillocks, numbered for reference. (Center) Formation of pinna during seventh week. Note migration of each hillock as signified by numbers. (Bottom) Adult pinna illustrating final shapes formed from hillocks, numbered as before.

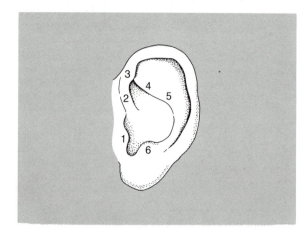
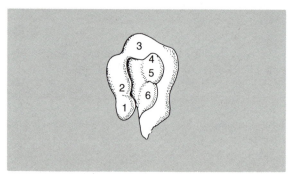
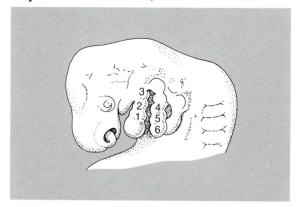

sification). By the twentieth week, the inner ear is complete.

Middle-ear formation begins early but is not complete until some time after birth. In the eighth week, cartilages take on peculiar shapes in the middle-ear region and form into the malleus and incus (hammer and anvil). Ultimately, they ossify and are held in place by a sophisticated suspension system. By the ninth week, the eardrum is forming into a three-layered diaphragm. The third middle-ear bone, the stapes, begins to appear in the fifteenth week and begins to ossify by the eighteenth week. In the twenty-first week, the ear canal begins to clear when a sealing plug of tissue disintegrates. Air begins to fill the middle-ear spaces in the twenty-first week. The malleus and incus complete their metamorphosis from cartilage to bone in the thirty-second week. The solid tissue posterior to the ear canal changes into a system of cavities (mastoid cells) during the thirty-fourth week. These cells receive air beginning in the thirty-fifth week, and the middle-ear structure is formed by the thirty-seventh week. At this time, although growth continues for years, the middle ear can be considered functionally complete.

Tissue formation for the external ear begins in the fourth week, but there is little similarity between the early structure and the finished product. A remarkable remolding process begins with the formation of hillocks (six bumps) on the first and second arches in the 11-millimeter six-week-old embryo. In the 15-millimeter embryo, in about the seventh week, these hillocks combine to give rough shape to the earflap. Final shaping is accomplished by the twentieth week, although growth continues into adulthood.

Bibliography

Anson, Barry, and James Donaldson: *Surgical Anatomy of the Temporal Bone and Ear*, 3d ed., W. B. Saunders, Philadelphia, 1981.

Holt, L. Emmett, and John Howland: *The Diseases of Infancy and Childhood*, D. Appleton and Co., New York, 1931.

Northern, Jerry L., and Marion P. Downs: *Hearing in Children*, 2d ed., Williams and Wilkins, Baltimore, 1978.

Warwick, Roger, and Peter L. Williams (eds.): *Gray's Anatomy*, 35th Brit. ed., W. B. Saunders, Philadelphia, 1973.

David M. Lipscomb

Anatomy

The auditory mechanism is subdivided into four regions: external ear, middle ear, inner ear, and the nerve of hearing. When sound encounters the ear, it is directed into the external auditory meatus (ear canal) where it strikes the tympanic membrane (eardrum), setting this thin membrane in motion. The first of three bones in the middle ear (the malleus or hammer) is directly connected to the tympanic membrane; thus the bone moves with the membrane. Two other bones, the incus (anvil) and stirrup (stapes), complete the chain of bones called ossicles. With movement of the malleus, the other two bones are also displaced. The ossicles transmit the vibrations across the middle ear to the inner ear. One important feature of the structure of the middle ear is the suspension system for the ossicular chain which is designed to negate the mass of the bones. Two muscles, one attached to the malleus and one attached to the stapes, are part of that suspension system.

The inner ear is filled with fluid. The organ of Corti in the inner ear contains sensory receptor cells that respond in many different ways, depending upon the sound character. An elaborate neural pathway leads from the inner ear to the central nervous system through as many as four way stations, each one adding to the perceptual value of the signal.

David M. Lipscomb

EXTERNAL EAR

The external ear, whose function is to receive sound waves, consists of the auricle and the external auditory meatus, which is a short tube bound medially by the tympanic membrane.

Auricle The auricle is made of an irregularly shaped plate of elastic cartilage 0.5 to 1 millimeter thick. The helix is the outer rim of the auricle; the concha is the well of the ear, and there is a small prominence anteriorly called the tragus.

The skin, which is firmly adherent on the anterior surface and looser on the posterior surface because of presence of subcutaneous tissue, is covered with fine hairs that are furnished with many sebaceous glands and a few sweat glands.

Three extrinsic muscles connect the auricle to the skull: the anterior, superior, and posterior auricular muscles. These muscles, if fully developed, are able to move the auricle. Six or more small rudimentary intrinsic muscles have been described in connection with the cartilage of the external ear, but they are of no apparent importance.

Both extrinsic and intrinsic muscles are supplied by branches from the temporal and posterior auricular branches of the facial nerve (cranial nerve VII).

The blood supply is from the external carotid artery through the posterior auricular and anterior temporal arteries to the posterior and anterior surfaces, respectively. The venous drainage is through the corresponding posterior auricular and superficial temporal veins. The posterior auricular vein drains into the external jugular vein, while the superficial temporal joins the posterior facial vein and drains into the internal jugular vein. The drainage

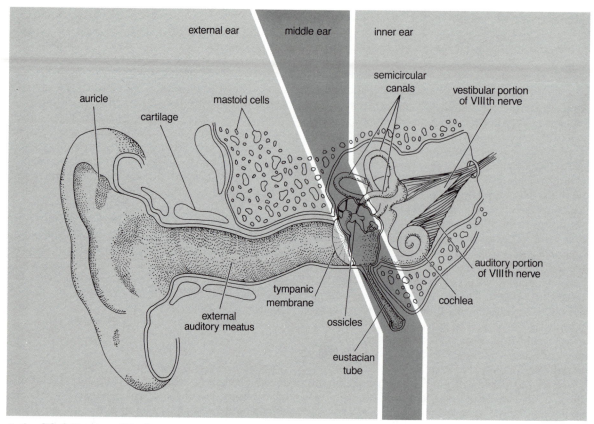

A simplified diagram of the human ear.

of posterior communicating branches into the mastoid emissary vein leads intracranially into the lateral venous sinus.

The sensory nerve supply of the external ear is by the greater auricular nerve to the lower third of both the anterior and posterior surfaces. The lesser occipital nerve supplies the rest of the posterior surface, and the auriculotemporal (cranial nerve V) supplies the rest of the anterior surface. The concavity of the concha between the area supplied by cranial nerve V and that supplied by cervical nerves is supplied by fibers of cranial nerves X, IX, and VII.

The lymphatic drainage from the upper part of the anterior surface of the auricle is to the parotid lymph node glands, while posteriorly it is to the glands at the mastoid tip and inferiorly to glands beneath the ear.

External Auditory Canal   The boundaries of the external canal are: (1) anteriorly: mandibular fossa and parotid gland; (2) posteriorly: mastoid; (3) superiorly: epitympanic recess medially and cranial cavity laterally; and (4) inferiorly: parotid gland.

The S-shaped external auditory canal has a shortened posterosuperior wall about 25 millimeters long and a longer anteroinferior wall, about 30 millimeters. It is elliptic in cross section. The lateral one-third is cartilaginous and directed upward, backward, and inward and has two anterior horizontal clefts, the fissures of Santorini. The medial two-thirds, which is bony, is directed inward, downward, and forward. The canal can be partially straightened by pulling the auricle outward, backward, and upward.

The bony portion of the canal is formed by the tympanic and squamous portions of the temporal bone and has a constriction (the isthmus) about 5 millimeters lateral to the drum. Another constriction in the external auditory canal is present at the bony and cartilaginous junction. The canal skin over the cartilage is relatively thick (1–1.5 millimeters) and adherent to it. It has hairs, sebaceous glands, and ceruminous glands. The sebaceous glands are similar to those in other parts of the body and open into the lumina of the hair follicles. The ceruminous glands lie in the deeper portion of the dermis. Their number is between 1000 and 2000 per human ear. The skin over the bony portion of the canal is very thin (0.1 millimeter) and firmly adherent to the underlying periosteum. It contains no hairs or glands except posterosuperiorly, where sebaceous glands and fine hairs may be present. Self-cleansing of the ear canal is effected by lateral migration of skin at a rate of 0.05 millimeter per day.

The nerve supply of the external auditory canal anteriorly and superiorly is through the auriculo-temporal nerve (cranial nerve V) and posteriorly and inferiorly through the auricular (Arnold's) nerve (cranial nerve X) and branches from the facial nerve and cranial nerve IX. The blood supply is provided by the posterior auricular and superficial temporal arteries as well as by the deep auricular artery, which is a branch of the first part of the maxillary (internal maxillary). Venous drainage is by way of the maxillary and external jugular veins and the pterygoid venous plexus. Lymphatic drainage is to the anterior, posterior, and inferior auricular nodes.

Robin T. Cotton

MIDDLE EAR

The middle ear is an air-filled cavity, interposed between the external ear canal and the fluid-filled spaces of the inner ear. The three compartments are separated from each other by air- and fluid-tight membranes. The middle ear has an approximate volume of 2 cubic centimeters, but communicates with an often larger system of interconnected air cells (pneumatic system of the ear) that extends mainly into the mastoid bone. (The outer surface of this bone can be felt behind the pinna or auricle.) The combined volume of the pneumatic spaces varies over a wide range. On the one extreme, it may be almost totally absent; on the other, it may have a volume as large as 25 cubic centimeters. The middle ear is further connected with the nasopharynx, the upper end of the pharynx, via the Eustachian tube, but this communication is normally closed; it can be opened by various maneuvers. The middle-ear spaces are separated from the cranial cavity, which houses the brain and associated tissues, by plates of relatively thin bone, through which middle-ear infections may be transmitted, leading to potentially serious endocranial complications.

Separating the middle ear from the external ear canal is the tympanic membrane or eardrum. It forms an exponential cone with its apex pointing inward. The membrane is thin and somewhat transparent, like a pane of frosted glass. Its outer layer consists of skin, continuous with that of the ear canal, and its inner layer of mucous membrane, which lines the entire middle ear. Between these two covering layers lies the membrana propria, consisting of two fibrous strata. The fibers of the outer stratum run predominantly in radial directions and those of the inner stratum mainly in circular directions. The handle of the malleus, a long slender process, is fairly tightly connected with this fiber system, its lower end being virtually woven into it. The latter coincides with the apex of the tympanic membrane cone, a place that is referred to as the umbo (navel).

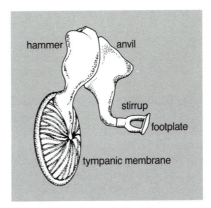

Tympanic membrane and ossicular chain.

The small section of the membrane above the handle of the malleus does not possess the membrana propria. There is only a very thin connective tissue layer without the typical fiber network. It is known as pars flaccida, in contrast to the lower pars tensa.

The blood vessels supplying the membrane normally are so fine that they are not visible to the naked eye. Mechanical or inflammatory irritations engorge them. Infections make them so diffuse that the whole membrane takes on a reddish hue; at the same time, it grows opaque as its tissues become edematous.

Lying in the middle-ear space are three ossicles, named for their respective shapes: malleus (hammer), incus (anvil), and stapes (stirrup). Their dry weights are 26 milligrams for the malleus or incus respectively, and about 3 milligrams for the stapes. The ossicles form a mobile chain connecting the tympanic membrane with the inner ear. There is an intimate relation between the tympanic membrane and the malleus handle. The malleus and incus are rather tightly joined with each other, and they are suspended between ligaments that permit them to rotate as a unit in the manner of a lever of the second class. The rotational axis lies ap-

The middle-ear system acting as a hydraulic lever (somewhat idealized).

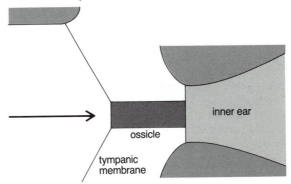

proximately in the horizontal plane, parallel to that of the tympanic membrane, which in turn faces toward the side of the head. The footplate of the stapes is fitted in an elastic but fluid-tight manner into an opening of the inner ear, called the oval window. Another inner-ear window, the round window, looks into the middle ear. It is closed by a membrane and serves as a pressure release for the fluid of the cochlea.

The reason for the existence of the obturator foramen, the hole in the middle of the stapes that gives it its characteristic shape, is that a large artery, the stapedial artery, passes through here during embryological life, supplying the side of the face. The function of this artery later is taken over by another one, and the stapedial artery degenerates in almost all but a few cases; the foramen, however, is retained for life.

Between any two adjacent ossicles are genuine joints, but they are not very strong, especially that between the slender lower end of the incus and the head of the stapes. Therefore, injuries to the ear frequently lead to ossicular dislocations. They rarely repair themselves on their own. Furthermore, infections may destroy parts of the ossicles, most frequently the long process of the incus. Such missing parts are never replaced during the healing process. In both cases the chain remains permanently defective.

Two tiny skeletal muscles, the smallest of the entire body, terminate at the neck of the malleus or that of the stapes respectively: the tensor tympani muscle and the stapedius muscle.

Running freely between the necks of malleus and incus, a slender nerve, the chorda tympani, traverses the middle ear. It carries taste fibers to the side of the tongue. This nerve is a branch of a larger one, the facial nerve, that mainly supplies motor fibers to the muscles of the face. It traverses the middle ear too, undergoing two sharp bends (first and second "knees") in the process. In contrast to the chorda tympani nerve, it is housed in a narrow bony canal that is not entirely closed toward the middle ear. Therefore, facial nerve paralysis is an occasional complication of middle-ear diseases, making the side of the face that the nerve supplies hang down in a characteristic, flaccid manner. Such paralyses also occur in the absence of middle-ear diseases. Often the paralyses persist because of the narrowness of the facial nerve canal that prevents the needed expansion of the tissues enclosed inside when they have become edematous or swollen. The nerve may recover spontaneously. If not, surgery may be required.

All structures housed in the middle ear—the ossicles, their ligamental suspensions, the two muscles, the two nerves—are wrapped up in their appropriate connective tissue coverings, such as the periosteum, fascia, or perineurium. These are in turn covered by mucous membrane. Because the walls of the middle-ear cavity also are lined by periosteum and mucous membrane (the mucoperiosteum), the remaining air space is constricted in some places, constituting a number of quite narrow passages. During middle-ear infections, they can become clogged by mucous membrane swelling, trapping infectious material behind them.

The mucous membrane carries a ciliated epithelium, although only on its nonmoving parts, that is, mainly on the tympanic walls. Each epithelial cell possesses a short, hairlike process (cilium) extending for a short distance into the middle-ear lumen. These cilia move in a concerted fashion so as to propel a thin blanket of mucus slowly but continuously toward the Eustachian tube orifice and from there into the pharynx, since the tube is clad by the same type of epithelium. This ciliary action removes cellullar debris, keeping the middle ear clean. It also drains it during mild infections, when secretions are accumulated within the middle-ear space. With more severe infections, the cilia may become paralyzed, or their cells are lost altogether. During the healing process, the cells usually reconstitute themselves and recover their function.

Following repeated and prolonged middle-ear infections, the mucous membrane may form dense networks of scar tissue in various parts of the middle ear, for instance around the ossicles. This process, known as tympanosclerosis, does not reverse itself on its own.

A disorder called otosclerosis may develop mainly at and around the stapes footplate. This insidious process starts gradually, usually in early middle life. It creates new bone, ultimately fixating the footplate rather rigidly in the oval window.

The various infectious and other pathologic processes result in hearing impairments of various degrees, but never in complete deafness. Many of the middle-ear structural disorders, including remnants of infections, can be surgically corrected, otosclerosis being a prime example. Hearing aids also serve well for alleviating the hearing handicap.

Juergen Tonndorf

EUSTACHIAN TUBE

An elongating, entodermally lined pouch between the first and second branchial arches in the embryo forms the primitive eustachian tube and tympanic cavity. Since it is an extension of the pharynx, the lining mucosa of the eustachian tube is similar to the ciliated respiratory mucosa of the nasopharynx. Extending from the middle ear to the nasopharynx, this tubular structure allows air to be transmitted to the middle ear, ensuring that the static pressure in the middle ear is close to atmospheric pressure, a condition that creates minimum opposition

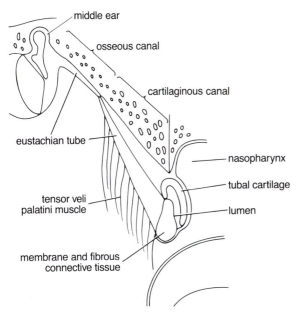

Configuration of the eustachian tube, which extends from the nasopharynx to the middle ear.

(impedance) to the flow of sound energy across the middle ear to the inner ear.

The configuration of the eustachian tube resembles an hourglass, with the isthmus roughly dividing the bony posterior one-third from the anterior two-thirds. The course is downward and medial from the tympanic ostium to the nasopharyngeal ostium, which lies posterior to the inferior nasal turbinate. The bony canal is a rigid osseous tubular structure that remains open, whereas the cartilaginous canal is incompletely surrounded by supporting cartilage, and in the resting state tends to collapse. In cross section the cartilaginous tube consists of an inverted J-shaped cartilage medially turning over the superior wall to contribute to the lateral wall, which is completed with fibrous connective tissue.

Some important anatomical differences exist between the eustachian tubes of infants and adults that may explain the vulnerability of infants to recurrent middle-ear infections. In the infant, the bony portion of the canal is relatively longer, and the axis of the tube is more nearly horizontal with the nasopharyngeal orifice located in the plane of the hard palate. Although the diameter of the nasopharyngeal orifice is smaller in the infant, the point of maximal constriction maintains a slightly larger lumen or opening. The eustachian tube in the infant is thus shorter, more horizontal, more rigid, and less constricted at the isthmus.

At rest, the lumen of the eustachian tube remains closed. The tensor veli palatini muscle is composed in part of a deep bundle of fibers that attach to the inferolateral fibroelastic tissue of the anterior eustachian tube. The entire muscle forms a sling around the hamulus of the pterygoid bone before inserting into the palate. During normal swallowing, sneezing, and yawning, contraction of this muscle allows the tube to open. Abnormal palatal anatomy, such as a congenital cleft, precludes normal function of this muscular action and predisposes the individual to middle-ear disease.

Charles N. Ford

COCHLEA

The cochlea is the portion of the inner ear responsible for hearing. Named for the snaillike shape of the membranous part, the cochlea is a small, complex inner-ear organ, containing over 20 different types of cells. The membranous part is surrounded by bone. There are two entrances into the bone: the oval window and the round window. The stapes is attached to the oval window by an annular ring or ligament that allows it to move and transfer the sound vibrations to a fluid channel of the cochlea called the scala vestibuli.

Fluid Channels   The many different types of cells in the cochlea combine to form a structure called the membranous cochlea. This structure separates the fluid channel called the scala vestibuli from the fluid channel called the scala tympani. The membranous cochlea is positioned between the scala vestibuli and the scala tympani like a spiral staircase running for 2½ turns from the base of the cochlea to the top (apex).

The perilymph fluid of the scala vestibuli is separated from the fluid of the membranous cochlea

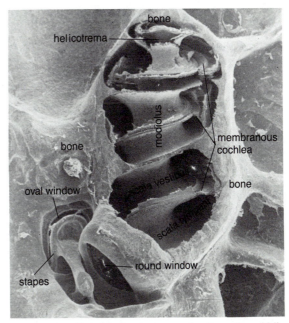

Section of cochlea showing its connection from the middle ear by the stapes.

(endolymph) by a membrane that is only two cells thick. This is known as Reissner's membrane and, like many structures in the cochlea, is named after the investigator who first reported it. This thin membrane is able to separate the sodium-rich perilymph fluid of the scala vestibuli from the potassium-rich endolymph fluid of the scala media and thereby to maintain a relative electrical charge of approximately 80 millivolts in the endolymph. This potential difference in the fluids is necessary for the sensory cells of the cochlea to function.

Sensory Cells   The sensory cells for hearing generally are called hair cells, because of the tuft of hairs properly known as stereocilia that appear in organized patterns on their upper surface. There are two distinct groups of hair cells. Three rows of outer hair cells spiral along the membranous cochlea from base to apex, a distance of approximately 33 millimeters. Each outer hair cell has a diameter of only 5 micrometers (5/1000 of a millimeter) and

has 100 to 150 stereocilia on its top formed in a W pattern. The average number of outer hair cells in a cochlea is 12,000.

There is only one row of inner hair cells, and it lies closer to the center or core of the cochlea than do the outer hair cells. Inner hair cells are separated from outer hair cells by a group of pillar cells, so named because of their supporting function. The approximately 3500 inner hair cells have a slightly greater diameter than outer hair cells. Each inner hair cell has 40–60 stereocilia on its top, where they form a shallow crescent pattern.

Organ of Corti   Both the hair cells and the pillar cells are part of the organ of Corti. This is a distinctive part of the membranous cochlea stretching from its base to its apex and resting on another part of the membranous cochlea called the basilar membrane. The basilar membrane has the perilymph fluid of the scala tympani on one side and the delicate organ of Corti on the other side. Move-

Diagram of cochlea as seen if a thin slice or cross section of the membranous cochlea is removed anywhere between the base and the apex.

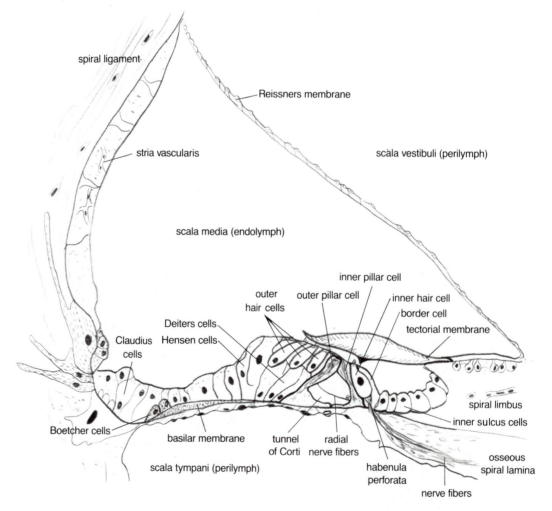

ments in the perilymph resulting from sound vibrations are transferred through the basilar membrane to the organ of Corti. The basilar membrane is constructed so that it is widest at the apical end of the cochlea and gradually tapers to its narrowest point at the basal end of the cochlea. The fibers that form the basilar membrane are much denser at the basal end than at the apical end. This construction means that the vibrations from high-frequency sounds will move the basilar membrane only at its basal end, and vibrations from sounds with a low pitch will move it most at the apical end of the cochlea. Because the organ of Corti rests on the basilar membrane, movements of the basilar membrane are passed to the organ of Corti and on to the hair cells that it contains.

A gelatinous tectorial membrane lies over the top of the organ of Corti, and the tips of the longest stereocilia on the outer hair cells are embedded in it. When a particular sound vibration causes a particular area of the basilar membrane to move, the tectorial membrane slides over the organ of Corti located on that area of the basilar membrane and thus moves the hair bundles on a small group of hair cells. Theoretically this causes a chemical reaction in those select hair cells on which the hair bundles have moved.

A number of nerve fibers are located at the base of each hair cell. Some of these nerve fibers bring messages to the cells, and some conduct messages in the form of electric signals away from the cells. The chemical reaction that has taken place in the hair cell due to the movement of the stereocilia or hair bundle becomes an electric signal in the nerve fibers attached to that hair cell. This is the electric signal that travels to the brain.

The complex membranous cochlea consists of many additional structures and cell types. Cells of the spiral ligament support the membranous cochlea and form a base for a structure known as the stria vascularis. The stria vascularis is rich in blood vessels and contains both light and dark cells. It is metabolically very active and is thought to give rise to the energy that supplies the 80-millivolt potential to the fluid of the endolymph directly in contact with it. Both Claudius cells and Boetcher cells rest on the basilar membrane and probably have a function in handling products related to the metabolic activity of the cochlea. Hensen cells, which structurally are part of the organ of Corti, also rest on the basilar membrane and probably perform functions similar to those of Claudius cells as well as a supporting function. Another important part of the organ of Corti is the Deiters' cells. They rest on the basilar membrane and both separate and support the outer hair cells that rest in cuplike depressions in the Deiters' cells. The outer and inner pillar cells also rest on the basilar membrane,

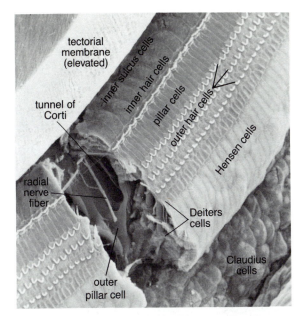

Highly magnified photograph of the organ of Corti.

and they join at their tops to form a fluid triangular space known as the tunnel of Corti. This space, through which the radial nerve fibers course to the bases of the outer hair cells, contains a fluid known as cortilymph. The composition of cortilymph is different from either the perilymph or the endolymph fluids discussed previously. It is the tops of the pillar cells that separate the three rows of outer hair cells from the single row of inner hair cells. The outer hair cells are surrounded by fluid spaces as they rest on the Deiters' cells; however, the inner hair cells are not surrounded by fluid but by other cells called border cells.

The tectorial membrane, which is attached on its underside to the hair tufts of the outer hair cells, is attached at its other end to the cells of the spiral limbus. The spiral limbus is separated from the inner hair cells by the cells of the inner sulcus. The inner sulcus rests on a bony ledge known as the osseous spiral lamina. It is through this bony shelf that the individual nerve fibers must travel to get the cochlear nerve that runs from the cochlea to the brain. On their way to and from the membranous cochlea, the individual nerve fibers travel through small holes in the bony shelf or osseous spiral lamina. These holes are known as the habenula perforata.

Cochlear Nerve When the fibers of the cochlear nerve leave the organ of Corti via the habenula perforata, they travel through spaces in the bone. The cell bodies of the nerve fibers lie together in an area known as the spiral ganglion. From the spiral ganglion the fibers continue on to the cochlear nerve. The cochlear nerve occupies the entire

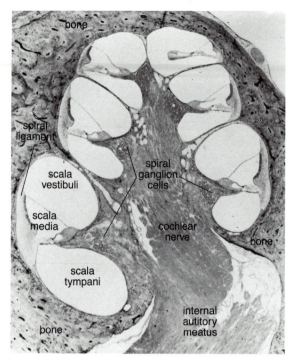

Section through the center of the cochlea.

center portion of the cochlea. It is completely surrounded by a bony sheath known as the modiolus. The low-frequency nerve fibers coming from the top of the cochlea occupy the center area of the cochlear nerve, with higher-frequency nerve fibers from the middle and basal turns of the cochlea joining on and making up the outer portion of the cochlear nerve. The cochlear nerve leaves the bony cochlea on its way to the brain through a hole known as the internal auditory meatus.

Bibliography
Ballantyne, J. C., and W. Friedmann (eds.): *Ultrastructural Atlas of the Inner Ear*, Butterworths, 1984.

Yost, W. A., and D. W. Nielsen (eds.): *Fundamentals of Hearing*, Holt, Rinehart, Winston, 1977.

I. Hunter-Duvar

AUDITORY NERVE
The auditory nerve, also referred to as the cochlear nerve, provides the sole connection between the sensory hair cells of the cochlea and the cochlear nucleus of the brainstem. It is therefore essential for hearing. The auditory nerve originates from cells of the spiral ganglion which, in humans, coils 2½ turns from base to apex within the bony axis of the cochlea and supplies the sensory innervation to hair cells in the corresponsing turns of the organ of Corti. This orderly base-to-apex sequence of connections between the hair cells and the spiral ganglion cells establishes within the auditory nerve an orderly representation of the base-to-apex frequency selec-

tivity of the cochlea. As seen in cross section, fibers in the nerve are arranged in a spiral; those from the apex of the cochlea are at the center and are tuned to low frequencies, whereas those from the base are on the outside and are tuned to high frequencies. The auditory nerve, accompanied by the vestibular and facial nerves, travels toward the brainstem in the internal auditory meatus of the temporal bone. In humans, the nerve is approximately 25 millimeters long and 2 millimeters in diameter, and contains an average of 32,000 myelinated nerve fibers. It terminates in the cochlear nucleus, a highly differentiated complex of auditory neurons situated at the junction of the pons and medulla oblongata. Within the cochlear nucleus, auditory nerve fibers branch and distribute themselves in an orderly topographic sequence, and thus transmit their selective frequency information to the corresponding cochlear nucleus neurons. Similar tonotopic arrangements prevail at each level of the auditory pathway from spiral ganglion to auditory cortex.

Innervation of the organ of Corti The innervation of the organ of Corti consists mainly of afferent fibers which, by definition, transmit auditory information to the brain. However, the auditory receptor also receives efferent fibers, which arise from neurons within the brain. These olivocochlear neurons are located in the superior olivary complex of the pons, and send their axons to the cochlea by way of the vestibular nerve, a slender branch of which ultimately joins the auditory nerve. Significantly, inner and outer hair cells are innervated by different kinds of afferent and efferent fibers. These fibers are most conveniently considered in relation to the specific hair cell type they innervate.

Inner Hair Cells In most species, some 90–95% of all spiral ganglion cells (type I) contact only inner hair cells, while the remainder (type II) contact only outer hair cells. Type I ganglion cells, which are bipolar in shape, have myelinated fibers both centrally in the nerve and peripherally up to their entry into the organ of Corti. Here, the peripheral fibers lose their myelin sheaths and become known as afferent radial fibers because each one takes a fairly direct path to the inner hair cell nearest to it and, without branching, makes contact with it. In the cat, each inner hair cell is contacted by about 20 radial fibers. However, given that there are some 3500 inner hair cells and an average of 32,000 myelinated cochlear nerve fibers, the number of radial fibers per cell may be lower in humans than in the cat. Nevertheless, the selective contact made by each of these fibers is consistent with their selective tuning to tonal stimulation. It is less clear what function is served by the multiple innervation of a single inner hair cell, but the redundancy may be more apparent than real because not all radial fibers are identical, in either their detailed structure or function.

The efferent innervation of the inner hair cell region arises from olivocochlear neurons located in the lateral part of the superior olivary complex. These fibers, which number about 1000 in humans, are thin and unmyelinated, and branch profusely in the region beneath the inner hair cells. Rather than contacting the inner hair cells themselves, they contact radial afferent fibers. Although this efferent innervation is found throughout the length of the organ of Corti, and thus presumably affects all radial afferent fibers, there is at present no clear understanding of its functional role in hearing.

Outer Hair Cells Type II ganglion cells, which comprise only 5–10 percent of the afferent fibers innervating the cochlea, make contact only with outer hair cells. The central and peripheral processes of these cells are thin and unmyelinated. The peripheral fiber travels with the radial afferent fibers to the organ of Corti, but rather than contacting an inner hair cell, it crosses the tunnel of Corti and turns basalward to become an outer spiral fiber. These course for a distance of 1 to 2 millimeters in the outer spiral bundle, giving off occasional branches which, in total, contact many outer hair cells (10–50). Each outer hair cell, moreover, is contacted by several outer spiral fibers. Thus, the relation between outer hair cells and type II ganglion cells is much more diffuse than that between inner hair cells and type I ganglion cells. Owing to the spiral-versus-radial course of the two kinds of afferent fibers, there is also a disparity in the place along the length of the organ of Corti innervated by adjacent ganglion cells of the two types. So far, it has not been possible to obtain recordings from type II ganglion cells or to determine their specific connections in the cochlear nucleus. Their function is unknown.

Perhaps better understood is the role of the efferent fibers that innervate the outer hair cells. These thick, myelinated fibers arise from some 400 olivocochlear neurons located in the medial part of the superior olivary complex. Because of extensive branching in the cochlea, the number of these fibers increases to several thousand by the time they enter the organ of Corti and pass directly to the outer hair cells, where they terminate. The distribution of contacts between these efferent fibers is not uniform. Contacts are greater in the first row of outer hair cells and tend to be few or absent at the extreme basal and apical ends of the organ of Corti. Functionally, electric stimulation of these efferent fibers results in a reduction in the activity of cochlear nerve fibers, but this inhibitory effect is detectable only at low and moderate levels of sound stimulation. It has been suggested that the mech-

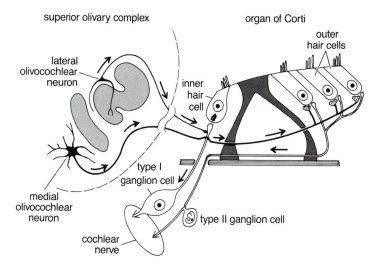

Simplified diagram illustrating the connections of the four types of nerve fibers innervating the organ of Corti of the cat.

anism underlying this effect is essentially mechanical and results from a change in the physical coupling between outer and hair cells, perhaps via the tectorial membrane or the endolymph.

Bibliography

Brodal, A.: *Neurological Anatomy*, 3d ed., Oxford University Press, New York, 1981.

Pickles, J. O.: *An Introduction to the Physiology of Hearing*, Academic Press, London, 1982.

W. Bruce Warr

CENTRAL AUDITORY MECHANISM

The auditory nerve, which carries information for hearing, and the vestibular nerve, which transmits balance information, are adjacent to each other as they travel through the internal auditory meatus of the ear and enter the skull together as the VIIIth cranial nerve. The auditory nerve enters the brainstem near the pontomedullary junction, and the individual fibers of the auditory nerve connect to the nerve cells of the cochlear nucleus complex. This is the first one of a series of nuclei through which auditory information is transmitted from the ear to the auditory cortex of the brain, where the patterns of nerve impulses are interpreted as sounds. These relay nuclei and the nerve fiber tracts that connect them constitute the ascending auditory pathway. While the cochlear nucleus is a relatively large structure in the small animals, such as guinea pigs, rats, and cats, that are frequently used in experimental studies of the auditory system, it is a relatively small structure in humans. It has been pushed backward by the expansion of the cerebrum and is now located underneath the inferior cerebellar peduncle.

The cochlear nucleus consists of at least three identifiable divisions, each of which receives nerve fibers from the entire auditory nerve. Each nerve fiber of the auditory nerve connects to several cells in each of these three divisions of the cochlear nucleus. Connections from the cochlear nucleus to higher auditory centers are through three different fiber tracts: the ventral stria (trapezoidal body), the intermediate stria (stria of Held), and the dorsal stria (stria of Monakow). All three fiber tracts cross to the opposite side of the brainstem, and the ventral and intermediate striae make connections with neurons in different parts of the second auditory relay nucleus, the superior olivary complex on both sides. From there, connections are made to the third main relay nucleus, the inferior colliculus, through the fiber tract of the lateral lemniscus. There are also neural connections between the right and left inferior colliculi.

The majority of the nerve fibers connecting the cochlear nucleus with higher nerve centers cross over to the other side, but some nerve fibers from the cochlear nucleus go directly from it to the inferior colliculus on the same side via the lateral lemniscus. This means that information from both ears is passed to both right and left higher auditory centers, making it difficult to determine the side on which a lesion in the auditory pathway is located when the lesion is more central than the superior olivary complex. Because the superior olivary complex is the first nucleus in the ascending auditory pathway where the impulses from each ear reach the same nerve cells, it is believed to play a major role in the ability to determine the direction of a sound source, a phenomenon based mainly on detecting small differences in the time that a sound arrives at the two ears. *See* PSYCHOACOUSTICS: Binaural Hearing.

The inferior colliculus connects to the fourth relay nucleus of the ascending auditory pathway, the medial geniculate body, which is located in the thalamus. The neurons of the medial geniculate body send nerve fibers to the auditory cortex via the auditory radiators. The primary cortical area receives its input from the anterior and medial parts of the geniculate body, whereas the other auditory cortical areas receive their input from the posterior part of the geniculate body.

The primary auditory cortex in humans is located in the temporal lobe on the middle part of the anterior transverse gyrus (gyrus of Heschl), which is buried in the floor of the lateral sulcus or Sylvian fissure. There are other areas, usually called association areas, of the cerebral cortex that also receive auditory input.

In addition to the ascending auditory pathway, there is an extensive descending pathway composed of at least two separate systems, the corticothalamic and the corticocochlear. The descending systems transmit information from the brain back to the ear (feedback). The best-understood portion of these descending systems is the olivocochlear system, which is the more peripheral part of the corticocochlear system. This system originates in the superior olivary complex and descends to the cochlea, and its fibers terminate on the hair cells, mainly outer hair cells. There is both a crossed and an uncrossed olivocochlear system.

Bibliography
Gelfand, S. A.: *Hearing: An Introduction to Psychological and Physiological Acoustics*, Marcel Dekker, New York, 1981.
Møller, A. R.: *Auditory Physiology*, Academic Press, New York, 1983.
Moore, B. C.: *An Introduction to the Psychology of Hearing*, 2d ed., Academic Press, London, 1982.
Pickles, J. O.: *An Introduction to the Physiology of Hearing*, Academic Press, London, 1982.

Aage R. Møller

Physiology

Although the ear is a biologic system, it is also a physical system and works according to various physical principles. The conducting apparatus, formed by the external and middle ears, provides the means by which sound is transformed into mechanical vibration, permitting sound energy to be transferred from air to the inner ear with reasonable efficiency. The inner ear is filled with fluid and has physical properties that are quite different from air. Thus, it is necessary to match the inner ear to air; otherwise hearing would be significantly less sensitive than it is. The conducting apparatus performs this matching function by acting as a physical transformer. Although this transformer is impressively efficient throughout a frequency range that encompasses speech, it becomes increasingly inefficient at very low and very high frequencies, thereby limiting human hearing to a range of approximately 20–20,000 hertz.

An alternative and, from a clinical viewpoint, interesting mode of "driving" the inner ear is via vibration of the bones of the skull. Airborne sound can do this but not very efficiently. Unless there is substantial blockage of the conducting apparatus, sound conducted by bone is normally of no consequence, except for listening to one's own voice. However, by vibrating the skull directly, a blockage can be effectively bypassed. This permits the sensitivity of the auditory system to be evaluated somewhat (but not completely) independently of the conducting apparatus. *See* AUDIOMETRY: Pure-Tone Audiogram.

The objective of the peripheral auditory system is to translate the physical stimulus of sound into a suitable physiologic signal. The hair cells, which react to bending of their hairs, are exquisitely sensitive devices for detecting the minute vibrations of the hearing organ. The sound energy transmitted to the inner ear causes a wavelike vibratory motion to be set up along the organ that, in turn, provides a mechanism for the separation of sounds of different frequencies. Thus, the peripheral mechanism conveys to the central nervous system not only information concerning the presence of sound and its intensity, but also information concerning its frequency content. Additionally, rather precise timing information is sent to the central nervous system.

Physically, the hair cells represent transducers that translate vibratory into electric energy. Their ability to do this depends upon a combination of intricate mechanical structures that serve to "funnel" the energy of the stimulus to the hair cells, and electrochemical systems. The normal functioning of the inner ear requires the proper chemical balance between the fluids of the bony and membranous labyrinths. Of course, oxygen and nourishment also must be brought in. These functions are served by the rich blood supply of the inner ear.

The vestibular apparatus, which is really the phylogenetic ancestor of the hearing mechanism, functions along similar (although not identical) lines. Naturally, the physical stimuli are different. Yet, the result of stimulation is again the bending of the delicate hairs atop the hair cells. Angular motion (such as rotation) is detected primarily by the semicircular canal organs, whereas linear motion and orientation in the earth's gravitational field are detected primarily by the saccule and utricle.

The peripheral auditory system serves not only to "pick up" sound but also to condition this stimulus so that the brain can process the information borne by it. (The same can be said of the peripheral vestibular system and corresponding stimuli.) This is not to say that auditory information is processed only at the level of the cortex. Once the information is encoded in the periphery and transmitted to the central nervous system, some degree of information processing occurs at each level (essentially each nucleus) within the central auditory system. Indeed, a great amount of auditory information processing takes place within the brainstem, for instance, the comparison of inputs from the two ears that makes precise sound location possible. Still, cognitive functions, such as understanding speech, clearly require the more elaborate processing mechanisms of the cerebral cortex. Such processing relies not only upon the elaborate auditory pathways and the interconnections between the neurons forming these pathways, but also upon the diversity of the types of auditory neurons, that is, their variety of structure and pattern of responses to sound stimulation.

John D. Durrant

AIR CONDUCTION MECHANISM

The middle ear receives sounds that enter the external ear canal and transmits them into the cochlea, the auditory portion of the inner ear. In this process, the middle ear acts as a transformer to match the low impedance of the air column in front of the tympanic membrane to the much higher impedance of the inner-ear fluids. The transformer function is mainly accomplished by the area ratio of the (large) tympanic membrane to the (smaller) stapes footplate; the action is that of a hydraulic lever. This action makes it possible to deliver an optimal amount of the incoming sound energy to the cochlea, providing it with high sensitivity. A number of nonlinear mechanisms activated at higher levels affords some protection for the delicate tissues of the inner ear.

Sound pressure exerted on the tympanic membrane forces it to vibrate in synchrony with the applied signal. At each given frequency, the magnitude and phase of the resulting displacements depend on the impedance of the membrane, or more precisely on the combined impedance of the entire peripheral system, because its members are closely coupled to one another. This includes even the inner ear, which also contributes to the middle-ear impedance, as seen through the tympanic membrane. The impedance is stiffness-controlled and is fairly well matched to that of the air column in the external ear canal so that the admission of audio-frequency energy, at least in the middle-frequency range that is important for speech reception, is close to optimal.

Even at low frequencies, the tympanic membrane is not displaced as a stiff plate. The manubrium of the malleus undergoes lesser excursions than the two membrane sections behind and in front of it. This mode of vibrations was first postulated by H. von Helmholtz.

This action of the membrane obeys the catenary principle, as exemplified by a chain (catena) suspended between two points. Under the effect of its own weight, such a chain hangs in a bight. If the bight is shallow, a pull is exerted at the two end points, which is larger than the weight load responsible for it. In fact, the pull increases the more tightly the chain is drawn. It would become infinitely large, if the chain could be made perfectly taut, which is of course impossible. Hence, the chain is seen to constitute a lever with a ratio that varies with its inverse curvature.

The vibrating tympanic membrane acts as a transformer—the function of a lever under the effect of a vibratory input. The fact that the displacements of the manubrium are smaller than those of the membrane indicates a proportional increase in force. Because the transformer ratio of a catenary-type transformer was said to vary with the in-

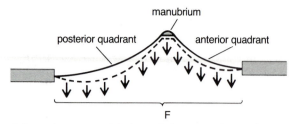

Schematic cross section through the tympanic membrane. Displacement is toward the outside during its vibrations in response to a force that is evenly distributed over its surface. Note that the center of each membrane section (posterior and anterior quadrants) is displaced more than the manubrium. (From J. Tonndorf and S. M. Khanna, "The Role of the Tympanic Membrane in Middle-Ear Transformation," *Ann. Oto. Rhino. Lar.*, 79:743–753, 1970)

verse curvature of the structure in question, the ratio must be higher in the upper regions of the tympanic membrane, where the curvature is small, and less near the umbo, where the curvature is stronger. On the other hand, the ratio of the ossicular lever, which when vibrating represents another transformer, is small when a force is applied at a point high on the manubrium (it may even be less than 1), but it grows progressively larger when the point of application is moved toward the umbo. Hence, for any given point along the manubrium and the appropriate sections of the membrane connected to it, the two transformers appear to complement each other so that the combined transformer ratio remains constant, probably not much higher than 1. Although this mechanism does not

Pars tensa of a left tympanic membrane of the cat. (a) Due to its exponential cone shape, the curvature of the membrane increases systematically toward the umbo, becoming largest in the inferior portion. (b, c) The two drawings illustrate in a schematic manner the reciprocal relation of the catenary membrane lever and the ossicular lever for two points along the manubrium. (From J. Tonndorf and S. M. Khanna, "The Role of the Tympanic Membrane in Middle-Ear Transformation," *Ann. Oto. Rhino. Lar.*, 79:743–753, 1970)

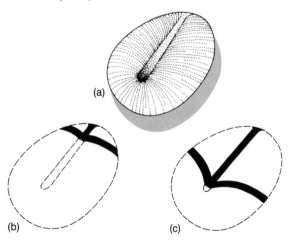

constitute the main transformer of the middle ear, it still fulfills an important task: it enables all sections of the tympanic membrane to contribute equally to the transmission of sound onto the ossicular chain.

At frequencies beyond 2.5 kilohertz (kHz), the displacement pattern of the tympanic membrane grows increasingly more complex, and its effectiveness in driving the manubrium decreases; therefore, the resulting manubrial displacement becomes progressively smaller. Eventually, at about 4 kHz, the membrane virtually ceases to drive the manubrium. However, the membrane still has an important task, to form a baffle around the manubrium so that the incident sound does not reach the manubrium from front and back, thus canceling its own effect. (Such cancellations occur when there are perforations in the tympanic membrane, reducing admission chiefly of low-frequency signals.)

Because it lacks the fiber network of the pars tensa, the pars flaccida hardly contributes to driving the malleus. However, when the malleus is rotated inward, its prominent lateral process, located just under the pars flaccida, juts farther out. This movement would be impaired if the pars flaccida were stiff and unable to stretch. This yielding appears to be its only significant task.

The elastic restoring force of the tympanic membrane is mainly given by the elasticity of the air trapped in the middle ear. In this respect the air cells of the mastoid play an important role. Driving air into and out of this cell system generates friction, which dampens the membrane displacements. One tangible consequence is that tympanic membranes are less likely to rupture under the effect of explosions when the pneumatic cell system is large than when it is small.

The tympanic membrane works optimally only when the air pressure on its two sides is equal. Otherwise, it yields to the higher pressure, that is, it is mechanically biased and its impedance increases. Maintenance and restoration of the air-pressure equilibrium is the task of the eustachian tube. Swallowing or yawning opens it, because the muscles fulfilling this task terminate in the soft palate. Sometimes, more forceful steps are required, such as the Valsalva maneuver, during which while holding the nostrils closed, one increases the air pressure in the respiratory tract. If the pressure differential is not greater than about 90 millimeters of mercury, this usually forces the tubes to open. People with well-trained tubes open them almost imperceptibly at lower differentials, even while sleeping.

Under the effect of sudden pressure changes, occurring for instance during explosions or during fast descents under water, too fast for the eustachian tubes to equalize pressure, the tympanic membrane fibers may be overextended, or overstretched, so that the membrane becomes flaccid and acquires a characteristic, crumpled look. Consequently, the membrane is partially decoupled from the manubrium. The decoupling attenuates energy transmission to the inner ear. The overstretched fibers require a few days to recover their proper length and tension and to restore their function.

If the change in environmental pressure is excessive, the tympanic membrane may even rupture. Such traumatic ruptures, as a rule, have a good tendency to heal. The tympanic membrane may also be ruptured during the course of infections, permitting discharge of mucus or pus accumulated behind it into the ear canal. After the infection subsides, small perforations usually heal again; larger ones often remain permanent.

The bulbous head of the malleus and the body of the incus represent counterweights to their lower, long and slender processes. The combined center of gravity of the two ossicles lies almost, but not quite, on their common axis of rotation, so that their masses, which are quite small to begin with, are rather well balanced and the moment of inertia is quite low. If this were not so, the ossicles would be set in motion when one shakes one's head; this would produce an audible noise. Furthermore, the larger effective mass would limit high-frequency transmission through the middle ear.

Malleus and incus were said to rotate together in response to audio frequencies, forming an almost rigid lever. Thus, when the malleus handle moves inward, the long crus of the incus does likewise, and vice versa. (How the ossicular lever combines with the transformer action of the tympanic membrane was already described.) However, the incudomallar joint is stiff and unyielding only at frequencies above approximately 100 hertz (Hz). At lower frequencies, the joint begins to slip, the more so the lower the frequency. This suggests that the joint may be friction-coupled. Together with the yielding of the tympanic membrane, this slippage serves to protect the inner ear to some degree against explosive pressure changes which, although large, occur relatively slowly when compared to those taking place during vibrations at audio frequencies.

When the two major ossicles rotate about their axis, they move the stapes along with them, displacing it with respect to the frame of the oval window. However, the footplate is not able to move into and out of this window like a piston, but can only swing around its posterior margin like a door around a hinge. At very high displacement amplitudes [at sound pressures in excess of 130 decibels (dB)], the curve described by the lower end of the incus around the rotational axis makes itself felt.

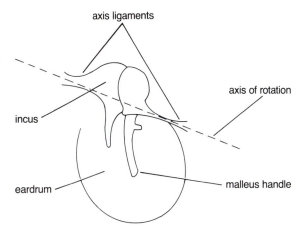

Major ossicles and their axis of rotation. Note that the axis lies in reality more nearly horizontal than indicated in this drawing. (From E. Barany, "A Contribution to the Physiology of Bone Conduction," *Acta Oto-Lar.*, suppl. 26:1–223, 1938)

The stapes head is moved not only toward and away from the oval window, but up and down as well, exactly twice per vibratory cycle. This introduces a frequency twice the signal frequency, that is, its second harmonic, but also reduces the effective displacement of the footplate.

The area of the footplate is considerably smaller than that of the tympanic membrane. This constitutes a hydraulic lever or, in response to alternating, audio-frequency signals, a transformer. The force density, the pressure, is increased from the larger tympanic membrane to the smaller footplate. However, the full area ratio, approximately 20:1, does not come to bear, since the tympanic membrane is not displaced as a stiff plate, as was already described.

There are thus a number of passive protective mechanisms provided by middle-ear structures. The two middle-ear muscles exert an active protection. When activated they attenuate sound transmission. The tensor tympani pulls the malleus inward, thereby tilting it slightly so that the tympanic membrane is tensed. This increases the impedance (lessens admission) of sound energy to a small degree. The stapedius pulls the stapes slightly out of the oval window, tilting it around its posterior margin. This partially disconnects the stapes from the incus, thus decreasing transmission. Both muscles are supplied by voluntary nerves; some people know how to contract these muscles voluntarily. More importantly, they are contracted by reflex action in response to sound signals in excess of approximately 70 dB sound pressure level, and also in response to tactile stimulation of the posterior wall of the external ear canal. The stapedius reacts faster and also more strongly than the tensor tympani. Short-lasting sounds produce attenuations of

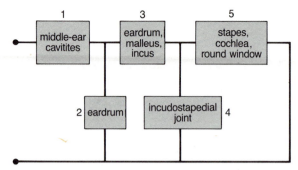

Block diagram of the middle-ear mechanism responding to air-conduction signals. Note that the middle-ear cavities are placed in series with the other elements, since they represent the elastic, restoring force of the tympanic membrane, the pneumatic air cells simultaneously providing some damping. Elements connecting to the ground bus indicate losses. In the guinea pig, Zwislocki evaluated quantitatively the properties of each element. (From J. J. Zwislocki, "Analysis of the Middle-Ear Function, I: Input Impedance," *J. Acoust. Soc. Amer.*, 34:1514–1523, 1962)

about 20 dB. On exposure to longer-lasting sounds, the muscles alternatingly contract and relax to avoid muscle fatigue. The attenuation varies accordingly. The neural center of this reflex mechanism is located in the inferior colliculus, an important nucleus or station of the central auditory pathways.

None of the four protective mechanisms mentioned is activated directly at the auditory threshold, but at considerably higher levels. This nonlinear action combines excellent transmission at low levels with some attenuation at higher levels, providing the organ with high sensitivity while affording some protection to it. With modern noise pollution, however, this protection seems hardly sufficient.

When both ears receive the same signal, a common image is perceived. If the signals arrive at exactly the same time at the two ears and are alike in intensity, the image is located in the middle of the head. If either the time of arrival is earlier in one ear or the intensity higher than in the other, the image is lateralized to that side. This is the basis of directional hearing.

BONE-CONDUCTION MECHANISM

The auditory organ responds not only to airborne signals but also to structural vibrations imparted to the skull when audio-frequency vibrations are directly transmitted to it. The resulting sensation is indistinguishable from that evoked by airborne signals. This mechanism, called bone conduction, constitutes an important audiologic tool for the differentiation of conductive hearing impairments from sensorineural ones.

Bone-conducted signals reach the auditory organ by several routes, in contrast to the singular one used by air-conducted signals which, after entering the ear canal, are simply transmitted through the middle ear into the inner ear. When the skull is set in vibrations, the flat bones of the cranial vault vibrate in a direction perpendicular to their own plane, like any other plates. The more massive bones at the skull basis, however, vibrate in a manner known as distortional, changing their shape in a complex three-dimensional manner.

Vibrations are transmitted throughout the skull from any point of contact, including the skull's interior; thus they reach the ear by at least two routes. They also reach both ears. The differences in time of arrival at and in intensity between the two sides is very small. Consequently, the common sound image in response to sustained sound signals usually is located in the middle of the head. When brief vibratory signals such as clicks are applied to both sides of the head, they are localized according to the difference in time of arrival at the ears or in intensity like air-conduction signals.

The vibrations of the temporal bone effect all three parts of the ear; the external, middle, and inner ear. Their induced vibrations eventually combine to excite the cochlea. The three components will be discussed separately.

External-Canal Component Vibrating skull bones radiate sound into the environment. The osseous and cartilaginous walls of the external ear canal participate in these vibrations, radiating sound into the canal lumen. At frequencies below approximately 1 kHz, some of that sound is drained off into the environment via the external canal opening, the more so the lower the frequency. For higher frequencies, there is no such drainage: the external opening is functionally closed, and the sound energy within the canal is picked up by the tympanic membrane and transmitted into the cochlea via the middle ear. That is, the canal acts as a high-pass filter. However, when the canal opening is firmly occluded, all sound is retained and eventually transmitted into the cochlea. An occluded ear, therefore, receives low frequencies at an intensity higher than at the other, nonoccluded ear. Hence, the common image, which normally was said to lie in the middle of the head, is lateralized into the ear in question. The test of Bing makes use of this occlusion effect and is employed clinically to demonstrate the functional intactness of the middle ear. When low-frequency bone-conduction signals are spontaneously lateralized, the middle-ear function on the side in question is shown to be impaired. Clinically, this is known as the test of Weber.

Middle-Ear Component Especially when the skull vibrates from side to side, perpendicularly to the axis of rotation of malleus and incus, the middle-ear ossicles participate in such vibrations. They do so, however, at amplitudes and phases of their own, because their moment of inertia is rather small and because they are only loosely coupled to the osseous walls of the middle ear. Forced by the vibrating incus, displacements of the stapes footplate relative to the oval window are set up, producing an input into the inner ear just as if the ossicular chain had been vibrated by air-conducted sound. Because of the mode of generation, this is often referred to as the inertial component of bone conduction.

Inner-Ear Component   The petrous portion of the temporal bone, which houses the inner ear, is a compact, dense bone. Therefore, it undergoes distortional vibrations. In this process, the two perilymphatic scalae of the cochlea alternatingly change their respective volumes: while scala vestibuli becomes larger, scala tympani becomes smaller, and vice versa. These out-of-phase volume changes force the cochlear duct to be displaced accordingly. A typical Békésy-type traveling wave is set up, and the organ is stimulated exactly as in response to an air-conduction signal. Formerly, this distortional

component of bone conduction was often referred to as the compressional mode.

It should be clear from the foregoing that the three quasi-independent components of external, middle, and inner ears generated by mechanical vibrations of the skull combine to produce a common input to the sense organ.

It is possible to cancel a bone-conduction signal by an air-conduction signal of the same frequency by careful adjustment of amplitude and phase of one of the signals. This experiment demonstrates that both types of input share some of the same mechanical pathways toward the end organ and that they stimulate it in the same manner.

When the bone-conduction and air-conduction audiograms are reduced by about the same amount, the function of the auditory receptor organ (or that of the central auditory pathways) is shown to be impaired; this is referred to as a sensorineural loss. However, when the bone-conduction audiogram is

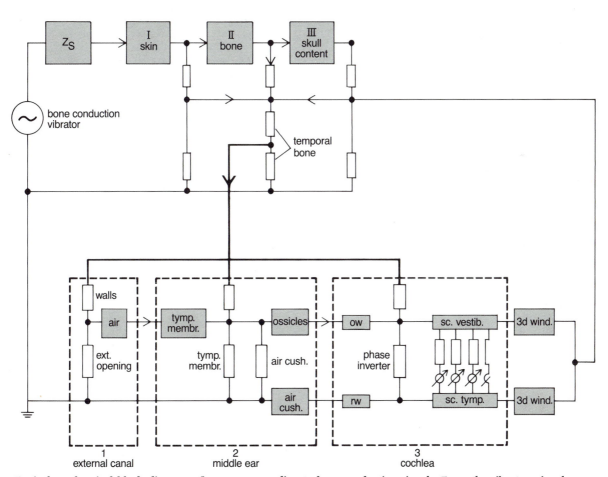

Equivalent electrical block diagram of an ear responding to bone-conduction signals. From the vibrator, signals are transmitted to all tissues of the head, including its interior. After arriving at the temporal bone, signals travel to the three anatomical parts of the ear, inducing quasi-independent vibrations. All three vibratory responses are eventually conducted toward the cochlea, where the auditory organ is excited in precisely the same manner as by air-conduction signals. (From J. Tonndorf, "A New Concept of Bone Conduction," *Arch. Otolar.*, 87:598–808, 1968)

near normal and definitely better than the air-conduction audiogram, middle-ear function is impaired, for instance due to an otosclerotic stapes fixation or an interruption of the ossicular chain; this is referred to as a conductive loss. The difference in magnitude between air- and bone-conduction can be demonstrated by the clinical tuning-fork test of Schwabach.

In the presence of conductive impairments, the bone-conduction audiogram is said to be near normal. The exception is the so-called Carhart's notch: The response at 0.5 kHz is reduced by about 5 dB, that at 1 kHz by about 10 dB, that at 2 kHz by about 15 dB, and that at 4 kHz once more by about 5 dB. This notch of the bone-conduction audiogram indicates that the contributions of the external and middle ears are prevented from reaching the sensory organ. The combined external-canal and middle-ear components happen to contribute maximally to the reception of bone-conduction signals in the range of 2 kHz. Hence, Carhart's notch is not a sign of a sensorineural loss, but of a purely mechanical impairment of middle-ear function.

Magnitude of Stimulus Response

In healthy ears, a sound pressure of about 40 micropascals is sufficient to produce a sensation of hearing if the frequency of the signal lies in the most sensitive region of the ear, around 3 kHz. This pressure can barely be read with sophisticated, modern measuring techniques. In response to such small-magnitude signals, the tympanic membrane executes displacements that, again around 3 kHz, are of the order of one-billionth of a centimeter. Even modern measuring techniques do not permit direct measurements at these levels. The results given represent extrapolations of measurements taken, under best conditions, at levels about 10,000 times higher.

Yet, there is every indication that these extrapolations are reasonably correct, the margin of error being considerably smaller than one order of magnitude. For one thing, the measurements were carried out well within the linear range of the auditory system, so that the extrapolations were permissible. Sceptics have stated that the displacement values could not be correct because they are too close to atomic dimensions; that is, they would be affected—if not completely masked out—by the background noise produced by the random motions of molecular and atomic particles. There are at least two answers to these objections: (1) The area of the tympanic membrane is so much larger than atomic dimensions that the noise thus generated would be spatially averaged out over the entire surface. (2) With the aid of laser holography, displacements of 30-billionths of a centimeter have

been directly measured in the center of the diaphragm of a condenser microphone in a very small spot, about 0.1 centimeter in diameter; there were no signs of an intervening noise. Nevertheless, the sound pressures as well as the resulting tympanic membrane displacements at the auditory threshold defy comprehension.

Tympanic membrane displacements, or those of the stapes footplate, are linear over an extremely large range. First signs of nonlinear displacements have been found at sound pressure levels in excess of 130 dB (see above). For a purely mechanical device, this is a large range, greater by a wide margin than that of any human-made device.

The displacements of the skull bones in response to vibratory inputs at audible levels are of comparable magnitudes, although the forces required to produce them are considerably higher. Air-conduction signals are favored in this respect by the impedance-matching properties of the middle ear.

Bibliography

Barany, E.: "A Contribution to the Physiology of Bone Conduction," *Acta Oto-Lar.*, suppl. 26:1–223, 1938.

Békésy, G. von: Experiments on Hearing, 1961.

Brodel, M.: *Three Unpublished Drawings on the Anatomy of the Human Ear*, 1946.

Carhart, R.: "Clinical Application of Bone Conduction Audiometry," *Arch. Otolar.*, 51:798–808, 1950.

Tonndorf, J.: "Bone Conduction," in W. Keidel and W. D. Neff (eds.), *Handbook of Sensory Physiology*, vol. V/3, pp. 37–83, 1976.

———: "A New Concept of Bone Conduction," *Arch. Otolar.*, 87:598–808, 1968.

——— and S. M. Khanna: "Mechanics of the Auditory System," in R. Hinchcliffe and D. Harrison (eds.), *Scientific Foundations of Otolaryngology*, chap. 16, 1976.

——— and ———: "The Role of the Tympanic Membrane in Middle-Ear Transformation," *Ann. Oto. Rhino. Lar.*, 79:743–753, 1970.

Zwislocki, J. J.: "Analysis of the Middle-Ear Function, I: Input Impedance," *J. Acoust. Soc. Amer.*, 34:1514–1523, 1962.

Juergen Tonndorf

Sensorineural Mechanism

The auditory sensorineural mechanism transforms (transduces) sound into neural impulses. The process takes place in the cochlea. Within the cochlea, the basilar membrane supports the organ of Corti, which contains two kinds of sensory receptor cells (hair cells) that transform mechanical vibration produced by sound into electrical potentials—a first step toward generation of nerve impulses in auditory nerve fibers that innervate the cells. The receptor cells are arranged in four rows running along the cochlear canal. The three outer rows contain one kind of hair cells—the outer hair cells; one inner row contains a different kind—the inner hair cells. Almost all nerve fibers that carry the auditory information from the cochlea to the brain, the afferent fibers, end on the inner hair cells; only about 5 percent continue to the outer hair cells. Because of this distribution, the inner hair cells are regarded as the direct transmitters of auditory information.

The role of the outer hair cells is not yet entirely clear. They receive the strong innervation of a system of efferent nerve fibers, called the crossed olivocochlear bundle, that carries information from the brain to the cochlea. Because stimulation of this bundle indirectly decreases the sensitivity of the inner hair cells, it appears that the outer hair cells affect the functioning of the cochlea either electrically, mechanically, or both ways. Another bundle of efferent fibers, the uncrossed olivocochlear bundle, innervates the afferent fibers ending on the inner hair cells. The effect of this bundle is not yet known.

The thick and fibrous tectorial membrane is suspended above the organ of Corti. It protrudes from a spiral bony outcropping, the spiral limbus, and is firmly attached to the longest stereocilia of the outer hair cells. The longest stereocilia of the inner hair cells appear to touch it, but not to be embedded in it. The tectorial membrane is believed to play an important role in hair cell stimulation.

The basilar membrane, the organ of Corti, and the tectorial membrane together constitute the flexible cochlear partition which controls the sound propagation in the cochlea. The thin Reissner's membrane, on the other hand, is mechanically unimportant. It serves as a chemical and electrical barrier between the perilymph and the endolymph, which have quite different chemical compositions and are at different electrical potentials. The perilymph is relatively rich in sodium ions and is approximately at zero potential. The endolymph is rich in potassium ions and is at a potential of about 80 millivolts. These differences are believed to be essential for the electromechanical sound transduction in the cochlea.

When sound reaches the cochlea through the middle ear and the oval window, it produces tranverse waves on the basilar membrane that travel from the vestibule toward the cochlear apex. The associated vibration of the organ of Corti and the tectorial membrane leads to excitation of the hair cells and, subsequently, the generation of impulses in the auditory nerve fibers. It has become increasingly evident that the mechanical events in the cochlea, rather than the neural ones, control the relation between the subjective pitch and sound frequency and make it possible to discriminate among different sounds. They also seem to affect the rate at which loudness grows with sound in-

tensity. Nevertheless, sound transduction in the hair cells and the mechanisms involved in the elicitation of the nerve impulses modify the outcome of the mechanical processes before the initial neural code for sound is established.

Cochlear Waves The sound analysis in the cochlea is achieved by the characteristic pattern of the waves on the basilar membrane. As the waves generated by a pure tone travel toward the helicotrema, their wave length gradually becomes shorter, but their amplitude increases to a maximum that is astonishingly sharp in a healthy cochlea, and then, almost abruptly, the amplitude decays to zero. The location of the maximum depends on sound frequency. At the low frequency of 100 hertz (Hz) it is located near the helicotrema. As the frequency is increased, the maximum moves toward the cochlear base and reaches the basal end of the basilar membrane between 10,000 and 20,000 Hz. Above 1000 Hz the maximum moves by about 6 millimeters in the human cochlea every time the frequency is doubled (changed by an octave). Thus, equal frequency ratios are translated into equal distances along the cochlea. Such a relation is called logarithmic—the distance along the cochlea is equal to the logarithm of a given frequency ratio. The same relation to sound frequency is followed by the subjective pitch, and it is believed that pitch is determined by the location of the vibration maximum. At low sound frequencies, both the location and pitch change more slowly with sound frequency. This leads to a decreased capacity for discriminating one frequency from another. When the hair cells in one part of the cochlea are damaged, a hearing loss results for sound frequencies producing vibration maxima in that part—sounds of corresponding pitches can be heard only when they are very intense. In the presence of a complex, multicomponent sound, the cochlear waves exhibit multiple amplitude peaks at locations corresponding to the frequencies of the components.

Hair Cell Stimulation Cochlear hair cells, like other sensory receptor cells of the body, carry an internal

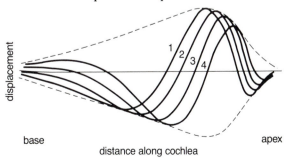

Cochlear wave at four different instants of time. Broken lines show the amplitude envelope.

electrical potential that is negative in relation to their environment. During excitation, the magnitude of this potential decreases by an amount depending on the strength of stimulation—the cells are partially depolarized. It has been found that cochlear hair cells, as well as hair cells in other sensory organs, are depolarized when their stereocilia are deflected in a specific direction determined by the anatomic structure of the cells. In the cochlea, this direction points radially away from the cochlear axis, the modiolus. Deflection of the stereocilia in the opposite direction produces hyperpolarization.

Because the tips of the stereocilia of the outer hair cells are held in the tectorial membrane, they can be deflected only through shear motion between this membrane and the reticular lamina that holds the apical parts of the cells. The shear motion must result from the transverse vibration of the basilar membrane. It was believed in the past, and is still believed by many scientists, that this happens simply because of the geometry of the system. The transverse motion of the basilar membrane under the organ of Corti is conceived as rotation of a rigid plate around an axis, the border of the spiral lamina; the motion of the tectorial membrane is conceived as rotation of another rigid plate around another axis, the edge of the spiral limbus. Because the two axes are at some distance from each other, a shear motion between the two plates must result. This concept of the shear motion is difficult to reconcile with the outcomes of many experiments, and it appears likely that the motion of the tectorial membrane is more complicated. In particular, the membrane is unlikely to behave as a rigid plate rotating around a fixed axis, and its relatively large mass that increases considerably toward the cochlear apex should play a role at sufficiently high sound frequencies. It is possible that this mass interacts with the elastic attachments of the membrane to the spiral limbus and, through the stereocilia of the outer hair cells, to the organ of Corti. Such interaction could produce a resonance whose location along the cochlea depends on sound frequency in roughly the same way as does the vibration maximum of the basilar membrane. The resonance could enhance the vibration maximum and increase in this way the cochlear frequency selectivity. In any event, it is well known that damage to the outer hair cells decreases dramatically this selectivity, and a good biologic state of the organ of Corti is essential for a sharp filter action. Such damage can be produced by excessive noise or certain drugs.

The cochlear frequency selectivity appears to be further enhanced by a biologic feedback that supplies energy to cochlear vibration and compensates for energy losses due to viscosity of the vibrating structures. Such losses are known to decrease the sharpness of mechanical resonating systems and filters in general. The nature of the feedback is not yet known, but the fact that the cochlea can supply energy to its vibrating structures has been well established by measurements of the resulting sound in the ear canal. The sound emitted spontaneously by the cochlea is present in many human ears but very few animal ears. In a normally functioning cochlea, the energy balance seems to be such that viscous energy losses are effectively compensated for, but no spontaneous vibration takes place. Partial damage to some crucial cochlear structures, such as the outer hair cells, can disturb the energy balance so that either the viscous losses are not sufficiently compensated for or an overcompensation results in spontaneous sound emission. The emissions may be audible as disturbing ear ringing, or tinnitus. However, not all tinnitus is produced by cochlear emissions. *See* TINNITUS.

In connection with the cochlear emissions of sound, the stereocilia of the hair cells have stiff cores consisting of actin filaments—the same material that is found in contractile muscle fibers. Muscle contraction occurs through an interaction between actin and myocin molecules. Because myocin is also found in the hair cells, it is possible that biochemical mechanisms similar to those of the muscle fibers produce motion of the stereocilia, or at least enhance it when it is produced externally.

Whereas the outer hair cells seem to have an effect on mechanical events in the cochlea, the stimulation of the inner hair cells appears to proceed passively. Their stereocilia are coupled to the tectorial membrane more loosely than those of the outer hair cells and do not follow exactly the shear motion between this membrane and the reticular lamina. As a result, the excitation of the inner hair cells can be out of step (out of phase) with that of the outer hair cells, depending on sound frequency. Damage to the inner hair cells does not appear to change the pattern of stimulation in the cochlea, but simply decreases the response in neural fibers that innervate the damaged cells.

Cochlear Distortions   In a linear sound-transmitting system, the output amplitude is directly proportional to the input amplitude. This is true in the cochlea only up to the vibration maximum of the basilar membrane. Beyond the maximum, toward the apex, the amplitude of basilar membrane vibration increases less rapidly. This amplitude compression is reflected in the responses of the hair cells and of the auditory nerve fibers. The mechanism underlying the compression is not known directly, but it seems to be abolished in the presence of malfunctions of the outer hair cells.

The compression means that the system functions in a nonlinear fashion. The output waveform is distorted, and new frequencies, called distortion products and not present in the input signal, are produced. When the signal is a pure tone consisting of one sound frequency, only higher harmonics of this frequency arise. But when it consists of more than one frequency, various combination tones of lower frequencies are added. Depending on their strengths and frequency relations, some of them can be heard. Their importance increases with sound intensity.

Whereas the compression manifests itself in the cochlear region between the vibration maximum and the cochlear apex, other nonlinear effects are evident between the maximum and the cochlear base. They are not evident in basilar membrane vibration, but clearly appear in the neural responses as distortions of the waveform. Whether they arise from a nonlinear mechanical stimulation of the inner hair cells, an electrical interaction between these cells and the outer hair cells, or a nonlinear process of neural stimulation is not yet clear.

The cochlear nonlinearities produce the suppression effect that modifies the cochlear frequency selectivity and may enhance it under some conditions. The effect manifests itself as suppression of neural excitation produced by one tone when another, stronger tone is added. The closer the frequencies of the tones, the stronger is the effect. Naturally, the effect must lead to suppression of weak frequency components of a multicomponent sound, such as speech, in favor of the strong ones. Because the suppression effect manifests itself already in the hair cell responses, it is assumed to have its origin in cochlear mechanics. It disappears when the outer hair cells are damaged.

Electromechanical Transduction As was mentioned above, deflection of the hair cell stereocilia away from the cochlear modiolus depolarizes the cells, and their deflection in the opposite direction hyperpolarizes them. Deflection of the stereocilia at right angles to this direction produces no effect. An oscillatory deflection to and from the modiolus produces an oscillatory receptor potential. In a linear electromechanical transducer, the voltage changes are directly proportional to changes in mechanical deflection or deformation. The hair cells are not linear transducers. In the presence of a symmetric, sinusoidal vibration, their depolarization amplitude exceeds the hyperpolarization amplitude. This means a strong distortion of the waveform and its partial rectification. At very low sound frequencies the oscillating receptor potential is much greater than the rectified direct potential. However, with increasing frequency the oscillating potential is shunted more and more by the electric capacitance of the cell membrane so that it gradually decreases and becomes smaller than the direct potential. Because the latter is essential at high frequencies for excitation of the afferent nerve fibers ending on the hair cells, the rectification serves

a useful purpose. The distortion of the waveform follows the cochlear sound analysis and occurs within filter channels. As a consequence, it does not affect directly the perceptual quality of sound.

The nonlinear transduction in the hair cells has two additional manifestations of note. At low sound intensities the direct receptor potential does not grow in direct proportion to the vibration amplitude but, rather, as its square. As the intensity increases, the growth decelerates, and large-intensity increments produce relatively small potential increments. The decreased rate of growth allows the hair cells to respond over a large intensity range of sound and contributes to the ability of the auditory system to cover an astonishing range of sound intensities. The largest intensity it can handle without incurring instant damage is a million million times larger than the smallest that can be perceived.

The mechanism of electromechanical transduction in the hair cells has not been ascertained beyond any reasonable doubt, but much indirect evidence points to electric resistance changes produced in the cell membrane by deflections of the stereocilia. The same membrane covers the cell bodies and the stereocilia, and it is not yet entirely clear where the resistance changes take place. Experimental evidence points to the stereocilia. The prevailing concept of electromechanical transduction in the hair cells can be summarized as follows. Because the stereocilia and the apical ends of the cells are bathed in the endolymph with a positive potential on the order of 80 mV, and the internal potential of the inner hair cells is on the order of -30 mV, a potential difference of about 110 mV exists across the cell membrane. Alternating deflections of stereocilia toward the modiolus and away from it produce asymmetrical oscillating resistance changes in the membrane covering the stereocilia. These changes modulate the electric current flowing across the membrane as the result of the existing electrical-potential difference. In turn, the current modulation produces the receptor potential represented by changes in the resting potential of the cell.

The process is assumed to be fundamentally the same for the inner and outer hair cells. However, more rectification takes place in the inner hair cells. The outer hair cells, on the other hand, are predominantly responsible for the so-called cochlear microphonics, an oscillating electrical potential that can be measured in the cochlear fluids and that represents a weighted sum of the receptor potentials of single hair cells. Cochlear microphonics have been useful in the investigation of cochlear processes, but their role in the processing of sound is not clear. The possibility cannot be excluded that they affect the synaptic transmission between the inner hair cells and the nerve fibers.

Synaptic Transmission About 15 to 20 afferent nerve fibers end on every inner hair cell, every fiber innervating only one cell. The fibers form synaptic boutons surrounding the base of each cell. Opposite every fiber ending, within the hair cell, there are special structures called synaptic bars or ribbons. They are surrounded by small vesicles containing the synaptic transmitter. When the hair cell is depolarized, the transmitter is released into the synaptic cleft separating the fiber membrane from the hair cell membrane. There, it acts on the fiber membrane, producing its depolarization. The depolarization is propagated passively along the fiber up to the habenula perforata, a bony shelf through which the nerve fibers reach the cochlea. There the depolarization produces a neural impulse that is propagated up the auditory nerve to the brain.

Nerve Impulses The rate of neural impulses in auditory nerve fibers, often called firing rate, is the code for sound intensity. Loudness appears to be directly proportional to the summed rate of all the fibers of the auditory nerve. How this proportionality arises is not entirely clear. Except at low sound intensities, the firing rates of single fibers are not directly proportional to loudness but saturate within about 30 dB, that is, when the intensity increases by a factor of about 1000. However, not all fibers have the same sensitivity. At sound intensities at which some fibers fire at their maximum rate, other fibers just begin to respond. It is also true that, for a given sound, not all fibers are equally stimulated. Where the vibration amplitude in the cochlea is relatively large, the fibers tend to respond at lower sound intensities than where the amplitude is relatively low. Correspondingly, in regions of relatively high vibration amplitude, the neural firing rates saturate at lower sound intensities than in regions of lower amplitudes. Further, not all fibers reach their maximum firing rates within a small intensity range. In many, the spike rate increases at a slow rate beyond the ordinary range. The occurrence of such nonsaturating characteristics depends to some extent on the location of the fiber endings in the cochlea relative to the vibration maxima. Clearly, the relations between the firing rates in single auditory nerve fibers and the total firing rate of the auditory nerve are quite complicated. They can be easily disturbed by cochlear damage. Typically, when a sufficient number of hair cells are killed, the auditory sensitivity is diminished severely. However, at high sound intensities the loudness appears unchanged, as a so-called loudness recruitment takes place. It corresponds to a faster increase in the total output of the auditory nerve than under normal conditions.

In general, the distribution of firing rates among the auditory nerve fibers reflects closely the spatial distribution of excitation of the inner hair cells, except for the phenomenon of rate saturation that tends to flatten the peaks in the excitation distribution. However, there are important differences in time pattern between the cochlear excitation and neural spike rates. Mechanical systems possessing sharp filter characteristics, like the cochlea, do not stop vibrating at once when the stimulating sound is turned off, but continue ringing for some time with a gradually decreasing amplitude. Such ringing has been observed in the cochlea. If it were perceived, it would probably be very disturbing by blurring sounds and making speech difficult to understand. Fortunately, it is completely abolished in neural responses. As a result of so-called adaptation processes, the nerve fibers are able to respond much more strongly at the onset of stimulation than during its continuation. The onset firing rate can be many times stronger than the steady-state firing rate. At the end of stimulation the neural sensitivity is strongly decreased and the fibers shut off their firing completely, while the cochlear mechanical ringing continues. By this device the auditory organ achieves the unique feat of providing a high-frequency resolution in the presence of a nearly perfect time resolution.

Bibliography
Békésy, G. v.: *Experiments in Hearing*, McGraw-Hill, New York, 1960.
Dallos, P.: *The Auditory Periphery*, Academic Press, New York, 1973.
Møller, A. R.: *Auditory Physiology*, Academic Press, New York, 1983.
Pickles, J. O.: *An Introduction to the Physiology of Hearing*, Academic Press, London, 1982.
Zwislocki, J. J.: "Five Decades of Research on Cochlear Mechanics," *J. Acoust. Soc. Amer.*, 67:1679–1685, 1980.
———: "How OHC Lesions Can Lead to Neural Hypersensitivity," *Acta Otolaryngol.* (Stockholm), 97:529–534, 1984.

Josef J. Zwislocki

VESTIBULAR SYSTEM

The function of the vestibular system is to provide awareness of the head's position and motion. It does this by means of five receptor organs located in the inner ear: the cristae of the three semicircular canals and the maculae of the utricle and saccule. Information from these receptors interacts in the central nervous system with that from the proprioceptive and visual systems to produce reflex responses that serve to maintain postural equilibrium, spatial orientation, and gaze.

Peripheral Vestibular System The vestibular system is phylogenetically the oldest of the sensory systems. The basic structure and function of the inner-ear receptors have remained essentially the same since the evolution of the modern fishes. Acting as transducers for the force associated with head accelerations, the maculae of the utricle and saccule detect linear acceleration in all directions of space including acceleration due to gravity, and the cristae of the three orthogonal semicircular canals detect angular acceleration in each of the corresponding space coordinates.

Basic Elements of Receptor Function. Hair cells on the receptor organs and their afferent nerve supply are the basic elements of vestibular receptor function. As with other hair cells, the physiologically effective stimulus is a force acting on the hair cell cilia parallel to the top of the cell that causes a bending of the hairs (a shearing force). Deflection of the cilia toward the kinocilium (the longest of the cilia) decreases the resting membrane potential (depolarization), while deflection away from the kinocilium increases it. These potential changes generate an electric current around the hair cell that produces the extracellular receptor potentials or microphonics.

The vestibular receptor organs are innervated by the posterior division of the VIIIth cranial nerve, the vestibular nerve. Peripherally, the vestibular nerve fibers make synaptic contact with the hair cells of the vestibular receptors, where they are excited by the electric current generated by the deflection of the cilia. The cell bodies of these fibers form an elongated mass of bipolar cells, Scarpa's ganglion, immediately outside the inner ear in the internal auditory canal. Centrally the projections synapse with neurons in the ipsilateral vestibular nucleus located in the brainstem.

An interesting aspect of the hair cell–nerve unit is the existence of a resting or spontaneous discharge: a continuous firing, even when there is no motion, of discrete action potentials (spikes) at rates of up to 70 to 90 per second.

Function of the Cristae and Maculae. The capacity of the cristae and maculae to function as sensors of linear and angular acceleration respectively rests on their anatomic configuration. The crista of each semicircular canal is located on the wall of the domelike ampullary expansion. The cilia of the hair cells extend upward from the crista into the cupula, a jellylike membrane. The cupula, having the same density as the surrounding fluid, forms a septum sealing the ampullary cavity. Because of the inertia of the canal fluid, rotation of the head around an axis perpendicular to the plane of the canal results in its displacement relative to the canal wall. The fluid motion deforms the cupula, bending the cilia and activating the hair cells.

Owing to the anatomic symmetry of the horizontal canal in each ear, rotation of the head in the horizontal (or yaw) plane produces displacement of fluid in opposite directions in the two canals. Motion of fluid toward the ampulla results in depolarization of the hair cell–nerve fibers in one

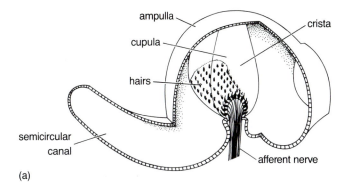

(a)

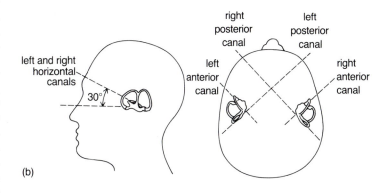

(b)

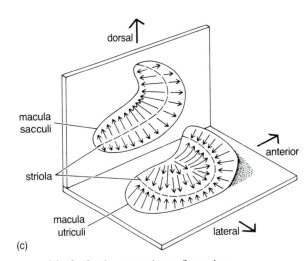

(c)

Vestibular system. (a) The basic anatomic configuration of the semicircular canals. (b) The semicircular canals in each side of the head. Broken lines indicate the plane of orientation of the individual canals. The parallel arrangement of the three synergistic pairs is apparent (left anterior canal and right posterior canal, right anterior canal and left posterior canal, right and left horizontal canals). (c) The orientation of the maculae, saccule, and utricle from one side. Arrows within the maculae indicate the orientation of the excitatory vector for the hair cells. (From H. O. Barber and C. W. Stockwell, *Manual of Electronystagmography,* **C. V. Mosby Co., 1976)**

canal. The opposite action takes place in the other canal. A similar situation occurs with the vertical canals, with the characteristic that the synergistic pairs are the anterior of one side and the posterior of the opposite side. Normally each canal works in a reciprocal mode to its opposite pair. Also, because of the high frequency of spontaneous activity in the nerve fibers, each canal organ is a bidirectional detector; that is, the activity of the fibers changes during both depolarization and hyperpolarization of the hair cells by, respectively, increasing or decreasing the number of spikes per second.

Each macula supports a "heavy load" of otoliths embedded in a gelatinous matrix attached to the macula and composed of a calcareous material with a density greater than that of the surrounding endolymph fluid. The position of this otolithic load depends on the direction of the gravitational or linear force. The saccule and utricle are composed of hair cells whose kinocilia are oriented so that those in the saccule are maximally sensitive to vertical displacement and those in the utricle to horizontal displacement, always with bidirectional capability. Also, as with the semicircular canals, the maculae of one inner ear operate synergistically with the maculae of the contralateral ear.

The bidirectional capability, together with the synergistic arrangement of the receptor organs, has important clinical implications. For example, damage to one inner ear may produce symptoms that suggest either inhibition of the receptors in that ear or excitation of the receptors on the contralateral side. This can make it difficult to infer the location of the lesion. A positive aspect of this property, however, is that even in cases of the complete destruction of one inner ear the brain can make use of the bidirectional capabilities of the remaining ear to obtain information about motion in opposite directions.

Frequency Range of Receptor Sensitivity. The magnitude of the responses arising from cilia displacement in the maculae and cristae does not exactly replicate the magnitude of the forces applied to these receptors; their sensitivity to sinusoidal accelerations decreases with increased frequency of the stimulus. This effect may be seen in the response of the semicircular canals to the forces associated with angular acceleration. Owing to the viscous elastic restraining forces of the cupula ligaments and those opposing the motion of the fluid in the narrow canals, the response of the crista is far from that of a perfect accelerometer. Instead, the magnitude of the change in frequency of spikes in the crista vestibular fiber is in phase and proportional to the velocity of the head for a wide range of frequencies of motion (0.05–10.0 hertz) which, interestingly, represent those of natural head movements. The semicircular canals, therefore, are often referred to as velocity detectors.

Central Vestibular System The basic elements of the vestibular reflex arc are the hair cells, an afferent bipolar neuron, an interneuron, and an effector neuron. The afferent bipolar neuron enters the brainstem, where it divides into an ascending and a descending secondary branch. Each of these gives off tertiary terminals that make contact with multiple interneurons in each of the four major nuclear groups of the ipsilateral vestibular nucleus. These are the superior, lateral, medial, and descending nuclei. The precise projection of the different receptors in each nucleus is not known in detail. There are interneurons that respond only to stimulation of a single vestibular receptor, others that respond to various vestibular receptors, and some that, in addition, respond to other sensory inputs such as vision and proprioception, hence providing the opportunities for multiple interactions.

An important anatomic connection in the vestibular reflex arc is made at this level. Ipsilateral interneurons receive inhibitory innervation from interneurons in the nucleus of the contralateral side connected to the contralateral synergistic receptors. Because of the reciprocity of action among receptor pairs, one effect of the cross-coupled connection is to enhance the input to each neuron, perhaps doubling its magnitude. Another effect is to connect the receptor from each ear to the vestibular nucleus of both sides. If one of the ears is damaged or destroyed, the remaining labyrinth is able, by its bidirectional capability, to detect motion in either direction and, further, because of the commissural connection, to activate the vestibular nuclei on both sides of the brain.

Vestibular Reflexes. The information from the vestibular nuclei is relayed through efferent vestibulospinal, vestibulocerebellar, and vestibuloreticular pathways to the muscles of the body so that balance and posture may be maintained. Because of the differences in neural connections, each vestibular nucleus has a dominant role in the production of different vestibular reflexes. The lateral and inferior vestibular nuclei are important for the production of vestibulospinal reflexes and control of muscle contractions in the neck and extremities. The superior and medial nuclei are important for the production of vestibulo-ocular reflexes. The medial nucleus is also important for commissural connections.

Vestibulo-Ocular Reflex. One of the most important vestibular reflexes is the vestibulo-ocular reflex, which involves the neurons innervating the extrinsic muscles of the eyes. Through this reflex the vestibular system contributes to the maintenance of gaze by moving the eyes in a direction opposite to that of the head movement, thus compensating for the angle of head motion. For large head rotations (greater than ± 20 degrees) the reflex takes the form of nystagmus—a back-and-forth eye movement consisting of a compensatory deviation, the slow component, interrupted by a flick in the opposite direction, the fast component.

Cerebral Cortex Center—Vestibular Subjective Sensation A connection has been demonstrated between the vestibular nucleus and the cerebral cortex through the thalamus. In humans this cortical area is located around the superior sylvian gyrus where direct electric stimulation results in the subjective sensation of motion. This area is believed to provide consciousness of motion. Interestingly, human subjects relate the movement of their head during rotations to the velocity, rather than the acceleration. Likewise, they misinterpret the direction of gravity during movement with a linear acceleration vector; they think they are falling backward when they are being pushed forward.

Bibliography

Baloh, R. W.: *Dizziness, Hearing Loss, and Tinnitus: The Essentials of Neurotology*, F. A. Davis Co., Philadelphia, 1984.

———— and V. Honrubia: *Clinical Neurophysiology of the Vestibular System*, F. A. Davis Co., Philadelphia, 1979.

Honrubia, V., and M. A. B. Brazier (eds.): *Nystagmus and Vertigo: Clinical Approaches to the Patient with Dizziness*, Academic Press, New York, 1982.

Vicente Honrubia

CENTRAL AUDITORY MECHANISM

Most knowledge about the physiology of the auditory nervous system has come from studying the responses of experimental animals to sounds. In most of these experiments the responses of single nerve cells to selected sounds have been recorded by using microelectrodes.

Microelectrodes can be glass pipettes filled with an electrically conductive solution or fine metal wires that are sharpened to very fine tips and are electrically insulated except at the tips. The tip size of microelectrodes ranges from a fraction of a micrometer (1/1000 of a millimeter) to a few micrometers. When placed close to a nerve cell or nerve fiber (neuron), microelectrodes record the electrical discharges given off by the individual neuron as it transmits the impulse. When a microelectrode is inserted into a nerve cell, the electrical potentials of the cell membrane that govern the discharges of the nerve fiber can be recorded. When the responses of an individual cell of the auditory nerve are recorded with microelectrodes, a picture is obtained of how a sound message is transformed in the ear. From studying the electrical patterns of the discharges of neurons in different parts of the auditory system, it is possible to map out how certain sounds are represented in the different parts of the auditory system.

Pure-Tone Coding When pure tones (sounds of only one frequency) are presented to an ear and the responses from single fibers in the auditory nerve are recorded, a prominent feature of the response is frequency tuning. This means that each nerve fiber is most sensitive to a certain frequency of sound. When the frequency of the tone is changed (a higher or lower tone is presented), the intensity of the sound (its loudness) has to be increased in order to reach the threshold of the neuron (the point at which the neuron fires off an impulse). The frequency at which the threshold has its lowest value is known as the fiber's characteristic frequency. A curve showing the thresholds at which a particular nerve fiber responds to different frequencies is known as the frequency threshold curve or tuning curve of that fiber. Single auditory nerve fibers have frequency tuning because the basilar membrane of the cochlea responds selectively to different frequencies.

Recording from cells in the cochlear nuclei has shown that cochlear nuclei cells also are tuned to the frequency of tones, but their tuning has been modified by neural processing and interaction between different nerve cells. Thus their frequency tuning curves are not all similar in shape, as are those of auditory nerve cells. Instead, some of their tuning curves are wider or narrower, or may have more than one peak. As information ascends the auditory pathway it is processed more and more, leading to increasing variety in the shapes of the tuning curves of the neurons. This change in the shape of tuning curves as information ascends the auditory nervous system is an indication that the information undergoes a transformation in the nuclei of the ascending auditory pathway. By the time this information has reached the auditory cortex, there is great variety in the shapes of the tuning curves, and curves may be further modified by the degree of wakefulness and attention of the animal.

Neurons in different nuclei of the auditory nervous system, including the cortex, are anatomically organized according to their characteristic frequencies. This is called tonotopic organization, and means that each neuron is located close to neurons tuned to similar frequencies, so that as a microelectrode is passed through a nucleus it will encounter neurons tuned to increasingly higher frequencies or increasingly lower frequencies. In other words, each nucleus has certain areas where impulses of certain frequencies pass through, similar to the cochlea where high frequencies are represented at the base and low frequencies at the apex. For this reason, tonotopic organization has also been referred to as cochleotopic organization. In the primary auditory cortex, tonotopic organization is quite precise: higher frequencies are found in the more frontal parts (rostally) and low frequencies are found caudally. In the association areas of the auditory cortex (area II), the tonotopic organization is reversed.

Tonotopic organization in the auditory system has been compared to the organization of the visual and somatosensory nervous systems, in which the visual field or the body surface is projected onto the surface of the respective cortices. However, these representations are two-dimensional, whereas frequency, as projected onto the surface of the auditory cortex, is a line (one-dimensional). What constitutes the other dimension of the auditory cortical surface has been a mystery until recently, when it was found that neurons that respond to binaural cues (differences in the time it takes for a sound to reach each of two ears and differences in the intensity of the sound at each ear) are located in an orderly fashion on the auditory cortex surface in a dimension perpendicular to the frequency dimension.

The first dimension of a tone, its frequency, is thus represented in the auditory nervous system in a way similar to the way it is represented in the cochlea: its anatomic location determines to which frequency it is sensitive. This is in accordance with the so-called place hypothesis of frequency discrimination, which states that each frequency has a specific place of maximal vibration. Similarly, each frequency activates neurons located in specific anatomic areas at each level of the auditory nervous system.

However, it has been known for a long time that the time pattern of a tone is also important for frequency discrimination. Thus, there must be some mechanism by which the time pattern of a tone is interpreted (decoded) by the auditory nervous system. While it is not yet known how temporal information is decoded, it has been known for decades that the temporal pattern of a sound is coded in the discharge patterns of individual nerve fibers in the auditory nerve. It is also known that this information is transmitted in the discharge patterns of cells in the cochlear nucleus and in the superior olivary complex, but it is not known how the information is interpreted in the central auditory nervous system. There are thus two ways in which the frequencies of pure tones can be coded in the auditory nervous system: by their anatomic location (place hypothesis) and by the temporal pattern of discharges of neurons.

Complex-Tone Coding Little study has been devoted to how the information in sounds that are more complex than pure tones is transmitted and interpreted. Natural sounds such as speech sounds vary rapidly in intensity (amplitude or loudness) and frequency (pitch). Studies have shown that the spectrum of vowel sounds seems to be represented in the discharge pattern of single auditory nerve fibers by the time pattern of the discharges and, to a lesser degree, by the place hypothesis. For this reason, investigators have studied how natural sounds are transformed in the auditory pathway by examining how animal auditory pathway neurons respond to tones with rapidly varying amplitude and frequency. The results show that the discharge patterns of single neurons in, for example, the cochlear nucleus change more in response to tones that change in amplitude and frequency than they do to steady tones, and that different neurons seem to prefer different specific rates of change. This response to changes in amplitude increases when more than one tone is presented at the same time, which indicates a preference for sounds that contain more than one frequency. In higher nuclei, such as the inferior colliculus, this specificity to changes is further developed. In this nucleus there are cells that respond only to changes in amplitude, while other respond to changes in both amplitude and frequency.

Although direct studies of the responses of the auditory pathway to speech sounds are few, it has been shown that vowel sounds are specifically coded in the neurons of these nuclei by their fundamental frequencies (how they are intoned) as well as by their spectra (formant structure). On the basis of studies of sounds that change in amplitude (amplitude-modulated sounds) and frequency, it may be assumed that the fundamental frequencies of the human vocal cords may be well represented in the discharge pattern of neurons in the nuclei of the auditory pathway, as should changes in the spectra of, for example, vowels (formant transitions). Changes in the spectra of speech sounds are known to be of great importance in speech perception. *See* SPEECH PERCEPTION.

DESCENDING AUDITORY PATHWAY FUNCTIONS
While not much is known about descending auditory pathway functions, it is known that when fibers of the olivocochlear bundle are stimulated electrically, the sensitivity of the hair cells decreases, and that when the ear is stimulated by sound, fibers of the bundle give off discharges. Although the specific purpose of the descending auditory system is not known, it is generally believed to play a role in the ability to focus on certain sounds and ignore others.

Bibliography
Gelfand, S. A.: *Hearing: An Introduction to Psychological and Physiological Acoustics*, Marcel Dekker, New York, 1981.

Møller, A. R.: *Auditory Physiology*, Academic Press, New York, 1983.

Moore, B. C.: *An Introduction to the Psychology of Hearing*, 2d ed., Academic Press, London, 1982.

Pickles, J. O.: *An Introduction to the Physiology of Hearing*, Academic Press, London, 1982.

Aage R. Møller

Pathology

The remainder of this article discusses pathologies of the ear related to hearing loss. They are arranged in anatomical sequence: external ear, middle ear, inner ear, and auditory nerve.

EXTERNAL EAR AND AUDITORY CANAL

Hearing loss is produced by several different categories of pathologic conditions of the external ear and ear canal: wax occlusion, inflammation, neoplasm, and both developmental and acquired anomalies. Basically, all of these disorders act in the same way—partially or completely blocking the passage of airborne sound waves to the eardrum and causing conductive hearing loss. With the exception of developmental abnormalities, hearing loss from disease of the ear canal generally is not permanent.

Wax Occlusion Wax occlusion is the most common external cause of hearing loss. Wax slowly builds up, hardens, and may become impacted. Sound waves simply cannot reach the eardrum. The otolaryngologist removes the impacted wax in a variety of fashions and in the process restores hearing.

Inflammation Another common temporary hearing loss is from inflammation of the external ear canal (external otitis). The skin of the ear canal becomes infected by bacteria or by fungus. In some cases this is localized to a furuncle or pimple near the opening of the ear canal. In other cases, the skin along the entire ear canal becomes tender, red, and swollen. Debris from the infection (secretions, pus, and dead skin), as well as swelling of the ear canal skin, acts to produce a hearing loss that disappears with proper treatment.

Benign Tumors Conductive hearing loss also can occur when the ear canal is blocked by tumor. The most common external auditory canal tumors are bony growths, osteomas, and exostoses. Exostoses, which are more often found in people who enjoy cold-water swimming, are firm, irregular, multiple masses of bone. Like osteomas, which are single lesions, these masses need to be removed only if they grow large enough to block the ear canal. Other benign tumors include lipomas (fatty tumors), myomas (muscle tumors), and angiomas (blood vessel tumors). If large enough, any of these can interfere with hearing.

Cholesteatoma of the ear canal is called keratosis obturans. Like cholesteatoma of the middle ear, this benign tumor refers to the buildup of desquamated cells (shed skin cells and debris). This can develop spontaneously or as a result of previous trauma or surgery. The condition can usually be treated by simple removal of the debris. In more extensive cases, radical treatment may be required.

Malignant Tumors Over 90 percent of external ear and ear canal malignancies are skin cancers; 60 percent of these are squamous cell carcinomas; 30 percent are basal cell carcinomas; and the remainder are melanomas, adenocarcinomas, or other tumors. Patients usually report ear pain and drainage. Squamous cell carcinoma and basal cell carcinoma are treated by wide surgical removal and postoperative radiotherapy when indicated. The prognosis for lesions of the ear canal remains poor, with a five-year survival rate of only 30 to 40 percent. Cancer of the outer ear has a five-year survival rate of over 90 percent.

Developmental and Acquired Anomalies Most anomalies of the pinna (external ear) are minor and do not interfere with hearing. Overly large ears (macrotia) and low-set ears are common abnormalities. Another familiar minor developmental anomaly, the lop or "Mickey Mouse" ear, actually improves hearing in the same fashion as does cupping of the ear by the hand. In contrast, many patients who have an external ear that may be only partly developed (or microtic) can expect to have a conductive hearing loss. This anomaly occurs in 1 in 20,000 to 30,000 live births. The microtic ear varies from a pinna that is small and slightly deformed to one that is only a nubbin of tissue. With the more severe external ear deformities, one also finds marked narrowing (stenosis) or even complete absence of the ear canal. As the ear canal opening decreases to smaller than 4 millimeters, a conductive hearing loss can be expected. The hearing loss gets worse as the opening gets smaller. Atresia (absence or narrowing of the external auditory canal) can occur independent of other ear abnormalities or can be associated with external- or middle-ear disorders. It can also be acquired as a result of infection, trauma, or tumor. Other defects, such as cleft palate, branchial cleft cysts, and kidney defects frequently occur in these patients along with sensory-neural hearing loss due to inner-ear abnormalities.

Congenital defects of the external auditory canal and external ear are evaluated carefully with audiometric studies and x-rays of the middle ear and temporal bone if atresia exists. Computerized tomography (CAT) scan or polytomography are normally used to give a radiographic picture of the area. Once properly evaluated, a child with bilateral ear deformities and hearing loss is begun on amplification and special training as soon as practical.

Cosmetic surgery of the external ear should be done before the child reaches school age. Severe malformations or complete lack of the external ear may be better treated with a prosthetic ear. Surgery to correct unilateral atresia or absence of the ear canal is generally delayed until the patient is old enough to give consent to the surgery. The first ear in a patient with bilateral atresia can be done at the age of four or five years, after the status of the ear canal and the middle ear and the risk of injury to the facial nerve have been determined. The other ear can be corrected one year later if the patient got a good result from the first surgery. Cosmetic and functional ear reconstruction must be coordinated between otologist and plastic surgeon. *See* AUDITORY DISORDERS, REMEDIATION OF: Surgical Treatment.

Bibliography

Bergstrom, Lavonne: "Anomalies of the Ear," in Gerald English (ed.), *Otolaryngology*, Harper and Row, Philadelphia, 1984.

Conley, J. J., and A. J. Novack: "The Surgical Treatment of Malignant Tumors of the Ear and Temporal Bone," *Arch. Otolar.*, 71:635–640, 1960.

Gates, George (ed.): *Clinical Auditory Evaluation*, American Academy of Otolaryngology, Rochester, 1981.

Goode, Richard: *Acoustic Aspects of Chronic Ear Surgery*, American Academy of Otolaryngology, Rochester, 1980.

Lee, K. J. (ed.): *Essential Otolaryngology*, 2d ed., Medical Examination Publishing Co., New York, 1977.

Shambaugh, George, and Michael Glasscock, III: *Surgery of the Ear*, 3d ed., W. B. Saunders, Philadelphia, 1980.

Judith N. Green

MIDDLE EAR

Most cases of conductive hearing loss are caused by abnormalities of the middle-ear sound transmission mechanism. Sound waves cause the eardrum to vibrate. This in turn sets the middle-ear ossicles (malleus, incus, and stapes) in motion. As the stapes moves, it pumps inner-ear fluid and thereby stimulates the sensory hair cells and the hearing nerve. A disorder anywhere in the middle-ear cavity would interfere with the sound transmission. Low-frequency hearing loss is produced by stiffness of the ossicles or eardrum or by fluid behind the eardrum that dampens vibration. High-frequency conductive hearing loss is produced by partial disruption of the ossicular chain or by an increase in mass in the middle-ear cavity. Hearing loss from middle-ear disease can be classified in several causative categories: acute and chronic inflammatory disease, congenital abnormalities, trauma, otosclerosis, and tumor.

Inflammatory Disease Eustachian tube dysfunction, acute and chronic infection of the middle ear and mastoid, and tympanosclerosis all may lead to hearing loss. The eustachian tube acts to drain fluid from the middle ear to the nasopharynx and to allow an influx of air into the middle-ear space. It can be blocked by swelling of the tube itself from allergy, viral infection and sinusitis, enlarged adenoids, tumor in the nasopharynx, and polyps or cholesteatoma in the middle ear. In patients with cleft palate or similar defects, the eustachian tube fails to open properly. The resultant negative pressure (partial vacuum) builds up in the middle-ear space. Fluid can then be drawn into the vacuum. This fluid acts to dampen sound transmission and cause a conductive hearing loss. The greater the amount of fluid, the worse the hearing. In most patients, especially many children and some older patients, eustachian tube dysfunction gives rise to chronic serous otitis media and later recurrent episodes of acute middle-ear infections.

The fluid in chronic serous otitis media is an excellent breeding ground for bacteria and causes many ear infections. Persistent negative pressure by itself causes a mild conductive hearing loss. Over a long period of time, a middle-ear vacuum or chronic serous otitis media can cause the eardrum to be drawn into the middle-ear cavity, forming small pockets. Cholesteatoma can form. Cholesteatoma refers to the buildup of shed, multiplying skin cells and debris in a loose matrix. As it enlarges, it fills the middle ear and mastoid spaces and can destroy the ossicles, causing a conductive hearing loss. If it becomes infected, inflammation of the bone with erosion can occur. These patients develop a foul ear drainage.

The tympanic membrane is affected in several ways by chronic ear disease. With prolonged negative pressure, it can eventually be drawn back and stuck to the inner wall of the middle ear, draping over the ossicles. Chronic negative pressure also can cause the eardrum to become flaccid or, in contrast, become so scarred (tympanosclerotic) from chronic inflammation that it vibrates poorly. Conductive hearing loss results.

Finally, a perforation or hole in the tympanic membrane also can occur from chronic middle-ear disease. The perforation can be dry or can continuously drain from infection. These perforations occur in the center, margin, or attic area (superior tympanic membrane). The margin and attic perforations are frequently associated with cholesteatoma as well. A perforation of greater than 1.5 millimeter will produce conductive hearing loss by interfering with tympanic membrane vibration and allowing sound waves to reach the round window directly and cancel sound transmitted through the normal channels. The larger the perforation, the greater the hearing loss. A hearing loss of 15 decibels results from a perforation of less than 20 percent of the vibrating surface, and a maximum conductive hearing loss of 40 to 45 decibels occurs if the tympanic membrane is completely gone but the ossicular chain is intact. Chronic otitis media and occasionally acute otitis media can cause sensory-neural hearing loss as well by spread of infection to the cochlea (inner ear).

Congenital Anomalies   Malformations of the middle ear range from minor abnormalities of the ossicles to major abnormalities involving the ossicles, tympanic membrane, facial nerve, and middle-ear muscles. The latter almost always are associated with stenosis or atresia of the ear canal. Defects of the Eustachian tube, vascular malformations, and congenital atresia also can occur and cause hearing loss. The origin of these disorders in most cases in unknown. Some are associated with chromosomal mistakes or congenital rubella.

Malformations of the stapes are the most common middle-ear defect. Movement of the stapes may be impaired by congenital fixation of the stapes footplate, contact of the stapes with the nearby bony wall, or by a stapes that is grossly deformed or even absent. The tendon of the stapes may be bony and fixed, rather than flexible. Absence of the oval or round window gives a significant conductive hearing loss because the sound waves are not transmitted well in the inner ear. A profound unilateral hearing loss is produced by absence of both oval and round windows.

The long process of the incus that connects it to the stapes may be missing. Obviously a conductive hearing loss results. Hearing loss also occurs if the malleus and incus are fused or if either ossicle is fixed to the nearby bony wall.

Vascular anomalies of the middle ear are rare and even more rarely cause hearing loss. Usually there is a pulselike noise in the middle ear. Conductive hearing loss can be caused by an aneurysm of the internal carotid artery or bulging of either the carotid artery or internal jugular vein into the middle-ear space. Motion of the ossicular chain is impeded by these vessels.

Abnormalities of the facial nerve frequently are found in association with other ear malformations. The Fallopian canal, which transmits the facial nerve in the middle-ear cavity, is lacking a complete bony covering in 50 to 60 percent of the population. It is thus vulnerable when repair of other congenital defects are attempted. The facial nerve itself only rarely interrupts the ossicular chain and causes a conductive hearing loss.

Otospongiosis (Otosclerosis)   In 1881 A. F. von Tröltsch coined the term otosclerosis to describe the disease in which the footplate of the stapes is firmly fixed in the oval window. It was thought that chronic middle-ear inflammation caused the secondary scarring (sclerosing) of the middle-ear tissue around the stapes; thus the term otosclerosis. Although it has long been known that this condi-

tion actually is caused by bone being reabsorbed and new loose spongy vascular bone (otospongiosis) being formed, the misnomer has stuck. Later in the course of the disease this spongy bone becomes calcified again and in its final mature state may be as dense as the surrounding bone.

Otospongiosis can involve almost any part of the temporal bone, but if vital areas are not affected, the patient remains asymptomatic. A focus (spot) of new spongy bone develops at a site just in front of the oval window in over 80 percent of cases and next to the round window in 40 percent. As this spot of otospongiosis next to the oval window grows, it gradually spreads to the oval window and then the footplate of the stapes. This acts to join the footplate to surrounding tissue and restrict movement of the stapes. Another common site of otosclerosis is the cochlea itself, with a resultant sensory-neural hearing loss.

Although otosclerosis is estimated to exist in 8 to 10 percent of white persons, it causes conductive hearing loss in only 1 percent of the population. It is rare in black and Asiatic people. Some women notice a worsening of an existing hearing loss or have the first symptoms of otospongiosis during pregnancy. In 75 to 80 percent of patients with otosclerosis both ears are involved.

While half of the people with otosclerosis have some family member with the disease, a definite genetic pattern of inheritance is not known. A child who has only one parent with otosclerosis has approximately a 20 percent chance of getting the disease.

There are two other bony disorders that involve the stapes in a very similar fashion. Paget's disease (osteitis deformans) commonly affects the whole skull and causes narrowing of the bony canal of the auditory (hearing) and facial nerves. If the hearing nerve is compressed enough, a sensory-neural hearing loss can develop. The stapes footplate also can be affected and fixed to surrounding bone with resultant conductive hearing loss.

Osteogenesis imperfecta is a bony disorder affecting the entire skeleton. The new bone that is laid down is brittle, and the patients suffer from many fractures. Half of these patients have hearing loss and a blue tinge to the whites of their eyes (sclera). In this condition, known as van der Hoeve's syndrome, this conductive hearing loss is thought to be caused by a process similar to otosclerosis that fixes the stapes footplate to surrounding bone. The patients also develop conductive hearing loss from fractures of the stapes itself.

In a typical case an individual with otospongiosis first notices a hearing loss between the age of 20 and 30 that slowly worsens with time. There is no ear pain or drainage. Hearing tests show conductive hearing loss that is greater in the lower frequencies. Tympanograms should demonstrate stiffness in the middle-ear system. The 512- and 1024-hertz tuning forks are heard better on the mastoid (bone conduction) than next to the ear (air conduction). As mentioned before, patients who develop cochlear otosclerosis as well as stapedial otosclerosis will also have a sensory-neural hearing loss.

Stapedectomy is the treatment of choice for patients with a sufficient conductive hearing loss who can medically tolerate surgery. It should never be performed on the only hearing ear. Patients who are not candidates for surgery find that hearing aids are very effective. *See* AUDITORY DISORDERS, REMEDIATION OF: Surgical Treatment.

Tumor   It is fortunate that tumors of the middle ear are rare because diagnosis is often delayed as these tumors remain asymptomatic until they are quite large. Both benign and malignant tumors generally cause a conductive hearing loss by filling the middle-ear cavity and external auditory canal, destroying the ossicles, and restricting movement of the eardrum. The sound transmission mechanism of the middle ear is thus interrupted. Sensory-neural hearing loss is more common in malignant tumors as they erode into the inner-ear system. Both can cause ear drainage, sudden bleeding from the ear canal, paralysis of the facial nerve, and dizziness. Constant deep ear pain is an alarming symptom and indicates possible malignancy.

There are many types of benign middle-ear and mastoid tumors, including choristoma, congenital cholesteatoma, dermoid cysts, meningioma, facial nerve neuroma, acoustic neuroma, glomus tympanicum, and glomus jugulare.

Choristomas are benign growths of salivary gland tumors that were misplaced to the middle ear in the embryo. They are often associated with other congenital middle-ear malformations. Like congenital cholesteatoma, discussed above, dermoid cysts are lesions that develop from "rests" of normal tissue misplaced during embryologic growth into the middle ear. Choristomas, congenital cholesteatomas, and dermoid cysts are treated by complete surgical removal.

Meningioma is a tumor that arises from a lining tissue of the brain. In the middle-ear cavity it may represent a brain tumor that has extended into the middle ear, or may be a primary middle-ear tumor. After careful evaluation with a computerized tomography (CAT) scan to determine the extent of tumor, these lesions are removed surgically by a mastoid or a middle-ear approach or by a combined approach if necessary. Neuromas (benign growths of nerve tissues) of the facial and hearing nerves can occur in the middle-ear space. In the case of the former, a facial neuroma generally causes facial paralysis and a conductive hearing loss due to the tumor occluding the middle-ear space. The

acoustic neuroma (neuroma of the hearing or auditory nerve) causes sensory-neural hearing loss by compression in the internal ear canal and displacement of the nerve.

Glomus tumors develop from clusters of nerve cells called paraganglioma that are involved in regulating various body functions. In the middle ear, one finds glomus jugulare tumors arising from the bulb of the jugular vein, and glomus tympanicum tumors arising from a nerve on the back wall of the middle ear. Much more common in women, they slowly enlarge and erode surrounding tissues. Hearing loss occurs as the tumor enlarges enough to fill the middle-ear space or if it erodes into the inner ear. The patients complain of a pulselike noise in the affected ear. After an appropriate workup, including a CAT scan or polytomography and vascular studies for advanced lesions, the tumors are treated with surgery and possible radiation.

The most common middle-ear malignancy is squamous cell carcinoma, a skin cancer. This usually starts in the external ear canal and invades the middle ear, thereby disrupting the sound transmission system. Radical surgery and radiation therapy combine to produce a five-year survival rate of only 25 to 30 percent. Melanoma and other malignancies rarely occur in the middle ear.

Bibliography

English, Gerald (ed.): *Otolaryngology*, Harper and Row, Hagerstown, 1976.

Gates, George (ed.): *Clinical Auditory Evaluation*, American Academy of Otolaryngology, Rochester, 1981.

Goode, Richard: *Acoustic Aspects of Chronic Ear Surgery*, American Academy of Otolaryngology, Rochester, 1980.

Goodman, M. L.: "Middle Ear and Mastoid Neoplasms," *Ann. Oto. Rhino. Laryngol.*, 80:419–422, 1971.

Montgomery, William: *Surgery of the Upper Respiratory Tract*, Lea and Febiger, Philadelphia, vol. 1, 1971.

Paradise, J. L.: "Otitis Media in Infants and Children," *Pediatrics*, 65:917, 1969.

Rosenwasser, Harry, and Simon Parisier: "Glomus Jugulare Tumors," in Gerald English (ed.), *Otolaryngology*, Harper and Row, Philadelphia, 1984.

Schuknecht, Harold (ed.): *Pathology of the Ear*, Harvard University Press, Cambridge, Massachusetts, 1974.

Shambaugh, George, and Michael Glasscock, III: *Surgery of the Ear*, 3d ed., W. B. Saunders, Philadelphia, 1980.

Judith N. Green

INNER EAR

The inner ear is an anatomically and physiologically complex system. Its structures and their functions are vulnerable to a host of diseases ranging from infections to damage by intense sound. The manifestations of these diseases can vary from total failure of the inner ear to develop (Michel's aplasia, a genetic, congenital disorder) to the very subtle signs encountered in early oxygen deprivation, such as a decrease in the normal electrical potential of endolymph, one of the fluids of the inner ear.

A hearing loss caused by disorder of the inner ear is called a sensory loss, although the term sensory-neural is more likely to be encountered, implying that some uncertainty exists concerning disorder location. Considerable research had been devoted to differentiating between inner-ear and cranial nerve VIII loci by hearing tests. The impetus for research was to improve diagnoses of tumors of cranial nerve VIII by noninvasive means. Differentiation is now important in the determination of eligibility for cochlear implantation, since adequate function of cranial nerve VIII is mandatory for candidacy. The separation of disease site by physical diagnosis is difficult. What appears to be a logical separation of parts of the auditory system for anatomical purposes becomes highly suspect when dealing with disease or lesions. For example, nearly all of the auditory nerve fibers leaving the inner ear degenerate when the sensory hair cells in the organ of Corti die. While the health of both of these types of cells may depend ultimately upon the viability of supporting cells in the organ of Corti, the fact remains that a lesion of the inner ear frequently is accompanied by a lesion of the VIIIth nerve. *See* COCHLEAR IMPLANTS.

Sensorineural hearing loss may be a symptom of a serious disease process like meningitis, a tumor, or syphilis. Once the primary disease has been treated as vigorously and comprehensively as possible, and if a hearing loss remains, it usually cannot be ameliorated medically or surgically. Then, emphasis is placed upon audiologic management—describing the sensations and perceptions caused by sound, and reducing or alleviating the social, educational, and emotional disability caused by the loss. Knowledge of lesion site seldom influences this management. However, understanding the damage that has been inflicted on the inner-ear structures by disease and correlating this with hearing-test results assists in explaining how the auditory system works. Indeed, advancements in designing prostheses for hearing-impaired persons are based upon such knowledge.

Diseases causing damage to the inner ear may be classified as congenital, traumatic, infectious, tumors (neoplasms), and those due to growth, aging, and unknown causes (idiopathic). The damage sustained by the inner ear for most of these diseases varies from patient to patient. The variability of damage from one patient to another suggests that hearing results may differ even when both suffered the same disease.

Congenital Diseases and Disorders Congenital pathologic conditions may be genetic in origin, may be caused by diseases during pregnancy such as maternal rubella, or caused by drugs taken by the mother during pregnancy. In the latter two cases, hearing losses are present at birth. Genetic inner-ear disorders, on the other hand, may be present at birth or delayed in onset, not becoming apparent until adulthood. It has been estimated that genetic factors account for at least one-half of all hearing losses in children. Abnormalities of the kidneys, skeleton, nervous system, and other body systems and processes frequently accompany congenital hearing problems. A collection of abnormalities in one individual due to the same causative factors is called a syndrome. Scores of congenital syndromes that include hearing loss have been described.

Numerous genetic hearing problems and their probable pattern of occurrence (recessive, dominant, or sex-linked) have been tabulated. Authorities have estimated that 1 in every 2000 school-aged children has a genetic hearing loss, and that it is one of the most prevalent causes of hearing problems in the population as a whole. *See* HEARING LOSS: Genetic Causes.

Certain drugs taken by a pregnant woman may be harmful to the developing auditory mechanism of the fetus. These include quinine, chloroquin, and Thalidomide. Infections sustained by the mother also can cross the placental barrier and cause serious, permanent damage to the inner ear of the fetus. The infections include rubella, mumps, cytomegalovirus, and syphilis, although the hearing loss due to congenital syphilis may not be present at birth but may develop later in life. The rubella epidemic in the United States in the early 1960s is claimed to have caused thousands of congenital hearing losses. Inner-ear damage also can be caused in newborns by genital herpes virus transmitted during birth.

Disorders Caused by Trauma Traumatic injuries to the inner ear vary from direct mechanical blows to the head (such as those sustained in automobile accidents) to those caused by sudden blasts such as gunfire.

Damage to the inner ear frequently accompanies skull fracture. This cause of hearing loss assumes important proportions when one considers the number of head injuries that occur daily. The head trauma may result in damage to one inner ear or to both. The consequent hearing loss may vary from complete to mild in degree, and it may be accompanied by dizziness due to coincident damage to the vestibular system. A common symptom is bleeding from the ear observed at the time of the accident.

Intense sound encountered in the workplace, at home, or in recreational pursuits (such as hunting and motorboating) can be hazardous to hearing as a result of damage to the inner ear. Hearing problems caused by a single sound exposure are said to result from acoustic trauma. They are relatively rare compared to those caused by repeated sound exposures. The latter problems are called noise-induced hearing loss. These by-products of a noisy civilization are insidious and progressive. These preventable losses may represent a devastating sensory deprivation. *See* HEARING LOSS: Noise-Induced.

Many types of chemicals in the environment (such as carbon monoxide, mercury, and lead) and chemicals used in the treatment of diseases can cause damage to the inner ear. These agents are referred to as ototoxic. They include such commonly used substances as salicylates (aspirin substances), aminoglycoside antibiotics (such as streptomycin, neomycin, gentamycin, and kanamycin), other antibiotics like chloramphenicol, and some diuretics (erthacrynic acid and furosemide). Physicians are well aware of the ototoxic nature of these substances, and they are prescribed only when necessary. Unfortunately, sensitivity to these ototoxic substances varies from one individual to another. The damage to the inner ear caused by these substances may be manifested by hearing loss, tinnitus, or dizziness.

Infectious Causes of Hearing Loss   Infectious diseases present two potential hazards to the inner ear: they can cause a hearing problem by directly acting in a detrimental fashion on inner-ear tissues, or they can be treated by drugs that themselves are poisonous to the inner-ear structures.

Bacterial infections of the middle ear may extend into the cochlea to attack the hearing organ; or bacterial and viral forms of meningitis may enter the inner ear to cause damage. Measles, mumps, and influenza are some of the more common infectious diseases that cause hearing loss through inner-ear damage. It is possible that some sudden hearing losses are due to viruses, because hearing losses may occur concomitantly with upper respiratory infections.

The hearing loss due to syphilis is often accompanied by severe dizziness. It frequently is progressive, but with early and appropriate prophylactic treatment it may be arrested or even reversed. However, profound hearing loss may occur.

Tumors   Tumors confined to the inner ear proper are especially rare, although tumors invading the internal auditory meatus, the bony canal through which cranial nerve VIII leaves the inner ear, occur more frequently. While the tumor of this nerve can interfere with cochlear blood supply and thus lead directly to changes in the cochlea, the initial symptoms usually reflect a neural source. Tumors of the labyrinth have been reported in von Recklinghausen's disease—multiple schwannomas.

Growth, Aging, and Other Causes of Hearing Loss
Otosclerosis, a disease usually confined to the middle ear, has been shown to invade the inner ear,

causing degenerative changes in some of the soft tissue structures. How frequently this occurs is unknown, but clinical experience suggests it may be unusual. Otosclerosis, commonly believed to be a genetic disease, usually becomes manifest in adulthood.

The hearing loss that results from aging is called presbycusis, a very imprecise term, because it now appears there are numerous causes for the decline in hearing seen in older people. Some of these causes are diseases known to produce organic lesions of the inner ear in persons of any age, and are discussed above. Particularly notable in this category is noise-induced hearing loss; persons now classified as aged were, a generation or two ago, the work force. Elderly people are particularly vulnerable to diseases, and as a result they receive prescriptions for numerous medications. Some of these medicines are ototoxic, and others appear to combine synergistically to produce a hearing disorder. Other causes for the decline in hearing noted in the elderly appear to be more closely related to changes in cognitive processing that accompany organic brain syndrome. *See* PRESBYCUSIS.

Which hair cells in the organ of Corti respond to sound is, in part, based on a correlation between the stiffness of the membrane on which the hair cells are located and the frequency of the sound. Age-related stiffness changes of this membrane could alter this tuning of specific hair cells to specific sounds. Likewise, it is possible that the hairs (cilia) of these sensory cells themselves change with advancing age, leading to altered cochlear function at micromechanical levels.

It has been theorized that biologic aging represents a weakening of the body's immune system. It may be assumed that genetics and environmental factors (such as diet) determine if and when such aging changes occur in a given individual. It appears that some older individuals retain quite robust hearing until very advanced ages. Thus, in spite of prevalent lay opinion, hearing loss is not an inevitable consequence of aging.

The cause of Ménière's disease is unknown, but the disease process, it is generally agreed, involves episodic swelling of the membranous (endolymphatic) inner-ear system. This distention of the scala media of the inner ear may be accompanied by rupture of some of the cochlear membranes, leading to a unfavorable mixture of cochlear fluids. This fluid mixture results in electrical changes in the cochlear potentials and, it is presumed, to failure of the hair cells to respond appropriately to sound. Thus, Ménière's disease is presumed to reflect a biochemical or metabolic malfunction of the inner ear.

Episodes of dizziness accompanied by hearing loss, fullness or pressure in the ears, and tinnitus typify Menière's disease. Although there is a great deal of individual variability demonstrated, the hearing loss may fluctuate early in the process but later it becomes permanent.

Slow leaks of perilymph, one of the inner-ear fluids, into the middle ear as a result of a perilymphatic fistula can result in a permanent, sensory-neural hearing loss. Early repair of the fistula may, however, lead to a recovery in hearing. Some of these fistulas are related directly to trauma or physical exertion (including sneezing and coughing), but others are due to unknown causes.

Bibliography

Beagley, H. A. (ed.): *Audiology and Audiological Medicine*, vol. 1, Oxford University Press, New York, 1981.

Konigsmark, B. W., and R. J. Gorlin: *Genetic and Metabolic Deafness*, W. B. Saunders, Philadelphia, 1976.

Paparella, M., and D. A. Shumrick (eds.): *Otolaryngology*, vol. 2: *The Ear*, W. B. Saunders, Philadelphia, 1980.

Tower, D. B. (ed.): *The Nervous System*, vol. 3: *Human Communication and Its Disorders*, ed. by E. L. Eagles, Raven Press, New York, 1975.

Jean M. Lovrinic; William S. Lovrinic

AUDITORY NERVE

Schwannomas, also known as neurilemmomas, are benign tumors that arise from the Schwann cell sheath of cranial or spinal nerve roots. These tumors constitute approximately 8 percent of all intracranial tumors and most commonly involve cranial (auditory) nerve VIII.

Almost all of the schwannomas arise within the internal auditory canal and have their origin from the vestibular division of the nerve. Occasional tumors arise from the facial nerve, and a smaller number may arise from the cochlear division of cranial nerve VIII. The tumors compress surrounding structures but do not invade.

Acoustic schwannomas occur more frequently in women, with a peak prevalence in the fifth and sixth decades. The tumors have a variable rate of growth. Small tumors may remain quiescent for a long time, and even cease to grow, without causing any symptoms. Small tumors, remaining within the internal auditory canal, occur more frequently in men. The large and giant-size lesions are more common in women.

The first symptoms to appear are unilateral tinnitus and a progressive high-frequency hearing loss. The cochlear nerve is generally normal histologically, even when profound deafness occurs. It has been shown experimentally in animals that up to 75 percent of the cochlear nerve fibers can be cut without hearing loss for pure tones. With acoustic schwannomas, the common auditory manifestation is a loss of speech discrimination out of proportion to the pure-tone hearing loss. It is thought that these symptoms are due to an interruption of the conduction capacity of the cochlear nerve by direct pressure effect of the tumor. Compression of blood vessels within the internal auditory canal by the tumor is also probably a cause of the decreased hearing by interfering with the blood flow to and from the cochlea.

Studies have also demonstrated that the blood vessels of the tumor itself are abnormal. Electron microscopic examination has demonstrated fenestrae and patent gap junctions between the lining cells of the blood vessel walls. This condition allows for leakage of serum through the wall and results in an increased concentration of protein in the cerebrospinal fluid and in the perilymph of the inner ear. Since smaller tumors are only minimally vascular, there would be less serum leakage, and, in general, the larger the tumor, the higher the protein level in the cerebrospinal fluid and inner ear.

As the tumor enlarges, the vestibular nerve cell bodies within the internal auditory canal progressively degenerate. This, however, is a slow process, and, although the brain largely compensates for vestibular dysfunction, the next symptom to appear may be unsteadiness or vertigo. The vestibular nerve has usually degenerated by the time that significant hearing loss occurs.

Involvement of the facial nerve within the internal auditory canal is somewhat less common and occurs later in the course of the disease. The symptoms consist of varying degrees of paralysis of the facial muscles.

The majority of acoustic schwannomas affect the size or shape of the internal auditory canal by erosion of the bone. This change can be determined by various x-ray techniques, among the more recent, computerized tomography (CAT), augmented by iodinated contrast material. The tumor, however, must be larger than 2 centimeters before it can be reliably demonstrated in this manner.

As the tumor becomes larger, it may extend out of the internal auditory canal and become located against the brain in an area bordered by the cerebellum and pons, referred to as the cerebellopontine angle. In this location, the tumor produces symptoms referable to compression of the brain and surrounding cranial nerves, so that it is both more dangerous and more difficult to remove.

Acoustic schwannomas are usually single. When multiple, they may be a manifestation of von Recklinghausen's neurofibromatosis. This disease is hereditary, and its transmission is a mendelian dominant. As a general rule, when the peripheral skin lesions of the disease are prominent, there are few, if any, intracranial lesions, whereas in patients with central nervous system lesions there are usually minimal peripheral lesions. In rare cases, the only manifestation of the disease may be bilaterally occurring acoustic schwannomas, although there are some investigators who consider this manifestation as separate from von Recklinghausen's disease.

The usual schwannoma is 1 to 4 centimeters in diameter, and rarely more than 8 centimeters, and is encapsulated. The cut surface may be firm and fibrous, focally hemorrhagic, necrotic, or cystic. Microscopically, two types of tissue are characteristic, referred to as Antoni A and Antoni B tissue. The Antoni A tissue corresponds to the fibrous areas observed grossly and consists of densely interlacing spindle cells with long oval nuclei, usually with their long axes parallel to one another. The characteristic palisading is due to clusters of cells with their nuclei in parallel rows. The Antoni B tissue consists of a variety of patterns, including loose areolar connective tissue, thick hyalinized blood vessels, large vessels containing thrombi, and cysts filled with proteinaceous fluid. Atypical cells may be seen, especially in tumors that have been present a long time, and these should not be interpreted as evidence of malignancy.

Schwannomas rarely, if ever, become malignant. In von Recklinghausen's disease, when a peripheral tumor becomes malignant, it is considered to be a neurofibrosarcoma rather than a malignant schwannoma, presumably deriving from the fibrous tissue cells of the tumor and not from the Schwann cells.

Bibliography

De Lozier, H. L., R. R. Gacek, and S. T. Dana: "Intralabyrinthine Schwannoma," *Ann. Oto. Rhino. Laryngol.*, 88:187–191, 1979.

Gussen, R.: "Pathology of Eighth Nerve Tumors and Petrosal Meningiomas," in D. B. Tower (ed.), *The Nervous System*, vol. 3, pp. 245–249, Raven Press, New York, 1975.

Kasantikul, V., et al.: "Intracanalicular Neurilemmomas," *Ann. Oto. Rhino. Laryngol.*, 89:29–32, 1980.

Martins, H., and J. T. Benitez: "Multiple Neurofibromatosis Involving the VIIIth Nerve," *J. Oto. Laryngol.*, 81:353, 1967.

Ruth Gussen

EAR AND HEARING

Ear and Hearing is published bimonthly and is the official professional journal of the American Auditory Society. The first issue was dated July/August 1975 and was titled the *Journal of the American Audiology Society*. When the society changed its name, the publication became *Journal of the American Auditory Society* with the September/October 1978 issue. *Ear and Hearing* replaced this title with the January/February 1980 issue.

J. Donald Harris was the editor in chief from 1975 through 1979. Ross J. Roeser held the position for *Ear and Hearing* from 1980 through 1984. Robert W. Keith took over in January 1985.

Ear and Hearing publishes papers of interest to clinicians, physicians, and educators who are dealing with the assessment, diagnosis, and management of auditory disorders. The journal is of primary interest to audiologists, otologists, educators of hearing-impaired persons, and designers and manufacturers of hearing aids. The goals of the journal follow the aims of the American Auditory Society—to increase knowledge of human hearing, to promote conservation of hearing, and to foster habilitation and rehabilitation of hearing-impaired people—with the primary purpose of the journal being to translate current research data into clinical concepts.

Active or associate membership in the American Auditory Society includes a subscription to *Ear and Hearing*. Active membership is open to individuals holding at least a baccalaureate degree from a certified college or university, while an associate member need only support the aims of the society. Although associate members do not have voting privileges, they do receive all publications and have all other rights and privileges. The society is based primarily within the United States, but there is no geographic limitation on membership.

Ross J. Roeser

EAR, NOSE AND THROAT JOURNAL

The *Ear, Nose and Throat Journal (ENTJ)* was first published as the *Eye, Ear, Nose, Throat Monthly* in February 1922. The publisher was the Professional Press Inc. of Chicago. The first medical editor was Thomas G. Atkinson, M.D. The basic concept was to publish material of clinical interest to otolaryngologists and ophthalmologists, and to include advances or innovations in therapies, new techniques in surgery, review articles, abstracts of articles in other medical publications, book reviews and letters to the editor.

A second progenitor of *Ear, Nose and Throat Journal* was *Diseases of the Eye, Ear, Nose and Throat*. This journal was first published in 1941 under the auspices of the Physicians' Postgraduate Press of Chicago. Francis L. Lederer, M.D., was the chief editor for the otolaryngology section, while Samuel J. Meyer, M.D., was the chief editor for the ophthalmology section. The journal was published monthly for two years (1941–1942), and its format was similar to that of the *Eye, Ear, Nose, Throat Monthly*. Its basic philosophy was to monitor changing trends in medicine and improve standards of medical practice. It endeavored to keep the general practitioner as well as the specialist informed about the practical problems in ophthalmology and otolaryngology, and to analyze differing viewpoints in clinical medicine.

In 1943, *Diseases of the Eye, Ear, Nose and Throat* was merged into the *Eye, Ear, Nose, Throat Monthly*, and this merger was reflected in volume 22 of the monthly. The basic philosophies of the combined journal remained unchanged, and it was published 12 times yearly as a size B magazine (7¼ × 10 inches or 18 × 25 centimeters).

In 1976 the resources of the *Eye, Ear, Nose, Throat Monthly* were acquired by the Insight Publishing Company of New York City. At this time, the editor for the ophthalmology portion was Manuel L. Stillerman, M.D.; and Armand G. DiBiasio, M.D., was editor for otolaryngology. Although the monthly's 1975 subscribers comprised 10,232 ophthalmologists and 5279 otolaryngologists, the magazine was being distributed without cost to clinicians and was being sponsored by advertisement revenue. However, the publisher felt that a lesser professional interest was served in continuing the ophthalmology section. Consequently, the monthly was restructured as a primary otolaryngology publication as the *Ear, Nose, and Throat Journal*, which was redesigned into a size A publication (8 × 11 inches or 20 × 28 centimeters). Volume 55, Number 7, of the former monthly was officially published as the *Ear, Nose and Throat Journal* in July 1976.

Alan D. Kornblut, M.D., because the chief editor of *Ear, Nose, and Throat Journal* in January 1980, and the editorial staff was expanded to include distinguished clinicians and academicians involved in otolaryngology or head and neck medicine and surgery in the United States, the United Kingdom, and Europe.

The *Ear, Nose, and Throat Journal* prints from 12,000 to 13,000 issues monthly. It is distributed to otolaryngologists in practice or residents in training, as well as to head and neck surgeons, allergists, pediatricians, and other clinicians concerned with disorders of the head and neck or ear, nose, and throat.

The *Ear, Nose and Throat Journal* is currently indexed in *Biological Abstracts*, *Chemical Abstracts*, *Excerpta Medica*, and *Index Medicus*.

The scope of the *Ear, Nose, and Throat Journal* comprises material of scientific merit or of timely interest to otolaryngology or head and neck medicine and surgery (inclusive of bronchoesophagology, allergy, audiology, and speech pathology). The journal publishes theme reviews and monographs on advances in the field as special issues prepared by guest editors from national or international medical centers. Contributed manuscripts are published in regular issues of the journal, and include papers describing original research, extensive clinical experiences, general reviews, and unusual case reports, as well as letters to the editor. Special sec-

tions of the journal are published as space allows, and they include commentaries, historical reviews, audiology columns, book reviews, new products, and a calendar of specialty-related events. Additionally, an annual otorhinolaryngological resident paper competition is held by the journal to encourage student or resident participation.

Manuscripts submitted should present experiences that are medically relevant or can be considered instructional. Subject matter that has been reported frequently in the past or contains insufficient clinical material is generally not acceptable for publication in the journal, although such may occasionally be adapted into an extended letter to the editor. Special consideration is given to manuscripts presented at local or national speciality-related meetings. All manuscripts will be refereed by members of *ENTJ*'s editorial staff, including the chief editor and the managing editor. Review criteria for acceptance of any material include originality, accuracy, appropriateness to clinical medicine, thoroughness of research, organization, and correctness of grammar.

Alan D. Kornblut

ECUADOR

Ecuador has experienced a series of changes since 1975 in the area of education of deaf people due to such diverse factors as population growth, increased interest in the field of educational investigations, advocacy movements led by the deaf community, and technical input from other countries. Educators, parents of deaf children, and deaf adults have become actively interested in and involved with improved educational and social equality.

DEMOGRAPHICS

In 1981 a landmark investigation was conducted by the National Commission for the International Year of the Disabled concerning Ecuador's disabled population. More than 1 million of Ecuador's 8.5 million citizens were identified as disabled, of whom 35 percent had a sensory (that is, visual or hearing) impairment. The total number of people with hearing impairments was estimated at almost 150,000; approximately 2 percent of the total population thus had some degree of hearing impairment.

This is a conservative estimate considering that the study only counted children or youths who were being served in schools or centers, and did not include children who had dropped out or never attended, nor many adults who were not affiliated with any formal organization. It is estimated that at the time of this investigation, less than 1 percent of all disabled persons were receiving formal rehabilitation or education and only approximately 50 percent had received any kind of specialized help at all. In 1980 there were less than 450 hearing-impaired students, out of an estimated 13,000 hearing-impaired children aged 4 to 15 years, who were enrolled in an educational or rehabilitation program. *See* DEAF POPULATION: Demography

There is no one reason to explain the large and consistent growth of deaf populations in Ecuador. The interplay between social, economical, and cultural factors creates a range of causes from careless accidents, unattended illnesses, and dietary deficiencies, to intermarriage among families, venereal diseases, and lack of pre- and postnatal care. Most of the losses are preventable. Although there is constant improvement being made in the areas of health care, education, and rehabilitation the majority of Ecuador's hearing-impaired individuals are still not being served. *See* HEARING LOSS.

EDUCATION AND REHABILITATION
Education and rehabilitation of deaf people is a pioneer field in Ecuador. Until the mid-1970s, most services available to deaf persons were offered by private, charitable organizations, often of a religious nature. In the late 1970s, special education became a concern addressed in the National Governmental Development Plan. Since then, there has been an increase in the number of programs offered for deaf children, their parents, and deaf adults.

According to the Ministry of Education study conducted in 1980 and an informal nationwide survey conducted by the Resource Center for Special Education in Quito in July 1984, there were approximately 20 schools or classes (academic programs); 7 of these served only hearing-impaired children, while the rest were classes of hearing-impaired children in special education schools which in addition may serve mentally retarded, learning-disabled, or blind children. Except for two residential schools, the rest had day schedules. If the hearing impairment is mild or if the parent can afford to pay the high registration fees of the private regular schools, a child may be "mainstreamed," but these cases are exceptions, and the child would not receive any support services. In these cases, the failures outweigh the successes.

Services for deaf people are concentrated in the two main cities of the country, Quito and Guayaquil. However, 9 out of 20 provinces of Ecuador have at least academic services available to hearing-impaired children. The majority of these schools provide a basic primary education with emphasis given to the development of oral skills. Very little emphasis is given in the area of prevocational education, although this is on the upswing. Over 50 percent of these schools are public and receive local

governmental aid. Teachers who work with hearing-impaired students, in general, are not specifically trained in deaf education. Most are regular school teachers, psychologists, speech therapists, or interested parents. The few trained professionals received their education outside Ecuador; there are no university programs in education of deaf pupils.

Other types of services found in Ecuador include three centers for professional training of adolescents and adults in the areas of carpentry, mechanics, shoemaking, weaving, sewing, and so on, which have limited job placement services; two diagnostic centers that offer neurological and audiometric evaluations to hearing-impaired students (about 20 per year); three rehabilitation centers with speech therapy services; several private practices which serve hearing-impaired children; and four organizations of deaf adults, three of which are informally organized and in initial stages with a total of 150 members, and one in Quito which is officially organized with 65 active participants. The Society of Deaf Adults in Quito offers services to hearing-impaired youths and adults, including nonformal adult education classes, sign language classes, and prevocational training. It also sponsors a theater of the deaf, organizes social events, and is in the process of publishing the first of several Ecuadorian Sign Language texts through a project, "Mano a Mano," funded by the InterAmerican Foundation. Presently, there are no established preschool or infant stimulation programs for hearing-impaired children, although some work is being done in individual cases by therapists, teachers, psychologists, or parents. No support services exist at the secondary or university levels for hearing-impaired students. There are very few hearing-impaired students attending regular high schools and no one with a severe hearing loss attending any university program in Ecuador. Some hearing-impaired young adults attend technical training centers to learn a trade.

COMMUNICATION METHODS
There is no nationally accepted method of communication among deaf people in Ecuador. Within the deaf community, sign language is used, but it differs slightly from region to region according to cultural, dialectical, and semantical differences. One of the purposes of the Quito Society of Deaf Adults' endeavor to publish sign language books is to make the sign language used in the different cultural regions in Ecuador available to teachers, parents, and deaf students.

According to research conducted by the Society of Deaf Adults in Quito, the origins of Ecuadorian signs can be traced to the commonly used gestural language of the Latin population, to iconic signs used among deaf individuals, and, since about 1980, to an influence of foreign sign languages: deaf travelers, North American Peace Corps volunteers, and returning deaf Ecuadorians who have been educated in Spain or Argentina.

Within the educational community, a controversy continues to exist between the oralists (who do not believe in teaching students any form of manual communication) and the proponents of total communication. There exist strictly "oral" schools in Ecuador, but the use of manual communication began to flourish in the 1980s as well as the acceptance and application of the teaching philosophy inherent in total communication. *See* EDUCATION: Communication.

SOCIOECONOMIC SITUATION
Information and statistics concerning the socioeconomic and employment status of deaf people are nonexistent in Ecuador. One may conclude by looking at the kind of jobs many hearing-impaired people hold (mechanics, parking lot attendants, craft workers, sewers, domestics, factory workers, carpenters, shoeshiners) that they are generally underemployed and that their average income is probably much lower than it is for the hearing population. There is also a large number of unemployed deaf people, especially women. In a very few cases, deaf people are teachers of deaf pupils or accountants. Until the educational and rehabilitation systems improve and employers' attitudes change, the socioeconomic situation of deaf people will continue to be too low.

FUTURE NEEDS
Ecuador finds itself at the beginning stages of what will be a long process of improving the lives of handicapped people, including those who are hearing-impaired. There are still many needs: more specialized teachers and professionals; better evaluative techniques and information to diagnose the hearing loss and to evaluate language development, cognition, and so on; more widespread utilization of hearing aids, especially at an early age; more emphasis on early intervention and preventive measures; more emphasis on supporting hearing-impaired students in regular schools; more parent organizations; a change in public attitudes toward deaf people (the label "mute" is still popular); broader acceptance of sign language; and a stronger lobbying voice with the Ecuadorian government.

Because there is a great amount of energy and interest directed toward attempting to meet these needs, the outlook for the future of hearing-impaired Ecuadorians is optimistic.

Bibliography
Hinojosa, J. R.: "La Problematica de la Educación Especial en el Ecuador," Ministerio de Educación y Cultura del Gobierno del Ecuador—Unidad de Educación Especial, UNESCO, 1980.

Labastida, E. R. de: *Los Impedidos en el Ecuador: Diagnostico de su Situación*, Instituto Nacional del Niño y la Familia, 1981.

Lalama, M.: "Interview," Centro de Investigaciones del Ministerio de Educación y Cultura del Gobierno del Ecuador, August 1984.

Montero, L.: "Informal Study of Schools, Organizations and Agencies Serving the Hearing Impaired Population of Ecuador," Resource Center for Special Education, July-August 1984.

Luisa Montero

EDUCATION

The education of deaf persons is unique in both special and general education in the United States today. Its unique character has existed since the establishment of the first school for deaf students in the United States in 1817 in Hartford, Connecticut. The singular nature of this education may be attributed primarily to two factors—the special educational characteristics of deaf learners and the low incidence of deafness in the general population.

The deaf child presents qualitatively different challenges to any educational system. The hearing child typically begins school with a highly developed auditory-vocal language system that will be the basis for classroom instruction and that will provide the foundation for the acquisition of reading and other academic skills. The deaf child does not have a developed auditory-vocal language system to serve as an instrument of learning. Since only a small percentage of deaf children have deaf parents, most deaf children also lack a visual-motor communication system such as American Sign Language (ASL) or one of the manual codes on English. Even though growing numbers of hearing parents are now learning and using some form of manual communication with deaf children, the initiation of such communication follows a process of identification of hearing loss and parental acceptance of deafness which might not be completed before the child is two years of age or older. Even after this, it will require time for the parents and other relatives to acquire skill in the use of manual communication. In general, it might be said of typical deaf children beginning the educational process that they have the same range of intellectual potential as hearing children; they have not mastered the auditory-visual system of English and, therefore, cannot use it as an instrument to acquire knowledge and academic skills; they have had relatively little, if any, exposure to American Sign Language or to a manual code on English; and because of the lack of effective, shared communication systems with parents, relatives, and other children, opportunities for experiential and incidental learning have been limited. *See* Manually Coded English; Sign languages: American.

Demographic Information

This section is primarily concerned with children who are classified as deaf for educational purposes. Because there has been confusion over the terms deaf, hard-of-hearing, and hearing-impaired, some general working definitions are necessary. The term hearing-impaired may be used to include the complete range of hearing loss, from very mild to no response to sound at all, and within this range may be found deaf and hard-of-hearing individuals. A deaf person is one whose hearing is disabled to an extent that precludes the understanding of speech through the ear alone. Some deaf people may hear environmental sounds, and even part of a speech signal, but not to the extent that they can process continuous speech through the auditory channel.

A hard-of-hearing individual is one whose hearing is disabled to an extent that makes difficult the understanding of speech through the ear alone, but does not preclude it. A hard-of-hearing person may not hear all of the speech sounds of a communication, but can hear enough to process messages through the auditory channel. There has been considerable disagreement over how to make a functional distinction for educational purposes between a person who is deaf and one who is hard-of-hearing. It is simple to classify a person who hears no speech as deaf and one who misses only a few sounds as hard-of-hearing. The problem of classification appears at the boundaries between the two, where it is difficult to determine when a loss becomes severe enough to constitute deafness.

One definition of deafness may overlap with another definition of hard-of-hearing. Previous attempts to use audiometric measures of hearing loss across the speech range in clinical settings have met with limited success when applied to educational environments. Two persons with identical hearing losses may function educationally quite differently, one as a deaf person and one as a hard-of-hearing person. There are many explanations for such variation, including age at onset of a hearing loss, ability to utilize a hearing aid, and presence of other handicapping conditions.

The numbers of hard-of-hearing children are much greater than the numbers of deaf children. On the other hand, hard-of-hearing children tend to need less intensive special educational programming, and some may require none at all. Federal government national incidence projections have estimated that there are approximately 50,000 deaf and 325,000 hard-of-hearing children in the American school-age population. More than 90 percent of the estimated population of deaf children and approximately 20 percent of the estimated hard-of-hearing population have been identified as receiving special educational services. This suggests that approximately 45,000 deaf children and 65,000 hard-of-hearing children are being identified and served. Although there is some overlap, deaf children generally receive more intensive, comprehensive, and special services. For hard-of-hearing children, special help tends to concentrate on speech-language therapy, with little or no direct additional academic support. Although there is growing evidence that hard-of-hearing children do, in fact, need more specialized educational services, this section concentrates on the types of programs specifically designed to provide educational services to deaf children. These are children whose hearing loss was present at birth or occurred before the onset of spoken language and is of such a nature as to preclude the ability to process spoken language through the ear alone, even with the use of a hearing aid. *See* Deaf population: Demography.

School Placement

Educational systems must make a series of decisions on placement, mode or modes of instruction, and academic emphasis. Each decision will be highly related to others and will entail either implicitly or explicitly questions of trade-offs or relative values. The question of school placement provides a relevant example. In the United States, although busing for racial integration has been relatively common, most elementary school-age children are educated in neighborhood schools, and most high school students attend schools within a local community. Parents of deaf children naturally prefer the same type of school attendance for their deaf children. However, given the low incidence of deafness, there may be no other deaf children within a particular elementary school attendance area. Even in large comprehensive high schools, the numbers of deaf children would be very small. Because of the small numbers and the need for special services, educational programs for deaf children may encompass several school districts, necessitating extensive travel to and from school on a daily basis. Where this is not available, an alternative may be enrollment at a residential school for deaf students with the child commuting home on the weekends. For many parents and educators, the question of placement represents a dilemma. The deaf child who attends a neighborhood school may not have access to the specialized services needed by a deaf learner and may be isolated because of difficulties in communicating with hearing classmates. A child who attends a regional program may spend time in transportation that detracts from time spent with the family and reduces contact with the neighborhood. A child who attends a residential school may have access to the most comprehensive educational services but less interaction with the family. Clearly, in deciding on school placement for an individual child, parents and educational personnel must balance a number of potential positive and negative factors. *See* Educational programs.

The general perception in the field of education of deaf persons—and in special education in general—has been that trends over the past 10 years have been such as to move education of deaf people from an enterprise essentially based in residential schools to one predominantly based in public schools with the children living at home. This reflects the impact of the mainstreaming movement in special education and the impact of Public Law 94-142, the Education for All Handicapped Children Act, enacted in 1975. The act mandated a free appropriate public education (FAPE) for all handicapped children and set forth guidelines to protect their rights. The legislation also stipulated that children must receive nondiscriminatory testing and that each child must have an individualized educational plan (IEP), which is to be reviewed on an annual basis. A key component of the act is the requirement that consideration must be given for placement of each child in the least restrictive environment (LRE) compatible with an individual's needs. *See* Educational legislation: Impact of Public Policy, Least Restrictive Environment.

The least restrictive environment provisions of P.L. 94-142 have led some observers to view it as a mainstreaming law. This is not the case. In fact, the term mainstreaming was deliberately excluded from the act, which clearly states that handicapped children should be educated with nonhandicapped children to the greatest extent possible and appropriate. The result has been that deaf children continue to have a number of options available to them, including instruction in regular classes supplemented by special services, resource rooms, special classes, special day schools, residential schools, and other settings such as programs for multiply handicapped children. Although there have been changes in the placements of children, the changes have not been as dramatic as some educators imagined. In fact, P.L. 94-142 probably has had as profound an impact on the proportions of children attending private and public schools as it has had on residential and day attendance. For example, in the 1972–1973 academic year one source identified more than 49,000 deaf children being served in educational programs. Of this number, somewhat more than 19,000 were in public residential schools for deaf students and about 18,000 were in public school day classes for deaf children. Of the remainder, a majority of more than 7000 were in public day schools for deaf people.

These numbers accounted for 90 percent of the placements of the 49,000 deaf children. By comparison, in 1982–1983, five years after the passage of P.L. 94-142, there were roughly 18,000 students in public residential schools, 21,000 in public day classes, and 3500 in public day schools out of a total of more than 46,000 students. For both academic years, approximately 39 percent of deaf students attended public residential schools, suggesting that the impact of P.L. 94-142 on residential schools has been less than expected. There was, however, a significant reduction in children identified as attending public day schools and an increase in those attending public day classes, with more children now in this placement than in public residential schools.

It is of interest to note that the greatest change over the 10-year period occurred in a placement that was relatively small to begin with—private residential schools for deaf students. In 1972–1973 there were 12 private residential schools identified, enrolling a total of 1353 deaf students. For 1982–1983 the same source reported 9 private residential schools enrolling a total of only 475 students. Thus, enrollment in private residential schools for deaf children in 1982–1983 had dropped to less than one-third of what it had been 10 years previously and included approximately 1 percent of deaf students. It appears then that the provisions of a free appropriate public education had a tremendous impact on private residential school programs, some of which are among the oldest and best known in the United States. This change took place in a relatively short period of time. Whether an equal reduction in enrollment at public residential schools will occur over a more protracted period of time is unclear, but the indications are that public residential schools will continue to educate a significant portion of the deaf students in America.

ACADEMIC ACHIEVEMENT

The question of academic orientation or focus ranks in importance with that of school placement. It has been established without serious question that the average six-year-old deaf child is disadvantaged—compared to the average six-year-old hearing child—in expression and reception of spoken language, in English grammatical skills, and in factual knowledge of the world. The deaf child begins school with some clearly identified deficits. Educators and parents must make some difficult choices. Traditionally, programs for deaf students have concentrated on remediating the speech and English grammar skills of deaf children. Special curriculum materials and procedures have been developed to help deaf children master the basic sounds of the language both receptively and expressively. Most programs, especially through the elementary school years, have special time set aside for individual or small group training in speech and use of residual hearing. Training sessions may also be incorporated into other parts of the school day, and classes in subjects such as history, social studies, or math may also be combined to some extent with training in vocal skills. The same thing is essentially true of training in English grammar, as most programs, choosing from among the several available alternates, employ some language curriculum to teach the children the fundamentals of English grammar. For the most part, the instruction is different from that provided hearing children in English classes; it is designed to teach English grammar to deaf children that hearing English-speaking children of a comparable age already know. As in training in vocal communication, the history, math, or social studies class may serve as the setting to teach the deaf student grammatical constructs such as subject-verb agreement, past tense, or passive voice.

Although it has not been widely discussed, the outcome for the deaf child is generally a school day in which there is relatively little time devoted to academic subjects, compared to the school day of the hearing child. There is evidence that as early as the preschool years deaf children spend less time on math or premath instruction than hearing children; by seven years of age their math achievement scores reflect this. Educational research in general is concerned with the concept of time on task, which states that the amount and quality of student learning in regard to a particular topic or subject matter is positively related to learning and mastery of content. The more time students spend on a subject, the more they will learn.

There are definite difficulties educators of deaf students face in organizing a school day, week, month, and year. Deaf children cannot realistically be expected to attend schools for longer periods of time during the day than hearing children. More time would be difficult to schedule, especially for those children in public school day classes. Of more importance, school learning itself may put more of a strain on deaf children, who have to maintain visual attention to learn. It is likely that school is more tiring for the deaf child compared to the hearing child, who does not need constant visual contact to understand the teacher and other students.

Most deaf children enter school with inadequately developed vocal skills and with imperfect mastery of English grammar. Much of the curriculum in programs for deaf students is designed to remediate these areas of weakness, and relatively little attention has been paid to academic content areas. The results have been discouraging. Despite the devotion of massive resources and years of intensive special instruction by speech and language therapists, most profoundly deaf individuals do not develop adequate vocal communication. Research indicates that expressive and receptive oral skills are heavily reliant on the amount of residual hearing an individual has, and there is little evidence that additional training improves the speech of deaf students after the onset of adolescence. The same is true of training in English grammar.

In addition to the unsatisfactory results in vocal communication and grammatical skills, the deaf child starts school at a disadvantage in factual knowledge of the world. Throughout the school years, the gap in achievement with hearing peers increases. By 17 years of age, when a child would be expected to be in twelfth grade, standardized tests of reading and English skills might show a fourth-grade achievement, and tests of arithmetic computation may be at the sixth-grade level.

For large numbers of deaf children, then, the years of their elementary and secondary education have had few beneficial effects. Concentration on vocal skills and English grammar have not produced the hoped-for results, and lack of attention to academic subject matter has led to unacceptably low levels of achievement. The complexity of the problem is illustrated by the fact that academic achievement is lowest in areas that rely on knowledge of English.

In the case of speech and grammatical development, then, the concept of time on task is not very useful. Increasing the already great amount of time invested in these areas by itself would probably result in little or no additional progress. After more than 400 years of direct instruction and generations of research, it must be acknowledged that educators still do not have the requisite knowledge and skills to help the majority of profoundly deaf children develop fluency in oral communication. Unless there is some unexpected breakthrough in research or technology, the situation probably will not alter substantially in the foreseeable future. *See* SPEECH TRAINING.

The prognosis in terms of academic achievement is somewhat more optimistic, although guarded. Research on national samples suggests that the academic attainments of deaf elementary and secondary students increased from the early 1970s to the early 1980s. There is also support for the argument that most standardized achievement tests, which assume a knowledge of standard English, are not appropriate for deaf children and may, in fact, underestimate their academic skills. The high rates of attendance and graduation of deaf students in postsecondary education programs, their demonstrated competence in a wide range of employment situations, and their ability to function successfully in a highly complex society lend support to this position.

There is reason to believe that increased concentration on academic subject matter can lead to increased achievement. However, this reorientation may be more difficult to achieve than seems apparent at first glance. First, the training of most present teachers of deaf children has emphasized vocal and grammatical skills at the expense of training in teaching of subject matter such as math, science, history, and social studies. In addition, most professionals involved in teacher training have had the same orientation. A reorientation and retraining of teachers and teacher trainers is necessary. The major thrust should be to develop teachers who have the speech and grammar teaching skills of traditional teachers of deaf students along with more expertise in specific content areas. Such an undertaking will require a complete restructuring of contemporary teacher-training programs. *See* TEACHING PROFESSION: Training.

The necessity for more emphasis on academic achievement has been made even more imperative by changes in education in general. Following evidence of a steady decline in overall academic achievement among American school children, educational systems, beginning in the late 1970s, moved to add intellectual vigor to the schooling process. Across the United States various reforms and innovations were tried, including merit pay for teachers, minimal competency tests for promotion and high school graduation, reduced emphasis on athletics and extracurricular activities, lengthening the school day, lengthening the school year, competency testing for teachers, and raising requirements for math, science, and foreign languages. It was clear by the early 1980s that the downward trend in achievement had been halted, and that achievement scores, at least in the elementary grades, were starting to improve. American elementary and secondary schools in the 1980s provided different intellectual and academic environments than those in the 1960s and 1970s. They were more demanding, rigorous, and achievement-oriented. Education of deaf pupils, as part of the American educational system, was influenced by these trends. There is already evidence that deaf students are achieving at higher levels than comparable deaf students 10 years previously. However, improvement is needed just to keep pace with the projected gains by hearing students that have been noted. To close the gap, educators of deaf children have to aim for a greater rate of improvement among deaf children than among hearing. The situation is especially critical among those public school programs that integrate deaf students into regular classrooms with interpreters. For deaf students to be successful, they must be able to meet increasingly demanding academic standards.

ETHNIC IDENTIFICATION OF DEAF STUDENTS

There have been some intriguing changes in the ethnic and racial composition of the deaf school-age population in the United States. Until the 1970s, it was believed that deafness was more common among Whites in the United States than among Blacks, and no serious attempts were made to identify the incidence of deafness among Hispanic Americans, Asian Americans, and Native Americans. Fortunately, beginning in the 1970s, more information was obtained on the ethnic status of deaf school children. Much of this information dealt with the two largest groups—Blacks and Hispanics. Because of the small numbers of Asian Americans and Native Americans in relation to the general population, less information was available. For example, one major study in 1975 of the ethnic distribution of 45,000 American deaf school children used only four categories: White, Black, Hispanic, and other. Asian-Americans and Native Americans were included in the "other" category. The ethnic breakdown of the students was reported to be 76 percent White, 15 percent Black, 7 percent Hispanic, and 2 percent other. The percentages were equivalent to the ethnic distribution of the general United States population of 18 years and younger, with a somewhat higher representation of Black students than might be expected. This was the first clear evidence that deafness was not less common among Blacks than the general population. Because the size of the Black deaf population has been underestimated, the needs have been underestimated, and have been minimized. Black children have been less likely to be diagnosed as deaf at early ages and to receive preschool training. They are more likely to be classified as mentally retarded.

Data indicate a continued rise in the percentage of deaf children who are of minority status in the school-age population. This reflects the growth in minority representation in the American school-age population due to immigration, higher minority birth rates in general, and a fall in the fertility rates for Whites. Still, minority representation in programs for deaf students reached 30 percent in the early 1980s, higher than in the general school-age population. Blacks, at 18 percent, again were overrepresented in relation to general population figures. Hispanics had increased to 9 percent, and in some large city programs constituted the largest single ethnic group. Asian-Americans represented 2 percent and Native Americans 1 percent, with the number of deaf Asian-American children projected to increase rapidly.

Very little attention has been devoted to the special characteristics of deaf Native American, Asian-American, Hispanic, and Black school children, and most teacher training programs have not provided special information or special training to meet the children's needs. There is a great discrepancy between the ethnic identity of teachers and the children they teach. While 30 percent of deaf school children are minorities, only 6 percent of the teachers are so. In a pluralistic society it is neither logical nor desirable to expect children always to be taught by a person of the same ethnic status. The point is that teachers of all ethnic backgrounds should be trained and available to teach children of all ethnic backgrounds. The necessity for meeting the needs of all children and for recruiting and training teachers of deaf students from all groups is a pressing one.

COMMUNICATION MODES IN THE CLASSROOM

Perhaps no issue in all of special education has received so much attention and generated so much bitter controversy as the question of how teachers and students should communicate in the classroom. In the United States the conflict has been magnified by a misunderstanding of the nature of American Sign Language (ASL) and its relationship both to spoken English and to manual codes on English. The devaluation of manual communication from ASL to manual English codes was accentuated by the consensus of linguists in the first half of the twentieth century that a true language can only be spoken. This consensus has been shattered, and linguists now accept the idea that manual languages exist that are of a richness and complexity equal to oral languages.

Prior to 1970 practically all preschool and elementary classes for deaf children were oral-only, that is, they did not permit the use of signs or fingerspelling. Many residential school programs allowed signs and fingerspelling to be used in classes with high school–age students, usually in coordination with speech. These schools were considered to employ a combined system, that is, they combined oral-only education for younger children with manual communication or simultaneously oral-manual communication for older children. The majority of residential schools, and apparently all day schools and day classes, however, used oral-only communication in all classes for all ages. The children frequently used manual communication among each other outside of the classroom. Depending on the circumstances, they used ASL or even invented their own esoteric systems.

The rationale for reliance on oral-only classroom communication arose from the belief that any form of manual communication would interfere with the development of speech and English grammatical abilities, thereby restricting access of the deaf child to the larger hearing community. It was argued that since signs were easier for a deaf child to use than speech, the child who used manual communication would not be motivated to develop speech skills. Even those schools that used manual communication with high school students banned it

from elementary classes, with the reasoning that all children should be first given the opportunity to learn orally. Signs were reserved for use at later ages with children who had not shown oral progress. *See* HISTORY: Sign Language Controversy.

The situation began to change as evidence accrued that oral-only education was not effective for a large proportion of the deaf population. In spite of intensive oral-only training, most deaf graduates did not possess fluent expressive and receptive oral skills, had difficulty with English grammar, and had unacceptably low levels of academic achievement. Results of several different research studies appeared that compared deaf children of deaf parents to deaf children of hearing parents in areas such as reading and writing, academic achievement, social adjustment, and speech. Deaf children of deaf parents consistently were shown to have better reading and written English skills, higher academic achievement, and superior social adjustment, with no differences in speech skills. Since the deaf children came from families in which deaf parents used manual communication with them from infancy, the reports caused educators to rethink their previously unquestioned assumptions about the negative effects of early manual communication on speech, English, and academic achievement. The evidence seemed to suggest that manual communication could enhance English skills and academic achievement and had no influence, either positive or negative, on functional oral communication.

Following the lead of educators such as David Denton in Maryland and Roy Holcomb in Delaware and California, programs for deaf students moved toward a more inclusive model of communication called total communication. Although numerous definitions have been advanced, total communication may be thought of in terms of the right of a deaf child to be exposed to and use, on the basis of the child's individual needs, any form of communication that can be effective in the classroom. This includes speech, speechreading, gestures, reading, writing, fingerspelling, manual codes on English, ASL, use of residual hearing, and any other means that are effective. This represents a major change in the philosophy behind education of deaf persons. In the past the goal was to fit all children to one mode of communication. Now the ideal is to fit the mode to the child. *See* SOCIOLINGUISTICS: Total Communication.

The majority of educational programs now use a manual code on English, usually in coordination with spoken English, for at least part of their school population. Several manual codes have been developed for instructional purposes (such as Signing Exact English, Seeing Essential English, Linguistics of Visual English, and Signed English), the systems differ from ASL and share a number of characteristics. First, they were designed to be used in coordination with speech and follow English word order, not ASL. The majority of vocabulary is drawn from ASL, with changes in handshape sometimes used to convey English words; for example, Signed English signs for "situation" and "environment" are the same except that for the right hand the S handshape is used with the former sign and the E handshape with the latter. Each of the manual codes also uses a number of invented signs for function words such as "the," "an," "she," "of," and for bound morphemes such as -ED, -LY, -EN, rather than rely on ASL mechanisms to convey the same information. There have been differences of opinion over the effectiveness of the invented codes. Many of them have been modified by use to incorporate grammatical features of ASL that are more efficient. It is likely that manual codes on English and their relation to ASL will be a matter of great interest and investigation in the future.

In education of deaf children, the 1970s may be viewed as a decade of change and the 1980s as one of consolidation. The underlying theme has been that of responding to individual needs, with growing flexibility in educational placement options and use of both oral and manual modes of communication. Indications are for increased academic achievement in deaf students, but continuing difficulties remain in helping deaf children achieve communication fluency in English and perform academically to the level of their intellectual potential.

Bibliography

Jordan, King, Gerilee Gustason, and Rosalyn Rosen: "An Update on Current Communication Trends at Programs for the Deaf," *American Annals of the Deaf*, 125:350–357, 1979.

Meadow, Kathryn: *Deafness and Child Development*, University of California Press, Berkeley, 1980.

Moores, Donald F.: *Educating the Deaf: Psychology, Principles and Practices*, Houghton Mifflin, Boston, 1982.

Wilbur, Ronnie B.: *American Sign Language and Sign Systems*, University Park Press, Baltimore, 1979.

Donald F. Moores

History

The nineteenth century was the most pivotal period in the education of deaf Americans. At the outset of the century, most Americans probably believed that deaf people were uneducable, but by 1900 most states and territories had established government-supported schools for their deaf citizens. Frequently, deaf individuals themselves either spearheaded the efforts to establish these schools or became the schools' first administrative officers. By the early twentieth century, the education of deaf people was an accepted principle, and schools were established or abolished as needs changed in particular locations.

COLONIAL AMERICA

The education of deaf children did not concern most colonial people, who viewed deafness as an unalterable act of God. Any attempt to change such an ordained condition was looked upon as sacrilege. Hence, in 1679 the inhabitants of Rowley, Massachusetts, viewed with misgivings Philip Nelson's attempt to teach speech to a young deaf-mute. Nelson's efforts stirred thoughts of sorcery and witchcraft; consequently, his attempts were summarily concluded.

The idea of teaching deaf people lay dormant among the colonials until 1771, when Colonel Thomas Bolling of Virginia sent his young deaf son John abroad to a Scottish school for deaf-mutes operated by Thomas Braidwood. The success of Braidwood's teaching was demonstrated to Bolling through his son's academic progress. As a consequence, in 1775 he placed his other two deaf children under Braidwood's instruction. During this same period Francis Green and his deaf son Charles moved to England where they sat out the American Revolution. In 1780 Charles too was enrolled in the Edinburgh school. *See* BRAIDWOOD, THOMAS.

Charles Green's progress over the next three years was sufficiently satisfactory that his father wrote a laudatory book regarding Braidwood's work, entitled *Vox Occulis Subjecta (The Voice Made Visible)*. After the Revolution, Green returned to the United States, and his interest in deaf education increased. Consequently, in 1801 he translated Abbé Charles Michel de l'Epée's book, *Education of the Deaf*, into English. He also wrote articles urging the introduction of education for deaf children in the United States. His efforts, however, were fruitless. Moreover, Green's political affiliations prior to and during the Revolution may well have prejudiced the public against his education proposals. *See* l'EPÉE, ABBÉ CHARLES MICHEL DE.

FIRST EDUCATION ATTEMPT (1812)

In addition to his three deaf children, Thomas Bolling had one hearing son, William, who subsequently became the father of two deaf children. With his familial background and knowledge, William was better prepared than his father had been to cope with the problem of deafness.

In May 1812 Bolling learned that John Braidwood, a grandson of the late Thomas Braidwood, was in the United States and was planning to establish a school for deaf children in Baltimore. Bolling encouraged Braidwood in his endeavor. However, Braidwood had a serious drinking problem, and he disappeared with Bolling's money. It was not until August 1812 that Bolling discovered that Braidwood had been jailed for his debts in New York City. For the sake of his children, Bolling covered Braidwood's debts and returned him to the family home as a tutor.

Bolling's extraordinary faith led him in 1815 to set up a school for Braidwood on his property, Cobbs Plantation. It was to be a boarding school with a promised income of $2000 to $2500 annually. Despite such assurances for success, John Braidwood continued to display his weakness for the bottle.

Finally, to preserve Braidwood's skill, Bolling arranged for him to train the Reverend John Kirkpatrick of Manchester, Virginia. Kirkpatrick, according to the agreement, was to conduct a class for deaf children in conjunction with a small private school that he operated. His presence was to provide the stability that it was hoped would keep Braidwood on course. Kirkpatrick continued to teach deaf pupils until 1819, when suddenly and without explanation his program ceased. Shortly thereafter, in 1820, John Braidwood, working as a bartender in Manchester, died and with him Bolling's dream of education for deaf people in the United States.

FIRST PERMANENT SCHOOL
FOR DEAF PEOPLE (1817)

Public education for deaf persons in the United States began in 1817 through the efforts of 28-year-old Thomas Hopkins Gallaudet, a minister in Hartford, Connecticut. Gallaudet's first interest in deaf people was sparked when he tried to teach a neighbor's deaf child, Alice Cogswell. The girl's father, Dr. Mason Cogswell, lent Gallaudet a book by the Parisian educator, Abbé Roch Ambroise Sicard. Following the procedures described, the young man began to teach the child vocabulary and sentences. Cogswell, observing Gallaudet's success with the child, arranged for him to be sent to Europe to study methods of teaching deaf students. *See* COGSWELL, ALICE; SICARD, ABBÉ ROCH AMBROISE CUCURRON.

Arriving in England, Gallaudet went to London, where he sought the opportunity for teacher training in the London School for the Deaf. The stated condition for such training was that Gallaudet would remain and teach at the school for three years. Gallaudet was anxious to return to the United States and begin his work, so he declined the offer. He then went north to the Braidwood School in Edinburgh to check on the training possibilities. Mr. Kinniburgh, the principal of the school, was carrying on the Braidwood tradition, including its policy of secrecy. John Braidwood's presence and mission in the United States was also known to Kinniburgh. Accordingly, perhaps to protect young Braidwood's interest, he imposed conditions Gallaudet could not accept.

Discouraged, Gallaudet returned to London where, fortuitously, the famous Abbé Sicard of the Pari-

sian National School for the Deaf was demonstrating the art of teaching deaf children. Gallaudet attended Sicard's lecture, met him, and received an invitation to come and study at the National School. Thus, after nine wasted months in England and Scotland, Gallaudet crossed the Channel to begin his studies with Sicard and his staff.

Sicard's two deaf master teachers, Jean Massieu and Laurent Clerc, worked with Gallaudet on Sicard's System of Ciphers, a language instruction system, and other techniques for teaching subject matter to deaf pupils. Clerc, the younger of the two mentors, established a good rapport with the American. *See* CLERC, LAURENT; MASSIEU, JEAN.

After three months of training, Gallaudet was ready to return to the United States. Before leaving, he asked the Abbé Sicard if he might take Laurent Clerc to America to assist him in establishing a school in Hartford. Reluctantly, Sicard agreed, and in June 1816 Gallaudet and Clerc set sail for the United States.

Meanwhile, Cogswell and other of Gallaudet's Hartford supporters had secured from the Connecticut legislature an Act of Incorporation for a school. In the fall of 1816, the legislature granted the sum of $5000 toward the support of the new institution.

Further money was raised by Gallaudet and Clerc, who traveled to various cities lecturing. Finally, on April 15, 1817, in Hartford, the American Asylum for the Deaf opened its doors, and soon a normal program was instituted to prepare teachers for the expanding staff. In turn, many of these instructors moved out to organize schools in various states. With that, education for deaf people was under way in the United States. *See* AMERICAN SCHOOL FOR THE DEAF; GALLAUDET, THOMAS HOPKINS.

1818–1843

Following the establishment of the American Asylum for the Deaf, interest increased on the behalf of education for deaf children. Over the next 25 years, six additional schools were established, and all but one imitated the Hartford model. These six early schools set a high standard for all educational institutions for deaf pupils.

The New York Institute for the Deaf was established in 1818, due in part to the efforts of a deaf Frenchman, F. Gard. A teacher in the Institution of Bordeaux, Gard sent a letter in 1816 addressed to the Philanthropists of the United States, which came to the attention of Samuel L. Mitchell, a New York physician. In the letter, Gard offered his services as a teacher of deaf pupils. With this impetus, Mitchell called two colleagues to discuss the possibility of starting a school for deaf children in New York City. After a series of meetings with interested citizens, four young deaf children were brought together on May 20, 1818, under the instruction of

Abraham O. Stansbury. Through the actions of various legislative committees over the following two years, the New York Institution for the Deaf was finally established as a publicly supported school. Gard, however, was not called upon to assist in the new program he had inspired, so he turned his efforts to Pennsylvania.

Gard wrote to several outstanding citizens of Philadelphia, expressing his desire to teach deaf people in the United States. His letters were again well received and influenced a number of citizens on his behalf. At the same time, Gallaudet and Clerc were lecturing in various American cities. Their presentations in Philadelphia impressed people considerably. As a result, it was believed that any attempt by Gard to establish a school would be competitive and would interfere with the efforts of the newly established American Asylum in Hartford; Gard was again rebuffed.

However, a Philadelphia shopkeeper, David G. Seixas, had gathered a group of street children whom he clothed and fed at his own expense. Among them were a number of deaf children. In the latter part of 1819 or early in 1820, Seixas organized his deaf charges, five boys and six girls, into a little school. Word of Seixas' educational efforts on behalf of the deaf children spread throughout the city, and a committee of interested citizens was organized in support of his program. On May 15, 1820, Seixas was appointed principal of the new Pennsylvania Institution for the Deaf, the third school for deaf people in the United States.

The fourth school, the Kentucky School for the Deaf, was established in Danville on December 7, 1822, by the state of Kentucky. Originally named the Kentucky Asylum for the Tuition of the Deaf and Dumb, the school had a shaky beginning. In the first year, two different persons assumed the principalship. The first proved to have misrepresented himself and was consequently fired; the second proved to be unqualified and was subsequently removed from his position.

Finally, in February 1824, John Adamson Jacobs, an 18-year-old student at Centre College, was appointed as assistant teacher. His success as a teacher quickly became obvious. Desirous to improve his teaching skills, Jacobs went to the American Asylum, where he studied with Gallaudet and Clerc. After 18 months of observation and practical teaching, Jacobs returned to Kentucky and found the school in disorder. He immediately set to work to organize it properly and was appointed principal, a position he held for 44 years, until his death in 1869. Jacobs is accordingly credited with the founding of this school.

The Ohio Institution for the Education of the Deaf, in Columbus, was the fifth school of its kind established in the United States. Its incorporating act was passed in 1827, after a long struggle on the part of the Reverend James Hoge to gain official recognition for the education of deaf children. The appointment of Horatio Hubbell as the first superintendent of the Ohio Institution marked the beginning of the program. In preparation for his task, Hubbell spent 18 months at the American Asylum in Hartford, Connecticut, studying instructional methods. In the fall of 1829, under Hubbell's direction, the school opened its doors.

The establishment of a school for deaf Virginians in 1838 marked a departure from earlier efforts, for this school was designed for both deaf students and blind students. Lewis Chamberlayne, a citizen of Richmond, Virginia, and the father of two deaf children, was instrumental in its establishment. He began his efforts by bringing to Virginia F. A. P. Barnard, an instructor in the New York Institution, along with some pupils from the school. Barnard conducted several teaching demonstrations for the benefit of the legislators and interested citizens of Richmond. This effort resulted in the passing of the first act toward the establishment of a state school for deaf children in Virgina. The Reverend Joseph D. Tyler, an experienced teacher in the American Asylum, was elected to serve as principal of the new school, called the Virginia School for the Deaf and Blind and located in Staunton, Virginia.

Chronologically, the next school established for deaf pupils was the Indiana School in 1843, which has the distinction of being the first school founded by a deaf individual, William Willard. An alumnus of the American Asylum for the Deaf and former teacher in the Ohio Institution, Willard went to Indiana for the purpose of establishing a private school for deaf children. Making contacts in Indianapolis, he soon assembled a sizable group of friends and supporters for his plan. In May 1843 a resolution was drawn up by a group of citizens advocating that Willard visit various parts of the state to create interest in the education of deaf people.

During the summer, Willard, at his own expense, traveled about the state collecting not funds but pupils for his proposed school, and in October 1843 opened his school with 12 pupils. In June 1846 the state appointed James S. Brown, a hearing man, to direct the affairs of the rapidly growing institution.

DEAF FOUNDERS OF AMERICAN SCHOOLS FOR THE DEAF (1843–1912)

As the educability of deaf children became apparent in the mid-nineteenth century, state residential schools were founded in fairly rapid succession. Some of the schools were established through the efforts of concerned parents of deaf children, humanely inclined legislators, or socially concerned citizens. Others were established by deaf people themselves.

Arkansas (1850) One of the schools established by a deaf individual was the Arkansas School for the Deaf in Little Rock, which was incorporated in 1868. The school's deaf founder, Joseph Mount, succeeded in his efforts only after several other individuals had failed. The first attempt was made by another deaf man, J. W. Woodward, who opened a school for deaf children in Clarksville in 1850. Although Woodward received an appropriation from the state legislature for his school, he was short of funds and was forced to close. Asa Clark, father of a deaf girl, also tried to open a school in Arkansas, this time in Fort Smith in February 1860. He, too, had to close his school, which was then reopened in January 1861 by Matthew Clark, a deaf graduate of the New York School. With the advent of the Civil War, this school closed for the second and final time.

Mount, a graduate of the Pennsylvania School, finally succeeded in keeping open an Arkansas school for deaf people in the post–Civil War period. On July 10, 1867, Mount persuaded the city of Little Rock to support an institution for deaf pupils. The next year the state legislature, at Mount's urging, agreed to incorporate the Little Rock school as the Arkansas Deaf-Mute Institution.

Kansas (1861) Philip A. Emery, a deaf man, was primarily responsible for founding the Kansas School for the Deaf. Previously a teacher at the Indiana School for the Deaf, Emery was unable to get an economic foothold in Kansas, and his funds were soon depleted. Poverty and starvation soon faced him and his family.

Emery's misfortunes were reversed, however, when Jonathan R. Kennedy, who had three deaf children, prevailed upon Emery to teach his youngsters. After some urging, Emery recognized this as being a call to service and also an opportunity to extricate himself and his family from pending disaster. At Kennedy's request, Emery decided to open a private school in Baldwin City, near Lawrence. On October 9, 1861, the school opened, but not one pupil entered until December 9. With her came a ham, some butter and eggs, and a wagonload of corn for which there was no demand. This bartering, customary in Kansas at that time, was to cover the $2.50 weekly board and tuition fee Emery charged. By April four more pupils had arrived.

Unknown to Emery, a minister appeared before the state legislature in Topeka and pleaded on Emery's behalf for an appropriation for the school year 1862–1863. In 1863 an assistant teacher, Joseph Mount, formerly of the Philadelphia Institute and later founder of the Arkansas school, joined Emery and his wife in their work. Emery was advised by the legislature to move his school to Topeka where it might be better cared for. From there it was moved in 1864 to Olathe, the school's present location. With the Kansas School for the Deaf successfully established and assured of regular appropriations, Emery resigned in 1864 and moved east, eventually settling in Chicago, where he developed a system of day schools for deaf children.

Western Pennsylvania (1869) The Western Pennsylvania Institution had its beginning in 1868, when a single deaf boy was brought to the Mission Sabbath School operated by the Third United Presbyterian Church of Pittsburgh. A deaf man, W. R. Drum, an alumnus of the Pennsylvania School in Philadelphia, was selected to teach the child. As word of Drum's work passed through the city, he soon had an additional 8 or 10 deaf children under his instruction. Another deaf graduate of the Pennsylvania School, Archie Woodside, was then appointed to assist Drum. Thereafter, Drum's name appears to have been dropped from the school's record in favor of Woodside and his hearing sister Sarah, who together were appointed teachers in the program by the local board of the first ward. They were then provided the use of a room in a public school building. Upon the program's opening in September 1869, the first day school for deaf pupils began. After six years, Woodside was succeeded by James H. Logan, an alumnus of the National Deaf-Mute College (Gallaudet College) and former teacher at the Illinois Institution in Jacksonville. It was during Logan's administration that the Western Pennsylvania Institution was expanded from a day into a residential facility.

Cincinnati (1875) For many years the parents of deaf children residing in and around Cincinnati had complained of the distance their children had to travel to reach the Ohio School for the Deaf in Columbus. It was not until 1875 that action was taken to provide a day school accommodation in the Cincinnati area.

The principal of the new Cincinnati Public School for the Deaf was a young deaf man, Robert P. McGregor, an 1872 graduate of the National Deaf-Mute College. For a couple of years McGregor encouraged state support for a plan of boarding those children who lived outside Cincinnati; however, this plan was abandoned in favor of the original day school concept. This decision reduced the school's population because many of the children lived too far away to commute. Nevertheless, the Cincinnati Public School for the Deaf prospered under McGregor's administration. However, in 1881 Robert P. McGregor abruptly resigned and moved west to the Colorado School for the Deaf.

Utah (1884) The Utah Territory in 1884 established a school for deaf children in Salt Lake City, which was first affiliated with the University of Deseret. The school's first instructor was an 1880 graduate of the National Deaf-Mute College, Henry C. White. The school, consisting of one room in the university building, was opened on August 26, 1884, with 1 pupil under White's instruction. By the end of the first month the school had 4 pupils and concluded the year with 14. The school operated for five years as a day school with the pupils boarding in various homes. This plan, however, was discovered to be unsatisfactory, and a common home for all of the pupils was determined to be the wiser plan.

In 1889 a residential school building was erected on the university campus. Frank W. Metcalf, a teacher in the Kansas School, was appointed principal and White was designated as the head teacher. The Utah School for the Deaf was by this time serving all of the deaf children in the territory.

Florida (1885) By 1882 Florida was the only state that had not yet provided an educational facility for its deaf children and youth. T. E. Coleman, a senior at the National Deaf-Mute College, attempted to resolve this situation by writing to Florida's governor and offering his services. The governor, W. D. Bloxham, was immediately interested.

After graduation Coleman moved to Mandarin, Florida, setting up a base of operations from which he could work effectively in the promotion of his idea of education for deaf children. Bloxham recommended legislation to further Coleman's cause. In 1884 St. Augustine was selected as the school's site. By early February 1885, the new institution was open to receive pupils, but none showed up. By the middle of May, however, deaf children were finding their way to St. Augustine, and the Florida School for the Deaf and the Blind became a functioning reality.

New Mexico (1885) On November 10, 1885, Lars M. Larson, an 1882 alumnus of the National Deaf-Mute College, called together in Santa Fe, New Mexico, his class of five deaf girls and boys to begin their education. This first effort to teach deaf children in New Mexico was begun as a private project and was supported by the charity of citizens. Finally, in 1887 the territorial legislature decreed $100 per month to be appropriated for the school's support. Later in that year the legislature passed a law designating the little adobe institution as the territorial school for deaf pupils and appointed Larson the superintendent and his mother, B. E. Larson, the school's matron. Shortly thereafter, owing to the depletion of the territorial treasury, Larson was able to keep his school in operation by resorting frequently to his private means. His triumph as an educator was clear when, in 1890, one student completed the entire course of study, graduated, and passed the entrance examination for the National Deaf-Mute College.

North Dakota (1890) Anson R. Spear, an 1880 alumnus of the National Deaf-Mute College and resident of Minneapolis, had long expressed an interest in the deaf people of the Dakota Territory.

He was also well informed as to the educational provisions stated in the 1889 enactment which divided the territory into the two sovereign states of North Dakota and South Dakota. It was this division that left the northern state without an educational facility for deaf children, and that brought Spear into action on behalf of education for deaf children in the new state of North Dakota.

The authors of the state constitution had realized the need for school facilities for the state's deaf population, and included not only a provision for educating deaf people but also designated the city of Devils Lake as the location for the school-to-be. With this progressive legislative vision in his favor, Spear found a fertile and receptive field for his educational proposal.

In September 1889 he went to Devils Lake in order to create an interest and an understanding among the citizens on behalf of educating deaf children. As a result of his efforts, the city of Devils Lake agreed to furnish Spear with a rent-free building for the school's first year. Spear then drew up a bill for the school's establishment and presented it in November to the state legislature in Bismarck. Although the bill was passed by both houses, it was ultimately vetoed by the governor. A legislative fight ensued, and the bill was finally passed over the governor's objections. A sum of $5000 was then appropriated for one year of the school's support, beginning on July 1, 1890. On August 10, 1890, Spear was appointed the school's first superintendent, and his wife was hired as the school's matron. According to schedule, the school opened on September 10, 1890. New pupils gradually appeared until there was a total of 23. At the end of March another teacher was employed to assist with the program. In 1893 Spear wrote that the school had the support and confidence of the people and of those who first doubted its necessity. *See* SPEAR, ANSON RANDOLPH.

Arizona (1912) Until 1912 the deaf children of Arizona attended educational facilities in Utah and California. In 1911 Henry C. White, the deaf founder of the Utah School, moved to Phoenix, Arizona, where he convinced the city's mayor to support the idea of establishing a school for deaf children in Arizona. White immediately established a class for deaf children in an unused storage area and began teaching. In 1912, with Arizona receiving statehood, G. W. P. Hunt was elected governor. Almost immediately Hunt received a letter from Governor Foss of Massachusetts recommending White as an outstanding deaf man and educator. Shortly thereafter, when the new legislature moved for the establishment of a school for deaf children, the governor appointed White its principal.

In the autumn of 1912, there were assembled 19 boys and girls to form the new Arizona School for the Deaf. White was joined by his hearing daughter, Harriet T. White, to serve as the school's matron. In 1919 the institution was expanded with the enrollment of blind children, and the school became known as the Arizona School for the Deaf and the Blind.

With the establishment of the Arizona School in 1912, the majority of the states were providing education for deaf children and youth. The school-founding phase in American education of deaf people was almost completed. States without schools at that time were Nevada, Wyoming, and Delaware; they have since met the educational needs of their deaf populations.

Bibliography

Brenner, Betty: "Deaf Man Began Mission 25 Years Ago," *Flint Journal*, Flint, Michigan, June 13, 1982.

Fay, Edward Allen (ed.): *Histories of American Schools for the Deaf: 1817–1893*, 3 vols., Volta Bureau, Washington, D.C., 1893.

Fourgon, Fernand: *Historique de la Pedagogie des Sourds-Muets*, 2 vols., Paris, 1957.

Hall, Percival: *Collected Papers*, Washington, D.C., ca. 1941.

Lane, Harlan: *The Wild Boy of Aveyron*, Harvard Press, Cambridge, 1976.

Morrow, Robert D.: *The Education of the Deaf and Blind in Arizona*, unpublished master's thesis, University of Arizona, Tucson, 1941.

Scouten, Edward L.: *Turning Points in the Education of Deaf People*, Interstate Press, Danville, Illinois, 1983.

Edward L. Scouten

Leaders

Educational leadership in the instruction of deaf students is believed to have been initiated in 721, when St. Bede wrote about St. John of Beverly teaching a deaf-mute to speak. In 1485 a book was written by Rudolphus Agricola about a deaf-mute who learned to read and write. In 1550 Pedro Ponce de Leon began his career as teacher of deaf students. Girolamo Cardano, in 1553, was the first physician to recognize the ability of deaf people to reason. *See* PONCE DE LEON, PEDRO.

In 1620 a Spaniard, Juan Pablo Bonet, wrote a book on the single-hand alphabet which he used to instruct deaf students. In 1653 John Wallis published *De Loquela*, presenting a method of teaching English and speech. In 1680 George Dalgarno of Scotland in his book *Deaf and Dumb Man's Tutor* expanded the concept of using the alphabet by pointing to 26 separate locations on the open palm, with the thumb and finger tips representing the vowels. Dalgarno had published an earlier book in 1661, *Art of Communication*. In 1690 John Conrad Amman, a Swiss medical doctor, wrote the book *The Talking Deaf Man*, in which he supported the concept of an oral approach for instructing deaf persons. In 1754 a German teacher of the deaf, Samuel Heinicke, adopted Amman's philosophy and expanded this teaching methodology throughout Germany. *See* HEINICKE, SAMUEL; PABLO BONET, JUAN.

In 1760 Charles Michel Abbé de l'Epée, a French priest who became intrigued with the learning needs of two deaf sisters, incorporated a language of methodical signs into his instructional methods for deaf students. He was the founder in 1755 of the National Institute of the Deaf in Paris, which was the first free school for deaf people in the world. The Abbé de l'Epée's successor, the Abbé Sicard, took over the school in 1789 and continued to refine and develop l'Epée's language signs into a more precise mode that would grammatically reflect the French language.

In 1760 Thomas Braidwood opened the first school for deaf pupils in England. Francis Green, an American who sent his son Charles Green to Braidwood's school in England, published an article recommending founding of a school for deaf children in America.

AMERICAN INNOVATORS

In 1815 Thomas Hopkins Gallaudet went to Europe in search of a proper teaching approach for deaf students in America after meeting a young deaf girl, Alice Cogswell. While in France he adopted the French system of signs as the American method. Upon his return to the United States, Gallaudet brought back a deaf French teacher, Laurent Clerc, who then aided him in establishing the first American school for deaf people, the Connecticut Asylum for the Education and Instruction of Deaf and Dumb Persons, in Hartford in 1817.

Bernard Engelsmann, who was a teacher of deaf people in Vienna, introduced the German method, an oral method of teaching deaf students, in a school for deaf children in New York City, which in 1867 led to the establishment of the first pure oral school for deaf people in the United States. The school is now known as the Lexington School. Clarke School for the Deaf in Northhampton, Massachusetts, was established in the same year through generous financial support by a Northhampton resident, John Clarke. *See* CLARKE SCHOOL.

In 1878 Zenas F. Westervelt introduced the Rochester method at a school for deaf students in Rochester, New York. This method is based on a system in which deaf students are taught to speak and fingerspell English simultaneously. Written English is also heavily stressed in this method.

LANGUAGE DEVELOPMENT SPECIALISTS

Several individuals have developed symbol systems and diagrams to assist deaf students in learning English. In 1836 F. A. P. Barnard developed six simple straight-line and curved-line symbols that represented word relationships that were "substantive, attributive, connective or showed assertion, influence, or time." Also about this time, Richard

Storrs devised 47 symbols for use in the study of grammar. They could be written above the words in a sentence to indicate such things as parts of speech, person, gender, tense, type, degree, and various inflections.

The Wing symbols were developed in 1883 by George Wing, a deaf teacher, to show forms, functions, and positions of parts of sentences. He grouped the symbols consisting of numbers and letters over words, phrases, or clauses into four categories: the essentials, modifying forms, correctives, and special symbols. There were eight essential symbols: subject, three verb modifications (transitive, intransitive, or passive), object, adjective complement, noun, and pronoun complement.

In 1899 Katherine Barry devised the Five Slate system, which is related to Sicard's theory of ciphers and similar to his five sentence parts. She utilized five large slates that were reserved for five categories: subject, verb, object of the verb, preposition, and object of the proposition. This method was used in every American school for deaf people by 1918.

In 1929 a deaf supervising teacher at the Texas School for the Deaf, Edith Fitzgerald, invented the Fitzgerald Key method, which helped countless deaf children to write English. This method provides children with rules by which they can generate correct English sentences as well as correct their own errors in composition. The method usually begins by placing individual words under appropriate headings with the following parts of speech and sentence functions: subject (who, what), verb and predicate words, indirect and direct objects (what, whom), phrases and words telling where, other phrases and word modifiers of the main verbs (for, from, how, how often, how much, and so on), and words and phrases telling when.

In 1968 Roy Holcomb, a supervisor of the program for deaf students at the James Madison Elementary School in Santa Ana, California, used the term total communication to designate a philosophy requiring the incorporation of appropriate aural, manual, and oral modes of communication to ensure effective communication with and among hearing-impaired persons. The Maryland School for the Deaf was the first residential school to adopt officially the total communication philosophy under the leadership of the superintendent David Denton. Margaret S. Kent defined total communication as "the right of every deaf child to learn to use all forms of communication so that he may have full opportunity to develop language competence at the earliest possible age."

In the late 1960s Dorothy Shifflett, a teacher and the mother of a deaf daughter, collaborated with a deaf teacher, Herbert Larson, to utilize the total approach in exposing deaf children to speech, speechreading, and auditory training as well as fingerspelling and signs in the education of deaf students in regular schools.

POSTSECONDARY EDUCATION

Gallaudet College was established in 1864 and was the world's only college for deaf students until 1967, when the National Technical Institute for the Deaf was established. President Abraham Lincoln signed an act of Congress to grant and confirm degrees in the liberal arts and sciences at Gallaudet College. The college started as the Columbia Institution of the Deaf and Dumb and the Blind as a result of donation of its existing land by Amos Kendall in 1856. Gallaudet College was named in honor of Thomas Hopkins Gallaudet in 1894. Edward M. Gallaudet was the first president of the college. *See* GALLAUDET, EDWARD MINER; GALLAUDET COLLEGE; NATIONAL TECHNICAL INSTITUTE FOR THE DEAF.

In the 1930s Peter N. Peterson, a deaf vocational teacher of the Minnesota School for the Deaf, proposed the establishment of a national technical institute for the deaf. But it was not until well after World War II, and as the result of major cooperative efforts from people in the field of deafness and congressional leadership, that the National Technical Institute for the Deaf (NTID) became a reality. Rochester Institute of Technology was picked as the site for NTID in 1967 by a committee chaired by S. Richard Silverman, who was the director of the Central Institute for the Deaf in St. Louis, Missouri. *See* CENTRAL INSTITUTE FOR THE DEAF.

D. Robert Frisina was appointed as the first director of NTID. He later became senior vice-president of Rochester Institute of Technology, the parent institution of NTID. William E. Castle, who was the institute's first dean, became director in 1977. Robert F. Panara was selected as the first deaf professor in 1967.

Under legislative authority, four federally funded regional postsecondary programs for deaf students have been established. These programs are situated at: California State University at Northridge led by Ray Jones, Seattle Central Community College directed by Ron Lafayette, St. Paul Technical Vocational Institute directed by Robert Lauritson, and the University of Tennessee led by William Woodrick. Malcomb Norwood, a deaf man who is the branch chief of Media Services and Captioned Services at the Office of Special Education, is the chief administrator of these regional postsecondary programs. *See* EDUCATIONAL PROGRAMS: Higher Education.

DEAF EDUCATIONAL ADMINISTRATORS

It has been only since 1975 that deaf people have regained leadership roles in schools for deaf students. In the 1800s there were quite a number of deaf individuals who founded schools and served as superintendents and principals of them. After the International Congress on Education of the Deaf in Milan, Italy, in 1880, many school educators and administrators put more emphasis on training deaf children to develop their oral skills. This affected deaf persons, who found themselves limited to certain positions, such as vocational training and dormitory supervision. There were, however, several deaf individuals who managed to serve as leaders in their own way. *See* HISTORY: Congress of Milan.

Many other deaf individuals with no administrative title have played significant leadership roles in various ways, that is, they have served as officers, or as members of a board of directors of a school or other educational organization. Many teachers have been actively involved in writing articles about teaching deaf students in professional journals and books. Some of them served as editors of their official school publications. Many deaf individuals who taught deaf students contributed to the field of educational leadership through consumer advocacy on the behalf of the deaf community, including the National Association of the Deaf. A selected number of deaf educators who did not have the opportunity to become administrators, but who made significant contributions to the field of deafness and who have definitely left an impact on education of the deaf will also be mentioned here.

Table 1 lists deaf persons who played a key role in founding a school. The last time a deaf person founded a school was in 1911, when Henry C. White established a school in Arizona after setting up one in Utah in 1884. Laurent Clerc, the first deaf teacher in America, played a key role in founding the first school for the deaf in Connecticut in 1817 with Thomas Hopkins Gallaudet. John J. Flournoy was instrumental in establishing the Georgia School for the Deaf with O. P. Fannin in 1846. In 1857 Flournoy was an advocate of a planned deaf community and proposed that one of the commonwealths or states in the nation be designated as a home territory for deaf people. In addition to Henry C. White, Philip Alfred Emery, and Anson R. Spear, there were other deaf leaders who each founded two schools. Emery founded schools in Kansas in 1861 and the Chicago Day School in 1875, and Spear founded a school in North Dakota in 1890 and a day school in Minneapolis in 1895. It was not until 1980 that Douglas J. N. Burke accomplished his dream to establish a college program for deaf students, the Southwest Collegiate Institute for the Deaf in Big Springs, Texas.

Table 2 provides a listing of deaf school superintendents. Some of these individuals became superintendents after founding the schools: Philip

Table 1. Founders of Schools for the Deaf

Name of School	Deaf Educational Leader	Year Founded
American School for the Deaf	Laurent Clerc	1817
Indiana School for the Deaf	William Willard	1843
Georgia School for the Deaf	John J. Flournoy	1846
Clarksville (Arkansas) School for the Deaf	John W. Woodward	1850
Kansas School for the Deaf	Philip Alfred Emery	1861
Western Pennsylvania School for the Deaf	James H. Logan	1869
Oregon School for the Deaf	William S. Smith	1870
New York State School for the Deaf—Rome	Alphonso Johnson	1875
Cincinnati Public School for the Deaf	Robert McGregor	1875
Chicago Day School for the Deaf	Philip Alfred Emery	1875
St. Louis Day School (Gallaudet)	Delos Albert Simpson	1878
Beverly (Massachussetts) School for the Deaf	William B. Swett	1879
New York State School for the Deaf—White Plains	William C. Smith	1880
Scranton (Pennsylvania) School for the Deaf	Jacob M. Koehler	1883
Northern New York School for the Deaf—Malone	Henry C. Rider	1884
Utah School for the Deaf	Henry C. White	1884
New Mexico School for the Deaf	Lars M. Larson	1885
Florida School for the Deaf and Blind	Thomas Hines Coleman	1885
Evansville (Indiana) School for the Deaf	Charles Kerney	1886
Eastern Iowa School for the Deaf	William DeCoursey French	1888
North Dakota School for the Deaf	Anson R. Spear	1890
Cleveland School for the Deaf	John H. Geary	1892
Minneapolis Day School for the Deaf	Anson R. Spear	1895
Oklahoma School for the Deaf	Ellsworth Long	1898
Virginia School for the Deaf—Hampton	William C. Ritter	1909
Arizona School for the Deaf and Blind	Henry C. White	1911
Several African Schools	Andrew Foster	1970
Southwest Collegiate Institute for the Deaf	Douglas J. N. Burke	1980

Table 2. Superintendents of Schools for the Deaf

Name of School	Deaf Educational Leader	Dates of Leadership Services
Texas District School—Houston	Larry Stewart	1975
Margaret Sterck School for the Hearing-Impaired	Roy Holcomb	1970s
North Dakota School for the Deaf	L. A. Long	1890s
Virginia School for the Deaf—Staunton	Joseph D. Tyler	
Mississippi School for the Deaf	John H. Gazly	1854–1855
	Mr. Menfort	1855–1856
Kansas School for the Deaf	Philip Alfred Emery	1861–1864
	Benajah Robert Nordyke	1864–1865
	Joseph Mount	1865–1867
New York State School for the Deaf—Rome	Alphonso Johnson	1875–?
Beverly (Massachusetts) School for the Deaf	William B. Swett	1879–1884
South Dakota School for the Deaf	James Simpson	1881–1903
Northern New York School for the Deaf—Malone	Henry C. Rider	1884–1902
New Mexico School for the Deaf	Lars M. Larson	1885–1906
North Dakota School for the Deaf	Anson R. Spear	1890–1895
Minneapolis Day School for the Deaf	Anson R. Spear	1895–1900
Minnesota School for the Deaf	James L. Smith	1905–1906
Virginia School for the Deaf—Hampton	William C. Ritter	1909–1937
Oregon School for the Deaf	Thure A. Lindstrom	1922–1923, 1925–1926
Washington State School for the Deaf	Archie Stack	1972–1982
Texas District School—Houston	Ralph White	1973–1974
Texas District School—El Paso	Douglas J. N. Burke	1973–1980
Illinois School for the Deaf	William Page Johnson	1976
Louisiana School for the Deaf	Harvey J. Corson	1978
Scranton (Pennsylvania) School for the Deaf	Victor H. Galloway	1979–1981
Texas School for the Deaf	Victor H. Galloway	1981
Oklahoma School for the Deaf	Ralph White	1982

Alfred Emery in Kansas, Henry C. Rider at Northern New York School in Malone, Anson R. Spear in North Dakota and Minneapolis, and William Ritter in Hampton, Virginia. The Kansas School for the Deaf had three deaf persons serving as the school's superintendents between the years 1861 and 1967. Harvey C. Corson is believed to be the first prelingually deaf superintendent; he served as principal and assistant superintendent of the Kentucky School for the Deaf before taking over the Louisiana School. Victor Galloway, the other prelingually deaf person, started a career as a systems engineer at Lockheed Aircraft Corporation and continued for 20 years before entering the education field. He is also one of the three who served as superintendents of two different schools; the others are Anson R. Spear and Ralph White.

Two deaf individuals, Robert Davila and Thomas Mayes, have served as vice-presidents of Gallaudet College, Davila as vice-president for precollege programs and Mayes for continuing education.

Philip Emery, Robert McGregor, Delos Albert Simpson, Jacob M. Koehler, Henry C. White, Ellsworth Long, William M. Decoursey French, and William Willard were the founders of the schools in which they subsequently served as school principals. James Denison was the only deaf representative from America (or indeed, the entire world) attending the Milan Congress in Italy in 1880. J. Schuyler Long, with an honorary doctorate, was a long-time principal in the Iowa School for the Deaf. He was a leader in the Convention of American Instructors of the Deaf (CAID) and an important contributor to the Teacher Certification Program that was adopted by the Conference of Educational Administrators Serving the Deaf in 1931. He was also the author of one of the earliest sign language books. *See* CONFERENCE OF EDUCATIONAL ADMINISTRATORS SERVING THE DEAF; CONVENTION OF AMERICAN INSTRUCTORS OF THE DEAF; SIGN LANGUAGE TEXTBOOKS.

Arthur L. Roberts and Robert Anderson, who were principals at Kendall Demonstration Elementary School and Illinois School, respectively, became presidents of the National Fraternal Society of the Deaf. Several principals and some superintendents, founders, and other administrators served as presidents of the National Association of the Deaf: Robert McGregor (1880–1883), Thomas F. Fox (1893–1896), Jacob M. Koehler (1896–1900), James L. Smith (1900–1904), James H. Cloud (1917–1923), Arthur L. Roberts (1923–1930), Tom L. Anderson (1940–1946), Byron B. Burnes (1948–1966), Jess M. Smith (1974–1976), Mervin D. Garretson

(1976–1978), Ralph White (1978–1980), T. Alan Hurwitz (1980–1982), Larry Forestal (1984–1986), and Larry Newman (1986–   ).

Larry Newman was named the 1968 California Teacher of the Year. James Cloud was the father of Dan Cloud, who served as superintendent of the residential schools in Kansas, in Illinois, and in White Plains, New York. Gertrude Scott Galloway, who serves as assistant principal at the Maryland School for the Deaf in Columbia, was the first female president of the National Association of the Deaf (1980–1982). *See* KENDALL DEMONSTRATION ELEMENTARY SCHOOL; NATIONAL FRATERNAL SOCIETY OF THE DEAF.

Robert Davila is the first educational administrator among deaf and hearing persons who served as president of CEASD, CAID, and CED. As president-elect of CAID in 1974, Davila was a member of the first Joint Administrative Committee of the National Office (JACNO) with the CEASD. Latham Bruenig is the only deaf person to serve as president of the Alexander Graham Bell Association. Gerilee Gustason and George Propp served as presidents of CAID. David Mudgett, a long-time deaf educator at the Illinois School for the Deaf, was among the founders of the Council on Education of the Deaf. *See* ALEXANDER GRAHAM BELL ASSOCIATION FOR THE DEAF; BREUNIG, H. LATHAM.

OTHER DEAF EDUCATIONAL LEADERS

Amos G. Draper was a professor at the National Deaf-Mute College (Gallaudet College). He entered as a student before the first class graduated and he joined the faculty immediately upon graduation. Thus he knew every graduate personally up to about the turn of the century. He gave one of the principal papers at the 4th International Congress in Chicago in 1893.

Warren Robinson was one of the early advocates of providing technical education opportunities to deaf students. He wrote an article on technical training, published in the *American Annals of the Deaf* in 1892, suggesting that a technical department be established at Gallaudet College.

George McClure was a long-time leader, exerting influence especially through his editing of the *Kentucky Standard*, the Kentucky School paper. When McClure was 100 years old, he renewed his subscription to the *Deaf American* (formerly the *Silent Worker*) for three years instead of one year because the rate was cheaper—and he lived for the full three years. *See* DEAF AMERICAN.

Several educational leaders used their writing talent to articulate their views on issues relating to education of deaf children. One was Edwin A. Hodgson, who established a printing department at the New York Institution for the Deaf (Fanwood) in 1876 and became an editor of the *Deaf-Mutes Journal* (*DMJ*), a weekly newspaper, after buying the company from Henry C. Rider. *DMJ* became one of the most popular, influential, and widely read newspapers of its day. George M. Teegarden, one of the head teachers at the Pittsburgh School for the Deaf, collaborated with his deaf principal, James H. Logan, in writing stories in a 32-page monthly magazine called the *Raindrop*, which was reprinted by the Volta Bureau. Teegarden was the founder and editor of the school publication, the *Western Pennsylvania*. James Logan resigned from the principalship of the Pittsburgh School to become publisher of the *Raindrop*. William M. Chamberlain was editor of the first magazine of the American deaf community, the *Gallaudet Guide and Deaf Mute's Companion*. He was also involved in two other publications for deaf people, the *National Deaf Mute's Gazette* and the *Deaf Mute's Friend*. As an instructor at the Central New York Institution, he started the school's publication, the *Register*, which he edited. Grover C. Farquhar, a long-time educator at the Missouri School for the Deaf, was associated with the *Missouri Record* for 47 years. In 1871 Melville Ballard, John B. Hotchkiss, Joseph B. Parkinson, and James Denison started the first literary magazine for deaf readers, the *Silent World*. *See* LITERATURE, Editors and Journalists in.

Olof Hanson, who was born in Sweden in 1862 and educated at the Minnesota School for the Deaf, was the architect for schools for deaf children in Pennsylvania, North Dakota, Washington, D.C., and Minnesota. He taught at the Minnesota School for two years before establishing his architectural business. *See* HANSON, OLOF.

Jean Massieu is believed to be the first deaf person to teach deaf children anywhere in the world. He was born deaf and had several deaf brothers and sisters. He taught Laurent Clerc in France, who went on to become the first deaf teacher of deaf people in the United States. He also taught many deaf students, some of whom went on to become principals of schools for deaf pupils in Lyon, Limoges, Besançon (all in France), Geneva (Switzerland), Cambray (France), Hartford (Connecticut), and Mexico City. He was the teacher of Thomas Hopkins Gallaudet, who came from America to learn how to educate deaf students. The Abbé Sicard, a hearing pioneer in the field of education of deaf children, was appointed director of the National Institution for Deaf-Mutes in Paris in 1790 largely on the strength of Massieu's performance. When he was denied an administrative position as a successor of the National Institution for Deaf-Mutes upon Sicard's death, he became a director and principal of a school for deaf students in Rodez, France.

Ferdinand Berthier, who was born deaf 20 years after Clerc, became dean of professors at a school for deaf people in Paris. He published numerous articles and books, documenting the struggles and advancing the welfare of deaf people. He also wrote many biographical articles about l'Epée and Sicard. *See* BERTHIER, JEAN-FERDINAND.

Bibliography

Bender, R. E.: *The Conquest of Deafness*, Case Western Reserve University Press, 1970.

Brill, R. G.: Personal notes, 1985.

Gannon, J.: *Deaf Heritage: A Narrative History of Deaf America*, National Association of the Deaf, Silver Spring, Maryland, 1981.

Lane, H.: *When the Mind Hears*, Random House, New York, 1984.

Moores, D.: *Educating the Deaf: Psychology, Principles and Practices*, Houghton Mifflin, Boston, 1978.

Quigley, S. P., and P. V. Paul: *Language and Deafness*, College-Hill Press, San Diego, 1984.

Ritter, A. L., and K. A. Hopkins: *A Deafness Collection: Selected and Annotated*, National Technical Institute for the Deaf, Rochester, New York, 1984.

Scouten, E.: *Turning Points in the Education of Deaf People*, Interstate Printers and Publishers, Danville, Illinois, 1984.

T. Alan Hurwitz

Teachers

In addition to the skills and knowledge required to teach nonhandicapped children or youths, teachers of hearing-impaired students must have unusual skills and special knowledge in order to be successful.

These are deaf people whose hearing loss is so great that they are unable to understand the spoken language through hearing, even with the help of hearing aids. If a loss of hearing occurred before birth (as a result of fetal injury caused by a mother's illness, for example) or in childhood prior to age two, the deaf child will never be able to develop normal communicative language by means of hearing alone. Acquisition of language and verbal communication skills will have to be acquired by this child mostly through other senses, and in almost all instances will require the assistance of a trained teacher. Parents may learn these skills and thereby assist or speed up the acquisition of a deaf child's communicative language. *See* HEARING LOSS: Prenatal Causes.

By contrast, a hard-of-hearing child, with the help of a hearing aid, has sufficient hearing to learn language and develop verbal communication skills primarily through audition alone. Teaching a hard-of-hearing child tends not to differ greatly from teaching a child without impaired hearing.

There are also children whose loss of hearing occurs after age two or three, when language has been acquired through hearing. These children will require a different approach to education because further language skills can be developed from the basics that were acquired before hearing was lost.

HISTORICAL NOTE

Teachers of deaf children in nineteenth-century schools in both Europe and the United States learned their skills by observing and working with master teachers already involved in schools or special programs developed for deaf children. Outstanding and successful teachers who were recognized leaders usually spent a lifetime working to perfect and record their experiences. Some guarded their skills in order to protect and ensure their means of livelihood, while others shared their information for the benefit of improving the instruction of other deaf students.

During the nineteenth century in the United States, programs for the professional training of teachers were generally located in state or privately operated residential schools for deaf students. Among these were the Clarke School for the Deaf in Northhampton, Massachusetts, Gallaudet College in Washington, D.C., the North Carolina School for the Deaf in Morganton, and the Central Institute for the Deaf in St. Louis, Missouri.

EARLIEST DEVELOPMENT OF STANDARDS

Standards for the formal training and professional preparation of teachers were first developed in the United States during the 1920s. The adoption of standards by an official organization and the development of a teacher certification program followed soon afterward. By 1928 there were 21 school-based teacher training programs whose personnel had agreed to adopt a commonly developed curriculum for such programs. This curriculum and set of requirements were later proposed for adoption by an organization known as the Conference of Superintendents and Principals.

By 1932 there had been 14 programs reviewed by a select committee of peers and approved as recognized centers for the preparation of teachers of deaf pupils. By September 1932 over 250 applications had been processed for certificates of recognition as teachers with special qualifications to work in this field.

ADMINISTRATION OF STANDARDS

Today, standards for the preparation of teachers, including a program for the certification of teachers by an organization of educators, are promoted and administered by a group of organizations known as the Council on Education of the Deaf. The council, representing more than 10,000 teachers, is an umbrella organization made up of representatives from the major organizations directly involved with and concerned about the education of deaf children. These include the Alexander Graham Bell Association for the Deaf, the Conference of Educational Administrators Serving the Deaf, and the Convention of American Instructors of the Deaf.

Table 3. Distribution of Teachers in Schools and Classes in the United States (1983)

	73 Public Residential Schools	9 Private Residential Schools	33 Public Day Schools	20 Private Day Schools	338 Public Day Classes (full-time)	121 Part-time or Itinerant	4 Private Day Classes (full-time)	1 Part-time or Itinerant	24 Facilities for Other Handicap(s)	TOTAL 623 Schools and Classes
Educational Administrators	536	19	93	29	359	65	3	0	28	**1,132**
Instructors	3708	116	705	115	2884	438	13	1	128	**8,108**
Teachers' Aides	671	23	292	35	1218	134	2	0	143	**2,518**
Clinical	716	17	201	30	1063	189	11	1	89	**2,317**
Media-Library	192	6	34	6	65	15	1	0	9	**328**
Deaf Teachers	792	9	113	10	225	33	1	0	11	**1,194**
Certified CEASD or CED	1501	80	307	76	688	99	5	0	27	**2,783**
Certified State Departments of Education	3509	105	613	125	2936	440	14	1	46	**7,789**
TOTAL STAFF	5823	181	1325	215	5589	841	30	2	397	**14,403**

The council is responsible for the development, adoption, and use of standards for both the preparation and the certification of teachers of deaf children. In addition, the council develops and implements a program for the evaluation of university-based programs for the preparation of teachers in this field. *See* TEACHING PROFESSION: Certification.

There are 13,000 to 15,000 teachers serving over 46,000 hearing-impaired children in schools, classes, and programs throughout the United States and Canada (Tables 3 and 4). These teachers serve the more than 24,000 deaf students attending programs in public schools sponsored by local school districts. Teachers involved in these programs serve deaf and hearing-impaired children in a variety of ways. Some serve as teachers of children in special classes. Others, working as itinerant instructors in a single school or several schools, serve more or less on a tutorial basis, and often as a special-resource person to regular classroom teachers. Some teachers serve as counselor-tutors for children mainstreamed into the general educational system. Additionally, teachers of deaf pupils may teach at the elementary, junior high school, and secondary education levels, each of which requires special skills and professional preparation. Teachers of deaf students are prepared to serve as specialists in early childhood education as well. Within this specialization there are two levels of service. The first is infant education, which may be located in either clinical or home teaching settings, both of which involve the education of parents along with the children. The second is at a preschool level with programs in kindergarten or nursery school settings. *See* TEACHING PROFESSION: Itinerant Teachers.

PROGRAMS EMPLOYING TEACHERS

The early schools (1817–1940) for deaf children in the United States were, for the most part, state-operated or state-supported residential schools. In the late nineteenth century, day schools for deaf children began to appear in local public school programs. Today, more than half of the children in schools are being educated in local public school programs that include a variety of educational delivery systems. More than 21,000 students are now enrolled in state-operated and state-supported special programs for deaf or hearing-impaired children, including both residential and day school enrollments. *See* EDUCATIONAL PROGRAMS: Day Schools, Residential Schools.

SPECIAL SKILLS

Teachers have received a bachelor's degree in the liberal arts, education, or speech and hearing, in addition to training in a special program focusing on the needs of deaf or hearing-impaired children. A part of the special training needed to teach deaf students focuses on a particular level or group of children the teacher plans to serve.

The special programs for training teachers of deaf students usually organize their curriculum around several general topics. One of these, sometimes referred to as trends in deaf education, includes information about the historical and current developments in deaf education; national and local issues, trends, and events that influence the education of hearing-impaired children; the variety of educational settings and service delivery models and the particular role of teachers in these various settings; deaf people in today's society and their special needs;

Table 4. Distribution of Students in Schools and Classes in the United States (1983)

	73 Public Residential Schools	9 Private Residential Schools	33 Public Day Schools	20 Private Day Schools	338 Public Day Classes (full-time)	121 Part-time or Itinerant	4 Private Day Classes (full-time)	1 Part-time or Itinerant	24 Facilities for Other Handicap(s)	TOTAL (623) Schools and Classes
Male	9,566	289	1860	360	10,768	1563	38	11	486	**24,941**
Female	7,578	228	1766	337	9,646	1449	34	3	340	**21,381**
Residential	11,013	324	0	0	5	0	0	0	714	**12,056**
Day	6,131	193	3626	697	20,409	3012	72	14	112	**34,266**
Mainstreamed	261	28	122	93	5,412	1193	15	3	5	**7,132**
Partially Mainstreamed	999	26	503	60	6,898	1042	9	2	14	**9,553**
TOTAL ENROLLMENT	17,144	517	3626	697	20,414	3012	72	14	826	**46,322**
Deaf-Blind	211	0	28	2	128	33	0	0	61	**463**
Deaf–Mentally Retarded	978	4	162	9	868	138	0	0	236	**2,395**
Deaf–Blind + Mentally Retarded	97	0	8	0	70	18	0	0	184	**377**
Deaf–Learning Disabled, Including Aphasic	1,182	25	384	26	1,034	131	3	0	18	**2,803**
Deaf–Socially or Emotionally Disturbed	797	10	63	3	313	51	0	0	19	**1,256**
Deaf–Other Multihandicapped	637	2	94	12	397	88	1	1	279	**1,511**
TOTAL MULTI-HANDICAPPED	3,902	41	739	52	2,810	459	4	1	797	**8,805**

and the implications and impact of hearing loss on psychological, sociological, vocational, and educational development.

A second unique part of the education of teachers of deaf pupils relates to parents. Teacher of deaf students, more than their counterparts in other educational settings, often are called upon to advise parents on a number of issues. Thus, teachers are trained to respond to issues, problems, and questions of parents of deaf children and to give basic guidance for additional assistance needed by parents.

A third important area that teachers of deaf students must be familiar with is speech and audiology. Teachers should have a thorough knowledge of human speech and auditory and visual mechanisms, including the anatomy of and common diseases affecting these mechanisms; the production, transmission, and reception of speech and other sounds; the effect of hearing loss upon the production of speech and the hearing of speech and other sounds; the procedures for testing hearing; the ability to interpret hearing test results; and the use of various types of amplifying equipment, instruments, and hearing aids. *See* AUDIOLOGY; SPEECH.

The fourth area in which teachers of deaf students must be prepared is language learning and the development of communication skills. The teacher must have knowledge of the structure of the English language, the use of language, and the relationship of these to learning by deaf children; disorders of language development; the commonly used methods of language instruction in use for deaf children; and the communication process, including the effects of hearing loss on communication, the various systems of communication, and the combinations of systems used in teaching hearing-impaired individuals to read, write, lipread, listen, and speak.

Finally, teachers should be able to plan, implement, evaluate, and measure the learning experiences of deaf children, and they must have the requisite skills to utilize the educational technology currently available. Specifically, teachers of deaf pupils ought to be able to use diagnostic tests to measure the ability and progress of their students; to use educational teaching equipment (computer, telephonic, visual display, and other instruments) designed for working with deaf learners; to effectively utilize paraprofessionals (teacher aides, volunteers, students, parents, and so on) in the classroom; and to participate effectively with a team of professionals, with deaf individuals, and with parents of deaf students.

Bibliography
Bender, R. E.: *The Conquest of Deafness*, Interstate Printers and Publishers, 1981.

American Annals of the Deaf, directory issue, Washington, D.C., 1984.

Hoag, R. L. (coord.): *Certification Standards for Professionals Involved in the Education of Hearing Impaired Children and Youth*, Council on Education of the Deaf, 1985.

————: *Standards for the Certification of Teachers of the Deaf*, Council on Education of the Deaf, 1974.

Scouten, E. L.: *Turning Points in the Education of Deaf People*, Interstate Printers and Publishers, 1984.

Ralph L. Hoag

Terminology

There are many distinctive terms commonly used in the literature and discussions about the education of deaf people that are not typical in other educational fields. The most relevant terms relate to degree of deafness, age at onset of hearing loss, communication, and educational placement.

DEAFNESS

In the education of deaf students the term deafness itself defies clear definition. Deafness can be defined from a number of perspectives, and all may have relevance for educational planning and services.

Most common are definitions of deafness based on severity of hearing loss as measured in decibels of pure-tone sounds necessary to hear across the frequency range of speech, usually reported for the ear with the better hearing.

Historically, children with hearing losses of 25–70 decibels (dB) have been considered hard-of-hearing, while those with hearing losses of 90 dB and greater have been considered deaf. Those with hearing losses in the 70–90 dB range are not so readily classified as deaf or hard-of-hearing. Many schools for deaf students have used 70 dB or thereabouts as a lower cutoff point for admission, but the average hearing loss of their students usually falls in the 90s. *See* AUDIOLOGIC CLASSIFICATION.

There is a strong movement to replace the traditional deaf/hard-of-hearing dichotomy with the more generic term hearing-impaired, whereby individuals with hearing losses in the 26–54 dB range are considered to be mildly hearing-impaired, those with hearing losses in the 55–69 dB range as moderately hearing-impaired, those in the 70–89 dB range as severely hearing-impaired, and those with losses of 90 dB and above as profoundly hearing-impaired. As a group, only those with profound hearing impairments should be considered deaf on the basis of pure-tone hearing loss alone, although

many with severe hearing impairments may present similar educational and communication needs.

The Conference of Educational Administrators Serving the Deaf (CEASD) has described a deaf person as "one whose hearing disability precludes successful processing of linguistic information through audition, with or without a hearing aid." This definition could be restated to indicate that a deaf person is one who depends essentially on vision for the successful processing of linguistic information.

AGE AT ONSET

Age at onset of hearing loss has major implications for the education of the deaf child. Earlier in the twentieth century, 50 percent or more of all students in educational programs for deaf children had become deaf through childhood diseases after their English language foundation had been established through hearing. Because of medical advances, this is no longer the case. Today a majority of deaf students have congenital deafness, meaning deafness is present at birth, as opposed to adventitious deafness, which indicates an onset of deafness sometime during childhood or adulthood. More relevant for educational purposes, and particularly for language acquisition, is whether deafness occurred before or after a language foundation could be established through hearing and the use of speech. Often the somewhat arbitrary age of three is used to distinguish between prelingual and postlingual deafness. CEASD has defined prelingual deafness as "deafness present at birth, or occurring early in life at an age prior to the development of speech or language."

It is of historical interest that some early schools for deaf pupils included "deaf-mutes" or "deaf and dumb" in their names. Those expressions were later dropped, but continue to be used by poorly informed persons. At the same time, many profoundly, prelingually deaf adults have unintelligible spoken language skills in spite of amplification and training throughout their education (most coming to rely strongly on sign language, reading, and writing for interpersonal communication). It would seem appropriate to use the term nonoral in describing these deaf persons as they reach late adolescence and adulthood.

COMMUNICATION

During the first 50 or 60 years of the twentieth century, the communication philosophies and practices of most programs for deaf students could be described as oral (or as pure oral among programs that adhere rigorously to the practice) or combined. Virtually all combined schools maintained an oral classroom environment for students throughout their preschool, primary, and early elementary years, but used the simultaneous method with most older students, incorporating both speech and signs for classroom instruction. A variation on the simultaneous method was the Rochester method, which featured the use of fingerspelling rather than signs, and is today more commonly known as Visible English. It should be noted that while reading, writing, and amplification were used extensively for classroom communication, the oral-manual dichotomy was highlighted.

In the late 1960s, a major movement began in the direction of total communication, and today this is the single most prevalent orientation in classes and schools for deaf people throughout the United States.

CEASD has defined total communication as "a philosophy incorporating appropriate aural, manual, and oral modes of communication in order to ensure effective communication with and among hearing-impaired persons." Parenthetically, this definition, like most published definitions of total communication, omits writing and reading as components of total communication, but presumably these are assumed.

Total communication bears some resemblance to what was once called the simultaneous method, with some notable exceptions. First, unlike the simultaneous method, it is advocated for all grade levels. Second, it has captured the attention of many parents and added a new sense of legitimacy to the use of signs in communicating with deaf children both in the classroom and in the home. Third, some definitions provide for the many technical developments available for communication and instruction with deaf students today, such as improved amplification and visual media.

The question arises as to whether total communication is an educational philosophy or a method. Like the oral method, it has features of both, but unlike the oral method, total communication remains to be translated into precise educational practices for a given child if indeed this is possible with such a global concept.

Paralleling and supported by the emergence of total communication, there has developed a new interest in the forms that manual communication should take in the education of deaf students. In general, these fall on a continuum from the precise representation of English through fingerspelling each letter and word (Visible English) to the use of American Sign Language (ASL). Seeing Essential English (SEE 1) and Signing Essential English (SEE 2) are two systems of signing in English that use existing signs but, in addition to following the order of English (unlike ASL), have added sign markers to indicate verb tense, articles, suffixes, and so on. Probably the most common form of manual communication used by teachers and parents with deaf students is Pidgin Signed English (PSE), which

loosely follows the word order of English without the more formal structure of other signed English codes. *See* SOCIOLINGUISTICS: Sign Language Continuum.

The attention to total communication and sign systems in this discussion of terminology should not lead the reader to conclude that oral and aural methods of communicating with deaf students are secondary. Oral programs remain strong throughout the United States.

PLACEMENT

The passage of Public Law 94-142, the Education for All Handicapped Children Act of 1975, and the postsecondary movement which began in the late 1960s greatly expanded provisions for the education of deaf students, and new terminology came into use. The term mainstreaming and its qualifiers, partial and full, largely replaced the former term integration to indicate that deaf students attend regular schools and classes, usually locally, for some or all of their instruction. The expression least restrictive environment came into use as a basis for the deaf student's placement in a particular educational environment, and the expression individualized education program (IEP) for planning the student's educational objectives and activities each year. New services were added to support the deaf student's participation in mainstream classes, including the services of interpreters.

Bibliography

Bess, F. H., and F. E. McConnell: *Audiology, Education, and the Hearing Impaired Child*, C. V. Mosby, St. Louis, 1981.

Frisina, D. R.: "Report of the Ad Hoc Committee to Define Deaf and Hard of Hearing," a report of the Conference of Educational Administrators Serving the Deaf, *American Annals of the Deaf*, 120(5):509–512, 1975.

Garretson, M. D.: "Committee Report Defining Total Communication," *Proceedings of the 49th Meeting of CEASD*, Rochester, New York, 1976.

———.: "Total Communication," in D. R. Frisina (ed.), *A Bicentennial Monograph on Hearing Impairment: Trends in the U.S.A.*, Alexander Graham Bell Association for the Deaf, Washington, D.C., 1976.

Moores, D. F.: *Educating the Deaf: Psychology, Principles, and Practices*, 2d ed., Houghton Mifflin, Boston, 1982.

Ross Stuckless

Communication

The broad topic of communication is subdivided here into communication in the classroom, outside the classroom, in the home, and in the administrative offices of the school and the school board. Each of these environments raises particular issues with respect to the education of deaf students. Only those related to the mode of communication will be considered here; questions bearing upon what is communicated are not discussed. The topic of language is entwined with communication, but it will be taken up only tangentially in this section. In the fourth subdivision of communication, the question of direct versus mediated communication in education will be presented, since it raises issues confronting educational administrators who deal with a majority of deaf students.

CLASSROOM

Educators of deaf students can choose among several methods of communication in the classroom. Each method must be viewed with respect to expression and reception. Each has a number of variations, and occasionally the same school may use more than one method. Furthermore, differences exist between the methods as described by their principal architects and as practiced in the classrooms. The daily use of a particular communication approach may be quite apart from the textbook description of its implementation. *See* SOCIOLINGUISTICS: Language Policy and Education.

Oral Method   The oral method places the communication burden on the deaf child. The instructor speaks, and the deaf student lipreads. In responding to the instructor, the deaf student is expected to speak. This "natural" method was most vigorously espoused by the German educator Samuel Heinicke, who in the late eighteenth century strongly opposed the manual methods of the Abbé de l'Epée. The controversy continued over a century until the International Congress on the Education of the Deaf held in Milan, Italy, in 1880, when the delegates voted in favor of the oral method of communication in the classroom. That single event typifies a change in the attitudes toward the use of signs in the instruction of deaf students that has evolved over two centuries. In the United States, from 1880 to 1960, the educational tide ran in favor of oralism, with a preponderance of schools professing to use that method of communication in the classroom. The ban on the use of sign was particularly forceful in the education of young deaf children. Even into the latter portion of the twentieth century, many schools continue to insist upon the oral method with preteen-age students. However, the proscriptions against manual communication have generally been relaxed for students in junior and senior high schools and beyond.

For the typical congenitally deaf and prelingually deafened students, good speech is very difficult to acquire, while those deafened after they have developed speech are usually successful in retaining it. Many prelingually deafened persons do not develop usable speech. Teachers of deaf students, however, usually develop considerable skill in interpreting what the student is saying in the classroom. They are aided by the fact that they are usually aware of the context in which the students are trying to express themselves. The intent of the method is, however, to force the deaf student to attempt to speak by denying the use of manual communication.

The art of lipreading comes most easily to those who have the greatest experience with the spoken language. Again, this means that the oral approach works better with later-deafened students. That is true especially for English, because only about half of its phonemes can be reliably discriminated on the lips; therefore, the lipreader is frequently forced to guess at what is being said. For example, the lip movements for saying time and dime are formed identically. Those most familiar with the language patterns can best determine from available situational and lip cues what is probably being said. The lipreader confronted with choosing between time and dime in the phrase "Give me the ____" must depend upon the context in which the order is given, since there are no differences in the lip configurations. Prelingually deaf students are, therefore, at a disadvantage because their experience with the English language is less than that of both their hearing and later-deafened peers. Some oral proponents accept the use of fingerspelling to assist with particularly difficult discriminations. This variation was approved by Alexander Graham Bell, who was a staunch supporter of the oral approach but believed that such fingerspelling did not violate its basic premises. *See* SPEECHREADING.

Acoustic Method   Originated by the Yugoslavian scientist Petar Guberina, the acoustic method relies entirely on the deaf students' residual hearing abilities. Powerful hearing aids, individual and group, are used to optimize whatever auditory capacity the students have retained. To develop their residual hearing, the students are given various physical exercises. The teacher uses speech to instruct, and the students listen. Visual aids such as lipreading and signing are discouraged in the hope that the students will take advantage of the auditory signals they receive, at least in their early years. The key to the method is the belief that, when denied all other sources of communication, the students will develop whatever residual hearing they have and learn to use it as normally hearing children do. In its pure form, the method is infrequently used in the United States, and then largely in preschool and elementary classes.

Cued Speech   Conceived by Orin Cornett, cued speech supplements the oral method with hand signals that differentiate the indiscriminable lip configurations. Three different placements of the hand while the individual is speaking would clearly indicate whether the word spoken is for, far, or fear, since the three words are identical on the lips. Cued speech also is thought to be useful in helping the prelingually deaf child shape speech. Using cued speech in the classroom, the students speak and cue at the same time, and the teacher responds in the same manner. The system has not been widely adopted in United States schools, just as a similar method developed at the beginning of the century in Denmark (the Hand-Mund system) has not had much popularity in Danish schools. *See* MOUTH-HAND SYSTEMS.

Rochester Method At about the time of the Milan Conference, Zenas Westervelt, superintendent of the Rochester (New York) School for the Deaf, developed a system that he considered midway between the oral and the manual approaches to communication. He suggested complete dependence upon fingerspelling. While the teacher spells to the students and they respond by spelling, they are also encouraged to speak. The teacher is also supposed to speak while spelling, thus giving the students practice in lipreading. The method has a few adherents, though its use tends to be limited to the early school years because the spelling becomes quite tedious as the length of messages increases. Consequently, in the upper grades of schools that use the Rochester method, either instruction becomes more oral or signs are introduced.

Simultaneous Method The simultaneous use of speech and sign, with occasional fingerspelling replacing signs, became the method of communication endorsed by Gallaudet College for use in its classrooms. It is an outgrowth of the French method of methodical signs, developed by the Abbé de l'Epée and brought to the United States in 1816 by Thomas Hopkins Gallaudet and the French master Laurent Clerc. The method is essentially visual: whatever can be done to optimize the visual expression is encouraged. To account for individual differences among deaf students, teachers not only speak (to provide for those who are proficient lipreaders) and sign or fingerspell (to provide for those who are more dependent on manual communication) but also write on the blackboard and use other visual media to enhance communication. This is done in as simultaneous a fashion as possible. Students are encouraged to speak as they express themselves manually, but they are not required to do so. In addition, the method as now practiced makes use of amplification, both group or individual. This method is now the one most commonly used in the classroom. *See* SOCIOLINGUISTICS: Simultaneous Communication.

Total Communication There are other approaches, but they are essentially hybrids of the five methods of communication described above. With this plethora of approaches, a philosophy of communication was espoused by Roy Holcomb which he named total communication. Holcomb proposed that deaf students be given the benefits of whatever means of communication are suitable and available. Though the descriptions of total communication sound very much like the simultaneous method, advocates of total communication point out that it is a philosophy of communication, not a method. Regardless, it has had considerable appeal for educators of deaf children, who have been faced by the fact that the students' academic achievements lag far behind those of their hearing peers, despite research that indicates that the deaf students, on the average, have intellectual endowments equal to those of the general population. Total communication also came into vogue at the same time that William Stokoe's research revealed American Sign Language (ASL) to be a true language and not simply a code for English. This renewed interest in the use of manual communication among educators. Paradoxically, the majority of them opted for Manual English, the representation in sign of spoken English, rather than the use of ASL. The philosophical shift from an oral to a total communication philosophy has been reflected in a more relaxed attitude toward communication in the classroom. However, some of the shifts in approach are more apparent than real.

Research done in 1979 shows a lack of correspondence between spoken and signed messages in presentations by teachers rated as expert in the use of simultaneous communication. The researchers videotaped classroom interchanges and then had independent transcriptions made of what the teachers said and signed. The comparisons showed that many of the classic deaf errors in the use of English—failure to use articles, deletion of plural markers, and so forth—were actually what the teacher was signing, not speaking. Since many of the students, especially those at the rear of the classroom, would be aware of the signs and not the speech, they were actually being taught improper English by the instructor's example. The classes studied by G. S. Marmor and L. Petitto were taught by teachers who were chosen because of their signing expertise. However, many teachers of deaf students enter total communication classes with only a semester's course in signing—hardly sufficient preparation for classroom instruction. Some schools have elected to undertake a total communication program without adequate preparation of the staffs. The resulting educational achievements of the students can be expected to be less than optimal.

Few individuals are able to sign simultaneously in ASL and speak in English, since the grammars of the two languages differ. This conflict has led some educators to suggest that schools use ASL for some subjects and then teach English as a second language accompanied by the appropriate Manual English equivalents. One difficulty with this approach will be finding certified teachers who also know ASL well enough to teach in it. From the students' point of view, such instruction would be unusual. Even schools that make use of manual communication do not have classes in ASL, or even in Manual English. The notion appears to be that the students will learn to sign by observing their teachers signing and by using it themselves, without any specific instruction in the articulation of signs, their grammar, or semantics. By contrast, English-speaking students in the United States receive at least 12 years' instruction in their native language; deaf students receive virtually none in what some consider to be their native language—ASL. Research by M. M. Maxwell challenges the belief that simply being exposed to English in manual form will be translated by the students into an improved use of that language. Indeed, Maxwell's findings suggest that the use of signs for English markers may only serve to confuse the students and inhibit their development of English proficiency. *See* SIGN LANGUAGE TEACHING.

As new hearing aids are being developed, students who formerly could not benefit from amplification may be able to do so. The individual aids can now be supplemented by more sophisticated group aids, including those that make use of infrared transmission. This electronic assistance can be expected to have some impact upon instructional practices. The cochlear implant—a device that provides direct electrical stimulation of the auditory nerve—also presents a challenge to educators. This prosthesis does not enable the implanted individual to hear, since electrical impulses are not adequate stimuli for the auditory nerve, but the cochlear implant does provide stimulation that is phased with external sounds. Teaching deaf persons to use such devices will require much skill and ingenuity from educators. Compared to the new hearing aids, however, the cochlear implants will have far less effect on classroom communication simply because the latter devices are prescribed only for the most profoundly hearing-impaired individuals. Those who have sufficient hearing to benefit from amplification—the majority of deaf students—are not recommended for the cochlear implant. *See* COCHLEAR IMPLANT; HEARING AIDS.

OUTSIDE THE CLASSROOM
During the day, deaf students spend six or fewer hours in the classroom. Outside of class they use sign language to communicate with other students on the playground, in the dormitories, on the school bus, and in many other informal situations. Deaf students in residential schools sign, even in those that insist upon strictly oral communication in the classroom. Signs are rarely taught in classes; they are passed from child to child.

In residential schools, budgetary constraints often keep administrators from employing highly skilled personnel as dormitory counselors. As a result, the communication policies of the classroom are often violated in the dormitories and on the playground. Educational administrators are aware of the problem and try to overcome it by holding training sessions for the extra-class personnel. However, enforcing communication regulations is a difficult task, made more difficult by the students' deafness.

HOME
A similar problem confronts the educator of deaf children who live at home. If the parents do not carry out the communication approach endorsed by the school in the home, then valuable hours are wasted and the students are placed in a conflicting situation. For hearing parents of deaf children, the oral approach has the greatest appeal, since it does not impose on the adult the task of learning new ways to communicate. Still, as the children grow into their teens, the weaknesses of conversations that are partially understood become more serious. Messages are more and more abstruse, placing heavier burdens on the communication process. At such times, the parent-child relations, which are stressful in normal families during the teens, become even more critical for deaf teen-agers. School counselors often find themselves spending a substantial part of their professional time mending the communication breakdowns between deaf students and their families.

EDUCATIONAL ADMINISTRATORS
Choosing which kinds of communication should be used in the classrooms confronts educational administrators and the school boards with a difficult task. Schools are assigned the task of preparing children to take their place in society as adults. Since the majority of the population can hear and speak, those who set educational policy usually support communication procedures that promise to make deaf children as much like others as possible. This does not mean, however, that these policymakers are insensitive to or ignorant of the problems in educating deaf children. Parents, too, often have strong preferences for one or another approach to the education of their deaf children. These attitudes, taken together, are the major reason why the arguments over methods of communication have persisted. Deaf students appear to communicate most easily by manual communication, but the general society and often their parents demand that their participation outside of the school be on an oral basis.

With the passage of the Rehabilitation Act Amendments of 1973, a change in the federal attitude has emerged. No longer are deaf, and other

Education **373**

disabled, persons required to adjust to whatever circumstances please the majority. Section 504 of Title V of the act forbids discrimination against persons because of their disability. While this act applies only to situations involving federal funds, its enactment has caused other authorities and the public to take notice of the difficulties faced by those who have physical impairments that preclude their enjoying the benefits of full citizenship. In practice this provision has meant that deaf persons have been entitled to have interpreters present at public meetings, in their court appearances, and at similar government-supported events.

Public Law 94-142, the Education of All Handicapped Children Act, has introduced a further novelty in the education of deaf people. The law requires that disabled students be educated in the least restrictive environment. This has meant that deaf students have been increasingly placed in settings with normally hearing students. Faced with the lack of teachers who have any expertise in communication with deaf students, educators have found it expeditious to employ oral or manual interpreters. These interpreters bridge the communication gap between the teacher who speaks and the child who does not hear. Since the teachers do not need to learn manual communication or otherwise adjust their instruction to fulfill their roles, most have welcomed the opportunity to teach deaf children.

The teacher-interpreter situation is not without its difficulties, however. A large problem is in finding qualified interpreters. Second, the supervision of interpreters places unusual strains on the administration. Since the staff does not know manual communication in most instances, the only immediate sources of information about the quality of communication are the deaf children—not generally a satisfactory position in which to place them. The situation also has the potential to arouse confusion with respect to authority. In the event of conflict of views, whom does the child obey? Very little research has been devoted to this aspect of educating deaf students "in the mainstream." *See* INTERPRETING.

In higher education for deaf students, interpreters have become commonplace. College instructors are typically subject-matter specialists not specifically prepared to be teachers. The interpreters' roles are usually well defined: they are there solely to put into sign what the instructors are saying. In the primary and secondary schools, interpreters are often called upon to be tutors as well. This dual role is seldom imposed upon interpreters in colleges and universities. Nonetheless, the administrator of these programs faces the same difficulties of finding suitable interpreters. The demands upon interpreters are substantial; they often move from a course in calculus to one in chemistry to one in

American history. To properly do their job, interpreters need, at a minimum, some acquaintance with the vocabularies used in the different subjects. Supervision may be considered less of a problem since the students are adults, but the inability of the average administrator to directly evaluate the interpreters' performances is a distinct limitation on their use.

Another response to personnel selection is to hire teachers who are themselves deaf. To do so has the virtue, it is hoped, of resolving the communication difficulties, with the added advantage of providing deaf children with suitable role models. The rationale for the oral method has changed little from Heinicke's arguments. "Deaf students must learn to live in a hearing world" is one of the often advanced reasons for supporting the oral approach to communication. A second point of view is that, if allowed to sign, deaf children will not learn to speak, as signing is so much easier for them than speaking. Rarely mentioned is the fact that it is the teachers who find signing difficult and speaking easy. This third point was quickly picked up by deaf teachers who, following the Milan Congress, helped to found the National Association of the Deaf (NAD). The association's defense of manual communication in the classroom was based, in part, on its desire to preserve employment for deaf teachers. By the beginning of the twentieth century, deaf teachers were virtually excluded from primary classes for deaf students and employed, if at all, in high school vocational classes. The advent of total communication has reopened the school doors for deaf teachers that the Milan Manifesto had closed.

The administrator of programs for deaf students must take into account the possibilities that the students have additional educationally significant disabilities; about one-third do. Emotional-behavioral disturbances lead the list, followed by mental retardation. Of great significance are visual anomalies, which occur more frequently in deaf students than students in general. Oddly, deaf students frequently go through their school years without adequate visual examinations, though they have undergone careful audiometry on a number of occasions. It is therefore likely that the reported rates for visual disabilities among deaf students, large as they are, actually underestimate the actual prevalence rates. The importance of these additional disabilities for the selection of communication modes in the classroom cannot be overestimated. Emotional and intellectual factors are obviously critical, as are visual abilities. Successful lipreading, for example, requires excellent visual acuity, especially if lighting and distance are not optimal, as in many classrooms. Reading fingerspelling, while it requires less acuity than lipreading, still makes substantial demands upon the individual's ability to see. Minor visual problems that would merely inconvenience an otherwise able-bodied individual can be seriously handicapping to a deaf person and should be considered in selecting methods of communication in the classroom.

Jerome D. Schein

Bibliography

Garnett, Jr., C. B.: *The Exchange of Letters Between Samuel Heinecke and Abbé Charles Michel de l'Epée*, Vantage Press, New York, 1968.

Marmor, G. S., and L. Petitto: "Simultaneous Communication in the Classroom: How Well Is English Grammar Represented?", *Sign Language Studies*, 23:99–136, 1979.

Maxwell, M. M.: "Simultaneous Communication in the Classroom: What Do Deaf Children Learn?", *Sign Language Studies*, 39:95–112, 1983.

Schein, J. D.: "Deaf Students with Other Disabilities," *American Annals of the Deaf*, 120:92–99, 1975.

————: *Speaking the Language of Sign: The Art and Science of Sign*, Doubleday, New York, 1984.

Walters, J. W., S. Quintero, and D. M. Perrigin: "Vision: Its Assessment in School-Age Deaf Children," *American Annals of the Deaf*, 127:418–432, 1982.

Research

Research in the education of deaf people generally has been conducted to investigate one of two major issues: the use of different modes of communication or the extent and efficacy of different educational placements. Because the emphasis has varied as a function of children's ages, the following discussion will address research within four separate categories: parent-child communication, early intervention–preschool education, elementary-secondary education, and postsecondary education.

PARENT-CHILD COMMUNICATION

Since the 1960s, there has been a stream of research indicating that deaf children of deaf parents are educationally and linguistically superior to deaf children of hearing parents. Further, studies of the interactions of deaf parents with their children have revealed that deaf mothers utilize a wide range of communication strategies, including speech, signing, fingerspelling, signing on the child's body, and physical manipulation. Also, deaf mothers interact with their deaf children functionally in the same ways that hearing mothers interact with hearing children, although deaf mothers use both oral and manual communication. The interactions of hearing mothers with their deaf children are less efficient, although those who use manual communication with their children come closer to the level of deaf mother–deaf child and hearing mother–hearing child communication than those hearing mothers who rely on oral-only communication.

PRESCHOOL EDUCATION

Coupled with the achievement of deaf children of deaf parents is a growing body of evidence of the lack of effectiveness of traditional oral-only preschool programs. The indicators are that children who attend oral-only preschools show no linguistic or academic superiority over children who do not attend preschool, and in some areas may be even weaker linguistically.

The combined impact of the demonstrated lack of effectiveness of traditional oral-only preschool programs and the demonstrated superiority of deaf children with deaf parents led to the establishment of simultaneous oral-manual or total communication preschool programs. The results of a longitudinal evaluation of seven preschool programs for deaf children across the United States supported a cognitive-academic emphasis over a socialization orientation. It was also found that: combined oral-manual communication is more beneficial than oral-only instruction; no clear differences are found between the Rochester method and total communication; class placement has no measurable effect on communication achievement; children are developing normally in cognitive skills and visual motor functioning; most programs do not train the children to utilize residual hearing effectively; pre-reading skills are strong but there are serious deficits in English; and arithmetic is underemphasized.

ELEMENTARY AND SECONDARY EDUCATION

There is less research on elementary-secondary programs than on the preschool and postsecondary years. One area that has generated great interest is the effectiveness of simultaneous oral-manual communication in the classroom. This has been of special interest since information has been disseminated documenting that the majority of programs in the United States now use total communication. The ability of teachers to produce grammatical manual representations of English under normal classroom conditions has been examined, comparing deaf teachers, experienced signing hearing teachers, and inexperienced signing hearing teachers. Deaf teachers delete far fewer signs and use more elements of American Sign Language (ASL), while the inexperienced hearing teachers do the reverse. Experienced hearing teachers are in the middle on all measures. One important implication for these findings is the apparently great amount of time required for hearing teachers to become efficient in manual communication.

A second area of interest is concerned with the teaching of reading to deaf children. Although there is a long history of research pointing to inadequacies of reading in deaf children, it is now suggested that perhaps existing standardized tests underestimate the reading abilities of deaf students. When the performance of deaf children reading in sign was investigated by using a miscue analysis approach, it was found that the reading process in deaf children is similar to that for hearing children and that deaf readers use context and prior knowledge to derive meaning from print.

The passage in 1975 of Public Law 94-142, the Education of All Handicapped Children Act, has accelerated the trend toward greater placement of deaf children in public schools and in integrated classrooms. The movement caused major changes in curriculum, the roles of teachers of deaf students, the use of interpreters, and the socialization of deaf children with hearing parents. However, there has been little research on the process.

POSTSECONDARY EDUCATION

Since 1965 alternatives for postsecondary training have expanded tremendously for deaf people. In 1960 Gallaudet College was the only institution for higher learning offering special programs for deaf students. During the ensuing 10 years, programs were established in such institutions as the Rochester Institute of Technology, California State University at Northridge, St. Paul Technical Vocational Institute, New Orleans Delgado Community College, and Seattle Community College. By the 1980s more than 100 programs in the United States provided postsecondary education and training for deaf students. Evaluation of three regional federally funded postsecondary programs for deaf students in Louisiana, Washington, and Minnesota has revealed that the programs in general were quite successful. The deaf students are able to compete effectively in regular classrooms with the aid of interpreters, and regular classroom teachers are supportive of having deaf students in their classes. The training is instrumental in helping deaf students achieve upward mobility in the job market. Deaf workers obtain high ratings from their immediate supervisors, although problems of communication raise barriers to advancement.

Bibliography

Craig, W.: "Effects of Preschool Training on the Development of Reading and Lipreading Skills of Deaf Children," *American Annals of the Deaf*, 109(3):280–296, 1964.

Ewoldt, C.: "A Psycholinguistic Description of Selected Deaf Children Reading in Sign Language," *Reading Research Quarterly*, 16(1):38–59, 1981.

Jordan, I., G. Gustavson, and R. Rosen: "An Update on Communication Trends in Programs for the Deaf," *American Annals of the Deaf*, 125(3):350–357, 1979.

Kluwin, T.: "The Grammaticality of Manual Representations of English," *American Annals of the Deaf*, 126(4):417–422, 1981.

Maestas y Moores, J.: "A Descriptive Study of Communication Modes and Pragmatic Functions Used by Three Prelinguistically Deaf Mothers with Their Infants One to Six Months of Age in Their Homes," unpublished doctoral dissertation, University of Minnesota, 1980.

McCroskey, R.: "Early Education of Infants with Severe Auditory Impairments," *Proceedings of the International Conference on Oral Education of the Deaf*, Alexander Graham Bell Association, Washington, D.C., pp. 1891–1905, 1967.

Meadow, K.: "*Deafness and Child Development*," University of California Press, Berkeley, 1981.

———: "The Effect of Early Manual Communication and Family Climate on the Deaf Child's Environment," unpublished doctoral dissertation, University of California, Berkeley, 1967.

——— et al.: "Interactions of Deaf Mothers and Deaf Preschool Children," *American Annals of the Deaf*, 126(4):454–468, 1981.

Moores, D.: "*Educating the Deaf: Psychology, Principles and Practices*," Houghton Mifflin, Boston, 1982.

———: "Education of the Deaf: Retrospectives and Prospectus," keynote address, biennial meeting of the Convention of American Instructors of the Deaf, Winnipeg, Manitoba, July 1983.

———, S. Fisher, and M. Harlow: "Post-Secondary Programs for the Deaf: Summary and Overview," Research Report no. 80, University of Minnesota Research and Demonstration Center in Education of Handicapped Children, Minneapolis, 1974.

———, K. Weiss, and M. Goodwin: "Early Intervention Programs for Hearing Impaired Children," *American Annals of the Deaf*, 123(8):925–936, 1978.

Julia Maestas y Moores

Evaluation

There are several ways to assess the academic achievement of hearing-impaired students. Assessment can be accomplished by standardized, nonstandardized, and informal measures which can be administered either individually or to groups of students. Standardized tests are commercially marketed, whereas nonstandardized devices are commercially marketed or systematically produced by teachers or teaching programs.

Informal evaluations, which are nonstandardized and nonsystematic, are frequently conducted by teachers who observe their students and infer what the students know. Teachers conduct informal observations by asking questions, giving cues to facilitate responses, requiring explanations, and by using many other approaches. While informal evaluations can be powerful and useful tools, they are not without flaws. Often, it is difficult for a teacher to explain exactly what is being evaluated to other professionals. Also, informal observations are dependent on the individual perceptions of each teacher. After observing the same student at the same time, two teachers may have totally different subjective evaluations regarding that student. Such informal observations can also be affected by teachers' personal prejudices.

STANDARDIZED TESTS

To eliminate the problems of informal evaluations, formal devices have been created to evaluate the progress of students. Formal devices for evaluating the educational progress of hearing-impaired students range from teacher-made tests to commercially produced, standardized achievement tests. Achievement tests are generally administered to groups of students on an annual basis and test a variety of academic skills which are appropriate to grade level. The most widely used achievement test with hearing-impaired students is the hearing-impaired version of the Stanford Achievement Test (SAT-HI). The SAT-HI has standardized instructions for deaf students as well as norms established on both deaf and normal-hearing students.

The SAT-HI is similar to other standardized achievement tests in that it has a multiple-skill battery, that is, it tests several areas of academic achievement. Some of the test areas that are investigated in achievement tests are math, vocabulary, reading comprehension, and spelling. Since relatively few items are required to produce stable ranking of students for the norm group, and to save both time and money, achievement tests do not test entire domains but instead sample narrowly from each. For example, to test the entire domain of two-digit addition, taken two at a time, would require a test that would have every possible two-digit addition combination, that is, 45 items. Such an approach would make testing so time-consuming that the process of education would not be possible.

When using the SAT-HI and other standardized tests to assess hearing-impaired students, the most critical problem may have its roots in the instructions themselves. Standardized achievement tests also have standardized instructions. It has been shown that deaf children who are given early and consistent exposure to sign language do better on achievement tests than deaf children who have not had such exposure. Perhaps part of the reason for the superior achievement of the deaf children who were given early sign language training is that these children understand the instructions and know better what is expected of them than those children with poorer levels of language. If the child does not understand the instructions to a test, the examiner is placed into a doublebind: if more explanations are given to the student the standardization of procedures have been violated, but if no clarification is made the hearing-impaired person may not be able to perform to the best of his or her abilities because of not knowing what to do.

Testing a deaf child becomes even more difficult when employing tests that are not designed for hearing-impaired populations. It is both inaccurate and inappropriate to use such tests. Popular tests such as the Wide Range Achievement Test, Metropolitan Achievement Test, and Peabody Individual Achievement Test are not appropriate for use with hearing-impaired groups because they have instructions that are too verbal (either written or oral) and place many deaf students at a severe disadvantage. Likewise, tests such as the Peabody Picture Vocabulary Test, which require no verbal response, should be avoided if they possess no standardized norms for hearing-impaired students.

Unless a test considers the language background of a hearing-impaired population, its results cannot be valid. Most tests are designed for administration to students who have had an early and consistent presentation of spoken language. Since this requirement is not consistently met by hearing-impaired populations, it is both logically and professionally improper to employ these tests with deaf people.

Achievement tests are generally norm-referenced tests, that is, the score obtained by a student is compared to a normalized or standardized group. The result is that the test score gives information about a student's performance relative to other students in the norm group. This comparison becomes a problem when testing hearing-impaired students since they are a heterogeneous group with wide ranges of communication skills, audiometric responses, intellectual abilities, and educational backgrounds. All of these factors should be taken into account in some fashion when comparing hearing-impaired students. Comparisons become even more dubious when trying to compare hearing-impaired students with populations of normal-hearing students.

Another problem with standardized tests is the scores that they yield. Since there is sampling error in obtained test scores, these scores are best approached as an indicative range of ability rather than an absolute appraisal of academic skills.

CRITERION-REFERENCED TESTS

The problems of comparison and test score error can be reduced through the use of criterion-referenced tests. Some criterion-referenced tests are commercially available, such as the Fountain Valley Teacher Support System in Reading, while the majority of such tests are produced by teachers. Criterion-referenced tests are an example of nonstandardized tests. This approach compares the obtained test scores to some predetermined standard, rather than to a normative group. For example, an individual is given a criterion-referenced test to investigate his or her ability to add two-digit numbers. The test consists of 10 problems requiring two-digit addition. The predetermined criterion for passing is arbitrarily set as obtaining the correct response on at least 90 percent of the 10 items. If the test taker meets this criterion, he or she progresses to more difficult material; if the criterion is not met, classroom activities are directed to enhancing those skills that are needed to meet it. In contrast to a norm-referenced achievement test, the test taker will be given criterion-referenced tests until able to meet the criterion.

The use of criterion-referenced tests is a good method for evaluating hearing-impaired populations in any class or school. Criterion-referenced tests can be more comprehensive than standardized achievement tests, better tailored to the needs of individual students, better related to what is actually happening in the classroom, and better able to avoid comparisons among a diverse group on parameters that are not relevant (such as communication skills when testing math skills).

A criterion-referenced test can be constructed by anyone who is interested in education. Some guidelines, as extrapolated from N. E. Gronlund, for constructing criterion-referenced tests include: (1) define the test domain specifically and carefully so that it can be covered systematically in the test; (2) define only domains that are important to the process of education; (3) have the test sample the domain with relevant items; (4) specify the performance criterion in absolute terms such as percent correct; and (5) readminister the test until the criterion is reached.

The problem of educational evaluation increases when the students are hearing-impaired. Standardized achievement tests should be viewed only as vague indicators of relative ability. Criterion-referenced tests, on the other hand, can be used as valuable aids in discovering the needs and abilities of hearing-impaired students.

Bibliography
Conrad, R.: *The Deaf Schoolchild: Language and Cognitive Function*, Harper and Row, London, 1979.

Gronlund, N. E.: *Constructing Achievement Tests*, Prentice-Hall, Englewood Cliffs, New Jersey, 1982.

Meadow, K. P.: *Deafness and Child Development*, University of California Press, Berkeley, 1980.

Moores, D. F.: *Educating the Deaf: Psychology, Principles and Practices*, 2d ed., Houghton Mifflin, Boston, 1980.

Nunnally, J: *Psychometric Theory*, McGraw-Hill, New York, 1978.

Joe D. Stedt

Trends
Several major trends have evolved during the history of deaf education. The most prominent has been the controversy over communication methods and related issues such as a misinterpretation of speech as language, a decline in the number of deaf teachers, residential school policy that ignored the sign knowledge of its youngest students, and an interpretation of mainstreaming as meaning public school placement rather than residential school placement.

BILINGUAL-BICULTURAL PRACTICES
Such trends run parallel to those experienced by other linguistic minorities in the United States. Consequently, research and practice from the field of bilingual education has been applied in several innovative programs for hearing-impaired children. Attitudes toward bilingual-bicultural policies have become more positive since the 1970s. University students in a midwestern hearing-impairment program and a related special-education teacher-training program, local teachers working in the field of hearing impairment, and local administrators of hearing-impairment programs agree that: bilingual language development is possible; American Sign Language is a nonoral language; hearing-impaired students should be given a chance to become bilingual-bicultural; and hearing-impaired students should be given a chance to demonstrate which language is the most beneficial language of instruction for learning English.

LANGUAGE CURRICULUMS
A major trend in the field is the focus on language as being central to the curriculum in academic programs for hearing-impaired students. The disproportionate attention once given to speech has been somewhat altered. Expressive speech ability, speechreading, and auditory training are still emphasized in oral-only and sign system programs, especially in the younger grades, but there is growing acceptance of those children who do not possess these abilities.

Teachers have also found that language curriculums dealing only with English syntactical features have not resulted in a command of oral or written language abilities, yet the focus on only this area of language goes back to the 1800s. Increasingly, some instructors are learning to focus on the teaching of semantic and pragmatic skills, combining analytical and natural methods of language learning. Other teachers are attempting to build English literacy skills on whatever knowledge of sign language a student might possess. Little research has been conducted to evaluate these attempts, and there is a desperate need for the development of theoretical frameworks and research focusing on teaching methodology and curriculum utilized in the classroom for hearing-impaired students.

HOLISTIC APPROACH

Another trend in the field of hearing impairment has been a mounting concern for the mental health of the hearing-impaired child. Previously, the deaf child was viewed as an imperfect human being (that is, a child who could not speak) and curriculum focused on that disability. However, the hearing-impaired child now appears to be viewed as capable of functioning in both the hearing and deaf societies, as becoming bilingual-bicultural, and the needs of the child are increasingly seen from a holistic perspective. Many hearing parents and educators now view the social-emotional environment that develops in a residential school or from consistent contact with deaf adults to be as important as speech goals. *See* PSYCHOLOGY: Mental Health.

MAINSTREAMING

In conjunction with the holistic trend, mainstreaming models are being evaluated in terms of the child's mental health as well as his or her academic progress. More hearing-impaired students are mainstreamed than in past years, and creative mainstreaming models include contained classrooms in public schools, residential students attending specific public school classes, and hearing-impaired students enrolled in public school classrooms with interpreter support. Residential schools continue to receive more of the difficult-to-teach, prelingually, multiply handicapped, or ethnic hearing-impaired population, while public schools are serving more students from white, middle-class families, with earlier-identified and milder aided losses. While there appears to be a greater need for teachers skilled in early childhood and multiply handicapped methodology, few college training programs are planning for these current needs.

Bibliography

Jordan, E., G. Gustavson, and R. Rosen: "Current Communication Trends at Programs for the Deaf," *American Annals of the Deaf*, 121:527–532, 1976.

Kannapell, B.: "Bilingualism: A New Direction in the Education of the Deaf," *Deaf American*, 119:9–15, 1974.

Kretschmer, R. R., and L. W. Kretschmer: *Language Development and Intervention with the Hearing Impaired*, University Park Press, Baltimore, 1978.

Leutke-Stahlman, B.: "A Positive Look at the Historical Similarities in Negative Attitudes Toward Linguistic Minorities," paper presented at the National Association for Bilingual Education (NABE), Detroit, April 1–9, 1982.

Meadows, K.: *Deafness and Child Development*, California University Press, 1980.

Moores, D. F.: *Educating the Deaf: Psychology, Principles, and Practices*, Houghton Mifflin, Boston, 1978.

———: "Nonvocal Systems of Verbal Behavior," in *Language Perspectives: Acquisition, Retardation, and Intervention*, University Park Press, Baltimore, 1974.

Prickett, H., and J. Hunt: "Education of the Deaf— The Next 10 Years," *American Annals of the Deaf*, 122(4):365–381, 1977.

Vernon, M.: "Deafness and Minority Group Dynamics," *Deaf American*, July-August, 1969.

Wilbur, R.: *American Sign Language and Sign Systems*, University Park Press, Baltimore, 1979.

Woodward, J.: "Some Sociolinguistic Problems in the Implementation of Bilingual Education for Deaf Students," in F. Cacamise and V. Hicks (eds.), *American Sign Language in a Bilingual, Bicultural Context*, NAD, Washington, D.C., 1980.

Barbara Luetke-Stahlman

Problems

Problems in the education of deaf people have increased mainly because the field of deaf education is in a state of change, influenced by pressures from many areas. Increases in technology and advancements in medicine have changed the population of deaf children; new laws have refocused educators' efforts about how to educate deaf children and, even more importantly, where they should be educated. The current increase in political awareness by deaf adults has begun to raise consciousness in professionals working with deaf and hearing-impaired individuals. This in turn has provided more information for parents to consider when their child has been diagnosed as deaf. This abundance of information requires parents to make far-reaching decisions affecting their child at a time when they are not adequately prepared to make these decisions.

MEDICAL ASPECTS

The deaf child born today is very different from the deaf child born in years past. Medical advancements have increased the survival rate of many children. More additional handicapping conditions are present in children who are deaf today. The use of medicine to control common childhood diseases such as scarlet fever which can cause deafness has reduced the number of postlingually deafened people (that is, people who become deaf after learning language). Although the percentage of deaf people in the general population has not changed, the average deaf child today has a greater hearing loss and its onset is much earlier. More deaf children are now prelingually deaf. This has caused the education of deaf people to become increasingly complex.

AUDIOLOGICAL ASPECTS

Audiological advances, although considerable in recent years, have not contributed to reducing significantly the time lag in identification of hearing loss. Because of its cost, equipment for the early identification of hearing loss is usually found only in large urban hospitals. Early identification of deafness is dependent on pediatrician awareness.

However, because of its low incidence, pediatricians do not usually suspect deafness early in the child's life. In addition, referrals to centers with sophisticated diagnostic procedures and equipment usually do not happen until later, when deafness creates noticeable behavioral changes in the child. The average age of identification is 20 months, causing a significant delay in the early development of the child.

EARLY INTERVENTION

Typically, the identification of deafness is made by a medical or audiological professional, who is likely to view the child from a medical perspective, that is, the child is "sick" and needs to be made "well." Compensatory or corrective procedures designed to make the deaf child "normal" are recommended to the family. Parents therefore invest a great deal of time and effort attempting to correct the problem of deafness instead of modifying their environment to balance out the differences. Parents are often counseled and encouraged to focus their energies on oral-aural communication. This approach tends to produce a fragmented vision effect in parents, causing them to view their deaf child in closed segments of time (0 to 3 years, 3 to 6 years, and so on) rather than over a period of years (adolescence through adulthood). Parents of young deaf children are usually not provided with an overall perspective on deafness. To prepare a young deaf child for a successful future, parents need extensive information about communication strategies, educational opportunities and alternatives, deaf adults, and the community in which they participate.

Early in deaf children's lives, their families are faced with a number of significant decisions that need to be made: what type of hearing aids are best, what can a deaf child do, what school should the child attend, how will a spouse or family react? All these issues require complex solutions, and stress within the family is easily created.

EDUCATIONAL ASPECTS

After the child is identified as deaf, one of the most important life events will be the educational opportunities pursued. The United States has an underlying historical premise that all people should eventually be mainstreamed into the dominant society. This melting pot philosophy led to the creation of Public Law 94-142, the Education for All Handicapped Children Act. P.L. 94-142 was designed to provide a better education for all handicapped populations. For many handicapped children (for example, blind or wheelchair-bound) in whom communication is not the one overriding barrier to access, this is probably a good law. However, its basic premise has created problems for the deaf child.

The following choices are available to parents in most states: a residential school for deaf children as either a residential or day placement, a day school established solely for deaf students, or a program that has separate classes for deaf students but is housed in a regular public school. In addition, many schools have programs where children may spend parts of the day with a teacher of deaf students in a resource room or in regular classes for hearing children. Finally, a deaf child may receive the services of an itinerant teacher of deaf children and spend the entire school day in hearing classes (sometimes with an interpreter using sign language). Numerous options are available (often dependent on geographical factors); however, the low incidence of deafness creates situations that require many school districts and towns to collaborate in establishing a program. Not all districts offer all options. Programming for deaf children in some school districts may depend on money. Schools may not have the appropriate staff to provide an adequate program, but are forced by law to provide an education as close to that of the nonhandicapped peers as possible. Additional pressure and stress is added to many families who are forced to accept legal educational programs that they feel are not beneficial for their children.

TEACHER TRAINING

The expansion of educational settings for the teaching of deaf children has created problems for college programs that train teachers. Traditionally, teachers in most university-based training programs were prepared as teachers for deaf students ranging from kindergarten through grade 12. This training was geared to prepare teachers for self-contained classrooms within large programs specifically for deaf children. Since the late 1980s, however, more teachers have been trained to fit into existing educational systems. They are not trained to create programs which, due to individual child needs, may need to be outside of the existing program structures and philosophies. The current trend is to train teachers under generic programs for children labeled exceptional or communicatively handicapped, instead of specifying that the disability is deafness. This generic view denies the special conditions and requirements of deaf children, and especially of deaf adults.

Changes in the field of deaf education have resulted in less emphasis on residential or large programs; there are no standard curriculum materials that are used from kindergarten through grade 12 in most programs. There has been a recognition of the need for high school teachers trained in specific high school subjects rather than in the traditional programming for kindergarten through grade 12. In addition, the advent of total communication requires teachers to learn signed language systems, and there has been an increase in knowledge about communication and its effect on learning. Deaf adults are also contributing more to the schooling process. These new pressures require that teachers be prepared as specialists, not as generalists. The changes have led to the Council on Education of the Deaf (the national certifying agency of teachers of deaf students) to institute procedures that certify teachers as preschool, elementary, or secondary teachers. While the changes have happened in the educational system, few states have actually instituted the new certifying procedures.

FUTURE OBJECTIVES

The future of the deaf education field depends on finding equitable solutions to the problems that accompany progress. Professionals must continue to focus on increasing the means for early identification of hearing loss, evaluating the effects of the medical model of deafness, determining the effects of P.L. 94-142 on programming for the young deaf child, and investigating the strengths and weaknesses of total communication. Finally, the field needs to incorporate more input from the deaf community. Competent, self-reliant, successful deaf adults are the goal of education. Having the skills and tools required to reach this goal is the daily responsibility of those who educate deaf children.

Robert J. Hoffmeister

EDUCATION OF THE HANDICAPPED ACT

The Education of the Handicapped Act (EHA) is the primary vehicle for federal funding and overseeing of special education services for handicapped children. It assures handicapped children access to adequate programs and services, skilled personnel, and fair procedures.

Under the EHA, the federal government offers financial commitments and incentives to state governments in exchange for specific promises on how educational services will be provided to handicapped children. In order to get federal funds, each state must demonstrate that it is complying with the act; otherwise, federal funds may be cut off. In addition, parents may enforce the law by using complaint procedures and private lawsuits to get specific services for individual children.

BACKGROUND

The federal government does not traditionally provide school services or establish educational policy. School systems are operated by local governments and financed by state and local taxes.

The federal government occasionally gives federal money to supplement local programs when necessary to advance national interests. The EHA is part of this tradition of federal involvement in local educational policy, to assure that handicapped children can get an education.

Federal policies also prohibit discrimination in the nation's schools. Constitutional principles of equal opportunity, embodied in the Fourteenth Amendment, justify federal intervention when school systems discriminate on the basis of race or sex. The EHA is based in part on a similar concept of equal educational opportunity. The Supreme Court has never had to determine whether there is a constitutional right to special education for handicapped children; the Court's cases related to education for handicapped children have been resolved on statutory grounds. Lower federal courts have relied on constitutional principles to find that handicapped children have a right to education. The landmark decisions of *Pennsylvania Association for Retarded Children (PARC) v. Pennsylvania* and *Mills v. Board of Education* influenced passage of key parts of the EHA which set out procedural protections and substantive educational rights for handicapped children.

HISTORY

The EHA was adopted on April 13, 1970, as P.L. 91-230. It authorized federal support for services and training programs to benefit handicapped children. EHA funding was described as a supplement or catalyst for improved state programs serving handicapped youth. But the EHA also provided major support for national and regional projects, research, and model programs. For example, the Captioned Films for the Deaf program in the Department of Health, Education and Welfare was expanded to meet the educational needs of deaf children as well as to produce entertainment films.

The first substantive changes in the law were the Education of the Handicapped Amendments of 1974, P.L. 93-380. These amendments incorporated the due process provisions of the *PARC* and *Mills* decisions, and included the concept that all handicapped children, regardless of the severity of their handicaps, are entitled to educational programming.

The most significant amendments were signed into law on November 29, 1975. The Education of All Handicapped Children Act (EAHCA), also known as P.L. 94-142, established procedures for states to follow in educating handicapped children between the ages of 3 and 18. The EAHCA also made substantive guarantees: every handicapped child is entitled to a free, appropriate, public education and to individualized programming, and must be educated with nonhandicapped children to the maximum extent appropriate. The major implementing regulations for this act went into effect on October 1, 1977, after extensive public hearings.

The EHA was amended again in 1978 by P.L. 95-461, and on December 2, 1983, by P.L. 98-199. Among other things, the 1983 amendments broadened the authority of the Secretary of Education, authorized special services for deaf-blind youth after age 21 to facilitate their transition from educational services to other services, and extended the age range for early education programs from birth to age 5.

SUBCHAPTER I—GENERAL PROVISIONS

In adopting the EHA, Congress made formal "findings" that the special educational needs of the nation's handicapped children were not being fully met by the states. Congress found that more than half of the 8 million handicapped children in the United States did not receive full equality of opportunity. One million were excluded entirely from public schools. Parents were often forced to provide services at their own expense. However, Congress found that, given appropriate funding, the needs of these children could be met by state and local educational agencies. School systems were failing to meet their responsibilities because of inadequate financial resources. Therefore, the federal government would assist state and local efforts to provide programs in order to assure equal protection of the law.

The purpose of the act is explicitly stated by Congress: "to assure that all handicapped children have available to them . . . a free appropriate public education which emphasizes special education and related services designed to meet their unique needs, to assure that the rights of handicapped children and their parents or guardians are protected, to assist States and localities to provide for the education of all handicapped children, and to assess and assure the effectiveness of efforts to educate handicapped children."

The following conditions are defined:

1. Handicapped children. The EHA covers children with handicapping conditions who "by reason thereof require special education and related services." The definition includes children who are mentally retarded, hard-of-hearing, deaf, speech- or language-impaired, visually handicapped, seriously emotionally disturbed, orthopedically impaired, or "other health impaired," and children with specific learning disabilities.

The EHA regulations define these conditions in more detail. In the area of hearing impairment, the regulations state:

"Deaf means a hearing impairment which is so severe that the child is impaired in processing linguistic information through hearing, with or without amplification, which adversely affects educational performance.

"Deaf-blind means concomitant hearing and visual impairments, the combination of which causes such severe communication and other developmental and educational problems that they cannot be accommodated in special education programs solely for deaf or blind children.

"Hard of Hearing means a hearing impairment, whether permanent or fluctuating, which adversely affects a child's educational performance but which is not included under the definition of 'deaf' in this section."

If a child's condition does not fit into the defined categories, the child is not entitled to services. In addition, if a child's physical or mental problem does not affect learning ability or require special education, the child is not entitled to services. For example, a child who is blind in only one eye may be able to participate in all school activities without any modifications. That child would not be considered a handicapped child for purposes of this act. Most disabilities have sufficient impact on some aspect of educational performance or learning ability to trigger EHA eligibility.

2. Special education. Special education means specially designed instruction, at no cost to parents or guardians, to meet the unique needs of a handicapped child. This definition requires school systems to look at each handicapped child as an individual. The school may not arbitrarily provide one program for all "deaf" children. Individualized programming is an essential component of the EHA guarantees.

3. Related services. The EHA defines related services to mean transportation and developmental, corrective, and other supportive services that may be required to assist a handicapped child to benefit from special education. The statute and regulations list illustrative services: speech pathology and audiology, psychological services, physical and occupational therapy, recreation, medical and counseling services, parent counseling and training, school health services, and social work services in schools.

An unlisted service may still be required by the act. For example, the act does not explicitly include interpreter services. Nevertheless, deaf children are entitled to interpreter services if they need them in order to benefit from their education.

4. Free appropriate public education. The heart of the EHA is the guarantee of a free appropriate public education to all handicapped children. The act defines this term to mean special education and related services that (1) are provided at public ex-

pense, under public supervision and direction, and without charge; (2) meet the standards of the state educational agency; (3) include an appropriate preschool, elementary, or secondary school education; and (4) are provided in conformity with an individualized education program. The mechanism for determining a free appropriate public education for an individual child is set out below.

5. Individualized education program. The act and its regulations do not specify appropriate services for every type of disability. Instead, parents, teachers, and school administrators must meet periodically and agree upon the necessary programming for each eligible child. This Individualized Education Program (IEP) is a signed, written agreement. It includes a statement about the child's current abilities, annual goals and short-term instructional objectives, specific services, extent of participation in regular educational programs, timetables, and objective criteria and evaluation procedures.

The IEP procedure is revolutionary in that it gives parents a voice in determining the type of education that an individual child will receive. The IEP provides an opportunity for resolving differences of opinion between parents and schools. It sets forth in writing a commitment of resources. Procedural protections assure that the agreed-upon services will be provided, and that the child will be properly and periodically evaluated.

SUBCHAPTER II—STATE ASSISTANCE

States apply for EHA funds by submitting to the United States Department of Education an acceptable state plan for special education services. Each state's grant is based upon a formula that counts the number of handicapped children in the state, multiplied by a percentage of the average per-pupil expenditure in public schools in the United States. This formula gives the states an incentive to identify nonhandicapped children as handicapped in order to increase their entitlement, so the EHA limits the number of children who may be counted to 12 percent of the number of all children in the eligible age group. The state remains responsible for serving all handicapped children it identifies, even if that number exceeds 12 percent. Each state must submit an annual report showing the number of children served, within age groups and by disability category.

The EHA calls for federal funds to pay a steadily increasing percentage of the additional cost of educating handicapped children, beginning with 5 percent for the 1978 fiscal year and increasing to 40 percent by 1982. However, the appropriation has never met these goals.

State Plan The state plan is intended to be a comprehensive policy and planning management tool.

Each plan must set out in detail how the state will meet the goal of "providing full educational opportunity to all handicapped children." The plan must include a detailed timetable and a description of the kind and number of facilities, personnel, and services necessary. It must be developed with input from an appointed advisory panel of experts and parents with opportunity for public hearings and public comment.

Least Restrictive Environment The state plan must also set out procedures to assure that, to the maximum extent appropriate, handicapped children are educated with children who are not handicapped. Special classes, separate schooling, or other removal of handicapped children from the regular educational environment is to occur only when the nature or severity of the child's handicap is such that education in regular classes with the use of supplementary aids and services cannot be achieved satisfactorily.

The least-restrictive-environment policy of the EHA is commonly known as mainstreaming. School systems must have a continuum of alternative placements, and must provide supplementary services that a handicapped child will need to succeed in regular classes. This preference for educating handicapped children in the mainstream of regular schools is difficult to apply to the needs of hearing-impaired children. The total communication environment, peer socialization, and the array of supportive services available in special programs for deaf children cannot easily be duplicated in local schools that do not have highly trained personnel and expertise in deafness.

Procedural Safeguards Disputes under the EHA are resolved by formal procedures. Generally, parents and handicapped children have a right of confidentiality and a right to examine all relevant records concerning the child. Parents who disagree with school evaluations may also obtain an independent evaluation of the child at public expense.

Parents are entitled to written notice in their native language prior to any change in the child's IEP, identification, evaluation, or placement.

Complaints and disagreements are resolved in formal due process hearings. Hearings are conducted by an impartial hearing officer who hears witnesses and takes evidence about the dispute. Parents and the school system have formal procedural rights, including the rights to be accompanied by counsel, to present evidence, and to confront and cross-examine witnesses. Parents may open the hearing to the public. The hearing officer's decision must be written, and it can be appealed to the state education agency by either party. Any party who is still dissatisfied with the decision may bring a civil court action in a state or federal court. During any dispute proceeding, unless the school and the parents agree otherwise, the child must stay in his or her present educational placement.

The act also sets out procedures to be used by the U.S. Department of Education when it determines that a state is not complying with the EHA or its state plan.

SUBCHAPTERS III AND IV—CENTERS AND SERVICES; TRAINING PERSONNEL

The EHA funds special programs for the education of handicapped children. For example, Regional Resource Centers are intended to assist state and local school systems in developing quality programs and services by providing consultation, technical assistance, and training.

Special funding is available for deaf-blind children and youth, including innovative programs in diagnosis, evaluation, adjustment, education, and training for such children and their families. The regulations establish extensive criteria for grants and services under this program. *See* DEAF-BLINDNESS.

Other grant programs fund projects for early education, severely handicapped children and youth, auxiliary activities, and postsecondary education programs (including regional centers for the deaf). Grants are made to institutions and agencies for training special education teachers, providers of related services, administrators, and other providers of special services. Grants are available to nonprofit organizations for parent education. The act authorizes national clearinghouses on education and postsecondary education to disseminate information and provide technical assistance to parents, professionals, administrators, and other interested parties.

SUBCHAPTER V—RESEARCH; INSTRUCTIONAL MEDIA

The EHA authorizes grants for research projects in improved techniques and devices for teaching handicapped children, development of appropriate curricula, application of new technologies to improve teaching, development of model programs, and dissemination of information on research and related activities.

Captioned film loan services for deaf persons and other special instructional media are funded by the EHA. Grants are also available for research and training in the use of film and educational media. Finally, contracts to establish and operate centers to facilitate the use of new technology in educational programs are available. The Secretary of Education gives preference under this part to applicants that can serve the educational technology needs of the Model Secondary School for the Deaf. *See*

MODEL SECONDARY SCHOOL FOR THE DEAF; NATIONAL CAPTIONING INSTITUTE.

Bibliography

Education of the Handicapped Act, 20 U.S.C. §§1401–1461.

Hull, K.: *An American Civil Liberties Union Handbook: The Rights of Physically Handicapped People*, 1979.

National Center for Law and the Deaf, *The Legal Rights of Hearing-Impaired People*, 1984.

Regulations promulgated under Education of the Handicapped Act (P.L. 91-230), as amended by the Education of All Handicapped Children Act (P.L. 94-142), 34 Code of Federal Regulations Parts 300-348.

Sarah S. Geer

ROWLEY V. BOARD OF EDUCATION

This case involved the effort of a deaf first-grader, Amy Rowley, and her parents, Clifford and Nancy Rowley, to secure the education they believed the child was entitled to under the Education for All Handicapped Children Act of 1975. The Rowleys were victorious in both federal courts below the Supreme Court. The school district then brought this case before the Supreme Court which, although sharply divided, adopted a conservative interpretation of the applicable law.

The Supreme Court reversed the lower court decisions and remanded the case to the district court for further consideration. The Rowleys may have succeeded again, but the case was dismissed as moot when the family moved to another state into a school district that provided Amy with the services the Rowleys sought.

Although not decided in the Rowleys' favor, this case was not without some positive results. The Supreme Court's decision affirmed the power of the courts to review and make substantive changes in the individual education programs established by school districts. And the Rowleys' efforts brought national attention to the problems of deaf and hearing-impaired children in the nation's schools.

Statutory Scheme The Education for All Handicapped Children Act is Title I of the Education of the Handicapped Act; it provides that each state receiving funds from the federal government for special education must provide each handicapped child with a free appropriate public education (FAPE). As defined by the act, "handicapped children" include children who are deaf or hard of hearing. Each recipient state must establish an advisory committee on the education of handicapped children which shall have members who are handicapped and members who are parents or guardians of handicapped children. The act provides that an individualized education program (IEP) shall be drafted for each handicapped child and that the child's parents shall participate in the development of this program. The U.S. Department of Education, the federal department assigned responsibility to administer the act, states that parents are "equal participants" in the development of their child's IEP.

Proceedings in School District Clifford and Nancy Rowley are both deaf, and graduates of Gallaudet College. Clifford Rowley is a chemist and Nancy Rowley is a certified teacher of deaf students. Their daughter, Amy, born in 1972, is also deaf. The Rowleys began training her in the use of total communication (lipreading, amplification, and sign language)—the mode of communication used in their home. When Amy was to begin first grade, the Rowleys, in the process of preparing Amy's IEP, asked the school district to provide Amy with a sign language interpreter when academic subjects were taught. *See* GALLAUDET COLLEGE; SOCIOLINGUISTICS: Total Communication.

The Rowleys provided their own testimony, as well as experts' opinions, to support their request for a sign language interpreter. The school district, rejecting these testimonies, declined their request. Instead, the school district provided Amy with a hearing aid (she had to take off her own hearing aids, which were better for her, and use the hearing aid provided by the school district, which worked only sporadically). A teacher of deaf pupils removed her from her classroom for one hour each day for personal instruction.

The Rowleys requested a hearing, asserting that the school district failed to provide their daughter with a FAPE and that it also failed to comply with the procedural requirements of the act. The hearing officer found for the school district. As an aggrieved party, the Rowleys appealed to the commissioner of education of New York, who affirmed the decision of the hearing officer. At that point, the Rowleys had exhausted all administrative remedies. According to the act, an aggrieved party who has exhausted all administrative remedies may initiate suit in a U.S. district court or a state court of competent jurisdiction. The Rowleys decided to file an action in a U.S. district court, suing the school district and the commissioner of education of New York.

Decisions of the Lower Federal Courts After a four-day trial, the district judge found for the Rowleys. Presented with two distinct programs, one developed by the school district and the other developed by the Rowleys, he determined that the program developed by the Rowleys was more appropriate. He found that Amy was a remarkably well-adjusted child; she was above-average in intelligence. Further, he found that Amy missed almost half of what was said in her classroom solely because of

her deafness. "[T]his information establishes that Amy is a very bright child who is doing fairly well in school. It also establishes that she understands considerably less of what goes on in class than she could if she were not deaf. Thus she is not learning as much, or performing as well academically, as she would without her handicap."

The judge concluded that "an 'appropriate education' could mean an 'adequate education' that is an education substantial enough to facilitate a child's progress from one grade to another and to enable him or her to earn a high school diploma. An 'appropriate education' could also mean one which enables the handicapped child to achieve his or her full potential. Between these two extremes, however, is a standard which I conclude is more in keeping with the regulations, with the Equal Protection decisions which motivated the passage of the Act, and with common sense. This standard would require that each handicapped child be given an opportunity to achieve his full potential commensurate with the opportunity provided to other children. . . . Since some handicapped children will undoubtedly have the intellectual ability to do better than merely progress from grade to grade, this standard requires something more than the 'adequate' education described above. On the other hand, since even the best public schools lack the resources to enable every child to achieve his full potential, the standard would not require them to go so far."

The district judge found that the education provided to Amy Rowley was not appropriate, and he therefore did not have to decide if the school district complied with the procedural requirements of the act in the development of her IEP.

The school district and the commissioner of education appealed this decision to the U.S. Court of Appeals for the Second Circuit. The court of appeals affirmed the decision of the district court, stating that "we are satisfied that the [district] court applied precisely the standard prescribed by Congress." The court emphasized the narrow scope of its decision. "This is not a class action in which the needs of all deaf children are determined. The evidence upon which our decision rests is concerned with a particular child, her atypical family, her upbringing and training since birth, and her classroom experience."

The school district then appealed the decision of the court of appeals to the Supreme Court of the United States.

Supreme Court Decision The Supreme Court split on its review of the lower courts' decision. The majority opinion was written by Justice Rhenquist, and was joined in by Justices Powell, Stevens, and O'Connor. The Supreme Court reversed the lower courts' decisions, taking a conservative approach as to the definition of a free appropriate public education.

The Supreme Court emphasized that an FAPE has four elements: (1) It must be at public expense and under public supervision and direction. (2) It must meet the state's educational standards, such as standards related to class size. (3) It must include an appropriate preschool, elementary, or secondary school education in the state. (4) It must be provided in accordance with the child's IEP.

The Supreme Court acknowledged that Congress derived its authority to enact the act from the equal protection clause of the Fourteenth Amendment to the Constitution. The Court stated, however, that equal protection does not necessarily mean equal opportunity. In the Court's view, an FAPE is one which is "sufficient to confer some educational benefit upon the handicapped child." The Court also noted that while the act encourages mainstreaming—such as educating handicapped children with nonhandicapped children—it does not absolutely require it.

The Court rejected the school district's contention that judicial scrutiny is limited to affirming or denying the district's IEP. Rather, a judge must determine (1) if the state has complied with the procedural requirements set forth in the act, including the development of the child's IEP in accordance with the law, and (2) if the individualized education program is reasonably calculated to enable the child to receive educational benefits. Only if the child's IEP had not been developed in accordance with the statutory requirements or if the education was not calculated to enable the child to receive educational benefits could judges concern themselves with questions of methodology.

In *Rowley*, the district judge found that the program developed by the Rowleys was "more appropriate" than the program developed by the school district; he found that the program developed by the Rowleys would provide Amy with an equal educational opportunity. The Supreme Court held that a plan would comply with the act if it provided any level of appropriateness, not necessarily an education "more appropriate" than another. Further, the Supreme Court held that the education need only provide some educational benefits, not necessarily an equal educational opportunity. Thus, the Supreme Court answered the second question in the affirmative: that the IEP developed by the school district was "reasonably calculated to enable the child to receive some educational benefits." An affirmative answer to the second question establishes that an education is appropriate, as defined by the Supreme Court.

A handicapped child is, however, entitled to an FAPE, which is more than just an "appropriate" education. Since there will be many educations that are "appropriate" for each handicapped child under the definition developed by the Supreme Court, the first question must be answered in the affirmative as well to establish that a handicapped child is receiving an FAPE. In *Rowley*, the Supreme Court remanded the case to the district court for the purpose of answering the first question: Was the plan developed in accordance with the requirements set forth in the act?

The Supreme Court decision offers some guidance in the resolution of suits brought under the act. First, the Court notes that there should be no presumption in favor of the educational program proposed by the school district. Second, judges are not entitled to study the subject on their own and determine the appropriate educational placement for the child. Rather, their decision must accord with the standards set forth in the *Rowley* decision: ensuring that a program was developed in accordance with the procedural requirements of the act—including full parental participation—and that the IEP is "reasonably calculated to enable the child to receive educational benefits."

Justice Blackmun took a more expansive view of the legislative history behind the act, stating his view that Congress intended to provide handicapped children with equal educational opportunity. Justice Blackmun concluded, however, that the school district provided Amy with "an educational opportunity substantially equal to that provided her non-handicapped classmates."

Justice White wrote a vigorous dissent, in which he was joined by Justices Brennan and Marshall. The dissent points out that the act itself "announces it will provide a '*full* educational opportunity to handicapped children.'" Further, the dissent notes, this goal is supported by quotations from the relevant congressional reports, as well as by numerous remarks of individual senators and representatives. Justice White wrote that, pursuant to the majority's test, the act's requirements would be satisfied if Amy was "given a teacher with a loud voice."

Conclusion The battle waged by Amy on behalf of all handicapped children is over, but it was only one battle. Many believe that it is now time to petition Congress to make explicit that handicapped children are entitled to the same opportunities to achieve their potential as nonhandicapped children. Also, it is advised that parents continue to press for the educational rights of their handicapped children. In a recent decision, the Supreme Court stated that services that "permit a child to remain at school during the day are no less related to the effort to educate than are services that enable the child to reach, enter, or exit the school."

Thus, the Court itself seems to now be taking a more expansive view of the act. Both legislation and judicial means must be utilized to obtain equal educational opportunities for handicapped children.

Bibliography

Rowley v. Board of Education of the Hendrick Hudson Central School District, 483 F. Supp. 528, 536 (SDNY, 1980), aff'd. 632 F. 2d 945 (Second Circuit, 1980), rev'd. and rem'd. 458 U.S. 176, 102 S. Ct. 3034 (1982).

Tatro v. Irving Independent School District, 703 F. 2d 823 (Fifth Circuit), aff'd. ——— U.S. ———, 104 S. Ct. 3371 (1984).

20 U.S.C. 1400 et seq.

Michael A. Chatoff; Barry G. Felder

EDUCATIONAL LEGISLATION

The first recorded instance of federal legislation in deafness education in the United States occurred in 1819, when Henry Clay introduced a bill in Congress granting 23,000 acres of Alabama land to the American Asylum for Deaf and Dumb Persons in Hartford, Connecticut. Passage of this legislation enabled this first permanent school for deaf children to sell the land, purchase property in Hartford, construct school buildings, and establish an endowment fund of $300,000. *See* AMERICAN SCHOOL FOR THE DEAF.

Amos Kendall, postmaster general in the cabinets of Presidents Andrew Jackson and Martin Van Buren, was interested in the education of deaf children in the District of Columbia, and had contributed a house on his estate as a residential school. On February 16, 1857, he was instrumental in congressional enactment of a law establishing the Columbia Institution for the Deaf, Dumb and Blind, which provided for 100 acres of land and buildings. Soon afterward, however, blind children were placed in a separate program. On April 8, 1864, a Civil War Congress passed another bill, signed by President Abraham Lincoln, establishing the National Deaf Mute College within the institution. *See* GALLAUDET COLLEGE.

Two years earlier, in 1862, the Morrill Act laid the groundwork for this legislation. This law provided grants of land to the states for the development of universities, opening the doors of higher education to all citizens, including women and minorities. The establishment of what later became Gallaudet College extended this land-grant principle to deaf Americans so that they too could share in the evolution and benefits of a higher liberal education.

Over the intervening years, federal educational legislation relating to deafness consisted almost entirely of the annual budget appropriations for Gallaudet College. In the 1950s, however, there began a new and broader thrust of federal involvement in hearing loss, for deaf people, and for professionals serving in the field.

VOCATIONAL REHABILITATION ACT

In 1954 Congress passed Public Law 88-565, the Vocational Rehabilitation Act, which provided a number of direct and indirect services to deaf persons as well as other disabled Americans. This act included service and funding for continuing education in either a university or a technical training facility and also funded research and demonstration grants that influenced deaf education as well as rehabilitation needs. One of the major projects funded under this law was the Leadership Training Program in the Area of the Deaf at San Fernando Valley State College in Northridge, California, which has since become California State University at Northridge. *See* CALIFORNIA STATE UNIVERSITY, NORTHRIDGE.

This legislation also paved the way for an unprecedented number of conferences and planning sessions for expansion of services to deaf people, mainly through the Deafness and Communication Disorders Office. Under the umbrella of the Rehabilitation Services Administration, this office was directed by Boyce R. Williams, a deaf graduate of Gallaudet College, with the enthusiastic support of Commissioner Mary E. Switzer. Seed money and other funding grants activated new projects and led to the establishment of organizations serving hearing-impaired persons—the Registry of Interpreters for the Deaf, the Professional Rehabilitation Workers with the Adult Deaf (which has since become the American Deafness and Rehabilitation Association), and the Council of Organizations Serving the Deaf. *See* AMERICAN DEAFNESS AND REHABILITATION ASSOCIATION; COUNCIL OF ORGANIZATIONS SERVING THE DEAF; REGISTRY OF INTERPRETERS FOR THE DEAF; WILLIAMS, BOYCE ROBERT.

The Vocational Rehabilitation Act Amendments of 1965 (P.L. 89-333) further extended federal support, which had bearing on education as well as rehabilitation, including provision of interpreter service for deaf persons in a wide variety of settings and situations.

The early success of the Soviet *Sputnik* provided impetus for further federal educational legislation, especially the National Defense Education Act of 1958 and the National Defense Education Act Amendments of 1964, which allocated funds for increased emphasis on the teaching of mathematics, science, and modern foreign languages. Summer institutes for math and science teachers of deaf pupils were held for a number of years at Gallaudet, Los Angeles State College, and other locations.

MEDIA SERVICES AND CAPTIONED FILMS

A significant law with far-reaching implications for deaf persons was P.L. 85-905, signed into law by President Dwight Eisenhower on September 2, 1958. This law created the Media Services and Captioned Films Branch of the Division of Educational Services in the Bureau of Education for the Handicapped of the U.S. Office of Education. Its intent was to enhance the educational and cultural advancement of deaf people and to provide increased accessibility to their environment through entertainment as well as educational films. Subsequent legislation, P.L. 87-715 and P.L. 91-230, expanded the services and functions of Media Services and Captioned Films. Within the amended laws was a provision for a national advisory committee on deaf education to advise the Secretary of Health, Education and Welfare. P.L. 91-230, the Education of the Handicapped Act (April 13, 1970), enlarged the focus of Media Services and Captioned Films from deaf individuals to all other disabled persons. The law also funded a National Center on Educational Media and Materials for the Handicapped, with the Ohio State University at Columbus awarded this contract.

TEACHER TRAINING

Public Law 87-276, sponsored by Senator Lister Hill of Alabama and Congressman John Fogarty of Rhode Island, was enacted September 22, 1961, to address the shortage of qualified teachers of the deaf. President John F. Kennedy signed the act, which provided stipends for both undergraduate and graduate study. As a result of this law, the number of approved university teacher training centers doubled. This law also established a national advisory committee, and inevitably, an amended 1963 law (P.L. 88-164) extended the provisions to fund teacher training and other services to all handicapped children.

Residential schools for deaf children were able to qualify for supplementary funding for their vocational departments under the Vocational Education Act of 1963, which applied to high schools with at least five different vocational fields of study. The 1968 amendments to the law required that at least 10 percent of the federal funds allocated be set aside for handicapped students.

On June 8, 1965, President Lyndon Johnson signed into law an act providing the establishment of a National Technical Institute for the Deaf (P.L. 89-36) with an advisory committee of 12 people. A total of 28 colleges and universities bid for the institute. In November 1966 it was announced that Rochester Institute of Technology, New York, had been selected. *See* NATIONAL TECHNICAL INSTITUTE FOR THE DEAF.

The monumental Elementary and Secondary Education Act of 1965 (P.L. 89-10) authorized more than $1.3 billion for improved classroom teaching. The act had a pronounced effect on handicapped and disadvantaged children. Later, Title 1 of the act was amended by P.L. 89-313 to provide for funding of state-operated schools for handicapped children in addition to regular public school programs.

BABBIDGE REPORT

Public Law 88-136, passed in October 1963, authorized the creation of an advisory committee on deaf education to be appointed by the Secretary of Health, Education and Welfare. Activated in March 1964, under the chairship of Homer Babbidge, the committee submitted its critical "Babbidge Report" to the Secretary in February 1965. Shortcomings and problems in deaf education were identified and analyzed, and recommendations were made for both administrative and legislative action. Partly as a result of this report, the Model Secondary School for the Deaf Act, P.L. 89-694, was passed in 1966, followed by Title VI of the Elementary and Secondary Education Act, also in 1966, which provided support for handicapped children enrolled in regular public schools. Under P.L. 91-230 this title was recodified as Part B of the Education of the Handicapped Act in April 1970. *See* MODEL SECONDARY SCHOOL FOR THE DEAF.

PUBLIC LAW 94-142

On November 29, 1975, President Ford signed into law the comprehensive Education for All Handicapped Children Act (P.L. 94-142), which guarantees an individually prescribed free appropriate public education for all handicapped children in the United States.

The new law had four purposes: (1) to assure the availability for all handicapped children of a free and appropriate public education which emphasizes special education and related services designed to meet their unique needs; (2) to assure that the rights of handicapped children and their parents or guardians are protected; (3) to assist states and localities with funding to provide for the education of all handicapped children; and (4) to assess and assure the effectiveness of efforts to educate handicapped children. *See* EDUCATION OF THE HANDICAPPED ACT.

REHABILITATION ACT OF 1973

It took a sit-down strike of handicapped persons in the Washington office and all regional offices of the Department of Health, Education and Welfare to get Secretary Joseph Califano to sign the regulations for implementing the Rehabilitation Act of 1973, with particular emphasis on Section 504, hailed as the "bill of rights" for disabled people in the United States.

The effective date of the regulations for Section 504 was June 3, 1977. A great deal of the language and intent of this section is similar to that of Title VI, the Civil Rights Act of 1964, and Title IX, the Education Amendments of 1972, one prohibiting discrimination on the basis of race and ethnic origin and the other prohibiting discrimination based on sex. *See* Rehabilitation Act of 1973.

Bibliography

Brill, Richard G.: *The Education of the Deaf*, Gallaudet Press, Washington, D.C., 1971.

Gannon, Jack R.: *Deaf Heritage (A Narrative History of Deaf America)*, National Association of the Deaf, Silver Spring, Maryland, 1981.

Mervin D. Garretson

Impact of Public Policy

Lawsuits and court decisions have caused a dramatic increase in federal attention to the rights of handicapped students since the 1970s. The 14th Amendment to the U.S. Constitution guarantees Americans the equal protection of the law. In *Brown v. Board of Education*, the famous desegregation case in 1954, the Supreme Court ruled, "In these days, it is doubtful that any child may reasonably be expected to succeed in life if he is denied the opportunity of an education. Such an opportunity, where the state has undertaken to provide it, is a right which must be made available to all on equal terms."

Almost 30 years later, the courts determined that equal education rights do apply to handicapped students as well as to minority groups. The *Pennsylvania Association for Retarded Children v. the Commonwealth of Pennsylvania* (1972) resulted in action against policies which excluded mentally retarded children from free, appropriate public education. The *Mills v. Board of Education* (1972) case in Washington, D.C., established the right of handicapped children to free, appropriate public education and the right of parents and students to be informed, to be heard, and to appeal through due process. By 1975 another 46 similar right-to-education cases were heard in 28 states, supporting educational rights of handicapped children.

Public Law 94-142 Because of data revealing that 4 million out of 8 million handicapped children were still receiving an inappropriate education and 1 million children were excluded from education, Congress issued legislation, P.L. 94-142, that would serve as an educational bill of rights for handicapped children and demonstrate governmental support and accountability.

This law stipulated that a free, appropriate public education would be available to handicapped children by September 1978 in elementary and secondary educational programs. Furthermore, the right to due process was assured to students and their parents in identification, nondiscriminatory evaluation, and placement procedures. The Individualized Education Program (IEP), developed in a meeting of educational professionals and parents, serves as the accountability tool for determining appropriate educational programming and placement. The IEP is an annual document stating the student's present level of skills, goals, and objectives; evaluation criteria; recommended placement; and support services needed.

Public Law 94-142 contains other important features. It authorizes a percentage formula for federal funding of special education based on handicapped child count, increasing from 5 percent in 1978 to 40 percent in 1982. It requires the state educational agencies to develop annual state plans for providing and monitoring free appropriate education and procedural safeguards for all handicapped children, personnel development, annual evaluations, and public participation in such planning. It requires accessibility to facilities and programs by removing architectural barriers, and also requires the provision of foreign language interpreters and interpreters for the deaf for parents and students, where appropriate. It stipulates employment of handicapped adults whenever possible in school programs and agencies. It requires a full continuum of placement options ranging from mainstreaming in regular classes to special schools in each state. The least restrictive environment (LRE) feature in the regulations encourages education in a program close to the student's home "where appropriate and without undue harm" to the student.

The interpretation of least restrictive environment has been problematic in the field of deaf education because of the low incidence of deaf students, inadequate knowledge and support services in some regular schools, differing opinions on appropriate education, and the high costs associated with providing quality education to deaf students.

The U.S. Department of Education has the responsibility for monitoring P.L. 94-142 processes and procedures in the states. The state educational agency (SEA) has primary responsibility in the state, working with local educational agencies (LEA) and intermediate educational units (IEU). Decisions of the state, local, and intermediate units may be challenged by parents through due process, civil lawsuits, or complaints to the U.S. Department of Education's Office of Civil Rights.

Section 504 Section 504 is part of the Rehabilitation Act of 1973, but for various political and substantive reasons the regulations were delayed for several years, becoming official only after various consumer groups successfully advocated for approval, publication, and implementation of 504 regulations in 1977. Because of this delay, the development of Section 504 regulations took into consideration the requirements of P.L. 94-142. The main differences between Section 504 and P.L. 94-142 are that 504 covers all ages, includes colleges or postsecondary education, and covers accessibility to employment and community services as well as education. Thus, Section 504 is considered much broader than P.L. 94-142.

Section 504 is a declaration of civil rights for all handicapped people. "No otherwise qualified handicapped individual in the United States . . . shall solely by reason of his handicap be excluded from the participation in, be denied the benefit of, or be subjected to discrimination under any program or activity receiving federal financial assistance."

The catchword in Section 504 is "qualified"; handicapped persons are not guaranteed jobs, services, or admission to college programs just because they are handicapped. Handicapped people are considered qualified if they meet the basic requirements and can perform satisfactorily with reasonable accommodations. Postsecondary education must be accessible to handicapped people and must not discriminate against them in recruitment, admissions, and programs.

Implications Public Law 94-142 and Section 504 provide equal opportunity and safeguards to handicapped people in the educational arena. In interpreting and implementing legislative requirements, it is important to provide assurance that educational placements, services, programs, and practices be appropriate to and meet the needs of individual students. A nonhierarchical continuum of options must be maintained to ensure appropriate placement in whatever environment is the least restrictive for the individual student, based on the student's abilities, goals, and needs, and on the program's ability to meet these needs. A full range of support services, qualified personnel, and parent education are needed. Networks of special schools, district programs, and state agencies are vital in sharing limited resources and funding to assure that educational services to handicapped persons in day and residential facilities are not only appropriately maintained, but also improved and enhanced.

Bibliography

Ballard, J., B. Ramirez, and F. Weintraub (eds.): *Special Education in America: Its Legal and Governmental Foundations*, Council for Exceptional Children, Reston, Virginia, 1982.

Gallaudet College: "P.L. 94-142 and Deaf Children," *Gallaudet Alumni Newsletter*, special issue, June 1977.

National Center for Law and the Deaf: *Legal Rights of Hearing Impaired People*, Gallaudet College Press, Washington, D.C., 1982.

————: *Information Sheet on Section 504 of the Rehabilitation Act of 1973*, Gallaudet College, Washington, D.C., 1978.

Rosen, R., and staff members of Kendall Demonstration Elementary School: *Parents' Guide to Individualized Education Program*, Precollege Programs, Gallaudet College, Washington, D.C., 1978.

Weintraub, F., et al.: *Public Policy and the Education of Exceptional Children*, Council for Exceptional Children, Reston, Virginia, 1976.

Roslyn Rosen

LEAST RESTRICTIVE ENVIRONMENT

The least restrictive environment provision of Public Law 94-142 requires "that, to the maximum extent appropriate, handicapped children, including children in public or private institutions or other care facilities, are educated with children who are not handicapped, and that special classes, separate schooling, or other removal of handicapped children from the regular educational environment occurs only when the nature or severity of the handicap is such that education in regular classes with the use of supplementary aids and services cannot be achieved satisfactorily."

The least restrictive environment does not refer specifically to deaf children, but tends to address all categories of handicapping conditions. Since deafness has such a low incidence rate compared to most other handicaps, placement decision makers, including some parents and special educators, tend to interpret the law in a manner that addresses the entire category of special education and ignores the unique needs of deaf children. In fact, most states have interpreted the least restrictive environment in a way that requires placement decision makers to consider alternatives from a hierarchical continuum. The mandate by which they operate requires placement to be made at the public school first (least restrictive) with the center school being located near the bottom of the continuum (most restrictive). The result of this model has been a large shift of deaf students from center schools (residential and day) to public school programs. *See* EDUCATIONAL PROGRAMS.

As with all handicapping conditions, hearing impairment may range from mild to profound losses; it may be present at birth (prelingual) or after language has been learned (postlingual); and it may be the sole handicap or one of many a child possesses. Each of the above variables should be considered when determining the needs of the hearing-impaired child, and the findings should dictate the child's most appropriate placement.

Educating hearing-impaired children successfully in the mainstream of public education correlates highly with the severity of hearing loss and other handicapping conditions. Hence, the milder the hearing loss, the more likely nonspecialized educational resources in the public school will be appropriate. Further, the more profound the hearing loss, the more expertise should be available to accommodate for the remediation of the deficits created by the loss.

The confusion in determining the least restrictive environment for a deaf child often comes when generalists in the field of special education and parents unacquainted with the profound effects of deafness apply to deaf students the criteria for determining the least restrictive environment for nondeaf students. For example, the vast majority of special education students have intellectual deficits. Their academic potentials are limited, which makes social interaction a primary goal of their educational programs. The least restrictive environment for these students would be their local schools and their home neighborhoods. Conversely, the deaf child's primary handicap is learning language and developing the skills for communicating unlimited intellectual concepts to others. For deaf students, social interaction with the general population of hearing individuals is possible only after special intensive educational services have been experienced over many years. This intervention is most often found in center schools (residential and day) that have brought together a sufficient number of deaf children to justify the employment of personnel whose primary training is in the area of deafness. The ingredients of a quality educational program for deaf students would include a sufficient number of students to ensure grouping by age, hearing level, academic achievement, and ability; qualified teachers of deaf students; knowledgeable supervisors; appropriate curricula; extracurricular activities; and vocational counseling and training.

The measure of the least restrictive environment should be related to the deaf child's ability and opportunities to communicate freely with others. Since most deaf children develop skills in using sign language, the least restrictive environment for them would be in a social or school setting with others possessing sign language skills. The most restrictive environment would be in a social setting or school where the deaf child would have no one available with whom he or she could communicate via sign language or other effective means.

Advocates for mainstreaming point to the acceptable academic success that integrated students achieve and to the need for children to be educated in their neighborhood schools. While some research supports this for selected deaf students, especially for those with less severe hearing losses, advocates for center school placement stress academic preparation with a strong specially trained support staff, deaf role models, and a social environment that assists students in learning leadership, citizenship, good sports behavior, and other needed skills.

While the intent of P.L. 94-142 is to protect the individual rights of deaf children, the least restrictive environment clause has frequently restricted the educational options open to them. For some, the law has resulted in deaf students being entered into mainstreamed programs where they are expected to keep pace with nondeaf students as they struggle to develop the language and other communication systems their hearing counterparts have already mastered. Deaf children would be better served if they were gradually mainstreamed into a competitive hearing environment after they had learned language.

Bibliography

Allen, Thomas, and Tamara Osborn: "Academic Integration of Hearing-Impaired Students: Demographic, Handicapping, and Achievement Factors," *American Annals of the Deaf*, April 1984.

DuBow, Sy: "Mainstreaming or Residential Schools for Deaf Students," *National Center for Law and the Deaf Newsletter*, Winter 1984.

———: "Special Education Law Since Rowley," *Clearinghouse Review*, January 1984.

Gregory, James, Timothy Shanahan, and Herbert Walberg: "Mainstreamed Hearing-Impaired High School Seniors: A Re-Analysis of a National Survey," *American Annals of the Deaf*, February 1984.

Gresham, Frank: "Social Skills and Self-Efficacy for Exceptional Children," *Exceptional Children*, vol. 51, no. 3, November 1984.

"Least Restrictive Environment and Quality Educational Program for Exceptional Children," resolution passed at Delegate Assembly, Council for Exceptional Children Convention, April 1980.

Karchmer, Michael, and Raymond Trybus: "Who Are the Deaf Children in Mainstreamed Programs?" series R, no. 4, Gallaudet College, Office of Demographic Studies, 1977.

Newman, Lawrence: "Perspectives: The Most Restrictive Environment," *California Palms*, Winter 1982.

Ogden, Paul, and Suzanne Lipsett: *The Silent Garden*, St. Martin's Press, 1982.

Wolk, Stephen, Michael Karchmer, and Arthur Shildroth: *Patterns of Academic and Non-Academic Integration Among Hearing-Impaired Students in Special Education*, series R, no. 9, Gallaudet College, Center for Assessment and Demographic Studies, 1982.

Gary L. Holman

MAINSTREAMING

Broadly defined, mainstreaming in education refers to the placement of disabled children in classrooms with regular public school children who are not handicapped. The term mainstreaming has also been used to mean integration into the majority culture. There are many definitions of mainstreaming as it relates to the education of hearing-impaired persons, depending on the degree or "intensity" of the integration. The mainstreamed deaf child may be: (1) fully enrolled in a public school class with normally hearing students, receiving occasional assistance from an itinerant speech pathologist or tutor several hours a week; (2) enrolled in a regular public school but in a separate classroom with other deaf students and a trained teacher of deaf pupils; contact with hearing students would be during physical education class, in the halls, on the playground, at recess, and at lunchtime; (3) enrolled in a regular class but with a resource room available, where the child spends part of the school day with a special teacher; (4) enrolled with other deaf children in a special classroom with a trained teacher but taking selected subjects in a regular classroom a portion of the day; (5) enrolled in a special classroom for deaf children and taking "nonacademic" classes with hearing children (art, vocational courses, physical education); (6) enrolled in a special program for deaf children in a separate wing of a public school building; or (7) enrolled in a special school for deaf children on the same grounds as a regular public school.

In practically all public schools in the United States by the 1980s, mainstreamed programs for deaf children had provided sign language interpreters for deaf children in an integrated classroom situation.

Mainstreaming of deaf children into regular public schools is not a new concept. Earliest recorded attempts go back to 1821, when Johann Graser of the province of Bavaria introduced an "integrated" program in the public school systems of a number of German states. The Graser approach began with a special department in each public school where deaf children were taught separately for 1½ to 2 years and then were incorporated fully into the mainstream of regular classes. At first, this idea was received with a great deal of enthusiasm and hopeful expectation, but after a few years of lackluster success it was abandoned.

Since that time, individual deaf children have been educated in public and private schools in every part of the world, including the United States. The number of hearing-impaired children in the public school system has continued to increase across the years. A number of these hearing-impaired students have been able to do fairly creditable academic work, others have barely made it, and for still others it has been a frustrating and traumatic experience.

In the United States, the main impetus for increased mainstreaming during the 1980s came from

enactment of Public Law 94-142, the Education of All Handicapped Children Act of 1975. However, the push for integration was appearing simultaneously in most nations of the world.

The concept of mainstreaming in general has been much more acceptable to parents and people with disabilities other than deafness. Among the hearing-impaired population, parents of deaf children, and professionals working in the area of hearing impairment, it has generated a great deal of controversy. It has been referred to as a simplistic solution to a complex problem, as ignoring the implications of the unwritten curriculum, as a situation where deaf children are dropped into a social and interactive vacuum because they do not hear what is occurring around them in the mainstream. Academics do not appear to be the main concern; instead it is the social isolation that most deaf children go through in a mainstreamed situation which affects their psychological, sociological, and emotional growth. Hard-of-hearing students appear to fare somewhat better, but unless they have an outgoing personality, they encounter many of the same problems as students with more severe hearing loss.

Bibliography
Brill, Richard G.: *Mainstreaming the Prelingually Deaf Child*, Gallaudet College Press, Washington, D.C., 1978.
Mervin D. Garretson

EDUCATIONAL PROGRAMS

Deaf education was the first type of special education to be established in the United States. In 1812 John Braidwood, an Englishman, established a school in Cobbs, Virginia, for the children of one family. This school lasted only a year. The first permanent school for deaf people was opened on April 15, 1817, by Thomas Hopkins Gallaudet in Hartford, Connecticut, with an enrollment of seven pupils. (It was not until 1837 that the first school for blind persons was established in the United States, and not until 1848 that the first program for the education of mentally retarded persons was established.) *See* AMERICAN SCHOOL FOR THE DEAF; GALLAUDET, THOMAS HOPKINS.

Today there is a broad spectrum of educational programs for deaf children in the United States. These range from programs that begin when the child is in infancy through continuing education programs for deaf adults. At each educational level parents and students have educational options. They may choose from several kinds of early childhood programs, day or residential and public or private schools at the elementary and secondary levels, and many postsecondary programs. This diversity, however, did not always characterize educational programs for deaf students.

PRIMARY AND SECONDARY SCHOOLS

In the nineteenth century most deaf children who received education did so at residential schools, like the one founded in 1817 in Hartford. The low incidence of deafness was the basic reason for this. Residential schools, unlike a typical day school, drew students from a broad geographical area, for the children both lived and studied at the school.

The overwhelming preponderance of students in residential schools ended in the twentieth century. Particularly following World War II, the percentage of deaf students in residential schools dropped. While residential schools had enrolled 90 percent of all deaf students in 1900, by 1983 enrollment was only 37 percent of all deaf students. Day schools, however, increased from 6 percent in 1900 to 58 percent in 1983.

The first day school for deaf children in the United States was established in Boston in 1869. In 1877 that school was renamed the Horace Mann School for the Deaf. The Chicago Day School for the Deaf was established in 1870, destroyed by the Chicago fire in 1871, and then rebuilt and reopened in January 1875.

The first private school for deaf children in the United States was the Whipple Home School for the Deaf in Mystic, Connecticut, established by Jonathan and Zerah Whipple in 1869. In 1873 the German Evangelical Lutheran Deaf Mute Institution was founded in Detroit, Michigan, as the first private denominational school for deaf children.

ENROLLMENT

In 1900 the official census of the United States reported a population of 75,994,575. The estimated population in 1983 was 228,000,000. While the population of the United States tripled over that 83-year period, the number of deaf children being educated more than quadrupled.

Two factors have affected enrollment in educational programs for deaf children. Advances in medicine have substantially reduced deafness caused by diseases of childhood. Whereas previously there was a high ratio of children who acquired deafness by diseases such as measles, mumps, and whooping cough, the development of antibiotics has almost eliminated this type of deafness. Before the advent of antibiotics in 1942, as many as 40 to 45 percent of those in schools for deaf students had become deaf after they were born, and a large proportion of these had become deaf after they had learned to talk. Now 90 percent of the children enrolled in most schools for deaf pupils became

deaf before they were old enough to learn to talk. *See* DEAF POPULATION: Demography.

However, while the percentage of deaf children in the general population has probably been decreasing, the number who are being enrolled in educational programs has been increasing. Included in this increased number are children who formerly were considered below school age, and deaf children with additional handicapping conditions. There are also children in local day programs whose families would not have sent them away from home to residential programs when no local program was available.

Before 1892 few schools in the United States admitted deaf children under seven years of age. That year Emma and Mary Garrett opened a home-school for young deaf children, and in 1893 the Pennsylvania legislature began support of this school, which lasted until 1933. This was the first early education program for deaf children. In 1918 the Central Institute for the Deaf in St. Louis began a program for children from three to six years of age. In more recent years, as exemplified by the John Tracy Clinic in Los Angeles, programs concerned with Early Childhood Education have devoted much of their time to educating the parents of preschool-age deaf children so that these parents can work with their own children. *See* CENTRAL INSTITUTE FOR THE DEAF.

Accreditation of schools for deaf students has been carried on both by the Conference of Educational Administrators Serving the Deaf (formerly the Conference of Executives of American Schools for the Deaf) and by regional accrediting agencies. The Conference of Education Administrators accredited its first school in 1963, and over the next 20 years accredited 28 schools, with 5 of them being reaccredited after a passage of time. *See* CONFERENCE OF EDUCATIONAL ADMINISTRATORS SERVING THE DEAF.

SPECIAL EDUCATION

The education of deaf-blind children received the attention of educators of deaf students as early as 1851. The incidence of this group was very small, and the education of such children was virtually on a tutoring rather than program basis, sometimes in a school for blind children and sometimes in a school for deaf pupils. *See* DEAF-BLINDNESS: EDUCATION.

It was in the 1950s that the number of deaf children with additional handicapping conditions began to be increasingly recognized in schools for deaf children. This situation was exacerbated by the rubella epidemic of 1963–1965. This greatly increased the number of deaf children with additional handicapping conditions, so that by the 1970s some studies indicated that as many as 25 percent of the enrollment of schools for deaf pupils was composed of multihandicapped deaf children. Thus, special programs for this group of students became necessary.

POSTSECONDARY

The higher education of deaf people began with the establishment of the National Deaf-Mute College (now known as Gallaudet College) in 1864 in Washington, D.C., with the enabling legislation signed by President Abraham Lincoln. Nearly 100 years later, other programs began that offered deaf students a variety of options. In 1962 California State University, Northridge (at that time known as San Fernando Valley State College), established a Leadership Training Program from which grew a Center on Deafness to provide a network of support for hearing-impaired students attending the university. In 1968 the National Technical Institute for the Deaf, which was built in conjunction with the Rochester (New York) Institute of Technology, admitted its first students. *See* CALIFORNIA STATE UNIVERSITY, NORTHRIDGE; GALLAUDET COLLEGE; NATIONAL TECHNICAL INSTITUTE FOR THE DEAF.

The program at Gallaudet College is primarily a liberal arts program granting the associate of arts degree, the bachelor's degree, the master's degree, and the doctor of philosophy degree. At the undergraduate level, nearly all students are deaf. The program at the National Technical Institute for the Deaf is one in which the deaf students have some classes by themselves and other classes with hearing students, where the deaf students use support services such as interpreters and notetakers. The students may work for an associate of arts degree, or a bachelor's or master's degree, primarily in business, science, or technology.

There are community college programs for deaf students as well. The first was established at Riverside (California) City College in 1961. A federal research and demonstration program resulted in the funding and establishment of the Delgado Community College program for deaf students in New Orleans in 1968 and programs at Seattle (Washington) Community College and the St. Paul (Minnesota) Technical Vocational Institute in 1969. Since then, community college programs that actively seek deaf students have proliferated, and a few Bible colleges have established programs for deaf pupils.

Bibliography
American Annals of the Deaf, vol. 129, no. 2, April 1984.

Brill, R. G.: *The Education of the Deaf: Administrative and Professional Developments*, Gallaudet College Press, 1974.

———: *International Congresses on Education of the Deaf*, Gallaudet College Press, 1984.

Davis, H., and S. R. Silverman (eds.): *Hearing and Deafness*, Holt, Rinehart and Winston, 1970.

Scouten, E. L.: *Turning Points in the Education of Deaf People*, Interstate Printers and Publishers, Danville, Illinois, 1984.

Richard G. Brill

ACCREDITATION

A school is accredited when it meets the required criteria established by an appropriate agency and completes the specified accrediting procedure. The primary purpose of accreditation is to improve educational quality through the process of self-evaluation. Self-evaluation gives candidate schools the opportunity to analyze thoroughly their general organization, program offerings, support services, physical plant, and overall fitness.

It is only since the 1960s that schools for deaf students have become accredited. One reason is that criteria used by regional accrediting agencies consisted of arbitrary standards that were designed primarily for academic high schools and were not appropriate for schools for deaf children. This was the case because deaf pupils rarely studied secondary-level academic subjects. In more recent years many schools for deaf people have raised the level of their secondary programs so that now there are many offering bona fide secondary programs for deaf students.

Another reason that accreditation by a regional accrediting agency was not appropriate was that a large majority of schools for deaf and severely hearing-impaired children were residential schools. Such schools provided for pupils of both an elementary and secondary age level, offered vocational training for the secondary age pupils, and provided a full residence hall program. Regional accrediting agencies were not designed to evaluate this type of school.

Therefore the Conference of Executives of American Schools for the Deaf (now known as the Conference of Educational Administrators Serving the Deaf), established its own accreditation program for residential schools. CEASD began working on developing an accreditation program in 1956, and in 1963 its first certificate of accreditation was issued to the New Mexico School for the Deaf.

Currently it is recognized that a school should provide each of its students with an education that is individually appropriate. The evaluation of a school now involves the entire school staff in making a self-evaluation study. Part of this self-evaluation study is specifying the objectives of the school and the kind of population it serves, and then determining how well the school is meeting its own objectives. After such a study, culminating in a self-evaluation document, a visitation team appointed by the accrediting agency tries to determine whether the school is doing what the self-evaluation study states. It is on this basis that a school becomes accredited.

The accreditation program of CEASD uses this self-evaluation method; the visitation team reviews the self-evaluation. Thus the accreditation is based on whether the school is providing an appropriate education for deaf children at all age levels, and in the residential components as well as the educational components.

Since 1978 CEASD has developed working relationships with many of the regional accrediting agencies throughout the country. As an alternative to only CEASD accreditation, a school may be evaluated by a regional association with a representative of CEASD on the visiting team, and then the school would complete the self-evaluation forms for both organizations. Thus, a school for deaf students can get accreditation from both the regional agency and the professional organization through this cooperative arrangement.

By July 1983 CEASD had accredited 28 schools for the deaf, with many in recent years getting joint accreditation.

Bibliography

Accreditation of Schools for the Deaf: A Guide for Self-Evaluation. Committee on Accreditation of Schools, Conference of Educational Administrators Serving the Deaf, Inc., June 1983.

Brill, R. G.: *Education of the Deaf: Administrative and Professional Developments*, Gallaudet College Press, 1974.

Richard G. Brill

EARLY CHILDHOOD

Early childhood education programs are for children under four years of age. Unlike programs for older children, early childhood programs often take place in the deaf child's home environment rather than a formal school setting.

Importance   The child born with a hearing impairment does not develop communication skill through hearing and thus requires special instruction to overcome this deficit. Because the most important years of language development are those of early childhood, programs should be started at the earliest possible age so that the communication problem will not be compounded by delaying special instruction until the child is of kindergarten or school age. A progam should begin at the same time as the hearing child begins to acquire language, as soon as possible after the hearing impairment is diagnosed. The very young hearing-impaired child should be provided with linguistic experiences that are as similar to those of the hearing child as possible. This means early and constant exposure to language. The hearing child gets this exposure by just listening, but it requires con-

scious adult intervention for the hearing-impaired child to receive a similar experience. *See* PSYCHOLINGUISTICS: Language Development.

Ideally, the hearing-impaired child should have as many meaningful linguistic experiences, using vision and amplification, as the hearing child has meaningful auditory experiences. Parents, who are generally with the child more than anyone else, can play a key role in providing this sort of linguistic experience.

Objectives   Special instructional programs for young hearing-impaired children can have different objectives. Some instruct parents on ways to facilitate their child's cognitive and communication development. Some concentrate on the affective area, offering parents help in dealing with their feelings about having a deaf child. Some offer support by answering questions about a variety of topics that are of concern to parents, such as child rearing problems, hearing aids use and function, and future schooling. Some programs are termed infant stimulation programs, and are designed to enrich the environmental stimulation of the child, thus facilitating cognitive development. Some emphasize socialization and integration with hearing children. Others combine a number of these objectives. *See* PARENT EDUCATION.

Early childhood services can be delivered in a number of ways, which include home visitors, the demonstration home, preschool programs, and correspondence courses.

Home Visitors   One way of helping the very young deaf child is to have a specially trained teacher visit the home to work with the parents and child. Parents and teachers develop an easier rapport when their meeting takes place in a home setting rather than in a classroom, and the parents feel more open about asking questions and discussing other concerns. Such discussions make it easier for the teacher to adjust the program to meet the individual parent's needs instead of following a set curriculum.

Demonstration Home   An alternative approach is to have the parents and child visit an educational program located in an actual home, apartment, or special homelike space constructed for that purpose within or adjacent to a school setting. The service offered can be similar to that offered by a home visitor. The demonstration home can also be an inexpensive way to get a program started, because it does not require construction of special educational facilities; any existing home or apartment can be used.

Preschool Program   The preschool program can be a regular program or one designed specifically for hearing-impaired children. Since one of the objectives of such programs is to provide the young deaf child with some group experience, the regular preschool program is often quite satisfactory, particularly if the regular preschool teachers know something about the special techniques used for language building in hearing-impaired children.

Correspondence Course For families who live in isolated areas where direct professional help is not available, there are several correspondence courses available without charge from the John Tracy Clinic in Los Angeles. These provide parents with instructions for implementing an early childhood program at home. Courses are available in both English and Spanish.

Bibliography

Kaurfman, B. A.: "Early Childhood Education and Special Education: A Study in Conflict," *Volta Review*, 82:15–24, 1980.

Lowell, E. L.: "Parent-Infant Programs for Preschool Deaf Children: The Example of John Tracy Clinic," *Volta Review*, 81:323–329, 1979.

Moores, D. F., K. L. Weiss, and M. W. Goodwin: "Early Education Programs for Hearing Impaired Children: Major Findings," *American Annals of the Deaf*, 123:925–936, 1978.

Edgar L. Lowell

DAY SCHOOLS

Day schools have day facilities only and are housed in buildings used primarily for deaf students. They are most frequently located in urban centers with a large population base. Services were provided to approximately 4400 deaf students by the 60 public and private day schools in North America during the 1982–1983 school year.

Historical Development The Boston School for Deaf-Mutes was established as the first day school in North America in 1869 by a group of parents who wanted an oral education for their children. Largely through the efforts of Alexander Graham Bell, who advocated an oral day school education for deaf children, the Boston day school model was replicated across North America as additional schools were established. The original day school in Boston was renamed the Horace Mann School for the Deaf in 1877 and is still in operation. *See* BELL, ALEXANDER GRAHAM; HISTORY: Sign Language Controversy.

In the century following the establishment of the first day school, the number of day schools grew slowly, to fewer than 30 throughout the United States and Canada. The greatly increased number of deaf children resulting from the 1963–1965 rubella epidemic led to a rapid expansion in the number of day schools. By October 1976 there were 100 day schools for deaf children in North America.

The least restrictive environment provision of the Education for All Handicapped Children Act (Public Law 94-142), the completion of the elementary school level by the rubella epidemic children, and the general decline in the birthrate resulted in a rapid reduction in the number of North American day schools to 60 as of 1983. The number of students served by day schools decreased by one-third during the five-year period, 1976-1981. *See* EDUCATIONAL LEGISLATION: Impact of Public Policy.

Rationale Several major arguments are made in support of the development and continuance of the day school option. A major impetus to the development of public day versus residential facilities has been the financial savings due to the elimination of afterschool care expenses.

In some areas, a lack of a particular educational approach or a perceived lack of quality services have served as motivations for the establishment of private day school facilities. A great many of the private day schools were founded by parents of deaf children.

Parents may seek out the day school option as one that is less disruptive to family life. It enables the child to live at home without being subjected to the rigor of dormitory life (loss of privacy, lack of individual ownership of pets, fewer opportunities for a paper route or other jobs, and so on). Parents of day school pupils are more easily involved in their children's educational program than is generally the case in residential schools. They are also more available for the resolution of any problems.

Day schools are located in population centers. Residential schools are usually found in smaller communities. Demographically, deaf adults tend to migrate to urban centers. One of the advantages frequently given for day schools is that students are growing up in the urban setting in which they will live as adults.

The low-incidence nature of deafness translates into a sparse and scattered population of students even in an urban setting. Inevitably, some children travel a considerable amount each day in order to attend a day school. In spite of the additional time needed for transportation by some pupils, the day school has been viewed as one that offers otherwise unattainable benefits for students who need a high concentration of specialized services and the nurture of family life.

The administrators of day schools for deaf pupils are knowledgeable in the field of the education of hearing-impaired children, and their area of responsibility is concentrated in that field. In contrast, educational administrators of day classes are frequently individuals who have not specialized in the education of hearing-impaired children and who have other areas of responsibility. Therefore, certain administrative strengths are seen to exist in the day school model.

Day school staff certification by the Council on Education of the Deaf (CED) or the Conference of Educational Administrators Serving the Deaf is comparable to that of instructional staff certification in residential schools and exceeds that of day class staff. Approximately 90 percent of day school instructors are certified by state departments or ministers of education (Canada).

Services   Day school programs in North America are largely focused on the preschool and elementary levels. Only 20 of the 60 schools operational in 1981 reported secondary level programming. Forty-three schools reported parent-infant home programs.

A significant majority of the schools have special programs for multihandicapped deaf students. The large day schools provide the concentration of specialized support services that are necessary to serve such students.

The day schools have implemented various mainstreaming provisions to further enhance the socioeducational placement of their students. Some day schools are located on the same campus as a regular school. In these instances, some hearing-impaired children integrate either as a class or individually with regular school classes. Individual hearing students may also receive assistance within the day school setting. This arrangement is usually informally negotiated by the two schools. Some day schools have established satellite classes for hearing-impaired students in schools for hearing children in order to facilitate integration.

Residential schools in North America almost universally enroll some day students. In some schools designated as residential, the number of day pupils outnumber those in residence. As both day schools and residential schools have expanded their programming, it has become increasingly difficult to categorize some schools.

Trends   There are some important trends that have the potential to affect the number of day school programs and the children served by them. The birthrate has continued to decline, which will reduce the overall numbers of deaf children in school attendance. The growth in the use of therapeutic abortions for high risk fetuses and the greater use of genetic counseling services are anticipated to reduce the number of children born deaf. *See* AUDITORY DISORDERS, PREVENTION OF: Genetic Counseling.

Countertrends in reduced funding and larger regular class sizes will reduce the availability of integrated placements for hearing-impaired students. The likelihood is a leveling off of the number of day schools and students served by them at the level found prior to the rubella epidemic.

Bibliography

Babbidge, Homer: *Education of the Deaf: A Report to the Secretary of Health, Education and Welfare*, U.S. Department of Health, Education and Welfare, Washington, D.C., 1965.

Bender, Ruth: *The Conquest of Deafness*, Press of Case Western Reserve University, Cleveland, 1970.

Craig, William, and Helen Craig (eds.): *American Annals of the Deaf*, vol. 122, no. 2, April 1977. and vol 128, no. 2, April 1983.

Mulholland, Ann: "The Day Program Movement in the Education of the Hearing Impaired," in Ann Mulholland and George Fellendorf (eds.), *Final Report of the National Research Conference on Day Programs for Hearing Impaired Children*, Alexander Graham Bell Association for the Deaf, Washington, D.C., 1968.

Taylor, Ian: "Medicine in Education," in *Report of Proceedings for Conference for Heads of Schools and Services for Hearing Impaired Children*, University of Manchester, September 1980.

Gary W. Nix

RESIDENTIAL SCHOOLS

A residential school is one in which all or some of the pupils live during the school week. Public residential schools serve all children who are eligible for admission in a specified geographical area, with no charge to the child's family.

History   The first permanent school for deaf people established in the United States, the American School for the Deaf in Hartford, Connecticut, was a residential school, as were most of the schools for deaf children established during the nineteenth century. Because of the low incidence rate of deafness, it was necessary to have a school serve a wide geographical area in order to have a sufficient number of deaf children to provide a proper educational program. Thus, residential schools would serve an entire state or a large part of the state.

Many of the early public residential schools were established by private groups and were governed by private boards of directors. The schools had agreements with the state whereby the state provided major financial support for the school, particularly for operating expenses. In turn, the school provided education for all deaf children within its geographical area.

The first school for deaf children actually established by a state rather than a private group was the Kentucky School for the Deaf. It was established in 1823 as the fourth school for deaf children in the United States. The three preceding ones had been founded by private boards.

By the 1980s, there were more than 70 public residential schools in the United States, with a total enrollment of over 17,000 children. The 9 private residential schools enrolled a total of approximately 500 children. About 65 percent of the pupils in the public residential schools lived in the schools during the week. The other students were day pupils. The day pupils live at home and attend the residential school on a daily basis, frequently with school bus transportation provided by their local school district.

Most of the 50 states, Puerto Rico, and the District of Columbia all have at least one residential school for deaf students. The 3 states without a residential school are Nevada, New Hampshire, and Rhode Island. Rhode Island, because of its small geographical size, is able to serve all children in the state on a day basis in a school in Providence that formerly was a residential school. New Hampshire has some day classes and pays tuition to send other pupils to a residential school in a neighboring state. Nevada has a day school program in Las Vegas.

Two of the small-population states, Alaska and Wyoming, list their schools as residential, but their residential pupils live in foster homes during the school year and not in school dormitories.

Several states have more than one residential school. In New York there are a total of five residential schools, one being administered directly by the state department of education, and the other four being administered by private boards of directors. In each case, the privately administered schools receive financial support for operating expenses from the state. Massachusetts has four residential schools, North Carolina three, and California two.

Advantages Benefits that come with size are among the major assets of a residential school. The larger number of pupils provides the opportunity for better homogeneous grouping. For example, a class of eight children can be composed of a group who are all approximately the same age, have approximately the same degree of hearing loss, and are all approximately at the same level of learning. Proper supervision can be provided for the teachers to aid them in their educational tasks. A larger school is better able to provide appropriate special educational equipment. On the secondary level there are a sufficient number of pupils to be able to have departmentalized teaching where teachers have specialized in certain subject areas as well as in teaching deaf students. Most residential schools offer a vocational program, or at least an opportunity to develop prevocational skills in their high school departments, in addition to their academic subjects.

The residential school, because of its numbers, can have other specialists, such as psychologists, audiologists, and guidance counselors, on its permanent staff, all of whom are trained and experienced in the needs of deaf children.

The school day is frequently longer in a residential school because there is not the need to start late and close early to allow for daily transportation of the pupils. In addition, the out-of-class study of the pupils is supervised by people who are familiar with deaf children's educational requirements.

Many of the day school classes rarely have a deaf teacher on the staff, while most residential schools have some deaf teachers and some deaf residence hall personnel. These deaf personnel serve as important role models for deaf students.

Generally the residential school provides many more extracurricular activities than a day school does, such as a complete athletic program, scout troops, clubs, and student government. All of the pupils have an opportunity to participate because the extracurricular activities are coached or guided by staff members who can communicate with deaf pupils. Many more deaf pupils have an opportunity to participate in these kinds of activities than is the case when the deaf student is trying to gain a place on a team or become an officer in a club when competing against hearing students. Thus the deaf student may have much broader opportunities for personal learning and self-fulfillment in a residential school.

Residence Hall Personnel The residential component of the school requires a staff of dormitory counselors or houseparents. During the nineteenth century and perhaps the early twentieth century the academic standards for these people were not particularly high. However, in more recent years these positions usually have been filled by people with a minimum of two years of college preparation and often with at least a bachelor's degree.

In earlier years dormitory or residence hall personnel were on duty an extremely large number of hours, but now residence hall personnel are generally scheduled for a 40-hour week, with added compensation for overtime.

Formerly many of the personnel lived in the school, but now most do not, and these more normal working conditions promote better mental health in the residence hall personnel. Residence hall personnel are frequently engaged in both formal and informal counseling of pupils and are often involved in many of the extracurricular activities.

In earlier years many of the pupils rarely went home on weekends, and some only when the school closed for Christmas and summer vacations. In recent years the majority of residential schools are closed every weekend, with all pupils going home every Friday and returning Sunday evening or Monday morning. This has resulted in a great strengthening of home ties and involvement in the hearing world.

Student Characteristics A study in California showed that the enrollment of the residential schools is composed of 94 percent who are classified as deaf and only 6 percent who are hard-of-hearing; the figures are probably somewhat representative of the states. This is in contrast with the enrollment in the day classes and day schools, where 61 percent are categorized as being deaf and 39 percent are hard-of-hearing. In the residential schools the few hard-of-hearing pupils generally come from small school districts where there was no provision for hard-of-hearing pupils. The larger proportion of deaf pupils allowed for more appropriate scheduling than was the case when many deaf and hard-of-hearing pupils were enrolled in the same program.

Legislation The Elementary and Secondary Education Act (Public Law 89-10, 1965) in its Title I provided federal financial assistance to local educational agencies for special education programs in areas having a high concentration of children from low-income families, all of whom were considered to be educationally deprived. Title I defined the educationally deprived child, and included those who are deprived because of handicapping conditions. Under the original legislation, because of its wording, funds had to be allocated to public school districts. Therefore, public residential schools for handicapped children could not qualify for benefits under the act. This was amended by P.L. 89-313 on November 1, 1965, and since that time residential schools for deaf students have received some federal money each year from the Elementary and Secondary Education Act.

With the passage of the Education for All Handicapped Children Act (P.L. 94-142) in 1975, which became effective in 1977, there have been some questions raised in regard to the location of the residential school, because of the statement in the regulations that children are to be placed in the "least restrictive environment." Many people have interpreted this phrase in a very literal sense as meaning that children should not attend a residential school because it is not the least restrictive environment. Many educators of deaf students point out, however, that the regulations also state that a child must be placed where the education is appropriate. Often the residential school is the only one that is large enough to provide an appropriate education for the deaf child. Many educators of deaf children also point out that lack of communication is often much more restrictive of the environment than of the physical placement. Deaf children who are placed in an environment where very few of their schoolmates and perhaps not more than one of their teachers, can really communicate with them are in a very restrictive environment. On the other hand, these children are in the least restrictive environment when they are in a school where all of their schoolmates and all of the faculty and staff can communicate with them. *See* EDUCATION OF THE HANDICAPPED ACT.

An official statement has been adopted and published by the Conference of Executives of American Schools for the Deaf in regard to least restrictive placements for deaf students. This statement says

in part: "(1) The Conference of Executives of American Schools for the Deaf (CEASD) supports the concept of placement of deaf children in the 'least restrictive' educational environment provided that this term applies only to alternatives for schooling which enable fulfillment of their academic and social potential and prepares them for a productive, well-adjusted adulthood. This determination is to be based on individual evaluations which provide both short- and long-term instructional objectives. (2) The quality and appropriateness of educational placement must be assessed in terms of both socialization and instruction. Initially, for some, a more segregated environment may be preferred; for others, complete integration may be best. More frequently, a combination—or a succession—of instructional settings may be desirable as young children mature, benefit from extensive intervention, and gain social, academic and vocational skills."

The role of the public residential school for deaf children in the future has been defined by B. L. Griffing as one which will be: (1) a comprehensive educational center; (2) a center providing child study or assessment services; (3) a learning resource center; (4) a demonstration school; and (5) a community or continuing education center.

As long as there are deaf children to be educated, it appears that there will be a place for the public residential school, although its role may change from what it has been in the past.

Bibliography

Brill, R. G.: "Interpretation of Least Restrictive Environment," *The Changing Role of School Programs for Deaf Children: Selected Papers*, compiled by the Conference of Executives of American Schools for the Deaf, Silver Spring, Maryland, 1977.

———: *The Education of the Deaf: Administrative and Professional Developments*, Gallaudet College Press, 1974.

Craig, William N.: "Statement on 'Least Restrictive' Placements for Deaf Students," *The Changing Role of School Programs for Deaf Children: Selected Papers*, compiled by the Conference of Executives of American Schools for the Deaf, Silver Spring, Maryland, 1977.

Griffing, B. L.: "Reshaping the Role of the State School for the Deaf in Public Education," *The Changing Role of School Programs for Deaf Children: Selected Papers*, compiled by the Conference of Executives of American Schools for the Deaf, Silver Spring, Maryland, 1977.

Richard G. Brill

PRIVATE SCHOOLS

Private schools have played an important part in the education of hearing-impaired children by exploring, initiating, and demonstrating effective educational practices that later become accepted patterns in the public schools serving the majority of children. The distinctive characteristic of private schools is that their governance derives from autonomously selected groups of individuals—often parents—who operate somewhat independently of the conventional legal and fiscal regulatory requirements placed on public schools.

Origins The establishment of private schools for hearing-impaired children antedated the beginning of public schools. The first school with a record of continuity was privately established in Paris in 1755. Its use of sign language, combined with emphasis on social development through residential living, was later adopted by most state-supported schools in the United States. The first enduring school in this country began in 1817 as the private Connecticut Asylum for the Education and Instruction of Deaf and Dumb Persons in Hartford, later to become the American School for the Deaf. The first college exclusively for deaf students, the National Deaf Mute College, was founded in 1864 on Kendall Green as the collegiate department of the then private Columbia Institution for the Deaf and Dumb and the Blind, and was later called Gallaudet College.

A number of today's publicly supported schools were originally established as private schools. The American School for the Deaf began in 1817, supported primarily by private donations, but by 1819 was given a federal land grant and was later supported by the State of Connecticut. The New York Institution for the Education of the Deaf and Dumb began in 1818 with private subscriptions and tuition, but soon attracted city and state support, later becoming the New York School for the Deaf. The Pennsylvania Institution for the Deaf and Dumb, begun privately in Philadelphia in 1820, had state support for some students by 1821 and eventually became the publicly supported Pennsylvania School for the Deaf. The Whipple Home School for Deaf Mutes, privately organized in 1869 in Ledyard, Connecticut, had state aid by 1879 and was a state school for Connecticut as the Mystic Oral School until its closure in 1980.

Status Several schools that have private charters are no longer completely independent because they depend very heavily upon public support. Both the Lexington School for the Deaf in New York and the Clarke School for the Deaf in Massachusetts enroll a majority of students whose tuition is paid entirely or in a large part by appropriations from the city or state in which they are located. Accountability for the use of public funds inevitably leads to increasing public regulation, resulting in hybrid public-private schools. All private schools organized as nonprofit corporations have the advantages of exemption from local property taxes, tuition for deaf children being considered a medical deduction on the state and federal income taxes of parents, and personal donations to the schools being considered

as tax deductible. Attempts to interpret these benefits of omission as tax support by various government agencies further threaten the independence of private schools. *See* CLARKE SCHOOL.

Advantages With the Education for All Handicapped Children Act (Public Law 94-142) mandating free public education for all handicapped children in the United States, private schools for deaf children can exist only if they become part of the public system as public-private hybrids, or if they can provide a program that will lead parents to choose them over public programs. The following are among reasons that parents have cited in choosing a private school over a public one. (1) Means of communication: the typical situation is that the private school offers the option of exclusively oral communication while local public schools often use a combination of oral and manual communication. (2) Quality of instruction: the private school has demonstrated a superior record of achievement, or provides instruction that the parents observe and judge superior to public programs. (3) Preferred environment: the private school offers either the day school or residential setting that parents prefer and that is not available in local public programs. (4) Religious instruction: the private school offers religious instruction, either in the classroom or in the dormitory, that is in accord with the parents' wishes. *See* EDUCATION: Communication.

Despite the difficulties of operating private independent schools in a society aggressively advocating public support of special education, they persist in numbers too great to list here, and new private programs are being formed in various parts of the country. Some private schools have joined one or both of the following organizations to reinforce their viability: the National Association of Private Schools for Exceptional Children (NAPSEC) and OPTION, an international organization of private auditory-oral schools for deaf children.

Private schools continue as change agents, establishing new models of practice and providing important options for parents in choosing the lifestyle of their children. Exclusively oral communication was introduced in the United States by the private New York Institution for Improved Instruction of Deaf-Mutes in 1867, later named the Lexington School for the Deaf. That same year, the Clarke Institution for Deaf Mutes was privately established in Massachusetts, introducing education for deaf children beginning as young as 5 years rather than at the ages of 8 to 10 prevalent at that time, and extending the number of years of education to 10. The beginning age of school enrollment was reduced to three years by the private Central Institute for the Deaf in 1914. Still earlier intervention for children from birth to age three was largely begun by private schools and hearing and speech centers, led by the John Tracy Clinic of Los Angeles, which also introduced correspondence courses for parents of young deaf children.

In addition to oral communication and early education, private schools were prominent in developing such innovations as intensive use of hearing aids coupled with audiology services, parent-infant programs focusing on the role of families, individualized instruction through low pupil/teacher ratios and efficient management systems, affiliations with universities and with research laboratories, involvement of various allied professions and disciplines in the education of hearing-impaired children, preparing the hearing-impaired students for enrollment in schools and colleges for students with normal hearing, and public education about deafness through relations with philanthropic groups.

Bibliography

Bender, Ruth E.: *The Conquest of Deafness*, 3d ed., Interstate Printers and Publishers, Danville, Illinois, 1981.

Scouten, Edward L.: *Turning Points in the Education of Deaf People*, Interstate Printers and Publishers, Danville, Illinois, 1984.

Donald R. Calvert

MULTIPLY HANDICAPPED

Education is considered an inherent right of all United States citizens, but to the deaf multihandicapped individual, education is just coming of age. For decades before legislation mandated a free appropriate public education for all, this particular segment of the deaf population was neglected. Because deaf multihandicapped persons constitute a low-incidence population with a high mortality rate, programming was scant. With the advent of medical technology, many individuals who would have died in infancy were being saved. The rubella epidemics of 1963, 1965, and 1969 increased this population. In addition, sophisticated educational testing tools were developed that aided in the identification of hidden disabilities that may accompany deafness. *See* HEARING LOSS.

Origins   In the 1960s and 1970s professionals in the field of deaf education began to focus on the programmatic needs of this unique population. The Pilot Project at the California School for the Deaf in Riverside was among the early programs for multihandicapped deaf children. Begun in 1964 with 40 students, it grew into a program serving over 100.

Other schools for deaf students, using components of the Pilot Project, established special programs to serve their multihandicapped deaf population. Symposiums and workshops were held throughout the United States to explore and define program needs of deaf multihandicapped students.

Although there is still confusion as to what is meant by the term deaf multihandicapped it is generally accepted that an individual who is deaf and has one or more other handicapping conditions is a deaf multihandicapped person. These handicapping conditions include mental retardation, learning handicaps, orthopedic handicaps, social or emotional disturbances, and other health-related impairments. The most common are mental retardation and social or emotional disturbances.

Policies   Education legislation enacted in the 1970s, especially the Rehabilitation Act of 1973 and the Education for All Handicapped Children Act (Public Law 94-142), influenced the services provided to multiply handicapped children. This legislation gives all handicapped children the inherent right to a free appropriate public education. Due to the complexity of the interrelationships of the handicapping conditions found in a deaf multihandicapped individual, programmatic needs are of an individual nature and deviate from traditional programming for deaf persons. Not only is the educational component of the program important, but the designated services provided by social service agencies are equally so. These agencies may include the Departments of Rehabilitation and Habilitation, Regional Centers, the Department of Public Social Services, or other state-operated children's services. All of these agencies work together as part of a total comprehensive program team for the deaf multihandicapped individual. The goal is to have the multihandicapped individual become as independent as possible.

The service delivery plan for deaf multihandicapped children varies from district to district and state to state. However, one of the clearest implications of P.L. 94-142 is the least restrictive environment clause. Philosophies vary on what is appropriate and least restrictive. In an attempt to clarify this visually, a researcher, E. Demo, developed the graphic cascade system of educational placement. This funnel-type graph scales the environments found in the educational system from regular classroom placement to "cluster" or self-contained schools found in most school districts, and ultimately to referral to agencies providing service that is governed by noneducational agencies. Although the cascade was criticized for overemphasizing "place," its intent was to make available special settings in which the student would be successful in learning. In many local school districts, the deaf multihandicapped students are placed in self-contained schools. If these schools are not successful in providing an appropriate program, referral is made to the state school for the deaf students for a suitable program. Once the student is on the site of the state school, the cascade system for placement is again reviewed. The least restrictive environment, however, is viewed as the regular school program with students who benefit from instruction in traditional deaf education methodology.

Placement ultimately narrows to a special unit separate from the main school departments. Research has shown that the deaf muiltihandicapped individual functions better in a small group, with program emphasis on functional skill development and vocational training. Instruction must take place in the natural setting with instructors and other staff adept in using total communication, and it must provide a strong behavior modification component. Finally, there must be cooperative programming among the home, school, and dormitory settings.

Future As medical advances increase, even more high-risk children will survive, and with sophisticated screening devices many profoundly handicapped children will be identified at birth. Therefore, more programs for multihandicapped students will be needed. In the future, there will be a need for improved coordination of all services among the agencies serving this population and for greater focus to be placed on teacher preparation and training. The time will come when some agreement as to the definition of "deaf multihandicapped" will be fully addressed, finalized, and accepted. With efforts by both local and state agencies, the program needs of this highly unique population will finally be met.

Bibliography

Brelje, William, and Bernard Wolff (eds.): *Summary Report*, 1969 Summer Institute Multiply Handicapped, Lewis and Clark College, Portland, Oregon.

Brill, Richard G.: *The Education of the Deaf*, Gallaudet College Press, Washington, D.C., 1974.

Experimental Classes for Multiply Handicapped Deaf Children, Indiana School for the Deaf, Indianapolis, Summer 1969.

Fine, Peter J. (ed.): *Deafness in Infancy and Early Childhood*, Medcom Press, Gallaudet College, 1974.

Flathouse, Virgil: *Multiply Handicapped Deaf Children and PL 94-142*, Council for Exceptional Children, 1979.

Haring, Norris (ed.): *Exceptional Children and Youth*, Charles E. Merrill, Columbus, Ohio, 1981.

Jensema, Carinne K.: "Issues in the Education of the Multi-Handicapped Hearing Impaired Children," *Directions*, vol. 3, no. 2, 1982.

Johnson, Judith, and Judy Harkins: "Stress and Teaching Hearing Impaired Children," *Perspectives*, vol. 2, no. 3, January 1984.

Jones, Thomas W.: "Issues in the Education of the Multi-Handicapped Hearing Impaired Children," *Directions*, vol. 3, no. 2, 1982.

Lennan, Robert K.: "The Deaf Multi-Handicapped Unit at the California School for the Deaf, Riverside," *American Annals of the Deaf*, June 1973.

Moulton, Robert, Robert A. Rath, and Billy Winney: "State Certification Standards and Reciprocity for Teachers of the Hearing Impaired," *American Annals of the Deaf*, vol. 128, no. 4, August 1983.

Rodriguez, Ramon: *Discussion of Educational Programs for the Multiply Handicapped, PL 94-142 Revisited*, Convention of American Instructors for the Deaf, 49th Biennial Meeting, selected papers, 1981.

Schein, Jerome, and Marcus T. Delk, Jr.: *The Deaf Population of the United States*, National Association of the Deaf, Silver Spring, Maryland, 1974.

Stewart, Larry (ed.): *Severely Handicapped Deaf People: A Perspective for Program Administrators and Planners, a Monograph of Selected Presentations from the Symposium "Foundations of Rehabilitation Planning with Deaf Persons Who Are Severely Handicapped"*, Tucson, Arizona, 1978.

Summer Workshop for Teachers of the Multi-Handicapped Hearing Impaired, Gallaudet College, Washington, D.C., June–July 1976.

Mary Ann Salem

COMMUNITY COLLEGES

In 1933 when the International Congress on the Education of the Deaf was held at West Trenton, New Jersey, the president of the Conference of Executives of American Schools for the Deaf proposed that a junior college for deaf students be established. This did not come about until 1961.

Riverside City College The first community college program established specifically for deaf students in the United States, and possibly in the world, was at Riverside, California, at Riverside City College in 1961. A two-year community college in California can serve one of two functions. There is an academic curriculum designed for the student who is going to transfer to a four-year college or university with full credit for the two academic years taken in the community college; there is also a vocational program for another and larger part of the student population.

The program for deaf students at Riverside City College is for students enrolled in the vocational program. It was not intended to prepare students academically for transfer to Gallaudet College. At Riverside City College the academic work required for the terminal vocational student includes work in English, history, health education, and psychology. A total of 64 units are required for the associate of arts degree. The balance of the units should be in vocational work. When the special program for deaf students was established, full-time instructors for deaf peole were hired. These instructors teach the more "verbal" courses, such as English and history, and then interpret in the other academic classes of health, psychology, and math, and carry on an extensive tutorial program following each lecture. Arrangements are made for some hearing students to provide special services such as notetaking and manual interpreting in the vocational courses. This program set the pattern for many subsequent community college programs for deaf students.

Following the successful establishment of the Riverside City College program, another junior or community college program for deaf students was not established until 1966. In that year a program began at the St. Petersburg (Florida) Junior College on the Clearwater campus.

Federal Support In 1967, guidelines were issued for a research and demonstration project jointly supported by the Bureau of Education of the Handicapped and the Vocational Rehabilitation Administration in the U.S. Department of Health, Education and Welfare. This project was entitled Improved Vocational Training Opportunities for Deaf People. The recipients of these grant awards were Delgado Junior College in New Orleans, Seattle Community College in the state of Washington, and St. Paul Technical-Vocational Institute in Minnesota. The University of Pittsburgh was the initial research component of the research and demonstration project. The University of Minnesota completed the research components of the project. Delgado Junior College opened its program with these federal funds in 1968, and Seattle Community College and St. Paul Technical-Vocational Institute opened their programs in 1969. The operating programs were initially five-year programs, with Delgado's federal funding lasting until 1973 and the other two until 1974.

Federal legislation provided further funding effective January 1, 1975. The programs for deaf students at St. Paul Vocational-Technical Institute and at the Seattle Community College continued their funding under this new authority, and Delgado Community College became funded again a year later. St. Paul and Seattle continue under federal funding adopted in 1983. Delgado still operates a program, but does not receive federal funding.

Evaluation Following the federal funding of the three community colleges, other programs, which were locally supported, began to open around the country. These programs proliferated rapidly, and there was some concern about the quality of many of them. In December 1971 a group of administrators representing eight postsecondary programs for deaf students met informally in St. Paul, Minnesota, to share information. A considerable effort was made to identify the current and projected postsecondary programs for deaf students, and a list was assembled of approximately 40 such programs. Certain basic criteria were established to identify what would truly constitute a program. These criteria were that: (1) the institution provide special services for the deaf student; (2) there be one or more full-time staff equivalent committed to deaf students in the institution, (3) there be cognizance of the communication needs of deaf stu-

dents, and (4) the program be available to deaf students directly upon graduation from a secondary program.

When these criteria were applied to the 40 programs, it appeared that there were 22 operational postsecondary programs for deaf students and 4 regional programs projected to open in September 1972.

Concern about the quality of community college programs resulted in a document being published and widely disseminated by the Conference of Executives of American Schools for the Deaf in 1973. Entitled *Principles Basic to the Establishment and Operation of Postsecondary Education for Deaf Students*, it was designed to function as a guide to institutions that might be contemplating services or programs for hearing-impaired students.

In 1977 a joint project of Gallaudet College and the National Technical Institute for the Deaf was the publication of *A Guide to College/Career Programs for Deaf Students*. This publication listed 74 programs serving hearing-impaired students. Programs listed did not have to meet any special criteria.

The April 1985 directory issue of the *American Annals of the Deaf*, in listing postsecondary programs for deaf students, specified that each postsecondary program listed must include at least one full-time instructional or support person for deaf students. There were a total of 57 two-year programs in community colleges. These 57 programs had a total of 2934 students. They varied greatly in size as indicated by the table.

There are four community colleges in Canada with programs for deaf pupils.

Analysis of Community Colleges Enrolling Deaf Students, 1984–1985 School Year

Number of Deaf Students in 57 Community Colleges

No. of students	100 or more	50–99	25–49	Under 25	Total
No. of programs	10	9	19	19	47

Number of Instructors Who Work Full Time with Deaf Students

No. of instructors in program	0	1	2	More than 2	
No. of programs	11	17	20	9	57

Note: Programs without full-time instructors may have other supportive staff such as interpreters or counselors specifically for deaf students.

Bibliography
    American Annals of the Deaf, vol. 130, no. 2, April 1985.
    Brill, R. G.: *The Education of the Deaf: Administrative and Professional Developments*, Gallaudet College Press, 1974.
    Proceedings of the International Congress on the Education of the Deaf, West Trenton, New Jersey, 1933, New Jersey School for the Deaf, West Trenton, 1933.
    Proceedings of the 44th Conference of Executives of American Schools for the Deaf, CEASD, Toronto, Ontario, Canada, 1972.

Richard G. Brill

HIGHER EDUCATION

The increase in the quality and quantity of postsecondary educational opportunities for deaf individuals was so rapid in the 20-year period from 1964 to 1984 as to constitute a virtual revolution. Gallaudet College, the only liberal arts college for deaf people in the world, was established in 1864. For the first 100 years of its existence, the college was essentially the only source of higher education for deaf students in the United States. Although there are reports of hearing-impaired individuals who graduated from other colleges during that period, their numbers were small and research suggests that typically they either had less than severe hearing losses or had lost their hearing after acquiring spoken language skills. Thus, because Gallaudet itself was a relatively small liberal arts college, college enrollment of deaf individuals across the United States probably never exceeded 400 in any given year until the 1960s. Because Gallaudet itself offered a five-year program for the majority of its students—a preparatory year in addition to the traditional four years—the number of deaf graduates of postsecondary programs probably never exceeded 50 to 60 annually. The attrition rates in college would suggest that even 50 is a somewhat high estimate.

Growth The situation began to change rapidly in the 1960s. Important factors contributing to the changes included federal support for postsecondary educational opportunities specifically for deaf students, legislation mandating equal access to education for disabled Americans, provision of vocational education money for disabled people, and a greater societal acceptance of and accommodation to diversity. In 1965 Congress authorized the establishment of the National Technical Institute for the Deaf (NTID), which was developed in affiliation with the Rochester (New York) Institute of Technology. The NTID program is a national program serving highly qualified deaf students. Most beginning students go through a program that offers career sampling, technical mathematics, science, English, and personal development. Training may lead to certification, a two-year associate degree, or a four-year baccalaureate degree. Interpreters and notetakers are provided for students taking classes with hearing peers.

Regional Centers Shortly following its legislation concerning NTID, Congress approved the establishment of three federally supported regional vocational technical programs which, like NTID, were to be developed within the framework of existing programs already serving hearing students. By 1969 programs were located at the Vocational Technical Institute in St. Paul, Minnesota; the Delgado Vocational Technical Junior College in New Orleans, Louisiana; and the Washington Community College in Seattle, Washington.

Each of the regional programs provides preparatory instruction in mathematics, English, and job sampling. The regional programs provide support services, including notetaking and interpreting in integrated classes; personal, social, and vocational counseling; and vocational placement.

Independent evaluation of the regional vocational technical programs produced strong evidence for their effectiveness in providing training and vocational placement for deaf students at a relatively low cost. Parents, students, and vocational rehabilitation counselors were favorable in their reactions to the programs. The immediate work supervisors of program graduates regarded deaf workers as desirable employees with high job performance, and the former students themselves reported high job satisfaction. The evidence also indicated an upward movement in the job market for students in the three programs. Significantly, many of the regular classroom teachers, who had little or no previous experience with deaf students, were enthusiastic about the programs, and were accepting of deaf students in their classes.

California State University at Northridge (CSUN) also began an educational program for deaf students in the 1960s, one that grew significantly. CSUN first accepted deaf graduate students into its National Leadership Training Program in the Area of Deafness in 1964. From there, CSUN developed support services for deaf students at undergraduate and graduate levels. The results were dramatic and led the federal government to provide CSUN support similar to that of the three regional vocational technical programs.

Enrollment The gains achieved in the 1960s have since been built upon and expanded. Additional impetus came from the provision under Section 504 of the Rehabilitation Act of 1973 that no otherwise qualified disabled applicant can be denied admission, solely on the basis of disability, to the services and programs of any educational institution receiving federal financial assistance. By 1983 the full-time enrollments of deaf students at Gallaudet (1077) and NTID (993) had increased tremendously. Almost 450 additional full-time students were enrolled at the Seattle, St. Paul, Delgado, and CSUN programs. Of equal importance was the growth of institutions of higher education offering special support services to deaf students. For the 1982–1983 school years, it was reported that more than 5500 full-time deaf students, including the 2500 students at the six national and regional programs, were found enrolled in 100 institutions of higher education in 31 states and the District of Columbia. Since the data only included programs with 15 or more deaf students, total enrollment in American postsecondary programs clearly is much higher.

It has been estimated that the college participation rate of young deaf students is now about 40 percent—a rate roughly equivalent to that of the general American young adult population. The postsecondary opportunities for deaf students also appear to encompass a wide variety of choices. These include certification-only, associate degree, undergraduate, and graduate training. Subject matter includes vocational, technical, liberal arts, and professional training.

Concern has been expressed over the proliferation of programs serving small numbers of deaf students, that is, less than 15 full-time students. The danger is that such programs will not be able to offer the specialized support services required by deaf students. On the whole, however, higher education opportunities now available in the United States for deaf individuals represent one of the greatest success stories in American education over the past generation.

Bibliography

Armstrong, David F., and Kurt Schneidmiller: *Hearing Impaired Students Enrolled in U.S. Higher Education Institutions: Current Status of Enrollments and Services*, Institutional Studies Report 83-3, Washington, D.C., Gallaudet College Office of Planning, 1983.

Moores, Donald F.: *Educating the Deaf: Psychology, Principles and Practices*, Houghton Mifflin, Boston, 1982.

————, Steven Fisher, and Mary Jane Harlow: *Post-Secondary Programs for the Deaf: Summary and Overview*, Research Report 80, University of Minnesota Research and Demonstration Center in Education of Handicapped Children, Minneapolis, 1974.

Rawlings, Brenda W., Michael A. Karchmer, and James J. DeCaro: *College and Career Programs for Deaf Students*, Gallaudet College, Washington, D.C., and National Technical Institute for the Deaf, Rochester, New York, 1983.

Donald F. Moores

CONTINUING EDUCATION

Adult continuing education, by a definition generally accepted by practitioners, is any learning activity more or less formally structured that provides participants with opportunities to acquire new skills, knowledge, or useful information important to their economic and social well being. The length of the learning activity may vary, ranging from an hour's lecture to a two-day seminar to a 16-week course. In the United States such programs are usually offered on a noncredit basis by colleges, public school systems, churches, businesses, corporations, and a variety of public and private agencies, and attract millions of adults each year. No official count has been made of the number of deaf adults enrolling in continuing education courses and programs, although sporadic efforts with a variety of experimental formats have been tried in different parts of the country since the early 1900s.

Period from 1900 to 1960 Early in the 1900s the Iowa and Minnesota state schools for deaf students initiated correspondence courses for former pupils, and the St. Louis Board of Education opened a special evening program in which deaf adults met twice a week for basic education classes in English, mathematics, and vocational subjects. The U.S. Department of Agriculture's extension services made agriculture and economics classes available to deaf people in rural North Carolina. The Works Progress Administration during the Franklin D. Roosevelt administration funded a variety of programs in Chicago, Newark, New Jersey, and Kansas City, with encouraging enrollments spurred by high unemployment during the depression. Generally these programs were set up for deaf people exclusively.

Since attendance is not compulsory, it is quite characteristic in adult education that attendance declines as a course progresses. This problem has been particularly conspicuous in programs for deaf adults, since the numbers are small and any drop in attendance becomes all the more noticeable.

Since 1960 The civil rights movement as well as the social reform programs under Presidents John Kennedy and Lyndon Johnson generated much attention to the educational needs of minorities, the underprivileged, and handicapped populations. Increased federal spending in education provided a thrust for adult education for disabled persons, with three projects drawing national involvement in planning and implementation. The first, in 1969, was a workshop in Kansas City sponsored by New York University under a grant from the Department of Health, Education and Welfare. Both deaf and hearing individuals representing a spectrum of educational interests reviewed past programs, identified current needs, and published recommendations for effective program sponsorship.

In 1979 California State University at Northridge (then San Fernando Valley State College) inaugurated the DAWN (Deaf Adults With Need) project that sought to familiarize selected deaf persons with methods and materials in adult education, with the objective of developing program leadership within the consumer population. Although three-month-long training sessions produced few programs, high national interest was generated, and the project established an awareness among state directors of adult education of the needs of the handicapped population.

The third and most extensive effort was the establishment at Gallaudet College in Washington, D.C., of a Center for Continuing Education. A liberal arts college for deaf students, with a great part of its financial support coming from federal appropriations, Gallaudet received a mandate in the 1970s to broaden its scope of services. It sought to meet educational needs of a nationwide constituency, including not only deaf adults but also parents of hearing-impaired children and youth, and professionals both in and outside the field of deafness whose services influenced the welfare of disabled individuals. Working in consortium with the established network of continuing education programs in the Washington metropolitan area, the center began in 1972 a demonstration program that differed from most programs introduced up to that time. Rather than offering courses specifically for deaf adults, the Gallaudet program attempted to mainstream hearing-impaired adults in existing courses for hearing adults on the theory that a great number of interest areas could be made available at a relatively low cost. To facilitate participation, the center offered orientation sessions to instructors with no previous experience in teaching deaf adults, and hired sign language interpreters to accompany deaf students in classes. Upon demand, special seminars or courses answering to particular interests of deaf persons—for example, communication training, basic education courses needing special teaching technologies, and teletype repair—have been offered. The center also produced some special teaching materials, mainly in language development.

By the early 1980s the Gallaudet Center, using its program as a laboratory setting, had trained interns sent by schools and colleges from various parts of the country. Subsequently, local programs built after the Washington model, using local resources and facilities, were initiated under the leadership of several schools for deaf pupils and community colleges, most notably the state schools in Fremont, California; Spartanburg, South Carolina; Morganton, North Carolina; Atlanta Area School for the Deaf in Georgia; St. Mary's School in Buffalo, New York; and the state school in Austin, Texas. Among postsecondary institutions adopting the plan were City Wide Colleges of Chicago, Johnson County Community College in Kansas, and Seattle Central Community College.

General Considerations Experience in continuing education for deaf adults indicates that many of the management technologies employed in providing programs for the general population apply to the management of programs for deaf people; similarly, obstacles and barriers to program growth are quite alike in both populations. However, the following considerations are pertinent: (1) More success is realized by programs in which deaf adults are themselves involved in the planning. (2) The use of volunteers in teaching, supervision, and management has realized little long-range success. (3) While formal needs assessments through mailed questionnaires or through person-to-person or group surveys often help in developing interest, they are generally no more effective in producing relevant programs than guesswork of experienced administrators. (4) Tuition charges and registration fees are more a deterrent to deaf people than to the hearing population, because the former tend to have lower average incomes. (5) Costs of interpreting, tutoring, and notetaking, as needed by many deaf students, are an additional burden to program managers and a stopgap to the growth and maintenance of courses for hearing-impaired persons. Few institutions are prepared for this fiscal responsibility. (6) Strong and constant promotion and advertising, however time-consuming and costly, are the best guarantees for building enrollments. (7) Correspondence courses and the use of electronic technology (television and computers) hold promise for reaching deaf adults in isolated rural areas; however, deaf people generally like to be in a group situation that allows for social interaction.

Bibliography

The Gallaudet College Continuing Education Center and Cooperating Institutions, Gallaudet College, Washington, D.C., 1972.

Luke, Robert A., and Carol Boggs: *Tricks of the Trade*, Gallaudet College, Washington, D.C., 1976.

Schein, J. C., et al: *Continuing Education of Deaf Adults*, Deafness Research and Training Center, New York, 1976.

Thomas A. Mayes

ENDEAVOR

The *Endeavor* is the official publication of the American Society for Deaf Children (ASDC; formerly the International Association of Parents of the Deaf, which evolved from the Parent Section of the Convention of American Instructors of the Deaf). Through all three group name changes, the *Endeavor* has remained the primary communicator among parents. The first issue was distributed in the fall of 1969. Since that time, the readership has increased from 6000 to 18,000 families with deaf children and the professionals who serve them. The *Endeavor* appears six times a year and has grown from a 4–6-page newsletter, to a 12–16-page issue. Although the format and length of the journal have changed, and advertisements and pictures are now included, the information in the *Endeavor* remains a constant source of support to families with children who are deaf or hard of hearing. The *Endeavor* supports the philosophy of total communication. *See* AMERICAN SOCIETY FOR DEAF CHILDREN; SOCIOLINGUISTICS: Total Communication.

FEATURES

The *Endeavor* has several regular columns. "The President's Corner," is written by the president of the executive board of ASDC, who has always been the parent of a deaf child. It includes information about ASDC and its activities, comments about the executive board, and personal experiences in raising a deaf child.

"The Editor's Corner" is also written by a parent and covers national issues as well as issues of personal concern to parents with deaf children.

"The Affiliate Corner" contains news of the activities of ASDC's affiliate groups throughout the United States and Canada. This column reflects local activities of parent groups. It gives ideas to other groups as to the kind of activities that can be accomplished by a local parent group.

"The Legislative Corner," written by lawyers who are experts in legal issues that affect deaf people and their families, provides updated information about pertinent legal cases and issues. Background information is given on established laws such as Public Law 94-142 (Education for All Handicapped Children) and the Rehabilitation Act of 1973, Section 504. Changes in laws affecting public schools, residential programs, and vocational programs are covered, and job training, employment, sports, accessibility, and technology are also included. *See* EDUCATION OF THE HANDICAPPED ACT; REHABILITATION ACT OF 1973.

A major article is a regular part of each *Endeavor*. Each issue also has a section called "Keeping Up," which covers news about the world of deafness in one or two sentences: information about captioned television programs, new organizations, technology, awards, changes, and innovations. Information for this section is gathered from newsletters, press releases, and special mailings from schools, organizations, government agencies, and private businesses in the United States and other countries.

Books of interest to parents are reviewed in most issues, with lists of "Good Reading" published during the summer and holiday issues. Books for children are also reviewed.

The *Endeavor* also includes poems written by children, deaf adults, and others; special short articles on such issues as "hearing ear dogs"; a calendar of meetings; letters from parents and professionals; hearing aid information; resolutions passed by organizations involved with deafness; special recognition to special people; publication of ASDC's position papers; and names of new members.

Special issues are periodically published. These have included a Summer Camp Directory (now published separately on an annual basis), an issue titled "Deafness and Learning Disabilities," and annual reports. There have also been special supplements devoted to deaf-blind children and their families.

The editor as well as many of the contributors to the *Endeavor* are parents with children who are deaf or hard of hearing. Professionals also contribute to the *Endeavor* in the Legislative Corner, in articles, and in occasional columns.

PUBLISHING HISTORY

The first issue of the *Endeavor* was printed and distributed in the fall of 1969. Mary Jane Rhoads was the first editor, and the National Association of the Deaf was the sponsor and publisher.

Jacqueline Z. Mendelsohn

ENGLAND, EDUCATION IN

The state system of education in England is essentially decentralized. Full-time education is compulsory for all children between the ages of 5 and 16 years. State education is free, but all parents have the right to have their children educated privately, in which case they are responsible for all costs involved. Generally, education up to the age of 11 years is termed primary education; primary schools may be separated into nursery (before 5 years), infant (5 to 7 years), and junior (8 to 11 years) schools, or they may cater to the whole age range up to 11 years. After their eleventh birthday, pupils normally transfer to secondary schools, where they remain until the minimum school-leaving age of 16 years. At this age, pupils may choose either to leave to find employment, to transfer to further education, or to remain at school for another two to three years. Most secondary schools are comprehensive, which means that they accept the full ability range of pupils, though in some areas a selective system remains, by which children of differing abilities attend different types of school, the more able pupils (approximately one-quarter) attending grammar schools.

The overall responsibility for carrying out the laws created by Parliament in its Education Acts rests with the 96 autonomous Local Education Authorities while the Department of Education and Science, the central body of national government, performs a regulatory, advisory, and monitoring role.

Classroom teachers in England traditionally enjoy a much higher degree of professional freedom than their European counterparts. The real power, however, rests with the headteacher who, working within the checks and balances provided by the boards of governors, the Local Education Advisory Service, and Her Majesty's Inspectors of Schools, is responsible for virtually all that happens within the school in terms of overall philosophy, the curriculum, the methods of teaching, the allocation of resources, the monitoring of standards, discipline and pastoral care, and general management. This system has resulted in a wide variety of practice and in a difference of emphasis and approach throughout England. Its strengths lie in its flexibility, its potential for meeting purely local needs, and the comparative ease with which innovation and experimentation may take place.

This pattern of difference, variety, and autonomy is also to be found in the system of educational provision for hearing-impaired children that has developed, and it is possible to understand this provision only against the background of the system that has developed for ordinary children. However, since there are relatively few hearing-impaired children thinly spread throughout the country, there is even greater variety of practice.

CLASSIFICATION
Formerly, children with a hearing loss were classified as either deaf or partial-hearing. The definitions of these terms are educational rather than audiological, and today they bear little relation to the degree of hearing loss. A very wide overlap exists between the two terms, and a significant number of children classified as partially hearing have less hearing than many of those classified as deaf. This has in part resulted from changes in the way in which children are educated, and it is likely that these terms will fall out of use, to be replaced by the term hearing-impaired. This term covers the whole spectrum of hearing loss, and it will probably be modified by an appropriate adverb such as profoundly, severely, moderately, slightly, as proposed by the British Association of Teachers of the Deaf, to indicate the severity of the hearing loss.

STATISTICS AND STATISTICAL TRENDS
It is difficult to give absolutely precise numbers of hearing-impaired children being educated in England; however, the number of hearing impaired children is small. Current trends indicate strongly that this number is reducing and will continue to do so, certainly into the 1990s. Evidence for this comes from various surveys. Numbers of children officially classified as deaf or partially hearing fell by 12.89 percent in the four years 1978–1981; the number of children aged between 11 and 16 years attending special schools is expected to fall by just over 40 percent between 1980 and 1986; in 1981

there were almost 55 percent fewer children identified as having a hearing loss at age 5 years than at age 15; 54 percent fewer children entered special schools or units for the hearing-impaired in January 1981, compared with January 1971.

Much of this reduction has resulted from the declining birthrate, which fell by 16 percent between 1973 and 1977. But this is not the sole cause. Due to medical advances, improved pre- and perinatal care, the rubella vaccination program, and an increase in therapeutic abortion for rubella contacts, there seems also to have been a reduction in the prevalence of congenital perinatal hearing-impairment. In 1978, for example, 10.82 per 10,000 children of school age were classified as deaf or partially hearing; in 1981 the rate was 9.75 per 10,000, a reduction in prevalence of almost 10 percent. A survey of total live births in the Greater Manchester area of England between 1975 and 1978 showed that only 1 child per 2077 had a severe or profound sensorineural loss—a prevalence equivalent to only 4.8 per 10,000. It is not known whether this finding is representative of the country as a whole, though there is no reason to believe that it should be radically different.

Changes such as these are having substantial effect on the educational services for hearing-impaired individuals. There have been closures of special schools and of units attached to ordinary schools; there have been early retirements and redundancies in a teaching force of qualified teachers of deaf people, which in 1976 was reported as being more than 30 percent understrength. It is likely that these trends will continue well into the 1990s, and there are likely to be major changes in the education service as a result.

SERVICES
Each Local Education Authority is responsible for the organization of the education services for hearing-impaired persons within its authority, but not all local Education Authorities are able to offer the full range of provisions. However, common patterns of provision have emerged. There are two broad sectors: the special schools and the External Services, which includes all forms of provision other than special school placement (such as special units attached to ordinary schools, children in ordinary classes supported by peripatetic teachers of deaf children, and parent-guidance services both home- and clinic-based).

Under Five: Preschool Service The responsibility for detecting and diagnosing hearing-impairment in infants and young children lies with the Area or District Health Authorities. It is normal practice for most babies to have screening tests of hearing before the age of one year. Screening and subsequent diagnostic tests are free, and if hearing loss is diagnosed, free hearing aids, earmolds, maintenance, and batteries are provided for life. Only certain models of aids are issued to adults, but children may be provided with any hearing aid that is available in England, though in practice the great majority are issued with aids from a range selected centrally by the Department of Health and Social Security (DHSS). Most children with bilateral loss are issued two aids. There is a growing tendency for preschool children to be issued radio aids in addition to their personal aids. These may be provided free by the Local Education Authority, by local charities, or be purchased privately. They are not yet provided by the DHSS. *See* HEARING AIDS.

Once a child has been diagnosed as hearing-impaired, the family is normally put onto a parent-guidance program, which is provided for parents usually in their own home by a peripatetic teacher. The frequency and duration of guidance sessions will vary according to need, but in the early days it is likely to be one or two sessions per week, reducing to perhaps one every two weeks. The role of the parents is now officially recognized as being vital in the early management of hearing-impaired children.

While only as recently as the early 1970s it was usual for children from the age of about three years with severe or profound losses to enter a special school, often as boarders, this practice is dying. Since 1979 it has been the official policy of the British Association of Teachers of the Deaf to place, wherever possible, hearing-impaired children under five in normal nursery schools with adequate support from the peripatetic services. This policy tended to reflect growing practice at the time rather than initiate it, and now relatively few children enter a special school before five.

Upon reaching the age of compulsory education at five years, a child must be placed in either a special school, a special unit attached to an ordinary school, or an ordinary school, depending upon need.

Special Schools   Depending on how they are financed, special schools are of three main types: maintained, nonmaintained, and independent. Maintained schools are funded and maintained entirely by the Local Education Authority. Nonmaintained schools are funded and maintained by charities administered by boards of governors and trustees. Costs are met from fees charged for each pupil. Supportive grants from central government are often given toward approved capital expenditure. These schools are nonprofit-making. Independent schools are funded and maintained privately by individuals or groups of individuals. Income is from fees, and profits may be made.

Special schools are further classified into schools for the deaf, schools for the partially hearing, and schools for the deaf and partially hearing, though this nomenclature has little meaning today. Schools may cater to children of primary age, to those of secondary age, or to a mixture of both. They may also offer day or residential placement. Residential schools usually cater to day pupils also. Less than one-third of the Local Education Authorities maintain special schools. The rest place children who need special school provision in an appropriate school, which may be either maintained by a different Local Education Authority, nonmaintained, or independent. The Local Education Authority in whose area the child has a permanent home is responsible for the child's education, for the payment of all fees, and for traveling expenses to and from school.

Normally, children are taught in classes with a maximum size of 10 children. In practice, there are usually only five or six children per class. Most classes of younger children also have either part-time or full-time classroom assistants. A few special schools have experimented with mainstreaming some of their pupils into ordinary schools, while a few others are closely associated with the special units in the locality. If the special school is a maintained school, it is reasonably easy to transfer from one placement to another should this be in the child's interests.

There are two selective secondary schools for able pupils, the Mary Hare Grammar School and Burwood Park School, which select their pupils by entrance examination, and two schools specifically for hearing-impaired children with additional handicaps. A number of other schools have small departments for the additionally handicapped.

Partially Hearing Units   Most Local Education Authorities provide special units for hearing-impaired children attached to ordinary schools. Often these are still called by their traditional title of partially hearing unit (PHU), but as most such units now contain some children with severe or profound losses this title is misleading. The number of these children has steadily increased since the 1950s and continues to do so, in spite of the reduction in the birthrate. The size of a unit may vary from 3 or 4 children to perhaps 30 or 40; most have between 8 and 12 pupils. Units may employ several teachers of deaf students, but most now have either one or two, and many units, particularly those for younger children, also have part-time classroom assistants.

Changes have taken place since the early 1970s in the pattern of placement of children into units. Whereas formerly only children with less severe losses and a fair degree of mastery of spoken language were given this type of placement, units today usually have children with a wide age range (for example, 5 to 11 years), a wide range of hearing loss, and a wide ability range. Consequently, class teaching, similar to the pattern of teaching that still prevails in many special schools, is rare. Children are more frequently taught in small groups of two and three, each grouping with its own curriculum and timetable. The majority of children in most units are integrated (mainstreamed) into the ordinary school for part of the week so that they have the opportunity to learn alongside hearing children. The patterns of integration vary enormously. Some children are integrated simply for activities such as art, physical education, games, and craft. Others will integrate for all subjects, spending most of their time in the ordinary class but being withdrawn on a regular basis into the unit for specialist help. Often an individual timetable and integration program is drawn up for each child, designed to meet the child's particular needs. In some units children are integrated only after they have gained a measure of linguistic competence; in others they are at least partially integrated from the time of school entry regardless of the degree of hearing loss or language ability.

With such a variety of practice and a dependence on only one or two teachers, some units will clearly be more successful than others. Generally, it is claimed that unit placement is better for the social development of the hearing-impaired children. The fact that there has been a continuous trend toward placing a greater proportion of such children in units and in employing more teachers in this sector suggests that Local Education Authorities as a whole regard unit provision as a successful development.
Peripatetic Teaching Service The duties of peripatetic teachers of deaf children are wide and varied. Not attached to any particular school, they are mostly employed by Local Education Authorities to visit and support hearing-impaired children who are placed in ordinary schools. By far the greatest number of hearing-impaired children are to be found in ordinary schools, but most of these will have only moderate losses. However, the number of children with severe and profound loss being educated in this way is growing steadily. Peripatetic teachers also run parent-guidance programs, participate in multidisciplinary diagnostic teams, support young people in further and higher education, and support hearing-impaired children in other types of special school, such as schools for the physically handicapped.

COMMUNICATION METHODOLOGY

Traditionally, hearing-impaired children in England have been educated with an oral approach. However, since the mid-1960s the question of communication methods has been at the forefront of discussion. As a result, a variety of manual methods aimed at assisting the communication process have appeared in the classroom. In 1982 the British Association of Teachers of the Deaf issued a policy document on the issue. It stated that "a fundamental aim of the education of hearing-impaired children must be the mastery of the English language in its spoken and written forms, with the goal of spoken English of prime importance." It recognized that some children might need additional manual methods to support English language learning, and expressed a preference for an oral approach supported by Signed English for these children. *See* EDUCATION: Communication.

The discussion has also highlighted the fact that there exist different oral practices which have been classified under the umbrella term "oral method." These practices fall into two broad groups, each based on different linguistic principles, natural oralism and structured oralism. The latter is based on the traditional approach which has developed in the special schools since the Conference of Milan. Natural oralism is a more recent development which places the emphasis on "meaningful acts of communication" rather than on linguistic form. A number of severely and profoundly hearing-impaired children have achieved considerable success through this approach, but it is not known whether it is applicable to the majority of such children. However, the British Association of Teachers of the Deaf recommends its use with preschool children. *See* HISTORY: Congress of Milan.

It seems probable that most existing Local Education Authorities are too small to make adequate provision themselves for children thought to need Signed English or other supportive systems. It is likely that a small number of geographically well-placed special schools will eventually take over this role.

FUTURE

The question of special education and of the special educational needs of children came under public review in England during the early 1980s. This process culminated in the report of the committee set up by the government entitled *Special Educational Needs* (the Warnock Report) and in the Education Act (1981). These far-reaching documents will have a significant effect on the way in which special education services develop; their influence will extend well into the twenty-first century. Generally, special education has been placed in a much wider framework. The 1981 act established the principle that all children who need special educational provision "are to be educated in ordinary schools, so far as it's reasonably practicable, and are to associate in the activities of the school with other children." Undoubtedly, this will gradually lead to a greater proportion of children being placed in ordinary schools, either mainstreamed or in special units. This will inevitably mean a further reduction in the number of special schools. It will also mean that an even greater proportion of the specialist teachers will be employed outside the special schools system. The rights of parents to be involved in decisions relating to their children's education are also considerably strengthened by the act, and since many will wish their children to be educated within the local community, the number of residential places needed, particularly at primary level, will greatly diminish.

It seems probable that by the turn of the century very few hearing-impaired children of primary age will receive the special education they need in special schools. Instead, it will be provided for them within the framework of the ordinary school. The special schools will probably cater to children from nonsupportive home backgrounds and to children with difficulties in addition to their hearing loss.

At the secondary level, a greater proportion of hearing-impaired pupils will probably attend special schools than at the primary stage, but the total number will still be smaller than is the case today. Although there will be fewer special schools, secondary departments will be larger. This will result from the need for the schools to be a certain minimum size in order to provide a wide, balanced curriculum, comparable with that provided in the ordinary school, and to offer the opportunity for pupils to participate fully in the public examination system.

For the students past age 16, there will be a rapid expansion into the field of further and higher education. There will be some increase in the courses available specifically for hearing-impaired students, but the greatest expansion will occur in the support services, with the aim of allowing such students to follow ordinary courses. While some colleges may come to specialize in catering for their needs within a normal college environment, it is very unlikely that a special college specifically for hearing-impaired students will emerge.

Bibliography

British Association of Teachers of the Deaf: "Audiological Definitions and Forms for Recording Audiometric Information," *Teacher of the Deaf*, 5(3): 83–87, 1981.

———: "Methodology in the Education of Hearing-Impaired Children," *Teacher of the Deaf*, 5(5):8–9, 1981.

———: "Methodology in the Education of Hearing-Impaired Children; A Structured Oral Programme; Natural Oralism—A Description; Signed English," *Teacher of the Deaf*, 4(4):4–12, 1980.

———: "A Survey of the Staffing and Salary Situation in Schools and External Services for the Hearing-Impaired," *Teacher of the Deaf*, 6(3):5–7, 1982.

Education Act, Her Majesty's Stationery Office, 1981.

Special Education Needs, Cmd 7212, a report of the Warnock Committee, Her Majesty's Stationery Office, 1978.

Taylor, I. G.: "Medicine and Education," *Teacher of the Deaf* 5(5):134–143, 1981.

Con Powell

Teacher Training

Since 1908 the government has required all teachers of deaf students to hold a specialist qualification for their work. Specialist training preceded this requirement and has its roots in the work of two private colleges founded in London in the 1870s. In the first half of the twentieth century, the work of teacher training was centered in the Department of Education of the Deaf in Manchester University and in the schools for deaf pupils that trained teachers for the in-service form of qualification offered by the National College of Teachers of the Deaf (now the British Association of Teachers of the Deaf). The shortage of trained teachers in the 1960s brought about an expansion of resources and created the present pattern of seven one-year postgraduate-postqualification courses, one four-year undergraduate course, and the part-time, in-service qualification offered by the British Association of Teachers of the Deaf. A period of consolidation of resources now seems inevitable as the decreasing child population alters the demand for specialist staff. The increasing commitment of educators to mainstream placement for hearing-impaired children and the effects of legislation concerned with special education (Education Act, 1981) will be influential factors in determining future patterns of development in the training of teachers of deaf pupils. *See* UNITED KINGDOM: Organizations.

1870–1920

The early courses of teacher training were developed within departments founded in schools for deaf children. The courses offered at the private college in Fitzroy Square (1872) and in Ealing (1877) in London were in schools and under the direction of two influential heads, Van Praagh and Kinsey. Thus, by the time of the Conference of Milan (1880), England had established two full-time courses of teacher training, both exclusively oral, both owing their techniques to Europe, and both—through their accompanying organization, the Association for the Oral Instruction of the Deaf and Dumb and the Society for the Training of Teachers of the Deaf and the Diffusion of the German System—intent upon promoting a particular form of educational practice. A third and very different body, the College of Teachers of the Deaf and Dumb, entered the work of teacher training five years later, in 1885. The college, which consisted of the headmasters of the institutions for deaf students, decided to train and examine entrants to the work and to award certificates to teachers who were proficient in either oral or manual methods of instruction. The training offered was similar to an apprenticeship and introduced the part-time, in-service strand of training which still exists.

Between 1880 and 1918 Fitzroy Square College, Ealing College, and the College of Teachers of the

Deaf and Dumb qualified between them some 700 teachers. Their training programs received government recognition in 1908, and from that time on their joint specialist qualification became a compulsory requirement for all teachers who sought to work with deaf students. From 1880 to 1907 the private colleges grew in strength, while the examination of the College of Teachers of Deaf and Dumb slowly established itself as a viable alternative to full-time training. The introduction of the joint examination in 1908 altered the pattern of growth, and for the next 10 years the size and influence of the private colleges decreased as the training offered by the College of Teachers of Deaf and Dumb became the major avenue of qualification. The examining right of the college survived the collapse of the Joint Examination Board in 1918 and became a feature of the new professional body, the National College of Teachers of the Deaf. The private colleges ceased their work at that time, and their few remaining students were transferred to the new full-time course established in 1919 in the University of Manchester.

1920–1965

The provision of training teachers of deaf pupils that existed in 1920 remained unchanged for nearly 50 years. The Department of Education of the Deaf in Manchester remained the only such department in England and thus retained its monopoly of full-time training, while the part-time, in-service qualification of the National College of Teachers of the Deaf grew in size and importance. Between 1920 and 1960 nearly 1500 teachers were qualified via the two bodies. The trend in the early years of this period, which made the diploma from the National College of Teachers of the Deaf the major source of qualification, was reversed by the time of World War II and by 1960 Manchester had trained nearly twice as many teachers as had the in-service method. By that time, the small course initiated by Irene Ewing, with less than 10 students in 1919, had grown to a full university department responsible for training 70–80 students a year.

By 1950 Manchester had also become recognized as an international center for the training of teachers of deaf pupils, and under the Ewings, teachers were trained from Australia, Canada, Ceylon, Cyprus, Hong Kong, Iceland, India, Indonesia, Eire, Iraq, Lebanon, Malaya, the Netherlands, Norway, New Zealand, Portugal, Singapore, South Africa, the West Indies, and the United States. During this period, the National College of Teachers of the Deaf also assumed a responsibility for overseas training, and in 1935 developed an overseas diploma which, unlike the home diploma, was awarded solely on the basis of a written examination. Between 1935 and 1960 most of the teachers who gained this diploma came from countries that were, or had been, part of the British Empire.

Thus, the period between 1920 and 1965 was characterized by two successful and complimentary forms of training and was dominated by two outstanding individuals. The Ewings not only created a highly successful training department but by pioneering an auditory oral practice established audiology as an academic discipline within teacher training.

1965–1980

The rapid expansion of the unit and peripatetic teaching force in the early 1960s exacerbated the already acute shortage of trained teachers of deaf people and was, in part, responsible for the expansion of the training resources which began in 1965. In that year, a one-year course was opened in London University, and four years later a further course was established at the Lady Spencer-Churchill College of Education, Oxford. The establishment of a course in a teachers college was a departure from previous practice and was motivated by the belief that student teachers of deaf people trained in such an environment would become more aware of current thought and practice in mainstream education. During this phase of development, Manchester University reduced the number of students on the one-year certificate course so as to allow for the establishment and growth of a four-year undergraduate course which included specialist training as a teacher of deaf students. In 1973 a total of 80 students completed their one-year training in the three departments: 33 in Manchester, 21 in London, and 26 in Oxford.

A further expansion took place in the mid-1970s with the creation of three additional one-year courses at Newcastle University (1973), Birmingham University (1976), and Bristol Polytechnic (1977). At this time, the course at London University was relocated and moved out to two colleges, one in Hertfordshire and one in West London. The course at Oxford also underwent a change due to the national policy of reorganization of higher education, and Lady Spencer-Churchill College of Education amalgamated to become part of the Oxford Polytechnic (1976).

Due to the overall shortage of teachers, particularly male teachers, and the need to recruit specialist teachers in secondary schools and departments, the in-service form of qualification was greatly used during this period. In the mid to late 1970s more candidates were seeking qualification each year via the in-service diploma of the National College of Teachers of the Deaf than were being trained in any one of the full-time centers. Between 1960 and 1975 the National College of Teachers of the Deaf sought to strengthen aspects of the diploma program and to overcome some of the problems associated with isolated part-time study. Regional training programs were developed along with vocation courses, and several special schools appointed senior teachers to be responsible for organizing training programs for the diploma examination. As unit provision expanded, permission was granted for teachers in units to study for the in-service examination if support was available from qualified and experienced teachers. By 1977 some 200 teachers a year were being trained via the full- and part-time courses; perennial shortage changed to near surfeit. Concerns about the need and relevance of the in-service qualification threatened its continuance. In 1978 a government report on special education (the Warnock Report) criticized aspects of the diploma with the result that the awarding body (the British Association of Teachers of the Deaf) began to review the form and content of the examination.

1980s

The size of the seven one-year courses varies: Oxford Polytechnic accepts 40–50 students for training each year; Manchester University, 30–40; West London Institute of Higher Education and the Hertfordshire College of Higher Education, 20–30 each; and Birmingham University, Newcastle University, and Bristol Polytechnic, less than 20 each.

The entry requirement for all the one-year courses, except at Manchester, is qualified teacher status. The Department of Audiology and Education of the Deaf at Manchester University also accepts into its one-year course graduates who complete additional practical work so as to gain qualification as teachers as well as teachers of deaf people. Three of the schools also stipulate teaching experience as an additional requirement for entry, while the remainder accept among their students some teachers straight from their initial teacher training courses.

The four-year course at Manchester University is a bachelor of arts combined honors program, which offers qualification as teacher and teacher of deaf people within the degree. In any four-year period there are over 70 students involved in the program.

The nomenclature of the one-year courses varies according to entry requirements and the tradition of the awarding institution and the validating body. Though the content and length of courses are fairly similar, some institutions offer the qualification at a certificate level while others award a diploma or advanced diploma. All courses seek to provide broadly based training and avoid overspecialization at the initial stage. There is thus no distinction between courses in terms of, say, their concentration on partially hearing as opposed to deaf children, or between preschool work and secondary work. Some of the newer courses like the one at Birmingham are situated within departments of special education; students benefit from a more generic training by being able to attend core lectures with students seeking specialist qualification in other areas. To this extent the courses can be seen to differ, although differences are more of emphasis and are dependent on the differing resources of institutions rather than on the fundamental differences in course structure or direction. The courses tend to concentrate on the oral education of hearing-impaired children, as this reflects the major educational practice in the country. However, nearly all of the courses inform their students about alternative and supportive practices, and a minority of them teach fingerspelling and signing skills to their students. *See* SIGNS: Fingerspelling.

Teachers from maintained schools can apply to their local education authority for approval on full salary in order to attend a course, while other students are eligible for either a mandatory continuation grant, if straight from initial training, or a discretionary grant, both of which are paid by their local education authority.

Since 1980 the number of students taking the diploma of the British Association of Teachers of the Deaf has rapidly decreased, and the examination was suspended for one year in 1984. This move allowed the association to assess future need and to decide whether it wished to be involved in initial or second-tier training in the future.

The fact that the majority of teachers of deaf people in England are women represents some problems in terms of staffing, especially in special schools, and causes a high level of absenteeism because of marriage or motherhood. While the training centers rarely exceed 10 percent per year for male students, the in-service form of training has consistently attracted more men, and between 1977 and 1980 one-fifth of those examined were men. Since the 1970s, some deaf teachers have qualified via the part-time courses and some of the full-time courses, though the total number is considerably less than 5 percent of the total working profession.

Facilities for advanced study are available at Manchester and Newcastle universities and at the Cambridge University Institute of Education. Manchester offers the widest range of options, one of the most significant being the diploma–master of science in audiology, which is the main source of qualified educational audiologists.

TRENDS

As the employment patterns for teachers of deaf students continue to diversify, future training courses will have to broaden their scope so as to include more of those skills required by teachers working in the support and peripatetic services rather than in the special school classroom. If total communication practices continue to proliferate in schools, teacher trainees in the future may have to question the traditional assumption that the acquisition of such skills by teachers is the role of second-tier rather than initial training. The move toward a generic teaching force in special education, following the passing of the 1981 Education Act, may well have its effect on specialist teacher training courses. If special schools and services are regionalized at some future date, then it is not inconceivable that training centers may well undergo something of the same process. *See* SOCIOLINGUISTICS: Total Communication.

Bibliography

Butterfield, P.H.: "The First Training Colleges for Teachers of the Deaf," *British Journal of Educational Studies*, vol. 19, no. 1, 1971.

Hodgson, K.W.: *The Deaf and Their Problems*, Watts and Company, 1953.

Pritchard, D.G.: *Education and the Handicapped*, Routledge and Kegan Paul, 1963

David M. Braybrook

Further Education

In England, the term further education is normally used to describe full- or part-time education offered within a college or similar educational establishment to persons older than age 16. These colleges are often called colleges of further education or technical colleges and offer general, vocational, or academic courses. General courses improve levels of literacy and numeracy and introduce students to different skills and to the work world. Vocational courses involve training for specific areas of employment, and can be full-time or part-time. Students taking part-time courses receive their practical training at work and attend college either on a day-release basis (one day a week) or on a block-release basis (for longer periods, perhaps a few weeks). The academic courses, generally those leading to the general certificate of education examinations at ordinary and advanced levels, are used to gain the necessary qualifications needed to go on to further study or to enter certain vocations.

The 1944 Education Act states that all people from 16 to 19 years of age are entitled to education, and that each Local Education Authority has a duty to provide suitable facilities for students with special educational needs, although it does not state whether this should be in the further education sector or within the school system. The choice here would seem to be that of the Local Education Authority and not the preference of the individuals or their parents.

The English system of education is a national but locally administered system. This may give rise to a great variety of provision, but not necessarily to a great deal of choice in provision. This fact should be considered when looking at further education provisions for hearing-impaired individuals. The type of further education available to individuals often depends less on what they need than on where they live.

HEARING-IMPAIRED PEOPLE

At one time, further education for hearing-impaired individuals was restricted to vocational training in a limited range of traditional occupations. Such training was commonly found in schools for deaf people. As a direct result of the increasing complexity of vocational training and of the changing attitudes toward employment opportunities, only one such training department still exists, and that now collaborates with local colleges of further education. Further education for hearing-impaired persons outside the school system is a comparatively recent development. For many deaf people, education ended when they reached school-leaving age and went into employment. The idea of going on to a college was not generally considered either by the teacher or by the deaf student.

Since the early 1960s, however, ideas have slowly changed, and many hearing-impaired students and their schools have started to look at further education as a viable possibility. With the growth in the demand has come a growth in provision, although it is difficult to determine which is the cause and which the effect.

NEEDS OF HEARING-IMPAIRED PEOPLE

Hearing-impaired students can be divided into several categories according to their needs. There are those who can integrate into a mainstream course with or without support. There are able students who, for whatever reason—poor linguistic level, limited communication skills, and so on—are unable to cope with ordinary courses for hearing students but who possess the intellectual ability to follow such a course. There are those who need some special course to raise their general level of attainment before proceeding to a further course. These students can often sample different courses or work possibilities which may involve them in some integration with hearing students. Finally, there are those of limited ability who need further education to prepare them for work and adulthood. Many hearing-impaired students need additional help after age 16 to mature and grow in independence. Continuing education in the same special school environment may not be appropriate; further education in a residential situation may be the correct solution.

PRESENT PROVISION

Further education provisions for hearing-impaired persons in England have developed on a piecemeal basis, usually according to the way the needs of the students in any one area are seen by the people living and working in that area. Such provision has not been planned, either on a regional or on a national basis, but has merely evolved, resulting in wide variety.

Provisions can be divided into two main categories, those of residential support and those of nonresidential support. The greater part of the residential support is provided by the schools, as colleges of further education normally exist only to serve a locality and therefore do not have residential accommodation. This has resulted in the anomaly of school-based residential provision for students in further education. It has also generally occurred in the nonmaintained schools, independent schools that are not directly controlled by the Local Education Authorities but by their own boards of governors.

Further education provisions can also be looked at for hearing-impaired persons in the light of the actual basis of any such provision, be it school-based, at a college, through peripatetic support, or a combination of any of these. School-based further education provision has already been mentioned. A school can be residential and provide a special course on school premises; a school may provide a support system for mainstreamed hearing-impaired students or offer special courses at local colleges; or some schools may provide a combination of any of these systems. Examples of school-based support systems can be found at the Yorkshire Residential School for the Deaf, Doncaster; the Royal School for the Deaf, Derby; Norfolk House College and Burwood Park School for the Deaf, Surrey; and Tewin Water School for the Partially Hearing, Hertfordshire, among others.

College-based provisions, however, are where teachers of deaf pupils are employed by a college, either to run specific courses for hearing-impaired students or to support hearing-impaired students who are integrating into nonspecific courses within the college or occasionally within other colleges in the locality. Examples of this kind of provision can be found at Bournville College of Further Education, Birmingham; North Nottinghamshire College of Further Education, Worksop; Shirecliffe College of Further Education, Sheffield (where the support extends outside the college to other colleges in the city); Tresham College of Further Education, Northamptonshire; and the Centre for the Deaf at the City Literary Institute in London (largest further education provision for hearing-impaired people in England).

At one time a hearing-impaired student integrating into a mainstream course may have been given some support by a local peripatetic teacher dealing mainly with preschool and school-age children. Specific appointments of peripatetic teachers to work with hearing-impaired students in further education have now been made in certain areas. For example, there is the Nottinghamshire Peripatetic Service for the Hearing Impaired in Further Education, where a team of teachers supports hearing-impaired students within the county.

TYPES OF COURSES

The kind of courses provided over the country as a whole varies considerably and reflects the needs of the different groups of hearing-impaired students. The majority of students are integrated into mainstream courses, including commerce, construction and building, engineering, horticulture, electronics, as well as into general education courses and into academic courses leading to the general certificate of education at ordinary and advanced levels. Some colleges and schools offer further education courses specifically for hearing-impaired persons that lead to a standard recognized qualification, so although the group is a special one, the course content and the final examination are the same as for other students. The City and Guilds Catering Course at the Burton-on-Trent Technical College in Staffordshire is an example. The City and Guilds Vocational Preparation Course at the Derby College of Further Education is an example of a semi-integrated course, where a group of hearing-impaired students comes together for certain elements of the course and is integrated for others. Such courses are of a general educational nature, with the opportunity to sample some vocational areas. Finally, there are the special courses for less able students; these may be in a school-based department of further education or in a college. Looking at provisions over the country as a whole, it can be seen that there is a wide spectrum of courses offered.

AVAILABLE SUPPORT

The most widely used form of support for students in mainstream courses is probably that of the tutorial system. A tutor, usually a teacher of deaf students, although the tutor may also be a subject specialist, is provided to assist the hearing-impaired student in understanding the language of the course. As deafness is a handicap that leads to language deprivation, deaf students generally do not have language skills to cope by themselves with the notes given and the books used in the course. A support tutor may also help the hearing-impaired student with the personal problems the student may experience when integrating with a hearing group. The tutor will also help and advise the lecturer, who may know little or nothing about deafness, and has received no special training. Support services often run training courses for lecturers who have deaf students, introducing them to the handicap and suggesting ways in which their teaching techniques can be adapted to help the hearing-impaired student.

Few professional educational interpreters exist in England. The Royal National Institute for the Deaf does provide a limited interpreting service, but otherwise any interpreting is carried out by the support tutor. The Council for the Advancement of Communication with the Deaf has started to define levels of interpreting, and to establish training courses leading to those different levels. It is hoped that this will lead to the training of educational interpreters who can be used in further education. *See* UNITED KINGDOM: Interpreting.

Students without interpreters get their lecture notes in a variety of ways: the lecturer may provide a copy of the lecture notes, may write all the necessary notes on the blackboard for the student to copy, or may have a hearing student make a duplicate set of notes using carbon paper, or the deaf student may copy the notes a hearing classmate has written. The last methods are only successful when the lecturer is asked to select a student who makes a good, clear set of notes. Recording the lecture and then having a hearing person transcribe it is very time-consuming and requires trained staff. It is, however, a system that is used occasionally. The use of a notetaker to go into the lecture with the hearing-impaired student specifically to take notes is not generally done in England.

Technical aids are used by many support services. Some college rooms have the inductance loop system installed. The most commonly used aid, however, is the radio aid. This helps to overcome the problem of distance when using a hearing aid, that is, the further away the speaker, the lower the volume of sound entering the hearing aid. It also helps to cut out much of the extraneous noise.

In addition to help with coursework, the hearing-impaired student may also require help in adjusting to studying and to working in a hearing community. Personal problems may arise, problems that a hearing student can discuss easily with friends or lecturers, but that the hearing-impaired student can discuss only after finding someone with whom to communicate. Most services will offer this form of support.

The level of support available to hearing-impaired students, however, varies greatly over the country as a whole. In some areas there is a wealth of support, in others very little or none at all. In some areas residential provisions are available. Some colleges offer special courses, but the number is relatively small. In country areas there may not be enough hearing-impaired students to justify financing the establishment of a support service. Elsewhere, the difficult financial situation may mean that a Local Education Authority has to establish priority areas, and a support service for hearing-impaired persons may not be one of them. The present provisions, although much better than 20 or even 10 years ago, are still diverse.

The demand from hearing-impaired young people for further education is growing and will continue to grow, but numbers are still relatively small. A full range of provisions in every local authority is not viable, but legislation is needed to ensure that the variety of provisions that are available nationally would be available to all hearing-impaired students. Suitable placement would not then depend upon where a student lived. The national system, although locally administered, needs to be nationally planned in order to ensure that each hearing-impaired student has access to an appropriate form of further education.

NATIONAL STUDY GROUP

The National Study Group on Further and Higher Education for the Hearing Impaired was formed in 1976 to bring together all those interested in or working in the field of further and higher education for hearing-impaired students. It seeks to promote the exchange of views and experiences of those working in this field, to monitor attitudes and considerations for public examinations taken by hearing-impaired individuals, and to improve the facilities and opportunities in further and higher education for them. Such an organization was called for, due to the relative isolation of those working with hearing-impaired persons in further education. It is still a young organization, but it has produced a number of publications relating to various aspects of the work with hearing-impaired people in further education, has held several one-day conferences, and has become accepted as an organization to which parents, students, and lecturers can turn for advice.

Bibliography

Department of Education and Science: *The Legal Basis of Further Education*, 1981.

Grant, A. C.: *The Further Education of the Hearing Impaired: Some Problems and Issues*, University of Sheffield, 1979.

Hatton, J., and D. Langley: *Post–6 Education for the Hearing Impaired*, paper given at the International Congress on Education of the Deaf, Hamburg, 1980.

Kell, M. D.: "Further Education for the Hearing Impaired," *Teacher of the Deaf*, 4:130–136, 1980.

National Bureau for Handicapped Students: *The Hearing Impaired Student in Tertiary Education*, 1977.

National Deaf Childrens Society: *After School: A Parents Guide to Further Education for Hearing Impaired Students*, 1982.

National Study Group on Further and Higher Education for the Hearing Impaired, Royal School for the Deaf, Derby.

John Hatton

L'EPÉE, ABBÉ CHARLES MICHEL DE
(1712–1789)

Charles Michel de l'Epée was born in Versailles, France, on November 24, 1712, the son of Françoise Marguerite (Varignon) and Charles François l'Epée, "regular surveyor of the king's buildings." The house where he was born was located at the corner of Bourbon and Clagny streets, the latter now named for the Abbé de l'Epée.

In 1729 and 1730 l'Epée attained the first degrees of the Catholic priesthood. A believer in the doctrines of Jansenism, which stressed moral determinism, he refused to adhere to the more orthodox view of the diocese of Paris. Consequently, his career within the church was hindered until he was befriended by Jacques Bénigne Bossuet, Bishop of Troyes. With Bossuet's patronage, l'Epée continued

Bust of the Abbé de l'Epée by Louis Auvray (1852), at the Insitut National, Paris.

his studies, becoming a priest in 1738, serving the church of Feuges, near Troyes.

His difficulties with the Catholic hierarchy were not over, however. In 1743, after the death of his benefactor, l'Epée was subjected to the censure of Christhophe de Beaumont, Archbishop of Paris, and was banned from preaching because of his friendship with a Jansenist bishop of Senez.

Now a frustrated cleric, l'Epée made a chance encounter that changed his life and the education of deaf persons. Called on business to a house on Fossés-Saint-Victor, he noticed young twin girls absorbed by their sewing work. When their mother revealed that they were deaf and mute, he was deeply disturbed. He learned that their private tutor was teaching them by means of pictures. Unassigned to specific clerical duties because of his theological beliefs, l'Epée decided to try to save the souls of those persons who were excluded from a faith transmitted by the sense of hearing. He believed that adherence of the soul to religion was not dependent upon the sense of hearing or the mastery of language. For his deaf students, signs would convey ideas.

To achieve his goals, l'Epée founded the first free public educational institution for deaf people in 1771. The school was located in his father's house on Moulins Street in Paris, and the family fortune initially paid its expenses. By comparison, Samuel Heinicke did not open the public "oralist" institution of Leipzig until 1778, with the financing of Frederick Augustus, Elector of Saxony. *See* HEINICKE, SAMUEL.

Eventually, three pensions (residential schools) for deaf girls and one for deaf boys were set up. Avoiding the private tutor-student relationship common among oral teachers, l'Epée taught 30 students with signs in 1771, 68 in 1783, 72 in 1785, and more than 100 in 1789.

Also in contrast to oral tutors of the eighteenth century, l'Epée did not keep his methods secret. He presented his students in public exercises in 1771, 1772, 1773, and 1774. In 1776 he published "The Instruction of Deaf and Mute Persons Using Methodical Signs; a Work Which Contains the Plan of a Universal Language Mediated by Natural Signs and Arranged According to a System," and in 1784 "The Correct Method of Instructing Deaf and Mute Persons Confirmed by Broad Experience." Shortly before his death, he also compiled a dictionary of signs.

In spite of writing an articulation manual, he perceived the learning of speech as a task which was tedious and very boring, purely mechanical, and unrewarding. Furthermore, he insisted that speech teaching did not require great talent, merely patience. He believed that teaching speech to deaf people "in a class of parrots" held them back from learning, because loosening a person's tongue nevertheless left the mind "in profound darkness."

At the start of his teachings, l'Epée used a fingerspelling alphabet for two hands. Later, he preferred the one-handed alphabet of Juan Pablo-Bonet, published in 1620 in Spain. *See* PABLO-BONET, JUAN; SIGNS: Fingerspelling.

L'Epée communicated with his students in an invented system he termed methodical signs, knowing nothing about indigenous Parisian Sign Language. Apparently such did exist, for in 1779 in "Observations of a Deaf Man on an Elementary Course of Education of Deaf and Mute Persons" the deaf writer Pierre Desloges affirmed: "We express ourselves on all subjects with as much accuracy and speed as if we enjoyed the faculties of speech and hearing." Desloges was referring to a natural language of signs that already existed when l'Epée began teaching, but l'Epée started off with an incomplete language, the language of children, and ignored that of deaf adults. *See* DESLOGES, PIERRE; SIGN LANGUAGES.

L'Epée believed that his iconic signs formed a natural and universal language that could express everything. His contemporary, the encyclopedist Denis Diderot, argued that at their inception oral languages could be only a "confused mixture of cries and gestures." Thus l'Epée's beliefs fit the intellectual climate of Enlightenment France. Ideas, he believed, exist before language, which is a representation of an analyzed thought broken down into successive elements. L'Epée thought he could develop a language in which the lexicon would be gestural and the syntax French. Certain signs were natural: to eat, drink, sleep, carry. Signs for ideas, however, were analytical. At times l'Epée broke down signs according to their etymology: "unintelligibility," for example, consisted of five signs, for interior, reading, possibility, abstract quality, and negation. Neither word nor sign, l'Epée thought, existed without an idea, and when the immediate meaning was lacking, one looked for the primitive roots from which the particular language derived.

For l'Epée it was necessary to learn the language completely or not at all. Since he wished his deaf students to learn French and other languages, he invented grammatical signs: the hand "at the hat" is masculine, while the hand "at the ear where the coiffure of a woman ends" is feminine; one finger is for singular, many for plural; the article is an articulation, the hooking of the index of the index finger; the adjective referring to the noun is the right hand, which one directs toward and lays on the left hand; for verbs, the past tenses are distinguished by the number of taps on the shoulder; the subjunctive mood is identified with the conjunction *que*, a double hooking of the index fingers; the imperative is the double command of the eyes and the hand; the active voice becomes the action of carrying a baby in one's arms. *See* SIGN LANGUAGES: French.

L'Epée advocated the learning of his system of signs by hearing people throughout the world within academies, which assured the spreading of his work, and he and his students were soon discovered by a curious Europe. In 1777 they were visited by the emperor of Germany, Joseph II, the brother of the French queen, Marie Antoinette. In 1780 Empress Catherine II offered sumptuous gifts to l'Epée if he would come to Russia. These he rejected, preferring to develop successors abroad. Disciples who would open similar schools visited him. They came from Vienna, Rome, Spain, Mainz, Holland, Zurich, and many cities in France.

L'Epée's decision to dedicate himself to teaching deaf children marked a radical departure in the history of deaf education. Unlike his predecessors, l'Epée was not interested in making a profit from or monopolizing his teaching techniques. The school he opened was public and free. He willingly trained others in his methods, and this factor set l'Epée apart.

He was the first teacher to insist upon the importance of sign language, rather than speech, as the most important tool for reaching the minds of deaf pupils. The long-continuing debate between proponents of speech and advocates of signs began when l'Epée and his rival Heinicke exchanged a series of letters arguing the merits of each approach. Moreover, l'Epée established a sign-language, or manual, tradition in the Paris Institution for the Deaf that would later be carried to the United States by Thomas Hopkins Gallaudet and Laurent Clerc, the individuals who founded the first permanent school for deaf people in the United States. *See* CLERC, LAURENT; GALLAUDET, THOMAS HOPKINS; HISTORY: Sign Language Controversy.

After his death on December 23, 1789, at the family home on Moulins Street, l'Epée was buried in the family chapel of the church of Saint-Roch, where he used to say mass with the friendly connivance of the parish priest.

Bibliography

Alard, Jean: *Controverse entre l'Abbé de l'Epée et Samuel Heinicke au sujet de la véritable manière d'instruire les sourds muets traduite en latin, et l'etat actuel de la question*, G. Pelluard, Paris, 1881.

Arnaud, Calixte: *l'Abbé de l'Epée et son oeuvre*, Imprimerie d'ouvriers sourds-muets, Paris, 1900.

Bélanger, Adolphe: *Etude bibliographique et iconographique sur l'Abbé de l'Epée*, G. Pelluard, Paris, 1886.

Berthier, Ferdinand: *L'Abbé de l'Epée, sa vie, son apostolat, ses tableaux, sa lutte et ses succès avec l'historique des monuments élevés à sa mémoire à Paris et à Versailles*, Michel Levy Frères, Paris, 1852.

Desloges, Pierre: *Observations d'un sourd-muet, sur un cours élémentaire d'éducation des sourds et muets, publié* en 1779 par m. l'Abbé Deschamps, chapelain de l'eglise d'Orléans, B. Morin, Amsterdam, 1779.

Diderot, Denis: *Lettre sur les sourds-muets, à l'usage de ceux qui entendent et qui parlent*, vol. 10, p. 241, Amsterdam, 1751.

L'Epée, Abbé Charles-Michel de: *Instruction des sourds et muets par la voie des signes methodiques, ouvrage qui contient le projet d'une langue universelle. Par l'entremise des signes naturels assujettis à une méthode*, Nyon l'Aîné, Paris, 1776.

————: *La véritable manigère d'instruire les sourds et muets confirmée par une longue expérience*, Nyon l'Aîné, Paris, 1784. [Dictionary of signs, undated manuscript.]

Valade-Gable, P. A.: *L'Abbé de l'Epée à Villereau, ouvrage inédit publié par Emile Mercier, président de l'Association Amicale des Sourds Muets de la Champagne*, Cercle de l'Abbé de l'Epée, Reims, 1903.

René Bernard

F

FABRAY, NANETTE
(1920–   )

If a poll were taken to name the person from the entertainment world who achieved the greatest success despite a hearing impairment, the name of Nanette Fabray would probably lead the rest. She not only won fame on stage, screen, and television but also earned numerous awards for her work with deaf and disabled people.

Nanette Fabray (born Ruby Nanette Fabares) made her debut in vaudeville at the age of four. Known as "Baby Nanette," she had a featured role in the popular *Our Gang Comedy* series on stage and screen. During her early teens, she developed a hearing impairment that was diagnosed as otosclerosis. Although she successfully masked her hearing loss, Fabray was to suffer emotionally as well as physically from its recurrent effects during her entire career. She remarked that it wrecked her first marriage, and throughout her life she experienced "a constant droning" in her ears. *See* EAR: Pathology.

The experience she gained while performing in vaudeville proved most valuable. She developed a versatile repertoire that included song, dance, and acting. Her first screen achievements came in her late teens when she appeared in various Hollywood productions. Among her film credits were: *Elizabeth and Essex* (1939), with Bette Davis and Errol Flynn; *A Child is Born* (1940), with Geraldine Fitzgerald and Jeffrey Lynn; the highly successful musical *The Band Wagon* (1953), costarring Fred Astaire and Cyd Charisse; *Happy Ending* (1969), with

John Forsythe and Jean Simmons; and *Harper Valley PTA* (1978), in which she costarred with Barbara Eden.

Harper Valley PTA was so successful when later released on national television that it became a

Nanette Fabray. (Public Information Office, NTID, Rochester, New York)

popular comedy serial. Unfortunately, Fabray could not continue her television role. While filming an episode in which she kidnaps a live elephant, she was accidentally attacked by the circus animal and suffered a concussion which affected her sense of balance for several years afterward. But this, along with the death in 1973 of her second husband, screenwriter and producer Ranald MacDougall, and four major operations at various times to restore her hearing to seminormalcy, did not end her career.

Fabray went on to make comebacks and breakthroughs time and again in the entertainment world. During World War II, she performed on Broadway in the musical comedy *Jackpot* (1944). As "Sally Madison" in this play, she danced and sang her way to win the hearts of a corps of Marines while selling U.S. War Bonds. In 1949 she won her first Tony Award for Best Actress in the musical comedy *Love Life*. In 1962 she was cast as "Nel Henderson," the First Lady, opposite Robert Ryan ("President Henderson") in the Irving Berlin–Howard Lindsay–Russell Crouse musical, *Mr. President*, which was directed by Joshua Logan and ran for almost a year. It earned her another Tony Award as Best Actress in a musical play.

However, Nanette Fabray may best be remembered for her song and dance acts, plus comic sketches, on television. She was Sid Caesar's partner as "Ann Victor" in the primetime television comedy series *Caesar's Hour* from 1954 to 1957. As the replacement for Imogene Coca, Fabray more than held her own with this "Saturday Night Live" version of comic skits, parodies of films and movie stars, and song and dance acts. In 1956 she won an Emmy Award as Best Supporting Actress in this show, as well as another Emmy for Best TV Comedienne of the year. In 1957 she earned a third Emmy for Best Comedienne in a Continuing Performance.

During the 1950s Nanette Fabray was much in demand. She was a popular guest star on the *Chevy Show* with hostess Dinah Shore. She also appeared often on the *Chevrolet Tele-Theatre*, a big-budget live dramatic series that presented an original play or adaptation weekly and featured some of the greatest stars of stage and screen.

As television matured and offered broader entertainment, including soap operas and quiz games, Fabray was a welcome guest and talented contributor. She appeared in *Love, American Style* in the 1970s, in the *Hollywood Squares* quiz game show, and in the *Love Boat* situation comedy series; and she played the role of "Grandma Romano" in the long-running series *One Day at a Time* during the 1970s and 1980s.

Fabray married screenwriter Ranald MacDougall in 1957. In time, MacDougall turned to directing and producing, as well as writing, many movies made for television. Among those in which Fabray played a feature role were: *Fame Is the Name of the Game* (1966), *But I Don't Want To Get Married* (1970), and *Magic Carpet* (1972). She also had the lead rold as "Nan McGovern" in *Westinghouse Playhouse Starring Nanette Fabray and Wendell Corey* (1961), which was written and directed by MacDougall and was based somewhat on Fabray's life story.

These appearances as one of the leading comedians of stage, screen, and television led to many friendships among her admirers and colleagues in the entertainment world. This was to become an advantage to her crusade in the service of deaf individuals, when she began to take an active role later in her career in the education and welfare of deaf and hearing-impaired persons.

Fabray was the first person to sing and sign a song on a primetime television show. She was invited to do so on the *Carol Burnett Comedy Hour* by her good friend Carol Burnett. Fabray's performance greatly helped to bring deaf awareness to television viewers, as did her role as hostess for the NBC-TV special *Experiment in Television* (1967), which spotlighted the National Theatre of the Deaf when this professional acting company was first formed and presented to the mass audience. Her presence and contribution helped to give credibility and visibility to the National Theatre of the Deaf and its objectives. *See* NATIONAL THEATERS OF THE DEAF: United States.

It was not long afterward that Fabray branched out to take an active and supportive role in furthering the education and welfare of deaf children and adults. A strong advocate of the deaf child's right to communicate by "doing what comes naturally," she championed the use of sign language and total communication in schools and educational programs for deaf children. To reinforce her beliefs, she starred in the Walt Disney film production *Amy* (1981), in which she was the head teacher "Malvina" who communicates by signs and fingerspelling, and who takes every opportunity to persuade the school's board of directors that this is the deaf child's natural mode of expression. *See* SOCIOLINGUISTICS: Total Communication.

Fabray also served on various advisory boards at the national and state level that deal with the needs of deaf and hearing-impaired consumers, such as closed captioned television programming, hearing aids, speech therapy, and both educational and research programs from kindergarten through college-age levels. For her dedicated efforts, she was given the Distinguished Service Award by President Nixon, the Eleanor Roosevelt Humanitarian Award, the Public Service Award from the American Academy of Otolaryngology, and the first Cogswell Award from Gallaudet College, which recognizes a lay person who has provided inspiration and valuable services on behalf of deaf people. From Gallaudet College, she also received an honorary doctor of humane letters degree, and from Western Maryland College an honorary doctor of fine arts degree. She served on the U.S. Office of Education's National Advisory Committee on Education of the Deaf for many years, in the National Captioning Institute, in the National Technical Institute for the Deaf, on the President's Committee on Employment of the Handicapped, and in the ·Better Speech and Hearing Institute. *See* GALLAUDET COLLEGE; NATIONAL TECHNICAL INSTITUTE FOR THE DEAF.

Fabray won the love and admiration of deaf and hearing-impaired people of all ages for her courageous battle against disability and for her equally courageous stand in support of better-quality-of-life programs in health, education, and welfare in all disabled persons.

Bibliography

Brooks, Tim, and Earle Marsh: *The Complete Directory to Prime Time Network TV Shows*, Ballantyne Books, New York, 1981.

Craig, Lissa: "Nanette Fabray," *NTID Focus*, Winter 1979.

Fehl, Fred: *On Broadway* (text by William and Jane Stott), University of Texas Press, Austin, 1978.

Fireman, Judy (ed.): *TV Book: The Ultimate Television Book*, Workman Publishing, New York, 1977.

Kaplan, Mike (ed.): *Variety Presents: The Complete Book of Show Business Awards*, Garland Publishing, New York, 1985.

Maax, Kenneth: *Star Stats: Who's Who in Hollywood*, Price/Stern/Sloan Publishers, Los Angeles, 1979.

Marill, Alvin H.: *Movies Made for Television*, Da Capo Press, New York, 1980.

NTID Advisory Group: *Directory of Board Members* (brochure), Rochester, New York, 1984.

Robert Panara

FAIRMOUNT THEATRE OF THE DEAF

In 1975 Brian Kilpatrick, a deaf actor, and Charles St. Clair, a hearing actor, founded the Fairmount Theatre of the Deaf as the first resident professional sign language and voice theater. This experiment in bilingual and bicultural entertainment has produced a wealth of theater works for deaf and hearing audiences in Cleveland, Ohio, as well as nationally.

PROGRAMS AND MANAGEMENT

Initially, the Fairmount Theatre of the Deaf was sponsored by the Fairmount Theatre Center, becoming an independent nonprofit tax-exempt organization in 1979. By then, the Fairmount Theatre of the Deaf had developed all of its major programs, including: (1) Mainstage productions: each season it presented three to five plays, each play running for three to four weeks, five to seven performances per week; (2) Morning matinee series: once or twice a week, visiting school students were provided with a morning performance of a mainstage play followed by a special discussion program; (3) Touring productions: mainstage plays and one-act plays were toured to several states, as well as to the Lincoln Center in New York City and the International Pantomime Festival in Czechoslovakia; (4) Arts-in-schools and young audience programs: 30–45 minute theater pieces were presented in schools throughout Cleveland to develop better understanding of deaf people and theater; and (5) Theatre school: evening classes were offered to the deaf and hearing community in American Sign Language and on various theater topics. *See* SIGN LANGUAGES: American.

In early years, the Fairmount Theatre of the Deaf was located in a library building that had been converted into offices, rehearsal space, costume and scene shops, and an 80-seat theater. In 1981 the Fairmount Theatre began staging its performances at the 160-seat Brooks Theatre of the Cleveland Playhouse, one of the oldest regional theaters in the United States. Administrative offices are located at the Cleveland Hearing and Speech Center.

The Fairmount Theatre of the Deaf has been supported primarily by a large board of trustees and by grants from numerous Cleveland and Ohio foundations and corporations, the National Endowment for the Arts, the National Committee, Arts for the Handicapped, and many other patrons. While the board and most of the administrative and technical staff of the Fairmount Theatre are hearing, about half of the acting company is deaf.

INNOVATIVE THEATRE PROGRAM

Besides being the first resident professional sign language and voice theater, the Fairmount Theatre of the Deaf is responsible for several other innovations.

First, it has created more than a dozen original full-length theater pieces. Early works dealt with deaf-hearing intercultural conflicts: *With These Hands* explored the struggle of a deaf theater artist in a hearing world; the musical *Alice in Deafinity* adapted Lewis Carroll's *Alice in Wonderland* into a vehicle about deafness; *Law of Silence* showed the oppression of deaf people in medieval times; *Silent Movie* chronicled the life of Albert Ballin, a deaf leader of the 1920s who proposed that sign language be substituted for title cards in silent films; and *Derrick* was modeled after the Donald Lang case, which involved a deaf lawyer's efforts to defend his deaf client.

More recent original works have involved innovative concepts of sign language and voice theater itself: Molière's *The Miser* was adapted into a wild-west comedy; Bram Stoker's novel *Dracula* was adapted for deaf theater; and a newer work, *Circus of Signs*, which won the Cleveland Critics Circle Award as best original play, made creative use of American Sign Language in a circus format.

A second innovative approach involved the Fairmount Theatre of the Deaf's strong bilingual focus. In addition to its original works, the theater staged bilingual versions of a wide variety of plays, including Tennessee Williams's *The Glass Menagerie*, Samuel Beckett's *Waiting for Godot*, Molière's *The Doctor in Spite of Himself*, and Neil Simon's *The Odd Couple*. In most of these plays, the individual characters were created through a collaboration between a deaf or hearing signing actor and a hearing voicing actor. The result was a nearly seamless union of two performers as one character.

The Fairmount Theatre's bilingual focus also applied to its audiences as the theater "opened a world of drama to the hearing impaired while also adding a new dimension to the theatrical experience of the hearing audience." The theater recruited previously inexperienced deaf people as patrons and supporters by using reduced ticket prices, special sold-out theater parties sponsored by deaf organizations, and afterplay discussion programs. At the same time, the Fairmount Theatre became a respected member of the Cleveland hearing theater community, and its plays were regularly reviewed by major newspaper and radio critics.

The Fairmount Theatre of the Deaf's third innovative approach involved the use of a professional translator who prepared scripts in both American Sign Language and English prior to the beginning of rehearsal. Not only did this permit the actors to spend more time developing their characters, but it also allowed the translator to create a more coherent play and to experiment in American Sign Language artistry. For example, in Arthur Schnitzler's *La Ronde*, 10 different levels of American Sign Language were created, ranging from the gutter language of a prostitute to the refined prose of a count. Edward Albee's *Seascape* required special three-fingered sign language for its lizard characters. For Paul Sills's *Story Theatre* and other musical and poetic works, special "rhyming" signs were incorporated into the translation. *See* SIGNS: Artistic.

As a fourth innovation, the Fairmount Theatre of the Deaf collaborated with WVIZ-TV in Cleveland to disseminate several productions. Three major programs, *With These Hands*, *Beauty and the Beast*, and *The Miser* (the latter two were nationally broadcast) won a total of five Emmy Awards.

THEATRE OF OPPORTUNITY

The Fairmount Theatre of the Deaf has provided professional opportunities for many deaf theater artists, including Don Bangs, Tony Benvenuto, Adrian Blue, Brian and Jacqueline Kilpatrick, Gregory Koppel, Susan Jackson, and Debbie Rennie. In describing his goals for the Fairmount Theatre, Brian Kilpatrick explained: "I wanted to show them the deaf can do theatre, art, and dancing . . . I wanted to say, "Look, we can do it. Just give us the opportunity.' "

Donald Bangs

FAMILY DYNAMICS

Family dynamics is the ongoing and ever-changing interaction among members of the family. The family is one of the most important units in society. Through the family, new members are brought into an ongoing society, learn the norms and values of that society, and become contributing members of the society. Family dynamics traditionally has been viewed from the psychological perspective, with the focus on the strengths and weaknesses each individual brings to the situation. The sociological perspective on family dynamics entails a broader meaning.

SOCIOLOGICAL PERSPECTIVE

The sociological perspective attempts to apply large-scale events in society to the more personal situations of individuals. This process has been referred to as the sociological imagination by C. Wright Mills, who stressed that neither the individual nor society could be understood without understanding both together. Thus, the sociological perspective helps show the interconnection between the self and the social world, between what happens to an individual and the social forces surrounding that individual.

FAMILY GROUPS

During their lifetimes, most persons are members of two family groups. The first is the family into which they are born and in which they grow up. This is called the family of orientation. The second is the family they help to establish as adults. This is called the family of procreation. It is particularly important to be aware of these two family groups when talking about deaf persons, because their family of orientation usually differs in important ways from the family of procreation.

Family of Orientation Most deaf people have hearing parents. Census figures since 1910 consistently indicate that over 90% of the deaf children born in the United States have hearing parents. With nine out of ten parents lacking personal experience with deafness, the majority of parents are not prepared for the diagnosis of deafness in their children. Some studies have indicated that the reaction of such parents to a deaf child is essentially negative. *See* DEAF POPULATION: Demography.

Families with hearing parents and deaf children tend to be larger than both families within the general population and families that include deaf adults. There appears to be no relationship between birth order of the deaf child and the pattern of births within families. In one study of the parents of children with one of five disabilities, including deafness, it was found that one-third of the disabled children were first-born children, one third were second-born, and one third were third- or fourth-born. In addition, the divorce rate is no higher among hearing parents with deaf children than among comparison families without deaf children. There is evidence, however, that where conflict exists between the hearing parents of a deaf child, the deaf child and his or her needs often become the issues underlying the conflicts.

Family of Procreation Although most deaf children are born into hearing families, when they become adults they tend to marry other deaf persons. Over 80 percent of the deaf adults in the United States have a deaf spouse. However, a smaller proportion of deaf persons than persons in the general population marry, and deaf persons marry at an older age. This is especially true for deaf males, who either marry at older ages or are more likely to remain single than are deaf females.

While most hearing parents are unprepared for the diagnosis of deafness in their children, deaf parents seem to expect the diagnosis and to accept it more readily. It should be noted, however, that of the children born to deaf parents, 88 percent have normal hearing. Even when both parents were born deaf, 81 percent of their children can be expected to have normal hearing. While hearing women with a deaf child tend to have more births than women in the general population, deaf women tend to have fewer births than women in the general population. Finally, the divorce rate among deaf women is higher than among hearing women. *See* HEARING LOSS: Genetic Causes.

SOCIOLOGICAL CHARACTERISTICS OF THE COMMUNITY

Although deaf parents are more likely to expect and accept a diagnosis of deafness in their child than are hearing parents, no one is ever fully prepared to be the parent of a disabled child. The accessibility and type of help available to parents have sociological implications that will influence the family dynamics. Nearly 30 percent of the adult deaf population in the United States was born in a rural area. These families may find few diagnostic and therapeutic services available to them. Even if the services are within range, the regular commuting that may be necessary to receive these services may make the process progressively wearing.

Even when the services may be readily available, as in most metropolitan areas, the sociological characteristics of the entire organizational structure of clinics and agencies operate to the advantage of certain children and their parents and to the disadvantage of others. For example, the child may be considered too young or too old, too severely disabled or not enough disabled, too bright or too retarded, at an income level too high or not high enough, to qualify for services. While parents may have comparatively little difficulty obtaining a diagnosis of disability, though deafness is not always diagnosed as soon as it should be, they are likely to encounter major problems obtaining therapeutic services. Depending on what is available within their area, parents may discover that their local school system does not have a program that can accommodate their child. The parents must then decide whether to place their child in a residential school away from home, to send their child to an out-of-state program, or to compromise what they want for their child with what is available. Once the decision has been made to place the child in a particular program, there is still the issue of the length of stay within the special classes and the inevitable time when the child outgrows the program. This process may be further compounded by the conflicting advice parents receive from the professionals they turn to for help. Each professional will present a particular point of view depending on area of expertise (medicine, audiology, education) and the orientation of the training received. *See* EDUCATIONAL PROGRAMS.

SOCIOLOGICAL CHARACTERISTICS OF THE FAMILY
The following factors are among those that contribute to the sociological dynamics of family interaction: the age at onset and the severity of the child's deafness; the income levels of the family; the educational setting of the deaf child; and the hearing status of the parents. Although each of these factors will be considered separately, they are interdependent.

Age at Onset and Degree of Hearing Loss The age at onset and the severity of the child's deafness are directly related to language development, the ability to speechread, and the quality of the deaf child's speech. Two useful categories for considering the influence of a hearing loss on individuals and their families are prelingual and postlingual deafness.

Postlingual deafness refers to those individuals who were born hearing and became deaf after they had acquired language. They tend to have better spoken language skills and speech than individuals born deaf.

Hearing and hard-of-hearing individuals tend to be better speechreaders than individuals with a severe hearing loss, because the former frequently have a good understanding of the spoken language and consequently know what to look for on the lips. Since speech and speechreading are the most commonly used modes of communication between deaf children and their hearing parents, the communication process will be less frustrating for those who lose their hearing after they have developed oral language skills and for those with a mild hearing loss because they are more likely to have better speechreading skills. There is also a major relationship between the extent of hearing loss and intelligibility of speech. The intelligibility declines as the severity of the loss increases, with an abrupt decline for those with a 70-decibel or greater loss. *See* SPEECH; SPEECHREADING.

Thus the age at onset and degree of hearing loss can have a profound impact on the sociological dynamics of family interaction. To the extent that families place a high value on spoken language skills, intelligible speech, and academic achievement, early onset of profound deafness may increase tension among members of the family.

Income It is well known that level of education and income are related. As a group, the hearing fathers of deaf children tend to be less well educated than the general population. Hearing mothers, however, tend to be slightly better educated. As a group, deaf adult males also tend to be less well educated than the general population, while deaf adult females tend to attain educational levels similar to the general population. According to the National Census of the Deaf Population, the median income for deaf individuals was 72 percent of that for individuals in the general population. Although fewer hearing mothers of deaf children work outside the home than in the general population, over one-third of hearing-impaired children do have working mothers. The smaller number of working mothers can be explained at least in part by the extra demands and special attention required by their hearing-impaired children. These same demands become a consideration for working mothers in terms of the amount of time they have to devote to their hearing-impaired child's school activities and the need for afterschool child care facilities. Overall, whether or not both parents are employed, hearing parents of deaf children are disproportionately represented in the lower income categories. *See* DEAF POPULATION: Socioeconomic Status.

Income is also associated with a number of other sociological characteristics of family dynamics. As family income increases, the proportion of deaf students who are members of an ethnic minority rapidly decreases. Of those deaf students who were either black or Hispanic, 79 percent were from families earning less than the median income in 1977. The proportion of deaf students who attend a preschool increases as family income increases. Also, as family income increases, there is a general decline in the proportion of deaf students in residential and day school programs and an increase in the proportion of deaf students enrolled in special education classes. Deaf students from higher-income families tend to use hearing aids more frequently than deaf students from lower-income families at home and in school.

The use of speech in parent-child interactions increases as income increases. The use of signs and fingerspelling remains essentially the same across income levels. Teacher-classroom interaction also increases as family income level increases. In teacher-student communication, speech is used more often with students from higher-income families. The proportion of students whose speech is rated intelligible or very intelligible also increases with family income. In addition, higher family income tends to be associated with better academic achievement.

Educational Setting Turning to the educational setting of the deaf child, the interrelatedness of the four factors (age at onset and severity of deafness, income, educational setting, and parents' hearing status) becomes more evident. Although the educational settings can be subdivided into several categories, they can be grouped into two major types, residential schools and nonresidential programs located within schools for hearing children. The obvious consequences of these two types for the sociological characteristics of family dynamics concern whether the child lives at home with the family or in a dormitory separated from the family unit, and the fact that in day classes deaf children constitute a minority group whereas in state residential schools the entire student population, as well as much of the staff, is deaf.

The literature on child development and socialization universally emphasizes the importance of the family. The role of the family and school are somewhat more complex for deaf children. Because of the special communication needs resulting from a hearing loss and the fact that most deaf children are born into hearing families that lack deaf role models, the consequences of living apart from the family in a dormitory may be somewhat ameliorated by homelike settings and the widespread use of manual communication. The importance of interaction between school and families has been demonstrated in studies focusing on a number of dimensions, including self-image, maturity, independence, and adjustment to deafness, in which the residential students with hearing parents scored or were rated lower than residential students with deaf parents on almost all of the comparisons.

Although studies have been conducted on the effects of being a member of a minority group based on sex or race, little systematic information has been gathered on the consequences of being a member of a minority group based on hearing loss within a regular school system. What information is available shows mixed results. While the extent of being accepted by the majority (hearing students) is associated with oral (speech and speechreading) skills, nearly all hearing-impaired adolescents in nonresidential programs expressed a feeling of isolation and loneliness seldom experienced by their counterparts in residential programs.

While nearly two-thirds of the children in residential schools are profoundly deaf, only 18% of those in nonresidential programs have a profound hearing loss. It is clear that as the severity of the hearing loss increases, the proportion enrolled in nonresidential or mainstream programs rapidly declines. The Annual Survey of Hearing Impaired Children and Youth found that while 82 percent of those students with a hearing loss of less than 27 decibels (considered to be within the normal range of hearing) in the better ear were in nonresidential programs, only 8 percent of those with a profound hearing loss in the better ear were in this type of program. It has also been determined that nonresidential programs enroll two to three times as many postlingually deaf children as do state residential programs. And finally, nonresidential programs enroll the highest proportion of children from high-income families and the lowest proportion from very low-income families.

Hearing Status of Parents   The hearing status of the parents has a number of implications when considering the sociological chracteristics of family dynamics. Three that have frequently been discussed relate to the parents' attitudes about deafness, both initial response to the diagnosis and their feelings about the child later on; knowledge of and attitudes toward manual communication during the early years of the deaf child; and differences in social and economic resources.

As noted above, census figures since 1910 consistently indicate that over 90 percent of the deaf children born in the United States have hearing parents. Hearing parents are much more likely than deaf parents to experience a long period of uncertainty about the precise nature of their child's difficulty. When the diagnosis is eventually made, hearing parents often experience shock, guilt, and grief. In addition, they may feel overwhelmed with

prescriptions for necessary auditory, speech, language, and speechreading training. Hearing parents may also place greater value on verbal skills than do deaf parents. These are the very skills most difficult for the deaf child to acquire. There is evidence that the gap between hearing parents' aspirations for their child and the deaf child's ability to perform in accordance with those expectations results in a lower self-image for the child.

In contrast, deaf parents almost never experience the debilitating effects of the diagnostic delay common to hearing parents. Although deaf parents may express a desire that their children be hearing, they adjust quickly to having a deaf child. They feel prepared to communicate with their deaf child and to help the child cope with deafness. One important advantage that deaf parents have over hearing parents is that they have a world in which they can imagine their deaf child will someday live. Not only may hearing parents be unaware of what is available for their deaf child, but when they do find out they may fear that their child may choose to live in an exclusively "deaf world." This fear is likely to be particularly evident when their deaf child reaches adolescence. During this period hearing parents are again reminded that their deaf children must make career choices and that they will soon be leaving home and establishing a family of their own. For many hearing parents this raises anew the whole question of "normalcy" for their children, the likelihood that their children will marry a deaf spouse, and the possibility of having deaf grandchildren.

Although there has been a steady increase in the number of hearing parents who are learning to communicate with their deaf children by using some form of manual communication, it is still the case that most deaf parents must intentionally learn sign language and fingerspelling and frequently do not learn it or use it until their children reach adolescence. Considerable evidence demonstrates that higher reading scores as well as written language scores are achieved by children with early manual communication. Other evidence shows that over four times as many deaf children with deaf parents go to college as compared to deaf children with hearing parents.

When the social, educational, and economic resources available to deaf and hearing parents are examined, it is clear that deaf parents lag behind hearing parents and may in fact be falling farther behind. Not only do studies of the educational achievement of deaf and hearing students generally report that deaf students compare unfavorably with their hearing peers, but there is evidence that the position of deaf people compared to the general population of the United States is less favorable now than earlier in the twentieth century. Likewise, it appears that the employment rate of deaf persons may have declined relative to their hearing counterparts. Although there has been a slight increase in the number of deaf persons in professional occupations since 1950, deaf persons are still overrepresented in skilled, semiskilled, or unskilled occupations, and underrepresented in professional and administrative positions. It is not surprising, therefore, that the incomes of employed deaf persons have not kept up with the general income increases enjoyed by the general population. If this trend continues, households headed by deaf adults will be disproportionately represented in the lower socioeconomic classes with fewer material resources to meet family needs.

SOCIOLOGICAL IMPLICATIONS

It is clear that deafness influences the family and family dynamics. However, no single perspective can hope to bring full understanding of all these influences. The sociological perspective is an attempt to look beyond the effects of deafness on the individual and to relate it to large-scale events in society. In addition to an individual's particular strengths and weaknesses, sociological factors such as race, age at onset, degree of hearing loss, availability of services, and socioeconomic and hearing status of parents have important implications relative to the child's ability to fulfill parental goals. By focusing on the sociological characteristics that influence family dynamics, it is possible to understand better the far-reaching implications of deafness as reflected in family interaction.

Bibliography

Barsch, Ray H.: *The Parent of the Handicapped Child*, Charles C. Thomas, Springfield, Illinois, 1968.

Christiansen, John B.: "The Socioeconomic Status of the Deaf Population: A Review of the Literature," in John B. Christiansen and Judy Egelston-Dodd (eds.), *Social Aspects of Deafness*, vol. 4: *Socioeconomic Status of the Deaf Population*, Department of Sociology and Social Work, Gallaudet College, Washington, D.C., 1982.

Henslin, James M.: *Introducing Sociology*, Free Press, New York, 1975.

Jensema, Carl J.: *The Relationship Between Academic Achievement and the Demographic Characteristics of Hearing Impaired Children and Youth*, Ser. R, No. 2, Gallaudet College, Office of Demographic Studies, Washington, D.C., 1975.

———, Michael Karchmer, and Raymond J. Trybus: *The Rated Speech Intelligibility of Hearing Impaired Children: Basic Relationships and a Detailed Analysis*, Ser. R, No. 6, Gallaudet College, Office of Demographic Studies, Washington, D.C., 1978.

Karchmer, Michael A., and Raymond J. Trybus: *Who are the Deaf Children in "Mainstream" Programs?*, Ser. R, No. 4, Gallaudet College, Office of Demographic Studies, Washington, D.C., 1977.

Meadow, Kathryn P.: *Deafness and Child Development*, University of California Press, Berkeley, 1980.

———: "Self-Image, Family Climate, and Deafness," *Social Forces*, 47(4):428–438, 1969.

Meisegeier, Richard W.: "Two Determinants for Perceiving Parents as Influential in the Development of Occupational Goals for Deaf Students," *Directions* (Gallaudet College), 2(4):29–34, 1982.

Mindel, Eugene D., and McCay Vernon: *They Grow in Silence: The Deaf Child and His Family*, National Association of the Deaf, Silver Spring, Maryland, 1971.

Rawlings, Brenda W., and Carl J. Jensema: *Two Studies of the Families of Hearing Impaired Children*, Ser. R, No. 5, Gallaudet College, Office of Demographic Studies, Washington, D.C., 1977.

Schein, Jerome D., and Marcus T. Delk, Jr.: *The Deaf Population of the United States*, National Association of the Deaf, Silver Spring, Maryland, 1974.

Richard W. Meisegeier

FAY, EDWARD ALLEN
(1843–1923)

Edward Allen Fay was a teacher, editor, administrator, and scholar at Gallaudet College from 1865 to 1923, a crucial period in the history of deaf Americans. Together with his friend Edward Miner Gallaudet and his sometime nemesis Alexander Graham Bell, Fay was one of the persons most responsible for shaping American attitudes toward deafness and deaf people during the late nineteenth and early twentieth centuries. He accomplished this quietly and calmly, possessing neither the political skills of Gallaudet nor the money and prestige of Bell. Fay's success resulted from a passionate commitment to scholarship, an open mind, a deep understanding of deaf people, and a remarkable capacity for work. *See* BELL, ALEXANDER GRAHAM; GALLAUDET, EDWARD MINER; GALLAUDET COLLEGE.

The oldest son of Barnabas and Louise Mills Fay, he was born on November 23, 1843, in Morristown, New Jersey, and grew up in an environment that stressed the importance of education for deaf persons. His father was a teacher at the New York School for the Deaf (Fanwood) until 1854, when he became the first principal of the Michigan School for the Deaf. Fay followed in his father's footsteps, teaching at the New York School after receiving his bachelor of arts degree from the University of Michigan in 1862. In 1865 he received a master's degree there, and was invited by Edward Miner Gallaudet to become the third member of the faculty at the National Deaf-Mute College (eventually renamed Gallaudet College), where he remained for 57 years. At Gallaudet College, Fay was a professor of languages, teaching French, German, and Latin, and from 1865 until 1920 served as vice president as well. In 1871 he married Mary Bradshaw. In 1881 he was awarded a doctor's degree in romance languages by Johns Hopkins University.

Fay's scholarship was impressive in quantity and breadth. In 1888 he published *Concordancia of the Divina Commedia*, written at the request of the Dante Society of Cambridge. He followed with *Histories of American Schools for the Deaf, 1817–1893*, edited by him and published by the Volta Bureau in 1893, and *Marriages of the Deaf in America* (1898) which he compiled and wrote between 1889 and 1895. Fay contributed about 150 articles to the *American Annals of the Deaf* and was editor for 50 years (1870–1920). In recognition of his scholarship he was honored with a doctor of science degree from the University of Michigan (1912) and a doctor of letters degree from Gallaudet College (1916). *See* AMERICAN ANNALS OF THE DEAF.

Marriages of the Deaf in America was perhaps his most important publication. *Marriages* was Fay's response to a paper A. G. Bell first delivered in 1883 titled "Memoir upon the Formation of a Deaf Variety of the Human Race." In this paper, Bell claimed that according to the supposed laws of heredity, as more deaf people married each other they were producing more deaf children. Bell asserted that deaf people should be segregated from each other and discouraged from using sign language to prevent them from intermingling and intermarriage.

With financial support from Bell's own Volta Bureau, Fay decided to test the validity of Bell's suppositions by examining all the marriages of deaf persons in the United States about which he could find information. Fay set for himself four goals in his study of marriages, to find "true answers" to the following questions: (1) Are marriages of deaf persons more liable to result in deaf offspring than ordinary marriages? (2) Are marriages in which both partners are deaf more liable to result in deaf offspring than marriages in which one of the partners is deaf and the other a hearing person? (3) Are certain classes of the deaf, however they may marry, more liable than others to have deaf children? If so, how are these classes respectively composed, and what are the conditions that increase or diminish this liability? (4) Aside from the question of the liability of the offspring to deafness, are marriages in which both of the partners are deaf more likely to result happily than marriages in which one of the partners is deaf and the other is a hearing person? Fay hoped that answers to these questions, drawn from scientific and dispassionate research, would resolve the controversy surrounding the education of deaf persons and the use of sign language. *See* HISTORY: Methods Controversy.

He analyzed 4471 marriages of deaf people in the United States between 1801 and 1894 and concluded that Bell's fears, in general, were misplaced. Deaf people, through intermarriages, were not producing a deaf race, for only 8.67 percent of the children born to two deaf parents were deaf. With characteristic intellectual honesty, however, Fay did write that marriages between two deaf partners were "far more liable to result in deaf offspring" than marriages between hearing partners. Nevertheless, the most important factor in genetic deafness, Fay concluded, was the presence of deaf relatives in the family of one or both of the marriage partners, whether the partners were hearing, adventitiously deaf, or congenitally deaf. *See* AUDITORY DISORDERS, PREVENTION OF: Genetics; HEARING LOSS: Incidence and Prevalence.

Fay's fourth goal in his study of marriages reveals a great deal about his attitude toward deaf people. Despite the fact that *Marriages* is crammed with numbers, Fay was interested in deaf people as individuals. While admitting that his data for divorces and separations were limited, he reached the significant conclusion that marriages between two deaf individuals were happier than those in which one partner was hearing and one deaf.

Fay explained in 1871 that his goal for the *Annals* was to include "everything . . . that tends to promote the physical, intellectual, or moral welfare of the deaf and dumb as a class, or that is of especial interest or value to teachers of deaf-mutes and others concerned for their elevation." More than any other editor, Fay succeeded in reaching this goal. For 50 years the *Annals* was a gold mine of information about deaf people in the United States and abroad, about research related to deafness, and about the many debates surrounding deaf people. Its issues included articles, book reviews, translations of European publications, news from schools for deaf people, reports of conferences, and meticulously compiled statistics about educational institutions and communication methods.

Moreover, the *Annals* provided a forum for deaf persons themselves. Fay encouraged deaf people to write for the *Annals* and to be involved in the great debates over sign language, deaf teachers, oral instruction, deaf clubs, and deaf intermarriage. Book reviews and translations were also solicited by Fay from qualified deaf persons.

Fay demonstrated similar sensibilities in the classroom. Students found him rigorous and thorough, but patient and never sarcastic or paternalistic. Moreover, he was a master of sign language, which he continually defended in the *Annals*.

George Veditz, former president of the National Association of the Deaf and a student of Fay's, summed up Fay's place in the history of deaf Americans. "I do not hesitate to name the two [Edward Miner Gallaudet and Fay] together, for where Gallaudet was our aggressive advocate and champion on the public platform, in conventions and otherwise, Fay's influence was equally powerful. The man of action and the man of thought were each the complement of the other, and, lacking either,

Edward Allen Fay. (Gallaudet College Archives)

American education of the deaf would not be what it is to-day." *See* NATIONAL ASSOCIATION OF THE DEAF; VEDITZ, GEORGE WILLIAM.

Throughout his lifetime, Fay, "the man of thought," epitomized the best characteristics of those hearing persons who helped shape the American deaf community. Unlike A. G. Bell or E. M. Gallaudet, whose mothers were both hearing-impaired, Fay had no deaf relatives. Still, growing up on the campuses of schools for deaf children, attaining thorough competence in sign language, and teaching at Gallaudet College for most of his career, he was comfortable with the deaf community. However, in contrast with some teachers of deaf students, he also was comfortable in the larger world of scholarship, and conducted path-breaking studies that were far ahead of their time. The conclusions he reached in *Marriages*—relative to the incidence of deafness among the children of deaf parents and the greater success of endogamous marriages among the deaf population—have remained valid in the face of more recent studies conducted with vast resources unavailable to Fay.

Fay died on July 14, 1923, in Washington, D.C.

Bibliography
"Edward Allen Fay Papers," Gallaudet College Archives, Washington, D.C.
Ely, Charles R.: "Edward Allen Fay: Educator of the Deaf," *Volta Review*, 25(11):483–487, November 1923.
Hall, Percival: "Fay, Edward Allen," *Dictionary of American Biography*, vol. 3, pp. 303–304, 1958.
Patterson, Robert: "Edward Allen Fay," *American Annals of the Deaf*, 67(4):258–266, September 1923.

John V. Van Cleve

FOLKLORE

An understanding of the concept of deaf culture and sociocultural values is important to the subject of deaf folklore. Though culture can be defined in many ways, the most appropriate definition is that culture refers to the distinctive ways of life of a particular group of people, with their customs, beliefs, values, material possessions, shared understandings, and sociocultural patterns of behavior that permit them to live together harmoniously but which separate them from others. Deaf culture can be related to the life-style of deaf people, which differs from that of hearing people in various ways. The same may be said of folklore. *See* DEAF POPULATION: Culture and Subculture.

Folklore is defined as jokes, stories, games, traditional beliefs, riddles, and legends that are passed on from one person to another "by word of mouth," or in the American deaf community, "by sign of hands." There are genres of deaf folklore, such as deaf jokes, riddles, cartoons, legends, personal experience narratives, signlore (signed puns, double-fingerspelling, alphabet and numbers stories, name signs, and so on), games, and stories about notable deaf persons. Examples of a riddle, a joke, a personal experience narrative, and a historical-literary anecdote follow.

EXAMPLES
A typical riddle takes advantage of the theme of deafness to solve a problem: Ten blackbirds were sitting on a telephone line; a hunter came and shot at them. Nine flew off and one stayed. Why? The answer is that nine blackbirds were hearing; one was deaf. Similarly, a well-known deaf joke emphasizes, by its very absurdity, the commonality of deafness: A woodcutter walked into a forest. He went to a tree and started to cut it with his ax. When the tree was ready to fall he yelled "timber!" and the tree came crashing down. He did the same thing with two more trees. He yelled "timber!" each time. He started to cut down a fourth tree. He yelled "timber!" but the tree did not fall. The woodcutter was perplexed. He cut some more and yelled "timber!" Still no success. The tree remained

standing. He tried once more but he had no luck. He decided to phone a tree doctor to come and check the tree. When the doctor arrived, he inspected the tree. After a diagnosis, he told the woodcutter, "The tree is deaf. You have to finger-spell 'T-I-M-B-E-R!' to it." Sure enough, the tree came crashing down!

Deaf folklore, in addition to satirizing the experience of deafness, frequently criticizes the hearing community, as in this personal experience narrative: Two well-dressed deaf men were conversing in sign language on a public bus. A stranger, awestruck, approached them and wrote a note to them: "Can you read?" One of the two deaf men, disgusted at this remark, took out an expensive pen and wrote on the note: "No, I can't, but can you write?"

Yet another form of deaf folklore is the historical anecdote: It is a well-known fact that a famous Philadelphian, Ben Franklin, discovered electricity with his kite-flying equipment. Few people know how this really happened. Ben Franklin's deaf printer had gone home early one evening and had gone to bed when Ben realized he just had to see his printer. Unfortunately the printer lived on the third floor and the front door was locked. So, how could poor Franklin get to his sleeping printer? The quick-thinking Franklin got the idea of flying his young nephew's kite near the window, hoping to get his printer's attention. (But his printer was asleep, so we assume that Franklin added a candle to the kite tail.) After the kite flew repeatedly back and forth past the window, the deaf printer awoke, stuck his head out the window, and saw Franklin on the ground three floors below. Franklin indicated that he had to talk to him and asked if he could come up. Rather than toss Franklin the key and perhaps lose it in the grass (he was too lazy to go downstairs and unlock the door) the printer tied it to the kite string. It was shortly afterward that lightning struck and Franklin became the discoverer of electricity—thanks to his deaf printer.

Folklore is important to the American deaf community for several reasons. It stimulates deaf children's and deaf adults' pride in their own deaf identity; it gives better understanding about the deaf community and deaf culture; it helps hearing people respect deafness as a cultural phenomenon with historical or literary backgrounds similar to their own; and it helps hearing people to understand how deaf people think and perceive the world.

PRESERVATION

Deaf folklore has been recorded by several deaf authors. Jack R. Gannon's *Deaf Heritage*, for example, has fine examples of cartoons, jokes, and classroom humor. Roy K. Holcomb's book *Hazards of Deafness* portrays the personal experiences that deaf people have had in their daily lives. The videotape "Off-hand Tales," made by Loy Golladay at the National Technical Institute for the Deaf, consists of short anecdotes dealing with deaf folklore. Two videotapes "American Folklore in the Deaf Community" and "Deaf Club Folklore," made by Simon J. Carmel, consist of deaf individuals' jokes, manual alphabet and numbers stories, personal experience narratives, and anecdotes. Edwin Allen Hodgson compiled many interesting anecdotes about deaf people in the nineteenth century in *Facts, Anecdotes and Poetry, Relating to the Deaf and Dumb*. This book was one of the earliest collections of deaf folklore.

Another movement involves a pilot project, started in 1979 and sponsored by the Clerc Cultural Fund Committee of the Gallaudet College Alumni Association. It was developed to record and collect archives of the genres of folklore of the American deaf community on videotape, and also to teach and encourage others to videotape such lore for deposit in the collection. This project is the first stage of a plan to create centralized archives of deaf folklore in the United States. The collected material will be filed in the archives of deaf folklore-folklife at the Gallaudet College Library, where it will be available to researchers and the general public. *See* GALLAUDET COLLEGE.

This collection will be a major resource for the study of deaf culture shared by the deaf community. It will be of importance to deaf and hearing people alike, and to professional folklorists and deaf specialists in public libraries, whose considerable interest in studying the folklore of deaf persons has been long hampered by the lack of any basic reference collection. The collection will provide a foundation on which the academic study of deaf folklore can be built.

CONCLUSION

The genres of deaf folklore have been duly passed on by deaf people's "sign of hands." These genres reflect the unique cultural patterns of behavior and, in particular, the strongly shared "deaf identity" within the deaf community, inside the predominantly hearing world.

Bibliography

"American Folklore in the Deaf Community" (videotape), Gallaudet College Media Services Catalog #V1882, Gallaudet College Library, Washington, D.C., 1981.

Brunvand, J. H.: *The Study of American Folklore*, 2d ed., W. W. Norton, New York, 1978.

Carmel, S. J.: "American Deaf Folklore," in Alice Hagemeyer (ed.), *Communicating with Hearing People: The Red Notebook*, National Association of the Deaf, Silver Spring, Maryland, 1982.

Cohen, E. N., and E. Eames: "The Anthropological Approach: Context, Comparison, and Theory," in *Cultural Anthropology*, Little, Brown, Boston, 1982.

"Deaf Club Folklore" (videotape), Gallaudet College Media Services Catalog, Gallaudet College Library, Washington, D.C., 1984.

Friedl, J.: "The Concept of Culture," in *The Human Portrait: Introduction to Cultural Anthropology*, Prentice-Hall, Englewood Cliffs, New Jersey, 1981.

Gannon, J. R.: *Deaf Heritage*, National Association of the Deaf, Silver Spring, Maryland, 1981.

Golladay, L.: "Off-hand Tales" (videotape), NTID Media Services Catalog #SRC Video 5371, National Technical Institute for the Deaf, Rochester, New York.

Hodgson, E. A.: *Facts, Anecdotes and Poetry, Relating to the Deaf and Dumb*, Deaf Mutes' Journal, 1891.

Holcomb, R. K.: *Hazards of Deafness*, Joyce Media, Northridge, California, 1977.

Kluckhohn, C.: "Queer Customs," in *Mirror for Man*, McGraw-Hill, New York, 1949.

Kroeber, A. L., and C. Kluckhohn: "Culture: A Critical Review of Concepts and Definitions," papers of the Peabody Museum of American Archaeology and Ethnology, Harvard University, Cambridge, Massachusetts, vol. 47, 1952.

Simon J. Carmel

FOSTER, ANDREW JACKSON
(1925–   )

Andrew Jackson Foster II is known as a pioneer, educator, and missionary in West Africa. He was born in Birmingham, Alabama, on June 27, 1925,

Andrew Jackson Foster.

the son of a coal miner, and became the first black person to graduate from Gallaudet College in recent times. In spite of numerous obstacles, he succeeded in his life-long ambition of establishing schools for deaf children in Africa. Foster is one of the persons most responsible for encouraging deaf Africans to pursue educational and leadership opportunities. In recognition of his unique accomplishments and service, Gallaudet College conferred upon him a doctor's degree in humane letters in 1970. *See* GALLAUDET COLLEGE.

Foster became profoundly deaf at the age of 11 from spinal meningitis. From age 12 to 16, he attended the Alabama School for the Colored Deaf in Talladega. When he was 17, he moved, alone, to Detroit, Michigan. Since he was a minor and his parents resided in Alabama, he was considered a nonresident and was denied admission to the Michigan School for the Deaf. This was in 1942, and Detroit's factories were booming with defense work. Undiscouraged by the school's refusal, he found jobs in several factories, continued his education through evening studies and correspondence courses, and became involved in religious activities for deaf people. After gaining his high school diploma, he received a congressional scholarship to attend Gallaudet College. He entered Gallaudet in 1951 and completed work for his bachelor's degree in education in three years by taking summer courses at Virginia's Hampton Institute. In preparation for his life's work, Foster earned his master's degree in special education from Eastern Michigan University in 1955 and a second bachelor of arts degree, this time in Missions, from Seattle Pacific College in 1956.

The establishment of schools for deaf Africans was Foster's boyhood dream. Though well qualified, Foster discovered that the doors of most mission boards were closed to black persons. Nevertheless, with the help of friends in Detroit and with the encouragement of Leonard M. Elstad, president of Gallaudet College, in 1956 in Detroit Foster founded the Christian Mission for Deaf Africans. Under its sponsorship, he headed for West Africa in 1957.

After surveying the possibilities of opening a school for deaf children in Monrovia, Liberia, Foster went to Ghana where, in a borrowed classroom, he established the Accra Mission School for the Deaf (later nationalized) on September 10, 1957. Later he established a residential school for deaf persons at Mampong-Akwagpim, 23 miles (37 kilometers) from Accra. In May 1960 he founded the first school for deaf Nigerians, the Ibadan Mission School for the Deaf (later taken over by the government). Since 1957, he has helped start numerous schools for deaf pupils in Liberia, Nigeria, Ghana, the Ivory Coast, Togo, Chad, Senegal, Benin, the Central Africa Republic, Cameroon, Gabon, Burundi, Zaire, and Kenya. *See* NIGERIA.

In addition to establishing schools for deaf Africans, Foster arranged training for teachers of deaf Africans. He has been instrumental in sending deaf Africans to Gallaudet College and several other higher-education institutions in the United States. Some of these individuals returned to Africa, assuming the responsibilities of teaching and training other deaf Africans.

Foster married a deaf woman, Bertha Zuther of West Germany, in 1961; they had five children.

Bibliography

Gallaudet College Archives, Washington, D.C.

Hairston, Ernest, and Linwood Smith: "Dr. Andrew Foster," in *Black and Deaf in America: Are We That Different*, pp. 66–67. T. J. Publications, Silver Spring, Maryland, 1983.

Valerie L. Dively

FRANCE

There is no census of the French deaf population, but claims have been made that there are about 3,500,000 hearing-impaired people in France. This number would include individuals who are slightly hard of hearing or deafened in old age; and of the approximately 800,000 persons who do not hear normal conversational speech (60 dB loss or more), there are between 50,000 and 100,000 deaf people who use sign language as their principal means of communication.

EDUCATION

Early diagnosis of deafness became a major preoccupation of the medical establishment during the early 1960s. The thrust of this effort was to recommend hearing aids as early as possible, with the idea of a preschool education (0–3 years) appearing later. Testing programs now exist in certain hospitals, in CAMPS (Center of Medico Pedagogical Action), and at individual speech therapy centers.

Under the provisions of the 1975 law that defines national guidelines for the affairs of handicapped people, each of continental France's 95 departments has its own departmental Commission of Special Education (CDES). The commission is responsible for decisions concerning the placement of handicapped children in special schools and the allocation of subsidies or grants. The majority of special schools for deaf children are the responsibility of the Ministry of Health, whose four major institutes have more than 700, mostly residential, students; other schools are under the National Education.

Among the special schools under the Health Ministry, the four large public national institutes

have the longest history: Institute at Paris (founded 1790), Bordeaux (1785), Chambery (1841), and Metz (1875). The Abbé Sicard was director at Bordeaux before he was chosen to direct the institute at Paris at its creation in 1790. Until the Congress of Milan, the Paris Institute was among the schools most attached to sign language. J. M. Itard, the institute's resident physician who taught the "wild boy" of Aveyron within its walls, fought for speech classes for the deaf children, and found himself in constant conflict with the teachers, some of whom were deaf. Among the teachers were Bebian, author of a notation system for sign language and defender of FSL (French Sign Language), Jean Massieu (deaf), Laurent Clerc (deaf), and Ferdinand Berthier. *See* BERTHIER, JEAN FERDINAND; CLERC, LAURENT; HISTORY; MASSIEU, JEAN; SICARD, ABBÉ ROCH AMBROISE CUCURRON; SIGN LANGUAGES.

Teacher training for the National Institutes consists of a two-year program: one year of theoretical courses and one year of on-the-job training.

The private sector consists mostly of a network of schools founded during the nineteenth century by religious groups, especially the Brothers of St. Gabriel and the Sisters of Sagesse. These schools functioned independently for a long period, making their own decisions on teacher training and curriculum development. In 1925, faced with the attempt of the Paris Institute to control teacher training for deaf students and the fear of being made accountable to the Ministry of Public Instruction, the private schools formed the Federation of Institutions of the Deaf and of the Blind of France (FISAF). The FISAF created a teacher training program, which was officially recognized after the war. It consisted of supervision of job training supplemented by several workshops a year of courses in theory.

The FISAF has 40 schools for hearing-impaired pupils (two specialize in deaf-blind students and two others in multihandicapped students), with vocational training stressed for the older students. FISAF schools accept almost 5000 students annually, 75 percent of whom live at school.

Among the remaining private schools are the centers created in the late 1960s. These nonresidential centers accept a limited number of students. They begin their program at a preschool level, use a higher quality and quantity of technical innovations than the more traditional schools, and represent a more medical approach to deaf education.

Another teacher training program was organized by the Ministry of National Education in 1963. Training leads to the Certificate of Aptitude for the Education of Deficient or Inadapted Children and Adolescents (CADEI). The teacher trainee can choose from 10 specialized subjects, one of which is called "hearing-impaired." Certified primary school teachers with five years of practice can obtain the CADEI after one year of additional training. The certificate qualifies the teacher for teaching in one of the four largest residential schools (Clermont-Ferrand, Rouen, Asnières, Lille) supervised by the Ministry of National Education, or in the growing number of mainstreamed classes in regular public schools.

Efforts to unify teacher training programs may increase as the idea of integrating deaf students in the regular public schools under the Ministry of National Education gains more and more ground.

SECONDARY EDUCATION AND VOCATIONAL TRAINING

There has almost always been a vocational training program in all residential schools. At first it consisted of hands-on training in trades useful for the day-to-day operations of the school—cooking, gardening, sewing, shoemaking, carpentry, and printing—supervised by master workers qualified to share their experience without worrying too much about curriculum constraints. Following World War II the range of such training programs was widened and became more diversified. Deaf students also began to take the same examinations as hearing students.

There have always been isolated cases of prelingual deaf children who followed, or tried to follow, a more liberal-arts-oriented program on the secondary level. The cost of such efforts was great, for they required continuous family support and private tutoring.

In the 1960s a private school with a limited number of students was opened to prepare deaf students for the baccalaureate, an exam required of 18-year-olds for many positions and for acceptance into a university. However, even today the number of deaf students who pass the bacclaureate is extremely small, and the number of deaf students accepted into a university even smaller.

Mainstreaming of deaf students is also done to a very limited extent. At the beginning of the 1980s, several junior high and high schools began accepting deaf students with some kind of support service, even interpreters. Or teachers in residential schools choose certain deaf students to mainstream, with some personal support by the teacher. Statistics indicate that in 1980, 346 deaf and 1326 hard-of-hearing students individually mainstreamed into public schools.

METHODS

Theoretically, the Milan Congress put an end to the debates, particularly notable in France, that centered on teaching methods. Schools for deaf students were officially oralist until the end of the 1970s. However, there were differences between the small residential schools, where signs were kept out of school, and the large residential schools, where it was simply not possible to prohibit signs except in the classroom. For a time the teachers lived with their students in school housing facilities, and they understood signs even if they did not use them in class. Signs were also tolerated with deaf students who were considered retarded, or with those in workshops for vocational training, the only area where deaf teachers were still found. After World War II, a new offensive was launched against sign language because hearing aids were becoming the new hope against deafness. Thus, when the movement for recognition of sign language appeared on the scene, few teachers remained who could understand signs.

It is difficult to predict what communication method will predominate in the future. An important indication of change on the "official" level is that all three teacher training programs now have an information-initiation to sign language. Signs are beginning to be seen in the classroom, but usually these limited experimental classes start from the presence of a deaf person, native in FSL, working side by side with a certified hearing teacher. *See* SOCIOLINGUISTICS.

THE WORK MARKET

A few prelingually deaf individuals are educated professionals—dentists, architects, pharmacists—but these cases are rare. There are also a few cases of deaf people managing small companies. More often, deaf women with some advanced education become laboratory assistants, while men are in computer fields or industrial drawing. Although statistics are not available, it is accurate to say that most deaf people are woefully underemployed at jobs that do not correspond to their training. Also, deafness limits chances for promotion, both because positions of responsibility are simply seen as the territory of hearing persons and because deaf people have a much harder time gaining access to continuing education. Unemployment has a greater impact on deaf people than on hearing people.

RECOGNITION OF FRENCH SIGN LANGUAGE

The movement for recognition of FSL, born just after the World Federation of the Deaf (WFD) Congress was held in 1975 in Washington, D.C., is opening new possibilities for deaf people in professional fields. Partly because of the development of interpreting services, deaf workers can begin to profit from vocational training and workshops in continuing education that were previously inaccessible. Teachers and dorm supervisors for deaf students, and teachers of sign language, are notable new sectors in the job market that have opened up for deaf people. *See* WORLD FEDERATION OF THE DEAF.

The French who attended the 1975 WFD Congress were impressed by the fact that American Sign Language (ASL) was recognized as a language and by the implications of that on the situation of the American deaf community. They returned home determined to change things in France. A few months later, through the efforts of the Union Nationale pour l'Insertion Sociale de Déficients Auditifs (UNISDA), signs appeared weekly on television, and the use of captions also became more frequent.

Systematic efforts to recognize the right of deaf people to have their own language were the result of a close collaboration between a small group of hearing and deaf individuals, both French and American. Several Americans moved to France for a few years; and exchanges between the two countries grew, especially as a result of summer workshops of French groups organized on the campus of Gallaudet College. *See* GALLAUDET COLLEGE.

Nonprofit associations appeared to fight for the institutional changes sought by the new movement. One of the most important associations was 2LPE (Two Languages for an Education, 1979) with 18 local and 7 regional chapters. With an orientation similar to the American Deaf Pride, 2LPE unites deaf people, parents, and professionals who promote the idea of a real bilingual education for deaf children. Though the association was not able to create new institutions immediately, it has acted as a pressure group and as a center for exchanging ideas. It organizes parents' workshops and participates in the development of FSL classes with other associations, notably with IVT (International Visual Theatre) and the ALSF (Academy of FSL) to train the new teachers of sign language. *See* ORGANIZATIONS.

The IVT and ALSF were, for the most part, responsible for the organization of FSL classes. Classes take place mainly outside schools; the teachers are almost exclusively native deaf signers who fight to retain their monopoly. Information from linguists, lessons gained from American and Swedish experiments, the slowness of the school establishment to accept signs, and perhaps the success of cued speech all contribute to explain why there has not been any concerted effort to create a French Sign Language book. The deaf teachers strive to teach FSL as a complete language rather than as a simple list of vocabulary.

Demand for interpreting services has risen considerably, and deaf people want more and better-quality interpreting. For meetings concerning social, political, and cultural affairs, and for professional training workshops, an interpreter has become a common requirement. The National Association of France of Interpreters for the Hearing Impaired (ANFIDA) was created in 1979, and awarded its first certificate in 1980. A more formal training session for interpreters was created for the region of Paris in 1982. However, interpreting services continue to be primarily the responsibility of volunteers without formal training (family members, teachers acting as social workers in their spare time, and so on). *See* INTERPRETING.

ASSOCIATIONS

The Union Nationale pour l'Insertion Sociale de Déficients Auditifs (UNISDA) is an umbrella organization created in 1973. It originated in the collaborative effort to prepare the Sixth Congress of the World Federation of the Deaf in Paris in 1971. Associations of deaf persons, parents of deaf children, persons deafened later in life, and oral deaf adults created it to serve as a clearing house for information, documentation, and joint research projects.

The Société Centrale d'Education et d'Assistance pour les Sourds-Muets de France, established in 1850, is a continuation of the Central Society founded in 1838 by Berthier. This association is the oldest organization in the world in the field of deafness. Although its objectives are not clearly defined, its action sporadic, and the membership very limited, for several years it published a newsletter which circulated some new ideas and played a significant role in the creation of UNISDA.

During the two decades following World War II, two federations of deaf associations found themselves in competition: the old Federation des Sociétés de Sourds-Muets, founded before the war, and the Union Nationale des Amicales d'Anciens Elèves des Institutions des Sourds de France (alumni of residential deaf schools), created in 1948. In general, the latter represented those from the religious schools of the FISAF, and the former the state schools.

The existence of the two federations attests to the importance of school, even into adulthood, in the deaf world. It also indicates the continuing importance of an opposition between the religious so-called conservative tradition and the progressive lay tradition during the Third Republic (though the opposition began to decrease after World War II).

The first effort at a union of the two federations did not last long. In 1955 the National Coordination Committee of Silent Societies was founded, but in 1961 the National Union of Alumni and the Federation of Societies (renamed National Federation of the Deaf of France) regained their independence.

In 1966 the two organizations put an end to their differences and combined to form the Confédération Nationale des Sourds de France (CNSF). The Federation Sportive des Sourds de France (established 1917) also participated in the founding of the confederation, though it retained its independence. In an effort to break with the tradition of associations that are based on alumni affiliations, the CNSF is divided geographically into eight regional federations representing 55 individual associations.

The CNSF officially represents the prelingually deaf population in government and bureaucratic decisions, acts as a deaf lobby, defends deaf people in social welfare problems, organizes and supports recreational and cultural activities for deaf people, and provides information for the general public.

Before the movement for the recognition of French Sign Language, certain members of the CNSF were requesting the use of signs in deaf schools. But the strong arguments between oralists and signers, and especially those between researchers in the fields of education, linguistics, and sociology which exploded at the end of the 1970s, made the confederation hesitate to pronounce an official position.

The Office of Coordination of the Association of Persons Deafened Later in Life (BUCODES), created in 1972, unites the associations, most of which were founded in the 1960s, of postlingually deaf persons and hard-of-hearing persons. Its activities and projects emphasize the fact that the postlingually affected individuals are different from, and more numerous than, prelingually deaf persons. The Office has organized lipreading courses, which are reimbursed by the social security system; is oriented toward working with the medical establishment for preventing deafness; and is trying for total reimbursement for hearing aids through social security. (The number of French deaf people with hearing aids, estimated at about 80,000, is one of the lowest percentage of hearing aid users in Europe.) The associations of postlingually deaf persons are leaders in the effort to install induction-loop bands in public places, to develop telex-type telephones for the deaf people, and to produce the decoder for television captioning.

The National Association of Parents of the Hearing Impaired (ANPEDA) was founded in 1965 as a result of parents' desires not to abandon their children to residential schools at an early age, and to contest the mediocre results obtained by the educational system, which limited their children's futures to menial tasks in the work market. Their militancy was met with hostility from the educational establishment, but parents were convinced that their children's ability to speak and integrate into a hearing society depended on early diagnosis, technical progress in the field of hearing aids, and new pedagogical methods. Their actions were oriented toward the medical and paramedical establishments. Unlike associations of parents of children with other handicaps, they neither created nor participated in the administration of schools for their children.

The association considers itself a center of exchange, analysis, documentation, and family services. It develops training workshops and regularly organizes national or international congresses of high quality. Some 40 regional associations, 34 departmental groups, and 20 local chapters participate in the association.

The National Federation of Associations of Parents of Students of Hearing Impaired Institutions (FNAPEDIDA) unites the associations of parents whose children go to FISAF schools, and was created in competition with the National Association of Parents, though through the years the two groups have reflected the same interests and have taken similar positions.

Bibliography

Bulletin de liaison, FNAPEDIDA, 12 rue Blanche, 75009 Paris.

Bulletin liaison et information, BUCODES, 254 rue st Jacques, 75011 Paris.

Communiquer, ANPEDA, 37 rue st Sébastien, 75011 Paris.

Coup d'Oeil, bulletin on sign language and communication, CEMS, 54 Bv Raspail, 75270 Paris CEDEX 06.

La voix du sourd, CNSF, 33 rue de la Roquète, 75011 Paris.

Revue générale de l'enseignement des Déficients auditifs, published by the Association Française des Enseignants Spécialisés dans la rééducation des Déficients du Langage et de l'audition (AFERLA), 254 rue st Jacques, 75005 Paris.

Bernard Mottez

FRAT

One of the oldest periodicals published by an organization of deaf people, *The Frat* is the official organ of the National Fraternal Society of the Deaf (NFSD). The periodical made its debut in February, 1904, less than two years after the idea of a fraternal society for deaf persons was conceived in Flint, Michigan. *See* NATIONAL FRATERNAL SOCIETY OF THE DEAF.

HISTORY

The records of the National Fraternal Society do not reveal just how the choice of the publication's name came about, but there has never been any attempt to change it. In fact, so well known has the name become that the society itself is often referred to as "The Frat."

The first issues contained four pages and were a modest 6 × 9 inches (15 × 22.5 centimeters). Although originally intended to be published monthly, for a subscription price of 60 cents per year, *The Frat* came off the press somewhat erratically during its first two years.

In 1907 an agreement was made with the National Association of the Deaf (NAD) for its official organ, *The Silent Worker*, to carry several pages devoted to the National Fraternal Society under the heading "The Frat Department." It was agreed at the society's 1907 convention that the society would receive greater exposure and save on printing costs under this arrangement. *The Silent Worker* (now known as *The Deaf American*) was then a publication of 20 pages measuring 11 × 14 inches (27.5 × 35 centimeters). The arrangement prevailed through July 1909, with *The Frat* printing its own four pages during August and September, when *The Silent Worker* did not publish. *See* NATIONAL ASSOCIATION OF THE DEAF; DEAF AMERICAN.

At the society's 1909 convention, it was mentioned that bids had been received from other publications, such as *The Silent Success* and *The Deaf American*, to carry "The Frat Department." Eventually, however, the society signed a contract with *The Southern Optimist*. This contract was canceled in mid-1911 at the request of the *Optimist* publisher. It should be noted that there were a number of periodicals for deaf readers in the early 1900s, but with the exception of *The Silent Worker*, their life-span was brief. *See* PERIODICALS: History.

Beginning with the August 1911 issue of *The Frat*, the society resumed publication of its official organ. Eight pages was the standard, but as the society continued to grow, pages varied between 8 and 16. In recent years, 16 pages has been the norm.

FORMAT AND POLICY

In the first issue of *The Frat* in 1904, the editorial stated that *The Frat* "would not only act as an interchange of ideas but also keep each and every member posted on the doings of individual brothers, the growth of the society, reports of officers, and all such matters that a knowledge of would aid in the promoting of the general welfare and that all-necessary and most valued asset of ours— HARMONY." It was further stated that the paper would reach out to members who were isolated from other sources of information possessed by members of the society's divisions.

Accordingly, for a good many years the contents of *The Frat* dwelled on matters related to the National Fraternal Society, its membership, its growth, and its efforts to build up confidence in the organization. Because of its turbulent early years, when deaf leaders were skeptical of the continued existence of the society, *The Frat* continually exhorted its members to defend the society, promote its growth, and bring in new members. There were reports of activities of the society's divisions, benefits paid to members, and new divisions being organized. In short, growing pains occupied the editorial pages of *The Frat*.

In the late 1920s and early 1930s, when the society began to grow, *The Frat* began to have as many as 24 pages per issue, and a wider variety of articles appeared therein. Although matters connected with the society's divisions and with insurance continued to dominate the pages, contributions (including poems) from members increased, as *The Frat* became a popular publication for members and nonmembers alike.

Between April 1928 and May 1931, "Questions and Answers on Parliamentary Law" became a steady feature. This column was written by Edwin M. Hazel, a society member and the first deaf person to become a member of the National and American Institutes of Parliamentarians. The most popular feature in *The Frat*, which started in 1930 and lasted until 1951, was James F. Meagher's "Spotlight." It appeared regularly, expanding and eventually covering a full page. Meagher was a versatile writer—witty, original, caustic, and provocative. He covered news from all over the world on just about every topic related to deafness and interspersed it with information that was not generally known. Meagher died suddenly in February 1951, and his column was taken over by Leonard Warshawsky, who was then conducting a column of his own, "Sport Sparks," in *The Frat*. Warshawsky continued to give worldwide news in abbreviated form, particularly as it related to deaf people and the field of deafness.

After "The Spotlight," the longest-running and regular contribution from a member of the society came from Guilbert C. Braddock. From 1937 to 1946, Braddock wrote a series of 97 brief biographical sketches under the heading "Notable Deaf Persons." The subjects, from all over the world, were chosen for their accomplishments, for having surmounted the handicap of deafness, and for having made some definite contribution to life. Later, the Gallaudet College Alumni Association assembled "Notable Deaf Persons" into book form. *See* GALLAUDET COLLEGE ALUMNI ASSOCIATION.

In 1944 and 1945, eight detailed articles were printed on the origin and progress of the National Fraternal Society of the Deaf under the heading "Lean Years and Lush." Although the byline says OLD FRAT, it is well known that the author was Arthur L. Roberts, editor of *The Frat* at that time.

The Frat has had very few editors since its beginning. Francis P. Gibson held the position from 1904 until his death in 1929. His successor, A. L. Roberts, served until his death in 1957. L. S. Cherry held the editorship until 1967 and was succeeded by F. B. Sullivan.

Until Roberts became editor, the editorial pages of *The Frat* seldom discussed issues of the time regarding deaf persons. Roberts took a strong stand against deaf peddlers, whom he labeled panhandlers, and also presented views on educational, vocational, social, and legal issues which concerned the deaf community. *The Frat* took a survey of deaf drivers in an effort to convince insurance companies that deaf drivers were good risks for automobile insurance. This policy continued with Roberts's successors, and today hardly an issue appears without some editorial comment on matters affecting deaf persons in general. *See* DRIVING RESTRICTIONS.

SUBSCRIBER INFORMATION

The Frat is free to the society's active members, to widows and widowers of members, as well as to schools for deaf children and to a number of foreign addresses. It is published bimonthly and has a circulation of 10,000. The change from monthly to bimonthly in 1955 was made because of the increase in printing costs. In its masthead, the phrase "Francis P. Gibson's Last Message: 'Carry on' " appears—the last words Gibson spoke to Roberts when leaving the office on his last day of work, and several days before his death.

Frank B. Sullivan

FRELICH, PHYLLIS
(1944–   )

Deaf Americans will remember the night in June 1980 when a deaf woman, Phyllis Frelich, won the Tony Award for Best Actress in the play *Children of a Lesser God*. It was the highest honor that a person could receive from the professional theater for acting on the Broadway stage.

Phyllis Frelich was born in 1944 in Devil's Lake, North Dakota, the first of nine children, all deaf from birth; her parents were also deaf. Like her father, she attended the North Dakota School for the Deaf. After graduation, she enrolled in Gallaudet College, where she fell in love with the theater. Her outstanding performances there in the Greek play *Medea*, in which she had the leading role, and also her role as the Leader of the Chorus in another Greek play, *Iphigenia at Aulis*, won her the Best Actress of the Year award. *See* GALLAUDET COLLEGE.

After graduating from Gallaudet College in 1967, Frelich was invited to join the National Theatre of the Deaf as one of its founding members. She met Robert Steinberg, a hearing man who had just graduated from the University of Rochester, and who became the stage manager for the National Theatre of the Deaf. Frelich taught him sign language, and together they went on tour with the National Theatre of the Deaf, with Frelich acting in various roles. In 1968 they were married, and during the next 10 years Frelich tried to combine two roles—mother of two and actress. *See* NATIONAL THEATERS OF THE DEAF: United States.

Phyllis Frelich. (Public Information Office, NTID, Rochester, New York)

In 1979 Frelich met playwright Mark Medoff, who thought of writing a play about the communication problems of deaf people in a hearing world. Medoff used Frelich and Steinberg as models for his characters, and developed the structure for *Children of a Lesser God*.

In January 1980 Medoff invited Frelich and Steinberg to his home in Las Cruces, New Mexico, where he served as chairperson of the theater department of the State University. The play began to take shape as Medoff found new insights into "the deaf experience," including the contrasting deaf and hearing experiences of the married couple. Often Frelich and Steinberg improvised scenes for the play, which is a fictional story about the romance between a speech therapist and a deaf woman student. Their later marriage problems are the result of communication breakdowns and her active involvement in deaf rights. Their difficulties, however, have universal appeal as they explore their individual need for independence. The play includes two other deaf characters in minor roles who also help provide a better understanding of deafness and deaf people.

When the script of the play was finally completed, Medoff first presented it in a workshop at the State University with Frelich as the deaf student, "Sarah Norman," and Steinberg as "James Leeds," the speech therapist.

Shortly afterward, the play was brought to Los Angeles by Gordon Davidson, the artistic director of the Mark Taper Theatre. Under his direction, the play went through more changes in rewriting and casting. The leading male role of "James Leeds" was taken over by John Rubinstein. It was a demanding role, as Rubinstein had to communicate in fluent signs with Frelich and at the same time speak her half of the dialogue. The setting of the play also challenged the imagination of the audience. To emphasize "the silent world" of deaf people, there was very little scenery, and even the props were mimed.

After a successful run in Los Angeles, the play opened on Broadway, March 30, 1980, at the Longacre Theatre, where it soon won the acclaim of audiences and critics. Tony Awards were given for Best Play, Best Actress (Phyllis Frelich), and Best Actor (John Rubinstein). The Outer Critics Circle named it "the most distinguished new play," and they hailed Frelich's acting as "an outstanding debut."

In the months that followed, the play performed to packed houses and the demand for tickets continued to increase. Another company was formed, the National Tour Company, to take the play on tour to major cities throughout the United States and Canada. Soon other groups were added: the Bus and Truck Company played in smaller cities of the United States; the London Company traveled to England, where it enjoyed a long run; and similar groups went to South Africa and Australia. In each of these touring companies, a deaf actress played "Sarah Norman," and by 1984 scores of deaf persons were employed in leading or supporting roles and as understudies. Also in 1984 a Hollywood motion picture company started moving toward an eventual film production.

Frelich continued to perform on Broadway in the original production of *Children of a Lesser God*, which ran continuously for over two years. She was honored by her native state of North Dakota when Governor Allen Olson presented her with the Theodore Roosevelt Rough Rider Award in 1981. In the same year, she was featured with Hal Linden on NBC-TV in a *Barney Miller* episode in which she played a deaf prostitute with sexy realism and humor. In March 1982 she participated in the ABC-TV spectacle *Night of 100 Stars* for the benefit of the Actors Fund of America.

In 1984 Frelich had the leading role in yet another new play written especially for her by Medoff. Titled *Hands of Its Enemy*, it was first workshopped in New Mexico by the American Southwest Theatre Company, a company created by Medoff, who is also its artistic director. Like *Children of a Lesser God*, it was later refined by director Gordon Davidson, who staged its formal showing at the Mark Taper Forum in Los Angeles early in October 1984.

Using the motif of "a play within a play," *Hands of Its Enemy* is about an inexperienced but ambitious deaf playwright, "Marietta Yerbt" (Frelich), whose first play is in rehearsal with a regional theater company. Her director, "Howard Bellman" (played by Hollywood film star Richard Dreyfuss), learns to communicate in sign language as the play unfolds. He has just returned from a drug and alcohol rehabilitation center and is using the play to regain his former status. Throughout the action, "Marietta's" best friend serves as her interpreter (played by Robert Steinberg), and through a clever use of interpreting and signing, the entire show is understood and enjoyed by both hearing and deaf theater-goers.

Hands of Its Enemy also makes a serious social comment, dealing with such contemporary topics as drug and alcohol addiction and rehabilitation, domestic violence, and the sexual abuse of children. Although it does not deal directly with deafness and deaf persons, it succeeded in sensitizing hearing audiences to "deaf awareness." This was largely due to the virtuoso performance of Frelich, who communicated the meaning and the spirit of the play so successfully.

With these two major stage triumphs, Frelich not only proved the capability and expertise of the talented deaf actress to perform with the best in the professional theater but also opened doors of opportunity for other deaf Thespians.

Bibliography
Panara, Robert, and John Panara: *Great Deaf Americans*, Silver Spring, Maryland, 1983.

Viertel, Jack: "Hands of Its Enemy" (review), *Los Angeles Herald Examiner*, October 1, 1984.

Robert Panara

G

GALLAUDET, EDWARD MINER
(1837–1917)

Born on February 5, 1837, in Hartford, Connecticut, Edward Miner Gallaudet was the youngest of eight children. His father, Thomas Hopkins Gallaudet, was founder and first principal of the American School for the Deaf in Hartford. It was the first publicly supported school for deaf students in the United States. The mother, Sophia Fowler, was deaf and had been a pupil of Thomas Hopkins Gallaudet. With this background, it is no wonder that Gallaudet's life-long work was in the field of deaf education. *See* AMERICAN SCHOOL FOR THE DEAF; GALLAUDET, THOMAS HOPKINS.

Gallaudet introduced a combined system that integrated oral methods into the strictly manual residential schools in the United States. He advocated the use of manual methods of instruction when most of the world had changed to oral instruction. He established the first college program for deaf students in the United States, and brought about the establishment of a graduate training program at Gallaudet College for teachers of deaf students. His profound sensitivity to the needs of deaf people and his understanding of their potential for educational advancement single him out in the history of deaf education in the United States.

EARLY YEARS
Gallaudet had not planned to be a teacher of deaf pupils; rather he had initially decided to be a businessman. When he was 12, his father first questioned him regarding his plans for the future, suggesting that working with deaf persons would provide a fulfilling life and would offer personal satisfaction. Gallaudet answered that he had no ambition to attend college, and was impatient to enter into a business life as soon as he had completed his high school course. His father said it would be alright to be a business person but warned that he should never be a banker because the work was too narrowing.

The father died shortly thereafter, on September 10, 1851, and Gallaudet supported himself as a clerk in the Phoenix Bank of Hartford. Soon afterward he felt the truth of his father's words and decided to enter Trinity College in Hartford to complete his education.

During his first year at Trinity, he was offered a position by W. W. Turner as an instructor in the American School for the Deaf. He began teaching at the American institution in December 1855, five months before his graduation from college. It was at this time Gallaudet formulated his plan for establishing a college for deaf people at some existing institution. He discussed his plans in depth with a fellow teacher, Jared A. Ayres, and they agreed to organize the college as soon as a millionaire could be found to endow it.

On two occasions Gallaudet felt he had been treated unjustly by the board of directors at the American School. He became unwilling to continue in their employ and, in the spring of 1857, decided to prepare himself for the ministry. His plans were to establish a mission in China for the education

Edward Miner Gallaudet. (Gallaudet College Archives)

of deaf people. These plans fell through, and he accepted a position in a Chicago bank at a salary that would enable him in a few years to carry out his purpose of establishing a mission. He resigned his position at the American School and was preparing to go to Chicago when he received a letter from Amos Kendall of Washington, D.C.

COLUMBIA INSTITUTION FOR THE DEAF

Then in his seventies, Kendall had served in Andrew Jackson's cabinet and was a multimillionaire, having made his fortune through investments in the telegraph system invented by his friend and business associate Samuel F. B. Morse. In 1856 Kendall and other wealthy individuals of Washington, D.C., were contacted by a person who had brought five deaf children from New York. These children, as well as other deaf children from the district, were being mistreated and abused by this individual. Kendall soon discovered this and sued successfully for their custody. He felt obligated to provide for their education and thus established the Columbia Institution for the Deaf with the support of an act of Congress. He was looking for a superintendent to take over maintenance of the school.

Gallaudet had been suggested to Kendall by Isaac Lewis Peet of the New York Institution. Kendall explained in his letter to Gallaudet that an act of Congress had allowed for the initial support of the institution. In addition, Kendall offered the first year's salary for the superintendent and donated two acres of land with a house which the institution could use for educating the children. Kendall also expressed an interest in having Gallaudet's mother accompany him to act as matron of the institution.

Kendall's offer presented the perfect opportunity to establish the college Gallaudet had dreamed of. Upon receiving Kendall's promise to support this venture, Gallaudet immediately accepted the position. He began his duties as superintendent of the Columbia Institution for the Deaf and Dumb and Blind on June 13, 1857. He was then only 20 years old and would continue with the school for 54 years.

Gallaudet soon added more students to the school. In 1859 he succeeded in having legislation passed by the state of Maryland that provided the maintenance and tuition of its deaf children in the Columbia Institution because Maryland had no similar school at that time.

Gallaudet was also able to secure $5000 in funds from an organization known as the Washington Manual Labor School and Male Orphan Asylum. This organization had never begun operation and had been founded by Gallaudet's grandfather, Peter Wallace Gallaudet, who had died in Washington in 1843. Gallaudet was able to secure the funds from its board of management so that the money could be used to teach manual labor to students at the Columbia Institution.

At this time Gallaudet felt pressure from friends and others who criticized him for being unmarried. On July 20, 1858, he married Jane Melissa Fessenden of Hartford, whom he had known from childhood.

GALLAUDET COLLEGE

The coming of the Civil War brought little comment from Gallaudet. Although he wanted to join a Connecticut regiment to defend the union, his friends convinced him that the school was in greater need of his services. He wrote little to document his experiences during the war even though the campus was surrounded by a military camp. He took advantage of this by convincing the military to put in a pipeline so that fresh water could be brought directly to the school.

During this time Gallaudet worked toward establishing a college for deaf students. Due to the language of the original act of corporation of the Columbia Institution, there was no age limit terminating a student's stay at the institution. Gallaudet was at liberty to allow students to remain until they had completed a collegiate course of instruction. He did not, however, have the ability to award degrees for completed course work. With this in mind, he submitted a bill to Congress that would enable the Columbia Institution to grant degrees. On April 8, 1864, this bill became law by the signature of President Abraham Lincoln.

Gallaudet proposed a preliminary course of study of two years in which students would prepare for collegiate study. Deaf people of that era did not have sufficient educational backgrounds to succeed in a collegiate course. Gallaudet felt two years of precollegiate coursework would prepare students to enter into the collegiate department of the Columbia Institution.

Kendall initially objected to this proposal. He felt students should enter the college as other normal students would enter other colleges across the country, in a four-year program. Although Kendall argued his point in a meeting with the board of directors, he finally agreed to Gallaudet's plan for a six-year program. On June 28, 1864, the college celebrated its inauguration and publicized that it was ready to receive pupils. In addition, the school awarded its first honorary degree to John Carlin, a deaf artist, who had received national recognition for his work. *See* CARLIN, JOHN.

The first student to enter the collegiate course was Melville Ballard of Maine, who had graduated from the high school class of the American School for the Deaf at Hartford in 1860. He had been serving as a teacher in the Columbia Institution since 1860 and voluntarily retired to enter into the special course of collegiate study begun September 1864. As Ballard was, strictly speaking, the only college student, certain remarks were made about him: "the 'college' has gone to the city," the 'college' has gone to bed," the 'college' is taking a bath," and so forth. Ballard was the first student to graduate from the college program, in 1866.

In the same year Gallaudet secured the services of Frederick Law Olmsted, the landscape architect, to design the layout of the campus. Olmsted had been a boyhood friend of Gallaudet in Hartford. Gallaudet also hired one of Olmsted's partners, Frederick Clarke Withers, to design the majority of the buildings which now make up the historic district of the college campus. *See* GALLAUDET COLLEGE.

On November 23, 1866, Gallaudet's wife Jane died after a long and distressing illness. She had borne two daughters, Katherine and Grace, and a son, Edward LeBaron, who had died shortly after birth, Gallaudet did not remarry until 1868.

COMBINED METHOD

In 1867 Gallaudet traveled to Europe to study the methods of teaching deaf students in the schools of Europe. This trip was made partly in reaction to the establishment of two oral-only schools, the Lexington School for the Deaf in New York City (formerly the New York Institution for Impaired Instruction), and the Clarke Institution for Deaf Mutes in Northampton, Massachusetts. Gallaudet realized that the oral methodology had great enticement for parents and the public at large. *See* CLARKE SCHOOL.

On his return from Europe, he presented a report to the board of directors of the Columbia Institution supporting the use of oral instruction as an additional method of educating deaf students. He strongly believed manual communication was equally important and should be used in a combined-method approach. Although there is great debate today regarding his definition of combined method, it appears Gallaudet had oral instruction established at his own school as a separate classroom subject. Courses in geometry, philosophy, English literature, and so on were taught by using sign language, the student's "natural" language. Students would then attend separate classes in articulation and lipreading. Those students who demonstrated little or no success in these classes were not forced to attend. *See* EDUCATION: Communication: HISTORY: Sign Language Controversy.

Gallaudet also called for a conference of principals of schools for the deaf across the country to meet at the Columbia Institution so that this and other issues could be discussed. Since 1861 the exchange of ideas and the discussion of problems had halted because of the Civil War. Gallaudet circulated an invitation to the principals of the institutions in the United States to meet at Kendall Green on May 12, 1868. Some controversy did arise in that no oral proponent was invited, but Gallaudet defended his selection of participants, saying that the conference was intended for only superintendents of schools for the deaf. Since the Clarke School and the Lexington School had no principals at that time, these schools could not be represented at the conference.

At the conference, Gallaudet presented his proposal for a combined-method approach which he hoped would act as a national method for educating deaf students. Gallaudet premised such a change in methodology on the fact that the schools had failed to teach their students to express themselves adequately in written English. Gallaudet was convinced that the chief aim of education of deaf persons was to provide this basic but essential skill. He also cited other factors which attributed to poor English language skills: the excessive use of sign language which did not follow English grammatical rules, poorly trained teachers in schools for deaf pupils, and a lack of adequate textbooks that could be used with deaf children.

Gallaudet reiterated these concerns at the Seventh Convention of American Instructors of the Deaf in 1870. Although he was an ardent proponent of sign language and considered it his mother tongue, he believed a combined-method approach would overcome the major obstacle prohibiting deaf students from acquiring acceptable written English skills.

Many supporters of sign language were outraged by the thought of having oral instruction introduced to the schools and believed it would only end in failure. However, many superintendents agreed to begin implementing this philosophy, and soon it became a national method for educating deaf persons. In this regard, Gallaudet played a pivotal role in gaining acceptance of a combined oral/manual philosophy.

On December 22, 1868, Gallaudet married Susan Denison, sister of James Denison, a teacher and principal of the elementary school at the Columbia Institution. Susan gave birth to three sons, Denison, Edson, and Herbert; and two daughters, Eliza and Marion.

EXPANDING THE COLLEGE

For the next 10 years Gallaudet spent most of his energies acquiring monies for the support of the institution and new construction. Gallaudet's own residence was completed in 1867. Three other houses for faculty were completed between 1867 and 1874. Chapel Hall was completed in 1870; College Hall in 1875; and the Gymnasium, which housed the second indoor swimming pool in the country, in 1880. All of the buildings were designed by Frederick Clarke Withers.

Acquiring monies from Congress for the continued support of the institution was by no means an easy task. This effort left Gallaudet many times near the point of exhaustion. In 1869 Gallaudet was forced to travel to Europe to escape the pressures. One senator in particular, Elihu B. Washburn from Illinois, attacked the appropriations of the college each year for almost 10 years. Ironically, the nephew of this senator, Cadwallader Washburn, later entered and graduated from the collegiate program of the Columbia Institution. Fortunately, Senator Washburn was appointed minister to France by President Grant in 1869. *See* WASHBURN, CADWALLADER LINCOLN.

Acquiring monies specifically for construction was equally difficult. In one meeting of the Committee of Appropriations, Senator Edmunds of Vermont looked at the stone ornamentations Gallaudet had planned for the college building. He asked Gallaudet how much the cost would be diminished if all the fancy brick work was omitted. Gallaudet admitted that $10,000 would be saved. At that moment a rap on the door was heard and a senate page stepped in to inform Senator Edmunds he was wanted for a caucus in an adjoining room. Edmunds rose smiling and addressed the entire board: "Well, gentlemen, you'll have to excuse me,

I will stand by any decision that you reach." Judge Niblack, who had supported appropriations for the institution, immediately moved that the plans be adopted. After the meeting was over, Judge Niblack said to Gallaudet with a laugh, "I thought it best to lose no time. There's no telling when Edmunds would come back."

Gallaudet was a shrewd politician. He made himself well known to Washington social circles by continually hosting parties, meetings, and receptions at his house on Kendall Green. In this way, he introduced senators, representatives, and others to the work of the institution. If he could lure individuals to the institution and show the work they were doing with deaf students, Gallaudet felt most would be convinced to support it. He was a charismatic, well-groomed, and well-mannered person who believed in making personal visits to present his invitations or discuss matters of importance.

Gallaudet met many important individuals in Washington through his involvement in various clubs and organizations. He was a founding member of the prestigious Cosmos Club and helped to establish the YMCA in Washington. He was a member of the Sons of the American Revolution and served as its historian general. He was also heavily involved with the Washington Literary Society. He strongly believed one should write prose and poetry, understand literature, and study art, but also used this affiliation to become better acquainted with prominent individuals in the Washington area. As a member of the Literary Society, he met Alexander Graham Bell, who had moved to Washington, D.C., in 1879. He became close friends with such individuals as John Nicolay, secretary to President Abraham Lincoln, and Joseph Henry, secretary of the Smithsonian Institution. Undoubtedly, Gallaudet used these contacts to the advantage of the institution.

Gallaudet's talents extended far beyond the areas of administration and lobbying. He was fluent in both French and German and could translate both languages into American Sign Language. He received honorary degrees from Trinity College (M.A., 1859; LL.D., 1869) and George Washington University (Ph.D., 1869). Yale University awarded him an LL.D. in 1895 for his book and articles on international law. He also carried a full course load at the college, teaching courses on ethics, moral philosophy, and jurisprudence. *See* SIGN LANGUAGES: American.

ORALISM AND A. G. BELL

In his work with educating deaf students, Gallaudet met one opponent with whom he was unable to compromise; this was Alexander Graham Bell. In his early years, Bell taught speech by using a system developed by his father, called Visible Speech, and demonstrated his methods at the Clarke and Hartford schools. Bell received a patent for his invention, the telephone, in 1876, and three years later moved to Washington, D.C., where he met Edward Miner Gallaudet.

Bell believed in a strictly oral methodology in educating deaf children and refused to compromise with the use of sign language. Bell felt that the use of sign language would prohibit a student from learning speech and lipreading. Although Bell and Gallaudet could not come to terms in their philosophies regarding deaf education, they did not become outspoken opponents until Gallaudet attempted to establish a graduate program in education, titled the Normal Department, at the college. In 1880 both were on such good terms that Bell received an honorary Ph.D. from the college.

In the summer of 1880 Gallaudet attended the International Congress of Instructors of the Deaf, in Milan, Italy. James Denison, the only deaf participant from the United States, accompanied Gallaudet. The vast majority of participants at the Milan Congress were from Europe. The largest group were Italians who vehemently supported the oral methodology for educating deaf students. The Congress approved several resolutions stipulating that the oral methodology was superior to the manual method of instructing deaf persons.

This action was based partly on demonstrations at the Congress by students taught with the oral method. Gallaudet complained that the students who demonstrated their speech skills were mainly postlingually deaf and had been tutored what to say before the actual demonstrations. Gallaudet also felt that the Congress was not in fact international in character, nor was its composition representative of international opinion. Only 21 of the 164 members of the Congress were from countries other than Italy and France. See HISTORY: Congress of Milan.

The Congress did, however, mark a turning point in the attitudes of educating deaf children in the United States. It was used successfully as a symbol of support for the oral methodology by oral propagandists, and by the end of the nineteenth century there were 18 strictly oral schools in America.

Gallaudet did not retreat in the face of this changing tide in support of oralism. He continued his support for a combined methodology which would satisfy the varying needs of children whose deafness fell into a variety of categories. In 1886 he was invited to appear before the Royal Commission of the United Kingdom for the Deaf and Dumb. Spurred by the declarations of the Milan Congress, the commission was established to investigate methods of educating deaf students of the United Kingdom. Gallaudet presented his testimony in support of the combined method and was well received.

Women students were admitted to the collegiate program in 1886. In order to provide suitable accommodations for them, Gallaudet gave up his residence on campus and moved his family to Hartford. Gallaudet remained half of the year with his family during this time. In September 1889 the women students were finally moved to other housing, and Gallaudet and family returned to Kendall Green.

Several requests were made to Gallaudet in 1890 to establish a Normal Department in the Columbia Institution, in which young men and women having all their faculties would be trained to be teachers of deaf students under the two principal methods being used. Gallaudet proposed to Congress in 1891 an appropriation that would establish the Normal Department. To Gallaudet's surprise, Bell asked to be heard by the House Appropriations Committee in opposition to the measure.

Gallaudet had a long conversation with Bell and found that his opposition to the establishment of the Normal Program was based on what he understood the purpose of the program to be, that is, to train deaf teachers. Gallaudet flatly denied this and assured Bell that no deaf person would be admitted to the Normal Department. Gallaudet also assured him that all of the students would be thoroughly trained in the oral method of teaching. Bell, however, appeared before the Appropriations Committee and asserted that the purpose of establishing this program was to train deaf teachers of deaf children. He opposed the establishment of the program specifically on this ground.

Gallaudet was appalled by Bell's interference, ignoring discussions that he and Bell had had together regarding the Normal Department. Bell's testimony before the House Appropriations Committee did not change their decision, but Bell carried the controversy over to the Senate Committee, securing petitions against the measure from a number of oral schools.

In the Senate Committee, Bell succeeded in getting the appropriation of $5000, which Gallaudet had requested, cut down to $3000 and given only for the payment for articulation teachers. Bell felt he had defeated the establishment of the Normal Department, but the appropriation was used by Gallaudet to carry forward the establishment of the Normal Department exactly as planned. Although Gallaudet and Bell did later attempt a reconciliation, Gallaudet stated in his diaries, "the hatchet is buried but I know where it is."

Further animosity developed over Gallaudet's proposal to merge their respective organizations: Bell's American Association to Promote the Teaching of Speech to the Deaf (AAPTSD) and Gallaudet's Convention of American Instructors of the Deaf (CAID). Bell initially seemed agreeable to the union and showed an interest in pursuing the matter at the AAPTSD meeting at Chautauqua, New York, in July 1894. *See* ALEXANDER GRAHAM BELL ASSOCIATION FOR THE DEAF; CONVENTION OF AMERICAN INSTRUCTORS OF THE DEAF.

By the end of the meeting, though, no agreement had been reached and several members had spoken openly against a merger. Gallaudet was especially irritated by Bell's enthusiasm to allow as members wealthy promoters who had no affiliation or expertise in deafness. Bell suggested committees be formed by the respective organization to discuss a proposal by the AAPTSD that would allow the creation of three distinct groups. Gallaudet considered the proposal absurd. He perceived these machinations by Bell to be deliberate attempts to lead him on, when in reality Bell had no intention of merging the two organizations.

Gallaudet decided to speak out openly against Bell and oralism and chose the July 1895 CAID meeting at Flint, Michigan, as his battleground. In his paper, read before the whole convention, Gallaudet summarized his dealings with Bell during the past five years. He accused Bell of fanaticism over the pure oral method and called him an outsider who had succeeded only in undermining the professionals working in deaf education. He stated openly that union of the two organizations failed due to Bell's autocratic manipulations of members of the AAPTSD. Gallaudet maintained that Bell's organization was unprofessional in character and "essentially a body of promoters," the majority of whom were not actual instructors of the deaf. Bell was given an opportunity the next day to respond, but Gallaudet viewed his statements as lame and impotent. Bell and Gallaudet made no further attempt to speak to one another until five years later. *See* BELL, ALEXANDER GRAHAM.

LATER YEARS

As Gallaudet neared the last years of his presidency, he tired of socializing to the point of calling it social racket. Instead, he busied himself with civic related activities, such as getting the streets of Washington paved or working to establish a vocational school for black children. In 1898 his wife Susan encouraged him to explore the possibility of acquiring some diplomatic position, but he tried unenthusiastically and unsuccessfully.

Gallaudet remained actively involved with the welfare of the institution throughout his later years. He succeeded in warding off an attempt by the Department of the Interior to control the disbursements of the institution, and convinced Congress to pass legislation that stipulated the institution's authority over its own disbursements.

On November 4, 1903, Gallaudet's second wife, Susan, died. This greatly affected Gallaudet, and in February 1910 he decided to tender his resignation at the age of 73. Gallaudet recommended Percival Hall, a graduate of the Normal Department, as his successor. That summer he made his last trip to Europe with his daughter Katherine. He lived to witness the centennial celebration of the American School, the school his father had established, and died in Hartford on September 26, 1917.

Bibliography

Ambrosen, Lloyd A.: *Contributions of Edward Miner Gallaudet to the Convention of American Instructors of the Deaf*, Master's Thesis, Gallaudet College, 1942.

Boatner, Maxine T.: *Voice of the Deaf: A Biography of Edward Miner Gallaudet*, Washington, D.C., 1959.

"Edward Miner Gallaudet Papers," Gallaudet College Archives, Washington, D.C.

"Edward Miner Gallaudet Papers," Manuscripts Division, Library of Congress, Washington, D.C.

Frater, Lorraine: *Dr. Edward Miner Gallaudet: His Views on the Oral Method, the Sign Language and the Manual Alphabet as a Means of Educational Instruction*, Master's Thesis, Gallaudet College, 1941.

Winefield, Richard M.: *Bell, Gallaudet and the Sign Language Debate: An Historical Analysis of the Communication Controversy in Education of the Deaf*, Doctor's Thesis, Harvard University, 1981.

David L. de Lorenzo

GALLAUDET, THOMAS HOPKINS (1787–1851)

While he is best remembered as a pioneer of American education of deaf persons, Thomas Hopkins Gallaudet would probably have described himself as foremost an evangelical Christian and secondly a philosopher of education. With the deaf French teacher Laurent Clerc, in 1817 Gallaudet founded the first public school for deaf students in the United States. Gallaudet served as the first principal of the institution, now known as the American School for the Deaf, in Hartford, Connecticut. His literary and oratorical prowess was instrumental in winning state and federal support for the fledgling institution. Under his leadership, the Hartford school served as a model and source of expertise for the establishment of other publicly supported educational institutions for deaf students throughout the United States. *See* AMERICAN SCHOOL FOR THE DEAF; CLERC, LAURENT.

Gallaudet's interest in educational reform was not limited to deaf people, however. After retiring as principal of the Hartford School in 1830, he turned his attention to a variety of benevolent endeavors. He wrote and lectured tirelessly for the American Colonization Society, arguing against slavery, and for the American Tract Society, spreading the doctrine of Protestantism. Turning down scores of offers to teach and head programs at universities and other educational institutions, Gallaudet preferred to remain in Hartford, serving as chaplain of the Retreat for the Insane and writing extensively on behalf of the many educational reforms of the period. His numerous articles and addresses supported education in the form of high schools, industrial schools, colleges for women, and continuing education (through the lyceum movement). A fundamental motive behind Gallaudet's efforts in the field of education was that as an evangelical Christian he saw in education the means of promoting moral reform and Christian benevolence.

The first of 12 children, Thomas Hopkins Gallaudet was born on December 10, 1787, to a firmly religious family in Philadelphia. His father, Peter Wallace Gallaudet, a merchant, traced his ancestry back to French Huguenot settlers of New York. His mother, Jane Hopkins, was a descendant of John Hopkins and of Thomas Hooker, a founder and first minister of Hartford. Though sickly as a child, and indeed throughout his life, Gallaudet was a brilliant student. He entered Yale at the age of 14 and graduated three years later, in 1805, at the top of his class. This was followed by a brief apprenticeship with a law firm and some independent study of literature before his return to Yale in 1808 as a tutor and graduate student. Earning a master of arts degree in 1810, Gallaudet was driven by poor health to seek the benefits of travel and activity in the form of work as a traveling sales agent in the western wilds of Ohio and Kentucky.

His diaries of this period portray an anguished and earnest young man, seeking to come to terms with his religious impulses, self-doubts, and yearnings for the right profession. By January 1812 he had reached a decision and enrolled in divinity school at Andover Theological Seminary, graduating with a license to preach in 1814. Reluctant to take on a full-time pastorship because of continued ill health, Gallaudet looked forward to serving as an itinerant preacher. However, a remarkable encounter with his young deaf neighbor, Alice Cogswell, in which Gallaudet broke through the communication barrier by teaching her the word "hat," led him to a different destiny. Alice's father, Mason Cogswell, a prominent Hartford physician, was eager for his daughter to be educated without having to be sent abroad. With the backing of wealthy Hartford citizens, Cogswell persuaded an at-first reluctant Gallaudet to cross the Atlantic and learn the European methods of instructing deaf people in order to establish a school in Connecticut. *See* COGSWELL, ALICE.

It seems likely that Gallaudet's original intention was to study both the British (oral) method and the French (manual) method of instruction in order to develop a combined approach. However, while

Thomas Hopkins Gallaudet, a daguerreotype from about 1842. (Archives, College Library, Gallaudet College)

in Britain he found the Braidwood family unwilling to quickly reveal their instructional methods to him, and in addition, he was dissatisfied with the results in those classes he was allowed to observe. Furthermore, in Edinburgh he met the distinguished Scottish mental philosopher Dugald Stewart. Stewart's study of sensory perception and language acquisition led him to argue convincingly to Gallaudet that a purely oral approach was an ineffectual way to teach language to deaf children. Though he did not get the specific training he had originally sought in Great Britain, Gallaudet did learn much that influenced his career as an educator. In addition to Stewart, he made the acquaintance of Dr. John Gordon, author of an article on deafness in Brewster's *Edinburgh Encyclopedia*, and attended a long series of lectures on the philosophy of the human mind by university professor Thomas Brown. *See* BRAIDWOOD, THOMAS.

In Paris, the Abbé Sicard, head of the Institut Royal des Sourds-Muets, gave Gallaudet a much warmer reception than had the Braidwoods. Gallaudet observed the methods used in each level of class, received private instruction on methodology from Sicard, and studied sign language with two teachers and prize graduates of the Paris institution: Jean Massieu and Laurent Clerc. Gallaudet's decision to hire Clerc as the first teacher of the proposed Hartford school was perhaps the most important one he made in behalf of education for deaf people. *See* MASSIEU, JEAN; SICARD, ABBÉ ROCH AMBROISE CUCURRON.

Accompanied by Clerc, Gallaudet returned to the United States in 1816, and to the task of rounding up public support and organizing the school for deaf Americans. The two men, sometimes accompanied by Mason Cogswell, toured New England towns, meeting legislators and prominent citizens and presenting lecture-demonstrations. Sometimes, Gallaudet preached at churches on behalf of deaf education. At public meetings Clerc would often prepare an address which Gallaudet would read to the audience, after which the two would answer questions. The presence of the deaf, yet well-educated, Clerc was proof that a school for deaf people in the United States could succeed. Thus the 1816 campaign to win support for the school was able to quell the doubts that some Americans still had about the possibility of educating deaf people. By 1817, the new school had been pledged some $5000 in individual contributions and another $5000 from the Connecticut General Assembly, marking the first time in United States history that public money had been appropriated for a benevolent institution.

Gallaudet was appointed principal of the school and continued in that capacity until 1830. Under his stewardship, the innovation of educating deaf people proved its viability. In addition to his administrative duties and full-time teaching, he tirelessly publicized the Hartford school and pleaded for public support through lectures, seminars, and writings. He continued to visit New England capitals, conducting exhibitions of the school's top students and lobbying governors and state legislators. As a result of his efforts, the New England states agreed to pay tuition for poor deaf students and the federal government provided land grants to support deaf education. Under his leadership, the Hartford school served as a model and source of expertise to fledgling institutions in other parts of the country. By 1830, the year of Gallaudet's retirement, five publicly supported schools for the deaf were in operation, and what had started as an educational innovation instigated and nurtured by Gallaudet had become an entrenched American institution, adopted by state governments as their responsibility.

Much of Gallaudet's success as leader of the American deaf education movement was the result of his rhetorical and literary skill. His reputation as a preacher was made early in his career with the 1818 publication of *Discourses on Various Points of Christian Faith and Practice*, a collection of sermons he had delivered in the Chapelle d'Oratoire (Chapel of the Oratory) while in Paris in 1816. A sampling of his published addresses shows the variety of benevolent causes Gallaudet spoke for, even

while fully engaged as an educator of deaf persons. In 1819 he delivered "An Address in Behalf of the Sandwich Island Mission." In 1820 his "Discourse, Delivered at the Annual Meeting of the Hartford Evangelical Tract Society" was published. His "Address on Female Education" was delivered in 1827 and published the following year. Three of Gallaudet's key addresses in behalf of deaf education are: "A Sermon Delivered at the Opening of the Connecticut Asylum," 1817; "A Discourse Delivered at the Dedication of the American Asylum," 1821; and "On the Duty and Advantages of Affording Instruction to the Deaf and Dumb," published in 1824.

This last address Gallaudet delivered at a number of occasions and places, including the principal towns of New England during his 1824 campaign for support for the Connecticut school, and again in 1828 to the U.S. House of Representatives. No less a critic than John Quincy Adams praised the sermon for its rational and emotive power. Indeed, the oration captures the means Gallaudet used to sway public opinion in behalf of education for deaf people, and helps account for his phenomenal success in this regard. In the sermon, Gallaudet portrayed the supporters of deaf education as Christian heroes. These saviors were freeing the heathen deaf who had been imprisoned in a dark dungeon of ignorance through no fault of their own. In this way, the sermon claimed, the biblical prophecy that "they that have not heard, shall understand" was coming true and thus the education of deaf Americans was a sign that the new Millennium, the Second Coming, was at hand.

Gallaudet's sermon captured much of the spirit of early-nineteenth-century America and an era of reform. Stimulated by the intellectual currents of evangelism, nationalism, and enlightenment philosophy, Americans banded together in benevolent organizations to foster social improvement, ranging from prison reform to asylums for the insane. While they addressed practical social problems, these benevolent undertakings were guided also by a religious motive: the goals of spiritual salvation and conversion to Christian beliefs. Reformers saw the growth of benevolence, the curing of social ills, and the conversion of the heathen as sure signs of a coming millennium marked by prosperity, righteousness, and the spiritual rule of Christ. Thus, the efforts to secure education of deaf Americans were part of the larger trend of benevolent social change. In this context, Gallaudet can be seen as a master of the rhetoric of early-nineteenth-century reform, promoting the cause of deaf education as one herald of America's millennial dream.

A prolific writer, Gallaudet pushed for education reform in print as well as from the pulpit and platform. He published widely in journals and magazines. Among his earlier writing is a series of articles published in the *Christian Observer*, a British monthly, in 1818 and 1819 and a second series in 1826. The first set of articles comprised Gallaudet's arguments in defense of the use of sign language for teaching deaf people. The later series is more of a treatise on language and its acquisition followed by the interesting suggestion that sign language could be of use to foreign missionaries in communicating abroad. *See* SIGN LANGUAGES.

Gallaudet did not write again on the subject of sign language until 1847. This time his forum was the newly created journal *American Annals of the Deaf and Dumb*. He wrote in an attempt to refute Horace Mann's well-publicized opinion that the European schools with their oral instructional methods were superior to those in the United States. The same journal also published Gallaudet's "Reminiscences of Deaf-Mute Instruction" in 1849. In 1858 the *American Annals of the Deaf and Dumb* posthumously published "Reading on the Lips," a brief description of an early encounter between Gallaudet and a deafened farmer.

Gallaudet's broad interest in education is reflected in some of his other writing. The series "Remarks on Seminars for Teachers" appeared in the *Connecticut Observer* newspaper beginning January 5, 1825. In 1830 he published the articles "Methods of Teaching to Read" and "Philosophy of Language" in the *American Journal* and *Annals of Education and Instruction*. The same year saw the publication of *The Child's Picture Defining and Reading Book*. This was followed in 1836 by *The Child's Book of the Soul*, the most popular of a number of widely distributed children's books on religion that Gallaudet wrote for the American Tract Society.

In 1831–1833 Gallaudet wrote the series "Language of Infancy" for the *American Annals of Education and Instruction*. In the same journal he published: the series "Family and School Discipline" in 1837; the article "Recollections of the Deaf and Dumb; To Illustrate the Principles of Family and School Discipline" in 1838; and the essay "On Attention" in 1839. In 1838–1839 he also published the series of articles "Female Teachers of Common Schools" for the *Connecticut Common School Journal*, followed in 1839–1840 by the series "Co-operation of Parents in Improving Common Schools." In 1839–1840 he also wrote the long series "Domestic Education at Table" for *Mother's Magazine*.

Gallaudet died on September 10, 1851, in Hartford. His interest in education and deafness was carried on by the work of his deaf wife, Sophia Fowler, one of the first graduates of the Hartford school, and by two of their children. The eldest, Thomas Gallaudet, became a minister to a deaf congregation at St. Ann's Church in New York City. The youngest, Edward Miner Gallaudet, became

the first president of Gallaudet College, which was named for his father, Thomas Hopkins Gallaudet. *See* EDUCATION: History; GALLAUDET, EDWARD MINER; GALLAUDET COLLEGE.

Bibliography

Barnard, Henry: *Tribute to Gallaudet*, 2d ed., F. C. Brownell, New York, 1859.

Fernandes, James J.: "The Gate to Heaven: T. H. Gallaudet and the Rhetoric of the Deaf Education Movement," unpublished doctoral dissertation, University of Michigan, 1980.

————: "Thomas Hopkins Gallaudet on Language and Communication: A Reassessment," *American Annals of the Deaf*, vol. 128, no. 4, August 1983.

Gallaudet, Edward Miner: *The Life of Thomas Hopkins Gallaudet*, Henry Holt, New York, 1888.

Humphrey, Heman: *The Life and Labors of the Rev. T. H. Gallaudet, LL.D.*, R. Carter, New York, 1857.

Mattingly, Paul H.: "Why NYU Chose Gallaudet," *New York University Education Quarterly*, pp. 9–15, Fall 1981.

James J. Fernandes

GALLAUDET COLLEGE

Gallaudet College is an accredited postsecondary institution functioning within the system of higher education in the United States. Serving primarily severely hearing-impaired students, it is known as the national college for the deaf. The college evolved from a small elementary school for deaf children established in 1856 into a liberal arts college. Eventually the liberal arts college became a multipurpose institution in the pattern of land-grant colleges and universities, and began to respond to many educational needs of deaf people nationwide.

The main campus of Gallaudet College, located in Washington, D.C., about a mile from the Capitol Building, consists of 99 acres of land. The campus is known as Kendall Green in recognition of one of the college's founders, Amos Kendall. The older part of the campus, now designated as a registered historic district, was landscaped by the famous nineteenth-century landscape architect Frederick Law Olmsted. The structures on the original site are mainly Victorian Gothic in style, and include College Hall, Chapel Hall, the Old Gymnasium, Fowler Hall, Dawes House, Kendall Hall, the Edward Miner Gallaudet Residence, the Ballard House, the Fay House, and the Denison House.

The remainder of the campus is characterized by several academic buildings and dormitories constructed in the mid-1950s. Campus facilities grew still further during the 1970s by the addition of a Learning Center (library, classrooms, and educational technology building), cafeteria, field house, central utilities building, and four dormitories. A Model Secondary School for the Deaf, opened in 1976, was constructed on 17 acres are the north-

Learning Center on Kendall Green. (Gallaudet College Photo Services)

western part of the campus, and a new Kendall Demonstration Elementary School, opened in 1980, was constructed on 6 acres in the northeastern part of the campus. *See* KENDALL DEMONSTRATION ELEMENTARY SCHOOL; MODEL SECONDARY SCHOOL FOR THE DEAF.

Gallaudet College obtained 8.7 acres of land and seven buildings, the campus of the former Marjorie Webster Junior College, from the federal government by an act of Congress signed into law by President Ronald Reagan on November 20, 1981. This campus was acquired primarily to accommodate expanding enrollments of the college due to the rubella epidemic of 1964 and 1965, which produced an estimated 17,400 deaf children. The college established a School of Preparatory Studies on this campus; however, the facilities are used for other college activities as space is available.

Gallaudet College is an associate member of the Consortium of Universities of the Washington Metropolitan Area. The universities composing the consortium are the American University, Catholic University of America, Howard University, Georgetown University, George Washington University, and University of the District of Columbia. Associate members, in addition to Gallaudet College, are Mount Vernon College and Trinity College. Membership in the consortium enables students, faculty, staff, and administrators to have access to many of the resources of the university community in Washington, D.C.

ORIGIN AND EARLY YEARS

Amos Kendall, postmaster general under Presidents Andrew Jackson and Martin Van Buren, established a small school for deaf and blind children in the District of Columbia in 1856. On February 16, 1857, Kendall encouraged Congress to incorporate the Columbia Institution for the Instruction of the Deaf, Dumb and Blind in a house which he donated along with two acres of land about a mile from the Capitol Building. Kendall and other prominent citizens in the District of Columbia served as trustees for the school, which opened with 16 students. In 1865 the blind students transferred to an institution for blind children in Maryland.

Kendall then employed Edward Miner Gallaudet, only 20 years old, as the first superintendent of the Columbia Institution. He was the son of Thomas Hopkins Gallaudet, who was the founder of the American School for the Deaf in Hartford, Connecticut, the first public residential school for deaf children in the United States. Gallaudet accepted the superintendency of the small institution because he had a vision of establishing a college for deaf persons. Gallaudet wrote in later years: "I visited Washington at once and had satisfactory interviews with Mr. Kendall. I unfolded to him my plan for a college and said that if he and his associates in the management of the proposed institution would support me in these plans, I would accept their offer. They met my overtures with alacrity, pleased with the idea of having what they had conceived of as no more than a small local school, grow ultimately into an institution of national importance and influence." *See* AMERICAN SCHOOL FOR THE DEAF; GALLAUDET, EDWARD MINER; GALLAUDET, THOMAS HOPINS.

When Gallaudet arrived in Washington, D.C., to take up his assignment as superintendent, Kendall was 68 years old. Kendall was an experienced journalist and politician, while Gallaudet, with a degree from Yale University, was a young, inspired educator of deaf people. On April 8, 1864, President Abraham Lincoln signed into law an enabling act that authorized the Columbia Institution to grant college degrees in the liberal arts and sciences. In the same year, Gallaudet became the president of the college division. Women were admitted to the college in 1887, and the training of teachers for deaf persons began in 1891 in the Normal Training Department. In 1894 the name of the college division of the institution was changed to Gallaudet College in honor of Thomas Hopkins Gallaudet.

Percival Hall, a graduate of Harvard University and the Normal Training Department of the college, became the second president of the college in 1910. During this administration, federal financial support for the institution continued and enrollment gradually increased.

PROGRESS IN THE 1950s

Leonard Elstad was named the third president of Gallaudet College in 1945. During Elstad's tenure the institution changed and grew. On June 18, 1954, the entire institution was named Gallaudet College by an act of Congress, and the board of directors was expanded in order to provide for national representation.

With a federal charter and strong authorizing legislation passed by Congress, Gallaudet College continued to obtain substantial federal financial support. The Department of Health, Education, and Welfare was established in 1953, and two officials of the new department, Nelson A. Rockefeller and Bradshaw Mintener, took a personal interest in Gallaudet College and supported its development. Federal funds were obtained by Elstad to construct a new library, student union building, classroom building, gymnasium, art building, four dormitories, and a new structure for the Kendall School, which functioned as a laboratory school for the teacher-training department. With these new facilities to offer, the enrollment of the college rose rapidly from approximately 200 students to 700. During Elstad's tenure, the college obtained full accreditation by the Middle States Association of Colleges and Schools.

GROWTH IN THE 1970S

In May 1969 Elstad signed an agreement with the Secretary of Health, Education, and Welfare in accordance with the Model Secondary School for the Deaf Act to establish and to operate a Model Secondary School for the Deaf. The legislation required that this school be established on the grounds of Gallaudet College to serve primarily an attendance area of the District of Columbia, Maryland, Virginia, West Virginia, Pennsylvania, and Delaware. The school was to demonstrate exemplary construction and innovative curricula. It was also charged with the development and testing of appropriate materials to serve adolescent deaf students in the Model Secondary School for the Deaf and in other programs throughout the United States. Although Elstad had entered into the agreement to establish and to operate the school, implementation of this agreement became the responsibility of Edward C. Merrill, Jr., who was appointed fourth president of Gallaudet College on July 1, 1969.

On December 24, 1971, President Richard M. Nixon signed the Kendall Demonstration Elementary School Act. This law authorized Gallaudet College to develop the existing Kendall School into a national demonstration day school similar in its role and function to the Model Secondary School for the Deaf. During the 1970s, both of these schools were established in response to the legislation for each. The Model Secondary School for the Deaf has a capacity of 450 to 500 students, and the Kendall Demonstration Elementary School can serve 250 to 300 students. A wide range of curriculum materials have been developed and tested by these schools

Kendall Demonstration Elementary School classroom. (Gallaudet College Photo Services)

and are available for use in other programs that are serving an estimated 60,000 to 70,000 hearing-impaired children and youth throughout the nation.

During the 1970s, Gallaudet College evolved into a multipurpose institution. The college established a Center for Continuing Education and began to open adult education programs for deaf people through its demonstration program. Gallaudet extension centers were negotiated with two community colleges, one in Kansas and one in Massachusetts, which extended the outreach of the college still farther. The college established a National Center on Law and the Deaf and saw the growth of the International Center on Deafness. The college began to focus national attention on the needs of deaf people through a wide variety of workshops, seminars, and research. For example, the first national conference on the status of deaf women was held, and studies were conducted concerning the occupational status of deaf persons in the nation's work force.

As these program developments occurred, the college completed construction of its new facilities, and several buildings were expanded, renovated, or restored. Enrollment during the 1970s and early 1980s rose to over 1500 undergraduate and graduate students.

During the seventies, the older buildings which had been built during the administration of Gallaudet were designated a national historic district by the Department of the Interior.

CHALLENGES OF THE 1980S

In the midsixties the United States experienced one of the worst epidemics of maternal rubella in its history. When this virus infects expectant mothers during the first trimester of pregnancy, the probability is high that the mother will bear a child who will be disabled, even multihandicapped. While the number of children deafened by all causes had averaged approximately 3000 per year, the number of early-deafened children was over 7000 in 1964 and over 5000 in 1965. This group of students taxed the resources of various local and state schools for special children. The babies of the 1960s became the young people of the 1980s who completed special programs throughout the nation. The number of deaf persons in the age group of 18–25 grew rapidly from approximately 25,000 in 1980 to 40,000 in the mideighties. Some of these young people moved directly into the labor force. Others sought a variety of vocational educational programs, where they learned specific marketable skills. Some students qualified to enter postsecondary programs. Although they demonstrated intellectual ability equal to or better than many hearing college students, they brought with them the usual academic problems which accompany early and profound deafness. They had language deficits and difficulty speechreading and expressing themselves orally. These students sought admission to Gallaudet College and other programs designed to provide the special services that they required in order to succeed academically. *See* HEARING LOSS: Incidence and Prevalence, Prenatal Causes.

As previously mentioned, Gallaudet College obtained facilities in northwest Washington that enabled it to open a School of Preparatory Studies. After appropriate renovations of the former junior college site, this facility enabled the college to expand its entering enrollment and to accept those rubella-deafened young people who qualified.

THE GOVERNING BODY

Congress incorporated the Columbia Institution on February 16, 1857. Ninety-seven years after the original incorporation of Gallaudet College, the 83d Congress enacted Public Law 420 amending the charter to change the name of the institution, defining its corporate powers, providing for its organization and administration, expanding the board of directors (later called the board of trustees), authorizing appropriations by Congress for the institution on a permanent basis, and defining the purposes of Gallaudet College to provide education and training to deaf persons and to further the education of deaf people. Congress later expanded the mission of Gallaudet College to include a Model Secondary School for the Deaf (P.L. 89-694) and the Kendall Demonstration Elementary School (P.L. 91-487.) These acts, together with other provisions of the law applicable to Gallaudet College, constitute the legal basis for the establishment and operation of the college.

The board of trustees exercises the corporate powers of the college provided by Congress. The function of the board is policy making, assurance of sound management, and active participation in obtaining necessary funds for the educational, research, and service programs. The board has initial and ultimate responsibility in determining general, educational, financial, and related policies deemed necessary for the administration and development of the college in accord with its stated purpose and goals for the education of deaf persons.

The board of trustees consists of 21 voting members and additional honorary, emeritus, and special members. Three voting members are public members, of whom one is a senator appointed by the President of the Senate and two are representatives appointed by the Speaker of the House of Representatives. Eighteen members, at least four of whom are deaf, are elected by the board of trustees. Among those elected by the board has been the Secretary of Education and the secretary's designated representative from the Department of Education.

RELATIONSHIP WITH THE FEDERAL GOVERNMENT

Gallaudet College has a unique relationship with the federal government resulting from the involvement of Congress and federal agencies since the establishment of the institution. Gallaudet College is a federally assisted private corporation. It is involved with the federal government in the annual federal appropriation, the budget process, and reporting requirements.

Although Gallaudet College has been partially, but substantially, funded annually by Congress since the establishment of the institution, specific authorizations for federal appropriations for the operation of the college were granted by enabling legislation in 1954 and in subsequent years.

ACCREDITATIONS

Gallaudet College is fully accredited and approved by the following agencies: the Middle States Association of Colleges and Schools; the National Council for the Accreditation of Teacher Education; the Educational Testing Board of the American Speech, Hearing and Language Association; the Council of Social Work Education; the Council of Rehabilitation Education; and the District of Columbia Licensure Board in Teacher Education.

DIPLOMAS AND DEGREES OFFERED

The Model Secondary School for the Deaf presents high school diplomas to those students completing secondary education requirements.

Gallaudet College offers an associate of arts degree in interpreting for hearing people who wish to become certified sign language interpreters. The college gives bachelor of science or bachelor of arts degrees in 26 major fields of study. The Graduate School offers two-year programs of study leading to the master of science degree in audiology and the master of arts degree in education, rehabilitation counseling, school counseling, educational technology, and linguistics. The Ph.D. degree in the administration of special programs is offered by the Graduate School in conjunction with the Consortium of Universities in the Washington area. The college also conducts extensive noncredit courses, workshops, seminars, and internships for which certificates are awarded.

ENROLLMENTS
The Model Secondary School for the Deaf annually enrolls over 400 students from its primary enrollment area and 20 other states. The Kendall Demonstration Elementary School enrolls annually approximately 200 day students from Washington, D.C., northern Virginia, and nearby Maryland counties. Typically, Gallaudet College enrolls about 1100 undergraduate students and 300 graduate students.

Through the Division of Public Services, the college provides a wide range of flexible programs and services touching between 25,000 and 30,000 people during the year. The management of a very busy summer session, which attracts around 4000 enrollments, is also the responsibility of this division.

CHARACTERISTICS OF STUDENTS
The Kendall Demonstration Elementary School accepts approximately 200 students from the onset of deafness through age 14. These children attend a day school program and reside in the District of Columbia, northern Virginia, and nearby Maryland counties. Among these children, 90 percent have a severe to profound hearing loss, and the other 10 percent have a severe to moderate loss. Approximately 30 percent of the children have a disability in addition to deafness. The Kendall School has a parent-infant program and four departments: preschool, primary, intermediate, and middle school. *See* AUDIOLOGIC CLASSIFICATION.

The Model Secondary School for the Deaf accepts hearing-impaired students from its primary attendance area, and students beyond this area may attend if there is no suitable program in their locality and enrollment maximums at the Model School have not been reached. The average hearing loss of students at the Model School is 94 decibels in the better ear. Approximately 80 percent of students at the Model School report birth as the time of onset of their deafness.

The college division accepts undergraduate students who are recommended by a local school district or special school, who have completed a secondary program, and who have indicated potential for postsecondary study on the Gallaudet entrance examination. Over 1400 students take the Gallaudet examination. Of this number, usually half qualify for admission. Of those who qualify, approximately 70 percent must take up to one year of preparatory studies before they earn admission to the first-year class. Approximately two-thirds of the students have a profound hearing loss, and over 25 percent have a severe loss. The average loss in the better ear over a five-year period is 93 decibels. Between 90 and 95 percent of the students lost their

Classroom scene. (Gallaudet College Photo Services)

hearing before school age. Since 1970 the median age of the onset of deafness has been birth.

The Graduate School accepts both hearing and hearing-impaired students pursuing master's degrees in counseling, education, educational technology, linguistics, and psychology. Hearing students are accepted for a master's degree in audiology. The Graduate School also offers a Ph.D. in the administration of special education. Generally, a third of the applicants are hearing-impaired.

The College of Continuing Education offers annual extension credit courses, summer programs, hearing-vision-impaired programs, and adult education. The college also provides resources for courses offered in extension centers. The full-time equivalent of students involved in continuing education averages around 2000. Other units of the Division of Public Services, such as the National Academy, sponsor numerous workshops and training programs.

In summary, Gallaudet serves hearing-impaired persons ranging from infants to deaf adults. These programs are not intended to be continuous or consecutive. However, they respond to a wide variety of educational needs, with students from the entire nation enrolling in programs.

A TYPICAL COLLEGE EXPERIENCE

By coming to Gallaudet College, the hearing-impaired student has an opportunity to have a typical college experience because the academic program responds to the needs of deaf students. Students feel that the collegiate environment is as normal as the usual campuses because, often for the first time in their lives, they have clear communication with virtually everyone. Finally, students have a wide choice of organizations and activities in which they may participate just as hearing students would on other campuses.

The college has an active student government and an independent student newspaper, *The Buff and Blue*, in which student opinion surfaces and campus, national, and world news appears. A student may join the staff of the *Tower Clock*, the yearbook, or choose to participate in the publication of *Manus*, a literary magazine which is published annually. A student with an inclination toward drama can participate in fall and winter productions which are presented in signs and voice and are open to the general public. On two occasions, in 1971 and in 1983, productions by Gallaudet College drama students won the eastern regional competition in the American College Theater Festival and appeared in national competition at the John F. Kennedy Center in Washington, D.C.

The college has three sororities (Chi Omega Psi, Delta Epsilon, and Phi Kappa Zeta) and three fraternities (Alpha Sigma Pi, Kappa Gamma, and

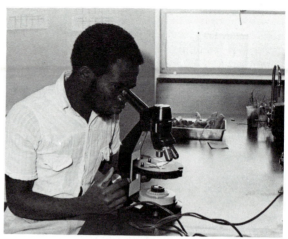

Laboratory facility. (Gallaudet College Photo Services)

Kappa Sigma). These sororities and fraternities, although not nationally affiliated, have the same traditions and practices as found on other college campuses. The college also has a colony of the Alpha Phi Omega national service fraternity. There are also intersorority and interfraternity councils.

Both the Model Secondary School for the Deaf and the college offer students an opportunity to participate in a wide variety of sports. The college competes with other collegiate teams in football, soccer, rugby, track, volleyball (men's and women's teams), basketball, baseball, field hockey (for women), tennis (for men and women), and golf. The percentage of students involved in athletic activities at Gallaudet College is far higher than student involvement in varsity athletics in many large institutions.

At the Model Secondary School for the Deaf, students have an opportunity to become involved in interest groups such as the photo club and home economics club. Students also participate in the preparation of the yearbook as well as service organizations such as a local chapter of the Junior National Association of the Deaf or a chapter of Junior Lions International.

With this range of organizations and activities, students at the Model Secondary School for the Deaf and Gallaudet College have remarkably typical high school and collegiate experiences.

COMMUNICATION: POLICY AND PRACTICE

Gallaudet College offers educational programs that are directed toward the same goals held by all elementary, secondary, and postsecondary institutions. The college and its various units are committed, however, to providing instruction through clear communication for early and profoundly deafened individuals. The primary or major communication strategy in the instructional setting is the simultaneous method of communication. This method requires the use of English grammar and syntax in spoken or mouthed form accompanied by signs and fingerspelled words. Audition, the use of residual hearing enhanced by amplification, is encouraged. The American Sign Language, which is a nonspoken native language of deaf persons, may be used on the campus to meet special needs. *See* EDUCATION: Communication; SIGN LANGUAGES: American; SOCIOLINGUISTICS: Simultaneous Communication.

INSTRUCTIONAL TALENT

Three faculties function on Kendall Green. The Kendall Demonstration Elementary School faculty, the Model Secondary School for the Deaf faculty, and the collegiate faculty. Requirements for faculty positions reflect faculty roles in the respective schools; however, there are common requirements for all faculty which respond to the special mission of the institution. In addition to appropriate academic credentials, faculty members must participate in an intensive orientation program. Faculty are also expected to demonstrate competence in expressive and receptive communication skills. Tenure is not awarded to a faculty member who cannot communicate clearly with students in an instructional setting by using simultaneous communication. Faculty members, particularly at the college level, are engaged in instruction, research, public service, and publishing; and many have become nationally known in their respective fields.

The collegiate faculty elects members to a Graduate Council which generally establishes the policies and operational procedures for the Graduate School. As in most colleges and universities, faculty members must qualify for teaching at the graduate level.

RESEARCH

Hearing impairment is a disability which, if severe, impedes an individual's ability to obtain education and employment. It also reduces the opportunity to participate in a variety of social activities. Research is essentially a problem-solving activity directed toward enhancing the lives of deaf people by addressing problems they experience in a hearing environment. The research efforts of Gallaudet College are focused within the Gallaudet Research Institute and its three centers.

The Center for Assessment and Demographic Studies evaluates instruments used with hearing-impaired children and conducts an annual survey of hearing-impaired children and youth. The Center for Studies in Language and Communication has conducted landmark research on the American Sign Language, is searching for a more complete picture of speech discrimination ability, is spon-

soring a new rehabilitation engineering project, and is testing an autocuer, a wearable device that will electronically produce cues in response to spoken language. The Center on Education and Human Development directs its attention to learning and cognitive studies, teaching, and child development studies, mental health projects, and Signed English research. These projects have resulted, for example, in the Signed English series of books for children and the Meadow/Kendall Social-Emotional Inventory.

The Division of Research at the college is recognized both nationally and internationally as a center where significant research focuses on the amelioration of the effects of deafness in learning and in life.

INSTITUTIONAL OUTREACH

Although Gallaudet College is essentially an educational institution, it endeavors to respond to requests for a wide variety of public services.

The Gallaudet College Press accepts manuscripts that have particular relevance and meaning to persons who are interested in hearing impairment. Some of the titles reflect the scope of these publications: *The Signed English Series*, *The Deaf Adult Speaks Out*, *Total Communication*, *Teachers of the Deaf*, *Hearing Impaired Children in the Mainstream*, and more specialized books in the fields of psychology, sign language, sociology, speech, audiology, language, and multiple-handicapping conditions. The college also provides periodicals: *The World Around Us* is for the school-age hearing-impaired child and has a circulation approaching 8000; *Perspectives* is for the teacher of the school-age child; *Directions* is a journal which provides an update on academic, professional, career, and research activities.

During the course of a year, the Information Center on Deafness within the Office of Institutional Advancement will respond to thousands of requests for general and technical information on deafness. The Visitor's Center of Gallaudet College is located in the Edward Miner Gallaudet Memorial Building and offers exhibits that introduce the uninitiated person to the nature of deafness, the educational needs of deaf people, technical assistance available to hearing-impaired people, and information about the wide range of accomplishments of deaf people within the larger society. The college has a National Academy which assists various professions to respond more fully to the needs of deaf people. For example, the National Academy sponsored workshops on the mental health needs of deaf people with the psychiatric divisions of various medical schools. The National Academy produced and distributed a videotape to inform nurses how to provide for the deaf patient in the hospital.

This same unit sponsored several seminars for deaf adults in the political process.

The National Center on Law and the Deaf provides limited clinical service to deaf people who encounter legal problems, and serves as an advocacy group for deaf citizens. The center files briefs on proposed legislation at both the state and national levels to ensure that the impact of such legislation on the deaf person is supportive. *See* LEGAL SERVICES.

Gallaudet College publishes a wide range of materials. The most basic of these are curriculum guides in subjects such as language, science, and mathematics. Other guides are for teachers of hearing-impaired students; they include such titles as *Evaluation of an In-Service Program* and *Guidelines to Writing or Rewriting Materials for Deaf Students*. The academic units of the college sometimes publish collections of papers that are in great demand.

ALUMNI

The Gallaudet College Alumni Association has 44 chapters within the United States. Alumni reside in most of the states and several foreign countries. The alumni are characteristically loyal to the institution and assemble every three years in an alumni meeting.

A survey of the alumni reveals the following characteristics: Of the graduates who responded, 85 percent are employed in professional, technical, and managerial occupations. Of the graduates, 39 percent had earned master's degrees and 3 percent had earned doctorates. During their lifetimes, graduates of Gallaudet College earned, on the average, more than deaf persons without a college degree.

The Gallaudet College Alumni Association sponsors the Laurent Clerc Graduate Fellowship Fund. Increments from this fund are awarded annually to deserving deaf persons for advanced study. Not only do the alumni provide nationwide leadership for many organizations serving the deaf, but they also are engaged in a wide variety of professions and occupations. *See* GALLAUDET COLLEGE ALUMNI ASSOCIATION.

INTERNATIONAL INVOLVEMENT

Foreign students receiving degrees from Gallaudet College have generally proved to be effective citizens in their native lands. In fact, a Gallaudet College graduate is often the only college-educated deaf person in the country to which he or she returns.

The International Center on Deafness is the administrative unit within the college that coordinates the involvement of the college in international affairs. This center names the delegates to international conferences, responds to requests for technical assistance, and sponsors seminars for professional staff members from other countries.

These seminars are offered in English, German, French, and Spanish. The International Center on Deafness also arranges itineraries for visiting professional persons from other countries and on occasion provides on-campus accommodations for them for limited periods of time.

THE CONTINUING MISSION

Although Gallaudet College is a unique institution, it represents accredited elementary, secondary, and postsecondary programs adapted to the needs of particular people. It has proved that people who are early and profoundly deafened can achieve a bona fide college degree if the mode of communication is clear. By accommodating the needs of the deaf person, the college makes available an education which is similar to the experience obtained by hearing students in other colleges. The deaf person participates in athletic programs, student government, and social organizations; develops a realistic self-perception, becomes a more independent thinker, learns about the external world, and develops an occupational interest and capability. Through appropriate educational opportunity, the individual largely overcomes the inconveniences of disability, leads a normal life, and, in most instances, makes a significant contribution to society.

Edward C. Merrill, Jr.

GALLAUDET COLLEGE ALUMNI ASSOCIATION

The Gallaudet College Alumni Association (GCAA) has over 4000 life members on record, representing more than 50 percent of the alumni of the four-year liberal arts college exclusively for deaf persons, located in Washington, D.C. *See* GALLAUDET COLLEGE.

FOUNDING

The GCAA was founded on June 27, 1889, during the third convention of the National Association of the Deaf (NAD) in Washington, D.C. The alumni met on the campus of the college (then called the National Deaf-Mute College) and formed an association. It was incorporated in the District of Columbia in 1909. *See* NATIONAL ASSOCIATION OF THE DEAF.

John B. Hotchkiss, a member of the class of 1869 and a Gallaudet faculty member, chaired the organizational meeting. Meville Ballard, the first and only graduate of the college in 1866, was elected president; John Hotchkiss, vice president; George W. Veditz, a member of the class of 1884, secretary; and Amos G. Draper, a member of the class of 1872 and a Gallaudet professor, treasurer. Thirty-one alumni paid their one-dollar annual dues that day and were recorded as charter members. That group represented Gallaudet classes of 1866 to 1889. *See* Veditz, George William.

PURPOSES

The GCAA was organized "to preserve and increase the prestige and influence of Gallaudet College as an institution of higher education for the deaf; to promote those concerns that affect the welfare of the deaf in general, especially those associated with education; and to perpetuate the friendships formed during college life and to promote social and fraternal relations among alumni of different college generations."

The GCAA has held triennial reunions, with a few exceptions. Most reunions have been held on the college campus, Kendall Green, but in the early years reunions were often held in various large cities in conjunction with other national meetings, such as the convention of the National Association of the Deaf or the Convention of American Instructors of the Deaf (CAID). *See* Convention of American Instructors of the Deaf.

MEMBERSHIP

There are four categories of membership in the GCAA: active, associate, honorary, and subscribing. Active members are those who have graduated from the college. Only active members may hold office in the GCAA. Associate members are those who have attended the college at least one year. Honorary membership is conferred by vote of the members; membership is conferred automatically upon those who receive an honorary degree from the college. Subscribing membership is open to friends and supporters of the college. New members pay a one-time life membership fee, the amount of which is determined by the board of directors.

AFFILIATIONS AND CHAPTERS

The GCAA is an associate member of the World Federation of the Deaf and a member of the American Coalition of Citizens with Disabilities. It was a founding member of the now defunct Council of Organizations Serving the Deaf. *See* Council of Organizations Serving the Deaf; World Federation of the Deaf.

The GCAA has 55 chapters in the United States and Canada. Most of these chapters were organized in the larger cities where there were significant concentrations of alumni or in the cities where there were residential schools for deaf students. The chapters were established to encourage young deaf students to attend Gallaudet College, to undertake projects in support of the college and the alumni association, and to perpetuate friendships established during college days. In the early days these organizations were called branches. The alumni in Minnesota were the first to form a branch

in 1895. Soon others followed and the number of chapters grew. The newest chapter was formed in Alaska in 1985. GCAA chapters have been very supportive of programs in schools for deaf children in their localities. They have raised funds for student loans, scholarships and other awards, athletic uniforms, and other needs. They have provided travel funds for students participating in leadership conferences and for needy students attending Gallaudet College. They have sponsored annual Gallaudet Day (December 10) programs and literary programs.

The chapters have contributed toward memorials, endowment funds, scholarship funds, and other fund-raising efforts conducted by the GCAA. They have collected and donated college memorabilia for the college archives and museum. A number of the chapters helped to launch the *Gallaudet Alumni Bulletin*, the GCAA's first publication.

HISTORY

In 1893, through efforts by the alumni, the name of the college was changed from National Deaf-Mute College to Gallaudet College in honor of Thomas Hopkins Gallaudet, one of the founders of the first permanent free school for deaf people in the United States and the father of the college's first president, Edward Miner Gallaudet. *See* Gallaudet, Edward Miner; Gallaudet, Thomas Hopkins.

In 1907 the alumni established the Edward Miner Gallaudet Fund on the occasion of Edward Miner Gallaudet's seventieth birthday and the fiftieth year of his work at Kendall Green. The fund grew over the years and, in the early 1950s, was used along with funds appropriated by the U.S. Congress to construct the Edward Miner Gallaudet Memorial Library. The library was completed in 1956 and helped toward the accreditation of the college in 1957 by the Middle States Association.

Alumni persuaded the college around 1915 to offer more technical courses of study in response to a changing industrial labor market. These courses led to the establishment of a technical department at the college. In the 1940s GCAA was successful in helping the college to win federal civil service status for its employees. In 1947 GCAA prevailed upon the college board of directors to add an alumni representative. Boyce R. Williams was chosen as the first alumni representative on the board. Today four alumni serve on the Gallaudet board of trustees. *See* Williams, Boyce Robert.

Over the years many portraits, busts, bas reliefs, and other memorials have been collected and hung in the college's Chapel Hall, a national landmark on the Gallaudet campus. The GCAA has a significant role in the growth and preservation of this collection. These memorials honor some of the world's leading educators of deaf people, faculty and staff members of Gallaudet College, and outstanding alumni. The collection includes a bust of the Abbé Charles de l'Epée, the founder of the first free school for the deaf people in the world (in Paris). There is a statue of Edward Miner Gallaudet by Pietro Lazzari, presented to the college by the GCAA in 1969. There is a bust of President James A. Garfield by Daniel Chester French. Garfield was a staunch supporter of higher education for deaf persons during his tenure in the U.S. Congress and as president. A bronze and marble tablet honors President Abraham Lincoln, who signed the college's charter in 1864 and who was the first United States President to be patron of Gallaudet College, a tradition that has continued to this day. *See* L'EPÉE, ABBÉ CHARLES MICHEL DE.

FUND RAISING

In 1960 the GCAA membership voted to launch an aggressive national drive to raise funds to present to the college during its centennial in 1964. David Peikoff, president of the GCAA at that time, was asked to head the drive. He resigned his position as president to become chairperson of the Centennial Fund Committee. During the ensuing seven years, he and his wife Pauline traveled over 56,000 miles by car and visited every state and many parts of Canada, soliciting contributions from alumni and friends. More than 5600 persons gave to the fund, and when it was officially presented to the college in June 1967, it totaled a half million dollars in cash and pledges.

It was agreed between the GCAA and the college that the Centennial Fund would be used to establish three permanent endowment funds: (1) half for the Graduate Fellowship Fund, to provide financial assistance to deaf graduates of Gallaudet College and other accredited colleges and universities seeking advanced degrees; (2) one-fourth for the Laurent Clerc Cultural Fund, named in honor of the first deaf teacher of deaf people in the United States, to promote projects and activities that would lead to the cultural enrichment of the deaf community; (3) one-fourth for an Alumni House Fund, to erect and maintain a multipurpose building on the college campus or in the immediate vicinity. *See* CLERC, LAURENT.

Each year the Graduate Fellowship Fund (GFF) awards grants in varying amounts to qualified deaf students pursuing doctoral degrees. Since 1968, when it began awarding grants, more than $200,000 has been given to 60 candidates studying in a range of fields. More than half of them have completed their doctorates.

The Laurent Clerc Cultural Fund annually presents four awards to individuals who have made significant contributions to the deaf community, namely: the Edward Miner Gallaudet Award to international or national leaders, deaf or hearing, working to promote the well-being of deaf people of the world; the Laurent Clerc Award for outstanding social contributions by a deaf person; the Alice Cogswell Award for valuable service on behalf of deaf people; and the Amos Kendall Award to a deaf person for notable excellence in a professional field not related to deafness.

The amount set aside for construction of an alumni house was insufficient to erect a new building, and inflation and construction costs escalated and outstripped the income earned by the endowment. In 1978 the college and the GCAA decided to use this fund to restore the college's old gymnasium located in the historic section of the campus and to convert it to an alumni house. This saved one of the few remaining examples of Queen Anne architecture in Washington, D.C., and the only remaining physical education facility in the District of Columbia built in the nineteenth century. Fondly called "Ole Jim" by the alumni, this building was designed by Frederick Withers, the renowned architect and founder of the American Institute of Architecture (AIA). The building was begun in 1879 and completed in 1881 at a cost of $14,400, appropriated by Congress. It was the largest wooden structure Withers had ever attempted.

Since funds were still needed to complete the "Ole Jim" restoration, a goal of $1.3 million was set by the college and the GCAA in 1979. Within three years the necessary funds were raised and the restoration project underway. The renovation was completed in time for a ribbon-cutting ceremony on June 25, 1982, during GCAA's thirty-first reunion. "Ole Jim" has offices, conference rooms, a kitchen, and a large dining/lounge area for luncheons, dinners, banquets, and social events.

In 1968 the college, in cooperation with the GCAA, established a permanent alumni office on the campus and hired Jack R. Gannon as the first director of alumni relations and as the executive secretary of the GCAA. Gannon was a teacher, coach, and editor of the school publication at the Nebraska School for the Deaf.

Until 1976 the elections of association officers were held during the reunions. In 1973 the GCAA membership voted to begin electing officers by a national ballot system instead of at triennial reunions, thus giving all members the opportunity to participate in elections instead of just those alumni attending a reunion. Chapters were invited to volunteer to serve as the screening committee and oversee the election process. In 1976 the association conducted its first mail ballot, with the Kentucky chapter in charge.

The GCAA proposed placing a memorial in the village of La Balme, France, to commemorate the birth of Laurent Clerc. In the fall of 1980 five deaf Americans were invited to France as guests of the French National Association of the Deaf. They toured the country, visiting schools, clubs, and organizations of deaf people. The tour culminated in La Balme, a quiet village in the foothills of the French Alps, where a large bronze plaque was formally presented to the mayor and hung in city hall.

Many attempts had been made over the years to get the U.S. Postal Service to issue a stamp commemorating Thomas Hopkins Gallaudet's work on behalf of deaf people. In the early 1980s, a GCAA committee chaired by Kenneth Rothschild succeeded in persuading the Postal Service's Citizens Stamp Advisory Committee to designate a first-class stamp in the Great American series in honor of Thomas Hopkins Gallaudet. The unveiling of the Gallaudet stamp design took place on Kendall Green during the thirty-first GCAA triennial reunion in June 1982. Postmaster General William F. Bolger was the featured speaker and formally unveiled the design. In June 1983 the first-day-of-issue ceremony of the Gallaudet stamp was held at the American School for the Deaf in West Hartford, Connecticut—the school that Gallaudet had established in 1817. Bolger again participated in the program along with American School headmaster Winfield McChord, Gallaudet College president Edward C. Merrill, Jr., and other dignitaries. A number of Gallaudet's descendants were present at the ceremony. *See* AMERICAN SCHOOL FOR THE DEAF; PHILATELY.

In April 1985 the GCAA and Gallaudet College formally dedicated a memorial garden at the Cosmos Club, an exclusive men's club in downtown Washington, D.C., in memory of Edward Miner Gallaudet, the college's first president. Gallaudet was one of the founders and the fifth president of the Cosmos Club. The garden project was initiated by the Laurent Clerc Cultural Fund committee and was a gift to the Cosmos Club from Gallaudet College and the GCAA.

CURRENT ACTIVITIES

Besides maintaining the Alumni Office, representing alumni interests on the campus, and working closely with its 55 chapters, the GCAA carries on several other activities. One is publishing the *Gallaudet Alumni Newsletter* twice monthly, except in June, July, August, and December. The GCAA also coordinates Charter Day, homecoming events, association and class reunions, and special alumni events on the campus; conducts an alumni leadership training program; assists in recruiting, fund raising, and public relations on behalf of the college; cosponsors with Gallaudet College the Gallaudet Journalism Award, which recognizes and commends outstanding efforts of professional writers reporting on deafness and deaf people; publishes

jointly with the National Information Center on Deafness a directory of national organizations and centers of and for deaf persons as a public service; and cosponsors with the Alexandria-Potomac Lions Club a national Outstanding Young Alumnus Award.

INFLUENTIAL INDIVIDUALS

Many individuals have played significant roles in the history of the GCAA. Only four can be mentioned here.

Charles D. Seaton, a teacher at the West Virginia School for the Deaf, was treasurer of the GCAA for seven consecutive terms, spanning a total of 30 years. He served the GCAA as an officer longer than any other individual. Benjamin M. Schowe, a labor specialist with the Firestone Rubber and Tire Company in Akron, Ohio, assumed the presidency of the GCAA in 1945. During his administration the GCAA experienced a surge in growth and activity: the alumni became more directly involved with the college, the GCAA began publication of the *Gallaudet Alumni Bulletin*, fifteen new alumni chapters were organized, and the first alumni representative was appointed to the college board of directors. *See* SCHOWE, BENJAMIN MARSHALL, SR.

In his role as chairperson of the Centennial Fund committee, David Peikoff brought national visibility to the GCAA and helped to propel the organization into a leadership role within the national deaf community. The success of this fund-raising effort by Peikoff and his team made an important impact on Gallaudet College and succeeding generations of deaf people. James N. Orman was a guiding force behind the GCAA. Beginning as its secretary in 1947 and concluding as a board member in 1976, Orman served the GCAA for 29 consecutive years. He was president for two terms and guided the GCAA through one of its stormiest relationships with Gallaudet College—a period when the role of higher education of deaf persons was coming under close scrutiny. The alumni and the college disagreed over the direction Gallaudet College should take. The alumni were concerned over expansion plans which they considered overly ambitious. They wanted to see additional postsecondary opportunities provided for deaf students in areas other than at Gallaudet College. The college administration felt that Gallaudet College should serve a greater number of deaf students. Orman was a strong, courageous leader during this period of disagreement, and it was to his credit that the GCAA emerged from the conflict a stronger and more influential national organization with far-reaching goals. One by-product of this disagreement was the Babbidge Report, a federal study of education of deaf people in the United States. It influenced the establishment of the National Technical Institute for the Deaf in Rochester, New York, and other postsecondary programs for deaf students. *See* NATIONAL TECHNICAL INSTITUTE FOR THE DEAF.

PUBLICATIONS

In May 1946 the GCAA began publishing its own paper, the *Gallaudet Alumni Bulletin.* Prior to that time, reunion proceedings and reports of organization activities had been published in the college student publication, *The Buff and Blue.* The GCAA had very limited funds in those days, so many of the chapters helped cover the cost of publishing the *Bulletin* by taking turns sponsoring an issue. The *Bulletin* appeared in a variety of formats but later became a newsmagazine and continued until 1966 when it was replaced by a monthly newsletter of four to six pages called the *Gallaudet Alumni Newsletter.* Today the *Newsletter* is published twice monthly and has a circulation of around 22,000 and an estimated readership of 35,000, making it one of the most widely read publications of deaf people in the United States. In keeping with the GCAA's objectives to increase the influence of Gallaudet College and to promote those concerns that affect the welfare of deaf people, the *Newsletter* is sent to all Gallaudet College alumni and, upon request, to interested individuals.

Between 1961 and 1964 when the GCAA was involved in raising funds for the Centennial Fund, the association published the *Gallaudet Centennial Newsletter* to keep contributors informed of the progress of the drive.

The GCAA has published five books: *The Silent Muse, An Anthology of Prose and Poetry by the Deaf,* (1960), *Our Heritage, 1864–1964* (1964), *The Gallaudet Almanac* (1974), *Notable Deaf Persons* (1975), and *Interesting Deaf Americans* (1985).

Bibliography

Crammatte, Florence, and Judy Mannes: "Ole Jim—Its History."

Gallaudet College Survey of Alumni, 1981.

GCAA: Acts of Incorporation and By-Laws.

————: Minutes and Proceedings, 1889–1920 (bound copies of *The Buff and Blue*).

————: Reports, 1920–1936 (bound copies of *The Buff and Blue*).

————: Reunion Proceedings, 1939–1960 (scrapbook).

Jack R. Gannon

GERMANY, FEDERAL REPUBLIC OF

The Federal Republic of Germany places great emphasis on the integration of deaf people with the hearing community. Traditionally, since Samuel Heinicke's early efforts, this has meant a strong oral emphasis in schools for deaf pupils and in communication situations. More recently, major strides have been made in differentiating individuals according to degrees or types of hearing loss, in the provision of various sensory aids, and in studies of language development. *See* HEINICKE, SAMUEL.

EDUCATIONAL SYSTEM

In understanding the current educational system, it must be recognized that owing to the destruction of the institutions during World War II and the partition of Germany, the schools and organizational structures could be or had to be reconstructed.

School System After the war, for example, there was mostly new construction of large school systems for hearing-impaired pupils, at first primarily in organizational units. The objective was a better differentiation according to the type and the degree of the hearing loss. The school system for elementary and junior high schools encompasses more than 60 schools with at least a fully developed one-track system (many with even a two- or three-track system) of at least nine grades, including educational counseling centers, early education, and kindergartens. In addition, there are 2 fully developed high schools for deaf students, 3 schools with high school classes for deaf pupils, and 12 schools with high school classes for hard-of-hearing pupils. Three schools have academic high school or junior college classes for hearing-impaired students, and there are eight institutions for multiply handicapped hearing-impaired students. Approximately 15,000 deaf and hard-of-hearing students per year attend these schools. A survey of a representative sample of deaf and hard-of-hearing children of a specified age (all of whom attended classes in the above-mentioned schools) was conducted in 1982 by the Research Center for Applied Linguistics for the Rehabilitation of the Disabled at Heidelberg. The survey revealed the following data: 42 percent of the hearing-impaired adolescents are profoundly deaf (more than 90 dB hearing loss); 33 percent have a severe or moderately severe hearing loss (60–90 dB); 21 percent have a moderate or mild hearing loss (30–60 dB); 5 percent have normal hearing or light impaired hearing (less than 30 dB loss).

On the day the survey was conducted, of the students in vocational training, only one of three profoundly deaf students, three of four severely or moderately hearing impaired, and three of five moderately or mildly hearing impaired used a hearing aid, although the objective is generally that all children wear hearing aids when in school. The data also revealed that among the vocational training students surveyed the ratio of males to females was considerably higher within the head-of-hearing group than the ratio found in the deaf group or in the normal hearing group. The same condition is also found for the exceptionally gifted moderately and mildly hearing-impaired students, who, based upon their acoustic and cognitive abilities, significantly more often receive their educaiton in integrated systems with hearing students.

Differentiating Between Deaf and Hard-of-Hearing Pupils The organizational structures have been redirected since about 1965 toward emphasis on conceptual (that is, didactic and methodological) as well as organizational autonomy, through a clearer differentiation between schools for the deaf and schools for the hard-of-hearing (for example, in the German states North Rhine Westfalia, Hamburg, Bavaria, and Hesse). The objective has been a stronger focus on methods tailored to fit varying degrees and types of impairment through a more differentiated separation of deaf and hard-of-hearing pupils, particularly to discourage the use of manual signs by hard-of-hearing pupils. The basis for this differentiation is the increasing awareness of mild hearing loss as a separate disability and the recognition of hard-of-hearing persons as a group with separate goals which necessitate separate organizational forms. *See* DEAF POPULATION: Hard-of-Hearing.

Early Education General psychological and cognitive development as well as speech and language development have gained increased importance in the early education of hearing-impaired children. Since 1958 a systematic increase in home training, kindergarten, and preschool education has taken place. In the 1980s early education became especially marked by the diagnosis of hearing impairment at an earlier age, and today almost all deaf children are identified as such before age one and most hard-of-hearing children before age three.

Parents' Participation (Cotherapy) Parallel to the development of the early education centers there has been a consistent growth in the participation of the parents with the development of systematic parent roles and participation in early education; foundation of local parent organizations and the formation of national organizations; legally based parental participation in the schools; foundation of private preschools by parents (since the beginning of the 1980s), with emphasis on the pure oral method and the discouragement of any manual signing; and advocation of the use of Manual German in early education by some groups of parents.

Mainstreaming Mainstreaming hearing-impaired people has gained importance along with the efforts to integrate persons with other disabilities, such as those who are learning-impaired or physically impaired. The existence of a well-structured school system for hearing-impaired students has resulted in only partial integration of deaf pupils into the regular school systems. Due to the lack of longitudinal research in this problem area, arguments about its successes or failures tend to be ideologically rather than scientifically oriented.

Continuing General Educational Schools A slow but systematic increase in continuing general educational schools (high schools, junior colleges, vocational high schools) is under way. Deaf students, frequently with hard-of-hearing students, can attend high schools or classes at high schools or junior colleges. There is a junior college at a special vocational school for deaf people, but special universities or colleges like Gallaudet College or the National Technical Institute for the Deaf do not exist in the Federal Republic. In rare cases, deaf students have attended universities and completed courses of study. *See* GALLAUDET COLLEGE; NATIONAL TECHNICAL INSTITUTE FOR THE DEAF.

Vocational Training The systematic increase and conscious centralization of institutions for the vocational training of hearing-impaired persons in the German states and on a national level has produced three types of vocational training: (1) 18 special vocational schools or vocational school classes for hearing-impaired students in the dual system (for example, with an average of 10 hours of classroom instruction per week combined with vocational training on the job in a hearing environment); (2) employment training institutions (primarily for the less talented students) integrating theoretical and practical education in one organizational form, using workshops and vocational training, permanent contact with the training supervisor and teacher, and theoretical and practical instruction; and (3) regular vocational schools (dual system).

Attendance at one of the two types of vocational training is influenced by the following factors: (1) The proximity of a vocational training institution. (2) The degree of hearing loss: 60 percent of the deaf students prefer the dual system (Type 1), 34 percent prefer the employment training institutions (Type 2), and 6 percent prefer the regular dual-system vocational schools (Type 3). The severely or moderately severe hearing-impaired students are divided among the three types of institutions in the ratio of 40:36:24. (3) The fact that an increasing number attend vocational schools along with hearing students. The moderately or mildly hearing-impaired students who have attended nine years of elementary and junior high school for hearing-impaired students attend the three types of vocational training schools in a ratio of 30:20:50 which means that every second student attends a regular fully integrated vocational school. (4) The level of school completion. Hearing-impaired students who have not completed the elementary school level of nine years of schooling receive their vocational training mostly in employment training institutions (Type 2) together with hearing-impaired students only; the ratio is 29:59:12. Hearing-impaired students who have completed elementary school attend the three types of vocational training in the ratio of 50:37:13, which means that every second student prefers training in a Type 1 dual system, that is, the practical education together with hearing students but the theoretical education with hearing-impaired students. Hearing-impaired pupils who have completed high school participate in the three types of vocational training in the ratio of 37:9:54, which means that the majority prefer the fully integrated form of the dual system, whereas only 37 percent attend the partially integrated form.

Hearing-impaired adolescents are trained in more than 100 different vocations. The 10 most frequent are dental technician (7 percent), technical drafter (7.2), garment worker or sewer (6.4), cabinetmaker (5.1), lathe operator (4.4), machinist or engine fitter (2.8), precision toolmaker (2.8), architectural drafter (2.8), housekeeper (2.8), and painter or lacquerer (2.3). Only machinist or engine fitter also belongs to the top 10 among hearing persons. Generally, hearing-impaired students opt for less communication-intensive vocations than those who hear.

Differentiated according to sex, among the 10 most frequent vocations chosen by hearing-impaired females (representing more than 60 percent of the females) are garment worker/sewer (14.5 percent), technical drafter (13.4), dental technician (11.1), housekeeper (5.8), architectural drafter (3.5), lady's tailor (3.5), fur sewer (2.9), office clerk (2.9), masseuse or medicinal bath attendant (2.9), and bookbinder (2.3). Among the males, every second student chooses one of the following 10 vocations: cabinetmaker (9.2 percent), lathe operator (10.8), machinist or engine fitter (5.1), dental technician (5.1), precision toolmaker (4.6), painter or lacquerer (4.2), machanic or fitter (3.7), toolmaker (3.7), art metalworker (2.8), and baker (2.8). Every third vocation selected by the hearing-impaired males is a "metal" vocation. The vocation of dental technician is particularly popular with deaf and profoundly hard-of-hearing individuals, more so among the females, who tend to come predominantly from the upper class and upper middle class, than the males. The second most frequent vocation, technical drafter, is also dominated by hearing-impaired females.

Generally, it can be said that the vocational training for deaf and hard-of-hearing students does not produce any academic professions in the Federal Republic. However, according to the type and number of the available and selected vocations since World War II, a continuously rising trend toward higher qualification can be observed. Also, despite their communication handicap, deaf and hard-of-hearing individuals, as a result of sound social welfare legislation, are provided with an opportunity comparable with hearing individuals to satisfactorily pursue a vocation.

Teacher Training   The education of teachers for deaf and hard-of-hearing pupils is scientifically based. Each teacher completes 8-10 semesters of studies at the universities of Cologne, Hamburg, Heidelberg, or Munich. During this time, required studies include general and special pedagogy; general and special psychology; general and applied linguistics, including phonetics; sociology of the handicapped; special diagnostics and special areas of medicine; psychopathology; and otology. A 1½-year special seminar practical training period, which varies according to the different German states, must be completed in the special schools after the university education. In the first 60 years of this century, the profession of teacher of the deaf was male-oriented, but since the mid-1960s, the proportion of female to male teachers has consistently increased.

Existing Deficiencies   The existing deficiencies in the educational system for deaf persons can be summarized as a lack of colleges and universities for hard-of-hearing and deaf students; a continuing partial deficiency in the early diagnosis of hearing impairment by doctors and pediatricians who practice privately and are not connected with audiological clinics and educational counseling centers, resulting in delayed onset of early education, particularly in the case of hard-of-hearing children; less than totally satisfactory cooperation between medical clinics and educational counseling centers, including the area of diagnosis and the lack of standardized terminology in this area; too little special or additional education for kindergarten personnel and nonteaching educators compared to that for teachers of deaf students despite 20 years of effort; and a shortage of interpreters.

COMMUNICATION METHODS

In both residential and integrated schooling in the Federal Republic, the oral-aural method is dominant. All discussion of communication skills centers, if not totally, at least partially, around the goal of this German method.

Residual Hearing and Vibration Systems   Since the 1960s residual hearing has been capitalized upon through the equipping of schools with hearing aid equipment, the earliest possible use of individual hearing aids, and the didactic and methodological development of auditory and speech training. Of all the technical and nontechnical systems that exploit vibrations as a supplement to or substitute for hearing, the mechanocutaneous Fonator System has been most successful, in classes, kindergarten groups, and home training. The Fonator System comprises the Mono-Fonator for individual speech therapy, the Mini-Fonator (completed in 1983) with wireless transmission as a communication aid at home, the Poly-Fonator for group training, and classroom hearing devices including vibrators. Each subsystem consists of an amplifier, a microphone, and a vibrator which can be worn like a wristwatch. Acoustic waves are transformed into vibrations, so that the deaf have access to phonetic and phonological speech information. Features (such as voiced versus voiceless or long versus short) of phonemes may be recognized, for example, in order to understand the differences between consonants and vowels, and between short plosives and longer fricatives. Vibratory feedback is a means of controlling speech, and of determining whether it is too high, too fast, or too slow, or too loud or too soft. *See* SENSORY AIDS.

Manual Systems   The use of manual signs has been discussed for 20 years. Some research has been done on fingerspelling or dactylology, and the system has been employed in some schools by some teachers. Essentially, however, this grapheme-oriented manual system has not been successful; its use is limited to a supplement to Manual German, for instance in television programs. Cued speech is known as a speechreading device; however, it is not widely used. The mouth-hand-system by Forchhammer is used by some teachers as a speechlearning aid. The phoneme-transmitting manual system (PMS), with visual motoric signs for each phoneme, was developed and evaluated between 1965 and 1972 and is used by about two-thirds of all teachers in the Federal Republic as a speech training device—its objective being to produce a speaking deaf child, not a signing one. The combination of residual hearing, lipreading, vibrotactile Fonator, and the PMS is widely used by teachers in many kindergartens and first grades of elementary schools for hearing-impaired students. *See* MOUTH-HAND SYSTEMS.

Manual German and Speech   Parallel to the development in the United States, there has been an increasing demand by deaf persons to use Manual German in the classroom and during leisure time; there also has been a demand that future teachers learn the signs of Manual German. The issue of the pure oral method as opposed to the combined method is controversial. A tentative agreement has been reached to use "manual signs that accompany speech." A further controversial issue is the question of whether, and to what extent, Manual German is a barrier to the integration of deaf persons into the hearing society in terms of mainstreaming, and whether the segregation into their own culture or group is to be preferred over integration into the hearing society. Teachers of deaf students, deaf people themselves, and interpreters for the deaf have collected the gestures commonly used in the Federal Republic and published a book of the gestures in order to standardize them. *See* SIGN LANGUAGES: German.

Reading and Writing   Writing seems to be an accepted information and communication aid between deaf and hearing persons. Reading and writing skills should thus be more strongly propagated and emphasized in the education of deaf students.

Language Development   The use of hearing aids and the better exploitation of residual hearing by profoundly deaf people, the use of Manual German as a communication aid, and the discussion of educating deaf children in residential schools or in partially or totally integrated schools have essentially led to two different schools of thought, both didactically and methodologically with respect to language development in the Federal Republic—a primarily "synthetic" and a primarily "comprehensive" approach. The synthetic approach emphasizes more systematic language and speech development, with the identification of language difficulties, a methodologically sound sequencing of language and speech structures, and aids for deaf people. The comprehensive approach involves teaching speech to deaf children as hearing native speakers would learn their mother tongue. This approach puts more emphasis on the psycholinguistic aspects of language development via conversation and less emphasis on the systematic acquisition of language structures.

A reasonable compromise between the primarily synthetic and the primarily comprehensive approaches seems to be emerging in practice, particularly since both methods have their advantages and disadvantages when considering the different cognitive structures of different deaf children. Widely accepted and presupposed, however, is the action-oriented communicative approach to language development and language instruction.

Bibliography

Braun, A., et al.: *Kommunikation mit Gehörlosen in Lautsprache und Gebärden*, München, 1982.

——— et al.: *Sprachunterricht an Schulen für Gehörlose*, Villingen, 1979.

Bund Deutscher Taubstummenlehrer: *Statistische Nachrichten*, Heidelberg, 1981.

Deutsche Gesellschaft zur Förderung der Gehörlosen und Schwerhörigen: *Die Gebärden der Gehörlosen*, Hamburg, 1977.

Günther, K.B.: *Schriftsprache bei hör- und sprachgeschädigten Kindern*, Heidelberg, 1982.

Günther, K.B., H.Ch. Strauss, and K. Schulte: *Soziale and personale Merkmale gehörloser und schwerhöriger Jugendlicher, Aussage zu Hörverlust, Intelligenz, Sozialstatus, Geschlecht, Erziehungsfeld, Schulerfolg*, Villingen-Schwenningen, 1984.

Jussen, H., and O. Kröhnert (Hrsg.): *Handbuch der Sonderpädagogik*, Band 3—*Pädagogik der Gehörlosen und Schwerhörigen*, Berlin, 1982.

Kröhnert, O.: *Die sprachliche Bildung der Gehörlosen*, Weinheim, 1966.

Lesen-Lire-Reading: *Bericht der Europäischen Föderation von Taubstummenlehrerverbänden, Oslo, 1979*, Heidelberg, 1981.

Rammel, G.: *Untersuchungen zur Zeichensystematik der Gebärden und der Gebärdensprachen*, Heidelberg, 1981.

Schlenker-Schulte, Ch.: "Speech-Teaching-Program: Speech Therapy for the Hearing Impaired," in *Proceedings of the International Congress on Education of the Deaf, Hamburg, 1980*, Heidelberg, 1982.

Schulte, K.: "The Communication Ability of the Deaf—How Can It Be Improved?" in *Proceedings of the International Congress on Education of the Deaf*, Stockholm, p. 727–739, 1970.

———— et al.: *Berufliche Bildung Hörgeschädigter in der Bundesrepublik Deutschland—Einflüsse von Hörgrad, Schichtzugehörigkeit, Intelligenzniveau, schulischer Sozialisation*, Villingen, 1983.

————, H.Ch. Strauss, and K.B. Günther: *Berufsbildung gehörloser und schwerhöriger Jugendlicher, Teilnahme an Berufsvorbereitenden Massnahmen, Besuch v. Berufl. Vollzeitschulen, Ausb. i. Berufsschule od. Berufsbildungswerk, Art u. Wahl d. Ausbildungsberufe*, Villingen-Schwenningen, 1985.

Schwinger, L.: "Phoneme Signs as Motoric Speech Reading Aids," in *Proceedings of the International Congress on Education of the Deaf, Hamburg, 1980*, Heidelberg, 1982.

Vetter, U., et al.: *Berufliche Bildung Hörgeschädigter–Informationen zur Struktur*, Villingen, 1982.

Periodicals: *Duetsche Gehörlosenzeitung; Hörgeschädigtenpädagogik; Hörgeschädigte kinder;* and *Sprache-Stimme-Gehör.*

Klaus Schulte

GESTURES

The modern word "gesture" derives from the Medieval Latin word *gestura*, meaning a way of carrying or a mode of action. In its earliest uses in English, it referred to the manner of carrying the body, or bodily bearing or deportment, especially within the context of religious ceremonial. Later it came to be used in treatises on rhetoric to refer to the way in which the body was employed in making speeches. This included specific actions of the limbs and face that are considered to be deliberately expressive of thought and feeling. It is in this sense that the word is most commonly used today. This article reviews the phenomenon of gesture as it may be observed in speakers, and considers its connections with spoken language, the development of gesture as an autonomous mode of expression, and its connection with sign languages.

STUDIES

The systematic study of how people employ bodily action either in conjunction with speech or without speech began in the seventeenth century, when several treatises on rhetoric appeared in which explicit descriptions were given of types of gestural expressions and when they should be used in speechmaking. In the eighteenth century, especially in France, the study of gesture was taken up by such writers as the Encyclopedist and philosopher Denis Diderot (1713–1784) and the philosopher Etienne Bonnot de Condillac (1715–1780), who thought the study of gesture would be important for an understanding of the nature of thought and the origin of language. This provided the philosophical climate that made it possible for the gestural expressions of deaf people to be studied seriously for the first time, as in the work of Abbé Charles Michel de l'Epée (1712–1789). *See* L'EPÉE, ABBÉ CHARLES MICHEL DE.

The study of gesture, including the study of gestural or sign languages, continued in the nineteenth century, notably in the work of E. B. Tylor (1832–1917), a founding father of anthropology, and Wilhelm Wundt (1832–1920), the founder of experimental psychology. Both Tylor and Wundt regarded gesture as an integral component of the process by which utterances are produced. They both argued that an understanding of the phenomenon of gesture has significant implications for the understanding of the nature of the human capacity for language.

In the twentieth century, gesture was little studied until about 1970, and since then has attracted increasing attention. Detailed work has been done on the interrelation of gesture and speech; there has been work done on the role of gesture in the development of language in infants and children; and there has been a great expansion in the study of sign languages.

The term "gesticulation" is used to refer to bodily movements which often are observed to accompany speech and which, even to a casual observer, are seen to be patterned in relation to it. These movements are usually considered to be part of a speaker's total expression. They may occur in all parts of the body, but most commonly remarked are those more or less complex movements of the hands and arms that are the most conspicuous features of "gesturing." Such bodily movements were considered an important part of the presentation of public speeches, and there are detailed discussions to be found within the tradition of rhetoric—notably in the works of the Spanish Roman Quintilian (ca. 15–96) and, in the modern period, beginning with work by such writers as John Bulwer (1644) and culminating in the highly influential textbook *Chironomia* by Gilbert Austin, published in 1806.

RELATION WITH SPEECH

The scientific study of gesticulation has been mainly concerned with how such movements are patterned in relation to speech in situations such as interviews or informal conversations. Analysis shows that gesticulation in the forelimbs and the head is organized into phrases in close association with the phrases of speech. The close match that has been found between phrases of gesticulation and phrases of speech suggests that speech and gesticulation are the products of a single underlying process. It appears that units of content may be expressed partly in speech and partly in gesture. Gesture phrases match speech phrases because both are components in the expression of a single unit of content.

There are many different ways in which content may be expressed in gesticulation. There are gesticulations that are simple in form and that function as markers of units of discourse. Complex gesticulations may present sketches or pantomimes, displaying aspects of the objects or actions that the speaker is talking about. They may have a metaphorical significance, as when a speaker uses containerlike gesticulations to suggest boundaries to the discussion, or provides gestures suggesting actions that can serve as concrete images for abstract processes. Speakers may also use gesticulation to clarify the meaning of a potentially ambiguous word, to complete spoken sentence fragments, or to convey aspects of meaning that are not conveyed directly in words.

The observation that a speaker may simultaneously present part of an utterance in verbal form and part in gesture means that the mental representation of the utterance cannot be exclusively verbal, as has sometimes been maintained. It is thought that the study of how gesticulation is related to speech will help to advance understanding of the nature of mental representation and of the processes by which such representation is translated into utterance form.

The intimate connection between gestural and spoken language expression is further revealed in developmental studies. The close relationship between hand movements and speech characteristic of adults is present at birth. Gestures, such as lifting the arms as a request to be picked up or pointing as a way of referring to objects, develop before speech, but they become more complex as speech develops. Gesticulations change in type and in their relation to speech as children grow. Five-year-olds tend to engage in elaborate enactments that serve instead of speech. Older speakers develop a more precise speech-gesture relation in which gesticulation occurs more selectively. There is an increasing use of abstract, discourse-making gesticulation. Certain forms of pantomimic gesticulation become more symbolic and more restricted in meaning.

Neurological studies also suggest that gesture and spoken language are part of the same system. Clinical neurologists have long recognized that patients suffering from brain damage that impairs speech (left hemisphere damage in most cases) also show impairment in their ability to use gestures. Some maintain that this can be understood as a result of interference with motor control; however, others believe that it is because the capacity for symbolization has been interfered with. Studies of gesticulation in aphasics suggest that the disorganization in gesticulation observed in these patients parallels closely the kind of disorganization observed in their speech. Studies of hand preferences in gesticulation in healthy people show that characterizing gesticulations are almost always produced by the dominant hand. Since the dominant hand is regarded as being under the control of the same side of the brain as the side controlling speech (left side in right-handed people), this finding has been taken as further evidence that gesticulation and speech are under the guidance of the same fundamental process.

Gesturing is thus an integral component of utterance production. When it accompanies speech, it is not organized as an autonomous system that may be explicitly learned, as a spoken or signed language may be learned. Furthermore, in gesticulation, expression is achieved through pantomimic or depictive action that is not articulated in recombinable component units, as spoken or signed utterances are.

CULTURAL VARIATION

Although gestural expression is universal, cultures vary considerably in the extent to which speakers employ gesturing and in the way they rely upon it as a source of information about what is being said. The best study suggesting this is still that of D. Efron, published in 1941. He undertook a comparative study of Southern Italian and East European Jewish immigrants in New York City and showed that there were marked differences in gesticulatory style between the two groups. Southern Italians were found to make much use of pictorial or pantomimic gesticulations, whereas East European Jewish immigrants employed gesticulation to portray visually the logical structure of what they were saying, but rarely used pictorial illustrative forms. Efron also showed that whereas the Italians had a rich repertoire of standardized gestures, the East European Jews did not. By comparing the gestural practices of the descendants of these two groups, Efron further showed that these differences decreased as the descendants were assimilated into English-speaking American life. This shows clearly that gestural style is learned as part of the culture.

AUTONOMOUS GESTURE

Many speaking communities rely on gesture as a mode of communication independent of speech.

Where this occurs, repertoires of gestural forms emerge that are standardized in the manner of their execution and relatively stable in meaning. Communities differ considerably in the extent to which they use such gestures and in the extent and nature of the repertoire used. A survey of a selected number of distinct gestural forms of this sort was undertaken by D. Morris and colleagues (1979) in 40 locations widely distributed from north to south in West Europe. The survey showed many differences in the number of forms recognized and in the meanings they were said to have.

Autonomous gestures (or emblems, as they have been termed by some writers) differ from gesticulations in that they have a standardized form, have a stable meaning, and are commonly one-handed, and many of them may be made in relation to a part of the face or other body part. In these respects they are rather like signs in a sign language. In most speaking communities such gestures are used singly and only occasionally. They constitute a repertoire of isolated forms, not a gestural system, and they are usually found to serve a quite restricted range of communicative functions. In a few communities, notably in Naples, Italy, such gestures are used extensively as an alternative to speech and may come to constitute a system not unlike a sign language. In some situations, for example in stock exchanges or in unmechanized sawmills where regular interaction is required but speech is impossible, gesture systems may emerge that serve the workers' communication requirements. In a few circumstances such gesture systems may become elaborate and serve as an alternative to speech in all circumstances. For instance, among the aboriginal women of the central Australian desert, complex sign languages have developed to permit verbal communication during periods of mourning, when speech may not be used. Less complex sign languages have developed in monasteries that follow the Rule of Silence of St. Benedict of the sixth century. Complex gesture systems or sign languages also developed among the Plains Indians of North America for use in ritual and in other circumstances when speech was avoided. *See* SIGN LANGUAGES: Australian Aboriginal, Plains Indian.

Gestural expression, then, is as fundamental a mode of expression as spoken language. Where speech is used, gesture plays a complementary role and does not become established as an autonomous system. Where circumstances make the use of speech difficult or impossible, however, gesture may be elaborated into languagelike systems. Gesture in the speaking community is thus continuous with the sign languages employed in communities of deaf people.

Bibliography

Efron, David: *Gesture, Race and Environment*, Mouton, The Hague, 1972 (original edition, 1941).

Ekman, Paul: "Biological and Cultural Contributions to Bodily and Facial Movement," in J. Blacking (ed.), *The Anthropology of the Body*, Academic Press, London, 1977.

————: "Movements with Precise Meanings," *Journal of Communication*, 26:3,14–26.

Kendon, Adam: "Did Gesture Have the Happiness to Escape the Curse at the Confusion of Babel?" in A. Wolfgang (ed.), *Nonverbal Behavior: Perspectives, Applications, Intercultural Insights*, C. J. Hogrefe, Lewiston, New York, 1984.

————: "The Study of Gesture: Some Observations on Its History," *Recherches Semiotique/Semiotic Inquiry*, 2:45–62, 1982.

Lock, Andrew (ed.): *Action, Gesture and Symbol: The Emergence of Language*, Academic Press, London, 1978.

McNeill, David: "So You Think Gestures Are Nonverbal?", *Psychological Review*, 92:350–371, 1985.

Morris, Desmond, et al.: *Gestures: Their Origins and Distribution*, Jonathan Cape, London, 1979.

Adam Kendon

Nonverbal Communication

The term "verbal," in its original sense, refers to the use of language and words. Thus the term "nonverbal communication" has been used to describe forms of expression and of exchanging information through means other than words. However, as linguistic research since the 1960s has shown, the signs in sign languages used by deaf people also have specific, conventional meanings and, in fact, are the functional equivalent of words in spoken languages. Signs therefore should also be considered as elements of verbal, not nonverbal, communication.

Gestures as nonverbal communication, then, refer not to signs but to other movements of the body that convey meaning and that may or may not be used along with speech. While gestures are commonly thought of as hand and arm movements, the term "gesture" also includes movements of the face, head, and other body parts. Some nonverbal researchers limit gestures to those body movements that are purposefully used by the communicator to express meaning. However, many scholars take a broader view of gestures, using the term for any body motions that express meaning to an observer, whether or not the meaning was intentionally expressed.

DEFINITION

The distinction between verbal and nonverbal communication is often unclear. When people communicate, they use both verbal and nonverbal cues in combination. Because the verbal and nonverbal aspects of communication can be so inseparable, some researchers refuse to use the terms "verbal" and "nonverbal" at all, and simply talk about "communication" or "face-to-face interaction." In considering nonverbal communication, it may be best to imagine the concept of nonverbalness as representing a continuum rather than a discrete category. At the verbal end of the continuum of hand gestures, for example, would be a sign, such as the sign TREE in American Sign Language (ASL). Slightly removed from it but in the same verbal vicinity would be an emblematic gesture (for example, the hitchhiking thumb signal) known to a particular cultural group. Toward the middle of the continuum would be placed an illustrative gesture that a speaker might use while describing something: holding the hands an appropriate distance apart while saying, "The fish was three feet long." At the nonverbal end of the continuum would be placed a movement such as scratching the head or rubbing the eyes, which might tell an observer about an individual's internal feelings (puzzled? tired? sleepy?), even though the movement was not made for the purpose of communication.

It should be noted that in moving from the nonverbal to the verbal end of the continuum, the gesture is employed more purposefully to communicate a message, and the meaning of the gesture can be more directly and specifically translated by a word or phrase.

In the context of signed communication as used by deaf people, the problem of defining nonverbal communication becomes even more difficult. Traditionally, in studying nonverbal communication among spoken language users, researchers have focused on the nonvocal aspects of interaction. However, the linguistic study of sign language since the mid-1960s indicates that not only are the manual aspects of signing a part of the language and therefore verbal, but even behaviors of the eyes, head, face, and body serve linguistic or verbal functions. Linguists have identified some nonmanual "signs" and a much larger number of nonmanual behaviors that accompany certain signs and function as adverbs or serve other grammatical purposes (such as differentiating between a question and an affirmation). *See* SIGN LANGUAGES: Facial Expressions.

Study of these nonmanual behaviors in signed languages leads to the conclusion that attempts to define nonverbal communication as behaviors distinct from the production of language are mistaken. Rather, the conception of what is linguistic or verbal in signed languages appears to be much broader than previously believed. And recent research on spoken languages has shown that facial and postural behaviors carry more verbal information than previously thought. In any case, there is general agreement that the particular content or meaning of nonverbal communication is related to feelings, attitudes, and internal states. Rather than employing words or signs to communicate feelings, people often use nonverbal cues.

CLASSIFICATIONS OF NONVERBAL BEHAVIORS
Most experts divide nonverbal behaviors into seven different categories: (1) physical characteristics, including height, weight, physical attractiveness, body shape, hair, and skin color; (2) touching behavior, which refers to the use of touch in stroking, hitting, greeting, and so on; (3) paralanguage, which includes changes in rate, rhythm, and pitch, and vocalizations such as laughing or crying—in other words, how something is said rather than what is said; (4) proxemics, which is the study of distance between communicators and how people react to spatial relationships; (5) artifacts, including anything a person wears on the body—clothes, makeup, hearing aids, eyeglasses; (6) environmental factors, which concern the influence that the setting (including furniture, lighting, colors, smells, and so on) has on the impressions that people form of each other and on the way they communicate; and (7) kinesics, which is the study of body motion, including facial expressions, eye behavior, posture, and gestures.

Semiotic Classification Researchers have classified gestures themselves in a number of different ways. One approach has been through semiotic classification, in which gestures are categorized according to how they convey meaning. Gestures that express meaning by pointing at something form one class. This type of gesture uses intrinsic coding, so called because the actual object referred to (that chair, this book) is directly or intrinsically indicated by the act of pointing to it. A second semiotic class of gestures includes those that depict or illustrate their meaning. (Imagine the type of gestures that would accompany statements like "The fish was three feet long" or "The road went up and down.") Such gestures employ iconic coding, by visually representing some physical feature of the object or concept they refer to. The third semiotic class of gestures is called symbolic. They have no obvious connection with the object or concept they represent. The meaning conveyed depends purely on an accepted but arbitrary convention; thus these gestures are said to employ arbitrary coding. (Why does the hitchhiker's raised thumb indicate that a ride is wanted? Simply because in the United States, that is the conventional meaning arbitrarily assigned to the gesture. In some African countries a similar gesture is interpreted as a gross insult!)

Functional Classification Other systems for classifying gestures are based on function rather than meaning. One widely used functional classification system developed by psychologists P. Ekman and W. Friesen includes five categories of body actions:

emblems, illustrators, affect displays, regulators, and adaptors.

Emblems. Emblems are gestures that can be directly translated with a word or phrase. They are typically used intentionally to communicate and can substitute for spoken words. The hitchhiker's thumb, the "okay" signal made by touching thumb and index finger to form a circle, the V sign for "peace" or "victory" are examples of emblematic gestures. There are also facial emblems, such as an exaggerated dropping of the jaw to indicate surprise, and eye emblems, such as the wink that might accompany the "okay" gesture. Most emblems are specific to a particular culture, but some are more universally used. For example, the gesture for eating (moving the hand toward the mouth) is understood by people of different cultures. Some cultures seem to use and recognize many more emblems than others: A study of Iranian emblems identified close to 300, while another study in the United States discovered less than 100 verified emblems. Emblems are usually used in isolation, and not strung together like words in a sentence. However, umpires, airplane mechanics, radio studio technicians, and other specialized groups have developed limited gesture systems that can be used in situations where speech is not possible. Such systems of emblems closely approach purely verbal communication, but differ from a true sign language by being limited to a particular context or communicative function and by lacking syntactic organization.

Illustrators. These are gestures that usually occur along with spoken language and that illustrate or help depict what is being said verbally. Pointing while giving directions, gestures that mimic the size or shape of an object, and gestures that demonstrate an action are examples of illustrators. They are intentionally used by communicators, but often less purposefully than emblems. Illustrators are used more frequently when a communicator is excited or having difficulty expressing ideas verbally. Thus they help in encoding meaning. Likewise, illustrators can help listeners decode or understand messages. People probably learn to use illustrators by observing others. The developmental psychologist Jean Piaget believed that for very young children gestures serve a communicative function equivalent to spoken language. Studies of the use of illustrators and other gestures by children support this view and show that as children grow older they make less use of simple and mimic gestures but increasingly use more complex and abstract gestures that tend to be precisely coordinated with speech.

Affect Displays. These gestures reveal the affective or emotional state of the communicator. For example, a person might, with flaring nostrils, pound a fist on the table in the midst of a heated argument, displaying intense emotion. Increased frequency, rate of movement, and intensity of gesture often reveal an aroused emotional state.

Regulators. These refer to nonverbal behaviors that help control or regulate turn-taking in communication. Through regulators, people let each other know when they wish to say something or continue talking, when they have finished talking and are ready to let the other person speak, or when they do not understand what the other person has said and require more explanation. While changes in eye contact, head nodding, and pauses are common regulators, hand gestures also can serve in this capacity. A raised finger or hand can signal when one wants the floor, and increased use of gesture often occurs when a communicator wants to keep talking and hold a listener's attention.

Adaptors. These movements, including picking, scratching, nail-biting, and rubbing, among others, are behaviors that at one time may have been used for self-comfort but have become unconscious habits. Adaptors are often associated with negative feelings, psychological discomfort, or anxiety. For example, public speakers who are experiencing stage fright may repeatedly adjust their glasses or brush back their hair. Researchers have found that people tend to exhibit more adaptors when in the act of lying, probably related to the increased anxiety that most people experience at such time. Although adaptors are usually performed unconsciously, they can communicate a nonverbal message to observers.

HISTORY OF THE STUDY OF GESTURES

Although the scientific study of gestures is fairly recent, they have been a subject of scholarly scrutiny for thousands of years. As early as 400 B.C. the Greek sophists were teaching the use of expressive gestures as an aid to public speakers. In a similar vein the Roman orator Cicero wrote about gesture in *Brutus*, one of his books on oratory, and recommended that the judicious stamping of a foot or smiting of a brow could help sway an audience. During the eighteenth and nineteenth centuries a number of writers, mostly British, who called themselves elocutionists described vocal and gestural behavior in great detail and made rather prescriptive recommendations on how public speakers should artfully employ both voice and gesture. With his publications of *The Expression of Emotion in Man and Animals* in 1872, Charles Darwin helped focus scientific attention on nonverbal communication, particularly facial expression.

The first scientific approach to the study of gesture is attributed to David Efron, who published *Gesture and Environment* in 1941. In 1952 Ray Birdwhistell's *Introduciotn to Kinesics* was a landmark work that applied the principles of linguistics to the study of body movement. Since then, the number of published studies of nonverbal communication by psychologists and communication scientists has grown vastly.

Bibliography

Baker, Charlotte: "On the Terms 'Verbal' & 'Nonverbal,' " in Inger Ahlgren and Brita Bergman (eds.), *Papers from the First International Symposium on Sign Language Research*, Swedish National Association of the Deaf, Stockholm, 1979.

Ekman, Paul, and Wallace V. Friesen: "The Repertoire of Nonverbal Behavior: Categories, Origins, Usage, and Coding," *Semiotica*, 1:49–98, 1969.

Kendon, Adam: "Gesture and Speech: How They Interact," in John M. Wiemann and Randall P. Harrison (eds.), *Nonverbal Interaction*, Sage, Beverly Hills, California, 1983.

Knapp, Mark L.: *Nonverbal Communication in Human Interaction*, 2d ed., Holt, Rinehart and Winston, New York, 1978.

LaFrance, Marianne, and Clara Mayo: *Moving Bodies: Nonverbal Communication in Social Relationships*, Brooks/Cole, Monterey, California, 1978.

Malandro, Loretta A., and Larry Barker: *Nonverbal Communication*, Addison-Wesley, Reading, Massachusetts, 1983.

Morris, Desmond, et al.: *Gestures: Their Origins and Distribution*, Stein and Day, New York, 1979.

James J. Fernandes

Non-Human Signing

People have long speculated about the capacity of great apes (chimpanzee, gorilla, and orangutan) to use sign language. As early as 1661 Samuel Pepys, a chronicler of London, recorded in his diary the arrival of a ship on the London docks carrying an animal that the sea captain claimed was a new species. Pepys stated in his diary that he viewed a great baboon much like a man in most things. Because of its similarity to humans, Pepys conjectured that it might be the offspring of a man and a she-baboon. From his description it can be safely assumed that the animal was probably a chimpanzee. Chimpanzees had not yet been discovered by the Europeans. Pepys went on to state that he believed the creature already understood much of the spoken English and might even be taught to speak or make signs. In 1747 the famous French philosopher Julien Onffray de la Mettrie proposed in his book *L'Homme Machine* that an anthropoid ape be taught to communicate by a teacher of deaf people. He stipulated that the ape should have an intelligent-looking face. In 1927 Robert Yerkes, a pioneer in the study of apes, stated that apes have plenty to talk about but lack the ability to use vocal speech to express their feelings. He suggested that they be taught the sign language used by deaf people.

EARLY ATTEMPTS TO TEACH APES LANGUAGE

The earliest attempts by scientists to establish communication with apes occurred in the first decades of the twentieth century. Surprisingly, they did not attempt to teach the apes sign language but insisted on vocal speech. In 1916 W. Furness attempted to teach an ape to speak. The results after years of work resulted in the orangutan producing two words: papa and cup. About that same time Nadie Kohts in Russia reared a chimpanzee in her home, but the chimpanzee failed to learn any spoken Russian. In the 1930s Winthrop Kellogg and his wife home-reared an infant chimpanzee, Gua, with their son Donald. It was rumored that Donald made more chimpanzee sounds than Gua made human sounds. Finally, in the late 1940s K. and C. Hayes home-reared a chimpanzee for six years, but she was able to learn only four vocal English words: mama, papa, cup, and up. These were largely voiceless, and she had a heavy "accent."

The problem with these attempts is that they were both anthropocentric in that the experimenters refused to accept the apes on their own terms. They tried to force the apes to produce something that is largely impossible for them: vocal human speech. Not only is the ape's vocal apparatus different from the human's, but apes lack the ability to control their vocalizations to the extent that humans do. Apes are limited almost entirely to emotional sounds elicited by stimuli in their environment.

WASHOE PROJECT

In 1966 R. Allen and B. T. Gardner began a project that was to prove to be the first successful attempt in which a chimpanzee was able to acquire parts of a human language. Their project took the best parts of the previous projects and changed those parts that were inappropriate for a chimpanzee. First, they reasoned that language is acquired in the enriched social environment of the family. So they raised their 10-month-old chimpanzee, Washoe, in an environment comparable to that of a human child. Washoe had human companions with her throughout the day. She lived in an 8 by 24 foot house trailer. She had a backyard to play in with a sandbox, a jungle gym, and a large tree. On weekends she was taken on outings.

The major change from the previous projects was that the Gardners adjusted the language to fit the nature of the chimpanzee. Because of the inability of chimpanzees to produce vocal speech and because chimpanzees in the wild use gestures to communicate with each other, it made a great deal of sense to use a human gestural language. The Gardners chose American Sign Language because it was both a gestural language and a human language. The experiment was a success, because in Washoe's infancy (her first four years) she acquired over 130 signs. This project pointed out the anthropocentric error of the early investigators.

Washoe used her signs in the manner in which she had acquired them: spontaneously and in correct social contexts. She carried on conversations with her human companions about events that occurred during the day. She would initiate conversations, comment on things in her environment, and question her human companions. Her vocabulary development compared very well to that of young human children. She would sign about things present as well as absent. For example, she would ask for friends who were not present. In addition, she generalized her signs to a variety of uses: for example, she used the sign "dog" not only to refer to real dogs, but pictures of dogs and the sound of barking dogs.

In 1970 R. Fouts continued to do research with Washoe as well as several other chimpanzees. Fouts examined the capacity of chimpanzees to use various aspects of language behavior. He studied such things as cross-modal transfer between auditory words and visual signs, comparison of individual differences between chimpanzees, generic and specific use of signs, comprehension and production of novel prepositional phrases, conceptual use of signs to describe classes of objects, and the metaphorical use of signs to describe novel objects. The evidence for a true cognitive continuity between humans and chimpanzees seemed to be well established. But the door was not closed on the issue.

OTHER STUDIES

In the mid-1970s other researchers began to study language acquisition in chimpanzees. A few of these ignored what had been done previously. Instead of raising their chimpanzees in an enriching social sign-language environment modeled after human language acquisition, they trained their charges in extensive drill sessions. One chimpanzee baby was drilled on signs in an empty 8 by 8 foot room for three to five hours each day. This continued for almost four years. The experimenter found that the chimpanzee would sign anything to get out of the situation. He argued that all chimpanzees, like his own, did not sign spontaneously, would only sign for rewards, and were cued by human trainers to sign. This research concluded that language was beyond the biological capacity of chimpanzees and therefore language was unique to humans.

Other psycholinguists in the late 1970s, after reviewing the data on signing apes, decided that the conclusions of the Gardners and others were unwarranted because the evidence was sparse and ambiguous. They argued that the form and structure of ape (signed) utterances showed almost no resemblance to signing in American Sign Language.

APES TEACHING APES

In 1978 Washoe was 12 years old and mature enough to have a baby. A project was designed to respond to the questions the critics had raised. It was decided to stop using signs around Washoe and her future infants except for seven signs: "who," "what," "want," "which," "where," "sign," and "name." Otherwise only vocal English was used to communicate with her. Fouts reasoned that if Washoe's infant acquired sign language from her, it would indicate a chimpanzee could spontaneously learn and use sign language.

Washoe's infant died at 2 months of age, but a 10-month-old male was found to replace it. When Loulis arrived, Washoe readily adopted him and eight days later Loulis began to use his first sign: "person." In 15 months he began using two sign combinations. Five years after his arrival, he was observed to use 54 different signs, all acquired from his chimpanzee mother and signing chimpanzee friends. Whereas Washoe was the first chimpanzee to acquire a human language, Loulis was the first to acquire a human language from other chimpanzees.

After 1980 Fouts acquired three more chimpanzees, Moja, Tatu, and Dar. These three were raised in their early years by the Gardners and were considered good signers. So, in addition to studying cultural transmission between mother and infant, Fouts began to examine the chimpanzee-to-chimpanzee conversations that occur spontaneously within this family of five. In order to control the possibility of human cueing and other influences, the chimpanzees were videotaped and observed on video monitors from a separate room. In other words, they were alone with the cameras. This was done in 20-minute segments randomly distributed three times each day for 15 days. In these 15 hours, 617 chimpanzee conversations were observed. In another study examining almost 6000 chimpanzee-to-chimpanzee conversations, it was found that almost 90 percent of these conversations had to do with the contexts of play, reassurance, and social interactions. Only 5 percent had anything to do with food.

SIGNIFICANCE

This research has had a direct impact on anthropology, philosophy, linguistics, language development, zoology, and psychology. In addition, it has had an influence on human welfare. Enriching chimpanzees' environments and studying their language acquisition may assist researchers in devising new approaches to the treatment of noncommunicative human children.

Bibliography

Fouts, R. S., D. H. Fouts, and D. Schoenfeld: "Sign Language Conversational Interactions Between Chimpanzees," *Sign Language Studies*, 42:1–12, 1984.

Gardner, B. T., and R. A. Gardner: "Two-Way Communication with an Infant Chimpanzee," in A. M. Schrier and R. Stollnitz (eds.), *Behavior of Nonhuman Primates*, vol. 4, pp. 117–184, Academic Press, New York, 1971.

Premack, D.: *Intelligence in Ape and Man*, Lawrence Erlbaum Associates, Hillsdale, New Jersey, 1977.

Rumbaugh, D. (ed.): *Language Learning in a Chimpanzee*, Academic Press, New York, 1977.

Seidenberg, M., and L. Petitto: "Signing Behavior in Apes: A Critical Review," *Cognition*, 7:177–215, 1979.

Terrace, H.: "Can an Ape Create a Sentence?", *Science*, 206:891–902, 1979.

Van Cantfort, T. E., and J. B. Rimpau: "Sign Language Studies with Chimpanzees and Children," *Sign Language Studies*, 34:15–72, 1982.

Roger S. Fouts

Seal of Central Institute for the Deaf.

GOLDSTEIN, MAX AARON
(1870–1941)

Max Aaron Goldstein was an otologist, educator, community leader, editor, author, collector, and a visionary who made his dreams a reality. Perhaps more than any other single American, he brought the benefits of otology and the developing field of audiology to the aid of deaf people.

Goldstein was the son of a wholesale merchant who migrated to St. Louis, Missouri, from northern Germany after the American Civil War. One of five children, he was born on April 19, 1870, in St. Louis. He received his early education in public schools there and graduated from Central High School. He was granted his doctor of medicine degree in 1892 by the Missouri Medical College, the department of medicine of Washington University in St. Louis. After internship at St. Louis City Hospital, Goldstein pursued postgraduate study in London and at the internationally renowned Vienna Polyclinic with Adam Politzer, the patriarch of modern otology.

At a meeting of the Medical Society of Vienna, Victor Urbantschitsch demonstrated his methods of improving the education of congenitally deaf children with apparent remnants of hearing by concentrating on the stimulation of what he termed a dormant auditory sense. This method intrigued Goldstein, and he joined Urbantschitsch in daily teaching sessions at the Döbling Institute for the Deaf. Because of Goldstein's enthusiasm and capability, Urbantschitsch exhorted him to introduce the methods to America, where they came to be called the acoustic method.

Goldstein returned to St. Louis in 1894 to establish a medical practice, and in 1895 he married Leonore Weiner. Anxious to apply what he had learned in Vienna, he began teaching a class of 16 deaf girls at St. Joseph's Institute for the Deaf and instructing the teachers on how to proceed with acoustic stimulation. He regularly devoted two afternoons a week to the supervision of this instruction, and demonstrated the class before meetings of eye, ear, nose, and throat specialists.

For the next 14 years Goldstein devoted his time to medical practice and teaching. He was professor of otology at Beaumont Hospital College of Medicine, which became St. Louis University College of Medicine in 1903. In 1896 he founded *The Laryngoscope*, and international journal concerned with diseases of the ear, nose, and throat, and served as editor until his death. (The journal continues publication in St. Louis.) At a meeting of the American Otological Society, Goldstein met Helen Keller and helped her increase the volume of her voice. He also taught her to dance the two-step in the ballroom of the Copley Plaza in Boston, Massachusetts. This led to a continuing friendship, and Miss Keller was the speaker at the twenty-fifth anniversary (1939) of Central Institute for the Deaf (CID), the school that Goldstein founded and directed. *See* CENTRAL INSTITUTE FOR THE DEAF; KELLER, HELEN; LARYNGOSCOPE.

In order to demonstrate his acoustic method, particularly as it applied to children younger than were then enrolled in schools, Goldstein needed a program directly responsive to his guidance and aspirations. CID opened as a school in rooms over his medical office in 1914. His receptionist served as the first teacher of the four pupils he enrolled, and Goldstein gave all the time he could spare to supervision and teaching. He realized he could not hope to reach many deaf children through his small school; therefore, well-trained teachers were needed to spread his methods throughout the country. Four teachers graduated from the program in 1915.

By 1916 Goldstein had attracted influential St. Louis citizens to be members of his board of trustees. Articles of incorporation were adopted and a petition for a charter approved. He designed the well-known seal of the school, which symbolized his philosophy of the cooperation of medicine and education by using two books surmounted by a chalice and the Aesculapian serpent. Goldstein demonstrated the speech and lipreading of his deaf children at meetings in private homes and in public auditoriums of St. Louis, Chicago, New York, and Philadelphia. The first school building, completed in 1917, is still in use today. *See* SPEECHREADING.

In 1917 Goldstein enlisted as a major in the Medical Officers Reserve Corps with the assignment to develop a national reeducation service to teach lipreading and correct the speech of soldiers made deaf by shell concussion. He organized and presided over the Society of Progressive Oral Advocates, with annual meetings of teachers and ear specialists beginning in 1918, and served as editor of *Oralism and Auralism*, the official publication. In 1940 the name was changed to the National Forum on Deafness and Speech Pathology, and in 1952 it merged with the Alexander Graham Bell Association for the Deaf. *See* ALEXANDER GRAHAM BELL ASSOCIATION FOR THE DEAF.

In order to conduct speech sounds and music to the ears of deaf children to stimulate their residual hearing, Goldstein devised the Simplex Tube. This consisted of a small funnel attached by surgical

Simplex Tube.

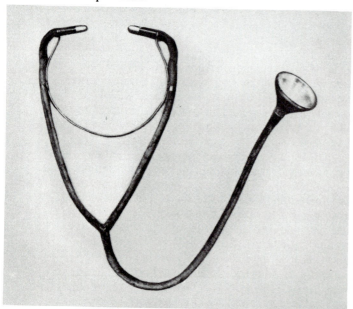

tubing to Y-shaped tubes that led to both ears. The Electrophone, the first electronic instrument for amplifying sound for a group of deaf children, was placed in a classroom by Goldstein in 1925. This was followed in 1939 by the first group hearing aid, called the Acouvox and designed at Goldstein's request by a professor of physics and an electrical engineer at Washington University. All classes at the school received instruction through auditory stimulation using this instrument. *See* HEARING AIDS.

In 1925 the Western Electric Company granted CID permanent loan of a new apparatus called the Audiometer. Goldstein demonstrated the use of this instrument with a range of frequencies from 16 to 32,000 dv (double vibrations) per second (now called hertz) to measure hearing, and predicted that it would replace tuning forks. To demonstrate the value of tactile impressions in developing speech perception and production, he used a megaphone with a paper diaphragm stretched tautly over the wide opening. This device enabled a 10-year-old deaf girl to answer questions received by feeling the vibrations of the diaphragm with her fingertips. *See* AUDIOMETRY.

A new building, attached to the original CID school in 1929, was constructed in three units—the school was in the center with a science wing on the south and a residence wing on the north. Concerned with encouraging deaf children to aspire to the arts, Goldstein imported tile from Europe for the dining room and for the patio which included a fountain with the seal of the institute as a backdrop.

Realizing the importance of a college degree for teachers in training, Goldstein began recruiting a college faculty that would lead to the first two-year professional training course in the United States. In February 1931 the chancellor of Washington University announced the affiliation of the Teachers' College of CID with University College, thereby establishing the first course for training teachers of deaf persons to be affiliated with an accredited university. After completing two years of a prescribed liberal arts course in an accredited university or college, students could be admitted for two years of professional training at CID and receive a bachelor of science degree in education from Washington University. In 1936 the board of graduate studies approved a program at CID leading to the master of science degree in education from Washington University. By 1947 the doctor of philosophy degree in audiology was part of the program. *See* AUDIOLOGY; TEACHING PROFESSION.

Max F. Meyer, head of the department of psychology at the University of Missouri, joined Goldstein as a member of the research staff. Charles E. Harrison, an electrical engineer, started his Technisonic Recording Studio at CID and recorded the

Max A. Goldstein.

speech of every child enrolled. Rafael Lorente de No, a distinguished neuroanatomist and senior assistant to Professor Raman y Cajal of the Cajal Institute in Madrid, was brought to the United States by Goldstein to be director of research.

Although Goldstein had published many papers in audiology and special education, his first book, *Problems of the Deaf*, was not published until 1933. This volume contained sections on the history of deafness and speech defects, the anatomy and physiology of the speech and hearing mechanism, tests for hearing, methods of instruction, advice for parents, antique hearing aids, quackery, and a concluding chapter on his personal research. Goldstein's second book, *The Acoustic Method for Training the Deaf and Hard-of-Hearing* (1939), represented his adaptation of the methods of Urbantschitsch to the education of American children using the improved electronic equipment of the time.

In 1933 Goldstein received the special gold medal of the American Laryngological, Rhinological and Otological Society for outstanding work with deaf persons, and for 40 years of study and effort for the rehabilitation of deaf people—only the third such award made by the society in 49 years. He was the second recipient of the St. Louis Award given in recognition of his achievements on problems dealing with deafness. Washington University awarded Goldstein the honorary degree of doctor of laws, with a citation referring to his eminence in the practice and teaching of otolaryngology, in professional literature, and to his pioneering instruction of deaf students.

Goldstein was a collector of stamps, coins, Indian relics, great works of art, antique hearing aids, and rare professional books, some dating to the fifteenth century. The 700-volume Max A. Goldstein Collection of rare books is housed in the Washington University Medical School Library Archives, where they are available to scholars. His collection of hearing aids is on display in the auditorium of the Clinic and Research building of CID.

In December 1940 Goldstein suffered a stroke resulting in paralysis of his left side. He was able to return to the school and attended the 1941 graduation and alumni reunion. While he was on vacation in Michigan, a second stroke took his life on July 27, 1941, in Frankfort. At his funeral service, the rabbi said, "Max Goldstein was both a dreamer and a doer. The dreamer has passed on, but the dream will live. The energetic doer has departed from our midst but his life work will continue."

This prophecy was true. The goals that Goldstein set to be accomplished through research and education have remained a challenge to the scientists, the teachers, the clinicians, and the parents and deaf children who make up today's Central Institute for the Deaf.

Bibliography

Goldstein, M.A.: *The Acoustic Method for the Training of the Deaf and Hard-of-Hearing*, Laryngoscope Press, St. Louis, 1939.

————: *Problems of the Deaf*, Laryngoscope Press, St. Louis, 1933.

Lane, H. S.: *The History of Central Institute*, chaps. 1, 2, 3, and 7, Central Institute for the Deaf, St. Louis, 1981.

Urbantschitsch, V.: *Auditory Training for Deaf Mutism and Acquired Deafness*, trans. by S. R. Silverman, Alexander Graham Bell Association for the Deaf, Washington, D.C., 1982.

Helen S. Lane

GÓMEZ FEU, ANTONIO
(1907–1984)

Antonio Nicolás Gómez Feu Morales, recognized by the contemporary Spanish art world as a master drafter, was born deaf on November 27, 1907, in Ayamonte, Huelva, Spain. He learned to draw before he could communicate verbally. He attributed his interest and skill in art to his deafness, believing that it gives a sense of isolation, vivid imagination, sensitivity to drawing, and great power to concentrate. Because of his ability to communicate with clients and students by speech, lipreading, and writing—resorting to sign language and fingerspelling only with other deaf persons—journalists have called him the "speaking deaf artist."

Gómez Feu began his education at age nine when he entered the School for the Deaf and Blind at Valencia. Within nine months he was speaking and

Antonio Gómez Feu's *Pescados y Mariscos*.

lipreading and had also grasped the fundamentals of reading and writing. In 1926 he entered the San Carlos Academy of Fine Arts, Valencia, and in 1931 at the San Fernando Academy of the Fine Arts, Madrid, he completed his formal schooling, qualifying for professorial rating.

In Lisbon during the Spanish Civil War and until 1942, he studied new techniques and matured as an artist by working on posters and magazines. He entered the field of fine arts as a portrait painter and, after receiving first prize in an exhibition, was offered his first professorship, provided he would assume Portuguese nationality, which he refused. In 1943, after a short sojourn in Ayamonte, he went to Seville to teach drawing at the School of Fine Arts. He held his first one-man show there in 1944, and another in Málaga in 1947. Finally he moved to Barcelona, where once again he won acclaim from several successful exhibitions and as a portraitist of many well-known people.

As a consequence of several commissions, his works reside in a number of museums. From 1953 to 1956 he executed a graphic documentary for the city of Barcelona of the picturesque and archeologically important focal points of its old section that was destined for demolition. These 40 drawings are on permanent exhibition at the Municipal Museum. Another group of drawings illustrating episodes from Cervantes' *Don Quixote* was placed on permanent exhibition in 1970 in the museum of Denia, Alicante. In September of the same year, Gómez Feu contributed background displays consisting of large-scale reproductions of antique maps and several original oil paintings for the Columbian Exhibition, a commercial enterprise in New York City.

Gómez Feu worked in a variety of media, including pencil, charcoal, sanguine crayon, watercolor, and oil pigments. His church interiors, noted for their arabesque details and filled with the interplay of tenuous shifting light, represent an aerial perspective that embodies mystical emotion. In his landscapes and scenes taken from the urban and folk life of Andalusia, he showed great patience, impeccable technique, and a neat interest in details. He also captured the very unusual light effect so characteristic of Ayamonte in Andalusia, his childhood milieu. He is perhaps best known for his portraits, which reveal the inmost core of each subject. In many instances he exaggerated or accented prominent outlines or a particular feature, solely to enhance the personality and temperament of the subject and never to an extent that detracts from the quality of the picture. Gómez Feu was also a master of composition, as shown by the oil painting *Pescados y Mariscos* (Fish and Seafood), in which his play of line imparts a subtle elegance to the composition.

In his works, Gómez Feu, a careful observer of nature, followed the classical canons of art (for which Velasquez was his master). His opinion with regard to abstract painting and the many "isms" of art was, first, that he was an artist imbued with Spanish realism and, second, that he preferred the classical approach to art, which admits the visual transfusion of sentiment. However, as a master interpreter of the fantastic (shown by his illustrations for such literary classics as Cervantes' *Don Quixote*, and by his purely imaginative works, such as *Danse Macabre*) Gómez Feu was influenced by Gustave Doré and constantly inspired by his colleague Segrelles. For Gómez Feu the fantasies stemmed from reality and, when finished, penetrated reality more often than would a literal rendition of the theme. In this respect his capacity to exceed normal imaginative limits has been compared to the literary creations of Edgar Allan Poe.

Gómez Feu died on November 27, 1984.

Bibliography

Bayona, José Mariá: "De Arte, Gómez Feu, Maestro del Retrato," *Hola* (magazine), clipping without date.

Gallaudet College Archives, Washington, D.C.

"Gómez Feu, Antonio," *Gran Enciclopedia de Andalucia*, Edicones Anel S.A., 1979.

"La Fisonomia De La Ciudad Vieja—cuando el lapiz es documental," *Destino*, no. 920, March 26, 1955.

Elva Fromuth Loe

GOODRICKE, JOHN
(1764–1786)

John Goodricke was an extraordinarily precocious English astronomer. Before his nineteenth birthday he discovered the periodicity of the variable star

Algol and correctly hypothesized the reason why the star varied in brightness. At age 19 he received the Copley Medal from England's Royal Society, and within three years he was made a Fellow of the Society. He also discovered the regular variations of the stars Delta Cephei and Beta Lyrae, publicizing his discoveries in four papers published in the *Philosophical Transactions of the Royal Society* between 1783 and 1786. He died at 21.

Goodricke was born on September 17, 1764, in Groningen, the Netherlands. His father, Henry Goodricke, a member of the English aristocracy, was on consular service in the Netherlands. There he had met and married Levina Benjamin Sessler. Goodricke apparently was named after his grandfather, Sir John Goodricke, of Ribston and Branhain Park, York County, England.

Goodricke was profoundly deaf and unable to speak intelligibly. The exact cause of his deafness is not known. He either was born deaf or lost his hearing in early infancy from illness. His parents realized that special provisions needed to be made for his education and, when he was eight years old, sent him to the famous Braidwood School for deaf children in Edinburgh, Scotland.

Like all the early private schools for deaf pupils, the Braidwood School surrounded in secrecy its techniques and the records of its students. Apparently Goodricke was exceptionally able, for he left Edinburgh in 1778 and entered the Warrington Academy, which made no accommodations for his deafness. He remained at this well-known private school in northern England for three years. The academy's records indicate that Goodricke did well in classics and especially well in mathematics before he returned in 1781 to York, where his family again resided. *See* BRAIDWOOD, THOMAS.

It was in York that Goodricke conducted his astronomical observations. Edward Piggott, a friend and neighbor, was the son of a surveyor and Fellow of the Royal Society who owned astronomical instruments that the boys worked with. Piggott also assisted Goodricke in setting his astronomical clock, synchronizing it every night with a cathedral clock whose striking was audible to Piggott but not to Goodricke. On November 16, 1781, Goodricke began keeping a journal of his astronomical observations, and about one year later he began paying close attention to a peculiar star named Algol.

Algol, also known as Beta Persei, is 459 trillion miles, or 78 light-years, away from the earth; is easily observable by the naked eye; and has a brightness of the second magnitude. On November 12, 1782, Goodricke observed that the brightness of Algol was only about the fourth magnitude, a sixfold decrease. His interest piqued, Goodricke watched the star every night for six weeks. During this period, it always shone with a brightness of the second magnitude, leading him to believe that his earlier observation had been a fluke due to poor eyesight or cloudy air. Then on the night of December 28, he again saw it at the fourth magnitude and watched the star continuously for three hours, during which it gradually brightened to its normal second magnitude.

Over the next five months Goodricke carefully observed Algol every night and recorded its variations. He discovered 11 nights when the star was dim, and ingeniously calculated that it began its dim phase every 2 days 20 hours 45 minutes. He also made the brilliant guess that Algol's variability was caused by another star revolving around it and thus regularly blocking some of its light from earth.

Goodricke recorded his observations and hypotheses and sent them to the Royal Society. Since Goodricke lacked speech, his letter was read during a Royal Society meeting on May 15, 1788, and was well received. The only previously recorded observation of Algol's variability had been made by an Italian astronomer, Gemaino Montanari, who in 1670 said that he had observed Algol to be abnormally faint. Neither Montanari nor anyone else before Goodricke, however, had established the periodicity of Algol's change in brightness or tried to explain it.

Goodricke's perspicacity in understanding Algol is remarkable. He later revised his calculations of the star's periodicity to a figure (four minutes nine seconds longer than his first calculation) that is virtually identical to that observed by modern instruments, although he used only his naked eye and his astronomical clock. Moreover, his hypothesis about the cause of Algol's variability was confirmed over 100 years later, in 1889, by German astronomer Hermann Vogel.

Although Goodricke's fame was established by his work on Algol, he discovered two other variable stars, Beta Lyrae and Delta Cephei, and reported these to the Royal Society. Hence, despite his youth, in April 1786 Goodricke was elected a Fellow of the Royal Society. Two weeks later on April 20, only 21 years old, Goodricke suddenly died. The cause of his death is not known, but it was attributed to overexposure to the cold night air, as he had spent night after night observing and recording the stars.

Bibliography

Hope, Geoffrey: "John Goodricke 1764–1786 Astronomer Extraordinary," *Talk*, no. 113, pp. 10–13, Autumn 1984.

Kopal, Zdenek: "Goodricke, John," in Charles C. Gillispie (ed.), *Dictionary of Scientific Biography*, vol. 5, Charles Scribner's Sons, New York, pp. 467–469, 1972.

Pannekoek, Antonie: *A History of Astronomy*, George Allen and Unwin, London, 1961.

Richardson, Robert S.: *The Star Lovers*, Macmillan, New York, 1967.

John V. Van Cleve

GORMAN, PIERRE PATRICK
(1924–   )

Pierre Patrick Gorman, only son of Eugene Gorman and Marthe (Vallée) Gorman, was born in Melbourne, Australia, on October 1, 1924. Gorman's outstanding academic career and distinguished contributions in the fields of librarianship, linguistics, and the education and rehabilitation of deaf and disabled persons can be attributed to three main factors: exceptional intelligence and strong resolve; the determination of his parents that he should live a normal life; and the excellence of his early teachers in enabling him to achieve a remarkable competence in language, speech, and lipreading.

When, early in infancy, it was discovered that Gorman had no usable hearing, his mother, a native of Paris, received educational guidance from Dr. Henriette Hoffer, then of the Centre Medico-Pedagogique in Paris. From about 2½ years old, Gorman was taught privately by Doreen Hugo, a teacher at the Victorian Deaf and Dumb Institution, Melbourne, who, with his parents, implemented the principles of Hoffer. By the age of six, Gorman had attained sufficient proficiency in communication to be admitted to Melbourne Church of England Grammar School. He remained there until 1942, when he satisfied the educational requirements for entry to Melbourne University, graduating bachelor of agricultural science in 1949 and obtaining an honors diploma in education. Gorman graduated bachelor of education in 1951. As part of the examination for the latter degree, he submitted an unpublished dissertation, *A Study of the Development in the Understanding of Social Concepts in Victorian School Children.*

From 1952 to 1969 Gorman lived in England. In 1951 he accepted an invitation from Professor Sir Alexander Ewing, then Ellis Llwyd Jones, Professor of Audiology and Education of the Deaf, to undertake postgraduate research into lipreading at Manchester University. Gorman found Manchester uncongenial, however, and later that year became a research student at Cambridge University, supervised by Robert Henry Thouless, Reader in Educational Psychology. Initially attached to Fitzwilliam House, Gorman became a member of Corpus Christi College, Cambridge, in 1954. Six years later he was awarded the degree of doctor of philosophy for a thesis entitled *Certain Social and Psychological Difficulties Facing the Deaf Person in the English Community.* This was the first academic study of the social and psychological consequences of profound hearing impairment for the individual deaf person to be undertaken in England. Gorman also thus became the first person born with no useful hearing to obtain a doctorate at a British university.

Gorman's work in the field of librarianship began in 1957 when he applied for the post of librarian to the now Royal National Institute for the Deaf, London. Initially a part-time appointment, the work rapidly expanded. When Gorman left the post in 1968, he was the institute's full-time chief librarian and information officer, and the library was internationally recognized as a leading center of information on any aspect of speech and hearing. In 1968 he also acted as visiting consultant for the information and library services of the Volta Bureau of the Alexander Graham Bell Association for the Deaf. His other assignments in librarianship include acting as consultant subject specialist in the disability area to the Commonwealth Parliamentary Library of Australia (1981) and as a member of the Victorian State Committee on Library and Information Services for Disabled Persons (beginning 1983). *See* Alexander Graham Bell Association for the Deaf; United Kingdom: Organizations.

Gorman's collaboration with Lady Grace Paget in the development of a communication system, then known as the New Sign Language, began in 1959. The language was originally devised by her husband, Sir Richard Paget, as a manual language for deaf or other pupils with mental or linguistic difficulties. Based on Paget's knowledge of sign gestures used by primitive peoples speaking none of the major world languages, the Paget-Gorman Systematic Sign Language is not a language in its own right. It may be described as a system or communication aiming to provide deaf children with a systematic, complete, and accurate visible pattern of spoken language, even if the children do not possess spelling or writing skills equal to the words being spoken. The system therefore seeks to provide a sign for every word normally spoken, except for proper names for which arbitrary signs of fingerspelling are used. Correctly used, the signs also convey verb tenses. A major advantage claimed for the Paget-Gorman system is that the transition from the language of school to that of home is facilitated. While used in some British schools for hearing-impaired pupils, the system has the disadvantage of lacking a base in the adult community. Difficulty in recruiting teachers or welfare workers with deaf persons skilled in the Paget-Gorman system is a further drawback.

After returning to Australia in 1969, Gorman was mainly engaged in research and education. He held temporary posts as director of a policy investigation project for the Victorian School for Deaf Children (1970–1971) and as Lankelly Foundation Scholar researching into the historical development of the Paget-Gorman system (1971–1972). Between 1972 and 1983 he held posts as research coordinator, lecturer, senior lecturer, and senior research fellow in the Educational Faculty, Monash University, in Melbourne. From October 1973 to February 1974 he was guest professor in the education of deaf children, Heidelberg University, West Germany. This lecturing has been supplemented by much published work, including papers delivered at congresses and seminars held at Zagreb (1955), Hong Kong (1968), Suva (1972), Washington (1975), and Tokyo (1975).

Gorman's contribution to the services of deaf persons is evidenced by his past and present participation in numerous committees. Past memberships included the Board of Management of the National Deaf Children's Society, London (1958–1969), the Executive Committee of the World Federation of the Deaf (1959–1962), and the Committee on Speech and Hearing of the International Society for the Rehabilitation of the Disabled (1961–1965). Later committees included the International Congress Committee on the Education of the Deaf (beginning 1975), the Social Educational and Employment Committee of the Deafness Foundation, Victoria (beginning 1977 and serving on the Foundation Executive beginning 1984), and the Victorian Committee of the Disabled Victorian Consultative Council on Rehabilitation (beginning 1982). He was director of the Association for Research in Deaf Education, London (from 1962), and the Eugene, Marthe and Pierre Gorman Foundation (from 1983). Among his professional memberships were the American Speech–Language–Hearing Society, the Australian Association of Speech and Hearing, the Australian and the British Association of Teachers of the Deaf, the Australian and British Psychological Societies, and the International Society of Audiology.

Gorman was deservedly the recipient of major distinctions: the Silver Cross of the Greek Red Cross (1960), the Gold Medal of the World Federation of the Deaf (1961), and the Returned Services League Anzac Award of the Year (1981). He became a Commander of the Most Excellent Order of the British Empire (Civil Division) in 1983.

Bibliography

"Deaf Adults," in *Proceedings of the International Congress on the Education of the Deaf*, pp. 120–122, Organising Committee of the International Congress on Education of the Deaf, Tokyo, 1976.

"Education of the Disabled Child in the South Pacific," occasional paper, School of Education, University of the South Pacific, 1972.

Epstein, J.: *No Music By Request: A Biography of the Gorman Family*, Collins, Sydney, 1980.

Gorman, Pierre: "Country Without Sound," in J. Hetherington, *Uncommon Men*, pp. 85–92, Cheshire, Melbourne, 1965.

"Organisation of Services for Deaf People," in *Proceedings of the 4th Pan-Pacific Rehabilitation Conference*, pp.

407–409, Joint Council for the Physically and Mentally Disabled, Hong Kong, 1969.

"Social Aspects of Deafness: The Senescent Years," in *Proceedings of the 7th World Congress of the World Federation of the Deaf "Full Citizenship for all Deaf People,"* pp. 428–431, National Association of the Deaf, 1976.

"Some Social and Psychological Difficulties Facing the Deaf School Leaver," in *Proceedings of the 2d World Congress of the Deaf, Zagreb, 23–27 August 1955*, pp. 324–328, Yugoslavia Federation of the Deaf, Belgrade.

Kenneth Lysons

GOYA Y LUCIENTES, FRANCISCO JOSÉ DE
(1746–1828)

Francisco Goya was one of Spain's greatest artists. Born on March 30, 1746, in Fuendetodos, Saragossa, Spain, Goya mastered various art forms — tapestry cartoons, traditional portraiture, aquatint etchings, historical prints, and lithographs — over a long, productive career. Generally optimistic in his early work, he became more satirical and embittered with humankind in later years, perhaps reflecting his deafness — which began when he was

Sebastian Martinez by **Francisco Goya. (Metropolitan Museum of Art, New York City)**

46 — or his dissatisfaction with the political turmoil and violence that wracked Spain in the years after the French Revolution.

Goya's artistic development began in the studio of José Luzán in the provincial capital of Aragon, where Goya worked on church pieces. Later he went to Madrid, where he twice failed in attempts to win a scholarship from the Royal Academy of Fine Arts of San Fernando, and traveled to Rome to study on his own. Returning to Madrid, in 1773 Goya married Josefa Bayeu, sister of the powerful court painter Francisco Bayeu. The marriage apparently aided Goya's career, for shortly afterward he was commissioned to paint cartoons for the tapestry factory of Santa Barbara, in which the Spanish king Charles III took a great interest.

From 1775 until 1788 Goya painted tapestry cartoons and studied technique, especially that of the seventeenth-century Spanish master Diego Velásquez, and his work received new recognition. In 1780 he was elected to the Academy of San Fernando, becoming its vice-director five years later. So honored, he began to receive commissions for both portraits and religious paintings, and in 1788, when Charles IV assumed the Spanish throne, Goya was made a court painter.

During this early period in his career, Goya became an accomplished portrait painter for the Spanish aristocracy. His portraits, such as that of the Marquesa de Pontejos (now in the National Gallery of Art, Washington, D.C.), reflected his attitude toward his subjects. The aristocrats are depicted as haughty, pompous, inexpressive, and even ugly. His portrait of his friend Sebastian Martínez (Metropolitan Museum of Art, New York City), completed just before the onset of the illness that left Goya deaf, demonstrates another characteristic of his work. Breaking with the formulas of conventional portraiture, Goya places the model in a closeup position, viewed from a low angle.

The exact nature of the illness that caused Goya's deafness is unknown, but it began in 1792 and apparently left him weakened until 1795. In 1794 and 1795 he executed the painting *Corral de Locos* (*The Lunatic Asylum Yard*; Meadows Museum, Dallas, Texas). It graphically portrays the agony which the artist was undergoing as he adjusted to the trauma of his deafness, and seems to represent a new, pessimistic attitude toward reality, one that is reflected in his later works as well.

Goya's deafness did not incapacitate him, however. It awakened new creative energies and caused him to give full rein to his keen observations and critical eye. Adjusting to his loss of hearing, Goya learned Spanish Sign Language at the Valencia Institute of Don Juan in Madrid, which today has a drawing with signs declaring it to be the work of Goya. In 1785 he was elected successor to his brother-

Corral de Locos (*The Lunatic Asylum Yard*) by Goya. (Meadows Museum, Dallas)

in-law, Francisco Bayeu, as director of painting at the Academy of San Fernando. Though he refused this honor, he was named honorary director by his fellow artists. *See* SIGN LANUGAGES: Spanish.

Goya's most productive period followed. In 1797 he published a series of aquatint etchings entitled *Caprichios* (*Caprices*). In 1799 he was named chief painter to the king. Napoleon's invasion of the Iberian Peninsula (1804–1814) provided more subjects for Goya's imagination, and the result was a second series of graphics, *Desastres de la guerra* (*Disasters of War*). In 1814, at the king's request, he executed two historical paintings, *May 2, 1808* and *May 3, 1808*.

To separate himself from the royal court, Goya purchased a country house on the banks of the Maganares River near Madrid. He named the house Quinta del Sordo (Villa of the Deaf One) and covered the walls with his cynical and pessimistic *Black Paintings*. At this time Goya produced a third and fourth series of prints entitled *Tauromaquia* (*Bullfighting*) and *Disparates* (*Follies*; sometimes called *Proverbios*).

With the return of Ferdinand VII to the Spanish throne and the threat of still another absolutist monarchy, an ailing and despondent Goya requested permission to move to France for the sake of his health. With permission granted, he gave Quinta del Sordo to his 18-year-old grandson, Mariano, and left for Paris. Goya stayed there only briefly before moving to Bordeaux, where he continued to work until his death on April 16, 1828.

Bibliography

Cheney, Sheldon: "The Challenge of the Romantics—and Goya," *The Story of Modern Art*, pp. 39–46, Viking, New York, 1961.

de Angelis, Rita: "Goya," *Maestros de la Pintura*, no. 48 and 51, Noguer, Rizzol.

Guidol, José: *Goya, 1746–1828: Biografía, estudio analitico y Catalogo de sus Pinturas*, Ediciones Poligrafa, 4 vols., Barcelona, 1970.

Elva Fromuth Loe

GRABILL, WILSON H.
(1912–1983)

Wilson H. Grabill was the most outstanding deaf social scholar of the twentieth century. An international authority on fertility and population statistics, he contributed numerous studies of American demography. Grabill's skills and personality drew him into positions of authority among his hearing peers, and he was an active, effective member of the deaf community as well.

He was born December 13, 1912, in Evansville, Wisconsin, to Dell Quincy Grabill, a Congregational minister in Fort Atkinson, and Elizabeth (Wilson) Grabill. Two sisters made up the balance of the family: one a twin born just 10 minutes before Wilson, the youngest child. At the age of five years, Grabill's hearing began to deteriorate until he became profoundly deaf.

After a few years in public schools, Grabill attended the Wisconsin School for the Deaf in Delavan, graduated in 1929, and entered the preparatory year at Gallaudet College that fall. The talent for mathematics that marked his career became evident at Gallaudet. He took all the mathematics courses offered and also studied advanced calculus at George Washington University. Later, Grabill earned a master of arts in statistics at American University and studied at the Department of Agriculture Graduate School and the National Bureau of Standards. Gallaudet College in 1963 conferred on him an honorary doctorate. *See* GALLAUDET COLLEGE.

After graduation from Gallaudet in 1934, Grabill found his first employment with the Federal Emergency Relief Agency (later called the WPA) as a junior statistical clerk. Seeking permanent status through the civil service examination process, he was the first deaf person to demonstrate the irrelevance of the then current requirement that every applicant be able to hear a watch tick at 15 feet.

Wilson H. Grabill in 1968.

In 1936, he married Edna Harbin of South Carolina, whom he had met at Gallaudet. A son, Michael Wilson, was born in 1950.

Grabill began his long career at the Bureau of the Census in 1939 when he was transferred there to be a calculating machine operator. Quickly rising through the bureaucracy, he became chief of the Bureau's Fertility Statistics Section in 1945, a position he held until 1957. From 1962 until his retirement he was chief of the Family and Fertility Statistics Branch of the Population Division. During his 44 years at the Bureau, Grabill earned the Department of Commerce's silver and gold medals for meritorious service, and he was cited for his "innovations in methodology and skill in developing subordinate professional workers."

Grabill's work on the fertility of the American people was a pioneering effort. He helped produce the Bureau's first decennial census report on fertility in 1940, remarking in one of his first memos with his typically dry humor: "The study of fertility is a virgin field."

Grabill was a productive scholar throughout his career, writing numerous reports for the Census Bureau and publishing widely. He coauthored three important books on fertility statistics: *The Fertility of American Woman* (1958), *Recent Trends and Variations in Fertility in the United States* (1968), and *Differential Current Fertility in the United States* (1970). Reviewers termed his first monograph "a monumental work" and "an indispensable source book." In addition, Grabill authored or coauthored eight articles that were published in various professional journals, and contributed one chapter to Donald Bogue's *The Population of the United States* (1959). His reputation as a fertility expert earned him guest lectureships at the University of Chicago and the East-West Population Institute in Honolulu, Hawaii.

Active in a variety of concerns, Grabill served on the boards of directors of two professional societies, the Population Association of America and the United States National Committee of the International Union for the Scientific Study of Population. In 1964, he became the second deaf person selected to the board of directors of Gallaudet College. He was the board's secretary for 10 years and chairperson of its honors committee. Grabill served his alma mater in other ways, too, as a member of the Laurent Clerc Cultural Fund and Graduate Fellowship Fund Committee.

A founding member of the National Health Care Foundation, Grabill served on its board and as its treasurer for 10 years. The foundation, supported entirely by deaf people and friends (until accepted into the United Fund), established and maintains a halfway house for deaf patients from St. Elizabeth's Hospital in the District of Columbia.

An active member of St. Barnabas Mission to the Deaf, Episcopal Diocese of Washington, D.C., Grabill was secretary, treasurer, and junior warden (chairperson) of the congregation. He was also treasurer of the Episcopal Conference of the Deaf, a national group, from 1964 to 1969. A member of the National Fraternal Society of the Deaf, Washington Division No. 46, and the Alexandria-Potomac Lions Club, he served the latter organization as treasurer. The Lions Club was the first in the nation with a majority of members who were deaf.

See NATIONAL FRATERNAL SOCIETY OF THE DEAF; RELIGION, PROTESTANT.

Wilson Grabill died of cancer at the age of 70 on January 30, 1983, in Clinton, Maryland.

Bibliography

"Alumni News: Recording the Population Explosion." *Gallaudet Today*, vol. 2, no. 3, Spring 1972.

Berg, Otto B.: "Wilson Grabill, 70 Dies: Noted Demographer and Churchman," *The Deaf Episcopalian*, vol. 59, no. 2, Winter 1983.

Gallaudet College Archives, Washington, D.C.

Alan B. Crammatte

GREATER LOS ANGELES COUNCIL ON DEAFNESS, INC.

The Greater Los Angeles Council on Deafness, Inc. (GLAD) is a nonprofit organization serving as an umbrella agency for over 45 organizations and agencies working in the area of deafness. It was founded in Los Angeles in August 1969. Its membership consists of social, recreational, and service clubs of deaf people; media groups; hospital programs; and educational, professional, and religious organizations; as well as 1500 hearing and deaf individuals.

FOUNDING

The council was established as the result of a recommendation made by Henry Klopping, then a postgraduate student in the National Leadership Program in the Area of the Deaf at California State University, Northridge (CSUN). As his graduate project, Klopping conducted a survey which showed the need for a community-based agency to provide services to deaf persons. A group of 25 individuals met at the invitation of CSUN and the California Association of the Deaf, and founded the Greater Los Angeles Council on Deafness with the purpose to disseminate information on deafness and to promote the social, economic, educational, and cultural welfare of hearing-impaired individuals. *See* CALIFORNIA STATE UNIVERSITY, NORTHRIDGE.

ORGANIZATION AND SERVICES

Council member organizations are represented in an Assembly of Delegates that meets quarterly. Individual members possess no voting authority but support the work of the council. The board of directors, most of whom are deaf (the president and vice-president must be deaf), is elected by the Assembly of Delegates and, in turn, appoints the executive director who is charged with administering the agency, which is the direct service arm of the council. The council provides leadership in the areas of communication, discrimination, employment, education, and the rights of deaf children and adults. It sponsors community workshops and educational forums; generates response from the community at quarterly general meetings; serves as a link between traditional social service agencies and the deaf community; and provides information and referral services, job development and placement, interpreter referral, telephone/TDD relay services, peer counseling, advocacy, and community education activities. The council's services were initiated in 1974 through an agreement with Information and Referral Services of Los Angeles County, an agency of the United Way, whereby a comprehensive data bank was made accessible to deaf people with the help of a council volunteer, a telephone, and a TTY. The services grew under an Innovation and Expansion Grant from the California Department of Rehabilitation, which also made possible the establishment of the nation's first sign language interpreter pool free to deaf people.

The council's facilities are housed in an administrative office and five outreach offices, with a staff that is half hearing-impaired and half nondeaf. Its hiring policy ensures that all staff possess the ability to communicate effectively in sign language, the oral method, gesticulation, and other modes as required. The involvement of hearing-impaired persons in the organizational structure of both the council and the agency allows for the development of deaf self-determination, promoting the philosophy "of, by, and for the deaf." The need for self-determination emerged as an outcome of a demonstration project conducted by the council and other deaf-administered service agencies in California. This project substantiated the hypothesis that deaf and hearing-impaired persons were not receiving adequate support services from traditional public social service agencies, and showed that deaf persons were not provided with the opportunity, on a comprehensive level, to be involved in the planning of their needs. Existing support systems established by nondeaf persons displayed paternalistic attitudes, which ultimately denied deaf people the right to self-determination and local community control. A turning point in the provision of services came in 1980 with legislation that created the Office of Deaf Access under the California State Department of Social Services, which provides funding for the council and four other agencies serving the deaf.

One of the council's most widely used services is the Interpreter Referral Program. With a pool of more than 200 qualified interpreters, communication accessibility is provided in a wide range of situations, such as job interviews, medical appointments, and legal situations. The council has developed a system for evaluating the skills of interpreters and also has established ethical standards of service. *See* INTERPRETING.

The council is active in establishing constructive dialogue with hospitals and police departments to make certain that hearing-impaired persons are afforded complete communication accessibility to those services. It also consults with various school districts that provide educational programs for hearing-impaired students and tries to ensure that hearing-impaired teachers in California are given testing and employment opportunities equal to that of their hearing peers. The council also lobbies for legislation that affects hearing-impaired individuals, such as bills on telecommunication, interpreters in courts, and deaf service agencies.

TELEVISION ACCESS

Since 1975 the council has been engaged in efforts to obtain access to television for hearing-impaired individuals under the Rehabilitation Act of 1973, which prohibits discrimination against qualified handicapped persons by recipients of federal financial assistance. Its efforts consisted of license renewal challenges against commercial and public broadcasting stations, and a separate class action suit against various government agencies and public broadcasting entities. The license renewal challenges reached the U.S. Supreme Court (*Community Television of Southern California vs Gottfried*) in 1983. The Court held that no television licensee could ignore the right of deaf and hearing-impaired individuals to access television, but until appropriate regulations were issued by the respective government agencies, including the Federal Communication Commission, the television stations were not in violation of the act. The concurrent class action suit attempted to compel the issuance of these regulations. *See* REHABILITATION ACT OF 1973: Gottfried v. Community Television of Southern California.

Located in the heart of the entertainment industry, the council is also available to act as consultant to television and movie producers in the planning of productions that involve deaf characters or stories related to deafness, and works closely with deaf media groups to see that deaf people are honestly portrayed and that deaf performers are hired whenever possible to portray deaf characters.

PUBLICATIONS

The council publishes the *Directory of Resources Available to Deaf and Hearing Impaired Persons in the Southern California Area*, a resource book containing over 900 listings ranging from "Audiological Services" to "Telecommunications" that is periodically updated. The *GLAD News Magazine*, a journal distributed to members, is published quarterly. The council also maintains a bookstore which carries collection of books on sign language and deafness, in addition to signal devices and telecommunication equipment such as TDDs.

Since its inception, many persons have played an important part in the council's development as a role model for deaf-administered agencies serving the deaf community. Leonard J. Meyer, past president, and Marcella M. Meyer, executive director, who volunteered her services to establish the agency, built the organization into a community-based group. Lawrence R. Fleischer, president, expanded advocacy into educational and communication fields. Leo Mouton, deputy director, a hearing person and a strong advocate of deaf self-determination, developed a method of delivering services sensitive to the needs of deaf persons. The council's legal needs and litigation in the field of communication have been provided pro bono by Attorney Abraham Gottfried, who has brought the issue of telecommunication access for hearing-impaired persons to the attention of the highest courts.

The council is a member of the National Association of the Deaf and has been commended by the City of Los Angeles and both houses of the California legislature. The California Assembly has recognized it as a "vital and necessary organization whose importance is attested by the great number of clients it effectively serves." *See* NATIONAL ASSOCIATION OF THE DEAF.

Bibliography

Klopping, H.: "A Survey of Prevalent Attitudes Among the Adult Deaf in Regards to the Establishment of a Counseling, Information and Referral Center in Los Angeles: A Report of Two Studies," unpublished graduate project, California State University, Northridge, 1969.

Meyer, L. J.: "The Greater Los Angeles Information and Referral Service for the Hearing Impaired," unpublished graduate project, California State University, Northridge, July 1974.

"Service to the Deaf Demonstration Project: Report to the Legislature by the Department of Social Services, March 15, 1980," prepared by Long Range Planning Bureau, William J. Rietdorf, Chief.

Marcella M. Meyer

GREECE

It is difficult to paint anything but a dismal picture when discussing facilities for handicapped persons—and, indeed, attitudes toward them—in Greece today. This generalization holds true for the deaf population in particular.

EDUCATION

Services for deaf persons are in their infancy. There is no state provision for the education of deaf people, although in January 1983 a national committee was assigned the task of developing a comprehensive educational program for all hearing-impaired children from infancy to 12 years old, with long-term planning provision for the 12–18 age group. There is room for optimism, therefore, that the future will be brighter.

The National Foundation for the Protection of the Deaf and Dumb, financially assisted by the state, is the most important provider of educational facilities for deaf children in Greece. With schools in Athens, Thessaloniki, Patras, Serres, Volos, and Kastella, Crete, in 1982 the Foundation served approximately 400 residential and day students, mostly at the elementary level.

There are two other schools for deaf children in Greece. One is the state-controlled school in Ekali, Athens, with classes for elementary school children (six grades), junior high school children (three grades beyond elementary), and high school children (a

further three grades). In 1982 the Ekali school served less than 100 residential and day pupils at all three levels. The other is a private day school in Athens, which, in 1982, enrolled less than 200 preschool, elementary, and high school students.

In 1982 a total of 640 children received some form of special education ostensibly directed toward meeting their needs. The Ministry of Health and Welfare estimate, on the basis of applications for benefits offered to hearing-handicapped children aged up to 18 years, indicated in 1982 that there were 1480 deaf children in the country. Since there is no Greek working definition differentiating between deaf and hard-of-hearing individuals, this figure is an imprecise indicator of the incidence of hearing impairment in Greece. Generally, however, only the most severe cases qualify for these benefits: children either diagnosed medically as very deaf or with gross spoken-language delays.

When the 1975 United States official estimate of 0.075% of the school-age population as deaf (no usable audition) is extrapolated onto Greek population figures, the result gives over 1600 such children (based on 1980 figures for children aged 5–19). By extending the projection to the hard of hearing (United States official estimate, 0.5% of the school-age population), the surmise is that there are at least a further 11,000 hard-of-hearing Greek pupils undiscovered either by the statisticians or by the social services.

The schools that exist are all oral, and no signing is used in the classrooms. Emphasis is given to the development of lipreading skills, together with a certain amount of auditory training. The overall aim is to develop speech and language skills to the point where children can follow the state curriculum for hearing children. The official state textbooks for the regular classroom are used at each grade level in all the schools. Children are integrated into regular schools wherever possible but, in the absence of state backup services, turn to private tutors for any additional support they need.

There is no provision for teacher training, and teachers of deaf students either have received some sort of training abroad or are regular classroom teachers.

There are no adult or higher education programs specifically open to deaf persons at present, although work has been carried out at the Ministry of Labor to create vocational training programs.

AUDIOLOGIC SERVICES

Certain hearing aids are subsidized by the state, but audiology is not a recognized profession in Greece. All aids are dispensed by commercial hearing aid dealers who may or may not have a background in audiology. By law, only ear, nose, and throat doctors are allow to carry out audiometric assessment.

EMPLOYMENT

No statistics are available that relate to the success of deaf persons in their careers as compared with the hearing population, nor indeed to the kind of jobs they hold. Since less than 44 percent of the officially counted deaf school-age population in Greece receive any formal education whatsoever, and of these only approximately 10 percent at a level beyond the elementary, it may be surmised that their total performance is considerably below average and that a very high proportion hold semi-skilled or unskilled jobs. (Education for hearing children is obligatory until age 15, or for at least nine years.)

COMMUNICATION

Deaf people communicate among themselves by means of Greek Sign Language. The Greek Deaf Union of Athens estimates that it is actively used by 30,000 deaf adults. Its roots lie with American Sign Language and French Sign Language, together with various indigenous sign-language systems, which jelled in their present form largely during the 1950s. This decade was marked by rapid urbanization and the congregation, for the first time on any sizable scale, of deaf people in the towns.

The Greek manual alphabet has 24 letters performed with 20 handshapes. However, initialized signs are not a very visible element of Greek Sign Language.

The present picture is one of restriction and poverty of choice available to deaf persons. However, there is indeed reason to be cautiously optimistic for a better tomorrow, both in the light of the plans for development of the social services mentioned above, and in the light of increased pressure from deaf persons themselves and their families for more opportunities, support, and encouragement.

Bibliography
Kourbetis, V.: *The Beginning of a Search for Greek Sign Language*, unpublished dissertation, Boston University, 1981.

A. Liambey

GREGG, JOHN ROBERT
(1867–1948)

John Robert Gregg invented the system of shorthand that bears his name. Born in Rockcorry, County Monaghan, Ireland, on June 17, 1867, he was the youngest of five children. An irate schoolmaster, considering Gregg a slow learner, boxed the child's ears, causing a permanent hearing loss.

Gregg's interest in shorthand was aroused indirectly through Mr. Annesley, who accompanied the Gregg family to church and took down the sermon in shorthand. After service the minister begged Annesley not to publish the sermon, which had been plagiarized. This incident led Gregg's father to decide that his children should learn shorthand. None succeeded apart from John, then aged about ten. He mastered several systems, including those of Taylor, Sloan-Duploye, and Pitman, but disliked the geometric basis and shading of the last method. In his early teens Gregg read a history of shorthand by Thomas Anderson, a member of the London Shorthand Society, who specified "Five Essentials of the Ideal Shorthand System": independent vowel and consonant characters; all characters written in one slope on one line; no shaded characters; few, simple and comprehensive rules for abbreviations. Gregg knew that no existing method met all these criteria and set out to invent a system that would. For his own guidance he laid down "Seven Basic Principles" inherent in a good shorthand system.

Gregg obtained employment as a clerk in Glasgow, Scotland. Here, aged 18, he published an unsuccessful method entitled *Script Phonography*. Afterward he moved to Liverpool, England, where he established a shorthand school, and in 1888 published a much improved method called *Light Line Phonography*. This was basically a cursive shorthand following the principle of Anderson that progress in shorthand would "be found in an attentive study of longhand writing." *Light Line Phonography* was gaining acceptance in England when Gregg's hearing suddenly, but temporarily, deteriorated further.

In 1893 Gregg emigrated to the United States, settling first in Boston and later in Chicago. There he succeeded in popularizing his system, renamed Gregg shorthand, largely through outstanding successes in public competitions of exponents of his method. Foreign language adaptations of Gregg shorthand appeared throughout America and Europe. Publications such as *The Gregg Writer* and the *American Shorthand Teacher* in the United States and the *Gregg Magazine* in England gave further impetus. In addition to the *Gregg Shorthand Manual*, which sold over 18 million copies, Gregg wrote numerous other shorthand books. He received many awards for his services to business education. These included honorary doctorates from Boston University (1930) and Elder College, Trenton, New Jersey (1942). Gregg died in New York City on February 23, 1948.

Bibliography
Symonds, F. Addington: *John Robert Gregg: The Man and His Work*, 1963.

Kenneth Lysons